NINTH EDITION

PORTRAIT OF AMERICA

COMPLETE VERSION

STEPHEN B. OATES
University of Massachusetts, Amherst

CHARLES J. ERRICO
Northern Virginia Community College

Houghton Mifflin Company
Boston   New York

PORTRAIT OF AMERICA, VOLUME ONE TO 1877, NINTH EDITION
by Stephen B. Oates and Charles J. Errico
Copyright © 2007 by Houghton Mifflin Company. All rights reserved.

PORTRAIT OF AMERICA, VOLUME TWO FROM 1865, NINTH EDITION
by Stephen B. Oates and Charles J. Errico
Copyright © 2007 by Houghton Mifflin Company. All rights reserved.

Publisher: Patricia Coryell
Sponsoring Editor: Sally Constable
Senior Development Editor: Jeff Greene
Senior Project Editor: Jane Lee
Editorial Assistant: Carrie Parker
Senior Art and Design Coordinator: Jill Haber
Senior Photo Editor: Jennifer Meyer Dare
Composition Buyer: Chuck Dutton
Associate Strategic Buyer: Brian Pieragostini
Senior Marketing Manager: Katherine Bates
Marketing Assistant: Lauren Bussard
Cover Design Manager: Anne S. Katzeff

ATLAS OF AMERICAN HISTORY
Copyright © 1999 by Rand McNally & Company. All rights reserved.

Project Manager: Carole Wicklander
Book Production Editor: Louise Frederiksen
Map Production Editor: Charles J. MacDonald
Managing Editor: Margaret McNamara
Digital Cartographers: Barbara Benstead-Strassheim, Elizabeth A. Hunt, Amy L. Troesch
Digital Cartography Project Manager: Thomas Vitacco
Cartographic Editorial: Robert K. Argersinger, Gregory P. Babiak, Jill M. Stift
Cartographic Production: Norma Denny, Jim Purvis
Manual Cartography Project Manager: David Zapenski
Designer: Donna McGrath
Production Manager: Robert Sanders
Typesetting: Yvonne Rosenberg

Text Credits: Excerpts from A MIDWIFE'S TALE by Laurel Thatcher Ulrich, copyright © 1990 by Laurel Thatcher Ulrich. Used by permission of Alfred A. Knopf, a division of Random House, Inc. From The Southern Lady: From Pedestal to Politics by Anne Frior Scott, pp. 4-21. Copyright © 1970 by The University of Chicago Press. Reprinted by permission. "Were the Puritans Puritanical?" from OUT OF OUR PAST: THE FORCES THAT SHAPED MODERN AMERICA by Carl N. Degler. Copyright © 1959, 1970 by Carl N. Degler. Reprinted by permission of HarperCollins Publishers, Inc. Copyright 1990 U.S. News & World Report, L.P. Reprinted with permission. Alexander Winston, "Sam Adams, Firebrand of the American Revolution," American Heritage, vol. 18, no. 3 (Apr. 1967). pp. 61-64, 105-108. Reprinted by permission of American Heritage Inc. 1967.

Art Credits: Page 5: © Bettman/CORBIS. Page 33 © Gibbes Museum of Art/Carolina Art Association.

Custom Publishing Editor: Sheila Ellis
Custom Publishing Production Manager: Christina Battista
Project Coordinator: Janell Sims

Cover Designer: Joel Gendron
Cover Image: PhotoDisc

This book contains select works from existing Houghton Mifflin Company resources and was produced by Houghton Mifflin Custom Publishing for collegiate use. As such, those adopting and/or contributing to this work are responsible for editorial content, accuracy, continuity and completeness.

Printed in the United States of America.

ISBN-13: 978-0-618-89571-7
ISBN-10: 0-618-89571-X
N-07691

2 3 4 5 6 7 8 9 – CM – 08 07 06

Houghton Mifflin
Custom Publishing

222 Berkeley Street • Boston, MA 02116

Address all correspondence and order information to the above address.

CONTENTS

remember the leading figures of history by their greatest
achievements or by their personal failures and peccadilloes.

PREFACE

Good history begins with a good story.
> —James West Davidson
> and Mark Hamilton Lytle

The ninth edition of *Portrait of America* is the work of two historians who care deeply about the teaching of American history. We realize that many students enter undergraduate history courses and advanced placement high school programs with the impression that the study of history entails little more than names and dates. We are convinced that the readings in *Portrait of America* demonstrate that this is a misconception and that studying history can in fact be a profoundly enriching experience. This is because *Portrait of America* stresses the human side of the American past, suggesting how the interaction of people and events shaped the course of American history. We chose selections for this anthology that make history live by telling a good story, and that were written for students, not for professional historians. The essays, narratives, and biographical portraits gathered here humanize American history, portraying it as a story of real people who actually lived, people with whom we can identify. We hope that the anthology is an example of humanistic history at its best, the kind that combines scrupulous and engaging scholarship with a compelling narrative style. Because college survey audiences are not professional ones, they might enjoy reading history if it is presented in an exciting and accessible form.

There is another reason why students will find *Portrait of America* edifying: it showcases the writings of some of America's most eminent historians. Volume One contains excerpts from critically acclaimed, best-selling books by David McCullough, Joseph Ellis, and Walter Isaacson, all famous authors. The prizes our contributors have won testify to their important places in the galaxy of American letters. Pulitzer Prize winners include Bruce Catton, David McCullough, Joseph Ellis, and Gordon Wood. In addition, Ira Berlin, John Demos, Eric Foner, John Hope Franklin, Page Smith, and Gordon Wood have all won the prestigious Bancroft Prize. Stephen B. Oates, an elected member of the Society of American Historians, won the Robert F. Kennedy Memorial Book Award, two Christopher Awards, and fellowships from the Guggenheim Foundation and the National Endowment for the Humanities. Both John Hope Franklin and Bruce Catton received the famed Presidential Medal of Freedom. Many other contributors also won significant literary and scholarly recognition. Thus *Portrait of America* offers readers a unique opportunity to learn from a lineup of historians and writers with national and even international reputations.

The ninth edition of Volume One has been extensively revised. It contains seven new selections of superior literary and historical merit. They make this the strongest edition of *Portrait of America* yet published. The new readings are:

- Walter Isaacson's portrait of the captivating personality of Benjamin Franklin, "the most identifiable and approachable of the founding fathers";
- David McCullough's exciting profile of John Adams, a patriot who courageously defended young British troops accused of perpetrating the Boston massacre and who became one of the great American leaders of the Revolutionary era;
- H. W. Brand's vivid description of "the miracle at Philadelphia"—the compromises achieved at the Great Convention of 1787 that created what would become the oldest written constitution in world history;

- Peter L. Bernstein's riveting account of the construction of the Erie Canal, one of the most significant technological achievements of the early nineteenth century that helped build a great nation;
- Stephen Yafa's story of the lives and working conditions of the young women who toiled in Lowell's thriving textile mills—a story Yafa tells through the perceptive eyes of a thirteen-year-old laborer;
- John Hope Franklin and Loren Schweninger's disturbing description of the brutal slave trade and of those African Americans who had the courage to try to escape the "hellish institution" of slavery while being chased by white patrols and howling dogs;
- James Oliver Horton and Lois E. Horton's graphic story of the black experience during Reconstruction, when the former slaves' dreams of true equality and a better life were obstructed by southern white violence and racial oppression.

The ninth edition retains the best and most popular selections of the previous edition. We hope that *Portrait of America* remains as balanced as ever, for it offers samplings of virtually every kind of history—men's and women's, black and white, social and cultural, political and military, urban and economic, national and local—so that students can appreciate the rich diversity of the American experience.

Portrait of America contains several important features that help students learn from its contents. Each selection is preceded by a glossary that identifies important individuals, events, and concepts that appear in the reading. Introductions set the selections in proper context and suggest ways to approach studying them. They also tie all the selections together so that they can be read more or less as connected episodes. Study questions following the selections raise significant issues and encourage students to

make comparisons and contrasts between selections. The questions also help students review the readings and suggest points for class discussion.

The anthology is intended for use largely in college survey courses. It could be used as a supplement to a textbook or to a list of paperback readings. Or it could serve as the basic text. *Portrait of America* could also be used effectively in advanced placement high school classes. The book is organized into fifteen parts according to periods or themes; each part contains two related selections. This organization allows readers to make comparisons and contrasts between different events or viewpoints.

With this edition, we are introducing a new website. On this website, instructors and students will find a number of selections that appeared in the seventh and eighth editions, but are not included in the ninth edition primarily for reasons of length. With this website, we can keep the printed version of *Portrait of America* to a reasonable length and still make available many popular selections from those editions.

We could not have assembled the ninth edition without the generous help of others. Robert Kinson, Elza M. England, and Denise Pattee Pargas assisted us at crucial points in preparing the manuscript, and we are most grateful to them. At Northern Virginia Community College, Alice Reagan aided us in identifying new selections, and Betty Pasqualini helped format the manuscript. Jay Boggis did a superb job of copyediting the manuscript, and we are most grateful to him. We also want to thank the following professors for taking time out from their busy schedules to review the volume: Richard Aquila, Pennsylvania State University, the Behrend College; Terri Halperin, University of Richmond; Gordon Patterson, Florida Institute of Technology; and Vivian Talbot, Weber State University.

S. B. O.
C. J. E.

PART ONE

The European Discovery

1 The American Holocaust: Columbus and the Conquest of the New World

DAVID E. STANNARD

Contrary to legend, the European discovery of America took place quite by accident. The story of that discovery begins in the fifteenth century, when the European world was slowly spinning its way out of the Middle Ages, slowly becoming aware of the treasures—and mysteries—of distant Asia. There were many who dreamed of the fabled Orient, but none with more enterprise than a Genoese sailor named Christopher Columbus, who was certain that he could reach the Orient by sailing westward across largely uncharted waters. The nation that financed his project, Columbus contended, would enjoy the shortest route to the riches of Japan and India—silks, gems, tapestries, and highly prized spices.

Since the Crusades, Europeans had bought these luxuries from Italian merchants, who got them from Arab traders in the Holy Land. But in the thirteenth and fourteenth centuries, travelers like Marco Polo reported that Asia was the source of the succulent goods the Italians brought out of the Near East. After the rise of Europe's nation states, Portugal sought an ocean route to Asia's fortunes; in the fifteenth century, its hardy navigators, pioneers of nautical astronomy, sailed around the African Cape and opened a sea route to India. Meanwhile, Columbus dreamed of a western route across the Atlantic—which was not infeasible, since intelligent Europeans in the fifteenth century knew the world was round. Finally, he persuaded the king and queen of Spain to commission him Admiral of the Ocean Sea and to provide money, men, and ships for his voyage. He would sail under the flag of Spain and would receive a share of the profits secured from whatever lands he reached in Asia.

Most of us have certain preconceptions about Columbus and his fabled voyage: every Columbus Day we commemorate the myth of the bold, visionary hero who defied contemporary superstition and plunged across a storm-tossed Atlantic against all odds, discovered America, and made the United States possible. In reality, of course, Columbus did not "discover" America; the Native Americans, or Indians, had done that some thirty thousand years before. And other Europeans had probably seen the New World before Columbus embarked on his voyage. What is more, Columbus never believed that he had found a new continent, instead insisting that he had seen islands of the Orient—proof of all his theories, goal of all his dreams. In sum, he realized none of his dreams save that of navigating the Atlantic. He died in 1506, unaware that his explorations had given Spain a claim to a vast New World and opened it for the profit and glory of the Old.

To be sure, Columbus had courage, imagination, and persistence, and he was a superior navigator. But his significance was considerably different from what most Americans realize. Named after Saint Christopher, the legendary pagan turned saint who became the "Christ-bearer," Columbus conceived it his destiny to carry Christianity across the ocean to the "pagan" countries of the Orient. In executing his divine mission, the great explorer was the flagbearer of European values and aspirations, which he unwittingly transported to the shores of the New World. In fact, Columbus's "Christian expeditionary force" established the first outpost of European civilization there, inaugurating three centuries of exploration and conquest that changed the course of modern history.

On the positive side, the European arrival led to "the Columbian Exchange," described by two authors as "a global swap of animals, plants, people, ailments and ideas" that had a profound impact on Europe, Africa, and the Americas. Among other things, this exchange sent American corn to Africa and American tobacco, potatoes, beans, squash, tomatoes, and peanuts to Europe. It also brought to the New World horses, cows, chickens, pigs, honeybees, coffee, wheat, and rice.

But there was another side to the European discovery of America, a dark side. From the viewpoint of the first Americans, to whom Columbus gave the name Indios, the European invasion of their world was a catastrophe. Columbus himself set the example for subsequent Europeans, initiating a policy of genocide, of enslavement and killing that was to result in the near extermination of the first Americans. David E. Stannard, author of the following selection, calls it "the American holocaust." To make matters worse, the Indians were not immune to the communicable diseases the Europeans carried to the New World. Epidemics of measles, typhoid, smallpox, dysentery, tuberculosis, and alcoholism were to sweep through the original Americans, killing them by the countless thousands. Modern demographers estimate that in 1492 some 12 million Indians inhabited the New World north of Mexico; in the ensuing centuries of white conquest, the number of Indians fell by about 90 percent.

What follows is a fresh, accurate, and vivid telling of the Columbus story and the beginnings of European genocide against the Indians. As you read this selection, how would you explain the treatment of the Indians? Was it all about greed for gold, land, and other riches? Was it prejudice toward a supposedly inferior race? Was it a terribly misguided conception of religious conversion on the part of the conquerors? Or was it a combination of factors?

GLOSSARY

INQUISITION Ferdinand and Isabella, the monarchs of Spain at the time of Columbus's explorations, established religious tribunals to impose Christianity on all of their subjects. Those who remained faithful to Islam or Judaism were exiled, tortured, or killed.

LAS CASAS Bartolomé de Las Casas was a young priest who transcribed Columbus's journals and became a severe critic of the Spanish cruelties against the native people they encountered. Las Casas is an important primary source in the documentation of Spanish attitudes and practices in the New World.

PEASANTS' WAR Perhaps as many as one hundred thousand people perished in 1524 as a result of this uprising. It was a product of famine, poverty, high taxes, and even the inspirational teachings of Martin Luther.

POOR'S HOLES Mass graves for the dead found in European cities during Columbus's time. Starvation and disease resulted in a high mortality rate even in the best of times. Droughts, crop shortages, and downturns in the economy drained fifteenth-century cities of their poverty-stricken population.

REPARTIMIENTO This system of Indian grants, initiated by Columbus, placed entire groups of native people under Spanish masters called *mineros* in the mines and *estancieros* on the plantations. The process encouraged further cruelty since the conquerors frequently worked the enslaved to death in order to receive "short-term material wealth."

REQUERIMIENTO An oath of allegiance to the Catholic church, the Pope, and the Spanish crown. It was read to the native people Columbus encountered in a language that they could not possibly understand. Failure to obey would lead to a holy war that would result in the confiscation of property, slavery, and/or death.

SWINE INFLUENZA (FLU) The domesticated pigs that Columbus took with him on his second voyage were the likely carriers of a highly infectious flu that killed massive numbers of natives and many Spanish.

The Spain that Christopher Columbus and his crews left behind just before dawn on August 3, 1492, as they sailed forth from Palos and out into the Atlantic, was for most of its people a land of violence, squalor, treachery, and intolerance. In this respect Spain was no different from the rest of Europe.

Epidemic outbreaks of plague and smallpox, along with routine attacks of measles, influenza, diphtheria, typhus, typhoid fever, and more, frequently swept European cities and towns clean of 10 to 20 percent of their populations at a single stroke. As late as the mid-seventeenth century more than 80,000 Londoners—one out of every six residents in the city—died from plague in a matter of months. And again and again, as with its companion diseases, the pestilence they called the Black Death returned. Like most of the other urban centers in Europe, says one historian who has specialized in the subject, "every twenty-five or thirty years—sometimes more frequently—the city was convulsed by a great epidemic." Indeed, for centuries an individual's life chances in Europe's pest-house cities were so poor that the natural populations of the towns were in perpetual decline that was offset only by in-migration from the countryside—in-migration, says one historian, that was "vital if [the cities] were to be preserved from extinction."

Famine, too, was common. What J. H. Elliott has said of sixteenth-century Spain had held true throughout the Continent for generations beyond memory: "The rich ate, and ate to excess, watched by a thousand hungry eyes as they consumed their gargantuan meals. The rest of the population starved." This was in normal times. The slightest fluctuation in food prices could cause the sudden deaths of additional tens of thousands who lived on the margins of perpetual hunger. So precarious was the existence of these multitudes in France that as late as the seventeenth century *each* "average" increase in the price of wheat or millet directly killed a proportion of the French population equal to nearly twice the percentage of Americans who died in the Civil War.

That was the seventeenth century, when times were getting better. In the fifteenth and sixteenth centuries prices fluctuated constantly, leading people to complain as a Spanish agriculturalist did in 1513 that "today a pound of mutton costs as much as a whole sheep used to, a loaf as much as a *fanega* [a bushel and a half] of wheat, a pound of wax or oil as much as an *arroba* [25 Spanish pounds]." The result of this, as one French historian has observed, was that "the epidemic that raged in Paris in 1482 fits the classic pattern: famine in the countryside, flight of the poor to the city in search of help, then outbreak of disease in the city following upon the malnutrition." And in Spain the threat of famine in the countryside was especially omnipresent. Areas such as Castile and Andalusia were wracked with harvest failures that brought on mass death repeatedly during the fifteenth century. But since both causes of death, disease and famine, were so common throughout Europe, many surviving records did not bother (or were unable) to make distinctions between them. Consequently, even today historians find it difficult or impossible to distinguish between those of the citizenry who died of disease and those who merely starved to death.

Roadside ditches, filled with stagnant water, served as public latrines in the cities of the fifteenth century, and they would continue to do so for centuries to follow. So too would other noxious habits and public health hazards of the time persist on into the future—from the practice of leaving the decomposing offal of butchered animals to fester in the streets, to London's "special problem," . . . "poor's holes." These were "large, deep, open pits in which were laid the bodies of the poor, side by side, row upon row. Only when the pit was filled with bodies was it finally covered over with earth." As one contemporary . . . delicately observed: "How noisome the stench is that arises from these holes so stowed with dead bodies, especially in sultry seasons and after rain."

Along with the stench and repulsive appearance of the openly displayed dead, human and animal alike, a modern visitor to a European city in this era would be repelled by the appearance and the vile aromas given off by the living as well. Most people never bathed, not once in an entire lifetime. Almost everyone had his or her brush with smallpox and other deforming diseases that left survivors partially blinded, pock-marked, or crippled, while it was the norm for men and women to have "bad breath from the rotting teeth and constant stomach disorders which can be documented from many sources, while suppurating ulcers, eczema, scabs, running sores and other nauseating skin diseases were extremely common, and often lasted for years."

Street crime in most cities lurked around every corner. One especially popular technique for robbing someone was to drop a heavy rock or chunk of masonry on his head from an upper-story window and then to rifle the body for jewelry and money. This was a time . . . when "it was one of the festive pleasures of Midsummer Day to burn alive one or two dozen cats," and when . . . "the continuous disruption of town and country by every kind of dangerous rabble [and] the permanent threat of harsh and unreliable law enforcement . . . nourished a feeling of universal uncertainty." With neither culturally developed systems of social obligation and restraint in place, nor effective police forces in their stead, the cities of Europe during the fifteenth and sixteenth centuries were little more than chaotic population agglomerates with entire sections serving as the residential turf of thieves and brigands, and where the wealthy were forced to hire torch-bearing bodyguards to accompany them out at night. In times of famine, cities and towns became the setting for food riots. And the largest riot of all, of course—though the word hardly does it justice—was the Peasants' War, which broke out in 1524 following a series of local revolts that had been occurring repeatedly since the previous century. The Peasants' War killed over 100,000 people.

As for rural life in calmer moments, Jean de La Bruyère's seventeenth-century description of human existence in the French countryside gives an apt summary of what historians for the past several decades have been uncovering in their research on rustic communities in Europe at large during the entire late medieval to early modern epoch: "sullen animals, male and female [are] scattered over the country, dark, livid, scorched by the sun, attached to the earth they dig up and turn over with invincible persistence; they have a kind of articulate speech, and when they rise to their feet, they show a human face, and, indeed, they are men. At night they retire to dens where they live on black bread, water, and roots."

To be sure, La Bruyère was a satirist and although, in the manner of all caricaturists, his portrait contains key elements of truth, it also is cruel in what it omits. And what it omits is the fact that these wretchedly poor country folk, for all their life-threatening deprivations, were not "sullen animals." They were, in fact, people quite capable of experiencing the same feelings of tenderness and love and fear and sadness, however constricted by the limitations of their existence, as did, and do, all human beings in every corner of the globe.

But what Lawrence Stone has said about the typical English village also was likely true throughout Europe at this time—that is, that because of the dismal social conditions and prevailing social values, it "was a place filled with malice and hatred, its only unifying bond being the occasional episode of mass hysteria, which temporarily bound together the majority in order to harry and persecute the local witch." Indeed, as in England, there were towns on the Continent where as many as a third of the population were accused of witchcraft and where ten out of every hundred people were executed for it in a single year. In one small, remote locale within reputedly peaceful Switzerland, more than 3300 people were killed in the late sixteenth- and seventeenth-century for allegedly Satanic activities. The tiny village of Wiesensteig saw sixty-three women burned to death in one year alone, while in Obermarchtal

fifty-four people—out of a total population of barely 700—died at the stake during a three-year period. Thus, while it is true that the Europeans of those days possessed the same range of emotions that we do, as Stone puts it, "it is noticeable that hate seems to have been more prominent an emotion than love. . . .

Throughout Europe, about half the children born during this time died before reaching the age of ten. Among the poorer classes—and in Spain particularly, which had an infant mortality rate almost 40 percent higher even than England's—things were much worse. In addition to exposure, disease, and malnutrition, one of the causes for such a high infant mortality rate (close to three out of ten babies in Spain did not live to see their first birthdays) was abandonment. Thousands upon thousands of children who could not be cared for were simply left to die on dungheaps or in roadside ditches. Others were sold into slavery. . . .

The wealthy had their problems too. They hungered after gold and silver. The Crusades, begun four centuries earlier, had increased the appetites of affluent Europeans for exotic foreign luxuries—for silks and spices, fine cotton, drugs, perfumes, and jewelry—material pleasures that required pay in bullion. Thus, gold had become for Europeans, in the words of one Venetian commentator of the time, "the sinews of all government . . . its mind, soul . . . its essence and its very life." The supply of the precious metal, by way of the Middle East and Africa, had always been uncertain. Now, however, the wars in eastern Europe had nearly emptied the Continent's coffers. A new supply, a more regular supply—and preferably a cheaper supply—was needed.

Violence, of course, was everywhere, as alluded to above; but occasionally it took on an especially perverse character. In addition to the hunting down and burning of witches, which was an everyday affair in most locales, in Milan in 1476 a man was torn to pieces by an enraged mob and his dismembered limbs were then eaten by his tormenters. In Paris and Lyon, Huguenots were killed and butchered, and their various body parts were sold openly in the streets. Other eruptions of bizarre torture, murder, and ritual cannibalism were not uncommon.

Such behavior, nonetheless, was not officially condoned, at least not usually. Indeed, wild and untrue accusations of such activities formed the basis for many of the witch hunts and religious persecutions—particularly of Jews—during this time. In precisely those years when Columbus was trekking around Europe in search of support for his maritime adventures, the Inquisition was raging in Spain. Here, and elsewhere in Europe, those out of favor with the powerful—particularly those who were believed to be un-Christian—were tortured and killed in the most ingenious of fashions: on the gallows, at the stake, on the rack—while others were crushed, beheaded, flayed alive, or drawn and quartered.

On the very day that Columbus finally set forth on his journey that would shake the world, the port of the city he sailed from was filled with ships that were deporting Jews from Spain. By the time the expulsion was complete between 120,000 and 150,000 Jews had been driven from their homes (their valuables, often meager, having first been confiscated) and then they were cast out to sea. As one contemporary described the scene:

It was pitiful to see their sufferings. Many were consumed by hunger, especially nursing mothers and their babies. Half-dead mothers held dying children in their arms. . . . I can hardly say how cruelly and greedily they were treated by those who transported them. Many were drowned by the avarice of the sailors, and those who were unable to pay their passage sold their children.

This was the world an ex-trader of African slaves named Christopher Columbus and his shipmates left behind as they sailed from the city of Palos in August of 1492. It was a world wracked by disease—disease that killed in massive numbers, but, importantly, that also tended to immunize survivors. A world in which all but the wealthy often could not feed themselves, and in which the wealthy themselves hungered after gold. It was a world, as well, of cruel violence and certainty of holy truth. Little wonder, then, that the first report back from that Atlantic

Far from idealizing Christopher Columbus as a bold adventurer, Ghirlandaio's portrait suggests instead a determined man of the Old World who brought destruction and violence into new lands that the explorer described in his journals as "beautiful and rich for planting." Columbus added that the natives in this Garden of Eden show "as much love as if they were giving their hearts." (© Scala/Art Resource, NY)

voyage, purportedly to the Orient, caused such sensations across the length and breadth of Europe.

In a letter composed aboard the *Niña*, as the returning ships passed through the Azores, Columbus described his discovery, during the previous fall and winter, of what he thought was the Indian Sea and its "many islands filled with people without number." One of the first major islands, which he called Juana, known to us today as Cuba, "was so long that I thought it must be the mainland, the province of [Cathay]." Another large island—the one we now know as Hispaniola, containing the nations of Haiti and the Dominican Republic—he called La Spañola. Columbus had reason to be impressed with the size of these two islands, since together they were two-thirds as large as his home country of Italy.

The Admiral continued his description of the wonders he had seen, in a passage that must be quoted at length if we are to achieve even a small understanding of the impact his voyage almost immediately had on the people of Europe, living under the wretched conditions of their time and just coming out of another cold and miserable winter:

As Juana, so all the other [islands] are very fertile to an excessive degree, and this one especially. In it there are many harbors on the sea coast, beyond comparison with others which I know in Christendom, and numerous rivers, good and large, which is marvelous. Its lands are lofty and in it there are many sierras and very high mountains, to which the island Tenerife is not comparable. All are most beautiful, of a thousand shapes, and all accessible, and filled with trees of a thousand kinds and tall, and they seem to touch the sky; and I am told that they never lose their foliage, which I can believe, for I saw them as green and beautiful as they are in Spain in May, and some of them were flowering, some with fruit. . . . And there were singing the nightingale and other little birds of a thousand kinds in the month of November, there where I went. There are palm trees of six or eight kinds, which are a wonder to behold because of their beautiful variety, and so are the other trees and fruits and plants; therein are marvelous pine groves, and extensive meadow country; and there is honey, and there are many kinds of birds and a great variety of fruits. Upcountry there are many mines of metals, and the population is innumerable. La Spañola is marvelous, the sierras and the mountains and the plains and the meadows and the lands are so beautiful and rich for planting and sowing, and for livestock of every sort, and for building towns and villages. The harbors of the sea here are such as you could not believe it without seeing them; and so the rivers, many and great, and good streams, the most of which bear gold.

If it sounded like Paradise, that was no accident. Paradise filled with gold. And when he came to describe the people he had met, Columbus's Edenic imagery never faltered:

The people of this island and of all the other islands which I have found and seen, or have not seen, all go naked, men and women, as their mothers bore them, except that some women cover one place only with the leaf of a plant or with a net of cotton which they make for that purpose. They have no iron or steel or weapons, nor are they capable of using them, although they are well-built people of handsome stature, because they are wondrous timid. . . . [T]hey are so artless and free with all they possess, that no one would believe it without having seen it. Of anything they have, if you ask them for it, they never say no; rather they invite the person to share it, and show as much love as if they were giving their hearts; and whether the thing be of value or of small price, at once they are content with whatever little thing of whatever kind may be given to them.

For years to come Columbus repeatedly would insist that his expeditions and adventures in the New World had nothing to do with "mere reason, mathematics, and maps," as two scholars of the subject put it, but rather that "his 'execution of the affair of the Indies' was a fulfillment of prophecies in Isaiah." In addition to helping explain, if taken seriously, why Columbus in many respects was a less successful navigator and helmsman than is commonly supposed (once into the Caribbean he rarely seemed to know where he was and routinely lost ships that were under his command), this rhetorical claim of biblical guidance is a clue to understanding the European reaction to his reported find. . . .

Numerous modern scholars have dissected and analyzed the effects of both biblical and classical myth on the minds of Europeans during this so-called Age of Discovery. But at least as strong as all the mixed-up imaginings of terrestrial heavens and Elysian fields, of lusty maidens and cannibalistic human beasts, was a fervent, and in many cases a truly maniacal, European craving for raw power and the wealth of gold and silver. Among the clergy, meanwhile, there was the promise of God's favor should they successfully introduce the New World's "pagan innocents" to the glory of his grace. It is not surprising, then, that in the very first sentence of his celebrated letter to the Spanish Crown Columbus says of the lands that he has found, "and of them all have I taken possession for Their Highnesses, by proclamation and with the royal standard displayed, and nobody objected." Consider the picture: standing alone with a few of his fellow officers in the white coral sand of a tiny island whose identification remains disputed to this day, an island "discovered" by Columbus despite the fact that it was well populated and had in fact been discovered by others thousands of years earlier, the admiral "took possession" of it—and of all the people it contained. And "nobody objected." Clearly, God was on the Spaniards' side.

So it went, from island to island, small and large, throughout the Caribbean. Wherever he went Columbus planted a cross, "making," as he said, "the declarations that are required," and claiming ownership of the land for his royal patrons back in Spain. Despite the fact that Columbus noted in his own journal of the voyage that "the people of these lands do not understand me nor I them," it seems to have been of particular satisfaction to him that never once did any of the onlooking Arawak-speaking islanders object to his repeated proclamations in Spanish that he was taking control of their lands away from them. Ludicrous though this scene may appear to us in retrospect, at the time it was a deadly serious ritual, similar in ways equally ludicrous and deadly to the other famous ritual the Spanish bestowed upon the non-Spanish-speaking people of the Americas, the *requerimiento.*

Following Columbus, each time the Spanish encountered a native individual or group in the course of their travels they were ordered to read to the Indians a statement informing them of the truth of Christianity and the necessity to swear immediate allegiance to the Pope and to the Spanish crown. After this, if the Indians refused or even delayed in their acceptance (or, more likely, their understanding) of the *requerimiento,* the statement continued:

I certify to you that, with the help of God, we shall powerfully enter into your country and shall make war against you in all ways and manners that we can, and shall subject you to the yoke and obedience of the Church and of Their Highnesses. We shall take you and your wives and your children, and shall make slaves of them, and as such shall sell and dispose of them as Their Highnesses may command. And we shall take your goods, and shall do you all the mischief and damage that we can, as to vassals who do not obey and refuse to receive their lord and resist and contradict him.

In practice, the Spanish usually did not wait for the Indians to reply to their demands. *First* the Indians were manacled; then, as it were, they were read their rights. As one Spanish conquistador and historian described the routine: "After they had been put in chains, someone read the *Requerimiento* without knowing their language and without any interpreters, and without either the reader or the Indians understanding the language they had no opportunity to reply, being immediately carried away prisoners, the Spanish not failing to use the stick on those who did not go fast enough.

In this perverse way, the invasion and destruction of what many, including Columbus, had thought was a heaven on earth began. Not that a reading of the *requerimiento* was necessary to the inhuman violence the Spanish were to perpetrate against the native peoples they confronted. Rather, the proclamation was merely a legalistic rationale for a fanatically religious and fanatically juridical and fanatically brutal people to justify a holocaust. After all, Columbus had seized and kidnapped Indian men, women, and children throughout his first voyage, long before the *requerimiento* was in use, five at one stop, six at another, more at others, filling his ships with varied samples of Indians to display like exotic beasts in Seville and Barcelona upon his return.

On at least one occasion Columbus sent a raiding party ashore to capture some women with their children to keep his growing excess of captured native males company, "because," he wrote in his journal, his past experience in abducting African slaves had taught him that "the [Indian] men would behave better in Spain with women of their country than without them." On this date he also records the vignette of "the husband of one of these women and father of three children, a boy and two girls," who followed his captured family onto Columbus's ship and said that if they had to go "he wished to come with them, and begged me hard, and they all now remain consoled with him."

But not for long. As a harbinger of things to come, only a half-dozen or so of those many captured native slaves survived the journey to Spain, and of them only two were alive six months later. On his second voyage Columbus tried an even more ambitious kidnapping and enslavement scheme. It is described by an Italian nobleman, Michele de Cuneo, who accompanied Columbus on this voyage:

When our caravels in which I wished to go home had to leave for Spain, we gathered together in our settlement 1600 people male and female of those Indians, of whom, among the best males and females, we embarked on our caravels of 17 February 1495, 550 souls. Of the rest who were left the announcement went around that whoever wanted them could take as many as he pleased; and this was done. And when everybody had been supplied there were some 400 of them left to whom permission was granted to go wherever they wanted. Among them were many women who had infants at the breast. They, in order the better to escape us, since they were afraid we would turn to catch them again, left their infants anywhere on the ground and started to flee like desperate people.

No one knows what happened to those six hundred or so left-over natives who were enslaved, on the Admiral's orders, by "whoever wanted them," or the four hundred or so who fled in terror, or their abandoned infants—but by the time Columbus's ships entered the waters outside Spain, of the 550 captured Indians he took with him two hundred had died. Says Cuneo: "We cast them into the sea." When they reached Cadiz, half of the remaining 350 slaves were sick and dying. Only a relative few survived much longer, because, Cuneo surmised, "they are not working people and they very much fear cold, nor have they long life."

This final point—"nor have they long life"—would not have been true a few years earlier: the health and life expectancy of the natives had been far superior to that of the Europeans prior to the Columbian invasion. But by the time Cuneo was writing he was certainly correct. Once the first Spanish settlements had taken root, the hold on life that any Indian had, at any given moment, was tenuous at best. Spanish diseases had begun their own invasion of the Americas almost from the moment Columbus and his crews first breathed upon their New World hosts. But the systematic, genocidal destruction of the Indians did not begin until Columbus's return.

Columbus's second voyage was the true beginning of the invasion of the Americas. The royal instructions authorizing the expedition had directed that the finest ships in Andalusia be outfitted for the trip and that they be commanded by the most expert pilots and navigators in the realm. Seventeen ships made the voyage and aboard those ships were more than 1200 soldiers, sailors, and colonists—including a cavalry troop of lancers and half a dozen priests. Along the way, at the Canary Islands, some other passengers were boarded: goats and sheep and cattle, and eight pigs, were placed on deck and in the holds below.

In early January of 1494 the fleet arrived at the place on the northern coast of Hispaniola that Columbus had chosen to build his New World capital, his town of Isabela. No sooner were the ships unloaded, however, than sickness broke out among the crews. It quickly spread among the natives, who had come to greet the ships with gifts of fish and fruits, "as if we had been their brothers," recalled one of the men on board. Within a few days, the Admiral's surgeon reported, a third of the Spaniards had fallen ill, while natives everywhere were dead. Columbus directed groups of the healthy among his crews to explore the island's inland regions and find the fabulous gold mines they all were sure existed. But many of those men returned to the ships, having come down with the mysterious illness along the way.

For years historians have speculated as to what the epidemic was that laid low so many Spaniards and killed so many native people. Carl Sauer thought it might have been some sort of intestinal infection, while Samuel Eliot Morison diagnosed it as either malaria or something caused by "drinking well water and eating strange fish." Most recently, Kirkpatrick Sale has opted for bacillic dysentery—although he too lists malaria or even syphilis as among the likely culprits. Others have thought it everything from smallpox to yellow fever. While it is possible (even probable) that more than one disease was causing the afflictions, the reported symptoms had nothing of the signs of syphilis, and malaria was not then present in the Indies or the Americas, nor would it be for many years to come. For the same reasons, it could not have been yellow fever or smallpox that was wreaking all this havoc, and it certainly did not derive from something the Spanish ate or drank, because it spread like wildfire not only among the Spanish, but with particular virulence among the Indian people all across the island. No, the most recent and original medically informed hypothesis—and the one that goes the furthest in explaining reported symptoms, including high mortality, and the extraordinary contagiousness—identifies influenza as the cause, influenza carried by those Canary Islands pigs.

If, as the Spanish physician and medical historian Francisco Guerra now contends, the epidemic that ravaged Hispaniola in 1494 was swine influenza, it would have been a pestilence of devastating proportions. For it now appears that it was swine flu that swept the world in 1918, killing off at least 20,000,000 people before it finally dissipated. Like other people in the Americas, and unlike the Spanish, the natives of Hispaniola had no previous exposure to the virus—nor to the numerous other diseases that historically, in other parts of the world, had spread from domesticated animal hosts. Other than small dogs in some locations and llamas in the Andes, few animals were domesticated anywhere in the hemisphere. And of the many plagues that in time would overwhelm the Americas' native peoples, influenza—of various types, from both humans and non-human vectors—was second only to smallpox and maybe measles as the most rapid epidemic killer of them all.

Whatever it was, in any case, the imported pathogen moved among the native people with a relentlessness that nothing ever had in all their history. "So many Indians died that they could not be counted," wrote Gonzalo Fernández de Oviedo, adding that "all through the land the Indians lay dead everywhere. The stench was very great and pestiferous." And in the wake of the plague they had introduced, the Spanish soldiers followed, seeking gold from the natives, or information as to where to find it. They were troubled by the illness, and numbers of them died from it. But unlike the island natives the European invaders and their forebears had lived with epidemic pestilence for ages. Their lungs were damaged from it, their faces scarred with pocks, but accumulations of disease exposure allowed them now to weather much. So they carried infections with them everywhere they went—burdensome, but rarely fatal, except to the natives that they met.

Following the Admiral's orders, reconnaissance parties were sent out across the island and off to Cuba, Jamaica, and to other nearby lands. The Spanish plagues raced on ahead. Still, the natives, as Columbus had observed during his first voyage, continued to be kind and generous to their guests, and so innocent in the use of dangerous weapons that when Columbus "showed them swords," he said, "they grasped them by the blade and cut themselves through ignorance."

Wherever the marauding, diseased, and heavily armed Spanish forces went out on patrol, accompanied by ferocious armored dogs that had been trained to kill and disembowel, they preyed on the local communities—already plague-enfeebled—forcing them to supply food and women and slaves, and whatever else the soldiers might desire. At virtually every previous landing on this trip Columbus's troops had gone ashore and killed indiscriminately, as though for sport, whatever animals and birds and natives they encountered, "looting and destroying all they found," as the Admiral's son Fernando blithely

Illustrated works like Pére Bartolomé de Las Casas' Very Brief Account of the Destruction of the Indies helped to spread the story of Spanish atrocities in the New World. The young priest described in his journals how the conquerors pursued the natives and "pitilessly slaughtered everyone like sheep in a corral." (Clements Library, University of Michigan)

put it. Once on Hispaniola, however, Columbus fell ill—whether from the flu or, more likely, from some other malady—and what little restraint he had maintained over his men disappeared as he went through a lengthy period of recuperation. The troops went wild, stealing, killing, raping, and torturing natives, trying to force them to divulge the whereabouts of the imagined treasure-houses of gold.

The Indians tried to retaliate by launching ineffective ambushes of stray Spaniards. But the combined killing force of Spanish diseases and Spanish military might was far greater than anything the natives could ever have imagined. Finally, they decided the best response was flight. Crops were left to rot in the fields as the Indians attempted to escape the frenzy of the conquistadors' attacks. Starvation then added its contribution, along with pestilence and mass murder, to the native peoples' woes.

Some desperate Hispaniola natives fled to other islands. One of these, a *cacique* named Hatuey, brought with him to Cuba as many of his surviving people as he could—and what little gold that they possessed. Once there, in a place called Punta Maisi, he assembled his followers together and displayed for them the treasures that they had, explaining that this was what the Spanish troops were after, that these apparently were objects of worship to the murderous invaders. Whereupon, to protect his people from the greed and savagery of these vile strangers, he threw the gold to the bottom of a nearby river.

It didn't work. The Spanish found Hatuey and his people, killed most of them, enslaved the others, and condemned their leader to be burned alive. Reportedly, as they were tying him to the stake, a Franciscan friar urged him to take Jesus to his heart so that his soul might go to heaven, rather than descend into hell. Hatuey replied that if heaven was where the Christians went, he would rather go to hell.

The massacres continued. Columbus remained ill for months while his soldiers wandered freely. More than 50,000 natives were reported dead from these encounters by the time the Admiral had recovered from his sickness. And when at last his health and strength had been restored, Columbus's response to his men's unorganized depredations was to organize them. In March of 1495 he massed together several hundred armored troops, cavalry, and a score or more of trained attack dogs. They set forth across the countryside, tearing into assembled masses of sick and unarmed native people, slaughtering them by the thousands. The pattern set by these raids would be the model the Spanish would follow for the next decade and beyond. As Bartolomé de Las Casas, the most famous of the accompanying Spanish missionaries from that trip recalled:

Once the Indians were in the woods, the next step was to form squadrons and pursue them, and whenever the Spaniards found them, they pitilessly slaughtered everyone like sheep in a corral. It was a general rule among Spaniards to be cruel; not just cruel, but extraordinarily cruel so that harsh and bitter treatment would prevent Indians from daring to think of themselves as human beings or having a minute to think at all. So they would cut an Indian's hands and leave them dangling by a shred of skin and they would send him on saying "Go now, spread the news to your chiefs." They would test their swords and their manly strength on captured Indians and place bets on the slicing

off of heads or the cutting of bodies in half with one blow. They burned or hanged captured chiefs.

At least one chief, the man considered by Columbus to be Hispaniola's ranking native leader, was not burned or hanged, however. He was captured, put in chains, and sent off by ship for public display and imprisonment in Spain. Like most of the Indians who had been forced to make that voyage, though, he never made it to Seville: he died en route.

With the same determination Columbus had shown in organizing his troops' previously disorganized and indiscriminate killings, the Admiral then set about the task of systematizing their haphazard enslavement of the natives. Gold was all that they were seeking, so every Indian on the island who was not a child was ordered to deliver to the Spanish a certain amount of the precious ore every three months. When the gold was delivered the individual was presented with a token to wear around his or her neck as proof that the tribute had been paid. Anyone found without the appropriate number of tokens had his hands cut off.

Since Hispaniola's gold supply was far less than what the Spaniards' fantasies suggested, Indians who wished to survive were driven to seek out their quotas of the ore at the expense of other endeavors, including food production. The famines that had begun earlier, when the Indians attempted to hide from the Spanish murderers, now grew much worse, while new diseases that the Spanish carried with them preyed ever more intensely on the malnourished and weakened bodies of the natives. And the soldiers never ceased to take delight in killing just for fun.

Spanish reports of their own murderous sadism during this time are legion. For a lark they "tore babes from their mother's breast by their feet, and dashed their heads against the rocks." The bodies of other infants "they spitted . . . together with their mothers and all who were before them, on their swords." On one famous occasion in Cuba a troop of a hundred or more Spaniards stopped by the banks of a dry river and sharpened their swords on the whetstones in its bed. Eager to compare the sharpness of their blades, reported an eyewitness to the events, they drew their weapons and

began to rip open the bellies, to cut and kill those lambs—men, women, children, and old folk, all of whom were seated, off guard and frightened, watching the mares and the Spaniards. And within two credos, not a man of all of them there remains alive. The Spaniards enter the large house nearby, for this was happening at its door, and in the same way, with cuts and stabs, begin to kill as many as they found there, so that a stream of blood was running, as if a great number of cows had perished. . . . To see the wounds which covered the bodies of the dead and dying was a spectacle of horror and dread.

This particular slaughter began at the village of Zucayo, where the townsfolk earlier had provided for the conquistadors a feast of cassava, fruit, and fish. From there it spread. No one knows just how many Indians the Spanish killed in this sadistic spree, but Las Casas put the number at well over 20,000 before the soldiers' thirst for horror had been slaked.

Another report, this one by a group of concerned Dominican friars, concentrated on the way the Spanish soldiers treated native infants:

Some Christians encounter an Indian woman, who was carrying in her arms a child at suck; and since the dog they had with them was hungry, they tore the child from the mother's arms and flung it still living to the dog, who proceeded to devour it before the mother's eyes. . . . When there were among the prisoners some women who had recently given birth, if the new-born babes happened to cry, they seized them by the legs and hurled them against the rocks, or flung them into the jungle so that they would be certain to die there.

Or, Las Casas again, in another incident he witnessed:

The Spaniards found pleasure in inventing all kinds of odd cruelties, the more cruel the better, with which to spill human blood. They built a long gibbet, low enough for the toes to touch the ground and prevent strangling, and hanged thirteen [natives] at a time in honor of Christ Our Saviour and the twelve Apostles. When the Indians were thus still alive and hanging, the Spaniards tested their strength and their blades against them, ripping chests open with one blow and exposing entrails, and there were those who did worse. Then, straw was wrapped around their torn bodies and they were burned alive. One man caught two children about two years old, pierced their throats with a dagger, then hurled them down a precipice.

If some of this has a sickeningly familiar ring to readers who recall the massacres at My Lai and Song My and other Vietnamese villages in the not too distant past, the familiarity is reinforced by the term the Spanish used to describe their campaign of terror: "pacification." But as horrific as those bloodbaths were in Vietnam, in sheer magnitude they were as nothing compared with what happened on the single island of Hispaniola five hundred years ago: the island's population of about eight million people at the time of Columbus's arrival in 1492 already had declined by a third to a half before the year 1496 was out. And after 1496 the death rate, if anything, accelerated.

In plotting on a graph the decline of Hispaniola's native population there appears a curious bulge, around the year 1510, when the diminishing numbers seemed to stabilize and even grow a bit. Then the inexorable downward spiral toward extinction continues. What that little blip on the demographic record indicates is not, however, a moment of respite for the island's people, nor a contradiction to the overall pattern of Hispaniola's population free-fall following Columbus's arrival. Rather, it is a shadowy and passing footnote to the holocaust the Spanish at the same time were bringing to the *rest* of the Caribbean, for that fleeting instant of population stabilization was caused by the importation of tens of thousands of slaves from surrounding islands in a fruitless attempt by the Spanish to replace the dying natives of Hispaniola.

But death seized these imported slaves as quickly as it had Hispaniola's natives. And thus, the islands of the Bahamas were rapidly stripped of perhaps half a million people, in large part for use as short-lived replacements by the Spanish for Hispaniola's nearly eradicated indigenous inhabitants. Then Cuba, with its enormous population, suffered the same fate. With the Caribbean's millions of native people thereby effectively liquidated in barely a quarter of a century, forced through the murderous vortex of Spanish savagery and greed, the slavers turned next to the smaller islands off the mainland coast. The first raid took place in 1515 when natives from Guanaja in the Bay Islands off Honduras were captured and taken to forced labor camps in depopulated Cuba. Other slave expeditions followed, and by 1525, when Cortés arrived in the region, all the Bay Islands themselves had been entirely shorn of their inhabitants.

In order to exploit most fully the land and its populace, and to satisfy the increasingly dangerous and rebellion-organizing ambitions of his well-armed Spanish troops, Columbus instituted a program called the *repartimiento* or "Indian grants"—later referred to, in a revised version, as the system of *encomiendas*. This was a dividing-up, not of the land, but of entire peoples and communities, and the bestowal of them upon a would-be Spanish master. The master was free to do what he wished with "his people"—have them plant, have them work in the mines, have them do anything, as Carl Sauer puts it, "without limit or benefit of tenure."

The result was an even greater increase in cruelty and a magnification of the firestorm of human devastation. Caring only for short-term material wealth that could be wrenched up from the earth, the Spanish overlords on Hispaniola removed their slaves to unfamiliar locales—"the roads to the mines were like anthills," Las Casas recalled—deprived them of food, and forced them to work until they dropped. At the mines and fields in which they labored, the Indians were herded together under the supervision of Spanish overseers, known as *mineros* in the mines and *estancieros* on the plantations, who "treated the Indians with such rigor and inhumanity that they seemed the very ministers of Hell, driving them day and night with

beatings, kicks, lashes and blows and calling them no sweeter names than dogs." Needless to say, some Indians attempted to escape from this. They were hunted down with mastiffs. When found, if not torn apart on the spot, they were returned and a show-trial was held for them, and for the edification of other Indians who were made to stand and watch. The escapees were

brought before the *visitador* [Spanish inspector-magistrate] and the accuser, that is, the supposedly pious master, who accused them of being rebellious dogs and good-for-nothings and demanded stiff punishment. The *visitador* then had them tied to a post and he himself, with his own hands, as the most honorable man in town, took a sailor's tarred whip as tough as iron, the kind they use in galleys, and flogged them until blood ran from their naked bodies, mere skin and bones from starvation. Then, leaving them for dead, he stopped and threatened the same punishment if they tried it again.

Occasionally, when slaves were so broken by illness, malnutrition, or exhaustion unto death that they became incapable of further labor output, they were dismissed from the mines or the fields where they worked. Las Casas estimated that perhaps 10 percent of the Indian conscripts survived long enough for this to happen. However, he continued:

When they were allowed to go home, they often found it deserted and had no other recourse than to go out into the woods to find food and to die. When they fell ill, which was very frequently because they are a delicate people unaccustomed to such work, the Spaniards did not believe them and pitilessly called them lazy dogs, and kicked and beat them; and when illness was apparent they sent them home as useless, giving them some cassava for the twenty- to eighty-league journey. They would go then, falling into the first stream and dying there in desperation; others would hold on longer, but very few ever made it home. I sometimes came upon dead bodies on my way, and upon others who were gasping and moaning in their death agony, repeating "Hungry, hungry."

In the face of utter hopelessness, the Indians began simply surrendering their lives. Some committed suicide. Many refused to have children, recognizing that their offspring, even if they successfully endured the Spanish cruelties, would only become slaves themselves. And others, wrote Las Casas,

saw that without any offence on their part they were despoiled of their kingdoms, their lands and liberties and of their lives, their wives, and homes. As they saw themselves each day perishing by the cruel and inhuman treatment of the Spaniards, crushed to the earth by the horses, cut in pieces by swords, eaten and torn by dogs, many buried alive and suffering all kinds of exquisite tortures . . . [they] decided to abandon themselves to their unhappy fate with no further struggles, placing themselves in the hands of their enemies that they might do with them as they liked.

Other natives, in time, did find ways to become reunited with whatever remained of their families. But when most wives and husbands were brought back together,

they were so exhausted and depressed on both sides that they had no mind for marital communication and in this way they ceased to procreate. As for the newly born, they died early because their mothers, overworked and famished, had no milk to nurse them, and for this reason, while I was in Cuba, 7,000 babies died in three months. Some mothers even drowned their babies from sheer desperation, while others caused themselves to abort with certain herbs that produced stillborn children. In this way husbands died in the mines, wives died at work, and children died from lack of milk, while others had not time or energy for procreation, and in a short time this land which was so great, so powerful and fertile, though so unfortunate, was depopulated.

By 1496, we already have noted, the population of Hispaniola had fallen from eight million to between four and five million. By 1508 it was down to less than a hundred thousand. By 1518 it numbered less than twenty thousand. And by 1535, say the leading scholars on this grim topic, "for all practical purposes, the native population was extinct."

In less than the normal lifetime of a single human being, an entire culture of millions of people, thousands of years resident in their homeland, had been exterminated. The same fate befell the native peoples of the surrounding islands in the Caribbean as well. Of all the horrific genocides that have occurred in the twentieth century against Armenians, Jews, Gypsies, Ibos, Bengalis, Timorese, Kampucheans, Ugandans, and more, none has come close to destroying this many—or this great a proportion—of wholly innocent people.

And then the Spanish turned their attention to the mainland of Mexico and Central America. The slaughter had barely begun.

This, of course, was only the beginning of the Indian holocaust perpetrated by the invading Europeans—first the Spaniards, then the Portuguese, then the British, and later the Anglo-Americans. Selection 21 will introduce you to the early Indian policy of the United States, and to President Andrew Jackson's ruthless treatment of the Cherokees.

QUESTIONS TO CONSIDER

1 Describe life in the big cities of Europe when Columbus set sail in 1492. What was "in-migration," and why did it save those early cities from extinction? Describe the great disparity that existed between the rich and poor in fifteenth-century Europe.

2 If one ventured outside the cities of Europe, was the quality of life better in the countryside? Given the graphic descriptions of living conditions pictured in this essay, explain why the people of Europe frequently turned on each other during witchcraft hysteria.

3 What perceived needs preoccupied the wealthy of Europe, and why were these desires an incentive for the voyages of Columbus and his contemporaries? Did the native people that Columbus encountered have an abundance of gold? Explain the system that Columbus

developed to encourage these people to find gold and the punishment he inflicted if they failed.

4 Describe Columbus's first impressions of the new land he "discovered" and the people who inhabited it. What significance did his landing in the New World have to the Catholic church in Spain?

5 In what way was the *requerimiento* only an excuse to treat native people brutally, confiscate their land, and enslave them? What was the likely disease that killed so many Native Americans when Columbus returned on his second voyage and established the town of Isabela? Why were the native people more vulnerable to this plague than the Spanish?

6 *Genocide* and *holocaust* are strong value-laden words that are usually associated with the horrible actions of Nazi Germany during World War II. Do these words apply to what the Spanish did to the native people they encountered? If so, what motivated such unpardonable actions—was it a conscious greed for gold or an unconscious disregard for human life?

2   From These Beginnings

PAGE SMITH

The European arrival in the Americas brought about a clash of imperial energies as Spain, Portugal, France, and eventually England vied with one another in staking claims to the "New World." For a time, it seemed that Spain would become the dominant imperial power in the New World. While Portugal received Brazil, thanks to an edict from the Pope in 1493, Spain claimed the rest of South and Central America and sent out explorers to look for gold and silver there. By the 1550s, powerful Spain had a sprawling colonial empire that comprised most of South America, Central America, Mexico, the Caribbean islands, Florida, and the American Southwest from Texas to California. As one historian pointed out, Spain established "the largest and most populous empire the western world had seen since the fall of Rome." The industrious Spaniards introduced to the New World the cattle ranch, horses, cattle, sheep, goats, burros, swine, and most of the lingo of the cowboy (rodeo, lariat, mustang, cinch, bronco, and chaps). The Spanish home government, thanks to the eloquent entreaties of Father Bartolomé de Las Casas, also tried to stop the brutal enslavement and extermination of the Native Americans, which the Spaniards themselves had begun.

Meanwhile French explorers searched eastern Canada for the Northwest Passage, a legendary waterway that was supposed to connect the Atlantic and Pacific Oceans and that, under France's control, would give France access to the luxuries of Asia. Unable to find such a passage, France was content to establish a fur-trading empire in Canada, with French explorers, traders, and missionaries advancing west to the Great Lakes and then southward down the Mississippi to New Orleans.

England, however, was slow to join the race for colonies, although John Cabot's voyage to North America in 1497 had given England a claim to the New World. Finally, under Queen Elizabeth, the English challenged Spain's rule of the oceans and domination of the New World. Adventurous "sea dogs" under John Hawkins raided Spanish commerce on both the Atlantic and the Pacific, and in 1588, in a dramatic sea battle, the English navy defeated the Spanish armada, a victory that gave England virtually undisputed control of the seas. Thanks to the persuasive arguments of Sir Walter Raleigh, Sir Humphrey Gilbert, and Richard Hakluyt, all champions of colonization, England at last began to build a New World empire. After an abortive attempt to found a colony on

Roanoke Island, North Carolina, Queen Elizabeth and her successor James I authorized private corporations called joint stock companies to establish the Virginia (first known as Jamestown), Plymouth, and Massachusetts Bay colonies.

From the outset, the Indians, from the Pequots of Massachusetts to the Powhatans of Virginia, posed the biggest obstacle to English conquest and settlement in North America. How to deal with them? The London-based leaders of Massachusetts and Virginia directed their settlers to treat the Indians "humanely," to christianize, feed, and clothe them, instruct them in "the manual arts and skills," and incorporate them into "the English community" so that they could enjoy the amenities of "civilization."

These instructions, of course, were based on the European misconception of the Indian as a savage. Although the Indians possessed a culture as old, as rich, and as religious as any in Europe, whites typically thought of them as "bad people, having little of humanity but shape, ignorant of civility or arts, or religion; more brutish than the beasts they hunt, more wild and unmanly than that unmanned wild country, which they range rather than inhabit." Racial prejudice fed that hostile attitude. In European eyes, these dark-skinned people were "pernicious creatures" and barbarians. Only violence would keep them in line. As one European man said, "Unless we bang the Indians stoutly, and make them fear us, they will never love us, nor keep the peace long with us."

And bang the Indians they did, killing off whole tribes and driving others into the interior, where they had to force their way into areas inhabited by other tribes. Some Indians—the Powhatans and Pequots, among them—resisted the colonists and were wiped out. Others, like the Piscataway Indians of Maryland, managed to accommodate themselves to the invaders and thus to preserve "their cultural integrity." Those Indians who did convert to Christianity and adopt the white man's way remained second-class citizens.

Writes historian James Freeman Hawke, "The white man took from the Indian what he could use. The Indian paths through the woods eventually became the settlers' ways and roads. Like the natives, they girdled trees to open up the forest to sunlight. They planted, harvested, and cooked native crops as the Indians did. The Indian taught them how to use snowshoes, how to convert animal pelts into warm winter clothing, how to make a dugout canoe and a pair of moccasins. . . . These borrowings helped to speed the white man's adjustment to the strange new world but did not fundamentally alter his culture." As we saw in the first selection, most of what the Indians got from the Europeans, especially their deadly diseases, virtually destroyed the Indian way of life.

As the number of colonies increased in the seventeenth century, a great migration began to English North America. That migration is the subject of this selection by historian Page Smith, who writes from the standpoint of the European immigrants, thus giving a different perspective from that in the opening selection. With a vivid pen and an eye for telling detail, Smith discusses the remarkable hodgepodge of humanity that streamed into the English colonies from more than a dozen European countries. Among them, of course, were hardy farmers, aspiring merchants, indentured servants, and visionary religious groups in search of better secular and spiritual lives. But the unfortunate and the disreputable came as well, ranging from English boys who were stolen and sold into bondage, to convicted felons and "rogues and vagabonds" shipped out to the colonies by the British government. As Smith explains, "rogues and vagabonds" included a variety of outlawed folk—beggars, prostitutes, drunkards, dancers, fiddlers, fencers, actors, jugglers, dice players, minstrels, fortunetellers, charlatans, tinkers, peddlers, and loiterers, all of whom played some part in the drama of colonization. From farmers to felons, this diverse assortment of individuals went on to seize the eastern coast of North America and to forge a new nation in the wilderness.

GLOSSARY

CALVINISTS   Those who subscribed to the religious teachings of John Calvin (1509–1664), a French theologian and a leader in the Protestant Reformation, who stressed God's sovereignty, the supremacy of the Scriptures, and predestination—the notion that one's fate was already determined by an all-powerful God and that human beings could do nothing to achieve their salvation or alter their fate.

DURAND   French Protestant who described the lovemaking of indentured servants during a passage to colonial America.

GREAT AWAKENING   Religious revival that swept the English colonies from about 1725 to 1770.

HUGUENOTS   French Protestants who fled from persecution in Catholic countries such as France.

INDENTURED SERVANT   A man or woman bound over to a master for a period of servitude; in exchange, the master paid the servant's way to the colonies and provided food and shelter.

MITTELBERGER, GOTTLIEB   German immigrant from Enzweiningen who provided a dramatic account of his voyage to America.

PENN, WILLIAM (1644–1718)   English Quaker who founded the colony of Pennsylvania as a refuge for Quakers.

REDEMPTIONERS   Bound servants similar to indentured servants, "they were carried to America by a ship captain with the understanding that after they reached the colonies, they would undertake to sell themselves to the highest bidder and then pay the captain the cost of their passage."

The American Colonists came from a variety of backgrounds. . . . What united them was the wilderness to which they came, a vast land . . . [that] was, literally, incomprehensible; it reached beyond the mind's imagining, threatening and promising, larger than all of Europe: coastal shelf and then mountains and endless plains and more mountains and, finally, the Pacific. No one could measure its extent. The English settlers for their part clung to its eastern margins, to the seacoast strip that faced the ocean highway to the Old World. Even here there were terrains, climates, and topographies as dramatically different as one could imagine—from the rocky, frigid shores of New Hampshire to the sunny beaches of South Carolina.

There was a kind of mad presumption about the whole venture: a few thousand, and then a few hundred thousand, and finally a few million souls scattered along almost two thousand miles of coastline. And in truth it could be said that those who made this strange odyssey to the New World were as diverse as the land they inhabited. Those from England itself represented every class and condition of men. And then there were the Swedes, who settled on the Delaware long before William Penn and his followers arrived, and the stolid and intractable Dutch, reputed to have bought Manhattan from the [Indians] for a few strings of beads—the most famous real estate deal in history. And the French Huguenots, Protestants fleeing from persecution in a Catholic country; the Catholics of Maryland, fleeing persecution in a Protestant country; the Quakers, fleeing the harassments of the Anglican establishment, the Church of England; and Germans from innumerable principalities, fleeing military draft and the various exactions of petty princes.

Within the British Isles themselves—Ireland, Scotland, England and Wales—there was striking diversity among the New World emigrants. The Separatists—the Pilgrims under William Bradford—wanted, in essence, to be separate; the Puritans wanted to found a Bible Commonwealth and redeem a fallen world. When Cromwell and the Puritans dominated England and beheaded Charles I, certain Royalists found refuge in Virginia and New York. When the restoration of the monarchy brought Charles II to the English throne and reestablished the Stuart line, the regicides—those

Page Smith, extracts from *A People's History of the American Revolution*, Vol. II: *A New Age Begins*, pp. 28–47, McGraw-Hill Publishing Company. Used by permission of the author.

involved in the execution of Charles I—found refuge in Puritan New England. When the Scottish Covenanters, or Presbyterians, so akin in spirit to the Puritans of New England, rose against the high-handed and tyrannical actions of the re-established monarchy, they were crushingly defeated . . . and cruelly repressed. Many, in consequence, came to America. And they continued to come for a hundred years. . . .

And then there were the Irish. They were a special case. They fled famine and rent-wracking landlords. . . . A Catholic people, they fled their Protestant masters. But above all they fled poverty, the poverty of a ruthlessly exploited peasantry. Generation after generation, the Irish came to the American colonies, primarily to Maryland and Pennsylvania, where they gravitated to the frontier areas. In addition to the Catholic Irish, Scotch-Irish Presbyterians came in substantial numbers to the colonies throughout the eighteenth century. The Scotch-Irish were those Covenanters, or militant Presbyterians, who had been forced by the bitter divisions in Scotland itself to seek the protection of the English armies in Northern Ireland (hence Scotch-Irish). For many of them, Ireland was little more than a way station to the colonies, where they showed a marked preference for Pennsylvania and settled, typically, on the frontier. . . .

So the immigrants came in an ever-growing tide—the hungry, the oppressed, the contentious, the ambitious, those out of power and out of favor, the losers, whether in the realm of politics or of economics. And America could accommodate them all: Irish peasant and his land-poor master, Scottish Highlander and Lowlander, persecuted Protestant and persecuted Catholic, fortune-seeker and God-seeker, they found their places, their kinfolk, the familiar accents of their home shires or counties or countries.

But the essence of them all, of all that human congress, the bone and marrow, the unifying principle, the prevailing and pervasive spirit was English. Like the others who came, the English came . . . for a number of reasons. Most of them shared some

particular expectation, whether for spiritual or material betterment or, happily, both. Many of those who came later shared, of course, the hopes of the original settlers. Many more came because conditions were desperately hard in England and Ireland for poor people, even for those who had not yet sunk into the pit of abandoned hopelessness that was the lot of the most wretched.

It has been estimated that London in the eighteenth century had 6,000 adult and 9,300 child beggars. In the entire country of some 10,000,000 persons, there were estimated to be 50,000 beggars, 20,000 vagrants, 10,000 idlers, 100,000 prostitutes, 10,000 rogues and vagabonds, 80,000 criminals, 1,041,000 persons on parish relief. Indeed, over half the population was below what we would call today "the poverty line," and many, of course, were profoundly below it—below it to the point of starvation. An estimate of the different classes—and class lines were almost impassable—in 1688 suggests that nobility, gentry, merchants, professionals, freeholders (those who held land on their own), craftsmen, and public officials constituted 47 per cent of the population; while common sailors and soldiers (recruited, for the most part, from the lowest levels of British society and enduring desperately hard conditions of service), laborers, servants, paupers, and all those other remarkable subdivisions that we have listed above such as rogues and vagrants made up 53 per cent of the population. The colonies, for their part, had a virtually inexhaustible demand for labor. Anyone willing to work could be put to worthwhile labor, and might (and often did) in a few years establish himself as an independent farmer or artisan.

Yet it was one thing to be an undernourished London apprentice who hated his master and another to find a way to get to America. Some indication of the situation of the working class in the larger cities may be discerned from the condition of pauper children in London in the early eighteenth century. Orphaned, or more frequently illegitimate and abandoned at birth, they were sent to workhouses and to parish nurses. A Parliamentary study found that of all such infants born or received in

German immigrants in Georgia. "The immigrants came in an ever-growing tide," Page Smith writes, "the hungry, the oppressed, the contentious, the ambitious, those out of power and out of favor, the losers, whether in the realm of politics or of economics." (New York Public Library, Rare Book Room, Astor, Lenox and Tilden Foundations.)

London's workhouses in a three-year period, only seven in every hundred were alive at the end of that time. As part of the "surcharge of necessitous people," orphaned and impoverished children who were public charges were sporadically dispatched to the colonies as indentured servants. People worked, typically, from six in the morning until eight at night for a pittance that barely supported life. They had no holidays except at Christmas, Easter, and on hanging days, when everyone might be entertained and edified by watching wretches hanged for crimes that, in many instances, would be classed as misdemeanors today.

Despite the cruelty of punishments, London had a large criminal class and was infested with prostitutes. The working class drowned its miseries in bad gin and beer. There were some 7,000 ginshops in the suburbs of London and, by 1750, 16,000 in the city itself (only 1,050 of which were licensed); most of them were in the poorest sections of the city, whose horrors are vividly recorded in Hogarth's etchings of Gin Lane. The hard liquor consumed in one year (1733) in London alone amounted to 11,200,000 gallons, or some 56 gallons per adult male.

2 FROM THESE BEGINNINGS   21

Next to public hangings, the principal entertainments available to the poor—and enjoyed by the rich as well—were cockfighting, bullbaiting, and badger baiting. In such circumstances there was ample incentive to emigrate almost anywhere. . . . But to the penniless, the question was: How? The growing need for labor in the colonies supplied the answer, and a system of indenture, based on the long-established apprenticeship, was devised. Agents paid for the ship's passage of improvident men and women who were willing to contract themselves in America to work off the cost of their transportation. By this means, tens of thousands of English and Irish workers of both sexes found their way across the ocean.

The system was easily and often abused. A class of men "of the lowest order," called spirits and crimps, arose, who spirited away unwilling lads and sold them into bondage. . . . One spirit boasted that he had been spiriting persons for twelve years at a rate of five hundred persons a year. He would give twenty-five shillings to anyone who would bring him a likely prospect, and he could sell such a one to a merchant at once for forty shillings. Often spiriting was a profitable sideline for a brewer, hostler, carpenter, or tavern keeper. The tavern keeper was in an especially advantageous position, since a drunken patron was an easy victim. So dreaded were these dismal agents that mothers frightened their children into obedience by warning them that a spirit would carry them off if they were bad. It was no idle threat. In 1653 Robert Broome secured a warrant for the arrest of a ship's captain charged with carrying off his son, aged eleven, who had been spirited aboard. A few years later, a commission going aboard the *Conquer* found that eleven out of nineteen servants had been "taken by the spirits." Their average age was nineteen. Not all spirits were depraved men, however, and even the worst of them often performed a useful service in arranging transportation for a servant who wished to emigrate to the colonies against the wishes of parents or a master. . . .

For a time it proved easier to get women servants than men servants. . . . Mathew Cradock, captain of the *Abraham,* sailing for Virginia, made elaborate preparations for carrying a shipload of servants, men and women alike, to Virginia on a four-year indenture. On his ship's arrival in various English ports, . . . he rounded up forty-one men and twenty women, the latter "from 17 to 35 yeares and very lustye and strong Boddied. . . ."

Clothing, "peppar and Gingar," and three-and-a-half pounds of tobacco for the men were all purchased before the ship set sail, and a midwife was hired to make sure none of the women were pregnant. Soon after the ship sailed it was driven into the harbor of Cowes, and it was a month before it got favorable winds. By that time, three of the women were pregnant and were sent home; some who were put ashore to do the washing ran away and had to be tracked down at a cost of ten shillings; and another was found "not fette to be entertained haveing the frentche dizeas [gonorrhea]" and was sent packing.

If a female indentured servant became pregnant during her service, her misdeed represented a loss to her master, so that an indentured servant guilty of bastardy was required to pay the usual charges levied against unwed mothers as well as to indemnify her master for the loss of her services during the later stages of her pregnancy and her lying-in. Not infrequently, the master was the culprit. In Maryland, Jacob Lumbrozo [of Portugal] . . . alias Dr. John, was charged with having made persistent overtures to his maid, Elisabeth Weales, and when rebuffed, "hee tooke her in his armes and threw her upon the bed she went to Cry out hee plucked out his handerchif of his pocket and stope her mouth and force her whether shee will or noe when hee know that she was with Child he gave her fickes to distroy it and for anything shee know hee would distroy her too. . . ." By the time the case came to court, Lumbrozo had married Elisabeth Weales, who became a prominent if contentious figure in the affairs of the county. In Virginia, a statute was passed to prevent a master who had impregnated his servant girl from claiming extra service from her beyond her indenture: "Late experiments shew that some dissolute masters have gotten their maides with child, and yet claime the benefitt of their service." However, the maid got off no better. After the end of her indenture she was to be sold by the church wardens for the use of the parish for two years. . . .

The terms of indenture required the master to provide food and clothing for his servants and, often in the case of German or Swiss servants, to take the responsibility for seeing that they learned English during the term of their indenture. At the end of their terms they were to be provided with a stated sum of money and a suit of presentable clothes so that they could make a proper start in life. South Carolina required that a female servant at the expiration of her service be given a waistcoat and petticoat, a new shift of white linen, shoes and stockings, a blue apron and two white linen caps. In some colonies, indentured servants received land at the end of their term of indenture. Thus in North Carolina during the proprietary period a servant's "freedom dues" were fifty acres of land and afterward three barrels of Indian corn and two new suits of a value of at least five pounds. . . ."

Whether wickedly abused or treasured and rewarded—and certainly they experienced both cruelty and kindness—indentured servants made up more than half the immigrants to the middle and southern colonies. During the twenty-five-year period between 1750 and 1775, some 25,000 servants and convicts entered Maryland, and a comparable number arrived in Virginia. Abbott Smith estimates that during the same period at least twice as many servants and redemptioners entered Pennsylvania, of whom perhaps a third were German and the rest, in large part, Irish. The Irish . . . were Catholics. To Protestants, this fact made the Irish the least desirable of all immigrant groups. The more substantial class of immigrants, especially the Germans and the Swiss, came as redemptioners. Redemptioners were carried to America by a ship captain with the understanding that after they reached the colonies, they would undertake to sell themselves to the highest bidder and then pay the captain the cost of their passage. Most of the redemptioners were craftsmen whose skills were much in demand in the colonies and who

could thus sell themselves on favorable terms to a master. If they could not sell themselves, it was the shipmaster's right to undertake to sell them, often at highly disadvantageous terms. Since a master could buy much cheaper from a ship captain, collusion between prospective buyers and the captain was not uncommon.

The story of indentured servants is one of the most dramatic in colonial America. While many of those who came under indenture were the "scum and offscourings of the earth"—convicts, paupers, runaway apprentices, prostitutes and the like—many, particularly among the non-English, were respectable and decent people who had fallen on hard times or simply wished to improve their fortunes. We also know that in the rude conditions of colonial life, many of the dissolute were redeemed.

In seventeenth- and eighteenth-century England, crime was endemic. The alarm of the more prosperous classes was expressed in cries for law and order. The penalty of death was prescribed for all felonies. In seventeenth-century England, almost three hundred crimes were classed as felonies; a conviction for anything, indeed, from housebreaking and the theft of goods worth more than a shilling must result in the sentence of death by hanging, since the judge had no discretionary power in felony cases. The benefit of clergy and royal pardon were the only mitigations. A convicted felon could "call for the book," usually a Bible, and if he could read it, he was freed of the penalty of death, branded on the thumb, and released. The practice stemmed from medieval times, when generally speaking only those in holy orders were able to read, and they were subject to their own ecclesiastical courts. The benefit of clergy was undoubtedly a great incentive to the development of a literate criminal class, but in a time when a vast majority of the poor were illiterate, it had little else to recommend it. The simple fact was that if you were poor and illiterate you might be hanged for stealing a few shillings' worth of cloth, while a villainous cutpurse who could decipher a simple text would be branded and then would go free. . . .

The royal pardon was the only amelioration of a murderous system. Again in a typically English accommodation, judges who thought sentences too severe could send up a list of those convicted felons they considered worthy of mercy, and these would be pardoned by the king. For many years more than half of those sentenced to hang were pardoned, and increasingly it came to be the practice to issue such pardons on the condition that the culprit agreed to leave the country. From the middle of the seventeenth century until early in the eighteenth, thousands of convicts left England under this arrangement. Of these, a substantial majority found their way to the English colonies in the West Indies and in North America. In 1717, Parliament passed a law permitting the "transportation" out of the realm of certain classes of offenders "in clergy." From 1619 to 1640 all felons reprieved by royal pardon were transported to Virginia to help make up the toll of those settlers lost by disease, and between 1661 and 1700 more than 4,500 convicts were dispatched to the colonies. In the years from 1745 to 1775, 8,846 convicts, 9,035 servants, and 3,324 slaves landed at Annapolis, Maryland.

Convicts were certainly not ideal settlers. In one contingent, twenty-six had been convicted for stealing, one for violent robbery, and five for murder. . . . The character of such settlers is indicated by the career of Jenny Voss, who was eventually hanged at Tyburn after having been transported to the colonies, where "she could not forget her old Pranks, but used not only to steal herself, but incited all others that were her fellow Servants to Pillfer and Cheat," so that her master was glad to be rid of her, the more so since "she had wheadled in a Son of the Planters, who used to Lye with her and supply her with Moneys. . . ."

Virginia and Maryland, which had been the principal outlets for transported felons, had passed laws forbidding their importation by the end of the seventeenth century. . . . But despite such [laws], Parliament in 1717 passed a statute that overrode colonial efforts to stem the tide of undesirables. A total of thirty thousand convicted felons were shipped from England in the fifty-year period prior to the Revolution, of whom the greater number apparently went to Maryland and Virginia. Since convicts were bound into servitude for seven or fourteen years, which often proved to be a lifetime, the colonists usually bid actively for the most likely ones. The men sold for from eight to twenty pounds or, roughly, twenty-five to fifty dollars. Women brought slightly less, while the old and infirm were given away or, if no taker could be found, a subsidy was paid to anyone who would take them in.

It was not a humane or enlightened system, and the most that can be said for it is that the majority of the transported felons who were sold into white semislavery were slightly better off alive than dead. For those who escaped their masters, fled to other colonies, and established themselves as respectable citizens, it was a handsome bargain. Those willing to work and fortunate enough to have a kind master, had a far better life than the one they had left behind in England. It is safe to surmise that a substantially higher proportion of women than men were redeemed to a decent life—from which it would presumably follow that a substantial number of Americans who trace their line of descent back to colonial times have an ancestress or two who arrived here as a convicted felon, a sneak thief, or a prostitute.

Three or four times a year, the convicts to be transported were marched in irons through the streets of London from Newgate Prison to Blackfriars. This procession provided, like hangings, a popular form of entertainment for mobs who would hoot at the convicts and, when the convicts replied with obscene epithets, sometimes pelt them with mud and stones. The more prosperous convicts could buy special privileges. Thus in 1736, four felons rode to the point of embarkation in two hackney coaches, and another, "a Gentleman of Fortune, and a Barrister at Law," convicted of stealing books from the Trinity College library, had a private coach to carry him in style. These men paid their own passage and shared a private cabin.

Besides the large number of convicted felons, there were many other Englishmen who fell in the rather commodious category of "rogues and vagabonds."

Although they came from a very different economic stratum, these were the hippies and dropouts of seventeenth- and eighteenth-century English society, the men and women so alienated from the dominant culture that they had devised their own. They lived on the margins of the law, devoted to preying in a thousand ingenious ways on the public. A statute of Parliament defined them as [beggars, drunkards, prostitutes, dancers, fiddlers, fencers, actors, jugglers, dice players, minstrels, fortunetellers, charlatans, tinkers, peddlers, and loiterers]. . . . Punishments were meant to be exemplary and painful. All beggars were to be stripped to the waist and whipped until they were bloody, then sent home or to the grim confines of a house of correction. Moreover, any rogue who appeared to be a hardened and dangerous character would be sent to such places beyond the seas as the Privy Council might designate.

By these provisions, incorrigible lawbreakers could be shipped out of the mother country even more readily than convicts throughout the colonial period. How "manie Drunkards, Tossepottes, whoremoisters, Dauncers, Fidlers and Minstrels, Diceplaiers, & Maskers" were dispatched to the colonies is not revealed by British court records. On the other hand, we know of enough charlatans, fortunetellers, minstrels, jugglers, tinkers, and actors in the colonies to assume that a good many of these roguish varieties made their way to America and provided lively if not always discreet entertainment for the less sophisticated colonists. What seems remarkable is that the colonies (like Virginia and Maryland) receiving the largest numbers of indentured servants and convicted felons were not utterly submerged and demoralized by these successive waves of human flotsam. Vicious and depraved as many of them must have been, the great majority made the adjustment to colonial life with reasonable success. Otherwise it is hard to see how these colonies could have survived, let alone prospered in their material and spiritual endeavors.

The transatlantic voyage from England to America was a terrible ordeal for most of those who made the crossing. Indentured servants signed up by crimps and spirits embarked on small, poorly equipped, and often dirty sailing vessels that took from one to as much as five months, depending on prevailing winds, to make the crossing. The *Sea-Flower,* with 106 passengers aboard, took sixteen weeks; forty-six of her passengers died of starvation, and of these, six were eaten by the desperate survivors. The long crossing meant bad food; the water stank and grew slimy, meat spoiled, and butter turned rancid. If the captain or owner was a profiteer, the food was often rotten to begin with. In small boats tossed by heavy seas, seasickness was commonplace. One passenger on such a crossing wrote a crude verse describing the effects of a storm on his fellow voyagers: Soon after the storm began, "there was the odest scene betwixt decks that I ever heard or seed. There was some sleeping, some spewing . . . some damning, some Blasting their legs and thighs, some their liver, lungs, lights and eyes. And for to make the scene the odder, some curs'd Father, Mother, Sister, and Brother."

A French Protestant named Durand sailed for Virginia after the revocation of the Edict of Nantes and the resumption of active persecution of the Huguenots. There were fifteen prostitutes on board ship, headed, hopefully, for a new life in the New World. During the passage, they spent their time singing and dancing and making love with the sailors and the indentured servants aboard. Durand, kept awake by their revels, wrote: "Certainly their insolence wrought a change in my nature, for my acquaintances would no doubt impute to me, as my greatest failing, an exaggerated love of the fair sex, & to tell the truth I must admit that in my youth there was no injustice in this accusation. Not that I was ever low enough or coarse enough to feel an affection for prostitutes, but I am obliged to confess I did not abhor their debauchery as I should have. . . . But when I saw those wenches behave so shockingly with the sailors and others, in addition to the distress caused by their songs and dances, it awakened within me so intense a hatred of such persons that I shall never overcome it." Durand's wife died at sea, the food ran out, and the captain proved to be a knave and a bully. Their voyage took nineteen miserable weeks, long enough for weakness and hunger to quiet the gaiety of the prostitutes.

In the German principalities, the counterparts of the English "spirits" were the Newlanders, agents who tried to persuade guileless countryfolk to set sail for America. Gottlieb Mittelberger, a German immigrant from Enzweiningen who arrived in Philadelphia in 1750, gave a vivid account of his crossing of the Atlantic. He was bitter about the "sad and miserable condition of those traveling from Germany to the New World, and the irresponsible and merciless proceedings of the Dutch traders in human beings and their man-stealing emissaries—I mean the so-called Newlanders. For these at one and the same time steal German people under all sorts of fine pretexts, and deliver them into the hands of the great Dutch traffickers in human souls." The trip meant "for most who undertake it the loss of all they possess, of freedom and peace, and for some the loss of their very lives and, I can even go so far as to say, of the salvation of their souls." Mittelberger's journey took six months, the people "packed into the big boats as closely as herring. . . ." The water distributed to thirsty passengers was often "very black, thick with dirt and full of worms." Mittelberger's description of conditions on the ship refers to "smells, fumes, horrors, vomiting . . . boils, scurvy, cancer, mouthrot . . . caused by the age and the highly-salted state of the food, especially of the meat. . . . Add to all that shortage of food, hunger, thirst, frost, heat, dampness, fear, misery, vexation, and lamentation . . . so many lice . . . that they have to be scraped off the bodies. All this misery reaches its climax when in addition to everything else one must suffer through two or three days and nights of storm . . . all the people on board pray and cry pitifully together." Under such circumstances, what little civility there might have been collapsed completely. People grew so bitter "that one person begins to curse the other, or himself and the day of his birth, and people sometimes come close to murdering one another. Misery and malice are readily associated, so that people begin to cheat and steal from one another." It is hardly surprising that America,

when the immigrants reached it, seemed a land of deliverance; "When at last after the long and difficult voyage the ships finally approach land," Mittelberger wrote, "for the sight of which the people on board had longed so passionately, then everyone crawls from below to the deck, in order to look at the land. . . . And the people cry for joy, pray, and sing praises and thanks to God. The glimpse of land revives the passengers, especially those who are half-dead of illness. Their spirits, however weak they had become, leap up, triumph, and rejoice. . . ."

As difficult as were the conditions under which indentured servants and redemptioners crossed the Atlantic, the circumstances of the prisoners were, as might be imagined, substantially worse. They were chained below decks in crowded, noisome ranks. One observer who went on board a convict ship to visit a prisoner wrote: "All the states of horror I ever had an idea of are much short of what I saw this poor man in; chained to a board in a hole not above sixteen feet long, more than fifty with him; a collar and padlock about his neck, and chained to five of the most dreadful creatures I ever looked on." Living conditions were little better than those obtaining on slave ships, and before the voyage was over it was not uncommon to lose a quarter of the human cargo, most frequently to the ravages of smallpox. (Only half as many women as men died on these hell ships, a fact attributed by merchants in the convict trade to their stronger constitutions.) Convicts so often arrived in the colonies more dead than alive that Parliamentary statutes finally set minimum allowances of bread, cheese, meat, oatmeal, and molasses per passenger—with two gills of gin issued on Saturdays.

The feelings of the colonists concerning the apparently endless stream of transported felons and vagabonds are indicated by a passage in the *Virginia Gazette* of May 24, 1751: "When we see our Papers fill'd continually with Accounts of the most audacious Robberies, the most cruel Murders, and infinite other Villanies perpetrated by Convicts transported from Europe," the correspondent wrote, "what melancholy, what terrible Reflections must it occasion!

What will become of our Posterity? These are some of thy Favours, Britain! Thou are called our Mother country; but what good Mother ever sent Thieves and Villains to accompany her children; to corrupt some with their infectious Vices and murder the rest? . . . In what can Britain show a more Sovereign contempt for us than by emptying their Jails into our Settlements. . . ." Whatever the colonists' feelings, the English were delighted with the practice of transporting their convicts to America. By such a procedure, the criminal was separated from evil companions and from the usually deplorable conditions that had induced him to take up a life of crime.

Not all convicts appreciated, by any means, the opportunity afforded them to start life over in the colonies. Not a few found their way back home (risking certain death, if caught) and declared that they would rather be hanged than return to America.

Servants and convicts who had served out their indentures often drifted to the frontier areas of the colonies, particularly to the southern frontier. Some took up cattle ranching in western Carolina, where the cattle were turned loose to graze, rounded up yearly into pens (hence Cowpens, South Carolina), and driven to the seacoast markets for meat and hides. Some, like the Hatfields and the McCoys, would in time feud with each other for decades; others lived lives of lawlessness and banditry, preying on staid planters in more settled areas and becoming, in some instances, the ancestors of the southern mountain folk, who for successive generations resisted the incursions of tax collectors.

A number, of course, gathered in the seaport towns of Baltimore, Philadelphia, New York, Charles Town, and Boston, where they drank excessively, did occasional labor, committed petty crimes, rioted, and formed the nucleus of revolutionary mobs. The truth was that with few exceptions, they belonged to that class of people whose feelings lie very close to the surface. Violent and passionate by nature, they were peculiarly susceptible to both religious conversion and revolutionary ardor. Restless and rootless, they were readily swept up by any emotional storm. Many of them were converted at the time of the Great Awakening [a series of Protestant revivals lasting from about 1725 to 1770] into pious Presbyterians, Methodists, and, somewhat later, Baptists. These denominations, with their emphasis on personal experience, were perfectly suited to the psychological needs of such individuals. Thus a substantial number of servants and ex-convicts accommodated themselves to the Protestant Ethic and became in time indistinguishable from their orthodox neighbors.

Less colorful, but equally important, were those settlers who came on their own initiative and at their own expense. By a process of natural selection, such individuals were usually aggressive, ambitious, and, as we would say today, highly motivated. Prominent among them were the Scotch-Irish. . . . [They were] independent yeoman farmers who were stout Presbyterians, often shared a common Scottish aversion to the British, and were now removed in turn to the congenial atmosphere of the colonies, particularly Pennsylvania. Hardy, enterprising Calvinists, they made their way in large numbers westward, where land was plentiful and cheap. There, serving as "the guardians of the frontier," they were constantly embroiled with eastern land speculators or various Indian tribes over ownership of land.

There was a special affinity between native Lowland Scots and the inhabitants of the middle and eastern colonies. This led to a substantial immigration of Scotch-Irish in the middle years of the eighteenth century preceding the Revolutionary crisis. Never large in numbers, the Scots nonetheless, like the Jews and Huguenots, played a disproportionately important role in colonial affairs and were prominent in the patriot cause.

The Rhineland country in present-day Germany was in the eighteenth century divided into a number of principalities, including the Rheinpfalz or Rhenish Palatinate, Württemberg, Baden, and Brunswick. These petty states were constantly embroiled in European conflicts, and many German peasants, most of them pious Lutherans, fled from the exactions of their princes: from conscription, heavy taxes, and a condition of chronic insecurity. The majority came to Pennsylvania, with some in

New York, Virginia, and the Carolinas. In Penn's colony, they established tight-knit, self-contained farming communities, where they clung to their language and their folk traditions. Travelers noted that they were stolid, hard-working, and usually more tidy than their English or Scotch-Irish neighbors. From *Deutsch,* they became Pennsylvania Dutch, developing their own patois and, by clinging stubbornly to their folk traditions, making their villages into small fortresses of cultural separatism. The most conspicuous and long-lived of the German immigrant groups that came to America were the Moravians, a pietist sect. . . . This group settled primarily in Salem, North Carolina, and Bethlehem, Pennsylvania, and to this day they preserve a rich tradition of church music, especially that of Johann Sebastian Bach. The Dunkers, who excelled in choral singing and bookmaking, and their close cousins the Mennonites also came largely to Pennsylvania. Today, forbidden by their religion to wear clothes with buttons, to drive cars, to use electricity, radios, or television, the Mennonite men with their chin hair, plain black clothes, and broad-brimmed black hats, and the women with their long skirts and bonnets, still farm the rich and carefully tended soil of central Pennsylvania and [have been] frequently embroiled with the state over their determination not to send their children to public schools. . . .

As Protestant England had persecuted its Catholics, so Catholic France persecuted its Protestants (known as Huguenots). In consequence many Huguenots looked to the New World. Since they were denied entry into New France, a number were strung out from Boston to Charles Town, favoring the toleration and commercial opportunities offered by these port towns. Peter Faneuil, the rich merchant who built Faneuil Hall, Boston's "Cradle of Liberty," and who was both a good patriot and a public benefactor, was of Huguenot ancestry, as were Paul Revere and—in South Carolina—the Rhetts, the Gadsdens, the Ravenels, the Laurenses, the Deveaux and the L'Enfants.

A handful of Jews came to the American colonies in the seventeenth and eighteenth centuries, with Pennsylvania and Rhode Island as the preferred locations. The first American synagogue was built in Providence, Rhode Island. Aaronsburg, Pennsylvania, was founded by Jewish settlers, and in Philadelphia the wealthy Gratz family contributed generously to the patriot cause. A Jewish scholar taught Hebrew at Harvard in the middle of the eighteenth century.

[Ultimately] . . . this collection of astonishingly diverse individuals, from a dozen countries and twice as many religious sects and denominations, spread out over a vast territory and coalesced into a nation and eventually into a united people. . . .

QUESTIONS TO CONSIDER

1 Sixteenth-century immigrants to the American colonies came from England, Scotland, Ireland, France, Germany, Holland, and Sweden. What characteristics does Page Smith suggest they had in common?

2 How did conditions in seventeenth- and eighteenth-century England fuel emigration to the colonies? Describe the system of indenture. How did convicted felons, rogues, and vagabonds end up coming to America?

3 Describe the ordeal of the ocean crossing for indentured servants and for convicts. If they arrived safely, how did these immigrants make their way in American society? In what ways did the system of indenture discriminate against women?

4 By the mid-eighteenth century, established colonists had begun to protest the dumping of England's human refuse on American shores. Why do you suppose the colonies were not simply overwhelmed by the flood of undesirables? Where did these and other colonial protests against English high-handedness eventually culminate?

5 Page Smith says that many of the felons, rogues, and vagabonds were converted to solid citizens in the religious revivals of the mid-eighteenth century. In what ways were these immigrants particularly susceptible to conversion?

PART TWO

The First Century

3 Black People in a White People's Country

GARY B. NASH

In 1619, a year before the Pilgrims landed at Plymouth Rock, a Dutch ship deposited "twenty Negars" on the wharf of Jamestown Colony, in what became Virginia. These were the first Africans to enter colonial America, but their exact status is unknown. Like Africans subsequently imported until 1660, they were probably indentured servants whose period of servitude was temporary. After 1660, however, most Africans who came to America were slaves, purchased through a heinous business operation, the international slave trade. By the eighteenth century, every English colony from Carolina to Massachusetts had enacted "slave codes," bodies of law that stripped black people of all rights and reduced them to pieces of property, or "chattel," with their children inheriting that status.

The troubling question is why the Africans were enslaved and white indentures were not. In the selection that follows, Gary B. Nash, one of the leading experts on colonial America, argues that the answer lies in a combination of racial prejudice and labor needs in early America, particularly in the southern colonies. When faced with the problem of cultivating labor-intensive crops, Nash writes, English settlers "turned to the international slave trade to fill their labor needs." That white colonists viewed Africans as uncivilized barbarians only made it easier "to fasten chains upon them." The Africans, of course, were no more barbaric than were the Native Americans. As Nash observes, the Africans had been stolen from richly complex and highly developed cultures. The English settlers, of course, knew nothing about such cultures beyond that they were neither white nor Christian and were therefore "uncivilized."

As more and more Africans were imported to the English colonies, racial fears intensified in direct proportion to the number of blacks in a given area. Such fears were worse in the southern colonies, where the extensive cultivation of labor-intensive crops necessitated the purchase of large numbers of slaves. In the northern colonies, as Nash points out, "slavery existed on a more occasional basis" because labor-intensive crops were not so widely grown there and far fewer Africans were imported. This is a crucial point. It helps explain why slavery later disappeared in the North, during and after the Revolution.

In the colonial period, meanwhile, every colony in the North and South alike enacted laws that severely regulated black people and made them slaves for life. Thus from the very outset, slavery served a twofold purpose: it was both a labor system and a means of racial control in a white people's country. This "mass enslavement of Africans," Nash points out, only reinforced racial prejudice in a vicious cycle. "Once institutionalized, slavery cast Africans into such lowly roles that the initial bias against them could only be confirmed and vastly strengthened."

To provide a fuller understanding of slavery in North America, Nash discusses the origins of African slavery itself and offers a graphic and painful portrait of the Atlantic slave trade, which involved "the largest forced migration in history" and was thus "one of the most important phenomena in the history of the modern world." Greed and profit kept the trade booming for four hundred years, with European entrepreneurs reaping fortunes at the expense of millions of human beings. The captain and crew of a slave ship, whether British, Dutch, Portuguese, or colonial American, had to be monstrously depraved and utterly inured to human suffering in order to carry out this brutal business. One such slave trader, Englishman John Newton, later repented, became a minister and an abolitionist, and wrote a hymn about his salvation, "How Sweet the Name of Jesus Sounds," popularly known as "Amazing Grace." Grace was indeed amazing, he said, to have saved "a wretch" like him.

The horrors of the middle passage, warns one historian, were "so revolting that a writer of the present day hesitates to give such details to his readers." On one slaver, said an eyewitness, "400 wretched beings" were chained and "crammed into a hold 12 yards in length . . . and only 3 1/2 feet in height." Because of the hold's "suffocating heat" and stench, the Africans panicked and in their torment tried in vain to escape. The next morning, the crew lifted "fifty-four crushed and mangled corpses up from the slave deck." To keep the survivors in line, the crew beat and murdered other Africans. Such atrocities were commonplace on slave ships, and the captains could not have cared less, because "insurance companies bore part of the loss, and profits were so high that heavy risks were cheerfully assumed."

Driven to madness in the rat-filled, claustrophobic bowels of the slave ships, many Africans maimed themselves or committed suicide. Others starved to death or died of some white man's disease. And the women, too many of them, were humiliated in unspeakable ways by their white captors. If the Africans somehow survived the Atlantic passage, they found themselves dumped into some fly-infested slave pen in a port of the New World. We can imagine such a group in chains on the wharves of colonial New York City or Baltimore. Sick, starving, and frightened, they had to find some way to endure the unendurable in a strange new land. That such Africans salvaged much of their heritage, transforming it into a distinctly African American heritage, was a tribute to their power "to keep on keeping on."

"Thus," writes historian Carl Degler, "began in the seventeenth century the Negro's life in America. With it commenced a moral problem for all Americans which still besets us at the close of the twentieth century." As Nash observes, the emergence of slavery in colonial America was "one of the great paradoxes in American history—the building of what some thought was to be a utopia in

the wilderness upon the backs of black men and women wrenched from their African homeland and forced into a system of abject slavery." That paradox, as we shall see, would persist through the American Revolution, the early Republic, and well into the nineteenth century, causing sectional tensions between the North and the South that finally plunged America into the most destructive war in its history.

GLOSSARY

BLACK CODES   Colonial laws that legalized and enforced slavery, depriving Africans of all rights and reducing them to pieces of property.

BLACK GOLD   The European expression for slaves.

DUTCH WEST INDIA COMPANY   A leading "international supplier of slaves."

GONÇALVEZ, ANTAM   Portuguese sea captain who made the first European landing on the west African coast south of the Sahara and brought back the first kidnapped Africans to Portugal in 1441.

MACKRONS   Africans considered too old or too infirm to make good slaves.

MIDDLE PASSAGE   The route across the Atlantic from the African coast to the New World.

ROYAL AFRICAN COMPANY   An English joint stock company chartered by the Crown to carry slaves to the English colonies.

SEQUEIRA, RUY DO   The Portuguese captain who began the European slave trade in 1472.

The African slave trade, which began in the late fifteenth century and continued for the next 400 years, is one of the most important phenomena in the history of the modern world. Involving the largest forced migration in history, the slave trade and slavery were crucially important in building the colonial empires of European nations and in generating the wealth that later produced the Industrial Revolution. But often overlooked in the attention given to the economic importance of the slave trade and slavery is the cultural diffusion that took place when ten million Africans were brought to the western hemisphere. Six out of every seven persons who crossed the Atlantic to take up life in the New World in the 300 years before the American Revolution were African slaves. As a result, in most parts of the colonized territories slavery "defined the context within which transferred European traditions would grow and change." As slaves, Africans were

Europeanized; but at the same time they Africanized the culture of Europeans in the Americas. This was an inevitable part of the convergence of these two broad groups of people, who met each other an ocean away from their original homelands. In addition, the slave trade created the lines of communication for the movement of crops, agricultural techniques, diseases, and medical knowledge between Africa, Europe, and the Americas.

Just as they were late in colonizing the New World, the English lagged far behind their Spanish and Portuguese competitors in making contact with the west coast of Africa, in entering the Atlantic slave trade, and in establishing African slaves as the backbone of the labor force in their overseas plantations. And among the English colonists in the New World, those on the mainland of North America were a half century or more behind those in the Caribbean in converting their plantation economies to slave labor. By 1670, for example, some 200,000 slaves labored in Portuguese Brazil and about 30,000 cultivated sugar in English Barbados; but in Virginia only 2,000 worked in the tobacco fields. Cultural

Gary B. Nash, *Red, White, and Black: The Peoples of Early North America*, 3e, © 1992, pp. 144–161, 208–225. Reprinted by permission of Prentice-Hall, Englewood Cliffs, New Jersey.

interaction of Europeans and Africans did not begin in North America on a large scale until more than a century after it had begun in the southerly parts of the hemisphere. Much that occurred as the two cultures met in the Iberian colonies was later repeated in the Anglo-African interaction; and yet the patterns of acculturation were markedly different in North and South America in the seventeenth and eighteenth centuries.

THE ATLANTIC SLAVE TRADE

A half century before Columbus crossed the Atlantic, a Portuguese sea captain, Antam Gonçalvez, made the first European landing on the west African coast south of the Sahara. What he might have seen, had he been able to travel the length and breadth of Africa, was a continent of extraordinary variation in geography and culture. Little he might have seen would have caused him to believe that African peoples were naturally inferior or that they had failed to develop over time as had the peoples of Europe. This notion of "backwardness" and cultural impoverishment was the myth perpetuated after the slave trade had transported millions of Africans to the Western Hemisphere. It was a myth which served to justify the cruelties of the slave trade and to assuage the guilt of Europeans involved in the largest forced dislocation of people in history.

The peoples of Africa may have numbered more than 50 million in the late fifteenth century when Europeans began making extensive contact with the continent. They lived in widely varied ecological zones—in vast deserts, in grasslands, and in great forests and woodlands. As in Europe, most people farmed the land and struggled to subdue the forces of nature in order to sustain life. That the African population had increased so rapidly in the 2,000 years before European arrival suggests the sophistication of the African agricultural methods. Part of this skill in farming derived from skill in iron production, which had begun in present-day Nigeria about 500 B.C. It

was this ability to fashion iron implements that triggered the new farming techniques necessary to sustain larger populations. With large populations came greater specialization of tasks and thus additional technical improvements. Small groups of related families made contact with other kinship groups and over time evolved into larger and more complicated societies. The pattern was similar to what had occurred in other parts of the world—in the Americas, Europe, the Middle East, and elsewhere—when the "agricultural revolution" occurred.

Recent studies of "pre-contact" African history have showed that the "culture gap" between European and African societies when the two peoples met was not as large as previously imagined. By the time Europeans reached the coast of West Africa a number of extraordinary empires had been forged in the area. The first, apparently, was the Kingdom of Ghana, which embraced the immense territory between the Sahara Desert and the Gulf of Guinea and from the Niger River to the Atlantic Ocean between the fifth and tenth centuries. Extensive urban settlement, advanced architecture, elaborate art, and a highly complex political organization evolved during this time. From the eighth to the sixteenth centuries, it was the western Sudan that supplied most of the gold for the Western world. Invasion from the north by the Moors weakened the Kingdom of Ghana, which in time gave way to the Empire of Mali. At the center of the Mali Empire was the city of Timbuktu, noted for its extensive wealth and its Islamic university where a faculty as distinguished as any in Europe was gathered.

Lesser kingdoms such as the kingdoms of Kongo, Zimbabwe, and Benin had also been in the process of growth and cultural change for centuries before Europeans reached Africa. Their inhabitants were skilled in metal working, weaving, ceramics, architecture, and aesthetic expression. Many of their towns rivaled European cities in size. Many communities of West Africa had highly complex religious rites, well-organized regional trade, codes of law, and complex political organization.

Of course, cultural development in Africa, as else-where in the world, proceeded at varying rates. Ecological conditions had a large effect on this. Where good soil, adequate rainfall, and abundance of minerals were present, as in coastal West Africa, population growth and cultural elaboration were relatively rapid. Where inhospitable desert or nearly impenetrable forest held forth, social systems remained small and changed at a crawl. Contact with other cultures also brought rapid change, whereas isolation impeded cultural change. The Kingdom of Ghana bloomed in western Sudan partly because of the trading contacts with Arabs who had conquered the area in the ninth century. Cultural change began to accelerate in Swahili societies facing the Indian Ocean after trading contacts were initiated with the Eastern world in the ninth century. Thus, as a leading African historian has put it, "the cultural history of Africa is . . . one of greatly unequal development among peoples who, for definable reasons such as these, entered recognizably similar stages of institutional change at different times."

The slave trade seems to have begun officially in 1472 when a Portuguese captain, Ruy do Sequeira, reached the coast of Benin and was conducted to the king's court, where he received royal permission to trade for gold, ivory, and slaves. So far as the Africans were concerned, the trade represented no strikingly new economic activity since they had long been involved in regional and long-distance trade across their continent. This was simply the opening of contacts with a new and more distant commercial partner. This is important to note because often it has been maintained that European powers raided the African coasts for slaves, marching into the interior and kidnapping hundreds of thousands of helpless and hapless victims. In actuality, the early slave trade involved a reciprocal relationship between European purchasers and African sellers, with the Portuguese monopolizing trade along the coastlands of tropical Africa for the first century after contact was made. Trading itself was confined to coastal strongholds where slaves, most of them captured in the interior by other Africans, were sold on terms set by the African sellers. In return for gold, ivory, and slaves, African slave merchants received European guns, bars of iron and copper, brass pots and tankards, beads, rum and textiles. They occupied an economic role not unlike that of the Iroquois middlemen in the fur trade with Europeans.

Slavery was not a new social phenomenon for either Europeans or Africans. For centuries African societies had been involved in an overland slave trade that transported black slaves from West Africa across the Sahara Desert to Roman Europe and the Middle East. But this was an occasional rather than a systematic trade, and it was designed to provide the trading nations of the Mediterranean with soldiers, household servants, and artisans rather than mass agricultural labor. Within Africa itself, a variety of unfree statuses had also existed for centuries, but they involved personal service, often for a limited period . . . rather than lifelong, degraded, agricultural labor. Slavery of a similar sort had long existed in Europe, mostly as the result of Christians enslaving Moslems and Moslems enslaving Christians during centuries of religious wars. One became a slave by being an "outsider" or an "infidel," by being captured in war, by voluntarily selling oneself into slavery to obtain money for one's family, or by committing certain heinous crimes. The rights of slaves were restricted and their opportunities for upward movement were severely circumscribed, but they were regarded nevertheless as members of society, enjoying protection under the law and entitled to certain rights, including education, marriage, and parenthood. Most important, the status of a slave was not irrevocable and was not automatically passed on to his or her children.

Thus we find that slavery flourished in ancient Greece and Rome, in the Aztec and Inca empires, in African societies, in early modern Russia and eastern Europe, in the Middle East, and in the Mediterranean world. It had gradually died out in Western Europe by the fourteenth century, although the status of serf was not too different in social reality from that of the slave. It is important to note that in all these regions slavery and serfdom had nothing to do with racial characteristics.

When the African slave trade began in the second half of the fifteenth century, it served to fill labor shortages in the economies of its European initiators and their commercial partners. Between 1450 and 1505 Portugal brought about 40,000 African slaves to Europe and the Atlantic islands—the Madeiras and Canaries. But the need for slave labor lessened in Europe as European populations themselves began to grow beginning late in the fifteenth century. It is possible, therefore, that were it not for the colonization of the New World the early slave trade might have ceased after a century or more and be remembered simply as a short-lived incident stemming from early European contacts with Africa.

With the discovery of the New World by Europeans the course of history changed momentously. Once Europeans found the gold and silver mines of Mexico and Peru, and later, when they discovered a new form of gold in the production of sugar, coffee, and tobacco, their demand for human labor grew astonishingly. At first Indians seemed to be the obvious source of labor, and in some areas Spaniards and Portuguese were able to coerce native populations into agricultural and mining labor. But European diseases ravaged native populations, and often it was found that Indians, far more at home in their environment than white colonizers, were difficult to subjugate. Indentured white labor from the mother country was another way of meeting the demand for labor, but this source, it soon became apparent, was far too limited. It was to Africa that colonizing Europeans ultimately resorted. Formerly a new source of trade, the continent now became transformed in the European view into the repository of vast supplies of human labor—"black gold."

From the late fifteenth to the mid-nineteenth centuries, almost four hundred years, Europeans transported Africans out of their ancestral homelands to fill the labor needs in their colonies of North and South America and the Caribbean. The most recent estimates place the numbers who reached the shores of the New World at about ten to eleven million people, although many million more lost their lives while being marched from the interior to the coastal trading forts or during the "middle passage" across the Atlantic. Even before the English arrived on the Chesapeake in 1607 several hundred thousand slaves had been transported to the Caribbean and South American colonies of Spain and Portugal. Before the slave trade was outlawed in the nineteenth century far more Africans than Europeans had crossed the Atlantic Ocean and taken up life in the New World. Black slaves, as one eighteenth-century Englishman put it, became "the strength and the sinews of this western world."

Once established on a large scale, the Atlantic slave trade dramatically altered the pattern of slave recruitment in Africa. For about a century after Gonçalvez brought back the first kidnapped Africans to Portugal in 1441, the slave trade was relatively slight. The slaves whom other Africans sold to Europeans were drawn from a small minority of the population and for the most part were individuals captured in occasional war or whose criminal acts had cost them their rights of citizenship. For Europeans the African slave trade provided for modest labor needs, just as the Black Sea slave trade had done before it was shut off by the fall of Constantinople to the Turks in 1453. Even in the New World plantations, slaves were not in great demand for many decades after "discovery."

More than anything else it was sugar that transformed the African slave trade. Produced in the Mediterranean world since the eighth century, sugar was for centuries a costly item confined to sweetening the diet of the rich. By the mid-1400s its popularity was growing and the center of production had shifted to the Portuguese Madeira Islands, off the northwest coast of Africa. Here for the first time an expanding European nation established an overseas plantation society based on slave labor. From the Madeiras the cultivation of sugar spread to Portuguese Brazil in the late sixteenth century and then to the tiny specks of land dotting the Caribbean in the first half of the seventeenth century. By this time Europeans were developing an almost insatiable taste for sweetness. Sugar—regarded by nutritionists today as a "drug food"—became one of the first luxuries

Once they arrived in the New World, slaves were auctioned to the highest bidder. Families were often divided and slaves were stripped of their clothes to show how little whipping they required. Having been poked and prodded, one captive compared the horrid experience to that of a horse being examined by a jockey. (Library of Congress)

that was transformed into a necessary item in the diets of the masses of Europe. The wife of the poorest English laborer took sugar in her tea by 1750 it was said. "Together with other plantation products such as coffee, rum, and tobacco," writes Sidney Mintz, "sugar formed part of a complex of 'proletarian hunger-killers,' and played a crucial role in the linked contribution that Caribbean slaves, Indian peasants, and European urban proletarians were able to make to the growth of western civilization."

The regularization of the slave trade brought about by the vast new demand for a New World labor supply and by a reciprocally higher demand in Africa for European trade goods, especially bar iron and textiles, changed the problem of obtaining slaves.

Criminals and "outsiders" in sufficient number to satisfy the growing European demand in the seventeenth century could not be found. Therefore African kings resorted to warfare against their neighbors as a way of obtaining "black gold" with which to trade. European guns abetted the process. Thus, the spread of kidnapping and organized violence in Africa became a part of maintaining commercial relations with European powers.

In the forcible recruitment of slaves, adult males were consistently preferred over women and children. Primarily this represented the preference of New World plantation owners for male field laborers. But it also reflected the decision of vanquished African villagers to yield up more men than women to raiding parties because women were the chief agriculturalists in their society and, in matrilineal and matrilocal kinship systems, were too valuable to be spared.

For the Europeans the slave trade itself became an immensely profitable enterprise. In the several centuries of intensive slave trading that followed the establishment of New World sugar plantations, European nations warred constantly for trading advantages on the West African coast. The coastal forts, the focal points of the trade, became key strategic targets in the wars of empire. The great Portuguese slaving fort at Elmina on the Gold Coast, begun in 1481, was captured a century and a half later by the Dutch. The primary fort on the Guinea coast, started by the Swedes, passed through the hands of the Danes, the English, and the Dutch between 1652 and 1664. As the demand for slaves in the Americas rose sharply in the second half of the seventeenth century, European competition for trading rights on the West African coast grew intense. By the end of the century monopolies for supplying European plantations in the New World with their annual quotas of slaves became a major issue of European diplomacy. The Dutch were the primary victors in the battle for the West African slave coast. Hence, for most of the century a majority of slaves who were fed into the expanding New World markets found themselves crossing the Atlantic in Dutch ships.

Not until the last third of the seventeenth century were the English of any importance in the slave trade. Major English attempts to break into the profitable trade began only in 1663, when Charles II, recently restored to the English throne, granted a charter to the Royal Adventurers to Africa, a joint-stock company headed by the king's brother, the Duke of York. Superseded by the Royal African Company in 1672, these companies enjoyed the exclusive right to carry slaves to England's overseas plantations. For thirty-four years after 1663 each of the slaves they brought across the Atlantic bore the brand "*DY*" for the Duke of York, who himself became king in 1685. In 1698 the Royal African Company's monopoly was broken due to the pressure on Parliament by individual merchants who demanded their rights as Englishmen to participate in the lucrative trade. Thrown open to individual entrepreneurs, the English slave trade grew enormously. In the 1680s the Royal African Company had transported about 5,000 to 6,000 slaves annually (though interlopers brought in thousands more). In the first decade of free trade the annual average rose above 20,000. English involvement in the trade increased for the remainder of the eighteenth century until by the 1790s England had become the foremost slave-trading nation in Europe.

CAPTURE AND TRANSPORT OF SLAVES

No accounts of the initial enslavement of Africans, no matter how vivid, can quite convey the pain and demoralization that must have accompanied the forced march to the west coast of Africa and the subsequent loading aboard ships of those who had fallen captive to the African suppliers of the European slave traders. As the demand for African slaves doubled and redoubled in the eighteenth century, the hinterlands of western and central Sudan were invaded again and again by the armies and agents of both coastal and interior kings. Perhaps 75 percent of the slaves transported to English North America came from the part of western Africa that lies between the Senegal and Niger rivers and the Gulf of Biafra, and most of the others were enslaved in Angola on the west coast of Central Africa. Slaving activities in these areas were responsible for considerable depopulation of the region in the eighteenth and nineteenth centuries.

Once captured, slaves were marched to the sea in "coffles," or trains. A Scotsman, Mungo Park, described the coffle he marched with for 550 miles through Gambia at the end of the eighteenth century. It consisted of 73 men, women, and children tied together by the neck with leather thongs. Several captives attempted to commit suicide by eating clay, another was abandoned after being badly stung by bees; still others died of exhaustion and hunger. After two months the coffle reached the coast, many of its members physically depleted by thirst, hunger, and exposure, where they were herded into fortified enclosures called barracoons.

The anger, bewilderment, and desolation that accompanied the forced march, the first leg of the 5,000-mile journey to the New World, was only increased by the actual transfer of slaves to European ship captains, who carried their human cargo in small wooden ships to the Americas. "As the slaves come down to Fida from the inland country," wrote one European trader in the late seventeenth century, "they are put into a booth or prison, built for that purpose, near the beach . . . and when the Europeans are to receive them, they are brought out into a large plain, where the [ships'] surgeons examine every part of every one of them, to the smallest member, men and women being all stark naked. Such as are allowed good and sound, are set on one side, and the others by themselves; which slaves so rejected are called Mackrons, being above 35 years of age, or defective in their lips, eyes, or teeth, or grown grey; or that have the venereal disease, or any other imperfection." Such dehumanizing treatment was part of the commercial process by which "merchandise" was selected and bargained for. But it was also part of the psychological process that attempted to strip away self-respect and self-identity from the Africans.

Cruelty followed cruelty. After purchase, each slave was branded with a hot iron signifying the company, whether Spanish, Portuguese, English, French, or Dutch, that had purchased him or her. Thus were members of "preliterate" societies first introduced to the alphabetic symbols of "advanced" cultures. "The branded slaves," one account related, "are returned to their former booths" where they were imprisoned until a full human cargo could be assembled. The next psychological wrench came with the ferrying of slaves, in large canoes, to the

The middle passage from the African coast to the New World was incredibly brutal. White slave traders preferred "tight packing" in cramped cargo holds filled with foul smells and poisonous air. When the weather permitted, the traders allowed the slaves to come on deck for meals and exercise. (© Bettmann/CORBIS)

waiting ships at anchor in the harbor. An English captain described the desperation of slaves who were about to lose touch with their ancestral land and embark upon a vast ocean that many had never previously seen. "The Negroes are so wilful and loth to leave their own country, that they have often leap'd out of the canoes, boat and ship, into the sea, and kept under water till they were drowned, to avoid being taken up and saved by our boats, which pursued them; they having a more dreadful apprehension of Barbadoes than we can have of hell." Part of this fear was the common belief that on the other side of the ocean Africans would be eaten by the white savages.

The kind of fear that inspired suicide while still on African soil was prevalent as well on the second leg of the voyage—the "middle passage" from the West

African coast to the New World. Conditions aboard ship were miserable, although it was to the advantage of the ship captains to deliver as many slaves as possible on the other side of the Atlantic. The preservation rather than the destruction of life was the main object, but brutality was systematic, both in pitching overboard any slaves who fell sick on the voyage and in punishing offenders with almost sadistic intensity as a way of creating a climate of fear that would stifle insurrectionist tendencies. John Atkins, aboard an English slaver in 1721, described how the captain "whipped and scarified" several plotters of rebellion and sentenced others "to cruel deaths, making them first eat the Heart and Liver of one of them killed. The Woman he hoisted up by the thumbs, whipp'd and slashed her with Knives, before the other slaves, till she died." Though the naval architects of Europe competed to produce the most efficient ships for carrying human cargoes to the New World, the mortality on board, for both black slaves below decks and white sailors above, was extremely high, averaging between 10 and 20 percent on each voyage.

That Africans frequently attempted suicide and mutiny during the ocean crossing provides evidence that even the extraordinary force used in capturing, branding, selling, and transporting them from one continent to another was not enough to make the captives submit tamely to their fate. An eighteenth-century historian of slavery, attempting to justify the terroristic devices employed by slavers, argued that "the many acts of violence they [the slaves] have committed by murdering whole crews and destroying ships when they had it in their power to do so have made these rigors wholly chargeable on their own bloody and malicious disposition which calls for the same confinement as if they were wolves or wild boars." The modern reader can detect in this characterization of enslaved Africans clear proof that submissiveness was not a trait of those who were forcibly carried to the New World. So great was this resistance that special techniques of torture had to be devised to cope with the thousands of slaves who were determined to starve themselves to death on the middle passage rather than reach the New World in chains. Brutal whippings and hot coals applied to the lips were frequently used to open the mouths of recalcitrant slaves. When this did not suffice, a special instrument, the *speculum oris,* or mouth opener, was employed to wrench apart the jaws of a resistant slave.

Taking into consideration the mortality involved in the capture, the forced march to the coast, and the middle passage, probably not more than one in two captured Africans lived to see the New World. Many of those who did must have been psychologically numbed as well as physically depleted by the experience. But one further step remained in the process of enslavement—the auctioning to a New World master and transportation to his place of residence. All in all, the relocation of any African brought westward across the Atlantic may have averaged about six months from the time of capture to the time of arrival at the plantation of a European slave master. During this protracted personal crisis, the slave was completely cut off from most that was familiar—family, wider kinship relationships, community life, and other forms of social and psychological security. Still facing these victims of the European demand for cheap labor was adaptation to a new physical environment, a new language, new work routines, and, most important, a life in which bondage for themselves and their offspring was unending.

THE DEVELOPMENT OF SLAVERY IN THE ENGLISH COLONIES

Even though they were long familiar with Spanish, Dutch, and Portuguese use of African slave labor, English colonists did not turn immediately to Africa to solve the problem of cultivating labor-intensive crops. When they did, it could have caused little surprise, for in enslaving Africans the English were merely copying their European rivals in attempting to fill the colonial labor gap. No doubt the stereotype of Africans as uncivilized made it easier for the English to fasten chains upon them. But the central fact remains that the English were in the New World, like the Spanish, Portuguese, Dutch, and French, to make a fortune as well as to build religious and political havens. Given the long hostility they had borne toward Indians and their experience in enslaving them, any scruples the English might have had about enslaving Africans quickly dissipated.

Making it all the more natural to employ Africans as a slave labor force in the mainland colonies was the precedent that English planters had set on their Caribbean sugar islands. In Barbados, Jamaica, and the Leeward Islands (Antigua, Monserrat, Nevis, and St. Christopher) Englishmen in the second and third quarters of the seventeenth century learned to copy their European rivals in employing Africans in the sugar fields and, through extraordinary repression, in molding them into a slave labor force. By 1680, when there were not more than 7,000 slaves in mainland North America and the institution of slavery was not yet unalterably fixed, upwards of 65,000 Africans toiled on sugar plantations in the English West Indies. Trade and communication were extensive between the Caribbean and mainland colonists, so settlers in North America had intimate knowledge concerning the potentiality of slave labor.

It is not surprising, then, that the North American colonists turned to the international slave trade to fill their labor needs. Africans were simply the most available people in the world for those seeking a bound labor force and possessed of the power to obtain it. What is surprising, in fact, is that the North American colonists did not turn to slavery more quickly than they did. For more than a half century in Virginia and Maryland it was primarily the white indentured servant and not the African slave who labored in the tobacco fields. Moreover, those blacks who were imported before about 1660 were held in various degrees of servitude, most for limited periods and a few for life.

The transformation of the labor force in the Southern colonies, from one in which many white

and a relatively small number of black indentured servants labored together to one in which black slaves served for a lifetime and composed the bulk of unfree labor, came only in the last third of the seventeenth century in Virginia and Maryland and in the first third of the eighteenth century in North Carolina and South Carolina. The reasons for this shift to a slave-based agricultural economy in the South are twofold. First, English entry into the African slave trade gave the Southern planter an opportunity to purchase slaves more readily and more cheaply than before. Cheap labor was what every tobacco or rice planter sought, and when the price of slave labor dipped below that of indentured labor, the demand for black slaves increased. Also, the supply of white servants from England began to dry up in the late seventeenth century, and those who did cross the Atlantic were spread among a growing number of colonies. Thus, in the late seventeenth century the number of Africans imported into the Chesapeake colonies began to grow and the flow of white indentured servants diminished to a trickle. As late as 1671 slaves made up less than 5 percent of Virginia's population and were outnumbered at least three to one by white indentured servants. In Maryland the situation was much the same. But within a generation, by about 1700, they represented one-fifth of the population and probably a majority of the labor force. A Maryland census of 1707 tabulated 3,003 white bound laborers and 4,657 black slaves. Five years later the slave population had almost doubled. Within another generation white indentured servants were declining rapidly in number, and in all the Southern colonies African slaves made up the backbone of the agricultural work force. "These two words, *Negro* and *slave*," wrote one Virginian, had "by custom grown Homogenous and Convertible."

To the north, in Pennsylvania, New Jersey, and Delaware, where English colonists had settled only in the last third of the seventeenth century, slavery existed on a more occasional basis, since labor-intensive crops were not as extensively grown in these areas and the cold winters brought farming to a halt. New York was an exception and shows how a cultural preference could alter labor patterns that were usually determined by ecological factors. During the period before 1664 when the colony was Dutch, slaveholding had been practiced extensively, encouraged in part by the Dutch West India Company, one of the chief international suppliers of slaves. The population of New York remained largely Dutch for the remainder of the century, and the English who slowly filtered in saw no reason not to imitate Dutch slave owners. Thus New York became the largest importer of slaves north of Maryland. In the mid-eighteenth century, the areas of original settlement around New York and Albany remained slaveholding societies with about 20 percent of the population composed of slaves and 30 to 40 percent of the white householders owning human property.

As the number of slaves increased, legal codes for strictly controlling their activities were fashioned in each of the colonies. To a large extent these "black codes" were borrowed from the law books of the English West Indies. Bit by bit they deprived the African immigrant—and a small number of Indian slaves as well—of rights enjoyed by others in the society, including indentured servants. Gradually they reduced the slave, in the eyes of society and the law, from a human being to a piece of chattel property. In this process of dehumanization nothing was more important than the practice of hereditary life-time service. Once servitude became perpetual, relieved only by death, then the stripping away of all other rights followed as a matter of course. When the condition of the slave parent was passed on to the child, then slavery had been extended to the womb. At that point the institution became totally fixed so far as the slave was concerned.

Thus, with the passage of time, Africans in North America had to adapt to a more and more circumscribed world. Earlier in the seventeenth century they had been treated much as indentured servants, bound to labor for a specified period of years but thereafter free to work for themselves, hire out their labor, buy land, move as they pleased, and, if they

wished, hold slaves themselves. But, by the 1640s, Virginia was forbidding blacks the use of firearms. In the 1660s marriages between white women and black slaves were being described as "shameful Matches" and "the Disgrace of our Nation"; during the next few decades interracial fornication became subject to unusually severe punishment and interracial marriage was banned.

These discriminatory steps were slight, however, in comparison with the stripping away of rights that began toward the end of the century. In rapid succession slaves lost their right to testify before a court; to engage in any kind of commercial activity, either as buyer or seller; to hold property; to participate in the political process; to congregate in public places with more than two or three of their fellows; to travel without permission; and to engage in legal marriage or parenthood. In some colonies legislatures even prohibited the right to education and religion, for they thought these might encourage the germ of freedom in slaves. More and more steps were taken to contain them tightly in a legal system that made no allowance for their education, welfare, or future advancement. The restraints on the slave owner's freedom to deal with slaves in any way he or she saw fit were gradually cast away. Early in the eighteenth century many colonies passed laws forbidding the manumission of slaves by individual owners. This was a step designed to squelch the strivings of slaves for freedom and to discourage those who had been freed from helping fellow Africans to gain their liberty.

The movement to annul all the slave's rights had both pragmatic and psychological dimensions. The greater the proportion of slaves in the population, the greater the danger to white society, for every colonist knew that when he purchased a man or woman in chains he had bought a potential insurrectionist. The larger the specter of black revolt, the greater the effort of white society to neutralize it by further restricting the rights and activities of slaves. Thus, following a black revolt in 1712 that took the lives of nine whites and wounded others, the New

York legislature passed a slave code that rivaled those of the Southern colonies. Throughout the Southern colonies the obsessive fear of slave insurrection ushered in institutionalized violence as the means of ensuring social stability. Allied to this need for greater and greater control was the psychological compulsion to dehumanize slaves by taking from them the rights that connoted their humanity. It was far easier to rationalize the merciless exploitation of those who had been defined by law as something less than human. "The planters," wrote an Englishman in eighteenth-century Jamaica, "do not want to be told that their Negroes are human creatures. If they believe them to be of human kind, they cannot regard them . . . as no better than dogs or horses."

Thus occurred one of the great paradoxes in American history—the building of what some thought was to be a utopia in the wilderness upon the backs of black men and women wrenched from their African homeland and forced into a system of abject slavery. America was imagined as a liberating and regenerating force, it has been pointed out, but became the scene of a "grotesque inconsistency." In the land heralded for freedom and individual opportunity, the practice of slavery, unknown for centuries in the mother country, was reinstituted. Following other parts of the New World, North America became the scene of "a disturbing retrogression from the course of historical progress."

The mass enslavement of Africans profoundly affected white racial prejudice. Once institutionalized, slavery cast Africans into such lowly roles that the initial bias against them could only be confirmed and vastly strengthened. Initially unfavorable impressions of Africans had coincided with labor needs to bring about their mass enslavement. But it required slavery itself to harden the negative racial feelings into a deep and almost unshakable prejudice that continued to grow for centuries. The colonizers had devised a labor system that kept the African in the Americas at the bottom of the social and economic pyramid. Irrevocably caught in the web of perpetual servitude, the slave

was allowed no further opportunity to prove the white stereotype wrong. Socially and legally defined as less than people, kept in a degraded and debased position, virtually without power in their relationships with white society, Afro-Americans became a truly servile, ignoble, degraded people in the eyes of the Europeans. This was used as further reason to keep them in slavery, for it was argued that they were worth nothing better and were incapable of occupying any higher role. In this long evolution of racial attitudes in America, nothing was of greater importance than the enslavement of Africans.

QUESTIONS TO CONSIDER

1 How did conditions in the New World transform the traditional character of the slave trade? Why? What crop had a particular effect, and why did it become so important in international trade?

2 What effects did the sudden growth of the slave trade in the seventeenth century have on conditions in Europe and in Africa? What had African culture been like before the seventeenth century? How had it compared with European culture?

3 Describe the conditions of the Atlantic slave trade. What was the purpose of physical cruelty in the slave trade? What do you think it would have been like to be an African stolen from his or her native land and taken across the middle passage? What might be the physical and psychological effects of such an experience?

4 By what process did black slavery gradually become established in the British North American colonies? How were the colonies unusual in this? Why did it develop less in the North than in the southern colonies? Why was New York an exception?

5 How does Gary Nash believe that slavery and racial prejudice influenced each other? What are the implications of his conclusions for the subsequent history of America up to the present day?

4 The Deerfield Massacre

JOHN DEMOS

The massacre of a western Massachusetts town by the French and Indians one night in 1704 was symbolic of the great struggle between France and England for supremacy in North America. To understand that terrible night requires that the English colonists in New England and the French in Canada be explained and contrasted. In 1630, the Puritans had founded the Massachusetts Bay colony and sought, under the leadership of their first governor, even-tempered John Winthrop, to create a model Christian commonwealth—"a city on a hill"—that would stand as a beacon of inspiration for others to emulate. Each town had its own congregation and its own minister, whose sermons rang with Calvinist precepts (see the glossary in selection 2). The system of local congregations that selected their ministers and ran their own affairs became known as the Congregational church. In their wilderness Zion, ministers and government officials worked together to maintain holiness, purity, and order. Only church members—the elect—could vote and hold political office. The government, in turn, protected the church by levying taxes to support it on members and nonmembers alike and by making church attendance compulsory. The Puritans, as historian Edmund S. Morgan said, "not only endeavored themselves to live a 'smooth, honest, civil life,' but tried to force everyone within their power to do likewise."

On the surface, the Puritans appeared to be pious, sedate folk living in peaceful villages. But as John Demos says in the following selection, Puritan New England "also had its share of discordant change, of inner stress and turmoil, and even of deadly violence." The Puritans believed, for instance, that Satan could seize people, especially women, and force them to practice witchcraft, which was a capital crime: those found guilty were hanged. As for the Native Americans in New England, as we have seen, the Puritans practiced a policy of killing the Indians off or driving them west or into Canada, where they formed alliances with the French.

The English had come to the New World to settle; the French had come not to settle, but to make money, by creating a fur-trading empire in Canada. Instead of exterminating the Indians, the French learned their language, traded, formed alliances, and even intermarried with them and sought to convert them to the Catholic faith. As imperial England and imperial France clashed on the American continent, the French army and its Indian allies fought a series of wars with the English army in America in which, as Demos says, the American colonials were "a junior partner." The motion picture, The Last of the Mohicans, *starring Daniel Day-Lewis and Madeleine Stowe, vividly illustrates this imperial conflict and the secondary role of the American militia in it. The film also shows how colonial civilians were often victims of the warfare between the two European nations.*

The citizens of colonial Deerfield were such victims. In Demos's skilled hands, the massacre of the town is an action-packed thriller, made all the more immediate because it is told in the present tense. When the French and Indian forces attack the little town, ordinary folk are slain, mutilated, or captured. One captive, the daughter of the town minister, does an incredible thing in the view of the survivors: she elects to remain with the Indians, marry a brave, and live out her life with them. Unfortunately, the author does not tell us why she found Indian life more attractive than Puritan life in Deerfield, Massachusetts. Perhaps she felt safer with the Indians: they would never have executed her on a charge of witchcraft. Perhaps, too, she found the Indians' spiritual views, which stressed the harmony of human beings with the sun, the moon, mother earth, and other living creatures, more meaningful and comforting to her than the implacable doctrines of Puritan theology.

GLOSSARY

GARRISON   Hired soldiers who manned a stockade.

NEW FRANCE   France's fur-trading colony in Canada.

WILLIAMS, EUNICE   The daughter of Deerfield's minister who was taken captive during the Deerfield raid. To the bafflement of her father and the other white survivors of

the attack, she elected to live with the Indians, married a warrior, and raised a family.

WILLIAMS, JOHN   Puritan minister of Deerfield who was captured during the Indian attack and subsequently returned to safety. He wrote a book about his experiences called *The Redeemed Captive Returning to Zion.*

Our traditional picture of colonial New England is essentially a still life. Peaceful little villages. Solid, strait-laced, steadily productive people. A landscape serene, if not bountiful. A history of purposeful, and largely successful, endeavor.

And yet, as historians are learning with ever-greater clarity, this picture is seriously at odds with the facts. New England had its solidity and purposefulness, to be sure. But it also had its share of discordant change, of inner stress and turmoil, and even of deadly violence. New England was recurrently a place of war, especially during the hundred years preceding the Revolution. The French to the north in Canada and the various Indian tribes on every side made determined, altogether formidable enemies. The roster of combat was long indeed: King Philip's War (1675–76), King William's War (1689–97), Queen Anne's War (1702–13), Father Rasle's War (1724–26), King George's War (1744–48), and the French and Indian War (1754–63). Most of these

were intercolonial, even international, conflicts, in which New England joined as a very junior partner. But there were numerous other skirmishes, entirely local and so obscure as not to have earned a name. All of them exacted a cost, in time, in money, in worry—and in blood.

Much of the actual fighting was small-scale, hit-and-run, more a matter of improvisation than of formal strategy and tactics. Losses in any single encounter might be only a few, but they did add up. Occasionally the scale widened, and entire towns became targets. Lancaster and Haverhill, Massachusetts; Salmon Fall and Oyster River, New Hampshire; York and Wells, Maine: Each suffered days of wholesale attack. And Deerfield, Massachusetts—above all, Deerfield—scene of the region's single, most notorious "massacre."

The year is 1704, the season winter, the context another European war with a "colonial" dimension. New France (Canada) versus New England. (New York and the colonies farther south are, at least temporarily, on the sidelines.) The French and their Indian allies have already engineered a series of devastating raids along the "eastern frontier"—the Maine and New Hampshire coasts. The English have counterattacked against half a dozen Abenaki

John Demos, "The Deerfield Massacre," from *The Unredeemed Captive* by John Demos. Copyright © 1994 by John Demos. Reprinted by permission of Alfred A. Knopf, a division of Random House.

Indian villages. And now, in Montreal, the French governor is secretly planning a new thrust "over the ice" toward "a little village of about forty households," a place misnamed in the French records "Guerrefille." (An ironic twist just there: Deerfield becomes "War-girl.")

Deerfield is not unready. Like other outlying towns, it has labored to protect itself: with a "stockade" (a fortified area, at its center, inside a high palisade fence), a "garrison" of hired soldiers, a "watch" to patrol the streets at night, and "scouts" to prowl the woods nearby. Indeed, many families are living inside the stockade. Conditions are crowded and uncomfortable, to say the least, but few doubt the need for special measures. The town minister, Rev. John Williams, conducts an extraordinary day of "fasting and prayer" in the local church—"possessed," as he reportedly is, "that the town would in a little time be destroyed."

The attack forces—French led, largely Indian in rank and file—set out in early February. Steadily they move southward, on frozen rivers and lakes, with one hard leg across the Green Mountains. They have snowshoes, sleds to carry their supplies, and dogs to pull the sleds. The lower part of their route follows the Connecticut River valley till it reaches a point near what would later become Brattleboro, Vermont. Here they will strike off into the woods to the south, leaving dogs and sleds for their return. They are barely a day's march—twenty miles—from their objective. The rest they will cover as quickly and quietly as possible. Surprise is their most potent weapon. The people of Deerfield, though generally apprehensive, know nothing of this specific threat. On the evening of February 28, the town goes to sleep in the usual way.

Midnight. Across the river to the west the attackers are making their final preparations: loading weapons, putting on war paint, reviewing plans. The layout of Deerfield is apparently known to them from visits made in previous years by Indian hunters and traders. Presently a scout is sent "to discover the posture of the town, who observing the watch walking in the street," returns to his comrades and "puts them to a stand." (Our source for the details of this sequence was a contemporary historian, writing some years after the fact.) Another check, a short while later, brings a different result. The village lies "all . . . still and quiet"; the watch evidently has fallen asleep. It is now about four o'clock in the morning, time for the attackers to move.

Over the river, on the ice. Across a mile of meadowland, ghostly and white. Past the darkened houses at the north end of the street. Right up to the stockade. The snow has piled hugely here; the drifts make walkways to the top of the fence. A vanguard of some forty men climbs quickly over and drops down on the inside. A gate is opened to admit the rest. The watch awakens, fires a warning shot, cries, "Arm!" Too late. The attackers separate into smaller parties and "immediately set upon breaking open doors and windows."

The townspeople come to life with a rush. Some find opportunities to escape by jumping from windows or roof lines. Several manage to flee the stockade altogether and make their way to neighboring villages. In half a dozen households the men leave families behind in order to rally outside as a counterforce. In others there is a frantic attempt to hide.

The minister's house is a special target, singled out "in the beginning of the onset"; later John Williams will remember (and write about) his experience in detail. Roused "out of sleep . . . by their violent endeavors to break open doors and windows with axes and hatchets," he leaps from the bed, runs to the front door, sees "the enemy making their entrance," awakens a pair of soldiers lodged upstairs, and returns to his bedside "for my arms." There is hardly time, for the "enemy immediately brake into the room, I judge to the number of twenty, with painted faces and hideous acclamations." They are "all of them Indians"; no Frenchmen in sight as yet. The minister does manage to cock his pistol and "put it to the breast of the first Indian who came up." Fortunately—for both of them—it misfires. Thereupon Williams is "seized by 3 Indians, who disarmed me, and bound me naked, as I was in my shirt"; in this posture he will remain "for near the space of an hour."

With their chief prize secured, the invaders turn to "rifling the house, entering in great numbers into every room." There is killing work too: "some were so cruel and barbarous as to take and carry to the door two of my children and murder them [six-year-old John, Jr., and six-week-old Jerusha], as also a Negro woman [a family slave named Parthena]." After "insulting over me a while, holding up hatchets over my head, [and] threatening to burn all I had," the Indians allow their captive to dress. They also permit Mrs. Williams "to dress herself and our children."

By this time the sun is "about an hour high" (perhaps 7:00 A.M.). The sequence described by John Williams has been experienced, with some variations, in households throughout the stockade: killings (especially of infants and others considered too frail to survive the rigors of life in the wilderness); "fireing houses"; "killing cattle, hogs, sheep & sacking and wasting all that came before them." In short, a village-size holocaust. When John Williams and his family are finally taken outside, they see "many of the houses . . . in flames"; later, in recalling the moment, he asks, "Who can tell what sorrows pierced our souls?"

The Williamses know they are destined "for a march . . . into a strange land," as prisoners. And prisoners are being herded together—in the meetinghouse and in a home nearby—from all over town. However, one household—that of the militia leader, Sgt. Benoni Stebbins—has mounted a remarkable resistance. Its occupants are well armed and fiercely determined; moreover, the walls of this house, "being filled up with brick," effectively repel incoming fire. The battle (as described in a subsequent report by local militia officers) continues here for more than two hours. The attackers fall back, then surge forward in an unsuccessful attempt "to fire the house." Again they retreat—this time to the shelter of the meetinghouse—while maintaining their fusillade all the while. The defenders return bullet for bullet, "accepting of no quarter, though offered," and "causing several of the enemy to fall,"

among them "one Frenchman, a gentleman to appearance," and "3 or 4 Indians," including a "captain" who had helped seize John Williams.

In the meantime, some of the attackers with their captives begin to leave the stockade. Heading north, they retrace their steps toward the river. Then a stunning intervention: A band of Englishmen arrives from the villages below (where an orange glow on the horizon "gave notice . . . before we had news from the distressed people" themselves). "Being a little above forty in number," they have rushed on horseback to bring relief. They stop just long enough to pick up "fifteen of Deerfield men." And this combined force proceeds to the stockade, to deliver a surprise of its own: "when we entered at one gate, the enemy fled out the other." Now comes a flat-out chase—pell-mell across the meadow—the erstwhile attackers put to rout. The Englishmen warm, literally, to the fight, stripping off garments as they run. (Later the same soldiers will claim reimbursement for their losses—and record details of the battle.) They inflict heavy casualties: "we saw at the time many dead bodies, and . . . afterwards . . . manifest prints in the snow, where other dead bodies were drawn to a hole in the river."

They make, in sum, a highly successful counterattack. But one that is "pursued too far, imprudently." For across the river the French commanders hear the tumult and swiftly regroup their own forces. The riverbank affords an excellent cover for a new stand; soon a "numerous company . . . [of] fresh hands" is in place there, concealed and waiting. On the Englishmen come, ignoring the orders of the officer "who had led them [and] called for a retreat." On and on—the river is just ahead, and the captives are waiting on the other side—into the teeth of the withering "ambuscade." Back across the meadow one more time, pursued and pursuers reversing roles. The English are hard pressed, "our breath being spent, theirs in full strength." Their retreat is as orderly as they can make it, "facing and firing, so that those that first failed might be defended"; even so, "many were slain and others wounded." Eventually the survivors regain the stockade and clamber inside, at which "the enemy drew off." They will appear no more.

It is now about 9:00 A.M. A numbness settles over the village. The fires are burning down. There is blood on the snow in the street. The survivors of the "meadow fight" crouch warily behind the palisades. The townspeople who had escaped start to filter back in through the south gate. Time to look after their wounded and count their dead.

Viewed from close up, the carnage is appalling. Death—by gunshot, by hatchet, by knife, by war club, grisly beyond words. And the torn bodies on the ground are not the whole of it [;] when the survivors poke through the rubble, they find more. Casualty lists have entries like this: "Mary, Mercy, and Mehitable Nims [ages, five, five, and seven, respectively] supposed to be burnt in the cellar." Indeed, several cellar hideouts have turned into death-traps; in one house ten people lie "smothered" that way.

And then the wounded. One man shot through the arm. Another with a bullet in his thigh. Another with a shattered foot. Yet another who was briefly captured by the Indians, and "when I was in their hands, they cut off the forefinger of my right hand" (a traditional Indian practice with captives). A young woman wounded in the Stebbins house. A second with an ankle broken while jumping from an upper-story window.

There are, too, the lucky ones, quite a number who *might* have been killed or injured (or captured) but managed somehow to escape. The people who ran out in the first moments and fled the town unobserved. A young couple and their infant son whose "small house" was so small that the snow had covered it completely. A woman who lay hidden beneath an overturned tub. A boy who dived under a pile of flax. Some of this is remembered only by "tradition," not hard evidence, but is too compelling to overlook. Here is another instance, passed through generations of the descendants of Mary Catlin: "The captives were taken to a house . . . and a Frenchman was brought in [wounded] and laid on the floor; he was in great distress and called for water; Mrs. Catlin fed

him with water. Some one said to her, 'How can you do that for your enemy?' She replied, 'If thine enemy hunger, feed him; if he thirst give him water to drink.' The Frenchman was taken and carried away, and the captives marched off. Some thought the kindness shown to the Frenchman was the reason of Mrs. Catlin's being left . . ." (Mary Catlin was indeed "left," the only one of her large family not killed or captured. And this is as plausible an explanation of her survival as any.)

Thus Deerfield in the immediate aftermath: the living and the dead, the wounded and the escaped. Tradition also tells of a mass burial in the southeast corner of the town cemetery. Another "sorrowful" task for the survivors.

Soon groups of armed men begin arriving from the towns to the south. All day and through the evening they come; by midnight there are "near about 80." Together they debate the obvious question, the only one that matters right now: "Should they follow the retreating enemy in order to retake their captive "friends"? Some are for it, but eventually counterarguments prevail. They have no snowshoes, "the snow being at least 3 foot deep." The enemy has "treble our number, if not more." Following "in their path . . . we should too much expose our men." Moreover, the captives themselves will be endangered, "Mr. Williams's family especially, whom the enemy would kill, if we come on."

The day after, "Connecticut men begin to come in"; by nightfall their number has swelled to fully 250. There is more debate on whether to counterattack. However, the "aforesaid objections" remain— plus one more. The weather has turned unseasonably warm, "with rain," and the snowpack is going to slush. They "judge it impossible to travel [except] . . . to uttermost disadvantage." Under the circumstances they could hardly hope "to offend the enemy or rescue our captives, which was the end we aimed at in all." And so they "desist" once again. They give what further help they can to "the remaining inhabitants"— help with the burials and with rounding up the surviving cattle. They prepare a report for the colony leaders in Boston, including a detailed count of casualties: 48 dead, 112 taken captive. (Another 140 remain "alive at home.") They leave a "garrison of 30 men or upwards" in the town. And the rest return to their home villages.

Meanwhile, the "march" of the captives, and their captors, is well under way: through the wilderness on to Canada. There is extreme privation and suffering on both sides. The French and Indians are carrying wounded comrades. The captives include many who are physically weak and emotionally stricken: young children, old people, pregnant women, lone survivors of otherwise shattered families. Food is short, the weather inclement, the route tortuous.

The captors, fearing a possible English pursuit, push forward as rapidly as possible. Any who cannot keep up must be killed and left by the trail "for meat to the fowls of the air and beasts of the earth." Among the first to suffer this fate is the minister's wife. Still convalescent following a recent pregnancy, she nearly drowns in a river crossing, after which, according to John Williams, "the cruel and bloodthirsty savage who took her, slew her with his hatchet at one stroke." In the succeeding days another seventeen of the captives will be similarly "dispatched."

Later in the journey the French and the Indians separate. And later still the Indians, who now hold all the captives, subdivide into small "bands." At one critical juncture Reverend Williams is marked for execution by revenge-minded kinsmen of the "captain" killed at Deerfield; a rival chief's intervention saves him. His five surviving children are scattered among different "masters" and, surprisingly, are "looked after with a great deal of tenderness."

There are two additional deaths—from starvation— as the various bands move farther north, but sooner or later ninety-two captives reach Canada. Some, like John Williams, are ransomed "out of the hands of Indians" by French officials; others are taken to Indian "forts" and encampments throughout the St. Lawrence River Valley.

Almost immediately their relatives and friends in New England begin efforts to secure their release. But the process is complicated, and progress is

The burning of Deerfield, Massachusetts. "Viewed close up," writes John Demos, "the carnage is appalling." (North Wind Picture Archives)

painfully slow. Eventually some fifty-three will be returned home, with John Williams as one of the last among them. His subsequent account of his experiences, published under the imposing title *The Redeemed Captive Returning to Zion,* will make him famous throughout the Colonies.

His daughter Eunice will become equally famous, but for a different reason: she declines to return and spends the rest of her long life among the Indians. She forgets her English and adjusts completely to Indian ways; she marries a local "brave" and raises a family. Another fifteen or so of her fellow captives will make a similar choice, and still others stay on with the French Canadians. These are the captives *un*redeemed: a source of sorrow, and of outrage, for the New Englanders.

In fact, efforts to bring them back will continue for decades. "Friends" traveling back and forth quite unofficially, and full-fledged "ambassadors" sent from one royal governor to the other, seek repeatedly to force a change. In some cases there are direct—even affectionate—contacts between the parties themselves. Eunice Williams pays four separate visits to her New England relatives. Each time they greet her with great excitement and high hopes for her permanent "return," but there is no sign that she even considers the possibility. She acknowledges the claims of her blood, but other, stronger claims draw her back to Canada. She has become an Indian in all *but* blood, and she prefers to remain that way. She will become the last surviving member of the entire "massacre" cohort.

The destruction of Deerfield came nearer the beginning than the end of the Anglo-French struggle for control of North America. And was barely a curtain raiser in the long, sorry drama of "white" versus "red." But it left special, and enduring, memories. Well into the nineteenth century New England boys played a game called Deerfield Massacre, complete with mock scalpings and captive taking. A curious bond grew between Deerfield and the descendants of those same Canadian Indians who had formed the attack party, with visits back and forth on both sides. And particular "massacre" memorabilia have been carefully—almost lovingly—preserved to the present day.

Indeed, Deerfield today recalls both sides of its former frontier experience. It remains an exquisitely tranquil—and beautiful—village, its main street lined with stately old houses (twelve of them open to the public). But its most celebrated single artifact is an ancient wooden door, hacked full of hatchet holes on that bitter night in the winter of 1704.

QUESTIONS TO CONSIDER

1 How was the Deerfield Massacre symbolic of the struggle between England and France for supremacy in North America? Why did the Indians side with the French and not the English?

2 Was Deerfield an isolated, defenseless town? What political and military objectives did the French and Indians hope to gain by raiding a community like Deerfield? Was the raid a success or a failure for the French and Indian forces?

3 Who was John Williams and what was his status in the community? What "terrible insults" did he suffer at the hands of his Indian captors? Why did the Indians take captives?

4 According to the author, Eunice Williams became as famous as her father. Why so? Why would she make the decision that earned her fame? Why would fifteen of her "fellow captives" do what she did?

PART THREE

Transformations

5 "The Empire of My Heart": The Marriage of William Byrd II and Lucy Parke Byrd

PAULA A. TRECKEL

In the lively and original selection that follows, Paula A. Treckel concludes "that the men and women of the past were, after all, only human." That is an eloquent statement of the entire approach of Portrait of America. *All too often students of history, confronted with a vast array of names in their textbooks, view them as people who were devoid of personality or passion. Few of you will continue to believe that after meeting the beautiful and irrepressible Lucy Parke Byrd and her unforgettable husband.*

Before we meet the Byrds of Virginia, it is necessary to place them in a proper historical context. By the eighteenth century, a farming and artisan society had emerged in the North, where slaves were few and most men were free and could boast of owning at least a fifty-acre farm. The abundance of available land allowed quite ordinary people to acquire property and aspire to fortunes and higher stations in life. Here the Protestant work ethic, which celebrated hard work, thrift, and individual economic enterprise, took hold.

In the South, by contrast, a slave-based, planter-dominated society had emerged. Only a relative few, about 5 percent, of southern white landowners were planters, that is, men who owned twenty slaves or more. Nonetheless, the ownership of slaves was a potent status symbol that made the planter a role model and an ideal that other white men sought to emulate. The eighteenth-century South, Treckel states, created a "hierarchy of race, class, and gender." At the top were the planters, who "wielded great authority over all in their domain—their wives, their servants, and their slaves." As in a play, all of them were required to know their parts. If someone forgot or chose not to remember his or her role, it could result in a chaotic situation that affected the entire production.

That sets the stage for the drama of William and Lucy Byrd. Lucy Parke, her maiden name, cer-
tainly looked the part of an English gentlewoman. She was graceful and elegant, the kind of woman
an important politician or planter would naturally select for the first dance at a fancy ball in colonial
Williamsburg. The problem was that Lucy had spirit and a sense of her own worth; she did not
want to repeat the role of her poor mother, who was so dutiful to her philandering husband that she
raised his bastard son. According to Treckel, "Lucy was unwilling to yield to her husband's author-
ity, and her desire for true intimacy within their marriage was in direct conflict with her husband's
need for power and control."

As you have doubtless guessed, there are fireworks in the following story. William and Lucy use
their defenseless slaves to release their anger at each other. There are even marital confrontations over
William's library. Like most women of her day, Lucy had only a limited education, and she real-
ized that the books that her husband treasured might help her gain access to the male-dominated
world beyond the Byrd plantation. The story of the Byrds is replete with arguments, jealousies,
love-making, and competition for power. As you profit from reading about the Byrd's fascinating,
dysfunctional marriage, you will learn a great deal about race, class, and gender in early eighteenth-
century America.

GLOSSARY

ALLESTREE, RICHARD   He wrote *Whole Duty of Man* and *The Ladies Calling*. These guidebooks instructed women to be modest, meek, compassionate, affable, and pious. Men were rational creatures who had an obligation to control the emotions of the women under their care. Elite southern men like William Byrd took these roles seriously and were not accustomed to challenges to their authority from independent women like Lucy.

DOWRY   Financial settlements, anything from money to cattle, that a woman's family would contribute to a new marriage. In the colonial period, people usually married within their own class, and the business arrangements sometimes meant more than true affection. "William was interested in Lucy's dowry as well as her beauty."

PATRIARCHAL FAMILY   A family structure in which the man dominated and made all of the important decisions. A firmly rooted concept in eighteenth-century England, it worked less effectively in the colonies, where labor shortages made wives and children a vital element in a family's survival.

SPOTSWOOD, ALEXANDER   The lieutenant governor of the Virginia colony who asked Lucy to dance with him at a Williamsburg ball. William was proud of his wife's beauty and the attention she received; after all, he thought of his wife as a mere extension of himself.

WESTOVER   This was the Byrd's estate on Virginia's James River. After spending most of his early years in England, William found his colonial home lonely and isolated compared to the intellectual and social stimuli of Europe.

The month was unusually cold, noted William Byrd II in his diary on 30 July 1710, "indeed the coldest that ever was known in [Virginia]." Could the weather, he wondered, have

caused the fever and headaches suffered by his people? Thank God none had died. On that chilly day he also "read a sermon in Dr. Tillotson and then took a little [nap]." In the afternoon Byrd had a "little quarrel" with his wife, Lucy, but "reconciled" their dispute "with a flourish. Then she read a sermon in Dr. Tillotson to me. It is to be observed," he recorded, "that the flourish was performed on the billiard table." After eating fish for dinner and reading

Paula A. Treckel, "'Empire of My Heart,' The Marriage of William Byrd II and Lucy Parke Byrd," *The Virginia Magazine of History and Biography*, vol. 105, no. 2 (Spring, 1997), pp. 125–156. Reprinted by permission.

Soon after William Byrd II posed for this portrait in London, he returned to his Virginia plantation. Thoroughly enamored with the beautiful Lucy Parke, he married her with the promise that she possessed "the empire of my heart." But William was an insecure and controlling husband, and frequent quarrels over power and finances marred this volatile yet sometimes loving relationship. (© Colonial Williamsburg Foundation)

a little Latin, Byrd and his wife "took a walk about the plantation." That evening, although he "neglected to say [his] prayers," he enjoyed "good health, good thoughts, and good humor, thanks be to God."

Most students of early American history are familiar with William Byrd II, the "great American gentleman," whose secret, coded diaries reveal the daily life of a member of Virginia's eighteenth-century planter elite. These journals have given generations of historians insights into the Chesapeake's changing economy, master-slave relations on early Tidewater plantations, and the development of plantation society and culture in the colonial South.

Byrd's remarkable candor in recording his most personal activities—the most infamous is his account of giving his wife a "flourish" on the billiard table—also provides a glimpse into the private world of a Virginia gentleman. In recent years, biographer Kenneth A. Lockridge used the diaries to psychoanalyze Byrd and trace his self-conscious struggle to construct an independent identity as a man and as an American. Historians Michael Zuckerman and Daniel Blake Smith also studied the diaries to shed light on familial mores in the eighteenth-century South. They argue that Byrd blurred the distinction between his public and domestic worlds and created a community, a web of relationships, in the region he ruled.

In addition to providing insights into individual development and the establishment of community in the Chesapeake, William Byrd's diaries give the modern reader an interior view of marriage and gender relations among the Virginia gentry during an important transitional period in American history. The journal entries illuminate Byrd's tempestuous relationship with his first wife, Lucy Parke Byrd, and reveal how at least one gentry couple struggled to reconcile their often conflicting notions of men's and women's proper roles in the colony's emerging plantation economy. The Byrd's stormy marriage was filled with tensions over power and intimacy, authority and love, reason and passion. The couple's slaves often found themselves the innocent victims of the Byrd's battles in the eighteenth-century war between the sexes.

The transformation of the Chesapeake economy from the seventeenth to the eighteenth century prompted modifications in the region's social structure. Although the concept of the patriarchal family was one that most English colonists brought with them to North America in the seventeenth century, harsh reality prevented them from realizing their ideal in Virginia. Because mortality was high and life expectancy low, family life was extremely fragile there. Men seldom lived long enough to assert their accustomed authority over their wives and children; labor shortages throughout most of the century meant that women often helped their husbands supply their families' basic needs. Wives who outlived their spouses were, of necessity, granted greater legal rights and responsibilities than their counterparts in northern colonies, where family life was more stable.

By the end of the century, demographic conditions improved, however, and it was possible for men and women to organize their families' lives in more familiar ways. Because men lived longer, they were able to assume their traditional role as household heads, directing the lives and organizing the labor of their wives and children. As the planter prospered, they began to invest in slave labor. Women whose husbands could afford slaves to work in their tobacco fields were free to devote themselves to bearing and rearing children and to their domestic tasks. A hierarchy based on race, class, and gender emerged in the early eighteenth century, and Virginia's affluent and aspiring planters looked to the mother country for refined models of behavior and family organization.

Yet, even as Chesapeake planters were finally able to replicate the patriarchal family that had long been their ideal, a new paradigm of family life emerged in England with the potential for softening the severity of men's authority and tempering its extremes. . . . This new family model emphasized the complementary nature of women's and men's roles and encouraged affection between husband and wife, parents and children. Although the man was still the head of the family, the woman, it was asserted, was the heart of the home; women's selfless love had the power to tame men's harsh passions and bring harmony to the domestic sphere.

This new ideal of family was a paradox for Englishwomen, however. They were told their real "freedom" rested in their subjugation to their husbands; their authority came through submission to their husbands' will. Only by completely subordinating themselves to their spouses did women have "power" to control them. The reward for their submission, obedience, and humility was security, protection, and happiness. These ideas about families, marriage, and men's and women's proper behavior provide the background for understanding the clash

of will between William and Lucy Byrd in early eighteenth-century Virginia.

William Byrd II was the son of Indian trader, public official, and planter William Byrd and his wife, Mary Horsmanden Filmer Byrd. Born in 1674, he was seven years old when his ambitious father sent him to England to receive a gentleman's education and learn firsthand the ways of the aristocracy. After attending Felsted Grammar School in Essex, he served an apprenticeship in the Netherlands with his father's commercial agents and later entered the Middle Temple to study law. The young William also developed friendships with members of the aristocracy, who elected him to membership in the Royal Society in 1696. Although Byrd spent most of his formative years in England and considered himself an Englishman, his colonial birth marked him as an outsider and both thwarted his efforts to marry into the aristocracy and limited his political potential. Finally, in 1705 he returned to Virginia to claim his sizable inheritance after his father's death.

The Chesapeake Byrd confronted when he returned to Westover, his estate on the James River in Charles City County, was a far cry from the England he had left behind, and he found it difficult to adjust to the isolation of his colonial home. To assuage his loneliness and increase his prospects, he began courting Lucy Parke. The beautiful younger daughter of Colonel Daniel Parke II and his wife, Jane Ludwell Parke, Lucy lived with her mother and her sister, Frances, at Queen's Creek in York County, near Williamsburg. Lucy's mother was the daughter of a prominent Virginia family. Her father was an ambitious, unscrupulous planter who had served in the House of Burgesses and on the governor's council. Parke's violent temper and reputation as a womanizer humiliated his wife and quite likely embarrassed his daughters; he lived openly with his mistress and fathered a son who was reared, at his insistence, by his wife. In 1697 Parke left his wife in charge of his estates and traveled back to England, where he joined the army, became aide-de-camp to the duke of Marlborough, and brought Queen Anne news of the Allied victory at Blenheim. On 29 March 1705, as reward for his military exploits, Parke was appointed governor of the Leeward Islands. . . .

William Byrd thought a connection with Daniel Parke, one of the few native-born Americans ever appointed governor of a British colony, could further his own political ambitions. To that end, Virginia's most eligible bachelor sought permission to court Parke's daughter, Lucy. "Since my arrival in this country I have had the honour to be acquainted with your daughters," he wrote his prospective father-in-law, "and was infinitely surpriz'd to find young ladies with their accomplishments in Virginia. This surprize was soon improv'd into a passion for the youngest for whom I have all the respect and tenderness in the world." William was interested in Lucy's dowry as well as her beauty. He discussed his financial status, because marriage was first and foremost an economic proposition in this era, and remarked, "I dont question but my fortune may be sufficient to make her happy, especially after it has been assisted by your bounty." Impressed, Parke agreed to the match and promised £1,000 as a marriage settlement.

William used the refined language and sophisticated manner of an English gentleman to woo Lucy. Recycling words he had employed before in his failed courtship of an Irish heiress and aping the literary conceits of the learned men he admired, he addressed Lucy as his "Fidelia" and styled himself "Veramour." Was she faithful to him? Was his love for her true? Or was William simply giving lip service to the new notion that affection should exist between husband and wife? "May angels guard my dearest Fidelia and deliver her safe to my arms at our next meeting," he wrote, "and sure they wont refuse their protection to a creature so pure and charming, that it would be easy for them to mistake her for one of themselves." "Fidelia," he swore, "possess[ed] the empire of my heart," and he longed to be hers forever.

What did nineteen-year-old Lucy Parke think of these effusive letters from her thirty-two-year-old suitor? Surely she was flattered, perhaps even awed, by the attentions of this mature, wealthy man, but

This portrait reflects the beauty and grace of Lucy Parke Byrd, but does not do justice to the young woman's powerful will. Far from the typical eighteenth-century plantation wife, she desired more intimacy in her marriage to William and access to the world of ideas that were in her husband's treasured library. (Virginia Historical Society)

did she respond in kind? Was she seduced by his attentiveness and urbane language or confused by his use of classical imagery and his flights of romantic allegory? Did she believe his profession that she had conquered the empire of his heart? Certainly Lucy's upbringing and education were provincial, far removed from the customs of the sophisticated English aristocrats whom William emulated. But her father's exploits and the Parke family's public humiliation may well have made her wise beyond her years, more knowledgeable than most young women her age of the ways of men and the world.

William Byrd had much to offer his "Fidelia." Undeniably the home he could provide was more stable and financially secure than the one in which she was reared. Was she seeking a strong, assertive, older man to care for her as her father had not? A gentleman of property and standing, respected and esteemed by his peers? A man ruled by cool reason rather than the hot passions and violence that governed her father's behavior? A man she could trust to be discreet in his indiscretions? Undoubtedly Lucy considered all of these things when she accepted William's proposal of marriage.

Did Lucy Parke love William Byrd, this man who vowed his eternal love for her? Did she believe that theirs would be a union bound by love, intimacy, and mutual esteem, a far cry from that of her parents? Although mutual affection became more important in mate selection as the century progressed, many elite couples in England and the colonies continued to base their marriages primarily on economic considerations. "I know it is the desire of all young people to be married," Daniel Parke dryly commented to his daughter, "and though very few are as happy after marriage as before, yet every one is willing to make the experiment at their own expense." Certainly Lucy and her sister knew that the choice of a husband was the most important decision in their lives; their father counseled them to "Consider who you marry is the greatest concern to you in the world."

On 4 May 1706, at the Parkes' Queen's Creek plantation, William Byrd wed Lucy Parke on the same day Frances Parke married John Custis IV. The Byrd's marriage, which lasted a decade, was a volatile, yet loving, union. The couple's quarrels and passionate reconciliations are recounted in the first extant volume of William's diary, which begins in 1709, three years after they wed and nearly two years after their daughter Evelyn's birth. The Byrd's marital difficulties were the consequence of their differing views of men's and women's proper roles. Their conflicts were also exaggerated by William's insecurities and exacerbated by the difference in their ages. A mature man, set in his ways, he envisioned himself as the patriarch of Westover, benevolently ruling over his lands and his household of family members, servants, and slaves. Clearly he thought he could mold his young wife—her thoughts, her actions, her appearance—to his liking. But Lucy had other ideas. As William struggled self-consciously to construct his identity as an English planter-patriarch, Lucy resisted his authoritarian, arbitrary ways. She demanded greater closeness and affection in their marriage and found it difficult to submit to his will. Her desire for intimacy threatened his need for authority and control. Could he surrender the "empire of [his] heart" to her and still be master of all in his domain? Could he share his deepest thoughts and fears with her, yet demand her submission to his will? In other words, the Byrds' marital difficulties centered on the age-old conundrum: Does loving someone place you in his or her power, or give you power over him or her? It is also possible that the Byrds' battle of wills and their attempts to resolve their problems reflected some of the fundamental conflicts inherent in the new model of English family life so eagerly embraced by the gentry in the eighteenth-century Chesapeake.

Lucy Parke Byrd's attitudes toward her role as a woman, a wife, and a plantation mistress, and her ideas about marriage as revealed in her husband's diary, also illuminate white women's role in the emerging plantation culture of the region. A charming, passionate woman who appears to have cared deeply for her husband, Lucy expressed her feelings openly; her laughter and sparkling personality enlivened and enriched William's life. Lucy's laughter, however, could quickly change to tears of sorrow. Her frustration with her husband, a consequence of her desire for greater intimacy and an unwillingness to submit to his will, sometimes resulted in expressions of rage. Sadly, she vented her anger not only on him but also on those doubly marked by their race and gender—the female slaves who served her family.

Was Lucy emotionally unstable, as many historians have concluded? Was she a "willful woman" of "Bad Disposition" or merely "fiery and free spirited"? Was she "spoiled and temperamental," or a loving, affectionate woman who simply refused to yield to her husband's authority, who balked at his despotic administration of their household and challenged his decisions? Or was her passionate expression of her feelings simply a reflection of the belief that women were naturally more emotional than men—a view held by most in the early eighteenth century?

The daughter of a tyrannical man who humiliated his obedient, compliant wife, Lucy often refused to emulate her mother and passively acquiesce to her demanding husband. Instead, she fought back. In doing so, she both embraced and violated notions of womanhood espoused by English family reformers and admired by William; although her actions were often ruled by her heart, not her head, Lucy refused to submit to her husband as women were instructed to do. What did William make of his passionate young wife who challenged his decisions, disagreed with his pronouncements, and refused to behave in the manner of a genteel Englishwoman? It must not have taken him long to see that his hope of creating a domestic patriarchy at Westover would never be realized.

To William, Lucy's emotional nature was emblematic of feminine weakness. His belief that men were naturally superior to women was typical of his day. . . . Men were rational beings, ruled by reason; women were governed by their emotions. "Female passions," wrote William Byrd, "require to be managed sometimes, to confine them within bounds and keep them, like a high-mettled horse, from runing away with their owner." Like most Enlightenment thinkers, he believed it was men's responsibility to rein in women's passions: The head must always rule the heart. Extremes in behavior must always be avoided; moderation, balance, and restraint were the edicts that governed Byrd's life. These were values expressed in John Tillotson's *Sermons Preach'd Upon Several Occasions* and Richard Allestree's *Whole Duty of Man,* works in the library at Westover.

Just as Byrd derived his model of gentlemanly behavior from these prescriptive works, he also probably read such guides as *The Ladies Calling,* also by Allestree, to provide insight into the behavior of women and their appropriate roles. The "final authority on the nature and duties of women" for more than a century, *The Ladies Calling* extolled the distinctly "feminine" virtues of modesty, meekness, compassion, affability, and piety.

"Modesty," Allestree proclaimed, ". . . [is] the most indispensable requisite of a woman; a thing so essential and naturall to the Sex, that every the least declination from it, is a proportionable receding from Womanhood." Meekness, too, was required because God had placed women in a position inferior to men. Women, however, were more compassionate than men, for, it was asserted, they had more tender natures. Affability was always expected of them because they were spared, by virtue of their sex, the cares and worries assumed by men.

A wife's chief responsibility was obedience to her husband—by virtue of her marriage vows and because it was ordained by God. She must protect her husband's reputation as her own and guard against jealousy. If her husband proved unfaithful, she should, according to Allestree, view this infidelity as a trial by God for some sin she might have committed. She must submit to it and not reproach her husband for his actions. "[T]he breaches of Wedlock will never be cemented by Storms and loud Outcries," Allestree warned. "Many men have bin made worse, but scarce any better by it: for guilt covets nothing more then an opportunity of recriminating; and where the Husband can accuse the Wive's bitterness, he thinks he needs no other apology for his own Lust."

Certainly Lucy's mother, silently submitting to her husband's flagrant infidelity, was the model of this philosophy. When Daniel Parke returned from England in 1692 with his mistress—he introduced her to the countryside as his "Cousin Brown"—Jane Parke welcomed her into their home. When "Cousin Brown" gave birth to a son shortly after her arrival in the colony, Jane quietly assumed responsibility for raising her husband's illegitimate child, christened Julius Caesar Parke. What did Lucy and her sister think of their father's blatant adultery? Did they witness any "Storms and loud Out-cries" in the privacy of their home or share their mother's bitterness at their father's behavior? Perhaps Lucy learned firsthand the value of Allestree's advice. Turning a blind eye to a husband's unfaithfulness was a way of dulling the pain of his betrayal.

Allestree also urged his female reader to be a good "huswife," skilled in all domestic tasks. As manager of her husband's household, she must "not . . . wast and embezle [his] Estate, but . . . confine her Expences within such limits as that can easily admit." She must be expert in "the well-guiding of the House" and must demand truth, fidelity, diligence, and industry of her servants. While overseeing the household, however, she must always remember that her authority was subordinate to her husband's.

Lucy Parke was probably familiar with this genteel idea of a gentlewoman's proper role. Her sphere, she had been taught, was the household, and she was responsible for its management. Lucy and her sister, Frances, were trained in needlework and cookery and had been taught all manner of housewifely accomplishments by their mother. It was considered unnecessary for them to receive a formal education; women who desired the same education as men were seen as defying their femininity. The Parke sisters most likely received only the most rudimentary schooling in reading, writing, and mathematics, although Jane Parke thought it important that her daughters receive tutoring in French and dancing to render them agreeable to prospective mates. Having watched her mother struggle to administer her father's estates and make them profitable, Lucy was probably content to leave such matters to her husband and turn all of her attention to her domestic tasks.

William, on the other hand, was loathe to delegate management of their household to his wife. Jealous of his authority, he did not even trust Lucy to "guide the house," and this interference was a cause of many quarrels in their marriage. Many of the couple's most violent arguments erupted not when she challenged his authority in his sphere but when he trespassed into what she clearly deemed her arena—the day-to-day operation of their home. All who dwelled on William's plantations, he believed, were his to command; all were members of his "family"—his wife, his children, his servants, his

slaves. . . . Viewing all the residents of his plantations as his subordinates, Byrd blurred the distinctions among them—distinctions based on race, gender, and class. Indeed, within the universe of his household he rarely conferred higher rank or priority of place on his wife and children. In his diaries he referred to Lucy as "my wife" and his children as "my son" and "my daughter." He seldom identified them by their given names, as he often did his house slaves. The words he used in reference to them underscored their relationship to him; William's choice of terms betrayed his belief that all at Westover revolved around him. In viewing his wife as his possession, subordinate to him, he jeopardized her position within their household.

Although in theory the planter-patriarch reigned supreme over his entire plantation, most Chesapeake planters delegated the day-to-day operation of the "great house" and supervision of household servants or slaves to their wives. William Byrd, however, was clearly reluctant to do so. Resentful of any encroachment on what he deemed his purview, he repeatedly criticized Lucy "for not minding her business," and his diary is a veritable litany of complaints. He reproached her for serving "new beef" before the old, "contrary to good management"; she improperly mended his shoes; he complained that she did not prepare his dish of stewed cherries correctly; he found fault with the cleanliness of their daughter's nursery; she did not govern her servants well.

William was especially angry when Lucy spent his money unwisely. Women's emergence as conspicuous consumers of their husbands' wealth was, ironically, a consequence of the new conception of the genteel English family. Charged with making houses into homes, women embellished the domestic sphere in which they were increasingly confined. In doing so they helped fuel the commercial revolution that transformed England into a nation of shopkeepers. Women also became avid consumers of fashion as a means of self-expression and a way of demonstrating their husbands' ability to pay. William Byrd, however, clearly shared Allestree's belief that a good wife should live within her husband's means, and a major quarrel ensued when William received "an invoice of things sent [for from England] by my wife which are enough to make a man mad." When the ship's captain delivered goods ordered by Lucy "to an extravagant value," William was "out of humor very much." In the end, he "made an invoice of the things my wife could spare to be sold." Lucy, understandably, "was in tears about her cargo," but a year later the argument was renewed. "[My] wife and I had a terrible quarrel about the things she had come in but at length she submitted because she was in the wrong," he noted. "For my part I kept my temper very well."

Reared in a household where money was tight and deprived of fine things during her childhood, Lucy probably hoped her wealthy husband would indulge her taste for silks and satins. Did she resent William's management of their finances? Were her self-indulgent shopping sprees a form of rebellion against his tightfistedness? Money was another emblem of a husband's power, and William controlled the purse strings at Westover. Lucy, on the other hand, had witnessed her mother's management of the family's accounts and knew such oversight was something women could do. Although Lucy's extravagance challenged her husband's authority, in the end she submitted to his will.

In criticizing Lucy for her spendthrift ways and domestic failings, William demonstrated his rule not only over the plantation as a whole, but over her as well. His standards, and only his, prevailed at Westover. One major source of contention was the couple's control of the labor and behavior of their chattels. Lucy had been well instructed by her parents in the treatment of her slaves. Daniel Parke taught his daughters to "Be Calm and Obligeing to all the servants, and when you speak doe it mildly Even to the poorest slave." He also warned them that "if any of the Servants committ small faults yt are of no consequence, doe you hide them. If you understand of any great faults they commit, acquaint yr mother, but doe not aggravate the fault." When William reproved Lucy in front of their servants and

slaves, however, he undermined her authority over them and made it more difficult for her to control them. Lucy's problems managing her house slaves illustrate the damaging effect of her husband's relentless criticism.

Lucy could be a cruel mistress. William disapprovingly recorded in 1710 that she "caused little Jenny to be burned with a hot iron." Later he reported a more disturbing incident: "In the evening my wife and little Jenny had a great quarrel in which my wife got the worst but at last by the help of the family Jenny was overcome and soundly whipped." Clearly Jenny refused to obey her mistress and fought back. That Lucy "got the worst" of their battle and had to be rescued by other slaves did not bode well for her authority over them, but the most violent confrontation between mistress and slave was yet to come.

"I had a terrible quarrel with my wife concerning Jenny that I took away from her when she was beating her with the tongs," William recalled. "She lifted up her hands to strike me but forbore to do it. She gave me abundance of bad words and endeavored to strangle herself, but I believe in jest only. However after acting a mad woman a long time she was passive again."

Again and again Jenny was the object of Lucy's wrath. Why? It was unusual for Lucy, or William for that matter, personally to correct the servants; ordinarily the Byrds ordered their punishment by others. Did Lucy believe that Jenny was her husband's mistress? Although William gives no evidence that she was, we cannot know what Lucy suspected. Was a clash of personalities between Jenny and Lucy perhaps to blame for their friction? Did Jenny's saucy behavior provoke her mistress's persecution? Or did Lucy project her rage against her husband onto her slave, a convenient, ever-present scapegoat? Female slaves, doubly marked by their race and gender as inferiors in a world ruled by white men, were especially vulnerable to abuse. In William's chilling account of their battle, Lucy wanted to strike him but directed her anger against herself instead. Because of this graphic expression of frustration, William called her "mad"—a word describing

Westover, the plantation on the banks of the James River, proved too isolated for William after he had experienced the cultural opportunities of England. Lucy also often felt lonely and unloved there. The luckless slaves felt the couple's wrath. William rebuilt the frame structure that his father constructed into the Georgian brick mansion seen in the above photograph and that still stands today. (Virginia Historical Society)

someone either angry (which Lucy clearly was) or mentally unbalanced. Eventually Lucy regained her composure and, as William says, "was passive again," a woman's proper state, in his view.

William understood that Lucy's ill-treatment of their slaves was her way of flouting his authority and an attempt to demonstrate her own. "My wife and I had a terrible quarrel about whipping Eugene while Mr. [Robert] Mumford was there," he recalled. ". . . [S]he had a mind to show her authority before company but I would not suffer it, which she took very ill." Not only did Lucy trespass on her husband's prerogative by publicly punishing his personal slave,

but she also abused those in her command in a futile attempt to win recognition of her authority over them. She and her slaves knew that William was the ultimate ruler of the household, and her mistreatment of them further proved her powerlessness.

Lucy also had her favorites among the Byrd family slaves. Anaka, her maid, probably came to Westover with Lucy when she married. Fond of drink, Anaka often stole from her master's supply. Lucy was more forgiving than her husband, who related he was "out of humor with my wife for trusting Anaka with rum to steal when she was so given to drinking." He whipped the slave for stealing his ale but later "forgave Anaka, on my wife's and sister's persuasion."

Both William and his wife vented their anger with each other on their defenseless slaves. William recorded that "my wife caused Prue to be whipped violently notwithstanding I desired not, which provoked me to have Anaka whipped likewise who had deserved it much more, on which my wife flew into such a passion that she hoped she would be revenged of me." William saw Anaka as Lucy's surrogate; whipping her was his way of punishing Lucy for her disobedience. He was so angered by his wife that even when she "came to ask my pardon and I forgave her in my heart," he "resent[ed], that she might be the more sorry for her folly."

Only rarely did Lucy invade William's sphere at Westover, but when she did, she felt his wrath. In the rambling house he inherited from his father, the intensely private man found sanctuary in the library, filled with books he imported from England and the Continent. There he retreated each morning to read works in French, Dutch, Hebrew, Latin, and Greek, settle accounts, and write in his diary. Behind his library's locked doors, William was transported from the cultural wilderness, the "silent country" of the Chesapeake, to other, far richer worlds. There he explored ancient Greece and Rome and toured the great cultures of Europe, Asia, and Africa. His exceptional library included books on travel, medicine, agriculture, and the arts, as well as classical works on law and politics. A connoisseur of books, William Byrd over the course of his lifetime amassed the largest and finest private library in colonial America.

In this private space Lucy was an unwelcome intruder. William often refused to let her borrow his books and was angry when she moved his personal papers. In locking Lucy out of his library, William shut her out of an important part of his life and revealed his fears of the emotional intimacy of marriage.

Lucy was persistent. Again and again she reached out to her husband. William, however, insisted on limiting and controlling his wife's access to the world of ideas that so delighted him. Although he owned a copy of Mary Astell's *Serious Proposal to the Ladies,* in which the author championed women's intellect, it is doubtful that William supported Astell's radical goal of equal education for women. More likely he agreed with Astell's argument that women's education made them better wives and mothers. To that end, he would decide what it was his young wife should know; he would mold her mind so that she would be his ideal companion. William quite likely applauded Richard Steele when the latter admonished his female readers to "learn in silence of your Husbands and spiritual Guides, read good Books, pray often, and speak little.". . .

Even as he controlled Lucy's access to the written word, William mocked his wife's lack of education. He laughed at her when she chastised him for speaking Latin with a visiting minister and excluded her from their conversation. It was bad manners, she cried. But it was more than that. He was just as furious when he caught her on the stairs listening to his conversations.

William understood knowledge was a source of his superiority and would not, could not, share its riches, or his innermost thoughts, with his wife who loved him. What did he fear? That she would discover he was not the man she thought him to be?

William Byrd's obsessive need to control his wife even extended to Lucy's appearance. As the couple prepared to travel to Williamsburg for the lieutenant governor's ball, William took issue with her decision to pluck her eyebrows. Proud of Lucy's beauty and aware of the impression she made on Virginia's powerful elite, he wanted her appearance to be exactly right. Her beauty and refined behavior were emblems of his position in the colony; she was an extension of him. "My wife and I quarreled about her pulling her brows. She threatened she would not go to Williamsburg if she might not pull them; I refused, however, and got the better of her," he smugly noted, "and maintained my authority." Lucy's presence at the social event of the year was important to her husband, and William was doubly honored when Lieutenant Governor Alexander Spotswood asked Lucy to be his partner in opening the ball. Although her husband's will prevailed, Lucy's threat showed she understood her value to him.

In disputing William's command throughout their marriage, Lucy threatened his manhood. William's anxieties about authority, his sense of inadequacy, and his doubts about his masculinity probably originated in his youth. It has been suggested that in order to curb his apprehensions and gain some control over his life, William obsessively followed a health regime based on regular sexual relations, proper diet, and exercise. Yet he also used sex to control and dominate his wife. His method of resolving disagreements and reconciling their quarrels was to "roger" Lucy or give her a "flourish." Subscribing to the sexual etiquette of the day in which men were the pursuers and women the pursued, William was, by his account, always the initiator and Lucy the passive but willing object of his desire. He took great pride in listing the variety of places they coupled—the billiard table, the trestle—and in noting when he performed "with vigor." Significantly, William also "rogered" Lucy more than once in his library, his domain, surrounded by the many volumes filled with the knowledge that empowered him and was denied to her.

It is likely William was a selfish lover. He noted having intercourse with his wife throughout her pregnancies, sometimes only days before she was delivered, and even when she felt ill or was indisposed. Their activities probably compromised her pregnancies and may even have precipitated her miscarriages. Only twice in the four years of his diary does he mention that he gave Lucy pleasure. In one of these instances, he observed, "I gave my wife a powerful flourish and gave her great ecstasy and refreshment." Was she always his willing partner? Perhaps Lucy understood that sexual union was the only way her husband knew to demonstrate his love for her. Realizing that their lovemaking was the only way she could achieve the kind of intimacy she desired with her husband, she willingly submitted to his overtures.

The tone of William's diaries is one of cool detachment, curiously devoid of emotion. His entries on his infant son's death, his daughter's near-fatal illness, and Lucy's miscarriages seem almost cruelly indifferent to the modern reader. It may well be, however, that William's journal was his way of taming his turbulent feelings; through writing he acquired the emotional detachment he longed for and struggled to achieve.

Like many men of his time, William was unfaithful to his wife. He occasionally "committed uncleanness" while in Williamsburg and recorded his transgressions with servants or prostitutes in his diary. He sometimes stole a kiss from a "Negro girl" or "made . . . good sport" with an Indian, but on most occasions he expressed remorse for his actions. Although Lucy suspected his infidelity, it is likely that she followed Allestree's advice and her mother's example and did not directly reproach her husband for his faithlessness. Growing up with her father's adultery and reared with her illegitimate brother, Lucy probably expected such behavior from men. Perhaps she had observed that in the calculus of marriage "a philandering husband abroad means greater wifely power at home."

When William flirted with a neighbor's wife in Lucy's presence, however, she was justifiably upset. "I played at [r-m] with Mrs. [Mary] Chiswell and kissed her on the bed till she was angry and my wife also was uneasy about it, and cried as soon as the company was gone," William recalled. Later, he "neglected to say my prayers, which I should not have done, because I ought to beg pardon for the lust I had for another man's wife." What made this episode so disturbing to Lucy was its public nature; her husband humiliated her before their friends. Although William regretted his actions, it was not because he had embarrassed his wife. Rather, he had stepped over the line of acceptable behavior for a gentleman. His public flirtation challenged Charles Chiswell's authority over his wife and jeopardized a friendship.

When William rebuffed Lucy's attempts at marital intimacy and asserted his authority over her, she turned to her sister, Frances, and a network of other women for support. The separation of men's and women's worlds, a consequence of their changing economic and social roles, led to the emotional estrangement of the sexes in the eighteenth-century Chesapeake, even as spousal affection was idealized. Women's domestic duties bound them to their homes, while men's responsibilities often took them into the larger world. Relatively isolated on plantations, mothers and daughters enjoyed close relationships, and sisters were often best friends. After her mother's death in 1708, Lucy confided in her sister and enjoyed the company of her female neighbors. The opportunity to visit their circle of friends was a much-anticipated break from plantation routine for southern women. Women's friendships were also reinforced by their domesticity and strengthened by the shared experiences of pregnancy and childbirth. Female friends and neighbors assisted Lucy during her confinements and comforted her when she suffered miscarriages.

In an age when a woman's worth was measured by her ability to bear and rear children, Lucy's difficult pregnancies were a source of worry and self-doubt. When she shared her fears with her husband, however, he did not know how to console her. "[M]y wife . . . was melancholy for her misfortunes and wished herself a freak," he recalled, "for which I rebuked her." But a rebuke was not what Lucy sought from her husband; William was emotionally incapable of providing her with the loving reassurance that she required. Consequently, Lucy turned to those with whom she shared the common bond of gender to meet her emotional needs.

Lucy's closest friend was Mary Jeffreys Dunn, the wife of a local minister. When Dunn's husband beat her and threatened to kill her, William offered her refuge at Westover. During her year-long residence there she became Lucy's confidante and constant companion. Although initially William welcomed her into his family, he soon regretted his hospitality. He came to view Dunn as a "Devil" whose purpose was to "infect" his wife with her ill humor. William feared that "if [she] tarry with us much longer my wife and I, who us'd to be envy'd for a happy couple, shall very probably come to extremitys." . . .

She encouraged Lucy's defiance and "bred very unpleasant controversys betwixt me & my wife." In addition to usurping his authority over his wife, Dunn appropriated William's command of his servants and slaves. "I will be master of my family," he thundered, "in spight of all the weak politiques practic'd to abuse my good nature."

Was Mary Dunn so evil, or did William exaggerate the threat she posed to his marriage? Always uncomfortable with his emotions and insecure in his command, he was jealous of this rival for his wife's affection. Lucy no longer confided in him or joined him in long, private walks around the plantation. Instead, she entrusted Dunn with her confidences and strolled with her. He blamed Dunn for his wife's defection and wanted Lucy to choose—him or Dunn. William voyaged to England at the height of their marital difficulties, either to jolt his wife into realizing their marriage was at risk or to flee a problem he was emotionally unable to resolve. Although Dunn's support gave Lucy comfort and the strength to defy her authoritarian husband, Lucy's love of William won out over their friendship, and the Byrds reconciled. But the couple's entanglement with Mary Dunn shows just how complex and competitive marital vows and the bonds of female friendship could be in the eighteenth-century South.

The marriage of Lucy Parke Byrd and William Byrd II survived their many battles and passionate reconciliations, and William anticipated a long and happy life with his engaging wife. Colonial matters required that he travel to England in 1715, but he urged his wife to join him when he realized his return to Westover would be delayed. Following the birth of their daughter Wilhelmina, Lucy set sail for England. Their loving reunion was tragically cut short by Lucy's sudden death from smallpox in November 1716. William was overwhelmed with grief and blamed himself for her death. "I little expected that I should be forced to tell you the very melancholy news of my dear Lucy's death," he wrote his brother-in-law, John Custis. ". . . Gracious God what pains did she take to make a voyage hither to seek a grave." Her death was punishment, he thought, for his pride in her beauty and accomplishments. "No stranger ever met with more respect in a strange country than she had done here, from many persons of distinction, who all pronounced her an honor to Virginia."

Lucy's death stunned William. He had never permitted himself to acknowledge how much he loved and depended on his infuriating, passionate, spirited wife. Just as her reception in England was a reflection on him, he saw her death as punishment for his faults—his pride in her, his vanity. She was an extension of him in death as in life. Her death was a form of abandonment, and in mourning her, he grieved for a lost part of himself.

Although William eventually remarried, his second wife, Maria Taylor Byrd, was far more conventional than his first. An English heiress, she understood the rules that governed English society and the relationship between husbands and wives and was comfortable with them. Unlike Lucy, she did not trespass on William's prerogative, challenge his authority, or defy his will. An excellent housewife, a successful mother, Maria was the epitome of the genteel, submissive English lady William had always wanted Lucy to emulate. Her manners were impeccable: she could be relied upon not to listen in on his private conversations or borrow books from his library. But Maria was not a woman he gave a "flourish" to on the billiard table or "rogered" in the library. She lacked the passion and emotion of Lucy, the light and love of William's life. Instead, the placid Maria was the model mistress to complement William's ideal gentleman-planter. She brought calm, order, and discipline to his household and his life.

One has to wonder if William Byrd, having finally gotten what he wanted—a docile, compliant, obedient wife to suit his cultivated estates—was happy. Or did he miss free-spirited, defiant, exciting Lucy who never gave up her efforts to defy his authority and achieve true intimacy with him? In their ongoing battle of wills, was she finally the victor? Did she, in the end, truly conquer the "empire of [his] heart"?

Lucy Parke Byrd's marriage to William Byrd II occurred during a transitional moment in the history of Virginia. As the Chesapeake was transformed into a plantation-based economy dependent on slave labor, women's and men's roles began to change. Aspiring gentlemen-planters such as Byrd tried to create a hierarchy of race, class, and gender in the region. These self-styled gentlemen-planters wielded great authority over all in their domain—their wives, their children, their servants, and their slaves. During the earliest years, however, their domestic patriarchies were sometimes imperfectly wrought, and the planters' power and authority was challenged by the women with whom they shared their lives.

The plantation mistress, modeled after the English gentlewoman, had a particular role to play within the region. Neither master nor slave, she was dependent on both for her status. Her authority was derived from the men of her household yet required her willingness to submit to their will. Some planters' wives, such as Lucy Parke Byrd, uneasily embraced the new ideal of conformable womanhood emerging in the Chesapeake and the corresponding separation of spheres, and alienation of affections, that it engendered. Lucy was unwilling to yield to her husband's authority, and her desire for true intimacy within their marriage was in direct conflict with her husband's need for power and control. These issues were central to the couple's marital difficulties and their battle for the empire of William Byrd's heart.

Although played out in the setting of the eighteenth-century Chesapeake, the drama of the Byrds' marriage—their struggle to reconcile their emotional needs with their conflicting ideals of family life—is curiously contemporary. It provides us with a poignant reminder that the men and women of the past were, after all, only human.

QUESTIONS TO CONSIDER

1 Were you surprised to read about such personal revelations, sometimes humorous and at times a bit

bawdy, in the diary of William Byrd? Like many couples, William and Lucy quarreled, reconciled, made love, and took long walks. Even though they lived almost two hundred years ago, did they have some of the same problems and joys that we see in contemporary marriages?

2 Both Lucy and William make for tempting psychological studies. In what ways did Lucy's philandering father and her humiliated mother influence Lucy and her expectations of marital bliss? Why was William so protective of his library and intent on controlling every aspect of his wife's life, even her appearance? Finally, why couldn't William give his young wife the intimacy she so desired?

3 What were the roles and attitudes that governed gender relationships among the plantation elite? How did William and Lucy fit that model, and in what ways did they break the mold? Although it was tumultuous, do you think that they had a good marriage? Do you think that William was happier with his more proper (and boring) second wife?

4 What does Treckel mean when she states that the "couple's slaves often found themselves the innocent victims of the Byrds' battles in the eighteenth century war between the sexes"? Why did William's criticism of his wife, with the slaves present, undermine Lucy's authority on this Virginia plantation? Does this help us understand Lucy's occasional violent bouts with the helpless labor force?

5 How were sexual relationships between a husband and wife symbolic of the greater roles that they were to play within Virginia's plantation society? Do you agree with Treckel that "William was a selfish lover" who had "anxieties about authority" and a sense of inadequacy about his own masculinity?

6 Men and women lived in separate worlds in the eighteenth-century Chesapeake, and this often compromised intimacy between husbands and wives. Who did Lucy turn to for friendship, and how did William react? Does Treckel's essay help you understand why women forged such close bonds with each other, a topic that will be explored further in selection 12?

6 Citizen Ben: A Worldly American's Seven Great Virtues

WALTER ISAACSON

Benjamin Franklin, who called himself "the printer of Philadelphia," was one of the most remarkable human beings colonial America ever produced. Historian Richard B. Morris called Franklin America's first pragmatist: he believed that "what was moral was what worked and what worked was moral." He also celebrated the Protestant work ethic in his bestselling Poor Richard's Almanack, *the advice in which became the maxims of Franklin's generation: "Early to bed, and early to rise, makes a man healthy, wealthy, and wise." "He that riseth late must trot all day, and shall scarce overtake his business at night." "Sloth makes all things difficult, but industry all easy." "Laziness travels so slowly, that poverty soon overtakes him." "Women and Wine, Game and Deceit, Make the Wealth Small and his Wants Great." Franklin not only personified the frugality, hard work, restlessness, and occasional irreverence of colonial Americans but came to symbolize their growing sense of nationality as well.*

In his long lifetime, Franklin tried his hand at virtually every trade and profession young America had to offer—among other things, he was a farmer, a printer, a scientist, an author, a philosopher, a statesman, a diplomat, and a connoisseur of women. In the last capacity, he composed an article on the cultivation of a mistress and became a legendary womanizer. He particularly enjoyed making love to older women, because sexual encounters, he said, made them "happy" and "so grateful." According to one anecdote, he fathered so many children that a colleague was moved to quip that it was not Washington but Benjamin Franklin who was "the real father of our country." Franklin would have appreciated the anecdote, for he had a consummate sense of humor. But above all, he had an unflagging love for liberty and the natural rights of people.

Still, Franklin was a complex and often contradictory person. Although he abhorred violence, he was a devious individual who rebelled against convention and authority, and in time became a leading American revolutionary. At the same time, Franklin regarded himself as truly a citizen of the world who hoped one day "that not only the love of liberty, but a thorough knowledge of the rights of man, may pervade all the nations of the earth, so that a philosopher may set his foot anywhere on its surface, and say, 'This is my country.'"

On the issue of slavery and race, however, Franklin was not always enlightened. In the 1730s, he held a low opinion of black people's intellectual abilities and even traded in slaves at his Philadelphia printing shop, either selling them for others or buying them as an investment. He once advertised that he had for sale "a breeding Negro woman about twenty years of age. Can do any household work." He also owned a slave couple, who worked with white servants in his home. By 1751, however, he had come to regard slavery as an economically unsound labor system. Twenty-one years later, a visit to an African American school was a revelation for him. What he saw convinced him that the schoolchildren were the equal of their white peers in intellectual capacity. That same year, Franklin publicly condemned the slave trade as "a detestable commerce" and damned slavery as a crime against humanity. After the Revolution, at the age of eighty-one, Franklin became the president of the Pennsylvania Society for the Abolition of Slavery. His evolution from slave trader to prominent American abolitionist demonstrated that people can become enlightened and can grow out of their prejudices.

In the following selection, based on his exciting new biography of Franklin, Walter Isaacson examines Franklin's values and offers brilliant insights into "the most identifiable and approachable of the founding fathers." A former editor of Time *magazine and chairman of CNN, Isaacson combined exhaustive research and a lively style of writing to produce a portrait of a charismatic, multifaceted man who was well built, stood six feet tall, and was "a bit of a playboy" in his younger years, as a recent History Channel program said. Isaacson even believes that Franklin would have felt comfortable living in our own fast-paced time. As he told PBS, "Franklin would relish the communication and digital revolution we're going through today, and I am sure he would have been one of the first people in America to have created a web site, and also probably created an on-line service so he could make money off the web site, because he loved the idea of spreading information, thoughts and discourse." As you read Isaacson's colorful portrait, decide if Franklin's seven great virtues are as relevant to the twenty-first century as they were to the eighteenth century. Do you agree with Isaacson that Franklin would have enjoyed the computer age?*

GLOSSARY

BAKER, POLLY   In one of Franklin's hoaxes, he created a fictitious woman who defended herself before a Massachusetts court, which had charged her with bearing five illegitimate children. Franklin wanted to make the point that it was unfair to condemn women for having children out of wedlock while absolving the men who had impregnated them. As Franklin told the story, Polly was found not guilty, and one of the judges married her.

DOGOOD, SILENCE   The pseudonym for the sixteen-year-old Franklin when he surreptitiously slipped essays, thirteen in all, under his brother's printing house door. Young Benjamin perfectly captured the cadence of the opinionated "slightly prudish widow," and was delighted when his brother published the essays in his newspaper.

FRANKLIN, JAMES   Benjamin's brother who was the editor of a Boston newspaper, the *New England Courant,* and who allowed his younger brother to serve as his apprentice. When James was jailed for criticizing the government, Benjamin temporarily took over the newspaper. Finding his brother overbearing, young Benjamin fled to Philadelphia.

FRANKLIN, WILLIAM   Benjamin's illegitimate son, who later became the British Governor of New Jersey. Differing views over the legitimacy of the American Revolution would eventually destroy the relationship between father and son.

JUNTO   A club consisting of Franklin's fellow tradesmen who met regularly to discuss contemporary issues and philosophical topics. Franklin insisted that their dialogues be nonconfrontational and respectful of the views of others. The Junto became involved in civic- improvement endeavors such as the establishment of America's first lending library.

LOUIS XVI   King of France when Franklin attempted to gain allies for the American Revolution. France would eventually support the American cause in the hope that this would weaken England. Revolutionary fervor later spread to Paris and cost the French monarch his life on the merciless guillotine.

PENNSYLVANIA GAZETTE   Franklin's newspaper in Philadelphia in which he expressed his profound belief in a free press. According to Franklin, a free press had an obligation to publish opposing viewpoints and not simply reflect the principles of its editor.

POOR RICHARD SAUNDERS   The fictional character in Franklin's immensely popular almanac, Poor Richard offered folksy advice on how to best lead a productive life.

READ, DEBORAH   This young woman, whom Franklin met when he came to Philadelphia, eventually became his wife. Despite his notorious womanizing, Franklin firmly believed in marriage. He contended that "a single man resembles the odd half of a pair of scissors."

ROUSSEAU, JEAN-JACQUES   Like Voltaire, a French philosopher and intellectual who was as immensely popular in Paris as Franklin.

VERGENNES, COMTE DE (CHARLES GRAVIER)   French foreign minister when Franklin was in Paris. Franklin influenced Vergennes with his calculations of the economic and strategic advantages that European nations would enjoy if America won its independence from Great Britain. Eventually France formed an alliance with America's revolutionary government. Franklin helped engineer the alliance that provided the American rebels with military support that helped them defeat the British and gain their independence.

His arrival in Philadelphia is one of the most famous scenes in autobiographical literature: the bedraggled 17-year-old runaway, cheeky yet with a pretense of humility, straggling off the boat and buying three puffy rolls as he wanders up Market Street. But wait a minute. There's something more going on here. Peel back a layer and we can see him as a 65-year-old wry observer, sitting in an English country house, writing this scene, pretending it's part of a letter to his son, an illegitimate son who has become a Royal Governor with aristocratic pretensions and needs to be reminded of his humble roots.

A careful look at the manuscript peels back yet another layer. Inserted into the sentence about his pilgrim's progress up Market Street is a phrase, written in the margin, in which he notes that he passed by the house of his future wife Deborah Read and that "she, standing at the door, saw me and thought I made, as I certainly did, a most awkward ridiculous appearance." So here we have, in a brief paragraph, the multilayered character known so fondly to his author as Benjamin Franklin: as a young man, then seen through the eyes of his older self and then through the memories later recounted by his wife. It's all topped off with the old man's deft little affirmation—"as I certainly did"—in which his self-deprecation barely cloaks the pride he felt regarding his remarkable rise in the world.

Benjamin Franklin is the founding father who winks at us. George Washington's colleagues found it hard to imagine touching the austere general on the shoulder, and we would find it even more so today. Jefferson and Adams are just as intimidating. But Ben Franklin, that genial urban entrepreneur, seems made of flesh rather than of marble, addressable by nickname, and he turns to us from history's stage with eyes that twinkle from behind those newfangled spectacles. He speaks to us, through his letters and hoaxes and autobiography, not with orotund rhetoric but with a chattiness and clever irony that is very contemporary, sometimes unnervingly so. We see his reflection in our own time.

He was, during his 84-year life, America's best scientist, inventor, diplomat, writer and business strategist, and he was also one of its most practical, though not most profound, political thinkers. He proved by flying a kite that lightning was electricity, and he invented a rod to tame it. He devised bifocal glasses and clean-burning stoves, charts of the Gulf Stream and theories about the contagious nature of the common cold. He was a pioneer of do-it-yourself civic improvement, launching such schemes as a lending library, volunteer fire corps, insurance association and matching-grant fund raiser. He helped invent America's unique style of homespun humor and philosophical pragmatism. In foreign policy, he created an approach that wove together idealism with balance-of-power realism. In politics, he proposed seminal plans for uniting the colonies and creating a federal model for a national government. And he was the person most responsible, of all the Founders, for instilling in the new nation the virtue that is central to its role in the world struggle: that of tolerance, specifically religious tolerance.

Instinctively more comfortable with democracy than were his fellow Founders and devoid of the snobbery that later critics would feel toward his own shopkeeping values, he had faith in the wisdom of the common man and felt that a new nation would draw its strength from what he called "the middling people." Through his self-improvement tips for cultivating personal virtues and through his civic-improvement schemes for furthering the common good, he helped to create, and to celebrate, a new ruling class of ordinary citizens who learned to be tolerant of the varied beliefs and dogmas of their neighbors.

Franklin has a particular resonance in 21st century America. A successful publisher and consummate networker with an inventive curiosity, he would have felt right at home in the information revolution. We can easily imagine having a beer with him after work, showing him how to use a Palm Pilot, sharing the business plan for a new venture or discussing Bill Clinton's foibles and George Bush's foreign policy. He would laugh at the latest joke about a priest and a rabbi or about a farmer's daughter. We would admire both his earnestness and his self-aware irony. And we would relate to the way he tried to balance, sometimes uneasily, a pursuit of reputation, wealth, earthly virtues and spiritual values.

Some who see the reflection of Franklin in the world today fret about a shallowness of soul and a spiritual complacency that seem to permeate a culture of materialism. They say that he teaches us how to live a practical and congenial life but not an exalted existence based on great spiritual passions. Others see the same reflection and admire the basic middle-class values and democratic sentiments that now seem under assault from élitists, radicals, religious fanatics and other bashers of modernity and the bourgeoisie. His admirers look upon Franklin as an examplar of the personal character and civic virtue that are too often missing in today's world.

Much of the admiration is warranted, and so too are some of the qualms. But the lessons from Franklin's life are more complex than those usually drawn by either his fans or his foes. Both sides too often confuse him with the striving pilgrim he portrayed in his autobiography. They mistake his genial moral maxims for the fundamental faiths that motivated his actions.

His morality was built on a sincere belief in leading a virtuous life, serving the country he loved and hoping to achieve salvation through good works. That led him to make the link between private virtue and civic virtue and to suspect, based on the meager evidence he could muster about God's will, that these earthly virtues were linked to heavenly ones as well. As he put it in the motto for the library he founded, "To pour forth benefits for the common good is divine."

It is useful for us to engage anew with Franklin, for in doing so we are grappling with a fundamental issue: How does one live a life that is useful, virtuous, worthy, moral and spiritually meaningful? For that matter, which of these attributes is most important? These are questions just as vital for a self-satisfied age as they were for a revolutionary one.

A methodical and wry man, Franklin loved making lists. He made lists of rules for his tradesmen's club, of synonyms for being drunk, of maxims for matrimonial happiness and of reasons to choose an older woman as a mistress. Most famously, as a young man, he made a list of personal virtues that he determined should define his life. Following his method, we can get a glimpse of his influence on the American character by looking at the seven defining virtues and traits that he, more than anyone, helped to imprint onto our national fabric.

---

1. AN AVERSION TO TYRANNY

At age 12, Franklin became an apprentice at the printshop of his older brother James, who tended to be quite tough as a master. "I fancy his harsh and tyrannical treatment of me," Franklin later speculated, had the effect of "impressing me with that aversion to arbitrary power that has stuck to me through my whole life." That was a bit unfair to poor James, whose newspaper in Boston was the first feisty and independent publication in the colonies and who taught young Benjamin how to be cheeky about establishment authority.

Franklin knew that his brother would never knowingly print his pieces. So one night he invented a pseudonym, disguised his handwriting and slipped an essay under the printing-house door. The cadre of his brother's friends who gathered the next day lauded the anonymous submission, and Franklin had the "exquisite pleasure" of listening as they decided to feature it on the front page of the next issue.

The literary character Franklin invented was a triumph of imagination. Silence Dogood was a slightly prudish widow from a rural area, created by a spunky unmarried Boston 16-year-old who had never spent a night outside of the city. He imbued Mrs. Dogood with that spirited aversion to tyranny that he would help to make part of the American character. "I am," she wrote, "a mortal enemy to arbitrary government and unlimited power. I am naturally very jealous for the rights and liberties of my country; and the least appearance of an encroachment on those invaluable privileges is apt to make my blood boil exceedingly." It was as good a description of the real Benjamin Franklin—and, indeed, of a typical American—as is likely to be found anywhere.

Franklin used Mrs. Dogood to attack the theocratic rule of the Puritan establishment and the link between church and state that was then the very foundation of Massachusetts government. At one point she asks, "Whether a Commonwealth suffers more by hypocritical pretenders to religion or by the openly profane?" Unsurprisingly, she concludes the former is worse, and singles out the Governor, a minister who had become a politician, as an example. "The most dangerous hypocrite in a Commonwealth is one who leaves the gospel for the sake of the law. A man compounded

Franklin enjoyed poking fun at himself and had little patience for those who took themselves too seriously. He displayed the American sense of humor, Isaacson observes, that includes "the wry, homespun mix of folksy tales and pointed observations that was perfected by such Franklin descendants as Mark Twain and Will Rogers." (© Drew Friedman)

of law and gospel is able to cheat a whole country with his religion and then destroy them under color of law."

Throughout his life, Franklin would be willing to compromise on many matters but not on his aversion to tyranny. After he became an editor on his own in Philadelphia, he led the fight against arbitrary taxes imposed from England. As early as 1755, when most of his fellow colonists were content to go along with such taxes, he wrote a scathing denunciation that concluded with what would eventually become an American rallying cry: "Those who would give up essential liberty to purchase a little temporary safety deserve neither liberty nor safety."

2. A FREE PRESS

The surest guard against tyranny and arbitrary power, Franklin came to believe, was free expression, the free flow of ideas and a free press. No tyrannical society can long exist, he felt, when it cannot control the flow of information and ideas.

After he had run away from his apprenticeship in Boston and begun publishing his own paper, the *Pennsylvania Gazette,* he expressed this credo in a famous editorial, "Apology for Printers," which remains one of the best defenses of a free press. The opinions people have, Franklin wrote, are "almost as various as their faces." The job of printers is to allow people to express these differing opinions. "There would be very little printed," he noted, if publishers produced only things that offended nobody. At stake was the virtue of free expression, and Franklin summed up the Enlightenment position: "Printers are educated in the belief that when men differ in opinion, both sides ought equally to have the advantage of being heard by the public; and that when Truth and Error have fair play, the former is always an overmatch for the latter."

"It is unreasonable to imagine that printers approve of everything they print," he went on to argue. "It is likewise unreasonable what some assert, That printers ought not to print anything but what they approve; since . . . an end would thereby be put to free writing, and the world would afterwards have nothing to read but what happened to be the opinions of printers."

It was not in Franklin's nature, however, to be dogmatic or extreme about any principle; he generally gravitated toward a sensible balance. The rights of printers, he realized, were balanced by their duty to be responsible. Thus, even though printers should be free to publish offensive opinions, they should exercise discretion. "I myself have constantly refused to print anything that might countenance vice or promote immorality, though . . . I might have got much money. I have also always refused to print such things as might do real injury to any person."

One such example involved a customer who asked the young printer to publish a piece in the *Gazette* that Franklin found "scurrilous and defamatory." In his effort to decide whether he should take the customer's money even though it violated his principles, Franklin subjected himself to the following test:

"To determine whether I should publish it or not, I went home in the evening, purchased a twopenny loaf at the baker's, and with the water from the pump made my supper; I then wrapped myself up in my great-coat, and laid down on the floor and slept till morning, when, on another loaf and a mug of water, I made my breakfast. From this regimen I feel no inconvenience whatever. Finding I can live in this manner, I have formed a determination never to prostitute my press to the purposes of corruption and abuse of this kind."

It is important to remember, when people complain about the irresponsibility of the press today, that back then it was much more raucous. In the Pennsylvania Assembly election of 1764, for example, all sorts of vicious articles and pamphlets were printed attacking Franklin, who was a candidate.

One such piece, titled "What is Sauce for a Goose is also Sauce for a Gander," raked up every possible allegation against Franklin—including that he had bought his honorary degrees, sought a royal governorship and stolen his electricity experiments from others, all of which were false. It also alleged that his son William was the bastard child of a "kitchen wench," which had some truth to it. Another broadside painted him as an excitable lecher:

> *Franklin, though plagued with fumbling age,*
> *Needs nothing to excite him,*
> *But is too ready to engage,*
> *When younger arms invite him.*

Modern election campaigns are often criticized for being negative, and today's press is slammed for being scurrilous. But the most brutal of modern attack ads pale in comparison with the barrage of pamphlets in the 1764 Assembly election. Pennsylvania survived them, as did Franklin, who never considered suing. And America's democracy learned that it could thrive in an atmosphere of unrestrained, even intemperate, free expression. Indeed, its democracy was built on a foundation of unbridled free speech. In the centuries since then, the nations that have thrived, economically and politically, have been those, like America, that are most comfortable with the cacophony, and even occasional messiness, that come from robust discourse.

———

3. HUMOR

By creating Silence Dogood, Franklin invented what became the quintessential genre of American folksy humor: the wry and self-deprecating homespun character whose feigned innocence and naiveté are disarming but whose wicked little insights poke through the pretensions of the élite and the follies of everyday life. "I am courteous and affable, good humored (unless I am first provoked) and handsome, and sometimes witty," she declares, flicking in the word "sometimes" with a dexterity uncommon in a 16-year-old. "I have likewise a natural inclination to observe and reprove the faults of others, at which I have an excellent faculty." It was a style adopted by such descendants as Mark Twain and Will Rogers.

Among the things Mrs. Dogood dared to make fun of was the college Franklin had planned to attend until his father decided it wasn't worth the cost. She recounts falling asleep under an apple tree while considering whether to send her son to Harvard. As she journeys in her dream toward this temple of learning, she notices that the gate is guarded by "two sturdy porters named Riches and Poverty," and only those who met the approval of the former could get in. Most of the students are content to dally with the figures called Idleness and Ignorance. "They learn little more than how to carry themselves handsomely, and enter a room genteelly (which might as well be acquired at a dancing school), and from thence they return, after abundance of trouble and charge, as great blockheads as ever, only more proud and self-conceited."

Franklin created a similar character in Poor Richard Saunders, the pseudonym he used when he began to publish an annual almanac. The beauty of inventing a fictional author was that he could poke fun at himself by admitting, only half in jest, that

money was his main motivation. "I might in this place attempt to gain thy favor by declaring that I write almanacks with no other view than that of the public good; but in this I should not be sincere," Poor Richard began his first preface. "The plain truth of the matter is, I am excessive poor, and my wife . . . has threatened more than once to burn all my books and Rattling-Traps (as she calls my instruments) if I do not make some profitable use of them for the good of my family."

In his first edition, Poor Richard predicts "the inexorable death" of his rival almanac writer Titan Leeds, giving the exact day and hour. It was a prank borrowed from Jonathan Swift. Leeds fell into the trap, and in his own almanac for 1734 (written after the date of his predicted death) called Franklin a "conceited scribbler" who had "manifested himself a fool and a liar." Poor Richard responded that all of these defamatory protestations indicated that the real Leeds must indeed be dead and his new almanac a hoax by someone else. "Mr. Leeds was too well bred to use any man so indecently and scurrilously, and moreover his esteem and affection for me was extraordinary."

Poor Richard's delightful annual prefaces never, alas, became as famous as the maxims and sayings that Franklin scattered in the margins of his almanacs each year, such as the most famous of all: "Early to bed and early to rise, makes a man healthy, wealthy and wise." Franklin would have been amused by how faithfully these were praised by subsequent advocates of self-improvement, and he would likely have been even more amused by the humorists who later poked fun at them. In a sketch with the ironic title "The Late Benjamin Franklin," Mark Twain gibed, "As if it were any object to a boy to be healthy and wealthy and wise on such terms. The sorrow that that maxim has cost me, through my parents experimenting on me with it, tongue cannot tell. The legitimate result is my present state of general debility, indigence, and mental aberration. My parents used to have me up before nine o'clock in the morning sometimes when I was a boy. If they had let me take my natural rest where would I have been now? Keeping store, no doubt, and respected by all." Groucho Marx, in his memoirs, also picked up the theme. "'Early to bed, early to rise, makes a man you-know-what.' This is a lot of hoopla. Most wealthy people I know like to sleep late, and will fire the help if they are disturbed before three in the afternoon."

Franklin's favorite device for poking fun at social mores and political outrages was the hoax. . . . Franklin's satires were meant to be playful and to make a moral point, although they did occasionally deceive. "The Speech of Polly Baker," for example, purports to recount the speech of a young woman on trial for having a fifth illegitimate child. Franklin, who had fathered an illegitimate child but taken responsibility for him, was particularly scathing about the double standard that subjects her, but not the men who had sex with her, to humiliation. As Polly says, "I readily consented to the only proposal of marriage that ever was made me, which was when I was a virgin; but too easily confiding in the person's sincerity that made it, I unhappily lost my own honor by trusting his; for he got me with child, and then forsook me. That very person you all know; he is now become a magistrate of this county." By doing her duty to bring children into the world, despite the fact that no one would marry her, and being willing to do so despite the public disgrace she argues that she deserved, "in my humble opinion, instead of a whipping, to have a statue erected to my memory." The court, Franklin wrote, was so moved by the speech that she was acquitted, and one of the judges married her the next day. Only years later, after the account was reprinted in both America and England, did Franklin reveal it was a hoax. As Franklin knew, humor was the gentlest yet most powerful way to make political points, and America would always be strongest when it was confident enough, and self-aware enough, to laugh at itself.

Or gig its tormentors. When he went to England to lobby for the American cause, he made his point with another widely reprinted hoax, "An Edict by the King of Prussia." In it the King declared that the Germans had colonized Britain years ago, protected it during wars and had now decided they had the right to levy taxes and restrict British trade. The edict added that the felons in German jails "shall be emptied out" and sent to England "for the better peopling of that country." Lest anyone be so thick as to miss the point, it concluded by noting that all of these measures should be considered "just and reasonable" in England because they were "copied" from the rules imposed by the British Parliament on the American colonies.

When his "Edict" appeared, Franklin had the pleasure of being a guest at the country estate of a friend. Another guest "came running in to us out of breath" with the morning papers, Franklin recounted in a letter to his son. "Here's the King of Prussia claiming a right to this kingdom!" Franklin feigned innocence as the story was read aloud.

"Damn his impudence," one of those present proclaimed.

But as the reading neared its end, another guest began to sense the hoax. "I'll be hanged if this is not some of your American jokes upon us," he said to Franklin. The reading, Franklin noted, "ended with abundance of laughing and a general verdict that it was a fair hit."

4. HUMILITY

When Franklin made his list of personal virtues he was intent on acquiring, he very proudly showed it around to his friends, one of whom, a Quaker, pointed out that he had left one off. Franklin was often guilty of "pride," the friend said, citing many examples. So Franklin added "humility" to his list.

He never quite perfected the virtue. "There is perhaps no one of our natural passions so hard to subdue as pride; disguise it, struggle with it, beat it down, stifle it, mortify it as much as one pleases, it is still alive and will every now and then peep out and show itself." This battle against pride would challenge him— and amuse him—for the rest of his life. "Even if I could conceive that I had completely overcome it, I would probably be proud of my humility."

But as he cheerily admitted, he learned how to fake the virtue. "I cannot boast of much success in acquiring the *reality* of this virtue, but I had a good deal with regard to the *appearance* of it," he wrote. In showing off his feigned humility, Franklin was America's first great imagemaker. Even after he became successful, he made a display of personally carting the rolls of paper he bought in a wheelbarrow down the street to his shop rather than having a hired hand do it.

When he formed his discussion club of fellow tradesmen, known as the Junto, Franklin's first rule was to display humility in conversation. America was to become, as Tocqueville would later point out, a nation of joiners and club formers, and Franklin was the first and foremost of the breed. And although civil and political discourse has been coarsened in recent years, there is still a tradition of Rotary Clubs and high-minded councils dedicated to discussing the common good without resorting to partisan fervor. Franklin decreed that Junto members should put forth their ideas through suggestions and questions, using (or at least feigning) naive curiosity to avoid contradicting people in a manner that could give offense. "All expressions of positiveness in opinion or of direct contradiction were," he recalled, "prohibited under small pecuniary penalties." It was a style he would urge upon the Constitutional Convention 60 years later, and he would wryly say of disputing: "Persons of good sense, I have since observed, seldom fall into it, except lawyers, university men and men of all sorts that have been bred at Edinburgh."

In a newspaper piece called "On Conversation," which he wrote shortly after forming the Junto, Franklin stressed the importance of deferring—or at least giving the appearance of deferring—to others. Otherwise, even the smartest comments would "occasion envy and disgust." His secret for how to win friends and influence people read like an early Dale Carnegie course: "Would you win the hearts of others, you must not seem to vie with them, but to admire them. Give them every opportunity of displaying their own qualifications, and when you have indulged their vanity, they will praise you in turn and prefer you above others. . . . Such is the vanity of mankind that minding what others say is a much surer way of pleasing them than talking well ourselves."

When he decided to use his Junto to launch the first subscription lending library in America, he realized that a show of humility would make it easier to raise funds. If he claimed the idea as his own, it would provoke jealousy. So he put himself, he said, "as much as I could out of sight" and gave credit for the idea to his friends. This method worked so well that "I ever after practiced it on such occasions." People will eventually give you the credit, he noted, if you don't try to claim it at the time. "The present little sacrifice of your vanity will afterwards be amply repaid."

President Bush, during his 2000 campaign, spoke of the need for America to have a little more humility in its dealings with the world. Sept. 11 changed that, and America felt the need to become more assertive. Nevertheless, Franklin would likely raise, in a gentle questioning way, whether it might make sense now to display just a bit of humility, or at least the appearance of it on occasion.

5. IDEALISM IN FOREIGN POLICY

When he went to Paris as an envoy during the Revolution, Franklin proved himself a master of the diplomatic doctrine of realism by playing an adroit balance-of-power game between France, Spain, the Netherlands and later Britain. In a memo he wrote to the wily French Foreign Minister Vergennes, whose realist outlook was summarized by his maxim that "the influence of every power is measured by the opinion one has of its intrinsic force," Franklin emphasized the cold calculation of national interests that he knew the minister would appreciate. If France and her ally Spain joined the American cause, Britain would lose her colonies and the "commerce

Franklin enjoyed flirting with the ladies of Paris. His scientific achievements made him a living legend in France and no social gathering was complete without his presence. This painting shows

Franklin surrounded by his admirers at the court of King Louis XVI and Marie Antoinette (who are seated on the right). (© The Art Archive/Culver Pictures)

that has rendered her so opulent," and America would guarantee that its allies could keep any Caribbean islands Britain lost. However, if France balked, then America might be "reduced to the necessity of ending the war by an accommodation" with Britain.

But Franklin realized that appealing to a calculus of power was only part of the equation. So even as he catered to France's calculation of her national interest, he also played the rousing chords of America's exceptionalism, the sense that America stands apart from the rest of the world because of its virtuous nature and ideals. Both the hard power that came from its strategic might and the soft power that flowed from the appeal of its liberty and democracy would, he realized, be equally important in assuring its influence.

On the private press he built at his home near Paris, Franklin printed the inspiring documents

coming out of America—the Declaration, the constitution he had written for Pennsylvania—as a way of winning hearts and minds in France and elsewhere. In a letter to Congress explaining his tactics, he gave a classic formulation of the lure of America's ideals: "Tyranny is so generally established in the rest of the world that the prospect of an asylum in America for those who love liberty gives general joy, and our cause is esteemed the cause of all mankind." He ended by echoing the shining "city upon a hill" metaphor used by the great American exceptionalists from John Winthrop to Ronald Reagan. "We are fighting for the dignity and happiness of human nature," he proclaimed. "Glorious it is for the Americans to be called by Providence to this post of honor."

Ever the great imagemaker, he cast himself to the French public as a symbol both of the virtuous frontier freedom romanticized by Rousseau and of the

Enlightenment's reasoned wisdom championed by Voltaire. In a clever and deliberate manner, leavened by the wit and joie de vivre the French so adored, he portrayed the American cause, through his own personification of it, as that of the natural state fighting the corrupted one. He made a point of eschewing powdered wigs and formal dress, instead wearing a fur cap he had picked up years earlier on a trip to Canada. The cap, like that worn by Rousseau, served as his badge of homespun purity and virtue, just as his ever present spectacles became an emblem of wisdom. It helped him play the part that Paris imagined for him: that of the noble frontier philosopher and simple backwoods sage—even though he had lived most of his life in Philadelphia and London.

It worked. Medallions of his fur-capped head were struck, engravings were hung in homes, and his likeness graced snuffboxes and signet rings. The fad went so far as to mildly annoy, though still amuse, King Louis XVI himself. He gave a lady of his court, who had bored him often with her praise of Franklin, a Sèvres porcelain chamber pot with Franklin's cameo embossed inside. Neither the King nor his ministers were instinctive champions of America's desire, which they correctly feared might prove contagious, to cast off hereditary monarchs. But the combination of Franklin's realist and idealist appeals eventually brought France into the war on America's side, which proved critical to its victory in the Revolution. It also showed that even France, at least back then, could be charmed.

When Franklin visited Versailles to receive the King's formal assent to the treaties, he declined to wear the ceremonial sword and regalia that were considered de rigueur at court. Seeing no reason to abandon the simple style that had served him well, he dressed in a plain brown suit with his famous spectacles as his only adornment. His one fashion concession was that he did not wear his fur cap and instead carried a hat of pure white under his arm. "Is that white hat a symbol of liberty?" asked an aristocratic woman at whose salon Franklin had worn his fur cap. Whether or not he meant it to be, white hats for men were soon in vogue in Paris.

After the ceremony, Franklin had the honor, if not pleasure, of being allowed to stand next to the Queen, the famously haughty Marie-Antoinette, as she played at the gambling tables. Alone among the throng at Versailles, she seemed to have little appreciation for the man who, she had been told, had once been "a printer's foreman." As she noted dismissively, a man of that background would never have been able to rise so high in Europe. Franklin would have proudly agreed.

Better than most diplomats in the nation's history, Franklin understood that America's strength in world affairs would come from a mix that included idealism as well as realism. When woven together, as they would be in policies ranging from the Monroe Doctrine to the Marshall Plan, they were the warp and woof of a sturdy foreign policy. And when countries such as France felt that the soft suasion of idealism was lacking, as has recently been the case, it proved harder to attract them to a cause. "America's great historical moments," historian Bernard Bailyn has noted, "have occurred when realism and idealism have been combined, and no one knew this better than Franklin."

6. COMPROMISE

When he returned from France to become the sage at the Constitutional Convention, Franklin was not America's most profound political theorist. But he did embody one crucial virtue that was key to the gathering's success: a belief in the nobility of compromise. Throughout his life, one of his mantras had been, "Both sides must part with some of their demands." He used this phrase many times, but never more notably than when the Constitutional Convention became deadlocked on the issue of whether the new Congress should be proportioned by population or have equal votes for each state.

Franklin had been among the first to develop, 30 years earlier, the concept of a federal compromise, where both the national government and the state governments could have sovereign powers. And as the Constitutional Convention was about to break down in the hot Philadelphia summer of 1787, he set in motion the process that would break the impasse and, to a large extent, shape the new nation.

First Franklin succinctly stated the problem: "The diversity of opinions turns on two points. If a proportional representation takes place, the small States contend that their liberties will be in danger. If an equality of votes is to be put in its place, the large States say their money will be in danger."

Then he gently emphasized, in a homespun analogy that drew on his affection for craftsmen and construction, the importance of compromise: "When a broad table is to be made, and the edges of planks do not fit, the artist takes a little from both, and makes a good joint. In like manner here, both sides must part with some of their demands."

Finally, he incorporated some compromises suggested by others into a specific motion. Representatives to the lower House would be popularly elected and apportioned by population, but in the Senate "the Legislatures of the several States shall choose and send an equal number of Delegates."

For Franklin, who personally believed in proportional representation, compromise was not only a practical approach but a moral one. Tolerance, humility and a respect for others required it. The near perfect document that arose from his compromise could not have been approved if the hall had contained only crusaders who stood on unwavering principle. Compromisers may not make great heroes; but they do make great democracies.

---

7. TOLERANCE

The great struggles of the 20th century were against fascism and then communism. As was made clear on Sept. 11, the great struggle of the 21st century will be between the forces of fanatic fundamentalism and those of tolerance. It is important to remember that America was not born with the virtue of religious tolerance, but had to acquire it. One of the myths is that the first settlers were advocates of religious freedom. In fact, the Puritans were very intolerant, not only of witches but also of any deviation from the tribal orthodoxy. The most arcane antinomian dispute ended up forcing people to move and found a new state like Rhode Island.

Among those who ran away from the intolerant orthodoxy of Boston was Franklin. He ended up in Philadelphia, a place unlike much of the world. There were Lutherans and Moravians and Quakers and even Jews, as well as Calvinists, living side by side in what became known as the City of Brotherly Love. Franklin helped formulate the creed that they would all be better off, personally and economically, if they embraced an attitude of tolerance.

Franklin believed in God and in the social usefulness of religion, but he did not subscribe to any particular sectarian doctrine. This led him to help raise money to build a new hall in Philadelphia that was, as he put it, "expressly for the use of any preacher of any religious persuasion who might desire to say something." He added, "Even if the Mufti of Constantinople were to send a missionary to preach Mohammedanism to us, he would find a pulpit at his service."

He also wrote parodies that poked fun at Puritan intolerance. In one of them, called "A Witch Trial at Mount Holly," a couple of accused witches were subjected to two tests: weighed on a scale against the Bible, and tossed in the river with hands and feet bound to see if they floated. They agreed to submit—on the condition that two of the accusers take the same test. With colorful details of all the pomp, Franklin described the process. The accused and accusers all succeed in outweighing the Bible. But both of the accused and one of the accusers fail to sink in the river, thus indicating that they are witches. The more intelligent spectators conclude that most people naturally float. The others are not so sure and resolve to wait until summer when the experiment could be tried with the subjects unclothed.

Franklin's freethinking unnerved his family. When his parents wrote of their concern over his "erroneous opinions," Franklin replied with a letter that spelled out a religious philosophy based on tolerance that would last his life. It would be vain for any person to insist that "all the doctrines he holds are true and all he rejects are false." The same could be said of the opinions of different religions. He had little use for the doctrinal distinctions his mother worried about. "I think vital religion has always suffered when orthodoxy is more regarded than virtue. And the Scripture assures me that at the last day we shall not be examined by what we *thought,* but what we *did* . . . that we did good to our fellow creatures. See *Matthew 26.*" (His parents, a bit more versed in the Scripture, probably caught that he meant *Matthew 25.*)

By the end of his life, he had contributed to the building funds of each and every sect in Philadelphia, including £5 for the Congregation Mikveh Israel for its new synagogue in April 1788. During the July 4 celebrations that year, he was too sick to leave his bed, but the parade marched under his window. For the first time, as per arrangements that Franklin had overseen, "the clergy of different Christian denominations, with the rabbi of the Jews, walked arm in arm."

And when he was carried to his grave two years later, his casket was accompanied by all the clergymen of the city, every one of them, of every faith.

In a world that was then, as alas it still is now, bloodied by those who seek to impose theocracies, Franklin helped to create a new type of nation that could draw strength from its religious pluralism. This comfort with the concept of tolerance—which was based on an aversion to tyranny, a fealty to free expression, a willingness to compromise, the morality of respecting other individuals and even a bit of humor and humility—is what most distinguishes America and its like-minded allies in the messy struggles that confront a new century.

QUESTIONS TO CONSIDER

1 After chronicling Franklin's accomplishments, Isaacson observes that he was "the founding father who winks at us." What made Franklin approachable and identifiable ("made of flesh rather than of marble")? How does Franklin's personality differ from that of Thomas Jefferson (selection 8) and George Washington (selection 10)?

2 How did Silence Dogood, one of Franklin's fictitious characters, represent the "typical American" in her dislike of tyranny?

3 In what ways did Franklin effectively use humor to make important points? For example, how did he express his opinion on the responsibility that men share with women when fathering illegitimate children? How did Franklin's British friends learn of his views on England's policies toward its faraway colonies?

4 How did Franklin use realism and idealism to help win support for the revolutionary cause? In what ways did Franklin modify his attire to play to the sympathies of the French?

5 Franklin avoided conflict and championed freedom of religion in a world in which people were often intolerant of those with different opinions and faiths. In what ways did Franklin promote religious diversity in his "City of Brotherly Love"? How did Franklin's appeal for compromise help resolve dissent between the large and small states at the Constitutional Convention?

6 Franklin's seven virtues helped him answer the question: "How does one live a life that is useful, virtuous, worthy, moral and spiritually meaningful?" Do these virtues only reflect the "shopkeeping values" of Franklin's time or do they have as much meaning for us today?

PART FOUR

"When in the Course of Human Events ..."

7 John Adams and the Coming of the Revolution

DAVID McCULLOUGH

Until 1765, Benjamin Franklin remained an ardent defender of the British Empire. Most other colonists shared his pride in the empire and saw no reason to break away from it. But after 1765—and the date is significant, as we shall see—Franklin and many others marched steadily down the path toward revolution. By 1775, as one historian has noted, the relationship between the American colonials and their English rulers had become "so strained, so poisoned, so characterized by suspicion and resentment that the once seemingly unbreakable bonds of empire were on the verge of dissolution." That same year, in fact, Minutemen at Lexington and Concord fired the opening shots of the war that resulted in American independence.

What were the causes of the American Revolution? What had so poisoned American-English relations that armed conflict broke out? Most experts agree that the roots of the Revolution are to be found in the previous century, when American colonists began developing their own institutions and ideas—particularly ideas about constitutions, taxation, and representation—that significantly diverged from those in England. This "first American revolution," as Clinton Rossiter called it, took place during a period of "salutary neglect," when the British imperial government allowed the colonies to develop without rigid and consistent government control. After 1763, however, all that changed. Reacting to new circumstances inside England and to the enormous cost of a recent war with France (the French and Indian War) for supremacy in North America, the imperial government abandoned salutary neglect and attempted to do what it had every legal right to do: rule the empire, including the North American colonies, forcefully and consistently for the benefit of the mother country. Among other measures, the Stamp Act of 1765 reflected the new imperial approach: it taxed newspapers, pamphlets, and other printed documents in the colonies for the purpose of making the colonies pay a third of the cost of England's protecting them. Unaccustomed to such interference from faraway London, colonial Americans protested, first with restraint, then with rising anger and bitterness, every new measure imposed on them from abroad. By 1775, a sizable and outspoken group of colonists had become profoundly disillusioned with imperial rule, and in 1776 they struck for independence.

In the following selection, David McCullough tells the story of the coming of the American Revolution through the life and deeds of John Adams. A Pulitzer Prize–winning biographer and a skilled and eloquent narrator in PBS's American Experience *series and Ken Burns's legendary television series on the Civil War, McCullough is eminently qualified to tell the story of John Adams. The author's biographical approach personalizes events; it elicits from cold fact the warmth of a living man who stood at the forefront of colonial resistance to perceived British tyranny that led to the American Revolution. The Adams you will meet here is a portly man with a round, clean-shaven, and "very English face." His enemies called him "His Rotundity." A Harvard graduate and a brilliant lawyer, Adams was in McCullough's words "a great hearted, persevering man of uncommon ability and force." Unlike his hot-headed kinsman, Sam, John Adams abhorred mob agitation and violence, even against the hated Stamp Act of 1765. Five years later, he boldly defended the British soldiers charged with killing five colonial civilians in the Boston Massacre. Adams would remember this as "one of the most gallant, generous, manly and disinterested actions of my whole life." Despite his dislike of mob action, he reveled in the Boston Tea Party. He went on to serve with distinction in the Continental Congress of 1774 and to stand as one of the great American leaders when the Revolution began. "That such has come to pass," wrote his wife Abigail "was surely the work of the Lord and 'marvelous in our eyes.'"*

Because of his great achievements in politics and the law during the revolutionary period, Adams became George Washington's vice president, serving from 1789–1797. He was also one of the leaders of the Federalist Party and in 1797 was elected president in his own right. He served one term, leaving office in 1801.

In 1812, now in retirement in Quincy, Massachusetts, Adams initiated a correspondence with his long-time political adversary, Thomas Jefferson. Jefferson replied from his Virginia plantation, and the two former presidents became warm friends, exchanging 158 letters over the ensuing fourteen years. In 1818, when Abigail Adams died of typhoid, Adams wrote Jefferson in anguish: "The dear partner of my life for fifty-four years as a wife, and for many years more as a lover, now lies in extremis, forbidden to speak or be spoken to." Jefferson could sympathize with his friend, for he had lost his own wife many years before. He wrote Adams: "I know well and feel what you have lost, what you have suffered, are suffering. . . . It is of some comfort to us both that the term is not very distant when we are to deposit . . . our sorrows and suffering bodies, to ascend in essence to an ecstatic meeting with the friends we have loved and lost and shall still love and never see again."

By 1820, they were the last of the founding fathers still alive, the last of the revolutionary leaders and nation-builders who had forged the American Republic. "I look back with rapture," Adams wrote Jefferson, "to those golden days when Virginia and Massachusetts lived and acted together like a band of brothers. While I breathe I shall be your friend."

In 1826, Jefferson, now eighty-three, and Adams, now ninety, died on the same day. It was July 4, the fiftieth anniversary of the signing of the Declaration of Independence.

GLOSSARY

ADAMS, ABIGAIL   John's devoted wife was intelligent, supportive of her husband, an opponent of slavery, and an early convert to the cause of revolution. Conscious of the inferior status of women in the early national period, she reminded her husband to "Remember the Ladies" when championing liberty and equality.

ADAMS, SAMUEL   John's older second cousin. Samuel was the leader of Boston's hot-headed radicals and one of the foremost opponents of perceived British tyranny in all of the colonies. A true agitator, he was in the thick of colonial resistance to the Stamp Act and led his "boys" in the Boston Tea Party.

BASS, JOSEPH   John's neighbor, a shoemaker, who served as Adams's assistant and frequent traveling companion during his many journeys away from home.

BOSTON MASSACRE (1770)   An angry Boston mob converged on the Customs House and taunted the nine British guards, throwing snowballs and oyster shells at them. The guards panicked and fired their muskets into the crowd, killing five.

BOSTON TEA PARTY (1773)   When Parliament allowed the East India Company to dump its stockpile of tea on the American colonies, a band of Bostonians disguised as Mohawk Indians boarded a British ship and threw the entire cargo into the bay. Parliament retaliated by closing the port of Boston and ordering other harsh changes, all of which became known as the Intolerable Acts.

BUNKER HILL (1775)   Legendary battleground between British troops and colonial militia. The battle actually took place on nearby Breed's Hill, Charlestown, Massachusetts. The British captured the hill, but suffered a far higher casualty rate than the colonial militia that opposed them. General Thomas Gage observed that the Americans displayed "a conduct and spirit against us, they never showed against the French."

***COMMON SENSE* (1776)**   Thomas Paine, an English immigrant to the colonies, wrote this pamphlet in which he urged Americans to seek their independence from Great Britain and its "royal brute," King George III. Paine asserted that "the birthday of a new world is at hand." He directed his message to the common man, and his inspirational words sold 120,000 copies of the pamphlet in just three months.

CONTINENTAL CONGRESS (1774)   Delegates from all of the colonies except Georgia attended this assembly in Philadelphia. Sam and John Adams were among the Massachusetts representatives. The Congress pledged not to obey the Intolerable Acts and, while promising obedience to the King, denied Parliament's right to tax the colonies.

FRENCH AND INDIAN WAR (1754–1763)   The French with their Iroquois allies fought Great Britain for control of North America. In the treaty ending the war, the French ceded Canada to Great Britain, along with all other French possessions east of the Mississippi River except for New Orleans.

GERRY, ELBRIDGE   A Massachusetts delegate to the Continental Congress and the son of a wealthy merchant who shipped fish abroad. He later served as an American envoy in the infamous XYZ Affair.

GRIDLEY, JEREMIAH   One of Boston's most able attorneys. Adams became his protégé and admired him for his "grandeur" and "lordly" manner in the courtroom. Gridley, in turn, advised Adams to "pursue the study of the law itself, rather than the gain of it."

HUTCHINSON, THOMAS   Conservative, pro-English lieutenant governor (later acting governor) of Massachusetts whom John Adams opposed and Samuel Adams smeared. Hutchinson was slandered when his letters were read out of context before the Massachusetts House and then suffered further when his elegant home came under attack from a Boston mob.

OLIVER, ANDREW   The Boston stamp distributor who enforced the Stamp Act. Irate colonists burned him in effigy and stoned his residence. He resigned his position, a victim of the local outrage against the Stamp Act.

OTIS, JAMES   John greatly admired this fiery Massachusetts revolutionary, who led the radical wing of colonial resistance to British policy. In fact, he was one of the first colonists to oppose British policy in the open because it deprived Americans of "the right of assessing their own taxes."

REVERE, PAUL   A silversmith and revolutionary whose engraving of the Boston Massacre misrepresented the actual events and inspired further animosity against the British. Later, he became famous for warning the militiamen at Lexington and Concord that the redcoats were coming.

SEWALL, JONATHAN   Like Adams, Sewall was a graduate of Harvard and a skilled attorney. Unlike Adams, he supported British policy. His decision to oppose the American Revolution greatly strained his friendship with Adams. Eventually, Sewall would in Adams's words, "quit America" and leave with his family for England, never to return.

The first news of the Stamp Act reached the American colonies during the last week of May 1765 and produced an immediate uproar, and in Massachusetts especially. Starting in November, nearly everything written or printed on paper other than private correspondence and books—all pamphlets, newspapers, advertisements, deeds, diplomas, bills, bonds, all legal documents, ship's papers, even playing cards—were required to carry revenue stamps, some costing as much as ten pounds. The new law, the first British attempt to tax Americans directly, had been passed by Parliament to help pay for the cost of the French and Indian War and to meet the expense of maintaining a colonial military force to prevent Indian wars. Everyone was affected. The *Boston Gazette* reported Virginia in a state of "utmost consternation." In August, Boston mobs, "like devils let loose," stoned the residence of Andrew Oliver, secretary of the province, who had been appointed distributor of the stamps, then attacked and destroyed the house of Lieutenant Governor Thomas Hutchinson, wrongly suspecting him of having sponsored the detested tax.

[John] Adams, who had earlier joined a new law club in Boston started by Jeremiah Gridley, had, at Gridley's suggestion, been working on an essay that would become *A Dissertation on the Canon and the Feudal Law*. It was his first extended political work and one of the most salient of his life, written at the age of thirty. Now, at the height of the furor, he arranged for its publication as an unsigned, untitled essay in the *Gazette*. (It would be published in England later, in a volume titled *The True Sentiments of America*.) It was not a call to arms or mob action—with his countryman's dislike of the Boston "rabble," Adams was repelled by such an "atrocious violation of the peace." The Stamp Act was hardly mentioned. Rather, it was a statement of his own fervent patriotism and the taproot conviction that

American freedoms were not ideals still to be obtained, but rights long and firmly established by British law and by the courage and sacrifices of generations of Americans. Years later Adams would say the Revolution began in the minds of Americans long before any shots were fired or blood shed.

"Be it remembered," he wrote in his *Dissertation*, "that liberty must at all hazards be supported. We have a right to it, derived from our Maker. But if we have not, our fathers have earned and bought it for us at the expense of their ease, their estates, their pleasure, and their blood. . . ."

The essay began appearing in the *Gazette* on August 12, 1765, and it struck an immediate chord. "The author is a young man, not above 33 or 34, but of incomparable sense," wrote Boston's senior pastor, Charles Chauncey, to the learned Rhode Island clergyman and future president of Yale College, Ezra Stiles. "I esteem that piece one of the best that has been written. It has done honor to its author; and it is a pity but he should be known."

Soon afterward Adams drafted what became known as the Braintree Instructions—instructions from the freeholders of the town to their delegate to the General Court, the legislative body of Massachusetts—which, when printed in October in the *Gazette*, "rang" through the colony. "We have always understood it to be a grand and fundamental principle of the [English] constitution that no freeman should be subject to any tax to which he has not given his own consent." There must be "no taxation without representation"—a phrase that had been used in Ireland for more than a generation. And in rejecting the rule of the juryless Admiralty Court in enforcing this law, the instructions declared that there must be a trial by jury and an independent judiciary.

In amazingly little time the document was adopted by forty towns, something that had never happened before.

Now fully joined in Boston's political ferment, Adams was meeting with Gridley, James Otis, Samuel Adams, and others. Observing them closely, he concluded that it was his older, second cousin, Samuel Adams who had "the most thorough understanding of

---

From *John Adams* by David McCullough. Copyright © 2001 by David McCullough. Abridged by permission of Simon & Schuster Adult Publishing Group. First published in Great Britain by Simon & Schuster UK Ltd.

liberty." Samuel Adams was "zealous and keen in the cause," of "steadfast integrity," a "universal good character." The esteemed Otis, however, had begun to act strangely. He was "liable to great inequities of temper, sometimes in despondency, sometimes in rage," Adams recorded in dismay.

Otis, a protégé of Gridley, had been for Adams the shining example of the lawyer-scholar, learned yet powerful in argument. Now he became Adams's political hero, just as Thomas Hutchinson became Adams's chief villain. A lifetime later, Adams would vividly describe Otis as he had been in his surpassing moment, in the winter of 1761, in argument against writs of assistance, search warrants that permitted customs officers to enter and search any premises whenever they wished. Before the bench in the second-floor Council Chamber of the Province House in Boston, Otis had declared such writs—which were perfectly valid in English law and commonly issued in England—null and void because they violated the natural rights of Englishmen. Adams, who had been present as an observer only, would remember it as one of the inspiring moments of his life, a turning point for him as for history. The five judges, with Hutchinson at their head as chief justice, sat in comfort near blazing fireplaces, Adams recalled, "all in their new fresh robes of scarlet English cloth, in their broad hats, and immense judicial wigs." But Otis, in opposition, was a "flame" unto himself. "With the promptitude of classical illusions, a depth of research . . . and a torrent of impetuous eloquence, he hurried away all before him." By Adams's account, every one of the immense crowded audience went away, as he did, ready to take up arms against writs of assistance. "Then and there was the first scene of the first act of opposition to the arbitrary claims of Great Britain," Adams would claim. "Then and there the child independence was born."

But by 1765 it was the tragic decline of James Otis that gripped Adams. At meetings now, Otis talked on endlessly and to no point. No one could get a word in. "Otis is in confusion yet," Adams noted a year or so later. "He rambles and wanders like a ship

without a helm." Adams began to doubt Otis's sanity, and as time passed, it became clear that Otis, his hero, was indeed going mad, a dreadful spectacle.

"The year 1765 has been the most remarkable year of my life," Adams wrote in his diary that December. "The enormous engine fabricated by the British Parliament for battering down all the rights and liberties of America, I mean the Stamp Act, has raised and spread through the whole continent a spirit that will be recorded to our honor, with all future generations."

"At home with my family. Thinking," reads the entry of a few nights later.

"At home. Thinking," he wrote Christmas Day.

With the repeal of the Stamp Act by Parliament in the spring of 1766, and the easing of tensions that followed in the next two years, until the arrival of British troops at Boston, Adams put politics aside to concentrate on earning a living. He was thinking of politics not at all, he insisted.

He was back on the road, riding the circuit, the reach of his travels extending more than two hundred miles, from the island of Martha's Vineyard off Cape Cod, north to Maine, which was then part of the Massachusetts Bay Province, to as far west as Worcester. As recalled in the family years later, he was endowed for the profession of law with the natural gifts of "a clear and sonorous voice," a "ready elocution," stubbornness, but with the "counter-check" of self-control, and a strong moral sense. He handled every kind of case—land transfers, trespass, admiralty, marine insurance, murder, adultery, rape, bastardy, buggery, assault and battery, tarring and feathering. He defended, not always successfully, poor debtors, horse thieves, and smugglers. He saw every side of life, learned to see things as they were, and was considered, as Jonathan Sewall would write, as "honest [a] lawyer as ever broke bread."

In 1766, like his father before him, Adams was elected selectman in Braintree. But so active had his Boston practice become by 1768 that he moved the family to a rented house in the city, a decision he did not like, fearing the effect on their health. He established a Boston office and presently admitted two young men, Jonathan Austin and William Tudor, to read law with him, in return for fees of 10 pounds sterling. "What shall I do with two clerks at a time?" Adams speculated in his diary, adding that he would do all he could "for their education and advancement in the world," a pledge he was to keep faithfully. When Billy Tudor was admitted to the bar three years later, Adams took time to write to Tudor's wealthy father to praise the young man for his clear head and honest heart, but also to prod the father into giving his son some help getting started in his practice. Adams had seen too often the ill effect of fathers who ignored their sons when a little help could have made all the difference.

With the death of Jeremiah Gridley the year before and the mental collapse of James Otis, John Adams, still in his thirties, had become Boston's busiest attorney. He was "under full sail," prospering at last, and in the Adams tradition, he began buying more land, seldom more than five or ten acres of salt marsh or woodland at a time, but steadily, year after year. (Among his father's memorable observations was that he never knew a piece of land to run away or break.) Eventually, after his brother Peter married and moved to his wife's house, John would purchase all of the old homestead, with its barn and fifty-three acres, which included Fresh Brook, to Adams a prime asset. In one pasture, he reckoned, there were a thousand red cedars, which in twenty years, "if properly pruned," might be worth a shilling each. And with an appreciative Yankee eye, he noted "a quantity of good stone in it, too."

He was becoming more substantial in other ways. "My good man is so very fat that I am lean as a rail," [his wife] Abigail bemoaned to her sister Mary. He acquired more and more books, books being an acknowledged extravagance he could seldom curb. (With one London bookseller he had placed a standing order for "every book and pamphlet, of reputation, upon the subjects of law and government as soon as it comes out.") "I want to see my wife and children every day," he would write while away on the court circuit. "I want to see my grass and blossoms and corn. . . . But above all, except the wife and children, I want to see my books."

In the privacy of his journal, he could also admit now, if obliquely, to seeing himself as a figure of some larger importance. After noting in one entry that his horse had overfed on grass and water, Adams speculated wryly, "My biographer will scarcely introduce my little mare and her adventures."

He could still search his soul over which path to follow. "To what object are my views directed?" he asked. "Am I grasping at money, or scheming for power?" Yes, he was amassing a library, but to what purpose? "Fame, fortune, power say some, are the ends intended by a library. The service of God, country, clients, fellow men, say others. Which of these lie nearest my heart? . . .

With Boston full of red-coated British troops—sent in 1768 to keep order, as another round of taxes was imposed by Parliament, this time on paper, tea, paint, and glass—the atmosphere in the city turned incendiary. Incidents of violence broke out between townsmen and soldiers, the hated "Lobsterbacks."

The crisis came in March of 1770, a year already shadowed for John and Abigail by the loss of a child. A baby girl, Susanna, born since the move to Boston and named for John's mother, had died in February at a little more than a year old. Adams was so upset by the loss that he could not speak of it for years.

On the cold moonlit evening of March 5, 1770, the streets of Boston were covered by nearly a foot of snow. On the icy, cobbled square where the Province House stood, a lone British sentry, posted in front of the nearby Custom House, was being taunted by a small band of men and boys. The time was shortly after nine. Somewhere a church bell began to toll, the alarm for fire, and almost at once crowds came pouring into the streets, many men, up from the waterfront, brandishing sticks and clubs. As a throng of several hundred converged at the Custom House, the lone guard was reinforced by eight British soldiers with loaded muskets and fixed bayonets, their captain with drawn sword. Shouting, cursing, the crowd pelted the despised redcoats with

This popular print by Paul Revere depicts British soldiers firing on a defenseless and non-threatening gathering of Bostonians. It is an excellent example of propaganda designed to distort the truth and inflame tensions against the British "Lobsterbacks." Adams, arguing that "facts are stubborn things," proved in court that, despite Revere's portrayal, there was no massacre in Boston. (Library of Congress)

snowballs, chunks of ice, oyster shells, and stones. In the melee the soldiers suddenly opened fire, killing five men. Samuel Adams was quick to call the killings a "bloody butchery" and to distribute a print published by Paul Revere vividly portraying the scene as a slaughter of the innocent, an image of British tyranny, the Boston Massacre, that would become fixed in the public mind.

The following day thirty-four-year-old John Adams was asked to defend the soldiers and their captain, when they came to trial. No one else would take the case, he was informed. . . . Adams accepted, firm in the belief, as he said, that no man in a free country should be denied the right to counsel and a fair trial, and convinced, on principle, that the case was of utmost importance. As a lawyer, his duty was clear. That he would be hazarding his hard-earned reputation and, in his words, "incurring a clamor and popular suspicions and prejudices" against him, was obvious, and if some of what he later said on the subject would sound a little self-righteous, he was also being entirely honest.

Only the year before, in 1769, Adams had defended four American sailors charged with killing a British naval officer who had boarded their ship with a press gang to grab them for the British navy. The sailors were acquitted on grounds of acting in self-defense, but public opinion had been vehement against the heinous practice of impressment. Adams had been in step with the popular outrage, exactly as he was out of step now. He worried for Abigail, who was pregnant again, and feared he was risking his family's safety as well as his own, such was the state of emotions in Boston. It was rumored he had been bribed to take the case. In reality, a retainer of eighteen guineas was the only payment he would receive.

Criticism of almost any kind was nearly always painful for Adams, but public scorn was painful in the extreme.

"The only way to compose myself and collect my thoughts," he wrote in his diary, "is to set down at my table, place my diary before me, and take my pen into my hand. This apparatus takes off my attention from other objects. Pen, ink, and paper and a sitting posture are great helps to attention and thinking."

From a treatise by the eminent Italian penologist and opponent of capital punishment Cesare, Marchese di Beccaria, he carefully copied the following:

If, by supporting the rights of mankind, and of invincible truth, I shall contribute to save from the agonies of death one unfortunate victim of tyranny, or of ignorance, equally fatal, his blessings and years of transport will be sufficient consolation to me for the contempt of all mankind.

There were to be two conspicuously fair trials held in the new courthouse on Queen Street. The first was of the British captain, Thomas Preston, the opening of the trial being delayed until October when passions had cooled. The second was of the soldiers. In the first trial Adams was assisted by young Josiah Quincy, Jr., while the court-appointed lawyer trying the case was Josiah's brother, Samuel, assisted by Robert Treat Paine. Whether Captain Preston had given an order to fire, as was charged, could never be proven. Adams's argument for the defense, though unrecorded, was considered a virtuoso performance. Captain Preston was found not guilty.

Adams's closing for the second and longer trial, which was recorded, did not come until December 3, and lasted two days. The effect on the crowded courtroom was described as "electrical." "I am for the prisoners at bar," he began, then invoked the line from the Marchese di Beccaria. Close study of the facts had convinced Adams of the innocence of the soldiers. The tragedy was not brought on by the soldiers, but by the mob, and the mob, it must be understood, was the inevitable result of the flawed policy of quartering troops in a city on the pretext of keeping the peace:

We have entertained a great variety of phrases to avoid calling this sort of people a mob. Some call them shavers, some call them geniuses. The plain English is, gentlemen, [it was] most probably a motley rabble of saucy boys, Negroes and mulattoes, Irish teagues and outlandish jacktars. And why should we scruple to call such a people a mob, I can't conceive, unless the name is too respectable for them. The sun is not about to stand still or go out, nor the rivers to dry up because there was a mob in Boston on the 5th of March that attacked a party of soldiers. . . . Soldiers quartered in a populous town will always occasion two mobs where they prevent one. They are wretched conservators of the peace.

He described how the shrieking "rabble" pelted the soldiers with snowballs, oyster shells, sticks, "every species of rubbish," as a cry went up to "Kill them! Kill them!" One soldier had been knocked down with a club, then hit again as soon as he could rise. "Do you expect he should behave like a stoic philosopher, lost in apathy?" Adams asked. Self-defense was the primary canon of the law of nature. Better that many guilty persons escape unpunished than one innocent person should be punished. "The reason is, because it's of more importance to community, that innocence should be protected, than it is, that guilt should be punished."

"Facts are stubborn things," he told the jury, "and whatever may be our wishes, our inclinations, or the dictums of our passions, they cannot alter the state of facts and evidence."

The jury remained out two and a half hours. Of the eight soldiers, six were acquitted and two found guilty of manslaughter, for which they were branded on their thumbs.

There were angry reactions to the decision. Adams was taken to task in the *Gazette* and claimed later to have suffered the loss of more than half his practice. But there were no riots, and Samuel Adams appears never to have objected to the part he played. Possibly Samuel Adams had privately approved, even encouraged it behind the scenes, out of respect for John's fierce integrity, and on the theory that so staunch a show of fairness would be good politics.

As time would show, John Adams's part in the drama did increase his public standing, making him in the long run more respected than ever. Years later, reflecting from the perspective of old age, he himself would call it the most exhausting case he ever undertook, but conclude with pardonable pride that his part in the defense was "one of the most gallant, generous, manly and disinterested actions of my whole life, and one of the best pieces of service I ever rendered my country."

A second son, Charles, was born that summer of 1770, and for all the criticism to which he was being subjected, Adams was elected by the Boston Town Meeting as a representative to the Massachusetts legislature. It was his first real commitment to

This John Singleton Copley oil painting shows Adams at age forty-three. Short and rotund, he did not have the presence of Washington or Jefferson. Yet his courage and dedication to the cause of liberty made him one of the most important figures of the early national period. (© Bettmann/CORBIS)

politics. Inevitably it would mean more time away from his practice, and still further reduction in income. When, the night of the meeting, he told Abigail of his apprehensions, she burst into tears, but then, as Adams would relate, said "she thought I had done as I ought, she was very willing to share in all that was to come."

But the complications and demands of both the law and politics became too much and Adams suffered what appears to have been a physical breakdown. "Especially the constant obligation to speak in public almost every day for many hours had exhausted my health, brought on pain in my breast and complaint in my lungs, which seriously threatened my life," he would later write. In the spring of 1771, he and the family moved back to Braintree, to "the air of my native spot, and the fine breezes from the sea," which "together with daily rides on horseback," gradually restored him.

Another child, Thomas Boylston, was born in September of 1772, and again Adams was off on the "vagabond life" of the circuit, carrying a copy of *Don Quixote* in his saddlebag and writing Abigail sometimes as many as three letters a day.

Business was good in Massachusetts in the calm of 1772 and Adams prospered once again. He appeared in more than two hundred Superior Court cases. Among his clients were many of the richest men in the colony, including John Hancock. At the conclusion of one morning in court, Adams was told people were calling him the finest speaker they had ever heard, "the equal to the greatest orator that ever spoke in Greece or Rome."

He could speak extemporaneously and, if need be, almost without limit. Once, to give a client time to retrieve a necessary record, Adams spoke for five hours, through which the court and jury sat with perfect patience. At the end he was roundly applauded because, as he related the story, he had spoken "in favor of justice.". . .

At the same time, he was vowing, at least in the privacy of his diary, to devote himself wholly to his private business and providing for his family. "Above all things I must avoid politics. . . ." But as tensions in the colony mounted, so did his pent-up rage and longing for action. On an evening with the Cranches, when a visiting Englishman began extolling the English sense of justice, Adams exploded, taking everyone by surprise, and Adams as much as any. "I cannot but reflect upon myself with the severity of these rash, inexperienced, boyish, raw and awkward expressions," he wrote afterward. "A man who has not better government of his tongue, no

more command of his temper, is unfit for everything but children's play and the company of boys." There was no more justice in Britain than in hell, he had told the Englishman.

By the time of the destruction of the tea, what was later to become known as the Boston Tea Party in December 1773, he had again moved the family to Boston. His hatred of mob action notwithstanding, Adams was exuberant over the event. In less than six months, in May 1774, in reprisal, the British closed the port of Boston, the worst blow to the city in its history. "We live, my dear soul, in an age of trial," he told Abigail. Shut off from the sea, Boston was doomed. It must suffer martyrdom and expire in a noble cause. For himself, he saw "no prospect of any business in my way this whole summer. I don't receive a shilling a week."

Yet she must not assume he was "in the dumps." Quite the contrary: he felt better than he had in years.

In 1774, Adams was chosen by the legislature as one of five delegates to the First Continental Congress at Philadelphia, and with all Massachusetts on the verge of rebellion, he removed Abigail and the children again to Braintree, where they would remain.

In July he traveled to Maine, for what was to be his last turn on the circuit before leaving for Philadelphia. During a break from the court at Falmouth (later Portland), he and Jonathan Sewall, who was still attorney general, climbed a hill overlooking the blue sweep of Casco Bay, where they could talk privately.

Their friendship had cooled in recent years, as had been inevitable under the circumstances. In his diary Adams had grieved that his best friend in the world had become his implacable enemy. "God forgive him for the part he has acted," Adams had written, adding, "It is not impossible that he may make the same prayer for me." Now Sewall pleaded with Adams not to attend the Congress. The power of Great Britain was "irresistible" and would destroy all who stood in the way, Sewall warned.

As long as they lived, neither man would forget the moment. Adams told Sewall he knew Great

Britain was "determined on her system," but "that very determination, determined me on mine." The die was cast, Adams said. "Swim or sink, live or die, survive or perish, [I am] with my country . . . You may depend upon it."

Less than a year later, after the battle of Bunker Hill, Sewall would choose to "quit America." With his wife and family he sailed for London, never to return. "It is not despair which drives me away," he wrote before departure. "I have faith . . . that rebellion will shrink back to its native hell, and that Great Britain will rise superior to all the gasconade of the little, wicked American politicians."

Not long afterward, in a series of letters to the *Boston Gazette* that he signed "Novangelus"—the New Englander—Adams argued that Americans had every right to determine their own destiny and charged the Foreign Ministry in London with corruption and venal intent. America, Adams warned, could face subjugation of the kind inflicted on Ireland. Unless America took action, and at once, Adams wrote, they faced the prospect of living like the Irish on potatoes and water.

With Joseph Bass at his side, Adams crossed Long Bridge over the frozen Charles River and rode into Cambridge in the early afternoon of January 24, 1776, in time to dine with General Washington at the temporary quarters of Colonel Thomas Mifflin near Harvard Yard. Mifflin, a wealthy young Philadelphia merchant who served with Adams in the Continental Congress, had been one of the first to welcome Adams on his arrival in Philadelphia. As a "fighting Quaker," he had since become Washington's aide-de-camp.

Martha Washington was present with her husband, as were General Horatio Gates and his lady. When Martha Washington and Elizabeth Gates arrived in Cambridge by coach in December, it was remarked that they would surely be a welcome addition "in country where [fire] wood was scarce." Gates, a former British officer, was an affable, plain-faced man who, like Washington, had served during the French and Indian War on the disastrous

Braddock expedition. As adjutant general he was Washington's right hand at Cambridge.

Washington and Adams were nearly the same age, Washington, at forty-three, being just three years older. Powerfully built, he stood nearly a head taller than Adams—six feet four in his boots, taller than almost anyone of the day—and loomed over his short, plump wife. The three officers, in their beautiful buff and blue uniforms, were all that Adams might imagine when picturing himself as a soldier.

Yet even they were upstaged by the main attractions of the gathering, a dozen or more sachems and warriors of the Caughnawaga Indians in full regalia who had been invited to dine, together with their wives and children. Adams had been fascinated by Indians since boyhood, when the aged leaders of the Punkapaug and Neponset tribes had called on his father. But he shared with Washington and Gates a dread fear of the British unleashing Indian war parties on the frontiers, as had the French twenty years before. Recalling what he had read and heard, Adams had earlier written to a friend, "The Indians are known to conduct their wars so entirely without faith and humanity that it would bring eternal infamy on the Ministry throughout all Europe if they should excite those savages to war. . . . To let loose these blood hounds to scalp men and to butcher women and children is horrid." Yet finding himself now unexpectedly in the actual presence of Indians was another matter, and he had a very different reaction.

The dinner, starting at two o'clock, was a diplomatic occasion. The Caughnawagas had come to offer their services to the Americans, and, gathered all about him, they presented a spectacle that Adams, to his surprise, hugely enjoyed. "It was a savage feast, carnivorous animals devouring their prey," he wrote in his diary. "Yet they were wondrous polite. The general introduced me to them as one of the Grand Council Fire at Philadelphia, upon which they made me many bows and cordial reception." To Abigail he reported himself decidedly pleased by the whole occasion.

What he could not risk telling her by letter was that the command at Cambridge had received the most heartening news, indeed the only good news, of the long, grim winter. An expedition led by young Henry Knox, a former Boston bookseller and colonel in Washington's army, had been sent to Lake Champlain to retrieve the artillery captured by Ethan Allen at Fort Ticonderoga and haul the great guns back over the snow-covered Berkshire Mountains all the way to Boston, a task many had thought impossible. Now the "noble train" was at Framingham, twenty miles to the west. It was a feat of almost unimaginable daring and difficulty and, ironically, only made possible by the severity of the winter, as the guns had been dragged over the snow on sleds.

Mounted and on their way again the next morning, with the temperature still in the twenties, Adams and Bass were joined by a newly elected Massachusetts delegate to Congress, young Elbridge Gerry. They rode out past the pickets and campfires of Cambridge and at Framingham stopped to see for themselves the guns from Ticonderoga, Adams making careful note of the inventory—58 cannon ranging in size from 3- and 4-pounders to one giant 24-pounder that weighed more than two tons. Clearly, with such artillery, Washington could change the whole picture at Boston.

The three riders pressed on through the grey and white landscape, making twenty to twenty-five miles a day. A "cold journey," Adams wrote. The weather was persistently wretched. There was more snow, wind, and freezing rain.

With dusk coming on by four in the afternoon and the bitter cold turning colder still, the glow and warmth of familiar wayside taverns was more welcome than ever. Under normal circumstances, Adams nearly always enjoyed such stops. He loved the food—wild goose on a spit, punch, wine, bread and cheese, apples—and a leisurely pipe afterward, while toasting himself by the fire. He picked up news, delighted in "scenes and characters," as he said, enough "for the amusement of Swift or even Shakespeare."

It was in such places that he had first sensed the rising tide of revolution. A year before the first meeting of Congress in 1774, riding the court circuit, he had stopped one winter night at a tavern at Shrewsbury, about forty miles from Boston, and as he would recall for Benjamin Rush years afterward, the scene left a vivid impression.

. . . as I was cold and wet I sat down at a good fire in the bar room to dry my great coat and saddlebags, till a fire could be made in my chamber. There presently came in, one after another half a dozen or half a score substantial yeomen of the neighborhood, who, sitting down to the fire after lighting their pipes, began a lively conversation upon politics. As I believed I was unknown to all of them, I sat in total silence to hear them. One said, "The people of Boston are distracted." Another answered, "No wonder the people of Boston are distracted; oppression will make wise men mad." A third said, "What would you say, if a fellow should come to your house and tell you he was come to take a list of your cattle that Parliament might tax you for them at so much a head? And how should you feel if he should go out and break open your barn, to take down your oxen, cows, horses and sheep?" "What would I say," replied the first, "I would knock him in the head." "Well," said a fourth, "if Parliament can take away Mr. Hancock's wharf and Mr. Row's wharf, they can take away your barn and my house." After much more reasoning in this style, a fifth who had as yet been silent, broke out, "Well it is high time for us to rebel. We must rebel sometime or other: and we had better rebel now than at any time to come: if we put it off for ten or twenty years, and let them go on as they have begun, they will get a strong party among us, and plague us a great deal more than they can now. As yet they have but a small party on their side."

But now, at town after town, the atmosphere was edged with melancholy, the talk was of . . . the dire situation at Boston.

Snow lay deep most of the way. With drifts banked against buildings and stone walls, trees bare against the sky, the wind seldom still, no part of the journey was easy or uplifting to the spirits. Instead of welcoming committees and church bells, there was only the frozen road ahead.

The one bright note was young Gerry, who belonged to the so-called "codfish aristocracy" of Marblehead, his father having made a fortune shipping dried cod to Spain and the West Indies. Like Adams, indeed like every member of the Massachusetts delegation, Gerry was a Harvard graduate, a slight, birdlike man, age thirty-one, who spoke with a stammer and had an odd way of contorting his face, squinting and enlarging his eyes. But he was good company. Because of the family business, he had traveled extensively and was an ardent patriot. He and Adams talked all the way, making the journey, as Adams related to Abigail, considerably less tedious than it might have been. Their days together on the wintry road marked the start of what was to be a long, eventful friendship.

Like Adams, Gerry viewed mankind as capable of both great good and great evil. Importantly now, they were also of the same heart concerning what had to be done at Philadelphia.

Abigail had already said what John knew needed saying when, in November, a petition was circulated at home calling for reconciliation with Britain. "I could not join today in the petitions . . . for a reconciliation between our no longer parent state, by a tyrant state and these colonies," she wrote. Then, making a slight but definite dash mark with her pen before continuing, as if to signify her own break from the past, she said, "Let us separate, they are unworthy to be our brethren."

Passing through New York, Adams bought two copies of a small anonymous pamphlet, newly published under the title *Common Sense*. Keeping one, he sent the other on to her.

Adams and his two companions arrived at Philadelphia on Thursday, February 8, 1776, fifteen days after leaving Braintree.

His first letters from Abigail did not reach him until more than a month later and were filled with accounts of thrilling events. The American bombardment of Boston had begun March 2 and 3. "No sleep for me tonight," she wrote, as the house trembled about her. On March 5 she described a more thunderous barrage: "the rattling of the windows,

the jar of the house and the continuous roar of the 24-pounders."

The night before, working at great speed, Washington's men had moved the guns from Ticonderoga to commanding positions on the high ground of the Dorchester Peninsula, south of Boston, looking over Boston Harbor and the British fleet. With hundreds of ox teams and more than a thousand American troops at work, breastworks had been set up and cannon hauled into place, all in a night and to the complete surprise of the British. Abigail was told that the British commander, on seeing what they had accomplished, remarked, "My God, these fellows have done more work in one night than I could make my army do in three months."

Days of fearful tension followed until Sunday, March 17, St. Patrick's Day, when she went again to the top of Penn's Hill to see a spectacle such as no one could ever have imagined—the British were abandoning Boston. General William Howe had struck an agreement with Washington. If allowed to depart in peace, the army would not leave Boston in flames.

The entire fleet, "the largest fleet ever seen in America," was lifting canvas in a fair breeze and turning to the open sea. "You may count upwards of one hundred and seventy-sail," she wrote. "They look like a forest."

The British had been outwitted, humiliated. The greatest military power on earth had been forced to retreat by an army of amateurs; it was a heady realization. As would be said by the Duke of Manchester before the House of Lords, "The fact remains, that the army which was sent to reduce the province of Massachusetts Bay has been driven from the capital, and the standard of the provincial army now waves in triumph over the walls of Boston."

With the departing fleet sailed a thousand Loyalists, many well known to John and Abigail Adams, including John's first mentor in the law, James Putnam of Worcester, and Samuel Quincy, brother of Hannah and Josiah, and Adams's opposing counsel in the Boston Massacre trials.

That such had come to pass, wrote Abigail, was surely the work of the Lord and "marvelous in our eyes."

QUESTIONS TO CONSIDER

1 Why did the Stamp Act cause such a furor in the colonies? Why did Adams believe, in McCullough's words, that the movement toward revolution "began in the minds of Americans long before any shots were fired or blood shed"?

2 Why was the so-called Boston Massacre misnamed? In what ways did the local residents invite and provoke this incident? Why was Adams's defense of the troops both typical of his character and an act of courage?

3 How was Adams able to defend the British soldiers accused of killing five Boston citizens without destroying his reputation as an advocate of the revolutionary cause? How did the British practice of quartering troops in colonial homes inspire acts of violence?

4 McCullough leaves the reader guessing when he concludes that Adams, although abhorring mob violence, was "exuberant" when he heard that the colonists had dumped tea into Boston Harbor. How do you interpret this apparent inconsistency in Adams?

5 Describe Adams's mixed feelings as the revolution approached. For example, how did he react to the loss of his good friend Jonathan Sewall? Adams had always feared the violent character of the Indians, but what was his reaction toward the Caughnawaga Indians who attended a feast hosted by George Washington?

6 If Abigail Adams and a group of "substantial yeoman" in a Shrewsbury tavern are good examples, what was the position of the colonists at the outset of the American Revolution?

8 Thomas Jefferson and the Meanings of Liberty

DOUGLAS L. WILSON

The United States was conceived in idealism and in paradox. America joined the family of nations dedicated to the proposition that "all men are created equal," that all are endowed with the unalienable rights of life, liberty, and the pursuit of happiness, and that they have a natural right to rebel when those rights are denied. So said Thomas Jefferson in the American Declaration of Independence, summing up truths that Americans had learned in the eighteenth-century Enlightenment, or Age of Reason, a time of momentous intellectual and scientific advancements that began in Europe and spread to America. Enlightenment thinkers in Europe stressed a belief in natural law, human progress, and government as a rational instrument, ideas that profoundly influenced Jefferson, Benjamin Franklin, and most other American patriots. The ringing prologue of Jefferson's Declaration, in fact, drew much of its inspiration from English philosopher John Locke, who had held that all human beings were innately equal and good and were entitled to "life, liberty, and possessions."

Yet in 1776, enlightened America held some 500,000 Africans in chains. Jefferson himself and George Washington, the commander of the patriot army, were large slaveholders. Indeed, slavery existed in all thirteen states and was an indispensable labor force for the patriot cause. Even so, many northerners, in a burst of revolutionary idealism, moved to abolish the institution in their states. Vermont was the first to do so, in 1777. Massachusetts outlawed it by a judicial decision six years later. New Hampshire removed it by "constitutional interpretation," and Pennsylvania, Rhode Island, and Connecticut all adopted gradual emancipation programs. When New York and New Jersey finally freed their slaves, the institution of bondage became peculiar to the South—hence the term peculiar institution.

The story was dramatically different in the South. True, some individual masters, swept up in the spirit of the Revolution, voluntarily manumitted their slaves. But most southern planters and political leaders refused to follow the lead of the northern states. Because those states had so few slaves in relation to their white population, white southerners liked to ask what the northerners had to lose in adopting emancipation. Southern whites did not see how they could abolish slavery, not with their heavy concentration of slaves (in some places they outnumbered whites) and their correspondingly large investments. For white southerners of the Revolutionary generation, however, slavery was more than a labor system, more even than a means of race control in a region brimming with blacks. It was the foundation of an entire patrician way of life, so interwoven with the fabric of southern society—as a potent status symbol, as personal wealth, as inheritances and dowries—that it did not seem possible to remove it.

And what of Jefferson, perhaps the most enlightened southerner of his day? In Jefferson, we meet an American anomaly: the antislavery slaveholder. Jefferson truly hated slavery; he damned it as "this blot in our country," this "great political and moral evil," and he devised a specific plan to get rid of it in Virginia—by gradual emancipation and colonization of the freed blacks outside the state. Yet Virginia never adopted his plan, and Jefferson himself was so much a part of his slaveholding culture—and so much in debt—that he felt unable to free his own slaves while he was alive (he did, however, provide for the liberation of five of his skilled slaves upon his death). It is not unfair to point out that Jefferson's illustrious political career—among other things, he was Revolutionary governor of Virginia, United States minister to France, Washington's secretary of state, and the third president of the United States—was made possible by slave labor.

In this selection, a distinguished Jefferson scholar reflects on this "many-sided and multi-talented man," especially on his contradictions concerning slavery and race. In doing so, Douglas Wilson raises a crucial point about the perils of presentism—that is, of intruding today's values and attitudes upon the past. To do that, he warns, risks distorting history. What annoys him is that too many Americans today seem unable to discuss the past in its own terms, unable "to make appropriate allowances for prevailing historical conditions."

As an example of presentism, Wilson discusses the story of Jefferson's alleged liaison with his house slave, Sally Hemings. The author denies the story as wholly out of character for Jefferson. But Wilson is wrong. More recent studies of Jefferson, citing DNA tests and other evidence, maintain that the Sage of Monticello was in fact the father of Sally Hemings's children. For an astute analysis of the controversy, see Joseph J. Ellis, "A Note on the Sally Hemings Scandal," in Ellis's American Sphinx (New York: Vintage Books, 1998). Wilson goes on to argue that even if Jefferson did sire Hemings's offspring, does it matter? This leads Wilson to a profound question that all of us ought to ponder. "How should we remember the leading figures of our history?" he asks. "By their greatest achievements and most important contributions or by their personal failures and peccadilloes?" Wilson emphatically sides with the first position.

Of Jefferson's many achievements, Wilson contends that his "pre-eminent contribution to the world was the Declaration of Independence." In discussing that contribution, Wilson confronts even worse examples of presentism: the view of Jefferson as a ranting hypocrite for trumpeting liberty and equality, yet failing to free his own slaves, and as an inveterate racist for his observations about the traits of black people in his Notes on the State of Virginia. Frankly, those observations are offensive to read today. Yet Wilson reminds us that they were speculative, "a suspicion only," and maintains that Jefferson would have readily discarded them had he encountered an outspoken, literate

African American such as Frederick Douglass. Addressing the question of why Jefferson did not free his slaves, Wilson observes that the great Virginian faced formidable obstacles in the context of his time and place. Then Wilson turns the whole question around. Instead of asking why Jefferson continued to hold slaves, the question ought to be, "How did a man who was born into a slaveholding society, whose family and admired friends owned slaves, who inherited a fortune that was dependent on slaves and slave labor, decide at an early age that slavery was morally wrong and forcefully declare that it ought to be abolished?"

As for the Declaration of Independence, Wilson makes a convincing case that Jefferson meant to include both blacks and women in his philosophical conception of equality. The author goes on to establish a powerful connection between Jefferson's Declaration and Lincoln's address at Gettysburg during the Civil War. The Gettysburg Address, Wilson points out, "invested Jefferson's eighteenth-century notion of equality with an essentially new meaning and projected it onto the future of the nation." As a result, Americans today have a different view of the prologue of the Declaration than did Jefferson's generation.

This is a powerful, thought-provoking essay. Now that you are aware of the problem of presentism, how would you evaluate the other readings in Portrait of America? *Do they judge the past through the lens of the present, or do they assess historical figures and societies on their own terms, within the context of their times?*

GLOSSARY

HEMINGS, SALLY Jefferson's mulatto house slave, by whom he supposedly fathered seven children.

MONTICELLO Jefferson's Virginia estate.

***NOTES ON THE STATE OF VIRGINIA* (1785)** Jefferson's only published book, in which he made observations about the racial traits of blacks and also offered a plan of gradual emancipation and colonization; later, Henry Clay and

Abraham Lincoln (in his pre–Civil War career) would endorse that approach.

PRESENTISM The imposition of present-day values and assumptions on individuals and societies of the past.

SOCIAL DARWINISM A belief, based on Charles Darwin's theories of biological evolution, that only the fittest individuals and societies survive.

"Today, makes yesterday mean." Emily Dickinson's gnomic utterance contains at least one undoubted truth—that the perspectives of the present invariably color the meanings we ascribe to the past. Nothing confirms this so readily as the changing reputations of historical figures, whose status often appears indexed to present-day preoccupations. It may be inevitable that every age should refashion its historical heroes in a contemporary idiom, but doing so carries with it an obvious and inherent danger. In imposing Today's meanings on Yesterday, we run the risk of distorting it—whether willfully, to suit our own purposes, or unintentionally, by unwarranted assumptions and because of meager information. In this way we lose track of what might be considered the obverse of Emily Dickinson's remark: that Yesterday has meanings of its own that are prior to and necessarily independent of Today's.

Thomas Jefferson is one of the few historical Americans who need no introduction. Even the most

Douglas L. Wilson, "Thomas Jefferson and the Meanings of Liberty," originally published in *The Atlantic*, January 1991. Used by permission.

Thomas Jefferson, in an oil painting done in 1805 by Rembrandt Peale. Jefferson was tall and slender, with a freckled face, gray eyes, and short, powdered, red hair. The color of his hair inspired one correspondent to salute him as "You red-headed son of a bitch." Despite his aristocratic upbringing, he was largely indifferent about his clothes, which rarely fit him. A Federalist senator once mistook Jefferson for a servant, observing with a sniff that his shirt was dirty. (New York Historical Society)

great national hero. With the . . . two hundred and fiftieth anniversary of his birth, in 1743, it seems appropriate to note some of the ways in which Thomas Jefferson is remembered by the American public and to examine the historical lens through which the man and his contributions are seen.

Only a generation ago Jefferson was still considered to be and treated as an object of veneration, so closely identified with the spirit of America as to constitute a problem for the historian. In 1960 Merrill D. Peterson confronted this problem in one of the most revealing works of Jefferson scholarship, *The Jefferson Image in the American Mind,* which surveys what Jefferson has meant to succeeding generations of Americans. "Where the object is Jefferson," Peterson wrote,

the historian's obligation to historical truth is compromised, in some degree, by his sense of obligation to the Jefferson symbol. Jefferson occupies such an important place in the symbolical architecture of this nation that the search for the elusive *himself* from the vaunted summit, Objectivity, must not be allowed to empty the symbol of meaning for "Jefferson's children."

It is a measure of the change that has occurred in the past thirty years that the one thing Jefferson's children nowadays are most likely to associate with him, apart from his authorship of the Declaration of Independence, is a sexual liaison with one of his slaves, Sally Hemings. College teachers are often dismayed to discover that many if not most of their students now regard this as an accepted fact. But this is not all. In the prevailing ethos of the sexual revolution, Jefferson's supposed liaison is widely received with equanimity and seems to earn him nothing more reproachful than a knowing smile. For most, such a liaison is apparently not objectionable, and for some, its presumed reality actually seems to work in his favor, showing him to have been not a stuffy moralist but a man who cleverly managed to appear respectable while secretly carrying on an illicit relationship. In effect, something that before the 1960s would have been universally considered a shameful

abbreviated knowledge of American history, at home or abroad, includes the author of the Declaration of Independence. Identified around the world with democracy and human rights, Jefferson's name and words have been invoked for two hundred years in the cause of freedom and political reform. But here in his own country, where the name synonymous with democracy is exhibited everywhere—on counties, cities, schools, streets, and every imaginable form of institution, business, and product—it sometimes seems that the man himself is receding from view, and that what is commonly thought and said about him gets harder and harder to reconcile with the blot on Jefferson's character has become almost an asset. Confirming this state of affairs is the case of a prominent black civil-rights leader who complained not long ago that Jefferson's alleged relationship with Hemings is not forthrightly acknowledged by the proprietors of Monticello, Jefferson's residence, and who frankly confessed that this liaison had for him a positive effect in showing that, though a slaveholder, Jefferson was well disposed toward black people.

Although the charge that Jefferson had fathered several children by one of his slaves was first made public in his lifetime, by a vindictive journalist and office-seeker, James Callender, it was believed mainly by those who disparaged Jefferson for political reasons and was not credited by Jefferson scholars or the public at large. But that began to change in 1974, when Fawn M. Brodie published a widely read book on Jefferson in which she attempted to establish the truth of Callender's charge as a prime biographical fact. Brodie's thesis about Jefferson and Hemings is an embellished and controversial reading of the evidence, but what is more significant in the present context is that her story was well geared to the dispositions of her audience. She insisted that her object was not to pillory Jefferson or to make him out as a moral monster but merely to depict him as a man. If, as a widower, he fell in love with a beautiful slave girl and took her as a mistress when she was fourteen years old, it was "not scandalous debauchery with an innocent slave victim," she assured us, "but rather a serious passion that brought Jefferson and the slave woman much private happiness over a period lasting thirty-eight years." Brodie's benign version of the story has proved persuasive, and where previous versions had depicted such behavior as scandalous, hypocritical, or shameful, Jefferson and Hemings are represented as a pair of happy lovers, bravely defying the conventions of a sexually puritanical and racist society.

Compelling as this picture has proved to the American public, most Jefferson scholars and historians have remained unpersuaded. It is true that Jefferson was extremely protective of his personal life and went to considerable lengths to keep it private, but it does not follow, as Brodie would have us believe, that he must

therefore have had something to hide. In accounting for Jefferson's behavior in the context of his own time, rather than ours, it is difficult for knowledgeable authorities to reconcile a liaison with Hemings with much else that is known about him. Jefferson implicitly denied the charge, and such evidence as exists about the paternity of Hemings's children points not to Jefferson but to his nephews. It is, of course, impossible to prove a negative, but the real problem with Brodie's interpretation is that it doesn't fit Jefferson. If he did take advantage of Hemings and father her children over a period of twenty years, he was acting completely out of character and violating his own standards of honor and decency. For a man who took questions of morality and honor very seriously, such a hypocritical liaison would have been a constant source of shame and guilt. For his close-knit family, who worshipped him and lived too near to him to have been ignorant of such an arrangement, it would have been a moral tragedy of no small dimensions.

But haunted as he was by other troubles and difficulties, there is no sign of this sort of shame or guilt in Jefferson's life. That is why Brodie must present Jefferson and Hemings as a happy couple and their supposed life together as giving satisfaction and lasting pleasure. And whereas there are grounds for suspecting a liaison, such as the terms of Jefferson's will and the testimony of Hemings's son Madison, there are no grounds whatever for believing in what Brodie called the "private happiness" enjoyed by Jefferson and Hemings. That is pure speculation. Because Brodie's thesis deals in such unwarranted assumptions, the great Jefferson biographer Dumas Malone regarded it as "without historical foundation." But what makes it possible for the American public to take the Sally Hemings story to heart, even more than the suspicious circumstances, seems to be a prevailing presentism.

"Presentism" is the term that historians use for applying contemporary or otherwise inappropriate standards to the past. An awkward term at best, it nevertheless names a malaise that currently plagues American discussions of anything and everything concerning the past: the widespread inability to make appropriate allowances for prevailing historical conditions. The issue of presentism is hardly new, but it has perhaps been amplified of late by the debunking and revisionist spirit of the times and the effect this has had on public perceptions. As the uncritically positive and unabashedly patriotic approach that for so long characterized the teaching of American history in the public schools has abated, the emphasis has steadily shifted to the problems and failures of the past. The saga of the glories of the old West has thus given way to a saga of exploitation and greed. Pride in conquering the wilderness has yielded to the shame of despoiling the land and dispossessing the indigenous peoples. What seems to have happened is that a laudably corrective trend has predominated to such an extent that the emphasis seems somehow reversed, and parents complain that they scarcely recognize the history their children are taught.

With a built-in emphasis on what had previously been ignored or suppressed, it is hardly surprising that almost all the revisionist news, at least where traditional American heroes are concerned, is bad. A question that was once reasonably clear has become a muddle: How should we remember the leading figures of our history? By their greatest achievements and most important contributions or by their personal failures and peccadilloes? Can one category cancel out the other? In a sense these reversals of fortune are inevitable, inasmuch as nothing ever keeps its place in a world of incessant change. It is perhaps an instance of what the historian Henry Adams called the law of acceleration—the tendency of change to come faster and faster—that John F. Kennedy and Martin Luther King Jr., whose murders elevated them to martyrdom, should both come in for reappraisal while their memories and legacies are still fresh. Do the revelations about such things as Kennedy's womanizing, his not-so-heroic war record, and his non-authorship of a book for which he accepted the Pulitzer Prize detract from his positive accomplishments as President? Do the revelations about King's philandering and his plagiarism as a graduate student have any bearing on his conspicuous achievements as a civil-rights leader? Or is this a case of asking the question backward? Is it perhaps more appropriate and revealing to ask, Are the significant contributions of Kennedy and King, which affected the lives of millions of Americans, in any way diminished by subsequent revelations about their shortcomings and failings in other areas?

In this climate the difficulties of judging a figure like Thomas Jefferson by an appropriate standard are considerably compounded. One who writes voluminously over a long time may easily have his own words quoted against him or cited to prove that he held views later modified or abandoned. Jefferson was pre-eminently such a person. On this point Merrill D. Peterson has observed,

His speculative and practical sides were frequently confused. Few men took into account that Jefferson's private self, as expressed in his letters, might not coincide with his public self. Or that his opinion at one time might not represent his opinion under different circumstances. Or that a man of his intellectual temperament did not often bother to qualify felicitous generalizations.

In some ways that are little recognized, Jefferson is surprisingly modern and accessible to the present age. His pronounced notions about health, for example, which seemed somewhat odd to previous generations, appear nowadays in an entirely different light. He believed strongly that regular exercise was essential to physical and mental well-being. As a college student, he developed a regimen of daily running to keep himself fit, and he came to believe in later life that walking was the most salutary form of exercise for the ordinary person. On the subject of diet he also held strong views, which minimized meat and animal products and emphasized instead the prime importance of vegetables. For our own time, at least, Jefferson turns out to have been something of a health-food prophet.

Whether his leading ideas on politics and government will prove as resilient remains to be seen. In spite of his great reputation as a statesman, many of these have proved as counter to the prevailing currents of American history as his prejudice against large cities and manufacturing. He could never reconcile himself, for example, to the Supreme Court's deciding the constitutionality of laws and acts of the executive—a development he regarded as unwarranted and disastrous. His preference for a small central government and his insistence on the prerogatives of the states have been strongly rebuffed, if not virtually obliterated, by decisive turns in our national development. Although history cannot be reversed, the relative size and power of the central government is once more (or still) at issue, as is the proper scope and authority of the Supreme Court. Even Jefferson's views on the disadvantages of large cities have today a resonance that was unheard or unheeded by previous generations.

Because he was attracted to laborsaving devices and was an ingenious adopter and adapter of new gadgets, Jefferson has gained a reputation as an inventor, but aside from a few items—an innovative moldboard for a plough, a revolving book stand—he probably invented little. Though he used and enthusiastically promoted the polygraph, a machine for making simultaneous copies of a written document, he did not invent it, and could not even keep his own in repair. But the fact that Jefferson is perceived as an inventor tells us something about the way he is valued. Abraham Lincoln was much interested in inventions and even went so far as to have one of his own patented, but this fact has made little impression on his admirers and is entirely absent from the legend.

President Kennedy paid a famous tribute to the multiplicity of Jefferson's talents, but they have always been regarded as astonishing. James Parton, one of Jefferson's nineteenth-century biographers, gave his dazzling range of abilities a dramatic accent when he characterized his subject as a man who "could calculate an eclipse, survey an estate, tie an artery, plan an edifice, try a cause, break a horse, dance a minuet, and play the violin." And Parton was describing a young Jefferson who had not yet written the Declaration. When the world's leading scientist and explorer, Alexander von Humboldt, came to visit Jefferson in Washington in 1804, he came to see not the President of the United States so much as the president of the American Philosophical Society and the author of *Notes on the State of Virginia* (1785). Had he visited the President at his home in Virginia, he would have seen what was perhaps the finest private library in America, which later became the foundation of the Library of Congress.

Not all of Jefferson's extraordinary talents are fully recognized by the public at large. One that is not is his great achievement as an architect. Self-taught from books and, until he went abroad, almost without worthy architectural models to observe, Jefferson managed to design a number of memorable structures. The residence of his that crowns (and names) a small mountain in the Virginia Piedmont has become one of the most familiar objects in American iconography. And Jefferson can claim credit for not just one Monticello but two: the domed structure represented on the back of the nickel is his second version of the house, which superseded the first one on the same site, and is dramatically different.

Part of the evidence for Jefferson's distinction as an architect is found in his beautifully detailed drawings, some of which reveal fanciful structures that were never built. But his most original and most imaginative design, and the one recognized by professional architects as among the greatest of all American architectural achievements, is his "academical village"—the campus of the University of Virginia. In forming his conception Jefferson effectively reinvented the idea of the university, from the innovative curriculum to the unique arrangement and design of the buildings. Here those seeking his monument have only to look about them.

Although he was a many-sided and multi-talented man who left a lasting imprint on a number of endeavors, there seems to be little doubt that Jefferson's pre-eminent contribution to the world was the Declaration of Independence—particularly its enduring affirmations of liberty and equality. In the prologue of the Declaration these affirmations were made the axioms from which the rights of revolution and self-government could confidently be deduced. The idea of individual liberty was not, of course, original with Jefferson, or exclusively an American invention. It was fostered in Western Europe by philosophers, religious dissidents, and political rebels, but it took root tenaciously among transplanted Europeans in the New World and, with the founding of the American republic, received its most durable expression in the Declaration of Independence. To the Declaration's studious and deeply learned author, many of what had passed in the history of the world for the prerogatives of governmental power were arbitrary and intolerable restraints on individual freedom. In fact, it is not too much to say that Jefferson's reigning political passion was a hatred of tyranny. And although his fear of the tyrannous abuse of power has sometimes been judged excessive, it is hard to argue that tyranny has ever been, or is even now, in short supply.

If it is possible to reduce so complex an issue to its simplest terms, one might venture that for Jefferson the paramount political issue in the American Revolution was what he called liberty and what we now call personal freedom, or choice. It was and remains the virtual sine qua non of American culture, something that Americans from the first have been strongly conscious of and willing to fight for. But what has become the most familiar and the most quoted phrase in the Declaration—"all men are created equal"—is about something else. It is an intriguing fact that although Americans generally understand that the prologue to the Declaration is their charter of freedom, even more indelibly impressed upon their imagination is its affirmation of the ideal of human equality.

How could the man who wrote, that "all men are created equal" own slaves? This, in essence, is the question most persistently asked of those who write about Thomas Jefferson, and by all indications it is the thing that contemporary Americans find most vexing about him. In a recent series of some two dozen radio talk shows, I was asked this question on virtually every program, either by the host or by a

Isaac Jefferson, born in 1775, was a skilled slave on Jefferson's Monticello plantation. This daguerreotype was taken by John Plumbe circa 1845. (Tracy W. McGregor Library, Special Collections Department, University of Virginia Library)

caller. Most often, those who point to this problem admire Jefferson, and they appear as reluctant to give up their admiration as they would be to give up the principle of equality itself. But they are genuinely baffled by the seeming contradiction.

The question carries a silent assumption that because he practiced slaveholding, Jefferson must have somehow believed in it, and must therefore have been a hypocrite. My belief is that this way of asking the question, as in the cases of Kennedy and King, is essentially backward, and reflects the pervasive presentism of our time. Consider, for example, how different the question appears when inverted and framed in more historical terms: How did a man who was born into a slaveholding society, whose family and admired friends owned slaves, who inherited a fortune that was dependent on slaves and slave labor, decide at an early age that slavery was morally

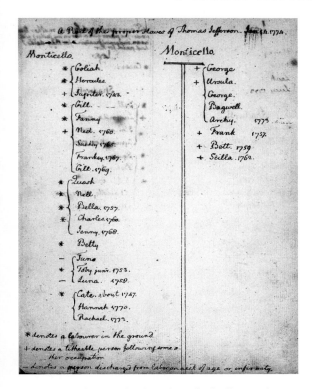

Twenty-nine slaves are listed on this roll of Jefferson's slaves at Monticello in 1774. In fact, Jefferson owned a total of 180 slaves and three large plantations, in addition to several smaller land holdings. The slaves listed on the roll without a footnote designation were under the age of ten. (Massachusetts Historical Society)

continue to hold them? This question, because of its underlying assumptions, is both harder and easier than the first. It is harder because we are at such a great remove from the conditions of eighteenth-century Virginia that no satisfactory explanation can be given in a nutshell. To come to terms with the tangle of legal restrictions and other obstacles faced by the eighteenth-century Virginia slaveholder who might have wished freedom for his slaves, together with the extraordinary difficulties of finding them viable places of residence and means of livelihood, requires a short course in early American history. But the question is easier in that there is no doubt that these obstacles to emancipation in Jefferson's Virginia were formidable, and the risk was demonstrably great that emancipated slaves would enjoy little, if any, real freedom and would, unless they could pass as white, be more likely to come to grief in a hostile environment. In short, the master whose concern extended beyond his own morality to the well-being of his slaves was caught on the horns of a dilemma. Thus the question of why Jefferson didn't free his slaves only serves to illustrate how presentism involves us in mistaken assumptions about historical conditions—in this case that an eighteenth-century slaveholder wanting to get out from under the moral stigma of slavery and improve the lot of his slaves had only to set them free.

wrong and forcefully declare that it ought to be abolished?

Though stating the same case, these are obviously different questions, focusing on different things, but one is framed in a historical context and the other ignores historical circumstances. The rephrased question reveals that what is truly remarkable is that Jefferson went against his society and his own self-interest to denounce slavery and urge its abolition. And, crucially, there is no hidden assumption that he must in some way have believed in or tacitly accepted the morality of slavery.

But when the question is explained in this way, another invariably follows: If Jefferson came to believe that holding slaves was wrong, why did he

The inevitable question about slavery and equality partly reflects the fact that most Americans are only vaguely familiar with the historical Jefferson, but delving into his writings and attempting to come to terms with the character of his thought, though illuminating, can create further consternation. The college student confronting Jefferson's one published book, *Notes on the State of Virginia,* is nowadays unprepared for and often appalled at what the author of the Declaration of Independence had to say about race. Thirty years ago college students were shocked to find Jefferson referring to the slave population as "blacks," a term that to them suggested racial insensitivity. But to those born after the civil-rights acts of the 1960s, it comes as a shock to discover that Jefferson, while firmly in favor of general emancipation, held out no hope for racial integration. Believing that an amalgamation of the races was not desirable and would not work, he advocated a plan of gradual emancipation and resettlement. Present-day students are even more shocked to find Jefferson concluding, albeit as "a suspicion only," that the blacks he had observed were "inferior to the whites in the endowments both of body and mind." Even his positive finding that blacks appeared to be superior to whites in musical ability rankles, for it comes through to students of the current generation as an early version of a familiar stereotype.

At a time like the present, when relations between the races are in the forefront of public discussion and desegregation is the law of the land, it is not surprising that college students should be sensitive to discrepancies between what they understand to be the prevailing ideals of their country and the views of its most prominent Founding Father. National ideals, however, spring not only from the beliefs and aspirations of founders but also, as this essay attempts to show, from the experience and efforts of subsequent generations. Though he foresaw that slavery could not prevail ("Nothing is more certainly written in the book of fate than that these people are to be free"), Jefferson can hardly be counted bigoted or backward for seriously doubting that a racially integrated society of white Europeans and black Africans was truly feasible. As the Harvard historian Bernard Bailyn has written, "It took a vast leap of the imagination in the eighteenth century to consider integrating into the political community the existing slave population, whose very 'nature' was the subject of puzzled inquiry and who had hitherto been politically nonexistent." Interestingly, the reasons that Jefferson gave for doubting the possibility of integration—"deep rooted prejudices entertained by the whites; ten thousand recollections, by the blacks, of the injuries they have sustained; new provocations; [and] the real distinctions which nature has made"—are the same reasons often cited by black separatists, who entertain the same misgivings.

But if Jefferson's being a separatist can be accounted for, what can be said about his invidious comparison of the natural endowments of blacks with those of whites, or with those of American Indians, whom he found to be on a par with whites? His own testimony suggests an answer, for he admitted that his acquaintance with blacks did not extend to the African continent and embraced only black people who had been born in and forced to live under the degrading conditions of slavery. "It will be right to make great allowances for the difference of condition, of education, of conversation, of the sphere in which they move," Jefferson wrote, but it is evident in the hindsight of two hundred years that his estimate of the capabilities of blacks failed to make sufficient allowances, particularly for the things he himself named. It is perhaps poetic justice that posterity should be liable to the same kind of mistake in judging him.

But if Jefferson's beliefs add up to a kind of racism, we must specify two important qualifications. First, that Jefferson offered his conclusions as a hypothesis only, acknowledging that his own experience was not a sufficient basis on which to judge an entire race. Had he lived long enough to meet the ex-slave Frederick Douglass or hear the searing eloquence of his oratory, he would have recognized intellectual gifts in a black man that were superior to those of most whites. Douglass's oratory brings us to the second qualification, which is a telling one. Attacking the justifications for slavery in 1854, Douglass observed,

Ignorance and depravity, and the inability to rise from degradation to civilization and respectability, are the most usual allegations against the oppressed. The evils most fostered by slavery and oppression are precisely those which slaveholders and oppressors would transfer from their system to the inherent character of their victims. Thus the very crimes of slavery become slavery's best defence. By making the enslaved a character fit only for slavery, they excuse themselves for refusing to make the slave a freeman.

Although we may find Jefferson guilty of failing to make adequate allowance for the conditions in which blacks were forced to live, Jefferson did not take the next step of concluding that blacks were fit only for slavery. This rationalization of slavery was indeed the common coin of slaveholders and other whites who condoned or tolerated the "peculiar" institution, but it formed no part of Jefferson's thinking. In fact, he took the opposite position: that having imposed the depredations of slavery on blacks, white Americans should not only emancipate them but also educate and train them to be self-sufficient, provide them with necessary materials, and establish a colony in which they could live as free and independent people.

But if going back to original sources and historical contexts is essential in discerning the meanings that Today has imposed on Yesterday, it is equally important in determining how Yesterday's meanings have colored Today's. The concept of equality that is universally recognized in our own time as a fundamental principle of American society only had its beginnings in the eighteenth century; it did not emerge full-blown from the Declaration of Independence.

Whenever he sent correspondents a copy of the Declaration, Jefferson transcribed the text in such a way as to show what the Continental Congress had added to his draft and what it had cut out. The process of congressional emendation was clearly a painful memory for him, and the deletion about which he probably felt the most regret was also the most radical of the passages, for it undertook to blame the King of England directly for the African slave trade. It begins,

He has waged cruel war against human nature itself, violating it's most sacred rights of life and liberty in the persons of a distant people who never offended him, captivating & carrying them into slavery in another hemisphere, or to incur miserable death in their transportation thither. . . . Determined to keep open a market where MEN should be bought & sold, he has prostituted his negative for suppressing every legislative attempt to prohibit or to restrain this execrable commerce.

Had this passage been ratified as part of the official Declaration, then a question often raised in the nineteenth century—Did Jefferson mean to include blacks in the language of the Declaration?—would have been susceptible of a clear-cut and demonstrable answer. For, as the political scientist Jean Yarbrough has recently pointed out, this passage says unmistakably that the Africans captured into slavery were not a separate category of beings but men, with the sacred rights of life and liberty that are said in the prologue of the Declaration to be the natural endowments of all men. It is precisely in having these same rights that the prologue asserts that all men are created equal.

This deleted passage also provides an answer to a question often raised in the twentieth century: Did Jefferson mean to include women in the phrase "all men are created equal"? Implicit in the passage is that "men" is being used in the broader sense of "mankind," for those who were cruelly transported to be "bought & sold" on the slave market were certainly female as well as male.

That blacks and women were meant to be included in the affirmations of Jefferson's Declaration at a time when they enjoyed nothing remotely like political and social equality underscores a source of continuing confusion for contemporary Americans—the difference between a philosophical conception of natural rights and a working system of laws and societal values which allows for the fullest expression of those rights. In our own time the stubbornly persistent disparity between these two is often a source of cynicism and despair, but a Jeffersonian perspective would put more emphasis on the considerable progress made in closing the gap. Jefferson himself was sustained by a profound belief in progress. His unshakable conviction that the world was steadily advancing, not only in the material but also in the moral sphere, is abundantly evident in his writings. Though sometimes criticized as being naive in this regard, he was fully aware that his belief embraced the prospect of recurrent political and social transformations. Writing from retirement at the age of seventy-three, he told a correspondent that "laws and institutions must go hand in hand with the progress of the human mind."

As that becomes more developed, more enlightened, as new discoveries are made, new truths disclosed, and manners and opinions change with the change of circumstances, institutions must advance also, and keep pace with the times. We might as well require a man to wear still the coat which fitted him when a boy, as civilized society to remain ever under the regimen of their barbarous ancestors.

One way of looking at American history from Jefferson's day down to our own is as the series of changes and adjustments in our laws and institutions necessitated by the ideals implicit in Jefferson's Declaration. Sometimes the effect of these ideals has been simply to prevent other, incompatible ideals from gaining ascendancy, as in the case of Social Darwinism, whose notions of the natural inferiority of certain racial and social groups were impeded by the prevalence and familiarity of the Declaration's precepts. But without doubt the most important event in the development of the American ideal of equality, after Jefferson's Declaration, was Abraham Lincoln's address at Gettysburg. Without any warrant from the founders themselves or from subsequent interpreters or historians, Lincoln declared that not only the essential meaning of the Civil War but also the national purpose itself was epitomized in Jefferson's phrase "all men are created equal."

As Garry Wills has cogently argued, Lincoln at Gettysburg was practicing not presentism but futurism. In the most stunning act of statesmanship in our history, he invested Jefferson's eighteenth-century notion of equality with an essentially new meaning and projected it onto the future of the nation. Transfigured in the context of civil war, and transformed by Lincoln into a larger and more consequential ideal, Jefferson's formulation would never be the same. Thanks in large part to Lincoln, Americans no longer understand the prologue of the Declaration as a philosophical expression of natural rights, but rather take it to be a statement about the social and political conditions that ought to prevail.

Jefferson's Declaration is thus remarkable not only for its durability—its ability to remain meaningful and relevant—but also for its adaptability to changing conditions. At a time when natural rights are widely proclaimed a nullity, the language of the Declaration is universally understood as affirming human rights, and is resorted to even by those who do not consciously associate their ideas or aspirations with Jefferson. When the black separatist Malcolm X underwent a change of heart about white people and publicly renounced the "sweeping indictments of one race," he told an audience in Chicago, "I am not a racist and do not subscribe to any of the tenets of racism. In all honesty and sincerity it can be stated that I wish nothing but freedom, justice, and equality; life, liberty, and the pursuit of happiness—for all people." Simply to name the most basic American ideals is to invoke the words of Jefferson.

QUESTIONS TO CONSIDER

1 Compare Thomas Jefferson and the Benjamin Franklin you met in selection 6. In what ways were they both representative of their time? Are there ways in which they were not?

2 How did the story of Jefferson and Sally Hemings first surface? What was the purpose of its publication? This story has been treated and interpreted in very different ways at different times. What do the varying interpretations say about the periods in which they originated?

3 Wilson says that one should not ask why Jefferson, author of the Declaration of Independence, did not free his slaves but rather how Jefferson, member of a slaveholding society, came to hate slavery. Do you agree with Wilson's point of view? During the Revolution and influenced especially by the Declaration of Independence, a number of southern slaveholders as well as the northern states did in fact free their slaves in the name of the liberty for which the American Revolution was being fought. So why did Jefferson not free his own? Is this question necessarily presentist?

4 The anthology entitles this selection "Thomas Jefferson and the Meanings of Liberty." What are the different meanings of liberty embodied in the Declaration of Independence? Which were most current in the eighteenth century? Which are most current today, and why have they changed?

5 Douglas Wilson raises the question of whether figures from the past should be remembered for their "greatest achievements" or for their "personal failures." What are the good sides and bad sides of revisionism that often stress the faults of great figures? What does this trend in historical writing say about the present?

PART FIVE

Birth of the Republic

9 Miracle at Philadelphia

H. W. BRANDS

Once the Revolution began, Americans set about creating the political machinery necessary to sustain an independent nation. The Second Continental Congress, called in 1775, continued as an emergency, all-purpose central government until 1781, when the Articles of Confederation were finally ratified and a new one-house Congress was elected to function as the national government. Wary of central authority because of the British experience, Americans now had precisely the kind of government most of them wanted: an impotent Congress that lacked the authority to tax, regulate commerce, or enforce its own ordinances and resolutions. Subordinate to the states, which supplied it with funds as they chose, Congress was powerless to run the country. Indeed, its delegates wandered from Princeton to Annapolis to Trenton to New York, endlessly discussing where they should settle.

Patriots such as James Madison of Virginia, Alexander Hamilton of New York, and the venerable George Washington fretted in their correspondence about the near paralysis of the central government and the unstable conditions that plagued the land. "An opinion begins to prevail, that a General Convention for revising the Articles of Confederation would be expedient," John Jay wrote Washington in March 1787. Washington agreed that the "fabrick" was "tottering." When Massachusetts farmers rose in rebellion under Daniel Shays, Washington was horror stricken. "Are your people getting mad? . . . What is the cause of all this? When and how is it to end? . . . What, gracious God, is man! that there should be such inconsistency and perfidiousness in his conduct? . . . We are fast verging to anarchy and confusion!"

Many of his colleagues agreed. There followed a series of maneuvers and meetings that culminated in the great convention of 1787, a gathering of fifty-five notables sent to Philadelphia to overhaul the feeble Articles of Confederation. Without authority, they proceeded to draft an entirely new constitution that scrapped the Articles, created a new government, and undoubtedly saved the country and America's experiment in popular government. As James MacGregor Burns has noted, it was a convention of "the well-bred, the well-fed, the well-read, and the well-wed." Most delegates were wealthy, formally educated, and youngish (their average age was the early forties), and more than a third of them were slave owners. The poor, the uneducated, the backcountry farmers, and women, blacks, and Indians were not represented. Throughout their deliberations, moreover, they compromised on the volatile slavery issue. "For these white men," wrote one scholar, "the black man was always a brooding and unsettling presence (the black woman, even more than the white woman, was beyond the pale, beyond calculation)." For most of the framers of the Constitution, order and national strength were more important than the unalienable rights of blacks or women. Like their countrymen, most could simultaneously love liberty, recognize the injustice of slavery, yet tolerate bondage as a necessary evil.

As we enter our third century under the Constitution, we need more than ever to remember that the framers were not saints but human beings—paradoxical, complex, unpredictable, and motivated by selfishness as well as high idealism. Yet, as H. W. Brands shows in the following selection, the founders were able to rise above petty self-interest to fashion what remains the oldest written national constitution, which in turn created one of the oldest and most successful federal systems in history.

Brands tells the story of the Constitutional Convention from the viewpoint of Benjamin Franklin, the oldest and perhaps the wisest of the delegates assembled there. As Franklin perused the list of delegates when the convention began, he declared himself extremely pleased. "We have here at present," Franklin said, "what the French call une assemblée des notables, *a convention composed of some of the principal people from the states of our Confederation." Reading over the same roster, Thomas Jefferson called the convention "an assembly of demi-gods."*

It was remarkable indeed that a new country of only about four million people produced an assembly of some of the most gifted statesmen in history. Yet only Franklin and George Washington, who presided over the convention, had national reputations. Both men sought to create a strong central government that would rise above the petty differences of the thirteen states. Other delegates feared such a government, especially one with a large standing army. Massachusetts delegate Elbridge Gerry spoke for many of his colleagues when he said that such an army might be misused, thus endangering their infant nation. Gerry compared a large standing army with a large standing penis. "An excellent assurance of domestic tranquility," he said, "but a dangerous temptation to foreign adventure." Franklin no doubt enjoyed a hearty laugh over the analogy. He would have reminded Gerry and the other delegates that "the wisdom of the common folks" would restrain both an overzealous chief executive and a strong standing army.

The most divisive dispute concerned the nature of representation. Franklin compared the dispute to that of a snake with two heads when confronting a bush. One head wanted to go on one side of the stem, Franklin said, but the other head insisted on the other side. "Neither of the heads would consent to come back or give way to the other," implying that the snake would starve to death if the heads could not reach an accommodation. The convention faced a similar problem: the delegates had to resort by necessity to accommodation and compromise, or their work would die of indecision. Fortunately for them and all succeeding generations of Americans, the delegates were able to fashion a new government through a series of painstaking compromises. By doing so, they ensured the survival of their new Constitution and the new government it created. A later historian called their achievement "the miracle at Philadelphia."

GLOSSARY

ARTICLES OF CONFEDERATION (1781–1789) The first American government after independence, it consisted of a weak central government that was subordinate to the states. There was a one-house congress that exercised all judicial, executive, and legislative functions but that lacked the power to levy taxes or to regulate currency.

BEDFORD, GUNNING A delegate from Delaware who believed that the large states had adopted "a dictatorial air" toward the small ones. He threatened succession if the individual states lost the sovereignty they had under the Articles of Confederation.

CUTLER, MANASSEH A Massachusetts clergyman and botanist who came to Philadelphia as a lobbyist for a group that was interested in receiving land grants in the Northwest Territory.

HAMILTON, ALEXANDER The brilliant New York delegate to the Constitutional Convention, Hamilton had earlier served as Washington's military aide during the American Revolution. Despite a humble background, Hamilton was an elitist who preferred monarchical government and distrusted the opinions of ordinary people.

JONES, JOHN PAUL During the American Revolution, Jones was an American naval officer who commanded the warship *Bonhomme Richard*. He raided British shipping and captured an English warship, which made him famous in America. During a desperate battle with another British warship, Jones's ship was severely damaged. When asked to surrender, he defiantly shouted: "I have not yet begun to fight."

MADISON, JAMES A Virginia delegate to the Constitutional Convention, this planter, slaveholder, and brilliant statesman was responsible for much of the substance of the new Constitution drafted there.

MORRIS, GOUVERNEUR A Pennsylvania delegate to the Constitutional Convention, Morris assumed the main responsibility for drafting the new Constitution. The preamble, which began, "We the people," was his inspiration and represented one of the single most important acts of the Constitutional Convention.

MORRIS, ROBERT Another Pennsylvania delegate to the Constitutional Convention, Morris was one of the richest men in America. He had earned a considerable reputation for his work in financing the American Revolution. While at the Constitutional Convention, Washington stayed at Morris's impressive mansion.

RANDOLPH, EDMUND A popular governor and a delegate from Virginia at the Constitutional Convention, Randolph championed the interests of the large states there, speaking in his trademark high-pitched voice Randolph wanted a legislature based on proportional representation (see the Virginia Plan in this glossary).

SHAYS'S REBELLION (1786) Poor farmers in western Massachusetts closed a county courthouse and threatened to seize a federal arsenal. Daniel Shays, who had fought at Bunker Hill, led a group of rural debtors who felt that the state government was insensitive to their needs. Shays's uprising was symptomatic of the weaknesses of the Articles of Confederation and the need for a stronger central government.

SOCIETY FOR POLITICAL INQUIRIES Formed by Benjamin Franklin, the society included George Washington, Thomas Paine, and many prominent Philadelphia residents. It met periodically to engage in lively discussions on, in Franklin's words, "the arduous and complicated science of government."

VIRGINIA PLAN Proposed by Edmund Randolph, the Virginia Plan called for a national executive with veto power, a national judiciary, and a two-house legislature. The lower house would be "elected by the people, and the upper house chosen by the lower." Delegates from the small states felt threatened by this proportional representation plan.

WILSON, JAMES A Pennsylvania delegate at the Constitutional Convention, Wilson advocated a strong national government and a legislature based on proportional representation. Wilson proposed that the southern states should count three-fifths of their slave populations when determining the number of representatives each slave state would have in the national House of Representatives.

[B]enjamin] Franklin had lived much longer than [James] Madison—much longer, in fact, than all but a handful of the other delegates to the constitutional convention. And he adopted a much less alarmist view of the future. He referred to [Daniel] Shays's rebellion as merely the work of "some disorderly people," and declared—this to a French friend, to whom he spoke candidly—"The rest of the states go on pretty well, except some dissensions in Rhode Island and Maryland respecting paper money."

Yet if he did not think doom at the door, Franklin heard its rumblings in the distance. Briefing [Thomas] Jefferson, still in France,* he wrote that from what he knew of the delegates, they seemed to be men of prudence and ability. "I hope good from their meeting." But the risks were great. "If it does not do good it must do harm, as it will show that we have not wisdom enough among us to govern ourselves, and will strengthen the opinion of some political writers that popular governments cannot long support themselves."

Anticipating the convention, Franklin organized a group called the Society for Political Inquiries, which met weekly in the library of his new home. Philadelphians made up the active membership, but the group enrolled various outside luminaries as honorary members. Among these was [George] Washington, who was thought to be favorably disposed to constitutional revision yet was also known to be reluctant to take a leading role. The former general cherished his exalted reputation and was correspondingly hesitant to involve himself in any divisive venture. At the same time, however, he hardly desired the undoing of the cause to which he had devoted eight years of his life. Nor did he wish to appear derelict in his duty. Franklin was among those telling Washington that duty called him to

Philadelphia. "Your presence will be of the greatest importance to the success of the measure," Franklin wrote. Washington allowed himself to be persuaded.

Washington's arrival in Philadelphia prompted a civic celebration the likes of which had not been seen since the end of the war. A cadre of his old officers rode out to greet him; the party crossed the Schuylkill on a floating bridge built by the British but abandoned intact at the evacuation of the city and since maintained by the locals. Church bells pealed as the hero passed; the leading citizens vied for his favor. Robert and Mrs. Morris won the prize of housing him, in their mansion on Market Street just east of Sixth. If the Morris house was any evidence, the financier's interests were thriving; besides a hothouse (for winter enjoyment), the compound boasted an icehouse (especially appreciated during the sweltering weeks of the convention) and a stable for twelve horses. (Yet, not content with a standard of living unsurpassed "by any commercial voluptuary of London," in the words of a French visitor, Morris subsequently speculated in western lands and lost all. He spent three years in a debtors' prison within wailing distance of his former mansion.)

On arrival Washington paid his respects to Franklin; the next day the general returned for dinner. The other delegates followed suit. Franklin's new dining room seated twenty-four; he now probably wished it bigger, for everyone insisted on seeing the man who was at once America's resident sage and, as Pennsylvania president, the convention's ex officio host. On Friday, May 18, he wrote a London brewer who had sent him a cask of porter [beer]. "We have here at present what the French call *une assemblée des notables,* a convention composed of some of the principal people from the several states of our confederation. They did me the honour of dining with me last Wednesday, when the cask was broached, and its contents met with the most cordial reception and universal approbation."

On this festive note the convention commenced its sober business. Only two men were even contemplated for president of the convention: Franklin and Washington. Franklin deferred to Washington,

From *The First American* by H. W. Brands, copyright © 2000 by H. W. Brands. Used by permission of Anchor Books, a division of Random House, Inc.
*At the time of the Constitutional Convention, Jefferson was serving as America's first minister to France.

Thomas Jefferson, although he was not present, called the men who gathered at Philadelphia to write the Constitution "an assembly of demi-gods." Most recognize in this Howard C. Christy painting the tall upright figure of the presiding officer, George Washington, and the slouched gout-stricken body of eighty-one year-old Benjamin Franklin. They were men of substance, of property—men who were about to draft what would become the longest-running constitution in the history of the world. ("Scene at the Signing of the Constitution" by Howard Chandler Christy. Courtesy Archives of the Capitol)

perhaps partly from concern that his health would not stand the wear of daily sessions, but at least equally from knowledge that the project would have the greatest chance of success under the aegis of the eminent general. (Washington's distance above mere mortals was already legendary. Several delegates were discussing this phenomenon when Franklin's Pennsylvania colleague, Gouverneur Morris, a hearty good fellow, suggested it was all in their minds. Alexander Hamilton challenged Morris: "If you will, at the next reception evenings, gently slap him on the shoulder and say, 'My dear General, how happy I am to see you look so well!' a supper and wine shall be provided for you and a dozen of your friends." Morris accepted the challenge and did what

Hamilton demanded. Washington immediately removed Morris's hand from his shoulder, stepped away, and fixed Morris with an angry frown until the trespasser retreated in confusion. Hamilton paid up, yet at the dinner Morris declared, "I have won the bet, but paid dearly for it, and nothing could induce me to repeat it.")

Franklin was right to worry about his ability to attend all the sessions. His mode of travel these days— to the limited extent he *did* travel—was via sedan chair, a seat mounted between two poles, which he had brought from France. Four prisoners from the Walnut Street jail hoisted the chair on their shoulders, and, if they walked slowly, Franklin's [kidney] stone did not pain him too much. Although the seat was covered, with glass windows, it was not really suited to foul weather, and when heavy rain doused the opening day of the convention, Franklin was forced to stay home. He had been planning to nominate Washington for convention president himself; instead the nomination was put forward by the Pennsylvania delegation. The gesture was appreciated all the same. "The nomination came with particular grace from Pennsylvania," recorded James Madison, "as Doctor Franklin alone could have been thought of as a competitor."

Before the convention most of the delegates knew Franklin only by reputation. His long absence from America rendered him something of a mystery; most wondered whether he would live up to all the good things said of him—or down to the few bad things. William Pierce of Georgia was one of the handful of delegates who recorded his impression:

Dr. Franklin is well known to be the greatest philosopher of the present age; all the operations of nature he seems to understand, the very heavens obey him, and the clouds yield up their lightning to be imprisoned in his rod.

But what claim he has to be a politician, posterity must determine. It is certain that he does not shine much in public council. He is no speaker, nor does he seem to let politics engage his attention.

He is, however, a most extraordinary man, and tells a story in a style more engaging than anything I ever heard. Let his biographer finish his character. He is 82 [actually 81] years old, and possesses an activity of mind equal to a youth of 25 years of age.

Franklin would have been the first to agree he was no orator, and in a gathering of fifty-five politicians, most of whom prided themselves on their forensic skills, he was content to let others carry the oratorical burden.

In fact he allowed others to carry even the burden of *his* statements. Very early the intentions of the organizers of the convention became evident: not merely to revise the Articles of Confederation but to draft an entirely new charter. The Virginians—especially Madison and Edmund Randolph—had

been busy, and on the third day Randolph revealed a comprehensive plan for a national government. The centerpiece of the Virginia plan was a powerful legislature of two houses, one house elected by the people, the other chosen by the popular house from nominations forwarded by the states. The legislature would name the executive and the judiciary, and it would possess a veto over state laws infringing its prerogatives.

Franklin had preferred a unicameral legislature for Pennsylvania, and he preferred it for America. He preferred an executive council, again on the Pennsylvania model, over a single president. But his first speech addressed another issue: how the executive was to be paid. Apologizing for the fact that his memory was not what it had been, he explained that he had written out his remarks. Franklin's Pennsylvania colleague James Wilson offered to read them, and Franklin accepted.

Franklin proposed that the executive, whether singular or plural, receive no compensation beyond expenses. "There are two passions which have a powerful influence on the affairs of men," he asserted. "These are ambition and avarice: the love of power, and the love of money: Separately, each of these has great force in prompting men to action; but when united in view of the same object, they have in many minds the most violent effects. Place before the eyes of such men a post of *honour* that shall at the same time be a place of *profit,* and they will move heaven and earth to obtain it." . . .

Some would call his proposal utopian, Franklin conceded; men must be paid for their labors. Yet he begged to differ, and he cited evidence. In English counties the office of high sheriff yielded no profit to its holder; on the contrary, the office cost its holder money. "Yet it is executed, and well executed, and usually by some of the principal gentlemen of the county." In France the office of counselor likewise exacted a cost of its holders, yet respectable and capable individuals vied for the distinction it conferred.

Nor did the members of the convention have to look across the ocean for examples of patriotic service untied to profit. They merely had to look across the room. "Have we not seen the great and most important of our offices, that of general of our armies, executed for eight years together without the smallest salary, by a patriot whom I will not now offend by any other praise?" If such was true amid the fatigues and distresses of war, would not the country be able to find men willing to give service during peace? "I have a better opinion of our country. I think we shall never be without a sufficient number of wise and good men to undertake and execute well and faithfully the office in question."

Perhaps Franklin misread from his own past into the future of his audience. Their very presence, combined with their youth, indicated they were not like him, who had delayed entering politics until he had made his fortune. Nor were any but a few as well off as Washington, who could afford to serve his country for eight years without compensation. These men might not place profit above honor, but few of them could ignore profit entirely.

Madison recorded the reaction to Franklin's speech: "The motion was seconded by Colonel [Alexander] Hamilton with the view, he said, of merely bringing so respectable a proposition before the committee, and which was besides enforced by arguments that had a certain degree of weight. No debate ensued, and the proposition was postponed for the consideration of the members. It was treated with great respect, but rather for the author of it than from any apparent conviction of its expediency or practicality."

Another Franklin proposal received equally short shrift. A month into the convention the body had made frustratingly little progress. Franklin noted that the delegates had searched history for guidance and looked to the governments of other countries. "How has it happened, sir, that we have not hitherto once thought of humbly applying to the Father of Lights to illuminate our understandings?" At the onset of the troubles with Britain, the Continental Congress, meeting in this very room, had daily requested divine help in finding its way. "Our prayers were heard, sir, and they were graciously answered. All of us who were engaged in the struggle must

have observed the frequent instances of a superintending Providence in our favour." Without Heaven's help the delegates would not be where they were, attempting what they were attempting. "Have we now forgotten that powerful Friend? Or do we imagine we no longer need its assistance?" Franklin remarked that he had lived a long time. "And the longer I live the more convincing proofs I see of this truth, *that God governs in the affairs of men.* And if a sparrow cannot fall to the ground without his notice, is it probable that an empire can rise without his aid?" . . .

This statement was as open as Franklin ever got in public about his religious beliefs. (And it was only partially public, the delegates having pledged themselves to confidentiality.) The delegates probably did not appreciate the unusual candor in Franklin's remarks; in any case they ignored them. His motion received a second, but Hamilton and others worried that, however laudable the practice of prayer might be, to commence it at this late date would convey a sense of desperation. Franklin responded that the past omission of a duty did not justify continued omission and that the public was just as likely to respond positively as negatively to word that their delegates were seeking God's blessing on their labors.

His argument failed. After Hugh Williamson of North Carolina pointed out that the convention lacked funds to pay a chaplain, Edmund Randolph offered an amendment to Franklin's motion. Randolph suggested hiring a preacher to give a sermon on Independence Day, less than a week off, and thereafter to open the sessions with a prayer.

Franklin accepted the amendment, but the delegates put off discussion by recessing for the day, and the proposition died. Franklin remarked with some wonder, at the bottom of the written copy of his speech, "The convention, except three or four persons, thought prayers unnecessary!"

Most delegates had more earthly matters in mind. The nature of the executive vexed the convention for weeks. At one extreme stood Alexander Hamilton, the former protégé of Washington—ambitious, arrogant, intolerant of those less gifted than he. A certain mystery surrounded his West Indian birth; John Adams, ever uncharitable, called him the "bastard brat of a Scotch pedlar." He was small and lithe, with delicate features that made him look even younger than his thirty-two years. Yet the fire that burned inside him made him seem, to Jefferson at least (after Hamilton aimed his flames Jefferson's way), "an host within himself." Even on best behavior, as at the convention, he put people off. William Pierce, while granting that Hamilton was "deservedly celebrated for his talents," added, "His manners are tinctured with stiffness, and sometimes with a degree of vanity that is highly disagreeable."

Patriotic and courageous during the war, Hamilton nonetheless retained a decided partiality toward the British system of government. "I believe the British government form the best model the world ever produced," Hamilton told the convention. The secret of the British government was its strength, which allowed it to provide individual security. The British recognized a fundamental facet of human nature. "All communities divide themselves into the few and the many. The first are the rich and well born, the other the mass of the people. The voice of the people has been said to be the voice of God; and however generally this maxim has been quoted and believed, it is not true in fact." The people were turbulent and fickle; they rarely knew where their interests lay. "Give therefore to the first class a distinct, permanent share in the government. They will check the unsteadiness in the second, and as they cannot receive any advantage by a change, they therefore will ever maintain good government."

Hamilton's confidence in benign rule by society's betters led him to conclude that executive power ought to be vested in a single man, elected for life. "It may be said that this constitutes an elective monarchy." Let the fainthearted call it what they wished. "Pray, what is a monarchy? May not the governors of the respective states be considered in that light?" Hamilton allowed for impeachment of the executive in cases of egregious malfeasance; in this respect, he said, the executive-for-life fell short of being a

monarch. But he endorsed the basic principle of monarchy, that the holder of the office ought to be irresponsible to the people. Only then would he be free of the people's unruly passions. Earlier speakers had suggested a long term for the executive, perhaps seven years. Hamilton deemed this insufficient. "An executive is less dangerous to the liberties of the people when in office during life, than for seven years."

Franklin held just the opposite view. Not only did he rest far less faith in the British system—having, unlike Hamilton, observed its operations closely at first hand—but he had less confidence in what Hamilton (and many others) deemed the better elements in society. To place entire executive authority in one man was to court trouble. Even assuming the best of goodwill on the part of the executive, what would happen when he got sick? Physical frailty might not worry Hamilton and others in the prime of life, but, as Franklin could assure them, life lasted beyond one's prime. Eventually, of course, the executive would die; though Hamilton proposed a scheme for electing a successor, after many years under one man the government could not escape disruption.

Moreover, judgments varied from man to man, and each executive would seek to make his own mark. "A single person's measures may be good. The successor often differs in opinion of those measures, and adopts others; often is ambitious of distinguishing himself by opposing them, and offering new projects. One is peaceably disposed, another may be fond of war, &c. Hence foreign states can never have that confidence in the treaties or friendship of such a government, as in that which is conducted by a number."

The only conclusion Franklin could draw was that executive power was too potent to be entrusted to a single person. "The steady course of public measures is most probably to be expected from a number."

Ultimately the convention split the difference between Hamilton and Franklin, opting for a single executive of limited term. On another issue—the one on which the entire constitutional project threatened to founder—compromise finally came as well, but with greater difficulty.

Under the Virginia plan, election to the lower house of the legislature would be according to population, with larger states—such as Virginia—having greater representation than smaller states. Because the upper house would be chosen by the lower house, this advantage to the larger states would inform the actions of the legislature as a whole. The delegates from the larger states thought this only just, not least since they were expected to pay the largest portion of the expenses of the central government.

Predictably, delegates from the smaller states objected. Under the Articles of Confederation, each state possessed equal weight within the legislature, and the small-state delegates intended to preserve this principle. Indeed, the instructions of the delegates from Delaware forbade them from countenancing any tampering with equal representation by states. Accordingly, when the delegation from New Jersey proposed an alternative to the Virginia plan— an alternative enshrining the one-state, one-vote principle—the smaller states rallied to it.

Upon the question of representation hinged the essence of the new government. If representation remained by states, then the new government would remain, to a large degree, a government of the states, along the lines of the Confederation. By contrast, if representation shifted to population, then the new government would be a government of the people. The states might retain their existence, but they would have hardly more meaning than counties in England.

This was exactly what James Madison believed they should have. "Some contend that states are sovereign," Madison declared, "when in fact they are only political societies." The states had never possessed sovereignty, which from the start of the Revolution had been vested in Congress. "The states, at present, are only great corporations, having the power of making by-laws, and these are effectual only if they are not contradictory to the general confederation. The states ought to be placed under the control of the general government—at least as much as they formerly were under the king and British Parliament."

These were fighting words, or promised to be. Gunning Bedford of Delaware demanded, "Are not the large states evidently seeking to aggrandize themselves at the expense of the small? They think no doubt that they have right on their side, but interest has blinded their eyes." Bedford accused the large states of adopting "a dictatorial air" toward the smaller, of suggesting they could make a government of their own without the small states. "If they do," Bedford warned, "the small ones will find some foreign ally of more honour and good faith, who will take them by the hand and do them justice."

Bedford's threat elicited an even sharper response from Gouverneur Morris. The larger states would not brook such secessionist talk, Morris asserted. "This country must be united. If persuasion does not unite it, the sword will." Amplifying his point, he added, "The scenes of horror attending civil commotion can not be described, and the conclusion of them will be worse than the terms of their continuance. The stronger party will then make traitors of the weaker, and the gallows and halter will finish the work of the sword."

It was just this kind of acrimony that had elicited Franklin's call for the help of the Deity; that call having failed of the convention's approval, he now interposed himself. "The diversity of opinion turns on two points," he told the delegates. "If a proportional representation takes place, the small states contend that their liberties will be in danger. If an equality of votes is to be put in its place, the large states say their money will be in danger." The time had come to compromise. "When a broad table is to be made, and the edges of the planks do not fit, the artist takes a little from both, and makes a good joint. In like manner here, both sides must part with some of their demands in order that they may join in some accommodating purpose."

He thereupon laid before the members a motion:

That the legislatures of the several states shall choose and send an equal number of delegates, namely _____, who are to compose the second branch of the general legislature.

Franklin's motion became the basis for the grand compromise that saved the convention and made the Constitution possible. The large states would have their way with the lower house, to be called the House of Representatives, which would be selected according to population. The interests of the smaller states would be safeguarded in the upper house, called the Senate, which would be chosen by the legislatures of the states, with each state getting two—the number that filled in Franklin's blank—senators. (More than a century later, of course, the Constitution would be amended to provide for direct election of senators by voters of the states, but the principle of equal representation remained.)

On the eve of the final vote on the grand compromise, Franklin entertained a visitor to the city. Dr. Manasseh Cutler was a clergyman from Massachusetts, also a botanist (and later a member of Congress). "There was no curiosity in Philadelphia which I felt so anxious to see as this great man, who has been the wonder of Europe as well as the glory of America," Cutler wrote. "But a man who stood first in the literary world, and had spent so many years in the Courts of Kings, particularly in the refined Court of France, I conceived would not be of very easy access, and must certainly have much of the air of grandeur and majesty about him. Common folks must expect only to gaze at him at a distance, and answer such questions as he might please to ask." When delegate Elbridge Gerry of Massachusetts, who was on his way to Franklin's house, asked Cutler if he wished to come, Cutler said he certainly did—but, as he told a friend later, "I hesitated; my knees smote together."

What Cutler found in the Franklin garden was not in the least what he expected.

How were my ideas changed, when I saw a short, fat, trunched old man, in a plain Quaker dress, bald pate, and short white locks, sitting without his hat under the tree, and, as Mr. Gerry introduced me, rose from his chair, took me by the hand, expressed his joy to see me, welcomed me to the city, and begged me to seat myself close to him.

His voice was low, but his countenance open, frank, and pleasing. . . . I delivered him my letters. After he had read them, he took me again by the hand, and, with the usual compliments, introduced me to the other gentlemen, who were most of them members of the Convention.

Here we entered into a free conversation, and spent our time most agreeably until it was dark. The tea-table was spread under the tree, and Mrs. Bache, a very gross and rather homely lady, who is the only daughter of the Doctor, and lives with him, served it out to the company. She had three of her children about her, over whom she seemed to have no kind of command, but who appeared to be excessively fond of their Grandpapa.

The Doctor showed me a curiosity he had just received, and with which he was much pleased. It was a snake with two heads, preserved in a large vial. It was taken near the confluence of the Schuylkill with the Delaware, about four miles from this city. It was about ten inches long, well proportioned, the heads perfect, and united to the body about one-fourth of an inch below the extremities of the jaws. . . .

The Doctor mentioned the situation of this snake, if it was traveling among the bushes, and one head should choose to go on one side of the stem of a bush and the other head should prefer the other side, and that neither of the heads would consent to come back or give way to the other. He was then going to mention a humourous matter that had that day occurred in Convention, in consequence of his comparing the snake to America, for he seemed to forget that every thing in Convention was to be kept a profound secret; but the secrecy of Convention matters was suggested to him, which stopped him, and deprived me of the story he was going to tell.

Doubtless the story involved the dispute over representation, which was on the verge of resolution—without the snake's starving or either of the heads' being cut off. Yet the vote was not certain, and the other delegates present definitely did not want the loquacious host to make the compromise settlement any more difficult.

(Their concern also reflected their fear of the convention's president. During one early session, copies of the Virginia propositions were circulated, with the injunction that these were for the delegates' eyes only and must be guarded with strictest care. Some while later a copy was discovered on the floor of the State House and turned over to Washington. The general placed the copy in his pocket and said nothing until the end of that day's debates. Thereupon he rose from his seat and addressed the delegates in the sternest tones. "Gentlemen," he said, "I am sorry to find that some member of this body has been so neglectful of the secrets of the Convention as to drop in the State House a copy of their proceedings, which by accident was picked up and delivered to me this morning. I must entreat gentlemen to be more careful, lest our transactions get into the newspapers and disturb the public repose by premature speculations. I know not whose paper it is, but there it is." Throwing the paper down on the table, he concluded, "Let him who owns it, take it." Then he bowed, picked up his hat, and left the room—"with a dignity so severe that every person seemed alarmed," said William Pierce. Significantly, no one claimed the paper, although Pierce's heart leaped into his throat when, reaching in his pocket, he could not find his own copy. To his immense relief, it turned up later in the pocket of his other coat.) . . .

Cutler was entranced by his octogenarian host. "I was highly delighted with the extensive knowledge he appeared to have of every subject, the brightness of his memory, and clearness and vivacity of all his mental faculties, notwithstanding his age (eighty-four) [eighty-three and a half, actually]. His manners are perfectly easy, and every thing about him seems to diffuse an unrestrained freedom and happiness. He has an incessant vein of humour, accompanied with an uncommon vivacity, which seems as natural and involuntary as his breathing."

Breathing came easier that summer for Franklin, who was used to Philadelphia's climate, than for some of the delegates from out of town. The southerners arrived dressed for the heat, but the northerners, in their woolen suits, suffered badly. The State House was comparatively cool when the sessions began at ten in the morning, but by midday the green baize on the tables where the delegates sat began to show dark spots from their sweat. The windows had to be kept closed, partly against the prying eyes and ears of outsiders but mostly against the flies that battened on the horse dung in the streets and the offal in the gutters. "A veritable torture during Philadelphia's hot season" was how a French visitor described "the innumerable flies which constantly light on the face and hands, stinging everywhere and turning everything black because of the filth they leave wherever they light." There was no escape, even at night. "Rooms must be kept closed unless one wishes to be tormented in his bed at the break of day, and this need of keeping everything shut makes the heat of the night even more unbearable and sleep more difficult. And so the heat of the day makes one long for bedtime because of weariness, and a single fly which has gained entrance to your room in spite of all precautions, drives you from bed."

Franklin survived the heat better than many delegates far younger than he, and better than he had feared. To be sure, a three-day illness in mid-July left him "so weak as to be scarce able to finish this letter," he explained to John Paul Jones in Paris. (In this same letter Franklin asked Jones to convey regards to Jefferson "and acquaint him that the Convention goes on well and that there is hope of great good to result.") But on the whole his health held up, and he attended the sessions of the convention faithfully.

Though the compromise on representation assured the success of the convention, the members still had work to do. They had to define the powers of the executive and the extent of legislative checks upon him. Should the legislature be able to impeach and remove him during his term? Franklin thought so. He considered the power of removal a guarantee both for the people and for the executive. "What was the practice before this in cases where the chief magistrate rendered himself obnoxious? Why, recourse was had to assassination, in which he was not only deprived of his life but of the opportunity of vindicating his character. It would be the best way, therefore, to provide in the constitution for the regular punishment of the executive when his misconduct

A view of the Pennsylvania State House (Independence Hall), where the delegates to the Constitutional Convention assembled in May 1787. During these meetings the United States government, as we know it, took shape. In the tower of the State House hung the Liberty Bell, which tolled the news of the signing of the Declaration of Independence and of American victories in the Revolution. An impassioned motto girdled the bell: "Proclaim liberty throughout the land, and to all the inhabitants thereof." But given all the inhabitants excluded from the blessings of liberty, the motto seems more than a little ironic. (Public Domain)

should deserve it, and for his honourable acquittal when he should be unjustly accused."

Should the executive be eligible for reelection? Some members thought he must be, else he necessarily suffer the degradation of being returned to the body of the people. Franklin differed strenuously. Such an assertion was "contrary to republican principles," he said. "In free governments the rulers are the servants, and the people their superiors and sovereigns. For the former therefore to return among the latter was not to *degrade* but to *promote* them." Doubtless with that sly smile of his, he added, "It would be imposing an unreasonable burden on them to keep them always in a state of servitude and not allow them to become again one of the masters."

Who should be able to vote? Many delegates thought responsibility attached to property, and irresponsibility to its lack, and said suffrage should be restricted to freeholders. Franklin granted that the person least prone to political pressure was the one who tilled his own farm, but he would not endorse the proposed restriction. "It is of great consequence that we should not depress the virtue and public spirit of our common people, of which they displayed a great deal during the war, and which contributed principally to the favourable issue of it."

Such a restriction would rightly provoke popular upset. "The sons of a substantial farmer, not being themselves freeholders, would not be pleased at being disfranchised, and there are a great many persons of that description."

What should be the requirements for candidates to the national legislature? Many delegates again wanted to see proof of owning property. Again Franklin embraced the more democratic position. Once more he voiced his dislike of everything that tended "to debase the spirit of the common people." Besides, as his own long experience of politics and politicians had taught him, the proposed restriction was no guarantee of good government. "If honesty was often the companion of wealth, and if poverty was exposed to peculiar temptation, it was not less true that the possession of property increased the desire of more property. Some of the greatest rogues I ever was acquainted with were the richest rogues." Moreover, other countries were watching America. "This constitution will be much read and attended to in Europe, and if it should betray a great partiality to the rich, it will not only hurt us in the esteem of the most liberal and enlightened men there, but discourage the common people from removing to this country."

The opinion of Europe—to which, it was fair to say, Franklin was more sensitive than anyone else at the convention—informed his opinion on a related topic. How long should immigrants be required to live in America before becoming eligible for office? Some said as much as fourteen years. Franklin thought this excessive. He was "not against a reasonable time, but should be very sorry to see any thing like illiberality inserted in the constitution." The members were writing not simply for an American audience. "The people in Europe are friendly to this country. Even in the country with which we have been lately at war, we have now and had during the war a great many friends not only among the people at large but in both Houses of Parliament. In every other country in Europe all the people are our friends." How the proposed constitution treated foreign immigrants would have much to do with

whether America retained those European friends. In any case, justice dictated fair treatment of the foreign-born, for many had served valiantly during the war. The mere fact of immigrants' relocation to America should count for something. "When foreigners, after looking about for some other country in which they can obtain more happiness, give a preference to ours, it is a proof of attachment which ought to excite our confidence and affection."

As cooler weather approached, so did the end of the convention's work. Franklin had his way on some of the remaining issues, yielded on others. He advocated requiring not one but two witnesses to the same overt act of treason, on grounds that prosecutions for this highest crime were "generally virulent" and perjury was too easily employed against the innocent. The convention agreed. (This requirement of two witnesses would prove critical in the treason trial of Aaron Burr twenty years later.) Franklin seconded a motion calling for an executive council to assist the president. Still advocating a wider distribution of power, he said, "We seem too much to fear cabals in appointments by a number, and to have too much confidence in those of single persons." Colonial experience with bad governors should have shown the need to restrain a single executive, while his own experience as chief executive of Pennsylvania revealed the positive benefits a council could provide. "A council would not only be a check on a bad president but be a relief to a good one." The convention disagreed.

The thorniest of the final issues involved slavery. How should slaves be counted toward representation in the lower house? Naturally the delegates from the states with few slaves wanted to minimize the slave count; they pointed out that since slave owners considered slaves to be property, those same slaves should not be counted as persons. The delegates from states with many slaves objected, less on philosophical grounds than on the pragmatic one that without some allowance for slaves, their states simply would not accept the new constitution. James Wilson of Pennsylvania proposed that the new constitution adopt the expedient devised by the Confederation Congress in 1783, when the legislature allowed the states to count three-fifths of the total number of their slaves. This compromise made no one happy but none so upset as to bolt the convention, and it was accepted.

A similar makeshift disposed of the question of the slave trade. The new constitution would give Congress power to regulate commerce, but the heavily slaved states resisted infringement on the commerce in slaves. Franklin had been sharply critical of the slave trade when it was practiced by the British, and—as he would soon reveal—had come to detest the entire institution of slavery, but when the southern states made clear that the issue of the slave trade was another potential convention-breaker, he acquiesced in another compromise. For twenty years Congress could not bar the traffic in slaves; from 1808 it might do what it chose on the subject.

On September 17 the completed copy of the Constitution was ready for the members' signatures. Franklin addressed the convention for the last time. Again he spoke through James Wilson, who read his colleague's prepared remarks. "I confess that there are several parts of this constitution which I do not at present approve," Franklin said. "But I am not sure I shall never approve them, for having lived long, I have experienced many instances of being obliged by better information or fuller consideration to change opinions even on important subjects which I once thought right but found to be otherwise. It is therefore that the older I grow, the more apt I am to doubt my own judgment, and to pay more attention to the judgment of others."

Some people felt themselves possessed of all truth; so did most sects in religion. Franklin explained how the Anglican Richard Steele (upon whose writing, many years before, he had modeled his own) once penned a dedication to the Pope, in which he explained, in Franklin's paraphrase, that "the only difference between our churches in their opinions of the certainty of their doctrines is, the Church of Rome is infallible and the Church of England is never in the wrong." Franklin also quoted a Frenchwoman of his acquaintance who, in an argument with her sister, declared, "I don't know how it is, Sister, but I meet with nobody but myself that's always in the right."

As the chuckles subsided, Franklin made his point. "In these sentiments, Sir, I agree to this constitution with all its faults, if they are such; because I think a general government necessary for us, and there is no form of government but what may be a blessing to the people if well administered." He reminded once more that the strength of any government rested on the virtue of the people. . . .

Franklin doubted whether any convention could have done better. "When you assemble a number of men to have the advantage of their joint wisdom, you inevitably assemble with those men all their prejudices, their passions, their errors of opinion, their local interests, and their selfish views. From such an assembly can a perfect production be expected?" The wonder was how well the present assembly had done. "I think it will astonish our enemies, who are waiting with confidence to hear that our councils are confounded like those of the builders of Babel, and that our states are on the point of separation, only to meet hereafter for the purpose of cutting one another's throats. Thus I consent, sir, to this constitution, because I expect no better, and because I am not sure that it is not the best."

Franklin closed by suggesting that the confidentiality that had surrounded the proceedings ought to continue upon the members' parting. "The opinions I have had of its errors, I sacrifice to the public good. I have never whispered a syllable of them abroad. Within these walls they were born, and here they shall die." If each delegate, returning to his constituents, complained at this point or that of the new government, the total of the complaints would probably scuttle the project. On the other hand, unanimity would encourage ratification. "I hope therefore that for our own sakes as a part of the people, and for the sake of posterity, we shall act heartily and unanimously."

Achieving this unanimity required a final bit of finesse. Franklin knew full well that unanimity of delegates was not possible. Edmund Randolph was holding out, as were Elbridge Gerry and George

Mason. But unanimity of the states might be attained, by polling the members within each delegation and heeding the majorities therein. Gouverneur Morris framed a formula for the signing: "Done in Convention, by the unanimous consent of the States present the 17th of September." Franklin moved that the convention adopt this formula, and the motion carried.

George Washington signed first, followed by thirty-seven others, state by state. James Madison related the convention's close:

Whilst the last members were signing it, Doctor Franklin, looking towards the president's chair, at the back of which a rising sun happened to be painted, observed to a few members near him, that painters had often found it difficult to distinguish in their art a rising from a setting sun. I have, said he, often and often in the course of the session, and the vicissitudes of my hopes and fears as to its issue, looked at that behind the president, without being able to tell whether it was rising or setting. But now at length I have the happiness to know that it is a rising and not a setting sun.

The delegates to Philadelphia had been authorized only to modify the Articles of Confederation, but they had recognized that the Confederation was utterly unworkable. Deliberately exceeding their authority, they had scrapped the Articles and proceeded to create an entirely new Constitution and a new government. As a result, there was a great deal of opposition to the document. Indeed, the ratification of the Constitution was a slow, agonizing process with the vote extremely close in many states. In Virginia, Patrick Henry declared that he "smelled a rat" in Philadelphia, and George Mason, concerned about the absence of a bill of rights, announced that he "would sooner chop off his right hand than put it to the Constitution." Still, Virginia narrowly approved the document by a vote of 89 to 79. There was high drama in many other states, too, but brilliantly defended by Alexander Hamilton, James Madison, and John Jay in the Federalist Papers, *the Constitution was finally ratified by the nine necessary states, and it took effect in 1789.*

After the convention, when a woman asked Franklin what kind of government the delegates had devised, he replied: "A republic, madam, if you can keep it." The old gentleman would be proud to know that Americans have now kept it for more than two centuries.

QUESTIONS TO CONSIDER

1 Describe George Washington's doubts about attending the Constitutional Convention. As you read selection 10, reflect on some of the reasons why the general was often a reluctant participant in the political discussions that followed independence. Why was Franklin eager to have Washington present at the Constitutional Convention?

2 Describe Franklin's health at the time of the Constitutional Convention. Why does this selection give you the impression that age had not dulled Franklin's keen senses?

3 Explain Franklin's reasons for proposing that the members of the executive branch of the new government should serve without pay. Given the background of most of the delegates to the Constitutional Convention, why was Franklin's recommendation impractical? Why did Franklin's suggestion for daily prayers also meet with resistance? Compare Franklin's desire for prayers at the Constitutional Convention with Walter Isaacson's description of Franklin's views on religion in selection 6.

4 How did Hamilton and Franklin differ in their views of the power and length of service of the chief executive in the new government? Analyze Hamilton's and Franklin's contrasting opinions about the "common man." Why did the two men differ on this subject?

5 What role did Franklin play in brokering a compromise between the large and small states on representation in the legislative branch of the new government? Explain Franklin's fascination with the snake with two heads. Explain too, how it symbolized the problems faced by his fellow delegates?

6 Contrast the views of northern and southern delegates on the representation of the slave population in the lower house of the new legislature. How was the thorny issue of the continuation of the international slave trade resolved?

10 The Greatness of George Washington

GORDON S. WOOD

In recent polls, American historians and presidential scholars ranked George Washington as the third best president in American history (Abraham Lincoln was first and Franklin D. Roosevelt second). In the following selection, Gordon S. Wood challenges those polls and argues that Washington deserves first-place honors. More than any other statesman, specialists contend, Washington defined the presidency and set the standard for executive leadership. "It is no exaggeration to say that but for George Washington, the office of president might not exist," one historian maintains. Washington was so respected in his day, so much above factional bickering and regional jealousies, that he was probably the only leader behind whom the country could unite. "One of the problems with Washington," says writer Garry Wills, "is that we think of him in the wrong company, as a peer of Franklin and Jefferson, when he belongs in the select company of Caesar, Napoleon and Cromwell as a charismatic nation-builder who personified an epoch."

Not that Washington was a saint. Like all of us, the first president had human flaws—among them, an aloofness that made him a hard man to know. Uncomfortable among learned men, he developed the habit of listening carefully to what was being said, pondering it, but rarely expressing his own opinion. His reticence struck some as arrogance, what an Englishman described as "repulsive coldness." His formidable size contributed to his seeming aloofness: standing a "ramrod straight" six-feet, three inches, which made him a giant in his day, he looked down at everybody. A man of robust health and energy, he nevertheless suffered from chronic dental problems and had to wear false teeth made of ivory and wood.

Adapting himself to the slave-owning world in which he was born and raised, Washington became a wealthy Virginia planter who owned as many as 317 slaves and shared the racial prejudice of most whites of his time. He even brought slave "servants" to the president's house in Philadelphia. He said he regretted that slavery existed and wished it could be abolished but was unable to do anything about it beyond providing for the manumission of his own slaves upon his death.

Wood makes clear that "Washington's genius, his greatness, lay in his character." He cultivated the role of "classical hero" that required him to remain aloof. For example, he did not like to be touched and even felt that hand-shaking was too personal. When you came into his office, you stood in his presence unless he asked you to sit. As we learned in selection 9, one old friend, Gouverneur Morris, bet Alexander Hamilton that he could slap Washington on the shoulder and compliment him on his appearance. Hamilton, who knew the general all too well, retorted that he would treat Morris and his friends to dinner and wine if Washington allowed such familiarity. All eyes were on Morris when he dared to approach Washington at a reception. True to his word, Morris placed a hand on Washington's shoulder as he warmly greeted him. True to his character, Washington removed the hand and coldly stared as Morris escaped through the embarrassed bystanders.

In The First of Men *(1988), the best biography of Washington yet written, historian John E. Ferling reveals that Washington had a complex and contradictory character. He suffered from low self-esteem, struggled all his life to overcome feelings of worthlessness, and had a pathological need for the admiration and affirmation of other people. Yet, as Ferling reminds us, Washington was also a man of extraordinary personal courage. He demonstrated a rare ability for self-criticism, strove hard to better himself, proved to be an excellent organizer, and gave his family "tender love and abiding steadfastness." But his most significant achievement, Wood believes, was his voluntary abandonment of power, which established an important precedent for the infant nation. "Washington gained his power by his readiness to give it up." Retreating to his beloved Mt. Vernon only to have his countrymen plead that he return to public service, Washington was truly the indispensable man of the early national period.*

GLOSSARY

CINCINNATUS   The legendary figure of the Roman Republic who, after successful military campaigns, returned to his farm and private life. Washington's willingness to surrender his sword to the Continental Congress and return to Mt. Vernon seemed to many Americans to represent a similar renunciation of power.

ENLIGHTENMENT   This seventeenth- and eighteenth-century movement focused on the use of reason, the advancement of science, and the dignity of mankind. Jefferson's Declaration of Independence, Franklin's experiments with electricity, and Washington's moral code all owed much to this advanced body of thinking.

FEDERALISTS   One of the first political parties, formed around the personality and programs of Alexander Hamilton. It found Jefferson and his followers a threat to America's national security because of their pro-French attitudes. Washington, although he protested that he was above politics, was gradually drawn into the Federalist camp.

L'ENFANT, PIERRE   A French engineer, intelligent but temperamental, who conceived of the design of the nation's capital. Washington, unlike Jefferson, wanted a city that in its grand scale would match the respect and power that he hoped the infant nation would eventually achieve.

STUART, GILBERT   A respected American painter whose portrait of Washington did not measure up to his portraits of Adams, Jefferson, Madison, and Monroe. Washington's stiffness and formality worked against the artist's attempts to portray any sense of personality or feelings.

TRUMBULL, JOHN   One of the outstanding American painters of the early national period. Four of his famous paintings of the climactic moments during the American Revolution hang in the United States Capitol today.

WEEMS, PARSON   The first biographer of Washington. Weems was more concerned with perpetuating the image of his subject than achieving historical accuracy. He created the myth of the downed cherry tree and the brave boy who shouldered the blame.

George Washington may still be first in war and first in peace, but he no longer seems to be first in the hearts of his countrymen. Or at least in the hearts of American historians. A recent poll of 900 American historians shows that Washington has dropped to third place in presidential greatness behind Lincoln and FDR. Which only goes to show how little American historians know about American history.

Polls of historians about presidential greatness are probably silly things, but, if they are to be taken seriously, then Washington fully deserved the first place he has traditionally held. He certainly deserved the accolades his contemporaries gave him. And as long as this republic endures he ought to be first in the hearts of his countrymen. Washington was truly a great man and the greatest president we have ever had.

But he was a great man who is not easy to understand. He became very quickly, as has often been

Gordon S. Wood, "The Greatness of George Washington," *The Virginia Quarterly Review*, vol. 68, no. 2 (Spring, 1992), pp. 189–207. Reprinted by permission.

As the general who won the Revolutionary War, George Washington was the only person in the infant American nation who had support in every section of the country. He cultivated a stiff, impersonal image based on the "classic hero" he so admired. Wood concludes that, when Washington surrendered his sword to the Continental Congress, he shocked Europe by "gaining his power by his readiness to give it up." (The Metropolitan Museum of Art, Bequest of Charles Allen Munn, 1924)

the continuing efforts to humanize him—even at the beginning of our history. Parson Mason Weems, his most famous biographer, was less of a churchman than he was a hustling entrepreneur. He was ready when Washington died in 1799: "I've something to whisper in your lug," Weems wrote to his publisher Matthew Carey a month after the great man's death. "Washington you know, is gone! Millions are gaping to read something about him. I am very nearly primed and cocked for 'em." Weems had his book out within a year.

The most famous anecdotes about Washington's early life come from Weems. He wanted to capture the inner private man—to show the early events that shaped Washington's character, even if he had to make them up. Weems presumed that the source of Washington's reputation for truthfulness lay in his youth. He tells a story that he said he had heard from Washington's nurse. It was, he says, "too valuable to be lost, too true to be doubted." This was, of course, the story of the cherry tree about whose chopping down Washington could not tell a lie.

Despite the continued popularity of Parson Weems' attempt to humanize him, Washington remained distant and unapproachable, almost unreal and un-human. There have been periodic efforts to bring him down to earth, to expose his foibles, to debunk his fame, but he remained, and remains, massively monumental. By our time in the late 20th century he seems so far removed from us as to be virtually incomprehensible. He seems to come from another time and another place—from another world.

And that's the whole point about him: he does come from another world. And his countrymen realized it even before he died in 1799. He is the only truly classical hero we have ever had. He acquired at once a world-wide reputation as a great patriot-hero.

And he knew it. He was well aware of his reputation and his fame earned as the commander-in-chief of the American revolutionary forces. That awareness of his heroic stature and his character as a republican leader was crucial to Washington. It affected nearly everything he did for the rest of his life.

pointed out, more a monument than a man, statuesque and impenetrable. Even his contemporaries realized that he was not an ordinary accessible human being. He was deified in his own lifetime. "O Washington," declared Ezra Stiles, president of Yale, in 1783. "How I do love thy name! How have I adored and blessed thy God, for creating and forming thee, the great ornament of human kind! . . . Thy fame is of sweeter perfume than Arabian spices. Listening angels shall catch the odor, waft it to heaven and perfume the universe!"

One scholar has said that Washington has been "the object of the most intense display of hero worship this nation has ever seen." Which helps explain

Washington was a thoroughly 18th-century figure. So much so, that he quickly became an anachronism. He belonged to the pre-democratic and pre-egalitarian world of the 18th century, to a world very different from the world that would follow. No wonder then that he seems to us so remote and so distant. He really is. He belonged to a world we have lost and we were losing even as Washington lived.

In many respects Washington was a very unlikely hero. To be sure, he had all the physical attributes of a classical hero. He was very tall by contemporary standards, and was heavily built and a superb athlete. Physically he had what both men and women admired. He was both a splendid horseman at a time when that skill really counted and an extraordinarily graceful dancer. And naturally he loved both riding and dancing. He always moved with dignity and looked the leader.

Yet those who knew him well and talked with him were often disappointed. He never seemed to have very much to say. He was most certainly *not* what we would today call an "intellectual." We cannot imagine him, say, expressing his views on Plato in the way Jefferson and John Adams did in their old age. Adams was especially contemptuous of Washington's intellectual abilities. It was certain, said Adams, that Washington was not a scholar. "That he was too illiterate, unread for his station and reputation is equally past dispute."

Adam's judgment is surely too harsh. Great men in the 18th century did not have to be scholars or intellectuals. But there is no doubt that Washington was not a learned man, especially in comparison with the other Founding Fathers. He was very ill at ease in abstract discussions. Even Jefferson, who was usually generous in his estimates of his friends, said that Washington's "colloquial talents were not above mediocrity." He had "neither copiousness of ideas nor fluency of words."

Washington was not an intellectual, but he was a man of affairs. He knew how to run his plantation and make it pay. He certainly ran Mount Vernon better than Jefferson ran Monticello. Washington's

heart was always at Mount Vernon. He thought about it all the time. Even when he was president he devoted a great amount of his energy worrying about the fence posts of his plantation, and his letters dealing with the details of running Mount Vernon were longer than those dealing with the running of the federal government.

But being a man of affairs and running his plantation or even the federal government efficiently were not what made him a world-renowned hero. What was it that lay behind his extraordinary reputation, his greatness?

His military exploits were of course crucial. But Washington was not really a traditional military hero. He did not resemble Alexander, Caesar, Cromwell, or Marlborough; his military achievements were nothing compared to those Napoleon would soon have. Washington had no smashing, stunning victories. He was not a military genius, and his tactical and strategic maneuvers were not the sort that awed men. Military glory was *not* the source of his reputation. Something else was involved.

Washington's genius, his greatness, lay in his character. He was, as Chateaubriand said, a "hero of an unprecedented kind." There had never been a great man quite like Washington before. Washington became a great man and was acclaimed as a classical hero because of the way he conducted himself during times of temptation. It was his moral character that set him off from other men.

Washington fit the 18th-century image of a great man, of a man of virtue. This virtue was not given to him by nature. He had to work for it, to cultivate it, and everyone sensed that. Washington was a self-made hero, and this impressed an 18th-century enlightened world that put great stock in men controlling both their passions and their destinies. Washington seemed to possess a self-cultivated nobility.

He was in fact a child of the 18th-century Enlightenment. He was very much a man of his age, and he took its moral standards more seriously than most of his contemporaries. Washington's Enlightenment, however, was not quite that of Jefferson or Franklin. Although he was conventionally enlightened about religion, "being no bigot myself to any mode of worship," he had no passionate dislike of the clergy and organized Christianity, as Jefferson did. And although he admired learning, he was not a man of science like Franklin. Like many other 18th-century Englishmen, he did *not* believe, as he put it, that "becoming a mere scholar is a desirable education for a gentleman."

Washington's Enlightenment was a much more down-to-earth affair, concerned with behavior and with living in the everyday-world of people. His Enlightenment involved what eventually came to be called cultivation and civilization. He lived his life by the book—not the book of military rules but the book of gentility. He was as keenly aware as any of his fellow Americans of the 18th-century conventions that defined what a proper gentleman was.

Such conventions were expressed in much of the writing of the Enlightenment. The thousands of etiquette books, didactic stories, *Spectator* papers, Hogarth prints, gentlemanly magazines, classical histories—all were designed to teach Englishmen manners, civility, politeness, and virtue. Out of all this writing and art emerged an ideal of what it was to be both enlightened and civilized, and a virtuous leader. Our perpetuation of a liberal arts education in our colleges and universities is a present-day reminder of the origins of this ideal; for the English conception of a liberally educated gentleman had its modern beginnings in the 18th century.

An enlightened, civilized man was disinterested and impartial, not swayed by self-interest and self-profit. He was cosmopolitan; he stood above all local and parochial considerations and was willing to sacrifice his personal desires for the greater good of his community or his country. He was a man of reason who resisted the passions most likely to afflict great men, that is, ambition and avarice. Such a liberal, enlightened gentleman avoided enthusiasms and fanaticisms of all sorts, especially those of religion. Tolerance and liberality were his watchwords. Politeness and compassion toward his fellow man were his manners. Behaving in this way was what constituted being civilized.

Washington was thoroughly caught up in this enlightened promotion of gentility and civility, this rational rolling back of parochialism, fanaticism, and barbarism. He may have gone to church regularly, but he was not an emotionally religious person. In all of his writings there is no mention of Christ, and God is generally referred to as "the great disposer of human events." Washington loved Addison's play *Cato* and saw it over and over and incorporated its lines into his correspondence. The play, very much an Enlightenment tract, helped to teach him what it meant to be liberal and virtuous, what it meant to be a stoical classical hero. He had the play put on for his troops during the terrible winter at Valley Forge in 1778.

One of the key documents of Washington's life is his "Rules of Civility and Decent Behaviour in Company and Conversation," a collection of 110 maxims that Washington wrote down sometime before his 16th birthday. The maxims were originally drawn from a 17th-century etiquette book and were copied by the young autodidact. They dealt with everything from how to treat one's betters ("In speaking to men of Quality do not lean nor Look them full in the Face") to how to present one's countenance ("Do not Puff up the Cheeks, Do not Loll out the tongue, rub the Hands, or beard, thrust out the lips, or bite them or keep the Lips too open or too Close").

All the Founding Fathers were aware of these enlightened conventions, and all in varying degrees tried to live up to them. But no one was more serious in following them than Washington. It is this purposefulness that gave his behavior such a copybook character. He was obsessed with having things in fashion and was fastidious about his appearance to the world. It was as if he were always on stage, acting a part. He was very desirous not to offend, and he exquisitely shaped his remarks to fit the person to whom he was writing—so much so that some historians have accused him of deceit. "So anxious was he to appear neat and correct in his letters," recalled Benjamin Rush, that he was known to "copy over a letter of 2 or 3 sheets of paper because there were a few erasures on it." He wanted desperately to know what were the proper rules of behavior for a liberal gentleman, and when he discovered those rules he stuck by them with an earnestness that awed his contemporaries. His remarkable formality and stiffness in company came from his very self-conscious cultivation of what he considered proper, genteel, classical behavior.

Washington and Franklin, both children of the Enlightenment, had very different personalities, but among the Founding Fathers they shared one important thing. Neither of them went to college; neither had a formal liberal arts education. This deficiency deeply affected both of them, but Washington let it show. Washington always remained profoundly respectful of formal education. Colleges like William and Mary were always an "Object of Veneration" to him. His lack of a formal liberal arts education gave him a modesty he never lost. He repeatedly expressed his "consciousness of a defective education," and he remained quiet in the presence of sharp and sparkling minds. He was forever embarrassed that he had never learned any foreign languages. In the 1780's he refused invitations to visit France because he felt it would be humiliating for someone of his standing to have to converse through an interpreter. He said that it was his lack of a formal education that kept him from setting down on paper his recollections of the Revolution. It was widely rumored that his aides composed his best letters as commander-in-chief. If so, it is not surprising that he was diffident in company. Some even called it "shyness," but whatever the source, this reticence was certainly not the usual characteristic of a great man. "His modesty is astonishing, particularly to a Frenchman," noted Brissot de Warville. "He speaks of the American War as if he had *not* been its leader." This modesty only added to his gravity and severity. "Most people say and do too much," one friend recalled. "Washington . . . never fell into this common error."

Yet it was in the political world that Washington made his most theatrical gesture, his most moral mark, and there the results were monumental. The greatest act of his life, the one that made him famous, was his resignation as commander-in-chief of the American forces. This act, together with his 1783 circular letter to the states in which he promised to retire from public life, was his "legacy" to his countrymen. No American leader has ever left a more important legacy.

Following the signing of the peace treaty and British recognition of American independence, Washington stunned the world when he surrendered his sword to the Congress on Dec. 23, 1783 and retired to his farm at Mount Vernon. This was a highly symbolic act, a very self-conscious and unconditional withdrawal from the world of politics. Here was the commander-in-chief of the victorious army putting down his sword and promising not to take "any share in public business hereafter." Washington even resigned from his local vestry in Virginia in order to make his separation from the political world complete.

His retirement from power had a profound effect everywhere in the Western world. It was extraordinary, it was unprecedented in modern times—a victorious general surrendering his arms and returning to his farm. Cromwell, William of Orange, Marlborough—all had sought political rewards commensurate with their military achievements. Though it was widely thought that Washington could have become king or dictator, he wanted nothing of the kind. He was sincere in his desire for all the soldiers "to return to our Private Stations in the bosom of a free, peaceful and happy Country," and everyone recognized his sincerity. It filled them with awe. Washington's retirement, said the painter John Trumbull writing from London in 1784, "excites the astonishment and admiration of this part of the world. 'Tis a Conduct so novel, so unconceivable to People, who, far from giving up powers they possess, are willing to convulse the empire to acquire more." King George III supposedly predicted that if Washington retired from public life and returned to his farm, "he will be the greatest man in the world."

Washington was not naïve. He was well aware of the effect his resignation would have. He was trying to live up to the age's image of a classical disinterested patriot who devotes his life to his country, and he knew at once that he had acquired instant fame as a modern Cincinnatus. His reputation in the 1780's as a great classical hero was international, and it was virtually unrivaled. Franklin was his only competitor, but Franklin's greatness still lay in his being a scientist, not a man of public affairs. Washington was a living embodiment of all that classical republican virtue the age was eagerly striving to recover.

Despite his outward modesty, Washington realized he was an extraordinary man, and he was not ashamed of it. He lived in an era when distinctions of rank and talent were not only accepted but celebrated. He took for granted the differences between himself and more ordinary men. And when he could not take those differences for granted he cultivated them. He used his natural reticence to reinforce the image of a stern and forbidding classical hero. His aloofness was notorious, and he worked at it. When the painter Gilbert Stuart had uncharacteristic difficulty in putting Washington at ease during a sitting for a portrait, Stuart in exasperation finally pleaded, "Now sir, you must let me forget that you are General Washington and that I am Stuart, the painter," Washington's reply chilled the air: "Mr. Stuart need never feel the need of forgetting who he is or who General Washington is." No wonder the portraits look stiff.

Washington had earned his reputation, his "character," as a moral hero, and he did not want to dissipate it. He spent the rest of his life guarding and protecting his reputation, and worrying about it. He believed Franklin made a mistake going back into public life in Pennsylvania in the 1780's. Such involvement in politics, he thought, could only endanger Franklin's already achieved international standing. In modern eyes Washington's concern for his reputation is embarrassing; it seems obsessive and egotistical. But his contemporaries understood. All gentlemen tried scrupulously to guard their reputations, which is what they meant by their honor. Honor was the esteem in which they were held, and they prized it. To have honor across space and time was to have fame, and fame, "the ruling passion of the noblest minds," was what the Founding Fathers were after, Washington above all. And he got it, sooner and in greater degree than any other of his contemporaries. And naturally, having achieved what all his fellow Revolutionaries still anxiously sought, he was reluctant to risk it.

Many of his actions after 1783 can be understood only in terms of this deep concern for his reputation as a virtuous leader. He was constantly on guard and very sensitive to any criticism. Jefferson said no one was more sensitive. He judged all his actions by what people might think of them. This sometimes makes him seem silly to modern minds, but not to those of the 18th century. In that very suspicious age where people were acutely "jealous" of what great men were up to, Washington thought it important that people understand his motives. The reality was not enough; he had to *appear* virtuous. He was obsessed that he not seem base, mean, avaricious, or unduly ambitious. No one, said Jefferson, worked harder than Washington in keeping "motives of interest of consanguinity, of friendship or hatred" from influencing him. He had a lifelong preoccupation with his reputation for "disinterestedness" and how best to use that reputation for the good of his country. This preoccupation explains the seemingly odd fastidiousness and the caution of his behavior in the 1780's.

One of the most revealing incidents occurred in the winter of 1784–85. Washington was led into temptation, and it was agony. The Virginia General Assembly presented him with 150 shares in the James River and Potomac canal companies in recognition of his services to the state and the cause of canal-building. What should he do? He did not feel he could accept the shares. Acceptance might be "considered in the same light as a pension" and might compromise his reputation for virtue. Yet he believed passionately in what the canal companies were doing and had long dreamed of making a fortune from such canals. Moreover, he did not want to show "disrespect" to the Assembly or to appear "ostentatiously disinterested" by refusing this gift.

Few decisions in Washington's career caused more distress than this one. He wrote to everyone he knew—to Jefferson, to Governor Patrick Henry, to William Grayson, to Benjamin Harrison, to George William Fairfax, to Nathanael Greene, even to Lafayette—seeking "the best information and advice" on the disposition of the shares. "How would this matter be viewed by the eyes of the world?" he asked. Would not his reputation for virtue be harmed? Would not accepting the shares "deprive me of the principal thing which is laudable in my conduct?"

The situation is humorous today, but it was not to Washington. He suffered real anguish. Jefferson eventually found the key to Washington's anxieties and told him that declining to accept the shares would only add to his reputation for disinterestedness. So Washington gave them away to the college that eventually became Washington and Lee.

Washington suffered even more anguish over the decision to attend the Philadelphia Convention in 1787. Many believed that his presence was absolutely necessary for the effectiveness of the Convention, but the situation was tricky. He wrote to friends imploring them to tell him "confidentially what the public expectation is on this head, that is, whether I will or ought to be there?" How would his presence be seen, how would his motives be viewed? If he attended, would he be thought to have violated his pledge to withdraw from public life? But, if he did not attend, would his staying away be thought to be a "dereliction to Republicanism"? Should he squander his reputation on something that might not work?

What if the Convention should fail? The delegates would have to return home, he said, "chagrined at their ill success and disappointment. This would be a disagreeable circumstance for any one of them to be in; but more particularly so, for a person in my situation." Even James Madison had second thoughts about the possibility of misusing such a precious asset as Washington's reputation. What finally convinced Washington to attend the Convention was the fear that people might think he wanted the federal government to fail so that he could manage a military takeover. So in the end he decided, as Madison put it, "to forsake the honorable retreat to which he had

retired, and risk the reputation he had so deservedly acquired." No action could be more virtuous. "Secure as he was in his fame," wrote Henry Knox with some awe, "he has again committed it to the mercy of events. Nothing but the critical situation of his country would have induced him to so hazardous a conduct."

When the Convention met, Washington was at once elected its president. His presence and his leadership undoubtedly gave the Convention and the proposed Constitution a prestige that they otherwise could not have had. His backing of the Constitution was essential to its eventual ratification. "Be assured," James Monroe told Jefferson, "his influence carried this government." Washington, once committed to the Constitution, worked hard for its acceptance. He wrote letters to friends and let his enthusiasm for the new federal government be known. Once he had identified himself publicly with the new Constitution he became very anxious to have it accepted. Its ratification was a kind of ratification of himself.

After the Constitution was established, Washington still thought he could retire to the domestic tranquility of Mount Vernon. But everyone else expected that he would become president of the new national government. He was already identified with the country. People said he was denied children in his private life so he could be the father of his country. He had to be the president. Indeed, the Convention had made the new chief executive so strong, so kinglike, precisely because the delegates expected Washington to be the first president.

Once again this widespread expectation aroused all his old anxieties about his reputation for disinterestedness and the proper role for a former military leader. Had he not promised the country that he would permanently retire from public life? How could he then now assume the presidency without being "chargeable with levity and inconsistency; if not with rashness and ambition?" His protests were sincere. He had so much to lose, yet he did not want to appear "too solicitous for my reputation."

Washington's apparent egotism and his excessive coyness, his extreme reluctance to get involved in public affairs and endanger his reputation, have not usually been well received by historians. Douglas Southall Freeman, his great biographer, thought that Washington in the late 1780's was "too zealously attentive to his prestige, his reputation and his popularity—too much the self-conscious national hero and too little the daring patriot." Historians might not understand his behavior, but his contemporaries certainly did. They rarely doubted that Washington was trying *always* to act in a disinterested and patriotic way. His anxious queries about how this or that would look to the world, his hesitations about serving or not serving, his expressions of scruples and qualms—all were part of his strenuous effort to live up to the classical idea of a virtuous leader.

He seemed to epitomize public virtue and the proper character of a republican ruler. Even if John Adams was not all that impressed with George Washington, Adam's wife Abigail was certainly taken with him. She admired his restraint and trusted him. "If he was not really one of the best-intentioned men in the world," she wrote, "he might be a very dangerous one." As Gary Wills has so nicely put it, Washington gained his power by his readiness to give it up.

As president he continued to try to play the role he thought circumstances demanded. He knew that the new government was fragile and needed dignity. People found that dignity in his person. Madison believed that Washington was the only part of the new government that captured the minds of the people. He fleshed out the executive, established its independence, and gave the new government the pomp and ceremony many thought it needed.

Sometimes it had more pomp than even he enjoyed. His formal levees complete with silver buckles and powdered hair, were painful affairs for everyone. These receptions, held at first on Tuesday and Friday afternoons and later on only Tuesdays, were an opportunity for prominent men to meet the president. The invited guests, all men, entered the president's residence at three o'clock, where they found the president standing before the fireplace. Fifteen minutes were allowed for the guests to assemble in a circle. As each guest entered the room he walked to the President, bowed, and without speaking backed to his place in the circle. The only voice heard was that of a presidential aide softly announcing the names. Promptly on the quarter hour the doors were shut; the President then walked around the circle, addressed each man by name, and made some brief remark to him. He bowed but never shook hands. Washington thought that hand-shaking was much too familiar for the president to engage in; consequently he kept one hand occupied holding a fake hat and the other resting on his dress sword. When the president had rounded the circle, he returned to the fireplace and stood until, at a signal from an aide, each guest one by one went to him, bowed without saying anything, and left the room. However excruciatingly formal these levees were, Washington thought they would continue. He thus designed the bowed shaped of the Blue Room to accommodate them.

Although many critics thought that the levees smacked of the court life of kings of Europe, Washington was not a crypto-monarchist. He was a devoted republican, at heart just a country gentleman. Martha used to break up tea parties at 9:30 p.m. by saying that it was past the President's bedtime.

As president he tried to refuse accepting any salary just as he had as commander-in-chief. Still, he wanted to make the presidency "respectable," and he spared few expenses in doing so; he spent 7 percent of his $25,000 salary on liquor and wine for entertaining. He was especially interested in the size and character of the White House of the capital city that was named after him. The scale and grandeur of Washington, D.C., owe much to his vision and his backing of Pierre L'Enfant as architect. If Secretary of State Thomas Jefferson had had his way, L'Enfant would never have kept his job as long as he did, and the capital would have been smaller and less magnificent— perhaps something on the order of a college campus, like Jefferson's University of Virginia.

Washington was keenly aware that everything he did would set precedents for the future. "We are a young nation," he said, "and have a character to establish. It behooves us therefore to set out right, for first impressions will be lasting." It was an awesome responsibility. More than any of his contemporaries, he thought constantly of future generations, of "millions unborn," as he called them.

He created an independent role for the president and made the chief executive the dominant figure in the government.

He established crucial precedents, especially in limiting the Senate's role in advising the president in the making of treaties and the appointing of officials. In August 1789 he went to the Senate to get its advice and consent to a treaty he was negotiating with the Creek Indians. Vice President John Adams who presided read each section of the treaty and then asked the senators, How do you advise and consent? After a long silence, the senators, being senators, began debating each section, with Washington impatiently glaring down at them. Finally, one senator moved that the treaty and all the accompanying documents that the president had brought with him be submitted to a committee for study. Washington started up in what one senator called "a violent fret." In exasperation he cried, "This defeats every purpose of my coming here." He calmed down, but when he finally left the Senate chamber, he was overheard to say he would "be damned if he ever went there again." He never did. The advice part of the Senate's role in treaty making was dropped.

The presidency is the powerful office it is in large part because of Washington's initial behavior. He understood power and how to use it. But as in the case of his career as commander-in-chief, his most important act as president was his giving up of the office.

The significance of his retirement from the presidency is easy for us to overlook, but his contemporaries knew what it meant. Most people assumed that Washington might be president as long as he lived, that he would be a kind of elective monarch—something not out of the question in the 18th century. Some people even expressed relief that he had no heirs. Thus his persistent efforts to retire from the presidency enhanced his moral authority and helped fix the republican character of the Constitution.

He very much wanted to retire in 1792, but his advisors and friends talked him into staying on for a second term. Madison admitted that when he had first urged Washington to accept the presidency he had told him that he could protect himself from accusations of overweening ambition by "a voluntary return to public life as soon as the state of the Government would permit." But the state of the government, said Madison, was not yet secure. So Washington reluctantly stayed on.

But in 1796 he was so determined to retire that no one could dissuade him, and his voluntary leaving of the office set a precedent that was not broken until FDR secured a third term in 1940. So strong was the sentiment for a two-term limit, however, that the tradition was written into the Constitution in the 22nd amendment in 1951. Washington's action in 1796 was of great significance. That the chief executive of a state should willingly relinquish his office was an object lesson in republicanism at a time when the republican experiment throughout the Atlantic world was very much in doubt.

Washington's final years in retirement were not happy ones. The American political world was changing, becoming more partisan, and Washington struggled to comprehend these changes. During President Adams' administration he watched with dismay what he believed was the growing interference of the French government in American politics. For him the Jeffersonian Republican party had become "the French Party." It was, he said, "the curse of this country," threatening the stability and independence of the Untied States. He saw plots and enemies everywhere and became as much of a high-toned Federalist as Hamilton.

His fear was real; his sense of crisis was deep. He and other Federalists thought that the French might invade the country and together with "the French Party" overthrow the government. "Having Struggled for Eight or nine Years against the invasion of our rights by one power, and to establish an Independence of it," he wrote in 1798, "I could not remain an unconcerned spectator of the attempt of another Power to accomplish the same object, though in a different way." He thus listened attentively to all the urgent Federalist calls that he come out of retirement and head the army that the Congress had created to meet the French invasion.

Again he expressed reluctance, and asked whether becoming commander-in-chief would not be considered "a restless Act—evidence of my discontent in retirement." Yet in 1798 he was far more eager to step back into the breach and do his duty than he ever had been before. It was a measure of his despair with this "Age of Wonders"!

Before he could actually commit himself, however, President John Adams acted and, without his permission, appointed him commander of all the military forces of the United States. He accepted, but scarcely comprehended how it had all come about. The next thing he knew he was on his way to Philadelphia to organize the army. Events were outrunning his ability to control them or even to comprehend them, and he more and more saw himself caught up in "the designs of Providence." His command was a disaster. He wrangled over the appointments of the second in command, intrigued against Adams, and interfered with his cabinet. When neither the French invasion nor the American army materialized, Washington crept back to Mount Vernon thoroughly disillusioned with the new ways of American politics.

In July 1799 Governor Jonathan Trumbull of Connecticut with the backing of many Federalists urged Washington once again to stand for the presidency in 1800. Only Washington, Trumbull said, could unite the Federalists and save the country from "a French President." Finally Washington had had enough. In his reply he no longer bothered with references to his reputation for disinterestedness and his desire to play the role of Cincinnatus. Instead he talked about the new political conditions that made his candidacy irrelevant. In this new democratic era of party politics, he said, "personal influence," distinctions of character, no longer mattered. If the members of the Jeffersonian Republican party "set up a broomstick" as candidate and called it "a true son of Liberty" or "a Democrat" or "any other epithet that will suit their purpose," it still would "command their votes in toto?" But, even worse, he said, the same was true of the Federalists. Party spirit now ruled all, and people voted only for their party candidate. Even if he were the Federalist candidate, Washington was "thoroughly convinced I should not draw a *single* vote from the anti-Federal side." Therefore his standing for election made no sense; he would "stand upon no stronger ground than any other Federal character well supported."

Washington wrote all this in anger and despair, but, though he exaggerated, he was essentially right. The political world was changing, becoming democratic, and parties, not great men, would soon become the objects of contention. To be sure, the American people continued to long for great heroes as leaders, and from Jackson through Eisenhower they have periodically elected Washington-*manqués* to the presidency.

But democracy made such great heroes no longer essential to the workings of American government. And Washington, more than any other single individual, was the one who made that democracy possible. As Jefferson said "the moderation and virtue of a single character . . . probably prevented this revolution from being closed, as most others have been, by a subversion of that liberty it was intended to establish."

Washington was an extraordinary heroic man who made rule by more ordinary mortals possible. He virtually created the presidency, and gave it a dignity that through the years it has never lost. But, more important, he established the standard by which all subsequent presidents have been ultimately measured—not by the size of their electoral victories, not by their legislative programs, and not by the number of their vetoes, but by their moral character. Although we live in another world than his, his great legacy is still with us.

QUESTIONS TO CONSIDER

1 Why do you think that so many Americans, upon learning of Washington's death, were eager to read about him and would probably have not accepted any biographer who was in any way critical of the former president? What in Washington's background made him stand out from all of the other founding fathers?

2 Many of the founding fathers, Adams and Jefferson among them, were learned men with first-rate minds. Does Wood believe that Washington was an intellectual, a great conversationalist, or even a "military genius" in the same league with Caesar or Cromwell? How was Washington's behavior influenced by the fact that he had never attended college? From your reading of selection 6, would you argue that Franklin, the other founding father without a formal education, acted in a similar manner?

3 In what ways were Washington's moral code and personal behavior a product of the lessons he had learned from the writings of the Enlightenment? Wood observes that Washington was "always on stage, acting a part." Do you think that Washington was too interested in appearances? Given his value system, why was Washington anguished over the gift of shares in the canal companies and attendance at the Constitutional Convention?

4 Why did Washington's surrendering of his sword to the Continental Congress following the American Revolution astonish the world? Even in the twenty-first century, is it typical for military leaders of successful revolutions to relinquish power? Still later he refused to run for a third term as president. Why would Wood state that this "was an object lesson in republicanism at a time when the republican experiment throughout the Atlantic world was very much in doubt"?

5 How did the formal levees or receptions symbolize Washington's character, personality, and perception of what the presidency should represent? Would you have felt comfortable at such a gathering?

6 Near the end of his life Washington seemed disillusioned with public service because political parties mattered more than the moral fiber of their leaders. Is this a continuing problem in the history of our country?

PART SIX

Patterns of Society

11 The Personal Side of a Developing People

JACK LARKIN

The study of everyday life is one of the most fascinating new fields of American history. Like biography, it is firmly grounded in specific experience; it allows us to see ordinary people of the past going about the daily business of living, and it invites us to compare their patterns of behavior with our own. By allowing us to reach back and touch the people of a bygone time, and be touched by them, the new social history does much to preserve the human continuum.

The following essay focuses on broad patterns of social behavior in the young Republic. The difference between that America and ours can be astounding, but so can the similarities, and you will want to note those as you read. In his narrative, Jack Larkin, chief historian of Old Sturbridge Village in Massachusetts, relies on contemporary observers of the young nation to answer several fascinating questions: What were people then really like? What did they eat and drink? What did they wear? What did they do for amusement? How did they occupy their leisure time? How did they deal with tension and stress? How did they make love?

The picture that emerges is of a vibrant, busy, contentious people who grew taller than the average European, who spat tobacco, wore dour expressions, slept in bug-ridden beds, dumped their sewage in the streets, pursued the pleasures of the flesh more than we might have imagined, and drank too much liquor. Indeed, as Larkin reports, their per capita annual consumption is estimated "at the equivalent of three and one-half gallons of pure two-hundred-proof alcohol," which prompted one historian to term it the era of "the alcoholic Republic."

Larkin also discusses customs of courtship and marriage, sexual attitudes, and instances of premarital intercourse in the era of the young Republic. As Larkin points out, Americans of the early nineteenth century "were remarkably straitlaced about sexual matters in public and eager to insist upon the 'purity' of their manners." But their actual practices were a different matter. "Bundling," the custom of allowing a premarital couple to sleep together (they were supposed to keep their clothes on), was still being practiced. Moreover, pregnancy was a frequent "prelude to marriage." In the early colonial period, 20 percent of the native-born brides were with child. In rural New England in the last decades of the eighteenth century, the figure had risen to 30 percent. As Larkin points out, "the frequency of sexual intercourse before marriage was surely higher, since some couples would have escaped early pregnancy." For "reining in the passions," health specialists such as Sylvester Graham preached sexual restraint and prescribed a strict regimen of diet and exercise to control "animal lusts." What was more, there appeared in the 1830s a new theory of female sexuality, which held that "carnal passion" was not natural in a woman. In her role as mother and "guardian of the home," the theory went, she had no interest in sex beyond bearing children. Although Larkin does not say so, this new theory of female sexuality was linked to the concomitant doctrine of "sexual spheres," which arose to justify and perpetuate the practice of segregating women in the sphere of the home and men in politics and wage earning (this is discussed in detail in selection 22, "Women and Their Families on the Overland Trails"). Why do you suppose such theories emerged? As you study "the personal side of a developing people," note the significance of patterns of regional, ethnic, and class distinctiveness in the young Republic.

GLOSSARY

BUNDLING   The custom of allowing a premarital couple to sleep "on the same bed without undressing."

CHAMBER POTS   Saved early Americans a trip to the outhouse on cold, dark nights.

CHAMBER SETS   Matching basin and ewer (a pitcher with a wide spout) for private bathing, a cup for brushing the teeth, and a chamber pot with cover to minimize odor and spillage.

CLAPP, SUMNER G.   Minister who led a temperance campaign in Enfield, Massachusetts.

DRAMMING   Ritual of downing a glass of hard cider twice a day.

GRAHAM, SYLVESTER   Author and lecturer who preached sexual restraint and a strict regimen of diet and exercise to control physical passions; his call for dietary reform, for eating bread and water in place of animal flesh, coffee, and tea, spawned a dietary movement, the adherents to which called themselves Grahamites. The graham cracker is named after him.

HALL, MARGARET   Prominent Scottish visitor to America whose letters home complained about the bugs and filth she saw there.

MILLER-WEAVER FEUD   Protracted quarrel between two bellicose families in York, Pennsylvania.

DOUR VISAGES

Contemporary observers of early-nineteenth-century America left a fragmentary but nonetheless fascinating and revealing picture of the manner in which rich and poor, Southerner and Northerner, farmer and city dweller, freeman and slave presented themselves to the world. To begin with, a wide variety of characteristic facial expressions, gestures, and ways of carrying the body reflected the extraordinary regional and social diversity of the young republic.

When two farmers met in early-nineteenth-century New England, wrote Francis Underwood, of Enfield, Massachusetts, the author of a pioneering 1893 study of small-town life, "their greeting might seem to a stranger gruff or surly, since the facial muscles were so inexpressive, while, in fact, they were on excellent terms." In courtship and marriage, countrymen and women were equally constrained, with couples "wearing all unconsciously the masks which custom had prescribed; and the onlookers who did not know the secret would think them cold and indifferent."

Underwood noted a pervasive physical as well as emotional constraint among the people of Enfield; it was rooted, he thought, not only in the self-denying ethic of their Calvinist tradition but in the nature of their work. The great physical demands of unmechanized agriculture gave New England men, like other rural Americans, a distinctively ponderous gait and posture. Despite their strength and endurance, farmers were "heavy, awkward and slouching in movement" and walked with a "slow inclination from side to side."

Yankee visages were captured by itinerant New England portraitists during the early nineteenth century, as rural storekeepers, physicians, and master

craftsmen became the first more or less ordinary Americans to have their portraits done. The portraits caught their caution and immobility of expression as well as recording their angular, long-jawed features, thus creating good collective likenesses of whole communities.

The Yankees, however, were not the stiffest Americans. Even by their own impassive standards, New Englanders found New York Dutchmen and Pennsylvania German farmers "clumsy and chill" or "dull and stolid." But the "wild Irish" stood out in America for precisely the opposite reason. They were not "chill" or "stolid" enough, but loud and expansive. Their expressiveness made Anglo-Americans uncomfortable.

The seemingly uncontrolled physical energy of American blacks left many whites ill at ease. Of the slaves celebrating at a plantation ball, it was "impossible to describe the things these people did with their bodies," Frances Kemble Butler, an English-born actress who married a Georgia slave owner, observed, "and above all with their faces. . . ." Blacks' expressions and gestures, their preference for rhythmic rather than rigid bodily motion, their alternations of energy and rest made no cultural sense to observers who saw only "antics and frolics," "laziness," or "savagery." Sometimes perceived as obsequious, childlike, and dependent, or sullen and inexpressive, slaves also wore masks—not "all unconsciously" as Northern farm folk did, but as part of their self-protective strategies for controlling what masters, mistresses, and other whites could know about their feelings and motivations.

American city dwellers, whose daily routines were driven by the quicker pace of commerce, were easy to distinguish from "heavy and slouching" farmers attuned to slow seasonal rhythms. New Yorkers, in particular, had already acquired their own characteristic body language. The clerks and commercial men who crowded Broadway, intent on their business, had a universal "contraction of the brow, knitting of the eyebrows, and compression of the lips . . . and a hurried walk." It was a popular American saying in the 1830s, reported Frederick Marryat, an Englishman

Chapter 4, adapted, from *The Reshaping of Everyday Life in the United States 1790–1840* by Jack Larkin. Copyright © 1988 by Jack Larkin. Reprinted by permission of HarperCollins Publishers, Inc.

Country revelers at a quilting "frolic" in the days of the early Republic. This 1813 painting, by German-born John Lewis Krimmel, is conspicuous for its fine detail and racial contrasts. Notice how well dressed the newly arrived whites are in comparison with the fiddler. Krimmel's comic portrayal marked the start of an *almost constant popular association of blacks with music and music making. It also contributed to the development of degrading racial stereotypes: note that both the fiddler and the serving girl have toothy grins and oversized red lips. (Courtesy The Henry Francis duPont Winterthur Museum)*

who traveled extensively in the period, that "a New York merchant always walks as if he had a good dinner before him, and a bailiff behind him."

Northern and Southern farmers and city merchants alike, to say nothing of Irishmen and blacks, fell well short of the standard of genteel "bodily carriage" enshrined in both English and American etiquette books and the instructions of dancing masters: "flexibility in the arms . . . erectness in the spinal column . . . easy carriage of the head." It was the ideal of the British aristocracy, and Southern planters came closest to it, expressing the power of their class

in the way they stood and moved. Slave owners accustomed to command, imbued with an ethic of honor and pride, at ease in the saddle, carried themselves more gracefully than men hardened by toil or preoccupied with commerce. Visiting Washington in 1835, the Englishwoman Harriet Martineau contrasted not the politics but the postures of Northern and Southern congressmen. She marked the confident bearing, the "ease and frank courtesy . . . with an occasional touch of arrogance" of the slaveholders alongside the "cautious . . . and too deferential air of the members of the North." She could recognize a

New Englander "in the open air," she claimed, "by his deprecatory walk."

Local inhabitants' faces became more open, travelers observed, as one went west. Nathaniel Hawthorne found a dramatic contrast in public appearances only a few days' travel west of Boston. "The people out here," in New York State just west of the Berkshires, he confided to his notebook in 1839, "show out their character much more strongly than they do with us," in his native eastern Massachusetts. He compared the "quiet, silent, dull decency . . . in our public assemblages" with Westerners' wider gamut of expressiveness, "mirth, anger, eccentricity, all showing themselves freely." Westerners in general, the clergyman and publicist Henry Ward Beecher observed, had "far more freedom of manners, and more frankness and spontaneous geniality" than did the city or country people of the New England and Middle Atlantic states, as did the "odd mortals that wander in from the western border," that Martineau observed in Washington's political population.

A PUNGENT FOLK

Early-nineteenth-century Americans lived in a world of dirt, insects, and pungent smells. Farmyards were strewn with animal wastes, and farmers wore manure-spattered boots and trousers everywhere. Men's and women's working clothes alike were often stiff with dirt and dried sweat, and men's shirts were often stained with "yellow rivulets" of tobacco juice. The locations of privies were all too obvious on warm or windy days. Unemptied chamber pots advertised their presence. Wet baby "napkins," today's diapers, were not immediately washed but simply put by the fire to dry. Vats of "chamber lye"—highly concentrated urine used for cleaning type or degreasing wool—perfumed all printing offices and many households. "The breath of that fiery bar-room," as Underwood described a country tavern, "was overpowering. The odors of the hostlers' boots, redolent of fish-oil and tallow, and of buffalo-robes and horse-blankets,

the latter reminiscent of equine ammonia, almost got the better of the all-pervading fumes of spirits and tobacco."

Densely populated, but poorly cleaned and drained, America's cities were often far more noisome than its farmyards. Horse manure thickly covered city streets, and few neighborhoods were free from the spreading stench of tanneries and slaughterhouses. New York City accumulated so much refuse that it was generally believed the actual surfaces of the streets had not been seen for decades. During her stay in Cincinnati, the English writer Frances Trollope followed the practice of the vast majority of American city housewives when she threw her household "slops"—refuse food and dirty dishwater—out into the street. An irate neighbor soon informed her that municipal ordinances forbade "throwing such things at the sides of the streets" as she had done; "they must just all be cast right into the middle and the pigs soon takes them off." In most cities hundreds, sometimes thousands, of free-roaming pigs scavenged the garbage; one exception was Charleston, South Carolina, where buzzards patrolled the streets. By converting garbage into pork, pigs kept city streets cleaner than they would otherwise have been, but the pigs themselves befouled the streets and those who ate their meat—primarily poor families—ran greater than usual risks of infection.

PRIVY MATTERS

The most visible symbols of early American sanitation were privies or "necessary houses." But Americans did not always use them; many rural householders simply took to the closest available patch of woods or brush. However, in more densely settled communities and in regions with cold winters, privies were in widespread use. They were not usually put in out-of-the-way locations. The fashion of some Northern farm families, according to Robert B. Thomas's *Farmer's Almanack* in 1826, had long been to have their "necessary planted in a garden or other conspicuous place." Other countryfolk went even further in turning human wastes to agricultural account and built their outhouses "within the territory of a hog yard, that the swine may root and ruminate and devour the nastiness thereof." Thomas was a long-standing critic of primitive manners in the countryside and roundly condemned these traditional sanitary arrangements as demonstrating a "want of taste, decency, and propriety." The better arranged necessaries of the prosperous emptied into vaults that could be opened and cleaned out. The dripping horse-drawn carts of the "nocturnal goldfinders," who emptied the vaults and took their loads out for burial or water disposal—"night soil" was almost never used as manure—were a familiar part of nighttime traffic on city streets.

The humblest pieces of American household furniture were the chamber pots that allowed people to avoid dark and often cold nighttime journeys outdoors. Kept under beds or in corners of rooms, "chambers" were used primarily upon retiring and arising. Collecting, emptying, and cleaning them remained an unspoken, daily part of every housewife's routine.

Nineteenth-century inventory takers became considerably more reticent about naming chamber pots than their predecessors, usually lumping them with miscellaneous "crockery," but most households probably had a couple of chamber pots; genteel families reached the optimum of one for each bedchamber. English-made ceramic pots had become cheap enough by 1820 that few American families within the reach of commerce needed to go without one. "Without a pot to piss in" was a vulgar tag of long standing for extreme poverty; those poorest households without one, perhaps more common in the warm South, used the outdoors at all times and seasons.

The most decorous way for householders to deal with chamber-pot wastes accumulated during the night was to throw them down the privy hole. But more casual and unsavory methods of disposal were still in wide use. Farm families often dumped their chamber pots out the most convenient door or window. In densely settled communities like York, Pennsylvania, the results could be more serious. In 1801, the York diarist Lewis Miller drew and then described an event in North George Street when "Mr. Day an English man [as the German-American Miller was quick to point out] had a bad practice by pouring out of the upper window his filthiness . . . one day came the discharge . . . on a man and wife going to a wedding, her silk dress was fouled."

LETTING THE BEDBUGS BITE

Sleeping accommodations in American country taverns were often dirty and insect-ridden. The eighteenth-century observer of American life Isaac Weld saw "filthy beds swarming with bugs" in 1794; in 1840 [English novelist] Charles Dickens noted "a sort of game not on the bill of fare." Complaints increased in intensity as travelers went south or west. Tavern beds were uniquely vulnerable to infestation by whatever insect guests travelers brought with them. The bedding of most American households was surely less foul. Yet it was dirty enough. New England farmers were still too often "tormented all night by bed bugs," complained *The Farmer's Almanack* in 1837, and books of domestic advice contained extensive instructions on removing them from feather beds and straw ticks.

Journeying between Washington and New Orleans in 1828, Margaret Hall, a well-to-do and cultivated Scottish woman, became far more familiar with intimate insect life than she had ever been in the genteel houses of London or Edinburgh. Her letters home, never intended for publication, gave a graphic and unsparing account of American sanitary conditions. After sleeping in a succession of beds with the "usual complement of fleas and bugs," she and her party had themselves become infested: "We bring them along with us in our clothes and when I undress I find them crawling on my skin, nasty wretches." New and distasteful to her, such discoveries were commonplace among the ordinary folk with whom she lodged. The American children she saw on her Southern journey were "kept in such a state of filth," with clothes "dirty and slovenly to a degree," but this was "nothing in comparison with their heads . . . [which] are absolutely crawling!" In New Orleans she observed women picking through children's heads for lice, "catching them according to the method depicted in an engraving of a similar proceeding in the streets of Naples."

BIRTH OF THE BATH

Americans were not "clean and decent" by today's standards, and it was virtually impossible that they should be. The furnishings and use of rooms in most American houses made more than the most elementary washing difficult. In a New England farmer's household, wrote Underwood, each household member would "go down to the 'sink' in the lean-to, next to the kitchen, fortunate if he had not to break ice in order to wash his face and hands, or more fortunate if a little warm water was poured into his basin from the kettle swung over the kitchen fire." Even in the comfortable household of the prominent minister Lyman Beecher in Litchfield, Connecticut, around 1815, all family members washed in the kitchen, using a stone sink and "a couple of basins."

Southerners washed in their detached kitchens or, like Westerners in warm weather, washed outside, "at the doors . . . or at the wells" of their houses. Using basins and sinks outdoors or in full view of others, most Americans found anything more than "washing the face and hands once a-day," usually in cold water, difficult, even unthinkable. Most men and women also washed without soap, reserving it for laundering clothes; instead they used a brisk rubbing with a coarse towel to scrub the dirt off their skins.

Gradually the practice of complete bathing spread beyond the topmost levels of American society and into smaller towns and villages. This became possible as families moved washing equipment out of kitchens and into bedchambers, from shared space to space that could be made private. As more prosperous households furnished one or two of their chambers with washing equipment—a washstand, a basin, and a ewer, or large-mouthed pitcher—family members could shut the chamber door, undress, and wash themselves completely. The daughters of the Larcom family, living in Lowell, Massachusetts, in the late 1830s, began to bathe in a bedchamber in this way; Lucy Larcom described how her oldest sister started to take "a full cold bath every morning before she went to her work . . . in a room without a fire," and the other young Larcoms "did the same whenever we could be resolute enough." By the 1830s better city hotels and even some country taverns were providing individual basins and pitchers in their rooms.

At a far remove from "primitive manners" and "bad practices" was the genteel ideal of domestic sanitation embodied in the "chamber sets"—matching basin and ewer for private bathing, a cup for brushing the teeth, and a chamber pot with cover to minimize odor and spillage—that American stores were beginning to stock. By 1840 a significant minority of American households owned chamber sets and washstands to hold them in their bedchambers. For a handful there was the very faint dawning of an entirely new age of sanitary arrangements. In 1829 the new Tremont House hotel in Boston offered its patrons indoor plumbing: eight chambers with bathtubs and eight "water closets." In New York City and Philadelphia, which had developed rudimentary public water systems, a few wealthy households had water taps and, more rarely, water closets by the 1830s. For all others flush toilets and bathtubs remained far in the future.

The American people moved very slowly toward cleanliness. In "the backcountry at the present day," commented the fastidious author of the *Lady's Book* in 1836, custom still "requires that everyone should wash at the pump in the yard, or at the sink in the kitchen." Writing in 1846, the physician and health reformer William Alcott rejoiced that to "wash the surface of the whole body in water daily" had now been accepted as a genteel standard of personal cleanliness. But, he added, there were "multitudes who pass for models of neatness and cleanliness, who do not perform this work for themselves half a dozen times—nay once—a year." As the better-off became cleaner than ever before, the poor stayed dirty.

BESOTTED ERA

In the early part of the century America was a bawdy, hard-edged, and violent land. We drank more than we ever had before or ever would again. We smoked and chewed tobacco like addicts and fought and quarreled on the flimsiest pretexts. The tavern was the most important gateway to the primarily male world of drink and disorder: in sight of the village church in most American communities, observed Daniel Drake, a Cincinnati physician who wrote a reminiscence of his Kentucky boyhood, stood the village tavern, and the two structures "did in fact represent two great opposing principles."

The great majority of American men in every region were taverngoers. The printed street directories of American cities listed tavernkeepers in staggering numbers, and even the best-churched parts of New England could show more "licensed houses" than meetinghouses. In 1827 the fast-growing city of Rochester, New York, with a population of approximately eight thousand, had nearly one hundred establishments licensed to sell liquor, or one for every eighty inhabitants.

America's most important centers of male sociability, taverns were often the scene of excited gaming and vicious fights and always of hard drinking, heavy smoking, and an enormous amount of alcohol-stimulated talk. City men came to their neighborhood taverns daily, and "tavern haunting, tippling, and gaming," as Samuel Goodrich, a New England historian and publisher, remembered, "were the chief resources of men in the dead and dreary winter months" in the countryside.

City taverns catered to clienteles of different classes: sordid sailors' grog-shops near the waterfront were rife with brawling and prostitution; neighborhood taverns and liquor-selling groceries were visited by craftsmen and clerks; well-appointed and relatively decorous places were favored by substantial merchants. Taverns on busy highways often specialized in teamsters or stage passengers, while country inns took their patrons as they came.

Taverns accommodated women as travelers, but their barroom clienteles were almost exclusively male. Apart from the dockside dives frequented by prostitutes, or the liquor-selling groceries of poor city neighborhoods, women rarely drank in public.

Gambling was a substantial preoccupation for many male citizens of the early republic. Men played billiards at tavern tables for money stakes. They threw dice in "hazard," slamming the dice boxes down so hard and so often that tavern tables wore the characteristic scars of their play. Even more often Americans sat down to cards, playing brag, similar to modern-day poker, or an elaborate table game called faro. Outdoors they wagered with each other on horse races or bet on cockfights and wrestling matches.

Drink permeated and propelled the social world of early-nineteenth-century America—first as an unquestioned presence and later as a serious and divisive problem. "Liquor at that time," recalled the builder and architect Elbridge Boyden, "was used as commonly as the food we ate." Before 1820 the vast majority of Americans considered alcohol an essential stimulant to exertion as well as a symbol of hospitality and fellowship. Like the Kentuckians with whom Daniel Drake grew up, they "regarded it as a duty to their families and visitors . . . to keep the bottle well replenished." Weddings, funerals, frolics, even a casual "gathering of two or three neighbors for an evening's social chat" required the obligatory "spirituous liquor"—rum, whiskey, or gin—"at all seasons and on all occasions."

Northern householders drank hard cider as their common table beverage, and all ages drank it freely. Dramming—taking a fortifying glass in the forenoon and again in the afternoon—was part of the daily regimen of many men. Clergymen took sustaining libations between services, lawyers before going to court, and physicians at their patients' bedsides. To raise a barn or get through a long day's haying without fortifying drink seemed a virtual impossibility. Slaves enjoyed hard drinking at festival times and at Saturday-night barbecues as much as any of their countrymen. But of all Americans they probably drank the least on a daily basis because their masters could usually control their access to liquor.

In Parma, Ohio, in the mid–1820s, Lyndon Freeman, a farmer, and his brothers were used to seeing men "in their cups" and passed them by without comment. But one dark and rainy night they discovered something far more shocking, "nothing less than a *woman beastly drunk* . . . with a flask of whiskey by her side." American women drank as well as men, but usually much less heavily. They were more likely to make themselves "tipsy" with hard cider and alcohol-containing patent medicines than to become inebriated with rum or whiskey. Temperance advocates in the late 1820s estimated that men consumed fifteen times the volume of distilled spirits that women did; this may have been a considerable exaggeration, but there was a great difference in drinking habits between the sexes. Americans traditionally found drunkenness tolerable and forgivable in men but deeply shameful in women.

By almost any standard, Americans drank not only nearly universally but in large quantities. Their yearly consumption at the time of the Revolution has been estimated at the equivalent of three and one-half gallons of pure two-hundred-proof alcohol for each person. After 1790 American men began to drink even more. By the late 1820s their imbibing had risen to an all-time high of almost four gallons per capita.

Along with drinking went fighting. Americans fought often and with great relish. York, Pennsylvania, for example, was a peaceable place as American communities went, but the Miller and Weaver families had a long-running quarrel. It had begun in 1800 when the Millers found young George Weaver stealing apples in their yard and punished him by "throwing him over the fence," injuring him painfully. Over the years hostilities broke out periodically. Lewis Miller remembered walking down the street as a teenaged boy and meeting Mrs. Weaver, who drenched him with the bucket of water she was carrying.

LIFE IN AN AMERICAN HOTEL?

This British cartoon suggests the American propensity to violence in a hard-edged, hard-drinking era, when people fought often and with relish. Perhaps the irritable fellow with the gun spent a sleepless night battling the hotel's bed bugs. (Punch, June 28, 1856)

He retaliated by "turning about and giving her a kick, laughing at her, this is for your politeness." Other York households had their quarrels too; in "a general fight on Beaver Street," Mistress Hess and Mistress Forsch tore each other's caps from their heads. Their husbands and then the neighbors interfered, and "all of them had a knock down."

When Peter Lung's wife, Abigail, refused "to get up and dig some potatoes" for supper from the yard of their small house, the Hartford, Connecticut, laborer recalled in his confession, he "kicked her on the side . . . then gave her a violent push" and went out to dig the potatoes himself. He returned and "again kicked her against the shoulder and neck." Both had been drinking, and loud arguments and blows within the Lung household, as in many others, were routine. But this time the outcome was not. Alice Lung was dead the next day, and Peter Lung was arrested, tried, and hanged for murder in 1815.

In the most isolated, least literate and commercialized parts of the United States, it was "by no means uncommon," wrote Isaac Weld, "to meet with those who have lost an eye in a combat, and there are men who pride themselves upon the dexterity with which they can scoop one out. This is called *gouging*."

or stay of execution might disappoint a crowd intent on witnessing the deadly drama and provoke a riot, as it did in Pembroke, New Hampshire, in 1834.

PUBLIC PUNISHMENT

The penal codes of the American states were far less bloodthirsty than those of England. Capital punishment was not often imposed on whites for crimes other than murder. Yet at the beginning of the nineteenth century many criminal offenses were punished by the public infliction of pain and suffering. "The whipping post and stocks stood on the green near the meetinghouse" in most of the towns of New England and near courthouses everywhere. In Massachusetts before 1805 a counterfeiter was liable to have an ear cut off, and a forger to have one cropped or partially amputated, after spending an hour in the pillory. A criminal convicted of manslaughter was set up on the gallows to have his forehead branded with a letter M. In most jurisdictions town officials flogged petty thieves as punishment for their crime. In New Haven, Connecticut, around 1810, Charles Fowler, a local historian, recalled seeing the "admiring students of [Yale] college" gathered around to watch petty criminals receive "five or ten lashes . . . with a rawhide whip."

Throughout the United States public hangings brought enormous crowds to the seats of justice and sometimes seemed like brutal festivals. Thousands of spectators arrived to pack the streets of courthouse towns. On the day of a hanging near Mount Holly, New Jersey, in the 1820s, the scene was that of a holiday: "around the place in every direction were the assembled multitudes—some in tents, and bywagons, engaged in gambling and other vices of the sort, in open day." In order to accommodate the throngs, hangings were usually held not in the public square but on the outskirts of town. The gallows erected on a hill or set up at the bottom of a natural amphitheater allowed onlookers an unobstructed view. A reprieve

RISE OF RESPECTABILITY

At a drunkard's funeral in Enfield, Massachusetts, in the 1830s—the man had strayed out of the road while walking home and fallen over a cliff, "his stiffened fingers still grasping the handle of the jug"—Rev. Sumner G. Clapp, the Congregationalist minister of Enfield, mounted a log by the woodpile and preached the town's first temperance sermon before a crowd full of hardened drinkers. In this way Clapp began a campaign to "civilize" the manners of his parishioners, and "before many years there was a great change in the town; the incorrigible were removed by death, and others took warning." Drinking declined sharply, and along with it went "a general reform in conduct."

Although it remained a powerful force in many parts of the United States, the American way of drunkenness began to lose ground as early as the mid–1820s. The powerful upsurge in liquor consumption had provoked a powerful reaction, an unprecedented attack on all forms of drink that gathered momentum in the Northeast. Some New England clergymen had been campaigning in their own communities as early as 1810, but their concerns took on organized impetus with the founding of the American Temperance Society in 1826. Energized in part by a concern for social order, in part by evangelical piety, temperance reformers popularized a radically new way of looking at alcohol. The "good creature" became "demon rum"; prominent physicians and writers on physiology, like Benjamin Rush, told Americans that alcohol, traditionally considered healthy and fortifying, was actually a physical and moral poison. National and state societies distributed anti-liquor tracts, at first calling for moderation in drink but increasingly demanding total abstinence from alcohol.

To a surprising degree these aggressive temperance campaigns worked. By 1840 the consumption of alcohol had declined by more than two-thirds, from close to four gallons per person each year to less than one and one-half. Country storekeepers gave up the sale of spirits, local authorities limited the number of tavern licenses, and farmers even abandoned hard cider and cut down their apple orchards. The shift to temperance was a striking transformation in the everyday habits of an enormous number of Americans. "A great, though silent change," in Horace Greeley's words, had been "wrought in public sentiment." . . .

Closely linked as they were to drink, such diversions as gambling, racing, and blood sports also fell to the same forces of change. In the central Massachusetts region that George Davis, a lawyer in Sturbridge, knew well, until 1820 or so gaming had "continued to prevail, more and more extensively." After that "a blessed change had succeeded," overturning the scenes of high-stakes dice and card games that he knew in his young manhood. Impelled by a new perception of its "pernicious effects," local leaders gave it up and placed "men of respectable standing" firmly in opposition. Racecourses were abandoned and "planted to corn." Likewise, "bear-baiting, cock-fighting, and other cruel amusements" began to dwindle in the Northern countryside. Elsewhere the rude life of the tavern and "cruel amusements" remained widespread, but some of their excesses of "sin and shame" did diminish gradually.

Over the first four decades of the nineteenth century the American people increasingly made churchgoing an obligatory ritual. The proportion of families affiliated with a local church or Methodist circuit rose dramatically, particularly after 1820, and there were fewer stretches of the wholly pagan, unchurched territory that travelers had noted around 1800. "Since 1830," maintained Emerson Davis in his retrospect of America, *The Half Century*, ". . . the friends of the Sabbath have been gaining ground. . . . In 1800, good men slumbered over the desecration of the Sabbath. They have

since awoke. . . ." The number of Sunday mails declined, and the campaign to eliminate the delivery of mail on the Sabbath entirely grew stronger. "In the smaller cities and towns," wrote Mrs. Trollope in 1832, worship and "prayer meetings" had come to "take the place of almost all other amusements." There were still communities near the edge of settlement where a traveler would "rarely find either churches or chapels, prayer or preacher," but it was the working-class neighborhoods of America's larger cities that were increasingly the chief strongholds of "Sunday dissipation" and "Sabbath-breaking."

Whipping and the pillory, with their attentive audiences, began to disappear from the statute book, to be replaced by terms of imprisonment in another new American institution, the state penitentiary. Beginning with Pennsylvania's abolition of flogging in 1790 and Massachusetts's elimination of mutilating punishments in 1805, several American states gradually accepted John Hancock's view of 1796 that "mutilating or lacerating the body" was less an effective punishment than "an indignity to human nature." Connecticut's town constables whipped petty criminals for the last time in 1828.

Slaveholding states were far slower to change their provisions for public punishment. The whipping and mutilation of blacks may have become a little less ferocious over the decades, but the whip remained the essential instrument of punishment and discipline. "The secret of our success," thought a slave owner, looking back after emancipation, had been "the great motive power contained in that little instrument." Delaware achieved notoriety by keeping flogging on the books for whites and blacks alike through most of the twentieth century.

Although there were important stirrings of sentiment against capital punishment, all American states continued to execute convicted murderers before the mid–1840s. Public hangings never lost their drawing power. But a number of American public officials began to abandon the long-standing view of executions as instructive communal rituals. They saw the crowd's holiday mood and eager participation as sharing too much in the condemned killer's own brutality. Starting with Pennsylvania, New York, and Massachusetts in the mid-1830s, several state legislatures voted to take executions away from the crowd, out of the public realm. Sheriffs began to carry out death sentences behind the walls of the jailyard, before a small assembly of representative onlookers. Other states clung much longer to tradition and continued public executions into the twentieth century.

SEX LIFE OF THE NATIVES

Early-nineteenth-century Americans were more licentious than we ordinarily imagine them to be.

"On the 20th day of July" in 1830, Harriet Winter, a young woman working as a domestic in Joseph Dunham's household in Brimfield, Massachusetts, "was gathering raspberries" in a field west of the house. "Near the close of day," Charles Phelps, a farm laborer then living in the town, "came to the field where she was," and in the gathering dusk they made love—and, Justice of the Peace Asa Lincoln added in his account, "it was the Sabbath." American communities did not usually document their inhabitants' amorous rendezvous, and Harriet's tryst with Charles was a commonplace event in early-nineteenth-century America. It escaped historical oblivion because she was unlucky, less in becoming pregnant than in Charles's refusal to marry her. Asa Lincoln did not approve of Sabbath evening indiscretions, but he was not pursuing Harriet for immorality. He was concerned instead with economic responsibility for the child. Thus he interrogated Harriet about the baby's father—while she was in labor, as was the long-customary practice—in order to force Charles to contribute to the maintenance of the child, who was going to be "born a bastard and chargeable to the town."

Some foreign travelers found that the Americans they met were reluctant to admit that such things happened in the United States. They were remarkably straitlaced about sexual matters in public and eager to insist upon the "purity" of their manners. But to take such protestations at face value, the unusually candid Englishman Frederick Marryat thought, would be "to suppose that human nature is not the same everywhere."

The well-organized birth and marriage records of a number of American communities reveal that in late-eighteenth-century America pregnancy was frequently the prelude to marriage. The proportion of brides who were pregnant at the time of their weddings had been rising since the late seventeenth century and peaked in the turbulent decades during and after the Revolution. In the 1780s and 1790s nearly one-third of rural New England's brides were already with child. The frequency of sexual intercourse before marriage was surely higher, since some couples would have escaped early pregnancy. For many couples sexual relations were part of serious courtship. Premarital pregnancies in late-eighteenth-century Dedham, Massachusetts, observed the local historian Erastus Worthington in 1828, were occasioned by "the custom then prevalent of females admitting young men to their beds, who sought their company in marriage."

Pregnancies usually simply accelerated a marriage that would have taken place in any case, but community and parental pressure worked strongly to assure it. Most rural communities simply accepted the "early" pregnancies that marked so many marriages, although in Hingham, Massachusetts, tax records suggest that the families of well-to-do brides were considerably less generous to couples who had had "early babies" than to those who had avoided pregnancy.

"Bundling very much abounds," wrote the anonymous author of "A New Bundling Song," still circulating in Boston in 1812, "in many parts in country towns." Noah Webster's first *Dictionary of the American Language* defined it as the custom that allowed couples "to sleep on the same bed without undressing"—with, a later commentator added, "the shared understanding that innocent endearments should not be exceeded." Folklore and local tradition, from Maine south to New York, had American mothers tucking bundling couples into bed with special chastity-protecting garments for the young woman or a "bundling board" to separate them.

In actuality, if bundling had been intended to allow courting couples privacy and emotional intimacy but not sexual contact, it clearly failed. Couples may have begun with bundling, but as courtship advanced, they clearly pushed beyond its restraints, like the "bundling maid" in "A New Bundling Song" who would "sometimes say when she lies down/She can't be cumbered with a gown."

Young black men and women shared American whites' freedom in courtship and sexuality and sometimes exceeded it. Echoing the cultural traditions of West Africa, and reflecting the fact that their marriages were not given legal status and security, slave communities were somewhat more tolerant and accepting of sex before marriage.

Gradations of color and facial features among the slaves were testimony that "thousands," as the abolitionist and former slave Frederick Douglass wrote, were "ushered into the world annually, who, like myself, owe the existence to white fathers, and those fathers most frequently their own masters." Sex crossed the boundaries of race and servitude more often than slavery's defenders wanted to admit, if less frequently than the most outspoken abolitionists claimed. Slave women had little protection from whatever sexual demands masters or overseers might make, so that rapes, short liaisons, and long-term "concubinage" all were part of plantation life.

As Nathaniel Hawthorne stood talking with a group of men on the porch of a tavern in Augusta, Maine, in 1836, a young man "in a laborer's dress" came up and asked if anyone knew the whereabouts of Mary Ann Russell. "Do you want to use her?" asked one of the bystanders. Mary Ann was, in fact, the young laborer's wife, but she had left him and their child in Portland to become "one of a knot of whores." A few years earlier the young men of

York, Pennsylvania, made up a party for "overturning and pulling to the ground" Eve Geese's "shameful house" of prostitution in Queen Street. The frightened women fled out the back door as the chimney collapsed around them; the apprentices and young journeymen—many of whom had surely been previous customers—were treated by local officials "to wine, for the good work."

From medium-sized towns like Augusta and York to great cities, poor American women were sometimes pulled into a darker, harsher sexual world, one of vulnerability, exploitation, and commerce. Many prostitutes took up their trade out of poverty and domestic disaster. A young widow or a country girl arrived in the city and, thrown on her own resources, often faced desperate economic choices because most women's work paid too poorly to provide decent food, clothing, and shelter, while other women sought excitement and independence from their families.

As cities grew, and changes in transportation involved more men in long-distance travel, prostitution became more visible. Men of all ages, married and unmarried, from city lawyers to visiting country storekeepers to sailors on the docks, turned to brothels for sexual release, but most of the customers were young men, living away from home and unlikely to marry until their late twenties. Sexual commerce in New York City was elaborately graded by price and the economic status of clients, from the "parlor houses" situated not far from the city's best hotels on Broadway to the more numerous and moderately priced houses that drew artisans and clerks, and finally to the broken and dissipated women who haunted dockside grogshops in the Five Points neighborhood.

From New Orleans to Boston, city theaters were important sexual marketplaces. Men often bought tickets less to see the performance than to make assignations with the prostitutes, who sat by custom in the topmost gallery of seats. The women usually received free admission from theater managers, who claimed that they could not stay in business without the male theatergoers drawn by the "guilty third tier."

Most Americans—and the American common law—still did not regard abortion as a crime until the fetus had "quickened" or began to move perceptibly in the womb. Books of medical advice actually contained prescriptions for bringing on delayed menstrual periods, which would also produce an abortion if the woman happened to be pregnant. They suggested heavy doses of purgatives that created violent cramps, powerful douches, or extreme kinds of physical activity, like the "violent exercise, raising great weights . . . strokes on the belly . . . [and] falls" noted in William Buchan's *Domestic Medicine*, a manual read widely through the 1820s. Women's folklore echoed most of these prescriptions and added others, particularly the use of two American herbal preparations—savin, or the extract of juniper berries, and Seneca snakeroot—as abortion-producing drugs. They were dangerous procedures but sometimes effective.

REINING IN THE PASSIONS

Starting at the turn of the nineteenth century, the sexual lives of many Americans began to change, shaped by a growing insistence on control: reining in the passions in courtship, limiting family size, and even redefining male and female sexual desire.

Bundling was already on the wane in rural America before 1800; by the 1820s it was written about as a rare and antique custom. It had ceased, thought an elderly man from East Haddam, Connecticut, "as a consequence of education and refinement." Decade by decade the proportion of young women who had conceived a child before marriage declined. In most of the towns of New England the rate had dropped from nearly one pregnant bride in three to one in five or six by 1840; in some places prenuptial pregnancy dropped to 5 percent. For many young Americans this marked the acceptance of new limits on sexual behavior, imposed not by their parents or other authorities in their communities but by themselves.

These young men and women were not more closely supervised by their parents than earlier generations had been; in fact, they had more mobility and greater freedom. The couples that courted in the new style put a far greater emphasis on control of the passions. For some of them—young Northern merchants and professional men and their intended brides—revealing love letters have survived for the years after 1820. Their intimate correspondence reveals that they did not give up sexual expression but gave it new boundaries, reserving sexual intercourse for marriage. Many of them were marrying later than their parents, often living through long engagements while the husband-to-be strove to establish his place in the world. They chose not to risk a pregnancy that would precipitate them into an early marriage.

Many American husbands and wives were also breaking with tradition as they began to limit the size of their families. Clearly, married couples were renegotiating the terms of their sexual lives together, but they remained resolutely silent about how they did it. In the first two decades of the nineteenth century, they almost certainly set about avoiding childbirth through abstinence, coitus interruptus, or male withdrawal, and perhaps sometimes abortion. These contraceptive techniques had long been traditional in preindustrial Europe, although previously little used in America.

As they entered the 1830s, Americans had their first opportunity to learn, at least in print, about more effective or less self-denying forms of birth control. They could read reasonably inexpensive editions of the first works on contraception published in the United States: Robert Dale Owen's *Moral Physiology* of 1831 and Dr. Charles Knowlton's *The Fruits of Philosophy* of 1832. Both authors frankly described the full range of contraceptive techniques, although they solemnly rejected physical intervention in the sexual act and recommended only douching after intercourse and coitus interruptus. Official opinion, legal and religious, was deeply hostile. Knowlton, who had trained as a physician in rural

Massachusetts, was prosecuted in three different counties for obscenity, convicted once, and imprisoned for three months.

But both works found substantial numbers of Americans eager to read them. By 1839 each book had gone through nine editions, putting a combined total of twenty to thirty thousand copies in circulation. An American physician could write in 1850 that contraception had "been of late years so much talked of." Greater knowledge about contraception surely played a part in the continuing decline of the American birthrate after 1830.

New ways of thinking about sexuality emerged that stressed control and channeling of the passions. Into the 1820s almost all Americans would have subscribed to the commonplace notion that sex, within proper social confines, was enjoyable and healthy and that prolonged sexual abstinence could be injurious to health. They also would have assumed that women had powerful sexual drives.

Starting with his "Lecture to Young Men on Chastity" in 1832, Sylvester Graham articulated very different counsels about health and sex. Sexual indulgence, he argued, was not only morally suspect but psychologically and physiologically risky. The sexual overstimulation involved in young men's lives produced anxiety and nervous disorders, "a shocking state of debility and excessive irritability." The remedy was diet, exercise, and a regular routine that pulled the mind away from animal lusts. Medical writings that discussed the evils of masturbation, or "solitary vice," began to appear. Popular books of advice, like William Alcott's *Young Man's Guide,* gave similar warnings. They tried to persuade young men that their health could be ruined, and their prospects for success darkened, by consorting with prostitutes or becoming sexually entangled before marriage.

A new belief about women's sexual nature appeared, one that elevated them above "carnal passion." Many American men and women came to believe during the nineteenth century that in their true and proper nature as mothers and guardians of the home, women were far less interested in sex than men were. Women who defined themselves as passionless were in a strong position to control or deny men's sexual demands either during courtship or in limiting their childbearing within marriage.

Graham went considerably farther than this, advising restraint not only in early life and courtship but in marriage itself. It was far healthier, he maintained, for couples to have sexual relations "very seldom."

Neither contraception nor the new style of courtship had become anything like universal by 1840. Prenuptial pregnancy rates had fallen, but they remained high enough to indicate that many couples simply continued in familiar ways. American husbands and wives in the cities and the Northern countryside were limiting the number of their children, but it was clear that those living on the farms of the West or in the slave quarters had not yet begun to. There is strong evidence that many American women felt far from passionless, although others restrained or renounced their sexuality. For many people in the United States, there had been a profound change. Reining in the passions had become part of everyday life.

SMOKING AND SPITTING

"Everyone smokes and some chew in America," wrote Isaac Weld in 1795. Americans turned tobacco, a new and controversial stimulant at the time of colonial settlement, into a crucially important staple crop and made its heavy use a commonplace—and a never-ending source of surprise and indignation to visitors. Tobacco use spread in the United States because it was comparatively cheap, a homegrown product free from the heavy import duties levied on it by European governments. A number of slave rations described in plantation documents included "one hand of tobacco per month." Through the eighteenth century most American smokers used clay pipes, which are abundant in colonial archeological sites, although some men and women dipped snuff or inhaled powdered tobacco.

Where the smokers of early colonial America "drank" or gulped smoke through the short, thick stems of their seventeenth-century pipes, those of 1800 inhaled it more slowly and gradually; from the early seventeenth to the late eighteenth century, pipe stems became steadily longer and narrower, increasingly distancing smokers from their burning tobacco.

In the 1790s cigars, or "segars," were introduced from the Caribbean. Prosperous men widely took them up; they were the most expensive way to consume tobacco, and it was a sign of financial security to puff away on "long-nines" or "principe cigars at three cents each" while the poor used clay pipes and much cheaper "cut plug" tobacco. After 1800 in American streets, barrooms, stores, public conveyances, and even private homes it became nearly impossible to avoid tobacco chewers. Chewing extended tobacco use, particularly into workplaces; men who smoked pipes at home or in the tavern barroom could chew while working in barns or workshops where smoking carried the danger of fire.

"In all the public places of America," wrote Charles Dickens, multitudes of men engaged in "the odious practice of chewing and expectorating," a recreation practiced by all ranks of American society. Chewing stimulated salivation and gave rise to a public environment of frequent and copious spitting, where men every few minutes were "squirting a mouthful of saliva through the room."

Spittoons were provided in the more meticulous establishments, but men often ignored them. The floors of American public buildings were not pleasant to contemplate. A courtroom in New York City in 1833 was decorated by a "mass of abomination" contributed to by "judges, counsel, jury, witnesses, officers, and audience." The floor of the Virginia House of Burgesses in 1827 was "actually flooded with their horrible spitting," and even the aisle of a Connecticut meetinghouse was black with the "ejection after ejection, incessant from twenty mouths," of the men singing in the choir. In order to drink, an American man might remove his quid, put it in a pocket or hold it in his hand, take his glassful, and then restore it to his mouth. Women's dresses might even be in danger at fashionable balls. "One night as I was walking upstairs to valse," reported Margaret Hall of a dance in Washington in 1828, "my partner began clearing his throat. This I thought ominous. However, I said to myself, 'surely he will turn his head to the other side.' The gentleman, however, had no such thought but deliberately shot across me. I had not courage enough to examine whether the result landed in the flounce of my dress."

The segar and the quid were almost entirely male appurtenances, but as the nineteenth century began, many rural and lower-class urban women were smoking pipes or dipping snuff. During his boyhood in New Hampshire, Horace Greeley remembered, "it was often my filial duty to fill and light my mother's pipe."

After 1820 or so tobacco use among women in the North began to decline. Northern women remembered or depicted with pipe or snuffbox were almost all elderly. More and more Americans adopted a genteel standard that saw tobacco use and womanliness—delicate and nurturing—as antithetical, and young women avoided it as a pollutant. For them, tobacco use marked off male from female territory with increasing sharpness.

In the households of small Southern and Western farmers, however, smoking and snuff taking remained common. When women visited "among the country people" of North Carolina, Frances Kemble Butler reported in 1837, the "proffer of the snuffbox, and its passing from hand to hand, is the usual civility." By the late 1830s visiting New Englanders were profoundly shocked when they saw the women of Methodist congregations in Illinois, including nursing mothers, taking out their pipes for a smoke between worship services.

FROM DEFERENCE TO EQUALITY

The Americans of 1820 would have been more recognizable to us in the informal and egalitarian way they treated one another. The traditional signs of deference before social superiors—the deep bow, the "courtesy," the doffed cap, lowered head, and averted eyes—had been a part of social relationships in colonial America. In the 1780s, wrote the American poetess Lydia Huntley Sigourney in 1824, there were still "individuals . . . in every grade of society" who had grown up "when a bow was not an offense to fashion nor . . . a relic of monarchy." But in the early nineteenth century such signals of subordination rapidly fell away. It was a natural consequence of the Revolution, she maintained, which, "in giving us liberty, obliterated almost every vestige of politeness of the 'old school.'" Shaking hands became the accustomed American greeting between men, a gesture whose symmetry and mutuality signified equality. Frederick Marryat found in 1835 that it was "invariably the custom to shake hands" when he was introduced to Americans and that he could not carefully grade the acknowledgment he would give to new acquaintances according to their signs of wealth and breeding. He found instead that he had to "go on shaking hands here, there and everywhere, and with everybody." Americans were not blind to inequalities of economic and social power, but they less and less gave them overt physical expression. Bred in a society where such distinctions were far more clearly spelled out, Marryat was somewhat disoriented in the United States; "it is impossible to know who is who," he claimed, "in this land of equality."

Well-born British travelers encountered not just confusion but conflict when they failed to receive the signs of respect they expected. Margaret Hall's letters home during her Southern travels outlined a true comedy of manners. At every stage stop in the Carolinas, Georgia, and Alabama, she demanded that country tavernkeepers and their households give her deferential service and well-prepared meals; she received instead rancid bacon and "such an absence of all kindness of feeling, such unbending frigid heartlessness." But she and her family had a far greater share than they realized in creating this chilly reception. Squeezed between the pride and poise of the great planters and the social debasement of the slaves, small Southern farmers often displayed a prickly insolence, a

considered lack of response, to those who too obviously considered themselves their betters. Greatly to their discomfort and incomprehension, the Halls were experiencing what a British traveler more sympathetic to American ways, Patrick Shirreff, called "the democratic rudeness which assumed or presumptuous superiority seldom fails to experience."

LAND OF ABUNDANCE

In the seventeenth century white American colonials were no taller than their European counterparts, but by the time of the Revolution they were close to their late-twentieth-century average height for men of slightly over five feet eight inches. The citizens of the early republic towered over most Europeans. Americans' early achievement of modern stature—by a full century and more—was a striking consequence of American abundance. Americans were taller because they were better nourished than the great majority of the world's peoples.

Yet not all Americans participated equally in the nation's abundance. Differences in stature between whites and blacks, and between city and country dwellers, echoed those between Europeans and Americans. Enslaved blacks were a full inch shorter than whites. But they remained a full inch taller than European peasants and laborers and were taller still than their fellow slaves eating the scanty diets afforded by the more savagely oppressive plantation system of the West Indies. And by 1820 those who lived in the expanding cities of the United States—even excluding immigrants, whose heights would have reflected European, not American, conditions—were noticeably shorter than the people of the countryside, suggesting an increasing concentration of poverty and poorer diets in urban places.

Across the United States almost all country households ate the two great American staples: corn and "the eternal pork," as one surfeited traveler called it, "which makes its appearance on every American table, high and low, rich and poor." Families in the cattle-raising, dairying country of New England, New York, and northern Ohio ate butter, cheese, and salted beef as well as pork and made their bread from wheat flour or rye and Indian corn. In Pennsylvania, as well as Maryland, Delaware, and Virginia, Americans ate the same breadstuffs as their Northern neighbors, but their consumption of cheese and beef declined every mile southward in favor of pork.

Farther to the south, and in the West, corn and corn-fed pork were truly "eternal"; where reliance on them reached its peak in the Southern uplands, they were still the only crops many small farmers raised. Most Southern and Western families built their diets around smoked and salted bacon, rather than the Northerners' salt pork, and, instead of wheat or rye bread, made cornpone or hoecake, a coarse, strong bread, and hominy, pounded Indian corn boiled together with milk.

Before 1800, game—venison, possum, raccoon, and wild fowl—was for many American households "a substantial portion of the supply of food at certain seasons of the year," although only on the frontier was it a regular part of the diet. In the West and South this continued to be true, but in the Northeast game became increasingly rare as forests gave way to open farmland, where wild animals could not live.

Through the first half of the eighteenth century, Americans had been primarily concerned with obtaining a sufficiency of meat and bread for their families; they paid relatively little attention to foodstuffs other than these two "staffs of life," but since that time the daily fare of many households had grown substantially more diverse. . . .

Important patterns of regional, class, and ethnic distinctiveness remain in American everyday life. But they are far less powerful, and less central to understanding American experience, than they once were. Through the rest of the nineteenth century and into the twentieth, the United States became ever more diverse, with new waves of Eastern and Southern European immigrants joining the older Americans of Northern European stock. Yet the new arrivals—and even more, their descendants—have experienced the attractiveness and reshaping power of a national culture formed by department stores, newspapers, radios, movies, and universal public education. America, the developing nation, developed into us. And perhaps our manners and morals, to some future observer, will seem as idiosyncratic and astonishing as this portrait of our earlier self.

QUESTIONS TO CONSIDER

1 Compare Larkin's description of American urban conditions, crime, disorder, and drunkenness, with the conditions Page Smith found in seventeenth-century London (selection 2). Were these Americans worse or better off than their English forebears? How did the American legal response to crime and disorder compare with the earlier British model?

2 Bacterial pollution from animal and human wastes, offal, open drains, and contaminated water were major threats to American health in the early nineteenth century. Are we more fortunate nearly two centuries later, or have we found new ways to poison our environment? Which era do you think is the more deadly?

3 Larkin is a social and cultural historian. What sources has he used to compile his vivid account of everyday life among ordinary Americans in the early nineteenth century? What are the advantages of using these sources? What are the potential disadvantages?

4 Larkin points out that American women drank less than a third as much as American men at the turn of the nineteenth century and that alcohol consumption by slaves was also limited. A few decades later, women spearheaded the temperance movement in communities all over the country. What issues of social control do you suppose were in operation throughout this period?

5 In what personal ways are these ordinary nineteenth-century Americans different from us today? How are they similar? What distinctively American traits does Larkin suggest were born in this era?

12 "I'm Almost Worn Out in the Cause": Motherhood and Childbearing in the Old South

SALLY G. McMILLEN

White men of the early Republic were enterprising builders of farms and plantations, merchant shops and law firms, hard at work making their fortunes in a bustling, materialistic society. For white men, the opportunities for individual advancement and self-fulfillment were increasingly plentiful. But it was not so for white women, who, like African Americans, were excluded from the Revolutionary promise of freedom and equality. Although men like Alexander Hamilton, Benjamin Franklin, and John Jay worried about the discrepancy between the idealism of the Declaration of Independence and the reality of slavery, no statesmen of note thought to extend the equality doctrine to white women. Though not slaves in a legal sense, they were certainly not free. Women in the young Republic could not vote or hold political office. Unmarried women and widows could own landed property, but few occupations were open to them. Indeed, custom held that the only proper sphere for women was in the home. According to the women's magazines and religious journals, which reflected the pervasive attitudes of a male-dominated world, the ideal woman was not only domesticated, but pious, pure, submissive, and unopinionated. Once a woman married, she was expected to be "with child" within a year, since child rearing, along with duty to her husband, was her main purpose in life. A married woman soon discovered that the law treated her like a child. She could not own property or sue in court without her husband. If a married woman did work outside the home, her husband legally commanded her wages. He was also the sole guardian of their children. If he died without a will and there were children, the woman was entitled to only one-third of her husband's estate. In certain cases, she could keep only her dowry—the property she had brought to the marriage. If she wedded again (and widows usually did remarry in order to survive), she had to surrender her property to her new husband. If the woman was an African American, she faced a double wall of discrimination—one because she was a woman, the other because she was black. The underlying assumption behind the whole range of discrimination against the so-called "fairer sex" was that women were inferior to men.

Sally G. McMillen challenges the myth of female inferiority by discussing the courage, the pain and sorrow, associated with motherhood in the early Republic. Her focus is on the white and slave women of the Old South, but their experiences in birthing and childbearing were similar to those of women in the North and on the frontier. McMillen vividly recreates the experience of conception and birthing. She transports us back to the grand plantation houses and the squalid, drafty slave quarters, so that we are right there with the plantation lady or a slave woman when they endured the painful, often frightening, and dangerous act of bringing a child into the world. Even with midwives or physicians there to help, women and their babies frequently died during childbirth. If infants survived that event, they still faced a myriad of life-threatening diseases on their perilous journey to adulthood.

Still, families remained large in the Old South—children, after all, were a cheap and indispensable labor source. Gradually, as the skills of physicians improved, childbearing became less dangerous.

Although white women still had to endure the frequent deaths of their children, the love and companionship between mother and child were a rich comfort in an otherwise harsh life.

As McMillen makes clear, motherhood for slave women was a "mixed blessing." Pregnancy offered only a brief reprieve from the grueling labor in the field. A new African American mother might receive a dress or other gift from her owner, because she had just provided him with another slave. Like white mothers, slave women also had to endure the pain of childbirth and the frequent loss of children to malaria and cholera, even malnutrition. Although children provided a source of love in an otherwise cruel life under the whip, slave mothers knew only too well that their children could be "sold off" to distant plantations, in which case they may never see them again.

As you will see from reading McMillen's poignant essay, family life in the Old South had a brighter side. White and African American women bonded as they shared the common experience of birth and childcare. Extended families, moreover, were commonplace, as younger family members took in older relatives who could no longer care for themselves. All in all, family ties, whether black or white, were extremely close, perhaps more so than in our own time.

GLOSSARY

ABORTIFACIENT   A substance that induces an abortion; some pregnant women, for example, took quinine to relieve the symptoms of malaria and in the process lost their unborn child.

ABROAD MARRIAGE   Interplantation marriage in which men usually visited their wives only on weekends and the children became the property of the owner of the slave woman.

BLACKWELL, ELIZABETH   The first woman to become a licensed physician in the United States. After a number of medical schools rejected her application, she gained admission to Geneva Medical College in New York because the male students believed that a woman's presence was "amusing."

CALOMEL   A white tasteless compound that expectant mothers used to cleanse their system of impurities and to relieve tension.

CONJURER   A slave who had knowledge of herbs and other medicinal cures for pain and diseases. Much of this knowledge was derived from the conjurer's rich West African culture. Usually present on large plantations, the conjurer used fear of witchcraft, voodoo, and sorcery to gain power with both whites and fellow slaves.

INFANTICIDE   The willful and intentional killing of an infant; considering the high birthrate and the value placed on motherhood and families, this was probably a rare occurrence in the Old South.

LAUDANUM   A form of opium administered to the ill, laudanum served as one of the home medications that southern families stored for those in need. For some women, infant death and the resultant sorrow led to misuse and addiction.

MIDWIVES   Women in the community who assisted in the delivery of newborns. Some had read medical literature, but many more had learned from experience and "depended on luck and nature to bring a woman safely through her delivery."

MISCEGENATION   Sexual relationships between whites and African Americans that resulted in the birth of a mulatto child. Slave women were terribly vulnerable to rape and unwanted sexual advances from whites who held all of the power in the plantation South. Since the status of a newborn was the same as its mother, all of the children born in the slave quarters belonged to the planter.

SICKLE CELL ANEMIA   An often fatal disease that afflicted African Americans. Sickle cell anemia made African American women even more vulnerable to health problems during pregnancy. Poor nutrition and heavy work schedules were other reasons for the high infant mortality and death of women in their childbearing years within the slave quarters.

FERTILITY

Married women's lives were largely concerned with the bearing and rearing of children. Being a mother was a fulfilling goal for married women in the nineteenth century. Prescriptive literature, sermons, maternal advice books, and even school lessons encouraged white women to seek their sacred occupation as mothers. Motherhood held special meaning in the South, where family and kin were the foundation of the region's social and economic structure. Few other options provided women with more satisfaction or gained them a greater degree of public recognition than their maternal role.

Pregnancies, confinements, suckling babies, and nurturing infants were ceaseless and demanding activities for black and white women. Many began bearing children in their late teens and continued almost unabated until ill health, menopause, or death interceded. One slave woman, May, bore nineteen children, of whom four lived. Mrs. Rhea, at the age of thirty-seven, had borne sixteen offspring, and one friend observed wistfully, "Her family may yet be much larger." John Ball, Jr.'s first wife bore eleven children in twelve years of marriage, and when she died, he remarried and began another family.

American women proved to be extremely fertile, more so than their European counterparts. The first national census in 1790 showed that white women of childbearing age bore, on the average, 7.1 children. But most married women were pregnant more than seven times; the tabulated birthrate was lower than the actual number of pregnancies and births due to the frequency of miscarriages and infant deaths. Throughout the antebellum period, fertility decreased nationwide, declining to an average of 5.4 children by 1850 and 4.6 by 1860. However,

regional variations existed, and the number of live births was higher in the Old South than in the North.

There were many reasons why southern women bore more children than women in the Northeast. While some northern middle-class couples apparently recognized the advisability of restricting family size, there seemed little reason to limit the number of children in southern families, aside from the health concerns of the women who bore them. Instead, there were positive arguments for large families. For farm women, each child became a potential worker to assist with agricultural production and contribute to family survival. Often living in isolated circumstances, children became the principal source of companionship and socializing. Ann Holmes Blank of Leesburg, North Carolina, was a lonely young mother, writing in 1846 that "if my dear little Henry would talk so that I could have someone to talk with me, I would not mind it so bad but to stay morning until night and no one to say a word to you is lonesome." Within a few years, her home would be bustling.

Limited land and economic constraints often unconsciously induced a family to control its size. But these restrictions were hardly relevant in the booming South, where opportunities beckoned the bold and aggressive. Overcrowding, which also discouraged larger families, especially in urban areas, was an alien notion to antebellum southerners, who had plentiful land, especially on the frontier. By the 1840s some middle-class couples in the Northeast were practicing birth control, but southern women rarely did, at least judging by large southern families and the frequency with which white and slave women bore children. Religious constraints may have affected white southerners' reactions to birth control, though this issue was not discussed publicly. According to Anne Firor Scott in *The Southern Lady*, sometimes the only effective means for women to delay another conception was to travel home for extended visits with parents and childhood friends.

By marrying a few years earlier than northern women, southern women might bear two or more

Reprinted from *Southern Women: Black and White in the Old South*, by Sally G. McMillen, pp. 48–76. Copyright © 1992 by Harlan Davidson, Inc. Reprinted by permission.

additional children. And, with the positive attention heaped on motherhood and the personal achievement associated with childrearing, there was little reason, other than enormous health risks and high maternal and infant mortality, to limit family size. For a man, a large family reflected positively on his status, his masculinity, and his ability to support his dependents.

For slave women, bearing an infant was a mixed blessing, evoking love for the child, the thrill of creating a blessed and helpless being, but also the realization that the child could be sold at any time and might never know any life beyond slavery. Yet many slave women continually held out hope that they could purchase their children's freedom. Statistics indicate that slave women bore slightly more children than southern white women, probably because they started two or three years earlier. Still, slave families were smaller than southern white families due to higher infant mortality. In addition, slave women experienced frequent miscarriages, and such health risks apparently increased during the late antebellum period due to worsening conditions and greater work demands.

The high fertility rates among slave women appear to counter what one might expect under an oppressive system. It would seem that women might not want to bear children in a society where hardships were ever-present and the future dim. Anthropologists know that in societies that are overly repressive or where living conditions prove difficult, couples both consciously and unconsciously limit family size. Fertility declines because of poor diet and bad health, overwork, a shortage of men, or a conscious desire not to have children. But southern slave women actually bore more children than white women and more than their counterparts on Caribbean plantations. The natural increase of the southern slave population was enormous, leaping from nearly 1.5 million in 1820 to almost 4 million by 1860.

One explanation for this population surge could be the encouragement that slave women received from their masters. Plantation owners welcomed large slave families, for as stated earlier, each additional child enhanced a master's wealth. One owner reported happily that a twenty-two-year-old bondwoman had already borne five children. Slave owner Rachel O'Connor congratulated her sister on her luck in having five black babies born in a two-month period, with two more slave women expecting. Owners may not have considered such attitudes as opportunistic or profit-minded, but slave women saw it otherwise. "You see dey raised de chilluns ter make money on jes lak we raise pigs ter sell," stated one Tennessee woman. How significantly such encouragement fostered high birthrates cannot be assessed, but it certainly did not inhibit fertility. Slave women knew that their value increased with their ability to bear children and that their fertility often protected them against willful sale. Plantation owners expressed their approval by rewarding a new mother with a dress, a small amount of cash, a trinket and, of course, time off during pregnancy and after delivery. Commented one Louisiana mistress who promised dresses to each new slave mother, "I am now in debt to four that has young babes, and fine ones too. They do much better by being encouraged a little and I have ever thought they deserved it."

While white women rarely did anything to limit their fertility, slave women may have been more comfortable with the idea, though how often they aborted fetuses or resorted to infanticide is unknown. Certainly bondwomen had cause to contemplate such action, considering widespread miscegenation and the problems associated with raising children as slaves. Occasionally bondwomen found ways to end a pregnancy. One slave seamstress, Jane, successfully aborted every baby she conceived, even as late as six months into one pregnancy, causing her mistress tremendous sorrow. Jane may have felt discouraged before she became a mother and did not want to face possible heartache. Being single may have created problems for her. Plantation and medical accounts sometimes recounted cases of infanticide in which dead infants were discovered in the woods or behind a barn. Nevertheless, considering the high fertility rate among southern blacks, it is evident that most slave women desired children, whatever the risks of bearing and rearing them, and rarely interfered with their pregnancies. Most important, like all mothers, they discovered immense joy in a baby's birth and found fulfillment that was otherwise absent in their bleak existence as plantation laborers.

PREGNANCY

Pregnancy was a time of anxiety and ill health for many southern women. While one might imagine that mothers joyfully anticipated the birth of an infant, the months preceding confinement were filled with fears about the upcoming event. Poor health was also a common complaint among pregnant women as they struggled to remain vital and useful, and, if possible, follow judicious behavior to ensure a healthy infant.

The single greatest health problem that expectant white women endured was malaria, a disease endemic in most areas of the Old South. During the antebellum period, malaria was the major health concern of all Americans outside of New England, but it was pervasive in the Old South. Nearly everyone suffered "fever and ague" during the summer and early fall, experiencing symptoms that included high fever, chills, and debilitation. Some elite families migrated temporarily to higher elevations or to the North to avoid annual bouts of sickness. This disease was spread by the anopheles mosquito, the carrier of the malaria protozoa. No one during the antebellum period understood correctly its cause. Most southerners, including physicians, deduced that a miasm, or "bad air," caused the disease, for it seemed to affect those southerners living near marshy or damp areas. Southerners never understood that such damp areas were prolific breeding grounds for mosquitoes. Lucy Shaw, living in the frontier town of Galveston, Texas, found the mosquitoes overwhelming. She wrote her mother: "If you wish to know what will thrive best in a climate like this, I can tell you that I know of nothing quite equal to the fleas and mosquitoes. . . . [They are] double the size of New England mosquitoes." Lucy repeatedly described the swarms of mosquitoes that made life intolerable, but she had no idea that these bothersome insects also caused frequent bouts of malaria.

Families like the Shaws living in lowland coastal areas, along rivers, and in delta regions where cotton and sugar cane flourished were most vulnerable. Ironically, the wealthy seemed to be most affected by incidents of malaria, for poor farm families who often lived in higher, drier elevations encountered fewer mosquitoes and thereby suffered less than plantation families. It may be that farm women also had healthier pregnancies, fewer miscarriages, and easier deliveries since they were less likely to suffer from malaria.

Pregnant women were more susceptible to malaria than most southerners because their immune systems were weakened during the last trimester of pregnancy. They lost their partial resistance acquired over years of exposure. The alternating chills and fever (up to 104 degrees), anorexia, and anemia of malaria created major health problems in pregnant women. Miscarriages were common in areas where malaria was endemic. The accompanying high temperature in the womb created an environment too uncomfortable for the fetus. In addition, quinine, the most effective cure for malaria, was a known abortifacient, but expectant women took it, desperate to offset the disease's symptoms. Malaria also inhibited fertility rates by raising a male's scrotal temperature and creating infertile sperm during the disease's duration.

Antebellum women (and physicians as well) had little scientific understanding of conception. Americans were naïve about the process of pregnancy, believing that women were most fertile immediately before and after menstruation. Prenatal visits to a physician were not regarded as necessary, except to treat severe health problems such as hemorrhaging or convulsions. But as medical books of the period indicate, doctors exhibited increasing interest in the mysteries of pregnancy. They began to recognize the prenatal period as an important time in the infant's development and encouraged expectant mothers to take proper care of themselves in order to bear a healthy child.

For literate women, medical literature like *Gunn's Domestic Medicine, or Poor Man's Friend,* or Buchan's *Domestic Medicine* provided helpful advice for home treatment. Many southern white families, especially those living on the frontier and far from a doctor's care, found a medical advice book an essential item. Expectant farm and slave women also secured wisdom and support from family members and female friends. Many women used herbal cures or folk remedies and collected recipes in notebooks. Southern women knew that various teas eased heartburn. Gentle exercise such as walking, riding in a carriage, or brushing the skin stimulated the body. A bland diet apparently was most pleasing to the developing fetus; and reading books that would not provoke passion or excite the mind was highly recommended. Women shared not only information but also explicit, often scary, details about childbirth, fueling fears among friends who would have benefited from a state of calm before their forthcoming confinement.

Nearly all healthy southern women carried on a normal routine while pregnant, continuing to work, care for children, labor in the fields and around the house, visit, and attend church and Sunday school. However, many slave owners exhibited concern about the health of their expectant slaves and provided them extra days off as needed, especially during the last trimester. Researchers have noted a relationship between the number of days off slave women received and the success of their confinement and health of their infant. Some expectant bondwomen moved from field work to less strenuous chores, such as sewing or weaving. Some received lighter punishments when pregnant (although common also was the practice of digging a hole for a pregnant woman who would lie face down on the dirt to receive her lashes).

Horizontal rest was a rare privilege for pregnant women, except for the truly privileged or those who were ill. Expectant mothers had little choice but to maintain their daily routine, for what southern family could have survived with a wife and mother who chose to lie down through her numerous pregnancies? Although the medical profession classified pregnant women as ill and childbirth as a disease, few southerners saw this as cause for easing the female work load. Pregnancy was a normal condition (certainly true for those women who bore eight, ten, or fourteen children) that did not warrant a change in routine. Older children still needed watching, feeding, and nurturing; gardens and orchards required weeding and picking; food had to be prepared; houses needed occasional cleaning; and field work demanded extra hands. Southern women carried on as long as their health and energy held out.

Expectant mothers spent their months of pregnancy in a state of anxiety for good cause. Women in their childbearing years experienced a higher mortality rate than did men of comparable age. In the South, women had much to fear. As Sally McMillen relates in *Motherhood in the Old South,* statistics from the 1850 federal census demonstrate that southern white women were twice as likely to die in childbirth as women in the Northeast. An unhealthy climate, the prevalence of malaria, improper medical practices, and the comparably frequent childbearing of Southern women all contributed to the grim statistics. The medical profession was not yet proficient at delivering babies, for medical misperceptions about proper treatment and unsanitary practices persisted. A midwife depended on luck and nature to bring a woman safely through her delivery.

Today, walking through an old southern cemetery sadly reminds one of the tenuous existence of the many who died during or shortly after bearing a child. The health risks were enormous, and expectant southern women put their faith in God and shared their worries with friends and family. As their diaries and letters reveal, nearly all women entered each confinement expecting it to be their last moment on earth. A period of pregnancy was not a joyous time, however much mothers loved their children. Many expressed a desire for longer intervals between each birth and for fewer confinements.

CHILDBEARING

Birthing practices varied by race, class, and individual need. In the antebellum period, new medical practices also affected the process of childbearing. Who was present and where the birth occurred could reflect practical considerations or a conscious choice. Slave women generally gave birth in their cabins, though on large plantations a slave hospital might be available for birthing. Most farm women remained at home, having little means to travel elsewhere. Poor white and free black women living in cities might use a charity hospital, such as those associated with medical colleges in New Orleans, Charleston, or Lexington. Urban women who were destitute or who lived alone often delivered their baby in a hospital. Unfortunately, these institutions served as teaching facilities for medical students and were not known for quality care or cleanliness. Doctors who performed multiple deliveries and failed to wash their hands and instruments might unknowingly infect prospective mothers. Puerperal fever, an infection that could develop in the womb following birth and was usually spread by physicians unaware

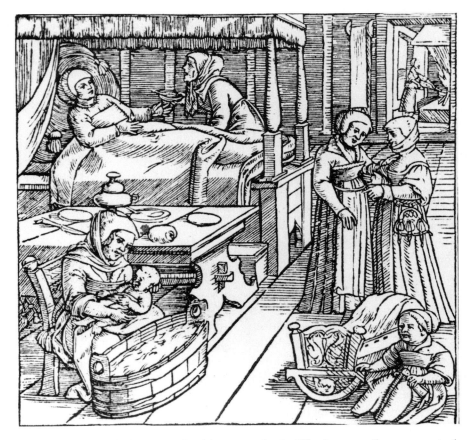

This early engraving shows the crowded birthing room where laboring women summoned mothers, sisters, aunts, friends, and neighbors to their bedside. The tragedies of women perishing in their childbearing years and infants and young children experiencing short and pain-ridden lives were all too common in the colonial period. Poor diets, harsh living conditions, and unrelenting work made childbirth even more precarious for slave mothers and their babies. (National Library of Medicine/History of Medicine Archive)

of proper sanitary procedures, was more common in women who bore babies in hospitals, though it occurred less frequently in the South than in the North and Europe.

Unless ill or weighed down by family responsibilities, some women traveled home to their mothers to bear their infant in familiar surroundings. Southern women were eager to have their mother present, especially with the birth of a firstborn. A surprising number of females made the effort to travel home, even those living far from civilization or hundreds of miles from their parents. In a familiar family setting, expectant women could bask in the attention of doting mothers, friends, and a trained medical assistant. Sometimes expectant women left their husbands three to four months before the infant was due (though often accompanied by a white or black escort, for southern women were not supposed to travel alone). Others arrived only a day or two before the infant emerged.

During the antebellum period, male doctors began to assume obstetrical duties traditionally handled by female midwives, reflecting a change that had begun in Europe and spread to America by the late eighteenth century. Since physicians classified childbirth as a disease, medical assistance was considered desirable. Medicine was not yet an elite occupation nor a particularly well-paid one, and doctors wanted to generate more income by acquiring new patients. Because of a growing emphasis on education and scientific inquiry, the educated and elite regarded female midwives and traditional domestic medical practices as old fashioned. Increasing numbers of men attended medical college as these institutions opened, but women and midwives were not admitted (at least until 1846, when Elizabeth Blackwell graduated from Geneva Medical College in New York, but her admission was apparently considered a joke by the students who voted to accept her).

Men gradually came to dominate obstetrical care, for they possessed the latest medical instruments, access to medical education, anesthetics, scientific testing, and professional literature. Antebellum doctors embarked on a campaign to denigrate the skills of female midwives and drive them out of a specialty that men wished to control. Despite their education and training, there is little evidence that doctors improved the survival rate of mothers and newborns, and, in fact, may have made confinements even riskier. Physicians were not particularly well prepared to deliver a baby, for their medical education and knowledge were rudimentary. Then too, medical schools were not very discriminating, and any white male who could afford the fees could attend medical college. Therefore, most physicians emerged with little actual experience and often delivered their first baby on the job. Doctors did their best to gain the confidence of female patients, though an advertisement by a Louisville physician in 1836 stating that "in cases of obstetrics, will be attended to without mutilation or instruments" could not have been too reassuring. Doctors proliferated in the South, taking advantage of the region's sickly population and its cheap land and economic opportunities. By 1860, the region had a higher proportion of physicians than the Northeast.

Doctors sometimes delivered slave babies; this practice reflected not as much the woman's choice as the desire of her owner. Plantation masters often hired a doctor to tend to all slave and family health problems, and delivering babies was included in the list of responsibilities. Owners believed that such measures provided slaves with good medical care. Also, a surprising number of slave owners had attended medical school and served as part-time physicians. Some southern fathers apparently regarded a medical education as excellent training for a son's future, giving him skills that would serve well on a plantation. Thus, medical care, however questionable in quality, was available in many rural and frontier areas during the antebellum period, for many ambitious young professionals migrated to such states as Alabama, Mississippi, Texas, and Arkansas seeking wealth.

It was more common for slave women to depend on midwives, friends, or a slave mistress rather than on a physician. Financial considerations often took precedence over professional care. Planters who had no doctor on contract preferred midwives, since their delivery fees, ranging from $1 to $4, were far less than the $5 to $25 that doctors charged. Rachel O'Connor wrote that she paid a black midwife $4 for each of four deliveries of slave babies, commenting that "it is better to pay that than to run any risk." A doctor was usually reserved for a medical emergency or prolonged confinement. Moreover, physicians who attended slave women were more inclined to experiment on them with drugs or radical surgery than they did on elite white women. Caesareans, which had been attempted for hundreds of years, were rarely successful because physicians knew little about proper suturing, cleanliness, or controlling blood flow. Still, a doctor might attempt to operate on a slave woman if her life was endangered and the fetus still viable. Since anesthesia was not used until the late antebellum period, the woman suffered excruciating pain. Invariably the woman and infant died, though apparently a handful of Louisiana doctors had a few successes during the antebellum period. Dr. J. Marion Sims of Alabama, who became one of the most respected gynecological physicians of the nineteenth century, developed a successful surgical cure for vesico-vaginal fistula (a tear of the vaginal tissue during birth) by experimenting on thirty slave women over a four-year period. Despite bondwomen's value to plantation owners, they were regarded as more expendable than white women when it came to medical experimentation.

Health conditions influenced slave women's ability to bear children. Considering the extent of female ills and poor diet, the high fertility rate among bondwomen is all the more remarkable. Inadequate nutrition weakened pregnant and lactating slave women and their infants (as it did impoverished white farm women who ate poorly). A typical slave diet of corn meal, pork, and molasses, supplemented by seasonal vegetables and an occasional helping of fruit or fish, provided women with adequate calories but insufficient nutrients. Some slave and poor white women ate clay to gain supplemental nutrients not available through their diet. No physician—nor any American for that matter—yet understood the

importance of vitamins and balanced meals. Slave women could only eat the food their masters provided and sometimes grew additional fare to relieve a monotonous diet.

Burdened by poor nutrition and heavy work demands, slave mothers often bore infants of low birth weight. In one sense this was positive, for a small baby led to shorter and less painful deliveries. (White southerners often misread the situation and concluded that slave women's apparent ease in bearing children was due to their vigorous activity as plantation laborers rather than poor diet and overwork.) Nevertheless a mother's nutritional deficiencies contributed to poorly developed bones and small pelvises which could foster difficult confinements. Slave women were less likely to suffer from malaria than white women and rarely experienced stillbirths caused by the dreaded disease. However, sickle cell anemia, a trait found almost exclusively in blacks and one that helped them resist the most common forms of malaria, increased the risk of chronic anemia and fostered susceptibility to other diseases.

White women who used doctors usually did so by choice, and according to Sally McMillen, by the Civil War probably about half of all elite women in the South depended on a male attendant for their confinements. Some white families planned ahead, estimating what they assumed to be the correct due date and scheduling the doctor. Other white women, both rich and poor, preferred midwives. Some mothers-to-be were sensitive to a male's presence in the birthing room. Tradition, expense, or the desire to depend totally on female support were other considerations. In many cases, women used whomever they could find, and family members often scrambled to locate an assistant when the baby arrived unexpectedly.

Considering the number of babies born in the South, and the many families who could not afford a physician or preferred not to use one, midwives still had a thriving business despite doctors' efforts to denigrate their skills. Some women purposely avoided physicians, fearing their dramatic cures and use of instruments and drugs. And however critical male doctors were of midwives, the two attendants often worked side by side to deliver an infant. Rarely did midwives interfere directly with what they regarded as a natural process, except to turn the baby or pull on the placenta to dislodge it after delivery. Female midwives, both black and white, calmed the patient, kept her upright as long as possible during contractions, administered soothing teas, pushed on the abdomen, and occasionally gave a medicine like ergot to enhance contractions.

Doctors may have identified childbirth as a disease, but like midwives, most hoped that nature would prove kind and ease the patient's delivery. Physicians, however, altered traditional procedures. They introduced scientific technology into the birthing chamber, speeding the process along artificially if necessary by assisting the infant's delivery with forceps, cathartics, and hooks. If the fetus was impacted, they might perform a craniotomy in which they used scalpels to chop up the baby's head inside the womb to remove it, sacrificing the infant to save the mother. Apparently, fewer southern doctors employed obstetrical instruments than their northern counterparts, perhaps because few felt competent enough to use them. Yet doctors still depended on heroic procedures during delivery, including an aggressive form of therapy to balance vascular tension. They bled women before and during delivery, lancing an artery or placing leeches on the temples or vagina to foster relaxation and lessen pressure. Purging a woman's system with calomel, a mercury chloride, was often deemed essential, and physicians also relied on ergot to hasten contractions. These techniques were performed in the name of science to balance the body's fluids, decrease blood pressure, and enhance relaxation.

By the 1850s, some doctors in the Northeast had successfully used ether and chloroform during confinements, allowing women a less agonizing experience by deadening most of the pain during delivery. But prior to the Civil War, few southern doctors used either anesthetic. Many were cautious or unfamiliar with the drugs, fearing the dangerous effect they could have on the mother and infant if administered improperly. Others believed it morally wrong to intervene with painkillers. They upheld the Biblical dictate, "In sorrow thou shalt bring forth children." For these physicians, the intensity of maternal pain corresponded to the depth of maternal love, and many believed that if a mother had an easy or painless delivery, she might ignore her newborn.

The ritual of childbirth fostered female bonding. Confinements could last for several hours or even a couple of days, as women watched, encouraged, and provided loving assistance. Male doctors changed this atmosphere with their presence, although most left the female support unit intact, recognizing it as too powerful and essential to ignore. But medical literature urged professionalization of the entire process, insisting on such details as a darkened room to preserve female delicacy, a horizontal birth position in case instruments were needed, proper bed clothing, and an absent husband. Doctors probably regarded female friends as necessary nuisances. They were not secure enough to dismiss them entirely and needed women to run errands and provide emotional support. Husbands were encouraged to be present in the home but never in the delivery room.

In the South, black and white women were often together during childbirth. If women of the two races ever shared any intimacies, it was during this important event. Childbirth was a rare time of mutual sharing, understanding, gratitude, and even affection. The meaning of birth, its pains and joys, drew common responses, whatever race or class. Many black women were highly skilled midwives who delivered white babies. In one instance, a Virginia woman was left in critical condition after two physicians struggled unsuccessfully for hours to deliver her baby. Her husband finally called Mildred, a black midwife, despite the doctors' objections. Mildred worked for the next seven hours. "I did ev'ything I knowed an' somethings I didn' know," she recalled, and successfully delivered a five-pound infant. The white mistress was extremely grateful, and even the physicians grudgingly acknowledged Mildred's skills. White women often were present when their slave women delivered babies and assisted with these births.

Four weeks seemed to be the prescribed recuperative period for white and slave women following delivery. Of course, many required a much longer period to regain good health, and some were ill for months following a confinement. A particularly profit-minded or mean-spirited master such as Pierce Butler of Georgia allowed his slave women only three weeks to rest and tend to their newborn.

Despite similar recovery periods, the subsequent activities of white and black women were markedly different. For slave women, the end of their month marked the resumption of plantation duties with little time to nurture their newborn. It was expected that elite white women at the end of their recuperative period would appear downstairs, dine with the family, stroll outside, and enjoy visitors. They continued to nurse and nurture their newborn. Farm women, like slaves, had little choice but to return to work as quickly as possible. For slave and farm women, balancing the demands as mothers, productive laborers, and family caretakers must have been more than many could handle.

Some slave mothers had no choice but to carry their infant to the field, placing the baby in a shady spot, strapping it to their backs or hanging it in a pouch on a tree, and breastfeeding it every few hours. No one, however, could constantly protect the baby from insects, snakes, heat, or inclement weather. Occasionally slave mothers had to leave young babies alone in their cabins without any care. They rushed back at prescribed times to nurse the infant. One bondwoman recounted sorrowfully that she believed her baby literally cried itself to death alone in the cabin. There was little she could do since her master insisted that she work unencumbered by a newborn. Larger plantations often offered a form of day care tended by an older slave woman (a granny) or adolescent girls who watched and fed both the babies and younger children. Sometimes plantation mistresses would care for newborn slaves, notwithstanding responsibilities to their own families and households.

Slave women, like most mothers, adored their babies, but the realities of their existence—a demanding or insensitive owner, long work hours, exhaustion, or poor health—interfered with the attention and care they could provide. Slave mothers and yeomen farm women had little free time or energy to nurture their young. Additional burdens fell on those mothers who had to raise their children without a husband present. In such cases, the support of other family members such as grandmothers or older children and friends must have been welcomed by overworked mothers. Few slave owners questioned the contradiction between the important role that the mother played during a child's early years and work demands which interfered with maternal responsibilities.

MOTHERHOOD AND CHILDREARING

Mothers were the principal caretakers of their children. White women received public encouragement for their responsibilities through maternal literature and public pronouncements acclaiming childrearing as women's sacred occupation. Typical of journalistic rhapsodizing was *The Magnolia,* a southern magazine for women that deemed motherhood the greatest profession on earth. "Who can estimate the power she exerts over the precious trust committed to her charge. How boundless her influence, how illimitable her sway; how irresistible the force of her instruction," noted one writer. Prescriptive literature celebrated mothers as the central figure in a child's upbringing. Few southern women ever questioned the accepted idea that they were the only parent fit to raise children. Fathers were busy with farm or plantation duties and apparently had little time or few nurturing skills to tend babies. Some men disdained the care of young children as an affront to their masculinity. And yet others assisted with childrearing, prescribing and administering medicine, lancing gums, imparting discipline, or relieving their wife when a sick child required round-the-clock attention.

Whether this domestic role provided women with a heightened sense of self-worth and power is open to question. As mothers and principal caretakers of their homes, women may have embraced their responsibilities with a heightened sense of dedication and found a degree of satisfaction. Some historians feel that this emphasis on domesticity encouraged women to believe in their roles as conservators and promoters of morality, roles they would take later into national reform movements. This appreciation may have enhanced their sense of self-worth. On the other hand, other scholars feel that such praise actually retarded women's desire to move into the public arena. By extolling domestic duties, men perhaps intended to prevent women from competing in the male world.

In farm families, a mother often delegated child-rearing responsibilities to older children so as to free herself for cooking or working in the fields. This experience also educated adolescents in practical child-rearing skills. In plantation families, slave children or maids tended to some of the duties of childrearing, but as a consequence white adolescents were left untrained in the complexities and demands of caring for a baby.

The majority of southern women breastfed their babies, contrary to mythical images that portrayed white babies suckling at the breasts of devoted black mammies. White women regarded breastfeeding as the most practical and healthiest means to feed a newborn. A mother also nursed her baby as an expression of maternal devotion and concern for its healthy future. Prescriptive literature supported her action. According to medical and maternal guidebooks, one of a mother's essential duties was to feed her baby, and such substitutes as wet nurses were regarded with a wary eye. Slave women generally fed their babies until they were one or two years old, perhaps a slightly longer weaning period than white children. (Many blacks have a lactose intolerance, ruling out cow's milk as an acceptable substitute.)

Supplemental baby food consisted of a mixture of bread, water, and molasses or sugar. As the infant aged, it might consume porridge or food chewed first by its mother.

Although few white women in the Old South willingly gave up suckling infants to black mammies, a sharing of maternal milk was not unusual. And feeding crossed racial lines. Childbirth often left women prostrate and in poor health, and some were too debilitated to nurse their babies. Some mothers had an inadequate milk supply or painful abscesses on their breasts. Mothers might die in childbirth, leaving a newborn without maternal sustenance. In such cases, a substitute feeder was essential for infants. On large plantations, finding a wet nurse to share milk was not too difficult because several slave women had probably given birth to babies recently and presumably were still nursing. In cities and towns, the situation was more problematic. White families often advertised for a wet nurse through the local newspaper, and some women earned money by sharing their milk. In rural areas, a farm wife might feed both her own and a neighbor's newborn; a sister might feed her infant nephew; and in rare but verified cases, a grandmother who had just delivered a baby might feed her grandchild. Sometimes strangers fed babies. One Tennessee woman, Virginia Shelton, who was traveling on a riverboat, noticed a motherless baby crying for sustenance, and she gave it milk from her breasts. It was also not unusual to have white women feeding black babies for the same reasons that black women sometimes nursed white babies. The most important consideration was to keep the infant alive during the most precarious time of life, giving whatever sustenance was required. Race was not an issue when a baby's life was at stake.

Bottle feeding was the least desirable means of feeding an infant, for bottles were not sanitary and fresh milk could be hard to find. Without refrigeration, bacteria proliferated in the bottles and caused diarrhea or other illnesses. In a few cases, an indulgent woman who was determined to regain her shapely figure or avoid the demands of a newborn altogether might find a mammy to suckle her new-born or resort to bottle feeding, but this was the exception. Nursing was one of the most important duties associated with rearing children.

Raising children involved years of commitment and endless energy. Bearing so many offspring prolonged the duties for southern women, and they often spent three decades or longer—from first pregnancy to the lingering problems of their children's adolescence—raising a family. Elite southern women gained a reputation as especially devoted and affectionate mothers, and perhaps they earned such accolades, thanks in part to the assistance of their domestic servants and their commitment to family. Wealthy southern mothers had more time to devote to their children than farm or slave women. Domestic servants allowed them more free time to read, write, and socialize, relieving them from the stresses of ceaseless maternal and domestic duties. Mrs. Tarry of North Carolina thanked her mother for lending her a slave woman, thereby preserving her energy and health. "I could ride out and never feel the least uneasiness about the children, for I knew she would take care of them," she wrote. Obviously the servant allowed her time to write letters as well. Privileged mothers could pick and choose the more enjoyable duties associated with childrearing. Slaves often performed the more tedious or less pleasurable tasks associated with babies, such as changing dirty diapers or entertaining a cranky infant, while mothers selected the more personally rewarding duties of breastfeeding and holding the baby when it was clean and happy.

The greatest worry facing both black and white mothers was the endless string of health problems associated with young children and the constant threat of an infant's death. The South deserved its reputation as an unhealthy place for all its residents, but infants suffered more than adults. Despite the immunities that newborns acquire naturally from their mothers, personal writings and medical statistics indicate that antebellum southern mothers had to be vigilant from the moment of their baby's birth. Census statistics in 1850 show that 17 percent of all deaths among whites occurred among children one year of age or younger and 38 percent to those five and under. Including black babies, these figures in 1860 were nearly 21 and 43 percent respectively. Such statistics alarmed physicians and mothers, but they had few proven means to combat high infant mortality other than attentive nursing. Considering the limitations of antebellum medicine and the usual failure of babies to respond positively to heroic treatment, it usually fell to parents to nurse and treat their youngsters. Mothers spent anxious years when their children were young, often sacrificing their own health and well-being to insure the lives of their offspring. Healthy babies were deemed cause for celebration, for the norm was to be ill. One Louisiana mother wrote that her children were well, despite the fact that one had an ear that was oozing, another had a sore throat, and a third was suffering from a fever. Apparently things could have been much worse.

Slave women had no choice but to tend to their own babies and sometimes relied on a conjurer or skilled older woman in the slave community for advice if an infant was sick. In desperate cases, a slave owner would call a physician to help an ill black baby. Slave mothers had more cause for worry, for according to the 1850 census, twice as many slave newborns died as white babies. Kenneth Kiple and Virginia Himmelsteib King in their medical study of blacks, *Another Dimension to the Black Diaspora*, suggest reasons for this frighteningly high mortality among slave babies, attributing many deaths to the poor health and diet of slave mothers and newborns. They suggest that a majority of slave infants were born with nutritional deficiencies. As noted earlier, slaves ate a monotonous and nutritionally deficient diet, heavy in carbohydrates and fats and low in calcium and iron. Babies inherited the deficiencies of their mothers. (Many poor white farm women ate no better, so these comments would apply to their children as well.) The quality of a mother's milk depended on her nutritional intake and gradually worsened during her childbearing years as each infant depleted her of stored nutrients. Since many blacks suffered from lactose intolerance, babies had to be weaned from breast milk to food and other liquids besides cow milk. Many slave children subsequently suffered from mild malnutrition, the usual symptoms of which were slight edema and pot bellies. The pudgy black youngsters seen on slave plantations were not necessarily well-fed ones, according to Kiple and King, but victims of poor nutrition. Malnutrition and low birth weight were medical problems not easily detectable or resolved by nineteenth-century medical knowledge. Most physicians lacked an awareness of preventive medicine. In addition, malnutrition made all slaves more susceptible to other diseases. Finally, not until later in the century did physicians learn the importance of incubating newborns. Slave mothers must have found it difficult to keep their infants warm when they had to be placed on the floor of damp cabins or on beds without adequate coverings.

Slave babies also suffered from diseases that typically affected newborns—measles, scarlet fever, cholera infantum, colic, whooping cough, and chicken pox. Slaves had natural immunities to some forms of malaria and to yellow fever, but they were more susceptible to pulmonary diseases like tuberculosis and pneumonia. Conditions in slave cabins were particularly dirty and damp. Not until the late antebellum period did agricultural reformers and some physicians initiate a campaign to improve living conditions for the South's slave population. Such reformers correctly understood the connection between good health and a clean living environment. Unfortunately, the campaign occurred at the same time that southerners were caught up in the cotton boom, and plantation profits often superseded concerns for better care of slaves.

Conditions in the slave quarters exacerbated ill health. Cabins, made from local materials such as logs, bricks, or stone, were simple structures, measuring from sixteen to twenty feet square, with a fireplace and door but often no window. The floor might be elevated, but just as likely was dirt. Keeping slave quarters clean and dry was impossible. Roofs leaked, animals wandered in, and lice, flies,

and mosquitoes were ever-present. Beds might be raised on frames, but many slaves slept on a mattress on the floor, with only a single blanket to cover them. And while slave communities fostered friendship and mutual support, close living exacerbated ill health. Contagious diseases spread quickly among a large population living in confined, damp quarters. That any slave, much less a newborn, remained healthy was a miracle.

Such conditions made it almost impossible for slave babies to escape illness. One of the most frightening of all newborn diseases was neonatal tetanus, reported to be far more common among slaves than whites. This form of tetanus occurred within the first two weeks of life, caused by bacteria infecting the umbilical cord. The affected infant displayed alarming symptoms including clenched fists, a rigid body and smile, and an inability to suckle, leading to death within a day or two. There was no effective treatment once symptoms occurred. According to Michael Johnson, sudden infant death syndrome (SIDS) was also more common among slave infants than white babies, with an estimated 82 percent of all cases affecting black babies. No one understood what caused an infant to die in its sleep, though owners sometimes accused the black mother of ignoring her child or rolling over and smothering it. Even today, doctors are still unsure what causes SIDS, but it has been suggested that nutritional deficiencies and overwork of the slave mother fostered the disease during the antebellum years.

For slightly older slave children, worms were a perpetual problem, as they were for whites. Usually shoes were worn only in winter, and hookworms could easily enter through the soles of the feet, especially when barefoot children walked in fields and gardens fertilized with human and animal fecal matter. Tapeworms were found in undercooked food or were spread by flies. For the malnourished child, worms could be fatal. Diarrhea was probably the most common health problem for all antebellum children. Water was frequently polluted, unlined latrines seeped into wells or streams, and unrefrigerated food could be tainted with bacteria. Rearing slave children was difficult for black mothers, for they were helpless against the ravages of disease, malnutrition, and ill health, especially considering the limited time they could give to each child.

White mothers often turned to maternal guidebooks for assistance in childrearing. Herb gardens provided necessary plants for homemade medicines, and a plantation medicine box usually stocked quinine, blue mass, calomel, laudanum, and perhaps arsenic for cleansing the system. Women nursing ill children relied on a combination of home cures, drugs, intuition, vigilance, and the assistance of a doctor. But physicians were not as valued in treating children as they were for attending deliveries. Many southern parents remained skeptical of doctors' abilities to cure their children and believed that death crossed the threshold when a physician entered the room. Doctors' heroic cures seemed unduly harsh for small constitutions, and much of what they tried was experimental or ineffective. Misidentifying and mistreating diseases was common. Maternal intuition often served children better than antebellum medical training.

Southern mothers had plenty of experience to guide them in caring for their sickly children, considering the frequency of illness among the many children they bore. They often made decisions about treating infants on their own, for their husbands might be absent or preoccupied. Mothers spent sleepless nights nursing sick children, perhaps aided by a kindly neighbor, domestic slave, or sympathetic husband. But when a child was ill, mothers assumed full responsibility and did not delegate nursing a sick youngster to a substitute.

White babies contracted most of the diseases that afflicted slave infants, though children born into elite families were less likely to suffer from diseases associated with filth, such as neonatal tetanus. Their houses were drier, brighter, and probably cleaner. Given the number of diseases that affected each child, southerners, except those living far from others, had acquired several immunities by the time they reached adulthood. The one disease that could be treated effectively during the antebellum period was smallpox.

Inoculations and vaccinations proved successful if administered properly, and southern mothers did not hesitate to have their infants treated against the dreaded disease.

Strangely, the medical experts of the day considered teething to be a grave childhood illness. Cultural or societal attitudes often affect perceptions of what a disease is, even when it has little to do with genuine pathology. Such was the case with teething, considered the most serious disease in a young child's life and lasting from approximately four months to two years of age, the time during which a child's teeth emerged. Because babies experienced diarrhea, high fevers, irritability, vomiting, and almost constant health problems, parents and doctors attributed all these illnesses to the most obvious change in the child's life—its emerging teeth. The "disease" demanded vigilance and action, and many young babies received quantities of calomel to cleanse their systems and relieve pressure, a periodic lancing of gums, and a variety of herbal remedies. Once teething passed, mothers breathed a sigh of relief that their child had survived the experience.

Few doctors understood the nature of contagious disease. Yet southern mothers displayed common sense in avoiding sickness, and they wisely kept a child at home if diseases like scarlet fever, whooping cough, or cholera were rumored to be in the vicinity. When yellow fever periodically hit such cities as Mobile or New Orleans, whites who could afford to leave fled the cities, leaving the poor behind. . . . The poor health of children was often a reason that southern families chose to migrate westward—and sometimes back home, if they found conditions to be worse than what they had left.

Babies were often sick throughout infancy or suffered prolonged and serious diseases that demanded enormous maternal sacrifices. An illness like whooping cough could last as long as six months. Rebecca Hall admitted that she scarcely slept at night when she nursed her three girls by herself, admitting "I am almost worn out in the cause." One child's illness could spread to every family member. Endless caretaking wore down the strongest of women.

With so many hardships to confront in insuring their infants' well-being, it becomes apparent that mothers could not always save their children. Many had to face the death of an infant. Grieving and learning to accept the death of a beloved child was a difficult but common experience for southern women. Some mothers spent later years recalling the birthdays of each child who succumbed. We know of their sorrow through the personal accounts of elite southern women, and undoubtedly the sentiments must have been similar for all mothers. Each departed child left an indelible mark. The death of a child is said to be the greatest loss that any parent can experience, and southern mothers became all too accustomed to grieving. The abundance of children in southern families did little to compensate for the suffering, nor did the commonness of infant mortality harden mothers to accept the inevitability of death. In fact, such bleak odds probably provided incentive for mothers to work long hours to insure the health of each child.

As personal correspondence and other sources indicate, infant illnesses and deaths were everyday occurrences in the antebellum South. Two cemeteries on Edisto Island, South Carolina, show a line of tiny gravestones belonging to two families that experienced eight and nine infant deaths, respectively. Caroline Mordecai Plunkett of North Carolina became an expert at nursing and grieving. She lost two children within three days; her husband died eight months later; she bore a baby three months after that, but the child lived only nine months. It is little wonder that Caroline spent her final years in an insane asylum. Another North Carolina family reported losing five infants to the same disease in a string of woeful years. Some women felt like giving up, like Sarah Screven, who mourned after her baby died, "I am a child of sorrow and never do I expect happiness on earth." "On the other hand, Lucy Shaw uttered a more typical reaction. She had lost two children and witnessed a friend bury four but nevertheless observed stoically, "It is strange how much we can bear and still live on and still feel an interest in things about us."

Southern mothers had no choice but to deal with their grief, which they did by expressing their feelings openly, writing about their sorrow, and sometimes by donning mourning clothes and anticipating the possibility that each sick child might die. Mothers relied on divine support and strength and eventually concluded that in God's ultimate wisdom, heaven would prove a kinder place for their child than a life of suffering on earth. Some believed that they would reunite with loved ones in heaven. Antebellum society permitted women to grieve openly, and many mothers did not hesitate to express their sorrow. They found strength in the support of their husbands, relatives, and friends, and especially from those women who also had experienced the death of a child.

Some privileged mothers depended on narcotics to drown their grief, and there was a close correlation between drug use among southern women and the sorrow associated with the death of a child. Many southern men drank alcohol; some southern women used drugs. Initially morphine or laudanum might have been taken innocently or only occasionally to get through a bad day, but this practice could turn into a destructive addiction. Obtaining opiates from a physician or apothecary was not difficult, and many plantation medicine boxes contained narcotics. Anne Cameron of North Carolina became addicted to morphine, opium, and laudanum as a result of her sorrow over the death of a young son, the ill health of another child, and her frequent bouts with malaria and headaches. She became so incapacitated that she was unable to perform her maternal duties, forcing her husband to deal with demanding family responsibilities and his wife's condition. Mary Chaplin, like several women, had a snuff habit which helped her endure her state of invalidism; it also affected her behavior and appearance. Whether slave women had access to narcotics is unknown, but the expense alone must have put them beyond reach. Some farm women smoked a pipe or chewed tobacco out of habit and pleasure, and a few elite women smoked small Cuban cigars. It is doubtful, however, that slave or white women enjoyed alcohol to the same degree that southern men did.

The complex combinations of children, stepchildren, and stepparents complicated motherhood for many women in the Old South. The death of a spouse, rather than divorce, was the most common reason for a white marriage ending. Men might lose two or three wives in childbirth; women who married older men might outlive a husband by two or three decades and remarry or remain single, depending on their economic circumstances and view of marriage. An existing family often regarded stepparents and stepsiblings as interlopers and accepted them with a measure of resentment. If a woman married a man with younger children, she might suffer ridicule and tension when she tried to nurture those children as her own. Such a situation was not an easy one, and women had to weigh the pros and cons before committing to marriage.

Slave mothers had other considerations, for many were single parents. While two-parent families were the norm in black communities, women were often forced to be the primary parent due to premarital pregnancy, rape, an "abroad" marriage, or because a partner had been sold or died. One slave woman overcame enormous odds to create a strong family, and she managed to live a remarkably independent life despite her status. Loren Schweninger relates the story of Sally, born around 1790 on the plantation of Charles Thomas, a wealthy Virginian. She was a field laborer, and at eighteen, suffered the sexual advances of a white man, probably Thomas's son. She bore a mulatto son in 1808 and another one a few years later. Her sons were automatically chattels despite the status and color of their father. When Thomas died in 1818, the slaves moved to Nashville with a new master. Sally received permission to hire out as a cleaning lady and to retain a portion of her earnings. She eventually rented her own home, converting the front room to a laundry. She built up a thriving business, and her sons found jobs as well. Sally saved her earnings, hoping to purchase freedom for her children. In 1827, she bore another mulatto son, this one fathered by a judge on the Tennessee Supreme Court. Two years later, Sally's oldest son was emancipated. Her second son escaped to the North, and shortly thereafter, Sally bought her third son's freedom. All three young men eventually prospered and became important members of their respective communities. The fact that Sally was not married, that her sons had white fathers, and that all three moved to other states would never have diminished for Sally the importance of her family. Her foremost duty was as mother to her children. Her sons remained devoted to their mother, writing and visiting her frequently.

Being a mother affected how a bondwoman functioned as a slave. Simply stated, they put their children first. Thus, it is easy to understand why few slave women ran away permanently and why antebellum slave women rarely participated in rebellions. Slave mothers could not abandon their children to seek freedom. Nor could they carry young children with them. Harriet Tubman, the famous Maryland fugitive slave who rescued between sixty and three hundred slaves (and at one point commanded a reward of $40,000 for her capture), probably would not have forayed bravely into the South so frequently had she borne any children. Slave women found other means to protest their oppression besides running away, for their children always commanded their untiring devotion.

QUESTIONS TO CONSIDER

1 Why were families so large, especially in the Old South? Why would McMillen state that "bearing an infant was a mixed blessing" for slave women? Describe the high risks to both mother and infant that were part of childbearing, and explain why those potential tragedies were far more frequent in the slave quarters.

2 Men seemed to want large families and fostered the concept that motherhood was the most important goal a woman could achieve. Why would southern men, especially slave owners, place such a high value on the birth of a child?

3 Describe the duties and responsibilities of pregnant women. Was there any knowledge of the importance

of prenatal care? Why would McMillen state that "expectant mothers spent their months of pregnancy in a state of anxiety"?

4 Describe the growing competition between midwives and male physicians. Who charged more, and who was more likely to attempt risky procedures on slave women? If you were a pregnant woman in the period covered by this selection, would you prefer that a midwife or a physician attend to you during childbirth? Explain your choice.

5 Why was childbirth an opportunity for white and slave women to share intimacies and to bond? About how long after the birth of the newborn were women expected to return to their normal duties? Given their grueling work in the field, how did slave women care for and nurse their babies?

6 Why do you think that the mortality rate for newborn slaves was twice as high as the figure for white babies? Describe the nutritional differences and the diseases bred by poor living conditions in the slave quarters.

PART SEVEN

The Nation Takes Shape

13 The Duel

JOSEPH J. ELLIS

Students of the past have long debated what determines the course of history. There are those who maintain that great "forces" shape the direction and composition of human societies; some even argue that people, individuals, are not important. There are others, however, who focus on the human side of the past, examining how the interaction of people and events dictates the course of subsequent events. From this view, human beings are not mere cogs in the engines of history; they can and do make a difference. Portrait of America *stresses the latter view of history. In the next two selections, the authors describe in human terms some major political and judicial developments in the young Republic, from the dawn of the nineteenth century to the turbulent 1820s.*

Let us pick up political events where Gordon S. Wood leaves off in his assessment of George Washington in selection 10. When John Adams replaced Washington as president in 1796, Federalist leaders were extremely apprehensive about the French Revolution and the anarchy and violence that seemed to characterize it. Might the French virus spread to America as it appeared to be spreading across Europe? Might a conspiracy already be under way in the United States to fan the flames of revolution, to unleash the American mob on Federalist leaders, to destroy the order and stability they had worked so hard to establish? Since 1793, when a Frenchman, Citizen Genêt, had tried to enlist American men and privateers for the French cause, the Federalists had feared revolution in their midst. Champions of a strong government to maintain order, apostles of elitist rule and the sanctity of private property, the Federalists soon equated the Republicans under Madison and Jefferson with revolution, chaos, and destruction. After all, did the Republicans not support the French? Did they not defend the mob here at home? Did they not call for more democracy in government (although many of their leaders paradoxically were southern slave owners)?

The harried Federalists barely fought off a Republican attempt to seize the government in 1796, when Adams defeated Jefferson by only three votes in the electoral college. Then, as though the Republican threat were not bad enough, trouble broke out with revolutionary France. In the notorious XYZ affair, French agents tried to extract a bribe from American representatives sent to negotiate about deteriorating Franco-American relations. Many Americans thought the nation's honor had been besmirched and demanded a war of revenge. In response, the Federalists undertook an undeclared sea war against France that lasted from 1798 to 1800. Using the war as a pretext to consolidate their power, bridle the Republicans, and prevent revolution in the United States, the Federalists passed the Alien and Sedition Acts. These, they declared, were necessary for the nation's security in the war with France.

The Alien Act severely restricted the rights and political influence of immigrants, who usually joined the Republicans after they were naturalized and who might be carrying the French virus. The Sedition Act made hostile criticism of Federalist policies punishable by fine and imprisonment. The Republicans, decrying such government censorship, launched a counterattack against Federalist "despotism." The Federalists were so discredited by the Alien and Sedition Acts, and so divided by an irreconcilable feud between Adams and Hamilton, that the Republicans were able to win the government in 1801. Their victory marked the decline and eventually the end of the Federalist party as a national political organization.

Jefferson liked to describe his rise to power as "the revolution of 1800." But was it really a revolution? True, the Republicans allowed the hated Alien and Sedition Acts to expire in 1801, reduced the residence requirement for naturalized citizenship from fourteen years to five so that America could again function as an "asylum" for "oppressed humanity," inaugurated a new fiscal policy of government frugality and efficiency, and strove to retire the national debt of $83 million in sixteen years. Jefferson also repudiated the idea of government by and for a political elite. Yet he and his top administrators were as educated, talented, and upper class as their Federalist predecessors. Moreover, while Jefferson embraced the laissez-faire principle that government is best which governs least, he found that reversing all Federalist commitments could cause confusion and consternation across the land. Therefore, he and his followers permitted the United States Bank to continue operating (it closed in 1811 when its charter ran out), and they maintained Federalist measures for refunding the national debt, stimulating American shipping, and assuming the states' Revolutionary War debts. Nor did Jefferson's "revolution of 1800" change the condition of America's enslaved blacks. As president, the author of the Declaration of Independence carefully avoided the subject of bondage.

"What is practicable," Jefferson said, "must often control what is pure theory." As Washington's secretary of state, Jefferson had demanded a strict construction of the Constitution, arguing that what was not specifically delegated to the federal government was reserved to the states. By that argument, he had opposed Secretary of the Treasury Alexander Hamilton's sweeping economic schemes. But when he became president and saw a chance to double the size of the United States by purchasing the Louisiana Territory, Jefferson abandoned strict construction and embraced the Federalist doctrine of "loose construction," for that was the only way he could justify the annexation of territory. As Jefferson proved, any president could stretch the Constitution in order to pursue an expansionist foreign policy—especially if his party controlled Congress. Indeed, later presidents did exactly that.

During Jefferson's presidency, two famous men, Alexander Hamilton and Aaron Burr, fought a duel that reveals much about Jefferson's America. In his award-winning new book, Founding Brothers,

Joseph J. Ellis tells the dramatic story of that duel, suggesting that the two principals were almost too alike ever to become friends. Intelligent, headstrong, and ambitious, Hamilton had helped build the Federalist party and, during Washington's presidency, devised an economic strategy that stabilized the economy of the new country. He had also manipulated behind the scenes to influence the presidential elections of both 1796 and 1800. Possessing many of the same qualities and flaws as Hamilton, Burr was a political chameleon who, as our story begins, was the controversial vice president of Thomas Jefferson. Both Hamilton and Burr were from New York and were veterans of many nasty political confrontations.

But political differences do not usually result in shots fired in anger on the dueling field. Ellis's compelling story raises many larger issues. One is the question of integrity: what kind of character moves our best leaders to put the interests of their country before their own political ambitions? Hamilton believed that Burr did not possess the quality of "character." Do you agree with Hamilton's assessment, or do you think that political motivation colored his feelings about Burr? The other issue involves the uniqueness of our country and the revolution that produced it. Revolutions in France and Russia, much like similar events in the Third World today, resulted in internal reprisals and bloody confrontations for power. What made the American experiment different? Perhaps part of the answer rests in the previous readings on Benjamin Franklin in selection 6 and George Washington in selection 10. These were "founding fathers" with both talent and character who sought stability after the Revolution and helped make the American experiment truly special.

GLOSSARY

ARNOLD, BENEDICT   After he killed Hamilton, Burr was compared to this Revolutionary War general, hero of the Canada and Saratoga campaigns, who turned traitor and earned the enmity of his countrymen.

CATILINE   A man who lacked virtue and whose treachery helped destroy the Roman Empire. Hamilton, when referring to Burr as a Catiline, was hurling the ultimate insult and branding him a threat to republican government.

CODE DUELLO   Defined the "etiquette" of dueling which, for example, allowed the person challenged (in this case Hamilton) the choice of weapons. These rules governing courtly violence by which two "gentlemen" settled questions of honor were quickly becoming illegal in most states, including New York.

HARTFORD CONVENTION   An assembly of New England states that discussed the possibility of secession during the War of 1812. If the death of Hamilton wounded the Federalist party and relegated it to only regional influence, the Hartford Convention delivered a mortal blow.

MORRIS, GOUVERNEUR   A Pennsylvania Federalist and friend of Hamilton who had earlier played a leading role at the Constitutional Convention and had served as minister to France. He delivered a moving funeral oration for his dead colleague at Trinity Church in New York.

PENDLETON, NATHANIEL   Hamilton's friend and second whose recollections of the duel are important in understanding the intentions and behavior of his soon-to-be-dead associate. The *code duello* authorized duelists to bring a second to make sure that the rules of the contest were equitably enforced.

VAN NESS, WILLIAM   Burr's close friend and colleague who served as his second on the fateful day of the duel.

The most succinct version of the story might go like this:

On the morning of July 11, 1804, Aaron Burr and Alexander Hamilton were rowed across the Hudson River in separate boats to a secluded spot near Weehawken, New Jersey. There, in accord with the customs of the *code duello*, they exchanged pistol shots at ten paces. Hamilton was struck on his right side and died the following day. Though unhurt, Burr found that his reputation suffered an equally fatal wound. In this, the most famous duel in American history, both participants were casualties.

While all the information in this version of the story is accurate, its admirable brevity creates some unfortunate historical casualties of its own. After all, if the duel between Burr and Hamilton was the most famous encounter of its kind in American history, we should be able to conjure up a mental image of this dramatic moment, a more richly textured picture of "The Duel." Only a fuller rendering will allow what was called "the interview at Weehawken" to assume its rightful place of primacy among such touted competitors as *Gunfight at the O.K. Corral* or the film classic *High Noon*. In matters of this sort, succinct summaries will simply not do. And so, in an effort to give this episode its requisite density of detail, to recover the scene in its full coloration, here is a more comprehensive version, which attempts to include all the available and indisputable evidence that survives.

Aaron Burr left his home on Richmond Hill near the southern end of Manhattan at first light on Wednesday, July 11, 1804. Although he slept that night on his couch and in his clothes, the vice president of the United States was a lifelong disciple of Lord Chesterfield's maxim that a gentleman was free to do anything he pleased as long as he did it with style. So Colonel Burr—the military title a proud

From *Founding Brothers* by Joseph J. Ellis, copyright © 2000 by Joseph J. Ellis. Used by permission of Alfred A. Knopf, a division of Random House, Inc.

emblem of his service in the American Revolution— was elegantly attired in a silklike suit (actually made of a fabric known as bombazine) and carried himself toward the barge on the bank of the Hudson River with the nonchalant air of a natural aristocrat strolling to an appointment with destiny.

His grandfather, the great theologian Jonathan Edwards, had once said that we were all depraved creatures, mere spiders hanging precariously over a never-ending fire. But Burr's entire life had been a sermon on the capacity of the sagacious spider to lift himself out of hellish difficulties and spin webs that trapped others. No one can be sure what was in Burr's mind as a single oarsman rowed him and William Van Ness, his devoted disciple and protégé, toward the New Jersey Palisades on the other side, but the judgment of posterity would be that Burr had finally trapped Hamilton in his diabolical web, and he was now moving in for the kill.

Meanwhile, just north of Richmond Hill, near present-day Wall Street, Hamilton was boarding a small skiff with two oarsmen, his physician, Dr. David Hosack, and his own loyal associate Nathaniel Pendleton. Like Burr, Hamilton was properly attired and also carried himself with a similar air of gentlemanly diffidence. He also carried a military title, thus outranking Burr with his honorary designation as "General Hamilton," based on his last appointment, that of inspector general of the New Army in 1799. At forty-nine, he was a year older than Burr and, like him, was a relatively short man—an inch taller, at five feet seven inches—with similarly small hands and feet, a somewhat delicate bone structure, and a truly distinctive head and face. He was called "the little lion of Federalism" because he was, in truth, little.

But the head was the place where God had seen fit to mark the two men as polar opposites. Burr had the dark and severe coloring of his Edwards ancestry, with black hair receding from the forehead and dark brown, almost black, eyes that suggested a cross between an eagle and a raven. Hamilton had a light peaches and cream complexion with violet-blue eyes and auburn-red hair, all of which came together to suggest an animated beam of light to Burr's somewhat

John Trumbull's painting captures the proud and intense Alexander Hamilton who, as Washington's secretary of the treasury, established brilliant programs that stabilized the infant nation's economy. He became the leader of the Federalist party until Aaron Burr abruptly ended his life in a duel. (© National Portrait Gallery, Smithsonian Institution/Art Resource, NY)

stationary shadow. Whereas Burr's overall demeanor seemed subdued, as if the compressed energies of New England Puritanism were coiled up inside him, waiting for the opportunity to explode. Hamilton conveyed kinetic energy incessantly expressing itself in bursts of conspicuous brilliance.

Their respective genealogies also created temperamental and stylistic contrasts. Unlike Burr's distinguished bloodline, which gave his aristocratic bearing its roots and biological rationale, Hamilton's more dashing and consistently audacious style developed as a willful personal wager against the odds of his impoverished origins. John Adams, who despised Hamilton, once referred to him as "the bastard brat of a Scotch pedlar." While intended as a libelous description, Adams's choice of words was literally correct.

Hamilton had been born on the West Indian island of Nevis, the illegitimate son of a down-on-her-luck beauty of French extraction and a hard-drinking Scottish merchant with a flair for bankruptcy. In part because of his undistinguished origins, Hamilton always seemed compelled to be proving himself; he needed to impress his superiors with his own superiority. Whether he was leading an infantry assault against an entrenched British strong point at Yorktown—first over the parapet in a desperate bayonet charge—or imposing his own visionary fiscal program for the new nation on a reluctant federal government, Hamilton tended to regard worldly problems as personal challenges, and therefore as fixed objects against which he could perform his own isometric exercises, which usually took the form of ostentatious acts of gallantry. Though he had not sought out the impending duel with Burr, there was nothing in Hamilton's lifelong pattern that would permit a self-consciously bland and supremely triumphant refusal of the challenge. He was moving across the nearly calm waters of the Hudson toward Weehawken, then, because he did not believe he could afford to decline Burr's invitation.

We actually know a good deal more about the thoughts in Hamilton's mind at this propitious moment. The previous evening he had drafted a personal statement, which he enclosed with his last will and testament, declaring that he had sincerely hoped to avoid the interview. Moreover, he claimed to feel "no *ill-will* to Col. Burr, distinct from political opposition, which, as I trust, has proceeded from pure and upright motives." What's more, he had decided to expose himself to Burr's fire without retaliating: "I have resolved, if our interview is conducted in the usual manner, and it pleases God to give me the opportunity, to *reserve* and *throw away* my first fire, and I have thoughts even of reserving my second fire—and thus giving a double opportunity to Col. Burr to pause and to reflect." He did not think of this course of action as suicidal, but as another gallant gamble of the sort he was accustomed to winning.

The usual description of the duel's location—the plains of Weehawken—is misleading. Indeed, if one were to retrace the Burr-Hamilton route across the Hudson and land just upstream from the modern-day Lincoln Tunnel, one would come face-to-face with a sheer cliff 150 feet high. Anyone attempting to scale these heights would hardly be capable of fighting a duel upon arrival at the top. The actual site of the duel was a narrow ledge, about ten feet wide and forty feet long, located only twenty feet above the water. It was a popular spot for duels precisely because of its relative isolation and inaccessibility. By prearranged agreement, the Burr party arrived first, just before 7:00 a.m., and began clearing away the incidental brush and rocks on the ledge.

Hamilton's party arrived shortly thereafter, and the two seconds, Van Ness for Burr and Pendleton for Hamilton, conferred to review the agreed-upon rules of the interview. It was called an "interview" because dueling was illegal in many states, including New York. Therefore, in addition to the established etiquette of the *code duello,* veteran duelists had developed an elaborately elusive vocabulary, what we would now call the "language of deniability," so that all participants could subsequently claim ignorance if ever brought to court. None of the oarsmen, for example, was permitted on the ledge to witness the exchange of fire. The physician, David Hosack, was also required to turn his back to the proceedings.

Because Hamilton had been challenged, he had the choice of weapons. He had selected a custom-made pair of highly decorated pistols owned by his wealthy brother-in-law, John Church. Apart from their ornate appearance, the weapons were distinctive for two reasons. First, they had been used in two previous duels involving the participants: once, in 1799, when Church had shot a button off Burr's coat; then, in 1801, when Hamilton's eldest son, Philip, had been fatally wounded defending his father's honor only a few yards from the site at Weehawken. Second, they also contained a concealed device that set a hair-trigger. Without the hair-trigger, the weapon required twenty pounds of pressure to fire. With the hair-trigger, only one pound of pressure was needed. While Hamilton knew about the hair-triggers, Burr almost certainly did not.

After Pendleton and Van Ness loaded the pistols, which were smoothbore and took a quite large .54-caliber ball, Pendleton whispered to Hamilton, "Should I set the hair-trigger?" Hamilton responded: "Not this time." As they prepared to take their

This popular image of the infamous duel at Weehawken circulated throughout the country and helped picture Burr as a murderer. The one-ounce ball that struck Hamilton created a two-inch hole *that caused dreadful damage to his rib cage, liver, diaphragm, and vertebra. Joseph Ellis concludes: "Given the limits of medical science then, there was no hope." (Corbis/Bettmann)*

designated places, then, both men were armed with extremely powerful but extremely erratic weapons. If struck in a vital spot by the oversized ball at such close range, the chances of a serious or mortal injury were high. But the inherent inaccuracy of a projectile emerging from a smoothbore barrel, plus the potent jerk required to release the cocked hammer, ignite the powder, and then send the ball toward its target, meant that in this duel, as in most duels of that time, neither party was likely to be hurt badly, if at all.

Burr and Hamilton then met in the middle to receive their final instructions. Hamilton, again because he was the challenged party, had the choice of position. He selected the upstream, or north, side, a poor choice because the morning sun and its reflection off the river would be in his face. The required ten paces between contestants put them at the extreme ends of the ledge. It was agreed that when both principals were ready, Pendleton would say, "Present"; then each man would be free to raise and

fire his weapon. If one man fired before the other, the non-firer's second would say, "One, two, three, fire." If he had not fired by the end of the count, he lost his turn. At that point, or if both parties had fired and missed, there would be a conference to decide if another round was required or if both sides agreed that the obligations of honor had been met.

Upon reaching his designated location, just before the final command, Hamilton requested a brief delay. He pulled his eyeglasses out of his breast pocket, adjusted them, then squinted into the glare, raised his pistol, sighted down the barrel at several imaginary targets, then pronounced himself ready. Burr waited with patience and composure through this delay. Not only is there no evidence that he had any foreknowledge of Hamilton's declared intention to reserve or waste his first shot, but Hamilton's behavior at this penultimate moment certainly suggested more harmful intentions. Why he would don his eyeglasses if he did not plan to shoot at Burr remains a mystery.

What happened next is an even greater mystery. In fact, the contradictory versions of the next four to five seconds of the duel might serve as evidence for the postmodern contention that no such thing as objective truth exists, that historic reality is an inherently enigmatic and endlessly negotiable bundle of free-floating perceptions. For our story to proceed along the indisputable lines established at the start, we must skip over the most dramatic moment, then return to it later, after the final pieces of the narrative are in place.

Two shots had rung out and Hamilton had just been hit. The one-ounce ball had struck him on the right side, making a hole two inches in diameter about four inches above his hip. The projectile fractured his rib cage, ricocheted off the rib and up through his liver and diaphragm, then splintered the second lumbar vertebra, where it lodged. Even with all the benefits of modern medical science, the internal damage would have made Hamilton a likely fatality, most certainly a lifetime cripple. Given the limitations of medical science available then, there was no hope. Hamilton himself recognized his own condition almost immediately. When Dr. Hosack rushed forward to examine him, Hamilton calmly declared, "This is a mortal wound, Doctor," then lapsed into unconsciousness.

Meanwhile, Burr seemed surprised and regretful at the outcome of his shot. He started toward the fallen Hamilton, but Van Ness stopped him and ushered him away from the scene and toward his boat, all the while shielding Burr behind an umbrella so that—the deniability motive again—the members of Hamilton's party could claim in some prospective court that they had never seen him. Halfway down the path toward the river, Burr stopped and insisted on going back. "I must go & speak to him," he pleaded. But Van Ness refused to comply and headed Burr into his barge and back across the river to New York.

Hosack half-expected Hamilton to die on the spot. After a few minutes of ministrations, however, it was clear that the unconscious Hamilton was breathing regularly, so they carried him down to the river. On the trip back, Hamilton recovered consciousness for a time and muttered to Hosack, "Pendleton knows I did not mean to fire at Colonel Burr the first time." When one of the oarsmen tried to move Hamilton's pistol, which lay on the seat, Hamilton warned him, "Take care of that pistol; it is undischarged and still cocked; it may go off and do harm," clearly indicating that Hamilton himself did not seem to realize the weapon had been fired. Upon arrival on the New York side, he was carried to the nearby home of James Bayard, a longtime friend and political disciple, where Hosack administered liberal doses of laudanum and waited for the end. Hamilton died at two o'clock on the afternoon of July 12, 1804, surrounded by the Episcopal bishop of New York, Benjamin Moore, as well as by David Hosack, Hamilton's wife, Elizabeth, and their seven surviving children.

The funeral two days later was an extravaganza of mourning. The mahogany coffin was trailed by Hamilton's gray horse, with his boots and spurs reversed astride the empty saddle. Behind it marched his widow and children, the political and legal leaders of the city, the students and faculty of Columbia College, bank presidents, army and navy officers, local clergy and foreign dignitaries, followed by several hundred ordinary citizens. Gouverneur Morris, an old family friend and Federalist colleague, delivered the funeral oration in an overflowing Trinity Church.

The overwhelming popular consensus was that Burr had murdered Hamilton in cold blood. The anti-Burr character of the newspaper stories fed the popular frenzy with concocted claims (for example, Burr had worn a suit, specially prepared for the duel, made of material that could deflect bullets) and melodramatic fabrications (for example, while Hamilton's widow and children shed tears over his dead body, Burr and his followers drank toasts to Hamilton's death in the local tavern, Burr only expressing regret that he had not shot him in the heart). A wax replication of the duel depicted Hamilton being shot by Burr and several hidden accomplices from ambush. The sign beneath the wax version read:

O Burr, O Burr, what has thou done?
Thou has shooted dead great Hamilton.
You hid behind a bunch of thistle,
And shooted him dead with a great hoss pistol.

With indictments pending against him for both dueling and murder, with newspaper editors comparing him to Benedict Arnold as the new exemplar of treachery, with ministers making his behavior the centerpiece for sermons against dueling as a barbaric throwback to medieval notions of justice, Burr fled the city in disgrace, not stopping until he reached Georgia.

So there you have it: Hamilton safely buried and assuming legendary proportions as a martyr; Burr slipping out of town, eventually headed toward bizarre adventures in the American West, but already consigned to political oblivion. This seems the most appropriate closing scene in our attempted recovery of "The Duel" as a famous and eminently visual story.

The missing ingredient in the story, of course, is the four- or five-second interval when the shots were actually fired. Postponing the recovery of this most crucial moment was not only unavoidable—there is no agreed-upon version to recover—but also matches the historical timing of the debate that generated the only evidence on which any narrative must be based. Which is to say that, in the wake of the actual duel, there was another duel of words between witnesses to the event, chiefly Pendleton and Van Ness, and then the inevitable collection of pro-Hamilton and pro-Burr advocates who filled up the newspapers and pamphlets of the day with corroborating testimony for their own conflicting versions.

But before the after-action accounts of the duel degenerated into a duel of its own, the only two eyewitnesses, Pendleton and Van Ness, published a "Joint Statement." Its chief purpose was to claim that both principals had conducted themselves in accord with the *code duello,* so that even though the practice of dueling was illegal, Burr and Hamilton had behaved according to the higher law of honor appropriate for proper gentlemen. Along the way to that principled point, however, Pendleton and Van Ness agreed on several significant particulars worthy of notice because of the light they shed on the looming disagreement over what, in fact, had happened.

First, Pendleton and Van Ness agreed that both principals fired their weapons. There were two shots, not one. This was an important fact to establish, because several published accounts of the duel by friends of Hamilton, undoubtedly influenced by various versions of his preduel pledge not to fire at Burr, had preemptively concluded that Hamilton had withheld his fire; that is, had not fired at all. Since the sound of the gunfire was audible to Hosack and the oarsmen, even though they did not see the exchange, no misrepresentation or falsification of this elemental point was feasible anyway, unless the two shots occurred simultaneously. And Pendleton and Van Ness agreed that they did not.

This led to the second and most intriguing agreement—namely, that an interval lasting "a few seconds" occurred between shots. Just how many seconds they could not agree on. They did concur, however, that a discernible gap of time separated the two shots. One of the two principals had fired first; the other had paused for a discreet and noticeable interval, and then he had fired. The two shots had not gone off instantaneously.

It is not easy to square what was to become the Hamiltonian version of the duel with this agreed-upon point. The crucial ingredient in the Hamiltonian account was that Burr fired first. If one began with the assumption, as Pendleton's and Hamilton's disciples insisted one should, that Hamilton arrived at Weehawken with a firm resolve not to fire at Burr, then it followed logically that Hamilton could not have fired first. Instead, Burr fired while Hamilton's pistol was still raised in the air. The impact of Burr's round then allegedly produced an involuntary jerk on Hamilton's trigger finger, which sent a round sailing harmlessly above Burr and into the trees. Van Ness claimed to have revisited the ledge the following day and found the severed branch of a cedar tree about twelve feet high and four feet to the side of where Burr had stood. This rendition of the story was also compatible with Hamilton's remark in the boat afterward, when he seemed to think his pistol was still loaded. He obviously had not realized that Burr's shot had caused an accidental firing of his own weapon. On the other hand, if one accepted the Hamiltonian version of the exchange, how could one explain the interval between the shots? In the Hamiltonian account, the exchange would have been nearly instantaneous.

Although the Burr version of what occurred presents some problems of its own, it is more compatible with the agreed-upon timing of the shots. According to Van Ness, Hamilton took aim at Burr and fired first, but missed. Burr then delayed his shot for "four or five seconds," waiting for the smoke to clear from around Hamilton and also waiting for Pendleton to begin the count—"One, two, three, fire." But Pendleton's attention had been fixed on his own chief and he apparently had lacked the wherewithal to say anything in this drawn-out moment of the drama. Burr then took it upon himself to fire rather than lose his shot. Hamilton fell instantly. Van Ness was adamant about the sequence of events: "It is agree'd I believe, by all who were within hearing, but particularly attested by Doctr. Hossack [*sic*], that several seconds intervened between the two discharges; and it is also agree'd that Gen. H. fell *instantly* on Mr. B's firing, which contradicts the idea that Mr. B. fired first." Van Ness went on to provide additional detail about Burr's behavior during the dramatic interval.

On the point of the first firing . . . I was never more confident of any matter subject to the examination of my senses. If any doubt had ever existed it would have been removed by the following circumstances: 1st When Genl. H fired I observed a jar or slight motion in Mr. B's body, from which I supposed he was struck; but seeing him immediately afterwards standing firm at his station—I concluded the wound could not be serious. Under the impression still, however, that he was wounded, as soon as I had the opportunity I enquired where he was struck?—and after explaining to him the reason of my impression, he

informed me that his foot had got upon a stone or piece of wood which gave him pain and had sprained his Ancle.

In other words, Burr's instinctive reaction to Hamilton's shot was a discernible flinch and an impulsive physical jerk that Burr, seeking afterward to emphasize his composure, blamed on a stone or piece of wood at his feet.

While the palpable detail of this version has the ring of truth, and while the contours of the Burr story align themselves more comfortably with the timing of the shots, two pieces of evidence do not fit. First, how does one explain Hamilton's obviously sincere conviction, delivered to Hosack and Pendleton in the boat afterward, that he had never fired his pistol? And second, if Hamilton did fire at Burr, how does one account for the severed branch so high above and off to the side of Burr's position?

There is a plausible and quite persuasive answer to the second question, which will then lead us to a plausible but more speculative answer to the first. The key insight, possessing the potential to unlock the mystery produced by the contradictory versions of what happened during the duel, is that both sides constructed their explanations around self-serving and misguided assumptions. The Hamilton side needed to claim that their fallen chief was a martyr who had arrived at Weehawken fully intending to expose himself to Burr's fire without shooting back. The Burr side needed to claim that their hero had behaved honorably, in accord with the principles of the *code duello,* and, after exposing his own life to Hamilton's pistol, had responded in kind but with better aim. The Hamiltonian story required a distortion in the sequence of the exchange in order to preserve Hamilton's posthumous reputation. The Burr story required a distortion of Hamilton's honorable intentions in order to justify Burr's fatal response. Both versions misrepresent what, in all likelihood, really happened.

Hamilton did fire his weapon intentionally, and he fired first. But he aimed to miss Burr, sending his ball into the tree above and behind Burr's location. In so doing, he did not withhold his shot, but he did waste it, thereby honoring his preduel pledge. Meanwhile, Burr, who did not know about the pledge, did know that a projectile from Hamilton's gun had whizzed past him and crashed into the tree to his rear. According to the principles of the *code duello*, Burr was perfectly justified in taking deadly aim at Hamilton and firing to kill.

But did he? This is not a question we can resolve beyond a reasonable doubt. In that sense the secret is locked forever in the vast recesses of Burr's famously enigmatic mind at that most pregnant moment. But consider the following pieces of circumstantial evidence: By killing Hamilton, Burr had nothing to gain and everything to lose, as he almost certainly knew at the time and as subsequent events confirmed quite conclusively; Burr's initial reaction to Hamilton's collapse, as described by both Pendleton and Van Ness, was apparent surprise and regret, followed soon thereafter by an urge to speak with the wounded Hamilton; moreover, in the latter stages of the preduel negotiations, when Hamilton's side proposed that David Hosack serve as physician for both parties, Burr had concurred that one doctor was sufficient, then added, "even that unnecessary"; finally, when duelists wished to graze or wound their antagonist superficially, the most popular targets were the hips and legs; Burr's ball missed being a mere flesh wound on the hip by only two or three inches, the damage to vital organs resulting from the ricochet off Hamilton's rib.

In the end, we can never know for sure. And it is perfectly possible that Burr's smoldering hatred for Hamilton had reached such intensity that, once he had his tormentor standing helplessly in his sights, no rational calculation of his own best interests was operative at all. What is virtually certain, and most compatible with all the available evidence, is that Hamilton fired first and purposely missed. The only plausible explanation for his remark in the boat about the pistol still being loaded is that he was semiconscious, in shock, and did not know what he was saying. Or, less likely, that Pendleton and Hosack made it up to support their version of the story. What is possible, but beyond the reach of the

available evidence, is that Burr really missed his target, too, that his own fatal shot, in fact, was accidental. Indeed, one of the most disarming features of the Burr version—a feature that enhances its overall credibility—is that it made Burr's shot a more deliberate and premeditated act. (Why emphasize the interval if one's intention was to diminish Burr's culpability?) In those few but fateful seconds, the thoughts racing through Burr's head would provide the ultimate answer to all questions about his character. But they are, like most of Burr's deepest thoughts, lost forever.

Our intense focus on what happened on that ledge beneath the plains of Weehawken makes eminent historical sense, for the elemental reason that the Hamilton version of the story has dominated the history books, and it is most probably wrong. But by straining to recover the factual ingredients in the story, we have inadvertently ignored the most obvious question—namely, what were these two prominent American statesmen doing on the ledge in the first place? Granted, they were there because Burr challenged Hamilton, and Hamilton concluded he could not refuse the challenge without staining his honor. But what had Hamilton done to so enrage Burr? And what was at stake for both men that was worth risking so much?

The short answer is that, just as there was a duel of words after the actual duel—won by Hamilton's advocates—there was also a duel of words beforehand, which Burr won with equivalent decisiveness. The somewhat longer answer is that the exchange of words that preceded the exchange of shots was itself merely a culmination of long-standing personal animosity and political disagreement that emerged naturally, in retrospect almost inevitably, out of the supercharged political culture of the early republic.

In the verbal exchanges before the duel, there can be no question that Burr fired first. On June 18, 1804, he called Hamilton's attention to a letter published almost two months earlier in the *Albany Register* in which the author, Dr. Charles Cooper, recalled a harangue Hamilton had delivered against Burr the preceding February. Burr was then running for governor of New York and Hamilton had attacked his qualifications. Exactly what Hamilton said was not reported in Cooper's letter, but it concluded with the following statement: "I could detail to you a still more despicable opinion which General HAMILTON has expressed of Mr. BURR." The offensive word was *despicable*. Burr wanted Hamilton to explain or disavow the word: "You might perceive, Sir, the necessity of a prompt and unqualified acknowledgment or denial of the use of any expressions which could warrant the assertions of Dr. Cooper."

Knowing as we do that Burr's request triggered a chain reaction that eventually produced the fatal explosion at Weehawken, it is instructive to note that neither Cooper's letter nor Burr's request mentioned any specific or clearly libelous statement by Hamilton. To be sure, *despicable* is hardly a compliment. But precisely what it referred to, or what Hamilton allegedly said about Burr, is unidentified. The core of the complaint was hollow. Therefore, all Hamilton had to do at this propitious moment was deny having said anything that could possibly fit that description, then express his personal regret that such slanderous insinuations had been attributed to him in the press. Burr would have had little choice but to accept his explanation.

Hamilton, however, chose to pursue another course. In effect, he used the inherent ambiguity of the offensive statement to evade any direct response to Burr. He could not, he explained, "without manifest impropriety, make the avowal or disavowal you seem to think necessary." What's more, the crucial word "admits of infinite shades, from the very light to very dark. How am I to judge of the degree intended?" After delivering a brief lecture on the vagaries of grammar and syntax, calculated to irritate Burr, Hamilton went on the offensive. He felt obliged to object "on principle, to consent to be interrogated as to the justness of *inferences,* which may be drawn by *others,* from whatever I have said of a political opponent in the course of a fifteen year competition." Burr's own letter, therefore, was a

gross insult in its arrogant insistence "upon a basis so vague as that which you have adopted." Hamilton was certain that, once Burr recovered his wits and sense, "you will see the matter in the same light as me." If not, then "I can only regret the circumstances, and must abide the consequences." If Burr's intention was to threaten him with the possibility of a duel, Hamilton was not disposed to submit passively to such threats. He would issue his own.

Hamilton's fate was effectively sealed once he sent this letter. Not only did he miss the opportunity to disown the offensive characterization of Burr; he raised the rhetorical stakes with his dismissive tone and gratuitously defiant counterthreat. Burr's response was incisively curt: "having Considered it attentively," he wrote, "I regret to find in it nothing of that sincerity and delicacy which you profess to Value." Then he raised the verbal game to yet a higher level of insult: "I relied with unsuspecting faith that from the frankness of a Soldier and the Candor of a gentleman I might expect an ingenuous declaration." But such expectations were obviously too much for such a duplicitous character as Hamilton, who lacked "the Spirit to Maintain or the Magnanimity to retract" his own words.

Moreover, Hamilton's complaint—that he could hardly be expected to remember everything he had said over "the course of a fifteen year competition"—inadvertently opened up a whole new and much larger field of conflict. In his instructions to Van Ness, who had become his designated representative in the exchange, Burr explained that the Cooper letter was merely the most recent libel against him by Hamilton. While Burr claimed that he had always restrained himself when criticized by his political enemies, "in regard of Mr. H there has been no reciprocity—for several years his name has been lent to the support of Slanders." Two years earlier, in fact, Burr had claimed to have confronted Hamilton with a personal complaint about incessant vilifications of his character, and Hamilton had acknowledged his indiscretion. Despite the apology and apparent promise to stop, Hamilton had then resumed his back-stabbing campaign. According to

Burr, the immediate incident only proved that Hamilton's libelous ways were incorrigible. Now, however, "these things must have an end."

As a result, the form of satisfaction Burr now demanded expanded beyond one single utterance reported in an Albany newspaper. Van Ness relayed the new terms on June 25, 1804: "Col: Burr required a General disavowal of any intention on the part of Genl Hamilton in his various conversations to convey impressions derogatory to the honor of M. Burr." Burr was now demanding a general apology for all past indiscretions. He acknowledged that this represented an escalation, but given Hamilton's arrogant evasiveness, "more will now be required than would have been asked at first." . . .

The answer, then, to the salient question—What were these two prominent American statesmen doing on that ledge beneath the plains of Weehawken?—is reasonably clear. Burr was there because Hamilton had been libeling him throughout their crisscrossing careers in public life. Despite earlier promises to cease this practice, Hamilton had persisted. Burr's patience had simply worn out.

Hamilton was there because he could not honestly deny Burr's charges, which he sincerely believed captured the essence of the man's character. What's more, Hamilton also believed, as he put it, that his own "ability to be in future useful, whether in resisting mischief or effecting good, in those crises of public affairs, which seem likely to happen, would probably be inseparable from a conformity with public prejudice in this particular." In other words, if he did not answer Burr's challenge, he would be repudiating his well-known convictions, and in so doing, he would lose the respect of those political colleagues on whom his reputation depended. This would be tantamount to retiring from public life. And he was not prepared to do that. If Burr went to Weehawken out of frustration, Hamilton went out of a combination of ambition and insecurity.

What did it mean? For those at the time it meant that Hamilton became a martyr to the dying cause of Federalism and Burr became the most despised

This John Vanderlyn painting portrays Aaron Burr who, with a single shot, killed both Alexander Hamilton and his own promising political career. The artist captures Burr's dark eyes, which "suggested a cross between an eagle and a raven." Like Hamilton, Burr was "ambitious, energetic," and an enormous risk taker. ("Aaron Burr" by John Vanderlyn)

national leader since Benedict Arnold. Indeed, less than a year after the duel, Burr made secret contact with British officials for the purpose of seizing some substantial portion of the trans-Mississippi territory and placing it under British control, presumably with Burr himself as governor. Perhaps Burr reasoned that, since he was being treated as a new Benedict Arnold, he might as well enjoy the fruits of a similar treason.

Meanwhile, clergymen, college presidents, and other self-appointed spokesmen for communal standards of morality seized upon the Burr-Hamilton encounter to launch a crusade against dueling throughout most of the northern states. What had once seemed an honorable if illegal contest of wills, bathed in a mist of aristocratic glamour and clad in the armor of medieval chivalry, came to be regarded as a patho-logical ritual in which self-proclaimed gentlemen shot each other in juvenile displays of their mutual insecurity. Though the practice of dueling survived in the South, and in its more democratic blaze-away version on the frontier of the West, the stigma associated with the Burr-Hamilton duel put the *code duello* on the defensive as a national institution. Not that it would ever die out completely, drawing as it did on irrational urges whose potency defies civilized sanctions, always flourishing in border regions, criminal underworlds, and ghetto communities where the authority of the law lacks credibility. Nevertheless, the Burr-Hamilton duel helped turn the tide against the practice of dueling by providing a focal point for its critics and serving as a dramatic object lesson of its self-destructive character. One of the reasons the Burr-Hamilton duel became legendary as the most famous duel in American history is its cautionary role as the most memorable example of how not to do it.

The chief reasons, however, for its legendary status, and the main reason why we can call it "The Duel" without much fear of being misunderstood, is the relative prominence of the two participants. Burr was the second-ranking official in the federal government. Hamilton was, after George Washington, the most powerful figure in the Federalist party and, his advocates would have added, the intellectual well-spring for all the political energy that Washington merely symbolized. Their fatal encounter represented a momentary breakdown in the dominant pattern of nonviolent conflict within the American revolutionary generation.

In the wake of other national movements—the French, Russian, and Chinese revolutions, as well as the multiple movements for national independence in Africa, Asia, and Latin America—the leadership class of the successful revolution proceeded to decimate itself in bloody reprisals that frequently assumed genocidal proportions. But the conflict within the American revolutionary generation remained a passionate yet bloodless affair in which the energies released by national independence did not devour its own children. The Burr-Hamilton duel represented the singular exception to this rule. Perhaps this is what Henry Adams had in mind when, in his inimitable style, he described the moment at Weehawken with its "accessories of summer-morning sunlight on rocky and wooded heights, tranquil river, and distant sky, and behind [it] all . . . moral gloom, double treason, and political despair," calling it "the most dramatic moment in the early politics of the Union." . . .

But that was only half the story. For the Federalist leaders in New England were interested in recruiting Burr as part of a larger scheme that aimed at nothing less than the dismemberment of the American republic. (This was really what Henry Adams was referring to by the phrase "the most dramatic moment in the early politics of the Union.") Their plan envisioned the secession of New England in the wake of Jefferson's reelection and the simultaneous capture of New York, which would then join the secessionist movement to create a Federalist-controlled confederacy of northern states. Burr, true to form, refused to make any promises to deliver New York to the secessionists, but he also would not repudiate the conspiracy.

Hamilton was aware of the Federalist plot, which was no half-baked scheme hatched by marginal figures, involving as it did several Federalist senators from New England and Timothy Pickering, the former secretary of state. "I will here express but one sentiment," Hamilton warned his Federalist colleagues, "which is, the Dismemberment of our Empire will be a clear sacrifice . . . without any counterballancing good." When apprised that the leading New England Federalists were waiting to hear that their old chief was committed to the secessionist plot, Hamilton made clear his opposition: "Tell them from ME, at MY request, for God's sake, to cease these conversations and threatenings about a separation of the Union. It must hang together as long as it can be made to." The last letter that Hamilton ever wrote, composed the night before the duel, was devoted to squelching the still-lingering

Federalist fantasies of a separate northeastern confederation, a dream that refused to die until the moribund effort at the Hartford Convention in 1815 exposed it as a fiasco.

What Hamilton seemed to see in Burr, then, was a man very much like himself in several respects: ambitious, energetic, possessing an instinctive strategic antenna and a willingness to take political risks. Hamilton understood the potency of Burr's influence because he felt those same personal qualities throbbing away inside himself. Both men also shared a keen sense of the highly fluid and still-fragile character of the recently launched American republic. The hyperbolic tone of Hamilton's anti-Burr comments derived not so much from intense personal dislike *per se* as from his intense fear that the precarious condition of the infant nation rendered it so vulnerable to Burr's considerable talents. Burr embodied Hamilton's daring and energy run amok in a political culture still groping for its stable shape.

The kernel of truth in Hamilton's distinction between personal and political criticism of Burr resides here. In a sense it was an accurate statement of Hamilton's assessment. Burr's reputation as a notorious womanizer or as a lavish spender who always managed to stay one step ahead of his creditors did not trouble Hamilton. What did worry him to no end was the ominous fit between Burr's political skills and the opportunities for mischief so clearly available in a nation whose laws and institutions were still congealing.

The problem with Hamilton's distinction, however, was that the putative barrier between personal and political criticism, or private and public behavior, kept getting overwhelmed by real choices. Personal character was essential in order to resist public temptations. In Burr's case, for example, the decision to support or betray Jefferson in 1801; or to conspire with Federalists promoting a northern secession in 1804; or, a few years later, to detach the American Southwest from the United States. Character counted in each of these choices, because the temptations being served up by the

political conditions in this formative phase of the American republic put the moral fiber of national leadership to a true test.

It was Burr's unique distinction, at least as Hamilton saw it, to fail every such test. Whereas no one else in the revolutionary generation wanted the role of Catiline, Burr seemed to be auditioning for the part at every opportunity. To put it somewhat differently, if the dispute between Burr and Hamilton had been settled in the courts rather than on the dueling grounds, and if one admitted the legal principle that truth constituted a legitimate defense against charges of libel (a principle, intriguingly, that Hamilton insisted on in the last case he ever argued), Hamilton would almost certainly have won.

It is difficult for us to fathom fully the threat that Burr represented to Hamilton because we know that the American experiment with republican government was destined to succeed. We know that a nation so conceived and so dedicated could and did endure, indeed flourish, to become the longest-lived republic in world history. Not only was such knowledge unavailable to Hamilton and his contemporaries, the political landscape they saw around themselves was a dangerously fluid place, where neither the national laws nor institutions had yet hardened into permanent fixtures. Or if one wished to think biologically rather than architecturally, the body politic had yet to develop its immunities to the political diseases afflicting all new nations. What seems extravagant and hyperbolic in Hamilton's critical description of Burr, then, was not a symptom of Hamilton's paranoia so much as a realistic response to the genuine vulnerability of the still-tender young plant called the United States. So much seemed to be at stake because, in truth, it was.

Our search for the full meaning of the duel has led us backward, past the purely personal jealousies, through the only partially resolvable mysteries of what happened beneath the plains of Weehawken on the fateful day, and beyond the history of dueling as a dying institution. It has become an excursion into the highly problematic political world of the newborn American republic, a place where real and not just imagined conspiracies were prevalent, where the endurance of the political entity called the United States was still very much up in the air. As is more or less true about any famous event that is deeply imbedded in the historical soil of a particularly fertile time and place, the real significance of the duel lies beyond the specific parameters of the event itself, beyond that narrow ledge above the Hudson River. It expands to encompass an entire but still-emerging world that Burr threatened and Hamilton believed himself to be defending.

Oliver Wendell Holmes once observed that "a great man represents a strategic point in the campaign of history, and part of his greatness consists of his being there." Both Burr and Hamilton thought of themselves as great men who happened to come of age at one of those strategic points in the campaign of history called the American revolutionary era. By the summer of 1804, history had pretty much passed them by. Burr had alienated Jefferson and the triumphant Republican party by his disloyalty as a vice president and had lost by a landslide in his bid to become a Federalist governor of New York. Hamilton had not held national office for nine years and the Federalist cause he had championed was well on its way to oblivion. Even in his home state of New York, the Federalists were, as John Quincy Adams put it, "a minority, and of that minority, only a minority were admirers and partisans of Mr. Hamilton." Neither man had much of a political future.

But by being there beneath the plains of Weehawken for their interview, they managed to make a dramatic final statement about the time of their time. Honor mattered because character mattered. And character mattered because the fate of the American experiment with republican government still required virtuous leaders to survive. Eventually, the United States might develop into a nation of laws and established institutions capable of surviving

corrupt or incompetent public officials. But it was not there yet. It still required honorable and virtuous leaders to endure. Both Burr and Hamilton came to the interview because they wished to be regarded as part of such company.

QUESTIONS TO CONSIDER

1 Since dueling was illegal in New York, what elaborate measures did the combatants, with their seconds, take to ensure that all participants could claim ignorance if this contest of honor was brought before a court?

2 The practice of dueling might lead some students to conclude that the early national period was a more violent time than we live in today. Would that be an accurate assessment? Why did most duelists survive their potentially dangerous encounter?

3 Hamilton wrote the day before the duel that he intended "to reserve and throw away my first fire." Why did Burr feel that Hamilton's intentions were to kill him?

4 Ellis states that the French, Russian, and Chinese revolutions produced violent tremors that resulted in bloody reprisals. How was the American Revolution different, thus making the Hamilton-Burr duel a unique episode in our nation's history?

5 Ellis concludes that Hamilton saw Burr as "a man very much like himself . . . ambitious, energetic, possessing an instinctive strategic antenna and a willingness to take political risks." Yet, given their similarities, why did Hamilton believe that his rival was such a tremendous threat to the stability of the infant nation?

6 By the time of the duel, both Hamilton and Burr were fading figures on the political landscape. Why then does Ellis state that the duel was a tragic event since both men, in effect, "suffered an equally fatal wound"?

14 The Great Chief Justice

BRIAN McGINTY

As the court of last appeal in all matters involving the Constitution, the United States Supreme Court may be the most powerful branch of the federal government. It has the authority to uphold or strike down federal and state legislation, overturn decisions by lower courts, and determine the rights of individuals. Consequently, as in the modern struggle over abortion, the Court often stands at the center of national controversy.

You may be surprised to read in this selection that the Court was not always supreme, that in the first decade of its existence it was a maligned junior branch of the federal government, ignored by lawyers and scorned by politicians. How did it change into the powerful national tribunal we know today? As Brian McGinty points out, Chief Justice John Marshall made the nation's high tribunal a court that is supreme in fact as well as in name. During his thirty-four years on the bench (from 1801 to 1835), Marshall, a dedicated Federalist, also read the basic tenets of federalism into American constitutional law: the supremacy of the nation over the states, the sanctity of contracts, the protection of property rights, and the superiority of business over agriculture.

If you fear you are about to read a dull and dreary essay on constitutional law, don't despair. McGinty's warm portrait of the chief justice personalizes the major currents of the period and captures Marshall the human being in vivid scenes. We see him doing his own shopping for groceries, frequenting taverns and grog shops (he loves wine so much that a colleague quips, "the Chief was brought up on Federalism and Madeira"), and carrying a turkey for a young man who is too embarrassed to do so in public. Marshall clashes repeatedly with Jefferson over fundamental political and constitutional issues; later, Marshall tangles with Andrew Jackson in defending the treaty rights of the Cherokee Indians, a subject to be treated in more detail in selection 21.

It was Marshall's Court decisions, however, that had the biggest influence on his country. As McGinty says, Marshall's ruling in Marbury v. Madison, *which established the principle of judicial review, was perhaps the most important decision ever to come from the United States Supreme Court. Judicial review empowered the Supreme Court to interpret the meaning of the Constitution and so to define the authority of the national government and the states. The system of judicial review helped ensure the flexibility of the Constitution—so much so that a document originally designed for a small, scattered, largely agrarian population on the East Coast could endure for two centuries, during which the United States became a transcontinental, then a transpacific urban and industrial nation. That the Constitution has been able to grow and change with the country owes much to John Marshall.*

GLOSSARY

BURR, AARON First United States citizen to be tried for treason; Marshall helped acquit him in his trial before the Supreme Court.

FEDERALISTS Those such as Washington, Hamilton, and Marshall who favored a strong federal government and a stable, well-ordered society run by the great landowners and merchants.

GIBBONS v. OGDEN (1824)   Case in which Marshall upheld federal jurisdiction over interstate commerce.

MARBURY v. MADISON (1803)   Case in which Marshall established the principle of judicial review, which empowered the Supreme Court to interpret the Constitution and thus to define the authority of the national government and the states.

McCULLOCH v. MARYLAND (1819)   Case in which Marshall ruled that the first United States Bank was constitutional and that the state of Maryland could not tax it.

STORY, JOSEPH   Associate justice on the Marshall Court and the chief justice's personal friend.

WORCESTER v. GEORGIA (1832)   Marshall's decision forbidding the state of Georgia to violate the treaty rights of the Cherokees.

WYTHE, GEORGE   Professor at the College of William and Mary in Virginia who was a mentor to Marshall, Jefferson, and Henry Clay; he was the first law professor in the United States.

He was a tall man with long legs, gangling arms, and a round, friendly face. He had a thick head of dark hair and strong, black eyes—"penetrating eyes," a friend called them, "beaming with intelligence and good nature." He was born in a log cabin in western Virginia and never wholly lost his rough frontier manners. Yet John Marshall became a lawyer, a member of Congress, a diplomat, an advisor to presidents, and the most influential and respected judge in the history of the United States. "If American law were to be represented by a single figure," Supreme Court Justice Oliver Wendell Holmes, Jr., once said, "sceptic and worshipper alike would agree without dispute that the figure could be but one alone, and that one John Marshall."

To understand Marshall's preeminence in American legal history it is necessary to understand the marvelous rebirth the United States Supreme Court experienced after he became its chief justice in 1801. During all of the previous eleven years of its existence, the highest judicial court in the federal system had been weak and ineffectual—ignored by most of the nation's lawyers and judges and scorned by its principal politicians. Under Marshall's leadership, the court became a strong and vital participant in national affairs. During his more than thirty-four

years as chief justice of the United States, Marshall welded the Supreme Court into an effective and cohesive whole. With the support of his colleagues on the high bench, he declared acts of Congress and of the president unconstitutional, struck down laws that infringed on federal prerogatives, and gave force and dignity to basic guarantees of life and liberty and property. Without John Marshall, the Supreme Court might never have been anything but an inconsequential junior partner of the executive and legislative branches of the national government. Under his guidance and inspiration, it became what the Constitution intended it to be—a court system in fact as well as in name.

Born on September 4, 1755, in Fauquier County, Virginia, John Marshall was the oldest of fifteen children born to Thomas Marshall and Mary Randolph Keith. On his mother's side, the young Virginian was distantly related to Thomas Jefferson, the gentlemanly squire of Monticello and author of the Declaration of Independence. Aside from this kinship, there was little similarity between Marshall and Jefferson. A son of the frontier, Marshall was a backwoodsman at heart, more comfortable in the company of farmers than intellectuals or scholars. Jefferson was a polished aristocrat who liked to relax in the library of his mansion near Charlottesville and meditate on the subtleties of philosophy and political theory.

The contrast between the two men was most clearly drawn in their opposing political beliefs. An advocate of limiting the powers of central government, Thomas

From "The Great Chief Justice" by Brian McGinty, *American History Illustrated* (September 1988), pp. 8–14, 46–47. Reprinted by permission of Cowles Magazines, publisher of *American History Illustrated*.

Chester Harding's 1829 portrait of John Marshall. The chief justice, writes Brian McGinty, "was a tall man with long legs, gangling arms, and a round, friendly face. He had a thick head of dark hair and strong, black eyes—'penetrating eyes,' a friend called them, 'beaming with intelligence and good nature.'" (Washington and Lee University, Virginia)

Jefferson thought of himself first and foremost as a Virginian (his epitaph did not even mention the fact that he had once been president of the United States). Marshall, in contrast, had, even as a young man, come to transcend his state roots, to look to Congress rather than the Virginia legislature as his government, to think of himself first, last, and always as an American. Throughout their careers, their contrasting philosophies would place the two men at odds.

Marshall's national outlook was furthered by his father's close association with George Washington and his own unflinching admiration for the nation's first president. Thomas Marshall had been a schoolmate of Washington and, as a young man, helped him survey the Fairfax estates in northern Virginia.

John Marshall served under Washington during the bitter winter at Valley Forge and later became one of the planter-turned-statesman's most loyal supporters.

Years after the Revolution was over, Marshall attributed his political views to his experiences as a foot soldier in the great conflict, recalling that he grew up "at a time when a love of union and resistance to the claims of Great Britain were the inseparable inmates of the same bosom—when patriotism and a strong fellow feeling with our suffering fellow citizens of Boston were identical;—when the maxim 'united we stand, divided we fall' was the maxim of every orthodox American . . ." "I had imbibed these sentiments so thoughroughly [*sic*] that they constituted a part of my being," wrote Marshall. "I carried them with me into the army where I found myself associated with brave men from different states who were risking life and everything valuable in a common cause believed by all to be most precious; and where I was confirmed in the habit of considering America as my country, and Congress as my government."

After Washington's death, Marshall became the great man's biographer, penning a long and admiring account of Washington's life as a farmer, soldier, and statesman, expounding the Federalist philosophy represented by Washington and attacking those who stood in opposition to it. Jefferson, who detested Federalism as much as he disliked Marshall, was incensed by the biography, which he branded a "five-volume libel."

Frontiersman though he was, Marshall was no bumpkin. His father had personally attended to his earliest schooling, teaching him to read and write and giving him a taste for history and poetry (by the age of twelve he had already transcribed the whole of Alexander Pope's *Essay on Man*). When he was fourteen, Marshall was sent to a school a hundred miles from home, where future president James Monroe was one of his classmates. After a year, he returned home to be tutored by a Scottish pastor who had come to live in the Marshall house. The future lawyer read Horace and Livy, pored through the English dictionary, and scraped at least a passing acquaintance with the "Bible of the Common Law," William Blackstone's celebrated *Commentaries on the Laws of England*.

In 1779, during a lull in the Revolution, young Marshall attended lectures at the College of William and Mary in Williamsburg. He remained at the college only a few weeks, but the impression made on him by his professor there, George Wythe, was lasting. A lawyer, judge, and signer of the Declaration of Independence, Wythe is best remembered today as the first professor of law at any institution of higher learning in the United States. As a teacher, he was a seminal influence in the development of American law, counting among his many distinguished students Thomas Jefferson, John Breckinridge, and Henry Clay.

Marshall did not remain long at William and Mary. It was the nearly universal custom then for budding lawyers to "read law" in the office of an older lawyer or judge or, failing that, to appeal to the greatest teacher of all—experience—for instruction. In August 1780, a few weeks before his twenty-fifth birthday, Marshall appeared at the Fauquier County Courthouse where, armed with a license signed by Governor Thomas Jefferson of Virginia, he was promptly admitted to the bar.

His first cases were not important, but he handled them well and made a favorable impression on his neighbors; so favorable that they sent him to Richmond in 1782 as a member of the Virginia House of Delegates. Though he retained a farm in Fauquier County all his life, Richmond became Marshall's home after his election to the legislature. The general courts of Virginia held their sessions in the new capital, and the commonwealth's most distinguished lawyers crowded its bar. When Marshall's fortunes improved, he built a comfortable brick house on the outskirts of the city, in which he and his beloved wife Polly raised five sons and one daughter (four other offspring died during childhood).

Marshall's skill as a lawyer earned him an enthusiastic coterie of admirers and his honest country manners an even warmer circle of friends. He liked to frequent the city's taverns and grog shops, more for conviviality than for refreshment, and he was an enthusiastic member of the Barbecue Club, which met each Saturday to eat, drink, "josh," and play quoits.

Marshall liked to do his own shopping for groceries. Each morning he marched through the streets with a basket under his arm, collecting fresh fruits, vegetables, and poultry for the Marshall family larder. Years after his death, Richmonders were fond of recalling the day when a stranger came into the city in search of a lawyer and found Marshall in front of the Eagle Hotel, holding a hat filled with cherries and speaking casually with the hotel proprietor. After Marshall went on his way, the stranger approached the proprietor and asked if he could direct him to the best lawyer in Richmond. The proprietor replied quite readily that the best lawyer was John Marshall, the tall man with the hat full of cherries who had just walked down the street.

But the stranger could not believe that a man who walked through town so casually could be a really "proper barrister" and chose instead to hire a lawyer who wore a black suit and powdered wig. On the day set for the stranger's trial, several cases were scheduled to be argued. In the first that was called, the visitor was surprised to see that John Marshall and his own lawyer were to speak on opposite sides. As he listened to the arguments, he quickly realized that he had made a serious mistake. At the first recess, he approached Marshall and confessed that he had come to Richmond with a hundred dollars to hire the best lawyer in the city, but he had chosen the wrong one and now had only five dollars left. Would Marshall agree to represent him for such a small fee? Smiling good-naturedly, Marshall accepted the five dollars, then proceeded to make a brilliant legal argument that quickly won the stranger's case.

Marshall was not an eloquent man; not eloquent, that is, in the sense that his great contemporary, Patrick Henry, a spellbinding courtroom orator, was eloquent. Marshall was an effective enough speaker; but, more importantly, he was a rigorously logical thinker. He had the ability to reduce complex issues to bare essentials and easily and effortlessly apply abstract principles to resolve them.

Thomas Jefferson (himself a brilliant lawyer) was awed, even intimidated, by Marshall's powers of persuasion. "When conversing with Marshall," Jefferson once said, "I never admit anything. So sure as you admit any position to be good, no matter how remote from the conclusion he seeks to establish, you are gone. . . . Why, if he were to ask me if it were daylight or not, I'd reply, 'Sir, I don't know, I can't tell.'"

Though Marshall's legal prowess and genial manner won him many friends in Richmond, his political views did little to endear him to the Old Dominion's political establishment. While Jefferson and his followers preached the virtues of agrarian democracy, viewing with alarm every step by which the fledgling national government extended its powers through the young nation, Marshall clearly allied himself with Washington, Alexander Hamilton, and John Adams and the Federalist policies they espoused.

Marshall was not a delegate to the convention that met in Philadelphia in 1787 to draft a constitution for the United States, but he took a prominent part in efforts to secure ratification of the Constitution, thereby winning the special admiration of George Washington. After taking office as president, Washington offered Marshall the post of attorney general. Marshall declined the appointment, as he did a later offer of the prestigious post of American minister to France, explaining that he preferred to stay in Richmond with his family and law practice.

He did agree, however, to go to Paris in 1798 as one of three envoys from President John Adams to the government of revolutionary France. He did this, in part, because he was assured that his duties in Paris would be temporary only, in part because he believed he could perform a real service for his country, helping to preserve peaceful relations between it and France during a time of unusual diplomatic tension.

After Marshall joined his colleagues Elbridge Gerry and Charles Pinckney in Paris, he was outraged to learn that the French government expected to be paid before it would receive the American emissaries. Marshall recognized the French request as a solicitation for a bribe (the recipients of the payments were mysteriously identified as "X," "Y," and "Z"), and he refused to consider it.

Thomas Jefferson, who was smitten with the ardor and ideals of the French Revolution, suspected that Marshall and his Federalist "cronies" were planning war with France to promote the interests of their friends in England. But the American people believed otherwise. When they received news of the "XYZ Affair," they were outraged. "Millions for defense," the newspapers thundered, "but not one cent for tribute!" When Marshall returned home in the summer of 1798, he was welcomed as a hero. In the elections of the following fall, he was sent to Congress as a Federalist representative from Richmond.

Jefferson was not pleased. He declined to attend a dinner honoring Marshall in Philadelphia and wrote worried letters to his friends. Though he deprecated his fellow Virginian's popularity, alternatively attributing it to his "lax, lounging manners" and his "profound hypocrisy," Jefferson knew that Marshall was a potentially dangerous adversary. A half-dozen years before the Richmonder's triumphal return from Paris, Jefferson had written James Madison a cutting letter about Marshall that included words he would one day rue: "I think nothing better could be done than to make him a judge."

In Congress, Marshall vigorously supported the Federalist policies of President John Adams. Adams took note of the Virginian's ability in 1800 when he appointed him to the important post of secretary of state, a position that not only charged him with conduct of the country's foreign affairs but also left him in effective charge of the government during Adam's frequent absences in Massachusetts.

John Marshall's future in government seemed rosy and secure in 1800. But the elections in November of that year changed all that, sweeping Adams and the Federalists from power and replacing them with Jefferson and the Democratic Republicans.

After the election, but before Adam's term as president expired, ailing Supreme Court Chief Justice

Oliver Ellsworth submitted his resignation. Casting about for a successor to Ellsworth, Adams sent John Jay's name to the Senate, only to have Jay demand that it be withdrawn. The thought of leaving the appointment of a new chief justice to Jefferson was abhorrent to Adams, and the president was growing anxious. He summoned Marshall to his office to confer about the problem.

"Who shall I nominate now?" Adams asked dejectedly. Marshall answered that he did not know. He had previously suggested that Associate Justice William Paterson be elevated to the chief justiceship, but Adams had opposed Paterson then and Marshall supposed that he still did. The president pondered for a moment, then turned to Marshall and announced: "I believe I shall nominate you!"

Adams's statement astounded Marshall. Only two years before, Marshall had declined the president's offer of an associate justiceship, explaining that he still hoped to return to his law practice in Richmond. "I had never before heard myself named for the office," Marshall recalled later, "and had not even thought of it. I was pleased as well as surprized [sic], and bowed my head in silence."

Marshall's nomination was sent to the Senate and promptly confirmed, and on February 4, 1801, he took his seat as the nation's fourth Chief Justice. As subsequent events would prove, it was one of the most important dates in American history.

With Thomas Jefferson in the Executive Mansion and John Marshall in the Chief Justice's chair, it was inevitable that the Supreme Court and the executive branch of the government should come into conflict. Marshall believed firmly in a strong national government and was willing to do all he could to strengthen federal institutions. Jefferson believed as firmly in state sovereignty and the necessity for maintaining constant vigilance against federal "usurpations." In legal matters, Jefferson believed that the Constitution should be interpreted strictly, so as to reduce rather than expand federal power.

Marshall, in contrast, believed that the Constitution should be construed fairly so as to carry out the intentions of its framers. Any law or executive act that violated the terms of the Constitution was, in Marshall's view, a nullity, of no force or effect; and it was the peculiar prerogative of the courts, as custodians of the laws of the land, to strike down any law that offended the Supreme Law of the Land.

Jefferson did not question the authority of the courts to decide whether a law or executive act violated the Constitution, but he believed that the other branches of the government also had a duty and a right to decide constitutional questions. In a controversy between the Supreme Court and the president, for example, the Supreme Court could order the president to do whatever the Court thought the Constitution required him to do; but the president could decide for himself whether the Supreme Court's order was proper and whether or not it should be obeyed.

As he took up the duties of the chief justiceship, Marshall contemplated his role with uncertainty. The Supreme Court in 1801 was certainly not the kind of strong, vital institution that might have been expected to provide direction in national affairs. There were six justices when Marshall joined the Court, but none (save the Chief Justice himself) was particularly distinguished. One or two men of national prominence had accepted appointment to the Court in the first eleven years of its existence, but none had remained there long. John Jay, the first Chief Justice, had resigned his seat in 1795 to become governor of New York. During the two years that John Rutledge was an associate justice, he had regarded the Court's business as so trifling that he did not bother to attend a single session, and he finally resigned to become chief justice of South Carolina. The Court itself had counted for so little when the new capitol at Washington was being planned that the architects had made no provision for either a courtroom or judges' chambers, and the justices (to everyone's embarrassment) found that they had to meet in a dingy basement room originally designed for the clerk of the Senate.

How could Chief Justice Marshall use his new office to further the legal principles in which he believed so strongly? How could he strengthen the weak and undeveloped federal judiciary when most of the nation's lawyers and judges regarded that judiciary as superfluous and unnecessary? How could he implement his view of the Supreme Court as the final arbiter of constitutional questions when the President of the United States—his old nemesis, Thomas Jefferson—disagreed with that view so sharply? It was not an easy task, but John Marshall was a resourceful man, and he found a way to accomplish it.

His opportunity came in 1803 in the case of *Marbury* v. *Madison*. William Marbury was one of several minor federal judges who had been appointed during the closing days of John Adams's administration. When Jefferson's secretary of state, James Madison, refused to deliver the commissions of their offices, the judges sued Madison to compel delivery. In 1789, Congress had passed a law granting the Supreme Court authority to issue writs of mandamus, that is, legally enforceable orders compelling public officials to do their legal duties. Following the mandate of Congress, Marbury and the other appointees filed a petition for writ of mandamus in the Supreme Court.

Marshall pondered the possibilities of the case. He was sure that Marbury and his colleagues were entitled to their commissions, and he was just as sure that Jefferson and Madison had no intention of letting them have them. He could order Madison to deliver the commissions, but the secretary of state would certainly defy the order; and, as a practical matter, the Court could not compel obedience to any order that the president refused to acknowledge. Such an impasse would weaken, not strengthen, the federal union, and it would engender unprecedented controversy. No, there must be a better way. . . .

All eyes and ears in the capitol were trained on the lanky Chief Justice as he took his seat at the head of the high bench on February 24, 1803, and began to read the Supreme Court's opinion in *Marbury* v. *Madison*.

The evidence, Marshall said, clearly showed that Marbury and the other judges were entitled to their commissions. The commissions had been signed and sealed before John Adams left office and were, for all legal purposes, complete and effective. To withhold them, as Jefferson and Madison insisted on doing, was an illegal act. But the Supreme Court would not order the secretary of state to deliver the commissions because the law authorizing it to issue writs of mandamus was unconstitutional: the Constitution does not authorize the Supreme Court to issue writs of mandamus; in fact, it prohibits it from doing so. And any law that violates the Constitution is void. Since the law purporting to authorize the Supreme Court to act was unconstitutional, the Court would not—indeed, it could not—order Madison to do his legal duty.

If historians and constitutional lawyers were asked to name the single most important case ever decided in the United States Supreme Court, there is little doubt that the case would be *Marbury* v. *Madison*. Though the dispute that gave rise to the decision was in itself insignificant, John Marshall used it as a springboard to a great constitutional pronouncement. The rule of the case—that the courts of the United States have the right to declare laws unconstitutional—was immediately recognized as the cornerstone of American constitutional law, and it has remained so ever since.

More than a half-century would pass before the Supreme Court would again declare an act of Congress unconstitutional, but its authority to do so would never again be seriously doubted. Marshall had made a bold stroke, and he had done so in such a way that neither Congress, nor the president, nor any other public official had any power to resist it. By denying relief to Marbury, he had made the Supreme Court's order marvelously self-enforcing!

Predictably, Thomas Jefferson was angry. If the Supreme Court could not issue writs of mandamus, Jefferson asked, why did Marshall spend so much time discussing Marbury's entitlement to a commission? And why did the Chief Justice lecture Madison that withholding the commission was an illegal act?

The president thought for a time that he might have the Chief Justice and his allies on the bench impeached. After a mentally unstable federal judge in New Hampshire was removed from office, Jefferson's supporters in the House of Representatives brought a bill of impeachment against Marshall's colleague on the Supreme Court, Associate Justice Samuel Chase. Chase was a Federalist who had occasionally badgered witnesses and made intemperate speeches, but no one seriously contended that he had committed an impeachable offense (which the Constitution defines as "treason, bribery, or other high crimes and misdemeanors"). So the Senate, three quarters of whose members were Jeffersonians, refused to remove Chase from office. Marshall breathed a deep sigh of relief. Had the associate justice been impeached, the chief had no doubt that he himself would have been Jefferson's next target.

Though he never again had occasion to strike down an act of Congress, Marshall delivered opinions in many cases of national significance; and, in his capacity as circuit judge (all Supreme Court justices "rode circuit" in the early years of the nineteenth century), he presided over important, sometimes controversial, trials. He was the presiding judge when Jefferson's political arch rival, Aaron Burr, was charged with treason in 1807. Interpreting the constitutional provision defining treason against the United States, Marshall helped to acquit Burr, though he did so with obvious distaste. The Burr prosecution, Marshall said, was "the most unpleasant case which has been brought before a judge in this or perhaps any other country which affected to be governed by law."

On the high bench, Marshall presided over scores of precedent-setting cases. In *Fletcher* v. *Peck* (1810) and *Dartmouth College* v. *Woodward* (1819), he construed the contracts clause of the Constitution so as to afford important protection for the country's growing business community. In *McCulloch* v. *Maryland* (1819), he upheld the constitutionality of the first Bank of the United States and struck down the Maryland law that purported to tax it. In *Gibbons* v. *Ogden* (1824), he upheld federal jurisdiction over interstate commerce and lectured those (mainly Jeffersonians)

who persistently sought to enlarge state powers at the expense of legitimate federal authority.

Though Marshall's opinions always commanded respect, they were frequently unpopular. When, in *Worcester* v. *Georgia* (1832), he upheld the treaty rights of the Cherokee Indians against encroachments by the State of Georgia, he incurred the wrath of President Andrew Jackson. "John Marshall has made his decision," "Old Hickory" snapped contemptuously. "Now let him enforce it!" Marshall knew, of course, that he could not enforce the decision; that he could not enforce any decision that did not have the moral respect and acquiescence of the public and the officials they elected. And so he bowed his head in sadness and hoped that officials other than Andrew Jackson would one day show greater respect for the nation's legal principles and institutions.

Despite the controversy that some of his decisions inspired, the Chief Justice remained personally popular; and, during the whole of his more than thirty-four years as head of the federal judiciary, the Court grew steadily in authority and respect.

Well into his seventies, Marshall continued to ride circuit in Virginia and North Carolina, to travel each year to his farm in Fauquier County, to attend to his shopping duties in Richmond, and to preside over the high court each winter and spring in Washington. On one of his visits to a neighborhood market in Richmond, the Chief Justice happened on a young man who had been sent to fetch a turkey for his mother. The youth wanted to comply with his mother's request, but thought it was undignified to carry a turkey in the streets "like a servant." Marshall offered to carry it for him. When the jurist got as far as his own home, he turned to the young man and said, "This is where I live. Your house is not far off; can't you carry the turkey the balance of the way?" The young man's face turned crimson as he suddenly realized that his benefactor was none other than the Chief Justice of the United States.

Joseph Story, who served as an associate justice of the Supreme Court for more than twenty years of Marshall's term as chief justice, spent many hours with the Virginian in and out of Washington. Wherever Story observed Marshall, he was impressed by his modesty and geniality. "Meet him in a stagecoach, as a stranger, and travel with him a whole day," Story said, "and you would only be struck with his readiness to administer to the accommodations of others, and his anxiety to appropriate the least to himself. Be with him, the unknown guest at an inn, and he seemed adjusted to the very scene, partaking of the warm welcome of its comforts, wherever found; and if not found, resigning himself without complaint to its meanest arrangements. You would never suspect, in either case, that he was a great man; far less that he was the Chief Justice of the United States."

In his youth, Marshall had been fond of corn whiskey. As he grew older, he lost his appetite for spirits but not for wine. He formulated a "rule" under which the Supreme Court judges abstained from wine except in wet weather, but Story said he was liberal in allowing "exceptions." "It does sometimes happen," Story once said, "the Chief Justice will say to me, when the cloth is removed, 'Brother Story, step to the window and see if it does not look like rain.' And if I tell him that the sun is shining brightly, Judge Marshall will sometimes reply, 'All the better; for our jurisdiction extends over so large a territory that it must be raining somewhere.'" "You know," Story added, "that the Chief was brought up upon Federalism and Madeira, and he is not the man to outgrow his early prejudices."

In Richmond, Marshall held regular dinners for local lawyers, swapped stories with old friends, and tossed quoits with his neighbors in the Barbecue Club. An artist named Chester Harding remembered seeing the chief justice at a session of the Barbecue Club in 1829. Harding said Marshall was "the best pitcher of the party, and could throw heavier quoits than any other member of the club." "There were several ties," he added, "and, before long, I saw the great Chief Justice of the United States, down on his knees, measuring the contested distance with a straw, with as much earnestness as if it had been a point of

law; and if he proved to be in the right, the woods would ring with his triumphant shout."

In 1830, a young Pennsylvania congressman and future president of the United States commented on Marshall's enduring popularity among his neighbors. "His decisions upon constitutional questions have ever been hostile to the opinions of a vast majority of the people in his own State," James Buchanan said, "and yet with what respect and veneration has he been viewed by Virginia? Is there a Virginian whose heart does not beat with honest pride when the just fame of the Chief Justice is the subject of conversation? They consider him, as he truly is, one of the great and best men which this country has ever produced."

Marshall was nearly eighty years old when he died in Philadelphia on July 6, 1835. His body was brought back to Virginia for burial, where it was met by the longest procession the city of Richmond had ever seen.

In the contrast between proponents of strong and weak national government, Marshall had been one of the foremost and clearest advocates of strength. The struggle—between union and disunion, between federation and confederation, between the belief that the Constitution created a nation and the theory that it aligned the states in a loose league— was not finally resolved until 1865. But the struggle *was* resolved. "Time has been on Marshall's side," Oliver Wendell Holmes, Jr., said in 1901. "The theory for which Hamilton argued, and he decided, and Webster spoke, and Grant fought, is now our cornerstone."

Justice Story thought that Marshall's appointment to the Supreme Court contributed more "to the preservation of the true principles of the Constitution than any other circumstances in our domestic history." "He was a great man," Story said. "I go farther; and insist, that he would have been deemed a great man in any age, and of all ages. He was one of those, to whom centuries alone give birth."

John Adams and Thomas Jefferson both lived long and distinguished lives, but neither ever gave an inch in their differences of opinion over Marshall. Jefferson went to his grave bemoaning the "cunning and sophistry" of his fellow Virginian. Adams died secure in the belief that his decision to make Marshall chief justice had been both wise and provident. Years later, Adams called Marshall's appointment "the pride of my life." Time has accorded Thomas Jefferson a great place in the affections of the American people, but, in the controversy over John Marshall, the judgment of history has come down with quiet strength on the side of John Adams.

QUESTIONS TO CONSIDER

1 John Marshall and Thomas Jefferson were both Virginians; they were also distant relatives. How did they turn out to be so different? How has McGinty's article altered or expanded your view of the Thomas Jefferson you met in selection 8?

2 *Marbury* v. *Madison* was a case of small immediate significance in 1803, a legal squabble over a few petty government appointments. How did it turn out to have such enormous consequences for America's governmental structure? What implications did Marshall's legal actions have for the Supreme Court's future, particularly when the Court was pitted against a popular president?

3 In *Marbury* v. *Madison* and in a few other cases, Chief Justice Marshall, a staunch Federalist, wrote decisions unfavorable to his party's interests. What elements in his character caused him to ignore party politics? Discuss the precedents that may have been set by his actions.

4 McGinty's biography alternates episodes from Marshall's famous legal career with anecdotes from his private life. Do you find this technique distracting, or does it help you to understand Marshall more fully? What sort of man do the personal anecdotes reveal? Are these traits evident in Marshall's long career as chief justice?

5 We live today under a strong central government that owes much to legal decisions written by Chief Justice Marshall more than 150 years ago. Discuss the ways in which the United States today is a "Federalist" rather than a "Republican" nation.

PART EIGHT

Woe If It Comes with Storm and Blood and Fire

15 The Fires of Jubilee: Nat Turner's Fierce Rebellion

STEPHEN B. OATES

While John Marshall was sitting on the bench, handing down judicial rulings aimed at stabilizing the Republic, there was another America, a black America, struggling on the underside of society to gain its freedom, its wholeness and humanity. Let us pick up the story of that struggle with the outbreak of the Revolution. The labor of slaves, as we have seen, was indispensable to the American cause. Hoping to disrupt the American war effort, the British invited the slaves to desert their American masters and join the British side, ultimately promising freedom if they did so. This promise horrified the American patriots. "Hell itself," one cried, "could not have vomited anything more black than this design of emancipating our slaves."

The Americans had reason to be worried, for their slaves went over to the British in ever increasing numbers. That blacks fought against the Revolution challenges the traditional notions of freedom and oppression in the Revolutionary era. From the view of fleeing slaves, the redcoats were the liberators, the American patriots the oppressors. To forestall mass slave defections, the Americans started recruiting blacks as soldiers too; some states even offered freedom in exchange for military service (South Carolina, however, offered white volunteers a bounty in slaves, in the form of one adult black to each private, three adult blacks and a child to each colonel). Altogether some 5,000 blacks served the American cause. But approximately 100,000 blacks, a fifth of the slave population in revolutionary America, were "loyalists," who sided with the British. When the war ended, General Washington, angry because some of his own slaves had fled, demanded that the defeated British return the black loyalists to their American masters. The British, however, asserted that the blacks had been emancipated in accordance with royal policy. In the end, the British did give up blacks who had been seized by royal forces and refugees who had come to British lines after the war had ended. Other black loyalists wound up in slavery in the British West Indies; 3,000 more were colonized in Nova Scotia, where they braved discrimination and established a community that still exists.

The black patriots, by contrast, gained a measure of freedom when the northern states abolished slavery. New Jersey even allowed them to vote—for a while. But most "free" blacks in the North languished in the twilight zone between bondage and full liberty. As Leon Litwack observes in North of Slavery *(1961), "Until the post–Civil War era, in fact, most northern whites would maintain a careful distinction between granting Negroes legal protection—a theoretical right to life, liberty, and property—and political and social equality. No statute or court decision could immediately erase from the public mind, North or South, that long and firmly held conviction that the African race was inferior and therefore incapable of being assimilated politically, socially, and most certainly physically with the dominant and superior white society." As a contemporary said of northern blacks, "Chains of a stronger kind still manacled their limbs, from which no legislative act could free them; a mental and moral subordination and inferiority, to which . . . custom has here subjected all the sons and daughters of Africa."*

There were northern blacks, of course, who overcame the obstacles against them and managed to lead prominent and influential lives. Phillis Wheatley of Boston was an internationally known poet, whose Poems on Various Subjects, Religious and Moral, *was the first book published by a black woman in America and only the second by an American woman. Prince Hall, one of several thousand blacks who fought for America in the Revolution, formed the first black Masonic lodge. And Benjamin Banneker, born a free black in slaveholding Maryland, became a well-known astronomer and the most famous African American in the young Republic.*

In the South, meanwhile, slavery took even deeper root with the invention of the cotton gin in 1793, and blacks on the booming plantations sank into bleak despair. Here "the human cattle moved," recalled Frederick Douglass, a former slave, "hurried on by no hope of reward, no sense of gratitude . . . no prospect of bettering their condition; nothing, save the dread and terror of the slave-driver's lash. So goes one day, and so comes and goes another." Yet, as Vincent Harding observes, the slaves were anything but passive drones, submitting to their lot without complaint. They resisted bondage every way they could: they ran away, faked illness, broke hoes, and resorted to other forms of sabotage. Inspired by the charismatic Toussaint L'Ouverture and the great slave rebellion he led on Santo Domingo in the Caribbean, southern blacks also plotted insurrection, something their masters most feared from them. In 1800 Gabriel Prosser plotted an insurrection in Richmond, but the authorities found out about it and hanged the conspirators. The same thing happened in Charleston in 1821 when house slaves told authorities that Denmark Vesey, a free black man, was plotting a giant slave rebellion. Vesey and his followers were all hanged.

Then in 1831, in an obscure county in southern Virginia, the worst fears of southern whites became a brutal reality when Nat Turner staged the bloodiest slave rebellion in southern history. It made him the most famous slave insurgent America had ever known, the victim of a violent system that struck back with retributive violence. His rebellion illustrates a profound truth. As black historian Lerone Bennett says, "Nat Turner reminds us that oppression is a kind of violence which pays in coins of its own minting. He reminds us that the first and greatest of all gospels is this: that individuals and systems always reap what they sow."

The following article attempts to transport you back into Nat Turner's time so that you might suffer with him and see the world through his eyes. That way you might gain melancholy insight into what it was like to be a slave. You might understand why Turner finally chose the sword as his instrument of liberation, and why he set out to fulfill the injunction in Exodus that "thou shalt give life for life, eye for eye, tooth for tooth, hand for hand, foot for foot, burning for burning." By placing Turner and his revolt in proper historical context, the article seeks to convey how the insurrection shocked the slave South to its foundations, exacerbated sectional tensions, and pointed the way toward civil war thirty years later.

GLOSSARY

BLUNT, SIMON   The last plantation attacked by Nat Turner's insurgents. Blunt's own slaves helped him repel Nat's attack.

FLOYD, JOHN   Governor of Virginia at the time of Nat Turner's insurrection and one of the first Virginians to blame Nat's rebellion on northern abolitionists.

FRANCIS, WILL   One of Nat Turner's confederates, a violent and angry slave who did much of the killing, only to be killed instead when Turner's force attacked Simon Blunt's plantation.

GRAY, THOMAS   Jerusalem lawyer and slaveholder who interrogated Nat Turner in his prison cell and published his "confession," which detailed the genesis and execution of the insurrection.

MOORE, PUTNAM   When Thomas Moore died, his nine-year old son, Putnam, became Nat Turner's legal owner.

MOORE, THOMAS   Nat Turner's third owner. Moore beat him in 1828 when Turner announced that the slaves ought to be free and would be "one day or other."

SOUTHAMPTON COUNTY   Obscure Virginia county on the North Carolina border where Nat Turner lived all his life and launched his insurrection.

TRAVIS, JOSEPH AND SALLY   After Thomas Moore's death, his widow, Sally, married Joseph Travis and took Putnam and the Moore slaves, including Nat Turner, to live at the Travis homestead. The Travis family was the first to die in Turner's insurrection.

TURNER, BENJAMIN   Nat's first owner and the source of his last name. All slaves had to take the last names of their owners; when they were sold, they had to assume the last names of their new owners. It is a measure of the respect Nat Turner commanded that he retained his initial last name despite being sold to Thomas Moore.

WHITEHEAD, MARGARET   The only white person Nat Turner himself killed during the revolt.

S
ome seventy miles below Richmond, in the southeastern part of Virginia along the North Carolina border, lay a little-known backwater called Southampton County. It was a rolling, densely forested area, with farms, plantations, and crossroad villages carved out of the woods. In 1831 most of the farms and smaller plantations were hardly

distinguishable from one another—the houses were charmless, two-story rectangles, surrounded by haystacks and corn and cotton patches. Around the "big house" were various satellite sheds, a one-room kitchen, a barn, and maybe some slave cabins. Out in back were pungent outhouses poised on the edge of a slope or a steep ravine. A typical homestead had a menagerie of dogs, chickens, hogs, cows, mules, and maybe a couple of horses. And it had an apple orchard, too, for the succulent fruit not only commanded a fair price at market, but was the source of Southampton's most cherished product—an apple

Stephen B. Oates, "The Fires of Jubilee: Nat Turner's Fierce Rebellion," adapted from Stephen B. Oates, *The Fires of Jubilee: Nat Turner's Fierce Rebellion*, New York: Harper & Row, 1975. Reprinted by permission of HarperCollins Publishers.

brandy potent enough to make a sailor reel. Not a homestead was complete without a brandy still, and the county's most popular citizens were those with well-stocked cellars.

The county seat or "county town" was Jerusalem, a smoky cluster of buildings where pigs rooted in the streets and old-timers spat tobacco juice in the shade of the courthouse. Consisting of some two thousand souls, Jerusalem lay on the forested bank of the Nottoway River some fifty or sixty miles from Norfolk and the Atlantic Ocean. To the west of Jerusalem was Bethlehem Crossroads and to the southwest a loose cluster of homesteads called Cross Keys. Such villages were the nerve centers of Southampton's social life—here on Sundays and holidays white families gathered to hear preaching, dance to fiddles, enjoy a communal barbecue, joke, gossip, cheer on a shooting match or a horse race, get drunk, talk about the weather or argue about politics in their distinct Virginia accent ("hoose" for house). Most political discussions focused on local issues, for Southampton had no newspapers of its own and people here lived in considerable isolation from the outside world. What news they received came mainly from travelers and express riders, who brought mail in from Petersburg, Norfolk, and Murfreesboro down in North Carolina.

Although Southampton was a remote, generally lackluster neighborhood, it did have a planter class and in that respect was no different from most other Southern tidewater communities. If you had to own at least 20 slaves to rank as a planter, then 96 of Southampton's 734 slaveholders—about 13 percent—could claim that coveted distinction. Some fifteen men, with names like Newsom, Worrell, and Briggs, owned fifty slaves or more—which theoretically classified them as aristocrats. And Thomas Ridley, old man Urquhart, and John Kelly possessed large plantations with 145 to 179 Negroes apiece, which, in terms of slave wealth, placed *them* among the Old South's elite. Evidently these backwater squires had inherited or married into most of their possessions and had bought the rest. Some enterprising fellows had even constructed homes that were impressive by

Southampton standards—with columned front porches and imported finery—and now found themselves hard-pressed to meet their mortgage payments. Still, Southampton's large planters lacked the tradition and prestige—and the majestic, landscaped mansions—that characterized Virginia's established gentry, especially the patricians along the great tidewater rivers in the more eastern and northeastern counties.

As was true of the rest of Dixie, most of Southampton's slaveowners resided on modest farms, some fighting to climb up the social and economic scale, others scratching out a hardscrabble existence from their crops and livestock. What is more, over one-third of Southampton's white families owned no slaves, none at all, and the average for the entire county was ten or eleven per slaveowning family. Many small slaveholders could not afford overseers and worked alongside their Negroes in the orchards and cotton patches. Though Virginia was no longer in a depression in 1831, the state had suffered over the past decade, as soil exhaustion and ruinous farm prices—particularly in the early 1820s—had plagued farmers and planters alike. In Southampton, assessed land values had declined sharply during the last twenty years, and a number of whites had moved on to new cotton lands in Georgia and Alabama, so that the county's population was now almost 60 percent black, with some 6,500 whites and 9,500 Negroes residing there. While most of the blacks were still enslaved, an unusual number—some 1,745, in fact—were "free persons of color." Only three counties in all of tidewater Virginia had more free Negroes than that.

By southern white standards, enlightened benevolence did exist in Southampton County—and it existed in the rest of the state as well. Virginians liked to boast that slavery was not so harsh in the Old Dominion as it was on the brutal cotton plantations in the Deep South. Sure, Virginians conceded, there might be occasional mistreatment in the form of a sadistic overseer or a licentious poor white who hankered after slave girls, but respectable Virginians convinced themselves that all was sweetness and sunshine in their master-slave relations. Why, on Sundays

Deep in the woods near Cabin Pond, Nat and his confederates, all field slaves, work out their plans for rebellion. From an old print published by J. D. Torrey, New York. (Culver Pictures)

Virginia masters even took their darkies to white churches, where they got to sit at the back or up in the balcony, murmuring a rehearsed *"Amen"* from time to time. After church, the slaves often gathered in a field—a shack or a shed—to conduct their own praise meetings, to shout and sing in an arcane language that aroused little interest among picnicking whites, who dismissed the noise as innocuous "nigger gabble."

Southampton whites, too, were pretty lax toward their slaves, allowing them to gather for religious purposes, visit other farms, and even travel to Jerusalem on market Saturdays to see relatives and friends. After all, what was there to worry about? Southampton's slaves were well treated, whites said, and apart from a few solitary incidents the county had never had any severe slave troubles. True, the Negroes did get a bit carried away in their praise meetings these days, with much too much clapping and singing. And true, some white evangelists were coming in from outside the county and "ranting" about equality at local revivals. But generally things

were quiet and unchanged in this tidewater neighborhood, where time seemed to stand as still as a windless summer day.

But all was not so serene as whites liked to believe. For a storm was brewing in Southampton's backwoods, in the slave cabins northwest of Cross Keys. It blew up with shattering suddenness, an explosion of black rage that struck Southampton County like a tornado roaring out of the Southern night. In the early morning hours of August 22, 1831, a band of slave insurgents, led by a black mystic called Nat Turner, burst out of the forests with guns and axes, plunging southeastern Virginia—and much of the rest of the South—into convulsions of fear and racial violence. It turned out to be the bloodiest slave revolt in Southern history, one that was to have a profound and irrevocable impact on the destinies of Southern whites and blacks alike.

Afterward, white authorities described him as a small man with "distinct African features." Though his shoulders were broad from work in the fields, he was short, slender, and a little knock-kneed, with thin hair, a complexion like black pearl, and large, deep-set eyes. He wore a mustache and cultivated a tuft of whiskers under his lower lip. Before that fateful August day whites who knew Nat Turner thought him harmless, even though he was intelligent and did gabble on about strange religious powers. Among the slaves, though, he enjoyed a powerful influence as an exhorter and self-proclaimed prophet.

He was born in 1800, the property of Benjamin Turner of Southampton County and the son of two strong-minded parents. Tradition has it that his African-born mother threatened to kill him rather than see him grow up in bondage. His father eventually escaped to the North, but not before he had helped inculcate an enormous sense of self-importance in his son. Both parents praised Nat for his brilliance and extraordinary imagination; his mother even claimed that he could recall episodes that happened before his birth—a power that others insisted only the Almighty could have given him. His mother and father both told him that he was intended for some great purpose, that he would surely become a prophet. Nat was also influenced by his grandmother, who along with his white masters taught him to pray and to take pride in his superior intelligence. He learned to read and write with great ease, prompting those who knew him to remark that he had too much sense to be raised in bondage—he "would never be of any service to any one as a slave," one of them said.

In 1810 Benjamin Turner died, and Nat became the property of Turner's oldest son Samuel. Under Samuel Turner's permissive supervision Nat exploited every opportunity to improve his knowledge: he studied white children's school books and experimented in making paper and gunpowder. But it was religion that interested him the most. He attended Negro religious meetings, where the slaves cried out in ecstasy and sang hymns that expressed their longing for a better life. He listened transfixed as black exhorters preached from the Bible with stabbing gestures, singing out in a rhythmic language that was charged with emotion and vivid imagery. He studied the Bible, too, practically memorizing the books of the Old Testament, and grew to manhood with the words of the prophets roaring in his ears.

Evidently Nat came of age a bit confused if not resentful. Both whites and blacks had said he was too intelligent to be raised a slave; yet here he was, fully grown and still in bondage. Obviously he felt betrayed by false hopes. Obviously he thought he should be liberated like the large number of free blacks who lived in Southampton County and who were not nearly so gifted as he. Still enslaved as a man, he zealously cultivated his image as a prophet, aloof, austere, and mystical. As he said later in an oral autobiographical sketch, "Having soon discovered to be great, I must appear so, and therefore studiously avoided mixing in society, and wrapped myself in mystery, devoting myself to fasting and prayer."

Remote, introspective, Turner had religious fantasies in which the Holy Spirit seemed to speak to him as it had to the prophets of old. "Seek ye the kingdom of Heaven," the Spirit told him, "and all things shall be added unto you." Convinced that he

"was ordained for some great purpose in the hands of the Almighty," Turner told his fellow slaves about his communion with the Spirit. "And they believed," Turner recalled, "and said my wisdom came from God." Pleased with their response, he began to prepare them for some unnamed mission. He also started preaching at black religious gatherings and soon rose to prominence as a leading exhorter in the slave church. Although never ordained and never officially a member of any church, he was accepted as a Baptist preacher in the slave community, and once he even baptized a white man in a swampy pond. There can be little doubt that the slave church nourished Turner's self-esteem and his desire for independence, for it was not only a center for underground slave plottings against the master class, but a focal point for an entire alternate culture—a subterranean culture that the slaves sought to construct beyond the white man's control. Moreover, Turner's status as a slave preacher gave him considerable freedom of movement, so that he came to know most of Southampton County intimately.

Sometime around 1821 Turner disappeared. His master had put him under an overseer, who may have whipped him, and he fled for his freedom as his father had done. But thirty days later he voluntarily returned. The other slaves were astonished. No fugitive ever came back on his own. "And the negroes found fault, and murmured against me," Turner recounted later, "saying that if they had my sense they would not serve any master in the world." But in his mind Turner did not serve any earthly master. His master was Jehovah—the angry and vengeful God of ancient Israel—and it was Jehovah, he insisted, who had chastened him and brought him back to bondage.

At about this time Nat married. Evidently his wife was a young slave named Cherry who lived on Samuel Turner's place. But in 1822 Samuel Turner died, and they were sold to different masters— Cherry to Giles Reese and Nat to Thomas Moore. Although they were not far apart and still saw each other from time to time, their separation was nevertheless a painful example of the wretched privations that slavery placed on black people, even here in mellowed Southampton County.

As a perceptive man with a prodigious knowledge of the Bible, Turner was more than aware of the hypocrisies and contradictions loose in this Christian area, where whites gloried in the teachings of Jesus and yet discriminated against the "free coloreds" and kept the other blacks in chains. Here slave owners bragged about their benevolence (in Virginia they took care of their "niggers") and yet broke up families, sold Negroes off to whip-happy slave traders when money was scarce, and denied intelligent and skilled blacks something even the most debauched and useless poor white enjoyed: freedom. Increasingly embittered about his condition and that of his people, his imagination fired to incandescence by prolonged fasting and Old Testament prayers, Turner began to have apocalyptic visions and bloody fantasies in the fields and woods southwest of Jerusalem. "I saw white spirits and black spirits engaged in battle," he declared later, "and the sun was darkened—the thunder rolled in the heavens, and blood flowed in streams—and I heard a voice saying, 'Such is your luck, such you are called to see, and let it come rough or smooth, you must surely bare it.'" He was awestruck, he recalled, but what did the voice mean? What must he bare? He withdrew from his fellow slaves and prayed for a revelation; and one day when he was plowing in the field, he thought the Spirit called out, "Behold me as I stand in the Heavens," and Turner looked up and saw forms of men there in a variety of attitudes, "and there were lights in the sky to which the children of darkness gave other names than what they really were—for they were the lights of the Saviour's hands, stretched forth from east to west, even as they extended on the cross on Calvary for the redemption of sinners."

Certain that Judgment Day was fast approaching, Turner strove to attain "true holiness" and "the true knowledge of faith." And once he had them, once he was "made perfect," then the Spirit showed him other miracles. While working in the field, he said, he discovered drops of blood on the corn. In the woods he found leaves with hieroglyphic characters and numbers etched on them; other leaves contained forms of men—some drawn in blood—like the figures in the sky. He told his fellow slaves about these signs—they were simply astounded—and claimed that the Spirit had endowed him with a special knowledge of the seasons, the rotation of the planets, and the operation of the tides. He acquired an even greater reputation among the county's slaves, many of whom thought he could control the weather and heal disease. He told his followers that clearly something large was about to happen, that he was soon to fulfill "the great promise that had been made to me."

But he still did not know what his mission was. Then on May 12, 1828, "I heard a loud noise in the heavens," Turner remembered, "and the Spirit instantly appeared to me and said the Serpent was loosened, and Christ had laid down the yoke he had borne for the sins of men, and that I should take it on and fight against the Serpent." Now at last it was clear. By signs in the heavens Jehovah would show him when to commence the great work, whereupon "I should arise and prepare myself, and slay my enemies with their own weapons." Until then he should keep his lips sealed.

But his work was too momentous for him to remain entirely silent. He announced to Thomas Moore that the slaves ought to be free and would be "one day or other." Moore, of course, regarded this as dangerous talk from a slave and gave Turner a thrashing.

In 1829 a convention met in Virginia to draft a new state constitution, and there was talk among the slaves—who communicated along a slave grapevine—that they might be liberated. Their hopes were crushed, though, when the convention emphatically rejected emancipation and restricted suffrage to whites only. There was also a strong backlash against antislavery publications thought to be infiltrating from the North, one of which—David Walker's *Appeal*—actually called on the slaves to revolt. In reaction the Virginia legislature enacted a law against teaching slaves to read and write. True, it was not yet rigorously enforced, but from the blacks' viewpoint slavery seemed more entrenched in "enlightened" Virginia than ever.

There is no evidence that Turner ever read anti-slavery publications, but he was certainly sensitive to the despair of his people. Still, Jehovah gave him no further signs, and he was carried along in the ebb and flow of ordinary life. Moore had died in 1828, and Turner had become the legal property of Moore's nine-year-old son—something that must have humiliated him. In 1829 a local wheelwright, Joseph Travis, married Moore's widow and soon moved into her house near the Cross Keys, a village located southwest of Jerusalem. Still known as Nat Turner even though he had changed owners several times, Nat considered Travis "a kind master" and later said that Travis "placed the greatest confidence in me."

In February, 1831, there was an eclipse of the sun. The sign Turner had been waiting for—could there be any doubt? Removing the seal from his lips, he gathered around him four slaves in whom he had complete trust—Hark, Henry, Nelson, and Sam—and confided what he was called to do. They would commence "the work of death" on July 4, whose connotation Turner clearly understood. But they formed and rejected so many plans that his mind was affected. He was seized with dread. He fell sick, and Independence Day came and passed.

On August 13 there was another sign. Because of some atmospheric disturbance the sun grew so dim that it could be looked at directly. Then it seemed to change colors—now pale green, now blue, now white—and there was much excitement and consternation in many parts of the eastern United States. By afternoon the sun was like an immense ball of polished silver, and the air was moist and hazy. Then a black spot could be seen, apparently on the sun's surface—a phenomenon that greatly aroused the slaves in southeastern Virginia. For Turner the black spot was unmistakable proof that God wanted him to move. With awakened resolution he told his men that "as the black spot passed over the sun, so shall the blacks pass over the earth."

It was Sunday, August 21, deep in the woods near the Travis house at a place called Cabin Pond. Around a crackling fire Turner's confederates feasted on roast pig and apple brandy. With them were two new recruits—Jack, one of Hark's cronies, and Will, a powerful man who intended to gain his freedom or die in the attempt. Around midafternoon Turner himself made a dramatic appearance, and in the glare of pine-knot torches they finally made their plans. They would rise that night and "kill all the white people." It was a propitious time to begin, because many whites of the militia were away at a camp meeting. The revolt would be so swift and so terrible that the whites would be too panic-stricken to fight back. Until they had sufficient recruits and equipment, the insurgents would annihilate everybody in their path—women and children included. When one of the slaves complained about their small number (there were only seven of them, after all), Turner was quick to reassure him. He had deliberately avoided an extensive plot involving a lot of slaves. He knew that blacks had "frequently attempted similar things," but their plans had "leaked out." Turner intended for his revolt to happen completely without warning. The "march of destruction," he explained, "should be the first news of the insurrection," whereupon slaves and free blacks alike would rise up and join him. He did not say what their ultimate objective was, but possibly he wanted to fight his way into the Great Dismal Swamp some twenty miles to the east. This immense, snake-filled quagmire had long been a haven for fugitives, and Turner may have planned to establish a slave stronghold there from which to launch punitive raids against Virginia and North Carolina. On the other hand, he may well have had nothing in mind beyond the extermination of every white on the ten-mile route to Jerusalem. There are indications that he thought God would guide him after the revolt began, just as He had directed Gideon against the Midianites. Certainly Turner's command of unremitting carnage was that of the Almighty, who had said through his prophet Ezekiel: "Slay utterly old and young, both maids and little children, and women. . . ."

The slaves talked and schemed through the evening. Night came on. Around two in the morning of August 22 they left the woods, by-passed Giles

Reese's farm, where Cherry lived, and headed for the Travis homestead, the first target in their crusade.

All was still at the Travis house. In the darkness the insurgents gathered about the cider press, and all drank except Turner, who never touched liquor. Then they moved across the yard with their axes. Hark placed a ladder against the house, and Turner, armed with a hatchet, climbed up and disappeared through a second-story window. In a moment he unbarred the door, and the slaves spread through the house without a sound. The others wanted Turner the prophet, Turner the black messiah, to strike the first blow and kill Joseph Travis. With Will close behind, Turner entered Travis' bedroom and made his way to the white man's bed. Turner swung his hatchet—a wild blow that glanced off Travis' head and brought him out of bed yelling for his wife. But with a sure killer's instinct Will moved in and hacked Travis to death with his axe. In minutes Will and the others had slaughtered the four whites they found in the house, including Mrs. Travis and young Putnam Moore, Turner's legal owner. With Putnam's death Turner felt that at last, after thirty years in bondage, he was free.

The rebels gathered up a handful of old muskets and followed "General Nat" out to the barn. There Turner paraded his men about, leading them through every military maneuver he knew. Not all of them, however, were proud of their work. Jack sank to his knees with his head in his hands and said he was sick. But Hark made him get up and forced him along as they set out across the field to the next farm. Along the way somebody remembered the Travis baby. Will and Henry returned and killed it in its cradle.

And so it went throughout that malignant night, as the rebels took farm after farm by surprise. They used no firearms, in order not to arouse the countryside, instead stabbing and decapitating their victims. Although they confiscated horses, weapons, and brandy, they took only what was necessary to continue the struggle, and they committed no rapes. They even spared a few homesteads, one because Turner believed the poor white inhabitants "thought

no better of themselves than they did of negroes." By dawn on Monday there were fifteen insurgents— nine on horses—and they were armed with a motley assortment of guns, clubs, swords, and axes. Turner himself now carried a light dress sword, but for some mysterious reason (a fatal irresolution? the dread again?) he had killed nobody yet.

At Elizabeth Turner's place, which the slaves stormed at sunrise, the prophet tried once again to kill. They broke into the house, and there, in the middle of the room, too frightened to move or cry out, stood Mrs. Turner and a neighbor named Mrs. Newsome. Nat knew Elizabeth Turner very well, for she was the widow of his second master, Samuel Turner. While Will attacked her with his axe the prophet took Mrs. Newsome's hand and hit her over the head with his sword. But evidently he could not bring himself to kill her. Finally Will moved him aside and chopped her to death as methodically as though he were cutting wood.

With the sun low in the east, Turner sent a group on foot to another farm while he and Will led the horsemen at a gallop to Caty Whitehead's place. They surrounded the house in a rush, but not before several people fled into the garden. Turner chased after somebody, but it turned out to be a slave girl, as terrified as the whites, and he let her go. All around him, all over the Whitehead farm, there were scenes of unspeakable violence. He saw Will drag Mrs. Whitehead kicking and screaming out of the house and almost sever her head from her body. Running around the house, Turner came upon young Margaret Whitehead hiding under a cellar cap between two chimneys. She ran crying for her life, and Turner set out after her—a wild chase against the hot August sun. He overtook the girl in a field and hit her again and again with his sword, but she would not die. In desperation he picked up a fence rail and beat her to death. Finally he had killed someone. He was to kill no one else.

After the Whitehead massacre the insurgents united briefly and then divided again, those on foot moving in one direction and Turner and the mounted slaves in another. The riders moved across the fields, kicking

On October 30, 1831, a Sunday, a white named Benjamin Phipps accidentally discovered Nat Turner in his hideout near *Cabin Pond. Since the white man had a loaded shotgun, Turner had no choice but to throw down his sword. (Brown Brothers)*

their horses and mules faster and faster, until at last they raced down the lane to Richard Porter's house, scattering dogs and chickens as they went. But the Porters had fled—forewarned by their own slaves that a revolt was under way. Turner knew that the alarm was spreading now, knew that the militia would soon be mobilizing, so he set out alone to retrieve the other column. While he was gone Will took the cavalry and raided Nathaniel Francis' homestead. Young Francis was Will's owner, but he could not have been a harsh master: several free blacks voluntarily lived on his farm. Francis was not home, and his pregnant young wife survived Will's onslaught only because a slave concealed her in the attic. After killing the overseer and Francis' two nephews Will and his men raced on to another farm, and another, and then overran John Barrow's place on the Barrow Road. Old man Barrow fought back manfully while his wife escaped in the woods, but the insurgents overwhelmed him and slit his throat. As a tribute to his courage they

wrapped his body in a quilt and left a plug of tobacco on his chest.

Meanwhile Turner rode chaotically around the countryside, chasing after one column and then the other, almost always reaching the farms after his scattered troops had done the killing and gone. Eventually he found both columns waiting for him at another pillaged homestead, took charge again, and sent them down the Barrow Road, which intersected the main highway to Jerusalem. They were forty strong now and all mounted. Many of the new recruits had joined up eager "to kill all the white people." But others had been forced to come along as though they were hostages. A Negro later testified that several slaves—among them three teen-age boys—"were constantly guarded by negroes with guns who were ordered to shoot them if they attempted to escape."

On the Barrow Road, Turner's strategy was to put his twenty most dependable men in front and send them galloping down on the homesteads before anybody could escape. But the cry of insurrection had preceded them, and many families had already escaped to nearby Jerusalem, throwing the village into pandemonium. By midmorning church bells were tolling the terrible news—*insurrection, insurrection*—and shouting men were riding through the countryside in a desperate effort to get the militia together before the slaves overran Jerusalem itself.

As Turner's column moved relentlessly toward Jerusalem one Levi Waller, having heard that the blacks had risen, summoned his children from a nearby schoolhouse (some of the other children came running too) and tried to load his guns. But before he could do so, Turner's advance horsemen swept into his yard, a whirlwind of axes and swords, and chased Waller into some tall weeds. Waller managed to escape, but not before he saw the blacks cut down his wife and children. One small girl also escaped by crawling up a dirt chimney, scarcely daring to breathe as the insurgents decapitated the other children—ten in all—and threw their bodies in a pile.

Turner had stationed himself at the rear of his little army and did not participate in these or any other killings along the Barrow Road. He never explained why. He had been fasting for several days and may well have been too weak to try any more killing himself. Or maybe as God's prophet he preferred to let Will and the eight or nine other lieutenants do the slaughtering. All he said about it afterward was that he "sometimes got in sight in time to see the work of death completed" and that he paused to view the bodies "in silent satisfaction" before riding on.

Around noon on Monday the insurgents reached the Jerusalem highway, and Turner soon joined them. Behind them lay a zigzag path of unredeemable destruction: some fifteen homesteads sacked and approximately sixty whites slain. By now the rebels amounted to fifty or sixty—including three or four free blacks. But even at its zenith Turner's army showed signs of disintegration. A few reluctant slaves had already escaped or deserted. And many others were roaring drunk, so drunk they could scarcely ride

their horses, let alone do any fighting. To make matters worse, many of the confiscated muskets were broken or too rusty to fire.

Turner resolved to march on Jerusalem at once and seize all the guns and powder he could find there. But a half mile up the road he stopped at the Parker farm, because some of his men had relatives and friends there. When the insurgents did not return, Turner went after them—and found his men not in the slave quarters but down in Parker's brandy cellar. He ordered them back to the highway at once.

On the way back they met a party of armed men—whites. There were about eighteen of them, as far as Turner could make out. They had already routed his small guard at the gate and were now advancing toward the Parker house. With renewed zeal Turner rallied his remaining troops and ordered an attack. Yelling at the top of their lungs, wielding axes, clubs, and gun butts, the Negroes drove the whites back into Parker's cornfield. But their advantage was short-lived. White reinforcements arrived, and more were on the way from nearby Jerusalem. Regrouping in the cornfield, the whites counterattacked, throwing the rebels back in confusion. In the fighting some of Turner's best men fell wounded, though none of them died. Several insurgents, too drunk to fight any more, fled pell-mell into the woods.

If Turner had often seemed irresolute earlier in the revolt, he was now undaunted. Even though his force was considerably reduced, he still wanted to storm Jerusalem. He led his men away from the main highway, which was blocked with militia, and took them along a back road, planning to cross the Cypress Bridge and strike the village from the rear. But the bridge was crawling with armed whites. In desperation the blacks set out to find reinforcements: they fell back to the south and then veered north again, picking up new recruits as they moved. They raided a few more farms, too, only to find them deserted, and finally encamped for the night near the slave quarters on Ridley's plantation.

All Monday night news of the revolt spread beyond Southampton County as express riders carried the alarm up to Petersburg and from there to the capitol in Richmond. Governor John Floyd, fearing a statewide uprising, alerted the militia and sent cavalry, infantry, and artillery units to the stricken county. Federal troops from Fortress Monroe were on the way, too, and other volunteers and militia outfits were marching from contiguous counties in Virginia and North Carolina. Soon over three thousand armed whites were in Southampton County, and hundreds more were mobilizing.

With whites swarming the countryside, Turner and his lieutenants did not know what to do. During the night an alarm had stampeded their new recruits, so that by Tuesday morning they had only twenty men left. Frantically they set out for Dr. Simon Blunt's farm to get volunteers—and rode straight into an ambush. Whites barricaded in the house opened fire on them at pointblank range, killing one or more insurgents and capturing several others—among them Hark Travis. Blunt's own slaves, armed with farm tools, helped in the defense and captured a few rebels themselves.

Repulsed at Blunt's farm, Turner led a handful of the faithful back toward the Cross Keys, still hoping to gather reinforcements. But the signs were truly ominous, for armed whites were everywhere. At last the militia overtook Turner's little band and in a final, desperate skirmish killed Will and scattered the rest. Turner himself, alone and in deep anguish, escaped to the vicinity of the Travis farm and hid in a hole under some fence rails.

By Tuesday evening a full-scale manhunt was under way in southeastern Virginia and North Carolina as armed whites prowled the woods and swamps in search of fugitive rebels and alleged collaborators. They chased the blacks down with howling dogs, killing those who resisted—and many of them resisted zealously—and dragging others back to Jerusalem to stand trial in the county court. One free black insurgent committed suicide rather than be taken by white men. Within a week nearly all the bona fide rebels except Turner had either been executed or imprisoned, but not before white

vigilantes—and some militiamen—had perpetrated barbarities on more than a score of innocent blacks. Outraged by the atrocities committed on whites, vigilantes rounded up Negroes in the Cross Keys and decapitated them. Another vigilante gang in North Carolina not only beheaded several blacks but placed their skulls on poles, where they remained for days. In all directions whites took Negroes from their shacks and tortured, shot, and burned them to death and then mutilated their corpses in ways that witnesses refused to describe. No one knows how many innocent Negroes died in this reign of terror—at least a hundred twenty, probably more. Finally the militia commander of Southampton County issued a proclamation that any further outrages would be dealt with according to the articles of war. Many whites publicly regretted these atrocities but argued that they were the inevitable results of slave insurrection. Another revolt, they said, would end with the extermination of every black in the region.

Although Turner's uprising ended on Tuesday, August 24, reports of additional insurrections swept over the South long afterward, and dozens of communities from Virginia to Alabama were seized with hysteria. In North Carolina rumors flew that slave armies had been seen on the highways, that one—maybe led by Turner himself—had burned Wilmington, butchered all the inhabitants, and was now marching on the state capital. The hysteria was even worse in Virginia, where reports of concerted slave rebellions and demands for men and guns swamped the governor's office. For a time it seemed that thousands of slaves had risen, that Virginia and perhaps the entire South would soon be ablaze. But Governor Floyd kept his head, examined the reports carefully, and concluded that no such widespread insurrection had taken place. Actually no additional uprisings had happened anywhere. Out of blind panic whites in many parts of the South had mobilized the militia, chased after imaginary insurgents, and jailed or executed still more innocent blacks. Working in cooperation with other political and military authorities in Virginia and North Carolina,

Floyd did all he could to quell the excitement, to re-assure the public that the slaves were quiet now. Still, the governor did not think the Turner revolt was the work of a solitary fanatic. Behind it, he believed, was a conspiracy of Yankee agitators and black preachers—especially black preachers. "The whole of that massacre in Southampton is the work of these Preachers," he declared, and demanded that they be suppressed.

Meanwhile the "great bandit chieftain," as the newspapers called him, was still at large. For more than two months Turner managed to elude white patrols, hiding out most of the time near Cabin Pond where the revolt had begun. Hunted by a host of aroused whites (there were various rewards totalling eleven hundred dollars on his head), Turner considered giving himself up and once got within two miles of Jerusalem before turning back. Finally on Sunday, October 30, a white named Benjamin Phipps accidentally discovered him in another hide-out near Cabin Pond. Since the man had a loaded shotgun, Turner had no choice but to throw down his sword.

The next day, with lynch mobs crying for his head, a white guard hurried Turner up to Jerusalem to stand trial. By now he was resigned to his fate as the will of Almighty God and was entirely fearless and unrepentant. When a couple of court justices examined him that day, he stated emphatically that *he* had conceived and directed the slaughter of all those white people (even though he had killed only Margaret Whitehead) and announced that God had endowed him with extraordinary powers. The justices ordered this "fanatic" locked up in the same small wooden jail where the other captured rebels had been incarcerated.

On November 1 one Thomas Gray, an elderly Jerusalem lawyer and slaveholder, came to interrogate Turner as he lay in his cell "clothed with rags and covered with chains." In Gray's opinion the public was anxious to learn the facts about the insurrection—for whites in Southampton could not fathom why their slaves would revolt. What Gray wanted was to take down and publish a confession from Turner that

would tell the public the truth about why the rebellion had happened. It appears that Gray had already gathered a wealth of information about the outbreak from other prisoners, some of whom he had defended as a court-appointed counsel. Evidently he had also written unsigned newspaper accounts of the affair, reporting in one that whites had located Turner's wife and lashed her until she surrendered his papers (remarkable papers, papers with hieroglyphics on them and sketches of the Crucifixion and the sun). According to Gray and to other sources as well, Turner over a period of three days gave him a voluntary and authentic confession about the genesis and execution of the revolt, recounting his religious visions in graphic detail and contending again that he was a prophet of Almighty God. "Do you not find yourself mistaken now?" Gray asked. Turner replied testily, "Was not Christ crucified?" Turner insisted that the uprising was local in origin but warned that other slaves might see signs and act as he had done. By the end of the confession Turner was in high spirits, perfectly "willing to suffer the fate that awaits me." Although Gray considered him "a gloomy fanatic," he thought Turner was one of the most articulate men he had ever met. And Turner could be frightening. When, in a burst of enthusiasm, he spoke of the killings and raised his manacled hands toward heaven, "I looked on him," Gray said, "and my blood curdled in my veins."

On November 5, with William C. Parker acting as his counsel, Turner came to trial in Jerusalem. The court, of course, found him guilty of committing insurrection and sentenced him to hang. Turner, though, insisted that he was not guilty because he did not feel so. On November 11 he went to his death in resolute silence. In addition to Turner, the county court tried some forty-eight other Negroes on various charges of conspiracy, insurrection, and treason. In all, eighteen blacks—including one woman—were convicted and hanged. Ten others were convicted and "transported"—presumably out of the United States.

But the consequences of the Turner revolt did not end with public hangings in Jerusalem. For southern whites the uprising seemed a monstrous climax to a whole decade of ominous events, a decade of abominable tariffs and economic panics, of obstreperous antislavery activities, and of growing slave unrest and insurrection plots, beginning with the Denmark Vesey conspiracy in Charleston in 1822 and culminating now in the worst insurrection Southerners had ever known. Desperately needing to blame somebody besides themselves for Nat Turner, Southerners linked the revolt to some sinister Yankee-abolitionist plot to destroy their cherished way of life. Southern zealots declared that the antislavery movement, gathering momentum in the North throughout the 1820's, had now burst into a full-blown crusade against the South. In January, 1831, William Lloyd Garrison had started publishing *The Liberator* in Boston, demanding in bold, strident language that the slaves be immediately and unconditionally emancipated. If Garrison's rhetoric shocked Southerners, even more disturbing was the fact that about eight months after the appearance of *The Liberator* Nat Turner embarked on his bloody crusade— something southern politicians and newspapers refused to accept as mere coincidence. They charged that Garrison was behind the insurrection, that it was his "bloodthirsty" invective that had incited Turner to violence. Never mind that there was no evidence that Turner had ever heard of *The Liberator;* never mind that Garrison categorically denied any connection with the revolt, saying that he and his abolitionist followers were Christian pacifists who wanted to free the slaves through moral suasion. From 1831 on, northern abolitionism and slave rebellion were inextricably associated in the southern mind.

But if Virginians blamed the insurrection on northern abolitionism, many of them defended emancipation itself as the only way to prevent further violence. In fact, for several months in late 1831 and early 1832 Virginians engaged in a momentous public debate over the feasibility of manumission. Out of the western part of the state, where antislavery and anti-Negro sentiment had long been smoldering, came petitions demanding that Virginia eradicate the "accursed," "evil" slave system and colonize all blacks at state expense. Only by removing the entire black population, the petitions argued, could future revolts be avoided. Newspapers also discussed the idea of emancipation and colonization, prompting one to announce that "Nat Turner and the blood of his innocent victims have conquered the silence of fifty years." The debate moved into the Virginia legislature, too, and early in 1832 proslavery and antislavery orators harangued one another in an unprecedented legislative struggle over emancipation. In the end most delegates concluded that colonization was too costly and too complicated to carry out. And since they were not about to manumit the blacks and leave them as free men in a white man's country, they rejected emancipation. Indeed, they went on to revise and implement the slave codes in order to restrict blacks so stringently that they could never mount another revolt. The modified codes not only strengthened the patrol and militia systems, but sharply curtailed the rights of free blacks and all but eliminated slave schools, slave religious meetings, and slave preachers. For Turner had taught white Virginians a hard lesson about what might happen if they gave slaves enough education and religion to think for themselves.

In the wake of the Turner revolt, the rise of the abolitionists, and the Virginia debates over slavery, the other southern states also expanded their patrol and militia systems and increased the severity of their slave codes. What followed was the Great Reaction of the 1830's and 1840's, during which the South, threatened it seemed by internal and external enemies, became a closed, martial society determined to preserve its slave-based civilization at whatever cost. If Southerners had once apologized for slavery as a necessary evil, they now trumpeted that institution as a positive good—"the greatest of all the great blessings," as James H. Hammond phrased it, "which a kind providence has bestowed." Southern postmasters set about confiscating abolitionist literature, lest these "incendiary" tracts invite the slaves to violence. Some states actually passed sedition laws and other restrictive measures that prohibited Negroes and whites alike from criticizing slavery. And slave

owners all across the South tightened up slave discipline, refusing to let blacks visit other plantations and
threatening to hang any slave who even looked rebellious. By the 1840's the Old South had devised
such an oppressive slave system that organized insurrection was all but impossible.

Even so, southern whites in the ante-bellum period never escaped the haunting fear that somewhere,
maybe even in their own slave quarters, another Nat
Turner was plotting to rise up and slit their throats.
They never forgot him. His name became for them a
symbol of terror and violent retribution.

But for ante-bellum blacks—and for their
descendants—the name of Nat Turner took on a
profoundly different connotation. He became a
legendary black hero who broke his chains and
murdered white people because slavery had murdered Negroes. Turner, said an elderly black man
in Southampton County only a few years ago, was
"God's man. He was a man for war, and for legal
rights, and for freedom."

QUESTIONS TO CONSIDER

1 Why did Nat Turner decide to strike back at the
slave system with retributive violence? Was he abused
as a slave? What role did the Old Testament, the
slave church, the slave underground, and extensive
fasting play in the genesis of Turner's insurrection?
Do you believe that he actually heard wind voices in
the trees, saw angels in the sky, and heard the call of
Jehovah?

2 Why did Turner command great respect in the
slave community? Why did he exclude privileged
house slaves from his plot? Who were his confederates, and why did they agree to follow him? When
did he finally decide to move? What do you think
was Turner's ultimate objective?

3 The details of the revolt—women hacked to death
with axes, children decapitated—are grisly indeed.
But the slave system was a brutal system that daily
maimed and murdered its victims. In light of that, do
you think Turner's actions were justifiable?

4 Why did most African Americans in Southampton
County refuse to join Turner's revolt? Why do you
think it failed? Or, to put it another way, how did
Nat and his followers, hopelessly outnumbered and
facing the tremendous firepower of the slave system,
manage to get as far as they did?

5 Why did the Virginia legislators debate and then
decide against abolishing slavery in their state? Who
or what did the governor and other white leaders
blame for the insurrection? How could they not put
the blame on the cruelties of the slave system? In
what ways do you think that the southern reaction
to the insurrection fueled sectional tensions and pre-
cipated the Civil War?

16 "I Will Be Heard!": William Lloyd Garrison and the Struggle Against Slavery

IRA BERLIN

*As we saw in the previous selection, southern whites blamed Nat Turner's insurrection on William
Lloyd Garrison, insisting that Nat had somehow acquired a copy of* The Liberator, *Garrison's
spirited abolitionist newspaper published in Boston. In the southern perception of events, the paper
had driven Nat mad and caused him to revolt. Nothing was further from the truth—there is no evidence that Nat had ever even heard of* The Liberator; *and Garrison himself said that Nat Turner*

had plenty of his own reasons to revolt. But southerners, unable to blame the insurrection on their own system, desperately needed a scapegoat. And so they pointed fingers at Garrison and his fellow northern abolitionists.

The following selection will introduce you to Garrison and the northern antislavery crusade. Garrison, however, was hardly the first abolitionist. Thomas Jefferson had hated slavery and advocated eradicating it by a gradual emancipation program. And southern and northern Quakers had opposed the institution since the colonial period. But in the 1820s—a decade of religious and political ferment—the antislavery movement truly took shape. Groups of Quakers and free blacks collected antislavery petitions and sent them to Congress, where intimidated southerners had them tabled, and Benjamin Lundy, a Baltimore Quaker, not only started publishing The Genius of Universal Emancipation *but organized antislavery societies in the South itself. At this time, most antislavery whites (a distinct minority of the population) were both gradualists and colonizationists such as Henry Clay. But by the 1830s, some had emphatically changed their minds. They renounced colonization, demanded immediate emancipation, organized a national antislavery society, and started an abolitionist crusade that would haunt the American conscience and arouse latent racism everywhere in the land.*

The best-known leader of the crusade was William Lloyd Garrison. A shy, intense, bespectacled young man who came from a broken home (his father had run away), he was raised by his mother as an ardent Baptist; later, he became a radical Christian perfectionist. Initially, Garrison too was a gradualist and a colonizer. But in 1829, after he went to work for Lundy's paper, Garrison renounced colonization and came out for immediate emancipation. In the columns of Lundy's paper, Garrison conducted a stunning moral attack against slavery and anybody who condoned or perpetuated it. For example, when he learned that a ship belonging to Francis Todd of Newburyport, Massachusetts (Garrison's hometown), was taking a cargo of slaves from Baltimore to New Orleans, Garrison castigated Todd as a highway robber and a murderer. The man, a highly respected citizen and a church deacon, slapped Garrison with a $5,000 libel suit. The court decided against Garrison and fined him $50, but he couldn't pay and had to go to jail. Later Garrison moved to Boston and established the abolitionist newspaper, The Liberator, *and went on to become the most prominent, and hated, leader of the crusade against slavery.*

Ira Berlin's essay captures the moral fervor of that momentous crusade and illuminates its origins. He takes us back to the Great Awakening, when people flocked to the churches to hear powerful preachers like George Whitefield, who told his flock that all human beings were equal in the eyes of God. Berlin reminds us that the democratic revolutions in America and France inspired a great many people to question the cruel practice of human bondage.

Even so, slavery by Garrison's time was firmly entrenched in the American South. Racial prejudice was prevalent in the North, too, where Berlin observes that free African Americans were denied the right "to vote, to sit on a jury, to testify in court, to carry a gun, and to travel freely." If they boarded a train, for example, white authorities forced them to sit in a segregated "colored car" in the rear.

To appreciate the incredible courage of William Lloyd Garrison, you need to understand the world in which he lived—a racist world in which the rights of property, including property in slaves, were often more important than human rights. It took a man of great inner strength to argue, in public, that the sweat and blood of African Americans had helped build this country, that slavery was a "sin" that must be abolished immediately, and that the emancipated blacks, after a period of instruction, must be assimilated into the American social order. These views were extremely unpopular in all parts of the country, and Garrison's life was constantly threatened. When he was on the platform, furious opponents of the abolitionist cause screamed at him and struck him with stones and rotten eggs. Once, in Boston, a mob threatened to hang him, dragging him through the street with a rope around his neck. Yet Garrison refused to temper his words or to renounce his cause. In the end, his noble crusade was successful.

GLOSSARY

ABOLITIONIST A person devoted to freeing the slaves, gradually with the cooperation of the South, immediately through nonviolent moral pressure (Garrison's methodology), or through bloodshed (the preferred approach of John Brown and David Walker). Those who sought an immediate end to slavery argued that they were assaulting a sinful institution.

ALLEN, RICHARD A former slave who eventually purchased his own freedom, he formed the first separate church in which African Americans could worship without facing discrimination. He opposed the American Colonization Society and argued that former slaves should stay in the country their labor had helped build.

AMERICAN ANTI-SLAVERY SOCIETY A national organization that Garrison helped form in 1833, it abandoned colonization and embraced immediate emancipation.

AMERICAN COLONIZATION SOCIETY A private organization founded in 1816 for the purpose of resettling "free persons of color" outside the United States. Although this was not an abolitionist enterprise, many members hoped to persuade the southern states to abolish slavery by promising to remove the liberated blacks to other lands. Liberia, on the western coast of Africa, was their most successful colonization site. Eventually twelve thousand African Americans sought refuge there.

BIRNEY, JAMES G. A Kentucky slaveowner and Alabama solicitor general who freed his slaves, relocated in the North, joined the abolitionist movement, and became the presidential candidate of the Liberty party in 1840 and 1844. He headed the first presidential platform dedicated to the elimination of slavery.

FEDERALIST This political party developed during the administration of George Washington. It supported a strong national government, a sound currency, and a pro-British foreign policy. The death of its leader Alexander Hamilton and its unpopular dissent during the War of 1812 relegated the party to only local influence in a few New England strongholds.

FORTEN, JAMES An African American leader and sail maker who resided in Philadelphia. His subscriptions to *The Liberator* helped launch Garrison's newspaper. Referring to the American Colonization Society as "a slaveholders' trick," he influenced Garrison to oppose the controversial organization.

GRADUAL EMANCIPATION See GRADUALISM.

GRADUALISM The idea that slavery should be eliminated over an extended period. In Garrison's day, there were various plans for gradual emancipation; many of them coupled with colonization of the freed blacks and fair compensation to slave owners for their loss. A Pennsylvania statute contained a variation of such a plan. The measure decreed that the children of slaves born in Pennsylvania after 1780 were to be freed when they reached their twenty-eighth birthday.

GREAT AWAKENING A Protestant revival movement that swept through the colonies in the eighteenth century and that was led by charismatic ministers like George Whitefield. As a result of this movement, church attendance dramatically increased; and Garrison's mother was one of many drawn to its evangelical brand of morality.

THE LIBERATOR Garrison's abolitionist newspaper, first published in Boston on January 1, 1831. Although it never had a circulation of more than a few thousand, its message frightened the slaveholding South and attracted reformers in the North to the antislavery cause.

LUNDY, BENJAMIN The Quaker publisher of *The Genius of Universal Emancipation* who took on Garrison as a "junior partner." Although their collaborative effort was short-lived, it gave Garrison an appreciation of the antislavery movement and the power of the printed word.

WALKER, DAVID A free African American revolutionary who wrote the *Appeal to the Colored Citizens of the World,* a pamphlet that urged slaves to revolt.

Save for the annual turning of the calendar, January 1, 1831, seemed little different than any other wintry day in Boston. There seemed nothing remarkable, for instance, about the slight balding young man who walked briskly past the Bunker Hill monument, Faneuil Hall, and other remembrances of America's revolutionary past. Nor did anyone notice that his pace quickened as he turned into Merchants' Hall, or that he mounted the stairs to a nondescript print shop with a mixture of determination and expectation. For more than a week, William Lloyd Garrison—along with his partner, Isaac Knapp, and several of their friends—had been setting type for a new journal that they all hoped would strike a blow at slavery, an evil that degraded millions of Americans and corrupted tens of millions more. For Garrison and his friends, chattel bondage denied the slaves' humanity and contradicted the principles of the Declaration of Independence as well as the precepts of Jesus Christ. *The Liberator,* they believed, would elevate the slaves and thus restore the nation's highest ideals.

Driven by the belief that all people were created equal and all created in God's image, Garrison worked on through the day, polishing his inaugural editorial. As he put the finishing touches on the first issue of *The Liberator,* Garrison reflected on the enormous task before him. Perhaps to steel himself as well as to assure readers of the depth of his commitment, he concluded the editorial with a ringing affirmation: "I am in earnest—I will not equivocate—I will not excuse—I will not retreat a single inch—AND I *WILL* BE HEARD."

When the issue was at last ready to go to press, Garrison emblazoned the masthead with the words, "OUR COUNTRY IS THE WORLD—OUR COUNTRYMEN MANKIND," capturing the universalism that would characterize his life's work. Now he needed only the cash for paper, ink, and a few other necessary supplies. Fortunately, the arrival of an advance payment

William Lloyd Garrison, celebrated abolitionist and editor of the controversial Liberator. *"I will be as harsh as truth, and as uncompromising as justice," wrote Garrison in his manifesto in the first issue of* The Liberator. *On the subject of slavery, "I do not wish to think, or speak, or write, with moderation. . . . I am in earnest—I will not equivocate—I will not excuse—I will not retreat a single inch—AND I WILL BE HEARD." (Department of Special Collections, Wichita State University Library)*

for some twenty-five subscriptions—courtesy of his friend James Forten, a black Philadelphia sail maker—made it possible for Garrison to proceed.

Publication of a radical abolitionist journal was a strange mission for the young man born in December 1805 in the small seaside town of Newburyport, Massachusetts. During the 1780s, through a series of judicial decisions, slavery had been abolished in Massachusetts. So, as a boy, Garrison could have had no direct knowledge of slavery. Nor could he have known many people of African descent, for scarcely a few dozen resided in his hometown. In addition,

Ira Berlin, "January 1, 1831, The Liberator." Reprinted from *Days of Destiny,* General Editors James M. McPherson and Alan Brinkley; Editor, David Rubel, by permission of DK Publishing. Copyright © 2001 Dorling Kindersley Ltd. All rights reserved. www.dk.com.

the tone of the first issue of *The Liberator* seemed out of character with the twenty-five-year-old who wrote it, for there was nothing in Garrison's physical appearance or demeanor to suggest the steadfast resolve that would lead him to press his beliefs to their logical conclusion.

The tensile strength that Garrison brought to *The Liberator* had been annealed in most unpromising beginnings. In the early nineteenth century, Adijah and Frances Garrison had migrated to Newburyport from the Maritime Provinces of Canada, seeking economic opportunity and a congenial community for their evangelical beliefs. They found little of the former but much of the latter, for Newburyport had been deeply touched by the Great Awakening and its aftermath. Sadly, though, the expansion of Boston had leached the town of its prosperity, making it increasingly difficult for Adijah Garrison to support his growing family. The maritime depression that accompanied the War of 1812 left him unemployed, impoverished, and depressed. He turned to drink and eventually deserted his family, leaving his wife and four young children destitute. Frances Garrison, fortified by her evangelical faith, labored mightily to sustain her children. But, in time, she was forced to place them with kindly neighbors and fellow congregants. Her youngest son, William, was apprenticed to the publisher of the *Newburyport Herald*.

Young William Lloyd Garrison loved the craft of printing as well as the world of words and ideas that sprang from the presses. He read voraciously, which compensated for his lack of formal education, and occasionally tried his hand at poetry and some fiction. But the *Herald* was a Federalist sheet that emphasized politics, and it was from the *Herald* that Garrison took his first political ideas, combining them with an exuberant idealism that had its roots in the radicalism of the American Revolution. (His first public utterance—delivered on July 4, 1824, at a meeting of the local debating society—celebrated the global expansion of American revolutionary principles as "freedom's awakening triumphant call.") Garrison's views were also shaped by his mother's

evangelical moralism and his own stiff-necked sense of rectitude. Principle, not expedience, would be his guide, and the identification and eradication of sin his quest.

This heady mixture manifested itself when, upon completing his apprenticeship in 1825, the nineteen-year-old Garrison took up the editorship of his own newspaper in Newburyport. Before long, he was denouncing Thomas Jefferson as "the great Lama of Infidelity" (for Jefferson's flirtation with deism) and proclaiming his own continuing attachment to the Federalist party, even though it had lost its electoral franchise nearly a decade earlier. In championing the candidacies of the few remaining Federalists, Garrison demonstrated his resolute commitment to loyalty no matter the cost, but as his candidates failed, so did his editorship. In 1828, with the collapse of his journalistic career in Newburyport, Garrison left for new opportunities in Boston.

While Garrison's unfashionable attachment to Federalism won him few new friends, his moralism gained him entry into Boston's expanding universe of benevolent reform. On the rise in Boston were Christian missionaries, temperance advocates, pacifists, vegetarians, and proponents of all manner of human betterment from feminism to socialism. As yet another foot soldier in the evangelical war against sin, Garrison quickly secured the editorship of a temperance journal and, when that publication also failed, attached himself to a kindly Quaker named Benjamin Lundy, the peripatetic publisher of an irregular antislavery sheet grandly entitled *The Genius of Universal Emancipation*.

For years, Lundy had traveled the slave states making the case for abolition. Carrying (almost literally) his press on his back, he lived from hand to mouth as he published his journal. For the most part, he labored in near-total anonymity, unnoticed except by like-minded members of the Society of Friends and appreciative people of color. Accepting Garrison as a junior partner marked a sharp break for Lundy, who was very much a loner. In fact, the association did not last long, but it was fateful, because in Lundy's cause Garrison found his life's work and in Lundy's methods he found his own metier. Garrison's egalitarianism and moralism gained a new, clearer direction as he came to appreciate through Lundy the evil that was chattel bondage.

Opposition to slavery was itself relatively new in the United States, as it was everywhere in the world. Until the end of the eighteenth century, slavery had few principled enemies. From antiquity onward, nearly every society practiced slavery, and every authority—religious and secular—sanctioned it, often with elaborate codes affirming the legitimacy of the slave master's rule. In a world where hierarchy was ubiquitous and inequality the norm, slavery had long been considered at one with God and nature, and few voices were raised against slave ownership.

The American and French revolutions changed that. The doctrine that "all men are created equal," asserted first in the American Declaration of Independence and then reiterated in the French Declaration of the Rights of Man, initiated a transformation of slavery from a universally accepted convention for extracting labor and assuring obedience into a hideous relic of the past. Henceforth, it was not equality that would be the anomaly but slavery. In the new United States, leading revolutionaries—Jefferson, Washington, and Franklin, to name just the most prominent—condemned slavery. Some, like Jefferson, bemoaned it while continuing to exercise the practice; others, like Washington, freed their slaves; still others, like Franklin, formed manumission societies and urged slavery's total liquidation.

Yet slavery survived and flourished, even as its legitimacy was called into question. At the end of the Revolution, it could still be found in every part of the new United States, deeply rooted at the base of the American economy and tightly woven into the fabric of society. Even in the northern states, opposition to slavery remained a novelty, and abolitionists moved with caution. Although slavery fell quickly in northern New England, where slaves were numerically few and their labor economically marginal, emancipation proved more difficult in southern New England and the middle-Atlantic states. The 1780 Pennsylvania Emancipation Act freed not a single slave on emancipation day—March 1 of that year—and proposed to eliminate slavery only by freeing the children of slaves born thereafter once they reached the age of twenty-eight. Moreover, at the time of the enactment of the Pennsylvania statute, the legal liquidation of slavery had not yet begun at all in Connecticut, Rhode Island, New Jersey, or the largest northern slave state, New York.

As in Pennsylvania, emancipationists in these states dared not challenge slavery directly; instead, they settled for the gradual, piecemeal emancipation of slaves, while assuring grumbling slaveholders of fair compensation for their lost property. Gradualism therefore guaranteed that the death of slavery in the North would take not years, or even decades, but generations to accomplish. More important, it signaled the impossibility of abolition in the South, where slaves were more numerous and believed to be an essential element of the plantation economy. Indeed, even as the work of abolition commenced, the number of slaves in the United States grew, increasing from about half a million at the beginning of the American Revolution to well over one million by 1810.

The feeble nature of the assault on slavery had much to do with the fact that slavery had become identified with people of African descent. Whatever white Americans thought of slavery in principle, they had no desire to live with black people who were free. As many white Americans explained it, circumstance—the very experience of enslavement—had degraded black people, making them unfit for full participation in the new republic. And some whites simply believed that black people ranked below them on the scale of civilization.

White slaveholders, who had a deep material interest in chattel bondage, made much of this perceived inferiority of black people as well as the feared destabilizing effects of emancipation. They promoted the ideas that free blacks would not work, that they would demand political rights and seize power, and that they would intermarry with whites and destroy white posterity. Perhaps even more telling is that many of the white opponents of slavery shared these sentiments. The very laws that liberated northern slaves often carried with them proscriptions regarding the liberty of former slaves, denying them the rights to vote, to sit on a jury, to testify in court, to carry a gun, and to travel freely. And where legislative enactments dared not tread, informal practice (newly established, but anointed with the force of custom) served the same function. By general consensus, white employers barred free blacks from trades they once practiced openly as slaves, and white citizens denied them entry into public places, excluding them from churches, schools, and militia musters. Some communities "warned out" free people of color, and when they would not leave voluntarily, they were often ridiculed and assaulted, physically as well as verbally. The desire to rid the nation of black people—particularly free blacks—spurred a movement to deport or "colonize" them, with Africa being the logical destination.

The obstacles faced by free blacks in the young republic led some opponents of slavery, styling themselves realists, to conclude that abolition was possible only upon removal—or, in their words, "pending repatriation." The realists denied any racial animus toward people of African descent. Indeed, they maintained that once repatriated, black people could enjoy without prejudice the rights promised by the Declaration of Independence. African Americans transported to Africa would not only regain their birthright, it was believed; they would also become agents of the expansion of American republicanism, Christianity, and commercial capitalism. With the founding of the American Colonization Society in 1817 and the establishment of the colony of Liberia soon thereafter, "Negro removal" became the central feature of American antislavery activity.

Yet colonization had other faces. Some advocates simply wanted to rid the United States of all its black people. Many of these were white supremacists who despised people of color. Other colonizationists were slaveholders who wanted to deport free blacks and thereby strengthen the institution of slavery. These people believed that eliminating free blacks would allow slaves to be content with their lot, making them better workers and more obedient servants. By depriving slaves of a model of black freedom, the threat of servile insurrection would also likely wither—assuring white slaveholders of economic prosperity, political stability, and an undiluted posterity.

For their part, black people had no doubt about the meaning of colonization. To them, colonization was little more than a plot to perpetuate chattel bondage and bolster white supremacy. Asserting their claims to American nationality, many denounced the logic of repatriation. "This is our home, and this is our country," proclaimed a coalition of black Philadelphians led by James Forten and Bishop Richard Allen of the African Methodist Episcopal Church. "Beneath its sod lie the bones of our fathers; for it some of them fought, bled, and died. Here we were born, and here we will die."

Like many other opponents of slavery, Benjamin Lundy was wedded to the colonizationist cause as the only practical means of securing the slaves' freedom. But Garrison had no such attachment, and as he accompanied Lundy around the nation, the pair of them proselytizing against slavery, Garrison discovered that the alleged beneficiaries of colonization wanted nothing to do with the scheme. He listened ever more attentively as men like Forten and Allen denounced colonization as a slaveholders' trick, and he found himself swept up by the power of their logic: If black people could be free and equal in Africa, why not in America? In this way, the African-American critique of colonization (and black people's demand for equality) became central to Garrison's understanding of slavery and race. He carried these ideas with him when he returned to Boston and made them his own. Thereafter, black people became his strongest supporters and most loyal allies.

The inaugural issue of *The Liberator* borrowed much from the protests of black leaders. Apologizing for his previous support of the "pernicious doctrine of *gradual* abolition"—a belief he now admitted to be "full of timidity, injustice, and absurdity"—Garrison demanded an immediate end to slavery and the resurrection of the principles asserted in the Declaration of Independence. In condemning slavery as a sin, he unsheathed the weapons that would become the signatures of his egalitarian campaign. There would be no groveling for political favor, with the implicit willingness to compromise—for the immoral nature of slavery would not allow for compromise. There would be no call for slaves to rise up and throw off their chains, with the explicit threat of bloodshed—for violence would beget only more violence. Instead, there would be relentless reassertion of the principle of human equality and persistent denunciation of the evil of slaveholding. White and black could not be distinguished in the eyes of God; therefore, they should not be distinguished in the eyes of the law. Is it possible that "all men are born equal, and entitled to equal protection, excepting those whose skins are black and hair wooly?" *The Liberator* editorialized. Garrison then concluded his opening editorial with this stern warning:

I will be as harsh as truth, and as uncompromising as justice. On this subject, I do not wish to think, or speak, or write, with moderation. No! No! Tell a man whose house is on fire to give a moderate alarm; tell him to moderately rescue his wife from the hands of the ravisher; tell the mother to gradually extricate her babe from the fire into which it has fallen;—but urge me not to use moderation in a cause like the present.

The first issue of *The Liberator* sparked a small fire that grew, as more issues were published, into a blaze extinguished only by civil war. In the process, Garrison forced a nation to confront, for the first time, its most pressing moral dilemma—race—and inspired a tradition of social commitment and moral agitation that became a model for others from Frederick Douglass to Martin Luther King Jr. He also personified the difference between conventional partisan politics (which seeks, through the process of compromise, to identify a mutually acceptable middle ground) and movement politics (which stakes out a principled

position on the periphery and then attempts to draw conventional politicians to its cause). Lastly, Garrison elevated the work of social reform into a profession, which men and women from Susan B. Anthony to Ralph Nader would find worthy as an occupation. On that New Year's Day in 1831, though, Garrison's work was just beginning.

When compared to the stirring editorial, the rest of *The Liberator's* first issue seems relatively tame. There were poems, short stories, meditations, and pleas for subscribers. Garrison published the text of a petition against slavery in the nation's capital, then being circulated in Boston, and urged readers to sign it. He also reprinted an article on the District of Columbia slave trade (taken from a Washington newspaper) that, like the petition, emphasized how slavery in the seat of their national government made hypocrites of all Americans. "That District," Garrison sneered, "is rotten with the plague, and stinks in the nostrils of the world." Elsewhere, he announced a fifty-dollar prize for the best essay on "The Duties of Ministers and Churches of all denominations to avoid the stain of Slavery." Garrison informed his readers of the arrival in North Carolina of *Appeal to the Colored Citizens of the World,* a pamphlet written by black revolutionary David Walker urging black people to rise up against slavery and racial subordination, and he took note of several other matters of local and national import. But the miscellany that filled the back pages of *The Liberator* hardly disguised its single-minded preoccupation.

The appearance of *The Liberator* challenged not only the institution of slavery in the South but also the antislavery movement in the North and the structure of racial inequality upon which both rested. In doing so, it naturally aroused opposition of the sort one might expect from such a radical assault on the foundations of American society and the conventions of master over slave, white over black. The same year that *The Liberator* appeared, the District of Columbia tried to prevent its circulation by prohibiting free blacks from removing copies from the post office. Meanwhile in Raleigh, North Carolina, a grand jury indicted Garrison for distributing incendiary literature, and the Georgia legislature offered a five-thousand-dollar bounty for anyone arresting Garrison and bringing him to the state to face charges of libel. Other threats emerged closer to home as Garrison was pelted with eggs and epithets; condemned as a fanatic, lunatic, and worse; and, according to one account, targeted for assassination. In October 1835, an antiabolitionist mob shouting "Hang him on the Commons" nearly lynched Garrison on the streets of Boston.

But Garrison did not frighten easily. Unmoved by the torrent of abuse, he gathered around him a small group of disciples attracted by the depth of his egalitarian commitment and his unshakable willingness to defend his principles against all comers. For the most part, his followers were young men and women—among them Lydia Marie Child, Abbey Kelly, Samuel May, and Henry C. Wright—who took seriously the promise of the American republic. Like Garrison, they were appalled by the nation's failure to practice the ideals it celebrated and by the rank injustice they believed was rooted in a government whose founding charter delayed the close of the slave trade for two decades, required the return of fugitive slaves, and assigned slaves the status of only three-fifths of a man. Using *The Liberator* as their platform, they denounced the republic, its founders, and its icons. Declaring the Constitution "a covenant with death and agreement with hell," they publicly burned copies to demonstrate their contempt for the government that most Americans believed represented the apotheosis of liberty.

Beyond this small coterie, at least at first, the Garrisonian assault on slavery won few converts. But the issuance of *The Liberator* broke the silence on slavery—for if Lundy's opposition to chattel bondage was barely audible, Garrison's broadcasts could not be escaped. *The Liberator* also removed colonization as a legitimate avenue of antislavery activity, eventually replacing it with the principle of immediate emancipation. Already by 1833, when the Garrisonians established the American Anti-Slavery Society, their leader had become the central figure in the war against chattel bondage and *The Liberator* the unparalleled voice of the antislavery movement.

In the years that followed, Garrison's influence extended beyond the radicals he had initially attracted into the moderate reform community at large. These newcomers to the antislavery cause included many who did not share Garrison's animosity toward both the American republic and conventional political partisanship. Rather than repudiate the Constitution, they embraced it and worked within its system to build political parties that might overturn slavery through electoral means. Noting that the Constitution never actually used the word *slave,* they aimed to restore what they claimed to be the Founding Fathers' antislavery intent. By 1840, political abolitionists such as Joshua Giddings of Ohio and William Slade of Vermont had used antislavery platforms to secure seats in Congress, and that same year James G. Birney ran for president as the candidate of the Liberty party, the first political party dedicated to the eradication of slavery.

Although Garrison distanced himself from politicians who wanted to ride the antislavery issue to power and blistered political abolitionists for their willingness to dance with the devil, he did nothing to discourage their assault on slavery. On occasion, he even raised a glass of ice water to toast their successes, making it clear for whom he would have voted (if he had considered it ethical to vote under the present system, which he did not). Likewise, antislavery politicians tended to keep their distance from Garrison and his followers; yet none would deny the strength they all drew from the assault on slavery he had unleashed on January 1, 1831. In late 1864, soon after his reelection, Abraham Lincoln invited Garrison to the White House. Later, the president was heard to remark that he considered himself "only an instrument" in the struggle for emancipation, adding, "The logic and moral power of Garrison and the antislavery people of the country and the army, have done it all." *The Liberator* had been heard.

QUESTIONS TO CONSIDER

1 Born in New England with no first-hand knowledge of slavery and little contact with individuals of African descent, Garrison had an unusual background for a man who so ardently opposed slavery. What do you think motivated Garrison to vigorously support a cause that was not popular even in the North?

2 Berlin states that until the end of the eighteenth century there were relatively few opponents of slavery. Many Americans, in fact, argued that the cruel institution was consistent with God and nature. How did the American and French Revolutions change attitudes toward slavery? Founding fathers like Jefferson, Franklin, and Washington all had their doubts about forced human bondage. Explain how each developed a different approach toward slavery.

3 How do we know that racial prejudice toward African Americans was not limited to the American South? Describe some of the restrictions faced by liberated northern slaves. Also describe the fears that southern whites had if emancipation ever became a reality.

4 The American Colonization Society was a controversial and greatly misunderstood organization. Why did most slaveowners support it and most African Americans oppose it? How did Garrison's opinion of it change as he preached against slavery across the country?

5 Why did Garrison oppose the gradual emancipation doctrine that other abolitionists supported? Did he feel that violence was necessary to end slavery? What was your reaction when you learned that the abolitionist movement varied greatly in strategy and tactics?

6 How did the South react to the publication of *The Liberator?* Was the mood of the North any less emotional? Why do you think that a newspaper with a relatively small circulation would cause such a great uproar?

PART NINE

The Age of Jackson

17 Andrew Jackson: Flamboyant Hero of the Common Man

JOHN F. MARSZALEK

The age of Jackson was a turbulent era—a period of boom and bust, of great population shifts into the cities and out to the frontier, of institutionalized violence and racial antagonisms, of utopian communities, reform movements, the abolitionist crusade, and the "great southern reaction" in defense of slavery. It was also a time of graft and corruption, of machine politics and ruthless political bosses. But above all, it was an age of the self-made man, a time when privilege and elitist rule gave way to the vestiges of popular democracy—at least for white males. Between the 1820s and the 1840s, America witnessed the rise of universal manhood suffrage for whites, long ballots, national nominating conventions, and grassroots political parties.

The man who gave the age its name was a self-made planter and slaveholder of considerable wealth. Like most aristocrats from the Tennessee country of his day, Andrew Jackson could not spell, he lacked education and culture, but he did aspire to wealth and military glory, both of which he won. Despite his harsh, gaunt features, he looked like a gentleman and a soldier, and in calm moods he could be gentle, even grave.

John F. Marszalek's lively essay captures the passion of a man who was more popular than any political figure since George Washington. Like Washington, Jackson established his early reputation in his military exploits against the British. Unlike the aloof Washington, Jackson was an emotional man who fought duels over his wife's honor and challenged corruption, real and perceived, in the political arena. His enemies—the British, Spanish, and the Indians—were the foes of the "common man" of his day, and Jackson successfully battled them all during his military career. Marszalek vividly describes Jackson's rough-and-tumble background, so different from that of the previous presidents and one that most Americans born without inherited privileges found vastly appealing.

Jackson's personality and rags-to-riches climb to the White House inspired a popular movement often called the Jacksonian revolution. This revolution moved America toward a more democratic system in which the government was responsive to the popular will. Jackson himself played a major role in the shift toward democracy—that is, toward a system of true majority rule, not just rule by a propertied elite. He set out to make the president and every other federal official answerable to the people. Thus, he favored abolishing the electoral college and rotating every elected office. He even challenged the role of the Supreme Court as the final arbiter in interpreting the Constitution, a subject covered in selection 14. Jackson also inaugurated the history of powerful executive leadership in this country. He used his veto power more than all his predecessors combined and asserted the right of the chief executive to initiate legislation, which altered the president's relationship with Congress and made the president the head of state.

Marszalek's portrait of Jackson presents the modern reader with puzzling dilemmas. We wonder how Jackson could be fiercely protective of white women yet massacre women of color and hold them as slaves. Could a slaveowner really be a man of the people? As you ponder this question, reflect on Douglas L. Wilson's warning about presentism in selection 8. Jackson himself would have answered this question with a resounding "yes" on two counts. First, the Jacksonian revolution ushered in universal white manhood suffrage in most states and created a true mass electorate. Second, "the people" in Jackson's day was a political concept that included all those who could vote. That meant white men almost exclusively. Women, slaves, and free blacks outside New England were all denied the electoral franchise and were excluded from the idea of "the people." They had no will to which Jackson or any other government official could be responsive.

Through the mode of biography, you are about to undertake a fascinating journey into a life and a world far removed from your own. The unique quality of biography is that it personalizes history. Biography connects the present with the past, allowing people of one age to reach back through the mists, to touch people of another age, and to understand. Perhaps that is what Irish poet William Butler Yeats meant when he said that "nothing exists but a stream of souls, that all knowledge is biography."

GLOSSARY

ADAMS, JOHN QUINCY   As President James Monroe's secretary of state, Adams negotiated the Adams-Oñis Treaty with Spain in 1819. Among other things, the treaty gave Florida to the United States. Adams's diplomatic triumph salvaged Jackson's reputation after the impulsive general had exceeded his orders and killed Seminoles and British citizens in Spanish Florida. One of America's finest secretaries of state, Adams was also largely responsible for the Monroe Doctrine. Later he served one term as president (1825–1829).

BATTLE OF NEW ORLEANS   America's greatest victory in the otherwise inglorious War of 1812, the nation's second war with Great Britain. The victory, however, had no effect on the outcome of the war, since a peace treaty had already been negotiated in Europe. Even so, the victory made Jackson the country's most celebrated war hero.

BENTON, THOMAS HART   This prominent Missouri politician served in the national Senate from 1821 to 1851. An outspoken champion of western development, he eventually shifted his allegiance to Jackson.

BURR, AARON   The man who killed Alexander Hamilton (see selection 13) resurfaces here as a schemer who encouraged Jackson to join him in a wild plot to seize and colonize Spanish territory in the Southwest. Jackson refused, and Burr wound up in jail on a charge of treason. He was found not guilty.

CALHOUN, JOHN C.   He served as vice president under both John Quincy Adams and Andrew Jackson and later as a prominent senator from South Carolina. A nationalist during the War of 1812, Calhoun subsequently turned his brilliant mind to a defense of slavery and the right of the South to nullify federal laws that failed to serve sectional interests.

CLAY, HENRY   A transplanted Kentuckian and a popular figure in the West, Clay served as speaker of the House of Representatives, where he opposed Jackson's actions in Spanish Florida and later threw his support to Adams in the presidential election of 1824. Since Jackson had won the popular vote and Clay became Adams's secretary of state, considered then as a steppingstone to the presidency, the outraged Jackson believed a "corrupt bargain" had robbed him of the White House.

DICKENSON, CHARLES   He made the fatal error of questioning Rachel Jackson's honor and faced the wrath of her husband, who challenged Dickenson to a duel. Jackson carried a bullet from Dickenson's dueling pistol in him for the rest of his life, but he had the satisfaction of killing his antagonist with the second shot.

DONELSON, RACHEL   Jackson's wife and "the abiding love of his life." She was outgoing and attractive and had only a limited education. Her first marriage to Lewis Robards failed miserably, and it ended officially more than two years after she took her wedding vows with her new husband.

He stood tall and thin, six feet one inch, yet weighed only 140 pounds. His face was narrow, his nose pointed, his wide forehead melting into his frizzy hair, once a sandy red, but by the time he became president of the United States, a whitish gray. His eyes were blue, and when he became angry, they blazed fire, or so contemporaries imagined. Nearly sixty-two years of age when he took the oath of office on March 4, 1829, the ravages of time were evident in the creases on his face and the stiffness of his gait. Still, his appearance was impressive: erect in posture and exuding strength and power.

Andrew Jackson was without doubt one of the most popular men ever elected president of the United States. Architect of the great victory over the British at New Orleans during the War of 1812, and the man who had crushed the Indians in the southeast, his execution of two British subjects in Spanish Florida only added to his appeal. Americans disliked the British and the Indians, two enemies they saw as barriers to the nation's progress. Because of Jackson's important victories over these groups, people began to refer to him as the "Old Hero." A Floridian said he believed something a friend had told him, "as much as if General Jackson, or Jesus Christ, had said it."

Despite his wide popularity, Jackson also became one of the nation's most reviled chief executives. To many Americans he appeared as the border ruffian from frontier Tennessee. He fought duels, he had a passion for horse racing and cockfighting, and his fiery temper seemed irrational and frightening. That the common people reacted to him so passionately provided even greater concern. He might be the "Old Hero" to some, but others saw him a dangerous demagogue, a threat to the very stability of the nation. A modern historian, though favorable to him, has written: "He was ill-educated, ill-tempered, opinionated, suspicious, unbending, dictatorial, . . . vindictive, and a fierce hater." A contemporary tried to find a middle ground: "If he was not as perfect and capable as his friends represented him to be, he was a better man than his enemies described him to be."

His beginnings themselves are in question; North and South Carolina both claim him as a native son because the exact location of his nativity is unknown. Without debate, however, all contemporaries and historians agree that he came from Scots-Irish frontier ancestry. His parents, Andrew and Elizabeth Jackson, had come to the British colonies from Ulster, Ireland, in 1765, eventually settling into the proverbial log cabin in the Carolinas. Andrew, the husband and father, died in March 1767, leaving behind a widow pregnant with the

Reprinted with permission of The Free Press, a division of Simon & Schuster, Inc. From *The Petticoat Affair: Manners, Mutiny, and Sex in Andrew Jackson's White House* by John F. Marszalek. Copyright © 1998 by John F. Marszalek.

Andrew Jackson's enormous popularity was a product of his military victories against the British, the Spanish, and Native Americans. The voters pictured him on horseback, not behind a desk. His enemies were the villains of the early national period. His humble background mirrored those of the great majority of the American electorate. (Library of Congress)

soon-to-be-born son. Upon the death of her mate, Elizabeth moved in with her sister and brother-in-law. She gave birth to Andrew, her third child, on March 15, 1767, and took over household duties for her sickly sister. Andrew Jackson, therefore, spent the first years of his life carrying his father's name but fatherless and without a home of his own, the youngest of eleven children under his mother's care.

The boy went to school and quickly gained the reputation of being the most obstreperous of the horde of children in his adopted home. He pushed his mother's patience to the limit with his furious horseback riding, swearing, and fighting. She hoped that religion would save him, but the American Revolution

proved to have the greater influence on his young life. The war forced him and his family to flee from the advancing British troops and their numerous Loyalist allies, people Andrew had known all his life. He and his two older brothers became soldiers, one brother soon becoming a war casualty.

In 1781, Andrew experienced a defining moment. The British captured him and his surviving brother, Robert, while wrecking their house. In the course of the pillaging, a British officer ordered Andrew to clean his boots. When the stubborn teenager boldly refused, the officer angrily swung his sword at the young boy, producing a deep cut and permanent scars on his head and on the fingers of his left hand, which he had thrown up to protect himself. Later, Andrew and Robert were thrown into prison in Camden, South Carolina, where they suffered from insufficient food and lack of medical attention. They would have died had it not been for their mother. Still nursing the sick and wounded as she had long been doing, she somehow convinced British authorities to include her sons in an exchange for some captive British soldiers.

Andrew's nightmare was hardly over, however. Robert died, and the debilitating fever of smallpox devastated his own body. His mother put him to bed at home. When he seemed out of danger, she hurried to Charleston to look after two nephews, both deathly ill on a prison ship in the harbor. Andrew never saw her again. In the fall of 1781, cholera struck her down as she nursed the sick.

His father, mother, and two brothers were all dead; his strong mother's departure was particularly devastating. A fearful, confused teenager, Andrew Jackson was forced to face the uncertain future alone. He grew angry and frustrated, no doubt developing his lifelong anger and dogged insistence on the unquestioning devotion of friends and relatives. All his life, Andrew Jackson wanted absolute assurance from those around him that they would always remain at his side. Having lost his family as a young man, he needed devoted permanent friends to take their place. He insisted on total loyalty, and he gave the same full measure.

Several severe physical maladies added to the young Jackson's problems. He apparently suffered from something known as the "big itch," a rash that affected his entire body. Equally, if not more embarrassingly, he did not stop "slobbering" until after he became an adult. Any derogatory remarks about either ailment provoked him into a no-holds-barred fight, the skinny young man refusing to quit no matter how he fared in the scuffle. Andrew Jackson had "a morbid fear of being made ridiculous."

Whether to test his perimeters or as a way of dealing with the losses and fears in his life, he became "the most roaring, rollicking, game-cocking, horse-racing, card-playing, mischievous fellow that ever lived in Salisbury" (North Carolina), where he settled after the war. Once, as a joke, he invited the town's well-known prostitutes to the Salisbury Christmas ball, feigning surprise when the respectable townspeople, particularly the women, had them escorted out. Early on, Andrew Jackson seemed unwilling or unable to understand society women and their protocol.

Jackson had moved to Salisbury to become a lawyer, though clearly he did not keep his nose buried in the books. Still, he was admitted to the bar in 1787. He argued his first case in 1788 in Jonesborough (now Jonesboro), Tennessee, his sensitivity toward any perceived insult becoming sensationally evident. He challenged the opposing lawyer to a duel for what he interpreted to be a slander of him. Having already demonstrated that he would not stand silent before any perceived insult about his appearance, he disclosed now that his sensitivity to affronts included character as well as looks.

That spring of 1788, Jackson left the Carolinas and moved west to Tennessee, his home for the rest of his life. He eventually settled in the Nashville area and rose quickly, becoming a lawyer, jurist, politician, land speculator, plantation and slave owner, militia leader, Indian fighter, and husband and father. He made fast friends among other young men on the make, individuals like John Overton and John Coffee, who smoothed the way for him in those early days. He impressed William Blount, the new state's leading politician and wheeler-dealer. He served as Tennessee's congressman and then United States senator from 1796 to 1798. Then the state's power brokers named him judge of the Superior Court of Tennessee, a post he held for the next six years. In 1801, he helped found the Tennessee lodge of Freemasons. The following year he was elected major general of the Tennessee militia. By the age of thirty-five he had become one of the leading figures in the frontier state.

Despite his political successes, opponents in Tennessee came to view him as an adulterer and a murderer, the two accusations resulting from the same root cause: his controversial marriage to Rachel Donelson, the abiding love of his life. As a youth he had suffered from the painful loss of his mother; now another woman would bring him pain anew.

Rachel Donelson was the daughter of one of the founders of Nashville, Colonel John Donelson. In 1780, Donelson had brought his family of eleven children from Virginia to the site he and others had already hacked out of the Tennessee wilderness. He had served in the Virginia House of Burgesses, so his move to Tennessee seemed less the result of desperation than the typical nineteenth-century American search for greater economic stature. Twelve years old at the time, Rachel still had not learned to read or write, skills she barely mastered in the next several years.

Not satisfied in Tennessee, Donelson decided to seek his fortune in another part of the frontier, in Mercer County, Kentucky. Here the pretty but untutored and flirtatious Rachel met a handsome, educated man named Lewis Robards. They fell in love and married in March 1785. Then disaster struck. Someone, Indian or white, killed Colonel Donelson during a trip between Kentucky and Tennessee. His widow took her unmarried children back to Tennessee, leaving Rachel and her husband behind in the home of Robard's mother. Among the other male boarders living there was John Overton, then studying the law in Kentucky and later to become one of Tennessee's leading justices and Andrew Jackson's closest friend.

It was obvious to anyone who spent any time at the Robards place that the young couple's marriage was a disaster. As family members watched, Lewis Robards proved "high-tempered, jealous hearted, . . . cruel [and] tyrannical." He accused his wife, an outgoing fun-loving girl, of sexual promiscuity with the young male boarders there. Actually he was the one having the affairs, rumors persisting that he regularly slept with slave women. No matter. He continued to blame her and finally threw her out of the house, convinced that her forward openness with men was inappropriate for a married woman. Samuel Donelson came for his sister in 1788 and took her home to their mother. Robards's own mother, hoping to salvage the marriage, urged John Overton, since he was returning to Nashville, to bring the couple back together again.

When Overton returned to Tennessee, he took up lodging with the Widow Donelson and soon brought up the possibility of the Robards's reconciliation. Rachel Robards agreed to try, and her husband moved to Tennessee and settled on land he owned in the area. Until the site was prepared, however, he and Rachel would live in her mother's house with the male boarders.

It was about this time, in 1789, that Andrew Jackson came to live on the Donelson property, sharing a small cabin with Overton. He had just arrived from North Carolina. He was immediately attracted to the vivacious Mrs. Robards. One of Andrew Jackson's enduring characteristics was his extreme gallantry toward women, manifested especially in his belief that they were innately weak and that men, as the stronger sex, were morally obligated to protect them. He no doubt displayed this solicitude toward Rachel Robards. Unfortunately, Jackson's attentions caused her husband to revert to the suspicious jealousy he had shown in Kentucky; he suspected Rachel and Andrew of having an affair. Jackson decided to move away to squelch any suspicions, but he confronted Robards first, insisting that the husband had no cause for jealousy. Robards exploded in fury, threatening to give Jackson a beating. Equally angry, Jackson suggested a duel instead. Both men backed off before

matters became even more heated, and Jackson peacefully moved away. He was prepared, however, to give battle for his honor and for a woman he insisted was only a friend.

This near-violent encounter only exacerbated the Robards's marriage problems. One day in May or June of 1789, Robards decided to go back to Kentucky, allegedly to bring back his furniture and other possessions. Yet sometime on the trip he told his travel mate that he had decided not to return at all. Rachel Robards remained married, but her husband, sure of her infidelity, had left her, without indicating just how permanent the separation might be.

In the fall of 1790, rumors filtered down to Nashville that Lewis Robards planned to force his wife to return to Kentucky with him. Taking the news seriously and unwilling to reconcile again, Rachel began making plans to escape to Natchez in Spanish Florida, where she could stay with friends until her husband's latest tirade subsided. She asked a Colonel Robert Stark, who was moving his family to that region, if she could travel with his party. Worried about the danger of Indian attack along the way, Stark looked around for another male escort. No Donelson relative seemed willing or able to go, so the obviously smitten Andrew Jackson foolishly, but predictably, volunteered his services, agreeing to travel as Rachel Robards's protector on her dangerous trip through the wilderness.

If Lewis Robards had held any doubts about Jackson's intentions before, they vanished now. Jackson must have realized how suspicious this looked to a jealous husband and an increasingly skeptical community, but he plunged ahead anyway, perhaps hoping to spur the hot-tempered husband to divorce the wife he suspected of wrong-doing and make her available to him. Jackson's gallantry toward females in general and his increasing affection for this woman in particular caused him to ignore the obviously suspicious circumstances surrounding this trip. Rachel, for her part, went along without question, displaying the womanly subservience Jackson no doubt expected from her.

There is no way of knowing just what went on as the party traveled to Bayou Pierre, some thirty miles north of Natchez. They arrived on January 12, 1790, Rachel Robards remaining there for two years and Jackson apparently visiting her every chance he had. No one knows if the two lived together during his visits, but clearly their closeness became more than platonic and was obviously suspicious to anyone who cared to notice it. The bachelor lawyer and the separated wife had developed a relationship strong enough for Jackson to brave the hard trip from Nashville to Natchez more than once.

Meanwhile, Lewis Robards was busy himself. Since Kentucky was a district of Virginia, he asked his brother-in-law, a member of the Old Dominion's legislature, to file divorce papers for him. At the same time, in the fall of 1790, he published his divorce plans in the press, claiming his wife had eloped with another man. On December 20, 1790, the Virginia legislature gave him authority to sue for divorce in a Kentucky court. Before any judicial action could be taken, however, the legislative resolution said that Rachel Robards had to be ordered, in eight issues of the *Kentucky Gazette,* to appear before the court and respond to charges of adultery. Apparently only Lewis Robards knew all these conditions attached to his successful petition, leaving everyone else to think that the Virginia legislature had simply granted a divorce. Jackson, a lawyer, never bothered to investigate the matter himself.

Robards's behavior, after he learned of the enabling legislation, only added to the confusion. He did not publish the first mandated order in the Kentucky newspaper until an entire year had passed. Perhaps plotting to ensnare Andrew and Rachel further, he did not file for divorce in the Mercer County, Kentucky, Court of Quarters Sessions until 1793. The final decree did not get promulgated until September 27 of that same year. By this time, Andrew and Rachel had been married for more than two years, Jackson's preeminent biographer arguing that they had actually taken this step even before they had learned of the December 1790 Virginia legislature's enabling act/divorce. They returned to Nashville in August of 1791 and lived openly as man and wife, they and their community ignoring the fact that Rachel Robards Jackson was clearly a bigamist.

Jackson did not learn of the recent Kentucky court divorce order until December 1793. John Overton, his close friend since their days together in the Donelson cabin, immediately counseled a legal remarriage. On January 24, 1794, a disturbed Rachel Robards Jackson and a stubbornly reluctant Andrew Jackson repeated their marriage vows; they became man and wife legally. The Nashville community ignored the complicated legality, and this confusing affair of the heart and courts had no impact on Jackson's solid political and economical standing in Tennessee.

Clearly, however, his marriage dispute bothered Jackson. He worried about its effect on his future. As an individual who would not tolerate criticism and who needed to feel secure in the permanence of his marriage, he reacted violently when two men threw it in his face. In 1803, John Sevier, Jackson's longtime political enemy, won election as governor of Tennessee. Still angry over some accusations Jackson had made against him in that campaign and during an earlier election for militia major general, Sevier accosted Jackson before a large crowd in front of the courthouse in Knoxville. "I know of no great service you have rendered the country except taking a trip to Natchez with another man's wife," Sevier yelled out. Jackson lunged at him, shouting: "Great God! Do you mention *her* sacred name?" The crowd had to pull the irate husband off his accuser. Before they did so, however, Jackson challenged Sevier to a duel. No one was going to impugn his wife's integrity (and, of course, his own) without paying the price.

Jackson arrived at the dueling grounds at the scheduled time, only to have to cool his heels for two days because Sevier and his seconds were nowhere to be found. When he finally saw them approaching, he charged his horse forward, seeking to use his cane as a lance. Sevier, trying to dismount from his horse, fell off in his haste, and Jackson frustratingly rode around, hoping to find someone, anyone, to gore. The two men canceled the duel by mutual agreement, but Jackson never forgave Sevier

DREADFUL FRACAS ATWEEN THE GINERAL AND THE BENTONS AT NASHVIL

This popular drawing shows Jackson embroiled in a fight with Missouri politician Thomas Hart Benton. Jesse, Benton's brother, *became involved in the fracas and shot Jackson in the arm and shoulder. (Library of Congress)*

for what he always considered a slanderous assault on the virtue of his beloved wife and on his own honor.

In 1806, another aspersion on Rachel Jackson's purity brought forth the same violent response. Jackson and Charles Dickinson became embroiled in an argument over a horse race. In his anger and apparently while under the influence of alcohol, Dickinson ridiculed Rachel for her lack of morality, though he later apologized for his words. Jackson was not appeased, and the harsh dialogue between the two men continued for months. Finally there seemed to be no other way out: there had to be a duel.

As the sun rose above the horizon on the early morning of May 30, 1806, Jackson and Dickinson met on the field of honor in nearby Kentucky. John Overton had convinced his reluctant friend to wear a loose-fitting coat, apparently hoping to camouflage his thin frame in the expansive cloth. Dickinson, allegedly the best shot in the state, fired first,

and Jackson's left hand reached for his chest, although he displayed no other sign of pain. Dickinson shrieked in fear, upset that he had not killed his opponent with the first shot. Jackson aimed his pistol, but it failed to fire. He then pulled the trigger a second time, and this time he drove Dickinson to the ground with a direct hit to the stomach. Jackson calmly walked away, blood flowing freely from a chest wound, but his stubborn will refused to give onlookers the satisfaction of acknowledging pain or injury. Dickinson died within the day.

Jackson never budged from his belief that he had only done what was right. He carried Dickinson's bullet where it lodged near his heart for the rest of his life, a constant reminder of his unbending resolve to protect his honor. The bullet also reminded him that his honor was inexorably intertwined with the virtue of the most important woman in his life, his wife Rachel. Any attack on her was an assault on him, too. Even in those days of the double standard for men and women, if his wife was a sexual sinner, so was he. The only difference was that he could defend himself and she could not. He had to do it for her even if it meant that he would have to dispute the appellation "murderer" for the rest of his days.

Jackson seemed convinced that martial exploits offered the best way to rehabilitate his reputation after the two duels. In 1805, he listened enthusiastically to Aaron Burr's nebulous scheme of military action against the Spanish Empire but then quickly became disenchanted with the whole idea. In 1812, just before the United States declared war on England, Jackson unsuccessfully tried to get Tennessee authorities to allow him to lead a military expedition against the Creek Indians. Thwarted and increasingly angered over apparent American impotence in the face of British assaults on land and sea and over his own inability to change it, he lashed out against an available target and once more defended a woman's honor.

In 1811, Silas Dinsmore, Indian agent in Mississippi's Choctaw region, tried to enforce a federal law requiring non-Indians passing through the territory to produce proper documentation. Slaveholders, for example, had to prove that slaves traveling with them were not fugitives. This administrative practice delayed the slaveholders on their travels to and from New Orleans, so they grew increasingly angry at the agent. When Jackson himself brought slaves from Louisiana to Tennessee, through Choctaw lands, he refused to obey Dinsmore's regulation and told anyone who would listen to him on his return to Nashville that his refusal had put a stop to further insults to lawful slaveholders.

Dinsmore had not backed down at all; indeed, he had only recently restrained a woman traveling with ten blacks through his territory. Angrily, Jackson wrote his congressman that the Indian agent had demonstrated *"lawless tyranny . . . over a helpless and unprotected female."* He threatened to march into Mississippi and personally thrash the offending official unless the government took action first. It was not his wife or his mother who needed protection now,

but rather a woman he did not even know. No matter, Andrew Jackson would not stand for an affront to any woman. Certainly Jackson's anger against Dinsmore concerned slavery and Indians more than it concerned this unknown female, but it is no accident that he expressed his frustrations by defending a seemingly wronged woman. To him, assault against any woman indicated the mark of unspeakable and unforgivable baseness and cowardice, and he would respond forcefully to thwart it.

Jackson found little satisfaction in his minispat with Dinsmore. His reputation still needed redemption, so he continued to feel frustrated at his lack of military action in the nation's recently declared war against England. He led a Tennessee militia to Natchez on his way to New Orleans to join the war, but he was shocked in February 1813 to receive a War Department order dismissing him and his men from the military service. Frustrated again, he refused to dismiss his soldiers, determined to force them to return to Tennessee as an organized unit. On the difficult return trip, his tough determination to drive his soldiers on, no matter the many obstacles, gained him the appellation "Old Hickory."

At this point, in September 1813, Jackson foolishly became embroiled in another bout of violence, this time with Thomas Hart Benton, later a prominent Missouri politician and supporter, and his brother, Jesse. Once again, Jackson believed it a matter of honor. He had acted as a second in a June duel between a member of his staff and Jesse Benton, and had become angry at Tom Benton's taunts over his role in the fiasco. Jackson physically attacked Tom at a Nashville hotel. Seeing his brother under assault, Jesse shot Jackson in the arm and shoulder. One bullet fractured a bone, and the other remained lodged in Jackson's left arm until it was removed years later during his presidency.

Although injured and in pain, Jackson was still determined to participate in the war that had broken out between the United States and England. In Alabama, the Creek Indians had begun a general uprising, and in August 1813 they overran Fort Mims, massacring many women and children. A horrified

Jackson angrily led his Tennessee militia into Alabama to avenge the slaughter, and three months later he led a massacre at the village of Talluhatchee. After the killing, someone brought Jackson an Indian baby from the battlefield, and he tried to get some Creek women to adopt the child. They refused, telling Jackson to kill the boy since all his relatives were dead. Jackson, probably remembering his own orphanhood during the American Revolution, adopted the baby himself, and he and his wife gave the child a good home until the boy died of tuberculosis in 1828.

After one more successful battle against the Indians, Jackson discovered he had an enemy in his own ranks. Malnourished from lack of food and reaching the end of their enlistments, some of his militia wanted to return home, an entire brigade rising in mutiny. Jackson stood down these defiant soldiers not once but several times, yet he still saw his force melt away. New recruits rushed to the colors, however, impressed by his determination to keep fighting. In March 1814, he slaughtered the Creeks, women and children included, at Horseshoe Bend, Alabama. This bloodbath broke the back of the Creek uprising, and later at the Treaty of Fort Jackson, the victorious Tennessean took most of the Indians' land. Promotion to brigadier general in the United States Army and command of the entire Gulf region quickly followed. Jackson's massacre of Indian women did not bother him; gallantry toward women extended only to white females and did not include Indians or blacks.

In late January 1815, Jackson led a motley collection of regular army men, militia, pirates, and free blacks to defeat an army of British regulars at New Orleans, a startling victory. He became the symbol of America's ability to stand up to the British, a hero whose stature equalled that of the leaders of the American Revolutionary generation. War gave him the status and the personal satisfaction for which he had been hungering. Importantly, too, it allowed him to rescue his dead mother from the shadow of the once conquering British, who had marched through their neighborhood and created the conditions that had resulted in her death and his orphanhood.

Andrew Jackson now became the nation's leading general. When he returned to Tennessee, it was clear that in his home state the Sevier and Dickinson duels were forgotten. Jackson was no longer a murderer, but a universally admired hero, the unusual circumstance of his marriage forgotten. Making sure this status stuck, John Henry Eaton, a little-known Nashville lawyer who had served with him in the army, completed a laudatory biography that only added to the Old Hero's fame. Meanwhile in Washington a young girl, later to be the biographer's wife and Jackson's maligned friend, survived the British sack of the capital and was growing into womanhood.

Jackson next negotiated several successful treaties with the southern Indians before the national government called on him to lead a campaign against recalcitrant Seminoles in Spanish Florida. These Indians were aiding runaway slaves from the United States, and Spanish authorities seemed powerless to stop them. Jackson's orders from President James Monroe and Secretary of War John C. Calhoun told him to pursue the Seminoles but not attack them if they took shelter in any Spanish fortification. Jackson quickly pushed into Spanish Florida, and just as quickly he went far beyond his instructions. In April and May 1818, he captured several Spanish towns, forced the Spanish governor to flee, and hanged two British subjects for allegedly aiding the Indians. Jackson's actions caused a major diplomatic flap and a serious disagreement in Monroe's cabinet. The majority of the president's inner circle, led by Calhoun, wanted to censure Jackson for going beyond his orders, and Speaker Henry Clay gave a scathing speech against Jackson on the House floor. The House itself refused to disapprove of Jackson's activities, however, and Secretary of State John Quincy Adams used this as a lever to force Spain to sell all of Florida to the United States. Adams's support in the cabinet kept any movement against Jackson from progressing very far. The Monroe administration knew their general had exceeded his authority, but it made good political sense just to let the matter drop. At that time and later, however, political opponents tried to use this so-called Seminole Affair against Jackson, and he took their partisan criticism personally, lashing out against it whenever it reared its head.

Andrew Jackson, the poor orphan boy of the American Revolution, had become one of the nation's most celebrated personalities as a result of the War of 1812 and his repeated successes against the Indians. Unfortunately, his activities in Florida revitalized the murder charges. His terrible health was another problem. His damaged left arm ached incessantly, and when he coughed, he often produced blood. The two bullets he carried in his body caused recurrent physical ailments, which would have killed most people, but Jackson's stubborn will kept driving him on. He continued to negotiate Indian removal pacts, he began building the Hermitage, and he spent an unhappy three months as governor of the Florida territory he had gained for the United States. He returned to Nashville in 1821, with public admiration for him growing. In July 1822, the Tennessee legislature nominated him for the presidency. . . .

In the November 1824 election, Jackson won the popular vote over John Quincy Adams, Henry Clay, and William H. Crawford by a wide margin. Since he did not gain a majority in the Electoral College, however, the election had to be resolved in the House of Representatives. Insisting that he was no politician, Jackson stood above the fray leading to the House vote. Others were not so altruistic and negotiated the best deal they could make for themselves and the candidates they supported. Henry Clay of Kentucky, like Jackson a candidate from the West and thus a major rival, threw his support to Adams. Clay could not stand Adams personally, but he found the New Englander's positions on public matters closer to his own than those of Andrew Jackson. On January 9, 1825, the House chose Adams to be the next president. Soon after, Adams chose Clay to be his secretary of state, the heir apparent to the presidency. Jackson roared in anger.

Throughout his life, whether it was the recurring matter of a woman's virtue, his own honor, or some public event, Jackson saw evil conspiracy and corruption in anything or anyone who stood in his way. In his own mind, his position, whatever it might be, was the correct one, the virtuous one; anyone who opposed him represented corruption. Just as Jackson was willing to duel whenever he believed someone called his honor as a gentleman into question, so he would fight to the finish whenever he believed he saw corruption. Consequently, the fact that he had won the popular vote for president, yet lost the election in the House, proved that he (and the people, his supporters) had been cheated. Adams and Clay had conspired together to thwart justice. A "corrupt bargain" had ensured that the people would not have the final say. "So you see," he shouted, "the *Judas* of the West has closed the contract and will receive the thirty pieces of silver . . . was there ever witnessed such a bare-faced corruption in any country before?"

Andrew Jackson, hurt before by the British and by the bullets of those who challenged his honor and that of his wife, had never quit before, and he would not do so now. He would conquer his corrupt adversaries as he had conquered Charles Dickinson. There was no half way; he determined to defeat this evil before it defeated him and through him destroyed the people and the nation.

In 1825, the Tennessee legislature passed a resolution nominating him once again for the presidency, even though the next election was three years away. His supporters in Tennessee and throughout the nation began to organize into a loose coalition of state organizations that eventually came to call itself the Democratic party. They attacked Adams, Clay, and their supporters at every turn in the Congress and on the local level. Democrats shouted their determination to overthrow the "corrupt bargain."

But it would not be so easy. The 1828 election campaign was one of the dirtiest in American history. Jackson's opponents combed through his past and attacked him viciously for his real and imagined transgressions. The so-called Coffin Hand Bill, the brainchild of John Binns of the *Philadelphia Press,* purported to document Jackson's alleged murders of twelve men in duels, executions, and various other war and peacetime activities. Charles Hammond of the *Cincinnati Gazette* launched a similar attack. High among the accusations against Jackson stood his alleged propensity for cockfighting, gambling, and cursing. Henry Clay castigated him as being a "military chieftain," who threatened American liberties. As one modern historian has phrased it: Jackson was "pictured as a bloody-minded tyrant who executed militiamen without trial, a sensualist who lived in sin with a woman to whom he had never been married, an ignorant, unreligious desperado who could scarcely write his own name."

On the most personal level, Jackson's opponents labeled his mother a British prostitute who had married a black man by whom she had given birth to Jackson, thus making him a black Englishman. Opponents dragged his own marriage through the mud, calling his wife a bigamist and an adulteress and accusing Jackson of being a wife stealer. "A vote for Jackson," an East Tennessee congressional candidate declared in an 1827 handbill, "meant a vote for a man who thinks that if he takes a fancy to his neighbor's pretty wife, he 'has nothing to do but to take a pistol in one hand and a horsewhip in another and . . . possess her.'" Shocked and angered at this attack, for political purposes, against his mother and beloved wife, Jackson wanted to lash out against his opposition, particularly Henry Clay, whom he thought especially responsible for such villainy. He told Duff Green, editor of the newly established Jacksonian newspaper in Washington, the *United States Telegraph,* to attack the opposition forthrightly but not unlimitedly. "Female character never should be introduced or touched by my friends," Jackson instructed, "unless a continuation of attack should continue to be made against Mrs. J. and then only, by way of *Just retribution* upon the *known guilty. . . . I never war against females,* and it is only the base and cowardly that do so." But Jackson wished he could battle against those who dared attack his beloved Rachel, but he knew that, for once in his life, he had to remain silent.

As Jackson seethed, his supporters grew in numbers and became more unified. John Quincy Adams's

vice president, John C. Calhoun of South Carolina, and New York political boss Martin Van Buren joined the Jacksonian bandwagon, as did Thomas Hart Benton, now a senator from Missouri. . . .

The closer it came to election time in November 1828, the more confident Jackson and his supporters became. Only Rachel Jackson seemed unhappy. The attacks on her reputation stung her, and her health appeared to worsen. In June, Lyncoya, the Indian boy her husband Andrew had rescued from an Alabama battlefield and adopted as his own, died at the age of sixteen. Rachel did all she could to save her son and, when she failed, she was devastated by his death.

She especially worried about becoming the president's wife and living in Washington, having to face the torments of public life. "I had rather be a doorkeeper in the house of God than to live in that palace at Washington," she lamented. No longer the attractive woman of her youth, she was, according to a contemporary description, "a coarse-looking, stout little old woman." She had a dark complexion at a time when the mark of beauty was to be pale. Yet she was "so good natured and motherly" that people felt "immediately . . . at ease with her." She was a plain but charming woman, "benevolent" being the word usually applied to her. Though worried about handling the duties of first lady, she determined to trudge ahead, to be the faithful, supportive wife that she had always been and that society expected of its women.

Jackson's great desire and his wife's deeply felt dread came to fruition when he defeated John Quincy Adams to become the seventh president of the United States, winning a smashing victory in the Electoral College, 178 to 83. Eight hundred thousand more males voted in the election of 1828 than had participated in 1824. The "Old Hero" from frontier Tennessee defeated the incumbent president, son of a previous officeholder and representative of rock-ribbed New England and the elite tradition of the presidency. The elite were out, the people were in.

The nation had undergone a massive political change. The party of Thomas Jefferson, James Madison, and

James Monroe, which, since the Federalist party demise after the War of 1812 was the only national political organization left, split in two. The Democrats of Andrew Jackson harkened back to the states' rights position of the original Jeffersonians, while the National Republicans of John Quincy Adams and Henry Clay supported the federal government supremacy that Adams had attempted to establish during his term.

The two-party system was born with a vengeance. The National Republicans represented the traditional elites, while the Jacksonians advertised themselves as the representatives of the common people. To argue that this party development was philosophical, however, would misrepresent the issue. There were National Republicans who were common men, and there were Jacksonians who were members of the elite. Party efforts revolved around electing candidates more than implementing ideology. Consequently, the era saw the birth of the politics of personality. Politicians attacked one another more than they battled over specific issues. In fact, they consciously obfuscated differences to prevent alienating any block of voters. Attacking one's opponent, tarring him with the brush of corruption, produced electoral success. Earlier on, when politics was the avocation of gentlemen, such attacks against an opponent's character were considered inappropriate. This attitude changed dramatically in the 1820s.

As far as Andrew Jackson and his supporters were concerned, therefore, they had won a victory in 1828 over major corruption. The main point of dispute during the Adams administration, after all, had been the "corrupt bargain" of 1824. This issue represented to the Jacksonians what was wrong with American society and politics overall. Corrupt elitists used the government for their own betterment, Jacksonians insisted, and the people suffered as a result. Jackson, as the tribune of the people, smashed such corruption in the election of 1828, the argument ran, and he could be counted on to root out all its manifestations in the national government and its offices. The people would no longer be fleeced, as they had been under Adams. They would have honest government for the benefit of all—through the agency of Andrew Jackson, the people's representative and the agent of reform.

But not every Jacksonian viewed reality this way. John C. Calhoun, for example, was Andrew Jackson's running mate less because he wanted to reform the Adams administration (of which he was the vice president after all) than because he saw an excellent opportunity to become president when Andrew Jackson retired from office, or more probably when he died during his term. This was no treachery; it was simply reasonable, practical politics. Calhoun, the great nationalist of his early years in Congress, was moving toward becoming the philosopher of states' rights, so he felt more comfortable with Jackson's localism than he did with Adams's nationalism. He easily took his stand at Jackson's side. His native state of South Carolina was growing increasingly worried about threats to its slave system, so it viewed states' rights as a logical and effective defense against national encroachment on the institution.

Jacksonians, although they were hardly unified as a party, were pleased at the great victory of 1828. They were clearly in the ascendancy, and the future looked full of political promise. Only Rachel Jackson seemed withdrawn. She was pleased for her husband's sake, but concerned about her own future. She wondered whether she should even accompany her husband to Washington, only reluctantly accepting John Henry Eaton's advice that she not give in to those who had been attacking her. Women in Nashville began preparing a wardrobe for her, and the city scheduled a great day of celebration prior to the Jacksons' departure for the inauguration.

Feeling little enthusiasm and even less strength, Rachel Jackson bestirred herself to prepare for her travel to the nation's capital. She went to Nashville to do some shopping and there stumbled upon a pamphlet defending her virtue against opposition attacks. She had known before of the attacks against her and her husband, but had never realized the extent of their vehemence. She broke down, trying to hide her panic when she returned home, before finally telling Andrew Jackson of her discovery.

A few days later, she had a heart attack. She rallied briefly, but on December 22, 1828, to her husband's unbelieving horror, she suffered another massive attack and died. Jackson kept hoping that she would somehow still recover, but he was doomed to tearful disappointment. He stayed near her dead form all that night and through the next day, finally and reluctantly pulling himself away. His beloved Rachel was indeed dead, and there was nothing he could do about it. He could not fight for her any longer. After her funeral, he could only pray "that I may have the grace to enable me to forget or forgive any enemy who has ever maligned that blessed one who is now safe from all suffering and sorrow, whom they tried to put to shame for my sake!" Convinced that his political enemies had killed his wife with their slanderous attacks in order to get him, by his lifelong code he had to vindicate her by punishing them. He may have prayed for grace to forgive, but in his heart he coveted revenge.

Andrew Jackson's chivalrous defense of women, in part the product of the slanderous remarks directed at his wife, erupted into the so-called "petticoat affair." John Eaton, Jackson's secretary of war, had recently married the daughter of a boarding house owner who was a woman of questionable virtue. Cabinet members' wives and the spouse of the vice president, John C. Calhoun, snubbed the Eatons. Predictably, "Old Hickory" came to the wronged woman's defense, and the resulting uproar led to the reorganization of the cabinet and increased hostility toward Calhoun. The favorite toast of Washington barbs soon became: "To the next Cabinet, may they all be bachelors, or leave their wives at home."

QUESTIONS TO CONSIDER

1 Andrew Jackson was more popular than any other president since George Washington. Why were the American people, especially the "common man," so attracted to him? Contrast his appeal with that of Washington, whom you met in selection 10. Would the two men have been comfortable in each other's company?

2 With the exception of John Adams and John Quincy Adams of Massachusetts, all of the previous presidents before Jackson were Virginia planters of significant wealth. How did Jackson's background differ from that of the presidents who came before him? Describe Jackson's early years and what Marszalek calls the "defining moment" in his life.

3 Explain Jackson's attitude toward and defense of women. Do you think that these deep-seated feelings were a product of his childhood and the loss of his mother?

4 In many ways, Jackson seemed to represent a number of troubling contradictions. For example, how do you explain the fact that his protectiveness toward women did not extend to those who were slaves or Native Americans? He massacred the Creeks, including women and children, at Horseshoe Bend, but why would he and his wife later adopt an Indian child and provide it with a loving home?

5 Character assassination and negative campaigning have characterized recent American politics. How did you react when you saw the same factors in the presidential election of 1828? What were some of the slanderous charges that Jackson's opponents directed at him, and how did the general react?

18 A Giant of Contradictions: The Irrepressible Sam Houston

JOE B. FRANTZ

The following selection, dramatically written by Joe B. Frantz, reads like a Hollywood script filled with political intrigue, violence, romance, and lost dreams. If after reading the previous selection you felt that Andrew Jackson could frequently be out of control, wait until you meet "the Raven"—Sam Houston. Actually, Jackson and Houston had much in common. Both lifted themselves up from humble beginnings, and both used their battlefield exploits to win national recognition. Little wonder that Houston viewed the older man as his mentor and Jackson, in turn, did all he could to promote his protégé's political career. But there were also significant differences between the two men. Whereas Jackson devoted himself to one woman during his long life, Houston loved many women, including an Indian maiden. According to Texas folklore, Frantz says, you could trace Houston's travels by the number of blue-eyed Indian babies found along the way. Houston's romantic misadventures included a divorce from his youthful first wife. Declaring himself "a ruined man," Houston resigned as governor of Tennessee in disgrace and went into exile with the Cherokees.

As you read this portrait of Houston, ponder the often contradictory behavior that southerners like Jackson and Houston displayed toward Indians. Jackson could slaughter tribes and yet adopt an Indian child and raise him as his own. Houston killed a number of Indians at the Battle of Horseshoe Bend but often lived with the Cherokees and even took the chief's daughter as his bride. What was there about the American experience that produced for whites like Jackson and Houston a love-hate relationship with the Indians?

The life of Sam Houston spanned seventy turbulent years of American history, from the start of Washington's second administration in 1793 to just after the battle of Gettysburg in 1863. Houston moved west as the nation did, from Virginia to Tennessee and finally to Texas. His personality, rowdy and unpredictable, fit that of many of the other legendary figures who streamed into Texas—men like Stephen F. Austin, Jim Bowie, and Davy Crockett. The new Mexican nation invited these raucous characters into Texas if they would promise to renounce their American citizenship and adopt Catholicism. It never worked. There was a constant state of friction between the newly transplanted Americans in Texas and the far-off government in Mexico City. Houston was one of the leaders in the Texas revolution and the military hero of the hour at San Jacinto. Once again, Houston had reinvented himself. The disgraced former governor of Tennessee was now the most prominent Texan of his century. He helped engineer Texas annexation to the United States, dreamed of new territorial conquests, and fought against the secessionists who wanted to break away from the Union.

Houston was a visionary whose flaws were as great as his strengths. In the following profile, Frantz brings to life this "Texas giant of contradictions" against a sweeping historical backdrop.

GLOSSARY

ALLEN, ELIZA   Houston's first wife, who, after the marriage dissolved, sent the Raven's political career into a downhill spiral. The author speculates that the divorce was caused by an age difference, another male suitor, or parental pressure to have a daughter wedded to the famous governor of Tennessee.

AUSTIN, STEPHEN F.   In the 1820s, at the invitation of the newly independent Republic of Mexico, he led hundreds of Americans into Texas. Known as the "father of Texas," he was more reluctant than Houston to begin a revolution against Mexico.

BATTLE OF HORSESHOE BEND   In March of 1814, Andrew Jackson's militia crushed the Creek Indians who had resisted the steady encroachment on their land by white settlers. Houston fought bravely in spite of serious injuries to his shoulder and leg. He also won the admiration of Jackson, and this began a lifelong friendship.

CALHOUN, JOHN C.   As James Monroe's secretary of war, he criticized Houston's Indian garb and unfairly accused the Raven of slave smuggling. Calhoun, from South Carolina, would later serve as vice president in the John Quincy Adams and Jackson administrations and become a leading advocate of states' rights, through which the South could protect its ownership of slaves.

FILIBUSTERING   Efforts made by soldiers of fortune to move into foreign nations, overturn their governments, and perhaps eventually bring them under the "protection" of the American flag. In the mid-nineteenth century, Mexico, Cuba, and Central America were targeted for filibustering operations.

JACKSON, ANDREW   Houston greatly admired the older man whom we met in selection 17, and he fought alongside Jackson at the Battle of Horseshoe Bend. He hoped to copy Old Hickory's rise from humble beginnings to the occupancy of the Oval Office.

KEY, FRANCIS SCOTT   The author of the "Star Spangled Banner," he served as Houston's lawyer when the Raven was asked to explain his attack on Congressman Stanbery before the House of Representatives.

LEA, MARGARET   Houston finally found a lasting love with this young woman from Alabama. Despite their age difference, the marriage worked. She became the first lady of Texas and the only woman to have a settling influence on the flamboyant Houston.

LECOMPTON CONSTITUTION   An attempt to bring Kansas into the Union as a new slave state. Houston supported it, but most of the residents of "Bleeding Kansas" did not, and they ultimately rejected it by a margin of six to one.

ROGERS, TIANA   The daughter of the Cherokee chief and a widow, she and Houston lived as man and wife for about a year. During this time Houston suffered from bouts with alcoholism and Indians nicknamed him the "Big Drunk."

SAN JACINTO   Fought in April of 1836, this was the decisive victory for the Texans in their war against Mexico, and it made Houston the hero of the hour.

SANTA ANNA   In 1834, General Antonio López de Santa Anna declared himself the dictator of Mexico and opposed the movement of Americans into the Texas territory. Victorious at the Alamo and defeated at San Jacinto, he remains a controversial figure in Mexican history.

STANBERY, WILLIAM   The congressman from Ohio who mistakenly accused Houston of misusing government funds to purchase Indian rations. The two men fought on a Washington street, and the feud provided Houston with the opportunity to resurrect his political career.

He was a man of extremes.

A giant of a man by the standards of the nineteenth century, Sam Houston would be a big man nowadays. Six feet two, says his army record; six feet six, said an admirer. No matter, he was large. He bore himself like a titan, always a commanding presence without being overbearing. A two-fisted drinker through half of his life, he turned abstemious after his third marriage and gave frequent temperance lectures during his remaining years. A storied Indian fighter, he lived with the Cherokees as a boy and returned to them after he exiled himself from Tennessee. A hater of Mexicans with continuing plans to take over their nation, he treated his captured enemy,

Joe B. Frantz, "Sam Houston, Grand Designer," *American West*, vol. 17, no. 4 (July/August, 1980), pp. 4–13. Reprinted by permission of the Western History Association.

General Antonio López de Santa Anna, with magnanimity at a time when Texans were crying for the Mexican generalissimo's blood.

He was a man of contradictions.

According to Texas folklore, you could trace Old Sam's route through the countryside nine months or more after he traveled past: every thirty miles (or a day's journey) you could find a blue-eyed Indian, a sure sign that Sam had camped there. He married an Indian woman while he had an undivorced wife back in Nashville. He married a teen-aged girl when he was a bachelor in his mid-thirties, and he married a girl who was barely twenty when he was pushing fifty.

Nothing in his early life indicated that Houston was headed for empire building. Born on March 2, 1793, near Timber Ridge Church toward the southern end of upland Virginia's Shenandoah Mountains (his home county, Rockbridge, still had only 16,637 inhabitants in 1970), he attended school sporadically until his widowed mother moved her nine children to a wilder frontier west of Maryville, Blount County, Tennessee, in 1807. The teen-ager showed no aptitude for farming or clerking, soon ran away to the far side of the Tennessee River to live with the Cherokees for a year, returned home (apparently less repentant than the Prodigal Son), was fined for beating a drum with such fervor that he upset the workings of a local court, and ducked out on the fine by returning to the Indians, who promptly adopted him and gave him a name, "the Raven." Up to this point Houston sounds like an 1810 version of any rebellious youth of the past twenty years, the worry of his mother, and the despair of her established, nosy neighbors.

Houston again left the Indians to teach school between May and November in 1812. Although he probably had no more than a year of schooling himself, he seems to have been a successful teacher (which ought to give certification boards some pause). But he could spell and he could read, though he was deficient in mathematics, and he had educated himself in frontier lore and military tactics, which should have kept his back-country kids in awe, if nothing else.

In March of 1813 Houston joined the Creek Indian War by enlisting as a private in the Thirty-ninth Infantry, and began a fairly rapid rise to officer status. A year later he met General Andrew Jackson, a man who would give as much direction as anyone could to the erratic flight of this Raven. When in late March, 1814, Houston showed extraordinary leadership at the Battle of Horseshoe Bend, Jackson commended his young third lieutenant, his words undoubtedly helping to assuage the pain of Houston's severe shoulder and leg wounds. The injured shoulder would pain him periodically for the remainder of his life.

After furloughs for his health and a stint on the state adjutant's staff in Nashville, Houston was named subagent to the Cherokees. An unexpected spin-off from this assignment resulted in a lifelong dislike for one of the South's sainted heroes, John C. Calhoun. After the secretary of war had received Houston and a Cherokee delegation to Washington with his outward southern courtesy, he called the young officer aside to upbraid him for appearing before a cabinet officer in the dress of a savage. Houston's retort that the Indians were more likely to accept him as a true son if he dressed as they did made no dent on Calhoun's rigid sense of etiquette.

Shortly Calhoun summoned Houston to charge him with complicity in slave smuggling. Houston's answer that, far from smuggling, he had actually attempted to break up a smuggling ring brought an investigation that exonerated him but implicated several congressmen friendly with the ring. When Calhoun failed to follow up on the disclosures or even to express regret to Houston for having accused him wrongly, Houston in a huff (not his last one) resigned his commission in the army, renouncing a career that he had apparently intended to follow for life. Such impulsiveness would not disappear with age.

To many of his friends, Sam Houston was through. His beloved Cherokees were being moved to the Arkansas River, his army commission was gone, and at the age of twenty-five he owed a hatful of debts.

The Raven promptly sold his possessions to liquidate his indebtedness, returned to Nashville, and at an age when most men were getting entrenched in their careers, started to read law in the office of Judge James Trimble in 1818. Although the reading should have required a minimum of eighteen months, Houston passed admission to the bar six months later. Meanwhile he played several roles in productions of Nashville's Dramatic Club, including one prophetic run as a drunken porter that brought praise from the audience and the press. In the words of the club's stage manager, Noah M. Ludlow, he had "never met a man who had a keener sense of the ridiculous . . . nor one who could more readily assume the ludicrous or the sublime." Forty years later both his Texas critics and admirers would have repeated this verdict.

After a brief fling as a lawyer in Lebanon, thirty miles east of Nashville, where he existed at first on near charity, he returned to Nashville as state adjutant general, with the rank of colonel. Less than three years later his fellow field officers would elect him major general. Meanwhile in October, 1819, with Jackson's help, Houston was named attorney general for the Nashville district, after having turned down an offer from the despised Secretary Calhoun, again recommended by Jackson, to be agent to the Cherokees. With Jackson's assistance Houston was becoming a man to notice.

Houston was paying back the old Chief's sponsorship by loyal support of Jackson's presidential ambitions. He stood for Congress, unopposed, in the late summer of 1823, in part to have a wider forum from which to present Jackson's record to the people. Foreshadowing a later stand, he made his maiden speech in Congress a call for recognition of Greek independence. As Llérena Friend, Houston's most nearly definitive biographer, so succinctly summed up, "In general, he supported in the House the measures which Jackson approved in the Senate." When Houston's first term was completed, he was easily reelected. He had not been an outstanding congressman on the issues of the day, but he had been devoted to his constituency and to his mentor. That type of congressman gets returned forever.

Houston tried to marry about this time, and traveled all the way from Washington to South Carolina for the event. There a Miss M— was waiting, but the couple decided to postpone such a step until Houston could quit campaigning for reelection and settle some "*personal* difficulties." Later he wrote a relative that he was continuing "the full enjoyments of the sweets of single blessedness." History does not record what became of the romance, except that it never came off.

In 1827, when he was thirty-four years old, Houston decided to make his big jump. With Jackson's support he announced for governor of Tennessee. Basically he ran a one-issue campaign; like most westerners he believed that his section was suffering for lack of internal improvements. Houston was elected governor handily by a four-to-three margin (57 percent) over his opponent. Meanwhile he pushed Jackson's candidacy for president. He was achieving a reputation as the one man who could handle the fractious Jackson. In one case, for instance, he refused to deliver a letter from Jackson to Samuel L. Southard, secretary of the navy, because he thought the old Chief was unnecessarily inflammatory. Like an obedient pupil, Jackson rewrote a milder version acceptable to his protégé.

Houston's first term as governor, while not spectacular, moved along harmoniously enough so that he was considered a shoo-in for a second term. In fact, his name was being bandied about as a possible successor to Andrew Jackson as president whenever Old Hickory should be elected and serve out his years. The idea was not far fetched. Tennessee, a developing western state, had captured the public's imagination. Over the next several decades three Tennesseeans would advance to the White House— Jackson, James K. Polk, and Andrew Johnson. In the late 1820s Houston's star shone as brightly as any of them except Jackson's. The governorship of the Volunteer State just might lead to the presidency, as it did for one of Houston's contemporaries, Polk. Why not the same path to national greatness for Houston?

The roadblock was romance. First, the American electorate does not like bachelors for its leaders, especially those with a reputation for being attractive to the ladies. As Houston wrote once in exasperation, "What the devil is the matter with the gals I can't say but there has been hell to pay and no pitch hot!" Everyone had a candidate for his marriage vows; he was, as a thirty-six-year-old bachelor governor, the catch of Tennessee, perhaps of the nation.

Before he completed his campaign, unopposed, for a second term, Houston fell in love. The affair was the kind that Victorian novelists often mooned about—an older half saint, half devil just waiting to be gentled by a pure woman barely come of age. The plot was straight out of *St. Elmo*. For years Houston had dropped by the home of Colonel John Allen at Gallatin during his travels through upper middle Tennessee. At first Colonel Allen had a thirteen-year-old daughter, Eliza, described as having "large blue eyes and yellow hair." Houston, ever gallant, undoubtedly talked to little Eliza each time he visited her father.

The trouble with thirteen-year-old girls is that they grow up, and one day when she was eighteen, Houston, according to one of his biographers, "looked into Eliza's blue eyes and ceased to speak to her of childish things." Despite the disparity of age, Eliza's parents and other relatives were undoubtedly thrilled by the prospect of the attraction becoming serious. At eighteen Eliza could be the first lady of Tennessee; in her middle twenties she might be the first lady of the United States. Few parents ambitious for good marriages for their offspring could resist being swept up in the enthusiasm of such prospects.

Today Eliza would have laughed and said, "Forget it, you dirty old man." But those were the days when daughters did as their parents bade them; in addition, every old crone in Gallatin was advising Eliza that a brilliant future was unfolding. Apparently Eliza confused prospects with love. She gave Houston her hand. On January 22, 1829, they were married by candlelight in a Presbyterian ceremony in Gallatin, and moved to the Nashville Inn where Houston continued his campaign for a second gubernatorial term. Aside from Houston's political necessities, he seemed to be the most attentive of husbands, and the two of them made a most affectionate couple. They went

out little socially, evidently content in each other's company.

But in mid-April it was all over. Houston took his bride, "the only earthly object dear to me," back to her parents and announced that he would never disclose the reasons "to a living person." As he told a boyhood friend, Willoughby Williams: "I can make no explanation. I exonerate this lady [Eliza] freely, and I do not justify myself. I am a ruined man." He promptly resigned as governor of Tennessee. The express to the White House had been derailed.

His silence has left gossips and historians frustrated for a century and a half. They still don't know what happened. A good guess is that Eliza told Houston that she had actually been in love with another man when she had been dazzled by his proposal of marriage, and that she did not love her husband. In keeping silent throughout the remainder of his life, Houston showed restraint that few other heads of households or heads of state would have observed, then or now. His silence is particularly noteworthy in an era when the male was king, and this particular male was the kingliest in his state.

Human nature in the 1820s was not different from human nature in the 1980s. Most of Houston's friends rushed to see who could desert him most quickly. A "howling crowd" burned him in effigy on Gallatin's courthouse lawn. Tennessee buzzed, and the nation quivered with the excitement of a good scandal. The *Richmond* (Virginia) *Inquirer* wrote of "rumors about Gen. Houston . . . too unpleasant . . . to be repeated." *Niles' Register* in Washington was more sympathetic as it lamented his "deeply wounded spirit."

And what of Eliza Allen? None of Houston's more than fifty biographers has probed her feelings. After all, she was a mere eighteen years old, thrown out—in effect—by her governor-husband. But Eliza was no teen-aged slender reed. Like Houston she too could keep silent, and did. The feeling persists that she may have been the one who spurned Houston, rather than the other way around. Houston wrote to his father-in-law after the separation: "I . . . do love Eliza . . . she is the only earthly object dear to me God will bear witness."

After the unexplained break with his wife, Houston resigned as governor and exiled himself to live with the Cherokees again, this time beyond the western end of Arkansas, not far from the kicker grounds of today's Okies from Muskogee. As *Niles' Register* noted at the end of May, 1829, Houston had "caused much surprise among the people." Or as William Carroll, a former supporter turned enemy, observed: "His conduct, to say the least, was very strange and charity requires us to place it to the account of insanity. I have always looked upon him as a man of weak and unsettled mind . . . incapable of manfully meeting a reverse of fortune."

The Cherokees received Houston as a brother, a restless soul who had gone away to the white man's world, who had succeeded by the white man's standards, who had drunk the bitter tea of white perfidy, and who had returned to relatives who asked no questions and demanded no justifications. To them, his broken marriage to Eliza Allen did not matter, for in the Cherokee world a marriage to a white woman was no marriage at all, just a temporary convenience. The Cherokees' basic attitude was similar to the whites', which held that a marriage to a red woman (or later, to a Japanese or a Nicaraguan or a Vietnamese) was a convenience to be ignored whenever the Yankee returned to his homeland. As a boy Sam Houston had learned freedom and acceptance from the Cherokees. Now as a man who had lost his compass—a man with no goals, no future, no love, and few friends—he turned to his Indian companions again.

At once Houston found friends. Almost as quickly he found love. He had known Tiana Rogers on that first sojourn—as the ten-year-old, half-naked, half-sister of his closest Cherokee boyhood chums, John and James Rogers. Now she was a tall, graceful "widow" of thirty, somewhat mysterious herself, for no one knew what had become of her first husband, David Gentry. Perhaps he was dead, killed in a fight against the Osage; perhaps the pair had split the blanket. Never mind. She was eligible, and Houston was in no position to ask questions.

In Cherokee society it was a splendid marriage for Houston. Tiana (to use just one of a dozen variations

of her name) was the daughter of the Supreme Chief, Ol-loo-te-ka, who himself was descended in part from a British soldier of the Revolution. And Houston was his adopted son. Tiana's half-brother John would be the next head chief, and her grand-nephew, William Charles Rogers, would become the last chief of the Cherokee nation. Although no official record exists of the marriage, the Cherokees accepted Houston and Tiana as man and wife rather than a temporary liaison.

So Houston married into the inner, upper councils of the Cherokee. He and Tiana set up in a large log house near the Neosho River, planted an apple orchard, and started living in Houston's accustomed good style, entertaining and trading. He began to write articles for the *Arkansas Gazette* over in Little Rock (a fine paper then, a superior one today), inveighing against the systematic defrauding of the Cherokees by the white man. These repeated charges did not endear Houston to Americans along the frontier, many of whom thought he ought to be lynched as a bigamist anyway. Although he signed his articles "Standing Bear," no one doubted Houston's authorship.

When official Washington reached out to demand that Houston comply with requirements that all American traders with Indians be licensed, Houston refused. American laws had no validity where he was concerned, he retorted. He was no longer a citizen of the United States. He was a Cherokee. To extend the law to him would be to enter a wedge whereby a free Cherokee nation might eventually succumb to vassalage. First the attorney general in Washington and then the United States Supreme Court, in a parallel case, declared that Houston's position was untenable.

For a year Houston was a model Indian and husband. Then in 1831 without warning, grief from his troubled life overflowed, and for six months he tried to drink his way to oblivion. He dueled with an employee; he struck his father-in-law and was beaten unconscious by bystanders, only to have the chief bathe and nurse him. The Indians gibed at him. They nicknamed him "Big Drunk." Perhaps it was because he would never drink with them.

Sam Houston loved the stage and was always at his best before an audience. As a young man, he played a number of parts for the Nashville Dramatic Club. Later, he salvaged his career with a much-praised speech before Congress. As Houston observed: "I was dying out and had they taken me before a justice of the peace and fined me ten dollars it would have killed me, but they gave me a national tribune for a theatre, and that set me up again. ("Sam Houston as Marius Among the Ruins of Carthage" by Orlando Rouland. The State Preservation Board, Austin, TX.)

And then in September Sam went to the bedside of his dying mother in Tennessee. He left the funeral sober. The Raven was ready to fly again.

Three months later he was back in the East, an unofficial member of a Cherokee delegation to present grievances to President Jackson. On this trip, in 1831, Congressman William Stanbery of Ohio wrongly accused Houston of having connived with Secretary of War John Eaton on a fraudulent contract for Indian rations. Houston sent Representative Cave Johnson of Tennessee to Stanbery to open negotiations for a duel. When Stanbery retorted that he did not recognize Sam Houston, the Raven announced, "I'll introduce myself to the damned rascal."

Chancing on Stanbery on a Washington street one night, Houston proceeded to cane the congressman about the head. When Stanbery drew a pistol which misfired against Houston's chest, Houston lifted Stanbery's feet in the air and "struck him elsewhere," which must be interpreted as a Victorian euphemism.

The affray brought Houston before the House of Representatives, though he was not a member. Francis Scott Key, the poet-lawyer, represented him before Congress. Meanwhile, Houston gave Washington society and its press the sort of sideshow in which it glories to this day.

Typically for that period in his life Houston sat up drinking with friends on the night before his own appearance before the House. The next morning he couldn't even hold down coffee. But when his turn came to speak, he stood straight and faced a standing-room-only crowd that included the diplomatic corps, the military, and highly placed civilians. Houston spoke without straining: "I can never forget that reputation, however limited," he said in an almost conversational tone that reached to the galleries, "is the high boon of heaven. . . . Though the plowshare of ruin has been driven over me and laid waste to my brightest hopes . . . I have only to say . . . 'I seek no sympathies, nor need;/The thorns which I have reaped are of the tree/I planted; they have torn me and I bleed.'"

The gallery was with him. One woman was heard to say, "I had rather be Sam Houston in a dungeon than Stanbery on a throne!" For half an hour Houston talked seriously, intensely, showing no evidence of a monumental hangover. He cited Julius Caesar, Oliver Cromwell, Napoleon Buonaparte, William Blackstone, and St. Paul; he retraced the tyrannies that had brought down Greece and Rome. He had committed, he said, only a crime of "impulse" after being almost driven to it by his opponent's charges. Otherwise he was guilty of no crime for which Congress could punish him without invading his private rights.

Finally, as Houston gazed at the American flag framing Lafayette's portrait, his declamation soared to new heights: "So long as that flag shall bear aloft its glittering stars . . . so long . . . shall the rights of American citizens be preserved safe and unimpaired—till discord shall wreck the spheres—the grand march of time shall cease—and not one fragment of all creation be left to chafe the bosom of eternity's waves."

At this point the gallery would have given Houston the White House. But Congress, more deliberate, debated four days before deciding that Sam Houston should be reprimanded. The Speaker announced, "I do reprimand you accordingly."

Stanbery wasn't through. He brought criminal charges of assault and then chaired an investigating committee into the fraud charge. For the assault Houston was fined $500, which he never paid. By a split decision the investigating committee acquitted him of fraud in a protracted trial that threatened to become the Watergate of the 1830s.

Stanbery lost more than just two cases out of three. He resurrected Sam Houston. Before the trials Houston was, in his terms, "a man of broken fortune and blasted reputation." But Houston, who had an actor's and a politician's (redundant terms possibly?) instinct for knowing when an audience turns in one's favor, later observed: "I was dying out and had they taken me before a justice of the peace and fined me ten dollars it would have killed me; but they gave me a national tribune for a theatre, and that set me up again." With his trial Sam Houston had returned in triumph to the white man's world. Redemption was his.

While Houston was on trial for caning Stanbery, he annoyed President Jackson's enemies by coming and going at will in the White House. If the president's relationship was not that of a surrogate father, it was at least avuncular and sponsoring, as it had

been since the two men had endured the Indian wars together earlier in the century.

The other place that Houston seemed to come and go at will was Texas, which was geographically intimate with Houston's new residence in Arkansas Territory. What was he doing there? The answers are as numerous as the people interrogated. He wrote a Tennessee cousin that he had business in Texas "of importance to his pecuniary interest," and that "I will practice law, and with excellent prospects of success." He also wrote of "several minor matters I am engaged in." Houston knew how to write and talk without really revealing anything. Today's press would have had a field day interviewing him; he would have raised all kinds of possibilities, filling newspapers and the air with speculations while seldom contributing any hard news.

In one memoir Houston is quoted as intending to become a herdsman and spend the rest of his life "in the tranquillity of the prairie solitudes." He could no more have tolerated a herdsman's life than his twentieth-century opposite number Lyndon Johnson could have remained a lifetime, high school debate coach. Houston was created for action.

"Several minor matters" were the operative words in Houston's remark above. Results of the "minor matters" are too well known to detail. Sam Houston showed up in Texas in time for a fight. He had been in the region only a few months when he was chosen to represent Nacogdoches as one of five delegates to a convention to decide on Texas policy toward mother Mexico. At the convention of 1833 he aligned himself with the "war party" opposed to Stephen F. Austin, often hailed as the "father of Texas," though a bachelor. Austin advocated a patient policy toward Mexico. Houston was named chairman of the committee to frame a constitution for a state of Texas, if it should be separated from its current status as an appendage of Coahuila. And he reflected the antibank bias of his mentor, Jackson, by helping to obtain a provision in the proposed constitution that no bank or any other moneyed corporation should be chartered. (In fact, Texas did not legalize banking until the end of Reconstruction, so deep was the antibank feeling.)

As the rift between Mexico and Texas deepened, Houston began urging his fellow Texans to break their connections with Mexico City. Older Texans urged moderation, believing that Mexico's excesses were caused by its inability to stabilize its own government and pointing out that the Mexicans had been unbelievably generous and usually tolerant toward the Anglo-American settlers. But the newer Texans had little patience, coupled with a huge dosage of yanqui intolerance for anything and anybody who was different. Although Houston could be extremely understanding of Indian inconsistencies, he detested the erratic Mexican government and joined the hotspurs in demanding separation.

By the spring of 1836 many Texans were ready to declare their independence of Mexico. Houston's name was put up as a delegate to represent Nacogdoches at the independence convention to be held at the beginning of March. He was defeated. But he was elected as a delegate from Refugio, more than three hundred miles away, despite his having been there only once as a military scout. Thus does chance intervene to forward careers.

When at the beginning of February Houston arrived at Washington-on-the-Brazos, where the convention was to be held, he "created more sensation than . . . any other man. He . . . seems to take pains to ingratiate himself with everybody." The convention met while Santa Anna was besieging the Alamo, whose defenders thought they were fighting for restoration of the liberal Mexican constitution of 1824. But the delegates, 150 miles behind the battle line, had their eyes on independence. They made their declaration on March 2, 1836, Houston's forty-third birthday, and presented Old Sam with a birthday present of the rank of major general and a mandate to organize and command an army, plus an intimation that he was to hold that command until he had defeated the Mexicans. As a leading newspaper in Texas observed, "No general ever had more to do."

Again, Houston provoked controversy. The jury is still out on his abilities as a field commander. At first he was roundly denounced, for all he did was retreat and avoid battle, which as subsequent leaders have discovered, does not fit the yanqui psyche. Did he withdraw, Fabian fashion, until he lured Santa Anna into a trap? Or did he retreat until he had nowhere else to hide, after which the luck of the cornered took over? Whichever side you choose, the one indisputable fact is that Sam Houston led his troops to their only significant victory in the Texas revolution, but it proved to be the last battle—at San Jacinto in a bayou bend twenty-five miles east of present-day Houston on April 21, 1836. In eighteen brief minutes the Texans captured 730 and killed 630 Mexicans against 9 of their own killed and 34 wounded. The next day Santa Anna himself was taken, the war was over, Texas was actually if not officially free, and Sam Houston was being idolized by most Texans and once again by a host of people back in the United States.

The eighteen minutes at San Jacinto rescued Houston once and for all from the oblivion that had faced him when he walked out of the governor's chair in Tennessee and out of the United States. For years more sedate people east of the Mississippi had clucked about how he had chucked his one golden opportunity. Now at forty-three years of age he was back as a man of action, a noticeable man. Again, redemption, as the Victorians viewed it, was his. While the idolatry ran high, Houston became the first president of the infant Republic of Texas.

And now that Houston was a Texan his Cherokee marriage to Tiana Rogers was no longer observed. With a private divorce from Eliza Allen following shortly, he was a free man. Most of his advisers thought he should remain that way.

However, Houston's third marriage, in 1840, proved happy and lasting. He really got two women for the price of one. On a swing through Alabama he met Margaret Lea, tall, brown-haired, violet-eyed and twenty. He was forty-seven. They both fell, though evidence exists that Margaret had kept an eye on Houston ever since he had debarked on crutches in New Orleans amid a wild demonstration of welcome a month after his victory at San Jacinto. He had been dressed in tatters, with a stinking rag wrapped around his still-bloody ankle wound. As attendants tried to lift him onto a litter, he had fainted. Instead of being repulsed by his dishevelment, Margaret had found him romantic. Evidently she had decided that this wild man was fated for her, though the odds against a young girl from Alabama getting acquainted with the hero of far-off Texas were almost insurmountable, akin to those of all the young girls in Ogallala and Ogden who know that the Prince of Wales remains a bachelor because he was meant for one of them.

But a couple of years later Houston and Margaret did meet through relatives, and the only barrier to their pursuit of happiness was Margaret's mother, Nancy, widow of a Baptist minister, who did not want anyone with as storied a past as Houston hanging around her daughter. After an intensive exchange of love letters, the couple decided to wed. Margaret wrote Houston that she was coming to Texas and named the boat. Houston was in Galveston to meet it. As he stepped from a dory to greet his intended, he saw only his prospective mother-in-law. Where was Margaret? In Alabama still. "General Houston, my daughter . . . goes forth in the world to marry no man. The one who receives her hand will receive it in my home," said Nancy.

And so Houston wound up in Marion, Alabama, where Margaret was firm in her intention to marry this rascal. The fact was, her mother liked Houston. But unlike the Allen parents, she saw the pitfalls as clearly as she felt the glamour of such a union. As the wedding was about to take place in the Lea residence on May 9, 1840, still another Lea relative pulled Houston aside to say that no wedding would take place until Houston explained the Eliza Allen debacle. The fiddlers were already tuned and ready to start the wedding music. But Houston told Margaret's relative to "call his fiddlers off." He would never break his silence on that subject.

Margaret did not care about Eliza, at least not enough to deny herself Sam Houston as a husband. The wedding took place, and Houston gave Texas a new heroine. Bernard Bee, Houston's former secretary of war, predicted the marriage wouldn't last six months. "In all my acquaintances with life," he wrote to a friend, "I have never met an Individual more totally disqualified for domestic happiness" than Houston.

Bee was wrong. Margaret and Sam lived together until his death a quarter of a century later, Nancy proved to be a doting if somewhat dictatorial mother-in-law, and Houston quit his notorious carousing habits. The raven was finally caged, and he liked it.

As president of the Republic of Texas, Houston showed a talent for organization and an ability to keep problems from aggravating into major quarrels. Most Texans felt he was too lenient with the captive Santa Anna. They wanted the Mexican leader hanged, quartered, stoned, anything but alive. Houston saw Santa Anna as an extension of Texan diplomacy and sent him to Washington under guard as a representative of Texas's hopes for independence. Nor could most Texans ever figure where Houston stood on annexation to the United States; most still can't.

After lying out a term, as required by the constitution of the Republic of Texas, Houston came back for a second round as president at the beginning of the 1840s, with annexation to the United States the crucial topic in most people's minds. By now Jackson was long gone as president, which considerably reduced Houston's influence in Washington. When Houston's second term ended, he was succeeded by Dr. Anson Jones, his hand-picked choice, while in Washington James K. Polk, another Tennessean and Jacksonian, was bearing down on the American presidency. The good-old-boy system is not a twentieth-century invention.

Uneven as ever, Houston refused to encourage a filibustering expedition into Mexico and turned down requests—nay, demands—to rescue Texans held prisoner as a result of the Mier foray below the

Rio Grande. Observed Houston, "The true interest of Texas is to maintain peace . . . and to cultivate her soil." When an outbreak of citizens' meetings insisted that Houston had the wide discretionary powers to order an invasion, Old Sam retorted, "The indulgence of intemperate expressions and feelings can produce no possible good." Indeed, he insisted, "No calamity has ever befallen Texas . . . but what has been caused by a disregard of law and substituting in its place a 'wide discretion.'" Still he called the Mexicans "an imbecile and ignorant people," too "vain" to consider consequences.

Truth was, though Texas was the size of continental France with considerably more geographical resources, the republic was having a hard time staying afloat. It needed the United States more than the United States needed it, and Houston was pragmatist enough to realize the situation. Houston threatened. Either annex Texas now or forget it, he warned.

Still his dream of a Texas empire persisted. In May, 1844, he wrote William S. Murphy, the United States chargé to Texas, of his vision of Texas's destiny—a nation of Europeans, all committed to working and planting, stretching across northern Mexico all the way to Oregon. Oh, what a nation that could be! But in 1845 Texas joined the United States, and Houston saw it become just another star in a flag that now contained twenty-eight such stars. The dream should have died. Still, like many Americans, he couldn't resist the idea that "the Anglo-Saxon race [must] pervade the whole southern extremity of this vast continent."

After Texas became a state, Houston served as one of its United States senators, and was regularly touted for the presidency by people, both North and South, who favored strong leadership. He was caught up in national issues, particularly the Compromise of 1850 and the Kansas-Nebraska bill. He regularly voted opposite to the thinking of his natural constituency, which had a strong southern drift. Most southern politicians in Washington looked on him as a traitor to his section, but he always replied that Texas had joined the United States, not the South. Furthermore, he was explicit in branding southern radicals as unfit for leadership.

And in 1858 Houston set the Senate's teeth on edge when he introduced a resolution proposing that the United States establish a protectorate over Mexico and Central America. Piously he told his fellow senators that he did not offer "this resolution . . . with a view to extending our dominion, but with a view of improving our neighborhood. The mixture of races [in the United States] causes an irresistible impetus, that must overshadow and overrule that whole region" from Mexico through Costa Rica. The resolution never reached a vote. But he kept bringing it up, like a small boy pestering his mother for more cookies.

So incensed were members of the Texas legislature by his constant ridiculing of Jefferson Davis, the secretary of war, and by his stand for union that despite his vote for the proslavery Lecompton Constitution of Kansas in 1858, they chose his successor as senator ahead of the usual election time. It was a studied insult to the old leader. Texans then overruled their legislature by electing Houston as governor, where he again fell quickly into disfavor because he opposed secession. To him, the United States came first. In the interim between his deposition as senator and his election as governor, Houston resumed talk of pastoral pursuits but still dreamed of being president. He saw two ways to achieve that honor, by saving the Union from the suicide of secession and fratricidal war, and by extending the power of the United States over Mexico.

Houston hid his grand designs behind a cloak of reason—Mexico by 1858 was in the throes of its fourteenth revolution in a little more than a third of a century of existence. (Houston alleged twenty-five revolutions, but he was making a point.) The United States, he argued, could bring Mexico into good government and the good life that goes with such an institution. Despite his adamance against southern secession, he hinted at Texas secession to carry out his plan if the United States should be indisposed to go along. When the Senate refused to vote on his resolution advocating a protectorate, he not only threatened independent Texas action but a movement by unidentified "human men" who would be willing to "arrest the cruelties on, and to stop the murders of, a defenseless people."

On another occasion, when a Pacific railroad bill was under consideration in 1859, Houston interjected a prediction that Texas would soon extend its borders to Mexico City, where it would run into California moving down the Pacific coast to the same terminus. He further predicted a harmonious union of the two potential empires.

Texas newspapers took up the cry in behalf of Houston's plan, as did English holders of Mexican bonds (Mexico was in arrears on payments of interest). Encouraged, Houston made a speech, the only one in his gubernatorial campaign of 1859, in which he asserted that a protectorate over Mexico would show the United States as "a nationality in which freedom exists" with "strength to maintain it."

Mexico was vulnerable to filibustering at this point. Mexican liberals under Benito Juárez were attempting to overthrow a reactionary central government, while Juan Cortina was depredating both sides of the Texas-Mexico border without declaring for much of anyone except himself. Houston knew he could get money to mount an expedition; could he get the men and materiel? The Texas Rangers were a possibility, and he had always kept the Indians in his camp.

The Rangers may have staved off a Texas invasion of Mexico by pacifying the border in late 1859 and early 1860. But in February, 1860, Houston sent two emissaries to sound out Colonel Robert E. Lee, then in command of federal troops in the area, whether he would be "willing to aid . . . to pacificate Mexico" as a protector in case Houston became president of the United States. Lee, ever correct, replied that he was opposed to filibustering and would act only "in conformity to the Constitution and laws of the country." Despite this refusal, which was really a rebuke from the high-minded Lee, Houston kept the heat on Washington, sending men and letters indicating that Texas would raise ten thousand men on thirty days' notice, and suggesting that the federal government should send proportionately more.

From Kentucky, from Pennsylvania, from New Jersey came offers to help Houston lead troops into Mexico, each with a prediction that such a grand filibuster would so inflame the American spirit as to promote its originator to the nation's highest office. Volunteers applied from most of the northern states and some of the southern ones. A man in New Orleans volunteered ten thousand muskets; a man in Philadelphia, $50,000. Another group promised that an expedition would be financed by British capitalists, who in addition would grant an annuity to Houston's wife. Houston had struck a national, even an international, chord, and he must have been mesmerized by the sound. The cause of empire was a sacred charge throughout the nineteenth century.

But there in the late spring of 1860 the threat ended. Whether Houston was sincere in wishing to extend the American flag over Mexico or whether he was fanning a fire of manifest destiny into a presidential draft cannot be ascertained. A disruptive fire that was smoldering within the United States would create a convulsion more nearly justifying Mexico's establishing a protectorate over the United States than the reverse.

Houston would go down fighting, augmenting his pragmatic, patriotic oratory of the 1850s with new bursts of rhetoric supporting the Union. The legislature demanded a special session to denounce the federal and northern state governments, but Houston stood firm. One reporter from the *Galveston News* obtained the statement from Houston that while he had rescued Texas several times in the past, this time it could go to hell by itself; "he would not go with her."

Houston took one last look at empire. To the burgeoning Confederacy he issued the warning that sooner than join the disunionists, Texas would travel in a third direction—her own "separate Nationality. . . . Texas has views of expansion not common to many of her sister States. Although an empire within herself, she feels that there is an empire beyond, essential to her security. She will not be content to have the path of her destiny clogged. The same spirit of enterprise that founded a Republic here, will carry her institutions Southward and Westward." When that sentiment became known, Houston lost the support of both the secessionists and the federal-minded.

But Texas was hell-bent on destruction along with the other secessionists, and in early 1861 left the Union. Undoubtedly Houston, although sixty-eight years old, could have mustered support for separate nationhood, but he did not want to shed the blood of brothers. Rumor held that the new president, Abraham Lincoln, would offer the old warrior a position in his cabinet, perhaps secretary of war, as a reward for his steadfast unionist sentiments. And Lincoln did offer troops to keep the governor in office. But Houston was tired of Texans' rebellious inclinations and determined to leave office and let the state sink without him. And sink it did, along with the other ten states of the Confederacy.

Out of office, Houston came around. Two months after being deposed as governor, he said in a speech at Independence, Texas, "The time has come when a man's section is his country. I stand by mine."

He had two more years, holding his family together by selling firewood. Sometimes Houston was mentioned as the next governor, but he was getting too old and ill for the political wars. Right after Vicksburg and Gettysburg, on July 26, 1863, he died of pneumonia. One of his everlasting enemies, E. H. Cushing, summed him up in an editorial in the *Houston Tri-Weekly Telegraph:* "He has not always been right, nor has he always been successful, but he has always kept the impress of his mind upon the times in which he has acted."

That he did.

Big Drunk. Big Dealer. Big Dreamer. Great Designer, in Llérena Friend's phrase. From the 1820s to 1861 Sam Houston was like a larger-than-life stink bug in America's life. No matter how many times you plugged his hole and pressed him down, he always reappeared somewhere else, as tangible a factor as ever. With his cool blue eyes, his Roman senator's brow, and his oversize but graceful frame, he could stare down the most formidable antagonist. But he had a dreamer's heart connected with a doer's organizational

skill, and each shared in making him Texas's most noteworthy adopted son.

No, that's wrong. Typically Houston adopted Texas, for in many ways he was larger than the infant republic and the fledgling state. He was the parent, and Texas was his offspring. As a parent, though he himself was often personally undisciplined, he scolded, spanked, cajoled, and threatened Texas until he shaped it into a wayward entity that still hasn't lived up to the standards and images he set for it.

QUESTIONS TO CONSIDER

1 Explain some of the contradictions that marked Houston's career. Reflect on the previous selection on Jackson. Did Jackson share Houston's love-hate relationship with the Indians? Compare the lives, accomplishments, and failures of the two men.

2 Describe the rise and fall of Houston as governor of Tennessee. What were Houston's aspirations at this juncture of his career, and how did Jackson fit into those plans? What part did Eliza Allen play in Houston's downfall? Can you guess the reasons for Houston's marital breakup?

3 Explain how Congressman Stanbery unwittingly brought Houston back into the public spotlight and revived the Raven's political career. How did Houston prepare for his important speech before the House of Representatives? What reaction did he receive from visitors in the gallery?

4 What role did Houston play in the Texas revolution against Mexico? After Texas entered the Union, did Houston believe that his first obligation was to the South or to the nation at large?

5 In the 1850s, as a senator and governor, Houston still longed to be president. What actions did he contemplate to gain this lofty goal? Was Robert E. Lee eager to join in his planned assault on Mexico?

6 What nickname best suits Houston—Big Drunk, Big Dealer, Big Dreamer, or Grand Designer? Explain your choice. Do you think a person of his character could be successful in modern American politics?

PART TEN

The Growth of Technology

19 The Erie Canal: The Waterway that Shaped a Great Nation

PETER L. BERNSTEIN

In the following selection, Peter L. Bernstein tells the story of the great Erie Canal, which opened in 1825 and which ran from Buffalo on Lake Erie to Albany on the Hudson River. Commerce from the west then moved south to "the harbor of New York City and its well-developed port facilities." Thus the Erie Canal provided a link between the Atlantic coast and the enormous untapped resources west of the Appalachian Mountains. In the modern era of giant rockets, space shuttles, and satellite probes of other planets, it is easy to dismiss the men and the technology that built this artificial waterway. In point of fact, the Erie Canal was one of the greatest technological achievements of the early nineteenth century. To Americans at that time, it was "the marvel of its age."

In his riveting narrative, Bernstein introduces us to the indefatigable surveyors, engineers, work crews, and politicians who made the canal a reality. He describes how a commission of New York politicians—chief among them, De Witt Clinton, the most powerful New York politician in the early 1800s—supervised the construction of the canal, which was financed by the New York legislature, thus earning New York the title of the Empire State. Beginning in 1817 when James Monroe was president, engineers and work crews relied on their Yankee ingenuity to develop "striking inventions and technological improvisations" to dig the gigantic waterway. They "hacked through dense forests and built over rivers and valleys with nothing more than bare hands, shovels and axes, mules, explosive powder, and crude but ingenious inventions to pull down trees and yank up their roots." An example of the "ingenious inventions" was the waterproof cement they devised to seal "the spaces between the neatly arranged stones lining the sides of the excavation, the locks, the culverts, and the aqueducts."

The completed canal, 363 miles long, caused an economic boom in America, as a "cornucopia of western agricultural products moved eastward toward the Atlantic, while manufactured goods . . . traveled westward to the limitless undeveloped lands lying in wait" beyond the mountains. The canal's agricultural products soon reached European markets, thus elevating the United States into an international economic power. Summing up the profound significance of the waterway, Bernstein writes: "By bringing the interior to the seas and the seas into the interior, the Erie Canal would shape a great nation, knit the sinews of the Industrial Revolution, propel globalization—extending America's networks outside our own borders—and revolutionize the production and supply of food for the entire world."

It is an amazing story, and Bernstein recounts it so vividly that we feel as though we are there with the workers as they cut through dark forests infested with malaria-carrying mosquitoes to excavate a ditch that "would meld forest, farm, and industry into a combination of extraordinary power." Addressing the triumphant work, Gouverneur Morris, one of the canal's commission of politicians, was moved to ask: "Does it not seem like magic?"

GLOSSARY

AQUEDUCT   This structure creates a man-made channel that conveys water from one location to another. There were eighteen aqueducts on the Erie Canal.

CLINTON, DE WITT   Born and raised in the Hudson River Valley of New York, Clinton ran as an antiwar candidate in the presidential election of 1812. He received eighty-nine electoral college votes, but lost to James Madison. Clinton also served as a United States senator, mayor of New York City, and governor of New York state from 1817 to 1828. As governor, this ambitious and farsighted politician was an outspoken advocate of building the Erie Canal.

CULVERT   A transverse drain that permits water to flow along a specific route.

FULTON, ROBERT   In 1807, Fulton's ship, the *Claremont,* was the first steamboat to sail up the Hudson River. Skeptics referred to the 150-mile journey as "Fulton's Folly." But the enterprising inventor's fleet of steamboats soon turned a profit by increasing the speed and reducing the cost of river transportation.

HAINES, CHARLES GLIDDEN   Clinton's protégé and personal secretary, Haines predicted that constructing the Erie Canal would stimulate the economy of New York and that of the entire nation.

LAFAYETTE, MARQUIS DE   A young French nobleman, Lafayette fought in the American Revolution on the patriots' side and was wounded in the battle of Brandywine. George Washington admired his courage in combat, remarking that "the Marquis is determined to be in the way of

danger." Lafayette became a popular figure in America and symbolized France's support of the American cause during the Revolution.

LOCKS.   These were enclosures with gates at either end. The locks raised or lowered boats as they moved from one level of a canal to another. The Erie Canal had eighty-three locks.

MORRIS, GOUVERNEUR   A Pennsylvania representative to the Constitutional Convention of 1787, Morris is credited with crafting the Constitution's famous preamble, "We the People of the United States," and making other important stylistic changes to the final document. Morris became an advocate of a waterway across New York and served as senior member of the commissioners who designed the Erie Canal.

PATOWMACK CANAL COMPANY   George Washington supported this project to build a canal on the Potomac River from Alexandria, Virginia, to the Appalachian Mountains. Bernstein concludes: "Washington's canal was an engineering achievement but a financial failure."

POLING   Through the use of a long pole made from resilient wood, poling allowed one person to push a boat or a barge in the desired direction.

SCHUYLER, PHILIP   Alexander Hamilton's father-in-law and a general during the American Revolution, Schuyler had visited England and studied its canal system. He was the chief engineer of a failed attempt to construct a navigable waterway from Albany on the Hudson River to the western interior of New York.

TACKING   The maneuver that changes the direction of a ship by turning the bow through the wind and shifting the sails so that the wind moves from one side of the sails to the other.

TAMMANY HALL   This Democratic party organization controlled New York politics from the 1850s to the 1930s.

TOWPATH   A path where horses or mules pull boats along a canal. On the Erie Canal, the towpath was about fifteen feet above the waterline. A boy would usually ride the animals while a man would steer the boat. Bernstein writes: "Although this sounds like a poky, primitive means of locomotion, in reality it was the critical technological advantage over travel by road or by river."

VAN BUREN, MARTIN   A New York Democrat, Van Buren was Andrew Jackson's vice president from 1833 to 1837. Van Buren served as president from 1837 to 1841. An economic collapse in 1837 was primarily responsible for his failure to win reelection in 1842.

WATSON, ELKANAH   Watson was an advocate of waterway projects that would "assist nature" and reap huge profits for investors. He claimed to be the first person to conceive of what became the Erie Canal.

WHITE, CANVAS   A wounded veteran of the War of 1812, White made a detailed study of the English canal system. As an engineer for the Erie Canal, White designed its locks, gates, and boats. His development of waterproof cement that could be produced in New York was crucial to the successful construction of the Erie Canal.

WRIGHT, BENJAMIN   A New York assemblyman, Wright was a surveyor and engineer who helped build the Erie Canal.

We live today in a time of widespread concern and fascination with technological innovation, the system of networking, and the influence of both on globalization in the twenty-first century. We also live in a time when the United States faces bewildering questions about its role in the world and, indeed, the vision of its long-term future. This acceleration in change has affected our political system, our society, the economy, and the world of finance in ways we are only beginning to comprehend. . . .

[T]he story of the Erie Canal . . . illuminate[s] the turbulent and exciting present with a great but unfamiliar history of how a revolutionary technological network molded the triumph of the United States as a continental power and as a giant in the world economy. The Erie Canal was the child of many dreamers and a host of surveyors, engineers, and politicians, most of whom had never seen a canal before and few of whom had any experience in designing, building, or operating a canal. But the heroes of this story had the foresight to change the face of the earth, not only literally but in a much more fundamental sense. They understood that the process they launched would alter every aspect of how people lived their lives.

When the canal was completed in October 1825 and Governor De Witt Clinton could celebrate the Wedding of the Waters by pouring a keg of water from Lake Erie into the Atlantic Ocean, he opened an uninterrupted navigable waterway through the imposing barrier of the mountain range extending from Maine all the way down to Georgia. The end result would lead to an historic explosion of commerce, ideas, and technological change. By bringing the interior to the seas and the seas into the interior, the Erie Canal would shape a great nation, knit the sinews of the Industrial Revolution, propel globalization—extending America's networks outside our own borders—and revolutionize the production and supply of food for the entire world. That was by no means all. In time, this skinny ditch in upstate New York would demonstrate that trade and commerce are the keys to the expansion of prosperity and freedom itself.

The notion of a canal connecting the eastern seaboard to the west had been an active topic of discussion for more than twenty years before construction actually began in 1817. The Appalachian mountain range posed a formidable barricade between the narrow line of states touching the Atlantic Ocean and the almost boundless lands on the other side of the mountains. While rivers often lead the people on opposite sides of their banks to join in forming one community, populations divided by mountains tend to become separate nations unless some easy means of communication exists between the two.

George Washington was keenly aware of this risk. Even before the Revolution, in 1775, he had expressed his concerns about the peril of losing the lands on the western side of the Appalachian Mountains to either France or Canada, or both, unless the mountain barrier could be pierced—and soon. The pioneers moving west had little allegiance to the lands they left behind. If nothing were done, the young United States would be left squeezed between the mountains and the sea, a constricted minor-league nation compared with the growth and power developing on the other side of the mountains.

Ink on the peace treaty declaring American independence was barely dry before Washington was organizing the Patowmack Company to convert the Potomac River into a canal running from the seacoast at Alexandria, Virginia, all the way up to the mountains. Washington's canal was an engineering achievement but a financial disaster. It was still under construction when he died in 1799 and fell into bankruptcy before work on the Erie Canal had even begun.

The geography for crossing the mountains was much more favorable in New York than in Virginia, but New Yorkers appeared to be in less of a hurry to capitalize on what nature had bestowed upon them. There was a succession of frustrating efforts over a period of some twenty-five years before they would finally break ground for the Erie Canal in 1817. The visionaries and supporters were determined to pursue their dream. Their opponents were stubborn in their skepticism about the feasibility of such a gigantic engineering venture, and many were also frightened by the prospect of spending so many millions of dollars of the state's money with no assurance that the canal would actually pay its way.

To Americans in the early days of the Republic—in what was then, in today's parlance, an "emerging economy" in which 93 percent of the population still lived on farms—the very idea of connecting the east to the west by means of a gigantic artificial waterway appeared as fantastic as sending a rocket to the moon. In January 1809, Thomas Jefferson judged it to be "little short of madness." Without the gritty determination of a small group of men convinced of the prospect of a great nation, an unquenchable enthusiasm to make it reality, and a keen sense of how to deploy power, the Erie Canal would not have been built and the western territories would in all likelihood have broken away.

New York's first attempt to develop an effective passage through the mountains was, like Washington's Patowmack Company, a privately financed venture; it was established in 1792 under the leadership of General Philip Schuyler, a hero of the Revolutionary War, and a merchant named Elkanah Watson who had all the right political connections. Rather than build a canal, the designers of this ill-fated effort attempted to transform the Mohawk River's many rapids, falls, and shallow stretches into a navigable waterway over about a hundred miles from Albany on the Hudson to the western interior of New York State. Engineering this project was difficult enough, but the lack of sufficient revenue to cover the enormous maintenance expenses turned out to be an even greater hurdle. Like the Patowmack Company—and for many of the same reasons—this endeavor ended in financial failure.

A few New Yorkers kept the faith and continued the struggle. There were those, such as the irrepressible optimist Gouverneur Morris, who proclaimed with remarkable clarity both the possibilities and huge benefits that a canal would bestow on the state and nation. Two members of the state legislature began to press for a canal around 1805, but most people tended to agree with Thomas Jefferson that huge financial costs and the scale and audacity of the engineering were insuperable obstacles.

Finally, in 1810, a small cadre of enthusiasts from the state legislature enlisted the support of De Witt

Clinton, the most powerful politician in the state at that moment. A serious intellectual and amateur scientist, Clinton was an insider's insider in the world of politics with a well-honed instinct for the uses of power. He had been the secretary for his uncle George Clinton, the nine-term governor of New York State who was then vice president of the United States. He had served as a U.S. senator, had been mayor of New York City for six years, and was now a state senator. He was about to become lieutenant governor.

Clinton's decision to participate was the pivotal moment in this story. He was the one individual with the political skill and intellectual authority to turn Morris's bold vision into a reality. Once he considered the possibilities, Clinton was willing to put his entire future on the line for the canal, without reservation and without fear of the political turmoil looming before him. Despite his high-handed mannerisms and unquenchable ambitions for high office, which tended to spawn enemies among politicians even in his own party, Clinton's firm leadership of a reluctant electorate, his extraordinary eloquence, and his brilliant analytical capabilities brought the boundless benefits of the canal to New York State and, ultimately, to the United States of America. There might never have been an Erie Canal without his unwavering support and readiness to risk his career on the canal's success.

The political battles and intrigues fought out in New York State over the fate of the Erie Canal were as fierce as any in its history. Politicians high and low, and from all parties, engaged in this struggle tirelessly and with great zest. The controversies engaged not only eminent leaders like De Witt Clinton and Martin Van Buren—both of whom made no effort to disguise their presidential aspirations—but the bare-knuckled forces of Tammany Hall as well. On more than one occasion, victory seemed within grasp only to be dashed by the resiliency of the opposition and the incredulity of the timid. In many ways, it was a lot easier for the engineers to improvise this stupendous technological achievement than

it was for De Witt Clinton and his allies to subdue their political opponents.

And as the time finally arrived when, as one protagonist put it, "it was impossible for stupidity itself [not] to stretch their opaque minds from Erie to the ocean," the former opponents of the canal turned themselves right around and claimed to be the true guardians of its future. Now the canal developed into a kind of religious totem, perceived as above and beyond the rambunctious political arena. . . .

The first step in building the Erie Canal took place when the crews defined the area to be cleared of the forest by driving red stakes sixty feet apart along the whole line of the proposed canal and then another set of stakes precisely forty feet apart to mark off the area to be excavated for the canal itself. The difference left room for the towpath and the berm (the side of the canal opposite the towpath).

The basic design of the canal recognized that it would be too shallow and probably too narrow for the kinds of steamboats then in operation, whose side wheels would churn up the muddy bottom only four feet below the surface while the wake would damage the canal walls from the constant waves banging against them. Sail power would be inappropriate because winds in one direction would not be suitable for boats moving against the wind and the canal would be much too narrow to leave any room for tacking. Poling would be too slow and impossible for heavy loads.

The only practical form of motive power was horses and mules to tow the boats along behind them, the same method the English had adopted for their canals. The need for a towpath along the entire length of the canal explains why the total width was designed to be twenty feet wider than the ditch itself. The towpath was often narrower than twenty feet, but the berm also had to be provided for to the extent possible so that people could move on the other side as well.

As originally planned, the middle section would be the easiest to build. Part of it, the so-called Long Level along the relatively flat country from Utica to Syracuse, was a stretch of fifty-nine miles, designed

The Erie Canal was the technological achievement of its age. The creators of the canal used brute force and ingenious inventions to cut a 363-mile swath through forests and mountains. This "wedding of the waters" between Lake Erie and the Hudson River created a pathway to the riches of the American west. (The Granger Collection, New York)

to be built without a single lock. This stretch was the longest canal level in the world without locks. Early progress was everything anyone had hoped for. When the first snowfalls forced work to halt at the end of 1817, the commissioners could report, "Much useful experience has been acquired in the course of the season."

The formal language obscured the drama of striking inventions and technological innovations the crews on the job developed to meet problems whose magnitude no one had ever encountered before. The most interesting achievements involved what the commissioners described, again with notable understatement, as "many valuable improvements . . . made in the method of grubbing standing timber." Grubbing—digging up or digging out . . . [the] "vast

confusion [of] generations of trees"—was the most important element of the process. Not a yard of ditch could be dug until the workers had cut down the countless thousands of trees, chopped them up into movable sizes, uprooted the stumps, and then carted away the staggering mess of logs, branches, and leaves.

Neither scientists nor engineers devised the ingenious laborsaving solutions to these tasks. Rather, the inventors were the men doing the hard work on the job. They remain anonymous. When the great celebrations at the completion of the canal took place, these men would continue to be unheralded. Yet the scale of their achievements was not to be denied.

Most of these remarkable laborsaving innovations on the canal owed their success to the principles of

Archimedes, the great inventor and mathematician of ancient Greece, who has received the credit for inventing the lever—a device based on the theory that a small amount of force moving a relatively large distance could translate into a greater amount of power delivered over a smaller distance. Most levers are boards set on a fulcrum nearer one end than the other—a kind of unbalanced seesaw—or are gears where a small wheel turns faster than a larger wheel to which it is connected.

One such clever invention on the Erie Canal dramatically reduced the time-consuming labor needed to chop down the massive trees in the forests, which would often have involved more than a hundred swings of an axe before the job was done. This gadget consisted of a wheel wound around with a cable and mounted so it could spin freely. When the loose end of the cable was attached to the top of a tree, one man all by himself could fell it by turning the wheel until the cable bent the tree over so far it finally broke free of its stump and crashed to the ground.

But the stump was still there, its thick roots reaching in all directions under the surface of the earth. The contraption contrived to uproot the stump was a truly formidable device. The basic machinery consisted of two wheels, each sixteen feet in diameter, set on either side of a huge axle thirty feet long and twenty inches in diameter. Another wheel, with a diameter of fourteen feet, was mounted in the middle of the axle. As the diameter of this wheel was two inches smaller than the outside wheels, it did not touch the ground and could spin freely. In order to drag a stump and its roots completely out of the earth, the men first braced the two outside wheels of the axle with heavy rocks so that the device would be stationary. Then they wound a chain around the axle and fastened the chain to the stump. After wrapping one end of a strong rope several times around the fourteen-foot wheel in the center of the axle, the men attached the other end of the rope to a team of horses or oxen. As the animals moved forward, pulling the rope behind them and turning the wheel, the tremendous pressure on the chain yanked the stump and its roots free of the earth. According to one authority, one of these contrivances with a team of four horses and seven laborers could grub thirty to forty large stumps a day.

After all this, the ground was ready for the excavation to begin, but no one had built anything as enormous as the Erie Canal before. In the early stages, the men followed the so-called European method of digging with spades and carting the excess earth away on wheelbarrows, an approach hallowed by thousands of years of use. Pressed to find more efficient ways to dig and remove the excavated earth, the men discovered they could save a lot of time and effort by replacing spades with horse-drawn plows. These plows carried heavy and sharpened pieces of iron that sliced through the roots as they were pulled along, tearing apart the earth. In addition, the teams of horses constantly carrying away heavy loads of excavated earth were packing down the ground along the side of the canal into solid banks much less vulnerable to leakage than with the traditional method.

All of this engineering improvisation by untrained talents would one day be known as Yankee ingenuity. But these innovations had an awesome quality as well, as signs of the growing force of man over nature in the budding Industrial Revolution. Cadwallader D. Colden, the grandson of the first man to dream of an Erie Canal nearly a hundred years earlier, put it this way in 1825: "Indeed, to see a forest tree, which had withstood the elements till it attained maturity, torn up by its roots, and bending itself to the earth, in obedience to the command of man, is a spectacle that must awaken feelings of gratitude to that Being, who has bestowed on his creatures so much power and wisdom."

De Witt Clinton was eager to use the impressive achievements of the first season as a base for pressing forward aggressively during the year ahead. Promising that "the completion of these stupendous works [would] spread the blessings of plenty and opulence [to] the most distant parts of the Union and command the approbation of the civilized world," he insisted that "we are required to persevere." As he saw it, there was not a moment to lose: he had his heart set on the ambitious target of a complete and fully operational canal by the end of 1824. It was no coincidence that 1824 would also be James Monroe's last full year as president (on the likely assumption he won reelection in 1820), bringing to an end the Virginia dynasty that had accounted for four of the first five presidents of the United States. The presidential contest in 1824 was wide open.

Clinton's secretary and friend, Charles Glidden Haines, provided strong support for Clinton's promises in his extended pamphlet of October 1818. Early in this document, Haines echoes George Washington's concerns as the prime motivation for building the Erie Canal: "Our mountains must be politically annihilated. Our sectional barriers must be swept away by a moral arm, whose power is resistless. . . . Nothing but this, can perpetuate that union which is to guarantee our future national greatness. Nothing but this, can preserve those popular institutions which are sealed with our fathers' blood."

The canal commissioners responded. Paperwork moved ahead smoothly in 1818. By the late summer, contracts had been signed for the entire length of the canal except at a few spots around projected structures like aqueducts or bridges. In anticipation of the great day when the waterway would be approaching completion, Clinton arranged for a survey and drawing of plans for a harbor at the mouth of Buffalo Creek on the shores of Lake Erie.

At the construction site, however, the hard work on the canal did not move ahead smoothly, at least not at first. The winter snows had been unusually heavy, which meant a late melt. The melting had barely begun when the heavens dumped so much rain over New York that the crews could not resume full operations until late May. All the work had to wait until the mud and puddles dried out. But after that, the advance moved along at such a vigorous pace that most of the lost time was made up, with nearly four thousand men and fifteen hundred horses engaged by the time the digging season came to an end with the return of winter weather. Progress was so convincing the commissioners were willing to project completion of the whole middle section by the end of the next digging season in 1819.

Although the clearing of the land and the excavation of the canal were now making satisfactory headway, the canal staff had not yet found a totally waterproof material, good for all seasons, to seal the spaces between the neatly arranged stones lining the sides of the excavation, the locks, the culverts, and the aqueducts. The available common quicklime in use was unstable, breaking down under any sustained pressure. As a consequence, leaks as well as rot were already making their appearance in the canal walls and the sides of the locks, requiring constant relining of the surfaces. Without a replacement for the quicklime, the canal could conceivably end up as nothing more than a pile of mush. Clinton, ever the voracious reader, had come upon a Roman cement for this purpose in *The Repository of the Arts* and obtained some samples from Italy. This material appeared to do the trick, but importing massive amounts of it across the Atlantic Ocean would have been prohibitively expensive.

Then the young engineer Canvass White heard that the contractors responsible for building culverts and aqueducts on the stretch between Syracuse and Rome might have come upon an answer to the puzzle in the vicinity of Chittenango, a little village about twenty miles east of Syracuse.* They were using local limestone that would not "slack"—that is, it would not disintegrate when wet—unlike all other limestone tried so far. White and Benjamin Wright traveled to Chittenango as soon as they received this news and set up a meeting with a local scientist named Andrew Barto in order to perform a full experiment with the material.

The encounter took place at Elisha Carey's barroom in the middle of town, an unlikely locale for a scientific experiment but a good place for the impatient spectators to calm their nerves.† Dr. Barto

---

*Chittenango is the birthplace of L. Frank Baum, author of *The Wizard of Oz*. A yellow brick road runs through the center of town.

†In a nice bit of irony, the site of Elisha Carey's tavern is now an engineering school.

arrived with a handful of moist mortar made from the limestone, which he now mixed with sand, rolled into a ball, and deposited into a pail of water, where it would sit overnight. When the group gathered at Elisha Carey's the next morning to examine the ball of cement, they found they could roll the ball across the room. It was hard and solid as a rock. Dr. Barto declared this cement was equal to anything they could find in Italy or Holland.

White conducted more experiments with the Chittenango cement until he was satisfied he had the perfect mixture to make it waterproof under all conditions. Then he saw to it that a factory was set up just outside of Chittenango to grind and manufacture the material, at a price to the commissioners of $3.50 for a barrel of five bushels of cement.

This was a development of the greatest importance. In addition to the 500,000 bushels of cement used in building the Erie Canal, the cement was exported in large quantities over the years to other states with similar needs. . . .

[Harsh weather had previously slowed construction of the canal.] The . . . year 1819 looked at first as though nature would be a troublemaker once again. The winter months were usually the easiest time to bring material and supplies up to the canal sites, because sleighs running smoothly on snow were a lot more efficient than wagons rattling along on rutty roads. But not in the winter of 1818–1819. At first the snowfall was too meager to permit sleighing. When the snows finally made their appearance, they arrived in what seemed to be one endless blizzard, blocking the sleighs until March. Although matters improved with an unusually dry spring, which was a big help, the extended summer heat and humidity were brutal and the mosquitoes a scourge, especially in the marshy country between Syracuse and the western end of the middle section at the Seneca River. The work crews had joked at first about the easy digging through the soft earth of the marshes, but the good cheer vanished when clouds of voracious mosquitoes descended on them. At least a thousand men came down with fevers, no doubt

including a high incidence of malaria, with medical care amounting to little more than snakeroot, green pigweed, or bleeding. Some jobs shut down completely until the cooler weather finally chased the mosquitoes away.*

The mosquitoes must have been a terrible curse everywhere in those years. In 1818, De Witt Clinton and his wife, Maria, who was already in poor health, planned to spend the summer months on Staten Island. The insects were merciless, and Maria fell gravely ill. In search of relief, the family moved up to Mt. Vernon in Westchester County but encountered swarms of mosquitoes there, too. Maria Clinton passed away at Mt. Vernon on July 30 at the age of forty-two, after twenty-two years of marriage.

Never one to let events overwhelm him, Clinton married for a second time nine months later. In between Maria's death and his remarriage, he took a terrible fall, which left him with a bad limp and limited physical activity for the rest of his life, but he maintained the frequency of his ceaseless travels of inspection by horse and by stage up and down the rough country along the path of the Erie Canal. . . .

When completed in 1825, the Erie Canal was the marvel of its age. As one of many tourists who came to see this technological triumph summed it up, "The truth is the canal is in everybody's mouth." Yet this completely man-made waterway was dug and hacked through dense forests and built over rivers and valleys with nothing more than bare hands, shovels and axes, mules, explosive powder, and crude but ingenious inventions to pull down trees and yank up their stumps.

The canal stretched 363 miles from Buffalo on Lake Erie, part of the Great Lakes system (referred to by Clinton as "our Mediterranean seas"), to Albany

---

*When construction by the United States began on the Panama Canal in 1904, the mosquito attacks were so violent and yellow fever and malaria so prevalent that the Americans employed over a thousand men just to cut grass and clear brush in order to make the working environment as inhospitable as possible to mosquitoes. See David McCullough, *The Path Between the Seas*, p. 573.

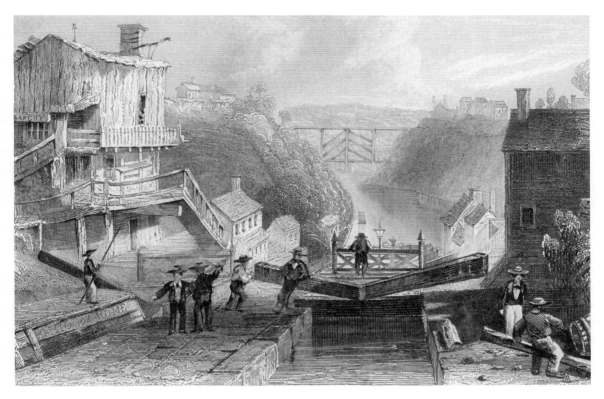

This scene depicts the breathtaking beauty that travelers enjoyed along the Erie Canal. The workers in the picture probably lived within the community. Bernstein relates that the "locals were most familiar with the countryside, knew best how and where to recruit a labor force, and would take greatest pride in building the stretch of canal near their homes." (© Bettmann/CORBIS)

on the Hudson River. From Albany, it was 150 miles down the Hudson to the vast harbor of New York City and its well-developed port facilities. Designed by a small group of surveyors with no civil engineering experience but a great talent for improvisation and innovation, the canal's eighty-three locks enabled boats to travel a total of 675 feet up and down from one end to the other, over hill and dale, and over eighteen aqueducts. One aqueduct more than three city blocks long carried the canal so far above the raging river below that the Marquis de Lafayette would describe it in wonder as "an aerial route." The canal was also crossed by hundreds of small bridges connecting the lands it sliced through on its path between Albany and Buffalo.

Once it was opened, the traffic on the canal expanded rapidly. A cornucopia of western agricultural products moved eastward toward the Atlantic while manufactured goods and, increasingly, immigrants and other pioneers traveled westward to the limitless undeveloped lands lying in wait. By replacing the rough roads, the Erie Canal slashed transport costs so radically that a shipment of flour could have traveled 2750 miles before the cost would exceed 50 percent of its ultimate proceeds. By road, the equivalent distance was only 130 miles. As a result, the tonnage of grain reaching Buffalo from the west in the mid-1840s was ten times what it had been just a decade earlier. The Erie Canal's agricultural cargoes soon found markets throughout Europe. In the process, the canal would influence such mighty decisions as the repeal of tariffs on food in Great Britain in 1846, freeing European labor for work in the factories and reducing costs of production throughout the European as well as the American economy.

The prosperity created by the canal earned New York the proud title of the Empire State and made New York City the greatest city in the nation and, some would argue, in the world. Indeed, the Erie Canal would have a compelling influence on the Industrial Revolution, as well as the perceptions, and the realities, of economic power. The canal counties of New York were early and sustained leaders in the number of patents issued in the United States each year. As late as 1852, freight tonnage carried on an enlarged Erie Canal was still thirteen times the traffic carried on all the railroads in New York State. When tolls were abolished in 1882, the canal was serving over twenty million people and had produced revenues of $121 million since 1825, more than quadruple its operating costs. And it was still going strong.

The financing of the Erie Canal was as original and brilliantly successful as its technological features. When the U.S. government in Washington finally rejected sponsorship of the canal in 1816—after repeated promises to contribute—New York State proceeded to finance the canal by selling its own bonds to the public at large and, with rising success, to financial markets abroad. The flow of revenues collected on the canal was so far in excess of operating expenses that the state was able to repay these bonds well ahead of the schedule.

Most important, Americans perceived the canal as an expression of faith in the potentials of a free society, a message of hope for a great young nation on the move. All of the leaders of the campaign for the canal—De Witt Clinton, Gouverneur Morris, Robert Fulton, as well as others less famous—shared a cloudless view of how the future would unfold if the commercial connection between east and west could be secured. Their foresight was remarkable: almost every feature of their wonderful dream came true.

"Does it not seem like magic?" Gouverneur Morris had asked a friend in December 1800, seventeen years before the first ground would be moved for construction of the canal. At the culmination of a trip to look over his own holdings of real estate across the raw backcountry of New York State, Morris went on:

. . . Hundreds of ships will in no distant period bound the billows of those inland seas. . . . As yet, my friend, we only crawl about on the outer shell of our country. The interior excels the part we inhabit in soil, in climate, in everything. The proudest empire in Europe is but a bauble compared to what America *will* be and *must* be, in the course of two centuries, perhaps of one. . . .

. . . As the Founding Fathers created a new nation to "secure the blessings of Liberty to ourselves and our Posterity," the Erie Canal cut a waterway through the mountains to bind that nation into one and to make possible a new economic system in America that would meld forest, farm, and industry into a combination of extraordinary power.

One of the most striking features of the whole story is how much of it was part of the early visions. From the prophecies of George Washington to the predictions of De Witt Clinton, the great prizes to be gained by cutting a waterway through the mountains were national unity and economic power. Washington understood with remarkable clarity that unity was impossible without the economic side, without "commerce." Clinton was convinced that unity would be an inevitable consequence of economic achievement. Both understood that huge capital investments like these—no matter how financed and managed—would work only if they helped to make private markets function better. The final results were a shining tribute to both men's keen sense of the shape of the future. That a canal would bind the United States to Europe as well as joining eastern Americans to the west was a bonus Washington and Clinton may have sensed but that neither explicitly articulated.

It is ironic, from the vantage point of the early twenty-first century, that the two efforts to achieve these objectives—Washington's Patowmack Company and Clinton's Ditch—were so fundamentally different in structure, concept, and ultimate operational success. Although Clinton had the great advantage of geography . . . Washington's waterway was financed and managed as private enterprise while Clinton's was a public improvement from start to finish.

Suppose we had to bet today on which project would turn out to be the more successful effort, geography aside: a profit-seeking venture controlled by one of the great executives and administrators of all time, or a state-financed project managed by a committee of politicians. The choice seems to be an obvious one. Thomas Jefferson had reminded George Washington in early 1784, "Nature then has declared in favor of the Potomac, and through that channel offers to pour into our lap the whole commerce of the Western world. [Moreover] public undertakings are carelessly managed, and much money spent to little purpose."

Yet the privately owned and operated Patowmack Company ended up a financial failure and finished way behind schedule, while the committee of politicians who managed the construction of the Erie Canal would oversee their novel, complex, and gigantic project with high success, bringing it to completion on schedule, at a mind-boggling level of expenditure that came in close to original estimates, and without a single significant blunder or failure along the way. The long odds would have come out the big winner on that bet.

This striking contrast in final outcomes is all the more amazing when we recall that Washington was a trained surveyor with engineering experience. . . . We might also note that Washington ended up with a labor force of slaves, while the Erie Canal employed free men, including those who contributed anonymously to the technological achievements of construction, such as the machines to pull down enormous trees and then uproot their massive stumps.

When the construction of the canal was complete, and it was at long last time to celebrate the Wedding of the Waters, De Witt Clinton—the heroic protagonist of this story—spoke with more brevity and

simplicity than with his usual flourishes. But he had the spirit of the occasion when he ended the ceremonies with these gentle words: "And may the God of Heavens and the Earth smile most propitiously on the work, and render it subservient to the best interests of the human race." His prayer was answered.

QUESTIONS TO CONSIDER

1 Explain Bernstein's conclusion that the Erie Canal "would lead to an historic explosion of commerce, ideas, and technological change." Why was it important for "this skinny ditch in upstate New York" to establish a link from the eastern seaboard to the lands west of the Appalachian Mountains? Why was there a chance that without the Erie Canal the United States might have lost its western frontier to France or Canada?

2 Who was De Witt Clinton? Why was Clinton's support of the Erie Canal crucial to its success?

3 Describe the technological innovations that the men who built the Erie Canal developed to remove trees and stumps. Where and how did the engineers who constructed the Erie Canal discover a local waterproof limestone to seal crevices between stones, locks, and culverts?

4 Imagine that you are one of the thousands of workers engaged in the arduous task of building the Erie Canal. Describe the working conditions, the backbreaking job of digging and removing tons of dirt, and the risks from the clouds of mosquitoes that plague your progress.

5 Describe the Erie Canal's impact on domestic transportation costs and trade with Europe. How did it affect the economy of New York?

6 Contrast the financing of George Washington's Patowmack Canal Company with the funding of the Erie Canal. Evaluate the success of the Erie Canal based on its record of meeting construction deadlines and cost estimates. Why does the author believe that a canal built by free labor had a greater potential for success than one constructed by slave labor?

20 Camelot on the Merrimack

STEPHEN YAFA

During the Jacksonian era, a group of Massachusetts businessmen formed the Boston Associates, an organization of financiers who built a model mill town in Massachusetts called Lowell. The story of Lowell—America's first planned industrial community—tells us a great deal about the dreams and realities of a nation already undergoing considerable industrial and urban growth. Stephen Yafa relates that story with a vivid pen—the landscaped town on the banks of the Concord and Merrimack Rivers that commanded worldwide attention, the healthy farm girls who worked its looms. In 1833, President Andrew Jackson and Vice President Martin Van Buren visited Lowell and watched transfixed as 2,500 mill girls, clad in blue sashes and white dresses, with parasols above their heads, marched by two abreast. "Very pretty women, by the Eternal!" exclaimed the president. Although they loathed Jackson, the members of the Boston Associates were pleased with his observation, for they were proud of their working girls—the showpieces of what they believed was the model of enlightened industrial management.

To their delight, Lowell became a famous international attraction. English visitors were especially impressed, because female workers in England's coal mines toiled in incredible misery: naked, covered with filth, they had to pull carts of coal on their hands and knees through dark, narrow tunnels. By contrast, as one historian has said, Lowell seemed a "female paradise." Equally impressive was the remarkable productivity of Lowell's "power-driven machinery." Before long, Lowell became (in historian Linda Evans's words) "the heart of the American textile industry and of the industrial revolution itself."

Lowell's relatively well-disciplined and well-treated work force seemed to demonstrate that industrial capitalism need not be exploitive. Even so, the Lowell system was paternalistic and strict. Sensitive to criticism that it was immoral for women to work, the mill bosses maintained close supervision over their female operatives, imposing curfews and compulsory church attendance. Nevertheless, the mill girls, as they were called, were transformed by their work experience. As historian Linda Evans says, "Most of these workers saw their mill work as a way to reestablish their value to the family," because they were no longer a burden to their parents (indeed, they could send money home now) and because they could save for their own dowries. "Soon," writes Evans, "it was hard to separate their sense of duty from their sense of independence." They felt a group solidarity, too, and in their boarding houses created "a working-class female culture." They also became aware of themselves as a working class with special problems, for they were powerless and had few options. They could not find other jobs, as could their male counterparts, could not become sailors or dockhands or work on construction gangs. For most of the women, mill work was their only option.

Yafa contends that it was a dismal option at best. In a brilliant tour de force, he tells the story of the mill girls and their lordly employers through the perceptive eyes of thirteen-year-old Lucy Larcom. For her and the other young girls, the long and tedious hours they spent tending to obstreperous machines robbed them of their childhood. And the mills they toiled in were grim-looking places. As Yafa says, "Nothing but the absence of bars on windows distinguished these cotton factories from prisons." The façade of Lowell that impressed President Jackson belied the inner reality of the "shining City of

Spindles." The title of this selection is ironic, for Lowell was no fairy tale Camelot—no "pristine embodiment of American enterprise in all its utopian glory." For the girls, life in Lowell's factories was unmitigated drudgery. And Francis Cabot Lowell, the visionary founder of the New England textile industry, was not an enlightened capitalist, but an "unapologetic thief." This is a sobering story, and the sad heroines are the young women of Lowell who had no political leverage with which to better their conditions.

As others have said, their very powerlessness led to the eventual demise of the paternalistic factory system. As more and more textile firms moved to Lowell and other towns, the pressure of competition led to overproduction, to the same cycles of boom and bust that plagued the entire national economy. Thanks to overproduction, many mills fell into decline; wages dropped, and working conditions deteriorated. In a display of solidarity, the mill girls organized a union and went on strikes to protest wage cuts and rising rents. In 1844, organized as the Lowell Female Labor Reform Association, they campaigned for a ten-hour workday and even took their grievances to the state legislature. The union failed, and the textile bosses eventually replaced most of their once-prized mill girls with another labor force—desperate immigrants, most from Ireland, who worked for lower wages and were far less demanding. By 1860, Lowell had become another grim and crowded mill town, another "squalid slum." As you ponder Lowell's story, consider what it suggests about the nature of American industrialization and about the special problems of women and labor in an industrializing society. Do you agree with Yafa that what happened in Lowell reveals some harsh truths about the incompatibility of democratic ideals and the profit motive?

GLOSSARY

APPLETON, NATHAN A Lowell family friend and a member of Boston's gentry elite, Appleton was a shrewd businessman and one of the principal investors in New England's first textile mills.

BOSTON ASSOCIATES Founders of the Lowell mill town, they built a textile empire that eventually comprised eight major firms, twenty mills, and more than six thousand employees.

BROWN LUNG DISEASE (BYSSINOSIS) This is a life-threatening illness that narrows a person's airways. Brown lung disease develops when workers inhale unprocessed cotton, flax, or hemp particles. Yafa writes: "Doctors frequently saw female workers vomiting up little balls of cotton."

DICKENS, CHARLES The reform-minded English novelist who authored *Oliver Twist,* Dickens was impressed with Lowell and the elevated status of the mill girls who worked there. Dickens informed his British readers that American textile mills had much better working conditions than their counterparts in Great Britain.

EMERSON, RALPH WALDO A native of Concord, Massachusetts, Emerson was a respected philosophical writer and lecturer who advocated the use of inner resources and self-reliance as the path to spiritual freedom. Emerson was one of the many eminent figures who visited Lowell and spoke to the mill girls.

JACKSON, PATRICK TRACY Lowell's brother-in-law, Jackson was the plant manager of the textile factory in Waltham, just outside of Boston, Massachusetts. Jackson would later build another mill along the Merrimack River where there was a better source of waterpower. He named the new and improved textile factory after Lowell.

LOWELL, FRANCIS CABOT After visiting English textile mills, Lowell formed the Boston Associates and pioneered a unique factory for the production of cotton goods at Waltham, Massachusetts. After his death, the Boston Associates established another mill village on the Merrimack River and named it Lowell. Yafa refers to Lowell's copying of English textile machinery as an early example of industrial espionage.

LOWELL OFFERING A monthly magazine edited and published by the Lowell mill girls, it impressed many noted writers with the quality of its contributions.

VERTICAL INTEGRATION   This meant controlling a product from the development of its raw materials through its sale as a finished commodity. The Lowell textile mills successfully practiced this management philosophy, thus increasing its profits and its dominance of the domestic market for cotton goods.

WATT, JAMES   In 1765, Watt invented the steam engine. By 1790, his technology was applied to driving textile machinery which, until then, depended on waterpower.

WHITNEY, ELI   In 1793, Whitney invented a device that removed seeds from raw cotton. This engine or "gin"

dramatically reduced the labor cost of producing southern cotton for the British and New England textile mills. Later on, Whitney helped pioneer the use of interchangeable parts, a concept that spurred the growth of manufacturing in his native New England.

WHITTIER, JOHN GREENLEAF   A popular New England poet, Whittier advocated women's rights and the abolition of slavery in America.

No person can be employed by the Company whose known habits are or shall be dissolute, indolent, dishonest, or intemperate, or who habitually absent themselves from public worship or violate the Sabbath. . . .

—POSTED MERRIMACK MANUFACTURING COMPANY REGULATION

Lucy Larcom did not need a watch to tell the time of day. From the age of eleven, she was awakened Monday through Saturday before sunrise by the loud, insistent pealing of the Lowell factory bell, giving young women and girls in the company boardinghouse just enough time to wash, dress, and walk a short distance over the canal footbridges, through a large gate, and into the mill yard. Another bell signaled the start of their workday at 5 a.m. Once inside the long, narrow five-story redbrick factories that rose up all around them, they set about their tasks.

Men began to blow forced air into the five-hundred-pound bales of raw cotton in the adjacent picking house to decompress and disentangle their fibers. In the mill's first-floor carding room workers using fine-toothed automated combs and rollers converted sheets of loose, raw cotton fiber into slivers, long fat tubes of cleaned parallel strands. Upstairs, as loud

machinery cranked into operation, Lucy and her coworkers in the spinning and weaving rooms, almost all women, filled the machines with raw material, mended broken threads, and tended to the hundreds of minute toilsome details of textile production. Below, the sun rose over the Merrimack River. It hardly mattered; they would not be allowed outside long enough to enjoy the day.

From five until seven in the morning, six days a week, these mill hands worked without food. A bell clanged at seven o'clock to announce a half-hour breakfast recess, another bell ended it, two more bells signaled the beginning and end of a half-hour lunch break at noon, and at the end of a fourteen-hour day, all but eighty or so minutes of it spent at work, a bell at seven in the evening sent them back to their boardinghouses for dinner. Afterward, if not too fatigued, they might attend a meeting of their Improvement Circles to hone educational and social skills, or they might read and gossip in the front parlor. Some went off in small groups to hear visiting speakers like eminent philosopher and writer Ralph Waldo Emerson at Lowell Hall. House-mothers enforced bedtime curfews. Contact with men was

---

"Camelot on the Merrimack," from *Big Cotton* by Stephen H. Yafa, copyright © 2005 by Stephen Yafa. Used by permission of Viking Penguin, a division of Penguin Group (USA) Inc.

carefully monitored. Church attendance on the Sunday Sabbath was mandatory.

In the opinion of some workers, like Lucy Larcom, what you made of your time at Lowell depended on what you intended to make of the rest of your life. Mill work tested patience; it demanded vigilance; it rewarded tenacity. Early-nineteenth-century Americans held firmly to a conviction that those virtues brought you closer to God. But for some young women fresh off the farms of northern New England, most between the ages of sixteen and twenty-one, nothing but the absence of bars on windows distinguished these cotton factories from prisons. "I am going home where I shall not be obliged to rise so early in the morning, nor be dragged about by the factory bell, nor confined in the noisy room from morning till night. I shall not stay here. . . . Up before day, at the clang of a bell . . . at work in obedience to that ding-dong of a bell—just as though we were so many living machines," one mill girl complained. She wasn't alone.

Three decades after [Eli] Whitney's invention, industrialization arrived in New England with the force of a sudden, turbulent storm. Winds of change blew through the multiplying cotton fields of the South, swept up mountains of lint, and deposited them into the newly minted textile factories of the North. This was all to the good—a new nation united by one cash crop grown and manufactured within its borders—but how to hire, train, organize, and regulate a large-scale industrial workforce where none yet existed in rural Massachusetts? The North improvised. Factory bells replaced cow bells: they soon sectioned off and parceled out time and labor like generals regimenting troops for combat.

For the first time in the short history of America, the mills at Lowell provided unmarried women with an opportunity to earn their own income away from home. Cotton was the catalyst. At Lowell, twenty-eight miles north of Boston, cotton created two cities—one real, the other a highly idealized fantasy bolstered by glowing accounts in the newspapers and magazines of that era. The first existed within the high thick walls of the daunting factory buildings that had rimmed the Merrimack since their construction started in the early 1820s, powered by water below and by human sweat above; the other Lowell, assembled from those same structures, took on a life of its own as the pristine embodiment of American enterprise in all its utopian glory. Three United States presidents and a host of foreign dignitaries visited, toured, and came away burbling with enthusiasm for this dynamic proof that enlightened capitalism worked. They looked on from a polite distance and saw what they wanted to, a shining City of Spindles. If they had chosen to probe further they would have discovered that inside the mills young female workers fought to maintain their mental and physical health for the better part of fourteen hours a day.

Raised on farms, Lowell's mill girls were used to hard work from a young age. They fed livestock, hoed, shoveled, raked, planted seed, swept, mended clothes, and stacked firewood, going about these and other chores at their own pace, often out of doors with rest breaks as needed. None of that applied to factory labor, they sadly discovered. Within the long, narrow brick buildings, the grinding, bone-aching tedium of mechanized production controlled their actions from dawn to dusk. Their workplace was an overheated, poorly ventilated room that filled an entire floor; it held as many as 200 machines. Screeching, clanking pulleys and levers and wheels roared with a deafening clatter; vibrations from the top-floor looms shook walls, ceilings, and floors as thousands of spring-loaded wood shuttles slammed against the side frames of looms, then back across at lightning speeds; they rattled and hammered without pause. Even at a distance, several floors below in the spinning and carding rooms, the mill girls lived with the explosive repetitive slap of those shuttles and the wheeze of whirring, straining metal wheels close by.

Only the most resourceful workers found escape. "In the sweet June weather," Lucy Larcom recalled, "I would lean out the window, and try not to hear the unceasing clash of sound inside. . . . I discovered, too, that I could so accustom myself to the noise that it became like silence to me. And I defied the machinery to make me its slave. Its incessant discords could not drown out the music of my thoughts if I would let them fly high enough."

Like Lucy, other factory women surrendered their personal freedom for the lure of independent income. In the words of one mill girl:

> Despite the toil we all agree,
> Out of the mill or in,
> Dependent on others we ne'er will be
> As long as we're able to spin.

That trade-off would motivate industrial American female labor in the decades to come. Also, until Lowell's mills opened, unmarried daughters had no way to contribute any significant earnings to their families. These new mills provided both opportunities. They offered the highest wages for working women in America, between $2 and $5 a week after deducting $1.25 for room and board, and they required few skills. Larcom was the daughter of a whaler who died young and left Lucy's mother to raise her eight children with no help. Out of necessity, Larcom and her older sister went into the cotton factories at a young age—Lucy, barely schooled at eleven, was about five years younger than almost anyone else. Mill work provided her with cash to send home and the license to dream; with scrupulous saving, she and her fellow workers had the funds for a new dress and jewelry to be seen in as they strolled up and down Lowell's shopping streets and through its groomed parks on a fine spring Sunday. More important to Lucy, a nascent writer, books from the Lowell circulating library were readily available, and she could join a group of coworkers after hours to read her latest poem, story, or essay aloud to an eager audience of boardinghouse mates.

Within the mills themselves, however, time slowed to a deadening crawl; fine hairs of cotton lint circulated through the hot air and mingled with particles of machine oil that gave off an acrid, burnt scent and seemed to coat walls, posts, and beams on every floor with a thin sheen. To maintain a high level of humidity to reduce thread breakage, managers often nailed windows closed. During summer months, temperatures soared. In balance, cotton's welfare mattered more than the workers'. Airborne lint hairs, one mill girl noted, fell as thickly "as snow falls in winter." They sometimes piled up on workers' clothing and hair; inhaled for more than twelve hours a day in the absence of fresh air, the lint caused frequent lung diseases that were difficult to diagnose and impossible to treat effectively.

One textile historian, William Moran, reports that women used nonsmoking tobacco, or snuff, as a defense against the lint they inhaled when sucking threads through the narrow endpassages of loom shuttles. They called their lip motion "the kiss of death." Doctors frequently saw female workers vomiting up little balls of cotton. Later, textile workers would be among the first diagnosed with brown lung disease, or byssinosis. Moran also notes that 70 percent of the early textile workers died of respiratory illnesses, as opposed to 4 percent of farmers in Massachusetts. Sick days meant lost wages: workers received no pay if they did not show up. Since the cost of using the factory's infirmary was deducted from your salary, many employees chose instead to work when ill, infecting others.

Then there was the work itself—sufficiently tedious to numb the mind, rarely challenging enough to stimulate it. In these mills, all of the brains were built into the machines, more technically advanced than in any other industry in America. No matter how bright you were, you were paid to tend the machines like the nannies of idiot savants who lacked all personal skills. When threads broke, as they did constantly, the machine stopped itself, but it could not repair its own severed strands. You tied a quick agile knot between loose ends as if lacing its shoe before restarting the gears in motion. . . .

. . . That was your lot in life. Eyeholes. Threads. Hosing down a pig trough took more skill. It also offered more diversion. And there were no supervisory positions for women anywhere in these mills.

For two or three years, the length of most of the mill girls' stay at Lowell, maintaining a healthy outlook became a second occupation. Friends helped.

Lucy and her close companion Harriet Hanson Robinson sometimes paused as time permitted to watch the new recruits arrive from isolated rural communities. They were "dressed in such an old-fashioned style that each young girl looked as if she had borrowed her grandmother's gown," Robinson later recalled. They clutched bandboxes that held all their worldly possessions, including love letters. "Years after, this scene dwelt in my memory, and wherever anyone said anything about being home-sick, there rose before me the picture of a young girl with a sorrowful face and a big tear in each eye, clambering down the steps at the rear of the great covered wagon, holding fast to a cloth-covered bandbox." Some wept openly. The sheer size of these massive factories stretching half a mile or more down river inspired an equal measure of terror and reverence at first sight, especially when the largest structure most of them had ever seen was a hay barn.

Surrounded by soaring walls of brick, they stared up with awe at the central belfry tower that rose high into the sky like a church spire. They'd soon learn, as Larcom and Robinson had, that the bell in that tower controlled the movements of their wak-ing hours as rigidly as phases of the moon controlled the tides. Some would make the best of a stultifying work regimen by exploring small ways to satisfy per-sonal needs. Although all books were banned in the mills, bibles included, Lucy had managed to paste re-cent newspaper clippings on the bright panes near her work space—her "window gems," as she called them—and she looked up from her spindles from time to time throughout the day to stay informed about the world beyond those walls. Others escaped into their imaginations, since conversations were dif-ficult to sustain over the thunderous racket of ma-chinery. These tactics worked intermittently at best. After two or so years in the mills, noticeable fatigue and poor health overtook many of these workers. There was a high turnover. "The daughter leaves the farm . . . a plump, rosey-cheeked, strong and laugh-ing girl . . . ," one female reformer wrote, "but alas, how changed!" after being tucked away inside these mills three hundred days a year. "This is a dark picture, but there are even darker realities, and these in no inconsiderable numbers."

Reformers seized on the oppressive working con-ditions to press their case for shorter hours and related improvements. In time these grievances combined with a depressed economy to create an irreparable rift between management and the first generation of New England's rural female employees, who were, all things considered, vastly better off than their bru-tally treated counterparts in Manchester, England. As one of that wave, Larcom initially spoke for many: "Certainly we mill girls did not regard our lot as an easy one, but we accepted its fatigues and discomforts as unavoidable, and could forgive them in struggling forward to what was before us." That tolerance would not last much past the first two decades. When it collapsed, Lowell's workforce swiftly and perma-nently changed character. By then, though, the am-bition, literary output, and jaunty public demeanor of these New England–born mill girls had already cast them as stars of an idyllic fairy tale set in the magical City of Spindles.

Celebrities, politicians, and foreign princes came to survey this Camelot for themselves. Citizens at all levels were emotionally invested in the dream of an American Industrial Revolution with Lowell as its spiritual and geographic center. Lowell had to be everything that Manchester, England, that septic tank of child enslavement, was not. One visitor, Captain Basil Hall, summed up the prevailing mood in his journal: ". . . [T]he village speckled over with girls, nicely dressed and glittering with bright shawls and gay bonnets, all streaming along . . . with an air of lightness, and an elasticity of step, implying an ob-vious desire to get to their work."

Hard evidence might dispute that point of view, but it hardly mattered: the creative capitalists who transformed these four square miles of rock-strewn farmland into an international symbol of American manufacturing power had accomplished their goal with brilliant audacity and in the process launched the nation's Industrial Revolution. They'd built the first fiber-to-fabric textile factories, an end-to-end system that converted raw cotton to finished goods.

They were feeding an inexhaustible market for cheap, lightweight, colorful cloth. More impressive still, they had done so with exceptional foresight. This group of men, called the Boston Associates, knew as much about human engineering as they did about rollers and heddles. Early on, before the first brick was mortared into place along the Merrimack River in 1821, they'd figured out how to repackage the drudgery of factory labor as the chance of a lifetime for self-improvement; they knew who to pitch and how to pitch. They knew, too, that if they succeeded they would be able to put together a diligent, dedicated workforce and gain the world's admiration for their efforts.

Francis Cabot Lowell, the man primarily responsible for realizing that vision, was to American cotton as Henry Ford would later be to automobiles. Although he died in 1817, a few years before the founding of the city that honored his name, Lowell had already fashioned both the machinery to produce finished cloth and the strategies that attracted an eager labor force to his factories. Shrewd and persuasive, he surrounded himself with capable industrialists and savvy financiers, and drew on family and social connections to raise capital. Lowell had something else going for him as well: he was an unapologetic thief. . . . Without bold acts of industrial espionage, cotton might never have progressed in the Western world beyond primitive spinning wheels and hand looms, but then again, capitalism's darlings have often been a rogue's gallery of impudent crooks.

Lowell arrived in Manchester, England, in 1810 on a prolonged tour of Europe intended to improve his poor health. Born to a prominent Boston mercantile family, he had gained respect as a successful businessman with interests in shipping, banking, foreign exchange, and real estate since graduating from Harvard the same year [1793] that Whitney invented the gin. Through family contacts he befriended English textile industrialists and gained access to their cotton mills after meeting up with a fellow Bostonian and family friend, Nathan Appleton. As a business courtesy, the British owners instructed their managers to provide details of their operations to the visiting Americans. Together, Appleton and Lowell spent days watching the elaborate spinning frames and automated looms of Lancashire convert loose shreds of fiber into substantial sheets of cloth. Driven by belts powered by steam engines that had by then replaced waterwheels, the frames and looms operated as many as twenty-three hours a day from Birmingham to Leeds. Lowell, a man with an advanced mechanical aptitude, learned everything he could about the design specifications of these miraculous machines—the power looms in particular.

. . . [H]e committed their functional operations to memory. That may not have been his first choice, but Lowell now knew he wanted to dedicate himself to automating cotton production in America. To do so he needed to license Manchester's machinery, raise capital, and build his own empire. Yet he found himself dealing with the same feisty British textile industrialists who had squelched all previous attempts to export their technology to potential competitors. Lowell's elevated social station mattered not a whit. He was still a Yankee, and America was still an impertinent renegade nation, so ill mannered it refused to bow down to Her Majesty. This made for sticky wickets all around. For Lowell, that might have ended the quest, but hasn't forbidden fruit always been the tastiest? Rather than retreat empty-handed, he decided to memorize as many of the working parts of the Manchester power loom as possible.

Enthralled by the dance of automated harnesses, sheds, reeds, heddles, and shuttles that moved simultaneously and efficiently in contrary directions, he committed himself to a massive feat of mental gymnastics. These components were choreographed through trial and error to synchronize precisely; any fluctuations or malfunctions in their split-second timing immobilized the entire machine. But a photographic memory, Lowell soon discovered, is an industrial spy's greatest ally. So, too, are secret compartments in steamer trunks where the spy might wedge a sketch or two. Although Lowell left no record of his trip to England, the consensus is that he smuggled back notes to aid his recollections; if so, they escaped the British customs officials who doggedly searched his belongings.

Equally important, during his prolonged stay in Manchester, Lowell experienced living conditions in one of the foulest cities on earth. Black day and night with overhanging clouds of choking, eye-watering smoke from coal used to fuel steam engines, Manchester epitomized the worst excesses of unregulated free enterprise. "Everywhere heaps of debris, refuse and offal; standing pools and gutters and a stench which alone would make it impossible for a human being in any degree civilized to live in such a district," wrote another visiting foreigner. . . . Manchester's cluttered, cramped, cold, and damp labor housing lacked sanitation or ventilation; its rivers ran brown with raw sewerage. Thousands of malnourished and filthy orphaned children, England's "parish wards," slept six or eight to a room and worked in these cotton mills for interminable hours under overseers who often beat and chained them.

A coal historian, Barbara Freese, pointed out that inventor James Watt believed "Nature can be conquered if we can but find her weak side." Manchester, she said, proved that in "looking for nature's weak side, we found our own." A brilliant observation at the very least. At one Parliamentary hearing, a deformed woman testified that she was strapped severely from the age of six. "You are considerably deformed in a consequence of this labor?" she was asked. "Yes, I am." "You were perfectly straight and healthy before you were in a mill?" "Yes, I was as straight a little girl as ever went up and down town." "Where are you now?" "In the poorhouse."

The average life expectancy among the poor in Manchester was seventeen years. More than 57 percent of newborns were dead by the age of five. Yet despite the unimaginable misery and squalor, the city itself gained stature for its manufacturing prowess.

French writer Alexis de Tocqueville best captured Manchester's paradoxical nature: "From this foul drain the greatest stream of human industry flows out to fertilize the whole world . . . here civilization works its miracles, and civilized man is turned back almost to a savage."

Francis Cabot Lowell knew he stood little chance of transplanting Manchester's mechanized industry to the United States unless he saved the broth and discarded the scum. Devout New England's farming families would never send their offspring to live and work in such a sordid environment. That meant clean living quarters for employees, excellent sanitation, no involuntary child labor, and fair wages. Sons were simply not expendable on family farms under any circumstances; Lowell's workers in the main would have to be single daughters. Coming from a similarly strict religious upbringing, he understood the concerns of those Puritan parents he would need to convince, and he shaped his pitch to address their anxieties. They would refuse to release their daughters to sample the lustful temptations of a large city without assurances that they would not stray. On the farm, strenuous physical labor was thought to exhaust a young woman's dangerously libidinous drives. In the factories, exhausting hours of day labor would have to be marketed to doubtful mothers and fathers as an equivalent preventative. Lowell would strive for an average age of twenty-one but would accept a few younger employees under special circumstances. And no one, male or female, would be beaten or otherwise brutalized in his mills. By taking these steps, Lowell introduced the corporate paternalism that would become the signature of his textile empire; it sat comfortably with his own humanistic beliefs.

As that workforce strategy gained focus, Lowell returned home to Massachusetts from England in 1812. He embarked at once on his plan to re-create a fully functional Manchester textile factory. . . .

With the help of merchant friends, Lowell obtained a charter to build his first cotton factory at Waltham, about ten miles up the Charles River from Boston. Its working power loom enabled the mill to integrate all of the cotton manufacturing processes under one roof to turn out cheap, coarse cloth. The $400,000 he'd raised was ten times as much as the money behind a typical Rhode Island mill. Lowell

Lowell, Massachusetts, was a model mill town located on the banks of the Concord and Merrimack Rivers. The community attracted worldwide attention because it presented a sharp contrast to the squalor of manufacturing centers in England and Europe. The *buildings stood in groups separated by trees, shrubs, and strips of lawn that were attractively landscaped and reminiscent of a college campus. (Corbis-Bettmann)*

built boardinghouses for the single women employees who came off the farms. To assuage their parents, he'd had them designed to closely resemble seminary dormitories; they were supervised by older housemothers who functioned as a kind of live-in morality police force. Churches went up nearby. God was everywhere, from loom to room. Knowing the power of money as well as probity to persuade, he also paid these women a higher salary than they could earn elsewhere for their fourteen-hour workdays. . . .

The mill soon began to make money, and by 1823 assets would grow from $39,000 to $771,000, a staggering increase. Lowell considered the initial boom in sales "too favorable to be credible." By 1815, more than 27 million pounds of raw cotton was being shipped from Southern plantations north for manufacture. But the calculating genius in all this was Lowell himself. Wrapping an American flag tightly around his business interests, he declaimed

before Congress in Washington, D.C., against the hated British. Lowell petitioned Congress to institute protectionist tariffs against English imports—"articles," he said, "that are made from very inferior materials and are manufactured in a manner calculated to deceive rather than serve the consumer." In the end he won an extraordinary victory: India cotton, manufactured in Britain and Waltham's only real competition, was taxed at 83.5 percent. . . .

A short time later, at the moment Lowell was on the brink of expanding his mill into a textile dynasty, his fragile health again failed. When he died young in 1817, at forty-two, he had in a few short years established the textile industry in America. Long before "vertical integration" became an MBA buzzword, Lowell practiced it by controlling cotton from raw material through the sale of finished goods; Lowell also efficiently managed the whole process with sufficient capital to carry it from concept to successful execution. Remarkably, he even found a way to bring his brother-in-law into the business without capsizing it in the process. It was that man, Patrick Tracy Jackson, in fact, who not only carried on as the head of the Waltham plant but vastly increased the family fortune by moving the mill in 1821 to a more suitable Massachusetts location about thirty miles north of Boston, where the Merrimack River fell thirty-two feet in elevation within one mile before converging with the Concord.

At that site, where the Pawtucket Falls and much swifter currents provided a far superior waterpower source, Jackson established the city named for his deceased brother-in-law. He and his Boston Associates wisely purchased a majority of shares in the adjacent Pawtucket Canal that skirted the falls, and secured surrounding farmlands and waterpower rights. Like Lowell, they envisioned an empire, not a solitary mill—as many as twenty thousand inhabitants at this location in the future, one of them speculated. . . .

. . . Lowell was a company town as much as any West Virginia mining community. Workers lived in company houses, spent their money in company stores, and prayed in company churches. For New England, Lowell represented corporate paternalism's finest hour. It had also become the nation's principal textile center and a source of vast wealth for its investors, now dubbed Lords of the Loom. The young country's insatiable demand for cotton translated to profits that averaged 24 percent annually for twenty consecutive years, until 1845. Close to 70 percent of the mill hands were single women. In the city's first two decades, its workers descended from the same Yankee blue-blood ancestors as the owners, with one significant difference: they were poor. "There was nothing peculiar about the Lowell mill girls," said Larcom, "except that they were New England girls of the older, hardier stock."

That contrast with the lowly mill girls in Europe, scorned by society as prostitutes, contributed to Lowell's reputation as a brand new chapter in the glorious chronicle of emerging America. The Lords of the Loom had produced and directed the country's first major industrial hit, a box office sensation and a patriotic triumph. That was the Lowell that

visitors from President Andrew Jackson to Davy Crockett read and heard about and traveled thousands of miles to view firsthand.

When Michel Chevalier, a French government official, visited Lowell, Massachusetts, and the surrounding Merrimack Valley in 1834, he portrayed a fresh, gleaming, bustling utopian town where apple orchards bloomed near steam locomotives and the buzzing of honeybees found their mechanical counterpart in the hum of spindles. Lilting bells called workers into the mills; young women on the streets were well-dressed. Chevalier commented on their comeliness—and their independence. To Chevalier, the abominable filth and stench of European factory cities made these clean and sunny sidewalks seem all the more like rainbows arched across the heavenly sky of a fabulous diorama: "A pile of huge factories, each five, six, or seven stories high and capped with a little white belfry, which strongly contrasts with the red masonry of the building. . . . By the side of these larger structures rise numerous little wooden houses, painted white, with green blinds, very neat, very snug, very nicely carpeted, with a few small trees around them, or brick houses in the English style; that is to say, simple, but tasteful without and comfortable within. . . ."

Lowell, he concluded, was "neat, orderly, quiet and prudent." During the previous decade schools and churches went up. Watchmakers and booksellers and other merchants opened shops, "every one of them as fresh and new as if the bricks had been in the mold but yesterday," Captain Basil Hall reported.

"Who shall sneer at your calling? Who shall count your vocation otherwise than noble and ennobling?" asked poet John Greenleaf Whittier rhetorically and rhapsodically about the mill hands. Lowell's "acres of girlhood," he burbled, were "the flowers gathered from a thousand hillsides and green valleys of New England. . . . Nuns of Industry, Sisters of Thrift, . . . dispensing comfort and hope and happiness around many a hearthstone. . . ."

Reading the published accounts of Whittier, Chevalier, and others, governments in Europe looked to Lowell as proof that industrial enterprise could prosper without grim enslavement and human suffering. Worker reform movements in Europe gained momentum. This tree-lined community became their darling: charming, productive, dignified, and above all, whistling while she worked.

By the time Chevalier arrived in 1834, there were nineteen five-story mills in operation containing 84,000 spindles and 3,000 looms. Workers now turned out an astonishing quantity of cheap cotton cloth—27,000,000 yards, or 15,698 miles, of it annually. Boat travel proved impractical at that volume; Patrick Jackson was busy laying track for a steam locomotive railroad line—one of the nation's first—to transport the finished cotton cloth to Boston and to carry raw cotton upriver from its docks. Domestic markets absorbed as much calico as they could produce. In addition, these mills were turning out considerable amounts of "Negro cloth"—coarse fabric purchased by Southern planters to clothe their slaves, who knew it as Lowell cloth.

Fearing they had sacrificed too much power to Northern industrialists, Southerners sought to build regional cotton mills for their own crops close to the fields: a sensible idea whose time would come, but not for another forty years. A few small cotton factories in South Carolina and elsewhere struggled to find a labor source; whites, no matter how poor, would not work side by side with slaves, and slaves were not trained for factory work. Planters considered it an inefficient use of resources. Competitive efforts failed. As hundreds of new plants opened in the North, producing everything from pig iron to shoe soles, the North's manufacturing clout now extended to a wide variety of finished goods and materials; it was going through one of the most prodigious industrial growth spurts in history, while the South depended ever more on its cotton, tobacco, rice, and sugar crops.

Within a decade of Lowell's founding, New England's textile aristocracy had gained so much wealth and political power that they had become uncrowned royalty. Their money built schools, hospitals, museums, churches, and parks in and around Boston,

a city they intended to glorify for posterity. Their success also encouraged other investment groups to open textile mills in New Hampshire, Massachusetts, and Maine.

These Lords of the Loom lived with their clans in an exclusive Boston enclave. When Appleton and Francis Cabot Lowell's son and relatives traveled to Lowell, which they frequently did during its early years, they soon departed. They were not about to make this mill community their home; while it served its purpose as their industrial showplace and cash cow, they considered it no place to socialize or to set down roots. You did not live downstairs with the help. . . .

The loom lords might be admired but they were not necessarily idolized by the general public. Too much wealth and power had accumulated to a chosen few. The masses identified more readily with young women who worked an average of seventy-three hours a week in these cotton factories yet eagerly absorbed culture by attending lectures and frequenting library reading rooms, still finding time to put out a magazine of their own. Their homespun magazine, *The Lowell Offering,* began life in 1840, and a year later it became a thirty-page monthly published by a young enthusiast, the Unitarian Reverend Abel C. Thomas. Readers could subscribe for six-and-a-quarter cents an issue: "A Repository of Original Articles, Written Exclusively by Females Employed in the Mills," read the banner line on every issue."

Quite quickly, *The Offering* became an international sensation, a symbol of brave new gender equality and an ode to self-improvement. All of the contents—stories, essays, verse, journal entries—were written by the mill hands and published without heavy editing. On his travels through America Charles Dickens visited Lowell and reported to his English audience, "I am now going to state three facts which will startle a large class of readers on this side of the Atlantic very much: First there is a joint-stock piano in a great many of the boardinghouses. Secondly, nearly all of these young women subscribe

Women factory workers at the Lowell mills were avid readers. They also formed self-improvement clubs and published their own monthly magazine, the Lowell Offering. *Yafa describes the magazine as "an international sensation, a symbol of brave new gender equality and an ode to self-improvement." (Lowell Historical Society)*

to circulating libraries. Thirdly, they have gotten up among themselves a periodical called *The Lowell Offering,* . . . written exclusively by females actively employed in the mills. . . ."

Dickens thought the contents of the magazine "compared advantageously with a great many English annuals." But what astonished him most was that many of its contributors were articulate women who wrote "after arduous labors of the day" about mill life. As the reform-minded author of *Oliver Twist* and essays that exposed Britain's despicable labor conditions, he was used to looking into workers' lives through a partially opened window—or grate— and supplying them with his own imagined speech, thought, and action. Not necessary here, he noted: "It is a pleasure to find that many of [*The Offering's*] tales are of the mills, and of those who work in them." One *Offering* contributor gave Dickens and others the lowdown on her boardinghouse mates:

One who sits on my right hand at table is in the factory because she hates her mother-in-law. . . . The next one has a wealthy father but like many of our country farmers, he is very penurious . . . the next is here because her parents are wicked infidels . . . the next is here because she has been ill-treated in so many families she has a horror of domestic service . . . the next has left a good home because her lover, who has gone on a whaling voyage, wishes to be married when he returns, and she would like more money than her father will give her. . . .

Each issue of *The Offering* combined informal, personal glimpses of factory life with literary efforts; among the most successful were the verses and essays of Lucy Larcom, who would go on to write eight books after leaving the mills and gain national prominence as an author.

A professor at the Collège de France in Paris devoted class lectures to the Lowell mill girls' magazine; a French politician brought a bound volume of *The Offering* to show the national Chamber of Deputies. Here were working women, expressing themselves with passion and clarity: there was no precedent for that, and there was much to learn in these pages about evolutionary social progress. The leaders and scholars of Europe and America looked on with an equal measure of bafflement and respect.

But if *The Lowell Offering* began as the inspirational voice of a new female labor class, it became a flash point for escalating unrest. Its well-meaning editors—two women, after the first few issues—did not foresee that within a few years worker loyalty to mill owners would be compromised by growing distrust. Workers were being pressured to accept lowered wages and ignored in their call for a shorter work day. That effort soon became known as the Ten Hour Movement. Activist mill hands wanted to use *The Offering* as their vehicle of protest. The female editors—older, more conservative—refused to criticize current conditions. . . .

Two decades after its founding, Camelot on the Merrimack was crumbling at its foundations. The rare sense of genuine camaraderie between owner and worker no longer seemed like paternalism so much as exploitation. When Ralph Waldo Emerson said, "The children of New England between 1820 and 1840 were born with knives in their brains," he was talking about these female mill workers, among others. They were too sharp to be easily manipulated. . . .

By then Lowell and the nation were in major transition. Cotton did more than mirror these social and economic convulsions: it motivated them. Locally, some factory women began wondering aloud if they could in good faith continue to earn their livelihood by the product of slavery. Antiabolitionist groups had moved from the fringe of society; they now claimed converts among leading families. Rallies erupted in the streets. Within the mills, worker organizers were threatening to take their reform demands to the state legislature. That didn't sit well with the Boston Associates. Might they not be better off not to rely so heavily on these New England farm girls with their astringent opinions and dangerous ideas? The investors turned their attention to the hordes of starving European peasants arriving daily in New York. Those foreigners desperately needed work; they would not dare to strike for better pay.

By the mid-1840s the Boston Associates had learned the hard way that cotton was above all else an agricultural crop, annually subject to nature's impulsive whims. Less than a decade previously, a Southern crop failure had coincided with a sudden slow-down in demand for raw plantation product by British textile mills, leading in part to the Panic of 1837—a collapse of the nation's credit structure. Its negative economic effects lingered on. That instability only intensified the risks of relying on unpredictable yields of a raw material dependent on weather and soil conditions. Cotton prices fluctuated severely. At the other end of the cycle, belt-tightening among consumers created a soft market for the Associates' finished goods. Feeling pressure from both sides, they welcomed cheaper immigrant factory labor. Although farm girls continued to seek employment in the mills until the mid-1850s, they became a minority in the workforce and learned quickly not to assert themselves. The owners by then were unwilling to tolerate any displays of worker agitation.

These Lords of the Loom were already doing battle with another formidable enemy—their own consciences. Slavery had made them rich. Still, the bible warned that no man had the right to lay claim to another as his property. For as long as possible, New England's textile barons had walked a fine line between religious conviction and business pragmatism. Slavery in existing states was an acceptable institution, they'd decided, but its expansion into new territories they could not abide. Now, with a massive migration west, the whole ugly mess rose up before them with such ferocious intensity that it could no longer be avoided. Whether they preferred to or not, they knew they would soon be forced to choose between principle and profit in the national arena, and between profit and paternalism locally: troublesome choices at every turn.

QUESTIONS TO CONSIDER

1 Imagine that you are one of the thousands of young women who worked in the Lowell textile mills. Describe your typical day, the working conditions in the mills, the boardinghouses, and the way you occupied your limited leisure time. How did the conditions in those sordid mills affect the young girls' health?

2 Why did many rural New Englanders hate the idea of America becoming an industrial nation?

What caused this bitter opposition to industrialization? How did the Lowell textile mills, at least in the early years, escape the evils many believed were inherent in urban industrial life?

3 Given the long hours and horrid working conditions in the textile mills, why did young girls come to the Lowell factory? Describe Lucy Larcom's background and how she reaped some benefits from toiling in the mills.

4 Who was Francis Cabot Lowell? How did he learn about the manufacture of finished cotton goods? Why would the author of this selection describe him as "an unapologetic thief"? What lessons did Lowell learn in Manchester, England, and how did he apply them in attracting a labor force to his textile mills?

5 Explain how the Lowell mills exemplified "one of the most prodigious industrial growth spurts in history." What factors made it impossible for the South to develop an industrial model equal to that of the North?

6 What was the *Lowell Offering* and why did it impress noted authors like Charles Dickens? Why did the mill girls start losing respect for the magazine? To whom did the Boston Associates turn when their female workforce began to view them as exploitative rather than paternalistic?

PART ELEVEN

Beyond the Mississippi

21 The Trail of Tears

DEE BROWN

One of the most unhappy chapters in American history is the way whites treated Indians. American Indian policy, however, must be seen in the context of the entire European conquest of the New World. That conquest began with Columbus, who gave the people the name Indios and kidnapped ten San Salvador Indians, taking them back to Spain to learn the white man's ways. In the ensuing four centuries, as Dee Brown writes in Bury My Heart at Wounded Knee, *"several million Europeans and their descendants undertook to enforce their ways upon the people of the New World," and when these people would not accept European ways, they were fought, enslaved, or exterminated.*

Whites in North America joined the conquest in the colonial period, when they drove most of the eastern tribes into the interior. This pattern of "Indian removal" continued through the eighteenth and nineteenth centuries. When Jefferson came to power, his administration began an official United States policy of Indian removal either by treaty or by outright warfare. During the next three decades, most tribes of the Old Northwest were "removed" in that manner to west of the Mississippi. When a thousand hungry Sac and Fox Indians recrossed the river into Illinois in 1832, militia and federal troops repelled the "invasion" in what became known as the Black Hawk War, in which young Abraham Lincoln commanded a militia company. The Sac and Fox retreated across the Mississippi into Wisconsin, but white soldiers pursued and needlessly slaughtered most of them.

The most forceful champion of removal was Andrew Jackson, whom the Indians called Sharp Knife. In their view, Jackson was an incorrigible Indian hater. In his frontier years he had waged war against the tribes in the South—the Cherokees, Choctaws, Chicasaws, Creeks, and Seminoles, known as the "Five Civilized Tribes," because most had well-developed agricultural societies. These tribes were still clinging to their tribal lands when Jackson took office. At once, he announced that the tribes must be sent away to "an ample district west of the Mississippi," and Congress responded with the Indian Removal Act, which embodied his recommendations. Under Jackson's orders, federal officials set about "negotiating" treaties with the southern tribes, with the implication that military force would be used if they did not consent to expulsion. In a subsequent act, passed in 1830, Congress guaranteed that all of the United States west of the Mississippi "and not within the states of Missouri and Louisiana or the Territory of Arkansas" would constitute "a permanent Indian frontier."

But settlers moved into Indian country before Washington could put the law into effect. So United States policymakers were obliged to shift the "permanent Indian frontier" from the Mississippi to the 95th meridian, again promising that everything west of this imaginary line would belong to the Indians "for as long as trees grow and water flows." In the late 1830s, United States soldiers rounded up the Cherokees in Georgia and herded them west into Indian country in what ranks among the saddest episodes in the sordid story of white-Indian relations in this country. Nor were the Cherokees the only Indians who were expelled. The other "civilized tribes" also suffered on the Trail of Tears to the new Indian Territory. What happened to the Cherokees is the subject of the next selection, written with sensitivity and insight by Dee Brown, a prolific historian of the West and of Native Americans.

By the time of Jackson, as Brown has said elsewhere, the Wampanoag of Massasoit "had vanished, along with the Chesapeakes, the Chicahominys, and the Potomacs of the great Powhatan confederacy. (Only Pocahontas was remembered.) Scattered or reduced to remnants were the Pequots, Montauks, Nanticokes, Madchapungas, Catawbas, Cheraws, Miamis, Hurons, Eries, Mohawks, Senecas, and Mohegans. . . . Their musical names have remained forever fixed on the American land, but their bones are forgotten in a thousand burned villages or lost in forests fast disappearing before the axes of twenty million invaders."

GLOSSARY

BOUDINOT, ELIAS   Coleader of a Cherokee delegation that agreed to resettlement in the West, he had established the Cherokees' first tribal newspaper, the *Cherokee Phoenix*.

CROCKETT, DAVY   Member of Congress from Tennessee who sympathized with the Cherokees' plight and damned the "cruel, unjust" way they were treated.

RIDGE, MAJOR   Coleader of a Cherokee delegation that agreed to resettlement in the West.

ROSS, JOHN   Cherokee leader who tried to save the Cherokee nation in Georgia; he protested to the federal government when the state of Georgia annexed all Cherokee lands within its borders.

SCOTT, WINFIELD   Commander of the army forces that rounded up the Cherokees and herded them to present-day Oklahoma.

TSALI   Aging Smoky Mountain Cherokee who resisted removal by force; Scott had him, his brother, and two of his sons executed by a firing squad.

UTSALA   Chief of the Cherokees who avoided removal by hiding in the Smoky Mountains.

In the spring of 1838, Brigadier General Winfield Scott with a regiment of artillery, a regiment of infantry, and six companies of dragoons marched unopposed into the Cherokee country of northern Georgia. On May 10 at New Echota, the capital of what had been one of the greatest Indian nations in eastern America, Scott issued a proclamation:

The President of the United States sent me with a powerful army to cause you, in obedience to the treaty of 1835, to join that part of your people who are already established in prosperity on the other side of the Mississippi. . . . The emigration must be commenced in haste. . . . The full moon of May is already on the wane, and before another shall have passed away every Cherokee man, woman and child . . . must be in motion to join their brethren in the west. . . . My troops already occupy many positions . . . and thousands and thousands are approaching from every quarter to render resistance and escape alike hopeless. . . . Will you then by resistance compel us to resort to arms? Or will you by flight seek to hide yourselves in mountains and forests and thus oblige us to hunt you down? Remember that in pursuit it may be impossible to avoid conflicts. The blood of the white man or the blood of the red man may be spilt, and if spilt, however accidentally, it may be impossible for the discreet and humane among you, or among us, to prevent a general war and carnage.

For more than a century the Cherokees had been ceding their land, thousands of acres by thousands of acres. They had lost all of Kentucky and much of Tennessee, but after the last treaty of 1819 they still had remaining about 35,000 square miles of forested mountains, clean, swift-running rivers, and fine meadows. In this country which lay across parts of Georgia, North Carolina, and Tennessee they cultivated fields, planted orchards, fenced pastures, and built roads, houses, and towns. Sequoya had invented a syllabary for the Cherokee language so that thousands of his tribesmen quickly learned to read

From "The Trail of Tears" by Dee Brown in *American History Illustrated,* June 1972. Reprinted by permission of Cowles Magazines, publisher of *American History Illustrated.*

and write. The Cherokees had adopted the white man's way—his clothing, his constitutional form of government, even his religion. But it had all been for nothing. Now these men who had come across the great ocean many years ago wanted all of the Cherokees' land. In exchange for their 35,000 square miles the tribe was to receive five million dollars and another tract of land somewhere in the wilderness beyond the Mississippi River.

This was a crushing blow to a proud people. "They are extremely proud, despising the lower class of Europeans," said Henry Timberlake, who visited them before the Revolutionary War. William Bartram, the botanist, said the Cherokees were not only a handsome people, tall, graceful, and olive-skinned, but "their countenance and actions exhibit an air of magnanimity, superiority and independence."

Ever since the signing of the treaties of 1819, Major General Andrew Jackson, a man they once believed to be their friend, had been urging Cherokees to move beyond the Mississippi. Indians and white settlers, Jackson told them, could never get along together. Even if the government wanted to protect the Cherokees from harassment, he added, it would be unable to do so. "If you cannot protect us in Georgia," a chief retorted, "how can you protect us from similar evils in the West?"

During the period of polite urging, a few hundred Cherokee families did move west, but the tribe remained united and refused to give up any more territory. In fact, the council leaders passed a law forbidding any chief to sell or trade a single acre of Cherokee land on penalty of death.

In 1828, when Andrew Jackson was running for President, he knew that in order to win he must sweep the frontier states. Free land for the land-hungry settlers became Jackson's major policy. He hammered away at this theme especially hard in Georgia, where waves of settlers from the coastal low-lands were pushing into the highly desirable Cherokee country. He promised the Georgians that if they would help elect him President, he would lend his support to opening up the Cherokee lands for settlement. The Cherokees, of course, were not citizens and could not vote in opposition. To the Cherokees and their friends who protested this promise, Jackson justified his position by saying that the Cherokees had fought on the side of the British during the Revolutionary War. He conveniently forgot that the Cherokees had been his allies during the desperate War of 1812, and had saved the day for him in his decisive victory over the British-backed Creeks at Horseshoe Bend. (One of the Cherokee chiefs who aided Jackson was Junaluska. Said he afterward: "If I had known that Jackson would drive us from our homes I would have killed him that day at the Horseshoe.")

Three weeks after Jackson was elected President, the Georgia legislature passed a law annexing all the Cherokee country within that state's borders. As most of the Cherokee land was in Georgia and three-fourths of the tribe lived there, this meant an end to their independence as a nation. The Georgia legislature also abolished all Cherokee laws and customs and sent surveyors to map out land lots of 160 acres each. The 160-acre lots were to be distributed to white citizens of Georgia through public lotteries.

To add to the pressures on the Cherokees, gold was discovered near Dahlonega in the heart of their country. For many years the Cherokees had concealed the gold deposits, but now the secret was out and a rabble of gold-hungry prospectors descended upon them.

John Ross, the Cherokees' leader, hurried to Washington to protest the Georgia legislature's actions and to plead for justice. In that year Ross was 38 years old; he was well-educated and had been active in Cherokee government matters since he was 19. He was adjutant of the Cherokee regiment that served with Jackson at Horseshoe Bend. His father had been one of a group of Scottish emigrants who settled near the Cherokees and married into the tribe.

In Washington, Ross found sympathizers in Congress, but most of them were anti-Jackson men and the Cherokee case was thus drawn into the whirlpool of politics. When Ross called upon Andrew Jackson to request his aid, the President bluntly told him that "no protection could be afforded the Cherokees" unless they were willing to move west of the Mississippi.

While Ross was vainly seeking help in Washington, alarming messages reached him from Georgia. White citizens of that state were claiming the homes of Cherokees through the land lottery, seizing some of them by force. Joseph Vann, a hard-working half-breed, had carved out an 800-acre plantation at Spring Place and built a fine brick house for his residence. Two men arrived to claim it, dueled for it, and the winner drove Vann and his family into the hills. When John Ross rushed home he found that the same thing had happened to his family. A lottery claimant was living in his beautiful home on the Coosa River, and Ross had to turn north toward Tennessee to find his fleeing wife and children.

During all this turmoil, President Jackson and the governor of Georgia pressed the Cherokee leaders hard in attempts to persuade them to cede all their territory and move to the West. But the chiefs stood firm. Somehow they managed to hold the tribe together, and helped dispossessed families find new homes back in the wilderness areas. John Ross and his family lived in a one-room log cabin across the Tennessee line.

In 1834, the chiefs appealed to Congress with a memorial in which they stated that they would never voluntarily abandon their homeland, but proposed a compromise in which they agreed to cede the state of Georgia a part of their territory provided that they would be protected from invasion in the remainder. Furthermore, at the end of a definite period of years to be fixed by the United States they would be willing to become citizens of the various states in which they resided.

"Cupidity has fastened its eye upon our lands and our homes," they said, "and is seeking by force and by every variety of oppression and wrong to expel us from our lands and our homes and to tear from us all that has become endeared to us. In our distress we have appealed to the judiciary of the United States, where our rights have been solemnly established. We have appealed to the Executive of the United States to protect those rights according to the obligation of treaties and the injunctions of the laws. But this appeal to the Executive has been made in vain."

This new petition to Congress was no more effectual than their appeals to President Jackson. Again they were told that their difficulties could be remedied only by their removal to the west of the Mississippi.

For the first time now, a serious split occurred among the Cherokees. A small group of subchiefs decided that further resistance to the demands of the Georgia and United States governments was futile. It would be better, they believed, to exchange their land and go west rather than risk bloodshed and the possible loss of everything. Leaders of this group were Major Ridge and Elias Boudinot. Ridge had adopted his first name after Andrew Jackson gave him that rank during the War of 1812. Boudinot was Ridge's nephew. Originally known as Buck Watie, he had taken the name of a New England philanthropist who sent him through a mission school in Connecticut. Stand Watie, who later became a Confederate general, was his brother. Upon Boudinot's return from school to Georgia he founded the first tribal newspaper, the *Cherokee Phoenix,* in 1827, but during the turbulence following the Georgia land lotteries he was forced to suspend publication.

And so in February 1835 when John Ross journeyed to Washington to resume his campaign to save the Cherokee nation, a rival delegation headed by Ridge and Boudinot arrived there to seek terms for removal to the West. The pro-removal forces in the government leaped at this opportunity to bypass Ross's authority, and within a few days drafted a preliminary treaty for the Ridge delegation. It was then announced that a council would be held later in the year at New Echota, Georgia, for the purpose of negotiating and agreeing upon final terms.

During the months that followed, bitterness increased between the two Cherokee factions. Ridge's group was a very small minority, but they had the full weight of the United States government behind them, and threats and inducements were used to force a full attendance at the council which was set for December 22, 1835. Handbills were printed in Cherokee and distributed throughout the nation, informing the Indians that those who did not attend would be counted as assenting to any treaty that might be made.

During the seven days which followed the opening of the treaty council, fewer than five hundred Cherokees, or about 2 percent of the tribe, came to New Echota to participate in the discussions. Most of the other Cherokees were busy endorsing a petition to be sent to Congress stating their opposition to the treaty. But on December 29, Ridge, Boudinot and their followers signed away all the lands of the great Cherokee nation. Ironically, thirty years earlier Major Ridge had personally executed a Cherokee chief named Doublehead for committing one of the few capital crimes of the tribe. That crime was the signing of a treaty which gave away Cherokee lands.

Charges of bribery by the Ross forces were denied by government officials, but some years afterward it was discovered that the Secretary of War had sent secret agents into the Cherokee country with authority to expend money to bribe chiefs to support the treaty of cession and removal. And certainly the treaty signers were handsomely rewarded. In an era when a dollar would buy many times its worth today, Major Ridge was paid $30,000 and his followers received several thousand dollars each. Ostensibly they were being paid for their improved farmlands, but the amounts were far in excess of contemporary land values.

John Ross meanwhile completed gathering signatures of Cherokees who were opposed to the treaty. Early in the following spring, 1836, he took the petition to Washington. More than three-fourths of the tribe, 15,964, had signed in protest against the treaty.

When the governor of Georgia was informed of the overwhelming vote against the treaty, he replied: "Nineteen-twentieths of the Cherokees are too ignorant and depraved to entitle their opinions to any weight or consideration in such matters."

The Cherokees, however, did have friends in Congress. Representative Davy Crockett of Tennessee denounced the treatment of the Cherokees as unjust, dishonest, and cruel. He admitted that he represented a body of frontier constituents who would like to have the Cherokee lands opened for settlement, and he doubted if a single one of them would second what he was saying. Even though his support of the Cherokees might remove him from public life, he added, he could not do otherwise except at the expense of his honor and conscience. Daniel Webster, Henry Clay, Edward Everett, and other great orators of the Congress also spoke for the Cherokees.

When the treaty came to a final decision in the Senate, it passed by only one vote. On May 23, 1836, President Jackson signed the document. According to its terms, the Cherokees were allowed two years from that day in which to leave their homeland forever.

The few Cherokees who had favored the treaty now began making their final preparations for departure. About three hundred left during that year and then early in 1837 Major Ridge and 465 followers departed by boats for the new land in the West. About 17,000 others, ignoring the treaty, remained steadfast in their homeland with John Ross.

For a while it seemed that Ross might win his long fight, that perhaps the treaty might be declared void. After the Secretary of War, acting under instructions from President Jackson, sent Major William M. Davis to the Cherokee country to expedite removal to the West, Davis submitted a frank report: "That paper called a treaty is no treaty at all," he wrote, "because it is not sanctioned by the great body of the Cherokees and was made without their participation or assent. . . . The Cherokees are a peaceable, harmless people, but you may drive them to desperation, and this treaty cannot be carried into effect except by the strong arm of force."

In September 1836, Brigadier General Dunlap, who had been sent with a brigade of Tennessee volunteers to force the removal, indignantly disbanded his troops after making a strong speech in favor of the Indians: "I would never dishonor the Tennessee arms in a servile service by aiding to carry into execution at the point of the bayonet a treaty made by a lean minority against the will and authority of the Cherokee people."

Even Inspector General John E. Wool, commanding United States troops in the area, was impressed by the united Cherokee resistance, and warned the Secretary of War not to send any civilians who had any part in the making of the treaty back into the Cherokee country. During the summer of 1837, the Secretary of War sent a confidential agent, John Mason, Jr., to observe and report. "Opposition to the treaty is unanimous and irreconcilable," Mason wrote. "They say it cannot bind them because they did not make it; that it was made by a few unauthorized individuals; that the nation is not party to it."

The inexorable machinery of government was already in motion, however, and when the expiration date of the waiting period, May 23, 1838, came near, Winfield Scott was ordered in with his army to force compliance. As already stated, Scott issued his proclamation on May 10. His soldiers were already building thirteen stockaded forts—six in North Carolina, five in Georgia, one in Tennessee, and one in Alabama. At these points the Cherokees would be concentrated to await transportation to the West. Scott then ordered the roundup started, instructing his officers not to fire on the Cherokees except in case of resistance. "If we get possession of the women and children first," he said, "or first capture the men, the other members of the same family will readily come in."

James Mooney, an ethnologist who afterwards talked with Cherokees who endured this ordeal, said that squads of troops moved into the forested mountains to search out every small cabin and make prisoners of all the occupants however or wherever they might be found. "Families at dinner were startled by the sudden gleam of bayonets in the doorway and rose up to be driven with blows and oaths along the weary miles of trail that led to the stockades. Men were seized in their fields or going along the road, women were taken from their spinning wheels and children from their play. In many cases, on turning for one last look as they crossed a ridge, they saw their homes in flames, fired by the lawless rabble that followed on the heels of the soldiers to loot and pillage. So keen were these outlaws on the scent that in some instances they were driving off the cattle and other stock of the Indians almost before the soldiers had fairly started their owners in the other direction."

Long afterward one of the Georgia militiamen who participated in the roundup said: "I fought through the Civil War and have seen men shot to pieces and slaughtered by thousands, but the Cherokee removal was the cruelest work I ever knew."

Knowing that resistance was futile, most of the Cherokees surrendered quietly. Within a month, thousands were enclosed in the stockades. On June 6 at Ross's Landing near the site of present-day Chattanooga, the first of many departures began. Eight hundred Cherokees were forcibly crowded onto a flotilla of six flatboats lashed to the side of a steamboat. After surviving a passage over rough rapids which smashed the sides of the flatboats, they landed at Decatur, Alabama, boarded a railroad train (which was a new and terrifying experience for most of them), and after reaching Tuscumbia were crowded upon a Tennessee River steamboat again.

Throughout June and July similar shipments of several hundred Cherokees were transported by this long water route—north on the Tennessee River to the Ohio and then down the Mississippi and up the Arkansas to their new homeland. A few managed to escape and make their way back to the Cherokee country, but most of them were eventually recaptured. Along the route of travel of this forced migration, the summer was hot and dry. Drinking water and food were often contaminated. First the young children would die, then the older people, and sometimes as many as half the adults were stricken with dysentery and other ailments. On each boat deaths ran as high as five per day. On one of the first boats to reach Little Rock, Arkansas, at least a hundred had died. A compassionate lieutenant who was with the military escort recorded in his diary for August 1: "My blood chills as I write at the remembrance of the scenes I have gone through."

When John Ross and other Cherokee leaders back in the concentration camps learned of the high mortality among those who had gone ahead, they petitioned General Scott to postpone further departures until autumn. Although only three thousand Cherokees had been removed, Scott agreed to wait until the summer drought was broken, or no later than October. The Cherokees in turn agreed to organize and manage the migration themselves. After a lengthy council, they asked and received permission to travel overland in wagons, hoping that by camping along the way they would not suffer as many deaths as occurred among those who had gone on the river boats.

During this waiting period, Scott's soldiers continued their searches for more than a thousand Cherokees known to be still hiding out in the deep wilderness of the Great Smoky Mountains. These Cherokees had organized themselves under the leadership of a chief named Utsala, and had developed warning systems to prevent captures by the bands of soldiers. Occasionally, however, some of the fugitives were caught and herded back to the nearest stockade.

One of the fugitive families was that of Tsali, an aging Cherokee. With his wife, his brother, three sons and their families, Tsali had built a hideout somewhere on the border between North Carolina and Tennessee. Soldiers surrounded their shelters one day, and the Cherokees surrendered without resistance. As they were being taken back toward Fort Cass (Calhoun, Tennessee) a soldier prodded Tsali's wife sharply with a bayonet, ordering her to walk faster. Angered by the brutality, Tsali grappled with the soldier, tore away his rifle, and bayoneted him to the ground. At the same time, Tsali's brother leaped upon another soldier and bayoneted him. Before the remainder of the military detachment could act, the Cherokees fled, vanishing back into the Smokies where they sought refuge with Chief Utsala. Both bayoneted soldiers died.

Upon learning of the incident, Scott immediately ordered that Tsali must be brought in and punished. Because some of his regiments were being transferred elsewhere for other duties, however, the general realized that his reduced force might be oc-cupied for months in hunting down and capturing the escaped Cherokee. He would have to use guile to accomplish the capture of Tsali.

Scott therefore dispatched a messenger—a white man who had been adopted as a child by the Cherokees—to find Chief Utsala. The messenger was instructed to inform Utsala that if he would surrender Tsali to General Scott, the Army would withdraw from the Smokies and leave the remain-ing fugitives alone.

When Chief Utsala received the message, he was suspicious of Scott's sincerity, but he considered the general's offer as an opportunity to gain time. Per-haps with the passage of time, the few Cherokees re-maining in the Smokies might be forgotten and left alone forever. Utsala put the proposition to Tsali: If he went in and surrendered, he would probably be put to death, but his death might insure the freedom of a thousand fugitive Cherokees.

Tsali did not hesitate. He announced that he would go and surrender to General Scott. To make certain that he was treated well, several members of Tsali's band went with him.

When the Cherokees reached Scott's headquar-ters, the general ordered Tsali, his brother, and three sons arrested, and then condemned them all to be shot to death. To impress upon the tribe their utter helplessness before the might of the government, Scott selected the firing squad from Cherokee pris-oners in one of the stockades. At the last moment, the general spared Tsali's youngest son because he was only a child.

(By this sacrifice, however, Tsali and his family gave the Smoky Mountain Cherokees a chance at survival in their homeland. Time was on their side, as Chief Utsala had hoped, and that is why today there is a small Cherokee reservation on the North Carolina slope of the Great Smoky Mountains.)

With the ending of the drought of 1838, John Ross and the 13,000 stockaded Cherokees began preparing for their long overland journey to the West. They assembled several hundred wagons, filled them with blankets, cooking pots, their old

people and small children, and moved out in sep-arate contingents along a trail that followed the Hiwassee River. The first party of 1,103 started on October 1.

"At noon all was in readiness for moving," said an observer of the departure. "The teams were stretched out in a line along the road through a heavy forest, groups of persons formed about each wagon. The day was bright and beautiful, but a gloomy thoughtful-ness was depicted in the lineaments of every face. In all the bustle of preparation there was a silence and stillness of the voice that betrayed the sadness of the heart. At length the word was given to move on. Going Snake, an aged and respected chief whose head eighty summers had whitened, mounted on his favorite pony and led the way in silence, followed by a number of younger men on horseback. At this very moment a low sound of distant thunder fell upon my ear . . . a voice of divine indignation for the wrong of my poor and unhappy countrymen, driven by brutal power from all they loved and cherished in the land of their fathers to gratify the cravings of avarice. The sun was unclouded—no rain fell—the thunder rolled away and seemed hushed in the distance."

Throughout October, eleven wagon trains de-parted and then on November 4, the last Cherokee exiles moved out for the West. The overland route for these endless lines of wagons, horsemen, and people on foot ran from the mouth of the Hiwassee in Tennessee across the Cumberland plateau to McMinnville and then north to Nashville where they crossed the Cumberland River. From there they followed an old trail to Hopkinsville, Kentucky, and continued northwestward to the Ohio River, crossing into southern Illinois near the mouth of the Cumberland. Moving straight westward they passed through Jonesboro and crossed the Mississippi at Cape Girardeau, Missouri. Some of the first parties turned southward through Arkansas; the later ones continued westward through Springfield, Missouri, and on to Indian Territory.

A New Englander traveling eastward across Ken-tucky in November and December met several

Trail of Tears, *an oil painting by Robert Lindneux. The first group of Cherokee started on their journey west on October 1, 1838. When all the groups had reached the new Indian Territory, as Dee Brown indicates, "the Cherokees had lost about four thousand by deaths—or one out of every four members of the tribe—most of the deaths brought about as the direct result of the enforced removal." (Woolaroc Museum, Bartlesville, Oklahoma)*

contingents, each a day apart from the others. "Many of the aged Indians were suffering extremely from the fatigue of the journey," he said, "and several were quite ill. Even aged females, apparently nearly ready to drop into the grave, were traveling with heavy burdens attached to their backs—on the sometimes frozen ground and sometimes muddy streets, with no covering for the feet except what nature had given them. . . . We learned from the inhabitants on the road where the Indians passed, that they buried fourteen or fifteen at every stopping place, and they make a journey of ten miles per day only on an average. They will not travel on the Sabbath . . . they must stop, and not merely stop—they must worship the Great Spirit, too; for they had divine service on the Sabbath—a camp meeting in truth."

Autumn rains softened the roads, and the hundreds of wagons and horses cut them into molasses, slowing movement to a crawl. To add to their difficulties, tollgate operators overcharged them for passage. Their horses were stolen or seized on pretext of unpaid debts, and they had no recourse to the law. With the coming of cold damp weather, measles and whooping cough became epidemic. Supplies had to be dumped to make room for the sick in the jolting wagons.

By the time the last detachments reached the Mississippi at Cape Girardeau it was January, with the river running full of ice so that several thousand had to wait on the east bank almost a month before the channel cleared. James Mooney, who later heard the story from survivors, said that "the lapse of over half a century had not sufficed to wipe out the memory of the miseries of that halt beside the frozen river, with hundreds of sick and dying penned up in wagons or stretched upon the ground, with only a blanket overhead to keep out the January blast."

Meanwhile the parties that had left early in October were beginning to reach Indian Territory. (The first arrived on January 4, 1839.) Each group had lost from thirty to forty members by death. The later detachments suffered much heavier losses, especially toward the end of their journey. Among the victims was the wife of John Ross.

Not until March 1839 did the last of the Cherokees reach their new home in the West. Counts were made of the survivors and balanced against the counts made at the beginning of the removal. As well as could be estimated, the Cherokees had lost about four thousand by deaths—or one out of every four members of the tribe—most of the deaths brought about as the direct result of the enforced removal. From that day to this the Cherokees remember it as "the trail where they cried," or the Trail of Tears.

QUESTIONS TO CONSIDER

1 Discuss Andrew Jackson's position on the Cherokees. Did he accurately reflect white attitudes toward and assumptions about the Indians?

2 How did factionalism within the Cherokee nation help the state of Georgia and the federal government to carry out their policy of Indian removal?

3 On December 29, 1835, a Cherokee treaty council signed away the Cherokees' tribal lands and agreed to the tribe's being moved west of the Mississippi. What methods did the United States government use to obtain this treaty? Discuss the paradox of how a nation such as the United States, founded on democratic principles of government, could justify signing such a fraudulent treaty.

4 The framers of the Constitution were men of property who also held republican ideals (see selection 9). The Boston Associates, who founded Lowell, Massachusetts, were also wealthy men who tried and ultimately failed to combine benevolent and materialistic ideas (see selection 20). How does the experience of Indian removal also illustrate America's conflict between benevolence and greed, idealism and pragmatism?

22 Women and Their Families on the Overland Trails

JOHNNY FARAGHER AND CHRISTINE STANSELL

After the War of 1812, America turned away from Old World entanglements and sought to extend its "natural sphere of influence" westward. Pioneers moved in sporadic waves out to the Mississippi River and beyond. Jefferson had made this westward movement possible by purchasing the vast Louisiana Territory from France in 1803. He had also begun American dreams of a transcontinental empire when he sent Lewis and Clark out to the Pacific and back. In the next two decades, Americans occupied the fertile Mississippi Valley, creating the new states of Louisiana, Indiana, Mississippi, Illinois, Alabama, and Missouri. At the same time, army explorers and scientists undertook expeditions up the Arkansas and Missouri Rivers, finding that the complex river systems offered tremendous possibilities for commerce and trade. In the Adams-Onís Treaty of 1819, Spain gave the United States its claims to the Oregon country, an expansive region lying north of the Red and Arkansas Rivers and the 42nd parallel. After Mexico revolted against Spain in 1822, the Mexican Republic also ratified the Adams-Onís Treaty, thus clearing the way for an American march to the Pacific.

American fur companies, operating out of St. Louis and Independence, Missouri, had already sent trappers and traders out into the awesome Rocky Mountains. These fabled mountain men blazed trails and explored rich mountain valleys across the Oregon country, reporting back that the region was excellent for settlement. In the 1830s and 1840s, Americans from the fringes of the South and the old northwestern states headed across the trails the mountain men had blazed, establishing American outposts in Oregon and California. Meanwhile, other settlers—most of them from the Border South—migrated into Mexican-held Texas, where they eventually revolted and set up an independent republic.

In the 1840s—an era of unprecedented westward expansion—the United States virtually doubled its territory. It annexed the Republic of Texas, drove the British out of Oregon with threats of violence, and acquired California and the rest of the Southwest in a highly controversial war with Mexico.

The "glacial inexorability" of this westward sweep, as historian T. H. Watkins phrased it, gave birth to a faith called Manifest Destiny, a belief that Americans had a natural, God-given right to expand their superior institutions and way of life across the continent. And woe indeed to anybody—British, Mexican, or Indian—who stood in the way. To clear the way for Anglo-American settlement, the government rescinded the "permanent" frontier it had granted the Indians west of the 95th meridian and in the 1850s adopted a policy of concentration, which forced them into specified areas in various parts of the West. To justify their broken promises and treaties, white Americans contended that they were the dominant race and so were responsible for the Indians—"along with their lands, their forests, and their mineral wealth." God wished the white men to have all the lands of the West, because they knew how to use the soil and the pagan Indians did not.

Still, as historian Bernard De Voto has reminded us, other energies besides Manifest Destiny thrust America westward. Some southerners, for example, desired the empty lands for southern expansion, in order to maintain an equilibrium of power in Washington between slave and free states. Both southern and northern interests sought to control the Middle West for political and economic gain; and American industrial interests exhibited a "blind drive" to establish ports on the West Coast, thereby opening the Pacific Ocean and distant Asia to United States commercial expansion. There was another story in America's inexorable westward march—the story of the people who made the grueling trek across the overland trails to start new lives. The pioneers—men and women alike—are stock figures in frontier mythology. What were they really like? In their discussion of the conditions of life for women and their families on the Oregon and California Trails, Johnny Faragher and Christine Stansell draw on contemporary diaries and letters to take us beyond the stereotypes. In the process, they raise some provocative questions. Did members of a westering family share the same attitudes? Was the women's experience different from the men's? Did the overland emigration alter eastern conventions about family structure and "proper" women's roles? In answering such questions, the authors paint a vivid and realistic portrait of daily life, family roles, work tasks, cultural expectations, and women's ties with one another as the wagons headed toward the Pacific.

GLOSSARY

BEECHER, CATHARINE A leading advocate of separate spheres of responsibility for men and women.

"CULT OF TRUE WOMANHOOD" Argued that the true place for the American woman was her home, where she enjoyed "real autonomy and control" in child rearing, household economy, and the moral and religious life of the family.

SEXUAL SPHERES The doctrine in Jacksonian America that justified segregating women in the home and men in politics and wage earning.

From 1841 until 1867, the year in which the transcontinental railroad was completed, nearly 350,000 North Americans emigrated to the Pacific coast along the western wagon road known variously as the Oregon, the California, or simply the Overland Trail. This migration was essentially a family phenomenon. Although single men constituted the majority of the party which pioneered large-scale emigration on the Overland Trail in 1841, significant numbers of women and children were already present in the wagon trains of the next season. Families made up the preponderant proportion of the migrations throughout the 1840s. In 1849, during the overwhelmingly male Gold Rush, the number dropped precipitously, but after 1851 families once again assumed dominance in the overland migration. The contention that "the family was the one substantial social institution" on the frontier is too sweeping, yet it is undeniable that the white family largely mediated the incorporation of the western territories into the American nation.

The emigrating families were a heterogeneous lot. Some came from farms in the midwest and upper South, many from small midwestern towns, and others from northeastern and midwestern cities. Clerks and shopkeepers as well as farmers outfitted their wagons in Independence, St. Louis, or Westport Landing on the Missouri. Since costs for supplies, travel, and

Examine the tired faces of this determined family on their long journey on the overland trails. Johnny Faragher and Christine Stansell write that "the trip West was exhausting, toilsome, and often grueling." The diaries of women reveal that their burden was often greater as they fought loneliness, cared for children, and helped their husbands move the wagons relentlessly forward. (Denver Public Library Photography Collection)

John Mark Faragher and Christine Stansell, "Women and Their Families on the Overland Trail to California and Oregon, 1842–1867" was originally published in *Feminist Studies,* Volume 2, Number 2/3 (1975): 150–166, by permission of the publisher, Feminist Studies, Inc.

settlement were not negligible, few of the very poor were present, nor were the exceptionally prosperous. The dreams of fortune which lured the wagon trains into new lands were those of modest men whose hopes were pinned to small farms or larger dry-goods stores, more fertile soil or more customers, better market prospects and a steadily expanding economy.

For every member of the family, the trip West was exhausting, toilsome, and often grueling. Each year in late spring, westbound emigrants gathered for the journey at spots along the Missouri River and moved out in parties of ten to several hundred wagons. Aggregates of nuclear families, loosely attached by kinship or friendship, traveled together or joined an even larger caravan. Coast-bound families traveled by ox-drawn wagons at the frustratingly slow pace of fifteen to twenty miles per day. They worked their way up the Platte River valley through what is now Kansas and Nebraska, crossing the Rockies at South Pass in southwestern Wyoming by mid-summer. The Platte route was relatively easy going, but from present-day Idaho, where the roads to California and Oregon diverged, to their final destinations, the pioneers faced disastrous conditions: scorching deserts, boggy salt flats, and rugged mountains. By this time, families had been on the road some three months and were only at the midpoint of the journey; the environment, along with the wear of the road, made the last months difficult almost beyond endurance. Finally, in late fall or early winter the pioneers straggled into their promised lands, after six months and over two thousand miles of hardship.

As this journey progressed, bare necessity became the determinant of most of each day's activities. The primary task of surviving and getting to the coast gradually suspended accustomed patterns of dividing work between women and men. All able-bodied adults worked all day in one way or another to keep the family moving. Women's work was no less indispensable than men's; indeed, as the summer wore on, the boundaries dividing the work of the sexes were threatened, blurred, and transgressed.

The vicissitudes of the trail opened new possibilities for expanded work roles for women, and in the cooperative work of the family there existed a basis for a vigorous struggle for female-male equality. But most women did not see the experience in this way. They viewed it as a male enterprise from its very inception.

Women experienced the breakdown of the sexual division of labor as a dissolution of their own autonomous "sphere." Bereft of the footing which this independent base gave them, they lacked a cultural rationale for the work they did, and remained estranged from the possibilities of the enlarged scope and power of family life on the trail. Instead, women fought *against* the forces of necessity to hold together the few fragments of female subculture left to them. We have been bequeathed a remarkable record of this struggle in the diaries, journals, and memoirs of emigrating women. In this study, we will examine a particular habit of living, or culture, in conflict with the new material circumstances of the Trail, and the efforts of women to maintain a place, a sphere of their own.

The overland family was not a homogeneous unit, its members imbued with identical aspirations and desires. On the contrary, the period of westward movement was also one of multiplying schisms within those families whose location and social status placed them in the mainstream of national culture. Child-rearing tracts, housekeeping manuals, and etiquette books by the hundreds prescribed and rationalized to these Americans a radical separation of the work responsibilities and social duties of mothers and fathers; popular thought assigned unique personality traits, spiritual capacities, and forms of experience to the respective categories of man, woman, and child. In many families, the tensions inherent in this separatist ideology, often repressed in the everyday routines of the East, erupted under the strain of the overland crossing. The difficulties of the emigrants, while inextricably linked to the duress of the journey itself, also revealed family dynamics which had been submerged in the less eventful life "back home."

A full-blown ideology of "woman's place" was absent in preindustrial America. On farms, in artisan shops, and in town market-places, women and children made essential contributions to family income and subsistence; it was the family which functioned as the basic unit of production in the colony and the young nation. As commercial exchanges displaced the local markets where women had sold surplus dairy products and textiles, and the workplace drifted away from the household, women and children lost their bread-winning prerogatives.

In Jacksonian America, a doctrine of "sexual spheres" arose to facilitate and justify the segregation of women into the home and men into productive work. While the latter attended to politics, economics, and wage-earning, popular thought assigned women the refurbished and newly professionalized tasks of child-rearing and housekeeping. A host of corollaries followed on the heels of these shifts. Men were physically strong, women naturally delicate; men were skilled in practical matters, women in moral and emotional concerns; men were prone to corruption, women to virtue; men belonged in the world, women in the home. For women, the system of sexual spheres represented a decline in social status and isolation from political and economic power. Yet it also provided them with a psychological power base of undeniable importance. The "cult of true womanhood" was more than simply a retreat. Catharine Beecher, one of the chief theorists of "woman's influence," proudly quoted Tocqueville's observation that "in no country has such constant care been taken, as in America, to trace two clearly distinct lines of action for the two sexes, and to make them keep pace with the other, but in two pathways which are always different." Neither Beecher nor her sisters were simply dupes of a masculine imperialism. The supervision of child-rearing, household economy, and the moral and religious life of the family granted women a certain degree of real autonomy and control over their lives as well as those of their husbands and children. . . .

At its very inception, the western emigration sent tremors through the foundations of this carefully compartmentalized family structure. The rationale behind pulling up stakes was nearly always economic advancement; since breadwinning was a masculine concern, the husband and father introduced the idea of going West and made the final decision. Family participation in the intervening time ran the gamut from enthusiastic support to stolid resistance. Many women cooperated with their ambitious spouses: "The motive that induced us

to part with pleasant associations and the dear friends of our childhood days, was to obtain from the government of the United States a grant of land that 'Uncle Sam' had promised to give to the head of each family who settled in this new country." Others, however, only acquiesced. "Poor Ma said only this morning, 'Oh, I wish we never had started,'" Lucy Cooke wrote her first day on the trail, "and she looks so sorrowful and dejected. I think if Pa had not passengers to take through she would urge him to return; not that he should be so inclined." Huddled with her children in a cold, damp wagon, trying to calm them despite the ominous chanting of visiting Indians, another woman wondered "what had possessed my husband, anyway, that he should have thought of bringing us away out through this God forsaken country." Similar alienation from the "pioneer spirit" haunted Lavinia Porter's leave-taking:

I never recall that sad parting from my dear sister on the plains of Kansas without the tears flowing fast and free. . . . We were the eldest of a large family, and the bond of affection and love that existed between us was strong indeed . . . as she with the other friends turned to leave me for the ferry which was to take them back to home and civilization, I stood alone on that wild prairie. Looking westward I saw my husband driving slowly over the plain; turning my face once more to the east, my dear sister's footsteps were fast widening the distance between us. For the time I knew not which way to go, nor whom to follow. But in a few moments I rallied my forces . . . and soon overtook the slowly moving oxen who were bearing my husband and child over the green prairie . . . the unbidden tears would flow in spite of my brave resolve to be the courageous and valiant frontierswoman.

Her dazed vacillation soon gave way to a private conviction that the family had made a dire mistake: "I would make a brave effort to be cheerful and patient until the camp work was done. Then starting out ahead of the team and my men folks, when I thought I had gone beyond hearing distance, I would throw myself down on the unfriendly desert and give way like a child to sobs and tears, wishing myself back home with my friends and chiding myself for consenting to take this wild goose chase." Men viewed drudgery, calamity, and privation as trials along the road to prosperity, unfortunate but inevitable corollaries of the rational decision they had made. But to those women who were unable to appropriate the vision of the upwardly mobile pilgrimage, hardship and the loss only testified to the inherent folly of the emigration, "this wild goose chase."

If women were reluctant to accompany their men, however, they were often equally unwilling to let them go alone. In the late 1840s, the conflict between wives and their gold-crazed husbands reveals the determination with which women enforced the cohesion of the nuclear family. In the name of family unity, some obdurate wives simply chose to blockbust the sexually segregated Gold Rush: "My husband grew enthusiastic and wanted to start immediately," one woman recalled, "but I would not be left behind. I thought where he could go I could and where I went I could take my two little toddling babies." Her family departed intact. Other women used their moral authority to smash the enterprise in its planning stages. "We were married to live together," a wife acidly reminded her spouse when he informed her of his intention to join the Rush: "I am willing to go with you to any part of *God's Foot Stool* where you think you can do best, and under these circumstances you have no right to go where I cannot, and if you do you need never return for I shall look upon you as dead." Roundly chastised, the man postponed his journey until the next season, when his family could leave with him. When included in the plans, women seldom wrote of their husbands' decisions to emigrate in their diaries or memoirs. A breadwinner who tried to leave alone, however, threatened the family unity upon which his authority was based; only then did a wife challenge his dominance in worldly affairs.

There was an economic reason for the preponderance of families on the Trail. Women and children, but especially women, formed an essential supplementary work force in the settlements. The ideal wife in the West resembled a hired hand more than a nurturant Christian housekeeper. Narcissa Whitman wrote frankly to aspiring settlers of the functional necessity of women on the new farms: "Let every young man bring a wife, for he will want one after he gets here, if he never did before." In a letter from California, another seasoned woman warned a friend in Missouri that in the West women became "hewers of wood and drawers of water everywhere." Mrs. Whitman's fellow missionary Elkanah Walker was unabashedly practical in beseeching his wife to join him: "I am tired of keeping an old bachelor's hall. I want someone to get me a good supper and let me take my ease and when I am very tired in the morning I want someone to get up and get breakfast and let me lay in bed and take my rest." It would be both simplistic and harsh to argue that men brought their families West or married because of the labor power of women and children; there is no doubt, however, that the new Westerners appreciated the advantages of familial labor. Women were not superfluous; they were workers. The migration of women helped to solve the problem of labor scarcity, not only in the early years of the American settlement on the coast, but throughout the history of the continental frontier.

In the first days of the overland trip, new work requirements were not yet pressing and the division of labor among family members still replicated familiar patterns. Esther Hanna reported in one of her first diary entries that "our men have gone to build a bridge across the stream, which is impassable," while she baked her first bread on the prairie. Elizabeth Smith similarly described her party's day: "rainy . . . Men making rafts. Women cooking and washing. Children crying." When travel was suspended, "the men were generally busy mending wagons, harnesses, yokes, shoeing the animals etc., and the women washed clothes, boiled a big mess of beans, to warm over for several meals, or perhaps mended clothes." At first, even in emergencies, women and men hardly considered integrating their work. "None but those who have cooked for a family of eight, crossing the plains, have any idea of what it takes," a disgruntled woman recalled: "My sister-in-law was sick, my niece was much younger than I, and consequently I had the management of all the cooking and planning on my young shoulders." To ask a man to help was a possibility she was unable even to consider.

The relegation of women to purely domestic duties, however, soon broke down under the vicissitudes of the Trail. Within the first few weeks, the unladylike task of gathering buffalo dung for fuel (little firewood was available *en route*) became women's work. As one traveler astutely noted, "force of surroundings was a great leveler"; miles of grass, dust, glare, and mud erased some of the most rudimentary distinctions between female and male responsibilities. By summer, women often helped drive the wagons and the livestock. At one Platte crossing, "the men drawed the wagons over by hand and the women all crossed in safety"; but at the next, calamity struck when the bridge collapsed, "and then commenced the hurry and bustle of repairing; all were at work, even the women and children." Such crises, which compounded daily as the wagons moved past the Platte up the long stretches of desert and coastal mountains, generated equity in work; at times of Indian threats, for example, both women and men made bullets and stood guard. When mountain fever struck the Pengra family as they crossed the Rockies, Charlotte relieved her incapacitated husband of the driving while he took care of the youngest child. Only such severe afflictions forced men to take on traditionally female chores. While women did men's work, there is little evidence that men reciprocated.

Following a few days in the life of an overland woman discloses the magnitude of her work. During the hours her party traveled, Charlotte Pengra walked beside the wagons, driving the cattle and gathering buffalo chips. At night she cooked, baked bread for the next noon meal, and washed clothes. Three successive summer days illustrate how trying these small chores could be. Her train pulled out early on a Monday morning, only to be halted by rain and a flash flood; Mrs. Pengra washed and dried her family's wet clothes in the afternoon while doing her daily baking. On Tuesday the wagons pushed hard to make up for lost time, forcing her to trot all day

to keep up. In camp that night there was no time to rest. Before going to bed, she wrote, "Kept busy in preparing tea and doing other things preparatory for the morrow. I baked a cracker pudding, warm biscuits and made tea, and after supper stewed two pans of dried apples, and made two loaves of bread, got my work done up, beds made, and child asleep, and have written in my journal. Pretty tired of course." The same routine devoured the next day and evening: "I have done a washing. Stewed apples, made pies and baked a rice pudding, and mended our wagon cover. Rather tired." And the next: "baked biscuits, stewed berries, fried meat, boiled and mashed potatoes, and made tea for supper, afterward baked bread. Thus you see I have not much rest." Children also burdened women's work and leisure. During one quiet time, Helen Stewart retreated in mild defiance from her small charges to a tent in order to salvage some private time: "It is exceeding hot . . . some of the men is out hunting and some of them sleeping. The children is grumbling and crying and laughing and howling and playing all around." Although children are notably absent in women's journals, they do appear, frightened and imploring, during an Indian scare or a storm, or intrude into a rare and precious moment of relaxation, "grumbling and crying."

Because the rhythm of their chores was out of phase with that of the men, the division of labor could be especially taxing to women. Men's days were toilsome but broken up at regular intervals with periods of rest. Men hitched the teams, drove or walked until noon, relaxed at dinner, traveled until the evening camp, unhitched the oxen, ate supper, and in the evening sat at the campfire, mended equipment, or stood guard. They also provided most of the labor in emergencies, pulling the wagons through mires, across treacherous river crossings, up long grades, and down precipitous slopes. In the pandemonium of a steep descent,

you would see the women and children in advance seeking the best way, some of them slipping down, or holding on to the rocks, now taking an "otter slide," and then a run til some natural obstacle presented itself to stop their accelerated progress and those who get down safely without a hurt or a bruise, are fortunate indeed. Looking back to the train, you would see some of the men holding on to the wagons, others slipping under the oxen's feet, some throwing articles out of the way that had fallen out, and all have enough to do to keep them busily occupied.

Women were responsible for staying out of the way and getting themselves and the children to safety, men for getting the wagons down. Women's work, far less demanding of brute strength and endurance, was nevertheless distributed without significant respite over all waking hours: mealtimes offered no leisure to the cooks. "The plain fact of the matter is," a young woman complained,

we *have no time for sociability*. From the time we get up in the morning, until we are on the road, it is hurry scurry to get breakfast and put away the things that necessarily had to be pulled out last night—while under way there is no room in the wagon for a visitor, nooning is barely long enough to eat a cold bite—and at night all the cooking utensils and provisions are to be gotten about the camp fire, and cooking enough to last until the next night.

After supper, the men gathered together, "lolling and smoking their pipes and guessing, or maybe betting, how many miles we had covered during the day," while the women baked, washed, and put the children to bed before they finally sat down. Charlotte Pengra found "as I was told before I started that there is no rest in such a journey."

Unaccustomed tasks beset the travelers, who were equipped with only the familiar expectation that work was divided along gender lines. The solutions which sexual "spheres" offered were usually irrelevant to the new problems facing families. Women, for example, could not afford to be delicate: their new duties demanded far greater stamina and hardiness than their traditional domestic tasks. With no tradition to deal with the new exigencies of fuel-gathering, cattle-driving, and cooking, families found that "the division of labor in a party . . . was a prolific

cause of quarrel." Within the Vincent party, "assignments to duty were not accomplished without grumbling and objection . . . there were occasional angry debates while the various burdens were being adjusted," while in "the camps of others who sometimes jogged along the trail in our company . . . we saw not a little fighting . . . and these bloody fisticuffs were invariably the outcome of disputes over division of labor." At home, these assignments were familiar and accepted, not subject to questioning. New work opened the division of labor to debate and conflict.

By midjourney, most women worked at male tasks. The men still retained dominance within their "sphere," despite the fact that it was no longer exclusively masculine. Like most women, Lavinia Porter was responsible for gathering buffalo chips for fuel. One afternoon, spying a grove of cottonwoods half a mile away, she asked her husband to branch off the trail so that the party could fell trees for firewood, thus easing her work. "But men on the plains I had found were not so accommodating, nor so ready to wait upon women as they were in more civilized communities." Her husband refused and Porter fought back: "I was feeling somewhat under the weather and unusually tired, and crawling into the wagon told them if they wanted fuel for the evening meal they could get it themselves and cook the meal also, and laying my head down on a pillow, I cried myself to sleep." Later that evening her husband awakened her with a belated dinner he had prepared himself, but despite his conciliatory spirit their relations were strained for weeks: "James and I had gradually grown silent and taciturn and had unwittingly partaken of the gloom and somberness of the dreary landscape." No longer a housewife or a domestic ornament, but a laborer in a male arena, Porter was still subordinate to her husband in practical matters.

Lydia Waters recorded another clash between new work and old consciousness: "I had learned to drive an ox team on the Platte and my driving was admired by an officer and his wife who were going with the mail to Salt Lake City." Pleased with the compliment, she later overheard them "laughing at the thought of a woman driving oxen." By no means did censure come only from men. The officer's wife as well as the officer derided Lydia Waters, while her own mother indirectly reprimanded teenaged Mary Ellen Todd. "All along our journey, I had tried to crack that big whip," Mary Ellen remembered years later:

Now while out at the wagon we kept trying until I was fairly successful. How my heart bounded a few days later when I chanced to hear father say to mother, "Do you know that Mary Ellen is beginning to crack the whip." Then how it fell again when mother replied, "I am afraid it isn't a very lady-like thing for a girl to do." After this, while I felt a secret joy in being able to have a power that set things going, there was also a sense of shame over this new accomplishment.

To understand Mrs. Todd's primness, so incongruous in the rugged setting of the Trail, we must see it in the context of a broader struggle on the part of women to preserve the home in transit. Against the leveling forces of the Plains, women tried to maintain the standards of cleanliness and order that had prevailed in their homes back East.

Our caravan had a good many women and children and although we were probably longer on the journey owing to their presence—they exerted a good influence, as the men did not take such risks with Indians . . . were more alert about the care of teams and seldom had accidents; more attention was paid to cleanliness and sanitation and, lastly, but not of less importance, meals were more regular and better cooked thus preventing much sickness and there was less waste of food.

Sarah Royce remembered that family wagons "were easily distinguished by the greater number of conveniences, and household articles they carried." In the evenings, or when the trains stopped for a day, women had a chance to create with few props a flimsy facsimile of the home.

Even in camp women had little leisure time, but within the "hurry scurry" of work they managed to re-create the routine of the home. Indeed, a female subculture, central to the communities women had left behind, reemerged in these settings. At night, women often clustered together, chatting, working, or commiserating, instead of joining the men: "High teas were not popular, but tatting, knitting, crocheting, exchanging recipes for cooking beans or dried apples or swopping food for the sake of variety kept us in practice of feminine occupations and diversions." Besides using the domestic concerns of the Trail to reconstruct a female sphere, women also consciously invoked fantasy: "Mrs. Fox and her daughter are with us and everything is so still and quiet we can almost imagine ourselves at home again. We took out our Daguerreotypes [photographs] and tried to live over again some of the happy days of 'Auld Lang Syne.'" Sisterly contact kept "feminine occupations" from withering away from disuse: "In the evening the young ladies came over to our house and we had a concert with both guitars. Indeed it seemed almost like a pleasant evening at home. We could none of us realize that we were almost at the summit of the Rocky Mountains." The hostess added with somewhat strained sanguinity that her young daughter seemed "just as happy sitting on the ground playing her guitar as she was at home, although she does not love it as much as her piano." Although a guitar was no substitute for the more refined instrument, it at least kept the girl "in practice with feminine occupations and diversions": unlike Mary Ellen Todd, no big whip would tempt her to unwomanly pleasure in the power to "set things going."

But books, furniture, knick-knacks, china, the daguerreotypes that Mrs. Fox shared, or the guitars of young musicians—the "various articles of ornament and convenience"—were among the first things discarded on the epic trash heap which trailed over the mountains. On long uphill grades and over sandy deserts, the wagons had to be lightened; any materials not essential to survival were fair game for disposal. Such commodities of woman's sphere, although functionally useless, provided women with a psychological lifeline to their abandoned homes and communities, as well as to elements of their identities which the westward journey threatened to mutilate or entirely extinguish. Losing homely treasures and memorabilia was yet another defeat within an accelerating process of dispossession.

The male-directed venture likewise encroached upon the Sabbath, another female preserve. Through the influence of women's magazines, by mid-century Sunday had become a veritable ladies' day; women zealously exercised their religious influence and moral skill on the day of their families' retirement from the world. Although parties on the Trail often suspended travel on Sundays, the time only provided the opportunity to unload and dry the precious cargo of the wagons—seeds, food, and clothing—which otherwise would rot from dampness. For women whose creed forbade any worldly activity on the Sabbath, the work was not only irksome and tedious but profane.

This is Sabath it is a beautiful day indeed we do not use it as such for we have not traveled far when we stop in a most lovely place oh it is such a beautiful spot and take everything out of our wagon to air them and it is well we done it as the flower was damp and there was some of the other ones flower was rotten . . . and we baked and boiled and washed oh dear me I did not think we would have abused the sabeth in such a manner. I do not see how we can expect to get along but we did not intend to do so before we started.

Denied a voice in the male sphere that surrounded them, women were also unable to partake of the limited yet meaningful power of women with homes. On almost every Sunday, Helen Stewart lamented the disruption of a familiar and sustaining order of life, symbolized by the household goods strewn about the ground to dry: "We took everything out the wagons and the side of the hill is covered with flower biscut meat rice oat meal clothes and such a quantity of articles of all discertions to

many to mention and childre[n] included in the number. And hobos that is neather men nor yet boys being in and out hang about."

The disintegration of the physical base of domesticity was symptomatic of an even more serious disruption in the female subculture. Because the wagon trains so often broke into smaller units, many women were stranded in parties without other women. Since there were usually two or more men in the same family party, some male friendships and bonds remained intact for the duration of the journey. But by midway in the trip, female companionship, so valued by nineteenth-century women, was unavailable to the solitary wife in a party of hired men, husband, and children that had broken away from a larger train. Emergencies and quarrels, usually between men, broke up the parties. Dr. Powers, a particularly ill-tempered man, decided after many disagreements with others in his train to make the crossing alone with his family. His wife shared neither his misanthropy nor his grim independence. On the day they separated from the others, she wrote in her journal: "The women came over to bid me goodbye, for we were to go alone, all alone. They said there was no color in my face. I felt as if there was none." She perceived the separation as a banishment, almost a death sentence: "There is something peculiar in such a parting on the Plains, one there realizes what a goodbye is. Miss Turner and Mrs. Hendricks were the last to leave, and they bade me adieu the tears running down their sun-burnt cheeks. I felt as though my last friends were leaving me, for what—as I thought then—was a Maniac." Charlotte Pengra likewise left Missouri with her family in a large train. Several weeks out, mechanical problems detained some of the wagons, including those of the other three women. During the month they were separated, Pengra became increasingly dispirited and anxious: "The roads have been good today—I feel lonely and almost disheartened. . . . Can hear the wolves howl very distinctly. Rather ominis, perhaps you think . . . Feel very tired and lonely—our folks not having come—I fear some of them ar sick." Having waited as long as possible for the others, the advance group made a major river crossing. "Then I felt that indeed I had left all my friends," Pengra wrote, "save my husband and his brother, to journey over the dreaded Plains, without one female acquaintance even for a companion—of course I wept and grieved about it but to no purpose."

Others echoed her mourning. "The whippor-wills are chirping," Helen Stewart wrote, "they bring me in mind of our old farm in pensillvania the home of my childhood where I have spent the happiest days I will ever see again. . . . I feel rather lonesome today oh solitude solitude how I love it if I had about a dozen of my companions to enjoy it with me." Uprootedness took its toll in debilitation and numbness. After a hard week, men "lolled around in the tents and on their blankets seeming to realize that the 'Sabbath was made for man,'" resting on the palpable achievements of miles covered and rivers crossed. In contrast, the women "could not fully appreciate physical rest, and were rendered more uneasy by the continual passing of emigrant trains all day long. . . . To me, much of the day was spent in meditating over the past and in forebodings for the future."

The ultimate expression of this alienation was the pressure to turn back, to retrace steps to the old life. Occasionally anxiety or bewilderment erupted into open revolt against going on.

This morning our company moved on, except one family. The woman got mad and wouldn't budge or let the children go. He had the cattle hitched on for three hours and coaxed her to go, but she wouldn't stir. I told my husband the circumstances and he and Adam Polk and Mr. Kimball went and each one took a young one and crammed them in the wagon, and the husband drove off and left her sitting. . . . She cut across and overtook her husband. Meantime he sent his boy back to camp after a horse he had left, and when she came up her husband said, "Did you meet John?" "Yes," was the reply, "and I picked up a stone and knocked out his brains." Her husband went back to ascertain the truth and while he was gone she set fire to one of the wagons. . . . He saw the flames and came running and put it out, and then mustered spunk enough to give her a good flogging.

Short of violent resistance, it was always possible that circumstances would force a family to reconsider and turn back. During a cholera scare in 1852, "women cried, begging their men to take them back." When the men reluctantly relented, the writer observed that "they did the hooking up of their oxen in a spiritless sort of way," while "some of the girls and women were laughing." There was little lost and much regained for women in a decision to abandon the migration.

Both sexes worked, and both sexes suffered. Yet women lacked a sense of inclusion and a cultural rationale to give meaning to the suffering and the work; no augmented sense of self or role emerged from augmented privation. Both women and men also complained, but women expanded their caviling to a generalized critique of the whole enterprise. Margaret Chambers felt "as if we had left all civilization behind us" after crossing the Missouri, and Harriet Ward's cry from South Pass—"Oh, shall we ever live like civilized beings again?"—reverberated through the thoughts of many of her sisters. Civilization was far more to these women than law, books, and municipal government; it was pianos, church societies, daguerreotypes, mirrors—in short, their homes. At their most hopeful, the exiles perceived the Trail as a hellish but necessary transition to a land where they could renew their domestic mission: "Each advanced step of the slow, plodding cattle carried us farther and farther from civilization into a desolate, barbarous country. . . . But our new home lay beyond all this and was a shining beacon that beckoned us on, inspiring our hearts with hope and courage." At worst, temporary exigencies became in the minds of the dispossessed the omens of an irrevocable exile: "We have been travelling with 25–18–14–129–64–3 wagons—now all alone—how dreary it seems. Can it be that I have left my quiet little home and taken this dreary land of solitude in exchange?"

Only a minority of the women who emigrated over the Overland Trail were from the northeastern middle classes where the cult of true womanhood reached its fullest bloom. Yet their responses to the labor demands of the Trail indicate that "womanliness" had penetrated the values, expectations, and personalities of midwestern farm women as well as New England "ladies." "Women's sphere" provided them with companionship, a sense of self-worth, and most important, independence from men in a patriarchal world. The Trail, in breaking down sexual segregation, offered women the opportunities of socially essential work. Yet this work was performed in a male arena, and many women saw themselves as draftees rather than partners. . . .

Nonetheless, the journals of overland women are irrefutable testimony to the importance of a separate female province. Such theorists as Catharine Beecher were acutely aware of the advantages in keeping life divvied up, in maintaining "two pathways which are always different" for women and men. The women who traveled on the Overland Trail experienced first-hand the tribulations of integration which Beecher and her colleagues could predict in theory.

QUESTIONS TO CONSIDER

1 How did necessity on the Overland Trail open up new work roles for women? Did women tend to regard these new "opportunities" to share in men's work as a gain or as a loss in status?

2 How did the sphere theory, which emerged in Jacksonian America, lead to a decline in woman's social, political, and economic status but a gain in her psychological and emotional status? Was the so-called cult of true womanhood simply a sexist ideology forced on oppressed American females?

3 Contrast the goals of men and women on the trail. Why did women feel particularly alienated by the migration experience?

4 How were women on the trail able to create a positive female subculture? What difficulties did they encounter?

5 Faragher and Stansell remind us that historians have often associated positive work roles for women with the absence of narrow definitions of a woman's place. Why is this association inaccurate in describing women's experiences on the Overland Trail?

PART TWELVE

"To Make Them Stand in Fear": The Slaveowning South

23 Runaways from a Hellish System

JOHN HOPE FRANKLIN AND LOREN SCHWENINGER

Thanks to the influence of the 1939 motion picture Gone with the Wind, *many white Americans still think of the Old South as a romantic land of magnolias and landscaped manors, of cavalier gentlemen and happy darkies, of elegant ladies and breathless belles in crinoline—an ordered, leisurely world in which men and women, blacks and whites, all had their destined place. This view of Dixie is one of America's most enduring myths* (Gone with the Wind *still commands huge audiences when it runs on television). The real world of the Old South was far more complex and cruel.*

Modern historical studies have demonstrated that antebellum Dixie was a rigidly patriarchal, slave-based social order that might have lasted indefinitely had not the Civil War broken out. At no time was slavery on the verge of dying out naturally. Tobacco cultivation may have become unprofitable by the Revolutionary period, but the invention of the cotton gin in 1793 stimulated cotton production immeasurably and created a tremendous demand for slave labor. Thanks to the cotton gin, slavery spread beyond the fertile black belt of Alabama and Mississippi, out to the Kansas-Missouri border, to the fringes of western Arkansas, and to south and east Texas. Although Congress outlawed the foreign slave trade in 1808 (it simply continued as an illicit traffic), the number of slaves rose dramatically so that by 1860 there were nearly 4 million in fifteen slave states, including Delaware and Maryland. Slavery remained profitable, too, as evidenced by the fact that in 1860 a prime field hand sold for $1,250 in Virginia and $1,800 on the auction blocks in New Orleans. A "fancy girl" went for as high as $2,500. Still, from the southern white's viewpoint, the profitability of slavery was not the crucial issue. Had slavery proved too costly in its plantation setting, southerners would have found other ways to use slave labor and keep blacks in chains, to maintain white male supremacy in the region.

The slaveholding South was a brutal system that sought to strip black people of all human rights, reducing them to the status of cattle, swine, wagons, and other "property." The slaveholders resorted to a complex "apparatus of control" by which they ruled the region. The symbol of their power was the ubiquitous whip, which, in the words of another historian, was calculated to make the slaves "stand in fear." Yet, as we saw in the portrait of Nat Turner (selection 15), the slaves created survival mechanisms in the form of their families, black religion, and a slave underground, which helped them "keep on keepin' on" in life under the lash. And they resisted, most of them did, by committing acts of terrorism (arson and sabotage) or day-to-day obstructionism, such as "accidently" breaking their hoes. As historian Deborah Gray White has pointed out, pregnant mothers sometimes conspired with midwives to abort their fetuses and even commit infanticide, so that their children would not suffer as they had. The slaves protested, too, in their songs and in their folk tales about how weak, clever animals (the slaves) could outwit larger, menacing animals (the masters).

To understand the antebellum South, one must remember that the region was divided into two distinct classes of white, slaveholders and non-slaveholders, with the latter constituting a majority of the white population. Non-slaveholders included poor whites—"po white trash," "rednecks," or "hillbillies," in the vernacular of the day—who lived on impoverished subsistence farms in the unproductive hill country and pine barrens. The class also included middle-class yeoman farmers who raised crops for market and city-dwelling merchants, artisans, and day-laborers. Since slaveholding was a potent status symbol and a great means of wealth, most of these individuals aspired to own slaves and rise up in the class scale.

Compared to the slaveholders, all non-slaveholding whites were relatively poor. Slaveholders owned more than 90 percent of the South's agricultural wealth; their average wealth was fourteen times greater than that of non-slaveholders. The planters, those who owned twenty or more slaves, were a minority in the slaveholding class—they numbered only 46,000 in 1860. Yet the planters owned most of the slaves and most of the agricultural wealth of their class and truly ruled the region. By stressing white racial supremacy and black inferiority and by playing on the fears of abolition, the ruling planters and their small slaveholding allies were able to unite poor whites, yeoman farmers and city dwellers behind the slave regime. In short, they successfully divided whites and blacks.

In the following selection, eminent African American historian John Hope Franklin and historian Loren Schweninger describe the horrors of slavery, particularly in the brutal domestic slave trade, which involved the selling of African Americans to slave traders on the open market. This diabolical practice often broke up black families, separating wives, husbands, children (including infants), and other relatives from each other. One husband and wife were sold to the slave traders after forty-three years of marriage. Indeed, the domestic slave trade so frequently separated African American couples that slave wedding vows had to be changed to read "until death or distance do you part." When slaves ran away, their masters employed bounty hunters, called "slave catchers," to track them down with vicious dogs. The story of the domestic slave trade will give you a better understanding of why Nat Turner revolted (selection 15) and why Harriet Tubman, a runaway, returned to Dixie many times to escort slaves to freedom on the Underground Railroad (selection 24).

Slavery left an indelible mark on both races. As African American historian Lerone Bennett Jr. wrote in his Confrontation: Black and White (1965): "Slavery, in sum, was a seed experience.

The significant dimensions of the race problem, the special dynamism that gave [the racial upheavals of the 1960s] their special harshness, are reflections of eddies that lie deep in the mind and deep in the past. The Negro is what he is today because he was once held in slavery by white people. And white people are what they are today because they cannot forget, because Negroes will not let them forget, what they did yesterday."

GLOSSARY

COFFLES Groups or "trains" of slaves who were being transported overland under the close scrutiny of white slave traders. Conditions were harsh during this forced march, and slaves were often bound to each other.

GULLAH An African dialect spoken by many slaves who lived in remote regions along the Georgia and South Carolina seacoast. Minimal contact with whites allowed those slaves to maintain their African linguistic patterns. For example, they often kept their African names and used groups of words to form adjectives, nouns, and verbs. For instance, they substituted "sweet mouth" for "flatter" and "day clean" for "dawn."

HIRING OUT Slave masters often loaned their slaves to neighboring plantations or to whites in urban areas of the South. Many of these slaves had marketable skills such as carpentry and bricklaying. The masters reaped the profit, keeping most and sometimes all of the wages their slaves earned.

KEMBLE, FRANCIS ANNE (FANNY) An English woman who married a Georgia planter, Kemble wrote a journal that contained detailed descriptions of the cruelties of slavery.

OLMSTED, FREDERICK LAW Olmsted was a northerner who traveled through the South in the 1850s. His published observations served as a firsthand indictment of the horrors of slavery.

OVERSEER The administrative assistant to masters on large plantations, the overseer was responsible for managing and disciplining the slaves.

PATROLS White paramilitary organizations that guarded the outskirts of plantations in order to capture runaways and prevent slave insurrections. One patroller commented that he could confiscate from slave cabins anything that "bore a hostile aspect, such as powder, shot." His job was also to "apprehend every negro whom we found from his home."

SLAVE CATCHERS Bounty hunters who tracked down runaways and returned them to their masters for a fee.

SMALL RICE Slave owners frequently made small rice a part of their slaves' diet. Small and poor in quality, such rice could not be sold on the open market.

Rachel O'Connor, the mistress of Evergreen Plantation in West Feliciana Parish, Louisiana, felt deeply about her servants. In her correspondence she spoke fondly of her slaves, and it was clear that her affection was deep and sincere. But she could not completely divorce her feelings of good fortune from the economic gain that came with the birth of each new black baby. At the time of her death, 84 percent of her estate was human property. She wrote in 1830:

I have sixteen little negro children a raising, the oldest of the sixteen a little turned of six years old, all very healthy children excepting my little favorite Isaac, he is subject to a cough but seldom sick enough to lay up, the poor little fellow is laying at my feet sound asleep. I wish I did not love him, as I do, but it is so, and I cannot help it.

Beset by creditors during the late 1820s, however, O'Connor transferred title of seventeen slaves to her half brother and future heir David Weeks, owner of the elegant Shadows Plantation in St. Mary Parish,

From *Runaway Slaves* by John Hope Franklin and Loren Schweninger, copyright © 1999 by John Hope Franklin and Loren Schweninger. Used by permission of Oxford University Press, Inc.

one hundred miles to the south. The longtime widow made the transfer to protect her slave property from confiscation and because she had already promised Weeks a portion of her estate. The slaves, however, would remain on her plantation. She had always prided herself on how well she treated her "black family," as she called them, and since her half brother owned many other slaves, she was confident that her black family would remain intact, at least during her lifetime.

But when Weeks established another plantation and asked her to send him some slaves, she did so. Her decision was not easy, but she weighed the economic needs of her half brother against the temporary dislocation of a few black families. As they were shipped down the Mississippi River, the young O'Connor slaves suffered great agony. They were leaving behind their parents as well as the place of their youth. As others followed, they, too, felt the wrenching pain of leaving mothers and other kin. Some of the young men who were sent off attempted to return to Evergreen. Despite the lack of experience in the swamp and bayou country, Harry, Eben, and Littleton made it as far as Baton Rouge in 1833 before being captured and returned. Not long afterwards, Harry absconded again, this time with Frank. They reached the O'Connor place and were reunited with their mothers. As punishment, however, they were sent to the remote island plantation of Grand Cote in the Attakapas region.

Even in this isolated wilderness, blacks struggled desperately to go and live with loved ones, but it was nearly impossible to get off the island. By 1840, runaway families had bonded together in secluded sections of the island, and when slaves absconded, they sometimes did so as entire families. "Linzy has taken to the woods with his wife and child he is well armed he has the little Double Barrelled gun and his butchers Knife," the plantation manager at Grand Cote wrote. He believed that Linzy would "Join the party" that had recently stolen a boat. He also observed "a great difference in the behaviour of several of the Blacks on the Island," and it was his opinion that they were being influenced by runaway bands.

He had little doubt that the runaway family had joined Linzy and that there was some clandestine correspondence "between them and the plantation." The anxious manager said that the neighbors should be alerted and that there should be a concerted effort to hunt down the runaways. It was the only way to save whites from the "miseries that those beings is capable of brin[g]ing down on [our] heads."

———

BREAKUP OF FAMILIES

The efforts of slaves to reunite with loved ones is well illustrated by the runaways on Louisiana's Grand Cote Island. Elsewhere the situation was quite different. Most slaves separated by sale or transfer could neither abscond in family units nor form colonies as in the Louisiana bayou country. Usually they were sold off and never saw members of their families again. The trauma of being separated forever from kith and kin can hardly be imagined. Most slaves were sold at one time or another during their lifetime, and often it was when they were young and would bring the highest price. Seldom were they sold together in family units of mother, father, and children. The separation of family members was common, especially after 1820, as whites poured into the Tennessee and Mississippi river valleys. In the Louisiana sugar parishes, 70 percent of the slaves purchased were male; traders from Virginia and Maryland scoured the countryside to send young black men to market. In the Upper South, forcible separations probably destroyed one out of three first marriages, and one out of three slave children under fifteen years of age was probably separated from one or both parents. As the prices for slaves in the west increased and the profits of the interregional trade mounted, men, women, boys, and girls were swept into the domestic slave trade. They were bought at private sales, auctions, and estate sales; transported to the west; and sold at a substantial profit. The buying and selling of children ages seven through twelve bore witness to the breaking up of families.

Although many owners denied they would ever engage in such practices, speculating in black youngsters was not uncommon. "What can be had for two (2) girls number one about seven (7) the other nine [?]" a slave trader asked. "I bought today a likely girl, I suppose she is 12 year old, 4 ft 10 inches high," another wrote Betts and Gregory, commission merchants in Richmond, Virginia, in 1861. "Do you think it a good time to sell. If so I will send her in." A third trader wrote the same firm inquiring if there was "anything doing in your negro Markette." He wanted to know what he could get for "a good girl 13 yrs old, one 12 yrs old, and a boy 10 yrs old, or wheather there wd be any certainty of my selling them at all."

At its extreme, the speculation involved black babies. In a suit filed by a Scott County, Kentucky, woman in 1845 against a Virginia trader heading to New Orleans, no mention was made of the parents of the two black children. The only relevant information provided was that the Kentucky woman had foolishly traded horses for two black babies represented as being healthy, one being six or seven months old and another who "could almost walk." In fact, she complained, the first child was six weeks old, the other four months old. Both were "extremely delicate, sickly and feeble, and it is very doubtful whether they can be raised at all." The black babies were in great risk of "dying before they pass the age of childhood, bringing their value down to nothing." It seems doubtful that a trader would carry two black babies from Virginia to Kentucky without their mother[s], or that the purchaser expected any short-term profits, but whatever the specific circumstances, the case shows the devastating impact of the domestic slave trade on black families.

The separation of families was an inherent part of the South's peculiar institution. Sales, trades, transfers, auctions, migration of slave-holders meant that mothers were taken from children, wives from husbands, children from parents, fathers from sons and daughters, and blood kin from one another. "I send you by Aaron *all* of Lucy's children," F. L. Hunt of Jackson, Mississippi, wrote a woman in Natchez, seeking to settle a debt. "I send them all down to be delivered on condition that you release me entirely from the whole matter." They were a "beautiful family of children," but if they were sold separately they could bring "a larger price."

The fear of being sold away from family and friends caused constant apprehension and worry. When the fateful moment arrived, as it often did, slaves pleaded with masters not to separate them from loved ones. When their appeals were ignored, slaves began an arduous journey away from the connections of their past, away from the kinship and family ties that had bound them together, away from the places and feelings of their youth. Since most slaves were sold at some time during their lifetime, even when they remained in the area of their birth they could still experience the grief and misery of living apart from loved ones.

A personal history narrated by Jenny reflected the changes that were occurring in the lives of other slaves. Described as "very black" and having lost her front teeth, she had been sold and resold at least six times by age sixteen or seventeen. She told her life's story in 1805 to a Scottsville, Virginia, jailer: she had been "raised" by William Gathright of Henrico County, who sold her to a Richmond butcher, who sold her to a man named Williamson, who sold her to "one Webster" of Buckingham County, who sold her to John Campbell of King and Queen County, who "left her" with a free black man in Powhatan County. She escaped from him and was later arrested and jailed.

Among the many causes of slaves running away, perhaps none was more poignant or pervasive than members of families seeking to reunite. They ran to neighboring plantations to be with husbands or wives, ran away to search for mothers and fathers, and all too often in vain for their children. It was especially traumatic for youngsters to be sold away from their parents or to see their parents sent away. . . .

Mere rumors of a possible sale could send slaves off and running. Slave owners planning to make a sale cautioned members of their own family to keep the matter confidential until the bargain was sealed to avoid possible flight. One Maryland owner put a mild mannered black woman and her child in jail prior to a private sale. Judging from the quick response of some slaves, such precautions were necessary. Sharper was a field hand working on a plantation across the Potomac River from Maryland. The moment he learned that he was to be turned over to a slave trader, he bolted out of the field and fled to his wife on a neighboring plantation. He remained at large nearly seven weeks, but in July 1831, he was apprehended, and by September he was on his way to a distant location. When she learned of the possible separation of her family in a pending sale, the Maryland slave Sophia gathered up her two children and ran to the District of Columbia. She too, was apprehended, jailed, returned, and auctioned off, along with her children. The money from the sale was used to care for her mistress, who, according to court records, suffered "great imbecility of mind." John Jones of Nash County, North Carolina, purchased "a negro fellow" and started with him to Georgia to sell him when "said negroe ran away" was captured and returned home.

The fate of most who absconded to avoid being sold was similar to that of Sharper and Sophia. Without time to plan, with few provisions, running to locations where slave owners would look first—where a spouse, child, or parent lived—most of this group were apprehended. Even those who remained out for many months discovered that living on the run was extremely difficult. They could remain with relatives for only short periods, and slaves on neighboring plantations took a substantial risk harboring a fugitive. Life on the run meant slaves could not stay in one place long, and they were often forced to live by thievery. Even the most resourceful among them found that it was difficult to remain undetected. In May 1799, "a very valuable Negro Fellow" in Charleston, South Carolina, was purchased by an up-country planter. Learning of his fate, he immediately bolted from the city. Stealing food from various plantations, he remained at large for seventeen months, but in the fall of 1800 he was arrested, jailed, charged with burglary, and executed.

It was not only the despair of being separated from loved ones that prompted slaves to abscond, but the fear of what awaited them in a new location. Purchased by Samuel Linton, who was traveling along the Eastern Shore looking for "a few young negroes," one Maryland slave escaped clutching her infant child. A year later she was apprehended in Delaware, returned to Maryland, and jailed until Linton could come up from South Carolina and take possession of his property. As soon as the North Carolina slave Delph learned she had been sold to a buyer from the Lower South, she ran away. She, too, remained at large for some months and during that time gave birth to a child. . . .

Being sold from a rural to an urban setting, from the Upper to the Lower South, from the east to the west, or even short distances across a river in the same state could cause enormous pain and suffering at the loss of family members. City slaves sent to plantations in remote or isolated locations often found the adjustments even more difficult. Lymus, a twenty-eight-year-old Charleston bricklayer, was sold to Thomas Butler King, a planter on St. Simons, a barrier island fronting on the Atlantic Ocean and surrounded by salt marshes and tidal streams. A few years later, the famous Englishwoman Frances Anne (Fanny) Kemble gave her impression of the condition of the slaves on St. Simons: the "filthy and wretched" quarters, the meals of corn grits and "small rice" (unfit for market), and the "inhumanity of allowing a man to strip and lash a woman, the mother of ten children; to exact from her, toil." Lymus discovered as well that the slaves on St. Simons were different from himself in dress, manner, beliefs, and speech, speaking Gullah with its African rhythm and inflections. A short time after his arrival, he managed to escape from the island and was seen on the road going from Darien to Savannah. He "will probably endeavor to make his way back to Charleston," King's agent wrote, hiring himself out at plantations along the way.

For a few, even the possibility of such dislocations was too much to bear. In 1820, Jane's Tennessee owner decided to move to Missouri. She expressed great unwillingness to leave the state "and was very anxious" to be sold "to some person in the neighbourhood." She had grown up in Rutherford County, was very close to her mother and siblings, and dreaded the prospect of leaving family and friends. She beseeched her owner to sell her to someone in the area, but he refused. A few days before she was scheduled to leave, she took her master's horse, rode off, and did not return. What went through her mind during the next twenty-four hours is difficult to say: Should she hide out? Try to escape? Go to her family for help? The following day, the horse was discovered near a mill pond, her shoes were set neatly a short distance from the shore, her handkerchief tied to the limb of a tree, and her footprints led down to the edge of the water. Sixteen days later, Jane's bloated corpse rose to the surface and was found bobbing near the edge of the pond by a local farmer.

[SLAVE CAPTURES]

The weeks following a sale were especially traumatic for slaves. Shackled and taken away, placed in holding pens, beginning the journey to an unknown location, they were driven overland in coffles, chained aboard riverboats, or confined to the hold of coastal vessels, under the constant surveillance of slave traders. Any attempt to seek liberty at this point would be dealt with harshly, as the men who conducted the interregional transfer of slaves were intent on delivering their human cargo in good condition and at the designated time. The passage was nearly unbearable for many slaves. The heartbreak of leaving a husband or wife, mother or father, child or loved one behind, whom they would probably never see again, created feelings of indescribable despair and anguish. . . .

[When slaves ran away, their masters advertised rewards for them on posters and in newspapers. At the same time, slave owners deployed armed patrols to guard the boundaries of their plantations and hired slave catchers to track down runaways with savage "negro dogs." The following story describes what happened to one slave when a brutal slave catcher set off after him.]

Slave catcher James C. Knox, of East Baton Rouge Parish, Louisiana, set out in July 1856 to capture Big Sandy, a slave owned by a local planter who had been hired out and had run away. A man of little means who owned no property, Knox had earned small amounts of extra cash on previous occasions hunting runaways. Borrowing a pack of hounds, he moved across the undulating countryside, along the dirt roads and into ravines, as his dogs lurched forward. An experienced hunter, Knox was confident that he could find Big Sandy, although he worried about how much resistance the black man might offer. He was confident that he could handle the situation, however, as he had on many previous occasions. He was equally confident that he would be able to collect a reward. He needed the money.

Pursuing Sandy, he accidentally came across another runaway, a field hand owned by planter Thomas Devall, and Knox interrupted his search for Sandy to take the newly found slave to Devall's overseer. Resuming his hunt, the dogs found Sandy hiding in a gully, but the slave had a Bowie knife and held the yelping hounds at bay. When Knox slid down into the gully, he slipped and fell, and Sandy leaped upon him. Even as the dogs tore at the slave's neck and arms, the black man raised his knife to stab his pursuer. "I then laid hold of the Knife with my left hand and held it," Knox said; and as they struggled he begged the black man to "get off of me and told him I would let him alone." Sandy refused, even as the dogs sunk their teeth into his back. Knox later testified:

I finally got the Knife in my right hand and then again told him to get off of me or I would Kill him with the knife—The first time I told the said Negro to get off of me he replied you have no business here and I will Kill you if I can.

The two men struggled for fifteen minutes, before Knox thrust the knife into Big Sandy's chest. The black man died a short time later.

The episode involving Knox and Big Sandy symbolized the determination of slave catchers and slave owners to recover runaways. Indeed, the entire system of slavery was predicated on the ability of whites to control their property. When a slave ran away, it was necessary to make every effort to recover the "miscreant." It seemed as if the peculiar institution itself was on trial when such "breaches" occurred. To control slaves, masters established rules and regulations on each farm and plantation, but they were also aided by an elaborate system of state and local laws, patrols, militia, vigilance committees, and individuals, like Knox, who specialized in tracking runaways. In the cotton country of southwest Mississippi, for example, thirty-one-year-old B. B. Boiken, who lived on another man's farm, told census takers that he was a full-time "Negro catcher."

As time passed, a sophisticated system evolved to assist slaveholders in recovering their lost property, a system that included slave catchers, patrols, traders, sheriffs, constables, jailers, justices of the peace, judges, and other state and local officials. To meet new exigencies, the laws were revised and the duties of persons involved in the process were clarified. How runaways were to be hunted, captured, jailed, and reclaimed, what the costs would be and who would pay them, and how the legal system would operate to dispose of unclaimed runaways were all questions that needed to be addressed. To examine how runaways were pursued, however, is to seek answers to questions about the fundamental nature of slavery. It reveals as well as any other focus the continual struggle between master and slave, a struggle that goes to the heart of slavery itself, a struggle that increased in intensity as the years passed. . . .

NEGRO DOGS

One of the most widespread methods of tracking runaways was to use highly trained so-called "negro dogs." Frederick Law Olmsted observed that no particular breed was used in the hunt—bloodhounds, foxhounds, bulldogs, Scotch staghounds, curs—but slave hunters and planters had a method of training each breed to be effective. The dogs were locked up and "never allowed to see a negro except while training to catch him." They were given the scent of a black man or woman's shoe or article of clothing and taught to follow the scent. Slaves were sent out as trainees, and when the dogs treed them, they were given meat as a reward. "Afterwards they learn to follow any particular negro by scent."

Despite Olmsted's assertions, specially bred bloodhounds were easily the dogs of choice. . . . The dogs were fierce hunters, and if not constrained at the end of the chase, they would tear a man to pieces.

"I had rather a negro would do anything Else than runaway," Louisiana planter David Barrow once admitted, but the "drives" he and his neighbors mounted to find runaways in West Feliciana Parish were sometimes undertaken "with the zest of sport." The "Negro hunters" would arrive in the morning with their dogs, the planters would mount their horses, and a band of hunters, planters, overseers would set out behind the pack of yelping hounds. They would ride at a gallop until the dogs began baying, and then they would slow to a trot. On one occasion they trailed a male slave "about a mile[,] *treed* him, made the dogs pull him out of the tree, Bit him badly, think he will stay home a while." On another occasion, Barrow said that the "dogs soon tore him naked, took him home Before the negro[es] at dark & made the dogs give him another overhauling."

Such vicious attacks were against the law in a number of states. The penal code of Georgia, for instance, provided that "any owner or employer of a slave or slaves, who shall cruelly treat such slave or slaves" shall be guilty of a misdemeanor. This included using attack dogs to track runaways. In 1855, in a case involving the drowning death of a fugitive fleeing from a pack of hounds, the Georgia Supreme Court ruled it was lawful "to track runaway negroes with dogs, and follow them up until they are caught, provided it be done with due degree of caution and circumspection." Dogs could

This 1861 oil painting, entitled "The Hunted Slaves," depicts "howling Negro dogs" catching up with runaways in the Great Dismal Swamp of North Carolina. Imported from Cuba, these vicious animals, "if not restrained at the end of the chase," could "tear a man to pieces." (Victoria and Albert Museum, London/Art Resource, NY)

be used if they did not "lacerate or otherwise materially injure the slave." In fact, however, most dogs trained to track runaways were vicious, fearsome beasts.

At times, slaves attempted to throw off the scent by going into streams or spreading pepper or spices on the ground, but these ploys usually were successful only in buying time. The dogs moved quickly up and down river banks or off in different directions to pick up the trail again. Even if slaves did escape for a time, they returned to see their families or obtain supplies, and as soon as this was learned, owners would "find their tracks and put the dogs on again." One master boasted that the longest period any of his slaves remained out was two months. He had "dogs trained on purpose to run after niggers, and never let out for anything else." A farmer in the cotton country of the Piedmont said that in his area

there were many men "who made a business of nigger-hunting," and they trained their horses and dogs to go over any fence. From the time they were pups, the "nigger dogs," as they were called, were trained to follow runaways. Usually only two were "kept kennelled all the time—these were old, keen ones, who led the rest when they were out; they were always kept coupled together with a chain, except when trailing."

Slave catchers who owned Negro dogs were quick to advertise the fact. Slave hunter David Turner, who lived a few miles from Bolivar, the county seat of Hardeman County, Tennessee, advertised in the *Western Tennessee Democrat*: "BLOODHOUNDS.—I have TWO of the FINEST DOGS for CATCHING NEGROES in the Southwest. They can take the trail TWELVE HOURS after the NEGRO HAS PASSED, and catch him with ease."

He ended: "I am ready at all times to catch runaway negroes." They were also quick to make certain that their charges reflected the fact that they possessed the finest dogs for catching runaways. Upon receiving word that a slave had escaped from a plantation owned by William L. Balfour in Yazoo County, Mississippi, in 1857, Thomas Hamberlin quickly set out in pursuit; within a short time, he apprehended and returned the fugitive. In presenting his bill to the estate, Hamberlin charged twenty dollars "for Catching with dogs—Negro *Ed,* upon the order of E D Cox, dated Nov, er 8th 1857, for the Estate of Dr. Balfour on Woodside plantation." During the 1850s, George W. Null, who owned three slaves, hired himself and his four "Negro Dogs" out to his neighbors to hunt runaways. He could earn five dollars a day to conduct his chases. When he died in early 1862, his wife sought permission to sell "a pack of Negro dogs which are now useless to his estate or family." When the sale occurred in May 1862, the four highly trained hounds were auctioned off to William B. Wilkerson for $300, a remarkably high price even considering the early inflation of Confederate currency.

Like Hamberlin, most dog-owning slave catchers worked as farmers or in other occupations, but were ready to respond at a moment's notice. Often slave owners and local sheriffs called on them when a slave ran away. In Laurens District, South Carolina, William W. Simpson was known to have "an uncommon and extraordinary dog for trailing." When a white man convicted of horse stealing and two black men sentenced to death for poisoning their master broke out of jail about 1823, Simpson on horseback with his "extraordinary dog" brought back the white man and one of the slaves. "[A] few days afterwards the negro broke gaol a second time," a report noted. Simpson and his dog "punctually attended and caught him again after a severe heat, and brought him back and he was executed according to his sentence."

Runaways had reason to fear the hounds following on their heels. If they caught up with them before the pursuers on horseback, a slave could receive severe injuries. One absentee planter in Philadelphia wrote his overseer in Alabama that, while he regretted a slave was off again in the woods, "I wish you to try to get him back, but dont want *dogs* to go and Ketch him. It is to dangerous. They may kill a man in a very short time. Last time they had nearly torn him up."

At times runaways were forced to stop and fight the dogs. One fleeing Mississippi slave who had assaulted a white man was taken "with much difficulty." The pursuers and the runaway had "quite a fight," and some of the dogs "were badly cut." Another slave who turned and fought was Peyton, who was hiding in an orchard behind the hotel in Columbiana, Alabama, until a fellow slave told whites where he was hiding. Late the same afternoon, ten men on horseback burst into the orchard behind a pack of dogs, and Peyton sprinted 400 yards when the dogs "bayed him." Peyton then drew his knife, quickly killed the lead dog, and ran off into a thicket. "He is so bold," a white woman commented; "Pate is a mean negro."

To teach "mean negroes" a lesson, planters often used dogs in the chase, and when they had a chance to show them what might happen if they tried to run away, they were quick to use their hounds for demonstration. Out with a large pack of dogs in a fox chase, two Alabama gentlemen accidentally came across a slave who had absconded several days before. The dogs surprised Toney, one of the gentlemen explained, "put him up a fence where he made a surrender—& upon learning who he belonged to—dogs were called off—but they escorted him home, with the *entire pack* of hounds to the horror of all the plantation—I hope it will have a good effect."

Hiring slave catchers and using "Negro dogs" were only two methods slaveholders employed to pursue runaways. They also corresponded with fellow slaveholders, kept records about the location of relatives and friends of their slaves, sent overseers and plantation managers in pursuit of runaways, advertised and offered rewards for the return of their property. . . .

In this 1860 drawing, entitled "Shooting Scene," slave patrols and their hounds have treed a hapless runaway. The artist depicts the enormous odds that runaways faced when fleeing from their owners. (Library of Congress)

INCARCERATION

Runaways who were not caught or did not surrender on their own were often captured and taken to the nearest jail. Each county seat had its jailhouse, usually near the courthouse. In cities, there were usually several public and private jails for holding slaves prior to sale and shipment. The private jails, called "pens," were sometimes clean and sanitary, but public jails were often dank, foul smelling, and filthy. Some jails proved to be death bins for runaways who refused to divulge the names of their owners. One anonymous runaway jailed in Kershaw District, South Carolina, steadfastly refused to divulge the identity of his master. The jailer asserted that "every exertion was made to discover the true owner of the said fellow, that letters were Written to those to whom he stated he belonged and that to some of those letters answers were Returned denying any Knowledge of the said fellow—that the usual and legal advertisements were inserted in the Camden Gazette, but no one appeared to claim the said fellow." Locked in a tiny, vermin-ridden cell—stiflingly hot in summer and icy cold in winter—the slave grew progressively weaker. In June 1819, after 170 days, he died. Staying in the same jail slightly longer—176 days—Jim also refused to give information about himself except that he came from Georgia. In March 1822, he, too, died.

Captured and jailed runaways who refused to reveal their owner's identity faced an uncertain future. Not only might they end up like the two men jailed in Kershaw District, South Carolina, but they were certain to remain in jail many months, sometimes a year or more, before being sold to pay expenses. Arrested in Chesterfield County, Virginia, in 1816, Hannibal lied about his place of origin. Although advertisements appeared in the *Richmond Enquirer,* no one claimed him, and after sixteen months, he was sold to a slave trader heading west. On his way, the trader stopped in Prince Edward County, and Hannibal confessed that he belonged to a store owner in Amelia County, but it was too late. The trader moved on with him to Nashville, then headed southwest toward Natchez and New Orleans.

Their refusal to return to their owners reveals the depth of despair of some slaves, many preferring to bide their time awaiting an opportunity to escape. In the early years, jails were often crudely built, sometimes with dirt floors, wooden windows, flimsy doors, and no guards during the night. To free his friend in Vicksburg in 1819, an outlying slave sneaked up to the Warren County jail several nights in a row "with an augur and other implements and did brake open the Doors of the Jail." Both slaves were caught, and the visitor had his ears cropped and received thirty-nine lashes. Two jailed runaways in Monroe County, Mississippi, fared better. According to the sheriff they "got out and made their escape so that they could not be got." The jail was "wholly insufficient to answer the ends of public justice." Much the same could be said for many other county facilities in the west.

Even when jails were more solidly constructed, ingenious slaves found ways to escape. Two Amherst County, Virginia, slaves dug their way to freedom. "In the construction of the room set apart for such prisoners," the jailer testified, "there was a deep sink dug out in the floor to be used for the purposes of a necessary." Ned and another runaway "got into this sink and by some means still unknown to any persons worked a hole under the Wall of the Jail and up to the surface of the ground on the outer side thereof." In 1854, shortly after being imprisoned in the Middlesex County jail, John burned the hinges

off the jailhouse door and made his escape. A witness said that "the Jail was burning, the front door was Standing a little open, the roof was on fire, near the center." John had covered the windows with a quilt and straw mattress, used a burning stick from the stove to ignite the facings next to the hinges on the door, and escaped either by prying the back of the door open or climbing through a large hole in the burning roof.

With its high brick walls and huge iron gate, Lynch's yard in St. Louis seemed virtually escape-proof. On Christmas night 1854, the slave Aaron, placed in the yard by the son of his owner because they believed he was plotting an escape, proved them right. Aaron neither scaled the wall nor assaulted the gatekeeper. He merely convinced a trusted fellow bondsman, who had been given the key to the front gate, to run away with him. Lynch "had entrusted the key of the yard to a slave he had bought sometime previous," the son of Aaron's owner testified,

his negro came to him (Lynch) about dusk in the evening & gave him a Key which Lynch thought was as usual the Key of the yard, he put it in his pocket and sometime after when he found that his own negro & the Plaintiff's had escaped together he found it was not the key of the yard.

In Charleston during the 1830s, escapes became so frequent that the city fathers passed an ordinance in 1839 to reorganize the workhouse. The statute provided for the establishment of a public market for the sale of slaves, stipulated that the master be required to admit and confine any slaves "delivered into his charge" and provided compensation to owners for blacks who broke out of jail. Not only would the owner be allowed "such damages as the owner of such Slave shall sustain by reason of his escape"—that is, for hiring slave catchers, sending agents, jail fees—but "also for the value of such Slave if the same be not apprehended within three months from the time of his or her escaping." Despite the law, breakouts continued and grew increasingly violent. When John, a slave owned by A. V. Toomer, escaped in 1849, he "grievously wounded" three white men before he was finally captured and executed.

As the runaway traffic increased along the lower Mississippi River, the jails in New Orleans, Baton Rouge, Natchez, and Vicksburg became so overcrowded and unhealthy that slave owners complained to public authorities. In some cases, the owners said, their slaves suffered greatly during the months they were incarcerated. Even when owners received prompt notification, runaways languished in the small, cramped jails. In 1829, the Mississippi legislature passed a special act permitting runaways jailed in Vicksburg to receive daily exercise by cleaning and repairing the streets. They would work, the law said, in chain gangs. By the 1840s, the rapidly growing trade center of Memphis was experiencing the same difficulties. On any given day, a group of residents asserted, eight or ten runaways were crowded into a few small, unhealthy cells. There were more runaways arriving in the city than at any other location in Tennessee. In 1841, Memphis leaders, too, asked the state legislature to pass a law permitting them to take jailed slaves outdoors to work in chain gangs.

Most incarcerated runaways, of course, did not face death, escape, or the chain gang. They were simply returned to their owners. The system that sent slaves back to their owners grew and expanded over the years as the number of patrollers increased, new jails were constructed, revised state and local laws were passed, and rewards were increased. James Knox was part of this system. A landless white, he received small rewards for hunting down runaways. Whatever the amount of the reward, however, his tenacious pursuit of Big Sandy went beyond profit. He, like Sandy's owner, was determined to keep order, maintain discipline, and curb resistance. The desperate struggle in the gully in East Baton Rouge Parish, Louisiana, in 1856 represented more than the confrontation between slave catcher and slave; it symbolized the struggle within slavery itself, a struggle involving hunters and the hunted.

QUESTIONS TO CONSIDER

1 Why was Rachel O'Connor, a plantation mistress, distressed over the deep affection that she felt toward many of her slave children? What was the fate of several members of her "black family"?

2 Explain why the slave trade often divided children from parents and husbands and wives from each other. Why would slaves bring a greater profit when sold individually rather than in family groups?

3 What purpose did slave catchers like James C. Knox serve southern slave owners? What cruel weapons did they employ to catch runaways? For example, how did such men train their "negro dogs"? Why do the authors maintain that the capture of runaways often had the spirit of a sporting event?

4 Describe the conditions that captured runaways had to endure in private slave "pens" and public jails in the South. Why was escape from incarceration sometimes an easy task?

5 Explain the authors' conclusion that the fight between James C. Knox and Big Sandy "symbolized the struggle within slavery itself, a struggle involving hunters and the hunted." Why did runaways damage the image of slavery that southern whites presented to the outside world? Why did masters try to walk a fine line between disciplining runaways and trying to guard them against death or permanent injury?

6 Imagine that you are a slave on a plantation somewhere in Dixie. How would you suffer from living under the lash of slavery and the constant threat of being sold off to slave traders? Would you accept the horrors of slavery and the domestic slave trade, finding ways to endure the unendurable? Or would you run away? If you choose to run, what would be your objective?

24 Let My People Go: Harriet Tubman and the Underground Railroad

BENJAMIN QUARLES

The fabled Underground Railroad consisted of secret routes that runaway slaves took to the North and freedom. Though one historian has argued that the Underground Railroad was never so highly organized as legend claims, the system did exist, and its conductors, always black, were brave men and women who stole into slave territory and escorted bands of slaves to the North, relying on black and white homesteads, called "stations," to hide and feed them along the way. Harriet Beecher Stowe said that she and her husband hid fugitives in their barn while they were living in Cincinnati, Ohio; and her great novel, Uncle Tom's Cabin, *drew on a real-life story in describing how Eliza Harris and her child escaped north on the Underground Railroad.*

For African Americans of the antebellum period, as Benjamin Quarles says in the following selection, the Underground Railroad was the most effective means of undermining the slave system and the white-coined myth of the slaves as obsequious Sambos who were happy with their lot. But since most of the northern states had black laws that discriminated against African Americans, denying them the right to vote, run for political office, sit on juries, attend public schools, marry whites, work at skilled jobs, and even be buried in white cemeteries, many fugitives went on to Canada, with the full approval of the Canadian government, where they could work as skilled laborers and enjoy a greater degree of freedom than they could in the United States. After the passage of the stringent new federal fugitive slave law in 1850, more runaways than ever sought refuge in Canada.

Harriet Tubman was the Underground Railroad's most famous conductor. Born a slave on Maryland's Eastern Shore, Tubman "stole" herself in 1849 by escaping to Philadelphia. In the years that followed, she slipped back into slaveholding Maryland, rifle in hand, at least fifteen times, and escorted some two hundred slaves, including her own parents, to freedom. In his marvelous book, Pioneers in Protest *(1968), Lerone Bennett, Jr., describes how Tubman operated once she was in slave territory: "She made her way to selected plantations where slaves were informed of her presence by code songs, prayers, or some other stratagem. Selected slaves were then apprised of the rendezvous area and the time of departure. Once the slaves were assembled, Harriet sized them up, searching them closely with her eyes. Satisfied, she placed the group under strict military discipline. During the trip, she was in absolute and total control and no one could question her orders. William Still, the black rebel who operated the key Philadelphia station of the Underground Railroad, said she 'had a very short and pointed rule of law of her own which implied death to anyone who talked of giving out and going back.' Once a slave committed himself to a Tubman escape, he was committed to freedom or death. On several occasions, slaves collapsed and said they were tired, sick, scared. Harriet always cocked her [rifle] and said: 'You go on or die. Dead Negros tell no tales.' Faced with a determined Harriet Tubman, slaves always found new strength and determination. During ten years of guerrilla action, the great commando leader never lost a slave through capture or return."*

Benjamin Quarles, one of our most eminent historians and an African American, offers a warm and sympathetic portrait of the great conductor, gently pulling back the legends that surround her to show us what she was like as a human being. Along the way, Quarles gives us judicious insights into the operations and significance of the Underground Railroad; and he concludes with a profound statement about Harriet Tubman as a symbol for the black struggle today.

GLOSSARY

BROWN, JOHN Militant white abolitionist who believed that slavery was too entrenched in the American system ever to be removed except by violent means. In 1859, he led a raid against the federal arsenal and armory at Harpers Ferry, Virginia, and seized the guns there. His goal was to destroy slavery by invading the South and inciting a vast slave uprising; or, failing that, by polarizing the sections and provoking a violent upheaval in which slavery would be wiped out. He was captured at Harpers Ferry and hanged.

GARRETT, THOMAS Delaware abolitionist and leader of the Society of Friends who assisted Harriet Tubman, providing money and shelter as she brought slaves north on the Underground Railroad.

SEWARD, WILLIAM H. United States senator from New York and a powerful leader of the all-northern Republican party.

STILL, WILLIAM Prominent free black who headed the General Vigilance Committee of Philadelphia and the Underground Railroad's "key station" in that city. He, too, assisted Harriet Tubman in her slave-liberating operations.

STOWE, HARRIET BEECHER Author of *Uncle Tom's Cabin* (1852), the most popular novel of the nineteenth century and a passionate indictment of the cruelties of the South's slave system.

TRUTH, SOJOURNER Like Tubman, "a deeply religious former slave" who was unlettered but eloquent. Truth was "primarily a women's rights activist" in the North.

" I grew up like a neglected weed—ignorant of liberty, having no experience of it." The speaker, a short, spare, black-skinned woman of thirty-five, was being interviewed at her home in St. Catherines, Ontario, in the summer of 1855. "Now, I've been free," she added, "I know what a dreadful condition slavery is." The speaker's interviewer, Benjamin Drew, a Boston school principal and a part-time journalist, made "verbal alterations" (as he put it) in the broken English of Harriet Ross Tubman, but he caught the animated spirit that would give meaning and purpose to a long career then in its budding stages.

From Benjamin Quarles, "Let My People Go: Harriet Tubman and the Underground Railroad," originally titled "Harriet Tubman's Unlikely Leadership," from Leon Litwack and August Meier (eds.), *Black Leaders of the Nineteenth Century* (Urbana: University of Illinois Press, 1988). Copyright © 1988 by the Board of Trustees of the University of Illinois. Used with permission of the University of Illinois Press.

A rescuer of slaves, Tubman had achieved nearly mythic status within ten years after her own dash for freedom. Save for the white South, contemporary references to her invariably bore a eulogistic ring. The author and reformer Thomas Wentworth Higginson dubbed her "the greatest heroine of the age," in a letter (June 17, 1859) to his mother. "Her tales of adventure are beyond anything in fiction and her ingenuity and generalship are extraordinary. I have known her for some time—the slaves call her Moses."

A present-day scholar, Larry Gara, holds that "the legendary exploits of Harriet Tubman are undoubtedly exaggerated." But it is equally undeniable that Tubman has resisted being demythologized. One who lived into her early nineties, she proved to be a legend that would not fade in the memory of her contemporaries and a figure who would find a niche in folk literature ("a heroine in homespun") as well as on the pages of the more formally written histories.

Whence the source of Tubman's imperishable legendary status? As the premiere conductor on a

Harriet Tubman (c. 1820–1913), known as "the Moses of her people" because of her heroic work on the Underground Railroad. She liberated some two hundred slaves in Maryland and escorted them north to freedom. (North Wind Picture Archives)

legendary liberty line, the Underground Railroad, Tubman might elude the sniffing dogs of the slave catchers but she could hardly escape the legends that would attach to her name. Tales of derring-do inevitably cluster around those whose operations, by their very nature, have to be clothed in secrecy. Moreover, in the case of the tight-lipped Tubman, legend had to fill in for her ingrained reticence about her activities, a circumstance growing out of her experiences as a slave and as a rescuer of slaves. Even after the crusade against slavery and its death in the Civil War, Tubman's modesty kept her from recounting her role in either occurrence; a brief, passing mention on a rare occasion was the extent to which she ever unburdened herself as to those

by-gone days. The Tubman legendry was also stimulated by her illiteracy, hearsay having to fill in for written records.

Contributing significantly to her fame, Tubman's legendary status played an important part in elevating her to a leadership level that she had not sought but did not spurn. Believing that her actions were preordained, she remained indifferent to whatever the sources of her power, whether stemming from her actual accomplishments or from a romancer's exuberance of spirit.

Even shorn of myth the existential Tubman compiled an impressive record, leaving her mark on our national history. This influence may be assessed by noting in turn her interrelationships with other blacks of her own day and time and her interaction with her white contemporaries, closing with a glance at her hold on the American mind since her death in 1913—an image that has not lost its luster.

Her basic story is readily grasped, furnishing background and providing us a glimpse into the Tubman psyche, her value system, and her vision of the world. Born in 1821 in Dorchester County, not far from the town of Cambridge on Maryland's Eastern Shore, she was one of the eleven children of Harriet Greene and Benjamin Ross, both slaves. Called Araminta as a baby, but later choosing the name of her mother, Harriet was put to work by the time she was five. For seven years she did general housework, including services as child's nurse and maid. Losing her house-slave status while still in her teens, Harriet then labored in the fields, a circumstance that would lead to her famed muscular strength and the physical endurance that belied her spare figure and habitually underfed look.

Two or three years after becoming a fieldhand, Harriet had an experience that marked her for life. She was struck on the head by a two-pound weight hurled at another slave, whom she was attempting to shield from a wrathful overseer. She never fully recovered from this nearly fatal blow. By swathing her head in a turban she could conceal the deep scar on her skull, but for the rest of her life she was prone to recurring seizures of deep, sudden sleep. She did regain her strength, however, and her capacity for manual labor rivaled that of a man by the time she was twenty.

Harriet's hard life in slavery was lessened a little by her marriage in 1844 to John Tubman. A free black, he lacked his wife's willpower and sense of mission and scoffed at her forebodings. Not fully reciprocating her deep affection for him, he did not join her after she made the dash for freedom; indeed, he soon took another wife. Losing the man, Harriet kept the name, even after taking a second husband in 1869.

One of Harriet Tubman's forebodings, the dread of being sold to the Deep South, took on a new intensity in 1849 upon the death of her master and the rumor that his estate would be broken up and his property dispersed. Impelled to delay no longer, she made her way to free-soil Pennsylvania. Upon her arrival she felt, she said, like she was in heaven.

Tubman's mood of exultation quickly gave way to a resolve to help others become free. As her schemes required money, she moved to Philadelphia and took work in a hotel, the first in a series of part-time jobs. After a year of penny-pinching frugality, she had saved enough to launch the first of her uniformly successful operations, a trip to Baltimore to rescue her sister, Mary Ann Bowley, and her two children.

To give a connected recital of Tubman's subsequent journeys into slavery locales is not possible. Insofar as she could, she operated in secret. Even had she been able to read and write, her sense of taking no unnecessary risks would have inhibited from her keeping a record of her movements. In some ten years of rescue work she made at least fifteen trips southward, personally escorting at least 200 freedom-bound slaves.

Tubman's traits of character and her methods of operation help to explain this extraordinary record. She was courageous, undeterred by the knowledge that there was a price upon her head. Her bravery was matched, moreover, by her coolness in a tight spot, her resourcefulness in a perilous situation. If the fugitives she led lacked her fearlessness, they were silenced by her blunt, no-nonsense manner. The rifle she carried while on rescue trips was not only for protection against slave catchers but also to intimidate any fugitive who became faint of heart and wished to turn back.

Her character molded by a deep reservoir of faith in God, Tubman felt that Divine Providence had willed her freedom and that a guardian angel accompanied her, particularly on her missions of deliverance. Gospel exhortations and spirituals came readily to her lips. When she was referred to as Moses, she did not demur.

If Tubman had complete trust in the Infinite, she also exercised great care in planning operations. She was unsurpassed in the logistics of escape—in anticipating the needs of her fugitive flocks, whether for food or clothes, disguises or forged passes, train tickets or wagons. Every precaution was carefully considered, down to carrying paregoric for fretful babies whose crying might jeopardize the escaping party. Well might she boast that she never lost a passenger.

Tubman was not a one-woman Underground Railroad, however, as this secretive mode of passage required a concerted effort. Her careful planning included full cooperation with others, and she worked hand in hand with two of the most dedicated stationmasters, Thomas Garrett in Wilmington, Delaware, and William Still in Philadelphia. Both assisted her by providing shelter for the fugitives she conducted and by making arrangements, if necessary, for their transportation further north. . . .

To blacks of the antebellum period, North and South, the central theme was the abolition of slavery. Of all the ways to bring this about the most direct, short of insurrection or war, and hence the most satisfying, was the Underground Railroad—the cooperative work of assisting slaves to run away and then assisting them to get a fresh start as free men, women, and children. In matters relating to fugitive slaves, blacks had a personal and vital interest, a particular sense of responsibility toward one another. In the process of striking at slavery, a black Underground Railroad operator was also striking at the conjoined caricature of a free black as a shiftless ne'er-do-well and of the slave as a submissive Sambo.

In the operations of the Underground Railroad the conductors, those who ventured into slave terrain seeking out prospective escapees, were invariably black, and none was better known than Harriet Tubman. To Afro-Americans she personified resistance to slavery as did no other single figure of her generation. She symbolized courage, determination, and strength.

In slave circles her status was unexcelled. The folklorist Harold Courlander points out that in the isolated communities in which many slaves were located Tubman's name was hardly likely to have been a household word, and when some slaves sang "Go Down, Moses," they must have done so "in the belief that Moses simply meant Moses." True enough. Yet Tubman's name was likely to have been an inspiration to thousands she never met, slave communities having their own systems of communication. Thomas Cole, a runaway slave from Huntsville, Alabama, said that during his escape he "was hopin and prayin all de time dat I could meets up wid dat Harriet Tubman woman." Whether in the flesh or as a symbol, Tubman made slave property less secure.

Tubman's sway over the slaves she sought to rescue was unquestionably absolute. In her relationships with those fugitives her unconscious and unstudied inclination toward self-dramatization came into its fullest sway. Communicating with slaves was easy for her. In overcoming the barrier of their mutual illiteracy, Tubman was verbally resourceful to the point of creativity, an unpolished eloquence being second nature to her. She was nothing if not action-bent, but to accomplish the deed she did not scorn the word. Far from empty, her rhetoric came from a well-stocked mind. As a slave she had developed her powers of recall, memorizing recited passages from the Bible. Her visual memory was no less acute, enabling her to interlard her discourses with homely details of earlier sights and scenes. She had the gift of tongue, a trait much admired by slaves and one that made a lasting impression on them.

Tubman had a strong singing voice, adding to her hold on the fugitives. Her repertoire consisted of those spirituals that bore a barely concealed freedom ring, abounding in code words and double meanings, such as "Didn't My Lord Deliver Daniel?" As used by Tubman, whether to announce her presence in some secluded spot or to keep up the group morale at strategically timed intervals while on the road, such songs became part of slave rescue apparatus. To those she escorted to freedom, one spiritual inevitably came to acquire a special significance. It was first sung some forty years before Tubman's birth, and to the runaways it took on the aspects of prophesy now come to pass. Having lodged itself in their hearts, it came readily to their lips:

> Go down, Moses,
> Way down in Egypt land.
> Tell ole Pharaoh
> Let my people go.

Obviously, too, Tubman's profound religious faith impressed the fugitives. Themselves church-oriented, they quickly recognized in her a deeper sense of Christian commitment than was customary and a great trust in Divine Providence. Praying frequently, spontaneously and with obvious conviction and expectation, Tubman seemed to find it easy to communicate with the Deity, and sometimes she seemed as though she had received a direct reply. Hence, although the biblically knowledgeable slaves knew that God was no respecter of persons, they might sometimes have wondered whether this held for Harriet Tubman.

If the slaves and fugitives revered her, the free blacks held her in the highest esteem short of worship. In the South her free black admirers would have to speak her praises privately and in hushed tones, but blacks north of slavery sang her name in full voice, removing any doubt as to their acclaim. The black in the best position to appraise Tubman and her work was the Philadelphia-based William Still, second only to Tubman herself as the leading black figure in the Underground Railroad. As secretary and executive director of the General Vigilance Committee, Still assisted the runaways reaching Philadelphia. Every major northern city had a similar vigilance committee, but the group in Philadelphia had no equal, in large part because of Still's energetic and resourceful leadership. From his many years of working in concert with Tubman, in 1872 Still offered this assessment of her: "A more ordinary specimen of humanity could hardly be found among the most unfortunate-looking farm hands of the South. Yet in point of courage, shrewdness and disinterested exertions to rescue her fellow-men, she was without equal. . . . Her like it is probable was never known before or since."

A similarly belated appraisal came from Frederick Douglass, like Tubman an escaped slave from Maryland. In a letter he told her that he had "wrought in the day" and to public attention and applause, whereas she had "wrought in the night," her witnesses the midnight sky and the silent stars. But, he went on, "excepting John Brown—of sacred memory—I know of no one who has willingly encountered more perils and hardships to serve our enslaved people than you."

In referring to Tubman, her northern-based black contemporaries readily used the term "heroine." When in April 1860 in Troy, New York, she led a group of rescuers that overpowered the officers and assisted Charles Nalle, a fugitive slave, to escape to Canada, *The Weekly Anglo-African* (May 12, 1860) praised her "intrepidity," capping their assessment with a complimentary comparison: "She acted like a heroine." During the Civil War, when the young schoolteacher Charlotte L. Forten visited Beaufort, South Carolina, she was ecstatic about Tubman, an entry in her diary for January 31, 1863, expressing her admiration: "We spent all our time at Harriet Tubman's. She is a wonderful woman—a real heroine." This theme recurs in a later notation in the diary for the same day: "My own eyes were full as I listened to her—the heroic woman."

Many antebellum blacks linked Tubman's name with that of Sojourner Truth, the two having much in common. Both were deeply religious former slaves. Like Tubman, the unschooled Truth had a rude eloquence, but unlike Tubman, she was a familiar figure on the lecture circuit, her six-foot frame and deep, resonant voice not without their effects on an audience. Primarily a women's rights activist, Truth played only a minor role in the Underground Railroad. Apparently the first time the two reformers met was in Boston in August 1864, Truth then assuring Tubman that President Lincoln was "our friend," in an effort to allay the latter's doubts on that score. . . .

"Not many of us are animated with the idea which seems to have possessed Harriet Tubman throughout her eventful life—to lay out time, talents, and opportunities for God's glory, and the good of our fellow-men," wrote schoolteacher Pauline E. Hopkins in 1902 in *The Colored American Magazine*. It was an evaluation that few blacks of her day would have questioned. Who among them, in a single person, had demonstrated more of a physical courage amounting to bravery, had lived a life more dedicated to the service of others, had exhibited more traits of an impeccable character, or had a deeper faith in the working of a Divine Providence?

An appraisal somewhat less celebratory and expansive characterized the reaction to Tubman by her white reformist allies. While singing her praises, white admirers hardly viewed her in the capacity of a leader or role model. While ever cordial and devoid of the person-to-person tensions so characteristic among black and white co-workers in reform movements, Tubman's experiences across the color line were not free of racial overtones, reflecting something of the prevailing patterns in race relations and attitudes. Her earliest experiences with white people were hardly reassuring. As a slave she had been constantly overworked and often whipped, whether by her master or those to whom she was hired out. She could never forget the angry overseer who had marked her for life, and she would have no fond memories of a kind and indulgent mistress. As she later explained, she had "heard tell" that there were good masters and mistresses but had not come across any of them.

Locating in Philadelphia after her escape, Tubman came in contact with a white population many of whom were in sympathy with runaway slaves and would incur any risk in assisting them. In 1775 the first organized society against slavery was founded there, its lengthy title indicating its broad program: the Pennsylvania Society for Promoting the Abolition of Slavery, the Relief of Free Negroes Unlawfully Held in Bondage, and for Improving the Condition of the African Race. Tubman became acquainted with abolitionist whites through her association with the General Vigilance Committee, which, though headed by William Still, was interracial in composition. White Underground Railroad operators in Pennsylvania and Delaware reflected a strong Quaker influence, as Tubman quickly found out.

The single white with whom Tubman worked most closely was Thomas Garrett of Wilmington, Delaware, a lifelong member of the Society of Friends. A key figure in slave rescue work along the mid-Atlantic corridor, Garrett gave much of his time and means and ran some risks to his personal safety, Delaware being a slave state. He provided shelter for the fugitives Tubman led and furnished her with the money to carry them on to Philadelphia and beyond. In August 1857, when Tubman's escaping parents were passing through Wilmington, Garrett gave them thirty dollars to pay their way to Canada. In soliciting funds for Tubman's trips, Garrett wrote to such well-wishers as the Edinburgh Anti-Slavery Society (Scotland), telling them of her exploits. "To our brave Harriet he often rendered most efficient help in her journeys back and forth," wrote Tubman's first biographer, Sarah Bradford. In a letter to William Still on the eve of the Civil War (December 1, 1860), Garrett made a typical reference to their co-worker: "I write to let thee know that Harriet Tubman is again in these parts. She arrived last evening from one of her trips of mercy to God's poor, bringing two men with her as far as New Castle. . . ."

Tubman's attitude toward white people was shaped by her contact with reformers like Garrett— men and women who raised money for her and also gave her a kind of affection and a measure of respect. As a rule, the reform-minded whites with whom she became acquainted liked her. The courage and daring of the runaways was a stimulus to the abolitionist crusade, and Tubman personified the heroic slave.

Whites also liked Tubman because in person-to-person contacts she did not make them feel uncomfortable, burdening them with a sense of guilt. Her language and manner were marked by an absence of bitterness. To whites she was nonthreatening, not pushy, not peer-basis-minded, not status conscious, and hence not given to self-pity or bent on upward mobility. In speaking in public she tended to be folksy, anecdotal, and given to reminiscence. "She spoke in a style of quaint simplicity," wrote a reporter in 1859. Tubman was not likely to pose questions a predominantly white audience would find awkward, such as Sojourner Truth's "Is God dead?" or the Frederick Douglass inquiry as to what the Fourth of July might or might not mean to the slaves.

By their financial support the white abolitionists expressed their kindly sentiments toward Tubman. In addition to raising money specifically for her slave rescue work, they assisted her in purchasing a home in Auburn, New York, for her parents. A befriender of Tubman's, Senator William H. Seward of New York, had sold her the home on liberal terms, and to pay for it she received unsolicited donations from other white supporters. At the annual meeting of the Massachusetts Anti-Slavery Society in 1859, its president, Thomas Wentworth Higginson, asked for a collection to assist her in buying the house so that "her father and mother could support themselves, and enable her to resume the practice of her profession!" Higginson's observation was greeted by "laughter and applause."

In private, as in public, Tubman and her white associates apparently had little trouble adjusting to each other. In their homes, as in their public gatherings, Tubman expected to be hospitably received, and to a greater extent than any other antebellum black she was. Unlike some former slaves, the uninhibited Tubman seems not to have felt ill at ease in a white household, however educated or affluent the family might be.

No white reformer held Tubman in higher respect and esteem than John Brown, who made it a point to establish personal contacts with black leaders. He regarded her as a kindred spirit, and she fitted into his plans as the shepherd of the slaves he proposed to run off, by force of arms, if necessary. He was well aware that Tubman was not gun-shy (Who in abolitionist circles had not heard of the long rifle she carried on her slave rescue trips?). Brown was also aware that the Tubman name would help him raise money from her white admirers, particularly those in Massachusetts. During the eighteen months before his raid on Harpers Ferry, Virginia, in October 1859, Brown met with Tubman on some half dozen occasions, one of them lasting nearly a week. His opinion of her fortified, he called her "General" and, according to his confidant and biographer, Franklin B. Sanborn, "she was fully conversant with his plans."

Apparently due to illness, Tubman did not accompany Brown to Harpers Ferry. Immediately after the abortive raid Frederick Douglass fled to Canada to avoid being served an arrest warrant issued against him as a Brown accomplice. No such warrant was issued for Tubman; even had there been legally admissible evidence of her complicity, an arrest warrant would hardly have been practical for someone whose whereabouts were a mystery.

Brown's hanging impelled Tubman to give his life a scriptural interpretation. She promptly confided to Sanborn that she had "been studying and studying upon it, and its clar to me, it wasn't John Brown that died on the gallows. When I think how he gave up his life for our people, and how he never flinched, but was so brave to the end; its clar to me it wasn't mortal man, it was God in him." The hanged Brown never left Tubman's memory. In an interview in 1912, reporter Anne Fitzhugh Miller quoted her as referring to Brown as "my dearest Friend.". . .

[During the Civil War, which she had predicted, Tubman served as a spy and a scout for the Union army, leading expeditions into the Confederate interior to liberate slaves from enemy plantations. Her services at the battlefront drew high praise from the white officers who fought with her. After the war, she devoted herself to charitable work for African Americans and was an outspoken advocate for women's rights. For her, women's liberation and racial liberation were "inseparably linked."]

Tubman's broad appeal, cutting across lines of race and class, age and gender, received public expression upon her death. The *New York Times* carried a two-paragraph obituary (March 14, 1913), and her funeral was attended by the local post of the Grand Army of the Republic. The city of Auburn, after a year's preparation, held a day-long memorial service on June 1914, unveiling a tablet in her honor. On that day many homes flew the Stars and Stripes, thereby demonstrating "that we are not forgetful of those who suffered for the cause of freedom," in the exhortatory accents of Major Charles W. Brister. At the evening exercises held in the city auditorium the featured speaker, Booker T. Washington, eulogized Tubman as one who "brought the two races together."

Beginning rather then ending with the observance at Auburn, the memorials to Harriet Tubman would continue over the years, taking a variety of forms and expressions. The national sentiment toward her was conveyed by agencies of the federal government. During World War II a liberty ship was christened the *Harriet Tubman*, prompting President Franklin D. Roosevelt to praise the U.S. Maritime Commission for having chosen so appropriate a name. In 1974 the Department of the Interior gave her Auburn home the status of a national historic landmark, and four years later the U.S. Postal Service issued a thirteen-cent Harriet Tubman commemorative stamp, the first in a "Black Heritage U.S.A. Series."

The mounting interest in women's history, a field sorely neglected until recent decades, has aided in keeping Tubman before us. Pointing out (in 1978) that black protest literature had focused largely on males, historian George P. Rawick advanced a corrective suggestion: "Why must we always use Nat as the name for the rebellious slave? Why not Harriet? The women's liberation movement has for some time used a poster that reproduces the image of Harriet Tubman with a long rifle. I think that might be a good symbol for the black struggle.". . .

QUESTIONS TO CONSIDER

1 What were Harriet's experiences in living under the lash in slaveholding Maryland? What factors prompted her to "steal" herself and escape to the North?

2 Why do you think Tubman invaded the South fifteen times to bring at least two hundred of her fellow slaves north to freedom? What was her incentive? Why was she so successful? What were the unique character traits of this extraordinary woman?

3 Quarles points out that Tubman was "not a one-woman Underground Railroad." What does he mean? In what ways was the Underground Railroad a cooperative operation? Name two prominent stationmasters who assisted Tubman in her slave-liberation expeditions. How did her operations and those of the Underground Railroad in general undermine the slave system and strike a blow at the white myth of the happy Sambo?

4 Who do you think is a more appropriate symbol for the rebellious slave, Nat Turner or Harriet Tubman? Explain the reasons for your choice.

5 The last two articles expose slavery as the brutal, totalitarian system that it really was. What facet of that system caused the strongest reaction in you both emotionally and intellectually? Explain your thoughts and feelings in detail.

PART THIRTEEN

The Death of Slavery

25 The Father of American Terrorism

KEN CHOWDER

Sectional conflict over slavery existed from the beginning of the Republic. It continued through the Federalist, Jefferson, and Jacksonian eras, becoming especially acute with the rise of the abolitionist crusade in the 1830s. Then, during the era of expansion and the Mexican War, the debate over slavery shifted to the western territories. By midcentury, as historian James M. McPherson says in Battle Cry of Freedom: The Civil War Era *(1988), "the greatest danger to American survival . . . was sectional conflict between North and South over the future of slavery." Indeed, from the 1840s on, every major sectional conflict involved the complex slavery issue, especially the expansion of slavery into the western territories and any future territories the United States might acquire. By 1848, slavery had become the central issue in American politics.*

The decade of the 1850s was a time of spiraling violence over slavery. In 1856, civil war between proslavery and antislavery pioneers broke out in the newly established Kansas Territory in the nation's heartland. When Americans started killing Americans in "Bleeding Kansas" over the future of slavery, it was a dress rehearsal for the national cataclysm a few years later.

The violent and bitter struggle over slavery reached a shattering climax in John Brown's raid at Harpers Ferry on a rain-swept October night in 1859. Brown's objective was to destroy slavery by inciting a massive, Nat Turner–style slave insurrection across the entire South. Or, failing that, he hoped that his raid would polarize the free states and slave states and lead to a blowup in which slavery itself would perish.

Brown's Harpers Ferry attack made him one of the most controversial figures in American history. When Virginia authorities captured and hanged Brown for his efforts, his admirers heralded him as an immortal American hero who (in the words of Ralph Waldo Emerson) "made the gallows as glorious as the cross." By contrast, his detractors damned Brown as a "mean, terrible, vicious man," a murderer and a maniac who sought to put the slaveholding South to the torch. For more than a century, Americans have engaged in such a heated controversy over whether Brown was right or wrong, sane or crazy, hero or fanatic, that scarcely anyone has taken the time to try to understand him.

For fifty-nine-year-old John Brown, a white man who had failed in virtually everything he had ever tried, the attack against Harpers Ferry was the supreme moment of his life, the moment he had been working for since he had committed himself to violence in the Kansas civil war in 1856. He and his handful of fellow revolutionaries—most of them young, five of them black—were going to liberate some four million human beings from bondage, thereby removing a monstrous wrong from American society. For Brown, slavery was an egregious "sin against God," a sin that violated the commandments of Jehovah, the angry God of the Old Testament. In Brown's eyes, slavery also contradicted the Declaration of Independence, which guaranteed all men the right to life, liberty, and the pursuit of happiness. Slavery violated Brown's secular views as well: his passionate commitment to the nuclear family (he had read about the brutal breakup of slave families), his belief in the right of all men to enjoy the fruits of their labor and to raise themselves above the condition of their birth.

Yet, instead of eradicating slavery, the United States had institutionalized that cruel institution, surrounding it with a network of constitutional and political safeguards quite as though the Declaration of Independence did not exist. Such hypocrisy enraged Brown. How could Americans sanction slavery and yet proclaim theirs the freest and most enlightened nation in the world? By 1859, he thought it impossible to remove slavery peacefully through regular political channels. As he pointed out, southerners and their northern allies dominated the crucial branches of the federal government and were using these agencies not only to preserve and perpetuate slavery, but also to extend it into the western territories. Moreover, in the infamous Dred Scott decision, the United States Supreme Court, controlled by proslavery southern Democrats, had denied African Americans the right of United States citizenship and had forbidden Congress or territorial legislatures to exclude slavery from the public lands. And in Brown's opinion few northerners seemed to care. Northern Democrats, he fumed, were all "doughfaces" who enjoyed licking up "Southern spittle." Republicans, he argued, were too "wishy-washy" about slavery to do anything about that institution, and the abolitionists were a bunch of "milk-and-water" pacifists who preferred talk to action. By the late 1850s, Brown asserted, slavery had become too entrenched in American life ever to be expunged by peaceful means. The only way to destroy this "hellish" institution was to annihilate it by revolutionary violence—and by the extermination of Brown's entire generation of men, women, and children, if that were the will of Jehovah. And Brown believed passionately that this was Jehovah's will, and that He had chosen Brown to be His special angel of death to root out slavery by the sword.

As it turned out, Brown's attack at Harpers Ferry traumatized the South as had no other event in history, and it spun the nation irreversibly toward civil war. White southerners viewed Harpers Ferry as a violent outgrowth of northern antislavery agitation, an act of "outside provocation" that caused them to equate Brown's style of revolutionary violence with Lincoln and the Republican party. Like the sinking of the battleship Maine *and the attack on Pearl Harbor, Brown's raid enflamed emotions to such intensity that rational dialogue was no longer possible. Sectional tensions over slavery had reached the breaking point.*

In the following essay, Ken Chowder raises troubling questions about Brown and his times. Do some historians condemn Brown as insane because he was a white man prepared to sacrifice his life for enslaved African Americans? Before branding Brown as mentally unstable because of his religious convictions, you might recall from selection 15 that Nat Turner also invoked the Bible and God's name to justify the bloodiest slave insurrection in southern history. Nor was Brown the only white figure of his day who thought himself a pawn in the hands of an all-wise, all-powerful God. Abraham Lincoln and Robert E. Lee, among many others, held such beliefs, yet few have ever called them maniacs or religious fanatics.

Consider a final question. Does the "violent, excessive, morally torn society" that produced Brown resemble the deeply troubled America of our own time? Chowder's title, "The Father of American Terrorism," suggests that Brown was the ancestor of modern American terrorists like Timothy McVeigh, who bombed the federal building in Oklahoma City in the 1990s because of his perceived grievances against the federal government. Do you think this is correct? Or is this an example of "presentism" discussed in selection 8—of imposing today's standards and difficulties on the people of the past? These are troubling questions, and we hope that discussing them in the class-room will give you a deeper understanding, not only of John Brown's world, but of your own.

GLOSSARY

BEECHER, HENRY WARD   A popular minister and an outspoken critic of slavery, Beecher contended that Brown's death made him a great martyr to the abolitionist movement. His sister, Harriet Beecher Stowe, wrote the best-selling novel *Uncle Tom's Cabin,* which converted countless readers to the antislavery cause.

BOOTH, JOHN WILKES   After witnessing Brown's execution, this prominent actor called Brown "a traitor," viewing him "with unlimited, undeniable contempt." A Maryland native, Booth had powerful pro-Confederate sympathies. Although he declined to fight in the rebel army, he did serve as a secret Confederate agent. In April 1865, he murdered President Lincoln at Ford's Theater.

BORDER RUFFIANS   Proslavery Missourians who crossed the border into neighboring Kansas, terrorizing free-state communities and voting illegally in Kansas elections; in 1855, they helped elect a proslavery territorial legislature in Kansas.

DOUGLASS, FREDERICK   A runaway slave, newspaper editor, and perhaps the most eloquent speaker on the abolitionist circuit. His powerful autobiography provided a first-hand account of the horrors of slavery.

GARRISON, WILLIAM LLOYD   A leading abolitionist and editor of the provocative antislavery newspaper, *The Liberator* (see selection 16).

JACKSON, THOMAS J.   A professor at the Virginia Military Institute, he was present at the hanging of John Brown. He would go on to become one of the Confederacy's greatest generals. He was nicknamed "Stonewall" after his heroics during the first battle of Manassas (also known as Bull Run).

KANSAS-NEBRASKA ACT (1854)   The brainchild of United States senator Stephen A. Douglas of Illinois, this controversial measure divided the northern section of the old Louisiana Purchase Territory into two new territories, Kansas and Nebraska. The act repealed the Missouri Compromise line (1820), which had divided the Louisiana Purchase, prohibiting slavery above the line and permitting it below the line. The act established popular sovereignty as the formula for dealing with slavery in the national lands; now the citizens of a territory would settle the status of slavery there by voting it in or out. Until the residents of Kansas and Nebraska voted on the slavery issue, southern slave owners were free to take their "chattel" into a vast northern domain once reserved for freedom. The Kansas-Nebraska Act was a monumental fiasco; it greatly intensified sectional tensions and brought about both the disintegration of the Whig party and the formation of a new, all-northern antislavery party, the Republicans, who pledged to halt the spread of slavery into the territories.

LEE, ROBERT E.   A Lieutenant Colonel in the United States Army at the time of Brown's raid, this prominent Virginian commanded the force of federal marines who captured Brown and a few of his surviving raiders in the fire engine house at Harpers Ferry. Like Brown, Lee considered slavery "a moral and political evil." Yet he condemned the abolitionists as "evil" people who had caused the nation's sectional troubles. In his judgment, the fate of slavery should be left to the wisdom of God. Initially he opposed secession, agreeing with President Buchanan that it was "nothing but revolution." But when the Civil War began, he sided with his beloved Virginia and joined the rebellion. He became the Confederacy's greatest general.

LOVEJOY, ELIJAH   An abolitionist editor who published an antislavery newspaper in Alton, Illinois. In 1837, a mob from Missouri, a slave state, murdered Lovejoy and threw his printing press into the Mississippi River. Lovejoy became the first martyr in the abolitionist cause.

POTTAWATOMIE MASSACRE (1856)   After proslavery Missourians sacked the free-state settlement of Lawrence, Brown and several antislavery followers retaliated by riding back to Pottawatomie Creek in eastern Kansas and hacking five proslavery settlers to death with broadswords. Since proslavery forces had murdered six free-state men and vowed to slaughter "every Goddamned abolitionist in Kansas Territory," Brown had about evened the score. The "massacre" ignited a civil war in Kansas, which left two hundred people dead and destroyed two million dollars in property. "Bleeding Kansas" proved to be a dress rehearsal for the national conflagration that followed five years later.

SUMNER, CHARLES   In May 1856, this prominent Republican senator from Massachusetts gave a provocative speech entitled, "The Crime Against Kansas." In retaliation, South Carolina congressman Preston Brooks attacked Sumner with a cane inside the Senate chamber, almost killing him with repeated blows to the head. This assault further polarized the country. For John Brown, the beating of Sumner provided one more reason to attack his proslavery foes on Pottawatomie Creek.

THOREAU, HENRY DAVID   His book about solitary life on Walden Pond near Concord, Massachusetts, eventually earned him a prominent place in American literature. Although Thoreau was a nonviolent abolitionist, he deified Brown after he was hanged, calling him "an angel of light" and comparing him to Christ.

TURNER, NAT   (see selection 15)

UNDERGROUND RAILROAD   The system by which runaway slaves escaped to the North. "Conductors" like Harriet Tubman (see selection 24) escorted the blacks out of the South, often just ahead of the slave patrols. "Station houses" along the way furnished the fugitives with food and shelter. Brown was active in Underground Railroad operations in Ohio and Massachusetts.

O n December 2, 1859, a tall old man in a black coat, black pants, black vest, and black slouch hat climbed into a wagon and sat down on a black walnut box. The pants and coat were stained with blood; the box was his coffin; the old man was going to his execution. He had just handed a last note to his jailer: "I John Brown am now quite *certain* that the crimes of this *guilty, land: will* never be purged *away;* but with Blood. I had . . . *vainly* flattered myself that without *very much* bloodshed; it might be done."

As he rode on his coffin, John Brown gazed out over the cornfields of Virginia. "This *is* a beautiful country," he said. "I never had the pleasure of seeing it before."

The United States in 1859 was a nation that harbored a ticking time bomb: the issue of slavery. And it

was a place where an astonishing number of men were willing to die for their beliefs, certain they were following a higher law. John Brown was one of those God-fearing yet violent men. And he was already more than a man; he was a legend. In fact, there were two competing legends. To slaveholders he was utter evil—fanatic, murderer, liar, and lunatic, and horse thief to boot—while to abolitionists he had become the embodiment of all that was noble and courageous.

After a lifetime of failure John Brown had at last found a kind of success. He was now a symbol that divided the nation, and his story was no longer about one man; it was a prophecy. The United States, like John Brown, was heading toward a gallows—the gallows of war.

A scaffold had been built in a field outside Charlestown, Virginia. There were rumors of a rescue attempt, and fifteen hundred soldiers, commanded by Col. Robert E. Lee, massed in the open field. No civilians were allowed within hearing range, but an

Ken Chowder, "The Father of American Terrorism," *American Heritage*, vol. 51, no. 1 (February/March, 2000), pp. 81–91. Reprinted by permission of *American Heritage*.

An African American photographer, Augustus Washington, took this early daguerreotype of John Brown around 1846. Ken Chowder concludes that the hanging of the radical abolitionist "was not the end of John Brown; it was the beginning." (© National Portrait Gallery, Smithsonian Institution/Art Resource, NY)

actor from Virginia borrowed a uniform so he could watch John Brown die. "I looked at the traitor and terrorizer," said John Wilkes Booth, "with unlimited, undeniable contempt." Prof. Thomas Jackson, who would in three years be known as Stonewall, was also watching: "The sheriff placed the rope around [Brown's] neck, then threw a white cap over his head. . . . When the rope was cut by a single blow, Brown fell through. . . . There was very little motion of his person for several moments, and soon the wind blew his lifeless body to and fro."

A Virginia colonel named J. T. L. Preston chanted: "So perish all such enemies of Virginia! All such enemies of the Union! All such foes of the human race!"

But hanging was not the end of John Brown; it was the beginning. Northern churches' bells tolled for him, and cannon boomed in salute. In Massachusetts, Henry David Thoreau spoke: "Some eighteen hundred years ago, Christ was crucified; This morning, perchance, Captain Brown was hung. . . . He is not Old Brown any longer; he is an angel of light."

John Brown's soul was already marching on. But the flesh-and-blood John Brown—a tanner, shepherd, and farmer, a simple and innocent man who could kill in cold blood, a mixture of opposite parts who mirrored the paradoxical America of his time—this John Brown had already vanished, and he would rarely appear again. His life instead became the subject for 140 years of spin. John Brown has been used rather than considered by history; even today we are still spinning his story.

As far as history is concerned, John Brown was genuinely nobody until he was fifty-six years old—that is, until he began to kill people. Not that his life was without incident. He grew up in the wilderness of Ohio (he was born in 1800, when places like Detroit, Chicago, and Cleveland were still frontier stockades). He married at twenty, lost his wife eleven years later, soon married again, and fathered a total of twenty children. Nine of them died before they reached adulthood.

At seventeen Brown left his father's tannery to start a competing one. "I acknowledge no master in human form," he would say, many years later, when he was wounded and in chains at Harpers Ferry. The young man soon mastered the rural arts of farming, tanning, surveying, home building, and animal husbandry, but his most conspicuous talent seemed to be one for profuse and painful failure.

In the 1830s, with a growing network of canals making barren land worth thousands, Brown borrowed deeply to speculate in real estate—just in time for the disastrous Panic of 1837. The historian James Brewer Stewart, author of *Holy Warriors,* says that "Brown was a typical story of someone who invested, as thousands did, and lost thousands, as thousands did as well. Brown was swept along in a current of default and collapse."

He tried breeding sheep, started another tannery, bought and sold cattle—each time a failure. When one venture lost money, Brown quietly appropriated funds from a partner in a new business and used it to pay the earlier loss. But in the end his farm tools, furniture, and sheep went on the auction block.

When his farm was sold, he seemed to snap. He refused to leave. With two sons and some old muskets, he barricaded himself in a cabin on the property. "I was makeing preparation for the commencement and vigorous prosecution of a tedious, distressing, wasteing, and long protracted war," Brown wrote. The sheriff got up a posse and briefly put him in the Akron jail. No shots were fired, but it was an incident people would remember, years later, when the old man barricaded himself at Harpers Ferry.

Brown's misadventures in business have drawn widely varying interpretations. His defenders say he had a large family to support; small wonder he wanted badly to make money. But others have seen his financial dreams as an obsession, a kind of fever that gave him delusions of wealth and made him act dishonestly.

Perhaps it was this long string of failures that created the revolutionary who burst upon the American scene in 1856. By that time Brown had long nurtured a vague and protean plan: He imagined a great event in which he—the small-time farmer who had failed in everything he touched—would be God's messenger, a latter-day Moses who would lead his people from the accursed house of slavery. He had already, for years, been active in the Underground Railroad, hiding runaways and guiding them north toward Canada. In 1837 he stood up in the back of a church in Ohio and made his first public statement on human bondage, a single pungent sentence: "Here before God, in the presence of these witnesses, I consecrate my life to the destruction of slavery." For years, however, this vow seemed to mean relatively little; in the early 1850s, as anger over slavery began to boil up all over the North, the frustrated and humiliated Brown was going from courtroom to courtroom embroiled in his own private miseries.

Finally it happened. The John Brown we know was born in the place called Bloody Kansas. Slavery had long been barred from the territories of Kansas and Nebraska, but in 1854 the Kansas-Nebraska Act decreed that the settlers of these territories would decide by vote whether to be free or slave. The act set up a competition between the two systems that would become indistinguishable from war.

Settlers from both sides flooded into Kansas. Five of John Brown's sons made the long journey there from Ohio. But Brown himself did not go. He was in his mid-fifties, old by the actuarial tables of his day; he seemed broken.

Then, in March of 1855, five thousand proslavery Missourians—the hard-drinking, heavily armed "Border Ruffians"—rode into Kansas. "We came to vote, and we are going to vote or kill every God-damned abolitionist in the Territory," their leader declared. The Ruffians seized the polling places, voted in their own legislature, and passed their own laws. Prison now awaited anyone who spoke against slavery.

In May, John Junior wrote to his father begging for his help. The free-soilers needed arms, "more than we need bread," he said. "Now we want you to get for us these arms." The very next day, Brown began raising money and gathering weapons and in August the old man left for Kansas, continuing to collect arms as he went.

In May 1856 a proslavery army sacked the free-soil town of Lawrence; not a single abolitionist dared fire a gun. This infuriated Brown. He called for volunteers to go on "a secret mission." The old man, in his soiled straw hat, stuck a revolver in his belt and led a company of eight men down toward Pottawatomie Creek. Proslavery people lived in the cabins there.

Late on the night of May 23, 1856, one of the group, probably Brown, banged on the door of James Doyle's cabin. He ordered the men of the family outside at gunpoint, and Brown's followers set upon three Doyles with broadswords. They split open heads and cut off arms. John Brown watched his men work. When it was over, he put a single bullet into the head of James Doyle.

His party went to two more cabins, dragged out and killed two more men. At the end bodies lay in the bushes and floated in the creek; the murderers had made off with horses, saddles, and a bowie knife.

What came to be called the Pottawatomie Massacre ignited all-out war in Kansas. John Brown, the aged outsider, became an abolitionist leader. In August some 250 Border Ruffians attacked the free-soil town of Osawatomie. Brown led thirty men in defending the town. He fought hard, but Osawatomie burned to the ground.

A few days later, when Brown rode into Lawrence on a gray horse, a crowd gathered to cheer "as if the President had come to town," one man said. The spinning of John Brown had already begun. A Scottish reporter named James Redpath had found Brown's men in their secret campsite, and "I left this sacred spot with a far higher respect for the Great Struggle than ever I had felt before." And what of Pottawatomie? Brown had nothing to do with it, Redpath wrote. John Brown himself even prepared an admiring account of the Battle of Osawatomie for Eastern newspapers. Less than two weeks after the fight, a drama called *Ossawattomie Brown* was celebrating him on Broadway.

That autumn, peace finally came to Kansas, but not to John Brown. For the next three years he traveled the East, occasionally returning to Kansas, beseeching abolitionists for guns and money, money and guns. His plan evolved into this: One night he and a small company of men would capture the federal armory and arsenal at Harpers Ferry, Virginia. The invaders would take the guns there and leave. Local slaves would rise up to join them, making an army; together they all would drive south, and the revolution would snowball through the kingdom of slavery.

On the rainy night of October 16, 1859, Brown led a determined little procession down the road to Harpers Ferry. Some twenty men were making a direct attack on the U.S. government; they would liberate four million souls from bondage. At first the raid went like clockwork. The armory was protected by just one man, and he quickly surrendered. The invaders cut telegraph lines and rounded up hostages on the street.

Then Brown's difficulties began. A local doctor rode out screaming, "Insurrection!," and by midmorning men in the heights behind town were taking potshots down at Brown's followers. Meanwhile, John Brown quietly ordered breakfast from a hotel for his hostages. As Dennis Frye, the former chief historian at Harpers Ferry National Historical Park, asks, "The question is, why didn't John Brown attempt to leave? Why did he stay in Harpers Ferry?" Russell Banks, the author of the recent John Brown novel *Cloudsplitter,* has an answer: "He stayed and he stayed, and it seems to me a deliberate, resigned act of martyrdom."

At noon a company of Virginia militia entered town, took the bridge, and closed the only true escape route. By the end of the day, John Brown's revolution was failing. Eight invaders were dead or dying. Five others were cut off from the main group. Two had escaped across the river; two had been captured. Only five raiders were still fit to fight. Brown gathered his men in a small brick building, the enginehouse, for the long, cold night.

The first light of October 18 showed Brown and his tiny band an armory yard lined with U.S. Marines, under the command of Col. Robert E. Lee. A young lieutenant, J. E. B. Stuart, approached beneath a white flag and handed over a note asking the raiders to surrender. Brown refused. At that Stuart jumped aside, waved his cap, and the Marines stormed forward with a heavy ladder. The door gave way. Lt. Israel Green tried to run Brown through, but his blade struck the old man's belt buckle; God, for the moment, had saved John Brown.

A few hours later, as he lay in a small room at the armory, bound and bleeding, Brown's real revolution began. Gov. Henry A. Wise of Virginia arrived with a retinue of reporters. Did Brown want the reporters removed? asked Robert E. Lee. Definitely not. "Brown said he was by no means annoyed," one reporter wrote. For the old man was now beginning a campaign that would win half of America.

He told the reporters: "I wish to say . . . that you had better—all you people of the South—prepare yourselves for a settlement of this question. . . . You may dispose of me very easily—I am nearly disposed of now; but this question is still to be settled—this negro question I mean; the end of that is not yet."

His crusade for acceptance would not be easy. At first he was no hero. Leaders of the Republican party organized anti-Brown protests; "John Brown was no Republican," Abraham Lincoln said. Even the *Liberator,* published by the staunch abolitionist William Lloyd Garrison, called the raid "misguided, wild, and apparently insane."

In the South the initial reaction was derision—the Richmond *Dispatch* called the foray "miserably weak and contemptible"—but that soon changed to fear. Stuart's soldiers found a carpetbag crammed with letters from Brown's supporters; a number of prominent Northerners had financed the raid. It had been a conspiracy, a wide-ranging one. But how wide?

A reign of terror began in the South. A minister who spoke out against the treatment of slaves was publicly whipped; a man who spoke sympathetically about the raid found himself thrown in jail. Four state legislatures appropriated military funds. Georgia set aside seventy-five thousand dollars; Alabama, almost three times as much.

Brown's trial took just one week. As Virginia hurried toward a verdict, the Reverend Henry Ward Beecher preached, "Let no man pray that Brown be spared! Let Virginia make him a martyr!" John Brown read Beecher's words in his cell. He wrote "Good" beside them.

On November 2 the jury, after deliberating for forty-five minutes, reached its verdict. Guilty. Before he was sentenced, Brown rose to address the court: "I see a book kissed here, . . . the Bible. . . . [That] teaches me to 'remember them that are in bonds, as bound with them.' I endeavored to act up to that instruction. . . . I believe that to have interfered . . . in behalf of His despised poor was not wrong, but right. Now, if it is deemed necessary that I should forfeit my life . . . , and mingle my blood further with the blood of my children and with the blood of millions in this slave country whose rights are disregarded . . . I say let it be done!"

For the next month the Charlestown jail cell was John Brown's pulpit. All over the North, Brown knew, people were reading his words. He wrote, "You know that Christ once armed Peter. So also in my case I think he put a sword into my hand, and there continued it so long as he saw best, and then kindly took it from me."

The author of the Pottawatomie Massacre was now comparing himself to Jesus Christ. And he was not alone. Even the temperate Ralph Waldo Emerson called him "the new Saint whose fate yet hangs in suspense but whose martyrdom if it shall be perfected, will make the gallows as glorious as the cross." There were rescue plans, but John Brown did not want to escape. "I am worth inconceivably more to hang than for any other purpose," he wrote.

He got that wish on December 2, and the mythologizing of the man began in earnest. Thoreau, Emerson, Victor Hugo, Herman Melville, and Walt Whitman all wrote essays or poems immortalizing him. James Redpath eagerly waited for the moment when "Old B was in heaven"; just a month after the execution, he published the first biography. Forty thousand copies of the book sold in a single month.

Less than a year and a half later, the guns began firing on Fort Sumter. If the country had been a tinder box, it seemed to many that John Brown had been the spark. "Did John Brown fail?" Frederick Douglass wrote. ". . . John Brown began the war that ended American slavery and made this a free Republic."

His reputation seemed secure, impermeable. The first biographies of the man James Redpath called the "warrior saint" all glorified him. But then, in 1910, Oswald Garrison Villard, grandson of the abolitionist William Lloyd Garrison, wrote a massive and carefully researched book that pictured Brown as a muddled, pugnacious, bumbling, and homicidal madman. Nineteen years later Robert Penn Warren issued a similar (and derivative) study. Perhaps the most influential image of John Brown came, not surprisingly, from Hollywood: In *Santa Fe Trail* Raymond Massey portrayed him as a lunatic, pure and simple.

It wasn't until the 1970s that John Brown the hero re-emerged. Two excellent studies by Stephen B. Oates and Richard Owen Boyer captured the core of the conundrum: Brown was stubborn, monomaniacal, egotistical, self-righteous, and sometimes deceitful; yet he was, at certain times, a great man. Boyer, in particular, clearly admired him: At bottom Brown "was an American who gave his life that millions of other Americans might be free."

Among African-Americans, Brown's heroism has never been in doubt. Frederick Douglass praised him in print; W. E. B. Du Bois published a four-hundred-page celebration of him in 1909; Malcolm X said he wouldn't mind being with white people if they were like John Brown; and Alice Walker, in a poem, even wondered if in an earlier incarnation she herself hadn't once been John Brown.

But, as Russell Banks points out, Brown's "acts mean completely different things to Americans depending upon their skin color." And the image that most white people today have of John Brown is still of the wild-eyed, blood-thirsty madman. After all, he believed that God spoke to him; he killed people at Pottawatomie in cold blood; he launched an attack on the U.S. government at Harpers Ferry with not even two dozen men. How sane could he have been?

Let's look at those charges one by one. First: *He conversed with God.* Brown's religious principles, everyone agrees, were absolutely central to the man. As a child he learned virtually the entire Bible by heart. At sixteen he traveled to New England to study for the ministry. He gave up after a few months but remained deeply serious about his Calvinist beliefs. Brown had a great yearning for justice for all men, yet a rage for bloody revenge. These qualities may seem paradoxical to us, but they were ones that John Brown had in common with his deity. The angry God of the Old Testament punished evil: An eye cost exactly an eye.

If God spoke directly to John Brown, He also spoke to William Lloyd Garrison and to the slave revolutionary Nat Turner. To converse with God, in Brown's day, did not mean that you were eccentric. In fact, God was on everyone's side. John Brown saw the story of Moses setting the Israelites free as a mandate for emancipation, but at the same time, others used the Bible to justify slavery (Noah did, after all, set an everlasting curse on all the dark descendants of Ham). It was all in the Bible, and Americans on both sides went to war certain that they were doing God's bidding. So it is that John Brown believed that God had appointed him "a special agent of death," "an instrument raised up by Providence to break the jaws of the wicked."

Second: *He killed in cold blood.* Brown was a violent man, but he lived in increasingly violent times. Slavery itself was of course a violent practice. In 1831 Nat Turner led seventy slaves to revolt; they killed fifty-seven white men, women, and children. A few years later a clergyman named Elijah Lovejoy was gunned down for speaking out against slavery. By the 1850s another distinguished clergyman, Thomas Wentworth Higginson, could lead a mob to the federal courthouse in Boston and attack the place with axes and guns. "I can only make my life worth living," Higginson vowed, "by becoming a revolutionist." During the struggle in Kansas Henry Ward Beecher's Plymouth Church in Brooklyn was blithely shipping Sharps rifles west; "there are times," the famous preacher said, "when self-defense is a religious duty." By the late fifties, writes the historian James Stewart, even Congress was "a place where fist fights became common . . . a place where people came armed . . . a place where people flashed Bowie knives." On February 5, 1858, a brawl broke out between North and South in the House of Representatives; congressmen rolled on the floor, scratching and gouging each other.

Brown's Pottawatomie Massacre was directly connected to this national chaos. On the very day Brown heard about the sacking of Lawrence, another disturbing report reached him from Washington: A Southern congressman had attacked Sen. Charles Sumner, a fierce abolitionist, on the floor of Congress, caning him almost to death for insulting the

South. When the news got to Brown's campsite, according to his son Salmon, "the men went crazy—*crazy*. It seemed to be the finishing, decisive touch." Brown ordered his men to sharpen their broadswords and set off toward Pottawatomie, the creek whose name still stains his reputation.

So it is that "Brown is simply part of a very violent world," according to the historian Paul Finkelman. At Pottawatomie, Finkelman says, "Brown was going after particular men who were dangerous to the very survival of the free-state settlers in the area." But Dennis Frye has a less analytical (and less sympathetic) reaction: "Pottawatomie was cold-blooded murder. [It was] killing people up close based on anger and vengeance."

To Bruce Olds, the author of *Raising Holy Hell,* a 1995 novel about Brown, Pottawatomie was an example of conscious political terrorism: "Those killings took place in the middle of the night, in the dark—that was on purpose. In his writings, [Brown] uses the word 'terror' and the word 'shock.' He intended to produce both of those, and he did."

Maybe Pottawatomie was insane, and maybe it was not. But what about that Harpers Ferry plan—a tiny band attacking the U.S. government, hoping to concoct a revolution that would carry across the South? Clearly *that* was crazy.

Yes and no. If it was crazy, it was not unique. Dozens of people, often bearing arms, had gone South to rescue slaves. Secret military societies flourished on both sides, plotting to expand or destroy the system of slavery by force. Far from being the product of a singular cracked mind, the plan was similar to a number of others, including one by a Boston attorney named Lysander Spooner. James Horton, a leading African-American history scholar, offers an interesting scenario. "Was Brown crazy to assume he could encourage slave rebellion? . . . Think about the possibility of Nat Turner well-armed, well-equipped. . . . Nat Turner might have done some pretty amazing things," Horton says. "It was perfectly rational and reasonable for John Brown to believe he could encourage slaves to rebel."

But the question of Brown's sanity still provokes dissension among experts. Was he crazy? "He was obsessed," Bruce Olds says, "he was fanatical, he was monomaniacal, he was a zealot, and . . . psychologically unbalanced." Paul Finkelman disagrees: Brown "is a bad tactician, he's a bad strategist, he's a bad planner, he's not a very good general—but he's not crazy."

Some believe that there is a very particular reason why Brown's reputation as a madman has clung to him. Russell Banks and James Horton make the same argument. "The reason white people think he was mad," Banks says, "is because he was a white man and he was willing to sacrifice his life in order to liberate black Americans." "We should be very careful," Horton says, "about assuming that a white man who is willing to put his life on the line for black people is, of necessity, crazy."

Perhaps it is reasonable to say this: A society where slavery exists is by nature one where human values are skewed. America before the Civil War was a violent society, twisted by slavery. Even sober and eminent people became firebrands. John Brown had many peculiarities of his own, but he was not outside his society; to a great degree, he represented it, in its many excesses.

The past, as always, continues to change, and the spinning of John Brown's story goes on today. The same events—the raid on Harpers Ferry or the Pottawatomie Massacre—are still seen in totally different ways. What is perhaps most remarkable is that elements at both the left and right ends of American society are at this moment vitally interested in the story of John Brown.

On the left is a group of historical writers and teachers called Allies for Freedom. This group believes that the truth about the Harpers Ferry raid has been buried by the conventions of history. Its informal leader, Jean Libby, author of *John Brown Mysteries,* says, "What we think is that John Brown was a black nationalist. His ultimate goal was the creation of an independent black nation." The Allies for Freedom believes, too, that far from being the folly of a lunatic, Brown's plan was not totally unworkable, that it came much closer to succeeding than historians have pictured. Libby thinks that many slaves and free blacks *did* join the uprising—perhaps as many as fifty. Why would history conceal the fact of active black participation in Harpers Ferry? "The South was anxious to cover up any indication that the raid might have been successful," Libby says, "so slaves would never again be tempted to revolt."

Go a good deal farther to the left, and there has long been admiration for John Brown. In 1975 the Weather Underground put out a journal called *Osawatomie*. In the late 1970s a group calling itself the John Brown Brigade engaged in pitched battles with the Ku Klux Klan; in one confrontation in Greensboro, North Carolina, in 1979, five members of the John Brown Brigade were shot and killed. Writers also continue to draw parallels between John Brown and virtually any leftist who used political violence, including the Symbionese Liberation Army (the kidnappers of Patty Hearst in the 1970s), the Islamic terrorists who allegedly set off a bomb in the World Trade Center in Manhattan, and Ted Kaczynski, the Unabomber.

At the same time, John Brown is frequently compared to those at the far opposite end of the political spectrum. Right-to-life extremists have bombed abortion clinics and murdered doctors; they have, in short, killed for a cause they believed in, just as John Brown did. Paul Hill was convicted of murdering a doctor who performed abortions; it was, Hill said, the Lord's bidding: "There's no question in my mind that it was what the Lord wanted me to do, to shoot John Britton to prevent him from killing unborn children." If that sounds quite like John Brown, it was no accident. From death row Hill wrote to the historian Dan Stowell that Brown's "example has and continues to serve as a source of encouragement to me. . . . Both of us looked to the scriptures for direction, [and] the providential similarities between the oppressive circumstances we faced and our general understandings of the appropriate means to deliver the oppressed have resulted in my being encouraged to pursue a path which is in many

ways similar to his." Shortly before his execution Hill wrote that "the political impact of Brown's actions continues to serve as a powerful paradigm in my understanding of the potential effects the use of defensive force may have for the unborn."

Nor was the murder Hill committed the only right-wing violence that has been compared to Brown's. The Oklahoma City bombing in 1995 was a frontal attack on a U.S. government building, just like the Harpers Ferry raid. Anti-abortion murders, government buildings, anarchist bombs in the mail—nearly every time political violence surfaces, it gets described in the press as a part of a long American tradition of terrorism, with John Brown as a precursor and hero, a founding father of principled violence.

He gets compared to anarchists, leftist revolutionaries, and right-wing extremists. The spinning of John Brown, in short, is still going strong. But what does that make *him*? This much, at least, is certain: John Brown is a vital presence for all sorts of people today. . . . Perhaps the violent, excessive, morally torn society John Brown represents so aptly was not just his own antebellum America but this land, now.

QUESTIONS TO CONSIDER

1 Chowder contends that John Brown represented "two competing legends"; one had meaning to the North and the other to the South. Why did slave-owners and abolitionists have such drastically different views of this controversial figure?

2 Describe Brown's life before he became embroiled in the antislavery movement. Why would Chowder conclude that "Brown was genuinely nobody until he was fifty-six years old"?

3 The Kansas-Nebraska Act authorized the residents of a territory not only to determine the status of slavery there, but to decide whether that territory would become a free or a slave state. Why did this solution fail and produce violence and bloodshed in Kansas? How do you view Brown's actions after the destruction of the free state town of Lawrence?

4 What was Brown's goal at Harpers Ferry? Did his plan, in your view, have a realistic chance of working? Why do you think that Brown stayed in Harpers Ferry and refused to try to escape into the mountainous terrain around him?

5 Chowder attempts to understand Brown through an examination of the values of the early nineteenth century, a time of violence when many people used the Bible and God's will to justify their actions. Do you find this a satisfactory explanation for Brown's actions? If violence against slavery had not taken place and resulted in civil war, do you think that the South would have soon voluntarily eliminated their peculiar institution? In other words, if Brown's actions were not right, what other strategy would have ended slavery without bloodshed?

6 Both liberals and conservatives have at times viewed Brown as both a role model and a villain. Why would Chowder state that Brown's world resembles our own? In your lifetime can you provide examples of individuals who have used violence and religion to justify their cause? Does this essay have greater meaning after the events of September 11, 2001?

26 Lincoln's Journey to Emancipation

STEPHEN B. OATES

Nobody was more upset about the troubles in Kansas than Abraham Lincoln. For him and his Republican colleagues, the Kansas-Nebraska Act, the Kansas civil war, and the Dred Scott decision were all part of an insidious design to spread slavery across the West and ultimately to nationalize that hated institution. From 1854 on, Lincoln was in the thick of the struggle to block slavery expansion, to keep the peculiar institution out of the territories by the force of national law. The first half of the next essay describes Lincoln's battles against both Stephen A. Douglas and proslavery southerners and discusses Lincoln's own solution to slavery before the Civil War, which was a modification of Jefferson's and Clay's plans. You will not only meet an eloquent public Lincoln with a vision of America's historic mission in the world but a private Lincoln troubled by doubts and insecurities, romantic difficulties, and an obsession with death. That same Lincoln, however, was as ambitious as he was deeply principled. He built up a remarkably successful law career, fought Douglas for his seat in the United States Senate, and carried the banner of slave containment all the way to the White House.

The second half of the essay traces Lincoln's evolving emancipation policy during the Civil War. Throughout the first year and a half of the conflict, Lincoln insisted that the North was fighting strictly to save the Union, not to free the slaves. But a combination of problems and pressures caused him to change his mind, and in September 1862 he issued the preliminary Emancipation Proclamation, to take effect on January 1, 1863. The proclamation announced that, after that date, Union military forces would liberate the slaves in the rebellious states.

How Lincoln approached the problem of slavery—and what he did about it—is one of the most written about and least understood facets of his presidency. Indeed, the subject has made Lincoln far more controversial than Andrew Jackson. Ever since he issued his proclamation, legends have flourished about Lincoln as the Great Emancipator—a man who dedicated himself to liberty and equality for all. On the other hand, counterlegends of Lincoln as a Great Racist eventually emerged among white segregationists and among many modern African Americans as well. Which view is correct? Should Lincoln be applauded as a great humanitarian, or was he just another white bigot, as one black historian recently contended? Or, as some of his contemporaries charged, was he an unscrupulous opportunist who sought to eradicate slavery merely for political and military expediency?

Drawing on modern scholarship about Lincoln's life and the times in which he lived, the author of this essay tries to answer the enduring questions about Lincoln and emancipation and to present a realistic portrait of one of the most mythologized human beings in American history. The author concludes that Lincoln truly hated slavery—"If slavery is not wrong," Lincoln thundered "nothing is wrong"—and that he attacked the peculiar institution in part because of deeply held moral principles. In the end, it was this tall and melancholy man who found in a terrible civil war the means of removing the paradox of slavery in "the land of the free."

GLOSSARY

CHANDLER, ZACHARIAH   One of three Republican senators who pressed Lincoln to free the slaves.

CONFISCATION ACT (SECOND)   Provided for the seizure and liberation of all slaves of people who supported or participated in the rebellion; the measure exempted slaveholders in the Confederacy who were loyal to the Union; most slaves would be freed only after case-by-case litigation in the federal courts.

DOUGLASS, FREDERICK   Eminent black abolitionist and editor who pressured Lincoln to free the slaves and enlist black soldiers.

EMANCIPATION PROCLAMATION (JANUARY 1, 1863)   Freed the slaves in the rebel states except for occupied Tennessee and certain areas in Virginia and Louisiana behind Union lines; announced that henceforth Lincoln's military forces would accept black men.

GEORGIA PEN   Slave-trading pen in Washington, D.C., that offended Lincoln.

LINCOLN, MARY TODD   Lincoln's wife and mother of four Lincoln boys, one of whom died in childhood and a second of whom (Willie) died during the Civil War.

REFUGEE SYSTEM   Installed by Lincoln's adjutant general in the Mississippi Valley in 1863; the adjutant enrolled all able-bodied black men in the army and put others to work as laborers in the military or on confiscated farms and plantations for wages.

SPEED, JOSHUA   Lincoln's intimate friend in whom he confided his romantic fears in the 1840s.

SUMNER, CHARLES   A personal friend of Lincoln's and a major Lincoln adviser on foreign affairs; one of three Republican senators who pressed Lincoln to free the slaves.

THIRTEENTH AMENDMENT   Ratified in December 1865, it guaranteed the permanency of Lincoln's Emancipation Proclamation by abolishing slavery everywhere in the country.

1

He comes to us in the mists of legend as a kind of homespun Socrates, brimming with prairie wit and folk wisdom. He is as honest, upright, God-fearing, generous, and patriotic an American as the Almighty ever created. Impervious to material rewards and social station, the Lincoln of mythology is the Great Commoner, a saintly Rail Splitter who spoke in a deep, fatherly voice about the genius of the plain folk. He comes to us, too, as the Great Emancipator who led the North off to Civil War to free the slaves and afterward offered his fellow Southerners a tender and forgiving hand.

There is a counterlegend of Lincoln—one shared ironically enough by many white Southerners and certain black Americans of our time. This is the legend of Lincoln as bigot, as a white racist who championed segregation, opposed civil and political rights for black people, wanted them all thrown out of the country. This Lincoln is the great ancestor of racist James K. Vardaman of Mississippi, of "Bull" Connor of Birmingham, of the white citizens' councils, of the Knights of the Ku Klux Klan.

Neither of these views, of course, reveals much about the man who really lived—legends and politicized interpretations seldom do. The real Lincoln was not a saintly emancipator, and he was not an unswerving racist either. To understand him and the liberation of the slaves, one must eschew artificial, arbitrary categories and focus on the man as he lived, on the flesh-and-blood Lincoln, on that flawed and fatalistic individual who struggled with himself and his countrymen over the profound moral paradox of slavery in a nation based on the Declaration of Independence. Only by viewing Lincoln scrupulously in the context of his own time can one understand the painful, ironic, and troubled

Reprinted from *Our Fiery Trial: Abraham Lincoln, John Brown, and the Civil War Era,* by Stephen B. Oates, copyright © 1978 by the University of Massachusetts Press.

journey that led him to the Emancipation Proclamation and to the Thirteenth Amendment that made it permanent.

2

As a man, Lincoln was complex, many-sided, and richly human. He was almost entirely self-educated, with a talent for expression that in another time and place might have led him into a literary career. He wrote poetry himself and studied Shakespeare, Byron, and Oliver Wendell Holmes, attracted especially to writings with tragic and melancholy themes. He examined the way celebrated orators turned a phrase or employed a figure of speech, admiring great truths greatly told. Though never much at impromptu oratory, he could hold an audience of 15,000 spellbound when reading from a written speech, singing out in a shrill, high-pitched voice that became his trademark.

He was an intense, brooding person, plagued with chronic depression most of his life. "I am now the most miserable man living," he said on one occasion in 1841. "If what I feel were equally distributed to the whole human family, there would not be one cheerful face on the earth." He added, "To remain as I am is impossible; I must die or be better."

At the time he said this, Lincoln had fears of sexual inadequacy, doubting his ability to please or even care for a wife. In 1842 he confided in his closest friend, Joshua Speed, about his troubles, and both confessed that they had fears of "nervous debility" with women. Speed went ahead and married anyway and then wrote Lincoln that their anxieties were groundless. Lincoln rejoiced, "I tell you, Speed, our forebodings, for which you and I are rather peculiar, are all the worst sort of nonsense." Encouraged by Speed's success, Lincoln finally wedded Mary Todd; and she obviously helped him overcome his doubts, for they developed a strong and lasting physical love for one another.

Still, Lincoln remained a moody, melancholy man, given to long introspections about things like death and mortality. In truth, death was a lifelong obsession with him. His poetry, speeches, and letters are studded with allusions to it. He spoke of the transitory nature of human life, spoke of how all people in this world are fated to die in the end—all are fated to die. He saw himself as only a passing moment in a rushing river of time.

Preoccupied with death, he was also afraid of insanity, afraid (as he phrased it) of "the pangs that kill the mind." In his late thirties, he wrote and rewrote a poem about a boyhood friend, one Matthew Gentry, who became deranged and was locked "in mental night," condemned to a living death, spinning out of control in some inner void. Lincoln retained a morbid fascination with Gentry's condition, writing about how Gentry was more an object of dread than death itself: "A human form with reason fled, while wretched life remains." Yet, Lincoln was fascinated with madness, troubled by it, afraid that what had happened to Gentry could also happen to him—his own reason destroyed, Lincoln spinning in mindless night without the power to know.

Lincoln was a teetotaler because liquor left him "flabby and undone," blurring his mind and threatening his self-control. And he dreaded and avoided anything which threatened that. In one memorable speech, he heralded some great and distant day when all passions would be subdued, when reason would triumph and "*mind, all conquering mind,*" would rule the earth.

One side of Lincoln was always supremely logical and analytical. He was intrigued with the clarity of mathematics; and as an attorney he could command a mass of technical data. Yet he was also extremely superstitious, believed in signs and visions, contended that dreams were auguries of approaching triumph or calamity. He was skeptical of organized religion and never joined a church; yet he argued that all human destinies were controlled by an omnipotent God.

It is true that Lincoln told folksy anecdotes to illustrate a point. But humor was also tremendous therapy for his depressions—a device "to whistle down sadness," as a friend put it. Lincoln liked all kinds of jokes, from bawdy tales to pungent rib-ticklers like "Bass-Ackwards," a story he wrote down and handed a bailiff one day. Filled with hilarious spoonerisms, "Bass-Ackwards" is about a fellow who gets thrown from his horse and lands in "a great *tow-curd,*" which gives him a "*sick of fitness.*" About "*bray dake,*" he comes to and dashes home to find "the *door* sick abed, and his *wife* standing open. But thank goodness," the punch line goes, "she is getting right *hat* and *farty* again."

Contrary to legend, Lincoln was anything but a common man. In point of fact, he was one of the most ambitious human beings his friends had ever seen, with an aspiration for high station in life that burned in him like a furnace. Instead of reading with an accomplished attorney, as was customary in those days, he taught himself the law entirely on his own. He was literally a self-made lawyer. Moreover, he entered the Illinois legislature at the age of twenty-five and became a leader of the state Whig party, a tireless party campaigner, and a regular candidate for public office.

As a self-made man, Lincoln felt embarrassed about his log-cabin origins and never liked to talk about them. He seldom discussed his parents either and became permanently estranged from his father, who was all but illiterate. In truth, Lincoln had considerable hostility for his father's intellectual limitations, once remarking that Thomas "never did more in the way of writing than to bunglingly sign his own name." When his father died in a nearby Illinois county in 1851, Lincoln did not attend the funeral.

By the 1850s, Lincoln was one of the most sought-after attorneys in Illinois, with a reputation as a lawyer's lawyer—a knowledgeable jurist who argued appeal cases for other attorneys. He did his most influential legal work in the Supreme Court of Illinois, where he participated in 243 cases and won most of them. He commanded the respect of his colleagues, all of whom called him "Mr. Lincoln" or just "Lincoln." Nobody called him Abe—at least not to his face—because he loathed the nickname. It did not befit a respected professional who'd struggled hard to overcome the limitations of his frontier background.

Frankly, Lincoln enjoyed his status as a lawyer and politician, and he liked money, too, and used it to measure his worth. By the mid–1850s, thanks to a combination of talent and sheer hard work, Lincoln was a man of substantial wealth. He had an annual income of around $5,000—the equivalent of many times that today—and large financial and real-estate investments.

Though a man of status and influence, Lincoln was as honest in real life as in the legend. Even his enemies conceded that he was incorruptible. Moreover, he possessed broad humanitarian views, some of them in advance of his time. Even though he was a teetotaler, he was extremely tolerant of alcoholics, regarding them not as criminals—the way most temperance people did—but as unfortunates who deserved understanding, not vilification. He noted that some of the world's most gifted artists had succumbed to alcoholism, because they were too sensitive to cope with their insights into the human condition. He believed that women, like men, should vote so long as they all paid taxes. And he had no ethnic prejudices. His law partner William Herndon, who cursed the Irish with a flourish, reported that Lincoln was not at all prejudiced against "the foreign element, tolerating—as I never could— even the Irish."

Politically, Lincoln was always a nationalist in outlook, an outlook that began when he was an Indiana farm boy tilling his father's mundane wheat field. While the plow horse was getting its breath at the end of a furrow, Lincoln would study Parson Weems's eulogistic biography of George Washington, and he would daydream about the Revolution and the origins of the Republic, daydream about Washington and Jefferson as great national statesmen who shaped the course of history. By the time he became a politician, Lincoln idolized the Founding Fathers as apostles of liberty (never mind for now that many of these apostles were also Southern slaveowners). Young Lincoln extolled the founders for beginning an experiment in popular government on this continent, to show a doubting Europe that people could govern themselves without hereditary monarchs and aristocracies. And the foundation of the American experiment was the Declaration of Independence, which in Lincoln's view contained the highest political truths in history: that all men are created equal and are entitled to freedom and the pursuit of happiness. Which for Lincoln meant that men like him were not chained to the condition of their births, that they could better their station in life and harvest the fruits of their own talents and industry. Thus he had a deep, personal reverence for the Declaration and insisted that all his political sentiment flowed from that document.

—————

3

Which brings us to the problem and paradox of slavery in America. Lincoln maintained that he had always hated human bondage, as much as any abolitionist. His family had opposed the peculiar institution, and Lincoln had grown up and entered Illinois politics thinking it wrong. But before 1854 (and the significance of that date will become clear) Lincoln generally kept his own counsel about slavery and abolition. After all, slavery was the most inflammable issue of his generation, and Lincoln observed early on what violent passions Negro bondage—and the question of race that underlay it—could arouse in white Americans. In his day, as I have said, slavery was a tried and tested means of race control in a South absolutely dedicated to white supremacy. Moreover, the North was also a white supremacist region, where the vast majority of whites opposed emancipation lest it result in a flood of Southern blacks into the free states. And Illinois was no exception, as most whites there were against abolition and were anti-Negro to the core. Lincoln, who had elected to work within the system, was not going to ruin his career by espousing an extremely unpopular cause. To be branded as an abolitionist in central Illinois—his constituency as a legislator and a U.S. congressman—would have been certain political suicide. At the same time, attorney Lincoln conceded that Southern slavery had become a thoroughly entrenched institution, that bondage where it already existed was protected by the Constitution and could not be molested by the national government.

Still, slavery distressed him. He realized how wrong it was that slavery should exist at all in a self-proclaimed free and enlightened Republic. He who cherished the Declaration of Independence understood only too well how bondage mocked and contradicted that noble document. Too, he thought slavery a blight on the American experiment in popular government. It was, he believed, the one retrograde institution that robbed the Republic of its just example in the world, robbed the United States of the hope it should hold out to oppressed people everywhere.

He opposed slavery, too, because he had witnessed some of its evils firsthand. In 1841, on a steamboat journey down the Ohio River, he saw a group of manacled slaves on their way to the cruel cotton plantations of the Deep South. Lincoln was appalled at the sight of those chained Negroes. Fourteen years later he wrote that the spectacle "was a continual torment to me" and that he saw something like it every time he touched a slave border. Slavery, he said, "had the power of making me miserable."

Again, while serving in Congress from 1847 to 1849, he passed slave auction blocks in Washington, D.C. In fact, from the windows of the Capitol, he could observe the infamous "Georgia pen"—"a sort of Negro livery stable," as he described it, "where droves of negroes were collected, temporarily kept, and finally taken to Southern markets, precisely like droves of horses." The spectacle offended him. He agreed with a Whig colleague that the buying and selling of human beings in the United States capital was a national disgrace. Accordingly Lincoln drafted a gradual abolition bill for the District of Columbia. But powerful Southern politicians howled in protest, and his own Whig support fell away. At that, Lincoln dropped his bill and sat in glum silence as Congress rocked with debates—with drunken fights and rumbles of disunion—over the status of slavery out in the territories. Shocked at the behavior of his colleagues,

Lincoln confessed that slavery was the one issue that threatened the stability of the Union.

What could be done? Slavery as an institution could not be removed, and yet it should not remain either. Trapped in what seemed an impossible dilemma, Lincoln persuaded himself that if slavery were confined to the South and left alone there, time would somehow solve the problem and slavery would ultimately die out. And he told himself that the Founding Fathers had felt the same way, that they too had expected slavery to perish some day. In Lincoln's interpretation, they had tolerated slavery as a necessary evil, agreeing that it could not be eradicated where it already flourished without causing wide-scale wreckage. But in his view they had taken steps to restrict its growth (had excluded slavery from the old Northwest territories, had outlawed the international slave trade) and so had placed the institution on the road to extinction.

So went Lincoln's argument before 1854. The solution was to bide one's time, trust the future to get rid of slavery and square America with her own ideals. And he convinced himself that when slavery was no longer workable, Southern whites would gradually liberate the blacks on their own. They would do so voluntarily.

To solve the ensuing problem of racial adjustment, Lincoln insisted that the federal government should colonize all blacks in Africa, an idea he got from his political idol, Whig national leader Henry Clay. Said Lincoln in 1852: if the Republic could remove the danger of slavery and restore "a captive people to their long-lost fatherland," and do both so gradually "that neither races nor individuals shall have suffered by the change," then "it will indeed be a glorious consummation."

4

Then came 1854 and the momentous Kansas-Nebraska Act, brainchild of Lincoln's archrival Stephen A. Douglas. The act overturned the old Missouri Compromise line, which excluded slavery from the vast northern area of the old Louisiana Purchase territory. The act then established a new formula for dealing with slavery in the national lands: now Congress would stay out of the matter, and the people of each territory would decide whether to retain or outlaw the institution. Until such time as the citizens of a territory voted on the issue, Southerners were free to take slavery into most western territories, including the new ones of Kansas and Nebraska. These were carved out of the northern section of the old Louisiana Purchase territory. Thanks to the Kansas-Nebraska Act, a northern domain once preserved for freedom now seemed open to proslavery invasion.

At once a storm of free-soil protest broke across the North, and scores of political leaders branded the Kansas-Nebraska Act as part of a sinister Southern plot to extend slave territory and augment Southern political power in Washington. There followed a series of political upheavals. A civil war blazed up in Kansas, as proslavery and free-soil pioneers came into bloody collisions on the prairie there—proof that slavery was far too volatile ever to be solved as a purely local matter. At the same time, the old Whig party disintegrated. In its place emerged the all-Northern Republican party, dedicated to blocking slavery extension and to saving the cherished frontier for free white labor. Then in 1857 came the infamous Dred Scott decision, handed down by the pro-Southern Supreme Court, which ruled that neither Congress nor a territorial government could outlaw slavery, because that would violate Southern property rights. As Lincoln and many others observed, the net effect of the decision was to legalize slavery in all federal territories from Canada to Mexico.

The train of ominous events from Kansas-Nebraska to Dred Scott shook Lincoln to his foundations. In his view, the Southern-controlled Democratic party—the party that dominated the Senate, the Supreme Court, and the presidency—had instituted a revolt against the Founding Fathers and the entire course of the Republic so far as slavery was concerned. Now human bondage was not going to die out. Now it was going to expand and grow and continue indefinitely,

as Southerners dragged manacled Negroes across the West, adapting slave labor to whatever conditions they found there, putting the blacks to work in mines and on farms. Now Southerners would create new slave states in the West and make slavery powerful and permanent in America. Now the Republic would never remove the cancer that infected its political system, would never remove the one institution that marred its global image, would never remove a "cruel wrong" that mocked the Declaration of Independence.

Lincoln waded into the middle of the antiextension fight. He campaigned for the national Senate. He joined the Republican party. He thundered against the evil designs of the "Slave Power." He spoke with an urgent sense of mission that gave his speeches a searching eloquence—a mission to save the Republic's noblest ideals, turn back the tide of slavery expansion, restrict the peculiar institution once again to the South, and place it back on the road to extinction, as Lincoln believed the Founding Fathers had so placed it.

By 1858, Lincoln, like a lot of other Republicans, began to see a grim proslavery conspiracy at work in the United States. The first stage was to betray the founders and send slavery flooding all over the West. At the same time, proslavery theorists were out to undermine the Declaration of Independence, to discredit its equality doctrine as "a self-evident lie" (as many Southern spokesmen were actually saying), and to replace the Declaration with the principles of inequality and human servitude.

The next step in the conspiracy would be to nationalize slavery: the Taney Court, Lincoln feared, would hand down another decision, one declaring that states could not prohibit slavery either. Then the institution would sweep into Illinois, sweep into Indiana and Ohio, sweep into Pennsylvania and New York, sweep into Massachusetts and New England, sweep all over the Northern states, until at last slavery would be nationalized and America would end up a slave house. At that, as George Fitzhugh advocated, the conspirators would enslave all American workers regardless of color. The Northern free-labor

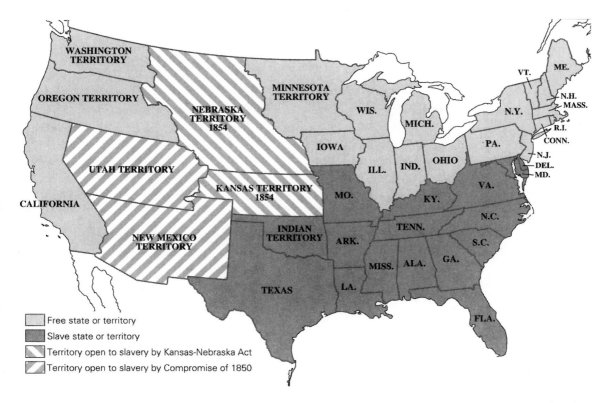

Free state or territory
Slave state or territory
Territory open to slavery by Kansas-Nebraska Act
Territory open to slavery by Compromise of 1850

The Kansas–Nebraska Act of 1854 exacerbated sectional tension over slavery in the territories. The measure nullified the Missouri Compromise line, which had prohibited slavery in the old Louisiana Purchase above the latitude of 36° 30′. Two new territories were now carved out of that northern region, and southerners were free to extend slavery there until such time as the residents voted to outlaw it.

system would be expunged, the Declaration of Independence overthrown, self-government abolished, and the conspirators would restore despotism with class rule and an entrenched aristocracy. All the work since the Revolution of 1776 would be obliterated. The world's best hope—America's experiment in popular government—would be destroyed, and mankind would spin backward into feudalism.

For Lincoln and his Republican colleagues, it was imperative that the conspiracy be blocked in its initial stage—the expansion of slavery into the West. In 1858 Lincoln set out after Douglas's Senate seat, inveighing against the Little Giant for his part in the proslavery plot and warning Illinois—and Northerners beyond—that only the Republicans could save their free-labor

system and their free government. Now Lincoln openly and fiercely declaimed his antislavery sentiments. He hated the institution. He hated slavery because it degraded blacks and whites alike. Because it prevented the Negro from "eating the bread which his own hand earns." Because it not only contradicted the Declaration, but violated the principles of free labor, self help, social mobility, and economic independence, all of which lay at the center of Republican ideology, of Lincoln's ideology. Yet, while branding slavery as an evil and doing all they could to contain it in the South, Republicans would not, could not, molest the institution in those states where it already existed.

Douglas, fighting for his political life in free-soil Illinois, lashed back at Lincoln with unadulterated

Dred Scott in 1858, a year after the Supreme Court decision that bore his name. Originally called Sam, Dred Scott, a slave, sought his freedom on the grounds that he had lived for a time in a free state and a free territory. His case led to one of the most infamous Supreme Court decisions in American judicial history. Bought and freed by a white benefactor in 1857, Scott became a porter at a St. Louis hotel and died in 1858. (Missouri Historical Society)

race-baiting. Throughout the Great Debates of 1858, Douglas smeared Lincoln and his party as Black Republicans, as a gang of radical abolitionists out to liberate all Southern slaves and bring them stampeding into Illinois and the rest of the North, where they would take away white jobs and copulate with white daughters. Again and again, Douglas accused Lincoln of desiring intermarriage and racial mongrelization.

Lincoln protested emphatically that race was not the issue between him and Douglas. The issue was whether slavery would ultimately triumph or ultimately perish in the United States. But Douglas understood the depth of anti-Negro feeling in Illinois, and he hoped to whip Lincoln by playing on white racial fears.

Forced to take a stand lest Douglas ruin him with his allegations, Lincoln conceded that he was not for Negro political or social equality. He was not for enfranchising Negroes, was not for intermarriage. There was, he said, "a physical difference" between blacks and whites that would "probably" always prevent them from living together in perfect equality. Having confessed his racial views, Lincoln then qualified them: if Negroes were not the equal of Lincoln and Douglas in moral or intellectual endowment, they *were* equal to Lincoln, Douglas, and "every living man" in their right to liberty, equality of opportunity, and the fruits of their own labor. (Later he insisted that it was bondage that had "clouded" the slaves' intellects and that Negroes were capable of thinking like whites.) Moreover, Lincoln rejected "the counterfeit argument" that just because he did not want a black woman for a slave, he necessarily wanted her for a wife. He could just let her alone. He could let her alone so that she could also enjoy her freedom and "her natural right to eat the bread she earns with her own hands."

Exasperated with Douglas and white Negrophobia in general, Lincoln begged American whites "to discard all this quibbling about this man and the other man—this race and that race and the other race as being inferior," begged them to unite as one people and defend the ideals of the Declaration and its promise of liberty and opportunity for all.

Lincoln lost the 1858 Senate contest to Douglas. But in 1860 he won the Republican nomination for president and stood before the American electorate on the free-soil, free-labor principles of the Republican party. As the Republican standard bearer, Lincoln was uncompromising in his determination to prohibit slavery in the territories by national law and to save the Republic (as he put it) from returning to "class, caste, and despotism." He exhorted his fellow Republicans to stand firm in their duty: to brand slavery as an evil, contain it in the South, look to the future for slavery to die a gradual death, and promise colonization to solve the question of race. Some day, somehow, the American house must be free of slavery. That was the Republican vision, the distant horizon Lincoln saw.

Yet, for the benefit of Southerners, he repeated that he and his party would not harm slavery in the Southern states. The federal government had no constitutional authority in peace time to tamper with a state institution like slavery.

But Southerners refused to believe anything Lincoln said. In Dixie, orators and editors alike castigated him as a black-hearted radical, a "sooty and scoundrelly" abolitionist who wanted to free the slaves at once and mix the races. In Southern eyes, Lincoln was another John Brown, a mobocrat, a Southern hater, a chimpanzee, a lunatic, the "biggest ass in the United States," the evil chief of the North's "Black Republican, free love, free Nigger" party, whose victory would ring the bells of doom for the white man's South. Even if Southerners had to drench the Union in blood, cried an Atlanta man, "the South, the loyal South, the Constitution South, would never submit to such humiliation and degradation as the inauguration of Abraham Lincoln."

After Lincoln's victory and the secession of the seven states of the Deep South, Lincoln beseeched Southerners to understand the Republican position on slavery. In his Inaugural Address of 1861, he assured them once again that the federal government would not free the slaves in the South, that it had no legal right to do so. He even gave his blessings to the original Thirteenth Amendment, just passed by Congress, that would have guaranteed slavery in the Southern states for as long as whites there wanted it. Lincoln endorsed the amendment because he thought it consistent with Republican ideology. Ironically, Southern secession and the outbreak of war prevented that amendment from ever being ratified.

When the rebels opened fire on Fort Sumter, the nation plunged into civil war, a conflict that began as a ninety-day skirmish for both sides, but that swelled instead into a vast and terrible carnage with consequences beyond calculation for those swept up in its flames. Lincoln, falling into a depression that would plague him through his embattled presidency, remarked that the war was the supreme irony of his life: that he who sickened at the sight of blood, who abhorred stridency and physical violence, was caught in a national holocaust, a tornado of blood and wreckage with Lincoln himself whirling in its center.

5

At the outset of the war, Lincoln strove to be consistent with all that he and his party had said about slavery: his purpose in the struggle was strictly to save the Union; it was not to free the slaves. He would crush the rebellion with his armies and restore the national authority in the South with slavery intact. Then Lincoln and his party would resume and implement their policy of slave containment.

There were other reasons for Lincoln's hands-off policy about slavery. Four slave states—Delaware, Maryland, Kentucky, and Missouri—remained in the Union. Should he try to free the slaves, Lincoln feared it would send the crucial border spiraling into the Confederacy, something that would be catastrophic for the Union. A Confederate Maryland would create an impossible situation for Washington, D.C. And a Confederate Missouri and Kentucky would give the rebels potential bases from which to invade Illinois, Indiana, and Ohio. So Lincoln rejected emancipation in part to appease the loyal border.

He was also waging a bipartisan war effort, with Northern Democrats and Republicans alike enlisting in his armies to save the Union. Lincoln encouraged this because he insisted that it would take a united North to win the war. An emancipation policy, he feared, would alienate Northern Democrats, ignite a racial powder keg in the Northern states, and possibly cause a civil war in the rear. Then the Union really would be lost.

But the pressures and problems of civil war caused Lincoln to change his mind, caused him to abandon his hands-off policy and hurl an executive fist at slavery in the rebel states, thus making emancipation a Union war objective. The pressures operating on Lincoln were complex and merit careful discussion.

First, from the summer of 1861 on, several Republican senators—chief among them, Charles Sumner of Massachusetts, Ben Wade of Ohio, and Zachariah Chandler of Michigan—sequestered themselves with Lincoln and implored and badgered him to free the slaves.[1] Sumner, as Lincoln's personal friend and one of his chief foreign policy advisers, was especially persistent. Before secession, of course, Sumner and his colleagues had all adhered to the Republican position on slavery in the South. But civil war had now removed their constitutional scruples about the peculiar institution. After all, they told Lincoln, the Southern people were in rebellion against the national government; they could not resist that government and yet enjoy the protection of its laws. Now the senators argued that the national government could eradicate slavery by the War Power, and they wanted Lincoln to do it in his capacity as commander-in-chief. If he emancipated the slaves, it would maim and cripple the Confederacy and hasten an end to the rebellion.

Second, they pointed out that slavery had caused the war, was the reason why the Southern states had seceded, and was now the cornerstone of the confederacy. It was absurd, the senators contended, to fight a war without removing the thing that had brought it about. Should the South return to the Union with slavery intact, as Lincoln desired, Southerners would just start another war over slavery, whenever they thought it threatened again, so that the present struggle would have accomplished nothing, nothing at all. If Lincoln really wanted to save the Union, he must tear slavery out root and branch and smash the South's planter class—that mischievous

class the senators thought had masterminded secession and fomented war.

Sumner, as a major Lincoln adviser on foreign affairs, also linked emancipation to foreign policy. On several occasions in 1861 and 1862, Britain seemed on the verge of recognizing the Confederacy as an independent nation—a move that would be calamitous for the Union. As a member of the family of nations, the Confederacy could form alliances and seek mediation and perhaps armed intervention in the American conflict. But, Sumner argued, if Lincoln made the obliteration of slavery a Union war aim, Britain would balk at recognition and intervention. Why so? Because she was proud of her antislavery tradition, Sumner contended, and would refrain from helping the South protect human bondage from Lincoln's armies. And whatever powerful Britain did, the rest of Europe was sure to follow.

Also, as Sumner kept reminding everyone, emancipation would break the chains of several million oppressed human beings and right America at last with her own ideals. Lincoln could no longer wait for the future to remove slavery. He must do it. The war, monstrous and terrible though it was, had given Lincoln the opportunity to do it.

Black and white abolitionists belabored that point too. They wrote Lincoln, petitioned him, and addressed him from the stump and in their newspapers. Foremost in that effort was Frederick Douglass, the most eminent African American of his generation, a handsome, eloquent man who had escaped from slavery in Maryland and become a self-made man like Lincoln, raising himself to prominence as an editor and reformer. From the outset, Douglass saw the end of slavery in this war, and he mounted a one-man crusade to win Lincoln to that idea. In his newspaper and on the platform, Douglass thundered at the man in the White House, playing on his personal feelings about slavery, rehearsing the same arguments that Sumner and his colleagues were giving Lincoln in person. You fight the rebels with only one hand, Douglass said. The mission of this war is the destruction of bondage as well as the salvation of the Union. "The very stomach of this rebellion is

---

[1] These "more advanced Republicans," as the *Detroit Post and Tribune* referred to Sumner and his associates, belonged to a powerful minority faction of the party inaccurately categorized as "radicals," a misnomer that has persisted through the years. For a discussion of this point, see my article, "The Slaves Freed," *American Heritage* (December 1980), 74–83.

the negro in the condition of a slave. Arrest that hoe in the hands in the negro, and you smite rebellion in the very seat of its life," he said. "The Negro is the key of the situation—the pivot upon which the whole rebellion turns," he said. "Teach the rebels and traitors that the price they are to pay for the attempt to abolish this Government must be the abolition of slavery," he said. "Hence forth let the war cry be down with treason, and down with slavery, the cause of treason."

The pressure on Lincoln to strike at slavery was unrelenting. In between abolitionist delegations came Sumner and his stern colleagues again, with Vice-President Hannibal Hamlin and Congressman Owen Lovejoy often with them. As the war progressed, they raised still another argument for emancipation, an argument Douglass and members of Lincoln's own Cabinet were also making. In 1862, his armies suffered from manpower shortages on every front. Thanks to repeated Union military failures and to a growing war weariness across the North, volunteering had fallen off sharply; and Union generals bombarded Washington with shrill complaints, insisting that they faced an overwhelming southern foe and must have reinforcements before they could win battles or even fight. While Union commanders often exaggerated rebel strength, Union forces did need reinforcements to carry out a successful offensive war. As Sumner reminded Lincoln, the slaves were an untapped reservoir of strength. "You need more men," Sumner said, "not only at the North, but at the South. You need the slaves." If Lincoln freed them, he could recruit black men into his armed forces, thus helping to solve his manpower woes.

On that score, the slaves themselves were contributing to the pressures on Lincoln to emancipate them. Far from being passive recipients of freedom, as Vincent Harding has rightly reminded us, the slaves *were* engaged in self-liberation, abandoning rebel farms and plantations and escaping to Union lines by the thousands. This in turn created a tangled legal problem that bedeviled the Lincoln administration. What was the status of such "contraband of war," as Union General Benjamin F. Butler designated them? Were they still slaves? Were they free? Were they somewhere in between? The administration tended to follow a look-the-other-way policy, allowing field commanders to solve the contraband problem any way they wished. Some officers sent the fugitives back to the Confederacy, others turned them over to refugee camps, where benevolent organizations attempted to care for them. But with more and more slaves streaming into Union lines, Sumner, several of Lincoln's Cabinet members, Douglass, and many others urged him to grant them freedom and enlist the able-bodied men in the army. "Let the slaves and free colored people be called into service and formed into a liberating army," Douglass exhorted the President, "to march into the South and raise the banner of Emancipation among the slaves."

Lincoln, however, stubbornly rejected a presidential move against slavery. It was "too big a lick," he asserted. "I think Sumner and the rest of you would upset our applecart altogether if you had your way," he told some aggressive Republicans one day. "We didn't go into the war to put down slavery, but to put the flag back; and to act differently at this moment would, I have no doubt, not only weaken our cause, but smack of bad faith. . . . This thunderbolt will keep."

Nevertheless, Lincoln was sympathetic to the entire range of arguments Sumner and his associates rehearsed for him. Personally, Lincoln hated slavery as much as they did, and many of their points had already occurred to him. In fact, as early as November and December 1861, Lincoln began wavering in his hands-off policy about slavery, began searching about for some compromise—something short of a sweeping emancipation decree. Again he seemed caught in an impossible dilemma: how to remove the cause of the war, keep Britain out of the conflict, cripple the Confederacy and suppress the rebellion, and yet retain the allegiance of Northern Democrats and the critical border?

In March 1862, he proposed a plan to Congress he thought might work: a gradual, compensated emancipation program to commence in the loyal border states. According to Lincoln's plan, the border states would gradually abolish slavery themselves over the next thirty years, and the federal government would compensate slaveowners for their loss. The whole program was to be voluntary; the states would adopt their own emancipation laws without federal coercion.

At the same time, the federal government would sponsor a colonization program, which was also to be entirely voluntary. Without a promise of colonization, Lincoln understood only too well, most Northern whites would never accept emancipation, even if it were carried out by the states. From now on, every time he contemplated some new antislavery move, he made a great fuss about colonization: he embarked on a colonization project in central America and another in Haiti, and he held an interview about colonization with Washington's black leaders, an interview he published in the press. In part, the ritual of colonization was designed to calm white racial fears.

If his gradual, state-guided plan were adopted, Lincoln contended that a presidential decree—federally enforced emancipation—would never be necessary. Abolition would begin on the local level in the loyal border and then be extended into the rebel states as they were conquered. Thus by a slow and salubrious process would the cause of the rebellion be removed and the future of the Union guaranteed.

The plan failed. It failed because the border states refused to act. Lincoln couldn't even persuade Delaware, with its small and relatively harmless slave population, to adopt his program. In desperation, Lincoln on three different occasions—in the spring and summer of 1862—pleaded with border-state congressmen to endorse his program. In their third meeting, held in the White House on July 12, Lincoln warned the border representatives that it was impossible now to restore the Union with slavery preserved. Slavery was doomed. They could not be blind to the signs, blind to the fact that his plan was the only alternative to a more drastic move against slavery, one that would cause tremendous destruction in the South. Please, he said, commend my gradual plan to your people.

But most of the border men turned him down. They thought his plan would cost too much, would only whip the flames of rebellion, would cause dangerous discontent in their own states. Their intransigence was a sober lesson to Lincoln. It was proof indeed that slaveowners—even loyal slaveowners—were too tied up in the slave system ever to free their own Negroes and voluntarily transform their way of life. If abolition must come, it must begin in the rebel South and then be extended into the loyal border later on. Which meant that the president must eradicate slavery himself. He could no longer avoid the responsibility. By mid-July 1862, the pressures of the war had forced him to abandon his hands-off policy and lay a "strong hand on the colored element."

On July 13, the day after his last talk with the border men, Lincoln took a carriage ride with a couple of his cabinet secretaries. His conversation, when recounted in full, reveals a tougher Lincoln than the lenient and compromising president of the legend-building biographies. Lincoln said he was convinced that the war could no longer be won through forbearance toward Southern rebels, that it was "a duty on our part to liberate the slaves." The time had come to take a bold new path and hurl Union armies at "the heart of the rebellion," using the military to destroy the very institution that caused and now sustained the insurrection. Southerners could not throw off the Constitution and at the same time invoke it to protect slavery. They had started the war and must now face its consequences.

He had given this a lot of grave and painful thought, he said, and had concluded that a presidential declaration of emancipation was the last alternative, that it was "a military necessity absolutely essential to the preservation of the Union." Because the slaves were a tremendous source of strength for the rebellion, Lincoln must invite them to desert and "come to us and uniting with us they must be made free from rebel authority and rebel masters." His interview with the border men yesterday, he said, "had forced him slowly but he believed correctly to this conclusion."

On July 22, 1862, Lincoln summoned his cabinet members and read them a draft of a preliminary Emancipation Proclamation. Come January 1, 1863, in his capacity as commander-in-chief of the armed forces in time of war, Lincoln would free all the slaves everywhere in the rebel states. He would thus make it a Union objective to annihilate slavery as an institution in the Confederate South.

Contrary to what many historians have said, Lincoln's projected Proclamation went further than anything Congress had done. True, Congress had just enacted (and Lincoln had just signed) the second confiscation act, which provided for the seizure and liberation of all slaves of people who supported or participated in the rebellion. Still, most slaves would be freed only after protracted case-by-case litigation in the federal courts. Another section of the act did liberate certain categories of slaves without court action, but the bill exempted loyal slaveowners in the rebel South, allowing them to keep their slaves and other property. Lincoln's Proclamation, on the other hand, was a sweeping blow against bondage as an institution in the rebel states, a blow that would free *all* the slaves there—those of secessionists and loyalists alike. Thus Lincoln would handle emancipation himself, avoid judicial red tape, and use the military to vanquish the cornerstone of the Confederacy. Again, he justified this as a military necessity to save the Union.

But Seward and other cabinet secretaries dissuaded Lincoln from issuing his Proclamation in July. Seward argued that the Union had won no clear military victories, particularly in the showcase Eastern theater. As a consequence, Europe would misconstrue the Proclamation as "our last shriek on the retreat," as a wild and reckless attempt to compensate for Union military ineptitude by provoking a slave insurrection behind rebel lines. If Lincoln must give an emancipation order, Seward warned, he must wait until the Union won a military victory.

Lincoln finally agreed to wait, but he was not happy about it: the way George B. McClellan and his other generals had been fighting in the Eastern theater, Lincoln had no idea when he would ever have a victory.

One of the great ironies of the war was that McClellan presented Lincoln with the triumph he needed. A Democrat who sympathized with Southern slavery and opposed wartime emancipation with a passion, McClellan outfought Robert E. Lee at Antietam Creek in September 1862, and forced the rebel army to withdraw. Thereupon Lincoln issued his preliminary Proclamation, with its warning that if the rebellion did not cease by January 1, 1863, the executive branch, including the army and the navy, would destroy slavery in the rebel states.

As it turned out, the preliminary Proclamation ignited racial discontent in much of the lower North, especially the Midwest, and led to significant Democratic gains in the off-year elections of 1862. Many Northern Democrats were already upset with Lincoln's harsh war measures, especially his use of martial law and military arrests. But Negro emancipation was more than they could stand, and they stumped the Northern states that fall, beating the drums of Negrophobia, warning of massive influxes of Southern blacks into the North once emancipation came. When the 1862 ballots were counted, the Democrats had picked up thirty-four congressional seats, won two governorships, and gained control of three state legislatures. While the Republicans retained control of Congress, the future looked bleak indeed if the war ground on into 1864.

Republican analysts—and Lincoln himself—conceded that the preliminary Proclamation was a major factor in the Republican losses. But Lincoln told a delegation from Kentucky that he would rather die than retract a single word in his Proclamation.

As the New Year approached, conservative Republicans begged Lincoln to abandon his "reckless" emancipation scheme lest he shatter their demoralized party and wreck what remained of their country. But Lincoln stood firm. On New Year's day, 1863, he officially signed the final Emancipation Proclamation in the White House. His hand trembled badly, not because he was nervous, but because he had shaken hands all morning in a White House reception. He assured everyone present that he was never more certain of what he was doing. "If my name ever goes into history," he said, "it will be for this act." Then slowly and deliberately he wrote out his full name.

In the final Proclamation, Lincoln temporarily exempted occupied Tennessee and certain occupied places in Louisiana and Virginia. (Later, in reconstructing those states, he withdrew the exemptions and made emancipation a mandatory part of his reconstruction program.) He also excluded the loyal slave states because they were not in rebellion and he lacked the legal authority to uproot slavery there. He would, however, keep goading them to obliterate slavery themselves—and would later push a constitutional amendment that liberated their slaves as well. With the exception of the loyal border and certain occupied areas, the final Proclamation declared that as of this day, all slaves in the rebellious states were *"forever free."* The document also asserted that black men—Southern and Northern alike—would now be enlisted in Union military forces.

Out the Proclamation went to an anxious and dissident nation. Later in the day an interracial crowd gathered on the White House lawn, and Lincoln greeted the people from an open window. The blacks cheered and sang, "Glory, Jubilee has come," and told Lincoln that if he would "come out of that palace, they would hug him to death." A black preacher named Henry M. Turner exclaimed that "it is indeed a time of times," that "nothing like it will ever be seen again in this life."

6

Lincoln's Proclamation was the most revolutionary measure ever to come from an American president up to that time. As Union armies punched into rebel territory, they would rip out slavery as an institution, automatically freeing all slaves in the areas and states they conquered. In this respect (as Lincoln said), the war brought on changes more vast, more fundamental and profound, than either side had expected when the struggle began. Now slavery would perish

as the Confederacy perished, would die by degrees with every Union advance, every Union victory.

Moreover, word of the Proclamation hummed across the slave grapevine in the Confederacy; and as Union armies drew near, more slaves than ever abandoned rebel farms and plantations and (as one said) "demonstrated with their feet" their desire for freedom.

The Proclamation also opened the army to black volunteers, and Northern free Negroes and Southern ex-slaves now enlisted as Union soldiers. As Lincoln said, "the colored population is the great *available* and yet unavailed of, force for restoring the Union." And he now availed himself of that force. In all, some 180,000 Negro fighting men—most of them emancipated slaves—served in Union forces on every major battlefront, helping to liberate their brothers and sisters in bondage and to save the Union. As Lincoln observed, the blacks added enormous and indispensable strength to the Union war machine.

Unhappily, the blacks fought in segregated units under white officers, and until late in the war received less pay than whites did. In 1864 Lincoln told Negro leader Frederick Douglass that he disliked the practice of unequal pay, but that the government had to make some concessions to white prejudices, noting that a great many Northern whites opposed the use of black soldiers altogether. But he promised that they would eventually get equal pay—and they did. Moreover, Lincoln was proud of the performance of his black soldiers: he publicly praised them for fighting "with clenched teeth, and steady eye, and well poised bayonet" to save the Union, while certain whites strove "with malignant heart" to hinder it.

After the Proclamation, Lincoln had to confront the problem of race adjustment, of what to do with all the blacks liberated in the South. By the spring of 1863, he had pretty well written off colonization as unworkable. His colonization schemes all floundered, in part because the white promoters were dishonest or incompetent. But the main reason colonization failed was because most blacks adamantly refused to participate in Lincoln's voluntary program. Across

Men of the Fifty-Fourth Massachusetts (Colored) Infantry Regiment. Organized after the Emancipation Proclamation, the Fifty-Fourth became the most famous black fighting unit in the Union Army. All the men in the regiment were volunteers, and nearly all were free blacks from the North. They enlisted for various reasons: to help free their brothers and sisters from bondage, to prove that black men were not inferior, and to help save the Union. The subject of the brilliant motion picture Glory (1989), *the Fifty-Fourth led the federal assault on Fort Wagner in Charleston Harbor, losing its white commander and almost half its men. Although the attack was repulsed, the men of the Fifty-Fourth proved that black soldiers could fight as well as white soldiers. All told, some 186,000 blacks served in the Union Army: they fought in 450 engagements and won twenty-one Congressional Medals of Honor. (Luis F. Emilio,* A Brave Black Regiment)*

the North, free Negroes denounced Lincoln's colonization efforts—this was their country too! they cried—and they petitioned him to deport slaveholders instead.

As a consequence, Lincoln had just about concluded that whites and liberated blacks must somehow learn how to live together in this country. Still, he needed some device for now, some program that would pacify white Northerners and convince them that Southern freedmen would not flock into their communities, but would remain in the South instead. What Lincoln worked out was a refugee system, installed by his adjutant general in the occupied Mississippi Valley, which mobilized Southern blacks in the South, utilizing them in military and civilian pursuits there. According to the system, the adjutant general enrolled all able-bodied freedmen in the army, employed other ex-slaves as military laborers, and hired still others to work on farms and plantations for wages set by the government. While there were many faults with the system, it was predicated on sound Republican dogma; it kept Southern Negroes out of the North, and it got them jobs as wage earners, thus helping them to help themselves and preparing them for life in a free society.

Even so, emancipation remained the most explosive and unpopular act of Lincoln's presidency. By mid–1863, thousands of Democrats were in open revolt against his administration, denouncing Lincoln as an abolitionist dictator who had surrendered to radicalism. In the Midwest, dissident Democrats launched a peace movement to throw "the shrieking abolitionist faction" out of office and negotiate a peace with the Confederacy that would somehow restore the Union with slavery unharmed. There were large antiwar rallies against Lincoln's war for slave liberation. Race and draft riots flared in several Northern cities.

With all the public unrest behind the lines, conservative Republicans beseeched Lincoln to abandon emancipation and rescue his country "from the brink of ruin." But Lincoln seemed intractable. He had made up his mind to smash the slave society of the rebel South and eliminate "the cruel wrong" of Negro bondage, and no amount of public discontent, he indicated, was going to change his mind. "To use a coarse, but an expressive figure," he wrote one aggravated Democrat, "broken eggs cannot be mended. I have issued the Proclamation, and I cannot retract it." Congressman Owen Lovejoy applauded Lincoln's stand. "His mind acts slowly," Lovejoy said, "but when he moves, it is *forward*."

He wavered once—in August 1864, a time of unrelenting gloom for Lincoln when his popularity had sunk to an all-time low and it seemed he could not be reelected. He confessed that maybe the country would no longer sustain a war for slave emancipation, that maybe he shouldn't pull the nation down a road it did not want to travel. On August 24 he decided to offer Confederate President Jefferson Davis peace terms that excluded emancipation as a condition, vaguely suggesting that slavery would be adjusted later "by peaceful means." But the next day Lincoln changed his mind. With awakened resolution, he vowed to fight the war through to unconditional surrender and to stick by emancipation come what may. He had made his promise of freedom to the slaves, and he meant to keep it so long as he was in office.

When he won the election of 1864, Lincoln interpreted it as a popular mandate for him and his emancipation policy. But in reality the election provided no clear referendum on slavery, since Republican campaigners had played down emancipation and concentrated on the peace plank in the Democratic platform. Nevertheless, Lincoln used his reelection to promote a constitutional amendment that would guarantee the freedom of all slaves, those in the loyal border as well as those in the rebel South. Since issuing his Proclamation, Lincoln had worried that it might be nullified in the courts or thrown out by a later Congress or a subsequent administration. Consequently he wanted a constitutional amendment that would safeguard his Proclamation and prevent emancipation from ever being overturned.

As it happened, the Senate in May of 1864 had already passed an emancipation amendment—the present Thirteenth Amendment—but the House had failed to approve it. After that Lincoln had insisted that the Republican platform endorse the measure. And now, over the winter of 1864 and 1865, he put tremendous pressure on the House to endorse the amendment, using all his powers of persuasion and patronage to get it through. He buttonholed conservative Republicans and opposition Democrats and exhorted them to support the amendment. He singled out "sinners" among the Democrats who were "on praying ground," and informed them that they had a lot better chance for the federal jobs they desired if they voted for the measure. Soon two Democrats swung over in favor of it. With the outcome still in doubt, Lincoln participated in secret negotiations never made public—negotiations that allegedly involved the patronage, a New Jersey railroad monopoly, and the release of rebels related to Congressional Democrats—to bring wavering opponents into line. "The greatest measure of the nineteenth century," congressman Thaddeus Stevens claimed, "was passed by corruption aided and abetted by the purest man in America." On January 31, 1865, the House adopted the present Thirteenth Amendment by just three votes more than the required two-thirds majority. At once a storm of cheers broke over House Republicans, who danced around, embraced one another, and waved their hats and canes overhead. "It seemed to me I had been born with a new life," one Republican recalled, "and that the world was overflowing with beauty and joy."

Lincoln, too, pronounced the amendment "a great moral victory" and "a King's cure" for the evils of slavery. When ratified by the states, the amendment would end human bondage everywhere in America. Lincoln pointed across the Potomac. "If the people over the river had behaved themselves, I could not have done what I have."

7

Lincoln conceded, though, that he had not controlled the events of the war, but that events had controlled him instead, that God had controlled him. He thought about this a great deal, especially at night when he couldn't sleep, trying to understand the

The strain of war: At left, Abraham Lincoln in Springfield, Illinois, on June 3, 1860. At right, after four years of war, Lincoln posed for photographer Alexander Gardner in Washington,

April 10, 1865. (Photo on left: Chicago Historical Society, photo on right: Brown University, McClennan Lincoln Collection)

meaning of the war, to understand why it had begun and grown into such a massive revolutionary struggle, consuming hundreds of thousands of lives (the final casualties would come to 620,000 on both sides). By his second inaugural, he had reached an apocalyptic conclusion about the nature of the war—had come to see it as a divine punishment for the "great offense" of slavery, as a terrible retribution God had visited on a guilty people, in North as well as South. Lincoln's vision was close to that of old John Brown, who had prophesied on the day he was hanged, on that balmy December day back in 1859, that the crime of slavery could not be purged away from this guilty land except by blood. Now, in his second Inaugural Address, Lincoln too contended that God perhaps had willed this "mighty scourge of War" on the United States, "until all the wealth piled by the bondman's two hundred and fifty years of unrequited toil shall be sunk, and until every drop

of blood drawn with the lash, shall be paid by another drawn from the sword."

In the last paragraph of his address, Lincoln said he would bind the nation's wounds "with malice toward none" and "charity for all." Yet that did not mean he would be so gentle and forgiving in reconstruction as most biographers have contended. He would be magnanimous in the sense that he wouldn't resort to mass executions or even mass imprisonment of Southern "traitors," as he repeatedly called them. He would not even have the leaders tried and jailed, though he said he would like to "frighten them out of the country." Nevertheless, still preoccupied with the war as a grim purgation which would cleanse and regenerate his country, Lincoln endorsed a fairly tough policy toward the conquered South. After Lee surrendered in April 1865, Lincoln publicly endorsed limited suffrage for Southern blacks, announcing that the intelligent ex-slaves and especially those who had served in Union military forces should have the vote. This put him in advance of most Northern whites. And it put him ahead of most Republicans as well—including many of the so-called radicals—who in April 1865 shrank from Negro suffrage out of fear of their own white constituents. True, Sumner, Salmon Chase, and a few of their colleagues now demanded that all Southern black men be enfranchised in order to protect their freedom. But Lincoln was not far from their position. In a line in his last political speech, April 11, 1865, he granted that the Southern black man deserved the vote, though Lincoln was not quite ready to make that mandatory. But it seems clear in what direction he was heading.

Moreover, in a cabinet meeting on Good Friday, 1865, Lincoln and all his Secretaries endorsed the military approach to reconstruction and conceded that an army of occupation might be necessary to control the rebellious white majority in the conquered South. During the war, Lincoln had always thought the military indispensable in restoring civilian rule in the South. Without the army, he feared that the rebellious Southern majority would overwhelm the small Unionist minority there—and maybe even reenslave the blacks. And he was not about to let the latter happen. The army had liberated the blacks in the war, and the army might well have to safeguard their freedom in reconstruction.

———

8

He had come a long distance from the young Lincoln who entered politics, quiet on slavery lest he be branded an abolitionist, opposed to Negro political rights lest his political career be jeopardized, convinced that only the future could remove slavery in America. He had come a long way indeed. Frederick Douglass, who interviewed Lincoln in the White House in 1863, said he was "the first great man that I talked with in the United States freely who in no single instance reminded me of the difference between himself and myself, of the difference of color." Douglass, reflecting back on Lincoln's presidency, recalled how in the first year and a half of the war, Lincoln "was ready and willing" to sacrifice black people for the benefit and welfare of whites. But since the preliminary Emancipation Proclamation, Douglass said, American blacks had taken Lincoln's measure and had come to admire and some to love this enigmatic man. Though Lincoln had taxed Negroes to the limit, they had decided, in the roll and tumble of events, that "the how and the man of our redemption had somehow met in the person of Abraham Lincoln."

But perhaps it was Lincoln himself who best summed up his journey to emancipation—his own as well as that of the slaves. In December 1862, after the calamitous by-elections of that year, in the midst of rising racial protest against his emancipation policy, Lincoln asked Congress—and Northern whites beyond—for their support. "The dogmas of the quiet past," he reminded them, "are inadequate to the stormy present. The occasion is piled high with difficulty, and we must rise with the occasion. As our case is new, so we must think anew, and act anew. We must disenthrall our selves, and then we shall save our country.

"Fellow-citizens, *we* cannot escape history. . . . The fiery trial through which we pass, will light us down, in honor or dishonor, to the latest generation. . . . In *giving* freedom to the slave, we *assure* freedom to the *free*—honorable alike in what we give, and what we preserve. We shall nobly save, or meanly lose, the last best, hope of earth."

QUESTIONS TO CONSIDER

1 Most of us are familiar with the story of "Honest Abe" Lincoln, the unambitious rail-splitting man of the people. How does Oates's biographical portrait of Lincoln reveal the complex human being behind this mythical image?

2 How was Lincoln able to reconcile his reverence for the founders and the Constitution with the moral

paradox of slavery in a free society? How did Lincoln hope to solve the problems of slavery and racial adjustment in America?

3 What was the so-called slave power conspiracy that Lincoln and many other Republicans feared by the late 1850s? How had the events of that crucial decade seemed to confirm their fears?

4 Oates says that the pressures and problems of fighting a civil war finally caused Lincoln to hurl an executive fist at slavery. What were the forces that led Lincoln to issue his Emancipation Proclamation?

5 Many of Lincoln's contemporaries as well as later scholars accused Lincoln of having made an empty gesture with the Emancipation Proclamation. How does Oates answer these accusations?

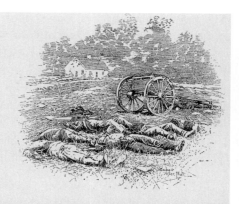

PART FOURTEEN

The Scourge of Civil War

27 The Ravages of War

STEPHEN B. OATES

The following essay challenges the long-held popular view of the Civil War as romantic and glorious. Calling the conflict "a killer war," Oates graphically describes the murderous weaponry that turned Civil War battlefields into slaughter pens, resulting in unbelievable and unprecedented casualties on both sides. But that is only part of this tragic story. Oates concludes that the Civil War wounded the spirit of the nation and left a legacy that fostered sectional bitterness and racial tension for years to come.

There were many reasons for this horrible war, but the existence of slavery in a country dedicated to freedom was the paradox that an entire generation could not resolve without resorting to bloodshed. That the new Confederacy was dedicated to saving slavery, both as a multibillion-dollar labor system and a means of race control, cannot be doubted. The Confederates wrote a constitution that closely resembled the United States Constitution save for one crucial difference: the Confederate document specifically guaranteed slavery and affirmed states' rights. In Savannah, Georgia, rebel vice president Alexander H. Stephens made it unmistakably clear what the Confederacy stood for. "Our new government is founded upon exactly the opposite idea [from that of equality in the Declaration of Independence]; its foundations are laid, its cornerstone rests, upon the great truth that the negro is not equal to the white man; that slavery—subordination to the superior race—is his natural and normal condition. This, our new government, is the first in the history of the world based upon this great physical, philosophical, and moral truth."

From the outset, this new government was beset with internal problems: it lacked sound money, guns, factories, food, railroads, and harmonious political leadership. Still, with its excellent generals and soldiers, the possibility of foreign intervention, and other advantages, the Confederacy faced better odds in its war for independence than had the American colonies. Why, then, did the Confederacy go down to defeat?

Slavery was not only the major reason for the war; it was ultimately an important factor in explaining the fall of the Confederacy. England, long committed to the concept of free labor, ended its flirtation with the Confederacy after Lincoln announced the Emancipation Proclamation. With this act the president captured the moral offensive, guaranteed European neutrality, and swelled the ranks of the Union Army with African Americans who were now fighting for a cause close to their hearts. The Union's superiority in manufacturing, railroads, financial resources, and even food production also wore down an increasingly divided Confederacy, which found that states' rights eroded the unity it needed in time of war.

Oates describes the final crippling blows as General Sherman's army "brought total war to the Deep South, contending as he did that modern wars were won by destroying the enemy's resources as well as his morale." In the short run, it produced ghostly pictures of ruined cities and destitute people. In the long run, it led to the death of slavery and the transformation of the country from a loose confederation of states into an indivisible nation.

GLOSSARY

ANTIETAM (MARYLAND) Robert E. Lee and George B. McClellan fought to a draw here in the bloodiest single day in American history. The battle ended Lee's first invasion of the North.

COLD HARBOR (VIRGINIA) The bloodiest hour of the war occurred as Ulysses S. Grant unsuccessfully tried an assault on Lee's army and lost 10,000 men in an effort to penetrate the rebel's entrenched defenses.

FREEDMEN'S BUREAU Established by congressional statute in March of 1865, the Bureau of Freedman, Refugees, and Abandoned Lands was supposed to provide food and schools for the former slaves, help them secure jobs, and make certain they received fair wages.

GETTYSBURG (PENNSYLVANIA) Lee's greatest reversal, in July of 1863, ended his second invasion of the North, best known for George Pickett's calamitous charge on the third day. Lee suffered such great losses that he could never again mount the offensive.

CONFEDERATE GENERALS:

BEAUREGARD, PIERRE GUSTAVE TOUTANT Led Confederate forces to victory at First Bull Run (or First Manassas), July 1861.

BRAGG, BRAXTON Quarrelsome commander of the Army of Tennessee, the Confederacy's main army in the western theater; lost the Battle of Perryville and the battles around Chattanooga, October–November 1863.

HOOD, JOHN BELL Led the Army of Tennessee to annihilation in the Battle of Nashville, December 1864.

JACKSON, THOMAS J. "STONEWALL" Defeated three separate Union forces in the Shenandoah Valley, spring 1862; became Lee's most brilliant divisional and corps commander; famous for his flanking march and attack at Chancellorsville, where he was mortally wounded by his own pickets.

JOHNSTON, ALBERT SIDNEY Many Confederates considered him the best general in the rebel army; commanded the western forces early in the war and was killed in the Battle of Shiloh, Tennessee, April 1862.

JOHNSTON, JOSEPH EGGLESTON Preferred to fight on the defensive; commanded the main Confederate Army in Virginia in the first half of 1862; fought against McClellan in the Peninsula campaign; was later sent west to coordinate rebel efforts to defend Vicksburg against Grant; contested Sherman's advance against Atlanta in 1864 and in the Carolinas in 1865.

LEE, ROBERT E. The best rebel commander; preferred to fight on the offensive; led the Army of Northern Virginia, the Confederacy's showcase army, from June 1862 to April 1865, when he surrendered to Grant; won the Seven Days Battles before Richmond, the Second Battle of Bull Run, Fredericksburg, and Chancellorsville against inferior Union generals; promoted to general in chief of all rebel military forces near the end of the war.

PEMBERTON, JOHN Rebel commander who surrendered Vicksburg, July 1863.

UNION GENERALS:

BURNSIDE, AMBROSE E. Inept commander of the Army of the Potomac, 1862–1863, who lost to Lee in the Battle of Fredericksburg, December 1862.

GRANT, ULYSSES S. The North's best general; captured Forts Henry and Donnelson in Tennessee in 1862 and the great river garrison of Vicksburg in 1863; won the battles around Chattanooga in December of that year; became general in chief of all Union forces in 1864, and led the Army of the Potomac against Lee in a series of ferocious engagements around Richmond, finally pinning Lee down in the siege of Petersburg.

HOOKER, JOSEPH Inept commander of the Army of the Potomac who lost to Lee at Chancellorsville, Virginia, May 1863.

McCLELLAN, GEORGE B. Commander of the Army of the Potomac, 1861–1862; orchestrated the glacial-paced Peninsula campaign against Richmond; was driven back by Lee in the Seven Days Battles and recalled to Washington; led the Potomac Army against Lee at Antietam and might have won the battle had he not been overly cautious; finally sacked by Lincoln on the grounds that the general had "the slows."

MEADE, GEORGE GORDON Led the Army of the Potomac in the Battle of Gettysburg, July 1863, and remained titular head of that army during Grant's great offensive against Lee, 1864–1865.

POPE, JOHN Blusterous, incompetent commander of the Union's Army of Virginia; decisively beaten by Lee and Jackson at Second Bull Run (Second Manassas), August 1863.

SHERMAN, WILLIAM TECUMSEH Grant's subordinate commander in the West, 1862–1863; became the Union's top general there when Grant was promoted to supreme command; led the Union's Western Army on its famous march through Georgia and the Carolinas, 1864–1865.

It began with a fanfare of bugles and patriotic oratory, with both sides promising that it would be over in ninety days. From Maine to Texas, volunteers flocked to recruiting centers and marched off to war as young women tossed flowers in their paths. Youths in uniform posed before exploding cameras and sent daguerreotypes of themselves back to their families and sweethearts. They gathered around glowing campfires and spoke in hyperbole about the excitement of battle and what they would do to the enemy when the shooting started. For the volunteers, for civilians in the North and South alike, it was all a picture-book war, a springtime of pomp and pageantry—of fierce drums and blaring bugles, of strutting drum majors and marching bands, of whipping banners and fluttering flags. It was a time when everybody was swept up in the romance of war, in the thrill and dreams of military glory.

What began as a ninety-day lark for both sides swelled instead into a national holocaust, a tornado of blood and wreckage that left scarcely a single family in North or South unscathed. Before it ended,

2.1 million men had gone to war for the Union, nearly 800,000 for the Confederacy. In Dixie, where most of the fighting took place, almost four-fifths of the white men of military age served the Rebel cause, "a *levée en masse*," wrote one historian, "made possible only by the existence of slavery."

There was nothing romantic about this killer war— a brothers' war, the worst kind of human conflict; it released a primordial fury still not understood. How can the cost of the war be reckoned? In numbers alone, the human devastation was staggering. Some 110,000 Federals and 94,000 Confederates lost their lives in combat or from mortal battle wounds. The injured often wished for a merciful bullet, for conditions in Civil War hospitals were ghastly. It was a medically ignorant time; both armies suffered from shortages of doctors and nurses; field hospitals were often pungent barns or chicken coops. In one infirmary a reporter found "the maimed, gashed, and dying" crowded together while a surgeon produced "a little heap of human fingers, feet, legs and arms" wherever he worked. After Gettysburg, Union surgeons consumed five days on amputations—more time than it took to fight the battle. Those who survived combat had to contend with an even deadlier foe: disease. Diarrhea, dysentery, "camp fevers" like malaria and typhoid, and other maladies plagued both armies and claimed more lives

Stephen B. Oates, "The Ravages of War," in *Touched by Fire: A Photographic Portrait of the Civil War*, vol. 2, ed. William C. Davis (Boston: Little Brown, 1996), pp. 239–243. Reprinted by permission of Stephen B. Oates.

The outcome of the Civil War was determined on the battlefield. This photograph shows Confederate dead after the 1862 Battle of Antietam, which repelled a rebel invasion of the North and forestalled European recognition of the Confederacy. (Chicago Historical Society).

than the battles did. On the Union side, diarrhea and dysentery alone killed 44,500 men. In round numbers, some 623,000 American servicemen—365,000 Federals and 258,000 Confederates—perished in the Civil War. The Union by itself lost more men than the United States did in World War II. Total Civil War casualties almost equaled the combined losses of all of America's other wars.

The fighting in the Civil War was savage beyond computation—a savagery made possible by the most murderous arsenal of destruction Americans had ever assembled. There were the versatile 12-pounder napoleons, the workhorse artillery of both armies, whose canister and grapeshot could obliterate entire lines of advancing infantry. There were the new rifled cannons, macabre guns with flat trajectories and immense hitting power. There were the muzzle-loading Springfield and Enfield rifles, which became the basic infantry weapons for both sides; far more accurate than the smoothbores they replaced, the single-shot rifles had an effective range of four hundred yards and could be loaded and fired three or four times a minute. Add to these the breech-loading repeaters, rudimentary machine guns, and ironclad warships introduced during the conflict, and one understands why experts call it the first modern war in which weapons and machines played a decisive role.

Such weapons turned Civil War battles into human slaughter pens. In one day at Antietam, the bloodiest single day in the annals of American warfare, 2,010 Yankees and 2,700 Rebels were killed and 18,440 combatants were wounded, 3,000 of them mortally. More Americans died that one day than in the War of 1812, the Mexican War, and the Spanish-American War put together. The 12,000 Confederate casualties were double those of U.S. forces on D day.

Losses in the Civil War grew more appalling with every campaign; 23,000 Federals and 28,000 Confederates mowed down or missing at Gettysburg, 64,000 Federals and 32,000 Confederates killed, wounded, or missing in the fighting from the Wilderness to Petersburg in 1864. When ordered to attack entrenched Rebels at Cold Harbor, Virginia, Union troops pinned strips of paper to their coats that gave their names and addresses, so that their bodies could be identified. One doomed Yankee scribbled in his diary; "June 3. Cold Harbor. I was killed." He and 7,000 other Union men were shot dead or wounded in less than an hour of fighting. That was surely the bloodiest hour of combat in all American history.

Gruesome though they are, casualty figures cannot convey what it was like to be in the Civil War. For that we turn to eyewitness accounts, which include some of the most vivid descriptions of the ravages of war ever recorded. Here a Union veteran recalls the horrors of Shiloh:

The ear-piercing and peculiar Rebel yell of the men in gray and answering cheers of the boys in blue rose and fell with the varying tide of battle and, with the hoarse and scarcely distinguishable orders of the officers, the screaming and bursting of shell, the swishing of canister, the roaring of volley firing, the death screams of the stricken and struggling horses and the cries and groans of the wounded formed an indescribable impression which can never be effaced from memory.

A Confederate officer on the Union bombardment of Fredericksburg:

Ten o'clock came, and the hammers of the church clocks were just sounding the last peaceful stroke of the hour, when suddenly, at the signal of a single cannon shot, more then 150 pieces of artillery, including some of the enemy's most ponderous guns, opened their iron mouths with a terrific roar and hurled a tempest of destruction upon the devoted town. The air shook, and the very earth beneath our feet trembled at this deafening cannonade, the heaviest that had ever yet assailed my ears. . . . The howling of the solid shot, the bursting of the shells, the crashing of the missiles through the thick walls and the dull sound of falling houses united in a dismal concert of doom. Very soon the site of the unhappy town was indicated, even through the fog, by a column of smoke and dust and the flames of burning buildings. . . . About noon the sun, breaking through the clouds, seemed to mock the smoking ruins it revealed.

A Union lieutenant on the second day at Gettysburg:

All along the crest everything was ready. Gun after gun, along the batteries, in rapid succession leaped where it stood and bellowed its canister upon the enemy. They still advanced. The infantry opened fire, and soon the whole crest, artillery and infantry, was one continuous sheet of fire. . . . All senses for the time were dead but the one of sight. The roar of the discharges and the yells of the enemy all passed unheeded, but the impassioned soul was all eyes and saw all things that the smoke did not hide. How madly the battery men were driving the double charges of canister into those broad-mouthed Napoleons! How rapidly those long blue-coated lines of infantry delivered their fire down the slope! . . . Men were dropping, dead or wounded, on all sides, by scores and by hundreds. Poor mutilated creatures, some with an arm dangling, some with a leg broken by a bullet, were limping and crawling toward the rear. They made no sound of pain but were as silent as if dumb and mute.

A Union war correspondent on the battlefield the night after Pickett's charge:

I became possessed by a nameless horror. Once I tumbled over two bodies and found my face close to the swollen, bloody features of the man who lay uppermost, judging from the position of other bodies. A shower of grape and canister must have torn the ranks of a regiment into shreds,

The summer and fall of 1863 resulted in Union victories at Gettysburg, Vicksburg, and Chattanooga. This scene depicts Robert E. Lee's defeat at Gettysburg, Pennsylvania, where Union forces were *able to take the tactical advantage of defending a position against an advancing and overextended army. (Courtesy of the Ann S. K. Brown Military Collection, Brown University Library)*

for 50 or 60 bodies lay there in a row. I came across the corpse of a drummer-boy, his arms still clasped around his drums, his head shattered by a shell. I realized what a price is paid for victories.

Noncombatants paid, too, as the storm uprooted whole communities. Before, during, and after battles, armies of homeless refugees clogged roads and byways. "I never saw a more pitiful procession than they made trudging through the deep snow," a Rebel soldier said of refugees from Fredericksburg.

I saw little children tugging along with their doll babies, holding their feet up carefully above the snow, and women so old and feeble that they could carry nothing and could barely hobble themselves. There were women carrying a baby in one arm and its bottle, clothes and covering in the other. Some had a Bible and a toothbrush in one and, a picked chicken and a bag of flour in the other. . . . Where they were going we could not tell, and I doubt if they could.

Another class of refugees suffered even more. These were the fugitive slaves, hundreds of thousands of whom abandoned Rebel homesteads and set out for the nearest Union army. In the embattled Mississippi Valley, where fugitives swamped Union lines, an Ohio chaplain wrote that "their condition was appalling. There were men, women and children in every stage of disease or decrepitude, often nearly naked, with flesh torn by the terrible experiences of their escapes." As Sherman's army marched through Georgia, some twenty-five thousand slaves followed it at one time or another—whole families trying to keep pace with the soldiers, with children tied to their parents by a rope. An Indiana officer noted that slave babies "tumbled from the backs of mules to which they had been told to cling, and were drowned in the swamps while mothers stood by the roadside crying for their lost children." Though most of the blacks fell away, too sick or exhausted to continue, seven thousand toiled after Sherman clear to the sea.

It was Sherman, of course, who brought total war to the Deep South, contending as he did that modern wars were won by destroying the enemy's resources as well as his morale. "We are not only fighting hostile armies," Sherman asserted, "but a hostile people, and must make old and young, rich and poor, feel the hard hand of war." That he did, as his army first burned Atlanta—"the workshop of the Confederacy"—while a regimental band played "John Brown's Body." A witness recalled that Yankee soldiers "took up the words wedded to the music, and, high above the roaring flames, above the clash of falling walls, above the fierce crackling of thousands of small-arm cartridges in the burning buildings, rose the triumphant refrain, 'His truth is marching on!'" Then sixty thousand Union troops cut a swath to Savannah 40 miles wide and 220 miles long, visiting war on civilians on a scale unprecedented in America. "We had a gay old campaign," remarked one soldier. "Destroyed all we could eat, stole their niggers, burned their cotton & gins, spilled their sorghum, burned & twisted their R. Roads and raised Hell generally." Sherman estimated the damage at $100 million. Smoldering Georgia was out of the war, her citizens in shock.

Sherman's army now stormed into South Carolina, tearing up railroads, burning down barns, pulverizing fields of corn and cotton, assassinating cows and chickens, wiping out everything that might sustain dwindling Rebel forces. Civilians fled their homes and evacuated their towns before Sherman's relentless columns. Columbia, the state capital, went up in an inferno of smoke, the conflagration started either by Confederates or Union troops. A Northerner wrote that

most of the citizens of Columbia had sons or relations in the Rebel army. Half of them were dead, and in the blackness of this terrible night their fortunes were all lost. Many wandered about wringing their hands and crying; some sat stolid and speechless in the street, watching everything that they had go to destruction. . . . Most of the people of Columbia would have been willing to die that night, then and there. What had they left to live for? *This, too, was war.*

By now Union forces were smashing up the Confederacy in East and West alike. In the Shenandoah, Philip Sheridan burned a broad path of devastation clear to the Rapidan River. In northwest Alabama, thirteen thousand Union horsemen launched the biggest and most destructive cavalry raid of the war; they crushed their Rebel opponents and burned and wrecked their way clear into southern Georgia. Such scorched-earth warfare earned Lincoln and his generals undying hatred in Dixie, but it brought them victory; within five months after Sherman began his march to the sea, the war was over.

The North suffered terrible human losses, but at least her economy was booming from war production. The South was not only defeated; she was annihilated. Half her men of military age were dead or wounded, two-fifths of her livestock wiped out, more than half her farm machinery demolished, her major cities in ruins, her railroads and industry desolated, her coastal and river ports out of commission, her commerce paralyzed, two-thirds of her assessed wealth, including billions of dollars in slaves, destroyed. "Have we not fallen on sad, sad times?" sighed a Georgia woman as she surveyed the misery around her. Perhaps Southerners now knew what Lincoln had meant when he vowed to teach them "the folly of being the beginners of war." Perhaps they could all—as a young Texas veteran expressed it—"fall down in the dust and weep over our great misfortune, our great calamities."

Across Dixie the physical damage was everywhere in evidence. Near fire-gutted Columbia, sixty-five horses and mules slain by Sherman's men rotted for six weeks because there were no shovels or other implements with which to bury them. The wreckage in the Tennessee Valley was typical of the dead Confederacy. Here an English traveler found "plantations of which the ruin is for the present total and complete," and a trail of war visible "in burnt up gin houses, ruined bridges, mills, and factories." He added, in reference to the vanquished slave-owning class, that "many who were the richest men . . . have disappeared from the scene."

Few Southerners were more destitute than the former slaves. Owning little more than the skin on their backs, they streamed by the thousands into Union army bivouacs or the nearest towns and cities. The Freedmen's Bureau set up relief camps and throughout the summer of 1865 distributed 100,000 daily rations to suffering blacks. But the camps were so crowded that epidemics killed a third of the people in them.

Whites were scarcely better off, as roving bands of thieves pillaged defenseless homes and famine and disease plagued the land. An official of the Freedmen's Bureau reported as "an everyday sight" women and children "begging for bread from door to door." The bureau gave out thousands of daily rations to whites too (total rations to whites and blacks came to 22 million between 1865 and 1870). Into "the vacuum of chaos and destruction," as one writer phrased it, came 200,000 occupation troops, who managed to restore some semblance of order to war-ravaged Dixie.

How much did the war cost both sections? Exact figures are hard to come by, especially for the Confederacy. Surviving records indicate that by October 1863 Confederate war expenditures had exceeded $2 billion. By 1879, according to one estimate, Union expenses growing out of the war were more than $6 billion. But these sums excluded the war debts of the states. Adding up estimates of those debts, Union and Confederate war expenses, total property loss, federal pensions to 1917, and interest to the national debt, one historian put the overall cost of the war at about $20 billion.

But this does not count the billions of dollars it took to rebuild the South. Nor does it include losses from reduced Southern production. The South's economy was so crippled that her per-capita output did not return to the antebellum level for more than fifty years after Appomattox. The South's per-capita income, 33 percent lower than the North's in 1860, was 40 percent lower in 1880 and stayed there until the twentieth century.

But dollars and percentages cannot gauge the full toll of the Civil War. One must look at the photographs to comprehend what it did to the land and the cities: the rubble of Richmond . . . the burned-out Gallego Flour Mills there . . . the fields of skull and bone . . . the maimed bodies of the wounded . . . the face of exhaustion in the North . . . the visage of defeat in Dixie.

But not even the photographs capture the emotional and psychological scars left by the conflict. Who knows what damage it did to the American spirit? Who can measure the mental anguish and human suffering that continued long after the guns were silent? Who can say how deep the bitterness and humiliation ran in the South, where millions of unrepentant whites embraced the legend of the lost cause and forged a bastion of white supremacy that lasted a century?

In time, though, some of the bitterness faded with the battle flags, and hard-bitten veterans of both armies, many with arms and legs gone, with eyes shot out and faces disfigured, marched in memorial parades and wept at speeches of remembered valor. And so in the veterans' reunions the war ended as it had begun—in an aura of glory.

But beyond the parades and reunions were grim reminders of what really happened in that war. There were the cemeteries in both sections, quiet fields where soldiers lay in ranks of white gravestones. There were the battlefield parks, with their polished cannons and statues of singular men frozen in marble. Here, if he listens closely, the visitor today can hear the echoes of the war—the rattle of musketry, the deadly whir of grapeshot, the ring of sabers, the shouts. He can almost see colliding lines of infantry and shell-torn flags in the smoke, can almost smell the acrid odor of gunpowder and the stench of death on the wind. The battlefields recall what madness beset Americans from 1861 to 1865 and what the nation paid, and paid dearly, for its survival. At every battle site there ought to be a shrine to those broken and blood-ied men, with the inscription "Lord God of hosts, Be with us yet, Lest we forget, Lest we forget. . . ."

QUESTIONS TO CONSIDER

1 Reflect on the early days of the Civil War when most viewed combat with feelings of romance and glory. Now compare these visions with the horrors that followed. Do you think that other American wars have witnessed a similar journey from hope to despair as the grim reality of combat became clearer?

2 Describe why the carnage of the Civil War was, in part, the product of medical treatment, disease, and the new weapons of mass destruction.

3 Civilians, both black and white, suffered in the Civil War, unlike any other military event in American

history. As you read about the path of destruction that General Sherman carved through Georgia and South Carolina, were you convinced that this was necessary to bring an earlier end to the war?

4 Oates describes how the southern economy was in ruins after the Civil War. Given the physical destruction of the cities and farms, do you think the victorious North should have helped rebuild the South, much like the United States aided in the recovery of Western Europe following World War II?

5 Oates concludes that "dollars and percentages can-not gauge the full toll of the Civil War." What im-pact did the war have on sectional tension between the North and South and racial friction between blacks and whites? Have these problems affected the American spirit in the twenty-first century?

6 Evidenced by the tourists who are drawn to the battlefields, the books sold, and even the popular PBS program by Ken Burns, the Civil War remains one of the most haunting and popular topics in American history. Why do you think it continues to interest and fascinate us?

28 Hayfoot, Strawfoot!

BRUCE CATTON

If the Civil War was won or lost on the battlefield, then it is important to acquaint ourselves with the soldiers who did the fighting. First of all, most of the 3 million soldiers in both armies were vol-unteers who lacked the training and the spit and polish of the professional soldiers of Europe. Second, they were young: a typical Civil War soldier, as James I. Robertson points out in Soldiers Blue and Gray *(1988), was between eighteen and twenty-nine years old; but some were as young as fourteen and others as old as seventy.*

Civil War soldiers endured harsh conditions in camp. Union men subsisted on hardtack, a kind of cracker that was often infested with weevils and so hard as to be inedible, and salt pork that was frequently tainted, and they washed it all down each day with three or four quarts of strong coffee apiece. That much caffeine must have fried their nervous systems. They drank their share of whiskey, too, which they called "bug juice," "rot gut," "bust skull," and consumed homemade con-coctions called, "Oh, be joyful" and "knockum stiff." Imbibing too much of such stuff would make you "fire and fall back" (vomit) and leave you "squashmolished" (plagued with a hangover). When soldiers of both armies secured cherished passes to leave camp and visit the nearest town or city, they often sought out the brothels, where they enjoyed "horizontal refreshments." Enterprising madams often offered lower prices to an entire company or regiment on a sort of group plan.

The sick and wounded of both armies suffered terribly in the dreaded field hospitals. Here a second war was going on that claimed more lives than the shooting war itself. Two-thirds of the Union deaths occurred in the hospitals, where surgeons and nurses, relying on primitive medical practices and dubious medicines, fought a losing battle to save wounded or diseased soldiers. Since nobody knew what caused infection, surgeons of both armies worked with unsanitary scalpels and saws in unsanitary conditions. Recalled one surgeon: "We operated in old blood-stained and often pus-stained coats, with undisinfected hands. We used undisinfected instruments and sponges which had been used in prior pus cases and only washed in tap water." The luckless soldier with a bone-breaking wound in the leg or arm faced certain amputation—it was the only way the surgeons knew to save his life. If he was in a well-stocked hospital, the surgeon would put him mercifully to sleep with chloroform or ether. If both were lacking (and they often were at battlefield hospitals), the poor victim might get a shot of whiskey, or simply a slab of leather placed between his teeth, before the surgeon applied the saw. Because of the horrible conditions in the hospitals and the lack of proper medical treatment, the mortality rate was appalling. Nearly every soldier with an abdominal wound died; some 60 percent of those with other wounds also died.

The real Civil War killer, however, was infectious disease. Dysentery and diarrhea were the worst, sending more men to the grave than bullets and shells on the battlefield. Doctors tried to combat diarrhrea/dysentery with laxatives, opium, castor oil, or Epsom salts, all of which, save the opium, exacerbated the condition horribly. Other killer diseases were malaria and typhoid, which the crude medicines of the day could do little to stop. Doing the best they could with the limited medical knowledge of the day, physicians treated abdominal pains with blisters and "hot fomentation" and intestinal ulcers with oral doses of turpentine, and they sometimes treated headaches with applications of leaches. As other historians have pointed out, a soldier's safety was more imperiled if he had to undergo treatment in an army hospital than if he had fought all three days at Gettysburg.

In his portrait of the Civil War fighting man, the late Bruce Catton, one of the most prolific and preeminent Civil War historians of all time, will introduce you to the daily life, routine, training, combat, and suffering of the soldiers of "the late unpleasantness," as they often called the war. He points out that outmoded battle tactics, combined with murderous new weaponry, turned Civil War battles into bloodbaths. Why did soldiers of the two sides volunteer to fight in such a brutal conflict? Catton touches on this, but two books by Civil War historian James M. McPherson, What They Fought For (1994) and For Cause and Comrades (1997), answer that question in depth. Suffice it to say, the Union soldiers fought to preserve the Union and its experiment in popular government; and when Lincoln issued the Emancipation Proclamation, they fought to free the slaves as a means of saving the Union and its free government. As one Union private said, "We have lived, prospered and been protected under a free government, and we wish to preserve the same for the welfare and happiness of our posterity. The welfare of millions yet unborn is dependent upon us, and it behooves us to do all in our power to sustain our government."

Confederates, on the other hand, fought to prevent the hated Yankee invaders from subjugating their region; they fought to protect their homes and families and to create an independent, slave-based nation, which, they believed, would ensure their liberty as white men. As McPherson points out, the *majority of rebel soldiers believed they were fighting "for liberty and slavery, one and inseparable." It did not matter that most Confederate soldiers were non-slaveholders; they were white and were as furiously opposed to the emancipation of black people, whom they hated and feared, as the planters were. As a captain of the Twenty-Eighth Mississippi wrote his wife: "I own no slaves and can freely express my notions without being taxed with any motive of self interest. I know that this country without Negro slave labor would be wholly worthless, a barren waste and desolate plain—we can only live and exist by this species of labor; and hence I am willing to fight to the last."*

Some 260,000 of his southern brothers did fight to the last in a doomed cause, while 360,000 Yankees died to make the United States a nation at last.

GLOSSARY

DRILL SERGEANT   Noncommissioned officer who had to teach the untaught and inexperienced volunteers how to march.

JOHNNY REB   Nickname for a Confederate soldier.

MILITARY TACTICS   Usually defined as "the art or science of disposing specific military or naval forces for battle and maneuvering them in battle."

REGIMENT   Basic army unit, which on paper consisted of about a thousand men divided into ten companies and commanded by a colonel. Four regiments, in turn, constituted a brigade; three or four brigades formed a division; three or more divisions made up a corps; and two or more corps constituted an army.

SPRINGFIELD RIFLE   Standard weapon for Civil War infantry, a .58-caliber muzzle-loading rifled musket that was far more accurate than the outmoded smoothbores.

SUTLER   Civilian merchant licensed by the army to sell additional rations to Union troops.

The volunteer soldier in the American Civil War used a clumsy muzzle-loading rifle, lived chiefly on salt pork and hardtack, and retained to the very end a loose-jointed, informal attitude toward the army with which he had cast his lot. But despite all of the surface differences, he was at bottom blood brother to the G.I. Joe of modern days.

Which is to say that he was basically, and incurably, a civilian in arms. A volunteer, he was still a soldier because he had to be one, and he lived for the day when he could leave the army forever. His attitude toward discipline, toward his officers, and toward the whole spit-and-polish concept of military existence was essentially one of careless tolerance.

He refused to hate his enemies—indeed, he often got along with them much better than with some of his own comrades—and his indoctrination was often so imperfect that what was sometimes despairingly said of the American soldier in World War II would apply equally to him: he seemed to be fighting chiefly so that he could some day get back to Mom's cooking.

What really set the Civil War soldier apart was the fact that he came from a less sophisticated society. He was no starry-eyed innocent, to be sure—or, if he was, the army quickly took care of that—but the America of the 1860s was less highly developed than modern America. It lacked the ineffable advantages of radio, television, and moving pictures. It was still essentially a rural nation; it had growing cities, but they were smaller and somehow less urban than today's cities; a much greater percentage of the population lived on farms or in country towns and villages than is the case now, and there was more of a

Bruce Catton, "Hayfoot, Strawfoot!" *American Heritage,* vol. 8, no. 3 (April 1957), pp. 30–37. Reprinted by permission of *American Heritage.*

backwoods, hay-seed-in-the-hair flavor to the people who came from them.

For example: every war finds some ardent youngsters who want to enlist despite the fact that they are under the military age limit of eighteen. Such a lad today simply goes to the recruiting station, swears that he is eighteen, and signs up. The lad of the 1860s saw it a little differently. He could not swear that he was eighteen when he was only sixteen; in his innocent way, he felt that to lie to his own government was just plain wrong. But he worked out a little dodge that got him into the army anyway. He would take a bit of paper, scribble the number *18* on it, and put it in the sole of his shoe. Then, when the recruiting officer asked him how old he was, he could truthfully say: "I am *over* eighteen." That was a common happening, early in the Civil War; one cannot possibly imagine it being tried today.

Similarly, the drill sergeants repeatedly found that among the raw recruits there were men so abysmally untaught that they did not know left from right, and hence could not step off on the left foot as all soldiers should. To teach these lads how to march, the sergeants would tie a wisp of hay to the left foot and a wisp of straw to the right; then, setting the men to march, they would chant, "Hay-foot, straw-foot, hay-foot, straw-foot"—and so on, until everybody had caught on. A common name for a green recruit in those days was "strawfoot."

On the drill field, when a squad was getting basic training, the men were as likely as not to intone a little rhythmic chant as they tramped across the sod—thus:

> March! March! March old soldier march!
> Hayfoot, strawfoot,
> Belly-full of bean soup—
> March old soldier march!

Because of his unsophistication, the ordinary soldier in the Civil War, North and South alike, usually joined up with very romantic ideas about soldiering. Army life rubbed the romance off just as rapidly then as it does now, but at the start every volunteer went into the army thinking that he was heading off to high adventure. Under everything else, he enlisted because

he thought army life was going to be fun, and usually it took quite a few weeks in camp to disabuse him of this strange notion. Right at the start, soldiering had an almost idyllic quality; if this quality faded rapidly, the memory of it remained through all the rest of life.

Early days in camp simply cemented the idea. An Illinois recruit, writing home from training camp, confessed: "It is fun to lie around, face unwashed, hair uncombed, shirt unbuttoned and everything un-everythinged. It sure beats clerking." Another Illinois boy confessed: "I don't see why people will stay at home when they can get to soldiering. A year of it is worth getting shot for to any man." And a Massachusetts boy, recalling the early days of army life, wrote that "Our drill, as I remember it, consisted largely of running around the Old Westbury town hall, yelling like Devils and firing at an imaginary foe." One of the commonest discoveries that comes from a reading of Civil War diaries is that the chief worry, in training camp, was a fear that the war would be over before the ardent young recruits could get into it. It is only fair to say that most of the diarists looked back on this innocent worry, a year or so afterward, with rueful amusement.

There was a regiment recruited in northern Pennsylvania in 1861—13th Pennsylvania Reserves officially, known to the rest of the Union Army as the Bucktails because the rookies decorated their caps with strips of fur from the carcass of a deer that was hanging in front of a butcher shop near their camp— and in mid-spring these youthful soldiers were ordered to rendezvous at Harrisburg. So they marched cross-country (along a road known today as the Bucktail Trail) to the north branch of the Susquehanna, where they built rafts. One raft, for the colonel, was made oversized with a stable; the colonel's horse had to ride, too. Then the Bucktails floated down the river, singing and firing their muskets and having a gay old time, camping out along the bank at night, and finally they got to Harrisburg; and they served through the worst of the war, getting badly shot up and losing most of their men to Confederate bullets, but they never forgot the picnic air of those first days of army life, when they drifted down a river through the forests, with a song in the air and the bright light of adventure shining just ahead. Men do not go to war that way nowadays.

Discipline in those early regiments was pretty sketchy. The big catch was that most regiments were recruited locally—in one town, or one county, or in one part of a city—and everybody more or less knew everybody else. Particularly, the privates knew their officers—most of whom were elected to their jobs by the enlisted men—and they never saw any sense in being formal with them. Within reasonable limits, the Civil War private was willing to do what his company commander told him to do, but he saw little point in carrying it to extremes.

So an Indiana soldier wrote: "We had enlisted to put down the Rebellion, and had to patience with the red-tape tomfoolery of the regular service. The boys recognized no superiors, except in the line of legitimate duty. Shoulder straps waived, a private was ready at the drop of a hat to thrash his commander—a thing that occurred more than once." A New York regiment, drilling on a hot parade ground, heard a private address his company commander thus: "Say, Tom, let's quit this darn foolin' around and go over to the sutler's and get a drink." There was very little of the "Captain, sir" business in those armies. If a company or regimental officer got anything especial in the way of obedience, he got it because the enlisted men recognized him as a natural leader and superior and not just because he had a commission signed by Abraham Lincoln.

Odd rivalries developed between regiments. (It should be noted that the Civil War soldier's first loyalty went usually to his regiment, just as navy man's loyalty goes to his ship; he liked to believe that his regiment was better than all others, and he would fight for it, any time and anywhere.) The army legends of those days tell of a Manhattan regiment, camped near Washington, whose nearest neighbor was a regiment from Brooklyn, with which the Manhattanites nursed a deep rivalry. Neither regiment had a chaplain; and there came to the Manhattan colonel one day a minister, who volunteered to hold religious services for the men in the ranks.

The colonel doubted that this would be a good idea. His men, he said, were rather irreligious, not to say godless, and he feared they would not give the reverend gentleman a respectful hearing. But the minister said he would take his chances; after all, he had just held services with the Brooklyn regiment, and the men there had been very quiet and devout. That was enough for the colonel. What the Brooklyn regiment could do, his regiment could do. He ordered the men paraded for divine worship, announcing that any man who talked, laughed, or even coughed would be summarily court-martialed.

So the clergyman held services, and everyone was attentive. At the end of the sermon, the minister asked if any of his hearers would care to step forward and make public profession of faith; in the Brooklyn regiment, he said, fourteen men had done this. Instantly the New York colonel was on his feet.

"Adjutant!" he bellowed. "We're not going to let that damn Brooklyn regiment beat us at anything. Detail twenty men and have them baptized at once!"

Each regiment seemed to have its own mythology, tales which may have been false but which, by their mere existence, reflected faithfully certain aspects of army life. The 48th New York, for instance, was said to have an unusually large number of ministers in its ranks, serving not as chaplains but as combat soldiers. The 48th, fairly early in the war, found itself posted in a swamp along the South Carolina coast, toiling mightily in semitropical heat, amid clouds of mosquitoes, to build fortifications, and it was noted that all hands became excessively profane, including the one-time clergymen. A visiting general, watching the regiment at work one day, recalled the legend and asked the regiment's lieutenant colonel if he himself was a minister in private life.

"Well, no, General," said the officer apologetically. "I can't say that I was a regularly ordained minister. I was just one of these——— ———local preachers."

Another story was hung on this same 48th New York. A Confederate ironclad gunboat was supposed to be ready to steam through channels in the swamp and attack the 48th's outposts, and elaborate plans were made to trap it with obstructions in the channel, a tangle of ropes to snarl the propellers, and so on. But it occurred to the colonel that even if the gunboat was trapped the soldiers could not get into it; it was sheathed in iron, all its ports would be closed, and men with axes could never chop their way into it. Then the colonel had an inspiration. Remembering that many of his men had been recruited from the less savory districts of New York City, he paraded the regiment and (according to legend) announced:

"Now men, you've been in this cursed swamp for two weeks—up to your ears in mud, no fun, no glory and blessed poor pay. Here's a chance. Let every man who has had experience as a cracksman or a safeblower step to the front." To the last man, the regiment marched forward four paces and came expectantly to attention.

Not unlike this was the reputation of the 6th New York, which contained so many Bowery toughs that the rest of the army said a man had to be able to show that he had done time in prison in order to get into the regiment. It was about to leave for the South, and the colonel gave his men an inspirational talk. They were going, he said, to a land of wealthy plantation owners, where each Southerner had riches of which he could be despoiled; and he took out his own gold watch and held it up for all to see, remarking that any deserving soldier could easily get one like it, once they got down to plantation-land. Half an hour later, wishing to see what time it was, he felt for his watch . . . and it was gone.

If the Civil War army spun queer tales about itself, it had to face a reality which, in all of its aspects, was singularly unpleasant. One of the worst aspects had to do with food.

From first to last, the Civil War armies enlisted no men as cooks, and there were no cooks' and bakers' schools to help matters. Often enough, when in camp, a company would simply be issued a quantity of provisions—flour, pork, beans, potatoes, and so on—and invited to prepare the stuff as best it could. Half a dozen men would form a mess, members would take turns with the cooking, and everybody had to eat what these amateurs prepared or go hungry. Later in the war, each company commander would usually detail two men to act as cooks for the company, and if either of the two happened to know anything about cooking the company was in luck. One army legend held that company officers usually detailed the least valuable soldiers to this job, on the theory that they would do less harm in the cook shack than anywhere else. One soldier, writing after the war, asserted flatly: "A company cook is a most peculiar being; he generally knows less about cooking than any other man in the company. Not being able to learn the drill, and too dirty to appear on inspection, he is sent to the cook house to get him out of the ranks."

When an army was on the march, the ration issue usually consisted of salt pork, hardtack, and coffee. (In the Confederate Army the coffee was often missing, and the hardtack was frequently replaced by corn bread; often enough the meal was not sifted, and stray bits of cob would appear in it.) The hardtack was good enough, if fresh, which was not always the case; with age it usually got infested with weevils, and veterans remarked that it was better to eat it in the dark.

In the Union Army, most of the time, the soldier could supplement his rations (if he had money) by buying extras from the sutler—the latter being a civilian merchant licensed to accompany the army, functioning somewhat as the regular post exchange functions nowadays. The sutler charged high prices and specialized in indigestibles like pies, canned lobster salad, and so on; and it was noted that men who patronized him regularly came down with stomach upsets. The Confederate Army had few sutlers, which helps to explain why the hungry Confederates were so delighted when they could capture a Yankee camp: to seize the sutler's tent meant high living for the captors, and the men in Lee's army were furious when, in the 1864 campaign, they learned that General Grant had ordered the Union Army to move without sutlers. Johnny Reb felt that Grant was really taking an unfair advantage by cutting off this possible source of supply.

If Civil War cooking arrangements were impromptu and imperfect, the same applied to its hospital system. The surgeons, usually, were good men by the standards of that day—which were low since no one on earth knew anything about germs or about how wounds became infected, and antisepsis in the operating room was a concept that had not yet come into existence; it is common to read of a surgeon whetting his scalpel on the sole of his shoe just before operating. But the hospital attendants, stretcher-bearers, and the like were chosen just as the company cooks were chosen; that is, they were detailed from the ranks, and the average officer selected the most worthless men he had simply because he wanted to get rid of men who could not be counted on in combat. As a result, sick or wounded men often got atrocious care.

A result of all of this—coupled with the fact that many men enlisted without being given any medical examinations—was that every Civil War regiment suffered a constant wastage from sickness. On paper, a regiment was supposed to have a strength ranging between 960 and 1,040 men; actually, no regiment ever got to the battlefield with anything like that strength, and since there was no established system for sending in replacements a veteran regiment that could must 350 enlisted men present for duty was considered pretty solid. From first to last, approximately twice as many Civil War soldiers died of disease—typhoid, dysentery, and pneumonia were the great killers—as died in action; and in addition to those who died a great many more got medical discharges.

In its wisdom, the Northern government set up a number of base hospitals in Northern states, far from the battle fronts, on the theory that a man recovering from wounds or sickness would recuperate better back home. Unfortunately, the hospitals thus established were under local control, and the men in them were no longer under the orders of their own regiments or armies. As a result, thousands of men who were sent north for convalescence never returned to the army. Many were detailed for light work at the hospitals, and in these details they stayed because nobody had the authority to extract them

and send them back to duty. Others, recovering their health, simply went home and stayed there. They were answerable to the hospital authorities, not to the army command, and the hospital authorities rarely cared very much whether they returned to duty or not. The whole system was ideally designed to make desertion easy.

On top of all of this, many men had very little understanding of the requirements of military discipline. A homesick boy often saw nothing wrong in leaving the army and going home to see the folks for a time. A man from a farm might slip off to go home and put in a crop. In neither case would the man look on himself as a deserter; he meant to return, he figured he would get back in time for any fighting that would take place, and in his own mind he was innocent of any wrongdoing. But in many cases the date of return would be postponed from week to week; the man might end as a deserter, even though he had not intended to be one when he left.

This merely reflected the loose discipline that prevailed in Civil War armies, which in turn reflected the underlying civilian-mindedness that pervaded the rank and file. The behavior of Northern armies on the march in Southern territory reflected the same thing—and, in the end, had a profound effect on the institution of chattel slavery.

Armies of occupation always tend to bear down hard on civilian property in enemy territory. Union armies in the Civil War, being imperfectly disciplined to begin with—and suffering, furthermore, from a highly defective rationing system—bore down with especial fervor. Chickens, hams, cornfields, anything edible that might be found on a Southern plantation, looked like fair game, and the loose fringe of stragglers that always trailed around the edges of a moving Union army looted with a fine disregard for civilian property rights.

This was made all the more pointed by the fact that the average Northern soldier, poorly indoctrinated though he was, had strong feelings about the evils of secession. To his mind, the Southerners who sought to set up a nation of their own were in rebellion against the best government mankind had ever

During the Civil War, there were often long intervals between battles when the soldiers of both sides drilled and relaxed in camp.

This photograph shows Union officers playing dominoes at Camp Winfield Scott, Yorktown, Virginia. (Corbis-Bettmann)

known. Being rebels, they had forfeited their rights; if evil things happened to them that (as the average Northern soldier saw it) was no more than just retribution. This meant that even when the army command tried earnestly to prevent looting and individual foraging the officers at company and regimental levels seldom tried very hard to carry out the high command's orders.

William Tecumseh Sherman has come down in history as the very archetype of the Northern soldier who believed in pillage and looting; yet during the first years of the war Sherman resorted to all manner of ferocious punishments to keep his men from despoiling Southern property. He had looters tied up by the thumbs, ordered courts-martial, issued any number of stern orders—and all to very little effect. Long before he adopted the practice of commandeering or destroying Southern property as a war

measure, his soldiers were practicing it against his will, partly because discipline was poor and partly because they saw nothing wrong with it.

It was common for a Union colonel, as his regiment made camp in a Southern state, to address his men, pointing to a nearby farm, and say: "Now, boys, that barn is full of nice fat pigs and chickens. I don't want to see any of you take any of them"—whereupon he would fold his arms and look sternly in the opposite direction. It was also common for a regimental commander to read, on parade, some [edict] from higher authority forbidding foraging, and then to wink solemnly—a clear hint that he did not expect anyone to take the order seriously. One colonel, punishing some men who had robbed a chicken house, said angrily: "Boys, I want you to understand that I am not punishing you for stealing but for getting caught at it."

It is more than a century since that war was fought, and things look a little different now than they looked at the time. At this distance, it may be possible to look indulgently on the wholesale foraging in which Union armies indulged; to the Southern farmers who bore the brunt of it, the business looked very ugly indeed. Many a Southern family saw the foodstuffs needed for the winter swept away in an hour by grinning hoodlums who did not need and could not use a quarter of what they took. Among the foragers there were many lawless characters who took watches, jewels, and any other valuable they could find; it is recorded that a squad would now and then carry a piano out to the lawn, take it apart, and use the wires to hang pots and pans over the campfire. . . . The Civil War was really romantic only at a considerable distance.

Underneath his feeling that it was good to add chickens and hams to the army ration, and his belief that civilians in a state of secession could expect no better fate, the Union soldier also came to believe that to destroy Southern property was to help win the war. Under orders, he tore up railroads and burned warehouses; it was not long before he realized that anything that damaged the Confederate economy weakened the Confederate war effort, so he rationalized his looting and foraging by arguing that it was a step in breaking the Southern will to resist. It is at this point that the institution of human slavery enters the picture.

Most Northern soldiers had very little feeling against slavery as such, and very little sympathy for the Negro himself. They thought they were fighting to save the Union, not to end slavery, and except for New England troops most Union regiments contained very little abolition sentiment. Nevertheless, the soldiers moved energetically and effectively to destroy slavery, not because they especially intended to but simply because they were out to do all the damage they could do. They were operating against Southern property—and the most obvious, important, and easily removable property of all was the slave. To help the slaves get away from the plantation was, clearly, to weaken Southern productive capacity, which in turn weakened Confederate armies. Hence the Union soldier, wherever he went, took the peculiar institution apart, chattel by chattel.

As a result, slavery had been fatally weakened long before the war itself came to an end. The mere act of fighting the war killed it. Of all institutions on earth, the institution of human slavery was the one least adapted to survive a war. It could not survive the presence of loose-jointed, heavy-handed armies of occupation. It may hardly be too much to say that the mere act of taking up arms in slavery's defense doomed slavery.

Above and beyond everything else, of course, the business of the Civil War soldier was to fight. He fought with weapons that look very crude to modern eyes, and he moved by an outmoded system of tactics, but the price he paid when he got into action was just as high as the price modern soldiers pay despite the almost infinite development of firepower since the 1860's.

Standard infantry weapon in the Civil War was the rifled Springfield—a muzzle-loader firing a conical lead bullet, usually of .58 caliber.

To load was rather laborious, and it took a good man to get off more than two shots a minute. The weapon had a range of nearly a mile, and its "effective range"—that is, the range at which it would hit often enough to make infantry fire truly effective—was figured at about 250 yards. Compared with a modern Garand, the old muzzle-loader is no better than a museum piece; but compared with all previous weapons—the weapons on which infantry tactics in the 1860's were still based—it was a fearfully destructive and efficient piece.

For the infantry of that day still moved and fought in formations dictated in the old days of smoothbore muskets, whose effective range was no more than 100 yards and which were wildly inaccurate at any distance. Armies using those weapons attacked in solid mass formations, the men standing, literally, elbow to elbow. They could get from effective range to hand-to-hand fighting in a very short time, and if they had a proper numerical advantage over the defensive line they could come to grips without losing

As Bruce Catton points out, Civil War armies had no cooks. When in camp, the soldiers received provisions like flour, beans, *or pork, and "prepared the stuff" however they could. These soldiers are cooking a meal over a makeshift fire. (Corbis-Bettmann)*

too many men along the way. But in the Civil War the conditions had changed radically; men would be hit while the rival lines were still half a mile apart, and to advance in mass was simply to invite whole-sale destruction. Tactics had not yet been adjusted to the new rifles; as a result, Civil War attacks could be fearfully costly, and when the defenders dug entrenchments and got some protection—as the men learned to do, very quickly—a direct frontal assault could be little better than a form of mass suicide.

It took the high command a long time to revise tactics to meet this changed situation, and Civil War battles ran up dreadful casualty lists. For an army to lose 25 per cent of its numbers in a major battle was by no means uncommon, and in some fights—the Confederate army at Gettysburg is an outstanding example—the percentage of loss ran close to one

third of the total number engaged. Individual units were sometimes nearly wiped out. Some of the Union and Confederate regiments that fought at Gettysburg lost up to 80 per cent of their numbers; a regiment with such losses was usually wrecked, as an effective fighting force, for the rest of the war.

The point of all of which is that the discipline which took the Civil War soldier into action, while it may have been very sketchy by modern standards, was nevertheless highly effective on the field of battle. Any armies that could go through such battles as Antietam, Stone's River, Franklin or Chickamauga and come back for more had very little to learn about the business of fighting.

Perhaps the Confederate General D. H. Hill said it, once and for all. The battle of Malvern Hill, fought on the Virginia peninsula early in the summer of 1862,

Because of deadly weaponry and outmoded infantry tactics, Civil War battles became gruesome bloodbaths. The wounded gathered around makeshift field hospitals, some sullen, others in shock.

These soldiers, two of them fresh off the amputating table, were casualties of the Virginia campaign of 1864. (© Hulton Archive/ Getty Images)

finished the famous Seven Days campaign, in which George B. McClellan's Army of the Potomac was driven back from in front of Richmond by Robert E. Lee's Army of Northern Virginia. At Malvern Hill, McClellan's men fought a rear-guard action—a bitter, confused fight which came at the end of a solid week of wearing, costly battles and forced marches. Federal artillery wrecked the Confederate assault columns, and at the end of the day Hill looked out over the battlefield, strewn with dead and wounded boys. Shaking his head, and reflecting on the valor in attack and in defense which the two armies had displayed, Hill never forgot about this. Looking back on it, long after the war was over, he declared, in substance:

"Give me Confederate infantry and Yankee artillery and I'll whip the world!"

QUESTIONS TO CONSIDER

1 Soldiers of both sides looted and pillaged, but in the Union army the practice evolved into economic warfare against civilians. Was this form of warfare effective? Was it justifiable? How did this form of warfare affect slavery?

2 Why did Confederate soldiers fight? Why did Union soldiers fight? What was the typical Union soldier's attitude toward emancipation? Think about modern military television commercials, urging young Americans to enlist in America's armed forces. Has the basic appeal of enlisting today changed from that of the Civil War period?

3 What was the biggest killer of the Civil War soldier? Why was this the case? Was the medical establishment equipped to handle disease and wounds? What single medical advance would have saved countless soldiers' lives?

4 During the Civil War, what was the difference between battlefield tactics and the advancement in modern weaponry? How did the discrepancy between tactics and weaponry affect Civil War battles? In your opinion, what advances were vital in bringing about a successful military strategy?

PART FIFTEEN

A Troubled Peace

29 "Call Me Mister": The Black Experience During Reconstruction

JAMES OLIVER HORTON AND LOIS E. HORTON

For African Americans in North and South alike, the Civil War had profound religious meaning from the beginning. Hundreds of thousands, writes historian Vincent Harding, "believed unwaveringly that their God moved in history to deliver his people, and they had been looking eagerly, praying hourly, waiting desperately for the glory of the coming of the Lord. For them, all the raucous, roaring guns of Charleston Harbor and Bull Run, of Antietam and Fort Pillow, of Shiloh and Murfreesboro and Richmond were the certain voice of God, announcing his judgment across the bloody stretches of the South, returning blood for blood to the black river." During the course of that war, African Americans believed, God did deliver them. He drove out the rebels and slaveholders, just as he had once driven out the Hittites and Canaanites. With the Confederacy's collapse, as one song went, "slavery chain done broke at last."

> *Slavery chain done broke at last!*
> *Broke at last! Broke at last!*
> *Slavery chain done broke at last!*
> *Gonna praise God till I die!*

Some reacted to their liberation with cautious elation. When a young Virginia woman heard her former masters weeping over the capture of Jefferson Davis, she went down to a spring alone and cried out, "Glory, glory, hallelujah to Jesus! I's free! I's free!" Suddenly afraid, she looked about. What if the white folks heard her? But seeing no one, she fell to the ground and kissed it, thanking

"Master Jesus" over and over. For her, freedom meant hope—hope that she could find her husband and four children who had been sold to a slave trader.

Others celebrated their liberation in public. In Athens, Georgia, they danced around a liberty pole; in Charleston, they paraded through the streets. Many African Americans, however, were wary and uncertain. "You're joking me," one man said when the master told him he was free. He asked some neighbors if they were free also. "I couldn't believe we was all free alike," he said. Some African Americans, out of feelings of obligation or compassion, remained on the home place to help their former masters. But others were hostile. When a woman named Cady heard that the war was over, she decided to protest the cruel treatment she had suffered as a slave. She threw down her hoe, marched up to the big house, found the mistress, and flipped her dress up. She told the white woman, "Kiss my ass!"

For Cady, for the young black woman of Virginia, for hosts of other African Americans, freedom meant an end to the manifold evils of slavery; it meant the right to say what they felt and go where they wanted. But what else did freedom mean to them? As black leaders of Charleston said, it meant that blacks should enjoy full citizenship, have the right to vote and run for political office. It meant federal protection from their former masters lest they attempt to revive slavery. And it meant economic security in the form of land, so that the blacks could exercise self-help and be economically independent of their former masters.

If the end of the war was a time of profound hope for black Americans, it was a monumental calamity for most southern whites. By turns, they were angry, helpless, vindictive, resigned, and heartsick. As we saw in "The Ravages of War" (selection 27), the Confederacy was devastated. Its towns and major cities, Richmond and Atlanta, were in rubble. Former rebel soldiers returning home found their farm and plantation houses ransacked and even burned down, their barns destroyed, their fields burned, and their livestock gone. As one historian says, "Many [white southerners] were already grieving over sons, plantations, and fortunes taken by war; losing their blacks was the final blow." Some masters shot or hanged African Americans who proclaimed their freedom. That was a harbinger of the years of Reconstruction, for most white southerners were certain that their cause had been just and were entirely unrepentant about fighting against the Union. A popular ballad captured the mood in postwar Dixie:

Oh, I'm a good ole Rebel, now that's just what I am
For this fair land of freedom I do not care a damn.
I'm glad I fit against it, I only wish't we'd won
And I don't want no pardon for nothin' what I done. . . .

I hates the Yankee nation and everything they do
I hates the Declaration of Independence too
I hates the glorious Union, 'tis dripping with our blood
And I hate the striped banner, I fit it all I could. . . .

I can't take up my musket and fight 'em now no mo'
But I ain't gonna love 'em and that is certain sho'
And I don't want no pardon for what I was and am
And I won't be reconstructed and I don't care a damn.

In Washington, Republican leaders were jubilant in victory and determined to deal firmly with southern whites in order to preserve the fruits of the war. But what about the new president, Andrew Johnson? A profane, hard-drinking Tennessee Democrat who bragged about his plebeian origins, Johnson had been the only southern senator to oppose secession openly. He had sided with the Union, served as war governor of Tennessee, and became Lincoln's running mate in 1864, on a Union ticket comprising both Republicans and War Democrats. As a result of the assassination of Lincoln, Johnson was now president, and he faced one of the most difficult tasks ever to confront an American chief executive: how to bind the nation's wounds, preserve African American freedom, and restore the southern states to their proper places in the Union.

Lincoln had contemplated an army of occupation for the defeated South, thinking that military force might be necessary to protect the former slaves and prevent the old southern leadership from returning to power. Now there was such an army in the conquered rebel states, and a great number of these Union troops were black.

In the following selection, historians James Oliver Horton and Lois E. Horton help you feel the soaring hope and terrible pain of emancipated blacks as they endured the transition from slavery to freedom in the postwar years. Instead of being passive and undeserving recipients of freedom (as an earlier generation of historians portrayed them), African Americans reached out and seized control of their destinies. They set about defining and exercising freedom for themselves, searched across the war-torn South for lost family members, established independent black churches, and struggled against an unrepentant white South determined to maintain white supremacy. With the acquiescence of President Johnson, white leaders in conquered Dixie adopted infamous black codes that severely restricted the freedom of the former slaves. In the story the Hortons tell, you will read about how southern African Americans had to endure Jim Crow segregation, poll taxes aimed at preventing blacks from voting, and the night-riding violence of the Ku Klux Klan. You will also read accounts of how African Americans had the courage to stand up to white prejudice and fight back.

For the blacks, the first troubled year of Reconstruction ended joyously with the ratification of the Thirteenth Amendment, which abolished slavery in America formally and forever. Nevertheless, as the Hortons remind us, "slavery still has an impact on Americans more than a century after its abolition. . . . As Americans, we must understand slavery's history if we are ever to be emancipated from its consequences."

GLOSSARY

BLACK CODES These were local laws adopted by white-dominated state governments early in Reconstruction in the conquered South. Such notorious statutes virtually kept the freedmen in a state of servitude. These laws placed severe restrictions on the ownership of land and the ability of the former slaves to move freely in order to seek better jobs. The black codes were a product of white southern governments that came into power under President Johnson's lenient Reconstruction plan. One historian described them as the "slave codes revisited."

BROWN, JOHN (selection 25) Brown had earned his reputation in "Bleeding Kansas" as an implacable antislavery warrior. Kansas, therefore, had a special appeal to African American migrants. Before the Civil War, free-state and proslavery settlers fought a vicious guerrilla war over the status of slavery there. The free-state majority finally won control of the territorial government. In 1861, Kansas entered the Union as a free state.

CARPETBAGGERS Northerners, including former soldiers, who migrated to the South in search of economic opportunities. Many were teachers and nurses who came to assist the freedmen. Named for the bags that carried their belongings, the carpetbaggers were resented by white southerners who resisted any changes in race relations.

DUNN, OSCAR J.   Black lieutenant governor of Louisiana, Dunn was born into slavery. He was self-educated and during Reconstruction became an outspoken advocate of black suffrage.

EXODUSTERS   Name given to some six thousand former slaves who fled the South for the freedom of the western frontier, where they hoped to obtain nominally free land under the Homestead Act. The Exodusters homesteaded twenty thousand acres of land, much of it only marginally productive. "I asked my wife did she know the ground she stands on," one Louisiana Exoduster remembered. "She said, 'No!' I said it is free ground, and she cried like a child for joy."

FIFTEENTH AMENDMENT (1870)   The right of United States citizens to vote could not be denied, this amendment said, "on account of race, color, or previous conditions of servitude." After Reconstruction, the white-dominated southern states used poll taxes, literacy tests, and grandfather clauses to prevent blacks from voting or holding political office. This rendered the great amendment meaningless for almost a century.

FOURTEENTH AMENDMENT (1868)   Despite President Johnson's opposition, the Republican majority in Congress approved this significant amendment, which prohibited individual states from depriving American citizens "of life, liberty, or property, without due process of law." The next selection recounts the "checkered history" of the Fourteenth Amendment.

FREEDMEN'S BUREAU   Established by congressional statute in March 1865, the Bureau of Freedmen, Refugees, and Abandoned Lands, popularly known as the Freedmen's Bureau, attempted to provide food and schools for the former slaves, to help them secure jobs, and to make certain they received fair wages.

GRANDFATHER CLAUSES   Sometimes called "understanding clauses" or "good character clauses," they were provisions built into southern state constitutions to ensure that poor and illiterate whites could vote, while blacks could not. Historian C. Vann Woodward referred to these "artfully devised" clauses as "loopholes" in the voting barriers "through which only white men could squeeze."

GRANT, ULYSSES S.   This former Union general served as president from 1869 to 1877. As chief executive, Grant did try to stop terrorist activities in the South, but otherwise did little to help the freedmen achieve true social, political, or economic freedom. As the Civil War ended, he advised President Johnson to remove the African American troops from the South.

HAMPTON, WADE   Governor of South Carolina and United States senator, Hampton represented white southerners who wanted to "redeem" the South by expelling carpetbaggers, scalawags, and freedmen from state governments and reestablishing white supremacy in Dixie.

HAYES, RUTHERFORD B.   Former governor of Ohio and a Republican, Hayes served as president from 1877 to 1881. Hayes defeated Democrat Samuel J. Tilden in the controversial presidential election of 1876. Tilden won the popular vote, but the outcome in the electoral college depended on disputed ballot counts in three southern states. The Republican and Democratic leaders agreed to a compromise in 1877 that awarded Hayes the presidency in exchange for removing federal troops from the South.

JIM CROW LAWS   Southern state and local laws that enforced segregation and discriminated against African Americans. The term "Jim Crow" derived from the name of a song sung by Thomas Rice in a black minstrel show before the Civil War.

JOHNSON, ANDREW   President from 1865 to 1869 and a product of the poor white South, Johnson had no sympathy for those who wanted to achieve true racial equality. He defied congressional Reconstruction measures and was impeached for political reasons. By one vote, the Senate failed to convict him, but Johnson was virtually powerless after the impeachment proceedings.

KU KLUX KLAN   Following the Civil War, this secretive paramilitary organization emerged in the South and used violence and intimidation to subdue the freedmen.

LIBERIA   In 1821, the American Colonization Society helped establish this settlement in West Africa as a haven for American black colonists. Over the next decade, several thousand free blacks voluntarily migrated to Liberia.

LITERACY TEST   In the years after Reconstruction, white southern leaders adopted literacy tests, which, like poll taxes, were designed to prevent freedmen from voting. Poor and illiterate whites were exempted from taking literacy tests because of carefully written "grandfather clauses." The Hortons sum up such discrimination against African Americans: "Starting in 1890 in Mississippi, and then spreading across the South, a constellation of laws restricted the [elective] franchise to whites only."

REVELS, HIRAM RHODES   In 1870, Revels, a minister and an educator, became the first African American to serve in the Unites States Senate. A Mississippi Republican, Revels left the Senate a year later to become president of Alcorn Agricultural College (now Alcorn University).

SCALAWAGS   Native southern whites who became Republicans during Reconstruction, scalawags resented being ruled by the planters and supported the legal and political rights of the freedmen.

SHARECROPPING   Lacking the money to acquire their own land in the South, many former slaves became sharecroppers. They rented plots of land from their former masters who paid them with shares of their crops. For African Americans, the sharecropping system was an odious form of exploitation. As the Hortons explain: "Unequal resources and power . . . led to white landowners' binding black sharecroppers to the land through real or contrived indebtedness."

SHERMAN, WILLIAM TECUMSEH   "Bill" Sherman, of course, was the Union general whose army cut a huge swath of destruction across the Confederacy in the last year of the war. But in the Hortons' story, he did something else that only made white southerners hate him all the more. On January 16, 1865, from his headquarters in Savannah, he issued Special Field Order 15, which confiscated certain portions of Confederate plantations and farms in the area for the exclusive use of the freedmen. Six months later, forty thousand black farmers were cultivating their own forty-acre plots along the coastal areas of Georgia and South Carolina. President Johnson later returned this property to its prewar white owners and expelled the former slaves from the land.

STANTON, EDWIN M.   Lincoln's Secretary of War, Stanton approved of Sherman's Special Field Order 15, which gave the freedmen an opportunity to farm confiscated Confederate land.

SOUTHERN HOMESTEAD ACT (1866)   Congress designated forty-four million acres of public land in five southern states for settlement by the freedmen and by whites who had remained loyal to the Union. Few benefited from this legislation. Much of the land was unsuitable for farming, and few former slaves had the resources to wait for the revenue that would follow their first successful crop.

TENURE OF OFFICE ACT (1867)   By the terms of this federal statute, no federal official confirmed by the Senate could be removed until the Senate had approved a successor. When President Johnson removed Secretary of War Stanton in 1868, he violated this law and was impeached as a consequence.

THIRTEENTH AMENDMENT (1865)   This momentous amendment ended slavery in the United States. Southern resistance to change and northern complacency would delay any significant improvement in race relations for another one hundred years.

A t the end of the war it was not clear how the reuniting America would define black freedom, although it was clear that slavery was dead. In January 1865, by a vote of 121 to 24, Congress passed the Thirteenth Amendment to the U.S. Constitution, providing for the total abolition of American slavery. Ratified before the year was out, it seemed to many whites and blacks to be the fulfillment of the American Revolution. At last all Americans would have the promise of liberty and justice found in the Declaration of Independence. First, however, the country faced the task of ensuring the survival of people made destitute by slavery and the war. The immediate needs of the freed people were great, greater than could be met by the efforts of the private philanthropies that had been active during the war. In March 1865, before the fall of Richmond, the government had established the Bureau of Refugees, Freedmen, and Abandoned Lands, placing it in the War Department. The Freedmen's Bureau established operations in every department of the occupied South and provided aid to impoverished whites as well as freed slaves. Bureau agents established schools for the freed people and registered legal marriages for former slaves. Attempting to restore order to the war-ravaged southern plantation economy, and to bring in tax money to support federal assistance, agents negotiated millions of labor contracts, many between freed people and their

Excerpts from James Oliver Horton and Lois E. Horton, *Slavery and the Making of America* (New York: Oxford University Press, 2005), pp. 207, 209–227, 230–231. Copyright © 2005 by Oxford University Press, Inc. Reprinted by permission of Oxford University Press, Inc.

Ratified in December, 1865, the Thirteenth Amendment guaranteed freedom to four million former slaves like those shown here. Most desired "forty acres and a mule"—that is, land and the tools to make it productive so that they could become economically self-sufficient. But most freedmen failed to achieve their dream when the sharecropping system, which replaced slavery, bound them to work land owned by white southerners. (Lightfoot Collection)

former owners. As state governments were reestablished, the Bureau also oversaw voter registration.

Freed people had definite ideas about the meaning of freedom. Some took new names to denote their new status, as some black people had done after they escaped from slavery before the war, calling themselves Freeman or Freedman, for example. Some dropped slave names given to them by their masters in favor of the names they had been known by in the slave quarters. Others who had been known by a succession of names as they were sold from owner to owner, settled on the name of the fairest or kindest master. Some took the names of masters they had when they were parted from family members. In this way, they hoped, it would be easier for husbands, wives, mothers, fathers, or children to find them.

Freedom meant keeping families together and finding lost family members. In slavery many people had tried to keep track of family members who were sold

away. Slaves and free blacks whose occupations let them travel through the South had provided important links, carrying information and messages between people separated by slavery. Many men, like Maryland's Charles Ball who had run away twice from farther south, had endured the hardships of escaping in order to return to wives and children whom they had been forced to leave behind. Even in the same area, husbands and wives owned by different planters had sometimes gone without sleep and risked harsh punishment in order to see their mates. Tamar Grandy and her husband were both slaves in eastern North Carolina in the early 1800s. She was sold to a Georgia trader but escaped and traveled a hundred miles to return to her husband and her mother. Her husband lived twenty-five miles away from where she was in hiding. For years he came to visit her, leaving home as soon as he finished his work, spending part of the night with his wife, and walking the long distance back in order to arrive home before sunrise, when he would be called to the fields.

With freedom came relief from the slaves' greatest fear—having family members sold away. Touching reunions occurred during and after the war. Ben and Betty Dodson found each other in a refugee camp. They had been sold to separate masters twenty years before, and he had spent all that time searching for her. One Virginia mother found her eighteen-year-old daughter in a refugee camp. The girl had been sold away when she was just an infant. Finding children who had been sold away when they were young or finding the parents who had been sold away when the children were young was exceedingly difficult. With each succeeding sale, a child may have been given a different name, and intervening years made it difficult to recognize the adult who was once someone's child. For such children to be able to find their families required a slave community that kept the children's family histories alive during long periods of separation. Even with the community's help, however, reuniting families was often impossible. Slave mortality was high, especially in the lower South, and it was likely that people sold down the river many years before had not survived until freedom came.

The seemingly insurmountable odds notwithstanding, freed people traveled great distances, tracking down every lead, in efforts to find their families. They questioned every person they met from the area where their relative was last heard of. Freedmen's Bureau teachers and missionaries wrote thousands of letters for the illiterate freed people, following every rumor that someone had seen or heard of their relatives. People placed advertisements in newspapers, giving information about the missing person's former life, personal characteristics, injuries, and scars. Nearly a generation after the Civil War, newspapers still carried such ads:

Information Wanted, of Caroline Dodson, who was sold from Nashville, Nov. 1st, 1862, by James Lumsden to Warwick, (a trader then in human beings), who carried her to Atlanta, Georgia, and she was last heard of in the slave pen of Robert Clarke, (human trader in that place), from which she was sold. Any information of her whereabouts will be thankfully received and rewarded by her mother. Lucinda Lowery, Nashville.

Land ownership was also important to the freed people. For many ex-slaves, the promise of self-sufficiency, independence, and opportunity that freedom represented rested on the ownership of land. Various military commanders had allowed former slaves to work land abandoned by fleeing Confederates, and rumors persisted that the federal government would eventually grant land to the freed people. On January 16, 1865, just months before the South's surrender, U.S. General William T. Sherman took time from his devastating Georgia campaign to meet with twenty black community leaders in Savannah and discuss the issue of confiscated Confederate land in Georgia, South Carolina, and northern Florida. Secretary of War Edwin M. Stanton joined the discussions and approved Sherman's Special Field Order 15, declaring that "the islands from Charleston south, the abandoned rice-fields along the rivers for thirty miles back from the sea, and the country bordering the St. Johns River, Florida, are reserved and set apart for the settlement of the [N]egroes now made free by the acts of war and the [Emancipation]

proclamation of the President of the United States." Each family was to be issued forty acres and an army mule to use in its cultivation. A few months later, the plan seemed confirmed by the government's placement of responsibility for refugees, freedmen, and abandoned lands in the same department.

In the spring of 1865, as the war came to an end, Vice President Andrew Johnson from Tennessee replaced the slain president in the oval office. Johnson had been Lincoln's wartime political choice, another strategy to hold the slaveholding border states, and was a political conservative. The new president spent the early days of his administration granting amnesty to former Confederate military leaders and handing out pardons wholesale to Confederates. White southerners needed simply to swear loyalty to the United States and agree to support the abolitionist provisions of the Thirteenth Amendment to have their property and general citizenship rights restored. Members of the southern aristocracy who had led the Confederacy in its war on the United States quickly applied for and received pardons. Thus, most of the land was returned to its prewar owners, and the former slaves who had been living on and cultivating the land during the last year of the war were expelled. Former abolitionists in Congress were never successful in their attempts to pass legislation granting former slaves land from the thousands of acres of confiscated Confederate land still under federal control. Ultimately, left without this foundation for independence, the freed people were forced to depend on former slaveholders to employ them or rent them land to farm.

Once pardoned and returned to political power, men from the planter class passed new laws reinstating much of their control over black people. In an attempt to re-create the southern racial etiquette of slave days, they punished black farm laborers for questioning white landlords, attacked black businessmen and their establishments for being too successful or competitive, attacked black students for displaying too much intelligence, confronted blacks who dressed too well or too neatly, and assaulted white people for encouraging black aspirations. Angered and distressed by the growing independence of their former slaves, planters complained that freed people were unwilling to work for what the planters considered reasonable wages. According to one Texas planter, the exorbitant wages offered by white employers with no sense of the "proper racial hierarchy" had spoiled the former slaves and led them to have outrageous expectations. Planters believed this had encouraged an inappropriate feeling of equality among the newly freed blacks.

After emancipation many African Americans did try to withdraw from the workforce. As a mark of their freedom, some men wanted their wives to be able to leave the fields and keep house for their families. Virtually all blacks wanted their children to be able to attend school, and some black people did demand respect from southern whites. As one former Georgia slave explained, many blacks vowed to take "no more foolishness off white folks." Long-standing customs and laws governing interracial contact in the South were designed to reinforce white supremacy. Whites addressed a black man as "boy" and a black woman as "girl" no matter how old they were, and either might be addressed as "nigger." The title of Uncle or Aunty that whites used for elderly blacks was the closest thing to respect an African American could expect. In Helena, Arkansas, after the war, when an elderly former slave addressed a white man on the street as "Mr." the white man followed the prewar convention and replied "Howdy uncle." The black man was insulted, made it clear they were not related, and demanded, "Call me Mister."

From the standpoint of former slaves, such confrontations were part of an effort to make freedom a reality of daily life in the South, a reality that white southerners were anxious to avoid. What ensued was a determined struggle between African Americans seeking dignity and respect and southern whites attempting to maintain the principle of white supremacy. White leaders argued that only strong restrictive measures would restore the black workforce to its prewar level of usefulness. Many southern states enacted black codes, limiting the freedom of former slaves and returning them to near slavery. Vagrancy

provisions imposed fines and jail time on unemployed African Americans, forcing former slaves into low-paying agricultural jobs and ensuring white planters a steady supply of cheap plantation labor. Without land, the ability to bargain for jobs, or the right to vote or hold office, southern blacks stood only marginally above their former slave position.

Almost all southern blacks were agricultural workers, and without land of their own, they had to depend on white landowners for work. After the war cash was in short supply in the South, so landowners offered shares of the crop instead of wages in return for black labor. Sharecropping, as this system was called, seemed an equitable solution to the problem. Sharecroppers lived on the land, worked it as if it were their own, brought in the crop, and were entitled to a portion of the harvest at the end of the season. For landowners this ensured an agricultural labor force without the need for cash, and for sharecroppers it offered an approximation of the independent family farm. Unequal resources and power, however, led to white landholders' binding black sharecroppers to the land through real or contrived indebtedness.

Essentially, the bonds of debt peonage replaced the chains of slavery, and planters could control their labor force almost as completely as slaveholders had controlled theirs. To purchase seed, tools, teams of mules or horses, and other supplies, impoverished sharecroppers were forced to rely on credit advanced against the following year's crop. They also purchased food, clothing, and other necessities on credit, either at stores operated by the landowner or at independently owned stores in the vicinity. Interest rates were generally high and sharecroppers found themselves falling further and further into debt each season. "[Landowners] didn't pay everything they promised," recalled one Arkansas sharecropper. When he attempted to appeal to local authorities, he found that a white man's accounting superseded any argument an African American could offer. "They said figures didn't lie," he reported. He understood that this could be a very dangerous situation, for any black man who questioned a white man's word was putting his life at risk. "You know how that

Before the Civil War, most southern states barred slaves from learning to read and write. During Reconstruction, the establishment of black schools made it possible for the former slaves, children and adults alike, to obtain an education. As the Hortons conclude, "education was an important mark of their freedom and represented their hope for a better future." (Cook Collection, Valentine Richmond History Center)

was," he explained, "You dassent dispute a [white] man's word then."

Henry Blacke sharecropped for much of his adult life. He later explained, "[N]o matter how good accounts you kept, you had to go by [the white landowners'] account, and—now brother, I'm telling you the truth about this—it has been that way a long time." White southerners seemed to operate with a different set of ethics when dealing with blacks. As one Freedmen's Bureau official put it, white "men who are honorable in their dealings with their white neighbors will cheat a Negro without feeling a single twinge of their honor." Whites argued that the survival of southern civilization demanded completely controlling blacks, and, as in slavery, any black person who showed signs of contesting their control must be brought into line immediately. A Freedmen's Bureau official described white attitudes toward blacks in the Reconstruction South saying, "Wherever I go . . . I hear the people talk in such a way as to indicate that they are yet unable to conceive of the Negro as possessing any right at all." Even among "honorable" white men, he noted, "to kill a Negro [white southerners] do not deem murder; to debauch a Negro woman they do not think fornication; to take the property away from a Negro they do not consider robbery."

The Republican-controlled Congress attempted to protect African American rights, but President Johnson fought efforts to strengthen and broaden the powers of the Freedmen's Bureau and to pass a Civil Rights Act nullifying the black codes and providing citizenship rights to black people. Johnson campaigned widely for Democratic candidates in the Congressional election of 1866. He spoke against Republican candidates, attacked programs to aid the former slaves, and referred to some of the strongest supporters of the U.S. war effort against the Confederacy as traitors to the nation. Even the most moderate Republicans were outraged, and, after Republicans made substantial gains in the election, they joined with their more radical colleagues in solid opposition to the president. The Republican Congress passed the Civil Rights Act of 1866 and the Fourteenth Amendment, which wrote its provisions guaranteeing black citizenship into the Constitution. They took control of reconstructing southern state governments, passing measures limiting the power of the old southern elites and calling for new state constitutions.

Congress also passed several measures to limit Johnson's power, including the Tenure of Office Act. According to that law, the president could not dismiss any cabinet member appointed with the advice and consent of the Senate until the Senate had approved a successor. In early 1868, Johnson violated this law, and the Republican-dominated House of Representatives voted to impeach him. Although Johnson was saved from being removed from office by one vote in the Senate, his presidency was so weakened that he ceased to be a significant obstruction to Congressional plans for reconstructing the South. Under Congressional Reconstruction, African Americans were allowed to participate in the state conventions that drew up the new constitutions, constitutions that gave blacks the right to vote. In South Carolina, Mississippi, Louisiana, and other southern states where blacks formed either a majority or a substantial proportion of the population, African Americans attained political power.

In 1866, pressured by abolitionists in Congress, the federal government passed the Southern Homestead Act, giving former slaves and whites who had remained loyal to the United States preferential access to 44 million acres of public land in five southern states for one year. The land, however, was poor—rocky, infertile, marshy, or otherwise unsuitable for farming. Penniless former slaves found it impossible to support themselves while waiting for the first crop, and few could take advantage of the program. A few blacks pooled their meager resources and bought some decent farmland. In Charleston two hundred freed people formed a land investment group called The Freemen's Land and Home Society and collectively purchased a 600-acre plantation on Remley's Point near the city, paying about ten dollars an acre. Many soldiers pooled their military pay and bought small plots, but the vast majority remained landless.

The ratification of the Fifteenth Amendment to the U.S. Constitution in 1870, outlawing the use of race to disenfranchise voters, brought more black men to the polls. Black women, too, were active in southern politics, even though, like white women, they could not vote. They attended political meetings and rallies and were a strong arm of the Republican Party, especially in the South where African American political power was most significant during Reconstruction. According to one historian, in South Carolina, "Freewomen as well as children left the rice fields when it was time to register, attended political meetings and rallies where their influence over the lowcountry vote was recognized and manipulated, and were found at the polls on election days." The presence of so many black women at political events apparently made some white Republicans uneasy. In Charleston, white Republicans attempted to convince black men to "leave their wives at their firesides, or, better still, to 'cut grass.'" The effort was apparently unsuccessful, for black women continued to be active advisers to their male representatives and participated in almost every phase of the voting process, except actually casting a ballot. Black leaders generally encouraged black women's participation in politics and recognized important, sometimes nontraditional, roles for them.

During the mid 1870s black women armed with clubs patrolled polling places in South Carolina to keep order and protect Republicans who came to vote.

With large numbers of freed African Americans in the South and 10 percent to 20 percent of southern white males still disqualified from voting because of their rebellion against the United States, blacks were a majority of the electorate in five southern states. Their votes provided the foundation for the Republican Party in the South, a party that had not existed there before the war. Blacks found allies among white Republicans from the North who came to the South during and after the war. Southern Democrats called these whites carpetbaggers after the bags in which many carried their possessions, denoting their newcomer status. Although generally characterized as political opportunists, most were teachers and nurses who came to aid and educate former slaves.

The southern Democrats' most venomous charges were leveled at those people called scalawags, white southerners who became Republicans or supported the Republican Party. Such southern whites who allied themselves with blacks were the targets of public ridicule and violence. This was especially true with the rise of such vigilante political terrorist groups as the Knights of the White Camilla, The Pale Face Brotherhood, and others organized in the mid- to late-1860s in an effort to frustrate Republican rule and force black people back to a place of servitude in southern society. The longest lasting and most notorious of these groups was a social club formed in Tennessee in 1866 that became the Ku Klux Klan. It was led by the former slave trader, Confederate general, and notorious commander of the Fort Pillow massacre, Nathan Bedford Forrest.

These groups used intimidation and violence to discourage blacks and white Republicans from voting. In the spring of 1866, whites invaded the black community in Memphis, Tennessee. When newly discharged black soldiers and local freedmen defended themselves against the marauding whites and city police, forty-six blacks and two whites died. The political motivation was clear when a local newspaper called the riot proof that "the southern men will not be ruled by the [N]egro." . . .

In 1868 Republican and former general Grant replaced Andrew Johnson as president. Congress reacted to the continuing southern violence in the early 1870s by enacting a number of anti-Klan measures, which the president signed into law. In 1871 Grant suspended the writ of habeas corpus in nine South Carolina counties where the Klan was particularly active, making it easier to arrest people suspected of terrorist activity, and sent in federal troops to augment the government's efforts to quell the violence. Congress launched an extensive investigation of the Klan and political terrorism in the South, and the federal officials arrested and indicted hundreds of whites in Mississippi, South Carolina, and North Carolina for their participation in terrorist activity. Some observers were surprised that, in addition to poor whites, many of those arrested for such crimes were professional men, doctors, lawyers, ministers, and college professors.

Seeing African Americans hold political office especially incensed white southern Democrats. They accused blacks of being ignorant, incompetent people attempting to rise above their naturally subservient place in society. The vast majority of southern blacks were illiterate at the end of the war, but most black political leaders were educated. Oscar J. Dunn, who became lieutenant governor of Louisiana, for example, was born a slave but had been able to educate himself. Many, like Dunn, were self-educated, but many others had been formally educated. Hiram Rhodes Revels, a freeborn North Carolina barber and an ordained African Methodist Episcopal minister, became America's first black U.S. senator in 1870. He was a Republican who represented Mississippi for one year, completing the term of Jefferson Davis, who had given up his Senate seat in 1861 to become president of the Confederacy. Revels was well educated, having attended a Quaker seminary in Indiana and Knox College in Illinois. After his term in the Senate, Revels served as president of Mississippi's Alcorn Agricultural College (now Alcorn University), the first land-grant college for black students. . . .

Hundreds of African Americans, former soldiers, abolitionists, businessmen, ministers, lawyers, and teachers, helped guide southern governments for a brief time in the turbulent years of Reconstruction. Many had been born in the South, had left to work and live in the North, in Canada, or in Europe, and returned to take advantage of the unprecedented opportunities for community service and black political leadership. Facing incredible economic and political problems, they worked with white Republicans and even some white Democrats to rebuild the South. In the years between the end of the Civil War and the first decade of the twentieth century, more than six hundred African Americans served in state legislatures, twenty were elected to the U.S. House of Representatives, and two were elected to the U.S. Senate.

During Reconstruction, federal and state government efforts held the promise of improving many people's lives in the South. The majority of the delegates to the South Carolina constitutional convention were black, and 57 out of the 124 blacks had been slaves. This convention passed a number of progressive measures in 1868: abolishing racial discrimination in voting, schools, and the militia; protecting married women's property rights; establishing the state's first divorce law and the first free public school system; providing for elected rather than appointed judges; and abolishing dueling, imprisonment for debt, and property requirements for voting and holding office. The Freedmen's Bureau established and ran more than four thousand schools in the South, open to whites as well as blacks. Many of these schools served areas where there had previously been no public education. The bureau ended most of its aid programs in 1868 but continued to operate schools that educated students from kindergarten to college until 1872. For the freed people, education was an important mark of their freedom and represented their hope for a better future. Since many slaves had been legally prohibited from learning to read and write, education was doubly important to them. About 95 percent of slaves were illiterate in 1863, but by 1877 more than six hundred thousand black children were in elementary schools. . . .

Southern Democrats were determined to reinstate the racial control of the prewar South and to further this aim tried to ensure black economic dependence and discourage black education. They used many methods in their postwar campaign, but violence became their signature. Outbreaks of racial violence, generally called riots but often seeming more like open rebellion, continued during the 1870s. Throughout the South, violence was the common political tool of those bent on returning to absolute and unquestioned white domination. Leading southern Democrats routinely rationalized the most heinous crimes if they helped "save southern civilization." Wade Hampton of South Carolina, who served as governor and U.S. senator, rallied his political colleagues by arguing that almost any illegal action, even murder, was completely acceptable if done in the name of white supremacy. He urged Democrats to do all in their power to "control the vote of at least one Negro, by intimidation, purchase, keeping him away or as each individual may determine, how may best accomplish it." Then he moved to the deadly specifics. "Never threaten a man individually. If he deserves to be threatened, the necessities of the times require that he should be killed."

African Americans did not meekly submit, however. They used whatever power they had to enforce the law and protect themselves and their communities. Black judges issued arrest warrants, and black sheriffs jailed white terrorists. Armed African Americans, especially war veterans, confronted white vigilante groups. Many black veterans had retained their military weapons, and some formed militia units to protect their communities. In Wilmington, North Carolina, black troops arrested the white chief of police when he refused to surrender his weapon as ordered, and in Victoria, Texas, blacks lynched the white killer of an African American townsman. In South Carolina, when a Confederate veteran stabbed a black Army sergeant for refusing to leave a railroad car in which white women were seated, black soldiers decided the veteran was guilty and shot him.

Southern whites quickly realized that racial intimidation could not be effective so long as these black militia units existed, and they tried to legally disarm and disband them. White Republican officials in the South were sometimes willing to accede to white petitions in order to gain the cooperation of prominent local citizens. As black militia units were disbanded, African American communities were left open to attack from the growing number of terrorist groups. Blacks were forced to depend on the law for protection, an increasingly unlikely possibility as conservative whites returned to power, or to defend themselves. In 1868, for example, black Mississippi politician Charles Caldwell was wounded by a white man. He shot and killed his assailant but was then charged with murder. Such confrontations were common, but Caldwell's acquittal by an all-white jury on the grounds of self-defense was unusual. . . .

Black voters in South Carolina constituted a majority, but white Democrats were determined to keep African Americans away from the polls. Blacks in some communities demanded their rights, and some whites chafed at what they considered African American arrogance. Such insults, the white southerners contended, "no white people upon earth had ever to put up with before." Whites in the small town of Hamburg on the Savannah River in South Carolina complained that they were forced to give way to black parades and were treated with disrespect and even arrested "on the slightest provocation" by the local black police. Tensions exploded during the country's centennial celebration on July 4, 1876, when a parading black militia company forced a local white farmer's son and son-in-law to halt their carriage. Although Dock Adams, the militia commander, opened the ranks to let them through after some contention, the next day the farmer brought charges against Adams for impeding his travel. The black militia confronted armed white men in the town, and a well-known Democratic politician demanded that Adams disarm his militia company. He refused, the men began fighting, and the black militiamen retreated to the armory. Hundreds of whites from Augusta, Georgia, just across the river, invaded Hamburg to answer the challenge, bringing a cannon to aid in avenging the insult to their racial honor. The whites killed the town's black marshal and killed at least five other blacks after they had been captured. Blacks killed one young white man. The white mob also looted and vandalized

African American homes and businesses. A grand jury indicted seven whites for murder and dozens more as accessories, but all were acquitted.

As the violence increased and it became clear that African Americans were not safe anywhere in the South, growing numbers of blacks began to reconsider colonization. African Americans from several southern states met in New Orleans in December 1875 to discuss migrating to the independent West African nation of Liberia. The racial troubles in America created substantial interest in Liberia, and not only among southern blacks. Northern blacks faced less continual violence but confronted discouraging racial discrimination in public places, in the job market, and in housing. In 1878, one colonization group in Pennsylvania received almost fifty thousand inquiries from African Americans considering migration possibilities.

Although many were interested in West Africa, many more African Americans looked to lands in the American West as a place of opportunity and a safe haven. A few people made their way to New Mexico, Arizona, Colorado, and Oklahoma. Groups of North Carolina and Mississippi blacks migrated to Nebraska, and others looked to the frontier state of Kansas. Exodusters, as migrants to the American frontier were called, led by such men as former slave Benjamin "Pap" Singleton from Tennessee, moved their families from the Deep South westward into Kansas during the 1870s. Kansas had a special appeal: it had plenty of unoccupied land and was associated in the minds of African Americans with the Underground Railroad and John Brown. For them, it was an abolitionist territory that had battled proslavery forces and finally entered the Union as a free state. By the mid-1870s many southern blacks were taken with "Kansas Fever" fueled by rumors of free land, free transportation, and free supplies. The reports were largely exaggerated, but they did draw thousands from the violent South to the promise of a new life. By 1878 the town of Nicodemus, Kansas, boasted a population of seven hundred African Americans, all recent migrants from the Deep South. In April of the next year, hundreds more Exodusters traveled up the Missouri River by steamboat to the eastern Kansas settlement of Wyandotte.

Most African Americans did not leave the South. They did not have the resources, debts bound them to the land on which they sharecropped, or family ties held them in place. The proportion of blacks living in the South had dropped from 94 percent at the start of the Civil War to 84 percent by 1880, but the vast majority were still southerners. For this vast majority of black people in America, their brief political influence was rapidly fading. In the presidential election of 1876, pitting Democrat Samuel J. Tilden against Republican Rutherford B. Hayes, both parties claimed victory in Louisiana, South Carolina, and Florida, and thus the presidency. When an electoral commission sustained Hayes's claim, Democrats in Congress refused to certify the election. After the chaos of civil war and the disruption of the Reconstruction, the nation was in no mood for such political uncertainty. From every quarter—business interests, state and local governments, churches, and universities—came the demand that the election be settled quickly. A series of meetings led to a compromise whereby the Republican, Hayes, would take the presidency. Democrats would not contest economic policies benefiting Republican business interests, and in return the Hayes administration would remove the last U.S. troops from the South, leaving southerners to handle civil stability and civil rights in their states. The compromise that saved the nation from uncertainty and placed the Republican in the White House had been struck at African Americans' expense.

In the following years Southern Democrats, assisted by rulings of the U.S. Supreme Court, removed federal protections for black rights in the South. The court weakened or struck down much of the preceding decades' civil rights legislation and placed the responsibility for enforcing the Fourteenth and Fifteenth amendments on the states. Southern blacks denied the right to vote or lacking legal protection found their only recourse was to state authority. As conservative Democrats moved into positions of power at all levels of southern state governments, there was little recourse at all. Starting in 1890 in Mississippi, and then spreading across the South, a constellation of laws restricted the franchise to whites only. Poll taxes generally put the vote financially out of reach for sharecroppers and other poor blacks. Literacy testing was often devised and administered so that no black person, no matter how educated, could qualify to vote. Meanwhile, a clause in state regulations safeguarded the voting rights of illiterate whites by waiving the literacy requirement for voters deemed people of good conduct or whose grandfathers had voted before 1860, a time when almost all southern blacks were slaves.

Other laws provided for racial segregation in public accommodations, transportation, and almost every phase of life. The Mississippi Plan, and the host of laws that followed in every southern state and many border states, were the foundation for the extensive southern system of racial segregation often called the Jim Crow system. The Jim Crow segregation system was named after a character played by white actor, Thomas Dartmouth "Daddy" Rice. In the 1840s and 1850s, Rice blackened his face and danced, playing Jim Crow, a racial stereotype born of the white imagination. By the mid-1890s it was clear that Reconstruction's promise of real freedom was coming to an end, and there seemed little blacks could do about it. . . .

. . . Yet Reconstruction was not a total failure. Slavery was ended, and black people no longer faced the awful prospect of having their children and other family members sold away from them. African Americans made great gains in literacy and education, and a few even managed to acquire land. The Constitution was changed: the Thirteenth Amendment abolished slavery, the Fourteenth Amendment guaranteed African Americans citizenship rights, and the Fifteenth Amendment forbade the denial of voting rights on account of race. Constitutional guarantees may not have been honored, but they established legal principles to which plaintiffs could appeal. African Americans had struggled before the Civil War to end slavery and during Reconstruction to attain citizenship rights, and they continued their struggle for full freedom through the twentieth century. . . .

Despite the progress made against racial injustice, slavery still has an impact on Americans more than a century after its abolition. Its legacy remains in the history and heritage of the South that it shaped, in the culture of the North where its memory was long denied, in the national economy for which it provided much of the foundation, and in the political and social system it profoundly influenced. Slavery and its effects are embedded in the national culture and in the assumptions and contradictory ideals of American society. The central issues under debate today—issues involving race, class, region, religion, and national identity—are all imperfectly understood without the historical context of American slavery and without an understanding of the means by which a freedom-loving people rationalized their tolerance of slavery's development. Although it is troubling to consider, it is nonetheless true that slavery was, and continues to be, a critical factor in shaping the United States and all of its people. As Americans, we must understand slavery's history if we are ever to be emancipated from its consequences.

QUESTIONS TO CONSIDER

1 Describe the accomplishments of the Freedmen's Bureau in helping blacks make the transition from slavery to freedom. Before the Civil War, the cruel domestic slave trade broke up black families. What actions did the freedmen take to find lost family members and what obstacles often impeded their efforts?

2 Why did the former slaves need to own land to achieve true independence? Contrast the actions of William Tecumseh Sherman and Andrew Johnson on the distribution of confiscated Confederate lands to the freedmen. Why did sharecropping prevent the freedmen from becoming independent landowners?

3 What immediate impact did the Fourteenth and Fifteenth amendments have on the rights of former slaves? How was this important legislation compromised by southern whites who feared and resisted any change in race relations?

4 In what ways did the carpetbaggers and scalawags try to help the freedmen? In what ways was the Southern Homestead Act supposed to benefit the former slaves? Did it benefit them? Describe the accomplishments of the Republican governments in the former Confederate states, governments in which African Americans participated. How did such governments keep "the promise of improving many people's lives in the South"?

5 What motivated some African Americans to migrate to Liberia and to the American frontier? Why did most of the former slaves remain in the South?

6 What was the compromise that settled the disputed presidential election of 1876? Why do the authors contend that it "had been struck at African American expense"? In what ways did poll taxes, literacy tests, and other Jim Crow measures severely restrict the freedom of the former slaves?

30 The Checkered History of the Great Fourteenth Amendment

ERIC FONER

In the following selection, Eric Foner, today's foremost historian of the Reconstruction era, recounts the dramatic and controversial history of the great Fourteenth Amendment. Because it promised equality of all Americans before the law, Foner states that it was "one of the most important lasting consequences of the immense changes produced by the war."

To place Foner's story in historical context, it would be well to pick up the Reconstruction story with what was transpiring in the nation's capital in 1865 and 1866. Andrew Johnson's soft, conciliatory reconstruction policy enraged Republican leaders on Capitol Hill. As we saw in the previous selection, the president not only opposed granting black men the right to vote but also allowed former Confederates to return to power in the southern states. Johnson also stood by when ex-rebel legislators enacted black codes that reduced blacks to a virtual condition of peonage, and he hotly opposed congressional interference in the reconstruction process. He even urged southern states to reject the Fourteenth Amendment, pushed through Congress by the Republicans, which would protect southern blacks. The amendment would prevent the states from adopting laws that abridged "the privileges or immunities of citizens of the United States." It would also bar the states from depriving "any person of life, liberty, or property, without due process of law," or from denying any person the "equal protection of the law." Johnson did more than just oppose the amendment; he damned Republican leaders like Charles Sumner of Massachusetts and Thaddeus Stevens of Pennsylvania, calling them tyrants and traitors. He even campaigned against the Republican party in the 1866 off-year elections. As a consequence, he alienated moderate as well as radical Republicans, who soon united against him. When the 1866 elections gave the Republicans huge majorities in both houses of Congress, they took control of Reconstruction and set about reforming the South themselves, granting blacks the right to vote and hold office.

Thus the stage is set for Foner's brilliant essay on one of the most important constitutional amendments in American history. In the short run, the equal protection clause had little effect on the lives of the former slaves. Southern white resistance and northern complacency resulted in what Foner calls "a new system of racial subordination" that sought to eliminate black voting, institute racial segregation, and place severe restrictions on "blacks' economic power."

Moreover, the great Fourteenth Amendment itself underwent a drastic reinterpretation. When Reconstruction ended in 1877, the United States entered what Mark Twain called the Gilded Age, a conservative era dominated by big businessmen and their corporate monopolies. In this period, reflecting the spirit of the times, the Supreme Court changed the original purpose of the Fourteenth Amendment: the Court's new interpretation turned it into an instrument for the protection of corporations. At the same time, the Court acquiesced in the ruthless oppression of black people in the white supremacist South.

But decades later, in the activist 1960s and 1970s, a progressive Supreme Court not only returned the Fourteenth Amendment to its original purpose, but also expanded it to protect the rights of "aggrieved groups of all sorts—blacks, women, gays, welfare recipients, the elderly, the disabled." More than a century after its ratification, this powerful amendment, first conceived in "imperfect compromise" during Reconstruction, has become today (in Foner's words) "the most important bulwark of the rights of American citizens." What follows is the fascinating story of how that came to be.

GLOSSARY

BLACK CODES   See glossary in previous selection.

BROWN v. BOARD OF EDUCATION OF TOPEKA (1954)   The Supreme Court's landmark decision that ruled that state-initiated racial segregation violated the equal protection

guarantee of the Fourteenth Amendment. This was because separation inherently meant inequality.

DRED SCOTT v. SANDFORD (1857)   With a majority of southerners as justices, the Supreme Court ruled that neither Congress nor the territories could outlaw slavery. Five justices maintained that to do so would violate the property rights clause of the United States Constitution. Since slaves were property, the Court said that they could not be United States citizens.

FIFTEENTH AMENDMENT   See glossary in previous selection.

JOHNSON, ANDREW   See glossary in previous selection.

PLESSY v. FERGUSON (1896)   This Supreme Court decision upheld "separate but equal" accommodations for whites and African Americans. The majority of justices argued that the ruling was consistent with the equal protection clause guaranteed by the Fourteenth Amendment.

RECONSTRUCTION ACT OF 1867   Provided the freedmen with the right to vote and "launched the short-lived period of Radical Reconstruction during which, for the first time in American history, a genuine interracial democracy flourished."

SANTA CLARA COUNTY v. SOUTHERN PACIFIC RAILROAD   In a strange twist the Supreme Court ruled in this case that a corporation was a person under the law. By this decision, the Fourteenth Amendment forbade states to interfere with a corporation's activities, like the regulation of working conditions.

STEVENS, THADDEUS   A Radical Republican leader in the House of Representatives, he devoted his career to the struggle against slavery and for the equal rights of the freedmen. He promoted the Fourteenth Amendment and the confiscation and distribution of former rebel lands to the newly freed slaves, and he was a major force in the impeachment trial of Andrew Johnson.

SUMNER, CHARLES   One of the leading Radical Republicans in the Senate, he too was a committed idealist who advocated complete civil and political equality for African Americans. "More than any of his political contemporaries," writes his biographer, David Herbert Donald, "Sumner realized that the future of American democracy depended on the ability of the white and black races to live together in peace and equality."

TRUMBULL, LYMAN   This Illinois senator and his colleague, Senator John Sherman of Ohio, thought that suffrage for the freedmen was "a political liability." Both men represented the moderate wing of the Republican party that desired a free labor economy in the South. They joined the Radicals who desired more drastic changes only after President Johnson opposed the Fourteenth Amendment and stuck adamantly to his prosouthern policy.

On June 13, 1866, Thaddeus Stevens, the majority floor leader in the House of Representatives and the nation's most prominent Radical Republican, rose to address his congressional colleagues. His subject was the Fourteenth Amendment to the Constitution—which, after months of deliberation and innumerable drafts and redrafts, was about to receive final approval by Congress. Its purpose was to secure the fruits of Union victory in the Civil War by guaranteeing equal civil rights for the freed slaves and loyal governments in the South.

Born during George Washington's administration, Stevens had enjoyed a public career that embodied, as much as anyone's, the struggle against the "Slave

"Equality Before the Law" by Eric Foner. Reprinted from *Days of Destiny*, General Editors James M. McPherson and Alan Brinkley; Editor, David Rubel, by permission of DK Publishing. Copyright © 2001 Dorling Kindersley Ltd. All rights reserved. www.dk.com.

Power" and for equal rights for black Americans. In 1837, as a delegate to Pennsylvania's constitutional convention, he had refused to sign the state's new frame of government because it abrogated the right of African Americans to vote. As a member of Congress during the 1850s, he had fought against the expansion of slavery and, during the secession crisis, opposed compromise with the South. Once the Civil War began, he was among the first to advocate the emancipation of slaves and the enrollment of black soldiers.

During the era of Reconstruction that followed the war, Stevens insisted that the South was a "conquered province," which Congress could govern as it saw fit. He was the most prominent advocate, for example, of distributing land to former slaves so that they might have an economic foundation for their freedom. Like other Radicals, he believed that Reconstruction was a golden opportunity to purge the

Thaddeus Stevens was the driving force behind the Fourteenth Amendment, but controversy followed this champion of the freedmen. In the superstitious nineteenth century, his clubfoot was deemed a sign of evil. Although he never married, there were many rumors about his relationship with an African American housekeeper with whom he lived for many years. (Library of Congress)

nation of the legacy of slavery and create a society whose citizens enjoyed equal civil and political rights, secured by a powerful and beneficent national government. "The whole fabric of southern society must be changed," he declared, "and never can it be done, if this opportunity be lost." Stevens's speech on June 13 was an eloquent statement of this political creed:

In my youth, in my manhood, in my old age, I had fondly dreamed that when any fortunate chance should have broken up for awhile the foundation of our institutions, and released us from obligations the most tyrannical that ever man imposed in the name of freedom, that the intelligent, pure and just men of this Republic . . . would have so remodeled all our institutions as to have freed them from every vestige of human oppression, of inequality of rights, of the recognized degradation of the poor, and the superior caste of the rich. . . . This bright dream has vanished [quoting Shakespeare's *The Tempest*] "like the baseless fabric of a dream." I find that we shall be obliged to be content with patching up the worst portions of the ancient edifice, and leaving it, in many of its parts, to be swept through by the . . . storm of despotism. Do you inquire why, holding these views and possessing some will of my own, I accept so imperfect a proposition? I answer, because I live among men and not among angels.

A few moments later, the Fourteenth Amendment was approved by the House. The result was never in doubt because, with the southern states still unrepresented, the Republican party commanded an overwhelming majority. The final vote was 120–32, well above the required two-thirds majority. Three days later, having been approved by the Senate shortly before the House vote, the amendment was sent to the states for ratification. It became part of the Constitution on July 28, 1868.

The Fourteenth Amendment prohibited the states from abridging the equality before the law of American citizens, provided for a reduction in representation in Congress should any state deprive male citizens of the right to vote, excluded Confederates who had previously taken a constitutional oath from holding state or federal office, and prohibited payment of the Confederate debt. It was one of the most important lasting consequences of the immense changes produced by the Civil War and the subsequent political crisis of Reconstruction, especially the struggle between the president and Congress over control of Reconstruction policy.

In late May 1865, six weeks after he succeeded the martyred Abraham Lincoln, Pres. Andrew Johnson announced his plan for reuniting the nation, launching the era of presidential Reconstruction. Although a staunch Unionist from Tennessee, Johnson was an inveterate racist and a firm defender of states' rights. The essentials of his Reconstruction plan allowed white southerners to establish new state governments—which were required by Johnson to abolish slavery, repudiate secession, and abrogate the Confederate debt but otherwise accorded a free hand in controlling local affairs. When these new governments quickly enacted the

Andrew Johnson from Tennessee remained loyal to the Union and became Lincoln's vice president at the end of the Civil War. The former senator was motivated by his devotion to the Constitution and his disdain for the planter class. With his poor southern white background, Johnson opposed granting political rights to the freedmen. His lenient Reconstruction program allowed former Confederates to take office in southern state governments, and he permitted these governments to enact the infamous black codes, which virtually reenslaved African Americans in the South. (Library of Congress)

abrogation of the Johnson-authorized state governments and the establishment of new ones based on equality before the law and universal manhood suffrage. The Radicals, however, didn't control the Republican party. Occupying the political middle ground was the moderate Republican majority, led in Congress by Sen. Lyman Trumbull of Illinois and Sen. John Sherman of Ohio. Unenthusiastic about black suffrage—which they viewed as a political liability in the North and an experiment whose outcome couldn't be predicted in the South—Trumbull, Sherman, and their allies were nonetheless fully committed to ensuring "loyal" governments in the former states of the Confederacy and protecting the elementary rights of freed slaves in a society organized on the basis of free labor rather than slavery. Eventually, however, Johnson's policies, and the actions of the state governments created under his supervision, drove them into the Radicals' arms, uniting the entire Republican party against the president.

Much of the ensuing debate over Reconstruction revolved around the problem, as Trumbull put it, of defining "what slavery is and what liberty is." The Civil War had greatly enhanced the power of the national state. Especially because of the service of two hundred thousand black men in the Union army and navy, the war had also put the question of black citizenship on the national agenda. By early 1866, moderates had concluded that equality before the law—enforced, if necessary, by national authority—had become an inevitable consequence of emancipation and a condition for restoring the South to full participation in the Union. These principles were embodied in the Civil Rights Act of 1866, a precursor to the Fourteenth Amendment that outlined the rights all Americans were to enjoy regardless of race. These included the rights to make contracts, bring lawsuits, and enjoy equal protection of the security of person and property. Johnson's veto of this measure and its repassage by Congress in April 1866 marked the final breach between the president and the Republican party. It was the first time in American history that a significant piece of legislation became law over a president's veto.

repressive Black Codes, most northern Republicans turned against the president. As one observer put it, the Black Codes seemed designed to "restore all of slavery but its name." Meanwhile, the election of "rebels" to leading offices in the South and reports of violence directed against both freed people and northern visitors reinforced the conviction that Johnson's plan played into the hands of the southern Democrats.

When the Thirty-ninth Congress (elected in November 1864) finally assembled in December 1865, Radical Republicans, led by Stevens, called for

Beyond impelling congressional Republicans to devise their own Reconstruction plan, Johnson's intransigence persuaded them to write their understanding of the consequences of the Civil War into the Constitution, there to be secure from shifting electoral majorities. The result was the Fourteenth Amendment, adopted by Congress after months of committee deliberations and a series of alterations on the House and Senate floors. Some Republicans wished to disqualify leading Confederates from voting; others wanted to include both "universal amnesty" for "rebels" and "universal suffrage" for black men. But these proposals failed to win the support of most Republicans. In its final form, the amendment was a compromise on which all Republicans could unite.

This process of compromise, however, as Stevens's June 13 speech suggests, resulted in a text that didn't fully satisfy the Radicals. The Fourteenth Amendment, as enacted, didn't abolish existing state governments in the South, nor did it guarantee blacks the right to vote; indeed, in one section, it offered each southern state, once readmitted to the Union, the alternative of allowing black men to vote and retaining the state's full representation in Congress or continuing to disenfranchise blacks and suffering a loss of representation proportionate to the black percentage of the state population. (No penalty applied, however, when women were denied the right to vote, an omission that led many advocates of women's rights to oppose ratification of the amendment.)

The Fourteenth Amendment had five sections in all, three of which have little importance today— those barring Confederates from office, dealing with the Confederate debt, and reducing a state's representation in Congress if men are denied the right to vote. (This last provision was never enforced, even during the decades when southern states disenfranchised most black voters.) Nonetheless, the Fourteenth Amendment has since become, after the Bill of Rights, the most important constitutional change in the nation's history. Its heart was Section 1, which declared that all persons born or naturalized in the United States were both national and state citizens. Section 1 also prohibited states from abridging the "privileges and

immunities of citizens"; depriving them "of life, liberty, or property without due process of law"; and denying them "equal protection of the laws." It thus established, as Thaddeus Stevens told the House, the principle that state laws "shall operate equally upon all." Later he added, "I can hardly believe that any person can be found who will not admit that . . . [it] is just."

In keeping with constitutional authority the principle that equality before the law, regardless of race, could and should be enforced by the national government, the Fourteenth Amendment permanently transformed the definition of American citizenship and refashioned relations between the federal government and the states as well as those between individual Americans and the nation. We live today in a legal and constitutional system shaped profoundly by the Fourteenth Amendment.

During the 1866 Congressional Elections, ratification of the Fourteenth Amendment became the central issue of the campaign. That fall, the president embarked on an unprecedented speaking trip across the North, known as the "swing around the circle." Its primary purpose was to drum up support for candidates associated with Johnson's National Union party—mostly northern Democrats who supported the president's Reconstruction policies. Yet Johnson also took the opportunity to rally whatever opposition to ratification he could. Again and again, he called for reconciliation between North and South, insisting that suffrage requirements and citizens' rights should be left to the states. Johnson also engaged in impromptu debates with hecklers, intimating that Stevens and the other Radicals were traitors. For their part, Republicans defended the amendment as necessary to secure the emancipation of the slaves and prevent Confederates from controlling the South.

The outcome of the midterm elections was continued Republican dominance in Congress and a clear mandate for Stevens and the Radicals. Johnson, however, continued his intransigent opposition to the amendment, urging southern legislatures to refuse to ratify it. And during the winter of 1866–1867, every southern state, except Tennessee, indeed rejected the amendment. With southern state governments thus having thoroughly discredited themselves in the eyes of nearly all Republicans, moderate and radical alike, party leaders concluded that only by establishing entirely new governments in the south could Reconstruction be accomplished. In March 1867, on the penultimate day of its post-election session, the Thirty-ninth Congress passed, over Johnson's veto, the Reconstruction Act of 1867. This gave the right to vote to black men in the South and launched the short-lived period of Radical Reconstruction during which, for the first time in American history, a genuine interracial democracy flourished. In March 1870, the Fifteenth Amendment, prohibiting any state from depriving citizens of the right to vote because of race, became part of the Constitution. What Republican leader Carl Schurz called "the great Constitutional revolution" of Reconstruction was complete. "Nothing in all history," exulted abolitionist William Lloyd Garrison, equaled "this wonderful . . . transformation of four million human beings from . . . the auction-block to the ballot-box."

In general, the Acts and Amendments of Reconstruction reflected the intersection of two products of the Civil War era: the newly empowered national state and the idea of a national citizenry enjoying equality before the law. In fact, rather than embodying a threat to liberty (as Jefferson had perceived it), the federal government had now become "the custodian of freedom," declared Charles Sumner, the abolitionist senator from Massachusetts. The rewriting of the Constitution during Reconstruction promoted a sense of the document's malleability and further suggested that the rights of individual citizens were intimately connected to federal power. This was a substantial departure from the pre–Civil War period, when disenfranchised groups were far more likely to draw inspiration from the Declaration of Independence than from the Constitution. (After all, the only mention of equality in the original Constitution came in the clause granting each state an equal number of senators.)

For example, the Bill of Rights, ratified in 1791, defined civil liberties in terms of state autonomy. Its language—"Congress shall pass no law . . ."—reflected the Jeffersonian belief that concentrated power was a threat to freedom. The Reconstruction amendments, however, which included the Thirteenth Amendment abolishing slavery, assumed that rights required political power to enforce them. These amendments, therefore, not only authorized the federal government to override state actions that deprived citizens of equality but also concluded with sections empowering Congress to "enforce" the amendments with "appropriate legislation." The Reconstruction amendments, especially the Fourteenth, transformed the Constitution from a document primarily concerned with federal-state relations and the rights of property into a vehicle through which members of vulnerable minorities could stake a claim to substantive freedom and seek protection against misconduct by all levels of government.

Limiting the privileges of citizenship to white men had long been intrinsic to the practice of American democracy. In 1857, in deciding *Dred Scott* v. *Sandford,* the Supreme Court had declared that no black person could be a citizen of the United States. Racism, federalism, a belief in limited government and local autonomy—Reconstruction challenged all these principles of nineteenth-century political culture. So deeply rooted were they, in fact, that only during an unparalleled crisis could they have been superseded, even temporarily, by the vision of an egalitarian republic embracing black Americans as well as white under the protection of the federal government. Indeed, it was precisely for this reason that the era's laws and constitutional amendments aroused such bitter opposition. The underlying principles—that the federal government possessed the power to define and protect citizens' rights, and that blacks were equal members of the body politic—were striking departures in American law. It isn't difficult to understand why President Johnson, in one of his veto messages, claimed that federal protection of African-American civil rights, together with the broad conception of national power that lay behind it, violated "all our experience as a people."

Frederick Douglass was a runaway slave, the author of a popular autobiography, the editor of the North Star, *perhaps the most dynamic of the abolitionist spokesmen, and the greatest black man of his generation. He was also a champion of the women's rights movement. (The National Archives)*

Reconstruction proved fragile and short lived. Its end is usually dated at 1877, when federal troops were withdrawn from the South (as a consequence of the contested 1876 presidential election) and white-supremacist Democrats regained control of southern state governments. But retreat from the idea of equality was already underway prior to 1877, as traditional ideas of racism and localism reasserted themselves during the early 1870s and violence disrupted the southern Republican party. This transition accelerated after 1877, when Supreme Court interpretation of the Fourteenth Amendment increasingly eviscerated its promise of equal citizenship. Deciding the 1873 Slaughterhouse Cases, for example, the Court severely restricted the rights protected under the amendment, ruling that these comprised only those rights that owed their existence to the federal government—such as traveling on navigable

waterways, running for federal office, and being protected on the high seas. Clearly, *these* rights were of limited concern to most former slaves. All other rights, the Court ruled, were derived from state, not national, authority, and with these the amendment had "nothing to do."

Next came the 1883 Civil Rights Cases, which invalidated a federal law prohibiting unequal treatment of blacks in public accommodations on the grounds that the Fourteenth Amendment barred only *legal* discrimination, not the actions of private individuals. Finally, the Court's famous 1896 decision in *Plessy* v. *Ferguson* decreed that state-mandated racial segregation didn't violate the Fourteenth Amendment's equal protection clause because "separate" could be equal. By the turn of the twentieth century, therefore, the states had been given carte blanche to nullify the Reconstruction amendments and civil rights laws. A new system of racial subordination was put in place in the South, centered on the elimination of black voting, racial segregation, and the severe restriction of blacks' economic opportunities. And these blatant violations of the Fourteenth and Fifteenth Amendments occurred with the acquiescence of the North, as reflected in the Supreme Court rulings.

Meanwhile, the Court made use of the Fourteenth Amendment in a manner that Thaddeus Stevens could never have imagined—as a barrier against governmental regulation of corporate behavior. In 1886, in *Santa Clara County* v. *Southern Pacific Railroad*, the Court declared that a corporation was a "person" under the law and thus couldn't be deprived of the "privileges and immunities" specified in the amendment's first section. This principle underpinned a long legal era during which the Court held that "liberty of contract"—the right of corporations to operate without state interference such as regulation of working conditions, limitation of working hours, and so on—was the real intention of the Fourteenth Amendment. Not until the late 1930s did the Court abandon this liberty-of-contract jurisprudence.

The Fourteenth Amendment's checkered history, however, is also the history of evolving American ideas about civil rights and civil liberties. During the first half of the twentieth century, the Court slowly took up the work of applying Fourteenth Amendment protections to the citizens' rights enumerated in the Bill of Rights. That is, the Court began to rule that states must respect the same civil liberties that the first ten amendments to the Constitution protect against federal intrusion. This process, called "incorporation" by legal historians, began shortly after World War I, when the Court responded to extensive censorship by wartime authorities with an opinion that obligated states under the Fourteenth Amendment to refrain from unreasonable restrictions on the freedoms of speech and of the press. Soon afterward, it invalidated state laws that required all students to attend public schools and prohibited teachers from instructing in languages other than English (measures directed against schools established by churches and immigrant groups). The amendment's guarantee of equal liberty, it declared, included the right to bring up children and practice religion free from governmental interference.

During the 1950s and 1960s, led by Chief Justice Earl Warren, the Court again turned to the Fourteenth Amendment as a source not only for the racial justice envisioned by its framers but also for a vast expansion of civil liberties for all Americans. In 1954, in the *Brown* v. *Board of Education* decision that overturned *Plessy,* the Warren Court ruled that state-sanctioned racial segregation violated the Fourteenth Amendment's equal protection clause because separation was inherently unequal. In subsequent decisions, it struck down state laws that sought to destroy civil rights organizations by requiring them to disclose lists of their members; and in *New York Times* v. *Sullivan* (1964), it greatly expanded the legal protections given newspapers and other media by requiring that plaintiffs in libel suits prove that the defamatory remarks in question were made out of either malice or a "reckless disregard" for the truth. Reversing its long history of compliance with racial injustice, the Supreme Court had become by the end of the 1960s the Congress's leading ally in the struggle for racial justice.

The Warren Court continued the process of incorporation until the states were required to abide by virtually every clause in the Bill of Rights—from such literal guarantees as protection against unreasonable searches and seizures and the right to a speedy trial to inferred rights, including the right of indigent defendants to publicly appointed legal counsel. During this period, the Court struck down numerous state and local measures, including some mandating prayer in public schools, that violated the First Amendment's ban on government support for religion.

Meanwhile, generating even greater controversy, it discovered under the aegis of the Fourteenth Amendment some entirely new rights that the states couldn't abridge. Most dramatic of these was the right to "privacy," embodied in the 1965 *Griswold* decision overturning a Connecticut law that prohibited the use of contraceptive devices and in *Roe* v. *Wade* (1973), which created the constitutional right to terminate a pregnancy. This "rights revolution" undertaken by the Warren Court elevated the status of the Fourteenth Amendment until it became the major constitutional provision to which aggrieved groups of all sorts—blacks, women, gays, welfare recipients, the elderly, the disabled—appealed in seeking to expand their legal rights and social status.

Today, amid the continuing controversies over abortion rights, affirmative action, the rights of homosexuals, and many other issues, the Court's interpretation of the Fourteenth Amendment remains a focus of judicial as well as political debate. An imperfect compromise when added to the Constitution during Reconstruction, the amendment has since become the most powerful bulwark of the rights of American citizens. We haven't yet created the "bright dream" of which Thaddeus Stevens spoke in his June 1866 speech, but thanks to the reinvigoration of the Fourteenth Amendment by the twentieth-century Supreme Court, more Americans enjoy more rights and more freedoms today than ever before in our history.

QUESTIONS TO CONSIDER

1 Consider the long career of Thaddeus Stevens. What issues did he champion and what frustrations

did he face? Why would Foner state that Stevens viewed Reconstruction as a "golden opportunity"?

2 Why would Foner describe the Fourteenth Amendment as "one of the most important lasting consequences of the immense changes produced by the Civil War and the subsequent political crisis of Reconstruction?" After its passage, do you think that race should have been a factor when determining legal equality? In what ways was its original purpose later compromised in Supreme Court rulings such as *Plessy* v. *Ferguson* and *Santa Clara County* v. *Southern Pacific Railroad?*

3 Why would Foner state that the Reconstruction amendments made the Constitution a document "through which members of vulnerable minorities could stake a claim to substantive freedom and seek protection against misconduct by all levels of government"? Before Reconstruction, why did the Declaration of Independence, more so than the Constitution, provide hope for the downtrodden and oppressed?

4 Why did the mood of the country in the conservative period following the fall of the Radical Republicans erode the original purpose of the Fourteenth Amendment? How would Thaddeus Stevens have viewed the Slaughterhouse Cases, the 1883 Civil Rights Cases, and the separate but unequal society that emerged?

5 The Fourteenth Amendment's checkered history reflected the changing values of the country. Explain how, during probusiness eras, it has protected corporations more than people. Why did it fail to prevent racial discrimination at the end of the nineteenth century? How did it help spark a "second reconstruction" nearly sixty years later, after a groundbreaking decision from the Warren Court?

6 The Fourteenth Amendment, initially passed to help guarantee equality under the law for the freedmen, became a vehicle in the twentieth century to help many other groups—women, gays, the elderly, and the disabled. Is this a violation or a natural extension of its original intent? Examine the rationale for decisions that applied the Fourteenth Amendment to issues like abortion, school prayer, and the rights of the accused. Are we now approaching that "bright dream" envisioned by Thaddeus Stevens?

PORTRAIT OF AMERICA

VOLUME 2 FROM 1865

CONTENTS

children making their way home after school. Laskin's vivid description of the blizzard is haunting. As he says, the storm was a tragic example of a dream gone wrong for pioneers who had moved west in search of a prosperous new life. For countless pioneer families, the promise of the Homestead Act proved to be a cruel joke. The storm that killed their children demonstrated "that the land they had desired so fervently and had traveled so far to claim wasn't free after all."

Theodore Roosevelt believed that she was one of those infamous muckrakers, more interested in filth than the truth. Tarbell ignored those insults. In 1906, her tenacity and willingness to make personal sacrifices resulted in a federal antitrust suit against the ignoble Rockefeller and his mighty Standard Oil Company.

depression in its history. Textbooks explain in detail the economic reasons for the crash of 1929 and the ensuing Depression, but none captures the human suffering and the failure of early relief efforts better than Watkins's prize-winning *The Great Depression,* a companion to the popular PBS television series, from which this selection is excerpted.

Roosevelt should have bombed the hideous gas chambers at Auschwitz and the railroad tracks leading to that murderous prison. The author contends that "mainstream Jewish opinion was against the whole idea." It is "abhorrent" to contemplate the number of helpless concentration camp prisoners that Allied bombs would have killed. Inmates already loaded into cattle cars would have perished from thirst and heat while waiting the "few days" the Germans needed to rebuild damaged track. Roosevelt believed that the best way to save Jewish lives was to win the war as swiftly as possible.

president despite his flaws and mistakes. McCullough argues that
Truman's most difficult decision was to enter the Korean War, that
his worst mistake was the sweeping loyalty oath test he instituted
for federal employment, and that he was at his best when the
Soviets blockaded West Berlin in 1948 and Truman saved the city
through a spectacular airlift.

the flesh-and-blood King from the dust of history. The selection traces King's intellectual and spiritual development that culminated in his philosophy of nonviolence; seeks to explore his personality, including his human flaws, with empathy and understanding; and assesses his accomplishments as an internationally acclaimed spokesman for the civil rights movement and the protest against the Vietnam War.

helped shape his performance in office. He was upbeat, witty, and supremely optimistic. But Reagan's other "salient traits" were his coldness, his inaccessibility, and his penchant for thinking only about the big picture and thus missing crucial details. Even so, Brookhiser credits Reagan with being the lead player in bringing about momentous historic events like the crumbling of the Berlin Wall, the collapse of the Soviet Union, the relegation of Communism to "the ash-heap of history," and the end of the Cold War that had plagued the planet for almost half a century.

PREFACE

Good history begins with a good story.

—James West Davidson
and Mark Hamilton Lytle

The ninth edition of *Portrait of America* is the work of two historians who care deeply about the teaching of American history. We realize that many students enter undergraduate history courses and advanced placement high school programs with the impression that the study of history entails little more than names and dates. We are convinced that the superb readings in *Portrait of America* demonstrate that this is a misconception and that studying history can in fact be a profoundly enriching experience. This is because *Portrait of America* stresses the human side of the American past, suggesting how the interaction of people and events shaped the course of American history. We chose selections for this anthology that make history live by telling a good story, and that were written for students, not for professional historians. The essays, narratives, and biographical portraits gathered here humanize American history, portraying it as a story of real people who actually lived, people with whom we can identify. We hope that the anthology is an example of humanistic history at its best, the kind that combines scrupulous and engaging scholarship with a compelling narrative style. Because college survey audiences are not professional ones, they might enjoy reading history if it is presented in an exciting and accessible form.

There is another reason why students will find *Portrait of America* edifying: it showcases the writings of some of America's most eminent historians. Volume Two contains excerpts from critically acclaimed, best-selling books by Margaret MacMillan and Doris Kearns Goodwin, both famous authors.

The prizes our contributors have won testify to their important places in the galaxy of American letters. Pulitzer Prize winners include Edmund Morris, David McCullough, James MacGregor Burns, Arthur M. Schlesinger, Jr., and Doris Kearns Goodwin. In addition, Eric Foner, John Lewis Gaddis, and Arthur M. Schlesinger, Jr., have all won the prestigious Bancroft Prize. Stephen B. Oates, an elected member of the Society of American Historians, received the Robert F. Kennedy Memorial Book Award, two Christopher Awards, and fellowships from the Guggenheim Foundation and the National Endowment for the Humanities. Many of the other contributors also earned significant literary and scholarly recognition. Thus *Portrait of America* offers readers a unique opportunity to learn from a lineup of historians and writers with national and even international reputations.

The ninth edition of Volume Two has been extensively revised. It contains seven new selections of superior literary and historical merit. They make this the strongest edition of *Portrait of America* yet published. The new readings are:

- James Oliver Horton and Lois E. Horton's graphic story of the black experience during Reconstruction, when the former slaves' dreams of true equality and a better life were obstructed by southern white violence and racial oppression;
- David Laskin's haunting description of the ferocious blizzard of 1888 that shocked migrants to the Dakota and Nebraska frontier and that killed hundreds of their children;
- William and Mary Lavender's vivid account of the suffragists who suffered cruel imprisonment for crusading for women's right to vote;

- Margaret MacMillan's inspired and insightful story of a sickly Woodrow Wilson and his losing struggle for American participation in the League of Nations;
- James West Davidson and Mark Hamilton Lytle's fascinating analysis of how the bigotry of native-born white Anglo-Saxon Protestants contributed to the execution of two obscure Italian immigrants named Sacco and Vanzetti;
- James MacGregor Burns's riveting account of the Great Depression of the 1930s and President Franklin D. Roosevelt's efforts to end it by bold and pragmatic experimentation;
- Richard Brookhiser's brilliant examination of Ronald Reagan's personality and of his role in such momentous events as the collapse of the Soviet Union and the end of the Cold War.

The ninth edition retains the best and most popular selections of the previous edition. We hope that *Portrait of America* remains as balanced as ever, for it offers samplings of virtually every kind of history—men's and women's, black and white, social and cultural, political and military, urban and economic, national and local—so that students can appreciate the rich diversity of the American experience.

Portrait of America contains several important features that help students learn from its contents. Each selection is preceded by a glossary that identifies important individuals, events, and concepts that appear in the reading. Introductions set the selections in proper context and suggest ways to approach studying them. They also tie all the selections together so that they can be read more or less as connected episodes. Study questions following the selections raise significant issues and encourage students to make comparisons and contrasts between selections. The questions also help students review the readings and suggest points for class discussion.

The anthology is intended for use largely in college survey courses. It could be used as a supplement to a textbook or to a list of paperback readings. Or it could serve as the basic text. *Portrait of America* could also be used effectively in advanced placement high school classes. The book is organized into fifteen parts according to periods or themes; each part contains two or three related selections. This organization allows readers to make comparisons and contrasts between different events or viewpoints.

With this edition, we are introducing a new website. On this website, instructors and students will find a number of selections that appeared in the seventh and eighth editions, but are not included in the ninth edition primarily for reasons of length. With this website, we can keep the print version of *Portrait of America* to a reasonable length and still make available many popular selections from those editions.

We could not have assembled the ninth edition without the generous help of others. Robert Kinson, Elza M. England, and Denise Pattee Pargas assisted us at crucial points in the preparation of the manuscript, and we are most grateful to them. At Northern Virginia Community College, Alice Reagan helped identify new selections, and Betty Pasqualini assisted with formatting the manuscript. Jay Boggis did a superb job of copyediting the manuscript, and we are most grateful to him. We also want to thank the following professors for taking time out from their busy schedules to review the volume: Richard Aquila, Pennsylvania State University, the Behrend College; Terri Halperin, University of Richmond; Gordon Patterson, Florida Institute of Technology; and Vivian Talbot, Weber State University.

S. B. O.
C. J. E.

PART ONE

A Troubled Peace

1 *"Call Me Mister"*: The Black Experience During Reconstruction

JAMES OLIVER HORTON AND LOIS E. HORTON

For African Americans in North and South alike, the Civil War had profound religious meaning from the beginning. Hundreds of thousands, writes historian Vincent Harding, "believed unwaveringly that their God moved in history to deliver his people, and they had been looking eagerly, praying hourly, waiting desperately for the glory of the coming of the Lord. For them, all the raucous, roaring guns of Charleston Harbor and Bull Run, of Antietam and Fort Pillow, of Shiloh and Murfreesboro and Richmond were the certain voice of God, announcing his judgment across the bloody stretches of the South, returning blood for blood to the black river." During the course of that war, African Americans believed, God did deliver them. He drove out the rebels and slaveholders, just as he had once driven out the Hittites and Canaanites. With the Confederacy's collapse, as one song went, "slavery chain done broke at last."

> *Slavery chain done broke at last!*
> *Broke at last! Broke at last!*
> *Slavery chain done broke at last!*
> *Gonna praise God till I die!*

Some reacted to their liberation with cautious elation. When a young Virginia woman heard her former masters weeping over the capture of Jefferson Davis, she went down to a spring alone and cried out, "Glory, glory, hallelujah to Jesus! I's free! I's free!" Suddenly afraid, she looked about. What if the white folks heard her? But seeing no one, she fell to the ground and kissed it, thanking "Master Jesus" over and over. For her, freedom meant hope—hope that she could find her husband and four children who had been sold to a slave trader.

Others celebrated their liberation in public. In Athens, Georgia, they danced around a liberty pole; in Charleston, they paraded through the streets. Many African Americans, however, were wary and uncertain. "You're joking me," one man said when the master told him he was free. He asked some neighbors if they were free also. "I couldn't believe we was all free alike," he said. Some African Americans, out of feelings of obligation or compassion, remained on the home place to help their former masters. But others were hostile. When a woman named Cady heard that the war was over, she decided to protest the cruel treatment she had suffered as a slave. She threw down her hoe, marched up to the big house, found the mistress, and flipped her dress up. She told the white woman, "Kiss my ass!"

For Cady, for the young black woman of Virginia, for hosts of other African Americans, freedom meant an end to the manifold evils of slavery; it meant the right to say what they felt and go where they wanted. But what else did freedom mean to them? As black leaders of Charleston said, it meant that blacks should enjoy full citizenship, have the right to vote, and run for political office. It meant federal protection from their former masters lest they attempt to revive slavery. And it meant economic security in the form of land, so that the blacks could exercise self-help and be economically independent of their former masters.

If the end of the war was a time of profound hope for black Americans, it was a monumental calamity for most southern whites. By turns, they were angry, helpless, vindictive, resigned, and heartsick. Their once-beloved Confederacy was devastated. Its towns and major cities, Richmond and Atlanta, were in rubble. Former rebel soldiers returning home found their farm and plantation houses ransacked and even burned down, their barns destroyed, their fields burned, and their livestock gone. As one historian says, "Many [white southerners] were already grieving over sons, plantations, and fortunes taken by war; losing their blacks was the final blow." Some masters shot or hanged African Americans who proclaimed their freedom. That was a harbinger of the years of Reconstruction, for most white southerners were certain that their cause had been just and were entirely unrepentant about fighting against the Union. A popular ballad captured the mood in postwar Dixie:

Oh, I'm a good ole Rebel, now that's just what I am
For this fair land of freedom I do not care a damn.
I'm glad I fit against it, I only wish't we'd won
And I don't want no pardon for nothin' what I done. . . .

I hates the Yankee nation and everything they do
I hates the Declaration of Independence too
I hates the glorious Union, 'tis dripping with our blood
And I hate the striped banner, I fit it all I could. . . .

I can't take up my musket and fight 'em now no mo'
But I ain't gonna love 'em and that is certain sho'
And I don't want no pardon for what I was and am
And I won't be reconstructed and I don't care a damn.

In Washington, Republican leaders were jubilant in victory and determined to deal firmly with southern whites in order to preserve the fruits of the war. But what about the new president, Andrew

Johnson? A profane, hard-drinking Tennessee Democrat who bragged about his plebeian origins, Johnson had been the only southern senator to oppose secession openly. He had sided with the Union, served as war governor of Tennessee, and became Lincoln's running mate in 1864, on a Union ticket comprising both Republicans and War Democrats. As a result of the assassination of Lincoln, Johnson was now president, and he faced one of the most difficult tasks ever to confront an American chief executive: how to bind the nation's wounds, preserve African American freedom, and restore the southern states to their proper places in the Union.

Lincoln had contemplated an army of occupation for the defeated South, thinking that military force might be necessary to protect the former slaves and prevent the old southern leadership from returning to power. Now there was such an army in the conquered rebel states, and a great number of these Union troops were black.

In the following selection, historians James Oliver Horton and Lois E. Horton help you feel the soaring hope and terrible pain of emancipated blacks as they endured the transition from slavery to freedom in the postwar years. Instead of being passive and undeserving recipients of freedom (as an earlier generation of historians portrayed them), African Americans reached out and seized control of their destinies. They set about defining and exercising freedom for themselves, searched across the war-torn South for lost family members, established independent black churches, and struggled against an unrepentant white South determined to maintain white supremacy. With the acquiescence of President Johnson, white leaders in conquered Dixie adopted infamous black codes that severely restricted the freedom of the former slaves. In the story the Hortons tell, you will read about how southern African Americans had to endure Jim Crow segregation, poll taxes aimed at preventing blacks from voting, and the night-riding violence of the Ku Klux Klan. You will also read accounts of how African Americans had the courage to stand up to white prejudice and fight back.

For the blacks, the first troubled year of Reconstruction ended joyously with the ratification of the Thirteenth Amendment, which abolished slavery in America formally and forever. Nevertheless, as the Hortons remind us, "slavery still has an impact on Americans more than a century after its abolition. . . . As Americans, we must understand slavery's history if we are ever to be emancipated from its consequences."

GLOSSARY

BLACK CODES   These were local laws adopted by white-dominated state governments early in Reconstruction in the conquered South. Such notorious statutes virtually kept the freedmen in a state of servitude. These laws placed severe restrictions on the ownership of land and the ability of the former slaves to move freely in order to seek better jobs. The black codes were a product of white southern governments that came into power under President Johnson's lenient Reconstruction plan. One historian described them as the "slave codes revisited."

BROWN, JOHN   Brown had earned his reputation in "Bleeding Kansas" as an implacable antislavery warrior. Kansas, therefore, had a special appeal to African American migrants. Before the Civil War, freestate and pro-slavery settlers fought a vicious guerrilla war over the status of slavery there. The free-state majority finally won control of the territorial government. In 1861, Kansas entered the Union as a free state.

CARPETBAGGERS   Northerners, including former soldiers, who migrated to the South in search of economic opportunities. Many were teachers and nurses who came to assist the freedmen. Named for the bags that carried their belongings, the carpetbaggers were resented by white southerners who resisted any changes in race relations.

DUNN, OSCAR J.   Black lieutenant governor of Louisiana, Dunn was born into slavery. He was self-educated and during Reconstruction became an outspoken advocate of black suffrage.

EXODUSTERS   Name given to some six thousand former slaves who fled the South for the freedom of the western frontier, where they hoped to obtain nominally free land under the Homestead Act. The Exodusters homesteaded twenty thousand acres of land, much of it only marginally productive. "I asked my wife did she know the ground she stands on," one Louisiana Exoduster remembered. "She said, 'No!' I said it is free ground, and she cried like a child for joy."

FIFTEENTH AMENDMENT (1870)   The right of United States citizens to vote could not be denied, this amendment said, "on account of race, color, or previous conditions of servitude." After Reconstruction, the white-dominated southern states used poll taxes, literacy tests, and grandfather clauses to prevent blacks from voting or holding political office. This rendered the great amendment meaningless for almost a century.

FOURTEENTH AMENDMENT (1868)   Despite President Johnson's opposition, the Republican majority in Congress approved this significant amendment, which prohibited individual states from depriving American citizens "of life, liberty, or property, without due process of law." The next selection recounts the "checkered history" of the Fourteenth Amendment.

FREEDMEN'S BUREAU   Established by congressional statute in March 1865, the Bureau of Freedmen, Refugees, and Abandoned Lands, popularly known as the Freedmen's Bureau, attempted to provide food and schools for the former slaves, to help them secure jobs, and to make certain they received fair wages.

GRANDFATHER CLAUSES   Sometimes called "understanding clauses" or the "good character clauses," they were provisions built into southern state constitutions to ensure that poor and illiterate whites could vote, while blacks could not. Historian C. Vann Woodward referred to these "artfully devised" clauses as "loopholes" in the voting barriers "through which only white men could squeeze."

GRANT, ULYSSES S.   This former Union general served as president from 1869 to 1877. As chief executive, Grant did try to stop terrorist activities in the South, but otherwise did little to help the freedmen achieve true social, political, or economic freedom. As the Civil War ended, he advised President Johnson to remove the African American troops from the South.

HAMPTON, WADE   Governor of South Carolina and United States senator, Hampton represented white southerners who wanted to "redeem" the South by expelling carpetbaggers, scalawags, and freedmen from state governments and reestablishing white supremacy in Dixie.

HAYES, RUTHERFORD B.   Former governor of Ohio and a Republican, Hayes served as president from 1877 to 1881. Hayes defeated Democrat Samuel J. Tilden in the controversial presidential election of 1876. Tilden won the popular vote, but the outcome in the electoral college depended on disputed ballot counts in three southern states. The Republican and Democratic leaders agreed to a compromise in 1877 that awarded Hayes the presidency in exchange for removing federal troops from the South.

JIM CROW LAWS   Southern state and local laws that enforced segregation and discriminated against African Americans. The term "Jim Crow" derived from the name of a song sung by Thomas Rice in a black minstrel show before the Civil War.

JOHNSON, ANDREW   President from 1865 to 1869 and a product of the poor white South, Johnson had no sympathy for those who wanted to achieve true racial equality. He defied congressional Reconstruction measures and was impeached for political reasons. By one vote, the Senate failed to convict him, but Johnson was virtually powerless after the impeachment proceedings.

KU KLUX KLAN   Following the Civil War, this secretive paramilitary organization emerged in the South and used violence and intimidation to subdue the freedmen.

LIBERIA   In 1821, the American Colonization Society helped establish this settlement in West Africa as a haven for American black colonists. Over the next decade, several thousand free blacks voluntarily migrated to Liberia.

LITERACY TEST   In the years after Reconstruction, white southern leaders adopted literacy tests, which, like poll taxes, were designed to prevent freedmen from voting. Poor and illiterate whites were exempted from taking literacy tests because of carefully written "grandfather clauses." The Hortons sum up such discrimination against African Americans: "Starting in 1890 in Mississippi, and then spreading across the South, a constellation of laws restricted the [elective] franchise to whites only."

REVELS, HIRAM RHODES   In 1870, Revels, a minister and an educator, became the first African American to serve in the Unites States Senate. A Mississippi Republican, Revels left the Senate a year later to become president of Alcorn Agricultural College (now Alcorn University).

SCALAWAGS   Native southern whites who became Republicans during Reconstruction, scalawags resented being ruled by the planters and supported the legal and political rights of the freedmen.

SHARECROPPING   Lacking the money to acquire their own land in the South, many former slaves became sharecroppers. They rented plots of land from their former masters who paid them with shares of their crops. For African Americans, the sharecropping system was an odious form of exploitation. As the Hortons explain: "Unequal resources and power . . . led to white landowners' binding black sharecroppers to the land through real or contrived indebtedness."

SHERMAN, WILLIAM TECUMSEH   "Bill" Sherman, of course, was the Union general whose army cut a huge swath of destruction across the Confederacy in the last year of the war. But in Hortons' story, he did something else that only made white southerners hate him all the more. On January 16, 1865, from his headquarters in Savannah, he issued Special Field Order 15, which confiscated certain portions of Confederate plantations and farms in the area for the exclusive use of the freedmen. Six months later, forty thousand black farmers were cultivating their own forty-acre plots along the coastal areas of Georgia and South Carolina. President Johnson later returned this property to its prewar white owners and expelled the former slaves from the land.

STANTON, EDWIN M.   Lincoln's Secretary of War, Stanton approved of Sherman's Special Field Order 15, which gave the freedmen an opportunity to farm confiscated Confederate land.

SOUTHERN HOMESTEAD ACT (1866)   Congress designated forty-four million acres of public land in five southern states for settlement by the freedmen and by whites who had remained loyal to the Union. Few benefited from this legislation. Much of the land was unsuitable for farming, and few former slaves had the resources to wait for the revenue that would follow their first successful crop.

TENURE OF OFFICE ACT (1867)   By the terms of this federal statute, no federal official confirmed by the Senate could be removed until the Senate had approved a successor. When President Johnson removed Secretary of War Stanton in 1868, he violated this law and was impeached as a consequence. The senate, however, failed to convict him.

THIRTEENTH AMENDMENT   (1865) This momentous amendment ended slavery in the United States. Southern resistance to change and northern complacency would delay any significant improvement in race relations for another one hundred years.

At the end of the war it was not clear how the reuniting America would define black freedom, although it was clear that slavery was dead. In January 1865, by a vote of 121 to 24, Congress passed the Thirteenth Amendment to the U.S. Constitution, providing for the total abolition of American slavery. Ratified before the year was out, it seemed to many whites and blacks to be the fulfillment of the American Revolution. At last all Americans would have the promise of liberty and justice found in the Declaration of Independence. First, however, the country faced the task of ensuring the survival of people made destitute by slavery and the war. The immediate needs of the freed people were great, greater than could be met by the efforts of the private philanthropies that had been active during the war. In March 1865, before the fall of Richmond, the government had established the Bureau of Refugees, Freedmen, and Abandoned Lands, placing it in the War Department. The Freedmen's Bureau established operations in every department of the occupied South and provided aid to impoverished whites as well as freed slaves. Bureau agents established schools for the freed people and registered legal marriages for former slaves. Attempting to restore order to the war-ravaged southern plantation economy, and to bring in tax money to support federal assistance, agents negotiated millions of labor contracts, many between freed people and their former owners. As state governments were reestablished, the Bureau also oversaw voter registration.

Freed people had definite ideas about the meaning of freedom. Some took new names to denote their new status, as some black people had done after they escaped from slavery before the war, calling themselves Freeman or Freedman, for example. Some

Excerpts from James Oliver Horton and Lois E. Horton, *Slavery and the Making of America* (New York: Oxford University Press, 2005), pp. 207, 209–227, 230–231. Copyright © 2005 by Oxford University Press, Inc. Reprinted by permission of Oxford University Press, Inc.

Ratified in December, 1865, the Thirteenth Amendment guaranteed freedom to four million former slaves like those shown here. Most desired "forty acres and a mule"—that is, land and the tools to make it productive so that they could become economically self-sufficient. But most freedmen failed to achieve their dream when the sharecropping system, which replaced slavery, bound them to work land owned by white southerners. (Lightfoot Collection)

important links, carrying information and messages between people separated by slavery. Many men, like Maryland's Charles Ball who had run away twice from farther south, had endured the hardships of escaping in order to return to wives and children whom they had been forced to leave behind. Even in the same area, husbands and wives owned by different planters had sometimes gone without sleep and risked harsh punishment in order to see their mates. Tamar Grandy and her husband were both slaves in eastern North Carolina in the early 1800s. She was sold to a Georgia trader but escaped and traveled a hundred miles to return to her husband and her mother. Her husband lived twenty-five miles away from where she was in hiding. For years he came to visit her, leaving home as soon as he finished his work, spending part of the night with his wife, and walking the long distance back in order to arrive home before sunrise, when he would be called to the fields.

With freedom came relief from the slaves' greatest fear—having family members sold away. Touching reunions occurred during and after the war. Ben and Betty Dodson found each other in a refugee camp. They had been sold to separate masters twenty years before, and he had spent all that time searching for her. One Virginia mother found her eighteen-year-old daughter in a refugee camp. The girl had been sold away when she was just an infant. Finding children who had been sold away when they were young or finding the parents who had been sold away when the children were young was exceedingly difficult. With each succeeding sale, a child may have been given a different name, and intervening years made it difficult to recognize the adult who was once someone's child. For such children to be able to find their families required a slave community that kept the children's family histories alive during long periods of separation. Even with the community's help, however, reuniting families was often impossible. Slave mortality was high, especially in the lower South, and it was likely that people sold down the river many years before had not survived until freedom came.

dropped slave names given to them by their masters in favor of the names they had been known by in the slave quarters. Others who had been known by a succession of names as they were sold from owner to owner, settled on the name of the fairest or kindest master. Some took the names of masters they had when they were parted from family members. In this way, they hoped, it would be easier for husbands, wives, mothers, fathers, or children to find them.

Freedom meant keeping families together and finding lost family members. In slavery many people had tried to keep track of family members who were sold away. Slaves and free blacks whose occupations let them travel through the South had provided

The seemingly insurmountable odds notwithstanding, freed people traveled great distances, tracking down every lead, in efforts to find their families. They questioned every person they met from the area where their relative was last heard of. Freedmen's Bureau teachers and missionaries wrote thousands of letters for the illiterate freed people, following every rumor that someone had seen or heard of their relatives. People placed advertisements in newspapers, giving information about the missing person's former life, personal characteristics, injuries, and scars: Nearly a generation after the Civil War, newspapers still carried such ads:

Information Wanted, of Caroline Dodson, who was sold from Nashville, Nov. 1st, 1862, by James Lumsden to Warwick, (a trader then in human beings), who carried her to Atlanta, Georgia, and she was last heard of in the slave pen of Robert Clarke, (human trader in that place), from which she was sold. Any information of her whereabouts will be thankfully received and rewarded by her mother. Lucinda Lowery, Nashville.

Land ownership was also important to the freed people. For many ex-slaves, the promise of self-sufficiency, independence, and opportunity that freedom represented rested on the ownership of land. Various military commanders had allowed former slaves to work land abandoned by fleeing Confederates, and rumors persisted that the federal government would eventually grant land to the freed people. On January 16, 1865, just months before the South's surrender, U.S. General William T. Sherman took time from his devastating Georgia campaign to meet with twenty black community leaders in Savannah and discuss the issue of confiscated Confederate land in Georgia, South Carolina, and northern Florida. Secretary of War Edwin M. Stanton joined the discussions and approved Sherman's Special Field Order 15, declaring that "the islands from Charleston south, the abandoned rice-fields along the rivers for thirty miles back from the sea, and the country bordering the St. Johns River, Florida, are reserved and set apart for the settlement of the [N]egroes now made free by the acts of war and the [Emancipation] proclamation of the President of the United States." Each family was to be issued forty acres and an army mule to use in its cultivation. A few months later, the plan seemed confirmed by the government's placement of responsibility for refugees, freedmen, and abandoned lands in the same department.

In the spring of 1865, as the war came to an end, Vice President Andrew Johnson from Tennessee replaced the slain president in the oval office. Johnson had been Lincoln's wartime political choice, another strategy to hold the slave-holding border states, and was a political conservative. The new president spent the early days of his administration granting amnesty to former Confederate military leaders and handing out pardons wholesale to Confederates. White southerners needed simply to swear loyalty to the United States and agree to support the abolitionist provisions of the Thirteenth Amendment to have their property and general citizenship rights restored. Members of the southern aristocracy who had led the Confederacy in its war on the United States quickly applied for and received pardons. Thus, most of the land was returned to its prewar owners, and the former slaves who had been living on and cultivating the land during the last year of the war were expelled. Former abolitionists in Congress were never successful in their attempts to pass legislation granting former slaves land from the thousands of acres of confiscated Confederate land still under federal control. Ultimately, left without this foundation for independence, the freed people were forced to depend on former slaveholders to employ them or rent them land to farm.

Once pardoned and returned to political power, men from the planter class passed new laws reinstating much of their control over black people. In an attempt to re-create the southern racial etiquette of slave days, they punished black farm laborers for questioning white landlords, attacked black businessmen and their establishments for being too successful or competitive, attacked black students for displaying too much intelligence, confronted blacks who dressed too well or too neatly, and assaulted white people for encouraging black aspirations. Angered and distressed by the growing independence of their former slaves, planters complained that freed people were unwilling to work for what the planters considered reasonable wages. According to one Texas planter, the exorbitant wages offered by white employers with no sense of the "proper racial hierarchy" had spoiled the former slaves and led them to have outrageous expectations. Planters believed this had encouraged an inappropriate feeling of equality among the newly freed blacks.

After emancipation many African Americans did try to withdraw from the workforce. As a mark of their freedom, some men wanted their wives to be able to leave the fields and keep house for their families. Virtually all blacks wanted their children to be able to attend school, and some black people did demand respect from southern whites. As one former Georgia slave explained, many blacks vowed to take "no more foolishness off white folks." Long-standing customs and laws governing interracial contact in the South were designed to reinforce white supremacy. Whites addressed a black man as "boy" and a black woman as "girl" no matter how old they were, and either might be addressed as "nigger." The title of Uncle or Aunty that whites used for elderly blacks was the closest thing to respect an African American could expect. In Helena, Arkansas, after the war, when an elderly former slave addressed a white man on the street as "Mr." the white man followed the prewar convention and replied "Howdy uncle." The black man was insulted, made it clear they were not related, and demanded, "Call me Mister."

From the standpoint of former slaves, such confrontations were part of an effort to make freedom a reality of daily life in the South, a reality that white southerners were anxious to avoid. What ensued was a determined struggle between African Americans seeking dignity and respect and southern whites attempting to maintain the principle of white supremacy. White leaders argued that only strong restrictive measures would restore the black workforce to its prewar level of usefulness. Many southern

states enacted black codes, limiting the freedom of former slaves and returning them to near slavery. Vagrancy provisions imposed fines and jail time on unemployed African Americans, forcing former slaves into low-paying agricultural jobs and ensuring white planters a steady supply of cheap plantation labor. Without land, the ability to bargain for jobs, or the right to vote or hold office, southern blacks stood only marginally above their former slave position.

Almost all southern blacks were agricultural workers, and without land of their own, they had to depend on white land-owners for work. After the war cash was in short supply in the South, so landowners offered shares of the crop instead of wages in return for black labor. Sharecropping, as this system was called, seemed an equitable solution to the problem. Sharecroppers lived on the land, worked it as if it were their own, brought in the crop, and were entitled to a portion of the harvest at the end of the season. For landowners this ensured an agricultural labor force without the need for cash, and for sharecroppers it offered an approximation of the independent family farm. Unequal resources and power, however, led to white landholders' binding black sharecroppers to the land through real or contrived indebtedness.

Essentially, the bonds of debt peonage replaced the chains of slavery, and planters could control their labor force almost as completely as slaveholders had controlled theirs. To purchase seed, tools, teams of mules or horses, and other supplies, impoverished sharecroppers were forced to rely on credit advanced against the following year's crop. They also purchased food, clothing, and other necessities on credit, either at stores operated by the landowner or at independently owned stores in the vicinity. Interest rates were generally high and sharecroppers found themselves falling further and further into debt each season. "[Landowners] didn't pay everything they promised," recalled one Arkansas sharecropper. When he attempted to appeal to local authorities, he found that a white man's accounting superseded any argument an African American could offer. "They said figures didn't lie," he reported. He understood

Before the Civil War, most southern states barred slaves from learning to read and write. During Reconstruction, the establishment of black schools made it possible for the former slaves, children and adults alike, to obtain an education. As the Hortons conclude, "education was an important mark of their freedom and represented their hope for a better future." (Cook Collection, Valentine Richmond History Center)

that this could be a very dangerous situation, for any black man who questioned a white man's word was putting his life at risk. "You know how that was," he explained, "You dassent dispute a [white] man's word then."

Henry Blacke sharecropped for much of his adult life. He later explained, "[N]o matter how good accounts you kept, you had to go by [the white landowners'] account, and—now brother, I'm telling you the truth about this—it has been that way a long time." White southerners seemed to operate with a different set of ethics when dealing with blacks. As one Freedmen's Bureau official put it, white "men who are honorable in their dealings with their white neighbors will cheat a Negro without feeling a single twinge of their honor." Whites argued that the survival of southern civilization demanded completely controlling blacks, and, as in slavery, any black person who showed signs of contesting their control must be brought into line immediately. A Freedmen's Bureau official described white attitudes toward blacks in the Reconstruction South saying, "Wherever I go . . . I hear the people talk in such a way as to indicate that they are yet unable to conceive of the Negro as possessing any right at all." Even among "honorable" white men, he noted, "to kill a Negro [white southerners] do not deem murder; to debauch a Negro woman they do not think fornication; to take the property away from a Negro they do not consider robbery."

The Republican-controlled Congress attempted to protect African American rights, but President Johnson fought efforts to strengthen and broaden the powers of the Freedmen's Bureau and to pass a Civil Rights Act nullifying the black codes and providing citizenship rights to black people. Johnson campaigned widely for Democratic candidates in the Congressional election of 1866. He spoke against Republican candidates, attacked programs to aid the former slaves, and referred to some of the strongest supporters of the U.S. war effort against the Confederacy as traitors to the nation. Even the most moderate Republicans were outraged, and, after Republicans made substantial gains in the election, they joined with their more radical colleagues in solid opposition to the president. The Republican Congress passed the Civil Rights Act of 1866 and the Fourteenth Amendment, which wrote its provisions guaranteeing black citizenship into the Constitution. They took control of reconstructing southern state governments, passing measures limiting the power of the old southern elites and calling for new state constitutions.

Congress also passed several measures to limit Johnson's power, including the Tenure of Office Act. According to that law, the president could not dismiss any cabinet member appointed with the advice and consent of the Senate until the Senate had approved a successor. In early 1868, Johnson violated this law, and the Republican-dominated House of Representatives voted to impeach him. Although Johnson was saved from being removed from office by one vote in the Senate, his presidency was so weakened that he ceased to be a significant obstruction to

Congressional plans for reconstructing the South. Under Congressional Reconstruction, African Americans were allowed to participate in the state conventions that drew up the new constitutions, constitutions that gave blacks the right to vote. In South Carolina, Mississippi, Louisiana, and other southern states where blacks formed either a majority or a substantial proportion of the population, African Americans attained political power.

In 1866, pressured by abolitionists in Congress, the federal government passed the Southern Homestead Act, giving former slaves and whites who had remained loyal to the United States preferential access to 44 million acres of public land in five southern states for one year. The land, however, was poor—rocky, infertile, marshy, or otherwise unsuitable for farming. Penniless former slaves found it impossible to support themselves while waiting for the first crop, and few could take advantage of the program. A few blacks pooled their meager resources and bought some decent farmland. In Charleston two hundred freed people formed a land investment group called The Freemen's Land and Home Society and collectively purchased a 600-acre plantation on Remley's Point near the city, paying about ten dollars an acre. Many soldiers pooled their military pay and bought small plots, but the vast majority remained landless.

The ratification of the Fifteenth Amendment to the U.S. Constitution in 1870, outlawing the use of race to disenfranchise voters, brought more black men to the polls. Black women, too, were active in southern politics, even though, like white women, they could not vote. They attended political meetings and rallies and were a strong arm of the Republican Party, especially in the South where African American political power was most significant during Reconstruction. According to one historian, in South Carolina, "Freewomen as well as children left the rice fields when it was time to register, attended political meetings and rallies where their influence over the lowcountry vote was recognized and manipulated, and were found at the polls on election days." The presence of so many black women at political events apparently made some white Republicans uneasy. In Charleston, white Republicans attempted to convince black men to "leave their wives at their firesides, or, better still, to 'cut grass.'" The effort was apparently unsuccessful, for black women continued to be active advisers to their male representatives and participated in almost every phase of the voting process, except actually casting a ballot. Black leaders generally encouraged black women's participation in politics and recognized important, sometimes nontraditional, roles for them. During the mid 1870s black women armed with clubs patrolled polling places in South Carolina to keep order and protect Republicans who came to vote.

With large numbers of freed African Americans in the South and 10 percent to 20 percent of southern white males still disqualified from voting because of their rebellion against the United States, blacks were a majority of the electorate in five southern states. Their votes provided the foundation for the Republican Party in the South, a party that had not existed there before the war. Blacks found allies among white Republicans from the North who came to the South during and after the war. Southern Democrats called these whites carpet-baggers after the bags in which many carried their possessions, denoting their newcomer status. Although generally characterized as political opportunists, most were teachers and nurses who came to aid and educate former slaves.

The southern Democrats' most venomous charges were leveled at those people called scalawags, white southerners who became Republicans or supported the Republican Party. Such southern whites who allied themselves with blacks were the targets of public ridicule and violence. This was especially true with the rise of such vigilante political terrorist groups as the Knights of the White Camilla, The Pale Face Brotherhood, and others organized in the mid- to late-1860s in an effort to frustrate Republican rule and force black people back to a place of servitude in southern society. The longest lasting and most notorious of these groups was a social club formed in Tennessee in 1866 that became the Ku Klux Klan. It was led by the former slave trader, Confederate general, and notorious commander of the Fort Pillow massacre, Nathan Bedford Forrest.

These groups used intimidation and violence to discourage blacks and white Republicans from voting. In the spring of 1866, whites invaded the black community in Memphis, Tennessee. When newly discharged black soldiers and local freedmen defended themselves against the marauding whites and city police, forty-six blacks and two whites died. The political motivation was clear when a local newspaper called the riot proof that "the southern men will not be ruled by the [N]egro.". . .

In 1868 Republican and former general Grant replaced Andrew Johnson as president. Congress reacted to the continuing southern violence in the early 1870s by enacting a number of anti-Klan measures, which the president signed into law. In 1871 Grant suspended the writ of habeas corpus in nine South Carolina counties where the Klan was particularly active, making it easier to arrest people suspected of terrorist activity, and sent in federal troops to augment the government's efforts to quell the violence. Congress launched an extensive investigation of the Klan and political terrorism in the South, and the federal officials arrested and indicted hundreds of whites in Mississippi, South Carolina, and North Carolina for their participation in terrorist activity. Some observers were surprised that, in addition to poor whites, many of those arrested for such crimes were professional men, doctors, lawyers, ministers, and college professors.

Seeing African Americans hold political office especially incensed white southern Democrats. They accused blacks of being ignorant, incompetent people attempting to rise above their naturally subservient place in society. The vast majority of southern blacks were illiterate at the end of the war, but most black political leaders were educated. Oscar J. Dunn, who became lieutenant governor of Louisiana, for example, was born a slave but had been able to educate himself. Many, like Dunn, were self-educated, but many others had been formally educated. Hiram Rhodes Revels, a freeborn North Carolina barber and an ordained African Methodist Episcopal minister, became America's first black U.S. senator in 1870. He was a Republican who represented Mississippi for one year, completing the term of Jefferson Davis, who had given up his Senate seat in 1861 to become president of the Confederacy. Revels was well educated, having attended a Quaker seminary in Indiana and Knox College in Illinois. After his term in the Senate, Revels served as president of Mississippi's Alcorn Agricultural College (now Alcorn University), the first land-grant college for black students. . . .

Hundreds of African Americans, former soldiers, abolitionists, businessmen, ministers, lawyers, and teachers, helped guide southern governments for a brief time in the turbulent years of Reconstruction. Many had been born in the South, had left to work and live in the North, in Canada, or in Europe, and returned to take advantage of the unprecedented opportunities for community service and black political leadership. Facing incredible economic and political problems, they worked with white Republicans and even some white Democrats to rebuild the South. In the years between the end of the Civil War and the first decade of the twentieth century, more than six hundred African Americans served in state legislatures, twenty were elected to the U.S. House of Representatives, and two were elected to the U.S. Senate.

During Reconstruction, federal and state government efforts held the promise of improving many people's lives in the South. The majority of the delegates to the South Carolina constitutional convention were black, and 57 out of the 124 blacks had been slaves. This convention passed a number of progressive measures in 1868: abolishing racial discrimination in voting, schools, and the militia; protecting married women's property rights; establishing the state's first divorce law and the first free public school system; providing for elected rather than appointed judges; and abolishing dueling, imprisonment for debt, and property requirements for voting and holding office. The Freedmen's Bureau established and ran more than four thousand schools in the South, open to whites as well as blacks. Many of these schools served areas where there had previously

been no public education. The bureau ended most of its aid programs in 1868 but continued to operate schools that educated students from kindergarten to college until 1872. For the freed people, education was an important mark of their freedom and represented their hope for a better future. Since many slaves had been legally prohibited from learning to read and write, education was doubly important to them. About 95 percent of slaves were illiterate in 1863, but by 1877 more than six hundred thousand black children were in elementary schools. . . .

Southern Democrats were determined to reinstate the racial control of the prewar South and to further this aim tried to ensure black economic dependence and discourage black education. They used many methods in their postwar campaign, but violence became their signature. Outbreaks of racial violence, generally called riots but often seeming more like open rebellion, continued during the 1870s. Throughout the South, violence was the common political tool of those bent on returning to absolute and unquestioned white domination. Leading southern Democrats routinely rationalized the most heinous crimes if they helped "save southern civilization." Wade Hampton of South Carolina, who served as governor and U.S. senator, rallied his political colleagues by arguing that almost any illegal action, even murder, was completely acceptable if done in the name of white supremacy. He urged Democrats to do all in their power to "control the vote of at least one Negro, by intimidation, purchase, keeping him away or as each individual may determine, how may best accomplish it." Then he moved to the deadly specifics. "Never threaten a man individually. If he deserves to be threatened, the necessities of the times require that he should be killed."

African Americans did not meekly submit, however. They used whatever power they had to enforce the law and protect themselves and their communities. Black judges issued arrest warrants, and black sheriffs jailed white terrorists. Armed African Americans, especially war veterans, confronted white vigilante groups. Many black veterans had retained their military weapons, and some formed militia units to protect their communities. In Wilmington, North Carolina, black troops arrested the white chief of police when he refused to surrender his weapon as ordered, and in Victoria, Texas, blacks lynched the white killer of an African American townsman. In South Carolina, when a Confederate veteran stabbed a black Army sergeant for refusing to leave a railroad car in which white women were seated, black soldiers decided the veteran was guilty and shot him.

Southern whites quickly realized that racial intimidation could not be effective so long as these black militia units existed, and they tried to legally disarm and disband them. White Republican officials in the South were sometimes willing to accede to white petitions in order to gain the cooperation of prominent local citizens. As black militia units were disbanded, African American communities were left open to attack from the growing number of terrorist groups. Blacks were forced to depend on the law for protection, an increasingly unlikely possibility as conservative whites returned to power, or to defend themselves. In 1868, for example, black Mississippi politician Charles Caldwell was wounded by a white man. He shot and killed his assailant but was then charged with murder. Such confrontations were common, but Caldwell's acquittal by an all-white jury on the grounds of self-defense was unusual. . . .

Black voters in South Carolina constituted a majority, but white Democrats were determined to keep African Americans away from the polls. Blacks in some communities demanded their rights, and some whites chafed at what they considered African American arrogance. Such insults, the white southerners contended, "no white people upon earth had ever to put up with before." Whites in the small town of Hamburg on the Savannah River in South Carolina complained that they were forced to give way to black parades and were treated with disrespect and even arrested "on the slightest provocation" by the local black police. Tensions exploded during the country's centennial celebration on July 4, 1876, when a parading black militia company forced a local white farmer's son and son-in-law to halt

their carriage. Although Dock Adams, the militia commander, opened the ranks to let them through after some contention, the next day the farmer brought charges against Adams for impeding his travel. The black militia confronted armed white men in the town, and a well-known Democratic politician demanded that Adams disarm his militia company. He refused, the men began fighting, and the black militiamen retreated to the armory. Hundreds of whites from Augusta, Georgia, just across the river, invaded Hamburg to answer the challenge, bringing a cannon to aid in avenging the insult to their racial honor. The whites killed the town's black marshal and killed at least five other blacks after they had been captured. Blacks killed one young white man. The white mob also looted and vandalized African American homes and businesses. A grand jury indicted seven whites for murder and dozens more as accessories, but all were acquitted.

As the violence increased and it became clear that African Americans were not safe anywhere in the South, growing numbers of blacks began to reconsider colonization. African Americans from several southern states met in New Orleans in December 1875 to discuss migrating to the independent West African nation of Liberia. The racial troubles in America created substantial interest in Liberia, and not only among southern blacks. Northern blacks faced less continual violence but confronted discouraging racial discrimination in public places, in the job market, and in housing. In 1878, one colonization group in Pennsylvania received almost fifty thousand inquiries from African Americans considering migration possibilities.

Although many were interested in West Africa, many more African Americans looked to lands in the American West as a place of opportunity and a safe haven. A few people made their way to New Mexico, Arizona, Colorado, and Oklahoma. Groups of North Carolina and Mississippi blacks migrated to Nebraska, and others looked to the frontier state of Kansas. Exodusters, as migrants to the American frontier were called, led by such men as former slave Benjamin "Pap" Singleton from Tennessee, moved their families from the Deep South westward into Kansas during the 1870s. Kansas had a special appeal: it had plenty of unoccupied land and was associated in the minds of African Americans with the Underground Railroad and John Brown. For them, it was an abolitionist territory that had battled proslavery forces and finally entered the Union as a free state. By the mid-1870s many southern blacks were taken with "Kansas Fever" fueled by rumors of free land, free transportation, and free supplies. The reports were largely exaggerated, but they did draw thousands from the violent South to the promise of a new life. By 1878 the town of Nicodemus, Kansas, boasted a population of seven hundred African Americans, all recent migrants from the Deep South. In April of the next year, hundreds more Exodusters traveled up the Missouri River by steamboat to the eastern Kansas settlement of Wyandotte.

Most African Americans did not leave the South. They did not have the resources, debts bound them to the land on which they sharecropped, or family ties held them in place. The proportion of blacks living in the South had dropped from 94 percent at the start of the Civil War to 84 percent by 1880, but the vast majority were still southerners. For this vast majority of black people in America, their brief political influence was rapidly fading. In the presidential election of 1876, pitting Democrat Samuel J. Tilden against Republican Rutherford B. Hayes, both parties claimed victory in Louisiana, South Carolina, and Florida, and thus the presidency. When an electoral commission sustained Hayes's claim, Democrats in Congress refused to certify the election. After the chaos of civil war and the disruption of the Reconstruction, the nation was in no mood for such political uncertainty. From every quarter—business interests, state and local governments, churches, and universities—came the demand that the election be settled quickly. A series of meetings led to a compromise where-by the Republican, Hayes, would take the presidency. Democrats would not contest economic policies benefiting Republican business interests, and in return the Hayes administration would remove the last U.S. troops from the South, leaving southerners to handle civil stability and civil rights in their states. The compromise that saved the nation from uncertainty and placed the Republican in the White House had been struck at African Americans' expense.

In the following years Southern Democrats, assisted by rulings of the U.S. Supreme Court, removed federal protections for black rights in the South. The court weakened or struck down much of the preceding decades' civil rights legislation and placed the responsibility for enforcing the Fourteenth and Fifteenth amendments on the states. Southern blacks denied the right to vote or lacking legal protection found their only recourse was to state authority. As conservative Democrats moved into positions of power at all levels of southern state governments, there was little recourse at all. Starting in 1890 in Mississippi, and then spreading across the South, a constellation of laws restricted the franchise to whites only. Poll taxes generally put the vote financially out of reach for sharecroppers and other poor blacks. Literacy testing was often devised and administered so that no black person, no matter how educated, could qualify to vote. Meanwhile, a clause in state regulations safeguarded the voting rights of illiterate whites by waiving the literacy requirement for voters deemed people of good conduct or whose grandfathers had voted before 1860, a time when almost all southern blacks were slaves.

Other laws provided for racial segregation in public accommodations, transportation, and almost every phase of life. The Mississippi Plan, and the host of laws that followed in every southern state and many border states, were the foundation for the extensive southern system of racial segregation often called the Jim Crow system. The Jim Crow segregation system was named after a character played by white actor, Thomas Dartmouth "Daddy" Rice. In the 1840s and 1850s, Rice blackened his face and danced, playing Jim Crow, a racial stereotype born of the white imagination. By the mid-1890s it was clear that Reconstruction's promise of real freedom was coming to an end, and there seemed little blacks could do about it. . . .

. . .Yet Reconstruction was not a total failure. Slavery was ended, and black people no longer faced the awful prospect of having their children and other family members sold away from them. African Americans made great gains in literacy and education, and a few even managed to acquire land. The Constitution was changed: the Thirteenth Amendment abolished slavery, the Fourteenth Amendment guaranteed African Americans citizenship rights, and the Fifteenth Amendment forbade the denial of voting rights on account of race. Constitutional guarantees may not have been honored, but they established legal principles to which plaintiffs could appeal. African Americans had struggled before the Civil War to end slavery and during Reconstruction to attain citizenship rights, and they continued their struggle for full freedom through the twentieth century. . . .

Despite the progress made against racial injustice, slavery still has an impact on Americans more than a century after its abolition. Its legacy remains in the history and heritage of the South that it shaped, in the culture of the North where its memory was long denied, in the national economy for which it provided much of the foundation, and in the political and social system it profoundly influenced. Slavery and its effects are embedded in the national culture and in the assumptions and contradictory ideals of American society. The central issues under debate today—issues involving race, class, region, religion, and national identity—are all imperfectly understood without the historical context of American slavery and without an understanding of the means by which a freedom-loving people rationalized their tolerance of slavery's development. Although it is troubling to consider, it is nonetheless true that slavery was, and continues to be, a critical factor in shaping the United States and all of its people. As Americans, we must understand slavery's history if we are ever to be emancipated from its consequences.

QUESTIONS TO CONSIDER

1 Describe the accomplishments of the Freedmen's Bureau in helping blacks make the transition from slavery to freedom. Before the Civil War, the cruel domestic slave trade broke up black families. What actions did the freedmen take to find lost family members and what obstacles often impeded their efforts?

2 Why did the former slaves need to own land to achieve true independence? Contrast the actions of William Tecumseh Sherman and Andrew Johnson on the distribution of confiscated Confederate lands to the freedmen. Why did sharecropping prevent the freedmen from becoming independent landowners?

3 What immediate impact did the Fourteenth and Fifteenth amendments have on the rights of former slaves? How was this important legislation compromised by southern whites who feared and resisted any change in race relations?

4 In what ways did the carpetbaggers and scalawags try to help the freedmen? In what ways was the Southern Homestead Act supposed to benefit the former slaves? Did it benefit them? Describe the accomplishments of the Republican governments in the former Confederate states, governments in which African Americans participated. How did such governments keep "the promise of improving many people's lives in the South"?

5 What motivated some African Americans to migrate to Liberia and to the American frontier? Why did most of the former slaves remain in the South?

6 What was the compromise that settled the disputed presidential election of 1876? Why do the authors contend that it "had been struck at African American expense"? In what ways did poll taxes, literacy tests, and other Jim Crow measures severely restrict the freedom of the former slaves?

2 The Checkered History of the Great Fourteenth Amendment

ERIC FONER

In the following selection, Eric Foner, today's foremost historian of the Reconstruction era, recounts the dramatic and controversial history of the great Fourteenth Amendment. Because it promised equality of all Americans before the law, Foner states that it was "one of the most important lasting consequences of the immense changes produced by the war."

To place Foner's story in historical context, it would be well to pick up the Reconstruction story with what was transpiring in the nation's capital in 1865 and 1866. Andrew Johnson's soft, conciliatory reconstruction policy enraged Republican leaders on Capitol Hill. As we saw in the previous selection, the president not only opposed granting black men the right to vote but also allowed former Confederates to return to power in the southern states. Johnson also stood by when ex-rebel legislators enacted black codes that reduced blacks to a virtual condition of peonage, and he hotly opposed congressional interference in the reconstruction process. He even urged southern states to reject the Fourteenth Amendment, pushed through Congress by the Republicans, which would protect southern blacks. The amendment would prevent the states from adopting laws that abridged "the privileges or immunities of citizens of the United States." It would also bar the states from depriving "any person of life, liberty, or property, without due process of law," or from denying any person the "equal protection of the law." Johnson did more than just oppose the amendment; he damned Republican leaders like Charles Sumner of Massachusetts and Thaddeus Stevens of Pennsylvania, calling them tyrants and traitors. He even campaigned against the Republican party in the 1866 off-year elections. As a consequence, he alienated moderate as well as radical Republicans, who soon united against him. When the 1866 elections gave the Republicans huge majorities in both houses of Congress, they took control of Reconstruction and set about reforming the South themselves, granting blacks the right to vote and hold office.

Thus the stage is set for Foner's brilliant essay on one of the most important constitutional amendments in American history. In the short run, the equal protection clause had little effect on the lives of the former slaves. Southern white resistance and northern complacency resulted in what Foner calls "a new system of racial subordination" that sought to eliminate black voting, institute racial segregation, and place severe restrictions on "blacks' economic power."

Moreover, the great Fourteenth Amendment itself underwent a drastic reinterpretation. When Reconstruction ended in 1877, the United States entered what Mark Twain called the Gilded Age, a conservative era dominated by big businessmen and their corporate monopolies. In this period, reflecting the spirit of the times, the Supreme Court changed the original purpose of the Fourteenth Amendment: the Court's new interpretation turned it into an instrument for the protection of corporations. At the same time, the Court acquiesced in the ruthless oppression of black people in the white supremacist South.

But decades later, in the activist 1960s and 1970s, a progressive Supreme Court not only returned the Fourteenth Amendment to its original purpose, but also expanded it to protect the rights of "aggrieved groups of all sorts—blacks, women, gays, welfare recipients, the elderly, the disabled." More than a century after its ratification, this powerful amendment, first conceived in "imperfect compromise" during Reconstruction, has become today (in Foner's words) "the most important bulwark of the rights of American citizens." What follows is the fascinating story of how that came to be.

GLOSSARY

BLACK CODES   See glossary in previous selection.

BROWN v. BOARD OF EDUCATION OF TOPEKA (1954)
The Supreme Court's landmark decision that ruled that state-initiated racial segregation violated the equal protection guarantee of the Fourteenth Amendment. This was because separation inherently meant inequality.

DRED SCOTT v. SANDFORD (1857)   With a majority of southerners as justices, the Supreme Court ruled that neither Congress nor the territories could outlaw slavery. Five justices maintained that to do so would violate the property rights clause of the United States Constitution. Since slaves were property, the Court said that they could not be United States citizens.

FIFTEENTH AMENDMENT   See glossary in previous selection.

JOHNSON, ANDREW   See glossary in previous selection.

PLESSY v. FERGUSON (1896)   This Supreme Court decision upheld "separate but equal" accommodations for whites and African Americans. The majority of justices argued that the ruling was consistent with the equal protection clause guaranteed by the Fourteenth Amendment.

RECONSTRUCTION ACT OF 1867   Provided the freedmen with the right to vote and "launched the short-lived period of Radical Reconstruction during which, for the first time in American history, a genuine interracial democracy flourished."

SANTA CLARA COUNTY v. SOUTHERN PACIFIC RAILROAD   In a strange twist the Supreme Court ruled in this case that a corporation was a person under the law. By this decision, the Fourteenth Amendment forbade states to interfere with a corporation's activities, like the regulation of working conditions.

STEVENS, THADDEUS   A Radical Republican leader in the House of Representatives, he devoted his career to the struggle against slavery and for the equal rights of the freedmen. He promoted the Fourteenth Amendment and the confiscation and distribution of former rebel lands to the newly freed slaves, and he was a major force in the impeachment trial of Andrew Johnson.

SUMNER, CHARLES   One of the leading Radical Republicans in the Senate, he too was a committed idealist who advocated complete civil and political equality for African Americans. "More than any of his political contemporaries," writes his biographer, David Herbert Donald, "Sumner realized that the future of American democracy depended on the ability of the white and black races to live together in peace and equality."

TRUMBULL, LYMAN   This Illinois senator and his colleague, Senator John Sherman of Ohio, thought that suffrage for the freedmen was "a political liability." Both men represented the moderate wing of the Republican party that desired a free labor economy in the South. They joined the Radicals who desired more drastic changes only after President Johnson opposed the Fourteenth Amendment and stuck adamantly to his prosouthern policy.

On June 13, 1866, Thaddeus Stevens, the majority floor leader in the House of Representatives and the nation's most prominent Radical Republican, rose to address his congressional colleagues. His subject was the Fourteenth Amendment to the Constitution—which, after months of deliberation and innumerable drafts and redrafts, was about to receive final approval by Congress. Its purpose was to secure the fruits of Union victory in the Civil War by guaranteeing equal civil rights for the freed slaves and loyal governments in the South.

Born during George Washington's administration, Stevens had enjoyed a public career that embodied, as much as anyone's, the struggle against the "Slave Power" and for equal rights for black Americans. In 1837, as a delegate to Pennsylvania's constitutional convention, he had refused to sign the state's new frame of government because it abrogated the right of African Americans to vote. As a member of Congress during the 1850s, he had fought against the expansion of slavery and, during the secession crisis, opposed compromise with the South. Once the Civil War began, he was among the first to advocate the emancipation of slaves and the enrollment of black soldiers.

During the era of Reconstruction that followed the war, Stevens insisted that the South was a "conquered province," which Congress could govern as it saw fit. He was the most prominent advocate, for example, of distributing land to former slaves so that they might have an economic foundation for their freedom. Like other Radicals, he believed that Reconstruction was a golden opportunity to purge the nation of the legacy of slavery and create a society whose citizens enjoyed equal civil and political rights, secured by a powerful and beneficent national government. "The whole fabric of southern society must be changed," he declared, "and never can it be done, if this opportunity be lost." Stevens's speech

Thaddeus Stevens was the driving force behind the Fourteenth Amendment, but controversy followed this champion of the freedmen. In the superstitious nineteenth century, his clubfoot was deemed a sign of evil. Although he never married, there were many rumors about his relationship with an African American housekeeper with whom he lived for many years. (Library of Congress)

on June 13 was an eloquent statement of this political creed:

In my youth, in my manhood, in my old age, I had fondly dreamed that when any fortunate chance should have broken up for awhile the foundation of our institutions, and released us from obligations the most tyrannical that ever man imposed in the name of freedom, that the intelligent, pure and just men of this Republic . . . would have so remodeled all our institutions as to have freed them from every vestige of human oppression, of inequality of rights, of the recognized degradation of the poor, and the superior caste of the rich. . . . This bright dream has vanished [quoting Shakespeare's *The Tempest*] "like the baseless fabric of a dream." I find that we shall be obliged to be content with patching up the worst portions of the ancient edifice, and leaving it, in many of its parts, to be swept through by the . . . storm of despotism. Do you inquire why, holding these views and possessing some will of my own, I accept so imperfect a proposition? I answer, be-cause I live among men and not among angels.

A few moments later, the Fourteenth Amendment was approved by the House. The result was never in doubt because, with the southern states still unrepre-sented, the Republican party commanded an over-whelming majority. The final vote was 120–32, well above the required two-thirds majority. Three days later, having been approved by the Senate shortly before the House vote, the amendment was sent to the states for ratification. It became part of the Con-stitution on July 28, 1868.

The Fourteenth Amendment prohibited the states from abridging the equality before the law of Ameri-can citizens, provided for a reduction in represen-tation in Congress should any state deprive male citizens of the right to vote, excluded Confederates who had previously taken a constitutional oath from holding state or federal office, and prohibited pay-ment of the Confederate debt. It was one of the most important lasting consequences of the immense changes produced by the Civil War and the subse-quent political crisis of Reconstruction, especially the struggle between the president and Congress over control of Reconstruction policy.

In late May 1865, six weeks after he succeeded the martyred Abraham Lincoln, Pres. Andrew Johnson announced his plan for reuniting the nation, launch-ing the era of presidential Reconstruction. Although a staunch Unionist from Tennessee, Johnson was an inveterate racist and a firm defender of states' rights. The essentials of his Reconstruction plan allowed white southerners to establish new state governments—which were required by Johnson to abolish slavery, repudi-ate secession, and abrogate the Confederate debt but otherwise accorded a free hand in controlling local affairs. When these new governments quickly en-acted the repressive Black Codes, most northern Re-publicans turned against the president. As one observer put it, the Black Codes seemed designed to "restore all of slavery but its name." Meanwhile, the election of "rebels" to leading offices in the South

Andrew Johnson from Tennessee remained loyal to the Union and became Lincoln's vice president at the end of the Civil War. The former senator was motivated by his devotion to the Consti-tution and his disdain for the planter class. With his poor south-ern white background, Johnson opposed granting political rights to the freedmen. His lenient Reconstruction program allowed former Confederates to take office in southern state governments, and he permitted these governments to enact the infamous black codes, which virtually reenslaved African Americans in the South. (Li-brary of Congress)

and reports of violence directed against both freed people and northern visitors reinforced the convic-tion that Johnson's plan played into the hands of the southern Democrats.

When the Thirty-ninth Congress (elected in No-vember 1864) finally assembled in December 1865, Radical Republicans, led by Stevens, called for abro-gation of the Johnson-authorized state governments and the establishment of new ones based on equality before the law and universal manhood suffrage. The Radicals, however, didn't control the Republican party. Occupying the political middle ground was the moderate Republican majority, led in Congress by Sen. Lyman Trumbull of Illinois and Sen. John Sherman of Ohio. Unenthusiastic about black suffrage—which they viewed as a political liability in the North and an experiment whose outcome couldn't be predicted in the South—Trumbull, Sherman, and their allies were nonetheless fully committed to ensuring "loyal" governments in the former states of the Confederacy and protecting the elementary rights of freed slaves in a society organized on the basis of free labor rather than slavery. Eventually, however, Johnson's policies, and the actions of the state governments created under his supervision, drove them into the Radicals' arms, uniting the entire Republican party against the president.

Much of the ensuing debate over Reconstruction revolved around the problem, as Trumbull put it, of defining "what slavery is and what liberty is." The Civil War had greatly enhanced the power of the national state. Especially because of the service of two hundred thousand black men in the Union army and navy, the war had also put the question of black citizenship on the national agenda. By early 1866, moderates had concluded that equality before the law—enforced, if necessary, by national authority—had become an inevitable consequence of emancipation and a condition for restoring the South to full participation in the Union. These principles were embodied in the Civil Rights Act of 1866, a precursor to the Fourteenth Amendment that outlined the rights all Americans were to enjoy regardless of race. These included the rights to make contracts, bring lawsuits, and enjoy equal protection of the security of person and property. Johnson's veto of this measure and its repassage by Congress in April 1866 marked the final breach between the president and the Republican party. It was the first time in American history that a significant piece of legislation became law over a president's veto.

Beyond impelling congressional Republicans to devise their own Reconstruction plan, Johnson's intransigence persuaded them to write their understanding of the consequences of the Civil War into the Constitution, there to be secure from shifting electoral majorities. The result was the Fourteenth Amendment, adopted by Congress after months of committee deliberations and a series of alterations on the House and Senate floors. Some Republicans wished to disqualify leading Confederates from voting; others wanted to include both "universal amnesty" for "rebels" and "universal suffrage" for black men. But these proposals failed to win the support of most Republicans. In its final form, the amendment was a compromise on which all Republicans could unite.

This process of compromise, however, as Stevens's June 13 speech suggests, resulted in a text that didn't fully satisfy the Radicals. The Fourteenth Amendment, as enacted, didn't abolish existing state governments in the South, nor did it guarantee blacks the right to vote; indeed, in one section, it offered each southern state, once readmitted to the Union, the alternative of allowing black men to vote and retaining the state's full representation in Congress or continuing to disenfranchise blacks and suffering a loss of representation proportionate to the black percentage of the state population. (No penalty applied, however, when women were denied the right to vote, an omission that led many advocates of women's rights to oppose ratification of the amendment.)

The Fourteenth Amendment had five sections in all, three of which have little importance today—those barring Confederates from office, dealing with the Confederate debt, and reducing a state's representation in Congress if men are denied the right to vote. (This last provision was never enforced, even during the decades when southern states disenfranchised most black voters.) Nonetheless, the Fourteenth Amendment has since become, after the Bill of Rights, the most important constitutional change in the nation's history. Its heart was Section 1, which declared that all persons born or naturalized in the United States were both national and state citizens. Section 1 also prohibited states from abridging the "privileges and immunities of citizens"; depriving them "of life, liberty, or property without due process of law"; and denying them "equal protection of the laws." It thus established, as Thaddeus Stevens told the House, the principle that state laws "shall operate equally upon all." Later he added, "I can hardly believe that any person can be found who will not admit that . . . [it] is just."

In keeping with constitutional authority the principle that equality before the law, regardless of race, could and should be enforced by the national government, the Fourteenth Amendment permanently transformed the definition of American citizenship and refashioned relations between the federal government and the states as well as those between individual Americans and the nation. We live today in a legal and constitutional system shaped profoundly by the Fourteenth Amendment.

During the 1866 Congressional elections, ratification of the Fourteenth Amendment became the central issue of the campaign. That fall, the president embarked on an unprecedented speaking trip across the North, known as the "swing around the circle." Its primary purpose was to drum up support for candidates associated with Johnson's National Union party—mostly northern Democrats who supported the president's Reconstruction policies. Yet Johnson also took the opportunity to rally whatever opposition to ratification he could. Again and again, he called for reconciliation between North and South, insisting that suffrage requirements and citizens' rights should be left to the states. Johnson also engaged in impromptu debates with hecklers, intimating that Stevens and the other Radicals were traitors. For their part, Republicans defended the amendment as necessary to secure the emancipation of the slaves and prevent Confederates from controlling the South.

The outcome of the midterm elections was continued Republican dominance in Congress and a clear mandate for Stevens and the Radicals. Johnson, however, continued his intransigent opposition to the amendment, urging southern legislatures to refuse to ratify it. And during the winter of 1866–1867, every southern state, except Tennessee, indeed rejected the amendment. With southern state governments thus having thoroughly discredited themselves in the eyes of nearly all Republicans, moderate and radical alike, party leaders concluded that only by establishing entirely new governments in the south could Reconstruction be accomplished. In March 1867, on the penultimate day of its postelection session, the Thirty-ninth Congress passed, over Johnson's veto, the Reconstruction Act of 1867. This gave the right to vote to black men in the South and launched the short-lived period of Radical Reconstruction during which, for the first time in American history, a genuine interracial democracy flourished. In March 1870, the Fifteenth Amendment, prohibiting any state from depriving citizens of the right to vote because of race, became part of the Constitution. What Republican leader Carl Schurz called "the great Constitutional revolution" of Reconstruction was complete. "Nothing in all history," exulted abolitionist William Lloyd Garrison, equaled "this wonderful . . . transformation of four million human beings from . . . the auction-block to the ballot-box."

In general, the Acts and Amendments of Reconstruction reflected the intersection of two products of the Civil War era: the newly empowered national state and the idea of a national citizenry enjoying equality before the law. In fact, rather than embodying a threat to liberty (as Jefferson had perceived it), the federal government had now become "the custodian of freedom," declared Charles Sumner, the abolitionist senator from Massachusetts. The rewriting of the Constitution during Reconstruction promoted a sense of the document's malleability and further suggested that the rights of individual citizens were intimately connected to federal power. This was a substantial departure from the pre–Civil War period, when disenfranchised groups were far more likely to draw inspiration from the Declaration of Independence than from the Constitution. (After all, the only mention of equality in the original Constitution came in the clause granting each state an equal number of senators.)

For example, the Bill of Rights, ratified in 1791, defined civil liberties in terms of state autonomy. Its language—"Congress shall pass no law. . ."—reflected the Jeffersonian belief that concentrated power was a threat to freedom. The Reconstruction amendments, however, which included the Thirteenth Amendment abolishing slavery, assumed that rights required political power to enforce them. These amendments, therefore, not only authorized the federal government to override state actions that deprived citizens of equality but also concluded with sections empowering Congress to "enforce" the amendments with "appropriate legislation." The Reconstruction amendments, especially the Fourteenth, transformed the Constitution from a document primarily concerned with federal-state relations and the rights of property into a vehicle through which members of vulnerable minorities could stake a claim to substantive freedom and seek protection against misconduct by all levels of government.

Limiting the privileges of citizenship to white men had long been intrinsic to the practice of American democracy. In 1857, in deciding *Dred Scott v. Sandford,* the Supreme Court had declared that no black person could be a citizen of the United States. Racism, federalism, a belief in limited government and local autonomy—Reconstruction challenged all these principles of nineteenth-century political culture. So deeply rooted were they, in fact, that only during an unparalleled crisis could they have been superseded, even temporarily, by the vision of an egalitarian republic embracing black Americans as well as white under the protection of the federal government. Indeed, it was precisely for this reason that the era's laws and constitutional amendments aroused such bitter opposition. The underlying principles—that the federal government possessed the power to define and protect citizens' rights, and that blacks were equal members of the body politic—were striking departures in American law. It isn't difficult to understand why President Johnson, in one of his veto messages, claimed that federal protection of African-American civil rights, together

Frederick Douglass was a runaway slave, the author of a popular autobiography, the editor of the North Star, *perhaps the most dynamic of the abolitionist spokesmen, and the greatest black man of his generation. He was also a champion of the women's rights movement. (The National Archives)*

with the broad conception of national power that lay behind it, violated "all our experience as a people."

Reconstruction proved fragile and short lived. Its end is usually dated at 1877, when federal troops were withdrawn from the South (as a consequence of the contested 1876 presidential election) and white-supremacist Democrats regained control of southern state governments. But retreat from the idea of equality was already underway prior to 1877, as traditional ideas of racism and localism reasserted themselves during the early 1870s and violence disrupted the southern Republican party. This transition accelerated after 1877, when Supreme Court interpretation of the Fourteenth Amendment increasingly eviscerated its promise of equal citizenship. Deciding the 1873 Slaughterhouse Cases, for example, the Court severely restricted the rights protected under the amendment, ruling that these comprised only those rights that owed their existence to the federal government—such as traveling on navigable waterways, running for federal office, and being protected on the high seas. Clearly, *these* rights were of limited concern to most former slaves. All other rights, the Court ruled, were derived from state, not national, authority, and with these the amendment had "nothing to do."

Next came the 1883 Civil Rights Cases, which invalidated a federal law prohibiting unequal treatment of blacks in public accommodations on the grounds that the Fourteenth Amendment barred only *legal* discrimination, not the actions of private individuals. Finally, the Court's famous 1896 decision in *Plessy* v. *Ferguson* decreed that state-mandated racial segregation didn't violate the Fourteenth Amendment's equal protection clause because "separate" could be equal. By the turn of the twentieth century, therefore, the states had been given carte blanche to nullify the Reconstruction amendments and civil rights laws. A new system of racial subordination was put in place in the South, centered on the elimination of black voting, racial segregation, and the severe restriction of blacks' economic opportunities. And these blatant violations of the Fourteenth and Fifteenth Amendments occurred with the acquiescence of the North, as reflected in the Supreme Court rulings.

Meanwhile, the Court made use of the Fourteenth Amendment in a manner that Thaddeus Stevens could never have imagined—as a barrier against governmental regulation of corporate behavior. In 1886, in *Santa Clara County* v. *Southern Pacific Railroad,* the Court declared that a corporation was a "person" under the law and thus couldn't be deprived of the "privileges and immunities" specified in the amendment's first section. This principle underpinned a long legal era during which the Court held that "liberty of contract"—the right of corporations to operate without state interference such as regulation of working conditions, limitation of working hours, and so on—was the real intention of the Fourteenth Amendment. Not until the late 1930s did the Court abandon this liberty-of-contract jurisprudence.

The Fourteenth Amendment's checkered history, however, is also the history of evolving American ideas about civil rights and civil liberties. During the first half of the twentieth century, the Court slowly took up the work of applying Fourteenth Amendment protections to the citizens' rights enumerated in the Bill of Rights. That is, the Court began to rule that states must respect the same civil liberties that the first ten amendments to the Constitution protect against federal intrusion. This process, called "incorporation" by legal historians, began shortly after World War I, when the Court responded to extensive censorship by wartime authorities with an opinion that obligated states under the Fourteenth Amendment to refrain from unreasonable restrictions on the freedoms of speech and of the press. Soon afterward, it invalidated state laws that required all students to attend public schools and prohibited teachers from instructing in languages other than English (measures directed against schools established by churches and immigrant groups). The amendment's guarantee of equal liberty, it declared, included the right to bring up children and practice religion free from governmental interference.

During the 1950s and 1960s, led by Chief Justice Earl Warren, the Court again turned to the Fourteenth Amendment as a source not only for the racial justice envisioned by its framers but also for a vast expansion of civil liberties for all Americans. In 1954, in the *Brown* v. *Board of Education* decision that overturned *Plessy,* the Warren Court ruled that state-sanctioned racial segregation violated the Fourteenth Amendment's equal protection clause because separation was inherently unequal. In subsequent decisions, it struck down state laws that sought to destroy civil rights organizations by requiring them to disclose lists of their members; and in *New York Times* v. *Sullivan* (1964), it greatly expanded the legal protections given newspapers and other media by requiring that plaintiffs in libel suits prove that the defamatory remarks in question were made out of either malice or a "reckless disregard" for the truth. Reversing its long history of compliance with racial injustice, the Supreme Court had become by the end of the 1960s the Congress's leading ally in the struggle for racial justice.

The Warren Court continued the process of incorporation until the states were required to abide by virtually every clause in the Bill of Rights—from such literal guarantees as protection against unreasonable searches and seizures and the right to a speedy trial to inferred rights, including the right of indigent defendants to publicly appointed legal counsel. During this period, the Court struck down numerous state and local measures, including some mandating prayer in public schools, that violated the First Amendment's ban on government support for religion.

Meanwhile, generating even greater controversy, it discovered under the aegis of the Fourteenth Amendment some entirely new rights that the states couldn't abridge. Most dramatic of these was the right to "privacy," embodied in the 1965 *Griswold* decision overturning a Connecticut law that prohibited the use of contraceptive devices and in *Roe* v. *Wade* (1973), which created the constitutional right to terminate a pregnancy. This "rights revolution" undertaken by the Warren Court elevated the status of the Fourteenth Amendment until it became the major constitutional provision to which aggrieved groups of all sorts—blacks, women, gays, welfare recipients, the elderly, the disabled— appealed in seeking to expand their legal rights and social status.

Today, amid the continuing controversies over abortion rights, affirmative action, the rights of homosexuals, and many other issues, the Court's interpretation of the Fourteenth Amendment remains a focus of judicial as well as political debate. An imperfect compromise when added to the Constitution during Reconstruction, the amendment has since become the most powerful bulwark of the rights of American citizens. We haven't yet created the "bright dream" of which Thaddeus Stevens spoke in his June 1866 speech, but thanks to the reinvigoration of the Fourteenth Amendment by the twentieth-century Supreme Court, more Americans enjoy more rights and more freedoms today than ever before in our history.

QUESTIONS TO CONSIDER

1 Consider the long career of Thaddeus Stevens. What issues did he champion and what frustrations did he face? Why would Foner state that Stevens viewed Reconstruction as a "golden opportunity"?

2 Why would Foner describe the Fourteenth Amendment as "one of the most important lasting consequences of the immense changes produced by the Civil War and the subsequent political crisis of Reconstruction?" After its passage, do you think that race should have been a factor when determining legal equality? In what ways was its original purpose later compromised in Supreme Court rulings such as *Plessy* v. *Ferguson* and *Santa Clara County* v. *Southern Pacific Railroad*?

3 Why would Foner state that the Reconstruction amendments made the Constitution a document "through which members of vulnerable minorities could stake a claim to substantive freedom and seek protection against misconduct by all levels of government"? Before Reconstruction, why did the Declaration of Independence, more so than the Constitution, provide hope for the downtrodden and oppressed?

4 Why did the mood of the country in the conservative period following the fall of the Radical Republicans erode the original purpose of the Fourteenth Amendment? How would Thaddeus Stevens have viewed the Slaughterhouse Cases, the 1883 Civil Rights Cases, and the separate but unequal society that emerged?

5 The Fourteenth Amendment's checkered history reflected the changing values of the country. Explain how, during probusiness eras, it has protected

corporations more than people. Why did it fail to prevent racial discrimination at the end of the nineteenth century? How did it help spark a "second reconstruction" nearly sixty years later, after a ground-breaking decision from the Warren Court?

6 The Fourteenth Amendment, initially passed to help guarantee equality under the law for the freedmen, became a vehicle in the twentieth century to help many other groups—women, gays, the elderly, and the disabled. Is this a violation or a natural extension of its original intent? Examine the rationale for decisions that applied the Fourteenth Amendment to issues like abortion, school prayer, and the rights of the accused. Are we now approaching that "bright dream" envisioned by Thaddeus Stevens?

PART TWO

Conquest of the West

3   Sitting Bull and the Sioux Resistance

ROBERT M. UTLEY

In the forty years after the Civil War, American pioneers conquered and exploited an immense inner frontier that lay between California and the Mississippi River. It was an area as diverse as it was expansive, a region of windy prairies, towering mountains, painted deserts, and awesome canyons. Heading east out of California or west from the Mississippi, Americans by the thousands poured into this great heartland, laying out cattle ranches and farms, building towns and mining camps, and creating a variety of local and state governments. People moved to the frontier for various reasons: to start a new life, seek glory and adventure, strike it rich in a single, fabulous windfall, and prevail over the West's challenging environment.

Still, the winning of the West was not all romance. Driven by the aggressive, exploitive imperatives of their culture, American pioneers—especially whites—infiltrated Indian lands and hunting grounds, and conflicts between settlers and Indians broke out all across the frontier line, thus opening a gruesome chapter in the westward movement after the Civil War. The fact was that white-dominated America tended to regard the Indians as savages who deserved violent treatment. If these "ignorant no-mads" blocked the advance of Christian civilization across the West, they should be "removed." And so, terrible fights erupted whenever whites and Indians came into contact. Trying to reduce the violence, the government sent out additional federal troops, including several African American regiments; instead of enforcing existing treaties, the soldiers usually defended whites who violated the pacts, which only provoked the Indians all the more.

In 1867, the federal government decided to confine the Indians to small, remote reservations in areas of the West spurned by United States settlers. Herein lies a paradox, for the whites' handling of the Indians in the late 1860s contrasted sharply with the way they treated southern blacks. The Congress that approved the small reservation policy, with its philosophy of strict segregation and inequality for western Indians, was the same Congress that attempted to give African American men in the South political rights equal to those of white men.

But many Indian bands refused to surrender their ancient hunting grounds, refused to be herded onto reservations and made to "walk the white man's road," and they fought back tenaciously. None did so with more resolve than the warrior elements of the proud, buffalo-hunting Lakota (or Sioux) of the northern Plains, who united behind Sitting Bull and vowed to throw the white invaders out of Lakota country. Sitting Bull, the great holy man and war chief of the Hunkpapa Lakota, is the subject of the selection by Robert M. Utley, a distinguished historian and biographer of the American West. Based on his biography, The Lance and the Shield: The Life and Times of Sitting Bull (1993), Utley's essay affords rare insight into Lakota culture and what happened to it when it collided with a rapacious, acquisitive invader whose superior military power, forked tongue, and deadly diseases brought doom to Native Americans everywhere.

As Utley points out, the government's small-reservation policy, which was implemented by treaties in 1868, split the Lakota into two camps. The agency Indians, under the leadership of Red Cloud of the Oglala Sioux, accepted reservation life and tried to adapt to it. The nonreservation Indians, headed by Sitting Bull, elected to fight the United States Army in a desperate attempt to save "the free life of old." Indeed, rising to the unprecedented position of head chief of all the Lakota, Sitting Bull assembled the most formidable Indian force in the West, one that on a hot June day in 1876 massacred George Armstrong Custer and 262 men of the United States Seventh Cavalry in the Battle of the Little Bighorn in Montana. But it was a Pyrrhic victory for the Lakota and their Cheyenne allies: in the fall, the army trapped them and compelled them to surrender. Sitting Bull escaped to Canada, and his followers ended up in out-of-the-way reservations in the Dakota Territory.

The other western tribes met the same fate. Overwhelmed by superior firepower and faced with starvation, because whites were exterminating the buffalo, the Indians' "commissary," the Native Americans had no choice but to abandon their way of life and submit to segregation on small reservations in the Dakotas, Oklahoma, New Mexico, Oregon, Idaho, and Montana. The federal government systematically obliterated Indian culture and tribal organization, placed the Indians on individual plots of land, and ordered them to become farmers and accept the culture of their conquerors. By 1890, thanks to generations of bloodletting and sickness, scarcely 200,000 Indians remained in the United States, compared with the 2 million Indians in North America at the time of the European discovery.

Meanwhile, Sitting Bull himself returned from Canada and surrendered to the military, which placed him on the Standing Rock Reservation as a prisoner of war. Here, as Utley says, the Indian agent—a petty tyrant—attempted to destroy Sitting Bull's reputation among his incarcerated people. Yet the great Lakota war chief and holy man remained indomitable: he accepted schooling for his offspring but rejected all other government efforts to make Indians into "imitation whites."

Defeated and broken in spirit, many reservation Indians turned to religion for comfort in a hostile world. First the Indians of Nevada, then the Lakota and other Plains Indians took up the Ghost Dance, a sacred ritual that reaffirmed tribal unity and prophesied the return of the old days, when the buffalo would be plentiful again and the Indians would be free of the white invaders. Intimidated by such a "frightful conglomeration of rituals and customs," as one white put it, the United States government outlawed the Ghost Dance. But Sitting Bull and his people kept on dancing. Indeed,

Sitting Bull became "the high priest of the religion at Standing Rock," which put him on a collision course with the Indian agent and his Lakota police. Utley recounts the violent, ironic climax to Sitting Bull's life and goes on to observe that he lost his struggle with white Americans, not because of any personal failing but because of "impersonal forces beyond his control or even his understanding." As you study Sitting Bull's life, the evolution of his three distinct personalities, and his tragic end, you might want to consider this question: Which do you think was the better way for the Indians to deal with the white invaders—the appeasement of Red Cloud, or the uncompromising resistance of Sitting Bull?

GLOSSARY

ARROW CREEK, BATTLE OF (AUGUST 13, 1872)   Here Sitting Bull performed a feat of bravery that awed his followers: he seated himself and calmly smoked his pipe within range of the soldiers' guns.

BLACK HILLS (SOUTH DAKOTA)   Sacred Lakota domain called Paha Sapa; gold miners invading the Black Hills helped ignite the Great Sioux War of 1876.

BROTHERTON, MAJOR DAVID H.   Accepted Sitting Bull's surrender in 1881.

CRAZY HORSE   An Oglala Lakota and the greatest of all the Sioux war chiefs, he also fought to drive the white invaders away and save the old ways.

CROW FOOT   Sitting Bull's favorite son, who died with him in the confrontation with Indian police in 1890.

CROWS   Plains Indian tribe and traditional enemy of the Lakota.

FORT LARAMIE TREATY (1868)   Set aside all of present-day South Dakota west of the Missouri River as the Great Sioux Reservation.

FOUR HORNS   Sitting Bull's uncle who was wounded in the Battle of Killdeer Mountain.

GHOST DANCE RELIGION   Begun by a Paiute messiah named Wovoca, the Ghost Dance movement swept the Plains Indians incarcerated on reservations; it prophesied the end of the white invaders and the return of the buffalo and all previous generations of Indians.

HUNKPAPA   Sitting Bull's division of the Lakota; the other six divisions were Miniconjou, Sans Arc, Two Kettle, Bruele, Oglala, and Blackfeet Sioux (not to be confused with the Blackfeet tribe that lived and hunted northwest of the Lakota).

KILLDEER MOUNTAIN, BATTLE OF (JULY 28, 1864)   A "calamitous" defeat for the Lakota that pointed up the futility of the Indians' fighting an open battle with well-armed soldiers.

LITTLE BIGHORN, BATTLE OF (JUNE 25, 1876)   More than two thousand Sioux warriors "massacred" Lieutenant Colonel George Armstrong Custer and his 265 men in this remote location in southeastern Montana.

LONG KNIVES   Indian name for white soldiers armed with rifles and bayonets.

McLAUGHLIN, JAMES   Agent of the Standing Rock Lakota Reservation who tried to shape the Indians into "imitation whites" and to destroy Sitting Bull's reputation.

RED CLOUD   Chief of the Oglala Sioux, Red Cloud led Indian resistance to the Bozeman Trail and the three forts that guarded it. The trail ran through Indian country in Montana and Colorado. Red Cloud's raids and the so-called "Fetterman Massacre" forced the United States in 1868 to abandon the trail and the forts and to "regard the Powder River country as 'unceded Indian country.'" As Utley says, Red Cloud had "won his war."

SULLY, GENERAL ALFRED   Commanded United States Army forces in the Battle of Killdeer Mountain.

SUN DANCE   The central ceremony in the sacred life of the Lakota; in it the dancers engaged in self-sacrifice and self-torture in order to gain the favor of the Great Mysterious and ensure a successful buffalo hunt.

WAKANTANKA   Lakota word for the Great Mysterious.

WICHASHA WAKAN   Lakota term for a holy man such as Sitting Bull.

Sitting Bull's fighting days ended on July 20, 1881, when he led his little band of faithful headmen into the cramped office of the commanding officer at Fort Buford, Dakota Territory. All were shabbily dressed and gaunt from the hunger of their Canadian exile. Sitting Bull, once the mightiest chief of the Lakota Sioux, wore a threadbare calico shirt and black leggings; a tattered, dirty blanket was loosely draped around his waist. Suffering a severe eye infection, he had tied a kerchief turbanlike around his head and drawn it partly across his eyes. Beneath, his dark seamed face with jutting nose and chin and perpetually downturned mouth registered both resignation and despair.

His men grouped behind him, the Sioux chief sat next to the blue-clad soldier chief. Placing his Winchester rifle beneath the chair, Sitting Bull drew to him his five-year-old son Crow Foot. Major David H. Brotherton opened the council by setting forth the terms on which the surrender would be received. In fact, they were no terms at all, since the U.S. government's adamant insistence on unconditional surrender had put off this day until starvation left no other recourse.

After the officer ceased speaking, Sitting Bull slumped in his chair, silent and glum. Brotherton invited him to speak. He sat motionless for five minutes—as if in a trance, thought one witness. He said a few words to his men, then gestured to Crow Foot, who picked up his father's rifle and handed it to the army officer. Then Sitting Bull spoke in words that the interpreter translated:

I surrender this rifle to you through my young son, whom I now desire to teach in this manner that he has become a friend of the Americans. I wish him to learn the habits of the whites and to be educated as their sons are educated. I wish it to be remembered that I was the last man of my tribe to surrender my rifle. This boy has given it to you, and he now wants to know how he is going to make a living.

"Sitting Bull" by Robert M. Utley, *MHQ: The Quarterly Journal of Military History,* Vol. V, No. 4 (Summer 1993). Reprinted by permission.

The ceremony at Fort Buford marked the end, at age fifty, of Sitting Bull's career as a warrior, war leader, and tribal war chief, a career that had begun at the age of fourteen, when he counted his first coup on a Crow Indian. He had achieved power and distinction in other fields, too—as a *wichasha wakan,* a holy man; as a band chief; and finally, a post unique in Sioux history, as supreme chief of all the Lakota tribes. His war honors and trophies, however, provided his greatest satisfaction. That he understood the tragic symbolism of giving up his rifle he betrayed in a song composed to connect what had been to what would be: A warrior / I have been / Now / It is all over / A hard time / I have.

What "had been" began in 1831 with Sitting Bull's birth into a distinguished family of the Hunkpapa tribe, one of the seven tribes of Teton or Lakota Sioux. A nomadic people, the Lakotas occupied the high plains between the Missouri River and the Bighorn Mountains while ranging north to the British possessions and south as far as the Platte and Republican rivers. Together, they numbered between 15,000 and 20,000 people. Other Sioux lived to the east—Yanktons and Yanktonais east of the Missouri River, and Dakotas, or Santees, in Minnesota.

At the age of fourteen, his name was not yet Sitting Bull but Jumping Badger, although his deliberate and willful ways had earned him the nickname Hunkesni, or "Slow." Much against his parents' counsel, Slow insisted on accompanying a war party of ten men striking westward from the Powder River in search of horses and scalps of the enemy Crow tribe. Unproven lads often tagged along on such expeditions as errand boys. They learned the ways of war without actually fighting.

On the third day out, crossing a divide, the party spotted a dozen mounted Crows gathered in conference beside a creek. Whooping and shouting, the Lakotas raced down the slope in a headlong charge. Startled, the Crows spread out to receive the attack. But one Crow spurred his horse to escape. Slow, mounted on a sturdy gray horse his father had given him, his naked body painted yellow from head to foot and hung with colorful strands of beads, shrieked a war cry and galloped in pursuit. The powerful gray swiftly overtook the quarry. Pulling abreast, Slow smashed his adversary with a tomahawk and knocked him from his mount. Another warrior hurried in to finish the act and count second coup. In fierce fighting, the Sioux killed all but four of the Crows, who fled the field.

In a jubilant ceremony at the home village, Slow donned his first white eagle feather, emblem of a first coup, and entered one of the world's most highly developed warrior societies. His mother presented him with the beaded, feathered lance that became his favorite offensive weapon. His father presented a shield bearing a sacred design that appeared to him in a dream. From his father also came his own name, to replace Slow and resonate in the history of not only the Sioux but their enemies as well: Tatanka-Iyotanka, Sitting Bull.

As Sitting Bull's adolescent years fell behind in the 1840s, he took on his adult build. With a heavy, muscular frame, a big chest, and a large head, he impressed people as short and stocky, although he stood five feet ten inches tall. His dark hair reached to his shoulders, often braided with otter fur on one side, hanging loose on the other. A severe part at the center of the scalp glistened with a heavy streak of crimson paint. A low forehead surmounted piercing eyes, a broad nose, and thin lips. Although dexterous afoot and superbly agile mounted, he was thought by some to be awkward and even clumsy.

In adulthood Sitting Bull developed into the Hunkpapa incarnate, the admired epitome of the four cardinal virtues of the Lakotas: bravery, fortitude, generosity, and wisdom. "There was something in Sitting Bull that everybody liked," one of his tribesmen recalled. "Children liked him because he was kind, the women because he was kind to the family and liked to settle family troubles. Men liked him because he was brave. Medicine men liked him because they knew he was a man they could consider a leader."

Sitting Bull evolved three distinct personalities. One was the superlative warrior and huntsman, adept at all the techniques of war and the hunt, boastful of

his deeds, laden with honors and ambitious for more, celebrated and rewarded with high rank by his people. Another personality was the holy man, suffused with reverence and mysticism, communing constantly with Wakantanka, the Great Mysterious, dreaming sacred dreams and carrying out the rites and ceremonies they mandated, entreating for the welfare of his people, offering sacrifices ranging from a buffalo carcass to his own flesh. A third was the good tribesman, a man of kindness, generosity, and humility, unostentatious in dress and bearing, composer and singer of songs, a friend of children and old people, peacemaker, sportsman, gentle humorist, wise counselor, and leader. That he excelled in all three realms testified to uncommon merit.

The Lakota culture was hardly a generation old at the time of Sitting Bull's birth. Only around the beginning of the nineteenth century did the Lakotas become fully mounted on horses and begin to acquire guns. Horses and guns enabled them to seize and defend their rich hunting grounds, to follow the great migrating herds of buffalo that shaped their distinctive way of life, and by the middle of the nineteenth century to evolve into the proud and powerful monarchs of the northern Great Plains. Ironically, by furnishing the horses and guns, white people made possible the Lakota way of life; then, in less than a century, they destroyed it.

In the years of Sitting Bull's youth, the Hunkpapas had little conception of the white world. The only whites they knew were traders based at posts along the Missouri River. From them, or other tribes acting as intermediaries, came the horses and guns, along with other useful manufactures. Whites in substantial numbers lived 500 miles to the southeast; the Hunkpapas sensed no threat from them. Their hostility was reserved for enemy tribes such as the Crows, Flatheads, Assiniboines, and Arikaras.

By Sitting Bull's thirtieth birthday, however, the white world had begun to intrude alarmingly on the Hunkpapas. Treaty makers, government agents, and soldiers had begun to appear along the upper Missouri in the 1850s, and by the 1860s the menace had grown

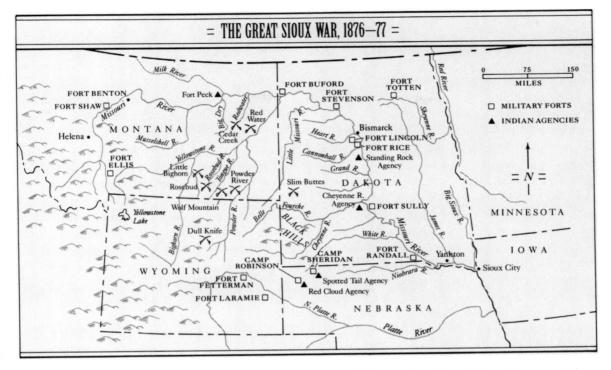

= THE GREAT SIOUX WAR, 1876–77 =

(From The Lance and the Shield *by Robert M. Utley. Maps by Jeffrey L. Ward. Copyright © 1993 by Jeffrey L. Ward.* Reprinted by permission of Henry Holt and Company, Inc.)

distressingly clear. Settlers fingered up the river valleys to the south. Emigrants bound for the gold mines of western Montana killed the buffalo and grazed their livestock on the choice grasses. The voracious boilers of the steamboats consumed the timber stands in the river valleys. The Hunkpapas began to add the whites to their list of enemies.

By this time Sitting Bull had participated in many war expeditions. These were usually limited both in objectives and in scale, though large-scale expeditions and pitched battles sometimes occurred. He had performed many feats of bravery that won the applause of his people and membership in the men's societies that played a major part in Lakota life. He became a war chief of the Hunkpapa tribe. His very name struck terror in the hearts of enemy warriors. Observing this effect, his comrades sometimes disconcerted an opponent by shouting, "Tatanka-Iyotanka tahoksila!"—"We are Sitting Bull's boys!"

Sitting Bull and his "boys" fought for a variety of motives. Where their range overlapped with that of others, they fought for control of hunting grounds. They fought in defense against the aggressions of others; for plunder, chiefly the horses that constituted the prime measure of wealth; for revenge of injuries real and fancied; for glory and the strictly prescribed war honors that determined prestige and leadership.

In any battle, whatever the scale, the Hunkpapas, like all Plains Indians, fought in time-honored fashion. Singly and in knots they galloped back and forth, firing arrows or musket balls at the enemy. Sometimes they gathered in bunches for a thrust aimed at overrunning their foes. Each man indulged in a variety of flashy escapades to display bravery; he followed a leader only when it suited his convenience or inclination. In any such encounter, Sitting Bull's role was chiefly, through exhortation and example, to inspire men to exhibit ever greater personal daring and to join with him in whatever tactical move circumstances seemed to dictate. Neither he nor any other chief "commanded," as whites used the term.

Typifying this mode of combat and Sitting Bull's part in it was the Lakotas' most memorable fight with an enemy tribe. This occurred in the winter of 1869–70, and they remembered it as the Thirty-Crows-Killed battle.

Sitting Bull's band wintered that year in Montana, along the Missouri River and Big Dry Creek. In the middle of the winter, amid bitter cold and deep snow, two Hunkpapa boys were returning from a day of hunting when a party of thirty Crows cut their trail in the snow. Except for two men mounted on one pony, the Crows were afoot. The two hurried to overtake the boys and succeeded in killing one. Wounded, the other escaped to carry word to the Hunkpapa village.

At once Sitting Bull organized a revenge expedition of about 100 warriors. Guided by the surviving boy, the men found their enemies posted behind rock breastworks at the head of Big Dry Creek. As dawn broke, the Hunkpapas attacked. A few on each side had firearms, but most had only bow and arrows. The Hunkpapas fought in the usual fashion, each man for himself, each striving for deeds of bravery and the coups that added to war honors. Although outnumbered more than three to one, the Crows enjoyed the advantages of defense from a fortified position. Steady in their own bravery, they sold their lives dearly. But as the morning hours slipped by, the Hunkpapas gradually took their toll on the Crows.

Like his warriors, Sitting Bull charged as chance presented and retreated when the fire grew too hot. Once he darted to the breastworks and reached across with his bow to count three coups. Finally, as noon approached, he and his comrades surged forward, leaped the walls, and in desperate hand-to-hand fighting killed the last of the Crows. Hunkpapa casualties were much lighter: Thirteen died and seventeen limped off with serious wounds.

This style of combat worked well enough against an enemy practicing the same style, as Crows, Assiniboines, and other Plains tribes did. Pursued in battles with white people, especially white soldiers, it had severe drawbacks.

Sitting Bull's Hunkpapas and other Lakotas of the upper Missouri had their first combat with United States troops in 1863–64. In two summer campaigns, Generals Henry H. Sibley and Alfred Sully led formidable expeditions to the Dakota plains, at first to round up Santee Sioux fugitives from the Minnesota uprising of 1862, then to punish Lakotas who had interfered with the migration to the newly discovered Montana mines.

Almost certainly, Sitting Bull fought in the battles of Dead Buffalo Lake and Stony Lake, July 26 and 28, 1863. He may have been at Whitestone Hill on September 3, 1863. He unquestionably played a leading part in the battles of Killdeer Mountain and the Badlands, July 28 and August 7–9, 1864. In all these fights, the Indians relied on their traditional techniques, and in all they suffered severe to calamitous defeats.

Killdeer Mountain should have shown the Sioux the perils of trying to take on the soldiers in open battle. As many as 1,400 lodges representing four Lakota tribes traced the southern edge of a low range of rugged, wooded mountains falling away on the north to the Little Missouri badlands. A series of buttes and ridges, separated by deep gorges, rose stairlike to the dominating mountain mass. In this natural fortress, emboldened by a force exceeding 2,000 warriors, the Sioux felt confident of routing the approaching army of General Sully.

With 2,200 cavalry and artillery, Sully advanced across the parched plains from the south. Judging the terrain too broken for mounted action, he dismounted and pushed forward on a broad front of skirmishers. Horseholders, then wagons and artillery, brought up the rear.

The Indians came out to meet him. Resplendent in paint and war costume, they sat their ponies in little clusters on every hill and ridge facing the blue lines and curling around their flanks. When within range, the two forces opened fire.

For five miles the fighting roiled northward toward the village at the foot of Killdeer Mountain, the Lakotas attacking in typical fashion. Despite their numbers, however, they could not slow the steady advance of the soldiers.

Mounted on a fast sorrel and armed with musket and bow and arrows, Sitting Bull fought with his usual bravery. As the soldiers launched a final assault aimed at the village itself, he saw a bullet slam into the back of his revered uncle, Chief Four Horns. "I am shot," yelled Four Horns, clinging grimly to his mount.

Sitting Bull dashed to the rescue, seized the horse's bridle, and, as his young nephew White Bull steadied the injured man, led the way into a sheltering thicket. There Sitting Bull gave Four Horns water to drink, applied medicine to the wound, and bandaged it. The bullet remained inside, Four Horns said; he could feel it and it hurt. (Later he recovered and explained that the bullet had dropped into his stomach and never bothered him again.)

While Sitting Bull doctored his uncle, the soldiers won final victory, scattering men, women, and children into the mountains and seizing the village. The next day they methodically destroyed everything that could benefit the Indians. Lodges, meat, robes, utensils—all went up in flames. The troops counted more than a hundred Sioux bodies left on the battlefield; how many dead and wounded were carried away is not known. By contrast, Sully reported casualties of two killed and ten wounded.

The Sibley-Sully campaigns, especially Killdeer Mountain, gave Sitting Bull his first taste of battle with the Long Knives. They did not, he discovered, fight like Indians. Instead they fought in organized formations, obedient to commands of their officers, and brought overwhelming firepower to bear. Their rifled muskets claimed greater range, accuracy, and hitting force than the feeble smoothbore trade muskets of the Indians. The soldiers' cannon in particular were frightening and deadly.

The lessons were clear: Acquire better firearms, and avoid open battle with the Long Knives, relying instead on the hit-and-run tactics at which the Sioux excelled. Sitting Bull's record suggests that he fully grasped the first lesson, only partly the second. Not surprisingly in view of the dictates of culture, neither he nor any other chief ever thought to fight in disciplined formations maneuvered by a hierarchy of command.

The Battle of Killdeer Mountain heralded two decades of conflict with the Long Knives. As whites edged onto the northern Great Plains, soldiers came to protect them. Their "war houses" on the Missouri River, along with the steamboats that carried people and merchandise to the Montana mines, infuriated the Sioux. No chief took a more uncomplicated or inflexible view of this invasion than Sitting Bull. Except for traders, he held, the whites must all get out of Lakota domain and quit traveling through it. If they would not go peaceably, they would be driven out.

It now fell to Sitting Bull to embody the spirit of Lakota resistance to the white threat. Throughout the late 1860s he led the Hunkpapa offensive against the whites. In this aggressive war, he wielded his favorite attack weapon, the lance, which symbolized his role as the offensive arm of the Hunkpapa tribe.

Principal objectives of the offensive were the military posts of the upper Missouri: Forts Rice, Stevenson, Totten, and Buford. Permanent abodes of the detested Long Knives, the forts stood for the resolve of the whites to possess Lakota territory. The campaign took the form mainly of raids near the forts. Logging details, stock herders, mail riders, and travelers bound for the mines periodically ran afoul of nearby war parties.

Sioux usually regarded direct assaults as risks not worth the prospective gain, but twice they launched such attacks, in each instance with Sitting Bull in the lead. The first occurred at Fort Rice on July 28, 1865. In four hours of desperate fighting, the garrison of "Galvanized Yankees"—Confederate prisoners enlisted for Indian duty—held the defenses and drove off the assailants with well-directed rifle and artillery fire. The second clash occurred on December 24, 1866, when Sitting Bull and his warriors seized the outbuildings of Fort Buford and battled their foes until routed by artillery and charging infantry.

Sitting Bull's offensive on the upper Missouri paralleled an even more determined one to the west, in the Powder River country, over the same issues. Spearheaded by Red Cloud's Oglala tribe, Lakotas fought to close the Bozeman Trail to the Montana mines and get rid of the three forts the army had built to guard travelers. Unlike Sitting Bull, Red Cloud won his war. In the Fort Laramie Treaty of 1868, the United States yielded the three forts and agreed to regard the Powder River country as "unceded Indian country." There the Sioux could live so long as the buffalo sustained their way of life.

The Treaty of 1868 profoundly shaped the destiny of both Red Cloud and Sitting Bull. Besides the unceded territory, it defined a Great Sioux Reservation—all the present state of South Dakota west of the Missouri—and bound all Sioux to settle there eventually. Within a few years Red Cloud and many of his followers had settled there, launching him on a career as mediator between his people and government authorities.

For his part, Sitting Bull scorned the treaty, the reservation, and everything else associated with the whites (except trade goods, especially arms and ammunition). He had not signed this or any other treaty, and never would. He intended to live as always, following the buffalo, raiding Crows and Assiniboines, and defending his homeland. "You are fools," he had lectured some agency Indians, "to make yourselves slaves to a piece of fat bacon, some hard-tack, and a little sugar and coffee."

In Red Cloud and Sitting Bull, the Treaty of 1868 personalized two powerful magnetic poles of leadership. Red Cloud emerged as the principal chief of the agency Lakotas, those who chose to live within the Great Sioux Reservation and accept government dole. Sitting Bull emerged as the principal chief of the nonreservation Lakotas, who ranged the plains country in the free life of old. Indeed, he had his followers proclaim him supreme chief of all the Lakotas. Such a post had never existed, but his force of personality gave it substance.

The Sitting Bull bands, the "northern Indians," the "hunting bands," or simply the "hostiles," in the white lexicon, numbered about 450 lodges, about 4,000 people including about 800 fighting men.

Sitting Bull in 1885, four years after his surrender. The great Lakota was both a holy man and a war chief who embodied the four cardinal virtues of his people: bravery, fortitude, generosity, and wisdom. The crucifix he wears in this photograph was supposedly presented to him by a Jesuit missionary in 1868. (Library of Congress)

Ranging the valleys of the Yellowstone River and its southern tributaries, many bands came together in the summer for the annual sun dance and perhaps a communal buffalo hunt and a big war expedition against an enemy tribe. In the winter they scattered to remote valleys to sit out the cold, hungry months. In the warm season their numbers swelled with reservation kin out for a summer's lark. In the frigid season their numbers dwindled as rations at the agencies beckoned.

In the aftermath of the Treaty of 1868, with the Lakotas increasingly divided into reservation and nonreservation factions, Sitting Bull called off his offensive against the Missouri River forts. From now on he would fight the white people only in defense of his homeland—the Powder and Yellowstone country that roughly coincided with the unceded territory of the treaty. Sitting Bull's last raid on Fort Buford occurred in September 1870. Now the shield instead of the lance symbolized his role among Lakotas.

Staunchly backing Sitting Bull in his new defense posture was the greatest of all Lakota war leaders— Crazy Horse of the Oglalas. He shared Sitting Bull's aversion to the reservation and the ways of the white people. To the hunting bands, he was a chief second in stature only to Sitting Bull.

Of more ambiguous conviction was another war chief, Gall of the Hunkpapas. Close to Sitting Bull since childhood, Gall tended to take counsel in expediency. Sometimes he even slipped into the Hunkpapa agency at Grand River to sample government rations.

The defensive policy expressed itself most forcibly in the opposition of the hunting bands to the Northern Pacific Railroad. In the summers of 1872 and 1873, they fought army units escorting company surveyors marking out a rail route in the Yellowstone Valley. This was the heart of Lakota hunting grounds and the more valuable to them because only recently wrested from the Crows at great cost in blood.

At the Battle of Arrow Creek on August 13, 1872, Sitting Bull performed one of his most memorable feats of bravery. Urged on by Sitting Bull and Crazy Horse, Lakota and Cheyenne warriors struck engineers and their cavalry guardians in the bend of a dry streambed in the upper Yellowstone Valley.

As the sun rose on the battlefield, all eyes turned in wonder to Sitting Bull, who staged a spectacle of bravery so imaginative that it surpassed all others that day. Getting his pipe and tobacco pouch from his horse, he walked from the bluffs out into the open valley to within enemy range. Seating himself on the ground, he shouted, "Who other Indians wish to smoke with me come." As Sitting Bull calmly and with studied deliberation filled the bowl with tobacco, his nephew White Bull, Gets-the-Best-Of, and two

Cheyennes ventured into the open and seated themselves beside the chief.

The "smoking party," as White Bull termed it, was a terrifying experience. After kindling the tobacco, Sitting Bull puffed placidly, then passed the pipe to his companions. With pounding hearts, each puffed vigorously and passed it quickly down the line. Throughout he said nothing, just looked around and smoked quietly as bullets kicked up dirt and sang through the air. When all the tobacco had burned, Sitting Bull picked up a stick, thoroughly cleaned the bowl, and stowed the pipe in its pouch. He rose and slowly walked back to the admiring knots of fellow tribesmen. The other smokers ran back.

This ingenious exhibition, so captivating to people who placed great emphasis on daring, added to Sitting Bull's long list of valorous deeds. It reinforced his reputation for bravery and answered those who, in the worsening factionalism of the early 1870s, mocked his pretensions. It was, White Bull remembered, "the bravest deed possible."

After 1873 the Northern Pacific faded from the Lakotas' list of grievances. In four inconclusive battles and a few skirmishes, they had expressed their violent opposition, but they had not stopped the railroad. The Panic of 1873 did that, and the railhead rested at Bismarck, on the Missouri, until after other events had neutralized the Sioux.

Although furious, the Sitting Bull bands offered no violent opposition to a far more blatant assault on their territory. Blazing the "Thieves' Road" into the Black Hills, the Custer Expedition of 1874 saw only a few Lakotas and fought none. But the discovery of gold set off a rush that doomed the Indians' possession of the hills.

It also confronted the administration of President Ulysses S. Grant with a hard dilemma. The Black Hills lay within the Great Sioux Reservation, inarguably guaranteed the Indians by the Treaty of 1868. Yet miners flocked to the hills, and the electorate demanded that the government legalize the invasion. In part because of intimidation by the Sitting Bull bands, however, the reservation chiefs refused to sell.

Not until the independent bands yielded to government control, federal officials concluded, could they buy the Black Hills.

A rationale was necessary to force the hunting bands onto the Great Sioux Reservation. They had not interfered with the gold rush, and although they had not signed the Treaty of 1868, it sanctioned their residence in the unceded territory. The defensive policy of Sitting Bull and Crazy Horse, furthermore, left only the thinnest pretext for military force. But their young men had raided Crows, Assiniboines, and Arikaras, as they had always done. They had also terrorized whites on the upper Yellowstone, more in fear of what might happen than of what had happened. In these treaty violations by people who had never subscribed to a treaty, the government found its excuse to order the Sitting Bull bands to the reservation or face military action. Such were the origins of the Great Sioux War of 1876.

Even when confronted with the government's ultimatum in their winter villages, Sitting Bull and his fellow chiefs did not understand that a war was brewing. They were minding their own business and had no plans to fight the white soldiers. Then, on March 17, 1876, cavalry stormed through a village on Powder River, killing two and wounding several others; now the hunting bands knew the Long Knives had declared war.

Sitting Bull drew the winter camps together for self-defense. As spring gave way to summer, reservation Indians began to make their way westward, to join in the defense. By late June his village had swollen from 3,000 to 7,000 people, from 800 to 1,800 warriors.

Now forty-five, Sitting Bull no longer took the lead on the battlefield. He was the "old man chief" and holy man whose judgment and counsel guided the policies and decisions of the allied tribes. Crazy Horse, Gall, and other fighters set the example in combat.

At a sun dance early in June, in supplication to Wakantanka, Sitting Bull gave 100 pieces of flesh from his arms. He also fasted and danced while gazing at the sun. Just below the sun he saw soldiers and horses bearing down on an Indian village. They rode upside down, their feet to the sky, their heads to the earth with hats falling off. A voice proclaimed: "These soldiers do not possess ears. They are to die." The vision and prophecy thrilled his people.

Soldiers were coming—three armies from three directions. They were led by General Alfred H. Terry, Colonel John Gibbon, and "Three Stars," George Crook. With Terry rode "Long Hair," George Armstrong Custer. On June 17, 1876, Sitting Bull's warriors confronted General Crook on the upper reaches of Rosebud Creek. Shoshone and Crow auxiliaries broke the Sioux charge and saved Crook's force from being overrun. Sitting Bull, his arms cut and useless from the sun-dance sacrifice, ranged the lines, exhorting the warriors. Crook limped back to his supply base.

The Battle of the Rosebud did not fulfill Sitting Bull's prophecy. Crook's soldiers had not fallen into the Sioux camp and died. But a week later, Long Hair Custer and his cavalrymen fell into the Sioux camp. It sprawled sleepily in the Little Bighorn Valley on that hot Sunday of June 25, 1876. As depicted in the sun-dance vision, many soldiers died.

A stunned white world gave Sitting Bull all the credit. The "Napoleon of the Sioux," the *New York Herald* labeled him two weeks later, and in subsequent issues self-appointed experts explained how such a catastrophe had happened. One of them declared that the famed Jesuit missionary Father Pierre-Jean De Smet had taught Sitting Bull to speak and read French; the chief had then studied French histories of the Napoleonic Wars and "modeled his generalship after the little Corsican corporal." An army officer, who should have known better, wrote, "The tactics of Sitting Bull seem to have been those pursued by the great Napoleon in his famous campaign of 1814, and were the same practiced by General Lee at Richmond in 1864–65." Soon the nation would be told that Sitting Bull, in a youthful guise, had attended West Point.

In such fantasies a dazed public and a mortified army sought explanations for the disaster that had befallen a supposedly elite regiment and its valiant commander. They wanted to believe that Custer's 7th Cavalry had been overwhelmed by superior numbers commanded by a military genius, the Napoleon of the Sioux.

The truth, of course, was that, as at Killdeer Mountain and all other encounters with Plains tribes, there had been no Indian general at the Little Bighorn. As one of his followers pointed out, "The chief might give orders to fight but he does not direct how to proceed."

The Indians did not win the battle because of generalship or even leadership. They won because they outnumbered the enemy three to one, because they were united, confident, and angry, and above all because the threat to their women and children fired every man with determination to save his family. The Indians won, too, because their foes let themselves be beaten in fragments. Both in the valley and on the battle ridge where the "last stand" occurred, command and control collapsed, discipline evaporated, and men panicked, which left the initiative to the Indians.

If whites ascribed Napoleonic genius to Sitting Bull in 1876, in less than a decade they had produced another interpretation. On the reservation, abetted by Indians currying favor with the Great Father, white officials now said Sitting Bull had not participated in the battle at all; he had remained in his teepee making medicine, or fled to the hills in terror, even abandoning his family, or skulked somewhere else safely out of danger.

In truth, at the Battle of the Little Bighorn, Sitting Bull was a chief several times over whose bravery no one questioned. He was far more valuable as a counselor than as a fighting man. Leave that to the young warriors striving for glory. Chiefs were expected to fight only to protect noncombatants, and that is what he did when soldiers led by Major Marcus Reno threatened the women and children at the upper end of the village.

After that threat receded, he could have withdrawn with honor. Instead he continued to fire at the soldiers and shout encouragement to the warriors, hovering on the edge of the fighting until everyone left to confront Custer downstream. Then he posted himself at the village's northern end, where many women and children had collected. More than enough men swarmed on the battle ridge to wipe out Long Hair, which they did in less than an hour.

Sitting Bull's significance at the Little Bighorn lay not in flaunting bravery, or directing the movements of warriors, or even inspiring them to fight. It lay instead in leadership so wise and powerful that it drew together and held together a muscular coalition of tribes, one so infused with his defiant cast of mind that it could rout Three Stars Crook at the Rosebud and rub out Long Hair Custer at the Little Bighorn. Never had the Sioux triumphed so spectacularly—and they never would again. For that triumph, more than any other chief they could thank Sitting Bull.

But the triumph contained the seeds of defeat. A stunned nation lashed back, and the Sioux country swarmed with regiments of "Custer avengers." By the spring of 1877, most of the hunting bands had surrendered and gone to the reservation, setting the stage for the government to seize the Black Hills and legalize the invasion.

Sitting Bull could not stomach such humiliation. With a die-hard following he crossed the "medicine road" into the land of the Grandmother. There he got along famously with the queen's redcoats, the North-West Mounted Police, and formed his first close ties to white men. But the buffalo were disappearing in Canada as they were in the United States, and "Bear Coat"—General Nelson A. Miles—watched the boundary like a hawk. After four years of hardship, starvation overcame humiliation, and young Crow Foot handed his father's rifle to Major Brotherton.

The final decade was one of despair. After nearly two years as a prisoner of war, Sitting Bull went to the reservation. At Standing Rock Agency, Agent

James McLaughlin's goal was to transform his charges into imitation whites. He sought to make them into tillers of the soil embracing Christianity, Americanism, and the customs and values of the white people. Sitting Bull refused to be made over. He accepted what he thought would be beneficial, such as schooling for his children and grandchildren, and rejected the rest. Finding him unpliable, McLaughlin launched the campaign of ridicule and derision that included the imputation of cowardice at the Little Bighorn.

Hunger, disease, a decade of cultural breakdown, and another land grab made the Sioux reservations fertile ground for the Ghost Dance religion that took root in 1890. It promised a new world, without whites, peopled by all the generations of Indians that had gone before, and stocked with an abundance of buffalo and other game. Whether Sitting Bull truly believed, he functioned as the high priest of the religion at Standing Rock. The government decided to remove him to a distant military post.

Irony and tragedy stalked Sitting Bull's final days. Not the Long Knives of old, but *ceska maza,* "metal breasts" (for their police badges) of his own tribe, closed in on their former leader. At dawn on December 15, 1890, a platoon of Indian policemen forced their way into his cabin on Grand River and placed him under arrest. Excited Ghost Dancers crowded around the cabin, and his own son Crow Foot, now fourteen, taunted him for giving up. The volatile confrontation blew up in a paroxysm of gunfire and hand-to-hand fighting. Sitting Bull went down, shot at close range in the chest and the back of the head by *ceska maza.* Crow Foot died too, beaten and shot by enraged policemen.

The Hunkpapas, even those who had forsaken the old ways, knew McLaughlin's portrait of Sitting Bull to be grotesquely flawed. They well remembered he had been a magnificent warrior, an inspiring war chief, a statesman and political leader of vast wisdom, a holy man of marvelous power, and to his last day a leader of compelling force.

The world remembers Sitting Bull not for what he achieved in his own culture but for his battle against the westward movement of the American people. It is this battle that gives him nearly universal name recognition beyond his own culture. In this struggle, as both lance and shield, his inflexibility served him well. He acted on faultless reasoning: The land of the Lakotas belonged to the Lakotas, and no whites had any right to be there. He fought to keep them out, and when that failed, he fought to defend his people and his territory from invasion. He lost not because of failings of leadership or, given his cultural outlook, failings of judgment, but because of impersonal forces beyond his control or even his understanding.

QUESTIONS TO CONSIDER

1 How did Lakota culture change during the nineteenth century? What effect did white settlers have on that culture throughout the century?

2 What was the traditional Lakota manner of fighting, and what values did it highlight? Why did this style of warfare not work against white troops, and what lessons does Robert Utley think Sitting Bull should have learned from this?

3 Describe Sitting Bull and his three "personalities." Discuss the stance he took toward whites, and compare it with that taken by Red Cloud. Which one of them do you think was right and why?

4 What were the principal interests of Americans in Sioux territory, and how did Americans generally react to Sitting Bull's effort at resistance? How did the United States government deal with the Lakota Sioux? How and on what pretext did they finally break the resistance of Sitting Bull's people?

5 What is the significance of the Ghost Dance religion and of Sitting Bull's tragic death? How do you feel about Utley's conclusion that Sitting Bull lost, not because of any personal or cultural failings but because of forces beyond his control?

4 Death on the Prairies: The Murderous Blizzard of 1888

DAVID LASKIN

With the Indians out of the way, Americans were free at last to conquer the vast Great Plains that reached from Texas to the Canadian border in the center of the country. Westering farmers had stopped at the edge of this enormous grassland because its arid climate and shallow topsoil seemed unsuited to agricultural techniques devised in the East. But after the Civil War came the development of new farming techniques and new machinery such as the windmill, the chilled-iron plow, and the combine—all of which made agriculture feasible on the windy prairies. As a consequence, farmers from east of the Mississippi swarmed there during the postwar years, some claiming 160 acres free under the 1862 Homestead Act, most buying their land from speculators or the railroads. In the 1880s alone, more than one million people poured onto the Great Plains from the Great Lakes states. Meanwhile, after the failure of Reconstruction, African Americans headed west as well; they were sodbusters, cowboys, speculators, miners, lawmen, desperadoes, and cavalrymen. Asian and Mexican Americans were present, too, all contributing to the drama of frontier conquest. The pioneers lived in all manner of homes—from dugouts to sod houses—battling tornadoes, hail, dust storms, blizzards, prairie fires, and grasshopper plagues in an endless struggle to make new lives for themselves on the nation's last frontier.

The westering experience tended to break down traditional male and female "spheres," which stripped women of all political and legal rights and restricted them to the home while their husbands had jobs and careers in the outside world and ran political affairs. As modern scholarship has demonstrated, frontier women were not chained to the home but were close to equal partners with their menfolk: in addition to their household chores, the women helped their husbands hunt, gather water and fuel, and plant and harvest.

As David Laskin points out in the following selection, male and female migrants to the Dakota and Nebraska frontier were shocked by its violent shifts in weather. Who back East or down South could have conceived of a land where the temperature could fall eighteen degrees in just three minutes? Who would have guessed that farmers and school children could start their days in shirtsleeves, without heavy overcoats, only to experience wind chills that night that were forty degrees below zero?

On January 12, 1888, the most murderous blizzard of that region suddenly struck the Dakota and Nebraska prairie. As Laskin says, "One moment it was mild, the sun was shining, a damp wind blew fitfully out of the south—the next moment frozen hell had broken loose." The ferocity of the storm killed hundreds of children making their way home after school. Thus it was called "the children's blizzard." Neither the children who survived the storm nor their parents would ever forget that terrible day.

Laskin's vivid description of the blizzard of 1888 will haunt you long after you have read his account. In Laskin's view, the storm was a tragic example of a dream gone wrong for pioneers who had migrated west in search of a prosperous new life. They learned that "the sudden storms, the violent swings from one meteorological extreme to another, the droughts and torrents and killer blizzards were not freak occurrences but facts of life on the prairie." For countless pioneer families, the promise of the Homestead Act proved to be a cruel joke. The storm that killed their children demonstrated "that the land they had desired so fervently and had traveled so far to claim wasn't free after all."

GLOSSARY

CARNEGIE, ANDREW   A Scottish immigrant and a self-made man, Carnegie founded the Carnegie Steel Company. In 1900, it became the largest industrial corporation in the world (see selection 5). In 1878, Carnegie won the steel contract to build the Brooklyn Bridge (see selection 6).

DEPRESSION OF 1893   The greatest economic depression the United States had yet experienced, the depression (or "panic") of 1893 was a product of agricultural and industrial expansion that had produced a surplus of goods. Railroad companies had built too many miles of track, and farmers had borrowed too heavily, forcing many to lose their land as crop prices fell.

EDISON, THOMAS ALVA   From his modern research laboratory in Menlo Park, New Jersey, Edison promised "a minor invention every ten days and a big thing every six months or so." Known as the "Wizard of Menlo Park," a man with little formal education, Edison produced two "big things": the phonograph in 1877 and the electric light, a product of experiments with carbon filaments, in 1879.

GALVESTON HURRICANE   This storm of September 8, 1900, was the deadliest hurricane in American history thus far. It devastated this southeastern Texas city, killing over ten thousand people. Galveston was left in ruins with $30 million damage ($700 million in today's dollars).

GARLAND, HAMLIN   A product of rural Iowa, Garland wrote novels such as *Son of the Middle Border* (1890) that described the bleak lives of settlers on the Great Plains.

HOMESTEAD ACT (1862)   Legislation that provided 160 acres of government land on the rugged prairie frontier to anyone who promised to live and work on it for five years.

The only requirement was a ten dollar registration fee. Between 1862 and 1900, almost six hundred thousand families received free homesteads on forty-eight million acres of land.

HYPOTHERMIA   A medical condition that occurs when a person's body temperature drops significantly below normal. Hypothermia starts when the core body temperature falls below 35 degrees Celsius (95 degrees Fahrenheit).

JOHNSTOWN FLOOD   On May 31, 1889, heavy rains forced the old South Fork Dam in Johnstown, Pennsylvania, to break, resulting in a deadly flood that killed over 2,209 people in that workingclass city.

MORGAN, J. PIERPONT   In the Gilded Age, Morgan was the most powerful and influential figure in the world of American finance. He established the first billion-dollar company, the United States Steel Corporation.

POWELL, JOHN WESLEY   An explorer and geologist, Powell was a professor at Illinois Wesleyan University and director of the United States Geological Survey.

ROCKEFELLER, JOHN D.   A Cleveland merchant, Rockefeller used ruthless and often illegal methods to build the Standard Oil Company that, by 1879, produced 90 percent of America's oil refining needs (see selection 8).

SCRIBNER, CHARLES   A New York publisher, Scribner started *Scribner's Monthly* in 1870. Eleven years later, he changed its name to the *Century Magazine*.

VANDERBILT, CORNELIUS   Nicknamed the "Commodore," Vanderbilt earned millions in the shipping business. Later in life, he built the New York Central Railroad that controlled over 4,500 miles of track from New York City to Chicago.

On January 12, 1888, a blizzard broke over the center of the North American continent. Out of nowhere, a soot gray cloud appeared over the northwest horizon. The air grew still for a long, eerie measure, then the sky began to roar and a wall of ice dust blasted the prairie. Every crevice, every gap and orifice instantly filled with shattered crystals, blinding, smothering, suffocating, burying anything exposed to the wind. The cold front raced down the undefended grasslands like a crack unstoppable army. Montana fell before dawn; North

Dakota went while farmers were out doing their early morning chores; South Dakota, during morning recess; Nebraska as school clocks rounded toward dismissal. In three minutes the front subtracted 18 degrees[*] from the air's temperature. Then evening gathered in and temperatures kept dropping steadily,

---

[*]All temperatures are Fahrenheit unless otherwise indicated.

Excerpt from pp. 1–8, 198–202, 267–271 from *The Children's Blizzard* by David Laskin. Copyright © 2004 by David Laskin. Reprinted by permission of HarperCollins Publishers.

hour after hour, in the northwest gale. Before midnight, windchills were down to 40 below zero. That's when the killing happened. By morning on Friday the thirteenth, hundreds of people lay dead on the Dakota and Nebraska prairie, many of them children who had fled—or been dismissed from—country schools at the moment when the wind shifted and the sky exploded.

Chance is always a silent partner in disaster. Bad luck, bad timing, the wrong choice at a crucial moment, and the door is inexorably shut and barred. The tragedy of the January 12 blizzard was that the bad timing extended across a region and cut through the shared experiences of an entire population. The storm hit the most thickly settled sections of Nebraska and Dakota Territory at the worst possible moment—late in the morning or early in the afternoon on the first mild day in several weeks, a day when children had raced to school with no coats or gloves and farmers were far from home doing chores they had put off during the long siege of cold. But the deadly quirks of chance went deeper and farther than circumstance or time of day. It was the deep current of history that left the prairie peculiarly vulnerable to the storm.

For nearly all of the nation's short life span, the grasslands at the heart of the country had been ignored, overlooked, skirted, or raced over. On maps the words *Great American Desert* hovered vaguely between the Mississippi River and the Rocky Mountains, and the rest was left blank or faintly labeled Indian Territory. But then, after the Civil War, when the swelling cities of the East Coast settled down to the serious business of industrial capitalism, the Great American Desert was reborn and rechristened. Suddenly this immense expanse of open land was not waste, but paradise—and like paradise, it was free, or all but free. Railroad companies flush with millions of acres of government land grants promised new settlers the sky and sold them the earth at irresistible prices. Under the Homestead Act, the U.S. government gave every comer 160 acres free and clear in exchange for the investment of a small filing fee and five years of farming. The dream of free land let loose a stampede. In the three decades after 1870, some 225 million acres of the continent's heartland

were broken, stripped of sod, and planted with crops—more land than had been "improved" in the preceding 263 years of white settlement in the United States. On the last frontier was enacted the greatest human migration the earth had yet endured.

It was late in the day to be an American pioneer. While Thomas Edison was making the first moving pictures in New Jersey, while electric lights shone from Chicago skyscrapers raised on steel skeletons, while Vanderbilts, Carnegies, Morgans, and Rockefellers were adorning their neo-Gothic and Renaissance palaces with the treasures of Europe, homesteaders in Dakota warmed themselves in sod huts at fires of buffalo bones. It wasn't that the sodbusters didn't know that elegant Pullman sleeping cars skimmed over the train tracks at the edges of their wheat fields or that the future price of that wheat depended on tycoons in New York and the number of mouths to feed in Russia. Whether they had come from Europe in the reeking steerage of immigrant ships or boarded converted cattle cars in Chicago, Saint Paul, or New York, they had witnessed with their own eyes the newborn marvels of the industrial world. Someday, they believed, these marvels would be theirs. If they worked hard enough, if their children worked hard enough, the land in time would provide.

And so the settlers of the prairie banked on the future and put their trust in land they loved but didn't really understand. They got down to work so quickly they didn't have time to figure out the vagaries of soil and climate, the cycles of the seasons, the fickle violent moods of the sky. Deprived of both the folk wisdom born of deep familiarity with a single place and the brash abstractions of the new science, the pioneers were vulnerable and exposed. There hadn't been time to put up fences. Children waded into tall grass and vanished. Infants were accidentally dropped in snowdrifts. Infections flourished in the primitive, unsanitary claim shanties.

Coded messages hummed through the telegraph wires strung alongside the train tracks, but settlers' farms were too far from the offices where the messages were received and decoded to do them any good. When the cloud descended from the northwest and filled the air with snow, they had no warning. Unaware of the risk, they wandered out in pursuit of a single precious cow and lost their way between sod hut and barn. Their fuel gave out, their roofs blew off, their animals suffocated. Their children froze to death in the furrows of their fields.

"All around no-one knew of any-one else's predicament," wrote a Dakota pioneer after the storm, "so each acted as he or she thought fit and people survived or died according to their temperament. You can't preach about it. If a young fellow had every penny of his cash tied up in an uninsured herd of cattle . . . what would most of us have done? No-one knew THEN that this was the day which was to be remembered when all the days of 70 years would be forgotten."

One of the many tragedies of that day was the failure of the weather forecasters, a failure compounded of faulty science, primitive technology, human error, narrow-mindedness, and sheer ignorance. America in 1888 had the benefit of an established, well-funded, nationwide weather service attached to the Army and headed by a charismatic general—yet the top priority on any given day was not weather, but political infighting. Forecasters—"indications officers," as they were styled then—insisted their forecasts were correct 83.7 percent of the time for the next twenty-four hours, but they were forbidden to use the word *tornado* in any prediction; they believed that America's major coastal cities were immune to hurricanes; they relied more on geometry and cartography than on physics in tracking storms; they lacked the means and, for the most part, the desire to pursue meteorological research. "[T]he promise of a science of profound interest to the scholar and of vast usefulness to the people is being rapidly realized," wrote explorer and geologist Major John Wesley Powell of meteorology in 1891. "While the science has not yet reached that stage when directions can be successfully given at what hour it is wise to carry an umbrella on a showery day, it has reached that stage when the great storms and waves of intense heat or intense cold can be predicted for all the

land in advance of their coming so as to be of great value to all industries of the land. All the discomforts of the weather cannot be avoided, but the great disasters can be anticipated and obviated." Mighty rhetoric—and many believed it. But in truth, when it came to weather prediction, government forecasters in the last decades of the nineteenth century were still relying more on empirical observations and even proverbs of the "red sky at night, sailor's delight" school than on a sound scientific understanding of the atmosphere. Many of the "great storms and waves of intense heat or intense cold" escaped them altogether—or were mentioned in their daily "indications" too late, too vaguely, too timidly to do anyone any good. When it came to "great disasters," they knew far less than they thought they knew.

It was the age of confidence. Arrogance was epidemic.

The officer in charge of the experimental indications office that had been established in Saint Paul for the express purpose of predicting blizzards and outbreaks of extreme cold on the prairie did not entirely miss the January 12 storm. He knew before midnight on January 11 that it would snow in Dakota Territory and Nebraska the following afternoon and get colder that night. His indications "verified." But they helped few, if any, people in the region escape or protect themselves. Warnings were not posted in time. No one reading the indications for that day would have guessed that an historic storm was bearing down on them. Those in positions of authority neither recognized nor cared about the forecasting failure. To the extent that knuckles got rapped as a result of the storm, it had to do with sleet-covered sugar plantations in the Deep South, not frozen children on the prairie.

It was the Gilded Age. Disaster meant financial ruin.

Even in a region known for abrupt and radical meteorological change, the blizzard of 1888 was unprecedented in its violence and suddenness. There was no atmospheric herald. No eerie green tinge to the sky or fleecy cirrus forerunner. One moment it was

January 12, 1888
The Advance of the Cold Wave

The settlers on the prairie were not prepared for the dramatic changes in weather conditions they faced in this new land. On January 12, 1888, a low-pressure system swept a frigid arctic air mass down from Canada. "The cold front raced down the undefended grasslands like a crack unstoppable army. Montana fell before dawn; North Dakota went while farmers were out doing their early morning chores; South Dakota, during morning recess; Nebraska as school clocks rounded toward dismissal. In three minutes the front subtracted 18 degrees from the air's temperature."

mild, the sun was shining, a damp wind blew fitfully out of the south—the next moment frozen hell had broken loose. The air was so thick with fine-ground wind-lashed ice crystals that people could not breathe. The ice dust webbed their eyelashes and sealed their eyes shut. It sifted into the loose weave of their coats, shirts, dresses, and underwear until their skin was packed in snow. Farmers who had spent a decade walking the same worn paths became disoriented in seconds.

The pioneers of the prairie, even those who had lived there only a few seasons, were accustomed to seeing hail rip open the bases of enormous black clouds and winds of summer fire stream out of the west. They had crouched by their stoves for dark days and nights while winter gales blew without ceasing. They had watched houses get sucked in whirling fragments up the bases of funnel clouds. But nobody had any idea that the atmosphere was capable of a storm like this.

The blizzard of January 12, 1888, known as "the Schoolchildren's Blizzard" because so many of the victims were children caught out on their way home from school, became a marker in the lives of the settlers, the watershed event that separated before and after. The number of deaths—estimated at between 250 and 500—was small compared to that of the Johnstown Flood that wiped out an entire industrial town in western Pennsylvania the following year or the Galveston hurricane of 1900 that left more than eight thousand dead. But it was traumatic enough that it left an indelible bruise on the consciousness of the region. The pioneers were by and large a taciturn lot, reserved and sober Germans and Scandinavians who rarely put their thoughts or feelings down on paper, and when they did avoided hyperbole at all costs. Yet their accounts of the blizzard of 1888 are shot through with amazement, awe, disbelief. There are thousands of these eyewitness accounts of the storm. Even those who never wrote another word about themselves put down on paper everything they could remember about the great blizzard of 1888. Indeed, it was the storm that has preserved these lives from oblivion. The blizzard literally froze

a single day in time. It sent a clean, fine blade through the history of the prairie. It forced people to stop and look at their existences—the earth and sky they had staked their future on, the climate and environment they had brought their children to, the peculiar forces of nature and of nature's God that determined whether they would live or die. . . .

"Everything changes; nothing does," the poet James Merrill wrote in a poem called "After the Fire." The effects of disaster, no matter how extreme, do not last forever. We bury our dead, nurse the wounded, rebuild, and get on with our lives. Today, aside from a few fine marble headstones in country graveyards and the occasional roadside historical marker, not a trace of the blizzard of 1888 remains on the prairie. Yet in the imagination and identity of the region, the storm is as sharply etched as ever: *This is a place where blizzards kill children on their way home from school.* To understand why and how the deadliest Midwestern blizzard happened the way it did is to understand something essential about the history of the American prairie—indeed about the history of America itself.

We'll never know how many spent that night out on the prairie. It had to be at least several thousand, most of them in the southern and eastern parts of Dakota Territory, in the eastern half of Nebraska, and in southwestern Minnesota. Northern Dakota was largely spared because the storm blew through so early that people remained home and kept their children in. Iowa, though it received the heaviest snow, also suffered relatively few casualties. The storm didn't hit there until late in the day, when evening was gathering and farmers and their children were back home. But in southern Dakota and Nebraska the timing could not have been worse. . . .

The catalog of their suffering is terrible. They froze alone or with their parents or perished in frantic, hopeless pursuit of loved ones. They died with the frozen bloody skin torn from their faces, where they had clawed off the mask of ice again and again. Some died within hours of getting lost; some lived through the night and died before first light. They were found standing waist deep in drifts with their hands frozen to barbed-wire fences, clutching at straw piles, buried under overturned wagons, on their backs, facedown on the snow with their arms outstretched as if trying to crawl. Mothers died sitting up with their children around them in fireless houses when the hay or coal or bits of furniture were exhausted and they were too weak or too frightened to go for more.

A young Dutch couple in Minnesota died kneeling side by side with their hands held high above their heads.

A nine-year-old Nebraska boy named Roman Hytrek was walking the prairie with his dog when the storm overtook them. That evening the dog turned up scratching at the door of a neighbor's house. Roman's empty coat was found in March. Eventually a search party recovered the boy's body. Roman had died alone leaning against the side of a hill. They speculated that he had unbuttoned his coat so that he could cradle his dog next to him in it and that the wind ripped it from his shoulders. . . .

William Klemp, a newly married Dakotan in the full vigor of young manhood, left his pregnant wife at home and went out in the storm to care for their livestock. He never returned. A few weeks later, Klemp's wife gave birth to a son. It was spring when they found his body in a sod shanty a mile from the house. Klemp's face had been eaten away by mice and gophers.

In the region that would soon become the state of South Dakota there were deaths in thirty-two of the forty-four counties east of the Missouri River. Every pioneer who wrote a memoir, every family that recorded its history included a story of someone who died in the blizzard. Every story is heartbreaking.

Lois Royce, a young teacher of a Nebraska country school, huddled on the open prairie all night with three of her pupils—two nine-year-old boys and a six-year-old girl. The children cried themselves to sleep. Lois stretched out on the ground, lying on her side with her back to the wind and the children cradled in the hollow of her body. She covered their sleeping bodies with her cloak. The boys died first. Lois felt one of the bodies cease to breathe and go cold. Then, a few hours later, the other. The boys went in silence. The little girl, Hattie Rosberg, had begged her teacher through the night for more covers to keep her warm. She died at daybreak deliriously crying, "I'm so cold, mama, please cover me up." When the air had cleared enough to see, Lois left the three dead children lying together and crawled on her hands and knees a quarter of a mile to the nearest farmhouse.

In Dakota's Beadle County . . . Robert Chambers, a farmer in his early thirties, was outside watering cattle with his two sons and their Newfoundland dog when the weather turned. The older boy, who was eleven, suffered from rheumatism, so Chambers sent him home before the storm got bad. He thought that he and nine-year-old Johnny could drive the cattle to the barn themselves. The dog would know the way. But . . . father and son were overtaken and bewildered. When Chambers realized there was no hope of finding their farmhouse, he burrowed into a drift, wrapped Johnny in his jacket and vest (neither of them had come out with overcoats), and told the boy to get into the hollow out of the wind. Robert Chambers stood in the storm shouting for help as long as his voice held. The dog barked frantically. But no one heard them over the wind.

By evening Chambers was too cold to do anything but lie down in the snow next to his son. He put the dog beside them for extra warmth. Johnny could feel how frigid his father's body was. He urged his father to get up and to look for the line of the trees they had planted by the house. But Chambers would not leave his son.

As the night wore on, father and son talked about death. Chambers assured Johnny that they would survive and repeated over and over that the boy must lie still. Johnny knew that his father was freezing to death. At some point the boy dozed off. When he woke, his father was still alive, but barely. Chambers told his son to pray and that he would pray with him.

At daylight a rescue party heard the Newfoundland barking and found them. The snow had drifted so deeply that Johnny was entirely buried but for a small opening by his mouth. The dog was standing guard. Robert Chambers was dead.

The Westphalen girls, Eda and Matilda, also died in the night. Though born five years apart, the daughters of German immigrants, the girls had grown close to each other in the tragedies that had befallen their family during the past few years. Diphtheria struck the Westphalens in the winter of 1883. Two days before Christmas, six-year-old Frederick died. Six weeks later, their father, Peter, deranged by grief, hanged himself. Since then their mother had managed alone with six children. The winter of the blizzard, Eda was thirteen, Matilda, eight. The storm hit when the girls were at their country school in a hilly section of eastern Nebraska near the railroad town of Scribner (named by an Eastern railroad official for his son-in-law, New York publisher Charles Scribner). The teacher, Nellie Forsythe, told the children to go home. Eda and Matilda left together. The schoolhouse was halfway up the side of a smooth rounded hill; their house was a mile due north at the bottom of a valley cut by a creek. Usually it was an easy walk downhill across the fields. But in the storm the girls had the wind in their faces. No matter how they struggled against it, the northwest wind pushed them east into a series of ravines. For a while they wandered in circles. Then they drifted east and south with the wind. Only when they came to a wire fence did Eda realize they had gone in the wrong direction. They needed to turn around—but turning meant walking into the wind. Matilda failed, and Eda took off her wraps and covered her younger sister.

Most victims of hypothermia curl up on their sides and die in a fetal position. Eda and Matilda died facedown. Very likely they dropped while fighting to walk into the wind. Once they fell, they must have lost consciousness very quickly. They lay on the snow a few feet apart on the side of a hill. The windward side. All night the wind blew snow over their bodies, covering them and laying them bare again.

In the course of the night, the haystack in which Etta Shattuck had taken refuge became her prison. The hay had become so compacted and heavy with drifting snow that it pinned Etta in the small hollow she had dug for herself. As the temperature plunged, the fibers tightened. Etta's torso stayed fairly warm, but the cave was so shallow that she was unable to shelter her legs or feet. Exposed to the cold, her legs turned to blocks of wood. She was powerless to escape.

Etta drifted in and out of consciousness, but she never fell into a deep sleep. She felt mice rustling through the stack and nibbling at her wrists and somehow that comforted her. It seemed miraculous that something else was alive in the storm. When she was most alert, Etta prayed. She moved her lips and tried to summon the voice to sing hymns. She ran the words through her mind, but the sound that came from her mouth was hardly more than labored breathing. She was glad as never before that she had found God. God had brought her to the haystack; she was sure of it. God would guide the steps of a rescuer. Etta had faith. She knew she would be saved.

At some point in the night the wind died down enough for her to hear coyotes howling. That keening yelp. Or maybe it was still the wind. Etta's eyes fluttered open and the air looked a little brighter. It must be morning. Whoever had forked the prairie grass into this stack would come. Etta tried her voice to see if she could cry out for help. She could move her mouth and neck and shoulders. But her body was caught in the vise of the frozen haystack and her legs were paralyzed. The hymns and prayers would keep her going until someone came and pulled her out.

If nothing else, as long as she could sing and pray, Etta could ward off deep sleep—the sleep from which she would never rouse herself. . . .

"I have seen the Dread of Dakota. A genuine blizzard and am now ready to leave anytime, that we can sell," pioneer wife Sadie Shaw wrote to relatives back east from her Dakota homestead in Douglas County. *"Oh, it was terrible.* I have often read about Blizzards but they have to be *seen* to be fully *realized."*

The Shaws did not sell. . . . There were many such threats and much misgiving after the blizzard of 1888, but few families left—at least not right away. The weather finally moderated. Summer came and the prairie turned hot and dry. Day after day the sun sucked the moisture out of the black soil of the prairie. Grieving families got on with their lives, prayed for rain, had more children.

The blizzard of January 12, 1888, did not put an end to the great white endeavor of settling and taming the prairie, but it did mark a turning point, a change of mood and direction. The Dakota boom had ended. Immigration to the prairie frontier slowed to a trickle in the last years of the 1880s. A time of reckoning and taking stock had set in. A new mood of caution, suspicion, and bitterness took hold. "Good bye, Lord, I am going west," Arthur Towne remembered the church deacon shouting as Dakota-bound families streamed out of their Vermont village in 1881. By the close of the decade the joy was gone and the Townes were exhausted. "It did seem as if the whole James River valley was just a dumping ground for blasted hopes," Towne's mother told him wearily. "The holiday spirit of eight years before had entirely vanished," wrote Hamlin Garland of the sullen mood of the decade's end. "The stress of misfortune had not only destroyed hope, it had brought out the evil side of many men. Dissension had grown common. Two of my father's neighbors had gone insane over the failure of their crops. . . . [S]omething gray had settled down over the plain. Graveyards, jails, asylums, all the accompaniments of civilization, were now quite firmly established. . . . No green thing was in sight, and no shade offered save that made by the little cabin. On every side stretched scanty yellowing fields of grain, and from every worn road, dust rose like smoke from crevices."

The truth was beginning to sink in: The sudden storms, the violent swings from one meteorological extreme to another, the droughts and torrents and killer blizzards were not freak occurrences but facts of life on the prairie. This was not a garden. Rain did not follow the plow. Laying a perfect grid of mile-sided squares on the grassland did not suppress the chaos of the elements. The settlers had to face the facts. Living here and making a living off this land was never going to be easy.

Weather that takes lives and destroys hopes presents a moral quandary. Call it an act of God or a natural disaster, somebody or something made this storm happen. But what? . . . Were the immigrant parents themselves to blame for uprooting their families from the relatively safe enclaves of the Ukraine, Vermont, Prussia, and Norway and exposing them to the brutal cold fronts and lows that sweep down off the Canadian Rockies?

Or should one condemn an economic system that gave some families mansions on Summit Avenue and left others so poor that they would risk their children and their own lives for the sake of a single cow? They called it "The School Children's Blizzard" because so many of the victims were so young—but in a way the entire pioneer period was a kind of children's disaster. Children were the unpaid workforce of the prairie, the hands that did the work no one else had time for or stomach for. The outpouring of grief after scores of children were found frozen to death among the cattle on Friday, January 13, was at least in part an expression of remorse for what children were subjected to every day—remorse for the fact that most children had no childhood. This was a society that could not afford to sentimentalize its living and working children. Only in death or on the verge of death were their young granted the . . . long columns of sobbing verse, the stately granite monuments. A safe and carefree childhood was a luxury the pioneer prairie could not afford.

"The dark, blinding, roaring storm once experienced, ever remains an actual living presence, that has marked its pathway with ruin, desolation and death," wrote South Dakota historian Caleb Holt Ellis in 1909. "The 12th of January, 1888, is, and long will be, remembered, not only by Dakotans, but by many in the northwest, not for the things we enjoy, love, and would see repeated; but for its darkness, desolation, ruin and death, spread broadcast; for

Homesteaders, many of whom were recent immigrants, took advantage of the free land offered by the federal government and moved west in hopes of finding a better life. The family shown here poses in their Sunday best against the background of their modest sod house. Alas, many of these families saw their dreams shattered by violent storms, voracious insects, and topsoil too shallow for growing crops. As David Laskin concludes, "the land that they had desired so fervently and had traveled so far to claim wasn't free after all." (© Bettmann-CORBIS)

the sorrow, sadness and heartache that followed in its train." To this day, nearly a century after Ellis wrote these words, the storm remains "an actual living presence" in the region. Mention the date to anyone whose family experienced the storm and you'll get a story of death or narrow escape. "There are those who say that that storm was no worse than others we have had," wrote Austen Rollag fifty years later, "but those who speak thus could not have been out of the house but sitting around the stove. I have seen many snowstorms in the more than sixty years I have

been living here, but not one can compare with the storm of January 12, 1888."

The memories still burn. They burn all the fiercer because sorrow, sadness, and heartache did indeed follow in the blizzard's train. Drought ravaged the prairie in the early 1890s. Thousands who had borrowed against their homesteads went bankrupt in the financial panic that inaugurated the depression of 1893. Farm income slipped steadily in the last decades of the nineteenth century. The price of corn fell by half between the mid-1870s and the 1890s. A great exodus commenced on the prairie. By the time the rains returned late in the 1890s, over 60 percent of the pioneer families had abandoned their homesteads. Settlers came back, tried to make a go of it in the Dakotas or even farther west—and once again got burned out, frozen out, and blown away. Outmigration is on the rise once more. Nearly 70 percent of the counties in the Great Plains states have fewer people now than they did in 1950. These days nearly one million acres of the plains are so sparsely populated that they meet the condition of frontier as defined by the Census Bureau in the nineteenth century. Seven of our nation's twelve poorest counties are in Nebraska. As whites flee to cities and coasts, Native Americans and the bison that sustained them for thousands of years are returning. Indian and buffalo populations have now reached levels that the region has not seen since the 1870s. The white farmers and townspeople who remain would shun you for daring to say it, but in large stretches of prairie it's beginning to look like European agricultural settlement is a completed chapter of history. "It's time for us to acknowledge one of America's greatest mistakes," wrote Nicholas D. Kristof on the op-ed page of the *New York Times,* "a 140-year-old scheme that has failed at a cost of trillions of dollars, countless lives and immeasurable heartbreak: the settlement of the Great Plains."

The blizzard of January 12, 1888, was an early sign of that mistake. In the storm that came without warning, the pioneers learned that the land they had desired so fervently and had traveled so far to claim wasn't free after all. Who could have predicted that the bill would arrive with a sudden shift of wind in the middle of a mild January morning? A thousand storms of dust and ice and poverty and despair have come and gone since then, but this is the one they remember. After that day, the sky never looked the same.

QUESTIONS TO CONSIDER

1 Why does Laskin state that the horrible blizzard of 1888 "hit the most thickly settled sections of Nebraska and Dakota Territory at the worse possible moment"? Describe the dramatic change in temperatures that accompanied this storm. Why were the humble people of this raw region of the prairie prone to take risks, even in the face of a devastating blizzard?

2 In the post–Civil War years, what factors encouraged the stampede of settlers into America's heartland, which earlier had been thought to be a worthless desert? Compare the lifestyle of these "sodbusters" to the luxuries enjoyed by the wealthy industrial tycoons back East.

3 Compare twenty-first-century weather forecasting (satellite imagery, the technology of the Weather Channel) with that of the late nineteenth century. What advance warning did the prairie settlers have of the blizzard of 1888?

4 This selection describes many personal stories of humble people who faced tragedy with an inner courage that is both compelling and memorable. Which of these stories touched you the most and why? Try to imagine yourself as a settler caught in the killer blizzard of 1888. Imagine what you and your children would have experienced, and explain whether you would have stayed or left that violent land.

5 Describe the change in "mood and direction" caused by the blizzard of 1888 on settlers living on the prairie and people who thought about moving there. Why does Laskin conclude "that most children had no childhood" on the bleak prairies?

6 Why do some historians conclude that "the settlement of the Great Plains" was "one of America's greatest mistakes"? How has the population of that rugged region changed over the past sixty years?

PART THREE

The New Industrial Order

5 The Master of Steel: Andrew Carnegie

ROBERT L. HEILBRONER

From the 1820s on, the United States industrialized at an impressive rate. But the real boost came during the Civil War, when the United States Congress created a national currency and banking system, enacted homestead legislation, and appropriated federal aid for a transcontinental railroad. Such measures, argues historian James M. McPherson, provided "the blueprint for modern America." From the crucible of civil war emerged a new America of big business, heavy industry, and commercial farming that became by 1880 "the foremost industrial nation" in the world. The federal government played a crucial role in the postwar boom. One Republican administration after another not only maintained a protective tariff to minimize foreign competition but gave away millions of dollars' worth of public land to railroad companies, adopted a hard-money policy that pleased big business, and—except for the Interstate Commerce and Sherman Antitrust Acts, both adopted because of popular unrest—cheerfully refused to regulate or restrict the consolidation of America's new industrial order.

It was during the Gilded Age (as Mark Twain called it), an era between Robert E. Lee's surrender at Appomattox and the turn of the century, that American capitalism, growing for decades now, produced mighty combinations that controlled most of the nation's wealth. The leaders of the new industrial order comprised a complex gallery of individuals popularly known as the robber barons. There had, of course, been many rich Americans before the Gilded Age, people who made fortunes from traffic in lands and goods. But the post–Civil War robber barons were a different breed, for they controlled the essential tools of the booming industrial economy itself: railroads (the nation's basic transportation system), banking, and manufacturing. They eliminated competition, set prices, exploited workers, and commanded the awe or fear of an entire generation. Enough of them were rags-to-riches individuals, the kind celebrated in the novels of Horatio Alger, to encourage the notion of the American dream at work, a dream that in the United States all who were capable could rise to the top. Some of the tycoons were gaudy vulgarians such as one H. A. W. Tabor. Finding a portrait of Shakespeare hanging in a Denver opera house that he had built, Tabor demanded that the portrait be replaced with his own, storming, "What the hell has Shakespeare done for Denver?" Others were industrial pirates such as Jay Gould, a consumptive rascal who made his money by various nefarious means.

But other entrepreneurs fit a different pattern: like the rapacious capitalist played by Michael Douglas in the movie Wall Street, *they were obsessed with the power that wealth brought them. An example was Cornelius "Commodore" Vanderbilt, who began his career as a ferryboatman, rose to ownership of riverboats (hence his nickname), and went on to become a railroad magnate who owned a transportation empire worth $80 million and lived in splendor in a Manhattan mansion. This rowdy, profane man loved to win in any way he could, once proclaiming, "Law? What do I care about the law. H'ain't I got the power?"*

Then there was John D. Rockefeller, a quiet, penny-pinching millionaire whose Standard Oil Company became one of the nation's most powerful monopolies. Indeed, Rockefeller's business methods, stressing the virtues of order, organization, and planning, set the example of modern business organization. Unlike other Gilded Age entrepreneurs, however, Rockefeller had little interest in money for money's sake. At the end of his life, through foundations named after him, he donated millions of dollars to religious activities, medical research, and higher education.

And then there was steel magnate Andrew Carnegie, the subject of the insightful portrait that follows. Another self-made man, Carnegie was at one time the richest person in the world. Perhaps more than any other tycoon, he embodied the spirit of the age, a man who not only created but advocated and celebrated industrial power. He defended democracy, capitalism, and the Anglo-Saxon race, and he even argued that evolution produced millionaires such as he, ignoring the fact that such folk enjoyed generous government benefits, not to mention the help of federal troops serving as strikebreakers. Yet Carnegie also acted on his own self-proclaimed sense of duty: having amassed a prodigious fortune, he proceeded to give almost all of it away during his lifetime. In him, Robert L. Heilbroner sees both the failures and the integrity of Gilded Age America.

GLOSSARY

ALGER, HORATIO   Gilded Age author whose heroes rose from poverty to greatness and thus fulfilled the "American dream."

AMERICAN FEDERATION OF LABOR   Organized in 1886 with Samuel Gompers as president, the AFL was an association of trade unions whose membership consisted exclusively of skilled workers.

CARNEGIE CORPORATION OF NEW YORK   After making his fortune, Andrew Carnegie established this "first great modern" philanthropic foundation.

CARNEGIE, McCANDLESS & COMPANY   Andrew Carnegie's British-American steel company and the nucleus of his steel empire.

FRICK, HENRY   Self-made millionaire who amalgamated his coke empire and Andrew Carnegie's steelworks and assumed "the active management of the whole." Frick, Captain William Jones, and Charles Schwab constituted "the vital energy" of the Carnegie empire.

GOSPEL OF WEALTH   Andrew Carnegie's philosophy (in a book of that title) that the millionaire has a duty to distribute wealth while still alive.

JONES, CAPTAIN WILLIAM   One of a "brilliant assemblage" of men around Andrew Carnegie, "a kind of Paul Bunyan of steel," who was inventive in handling machinery and talented at dealing with people.

KNIGHTS OF LABOR   America's first major labor union, founded in 1869. By 1886, its membership numbered more than 700,000.

MORGAN, J. P.   Wealthy banker who purchased the Carnegie steel empire in 1901 for $492 million; it became the core of the United States Steel Company.

PULLMAN, GEORGE   Developed the Pullman railroad sleeping car and joined forces with Andrew Carnegie to form the Pullman Palace Car Company.

SCHWAB, CHARLES   Assistant manager of Andrew Carnegie's Braddock plant and another of the brilliant men surrounding Carnegie.

SCOTT, THOMAS A.   Superintendent of the Pennsylvania Railroad and Andrew Carnegie's boss who first encouraged him to invest in stock.

UNITED STATES STEEL COMPANY   J. P. Morgan merged the Carnegie empire with other interests to create this huge corporation, which controlled more than 60 percent of America's steel production.

WOODRUFF, T. T.   When Andrew Carnegie bought a one-eighth interest in Woodruff's company, Woodruff began production of the first sleeping car for trains.

Toward the end of his days, at the close of World War I, Andrew Carnegie was already a kind of national legend. His meteoric rise, the scandals and successes of his industrial generalship—all this was blurred into nostalgic memory. What was left was a small, rather feeble man with a white beard and pale, penetrating eyes, who could occasionally be seen puttering around his mansion on upper Fifth Avenue, a benevolent old gentleman who still rated an annual birthday interview but was even then a venerable relic of a fast-disappearing era. Carnegie himself looked back on his career with a certain savored incredulity. "How much did you say I had given away, Poynton?" he would inquire of his private secretary; "$324,657,399" was the answer. "Good Heaven!" Carnegie would exclaim. "Where did I ever get all that money?"

Where he *had* got all that money was indeed a legendary story, for even in an age known for its acquisitive triumphs, Carnegie's touch had been an extraordinary one. He had begun, in true Horatio Alger fashion, at the bottom; he had ended, in a manner that put the wildest of Alger's novels to shame, at the very pinnacle of success. At the close

of his great deal with J. P. Morgan in 1901, when the Carnegie steel empire was sold to form the core of the new United States Steel Company, the banker had extended his hand and delivered the ultimate encomium of the times: "Mr. Carnegie," he said, "I want to congratulate you on being the richest man in the world."

It was certainly as "the richest man in the world" that Carnegie attracted the attention of his contemporaries. Yet this is hardly why we look back on him with interest today. As an enormous money-maker Carnegie was a flashy, but hardly a profound, hero of the times; and the attitudes of Earnestness and Self-Assurance, so engaging in the young immigrant, become irritating when they are congealed in the millionaire. But what lifts Carnegie's life above the rut of a one-dimensional success story is an aspect of which his contemporaries were relatively unaware.

Going through his papers after his death, Carnegie's executors came across a memorandum that he had written to himself fifty years before, carefully preserved in a little yellow box of keepsakes and mementos. It brings us back to December, 1868, when Carnegie, a young man flushed with the first taste of great success, retired to his suite in the opulent Hotel St. Nicholas in New York, to total up his profits for the year. It had been a tremendous year and the calculation must have been

---

"The Master of Steel: Andrew Carnegie" by Robert L. Heilbroner. Reprinted from *American Heritage*, August 1960, pp. 4–9, 107–111, by permission of the author.

extremely pleasurable. Yet this is what he wrote as he reflected on the figures:

Thirty-three and an income of $50,000 per annum! By this time two in years I can so arrange all my business as to secure at least $50,000 per annum. Beyond this never earn—make no effort to increase fortune, but spend the surplus each year for benevolent purposes. Cast aside business forever, except for others.

Settle in Oxford and get a thorough education, making the acquaintance of literary men—this will take three years of active work—pay especial attention to speaking in public. Settle then in London and purchase a controlling interest in some newspaper or live review and give the general management of it attention, taking part in public matters, especially those connected with education and improvement of the poorer classes.

Man must have an idol—the amassing of wealth is one of the worst species of idolatry—no idol more debasing than the worship of money. Whatever I engage in I must push inordinately; therefore should I be careful to choose that life which will be the most elevating in its character. To continue much longer overwhelmed by business cares and with most of my thoughts wholly upon the way to make more money in the shortest time, must degrade me beyond hope of permanent recovery. I will resign business at thirty-five, but during the ensuing two years I wish to spend the afternoons in receiving instruction and in reading systematically.

It is a document which in more ways than one is Carnegie to the very life: brash, incredibly self-confident, chockablock with self-conscious virtue—and more than a little hypocritical. For the program so nobly outlined went largely unrealized. Instead of retiring in two years, Carnegie went on for thirty-three more; even then it was with considerable difficulty that he was persuaded to quit. Far from shunning further money-making, he proceeded to roll up his fortune with an uninhibited drive that led one unfriendly biographer to characterize him as "the greediest little gentleman ever created." Certainly he was one of the most aggressive profit seekers of his time. Typically, when an associate jubilantly cabled: "No. 8 furnace broke all records today," Carnegie coldly replied, "What were the other furnaces doing?"

It is this contrast between his hopes and his performance that makes Carnegie interesting. For when we review his life, what we see is more than the career of another nineteenth-century acquisitor. We see the unequal struggle between a man who loved money—loved making it, having it, spending it—and a man who, at bottom, was ashamed of himself for his acquisitive desires. All during his lifetime, the moneymaker seemed to win. But what lifts Carnegie's story out of the ordinary is that the other Carnegie ultimately triumphed. At his death public speculation placed the size of his estate at about five hundred million dollars. In fact it came to $22,881,575. Carnegie *had* become the richest man in the world—but something had also driven him to give away ninety per cent of his wealth.

Actually, his contemporaries knew of Carnegie's inquietude about money. In 1889, before he was world-famous, he had written an article for the *North American Review* entitled "The Gospel of Wealth"—an article that contained the startling phrase: "The man who dies thus rich dies disgraced." It was hardly surprising, however, if the world took these sentiments at a liberal discount: homiletic millionaires who preached the virtues of austerity were no novelty; Carnegie himself, returning in 1879 from a trip to the miseries of India, had been able to write with perfect sincerity, "How very little the millionaire has beyond the peasant, and how very often his additions tend not to happiness but to misery."

What the world may well have underestimated, however, was a concern more deeply rooted than these pieties revealed. For, unlike so many of his self-made peers, who also rose from poverty, Carnegie was the product of a *radical* environment. The village of Dunfermline, Scotland, when he was born there in 1835, was renowned as a center of revolutionary ferment, and Carnegie's family was itself caught up in the radical movement of the times. His father was a regular speaker at the Chartist rallies, which were an almost daily occurrence in Dunfermline in the 1840's, and his uncle was an impassioned orator for the rights of

Andrew Carnegie, in his mid-twenties when photographed here in 1861, was the son of Scottish working-class radicals and the product of a stern religious upbringing. In his younger days, he thought that the amassing of wealth was "one of the worst species of idolatry." However, he abandoned his plans to retire at thirty-five in order to devote his energies to self-improvement and benevolent enterprises. Instead, he became one of the richest men the world had ever known. (Courtesy, Carnegie Corporation of New York)

From another uncle, George Lauder, Carnegie absorbed a second passion that was also to reveal itself in his later career. This was his love of poetry, first that of the poet Burns, with its overtones of romantic egalitarianism, and then later, of Shakespeare. Immense quantities of both were not only committed to memory, but made into an integral—indeed, sometimes an embarrassingly evident—part of his life: on first visiting the Doge's palace in Venice he thrust a companion in the ducal throne and held him pinioned there while he orated the appropriate speeches from *Othello*. Once, seeing Vanderbilt walking on Fifth Avenue, Carnegie smugly remarked, "I would not exchange his millions for my knowledge of Shakespeare."

But it was more than just a love of poetry that remained with Carnegie. Virtually alone among his fellow acquisitors, he was driven by a genuine respect for the power of thought to seek answers for questions that never even occurred to them. Later, when he "discovered" Herbert Spencer, the English sociologist, Carnegie wrote to him, addressing him as "Master," and it was as "Master" that Spencer remained, even after Carnegie's lavishness had left Spencer very much in his debt.

But Carnegie's early life was shaped by currents more material than intellectual. The grinding process of industrial change had begun slowly but ineluctably to undermine the cottage weaving that was the traditional means of employment in Dunfermline. The Industrial Revolution, in the shape of new steam mills, was forcing out the hand weavers, and one by one the looms which constituted the entire capital of the Carnegie family had to be sold. Carnegie never forgot the shock of his father returning home to tell him, in despair, "Andra, I can get nae mair work."

A family council of war was held, and it was decided that there was only one possible course—they must try their luck in America, to which two sisters of Carnegie's mother, Margaret, had already emigrated. With the aid of a few friends the money for the crossing was scraped together, and at thirteen Andrew found himself transported to the only country in which his career would have been possible.

the working class to vote and strike. All this made an indelible impression on Carnegie's childhood.

"I remember as if it were yesterday," he wrote seventy years later, "being awakened during the night by a tap at the back window by men who had come to inform my parents that my uncle, Bailie Morrison, had been thrown in jail because he dared to hold a meeting which had been forbidden . . . It is not to be wondered at that, nursed amid such surroundings, I developed into a violent young Republican whose motto was 'death to privilege.'"

It hardly got off to an auspicious start, however. The family made their way to Allegheny, Pennsylvania, a raw and bustling town where Carnegie's father again sought work as an independent weaver. But it was as hopeless to compete against the great mills in America as in Scotland, and soon father and son were forced to seek work in the local cotton mills. There Andrew worked from six in the morning until six at night, making $1.20 as a bobbin boy.

After a while his father quit—factory work was impossible for the traditional small enterpriser—and Andrew got a "better" job with a new firm, tending an engine deep in a dungeon cellar and dipping newly made cotton spools in a vat of oil. Even the raise to $3 a week . . . could not overcome the horrors of that lonely and foul-smelling basement. It was perhaps the only time in Carnegie's life when his self-assurance deserted him: to the end of his days the merest whiff of oil could make him deathly sick.

Yet he was certain, as he wrote home at sixteen, that "anyone could get along in this Country," and the rags-to-riches saga shortly began. The telegraph had just come to Pittsburgh, and one evening over a game of checkers, the manager of the local office informed Andrew's uncle that he was looking for a messenger. Andy got the job and, in true Alger fashion, set out to excel in it. Within a few weeks he had carefully memorized the names and the locations, not only of the main streets in Pittsburgh, but of the main firms, so that he was the quickest of all the messenger boys.

He came early and stayed late, watched the telegraphers at work, and at home at night learned the Morse code. As a result he was soon the head of the growing messenger service, and a skilled telegrapher himself. One day he dazzled the office by taking a message "by ear" instead of by the commonly used tape printer, and since he was then only the third operator in the country able to turn the trick, citizens used to drop into the office to watch Andy take down the words "hot from the wire."

One such citizen who was especially impressed with young Carnegie's determination was Thomas A. Scott, in time to become one of the colorful railway magnates of the West, but then the local superintendent of the Pennsylvania Railroad. Soon thereafter Carnegie became "Scott's Andy"—telegrapher, secretary, and general factotum—at thirty-five dollars a month. In his *Autobiography* Carnegie recalls an instance which enabled him to begin the next stage of his career.

One morning I reached the office and found that a serious accident on the Eastern Division had delayed the express passenger train westward, and that the passenger train eastward was proceeding with a flagman in advance at every curve. The freight trains in both directions were standing on the sidings. Mr. Scott was not to be found. Finally I could not resist the temptation to plunge in, take the responsibility, give "train orders" and set matters going. "Death or Westminster Abbey" flashed across my mind. I knew it was dismissal, disgrace, perhaps criminal punishment for me if I erred. On the other hand, I could bring in the wearied freight train men who had lain out all night. I knew I could. I knew just what to do, and so I began.

Signing Scott's name to the orders, Carnegie flashed out the necessary instructions to bring order out of the tangle. The trains moved; there were no mishaps. When Scott reached the office Carnegie told him what he had done. Scott said not a word but looked carefully over all that had taken place. After a little he moved away from Carnegie's desk to his own, and that was the end of it. "But I noticed," Carnegie concluded good-humoredly, "that he came in very regularly and in good time for some mornings after that."

It is hardly to be wondered at that Carnegie became Scott's favorite, his "white-haired Scotch devil." Impetuous but not rash, full of enthusiasm and good-natured charm, the small lad with his blunt, open features and his slight Scottish burr was every executive's dream of an assistant. Soon Scott repaid Andy for his services by introducing him to a new and very different kind of opportunity. He gave Carnegie the chance to subscribe to five hundred dollars' worth of Adams Express stock, a company which Scott assured Andy would prosper mightily.

Carnegie had not fifty dollars saved, much less five hundred, but it was a chance he could ill afford to miss. He reported the offer to his mother, and that pillar of the family unhesitatingly mortgaged their home to raise the necessary money. When the first dividend check came in, with its ornate Spencerian flourishes, Carnegie had something like a revelation. "I shall remember that check as long as I live," he subsequently wrote. "It gave me the first penny of revenue from capital—something that I had not worked for with the sweat of my brow. 'Eureka!' I cried, 'Here's the goose that lays the golden eggs.'" He was right; within a few years his investment in the Adams Express Company was paying annual dividends of $1,400.

It was not long thereafter that an even more propitious chance presented itself. Carnegie was riding on the Pennsylvania line one day when he was approached by a "farmer-looking" man carrying a small green bag in his hand. The other introduced himself as T. T. Woodruff and quite frankly said that he wanted a chance to talk with someone connected with the railroad. Whereupon he opened his bag and took out a small model of the first sleeping car.

Carnegie was immediately impressed with its possibilities, and he quickly arranged for Woodruff to meet Scott. When the latter agreed to give the cars a trial, Woodruff in appreciation offered Carnegie a chance to subscribe to a one-eighth interest in the new company. A local banker agreed to lend Andy the few hundred dollars needed for the initial payment—the rest being financed from dividends. Once again Andy had made a shrewd investment: within two years the Woodruff Palace Car Company was paying him a return of more than $5,000 a year.

Investments now began to play an increasingly important role in Carnegie's career. Through his railroad contacts he came to recognize the possibilities in manufacturing the heavy equipment needed by the rapidly expanding lines, and soon he was instrumental in organizing companies to meet these needs. One of them, the Keystone Bridge Company, was the first successful manufacturer of iron railway bridges. Another, the Pittsburgh Locomotive Works,

made engines. And most important of all, an interest in a local iron works run by an irascible German named Andrew Kloman brought Carnegie into actual contact with the manufacture of iron itself.

None of these new ventures required any substantial outlay of cash. His interest in the Keystone Bridge Company, for instance, which was to earn him $15,000 in 1868, came to him "in return for services rendered in its promotion"—services which Carnegie, as a young railroad executive, was then in a highly strategic position to deliver. Similarly the interest in the Kloman works reflected no contribution on Carnegie's part except that of being the human catalyst and buffer between some highly excitable participants.

By 1865 his "side" activities had become so important that he decided to leave the Pennsylvania Railroad. He was by then superintendent, Scott having moved up to a vice presidency, but his salary of $2,400 was already vastly overshadowed by his income from various ventures. One purchase alone—the Storey farm in Pennsylvania oil country, which Carnegie and a few associates picked up for $40,000—was eventually to pay the group a million dollars in dividends in *one* year. About this time a friend dropped in on Carnegie and asked him how he was doing. "Oh, I'm rich, I'm rich!" he exclaimed.

He was indeed embarked on the road to riches, and determined, as he later wrote in his *Autobiography,* that "nothing could be allowed to interfere for a moment with my business career." Hence it comes as a surprise to note that it was at this very point that Carnegie retired to his suite to write his curiously introspective and troubled thoughts about the pursuit of wealth. But the momentum of events was to prove far too strong for these moralistic doubts. Moving his headquarters to New York to promote his various interests, he soon found himself swept along by a succession of irresistible opportunities for money-making.

One of these took place quite by chance. Carnegie was trying to sell the Woodruff sleeping car at the same time that a formidable rival named George

Pullman was also seeking to land contracts for his sleeping car, and the railroads were naturally taking advantage of the competitive situation. One summer evening in 1869 Carnegie found himself mounting the resplendent marble stairway of the St. Nicholas Hotel side by side with his competitor.

"Good evening, Mr. Pullman," said Carnegie in his ebullient manner. Pullman was barely cordial.

"How strange we should meet here," Carnegie went on, to which the other replied nothing at all.

"Mr. Pullman," said Carnegie, after an embarrassing pause, "don't you think we are making nice fools of ourselves?" At this Pullman evinced a glimmer of interest: "What do you mean?" he inquired. Carnegie quickly pointed out that competition between the two companies was helping no one but the railroads. "Well," said Pullman, "what do you suggest we do?"

"Unite!" said Carnegie. "Let's make a joint proposition to the Union Pacific, your company and mine. Why not organize a new company to do it?" "What would you call it?" asked Pullman suspiciously. "The Pullman Palace Car Company," said Carnegie and with this shrewd psychological stroke won his point. A new company was formed, and in time Carnegie became its largest stockholder.

Meanwhile, events pushed Carnegie into yet another lucrative field. To finance the proliferating railway systems of America, British capital was badly needed, and with his Scottish ancestry, his verve, and his excellent railroad connections Carnegie was the natural choice for a go-between. His brief case stuffed with bonds and prospectuses, Carnegie became a transatlantic commuter, soon developing intimate relations both with great bankers like Junius Morgan (the father of J. P. Morgan), and with the heads of most of the great American roads. These trips earned him not only large commissions—exceeding on occasion $100,000 for a single turn—but even more important, established connections that were later to be of immense value. He himself later testified candidly on their benefits before a group of respectfully awed senators:

For instance, I want a great contract for rails. Sidney Dillon of the Union Pacific was a personal friend of mine.

Huntington was a friend. Dear Butler Duncan, that called on me the other day, was a friend. Those and other men were presidents of railroads . . . Take Huntington; you know C. P. Huntington. He was hard up very often. He was a great man, but he had a great deal of paper out. I knew his things were good. When he wanted credit I gave it to him. If you help a man that way, what chance has any paid agent going to these men? It was absurd.

But his trips to England brought Carnegie something still more valuable. They gave him steel. It is fair to say that as late as 1872 Carnegie did not see the future that awaited him as the Steel King of the world. The still modest conglomeration of foundries and mills he was gradually assembling in the Allegheny and Monongahela valleys was but one of many business interests, and not one for which he envisioned any extraordinary future. Indeed, to repeated pleas that he lead the way in developing a steel industry for America by substituting steel for iron rails, his reply was succinct: "Pioneering don't pay."

What made him change his mind? The story goes that he was awe-struck by the volcanic, spectacular eruption of a Bessemer converter, which he saw for the first time during a visit to a British mill. It was precisely the sort of display that would have appealed to Carnegie's mind—a wild, demonic, physical process miraculously contained and controlled by the dwarfed figures of the steel men themselves. At any rate, overnight Carnegie became the perfervid prophet of steel. Jumping on the first available steamer, he rushed home with the cry, "The day of iron has passed!" To the consternation of his colleagues, the hitherto reluctant pioneer became an advocate of the most daring technological and business expansion; he joined them enthusiastically in forming Carnegie, McCandless & Company, which was the nucleus of the empire that the next thirty years would bring forth.

The actual process of growth involved every aspect of successful business enterprise of the times: acquisition and merger, pools and commercial piracy, and even, on one occasion, an outright fraud in selling the United States government overpriced and underdone steel armor plate. But it would be as foolish to maintain that the Carnegie empire grew by trickery as to deny that sharp practice had its place. Essentially what lay behind the spectacular expansion were three facts.

The first of these was the sheer economic expansion of the industry in the first days of burgeoning steel use. Everywhere steel replaced iron or found new uses—and not only in railroads but in ships, buildings, bridges, machinery of all sorts. As Henry Frick himself once remarked, if the Carnegie group had not filled the need for steel another would have. But it must be admitted that Carnegie's company did its job superlatively well. In 1885 Great Britain led the world in the production of steel. Fourteen years later her total output was 695,000 tons less than the output of the Carnegie Steel Company alone.

Second was the brilliant assemblage of personal talent with which Carnegie surrounded himself. Among them, three in particular stood out. One was Captain William Jones, a Homeric figure who lumbered through the glowing fires and clanging machinery of the works like a kind of Paul Bunyan of steel, skilled at handling men, inventive in handling equipment, and enough of a natural artist to produce papers for the British Iron and Steel Institute that earned him a literary as well as a technical reputation. Then there was Henry Frick, himself a self-made millionaire, whose coke empire naturally complemented Carnegie's steelworks. When the two were amalgamated, Frick took over the active management of the whole, and under his forceful hand the annual output of the Carnegie works rose tenfold. Yet another was Charles Schwab, who came out of the tiny monastic town of Loretto, Pennsylvania, to take a job as a stake driver. Six months later he had been promoted by Jones into the assistant managership of the Braddock plant.

These men, and a score like them, constituted the vital energy of the Carnegie works. As Carnegie himself said, "Take away all our money, our great works, ore mines and coke ovens, but leave our organization, and in four years I shall have re-established myself."

But the third factor in the growth of the empire was Carnegie himself. A master salesman and a skilled diplomat of business at its highest levels, Carnegie was also a ruthless driver of his men. He pitted his associates and subordinates in competition with one another until a feverish atmosphere pervaded the whole organization. "You cannot imagine the abounding sense of freedom and relief I experience as soon as I get on board a steamer and sail past Sandy Hook," he once said to Captain Jones. "My God!" replied Jones. "Think of the relief to us!"

But Carnegie could win loyalties as well. All his promising young men were given gratis ownership participations—minuscule fractions of one per cent, which were enough, however, to make them millionaires in their own right. Deeply grateful to Jones, Carnegie once offered him a similar participation. Jones hemmed and hawed and finally refused; he would be unable to work effectively with the men, he said, once he was a partner. Carnegie insisted that his contribution be recognized and asked Jones what he wanted. "Well," said the latter, "you might pay me a hell of a big salary." "We'll do it!" said Carnegie. "From this time forth you shall receive the same salary as the President of the United States." "Ah, Andy, that's the kind of talk," said Captain Bill.

Within three decades, on the flood tide of economic expansion, propelled by brilliant executive work and relentless pressure from Carnegie, the company made immense strides. "Such a magnificent aggregation of industrial power has never before been under the domination of a single man," reported a biographer in 1902, describing the Gargantuan structure of steel and coke and ore and transport. Had the writer known of the profits earned by this aggregation he might have been even more impressed: three and a half million dollars in 1889, seven million in 1897, twenty-one million in 1899, and an immense forty million in 1900. "Where is there such a business!" Carnegie had exulted, and no wonder—the majority share of all these earnings, without hindrance of income tax, went directly into his pockets.

Nevertheless, with enormous success came problems. One of these was the restiveness of certain partners, under the "Iron-Clad" agreement, which prevented any of them from selling their shares to anyone but the company itself—an arrangement which meant, of course, that the far higher valuation of an outside purchaser could not be realized. Particularly chagrined was Frick, when, as the culmination of other disagreements between them, Carnegie sought to buy him out "at the value appearing on the books." Another problem was a looming competitive struggle in the steel industry itself that presaged a period of bitter industrial warfare ahead. And last was Carnegie's own growing desire to "get out."

Already he was spending half of each year abroad, first traveling, and then, after his late marriage, in residence in the great Skibo Castle he built for his wife on Dornoch Firth, Scotland. There he ran his business enterprises with one hand while he courted the literary and creative world with the other, entertaining Kipling and Matthew Arnold, Paderewski and Lloyd George, Woodrow Wilson and Theodore Roosevelt, Gladstone, and of course, Herbert Spencer, the Master. But even his career as "Laird" of Skibo could not remove him from the worries—and triumphs—of his business: a steady flow of cables and correspondence intruded on the "serious" side of life.

It was Schwab who cut the knot. Having risen to the very summit of the Carnegie concern he was invited in December, 1900, to give a speech on the future of the steel industry at the University Club in New York. There, before eighty of the nation's top business leaders he painted a glowing picture of what could be done if a super-company of steel were formed, integrated from top to bottom, self-sufficient with regard to its raw materials, balanced in its array of final products. One of the guests was the imperious J. P. Morgan, and as the speech progressed it was noticed that his concentration grew more and more intense. After dinner Morgan rose and took the young steel man by the elbow and engaged him in private conversation for half an hour while he plied him with rapid and penetrating questions; then a few

In his late years, Carnegie turned again toward the idealism of his youth. Declaring that his riches had come to him as a "sacred trust" to administer for the good of humanity, he endowed numerous philanthropies and managed to give away 90 percent of his wealth before he died. (Carnegie Corporation of New York)

weeks later he invited him to a private meeting in the great library of his home. They talked from nine o'clock in the evening until dawn. As the sun began to stream in through the library windows, the banker finally rose. "Well," he said to Schwab, "if Andy wants to sell, I'll buy. Go and find his price."

Carnegie at first did not wish to sell. Faced with the actual prospect of a withdrawal from the business he had built into the mightiest single industrial empire in the world, he was frightened and dismayed. He sat silent before Schwab's report, brooding, loath to inquire into details. But soon his enthusiasm returned. No such opportunity was likely to present itself again. In short order a figure of $492,000,000 was agreed on for the entire enterprise, of which Carnegie himself was to receive $300,000,000 in five per cent gold bonds and preferred stock. Carnegie jotted down the terms of the transaction on a slip of paper and told Schwab to bring it to Morgan. The banker glanced only briefly at the paper. "I accept," he said.

After the formalities were in due course completed, Carnegie was in a euphoric mood. "Now, Pierpont, I am the happiest man in the world," he said. Morgan was by no means unhappy himself: his own banking company had made a direct profit of $12,500,000 in the underwriting transaction, and this was but a prelude to a stream of lucrative financings under Morgan's aegis, by which the total capitalization was rapidly raised to $1,400,000,000. A few years later, Morgan and Carnegie found themselves aboard the same steamer en route to Europe. They fell into talk and Carnegie confessed, "I made one mistake, Pierpont, when I sold out to you."

"What was that?" asked the banker.

"I should have asked you for $100,000,000 more than I did."

Morgan grinned. "Well," he said, "you would have got it if you had."

Thus was written *finis* to one stage of Carnegie's career. Now it would be seen to what extent his "radical pronouncements" were serious. For in the *Gospel of Wealth*—the famous article combined with others in book form—Carnegie had proclaimed the duty of the millionaire to administer and distribute his wealth *during his lifetime*. Though he might have "proved" his worth by his fortune, his heirs had shown no such evidence of their fitness. Carnegie bluntly concluded: "By taxing estates heavily at his death, the State marks its condemnation of the selfish millionaire's unworthy life."

Coming from the leading millionaire of the day, these had been startling sentiments. So also were his views on the "labor question" which, if patronizing, were nonetheless humane and advanced for their day. The trouble was, of course, that the sentiments were somewhat difficult to credit. As one commentator of the day remarked, "His vision of what might

be done with wealth had beauty and breadth and thus serenely overlooked the means by which wealth had been acquired."

For example, the novelist Hamlin Garland visited the steel towns from which the Carnegie millions came and bore away a description of work that was ugly, brutal, and exhausting: he contrasted the lavish care expended on the plants with the callous disregard of the pigsty homes: "the streets were horrible; the buildings poor; the sidewalks sunken and full of holes. . . . Everywhere the yellow mud of the streets lay kneaded into sticky masses through which groups of pale, lean men slouched in faded garments. . . ." When the famous Homestead strike erupted in 1892, with its private army of Pinkerton detectives virtually at war with the workers, the Carnegie benevolence seemed revealed as shabby fakery. At Skibo Carnegie stood firmly behind the company's iron determination to break the strike. As a result, public sentiment swung sharply and suddenly against him; the St. Louis *Post-Dispatch* wrote: "Three months ago Andrew Carnegie was a man to be envied. Today he is an object of mingled pity and contempt. In the estimation of nine-tenths of the thinking people on both sides of the ocean he has . . . confessed himself a moral coward."

In an important sense the newspaper was right. For though Carnegie continued to fight against "privilege," he saw privilege only in its fading aristocratic vestments and not in the new hierarchies of wealth and power to which he himself belonged. In Skibo Castle he now played the role of the benign autocrat, awakening to the skirling of his private bagpiper and proceeding to breakfast to the sonorous accompaniment of the castle organ.

Meanwhile there had also come fame and honors in which Carnegie wallowed unashamedly. He counted the "freedoms" bestowed on him by grateful or hopeful cities and crowed, "I have fifty-two and Gladstone has only seventeen." He entertained the King of England and told him that democracy was better than monarchy, and met the German Kaiser: "Oh, yes, yes," said the latter worthy on being introduced. "I have read your books. You do not like kings." But Mark Twain, on hearing of this, was not fooled. "He says he is a scorner of kings and emperors and dukes," he wrote, "whereas he is like the rest of the human race: a slight attention from one of these can make him drunk for a week. . . ."

And yet it is not enough to conclude that Carnegie was in fact a smaller man than he conceived himself. For this judgment overlooks one immense and irrefutable fact. He did, in the end, abide by his self-imposed duty. He did give nearly all of his gigantic fortune away.

As one would suspect, the quality of the philanthropy reflected the man himself. There was, for example, a huge and sentimentally administered private pension fund to which access was to be had on the most trivial as well as the most worthy grounds: if it included a number of writers, statesmen, scientists, it also made room for two maiden ladies with whom Carnegie had once danced as a young man, a boyhood acquaintance who had once held Carnegie's books while he ran a race, a merchant to whom he had once delivered a telegram and who had subsequently fallen on hard times. And then, as one would expect, there was a benevolent autocracy in the administration of the larger philanthropies as well. "Now everybody vote Aye," was the way Carnegie typically determined the policies of the philanthropic "foundations" he established.

Yet if these flaws bore the stamp of one side of Carnegie's personality, there was also the other side—the side that, however crudely, asked important questions and however piously, concerned itself with great ideals. Of this the range and purpose of the main philanthropies gave unimpeachable testimony. There were the famous libraries—three thousand of them costing nearly sixty million dollars; there were the Carnegie institutes in Pittsburgh and Washington, Carnegie Hall in New York, the Hague Peace Palace, the Carnegie Endowment for International Peace, and the precedent-making Carnegie Corporation of New York, with its original enormous endowment of $125,000,000. In his instructions to the trustees of this first great modern foundation, couched in the simplified spelling of which he was an ardent advocate, we see Carnegie at his very best:

Conditions on erth [sic] inevitably change; hence, no wise man will bind Trustees forever to certain paths, causes, or institutions. I disclaim any intention of doing so . . . My chief happiness, as I write these lines lies in the thot [sic] that, even after I pass away, the welth [sic] that came to me to administer as a sacred trust for the good of my fellow men is to continue to benefit humanity . . .

If these sentiments move us—if Carnegie himself in retrospect moves us at last to grudging respect—it is not because his was the triumph of a saint or a philosopher. It is because it was the much more difficult triumph of a very human and fallible man struggling to retain his convictions in an age, and in the face of a career, which subjected them to impossible temptations. Carnegie is something of America writ large; his is the story of the Horatio Alger hero *after* he has made his million dollars. In the failures of Andrew Carnegie we see many of the failures of America itself. In his curious triumph, we see what we hope is our own steadfast core of integrity.

QUESTIONS TO CONSIDER

1 Robert L. Heilbroner suggests that Andrew Carnegie was interesting because of the contrasts in his character: the conflict between his Calvinist simplicity and his overpowering urge to accumulate wealth. What are the sources of Carnegie's contradictory character?

2 Describe Carnegie's personal "gospel of wealth." Did he live up to his own ideals? Why do you think he was attracted to the teachings of his "master," evolutionist Herbert Spencer?

3 All his life, Carnegie insisted upon his hatred of aristocratic privilege, yet he lived a life of magnificence in his Scottish castle, and he courted the acquaintance of famous politicians, scholars, and royal personages. How did he justify his actions? Did he

see himself as a different sort of aristocrat? Why did he go back to Britain to live?

4 Carnegie left a rich legacy of philanthropies, most notably the vast network of libraries that has developed into our present public library system. How was the money to fund these philanthropies obtained in the first place? Why do you think Carnegie—and many others—failed to see the contrast between the good money could do and the way it was made? How might wealthy people in the Gilded Age have viewed the lives of the working poor?

5 How does what Heilbroner calls the "failure" of Andrew Carnegie reflect the failure of America in the Gilded Age? What were the social and economic consequences of the *Gospel of Wealth* and of huge concentrations of capital in late nineteenth-century America?

6 The Brooklyn Bridge: A Monument to American Ingenuity and Daring

DAVID McCULLOUGH

Imagine the wide-eyed wonder of European immigrants, approaching New York City by ship, when they first glimpsed the towering Brooklyn Bridge across the East River. As David McCullough says in the following selection: "Its enormous granite towers loomed higher than anything anyone had ever seen, higher than the topgallant sails of the square-riggers coursing the river, higher than any building in New York, or any structure then on the North American continent."

This marvelous technological achievement was not only "the proudest symbol of America's greatest city," but also "much that is best about America." The late nineteenth century had produced many wonders, such as Thomas Edison's phonograph, George Eastman's Kodak camera, and Alexander Graham Bell's telephone. But nothing symbolized America's technological genius more than the enormous suspension bridge that stretched a mile across New York's East River. The bridge was all the more remarkable because it was free of the corruption, exploitation, and unfair business practices most often associated with the Gilded Age.

The story of the Brooklyn Bridge is also a tale of familial love and dedication. John A. Roebling, who had perfected the suspension bridge, designed the structure but died of "a freak accident" while surveying the Brooklyn shore. His son, Washington Roebling, a Civil War veteran on the Union side, took over his father's work, and it was this indomitable man and his persevering wife, Emily Warren Roebling, who saw the bridge through to its completion in 1883. The building of this magnificent structure involved more than steel and granite; it is a testament to a family's love and dedication to a common goal.

On another level, McCullough's portrait of the bridge and its builders represents urban history at its best. The labor force was remarkably diverse, including "men of every color and kind, from every corner of the globe." There were blacks up from the South, farm boys in from the countryside, and immigrants from across the sea. Such folk helped make New York the largest, most diverse, and most vibrant city in America.

In sum, the Brooklyn Bridge was a tremendous technological achievement, a family story, and a symbol of America's changing urban landscape. As you read the trilogy of essays in this section of Portrait of America, *think about how they are interrelated. It was the powerful steel industry of Andrew Carnegie, the subject of the previous selection, that furnished the steel for the bridge's cables. And it was the immigrants, treated in selection 7, who provided part of the manpower that built this American phenomenon.*

GLOSSARY

BATTLE OF THE LITTLE BIGHORN (JUNE 25, 1876)   See *Little Bighorn* in glossary in selection 3.

BENDS   A disease that results in extreme pain to the extremities, abdomen, and chest. Washington Roebling had made repeated dives into the strong currents of the East River to inspect the foundation of the bridge. He suffered the bends, caused by leaving the compressed air of deep water too quickly.

ROEBLING, EMILY WARREN   Washington's young wife, who helped supervise the construction of the Brooklyn Bridge after her husband was stricken with the bends. "In little time, she was conversant with every detail and became Washington's most valuable and trusted aide."

ROEBLING, JOHN A.   Builder who left Germany in the 1830s to make his fortune in America. His suspension bridges in Niagara, Pittsburgh, and Cincinnati were already completed when he started his project for a mammoth structure across New York's East River. He died of tetanus before finishing "his crowning work, his masterpiece."

ROEBLING, WASHINGTON   John's son and a Civil War hero. His dedication to completing the Brooklyn Bridge was partly motivated by his desire to build a monument to his father.

SCHUYLER, MONTGOMERY   The architectural critic who praised the Brooklyn Bridge as the most "durable monument" of its age—more important than a shrine, a fortress, or a palace.

TWEED RING   Corrupt political bosses were in control of many of the large cities in the late nineteenth century, but few were more powerful than William Marcy Tweed, who ran New York City at the time that the Brooklyn Bridge was being constructed. The three-hundred-pound Tweed and his Tammany Hall henchmen used graft to rob city treasuries of untold millions.

There is something particularly appealing about a bridge, almost any bridge, but the Brooklyn Bridge surpasses all.

In its day, it was the biggest, most famous bridge in the world, the most beautiful of suspension bridges, and the most dramatic testament yet to American technical ingenuity and daring. More than a mile long, it spanned New York's East River with "one great leap," as was said. Its enormous granite towers loomed higher than anything anyone had ever seen, higher than the topgallant sails of the square-riggers coursing the river, higher than any building in New York, or any structure then on the North American continent.

"You see great ships passing beneath it," wrote a visitor from abroad "and you will feel that the engineer is the great artist of our epoch and you will own that these people have a right to plume themselves on their audacity."

It was the thing everyone from the hinterlands was told not to miss seeing ("If ever you get to New York"), and the first New World spectacle beheld by tens of millions of immigrants as their inbound ships came up the harbor. As nothing else ever had, the bridge indicated that there was no place like New York, no place like America in the wondrous nineteenth century.

The heroic story of its construction is well known. Its position in American life is unrivaled, and as remarkable as anything about this infinitely unprecedented structure is that it has never lost that position. It remains not only the proudest symbol of America's greatest city and a thrilling work of architecture, but an enduring symbol of much that is best about America. And this, it happens, was just as its designer, the brilliant John A. Roebling, had promised from the start with characteristic immodesty.

If built according to his plans, he said, the bridge would stand down the ages as a stunning example of engineering and a great work of art.

That the bridge rose out of the Gilded Age, with its rampaging corruption, its infamous Tweed Ring and the Grant administration, the very heyday of

The Brooklyn Bridge was one of the most majestic and daring technological achievements of its age. In this 1912 photograph, New Yorkers enjoy the boardwalk, where they could escape "up and out and over the river, higher than they had ever been, to take in the spectacular panorama and breathe air fresh from the sea." (© The New York Times)

shoddy in nearly everything, makes the promise and its fulfillment all the more outstanding.

Himself an immigrant, Roebling had left Germany in the 1830s to find his destiny "in all that space" of America, and on arriving, he had taken the multitude of projects he saw under construction—highways, railways, canals—as the natural expression of an enlightened, self-governing people. It was John A. Roebling who perfected the suspension form, with bridges at Niagara, Pittsburgh, and Cincinnati. The bridge over the East River was to have been his crowning work, his masterpiece, but he died of tetanus in 1869, after a freak accident while making the initial surveys on the Brooklyn shore.

Only his son, Col. Washington Roebling, a Civil War hero, was qualified to take up the work in his place, and if dedication, high intelligence, decisiveness, and extraordinary courage are qualities to be especially admired, he was the most admirable of men. He carried on in the face of trials and setbacks never foreseen by his father, and with the ever-present knowledge that if the bridge succeeded, it would be his father's triumph, while should it fail, it would be his failure.

Washington Roebling had a gift for being always where he was needed, no matter the danger. In the crucial first stages, he was in and out of the great caisson foundation beneath Brooklyn tower, down below the river more often than anyone, to the point where he was stricken by the "bends," the dreaded caisson disease. The pain was excruciating and caused, as no one yet understood, by coming out of compressed air too rapidly.

As a result, he spent the better part of fourteen years in confinement, watching over the work with a telescope from a window in his house in Brooklyn Heights. To see that his orders were carried out, and to appraise progress on the bridge for him first hand, his wife, Emily Warren Roebling, went back and forth to the site several times daily. It was she who dealt with the press and the trustees of the project. In little time, she was conversant with every detail and became Washington's most valuable and trusted aide.

Nearly all of the work was exceedingly dangerous. How many others were eventually felled by the bends, how many were killed or maimed in building the towers or stringing the steel cables is not known—it is a measure of the time that nobody bothered to keep such records. But the cost in suffering and loss of life was considerable. Probably twenty-five or more were killed before the work ended.

The labor force was the epitome of "diversity," as we would say. Men of every color and kind, from every corner of the globe would later boast that they helped build the Brooklyn Bridge—New England farm boys new to the city, African Americans up from Maryland and Virginia, Irish and Italian immigrants in droves, English, Welsh, Swedes, Germans. Sailors proved particularly adept at the high-wire work.

Further, it was an enterprise led by youth, as suited a project that in concept and detail was virtually all pioneering and where physical stamina and creative energy counted for more than experience. Roebling, the only one who knew from experience how his father's bridges were built, was all of thirty-two when he took charge as chief engineer. The average age of the assistant engineers was thirty-one. Emily Roebling was twenty-six.

Because Roebling was never seen, rumors spread that he had lost his mind, and that if truth be known, this greatest, most daring of projects was in the hands of a woman.

The towers were completed the summer of 1876, the summer of the Centennial and the Battle of the Little Big Horn. The "spinning" of the cables commenced at once.

When the long span over the river was far enough finished for the first horse and carriage to cross, it was Emily Roebling who rode in it, carrying a rooster, as a symbol of victory, while from the rigging overhead

the men waved their hats and cheered. If ever I could go back in time to witness an event, it would be this.

Construction ended, the bridge was opened on May 24, 1883. It had taken fourteen years. The fireworks in celebration that night were the most spectacular ever seen.

On reflection, some saw this clearly as an achievement of far-reaching importance. "It so happens," wrote the architectural critic Montgomery Schuyler, "that the work which is likely to be our most durable monument, and to convey some knowledge of us to the most remote posterity, is a work of bare utility; not a shrine, not a fortress, not a palace, but a bridge."

Like other ambitious projects then under way in New York, such as the Metropolitan Museum and Central Park, the bridge was an emphatic commitment to the ideal of the city, intended as a grand-scale enhancement to city life.

On Sundays and holidays, people could escape from the narrow, congested streets of the city to walk the bridge, to go up and out over the river, higher than they had ever been, to take in the spectacular panorama and breathe air fresh from the sea. Thousands came, year in, year out, to stroll the famous pedestrian promenade, a boardwalk unlike any to be found on any bridge ever built. By design, it was placed above the vehicular traffic so as not to impede the view, the Roeblings being what might be called civilized civil engineers.

Initially, the bridge had been launched by Brooklyn people who saw that Manhattan was running out of space in which to expand. If a connection could be made, they thought, then surely the overflow would come Brooklyn's way. No one had yet imagined that a city might grow upward instead of out.

As it happened, it was the bridge itself, with its immense scale and use of steel, that marked the start of high-rise New York. Steel for girders and steel rope or cable for elevators would make possible the skyscraper and the vertical city of the twentieth century.

Though dwarfed by modern New York, and by the colossal Verrazano Bridge down the harbor, the Roebling masterpiece is still an American treasure beyond compare, beloved in a way nothing else built in America has ever been. Its towers are still the loftiest towers of stone to be seen. (The towers of the larger suspension bridges built since are of steel.) It is still acclaimed by architectural critics and figures time and again in movies, advertisements, and television commercials. Photographers find it irresistible. It is photographed, without cease, from every angle in all seasons, in every kind of light.

It remains a reminder of other days, yet serves still as an indispensable main artery. Trucks and automobiles, as unimaginable to the builders as were skyscrapers, stream across in both directions twenty-four hours a day.

And on good days, the crowds still come to walk the promenade and experience the thrill of the view, the same lift of spirits felt by so many for more than a century. It remains what it was, the greatest of bridges, the Brooklyn Bridge, made in America, its appeal defying time, a symbol now no less than ever of brave work nobly done.

QUESTIONS TO CONSIDER

1 Of all of the great technological achievements of the late nineteenth century, what made the Brooklyn Bridge the symbol of American accomplishment? As McCullough observes, the awe-inspiring structure convinced those who first viewed it to believe that "there was no place like New York."

2 In what sense was building the Brooklyn Bridge largely a product of a family's devotion to each other? What were the separate roles played by John, Washington, and Emily Warren Roebling?

3 Describe the ethnic and racial backgrounds of the young labor force that built the Brooklyn Bridge. Why does McCullough conclude that the giant steel and granite structure represented America's diversity?

4 Why was the Brooklyn Bridge "a grand-scale enhancement to city life"? How did average New Yorkers use it on Sundays and holidays to experience something they had never seen or felt before?

5 Reflecting on selection 5 on Andrew Carnegie, explain why the modern American city of the late nineteenth century could never have developed without the steel industry. Besides the Brooklyn Bridge, in what other ways did steel change the New York landscape?

6 Why does McCullough conclude that the Brooklyn Bridge is "a symbol now no less than ever of brave work nobly done"?

7 A Little Milk, a Little Honey

DAVID BOROFF

The Gilded Age witnessed an enormous surge of immigration from Europe, as the romantic lure of America seemed to draw more people than ever. For Europeans, as one historian has noted, "America was rich, America was good, America was hope, America was the future." They came over by the millions, crowding into American cities and swelling the bottom ranks of American labor. Between 1850 and 1910, some 22,800,000 immigrants arrived in the United States, more than three-fourths of them after 1881. There was also a significant shift in the source of immigration. The "old" immigrants were from western and northern Europe—Britain, Ireland, Germany, and the Scandinavian countries. But in the 1890s, most immigrants were from eastern and southern Europe—Russia, Serbia, Austria-Hungary, and Italy—and most were Jewish or Catholic. When these people arrived in America's northeastern cities, they invariably antagonized native-born Protestants, who unfairly blamed them for America's growing urban problems.

The major gateway of the new immigration was New York City, where the population swelled from 1.5 million in 1870 to a spectacular 5 million by 1915. The constant stream of new arrivals made New York the largest and most ethnically diverse city in America. In fact, by 1900, more than three-fourths of New York's citizenry was foreign born. Among them were several hundred thousand eastern European Jews, most of whom settled in the crowded and tumultuous Lower East Side, where they lived in conditions that contrasted sharply with the dream of America that had brought them here.

David Boroff provides a vivid picture of the Jewish immigrants, who first began arriving in New Amsterdam (later New York) in 1654. His focus, however, is on the period after 1880, when Jewish immigration was, as he puts it, "in flood tide." Boroff's lively narrative not only captures the immigrant experience but points out the influence of the Jewish immigrants on the United States and America's influence on them.

In significant ways, the Jewish immigrant experience mirrored that of other ethnic groups newly arrived in America. Italians, Poles, Slovaks, Greeks, and Irish also congregated in "immigrant ghettos" in which they tended to recreate the features of the Old World societies they had left behind. While the ghetto had its bleak side, it nevertheless afforded ethnic groups "a sense of belonging," of "cultural cohesiveness" that assuaged the pain of leaving their homelands and starting over in a strange, often overwhelming new land.

GLOSSARY

AUSWANDERERHALLEN   Emigrant buildings in Hamburg.

CANTOR   In a synagogue's religious service, this officer performs the liturgy and sings or chants the prayers.

CASTLE GARDEN   The huge building, situated at the foot of Manhattan, where immigrants were cleaned and interrogated after their arrival.

CHEDERS   Hebrew schools.

COFFEE HOUSE   The most popular cultural institution in the Jewish ghetto.

GEHENNA   Hell.

GENTILE   People who are not Jewish.

GREENHORN, OR GREENER   Pejorative term for newly arrived immigrants.

JEWISH DAILY FORWARD   Socialistic Yiddish newspaper, edited by Abraham Cahan.

LANDSLEIT   Jewish term for fellow townsmen.

MAX HOCHSTIM ASSOCIATION   Energetically recruited girls to work as prostitutes.

NEW YORK INDEPENDENT BENEVOLENT ASSOCIATION   An organization of pimps.

ORTHODOX JEW   One who adheres faithfully to traditional Judaism, who is devoted to the study of the Torah, attends synagogue daily, and takes care to observe the Sabbath, Jewish holy days, dietary laws, and religious festivals.

"PIG MARKET"   Functioned as the labor exchange on the Lower East Side.

POGROM   Organized massacre of Jews.

SHTETL   Typical small Jewish town in Europe.

WHITE PLAGUE   Immigrants' term for tuberculosis.

YIDDISH   The Hebrew-German dialect and the main vehicle for a Jewish cultural renaissance between 1890 and World War I.

ZHID   Yiddish word for "leave."

It started with a trickle and ended in a flood. The first to come were twenty-three Jews from Brazil who landed in New Amsterdam in 1654, in flight from a country no longer hospitable to them. They were, in origin, Spanish and Portuguese Jews (many with grandiloquent Iberian names) whose families had been wandering for a century and a half. New Amsterdam provided a chilly reception. Governor Peter Stuyvesant at first asked them to leave, but kinder hearts in the Dutch West India Company granted them the right to stay, "provided the poor among them . . . be supported by their own nation." By the end of the century, there were perhaps one hundred Jews; by the middle of the eighteenth century, there were about three hundred in New York, and smaller communities in Newport, Philadelphia, and Charleston.

Because of their literacy, zeal, and overseas connections, colonial Jews prospered as merchants, though there were artisans and laborers among them. The Jewish community was tightly knit, but there was a serious shortage of trained religious functionaries. There wasn't a single American rabbi, for example, until the nineteenth century. Jews were well regarded, particularly in New England. Puritan culture leaned heavily on the Old Testament, and Harvard students learned Hebrew; indeed, during the American Revolution, the suggestion was advanced that Hebrew replace English as the official language of the new country. The absence of an established national religion made it possible for Judaism to be regarded as merely another religion in a pluralistic society. The early days of the new republic were thus a happy time for Jews. Prosperous and productive, they were admitted to American communal life with few restrictions. It is little wonder that a Jewish spokesman asked rhetorically in 1820: "On what spot in this habitable Globe does an Israelite enjoy more blessings, more privileges?"

From David Boroff, "A Little Milk, a Little Honey," *American Heritage,* October/November 1966, Vol. 17, No. 6. Reprinted by permission of American Heritage, Inc. Copyright © Forbes, Inc., 1966.

The second wave of immigration during the nineteenth century is often described as German, but that is misleading. Actually, there were many East European Jews among the immigrants who came in the half century before 1870. However, the German influence was strong, and there was a powerful undercurrent of Western enlightenment at work. These Jews came because economic depression and the Industrial Revolution had made their lot as artisans and small merchants intolerable. For some there was also the threatening backwash of the failure of the Revolution of 1848. Moreover, in Germany at this time Jews were largely disfranchised and discriminated against. During this period, between 200,000 and 400,000 Jews emigrated to this country, and the Jewish population had risen to about half a million by 1870.

This was the colorful era of the peddler and his pack. Peddling was an easy way to get started—it required little capital—and it often rewarded enterprise and daring. Jewish peddlers fanned out through the young country into farmland and mining camp, frontier and Indian territory. The more successful peddlers ultimately settled in one place as storekeepers. (Some proud businesses . . . made their start this way.) Feeling somewhat alienated from the older, settled Jews, who had a reputation for declining piety, the new immigrants organized their own synagogues and community facilities, such as cemeteries and hospitals. In general, these immigrants were amiably received by native Americans, who, unsophisticated about differences that were crucial to the immigrants themselves, regarded all Central Europeans as "Germans."

Essentially, the emigration route was the same between 1820 and 1870 as it would be in the post-1880 exodus. The travellers stayed in emigration inns while awaiting their ship, and since they had all their resources with them, they were in danger of being robbed. The journey itself was hazardous and, in the days of the sailing vessels when a good wind was indispensable, almost interminable. Nor were the appointments very comfortable even for the relatively well to do. A German Jew who made the journey in

1856 reported that his cabin, little more than six feet by six feet, housed six passengers in triple-decker bunks. When a storm raged, the passengers had to retire to their cabins lest they be washed off the deck by waves. "Deprived of air," he wrote, "it soon became unbearable in the cabins in which six sea-sick persons breathed." On this particular journey, sea water began to trickle into the cabins, and the planks had to be retarred.

Still, the emigration experience was a good deal easier than it would be later. For one thing, the immigrants were better educated and better acquainted with modern political and social attitudes than the oppressed and bewildered East European multitudes who came after 1880. Fewer in number, they were treated courteously by ships' captains. (On a journey in 1839, described by David Mayer, the ship's captain turned over his own cabin to the Jewish passengers for their prayers and regularly visited those Jews who were ill.) Moreover, there was still the bloom of adventure about the overseas voyage. Ships left Europe amid the booming of cannon, while on shore ladies enthusiastically waved their handkerchiefs. On the way over, there was a holiday atmosphere despite the hazards, and there was great jubilation when land was sighted.

There were, however, rude shocks when the voyagers arrived in this country. The anguish of Castle Garden and Ellis Island was well in the future when immigration first began to swell. But New York seemed inhospitable, its pace frantic, the outlook not entirely hopeful. Isaac M. Wise, a distinguished rabbi who made the journey in 1846, was appalled. "The whole city appeared to me like a large shop," he wrote, "where everyone buys or sells, cheats or is cheated. I had never before seen a city so bare of all art and of every trace of good taste; likewise I had never witnessed anywhere such rushing, hurrying, chasing, running. . . . Everything seemed so pitifully small and paltry; and I had had so exalted an idea of the land of freedom." Moreover, he no sooner landed in New York than he was abused by a German drayman whose services he had declined. "Aha! thought I," he later wrote, "you have left home and kindred in order to get away from the disgusting Judaeo-phobia and here the first German greeting that sounds in your ears is hep! hep!" (The expletive was a Central European equivalent of "Kike.") Another German Jew who worked as a clothing salesman was affronted by the way customers were to be "lured" into buying ("I did not think this occupation corresponded in any way to my views of a merchant's dignity").

After 1880, Jewish immigration into the United States was in flood tide. And the source was principally East Europe, where by 1880 three-quarters of the world's 7.7 million Jews were living. In all, over two million Jews came to these shores in little more than three decades—about one-third of Europe's Jewry. Some of them came, as their predecessors had come, because of shrinking economic opportunities. In Russia and in the Austro-Hungarian empire, the growth of large-scale agriculture squeezed out Jewish middlemen as it destroyed the independent peasantry, while in the cities the development of manufacturing reduced the need for Jewish artisans. Vast numbers of Jews became petty tradesmen or even *luftmenschen* (men without visible means of support who drifted from one thing to another). In Galicia, around 1900, there was a Jewish trader for every ten peasants, and the average value of his stock came to only twenty dollars.

Savage discrimination and pogroms also incited Jews to emigrate. The Barefoot Brigades—bands of marauding Russian peasants—brought devastation and bloodshed to Jewish towns and cities. On a higher social level, there was the "cold pogrom," a government policy calculated to destroy Jewish life. The official hope was that one third of Russia's Jews would die out, one third would emigrate, and one third would be converted to the Orthodox Church. Crushing restrictions were imposed. Jews were required to live within the Pale of Settlement in western Russia, they could not Russify their names, and they were subjected to rigorous quotas for schooling and professional training. Nor could general studies be included in the curriculum of Jewish religious schools. It was a life of poverty and fear.

Nevertheless, the *shtetl,* the typical small Jewish town, was a triumph of endurance and spiritual integrity. It was a place where degradation and squalor could not wipe out dignity, where learning flourished in the face of hopelessness, and where a tough, sardonic humor provided catharsis for the tribulations of an existence that was barely endurable. The abrasions and humiliations of everyday life were healed by a rich heritage of custom and ceremony. And there was always Sabbath—"The Bride of the Sabbath," as the Jews called the day of rest—to bring repose and exaltation to a life always sorely tried.

To be sure, even this world showed signs of disintegration. Secular learning, long resisted by East European Jews and officially denied to them, began to make inroads. Piety gave way to revolutionary fervor, and Jews began to play a heroic role in Czarist Russia's bloody history of insurrection and suppression.

This was the bleak, airless milieu from which the emigrants came. A typical expression of the Jewish attitude towards emigration from Russia—both its hopefulness and the absence of remorse—was provided by Dr. George Price, who had come to this country in one of the waves of East European emigration:

Should this Jewish emigrant regret his leave-taking of his native land which fails to appreciate him? No! A thousand times no! He must not regret fleeing the clutches of the blood-thirsty crocodile. Sympathy for this country? How ironical it sounds! Am I not despised? Am I not urged to leave? Do I not hear the word *Zhid* constantly? . . . Be thou cursed forever my wicked homeland, because you remind me of the Inquisition. . . . May you rue the day when you exiled the people who worked for your welfare.

After 1880, going to America—no other country really lured—became the great drama of redemption for the masses of East European Jews. (For some, of course, Palestine had that role even in the late nineteenth century, but these were an undaunted Zionist cadre prepared to endure the severest hardships.) The assassination of Czar Alexander II in 1881, and the subsequent pogrom, marked the beginning of the new influx. By the end of the century, 700,000

Jews had arrived, about one quarter of them totally illiterate, almost all of them impoverished. Throughout East Europe, Jews talked longingly about America as the "goldene medinah" (the golden province), and biblical imagery—"the land of milk and honey"—came easily to their lips. Those who could write were kept busy composing letters to distant kin—or even to husbands—in America. (Much of the time, the husband went first, and by abstemious living saved enough to fetch wife and children from the old country.) Children played at "emigrating games," and for the entire *shtetl* it was an exciting moment when the mail-carrier announced how many letters had arrived from America.

German steamship companies assiduously advertised the glories of the new land and provided a one-price rate from *shtetl* to New York. Emigration inns were established in Brody (in the Ukraine) and in the port cities of Bremen and Hamburg, where emigrants would gather for the trip. There were rumors that groups of prosperous German Jews would underwrite their migration to America; and in fact such people often did help their co-religionists when they were stranded without funds in the port cities of Germany. Within Russia itself, the government after 1880 more or less acquiesced in the emigration of Jews, and connived in the vast business of "stealing the border" (smuggling emigrants across). After 1892, emigration was legal—except for those of draft age—but large numbers left with forged papers, because that proved to be far easier than getting tangled in the red tape of the Tzarist bureaucracy. Forged documents, to be sure, were expensive—they cost twenty-five rubles, for many Jews the equivalent of five weeks' wages. Nor was the departure from home entirely a happy event. There were the uncertainties of the new life, the fear that in America "one became a gentile." Given the Jewish aptitude for lugubriousness, a family's departure was often like a funeral, lachrymose and anguished, with the neighbors carting off the furniture that would no longer be needed.

For people who had rarely ventured beyond the boundaries of their own village, going to America was an epic adventure. They travelled with pitifully little money; the average immigrant arrived in New York with only about twenty dollars. With their domestic impedimenta—bedding, brass candlesticks, samovars—they would proceed to the port cities by rail, cart, and even on foot. At the emigration inns, they had to wait their turn. Thousands milled around, entreating officials for departure cards. There were scenes of near chaos—mothers shrieking, children crying; battered wicker trunks, bedding, utensils in wild disarray. At Hamburg, arriving emigrants were put in the "unclean" section of the *Auswandererhallen* until examined by physicians who decided whether their clothing and baggage had to be disinfected. After examination, Jews could not leave the center; other emigrants could.

The ocean voyage provided little respite. (Some elected to sail by way of Liverpool at a reduction of nine dollars from the usual rate of thirty-four dollars.) Immigrants long remembered the "smell of ship," a distillation of many putrescences. Those who went in steerage slept on mattresses filled with straw and kept their clothes on to keep warm. The berth itself was generally six feet long, two feet wide, and two and a half feet high, and it had to accommodate the passenger's luggage. Food was another problem. Many Orthodox Jews subsisted on herring, black bread, and tea which they brought because they did not trust the dietary purity of the ship's food. Some ships actually maintained a separate galley for kosher food, which was coveted by non-Jewish passengers because it was allegedly better.

Unsophisticated about travel and faced by genuine dangers, Jewish emigrants found the overseas trip a long and terrifying experience. But when land was finally sighted, the passengers often began to cheer and shout. "I looked up at the sky," an immigrant wrote years later. "It seemed much bluer and the sun much brighter than in the old country. It reminded me on [sic] the Garden of Eden."

Unhappily, the friendly reception that most immigrants envisioned in the new land rarely materialized. Castle Garden in the Battery, at the foot of Manhattan—and later Ellis Island in New York Harbor—proved to be almost as traumatic as the journey itself. "Castle Garden," an immigrant wrote, "is a large building, a Gehenna, through which all Jewish arrivals must pass to be cleansed before they are considered worthy of breathing freely the air of the land of the almighty dollar. . . . If in Brody, thousands crowded about, here tens of thousands thronged about; if there they were starving, here they were dying; if there they were crushed, here they were simply beaten."

One must make allowances for the impassioned hyperbole of the suffering immigrant, but there is little doubt that the immigration officials were harassed, overworked, and often unsympathetic. Authorized to pass on the admissibility of the newcomers, immigration officers struck terror into their hearts by asking questions designed to reveal their literacy and social attitudes. "How much is six times six?" an inspector asked a woman in the grip of nervousness, then casually asked the next man, "Have you ever been in jail?"

There were, of course, representatives of Jewish defense groups present, especially from the Hebrew Immigrant Aid Society. But by this time, the immigrants, out of patience and exhausted, tended to view them somewhat balefully. The Jewish officials tended to be highhanded, and the temporary barracks which they administered on Ward's Island for those not yet settled soon became notorious. Discontent culminated in a riot over food; one day the director—called The Father—had to swim ashore for his life, and the police were hastily summoned.

Most immigrants went directly from Castle Garden or Ellis Island to the teeming streets of Manhattan, where they sought relatives or *landsleit* (fellow townsmen) who had gone before them. Easy marks for hucksters and swindlers, they were overcharged by draymen for carrying their paltry possessions, engaged as strikebreakers, or hired at shamelessly low wages.

"Greenhorn" or "greener" was their common name. A term of vilification, the source of a thousand cruel jokes, it was their shame and their destiny. On top of everything else, the immigrants had to abide

Dated 1900, this photograph shows Hester Street in New York's Lower East Side at the peak of Jewish immigration from Eastern Europe. The Jewish neighborhoods were characterized by an integration of domestic life and commercial activity. One avenue of economic activity for these immigrants was the pushcart, which could be rented at low rates. Crowded and impoverished as it was, *the Lower East Side teemed with cultural vitality. It was, as author David Boroff puts it, "a vibrant community, full of color and gusto, in which the Jewish immigrant felt marvelously at home." (Seaver Center for Western History Research, Los Angeles County Museum of Natural History)*

the contempt of their co-religionists who had preceded them to America by forty or fifty years. By the time the heavy East European immigration set in, German Jews had achieved high mercantile status and an uneasy integration into American society. They did not want to be reminded of their kinship with these uncouth and impoverished Jews who were regarded vaguely as a kind of Oriental influx. There was a good deal of sentiment against "aiding such paupers to emigrate to these shores." One charitable organization declared: "Organized immigration from Russia, Roumania, and other semi-barbarous countries is a mistake and has proved to be a failure. It is no relief to the Jews of Russia, Poland, etc., and it jeopardizes the well-being of the American Jews."

A genuine uptown-downtown split soon developed, with condescension on one side and resentment on the other. The German Jews objected as bitterly to the rigid, old-world Orthodoxy of the immigrants as they did to their new involvement in trade unions. They were fearful, too, of the competition they would offer in the needle trades. (Indeed, the East

Europeans ultimately forced the uptown Jews out of the industry.) On the other side of the barricades, Russian Jews complained that at the hands of their uptown brethren, "every man is questioned like a criminal, is looked down upon . . . just as if he were standing before a Russian official." Nevertheless, many German Jews responded to the call of conscience by providing funds for needy immigrants and setting up preparatory schools for immigrant children for whom no room was yet available in the hopelessly overcrowded public schools.

Many comfortably settled German Jews saw dispersion as the answer to the problem. Efforts were made to divert immigrants to small towns in other parts of the country, but these were largely ineffective. There were also some gallant adventures with farming in such remote places as South Dakota, Oregon, and Louisiana. Though the Jewish pioneers were brave and idealistic, drought, disease, and ineptitude conspired against them. (In Oregon, for example, they tried to raise corn in cattle country, while in Louisiana they found themselves in malarial terrain.) Only chicken farming in New Jersey proved to be successful to any great degree. Farm jobs for Jews were available, but as one immigrant said: "I have no desire to be a farm hand to an ignorant Yankee at the end of the world. I would rather work here at half the price in a factory; for then I would at least be able to spend my free evenings with my friends."

It was in New York, then, that the bulk of the immigrants settled—in the swarming, tumultuous Lower East Side—with smaller concentrations in Boston, Philadelphia, and Chicago. Far less adaptable than the German Jews who were now lording it over them, disoriented and frightened, the East European immigrants constituted a vast and exploited proletariat. According to a survey in 1890, sixty per cent of all immigrant Jews worked in the needle trades. This industry had gone through a process of decentralization in which contractors carried out the bulk of production, receiving merely the cut goods from the manufacturer. Contracting establishments were everywhere in the Lower East Side, including

the contractors' homes, where pressers warmed their irons on the very stove on which the boss's wife was preparing supper. The contractors also gave out "section" work to families and landsleit who would struggle to meet the quotas at home. The bondage of the sewing machine was therefore extended into the tenements, with entire families enslaved by the machine's voracious demands. The Hester Street "pig market," where one could buy anything, became the labor exchange; there tailors, operators, finishers, basters, and pressers would congregate on Saturday in the hope of being hired by contractors.

Life in the sweatshops of the Lower East Side was hard, but it made immigrants employable from the start, and a weekly wage of five dollars—the equivalent of ten rubles—looked good in immigrant eyes. Moreover they were among their own kin and kind, and the sweatshops, noisome as they were, were still the scene of lively political and even literary discussions. (In some cigar-making shops, in fact, the bosses hired "readers" to keep the minds of the workers occupied with classic and Yiddish literature as they performed their repetitive chores.) East European Jews, near the end of the century, made up a large part of the skilled labor force in New York, ranking first in twenty-six out of forty-seven trades, and serving, for example, as bakers, building-trade workers, painters, furriers, jewellers, and tinsmiths.

Almost one quarter of all the immigrants tried their hands as tradesmen—largely as peddlers or as pushcart vendors in the madhouse bazaar of the Lower East Side. For some it was an apprenticeship in low-toned commerce that would lead to more elegant careers. For others it was merely a martyrdom that enabled them to subsist. It was a modest enough investment—five dollars for a license, one dollar for a basket, and four dollars for wares. They stocked up on pins and needles, shoe laces, polish, and handkerchiefs, learned some basic expressions ("You wanna buy somethin'?"), and were on their hapless way.

It was the professions, of course, that exerted the keenest attraction to Jews, with their reverence for learning. For most of them it was too late; they had to reconcile themselves to more humble callings. But it was not too late for their children, and between 1897 and 1907, the number of Jewish physicians in Manhattan rose from 450 to 1,000. Of all the professions it was medicine that excited the greatest veneration. (Some of this veneration spilled over into pharmacy, and "druggists" were highly respected figures who were called upon to prescribe for minor—and even major—ills, and to serve as scribes for the letters that the immigrants were unable to read and write themselves.) There were Jewish lawyers on the Lower East Side and by 1901 over 140 Jewish policemen, recruited in part by Theodore Roosevelt, who, as police commissioner, had issued a call for "the Maccabee or fighting Jewish type."

The Lower East Side was the American counterpart of the ghetto for Jewish immigrants, as well as their glittering capital. At its peak, around 1910, it packed over 350,000 people into a comparatively small area—roughly from Canal Street to Fourteenth Street—with as many as 523 people per acre, so that Arnold Bennett was moved to remark that "the architecture seemed to sweat humanity at every window and door." The most densely populated part of the city, it held one sixth of Manhattan's population and most of New York's office buildings and factories. "Uptowners" used to delight in visiting it (as a later generation would visit Harlem) to taste its exotic flavor. But the great mass of Jews lived there because the living was cheap, and there was a vital Jewish community that gave solace to the lonely and comfort to the pious.

A single man could find lodgings of a sort, including coffee morning and night, for three dollars a month. For a family, rent was about ten dollars a month, milk was four cents a quart, kosher meat twelve cents a pound, herring a penny or two. A kitchen table could be bought for a dollar, chairs at thirty-five cents each. One managed, but the life was oppressive. Most families lived in the notorious "dumbbell" flats of old-law tenements (built prior to 1901). Congested, often dirty and unsanitary, these tenements were six or seven stories high and had four apartments on each floor. Only one room in each three or four room apartment received direct air and sunlight, and the families on each floor shared a toilet in the hall.

Many families not only used their flats as workshops but also took in boarders to make ends meet. [Journalist and reformer] Jacob Riis tells of a two-room apartment on Allen Street which housed parents, six children, and six boarders. "Two daughters sewed clothes at home. The elevated railway passed by the window. The cantor rehearses, a train passes, the shoemaker bangs, ten brats run around like goats, the wife putters. . . . At night we all try to get some sleep in the stifling, roach-infested two rooms." In the summer, the tenants spilled out into fire escapes and rooftops, which were converted into bedrooms.

Nevertheless, life on the Lower East Side had surprising vitality. Despite the highest population density in the city, the Tenth Ward had one of the lowest death rates. In part, this was because of the strenuous personal cleanliness of Jews, dictated by their religion. Though only eight per cent of the East European Jews had baths, bathhouses and steam rooms on the Lower East Side did a booming business. There was, of course, a heavy incidence of tuberculosis—"the white plague." Those who were afflicted could be heard crying out, *"Luft! Gib mir luft!"* ("Air! Give me air!"). It was, in fact, this terror of "consumption" that impelled some East Side Jews to become farmers in the Catskills at the turn of the century, thus forerunning the gaudy career of the Catskill Borscht Belt resort hotels. The same fear impelled Jews on the Lower East Side to move to Washington Heights and the Bronx, where the altitude was higher, the air presumably purer.

Alcoholism, a prime affliction of most immigrant groups, was almost unknown among Jews. They drank ritualistically on holidays but almost never to excess. They were, instead, addicted to seltzer or soda water . . . which they viewed as "the worker's champagne." The suicide rate was relatively low, though higher than in the *shtetl,* and there was always a shudder of sympathy when the Yiddish press announced that someone had *genumen di ges* (taken gas).

The Lower East Side was from the start the scene of considerable crime. But its inhabitants became concerned when the crime rate among the young people seemed to rise steeply around 1910. There was a good deal of prostitution. The dancing academies, which achieved popularity early in this century, became recruiting centers for prostitutes. In 1908–9, of 581 foreign women arrested for prostitution, 225 were Jewish. There was the notorious Max Hochstim Association, which actively recruited girls, while the New York Independent Benevolent Association—an organization of pimps—provided sick benefits, burial privileges, bail, and protection money for prostitutes. The membership was even summoned to funerals with a two-dollar fine imposed on those who did not attend. Prostitution was so taken for granted that Canal Street had stores on one side featuring sacerdotal articles, while brothels were housed on the other.

Family life on the Lower East Side was cohesive and warm, though there was an edge of shrillness and hysteria to it. Marriages were not always happy, but if wives were viewed as an affliction, children were regarded as a blessing. The kitchen was the center of the household, and food was almost always being served to either family or visitors. No matter how poor they were, Jewish families ate well—even to excess—and mothers considered their children woefully underweight unless they were well cushioned with fat.

It was a life with few conventional graces. Handkerchiefs were barely known, and the Yiddish newspapers had to propagandize for their use. Old men smelled of snuff, and in spite of bathing, children often had lice in their hair and were sent home from school by the visiting nurse for a kerosene bath. Bedbugs were considered an inevitability, and pajamas were viewed as an upper-class affectation. Parents quarrelled bitterly—with passionate and resourceful invective—in the presence of their children. Telephones were virtually unknown, and a telegram surely meant disaster from afar.

The zeal of the immigrants on behalf of their children was no less than awe-inspiring. Parents yearned for lofty careers for their offspring, with medicine at the pinnacle. In better-off homes, there was always a piano ("solid mahogany"), and parents often spent their precious reserves to arrange a "concert" for their precocious youngsters, often followed by a ball in one of the Lower East Side's many halls.

To be sure, the children inspired a full measure of anxiety in their parents. "Amerikane kinder" was the rueful plaint of the elders, who could not fathom the baffling new ways of the young. Parents were nervous about their daughters' chastity, and younger brothers—often six or seven years old—would be dispatched as chaperones when the girls met their boy friends. There was uneasiness about Jewish street gangs and the growing problem of delinquency. The old folks were vexed by the new tides of secularism and political radicalism that were weaning their children from traditional pieties. But most of all, they feared that their sons would not achieve the success that would redeem their own efforts, humiliations, and failures in the harsh new land. Pressure on their children was relentless. But on the whole the children did well, astonishingly well. "The ease and rapidity with which they learn," Jacob Riis wrote, "is equalled only by their good behavior and close attention while in school. There is no whispering and no rioting at these desks." Samuel Chotzinoff, the music critic, tells a story which reveals the attitude of the Jewish schoolboy. When an altercation threatened between Chotzinoff and a classmate, his antagonist's reaction was to challenge him to spell "combustible."

The Lower East Side was a striking demonstration that financial want does not necessarily mean cultural poverty. The immigrant Jews were nearly always poor and often illiterate, but they were not culturally deprived. In fact, between 1890 and World War I, the Jewish community provides a remarkable chapter in American cultural history. Liberated from the constrictions of European captivity, immigrant Jews experienced a great surge of intellectual vitality. Yiddish, the Hebrew-German dialect which some people had casually dismissed as a barbarous "jargon," became the vehicle of this cultural renascence. Between 1885 and 1914, over 150 publications of all kinds made their appearance. But the new Yiddish journalism reached its apogee with the *Jewish Daily*

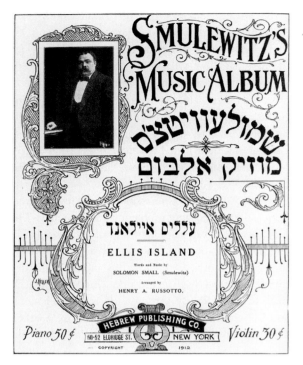

Yiddish sheet music from 1912. The song celebrates Ellis Island, which had replaced Castle Garden in 1892 as the point of entry for immigrants. A culture within a culture, Jewish New York had its own schools, newspapers, publishing houses, literary and musical circles, and a thriving Yiddish theater. (Sheet Music Collection, The John Hay Library, Brown University)

Forward under the long editorial reign of Abraham Cahan. The *Forward* was humanitarian, pro-labor, and socialistic. But it was also an instrument for acclimatizing immigrants in the new environment. It provided practical hints on how to deal with the new world, letters from the troubled (*Bintel Brief*), and even, at one time, a primer on baseball ("explained to non-sports"). The *Forward* also published and fostered an enormous amount of literature in Yiddish—both original works by writers of considerable talent, and translations of classic writers.

In this cultural ferment, immigrants studied English in dozens of night schools and ransacked the resources of the Aguilar Free Library on East Broadway. "When I had [a] book in my hand," an immigrant

wrote, "I pressed it to my heart and wanted to kiss it." The Educational Alliance, also on East Broadway, had a rich program designed to make immigrant Jews more American and their sons more Jewish. And there were scores of settlement houses, debating clubs, ethical societies, and literary circles which attracted the young. In fact, courtships were carried on in a rarefied atmosphere full of lofty talk about art, politics, and philosophy. And though there was much venturesome palaver about sexual freedom, actual behavior tended to be quite strait-laced.

But the most popular cultural institution was the café or coffee house, which served as the Jewish saloon. There were about 250 of them, each with its own following. Here the litterateurs sat for hours over steaming glasses of tea; revolutionaries and Bohemians gathered to make their pronouncements or raise money for causes; actors and playwrights came to hold court. For immigrant Jews, talk was the breath of life itself. The passion for music and theater knew no bounds. When Beethoven's Ninth Symphony was performed one summer night in 1915, mounted police had to be summoned to keep order outside Lewisohn Stadium, so heavy was the press of crowds eager for the twenty-five-cent stone seats. Theater (in Yiddish) was to the Jewish immigrants what Shakespeare and Marlowe had been to the groundlings in Elizabethan England. Tickets were cheap—twenty-five cents to one dollar—and theatergoing was universal. It was a raucous, robust, and communal experience. Mothers brought their babies (except in some of the "swellest" theaters, which forbade it), and peddlers hawked their wares between the acts. There were theater parties for trade unions and *landsmanschaften* (societies of fellow townsmen), and the audience milled around and renewed old friendships or argued the merits of the play. The stage curtain had bold advertisements of stores or blown-up portraits of stars.

There was an intense cult of personality in the Yiddish theater and a system of claques not unlike that which exists in grand opera today. The undisputed monarch was Boris Thomashefsky, and a theater program of his day offered this panegyric:

Tomashefsky! Artist great!
No praise is good enough for you!
Of all the stars you remain the king
You seek no tricks, no false quibbles;
One sees truth itself playing.
Your appearance is godly to us
Every movement is full of grace
Pleasing is your every gesture
Sugar sweet your every turn
You remain the king of the stage
Everything falls to your feet.

Many of the plays were sentimental trash—heroic "operas" on historical themes, "greenhorn" melodramas full of cruel abandonments and tearful reunions, romantic musicals, and even topical dramas dealing with such immediate events as the Homestead Strike, the Johnstown Flood, and the Kishinev Pogrom of 1903. Adaptability and a talent for facile plagiarism were the essence of the playwright's art in those days, and "Professor" Moses Horwitz wrote 167 plays, most of them adaptations of old operas and melodramas. The plays were so predictable that an actor once admitted he didn't even have to learn his lines; he merely had to have a sense of the general situation and then adapt lines from other plays.

There was, of course, a serious Yiddish drama, introduced principally by Jacob Gordin, who adapted classical and modernist drama to the Yiddish stage. Jewish intellectuals were jubilant at this development. But the process of acculturation had its amusing and grotesque aspects. Shakespeare was a great favorite but *"verbessert und vergrossert"* (improved and enlarged). There was the Jewish *King Lear* in which Cordelia becomes Goldele. (The theme of filial ingratitude was a "natural" on the Lower East Side, where parents constantly made heroic sacrifices.) *Hamlet* was also given a Jewish coloration, the prince becoming a rabbinical student who returns from the seminary to discover treachery at home. And *A Doll's House* by Ibsen was transformed into *Minna,* in which a sensitive and intelligent young woman, married to an ignorant laborer, falls in love with her boarder and ultimately commits suicide.

Related to the Jewish love of theater was the immigrant's adoration of the cantor, a profession which evoked as much flamboyance and egotistical preening as acting did. (In fact, actors would sometimes grow beards before the high holydays and find jobs as cantors.) Synagogues vied with each other for celebrated cantors, sometimes as a way of getting out of debt, since tickets were sold for the high-holyday services.

The Lower East Side was a vibrant community, full of color and gusto, in which the Jewish immigrant felt marvelously at home, safe from the terrors of the alien city. But it was a setting too for fierce conflict and enervating strain. There were three major influences at work, each pulling in a separate direction: Jewish Orthodoxy, assimilationism, and the new socialist gospel. The immigrants were Orthodox, but their children tended to break away. *Cheders* (Hebrew schools) were everywhere, in basements and stores and tenements, and the old custom of giving a child a taste of honey when he was beginning to learn to read—as symbolic of the sweetness of study—persisted. But the young, eager to be accepted into American society, despised the old ways and their "greenhorn" teachers. Fathers began to view their sons as "free-thinkers," a term that was anathema to them. Observance of the Law declined, and the Saturday Sabbath was ignored by many Jews. A virulent antireligious tendency developed among many "enlightened" Jews, who would hold profane balls on the most sacred evening of the year—Yom Kippur—at which they would dance and eat nonkosher food. (Yom Kippur is a fast day.) And the trade-union movement also generated uneasiness among the pious elders of the Lower East Side. "Do you want us to bow down to your archaic God?" a radical newspaper asked. "Each era has its new Torah. Ours is one of freedom and justice."

But for many immigrants the basic discontent was with their American experience itself. The golden province turned out to be a place of tenements and sweatshops. A familiar cry was *"a klug of Columbus!"* ("a curse on Columbus") or, "Who ever asked him, Columbus, to discover America?" Ellis Island was called *Tremindzl* (Island of Tears), and Abraham Cahan, in his initial reaction to the horrors of immigration, thundered: "Be cursed, immigration! Cursed by those conditions which have brought you into being. How many souls have you broken, how many courageous and mighty souls have you shattered." The fact remains that most Jewish immigrants, in the long run, made a happy adjustment to their new land.

After 1910, the Lower East Side went into a decline. Its strange glory was over. New areas of Jewish settlement opened up in Brooklyn, the Bronx, and in upper Manhattan. By the mid-twenties, less than ten per cent of New York's Jews lived on the Lower East Side, although it still remained the heartland to which one returned to shop, to see Yiddish theater, and to renew old ties. By 1924 Jewish immigration into the United States was severely reduced by new immigration laws, and the saga of mass immigration was done. But the intensities of the Jewish immigrant experience had already made an indelible mark on American culture and history that would endure for many years.

QUESTIONS TO CONSIDER

1 Compare the migration experience of Jewish immigrants to America in the periods before and after 1880. In what ways did the experience become easier or more difficult? How did the immigrants themselves change?

2 For some Jewish immigrants, America was "the land of milk and honey," whereas others cursed Columbus and called Ellis Island the "Island of Tears." Discuss the reality of the Jewish immigrant experience hidden behind both images of America.

3 Analyze the reasons for the ambivalent feelings and divisions that developed between newer eastern European Jewish immigrants and those Jews, usually of German origin, who had been settled in the United States for several generations.

4 The lure of land in the New World brought generations of Europeans to America. Why did the bulk of eastern European Jewish immigrants choose to remain in urban industrial centers such as New York City? Was there anything about their *shtetl* experience that made Jews more adaptable to city life?

5 Boroff says, "The immigrant Jews were nearly always poor and often illiterate, but they were not culturally deprived." What evidence is there to support this statement?

PART FOUR

Reform and Expansion

8 The Lady Versus Goliath: Ida Tarbell Takes on Standard Oil Co.

PAULA A. TRECKEL

In the Gilded Age, politics became a big business, too, as the mighty industrialists poured money into government circles at an unprecedented rate. Men now entered politics for the same reason they went into business: to make their fortunes. The new politics even derived much of its vocabulary from the world of industry. "A political party," contended American statesman William H. Seward, "is in one sense a joint stock company in which those who contribute the most direct the action and management of the concern." The United States Senate became known as the Millionaires' Club, because only the rich and powerful seemed able to get in. A sizable portion of both major parties not only vigorously defended the industrial barons but eagerly accepted their campaign contributions. A number of politicians shamelessly took bribes as well.

In the 1880s, the two national parties—the Republicans and Democrats—had a monopoly on American politics, and neither was responsive to the grassroots of America. The industrial consolidation had left many victims in its wake—workers, farmers, consumers, and small or aspiring business and professional people who wanted their share of opportunity and wealth. They had little chance for success as long as the wealthy captains of industry—men like Andrew Carnegie, J. Pierpont Morgan, and John D. Rockefeller—ruled the country, including its politicians. Such business moguls were determined to eliminate competition to their business empires by ruthless and sometimes illegal means.

Unable to persuade the federal government and the two major parties to redress their grievances, the victims of industrial consolidation launched their own reform movements. American farmers organized alliances to protect themselves against the big industrialists who ran the country. The alliance movement was an effort at cooperative agriculture to free farmers from "the furnishing merchants," banks, trusts, and railroads. The alliances, in turn, led to political organization, first in the People's party of Kansas (which drew men and women alike to its banners) and ultimately in the national People's party, or the Populist party, in 1892. According to Populist historian Lawrence Goodwyn, the agrarian revolt that culminated in the Populist crusade constituted "the largest democratic mass movement in American history." And the objective of that mass movement was to restore government to the people.

Another reform-minded group of the era was a cadre of investigative journalists associated with McClure's Magazine. *Founded by Samuel Sidney McClure, the journal was dedicated to exposing and finding solutions to the social and economic ills that plagued industrial America. Soon McClure gathered around him "a team of journalists" known popularly as "muckrakers." Theodore Roosevelt gave them that name because he thought them too obsessed with social evils, with raking up the muck, or filth, of American society.*

In the sprightly selection that follows, Paula A. Treckel tells the story of Ida Tarbell, "the foremost 'lady muckraker' of her time" Rejecting marriage because it would have restricted her freedom, Tarbell chose journalism as her profession (she also wrote a popular biography of Abraham Lincoln) and in 1894 joined McClure's Magazine *staff in New York City. There she became a member of McClure's "muckraking" team of investigative reporters—Ray Stannard Baker, Lincoln Steffens, and William Allen White. By now, the pressure for reform had led to the passage of the Sherman Anti-Trust Act of 1890, which outlawed monopolies and other restraints of trade. But, as Treckel says, the measure was difficult to enforce "against America's powerful industrialists."*

In 1903, Tarbell went after one of the country's mightiest trusts, Standard Oil Company, owned by millionaire John D. Rockefeller. When apprised that she was preparing an exposé of his company, Rockefeller derided her as "Miss Tarbarrel" and compared her to a worm that if ignored would disappear. But "Miss Tarbarrel" was undaunted. Through tenacity and painstaking research, she produced "The History of Standard Oil," which serialized in McClure's Magazine. *Her exposé helped the government break up Rockefeller's huge monopoly, and it made Tarbell one of the most celebrated women in the land. What follows is the tale of how this amazing woman slew the American Goliath.*

GLOSSARY

BAKER, RAY STANNARD   A writer for *McClure's Magazine* who examined corruption and violence in the labor union movement. He stated, "I learned that common human suffering and common human joy, if truly reported, never grow stale." In his introduction to *The Shame of the Cities,* he added that America's problems could be resolved through "good conduct in the individual, simple honesty, courage, and efficiency."

FEDERAL TRADE COMMISSION (1914)   One of the accomplishments of Woodrow Wilson's New Freedom, it represented a noble effort to oversee the practices of large corporations. It investigated complaints and could order companies to resolve the problems that surfaced. Many of its early members were conservatives who responded to only the most grievous of misdeeds.

McCLURE, SAMUEL SIDNEY   Irish immigrant who established an influential newspaper chain and a magazine, *McClure's Magazine,* that focused on the major problems of his day. Ida Tarbell was one of many talented young writers that McClure hired. Although his inexpensive mass circulation journal contained fiction, essays on science, and profiles of leading figures like Thomas Edison, investigative journalism became its most prominent feature.

MONOPOLY   A company or group of companies that controls a market so completely, as Carnegie did with steel or Rockefeller with oil, that a particular corporate entity can dictate supply and prices and thus destroy competition.

MUCKRAKER   Theodore Roosevelt inadvertently coined this word. He compared the young reform-minded writers who published articles for *McClure's Magazine* to the man in *Pilgrim's Progress* who was so busy raking the "muke" (filth) that he never noticed the celestial crown over his head. Nonetheless, the American people were enthralled with writing like Upton Sinclair's portrayal of the meat-packing industry, Ray Stannard Baker's lurid description of the labor movement, and Lincoln Steffen's tale of a corrupt alliance between business and politics.

OIL REFINERY   Rockefeller invested in this business, which converted crude oil to useful commodities such as kerosene that provided both light and heat for America's homes and businesses. His base of operation was Cleveland, Ohio, which was close to the oil fields of western Pennsylvania and abutted the shipping lanes of Lake Erie.

PROGRESSIVE MOVEMENT   A reform movement that started at the state level with governors like Robert LaFollette in Wisconsin and moved to the national level from 1901 to 1914 during the presidential administrations of Theodore Roosevelt, William Howard Taft, and Woodrow Wilson. In seeking railroad regulation and antitrust legislation, the progressives championed the interests of farmers, laborers, and consumers.

REBATES   Kickbacks to large corporations from the railroads. As public carriers, the railroads could not practice discrimination in the rates they charged, yet they depended on their better customers to stay in business. Rockefeller used this illegal strategy to gain favorable transportation rates that smaller companies could not demand.

SHERMAN ANTI-TRUST ACT (1890)   Under pressure from reformers and consumer advocates, Congress enacted this measure, which made it illegal for corporations to destroy competition or to be "in restraint of trade or commerce." Although it regulated some business combinations, its language was vague, and corporations continued to eliminate competition and form monopolies.

SIDDALL, JOHN   Tarbell's youthful assistant who helped her gather evidence on the illegal activities of the Standard

Oil Company. He and other employees at *McClure's Magazine* made certain that the accusations against the giant oil corporation were accurate and that Rockefeller could not charge the magazine with libel.

SOUTH IMPROVEMENT COMPANY   A Rockefeller enterprise that combined the largest and most powerful railroads and oil refineries. Its resources were so great that it destroyed competition.

STANDARD OIL COMPANY   It dominated the business of refining oil. By 1881, through illegal and sometimes cutthroat tactics, Rockefeller had 90 percent of this lucrative industry under his control and had established a monopoly that strangled competition. Tarbell's writings forced a reluctant federal government to dismantle this mammoth trust in 1911.

STEFFENS, LINCOLN   One of S. S. McClure's staff of investigative authors. He wrote a series of articles exposing corruption in Minneapolis that involved business and political leaders.

TARBELL, FRANKLIN   Ida's father, who hoped that he might profit through the manufacture of oil tanks that would transport the "black gold" to the refineries. Rockefeller used illegal rebates to destroy small operators like him. Ida learned from her father's misfortunes that "it was your privilege and duty to fight injustice."

TRUST   A method of combining resources that avoided the antimonopoly laws established by many states to prohibit one corporation from holding stock in another. Rockefeller, for example, had stockholders of various oil companies delegate their interests to Standard Oil "trustees" who made decisions that benefited the entire entity. Thus, one body managed and directed the interests of many companies.

TUTTLE, HENRY B.   A co-owner in a produce shipping firm, he gave Rockefeller a job as a bookkeeper and, in Treckel's words, "launched one of the most successful careers in American business."

WHITE, WILLIAM ALLEN   A well-known journalist and later a leading internationalist who argued for aid to the beleaguered democracies of England and France. The popularity of the Progressive movement surprised him. "The thing that constantly amazed me," noted White, "was how many people were with us."

The *Lion and the Mouse* made its Broadway debut on Saturday, November 25, 1905. The play told the tale of "the richest and the ablest and the hardest and the most unscrupulous" millionaire in America, John Burkett Ryder, and his confrontation with Miss Shirley Rossmore, a young woman of "clear moral intensity." The story opened with Miss Rossmore's father, a judge, accused of accepting securities from Ryder in exchange for making judicial decisions in the millionaire's favor. To prove her father's innocence, Miss Rossmore—the "mouse" to Ryder's "lion"—set out to expose the millionaire's criminal activities.

Unlikely as it may appear, the plot of this Broadway melodrama was snatched from the headlines of the day. It was loosely based on the story of Ida M. Tarbell and her investigation of millionaire John D. Rockefeller and his Standard Oil Company monopoly. Although it lacked the Broadway play's love story and happy ending, Tarbell's investigation of how Rockefeller achieved domination of the oil industry had more than its share of intrigue, crime, and corruption. Tarbell used her sense of moral outrage, passion for justice, and historian's eye for detail to reveal the inner workings of Rockefeller's business empire to the world. Her work helped lead to the prosecution of Standard Oil by the United States government and the company's subsequent dismantling in 1911.

Ida Minerva Tarbell was born on November 5, 1857, in the frontier town of Hatch Hollow, Pennsylvania, one of the rough and rowdy oil boomtowns of the region. Her father, Franklin Tarbell, hoped to make his fortune in the young industry by manufacturing tanks to hold the black gold taken from beneath the Pennsylvania hills. As a child, Ida saw how boom and bust cycles swept through the dirty, oil-slick communities that dotted the countryside and witnessed the horrors of accidents—fires and explosions—that plagued the industry.

This 1905 photograph shows Ida Tarbell at work in her study. The "lady muckraker" made the public aware of the corrupt and monopolistic practices of the Standard Oil Company. (Tarbell Archives, Pelletier Library, Allegheny College)

In 1872, suddenly and without warning, the region's railroads—the link necessary to bring the oil to market—doubled their shipping rates, deeply cutting the independent producers' profits. Then word leaked out that the railroads had favored a mysterious Cleveland-based outfit called the South Improvement Company by giving it rebates, in direct violation of federal law. Young Ida watched as her father and his friends crusaded against this menace to their livelihood. Violence swept the oil fields of western Pennsylvania as vigilantes destroyed the South Improvement Company's oil cars and burned out the men who joined or sold out to that organization. "It was my first experience in revolution," Tarbell recalled. She learned "it was your privilege and duty to fight injustice."

The force behind the threatened takeover of the region's oil production was John D. Rockefeller, a man who had risen from humble beginnings to become one of the nation's wealthiest and most powerful

"Lady Muckraker" by Paula A. Treckel. This article is reproduced from the June 2001 issue of *American History Illustrated* with permission of PRIMEDIA Special Interest Publications (History Group), copyright *American History Illustrated,* and the author.

industrialists. Born in upstate New York in 1839, Rockefeller was the son of con artist William Avery Rockefeller and his long-suffering wife, Eliza. The family's poverty soon taught John the importance of saving and investing money and fired his dreams of becoming wealthy. "Some day, sometime, when I am a man, I want to be worth a-hundred-thousand-dollars," he confided to a friend. "And I'm going to be, too—some day." The somber boy found spiritual comfort in the Baptist church, which instilled in him the values of self-reliance and self-improvement and the belief that hard work would be rewarded both on earth and in heaven. Throughout his life John turned to his church for practical lessons in living.

When the Rockefeller family moved to Cleveland, Ohio, 16-year-old John sought work to help support his family. "I did not go to any small establishments," he recalled. "I did not guess what I would be, but I was after something big." During a meeting with Henry B. Tuttle, partner in a produce-shipping firm, Rockefeller boldly stated, "I understand bookkeeping, and I'd like to get work."

"We'll give you a chance," Tuttle said, and he hired the boy to handle the company's books, thereby launching one of the most successful careers in American business.

John worked hard and invested his clerk's salary in local grain and livestock businesses. By age 18 he had made enough money to start his own produce business with Englishman Maurice Clark. When the Civil War dramatically increased the price of commodities, the young Rockefeller invested his profits in a local oil refinery. Refineries bought crude oil from the oil producers and processed it into products such as kerosene. Cleveland was then the center of the refining industry because it was close to the oil-rich fields of western Pennsylvania, and its location on Lake Erie provided an easy means of shipping the valuable commodities it produced. Over time John D. Rockefeller purchased several more refineries in the area; in 1870 he incorporated his holdings as Standard Oil.

As America's industry boomed in the years following the Civil War and railroads became an ever-more important force, Rockefeller used every advantage—legal and illegal—that the market allowed. One tactic was to secure reduced rates from railroads by guaranteeing them volume shipments on a regular basis. When other companies refused to join forces with Rockefeller or agree to control the production and price of oil, he drove them out of business. Ida Tarbell saw for herself the effect of Rockefeller's machinations when he formed an alliance between three of the most powerful railroads and a handful of oil refiners, called it the South Improvement Company, and used it as a tool to gain further dominance. Using such tactics, Standard Oil's 40 companies gained control of 90 percent of the nation's oil refining industry by 1881.

In addition to buying refineries, Rockefeller sought control of the oil fields themselves. He built his own transportation network of pipelines and tankers, and marketed his products both at home and abroad. Rockefeller's efforts produced added benefits as well. He introduced cutting-edge technology and efficiency to the oil industry. And as the cost of processing petroleum dropped, so too did prices for fuel oil and lighting products.

While John D. Rockefeller was ruthlessly cornering the nation's oil market, Ida Tarbell was attending college in western Pennsylvania. From an early age she had planned to become an independent, professional woman,. "I would never marry," she pledged. "It would interfere with my plan; it would fetter my freedom." In 1876 she enrolled as a freshman at Allegheny College in Meadville, Pennsylvania. She was the only woman in her class. Following her graduation in 1880, Tarbell taught for a year before joining the staff of the Meadville, Pennsylvania, *Chautauqua Assembly Herald,* a publication of the Chautauqua Assembly's Literary and Scientific Circle.

During her six years at the *Chautauquan,* Tarbell learned the art and craft of journalism. She started out as a researcher and eventually assumed the duties, if not the title, of managing editor. Nevertheless, Tarbell longed for more. In church one Sunday, a visiting minister thundered, "You're dying of respectability!" at his complaisant congregation and spurred Tarbell to action. In 1889 she decided to try supporting herself with her own pen. The young journalist left the *Chautauquan* and headed for France.

Tarbell was ready for a new beginning. In Paris she made friendships that lasted a lifetime and reinvented herself as a historian, researching the life of French Revolutionary heroine Madame Manon Phlipon de Roland. To support herself, Tarbell wrote articles on French life for American news syndicates. One story, "The Paving of the Streets of Paris by Monsieur Alphand," piqued the interest of editor Samuel Sidney McClure, founder of *McClure's Magazine*. McClure had emigrated from Ireland in 1866, and in 1884 he had established one of the earliest U.S. newspaper syndicates. A dynamic, energetic man—Rudyard Kipling described him as a "cyclone in a frock coat"—McClure launched his magazine in 1893 to campaign for solutions to the pressing problems of the day. He was always looking for fresh, talented writers to join his staff. On a trip to Paris in the summer of 1892, he bounded up the stairs of Ida Tarbell's apartment building and into her life, changing it forever.

McClure asked Tarbell if she would come to New York to work at his magazine. Reluctant to give up her hard-earned independence, she agreed only to submit occasional articles to *McClure's* while she completed her biography of Madame Roland. But by 1894, Tarbell was unable to financially support herself, and she returned to the United States with her unfinished Madame Roland manuscript and joined the staff of *McClure's* in New York.

Ida Tarbell returned to a nation still reeling from the panic caused by the stock market crash of 1893. More than 15,000 businesses had failed, and at least one third of all manufacturing workers had lost their jobs. Midwestern farmers also suffered as they faced rising interest rates and falling crop prices. Tarbell's own family's financial distress clouded her homecoming. Her father had become an independent oil producer just as Standard Oil forced an increase in the price of the region's crude oil. Refiners were reluctant to buy crude from small, independent producers like Franklin Tarbell, and he had to mortgage the family's

Titusville home to pay his debts. One of his friends committed suicide when his own business failed.

The nation as a whole was changing, evolving from a largely agrarian economy into a more industrial one. With the change came abuses—not just the great concentration of wealth in the hands of a few industrialists such as Andrew Carnegie and Rockefeller, but also urban corruption, boss politics, and child labor. The Progressive Movement emerged in response to these issues and prompted Congress to pass the Sherman Anti-Trust Act in 1890, making it illegal to monopolize or restrain trade through unfair collaborations or conspiracies. The law was vague, however, and authorities had difficulty enforcing it against America's powerful industrialists.

At *McClure's* a team of journalists—Tarbell, Lincoln Steffens, William Allen White, and Ray Stannard Baker—reflected Progressive concerns in their articles about some of the era's excesses. Yet not everyone approved of this new breed of journalism. Although he knew and befriended many of the magazine's writers, including Tarbell, President Theodore Roosevelt publicly complained that these journalists focused only upon society's evils. "In Bunyan's *Pilgrim's Progress*," he said, "you may recall the description of the Man with the Muck-rake, the man who could look no way but downward with the muck-rake in his hands; who was offered a celestial crown for his muck-rake, but who would neither look up nor regard the crown he was offered, but continued to rake to himself the filth of the floor." The president's comments gave a name to the new generation of investigative journalists, with Ida Tarbell the foremost "Lady Muckraker" of her time.

McClure's January 1903 issue epitomized the work of the muckrakers. Lincoln Steffens contributed an article about political corruption in Minneapolis, part of his "Shame of the Cities" series. Ray Stannard Baker wrote about corruption and violence in the labor union movement in a piece called "The Right to Work." The issue also included an installment in a series by Ida Tarbell on "The History of Standard Oil," one of the most important exposés of the twentieth century.

The proliferation of industrial trusts interested *McClure's* staff members. They decided the best way to approach the subject would be to tell "the story of a typical trust to illustrate how and why the clan grew," recalled Tarbell. "How about the greatest of them all—the Standard Oil Company?" Tarbell decided she wanted to tackle the project, and she traveled to Europe where Sam McClure and his family were vacationing while he recovered from exhaustion. Tarbell expected to stay only a week while she pitched her idea to the publisher, but he asked her to join them in their travels. Finally, after visiting Switzerland and Italy, McClure approved Tarbell's story idea. She later admitted, "It had been a strong thread weaving itself into the pattern of my life from childhood on." Tarbell later explained to critics who charged that her work was motivated by personal concerns, "We were undertaking what we regarded as a legitimate piece of historical work. We were neither apologists nor critics, only journalists intent on discovering what had gone into the making of this most perfect of all monopolies."

Tarbell had no shortage of material to draw upon. Congress had been investigating Standard Oil almost continually since the company's creation in 1870 when it was suspected of receiving rebates from railroads and violating free trade. In the years since, government investigators had generated volumes of testimony, a massive collection of documentary evidence, as well as countless newspaper and magazine articles. These resources provided Tarbell with the foundation for her work, although at first she found the sheer mass of material at her disposal overwhelming. "The task confronting me is such a monstrous one that I am staggering a bit under it," she lamented. Aided by a young, eager assistant, John Siddall, she spent a year researching her subject before *McClure's* announced the series to readers.

Initially Tarbell was going to write the story in three parts—in the end she wrote 19. Dissecting the inner workings of Standard Oil with the precision of a surgeon wielding a scalpel, she exposed espionage and industrial terrorism. In one example, Tarbell detailed the testimony of Mrs. Butts, whose

On his ninety-first birthday, John D. Rockefeller hardly looked like the ruthless oil magnate who called Tarbell "Miss Tarbarrel." He maintained a religious faith based on "dividends of righteousness." Like Andrew Carnegie, he gave much of his huge fortune away. (Courtesy of the Rockefeller Archive Center)

oil company had a regular customer in New Orleans. A Standard Oil representative approached the customer and "made a contract with him to pay him $10,000 a year for five years to stop handling the independent oil and take Standard Oil." Tarbell also told of a young office boy in a Standard Oil plant who was told to destroy some company papers when the name of his Sunday school teacher, an independent oil refiner, caught his eye. The records contained information, collected by railroad freight clerks in Standard Oil's pay, about his teacher's oil shipments. Armed with such inside knowledge, the great trust could act against its competition by sidetracking rail cars, interfering with or destroying rivals' shipments, or pressuring buyers to cancel orders. By showing how the corporation worked in collusion with the railroads and carefully explaining its elaborate system of rebates and "drawbacks," Tarbell meticulously built her case against the great monopoly.

Rockefeller himself refused to meet with the woman he privately called "Miss Tarbarrel," and he met her series with stony silence. One day, while strolling in the grounds of his Cleveland home, a friend asked Rockefeller why he did not respond to Tarbell's charges. "Not a word!" he interrupted. "Not a word about that misguided woman." Then he pointed to a worm on the ground nearby. "If I step on that worm I will call attention to it," Rockefeller said. "If I ignore it, it will disappear."

Tarbell understood Rockefeller's need for silence. "His self-control has been masterful," she said; "he knows, nobody better, that to answer is to invite discussion, to answer is to call attention to the facts in the case." This, she was confident, he would not do. She also never feared that Rockefeller would take steps to silence her. "What had we to be afraid of?" she declared.

The journalist's curiosity got the best of her, however, when John Siddall learned that Rockefeller planned to give a talk in October 1903 to the Sunday school at the Euclid Avenue Baptist Church in Cleveland. She could not resist the opportunity to get a peek at the man. On that crisp October morning, Tarbell and Siddall arrived early at the church and awaited Rockefeller's entrance. Tarbell vividly recalled the moment when she first saw him: "We were sitting meekly at one side when I was suddenly aware of a striking figure standing in the doorway. There was an awful age in his face—the oldest man I had ever seen, I thought, but what power!" She recalled that his voice was "Clear and utterly sincere. He meant what he was saying. He was on his own ground talking about dividends, dividends of righteousness." When the talk ended, Tarbell and Siddall slipped out to get a good seat in the gallery, from where they could see the Rockefeller pew. Tarbell noted, "It was plain that he, and not the minister, was the pivot on which the audience swung."

Tarbell's findings strengthened the United States government's case against Standard Oil. Following publication of her series, President Roosevelt decided to make an example of the great oil trust.

On November 15, 1906, the government charged the Standard Oil Company of New Jersey and its 70 affiliates with violating the Sherman Anti-Trust Act. The company and its trustees were eventually found guilty of creating a monopoly, conspiring to restrain and control interstate commerce through the use of railroad rebates and drawbacks, controlling pipelines, conducting industrial espionage, and illegally eliminating competition from the marketplace. Following a series of appeals, the Supreme Court upheld the original decision against Standard Oil in May of 1911, and the mighty monopoly was broken up. Rockefeller retained stock in Standard Oil of New Jersey and the 33 independent subsidiaries created by the Supreme Court's decision. Ironically, the break-up of the trust made Rockefeller the world's richest man with a net worth of $900 million in 1913. And by the time of his death at age 98 on May 23, 1937, John D. Rockefeller was more widely known as "the world's greatest philanthropist" than the great "Lion" of the industrial age.

In addition to prompting the government's suit against Standard Oil, Ida Tarbell's series, published in two volumes as *The History of the Standard Oil Company* in 1904, contributed to the passage of new laws to protect competition in the marketplace. In 1914 the government established the Federal Trade Commission to oversee business activities.

Despite an illustrious career—in 1922 the *New York Times* included her as one of the "Twelve Greatest Living American Women"—Ida Tarbell never equaled *The History of Standard Oil*. Historian and Rockefeller biographer Allan Nevins declared, "It was the best piece of business history that America had yet produced." Before Tarbell's death on January 6, 1944, a young history professor asked her, "If you could rewrite your book today, what would you change?"

"Not one word, young man," she proudly replied, "Not one word."

QUESTIONS TO CONSIDER

1 Compare Rockefeller's climb to financial fortune with that of Andrew Carnegie, the subject of selection 5. How had both men in their youth showed initiative and the ability to invest wisely? Do you admire them for their energy or condemn them for their ruthlessness in taking advantage of labor and destroying competition?

2 Rockefeller's control of an industry reduced prices for fuel oil and lighting products such as kerosene. Why then did the federal government conclude that his actions were destructive? Compare Rockefeller's business and the government's reaction to it with the present-day court actions against Bill Gates and the claim that Microsoft unfairly destroyed competition. (See selection 31 for a portrait of Gates.)

3 Describe the economic problems that plagued Ida Tarbell's America when she returned home from Paris. How did the young writers at *McClure's Magazine* hope to solve these problems? What was Theodore Roosevelt's opinion of their efforts?

4 How had the Standard Oil Company affected Tarbell's life? Do you think that her personal feelings motivated her attack on Rockefeller? What did she discover about the giant oil corporation?

5 What did Rockefeller mean when he discussed "dividends of righteousness" at the Euclid Avenue Baptist Church? Why do you think that Tarbell was so anxious to see him?

6 Once Tarbell's charges against Rockefeller's giant oil monopoly became widely known, what did the federal government do in response? Did Rockefeller's wealth increase or diminish as a result of Tarbell's claims and the resultant government action? Again, reflect back to selection 5 and compare Rockefeller's reputation with that of Carnegie when both men were in the twilight of their careers.

9 America's First Southeast Asian War: The Philippine Insurrection

DAVID R. KOHLER AND JAMES W. WENSYEL

The last quarter of the nineteenth century marked the second age of imperialism, a time when the industrial nations of Europe—Britain, Germany, France, Belgium, and Russia—claimed colonies in Africa and spheres of influence in distant China. The United States, flexing its imperial muscles in the 1890s, was also alive with "aggressive, expansionistic, and jingoistic" sentiments. In 1893, with the help of 150 marines from a United States cruiser, American residents in Hawaii deposed the queen of the islands, set up a provisional government, and clamored for annexation. In 1898, the United States formally annexed Hawaii, thus expanding American territory and interests in the Pacific. In 1898–1899, the United States gained additional Pacific possessions in a controversial war with Spain, by then a second-rate power whose old empire in the Americas had all but disintegrated.

American expansionists, cheered on by a truculent yellow press, did not cause the war with Spain. But American policymakers and business leaders did use it as a means to extend American economic and political power. The war itself grew out of deplorable conditions in Cuba, caused by decades of Spanish misrule. A series of Cuban revolts and Spanish atrocities, which the American press exaggerated, aroused Americans' sympathy for the Cubans, whose cause seemed identical to that of the American patriots in 1776. In February 1898, American sentiment turned to outrage when the United States battleship Maine *blew up in Havana harbor, killing 260 American sailors.*

The cause of the explosion was never established, but American expansionists—among them, Assistant Secretary of the Navy Theodore Roosevelt—blamed Spain and demanded war. Overnight a slogan caught the imagination of the country: "Remember the Maine! To hell with Spain!"

In March, President William McKinley demanded that Spain agree to negotiations that would grant independence to Cuba. Faced with the possibility of a disastrous war in a distant hemisphere, Spain tried to maneuver, declaring an armistice with Cuban insurgents but hedging on Cuban independence. By then, both President McKinley and Congress were prepared for war. When Congress adopted a resolution recognizing Cuban independence, Spain retaliated by declaring war on the United States; the next day, Congress responded in kind.

Less than a week later, the American Asiatic Squadron under Commodore George Dewey won a dazzling victory in Manila Bay in the Spanish-held Philippines. As it turned out, Roosevelt had secured the command for Dewey and had directed him to prepare for action two months before official hostilities commenced. The United States also invaded Cuba, where Theodore Roosevelt gained national fame as colonel of the Rough Riders. After ten weeks of fighting, Spain capitulated, giving up control of Cuba and surrendering Puerto Rico, Guam, and the Philippines to the United States. For Secretary of State John Hay, it had been "a splendid little war."

Much has been written about the Spanish-American War and the United States empire that emerged from it. Much less is known about an important offshoot of that war—an American military campaign against Philippine insurgents that lasted three years, involved 126,000 United States troops, and resulted in 7,000 American and some 216,000 Filipino casualties. The United States learned a number of hard lessons about fighting against nationalist insurgents in distant Asian jungles, but sixty years later another generation of Americans forgot those lessons when plunging into a similar conflict in Vietnam. In the selection that follows, David R. Kohler, a naval special warfare officer, and James W. Wensyel, a retired army officer and the author of several books, narrate American involvement in the Filipino insurrection of 1898–1902, showing how it grew out of the Spanish-American War and the American bid for empire. The authors point out the influence of the Indian wars on American tactics in the Philippines, and they draw several significant parallels between the Philippine conflict and America's involvement in Vietnam. It was the Philippine conflict that generated strategic hamlets, free-fire zones, and search-and-destroy missions—terms that were later seared into the history of American involvement in Vietnam. As experienced military men, Kohler and Wensyel contend that future American leaders should ponder the lessons of the Philippine and Vietnamese conflicts before embarking on similar adventures.

GLOSSARY

AGUINALDO Y FAMY, GENERALISSIMO DON EMILIO   Commander of the Filipino nationalists who fought the Spaniards and then the Americans in an effort to achieve Philippine independence.

BOLO KNIFE   This sharp-edged instrument was the Filipino revolutionary's main weapon.

DEWEY, COMMODORE GEORGE   Commander of the American Asiatic Squadron, which sank the Spanish fleet in the Battle of Manila Bay, May 1, 1898.

GRAYSON, WILLIAM "WILLIE" WALTER   The Philippine insurrection began when he and his fellow soldiers seized Filipino nationalists within their picket line and firing broke out between the American and Filipino camps.

GUERRILLA WARFARE   Like the Vietcong and North Vietnamese sixty years later, the Filipinos eschewed conventional, Western-style warfare of pitched battles and dispersed throughout the countryside conducting "hit-and-run operations by small bands."

MACABEBES   Filipino mercenaries from the central Luzon province of Pampanga who fought for Spain and the United States against their own countrymen.

MacARTHUR, GENERAL ARTHUR   Assuming command of United States forces in 1900, he initiated new tactics designed to isolate the Filipino guerrillas from the villages that supported them; his tactics gave rise to strategic hamlets, free-fire zones, and search-and-destroy operations.

MAHAN, ADMIRAL ALFRED THAYER   United States naval strategist who contended that sea power and overseas colonies were the keys to national power; his writings greatly influenced American imperialists such as Theodore Roosevelt and Henry Cabot Lodge.

MERRITT, MAJOR GENERAL WESLEY   Commanded the United States Philippine Expeditionary Force, sent to oust the Spaniards from the islands.

SANTAYANA, GEORGE   Spanish-born philosopher, poet, and educator who observed that those who do not learn from the mistakes of the past are doomed to repeat them.

SMITH, BRIGADIER GENERAL JACOB W. "HELL-ROARING JAKE"   Veteran of the Wounded Knee Sioux massacre of 1890; when the insurgents on Samar Island massacred fifty-nine American soldiers, "Hell-Roaring Jake" Smith ordered his men to burn and kill their way across the island in retaliation.

TAFT, WILLIAM HOWARD   Headed a United States civilian commission that took over the Philippine colonial government in 1901.

USS *MAINE*   The mysterious sinking of this American battleship was the catalyst of the Spanish-American War.

"WATER CURE"   American method of torture devised in retaliation for Filipino acts of terrorism (booby traps and assassination); a bamboo reed was placed in an insurgent's mouth, and water, often salted or dirty, was poured down his throat until he was so painfully bloated that he talked.

"WHITE MAN'S BURDEN"   Racist concept, popular among American imperialists, that whites had a "moral responsibility" to uplift and civilize supposedly inferior dark-skinned people such as the Filipinos.

G uerrilla warfare . . . jungle terrain . . . search and destroy missions . . . benevolent pacification . . . strategic hamlets . . . terrorism . . . ambushes . . . free-fire zones . . . booby traps . . . waning support from civilians at home. These words call forth from the national consciousness uncomfortable images of a war Americans fought and died in not long ago in Southeast Asia. But while the phrases may first bring to mind America's painful experience in Vietnam during the 1960s and '70s, they also aptly describe a much earlier conflict—the Philippine Insurrection—that foreshadowed this and other insurgent wars in Asia.

The Philippine-American War of 1898–1902 is one of our nation's most obscure and least-understood campaigns. Sometimes called the "Bolo War" because of the Filipino insurgents' lethally effective use of razor-sharp bolo knives or machetes against the American

expeditionary force occupying the islands, it is often viewed as a mere appendage of the one-hundred-day Spanish-American War. But suppressing the guerrilla warfare waged by Philippine nationalists seeking self-rule proved far more difficult, protracted, and costly for American forces than the conventional war with Spain that had preceded it.

America's campaign to smash the Philippine Insurrection was, ironically, a direct consequence of U.S. efforts to secure independence for other *insurrectos* halfway around the world in Cuba. On May 1, 1898, less than a week after Congress declared war against Spain, a naval squadron commanded by Commodore George Dewey steamed into Manila Bay to engage the Spanish warships defending that nation's Pacific possession. In a brief action Dewey achieved a stunning victory, sinking all of the enemy vessels with no significant American losses. Destroying the Spanish fleet, however, did not ensure U.S. possession of the Philippines. An estimated 15,000 Spanish soldiers still occupied Manila and the surrounding region. Those forces would have to be rooted out by infantry.

David R. Kohler and James W. Wensyel, from *American History Illustrated* (January/February 1990), 19–30. Original title: "Our First Southeast Asian War," Reprinted through the courtesy of Cowles Magazines, publisher of *American History Illustrated*.

President William McKinley had already ordered a Philippine Expeditionary Force of volunteer and regular army infantry, artillery, and cavalry units (nearly seven thousand men), under the command of Major General Wesley Merritt, to "reduce Spanish power in that quarter [Philippine Islands] and give order and security to the islands while in the possession of the United States."

Sent to the Philippines in the summer of 1898, this limited force was committed without fully considering the operation's potential length and cost. American military and government leaders also failed to anticipate the consequences of ignoring the Filipino rebels who, under Generalissimo Don Emilio Aguinaldo y Famy, had been waging a war for independence against Spain for the past two years. And when American insensitivity toward Aguinaldo eventually led to open warfare with the rebels, the American leaders grossly underestimated the determination of the seemingly ill-trained and poorly armed insurgents. They additionally failed to perceive the difficulties involved in conducting military operations in a tropical environment and among a hostile native population, and they did not recognize the burden of fighting at the end of a seven-thousand-mile-long logistics trail.

Asian engagements, the Americans learned for the first time, are costly. The enterprise, so modestly begun, eventually saw more than 126,000 American officers and men deployed to the Philippines. Four times as many soldiers served in this undeclared war in the Pacific as had been sent to the Caribbean during the Spanish-American War. During the three-year conflict, American troops and Filipino insurgents fought in more than 2,800 engagements. American casualties ultimately totaled 4,234 killed and 2,818 wounded, and the insurgents lost about 16,000 men. The civilian population suffered even more; as many as 200,000 Filipinos died from famine, pestilence, or the unfortunate happenstance of being too close to the fighting. The Philippine war cost the United States $600 million before the insurgents were subdued.

The costly experience offered valuable and timeless lessons about guerrilla warfare in Asia; unfortunately, those lessons had to be relearned sixty years later in another war that, despite the modern technology involved, bore surprising parallels to America's first Southeast Asian campaign.

ORIGINS

America's war with Spain, formally declared by the United States on April 25, 1898, had been several years in the making. During that time the American "yellow press," led by Joseph Pulitzer's *New York World* and William Randolph Hearst's *New York Journal,* trumpeted reports of heroic Cuban *insurrectos* revolting against their cruel Spanish rulers. Journalists vividly described harsh measures taken by Spanish officials to quell the Cuban revolution. The sensational accounts, often exaggerated, reminded Americans of their own uphill fight for independence and nourished the feeling that America was destined to intervene so that the Cuban people might also taste freedom.

Furthermore, expansionists suggested that the revolt against a European power, taking place less than one hundred miles from American shores, offered a splendid opportunity to turn the Caribbean into an American sea. Businessmen pointed out that $50 million in American capital was invested in the Cuban sugar and mining industries. Revolutions resulting in burned cane fields jeopardized that investment. As 1898 opened, American relations with Spain quickly declined.

In January 1898 the U.S. battleship *Maine* was sent to Cuba, ostensibly on a courtesy visit. On February 15 the warship was destroyed by a mysterious explosion while at anchor in Havana harbor, killing 262 of her 350-man crew. The navy's formal inquiry, completed on March 28, suggested that the explosion was due to an external force—a mine.

On March 29, the Spanish government received an ultimatum from Washington, D.C.: Spain's army in Cuba was to lay down its arms while the United States negotiated between the rebels and the Spaniards. The Spanish forces were also told to abolish all *reconcentrado* camps (tightly controlled areas, similar to the strategic hamlets later tried in Vietnam, where peasants were regrouped to deny food and intelligence to insurgents and to promote tighter security). Spain initially rejected the humiliation of surrendering its arms in the field but then capitulated on all points. The Americans were not satisfied.

On April 11, declaring that Spanish responses were inadequate, President McKinley told a joint session of Congress that "I have exhausted every effort to relieve the intolerable condition . . . at our doors. I now ask the Congress to empower the president to take measures to secure a full and final termination of hostilities in Cuba, to secure . . . the establishment of a stable government, and to use the military and naval forces of the United States . . . for these purposes. . . ."

Congress adopted the proposed resolution on April 19. Learning this, Spain declared war on the 24th. The following day, the United States responded with its own declaration of war.

The bulk of the American navy quickly gathered on the Atlantic coast. McKinley called for 125,000 volunteers to bolster the less than eighty-thousand-man regular army. His call was quickly oversubscribed; volunteers fought to be the first to land on Cuba's beaches.

The first major battle of the war, however, was fought not in Cuba but seven thousand miles to the west—in Manila Bay. Dewey's victory over Spanish Admiral Patricio Montojo y Pasarón (a rather hollow victory as Montojo's fleet consisted of seven unarmored ships, three of which had wooden hulls and one that had to be towed to the battle area) was wildly acclaimed in America.

American leaders, believing that the Philippines would now fall into America's grasp like a ripe plum, had to decide what to do with their prize. They could not return the islands to Spain, nor could they allow them to pass to France or Germany, America's commercial rivals in the Orient. The American press rejected the idea of a British protectorate. And, after four hundred years of despotic Spanish rule in which Filipinos had little or no chance to practice self-government, native leaders seemed unlikely candidates for managing their own affairs. McKinley faced a grand opportunity for imperialistic expansion that could not be ignored.

The debate sharply divided his cabinet—and the country. American public opinion over acquisition of the Philippines divided into two basic factions: imperialists versus anti-imperialists.

The imperialists, mostly Republicans, included such figures as Theodore Roosevelt (then assistant secretary of the navy), Henry Cabot Lodge (Massachusetts senator), and Albert Beveridge (Indiana senator). These individuals were, for the most part, disciples of Alfred Thayer Mahan, a naval strategist who touted theories of national power and prestige through sea power and acquisition of overseas colonies for trade purposes and naval coaling stations.

The anti-imperialists, staunchly against American annexation of the Philippines, were mainly Democrats. Such men as former presidents Grover Cleveland and Rutherford B. Hayes, steel magnate Andrew Carnegie, William Jennings Bryan, union leader Samuel Gompers, and Mark Twain warned that by taking the Philippines the United States would march the road to ruin earlier traveled by the Roman Empire. Furthermore, they argued, America would be denying Filipinos the right of self-determination guaranteed by our own Constitution. The more practical-minded also pointed out that imperialistic policy would require maintaining an expensive army and navy there.

Racism, though demonstrated in different ways, pervaded the arguments of both sides. Imperialists spoke of the "white man's burden" and moral responsibility to "uplift the child races everywhere" and to provide "orderly development for the unfortunate and less able races." They spoke of America's "civilizing mission" of pacifying Filipinos by "benevolent assimilation" and saw the opening of the overseas frontier much as their forefathers had viewed the western frontier. The "subjugation of the Injun" (wherever he might be found) was a concept grasped by American youth—the war's most enthusiastic supporters (in contrast to young America's opposition to the war in Vietnam many years later).

The anti-imperialists extolled the sacredness of independence and self-determination for the Filipinos. Racism, however, also crept into their argument, for they believed that "protection against race mingling" was a historic American policy that would be reversed by imperialism. To them, annexation of the Philippines would admit "alien, inferior, and mongrel races to our nationality."

As the debate raged, Dewey continued to hold Manila Bay, and the Philippines seemed to await America's pleasure. President McKinley would ultimately cast the deciding vote in determining America's role in that country. McKinley, a genial, rather laid-back, former congressman from Ohio and one-time major in the Union army, remains a rather ambiguous figure during this period. In his Inaugural Address he had affirmed that "We want no wars of conquest; we must avoid the temptation of territorial aggression." Thereafter, however, he made few comments on pacifism, and, fourteen weeks after becoming president, signed the bill annexing Hawaii.

Speaking of Cuba in December 1897, McKinley said, "I speak not of forcible annexation, for that cannot be thought of. That, by our code of morality, would be criminal aggression." Nevertheless, he constantly pressured Madrid to end Spanish rule in Cuba, leading four months later to America's war with Spain.

McKinley described experiencing extreme turmoil, soul-searching, and prayer over the Philippine annexation issue until, he declared, one night in a dream the Lord revealed to him that "there was nothing left for us to do but to take them all [the Philippine Islands] and to educate the Filipinos, and uplift, and civilize, and Christianize them." He apparently didn't realize that the Philippines had been staunchly Roman Catholic for more than 350 years under Spanish colonialism. Nor could he anticipate the difficulties that, having cast its fortune with the expansionists, America would now face in the Philippines.

PROSECUTING THE WAR

Meanwhile, in the Philippine Islands, Major General Wesley Merritt's Philippine Expeditionary Force went about its job. In late June, General Thomas Anderson led an advance party ashore at Cavite. He then established Camp Merritt, visited General Aguinaldo's rebel forces entrenched around Manila, and made plans for seizing that city once Merritt arrived with the main body of armed forces.

Anderson quickly learned that military operations in the Philippines could be difficult. His soldiers, hastily assembled and dispatched with limited prior training, were poorly disciplined and inadequately equipped. Many still wore woolen uniforms despite the tropical climate. A staff officer described the army's baptism at Manila: ". . . the heat was oppressive and the rain kept falling. At times the trenches were filled with two feet of water, and soon the men's shoes were ruined. Their heavy khaki uniforms were a nuisance; they perspired constantly, the loss of body salts inducing chronic fatigue. Prickly heat broke out, inflamed by scratching and rubbing. Within a week the first cases of dysentery, malaria, cholera, and dengue fever showed up at sick call."

During his first meeting with Dewey, Anderson remarked that some American leaders were considering annexation of the Philippines. "If the United States intends to hold the Philippine Islands," Dewey responded, "it will make things awkward, because just a week ago Aguinaldo proclaimed the independence of the Philippine Islands from Spain and seems intent on establishing his own government."

A Filipino independence movement led by Aguinaldo had been active in the islands since 1896 and, within weeks of Dewey's victory, Aguinaldo's revolutionaries controlled most of the archipelago.

Aguinaldo, twenty-nine years old in 1898, had taken over his father's position as mayor of his hometown of Kawit before becoming a revolutionary. In a minor skirmish with Spanish soldiers, he had rallied the Filipinos to victory. Thereafter, his popularity grew as did his ragtag but determined army. Aguinaldo was slight of build, shy, and soft-spoken, but a strict disciplinarian.

As his rebel force besieged Manila, Aguinaldo declared a formal government for the Philippines with himself as president and generalissimo. He proclaimed his "nation's" independence and called for Filipinos to rally to his army and to the Americans, declaring that "the Americans . . . extend their protecting mantle to our beloved country . . . When you see the American flag flying, assemble in numbers: they are our redeemers!" But his enthusiasm for the United States later waned.

Merritt put off Aguinaldo's increasingly strident demands that America recognize his government and guarantee the Filipinos' independence. Aguinaldo perceived the American general's attitude as condescending and demeaning.

On August 13, Merritt's forces occupied Manila almost without firing a shot; in a face-saving maneuver the Spanish defenders had agreed to surrender to the Americans to avoid being captured—and perhaps massacred—by the Filipino insurgents. Merritt's troops physically blocked Aguinaldo's rebels, who had spent weeks in the trenches around the city, from participating in the assault. The Filipino general and his followers felt betrayed at being denied a share in the victory.

Further disenchanted, Aguinaldo would later find his revolutionary government unrepresented at the Paris peace talks determining his country's fate. He would learn that Spain had ceded the Philippines to the United States for $20 million.

Officers at Merritt's headquarters had little faith in the Filipinos' ability to govern themselves. "Should our power . . . be withdrawn," an early report declared, "the Philippines would speedily lapse into anarchy, which would excuse . . . the intervention of other powers and the division of the islands among them."

Meanwhile, friction between American soldiers and the Filipinos increased. Much of the Americans' conduct betrayed their racial bias. Soldiers referred to the natives as "niggers" and "gugus," epithets whose meanings were clear to the Filipinos. In retaliation,

the island inhabitants refused to give way on sidewalks and muscled American officers into the streets. Men of the expeditionary force in turn escalated tensions by stopping Filipinos at gun point, searching them without cause, "confiscating" shopkeepers' goods, and beating those who resisted.

On the night of February 4, 1899, the simmering pot finally boiled over. Private William "Willie" Walter Grayson and several other soldiers of Company D, 1st Nebraska Volunteer Infantry, apprehended a group of armed insurgents within their regimental picket line. Shots were exchanged, and three Filipino *insurrectos* fell dead. Heavy firing erupted between the two camps.

In the bloody battle that followed, the Filipinos suffered tremendous casualties (an estimated two thousand to five thousand dead, contrasted with fifty-nine Americans killed) and were forced to withdraw. The Philippine Insurrection had begun.

GUERRILLA WARFARE

The Americans, hampered by a shortage of troops and the oncoming rainy season, could initially do little more than extend their defensive perimeter beyond Manila and establish a toehold on several islands to the south. By the end of March, however, American forces seized Malolos, the seat of Aguinaldo's revolutionary government. But Aguinaldo escaped, simply melting into the jungle. In the fall, using conventional methods of warfare, the Americans first struck south, then north of Manila across the central Luzon plain. After hard marching and tough fighting, the expeditionary force occupied northern Luzon, dispersed the rebel army, and barely missed capturing Aguinaldo.

Believing that occupying the remainder of the Philippines would be easy, the Americans wrongly concluded that the war was virtually ended. But when the troops attempted to control the territory they had seized, they found that the Filipino revolutionaries were not defeated but had merely changed strategies.

United States troops sent to the Philippines found the tropical climate and terrain "almost as deadly as combat." The first contingent of soldiers arrived wearing woolen uniforms. Thousands of *Americans fell victim to dysentery and malaria. (Keystone-Mast Collection, California Museum of Photography, University of California, Riverside)*

Abandoning western-style conventional warfare, Aguinaldo had decided to adopt guerrilla tactics.

Aguinaldo moved to a secret mountain headquarters at Palanan in northern Luzon, ordering his troops to disperse and avoid pitched battles in favor of hit-and-run operations by small bands. Ambushing parties of Americans and applying terror to coerce support from other Filipinos, the insurrectionists now blended into the countryside, where they enjoyed superior intelligence information, ample supplies, and tight security. The guerrillas moved freely between the scattered American units, cutting telegraph lines, attacking supply trains, and assaulting straggling infantrymen. When the Americans pursued their tormentors, they fell into well planned ambushes. The insurgents' barbarity and ruthlessness during these attacks were notorious.

The guerrilla tactics helped to offset the inequities that existed between the two armies. The American troops were far better armed, for example, carrying .45-caliber Springfield single-shot rifles, Mausers, and then-modern .30-caliber repeating Krag-Jorgensen rifles. They also had field artillery and machine guns. The revolutionaries, on the other hand, were limited to a miscellaneous assortment of handguns, a few Mauser repeating rifles taken from the Spanish, and antique muzzle-loaders. The sharp-edged bolo knife was the revolutionary's primary weapon, and he used it well. Probably more American soldiers were hacked to death by bolos than were killed by Mauser bullets.

As would later be the case in Vietnam, the guerrillas had some clear advantages. They knew the terrain, were inured to the climate, and could generally count on a friendly population. As in Vietnam, villages controlled by the insurgents provided havens from which the guerrillas could attack, then fade back into hiding.

Americans soon began to feel that they were under siege in a land of enemies, and their fears were heightened because they never could be sure who among the population was hostile. A seemingly friendly peasant might actually be a murderer. Lieutenant Colonel J. T. Wickham, commanding the 26th Infantry Regiment, recorded that "a large flag of truce enticed officers into ambushes . . . Privates Dugan, Hayes, and Tracy were murdered by town authorities . . . Private Nolan [was] tied up by ladies while in a stupor; the insurgents cut his throat . . . The body of Corporal Doneley was dug up, burned, and mutilated . . . Private O'Hearn, captured by apparently friendly people was tied to a tree, burned over a slow fire, and slashed up . . . Lieutenant Max Wagner was assassinated by insurgents disguised in American uniforms."

As in later guerrilla movements, such terrorism became a standard tactic for the insurgents. Both Filipinos and Americans were their victims. In preying on their countrymen, the guerrillas had a dual purpose: to discourage any Filipinos disposed to cooperate with the Americans, and to demonstrate to people in a particular region that they ruled that area and could destroy inhabitants and villages not supporting the revolution. The most favored terroristic weapon was assassination of local leaders, who were usually executed in a manner (such as beheading or burying alive) calculated to horrify everyone.

By the spring of 1900 the war was going badly for the Americans. Their task forces, sent out to search and destroy, found little and destroyed less.

The monsoon rains, jungle terrain, hostile native population, and a determined guerrilla force made the American soldiers' marches long and miserable. One described a five-week-long infantry operation: ". . . our troops had been on half rations for two weeks. Wallowing through hip-deep muck, lugging a ten-pound rifle and a belt . . . with 200 rounds of ammunition, drenched to the skin and with their feet becoming heavier with mud at every step, the infantry became discouraged. Some men simply cried, others slipped down in the mud and refused to rise. Threats and appeals by the officers were of no avail. Only a promise of food in the next town and the threat that if they remained behind they would be butchered by marauding bands of insurgents forced some to their feet to struggle on."

News reports of the army's difficulties began to erode the American public's support for the war. "To chase barefooted insurgents with water buffalo carts as a wagon train may be simply ridiculous," charged one correspondent, "but to load volunteers down with 200 rounds of ammunition and one day's rations, and to put on their heads felt hats used by no other army in the tropics . . . to trot these same soldiers in the boiling sun over a country without roads, is positively criminal. . . . There are over five thousand men in the general hospital."

Another reported that the American outlook "is blacker now than it has been since the beginning of the war . . . the whole population . . . sympathizes with the insurgents. The insurgents came to Pasig [a local area whose government cooperated with the Americans] and their first act was to hang the 'Presidente' for treason in surrendering to Americans. 'Presidentes' do not surrender to us anymore."

NEW STRATEGIES

Early in the war U.S. military commanders had realized that, unlike the American Indians who had been herded onto reservations, eight million Filipinos (many of them hostile) would have to be governed in place. The Americans chose to emphasize pacification through good works rather than by harsh measures, hoping to convince Filipinos that the American colonial government had a sincere interest in their welfare and could be trusted.

As the army expanded its control across the islands, it reorganized local municipal governments and trained Filipinos to take over civil functions in the democratic political structure the Americans planned to establish. American soldiers performed police duties, distributed food, established and taught at schools, and built roads and telegraph lines.

As the war progressed, however, the U.S. commanders saw that the terrorism practiced by Aguinaldo's guerrillas was far more effective in controlling the populace than was their own benevolent approach. Although the Americans did not abandon pacification through good works, it was thereafter subordinated to the "civilize 'em with a Krag" (Krag-Jorgensen rifle) philosophy. From December 1900 onward, captured revolutionaries faced deportation, imprisonment, or execution.

The American army also changed its combat strategy to counter that of its enemy. As in the insurgents' army, the new tactics emphasized mobility and surprise. Breaking into small units—the battalion became the largest maneuver force—the Americans gradually spread over the islands until each of the larger towns was occupied by one or two rifle companies. From these bases American troops began platoon- and company-size operations to pressure local guerrilla bands.

Because of the difficult terrain, limited visibility, and requirement for mobility, artillery now saw limited use except as a defensive weapon. The infantry became the main offensive arm, with mounted riflemen used to pursue the fleeing enemy. Cavalry patrols were so valued for their mobility that American military leaders hired trusted Filipinos as mounted scouts and cavalrymen.

The Americans made other efforts to "Filipinize" the war—letting Asians fight Asians. (A similar tactic had been used in the American Indian campaigns twenty years before; it would resurface in Vietnam sixty years later as "Vietnamization.") In the Philippines the Americans recruited five thousand Macabebes, mercenaries from the central Luzon province of Pampanga, to form the American officered Philippine Scouts. The Macabebes

had for centuries fought in native battalions under the Spanish flag—even against their own countrymen when the revolution began in 1896.

Just as a later generation of American soldiers would react to the guerrilla war in Vietnam, American soldiers in the Philippines responded to insurgent terrorism terrorism in kind, matching cruelty with cruelty. Such actions vented their frustration at being unable to find and destroy the enemy. An increasing number of Americans viewed all Filipinos as enemies.

"We make everyone get into his house by 7 P.M. and we only tell a man once," Corporal Sam Gillis of the 1st California Volunteer Regiment wrote to his family. "If he refuses, we shoot him. We killed over 300 natives the first night. . . . If they fire a shot from a house, we burn the house and every house near it."

Another infantryman frankly admitted that "with an enemy like this to fight, it is not surprising that the boys should soon adopt 'no quarter' as a motto and fill the blacks full of lead before finding out whether they are friends or enemies."

That attitude should not have been too surprising. The army's campaigns against the Plains Indians were reference points for the generation of Americans that took the Philippines. Many of the senior officers and noncommissioned officers—often veterans of the Indian wars—considered Filipinos to be "as full of treachery as our Arizona Apache." "The country won't be pacified," one soldier told a reporter, "until the niggers are killed off like the Indians." A popular soldiers' refrain, sung to the tune of "Tramp, tramp, tramp, the boys are marching," began, "Damn, damn, damn the Filipinos," and again spoke of "civilizing 'em with a Krag."

Reprisals against civilians by Americans as well as insurgents became common. General Lloyd Wheaton, leading a U.S. offensive southeast of Manila, found his men impaled on the bamboo prongs of booby traps and with throats slit while they slept. After two of his companies were ambushed, Wheaton ordered that every town and village within twelve miles be burned.

The Americans developed their own terrorist methods, many of which would be used in later Southeast

Asian wars. One was torturing suspected guerrillas or insurgent sympathizers to force them to reveal locations of other guerrillas and their supplies. An often-utilized form of persuasion was the "water cure," placing a bamboo reed in the victim's mouth and pouring water (some used salt water or dirty water) down his throat, thus painfully distending the victim's stomach. The subject, allowed to void this, would, under threat of repetition, usually talk freely. Another method of torture, the "rope cure," consisted of wrapping a rope around the victim's neck and torso until it formed a sort of girdle. A stick (or Krag rifle), placed between the ropes and twisted, then effectively created a combination of smothering and garroting.

The anti-imperialist press reported such American brutality in lurid detail. As a result, a number of officers and soldiers were court-martialed for torturing and other cruelties. Their punishments, however, seemed remarkably lenient. Of ten officers tried for "looting, torture, and murder," three were acquitted; of the seven convicted, five were reprimanded, one was reprimanded and fined $300, and one lost thirty-five places in the army's seniority list and forfeited half his pay for nine months.

Officers and soldiers, fighting a cruel, determined, and dangerous enemy, could not understand public condemnation of the brutality they felt was necessary to win. They had not experienced such criticism during the Indian wars, where total extermination of the enemy was condoned by the press and the American public, and they failed to grasp the difference now. Press reports, loss of public support, and the soldiers' feeling of betrayal—features of an insurgent war—would resurface decades later during the Vietnam conflict.

SUCCESS

Although U.S. military leaders were frustrated by the guerrillas' determination on the one hand and by eroding American support for the war on the other, most believed that the insurgents could be subdued.

Especially optimistic was General Arthur MacArthur, who in 1900 assumed command of the seventy thousand American troops in the Philippines. MacArthur adopted a strategy like that successfully used by General Zachary Taylor in the Second Seminole War in 1835; he believed that success depended upon the Americans' ability to isolate the guerrillas from their support in the villages. Thus were born "strategic hamlets," "free-fire zones," and "search and destroy" missions, concepts the American army would revive decades later in Vietnam.

MacArthur strengthened the more than five hundred small strong points held by Americans throughout the Philippine Islands. Each post was garrisoned by at least one company of American infantrymen. The natives around each base were driven from their homes, which were then destroyed. Soldiers herded the displaced natives into *reconcentrado* camps, where they could be "protected" by the nearby garrisons. Crops, food stores, and houses outside the camps were destroyed to deny them to the guerrillas. Surrounding each camp was a "dead line," within which anyone appearing would be shot on sight.

Operating from these small garrisons, the Americans pressured the guerrillas, allowing them no rest. Kept off balance, short of supplies, and constantly pursued by the American army, the Filipino guerrillas, suffering from sickness, hunger, and dwindling popular support, began to lose their will to fight. Many insurgent leaders surrendered, signaling that the tide at last had turned in the Americans' favor.

In March 1901, a group of Macabebe Scouts, commanded by American Colonel Frederick "Fighting Fred" Funston, captured Aguinaldo. Aguinaldo's subsequent proclamation that he would fight no more, and his pledge of loyalty to the United States, sped the collapse of the insurrection.

As in the past, and as would happen again during the Vietnam conflict of the 1960s and '70s, American optimism was premature. Although a civilian commission headed by William H. Taft took control of the colonial government from the American army in July 1901, the army faced more bitter fighting in its "pacification" of the islands.

As the war sputtered, the insurgents' massacre of fifty-nine American soldiers at Balangiga on the island of Samar caused Brigadier General Jacob W. "Hell-Roaring Jake" Smith, veteran of the Wounded Knee massacre of the Sioux in 1890, to order his officers to turn Samar into a "howling wilderness." His orders to a battalion of three hundred Marines headed for Samar were precise: "I want no prisoners. I wish you to kill and burn, the more you kill and burn the better it will please me. I want all persons killed who are capable of bearing arms against the United States." Fortunately, the Marines did not take Smith's orders literally and, later, Smith would be court-martialed.

On July 4, 1902, the Philippine Insurrection officially ended. Although it took the American army another eleven years to crush the fierce Moros of the southern Philippines, the civil government's security force (the Philippine Constabulary), aided by the army's Philippine Scouts, maintained a fitful peace throughout the islands. The army's campaign to secure the Philippines as an American colony had succeeded.

American commanders would have experienced vastly greater difficulties except for two distinct advantages: 1) the enemy had to operate in a restricted area, in isolated islands, and was prevented by the U.S. Navy from importing weapons and other needed supplies; and 2) though the insurgents attempted to enlist help from Japan, no outside power intervened. These conditions would not prevail in some subsequent guerrilla conflicts in Asia.

In addition to the many tactical lessons the army learned from fighting a guerrilla war in a tropical climate, other problems experienced during this campaign validated the need for several military reforms that were subsequently carried out, including improved logistics, tropical medicine, and communications.

The combination of harsh and unrelenting military force against the guerrillas, complemented by the exercise of fair and equitable civil government and civic action toward those who cooperated, proved to be the Americans' most effective tactic for dealing with the insurgency. This probably was the most significant lesson to be learned from the Philippine Insurrection.

LESSONS FOR THE FUTURE

Vietnam veterans reading this account might nod in recollection of a personal, perhaps painful experience from their own war.

Many similarities exist between America's three-year struggle with the Filipino *insurrectos* and the decade-long campaign against the Communists in Vietnam. Both wars, modestly begun, went far beyond what anyone had foreseen in time, money, equipment, manpower, casualties, and suffering.

Both wars featured small-unit infantry actions. Young infantrymen, if they had any initial enthusiasm, usually lost it once they saw the war's true nature; they nevertheless learned to endure their allotted time while adopting personal self-survival measures as months "in-country" lengthened and casualty lists grew.

Both wars were harsh, brutal, cruel. Both had their Samar Islands and their My Lais. Human nature being what it is, both conflicts also included acts of great heroism, kindness, compassion, and self-sacrifice.

Both wars saw an increasingly disenchanted American public withdrawing its support (and even disavowing its servicemen) as the campaigns dragged on, casualties mounted, and news accounts vividly described the horror of the battlefields.

Some useful lessons might be gleaned from a comparison of the two conflicts. Human nature really does not change—war will bring out the best and the worst in the tired, wet, hungry, and fearful men who are doing the fighting. Guerrilla campaigns—particularly where local military and civic reforms cannot be effected to separate the guerrilla from his base of popular support—will be long and difficult, and will demand tremendous commitments in resources and national will. Finally, before America commits its armed forces to similar ventures in the future, it would do well to recall the lessons learned from previous campaigns. For, as the Spanish-born American educator, poet, and philosopher George Santayana reminded us, those who do not learn from the past are doomed to repeat it.

QUESTIONS TO CONSIDER

1 How and why did the United States initially become involved in the Philippines? What, according to the authors, were the fundamental mistakes committed by the Americans in making that decision?

2 Why did the Americans decide to take over the Philippines? What were the different categories of American public opinion in reaction to this development? How were they different, and what attitudes did they share?

3 What military advantages did the Philippine insurgents have? What were American military tactics and goals, and how did they change in response to the conditions of the Philippine conflict?

4 How does the conflict in the Philippines compare with the Indian wars that preceded it? In particular, how did the American public and American soldiers differ in comparing the Philippine conflict with the Indian wars, and what were the results and significance of this difference?

5 What, according to the authors, are the lessons to be learned from our involvement in the Philippines? Have they been learned?

PART FIVE

Currents of the Progressive Era

10 Theodore Roosevelt, President

EDMUND MORRIS

Despite a long, enervating depression, American industry continued to expand and consolidate throughout the 1890s, and the rate of expansion was even faster in the first decade of the twentieth century. By then, economic concentration had resulted in a handful of giant combinations that were dominating each area of industrial activity. In 1909, 1 percent of American business enterprises produced 44 percent of the nation's manufactured goods. Money and property were so maldistributed that 1 percent of the United States population—the corporate magnates and their families—owned seven-eighths of the country's wealth. Middle-class families were getting by, although precariously. And the rest—industrial workers in America's teeming, dilapidated cities and debtor farmers in the South and West—lived in poverty.

The new Populist party, a third-party reform movement, posed the first serious challenge to the new industrial order and the corporate bosses who controlled it. The Populist insurgents made thousands aware of the need for reform—the need to correct the abuses of industrial monopolies and to protect the mass of the nation's people. So did liberal intellectuals and crusading journalists—the celebrated muckrakers who exposed glaring malpractices in business and in municipal governments. Thanks to these men and women, thanks to tensions caused by rapid and unmanaged industrial growth, and thanks to a genuine desire to revive humanitarian democracy, there emerged the complex Progressive movement, which lasted from the late 1890s through the First World War. For the most part, those who joined the ranks of progressivism were victims of monopolies and were anxious to dismantle the biggest of them and control the rest.

Progressivism transcended party labels, as Democrats and Republicans alike took up the banners of reform. In the Democratic party, William Jennings Bryan crusaded against the conservative Republican–big business alliance that ran the country; later Bryan passed the leadership of Democratic progressivism to Woodrow Wilson, the subject of selection 13. In the Republican party, "Fighting Bob" La Follette, governor of Wisconsin, made his state a model of progressivism. But the best-known Progressive Republican was the man who found himself elevated to the White House when an assassin murdered William McKinley in 1901. "Now look!" exclaimed a horrified Republican. "That damned cowboy is president of the United States."

That damned cowboy, of course, was Theodore Roosevelt, a whirlwind of a man whose motto was "Get action, do things; be sane, don't fritter away your time; create, act, take a place wherever you are and be somebody: get action." Get action he did, as he hunted big game on three continents, sparred with prizefighters, rode with cowboys, dashed off voluminous histories, knocked down a tough in a western saloon, led the celebrated Rough Riders during the Spanish-American War, terrorized a police force, ran the Empire State as governor, and rose to the nation's highest office. Never mind that he was an accidental president. Once in the presidency, he put on a performance—for surely that is the word for it—that held the nation spellbound.

What president since the Civil War had had such uninhibited gusto, such a sense of the dramatic? He conducted a vigorous foreign policy that made the United States a major presence in the world. He dispatched a fleet of white battleships around the globe and won a Nobel Peace Prize for mediating the Russo-Japanese War. In this hemisphere, he rattled the Monroe Doctrine, ordered American troops to Santo Domingo, stationed marines in Cuba, encouraged a revolution against the Republic of Colombia that established the new nation of Panama, and then acquired the rights to build a canal there that would furnish America with a lifeline to the Pacific. Roosevelt's actions in Panama were provocative, even unethical, but he didn't care. As he said later, "If I had followed traditional conservative methods I would have submitted a dignified state paper of probably two hundred pages to the Congress and the debate would be going on yet, but I took the Canal Zone and let the Congress debate, and while the debate goes on, the canal does also."

He was just as vigorous in his domestic policy. He trumpeted the cause of conservation, sent troops to protect strikers in the Pennsylvania coal mines, and thundered so violently against "the malefactors of great wealth" and "the criminal rich" that conservative Republicans were appalled. The first post–Civil War president to recognize the threat of monopolies and trusts to America's economic life, TR shook his fist in the face of banker J. Pierpont Morgan, and his attorney general initiated more antitrust suits than all previous attorneys general combined. As a result, TR won a reputation as a crusading "trust buster." In point of fact, he accepted business consolidation as an economic reality in America and, instead of crushing all business combinations, established a policy of government scrutiny and control. Thus, he attacked only "bad" or "evil" trusts and left the "good" ones alone. Indeed, as one scholar put it, "the first great wave of business consolidation" actually came to a climax during Roosevelt's presidency.

Behind Roosevelt's actions was a volatile personality that kept his legions of followers enthralled. And that personality, full of contradiction, of great charm and physical exuberance, of egotistical moralizing and militarism, fairly explodes off the pages that follow. In them, TR's Pulitzer Prize–winning biographer, Edmund Morris, makes us aware of the importance of personal qualities in shaping the conduct and careers of historical figures. As you read this spirited portrait, you may not always like Theodore Roosevelt, but you will never find him boring.

GLOSSARY

HANNA, MARK Chairman of the Republican National Committee who aspired to take over the White House after TR had finished his "caretaker" term.

LIVINGSTONE, ROBERT Journalist who praised TR's great "gift of personal magnetism."

ROOSEVELT, ALICE LEE TR's first wife, who died of Bright's disease (kidney inflammation) on the same day that TR's mother died of typhoid fever.

ROOSEVELT, MARTHA BULLOCH "MITTIE" TR's mother.

TEEDIE TR's boyhood nickname.

WASHINGTON, BOOKER T. The head of Alabama's all-black Tuskegee Institute whom TR invited to dine at the White House; "it was the first time that a president had ever entertained a black man in the first house of the land," and it enraged southern white supremacists.

Let us dispose, in short order, with Theodore Roosevelt's faults. He was an incorrigible preacher of platitudes. . . . He significantly reduced the wildlife population of some three continents. He piled his dessert plate with so many peaches that the cream spilled over the sides. And he used to make rude faces out of the presidential carriage at small boys in the streets of Washington.

Now those last two faults are forgivable if we accept British diplomat Cecil Spring-Rice's advice, "You must always remember the President is about six." The first fault—his preachiness—is excused by the fact that the American electorate dearly loves a moralist. As to the second and most significant fault—Theodore Roosevelt's genuine blood-lust and desire to destroy his adversaries, whether they be rhinoceroses or members of the United States Senate—it is paradoxically so much a part of his virtues, both as a man and a politician, that I will come back to it in more detail later.

One of the minor irritations I have to contend with as a biographer is that whenever I go to the library to look for books about Roosevelt, Theodore, they infallibly are mixed up with books about Roosevelt, Franklin—and I guess FDR scholars have the same problem in reverse. Time was when the single word "Roosevelt" meant only Theodore; FDR

himself frequently had to insist, in the early thirties, that he was not TR's son. He was merely a fifth cousin, and what was even more distant, a Democrat to boot. In time, of course, Franklin succeeded in preempting the early meaning of the word "Roosevelt," to the point that TR's public image, which once loomed as large as Washington's and Lincoln's, began to fade like a Cheshire cat from popular memory. By the time of FDR's own death in 1945, little was left but the ghost of a toothy grin.

Only a few veterans of the earlier Roosevelt era survived to testify that if Franklin was the greater politician, it was only by a hairsbreadth, and as far as sheer personality was concerned, Theodore's superiority could be measured in spades. They pointed out that FDR himself declared, late in life, that his "cousin Ted" was the greatest man he ever knew.

Presently the veterans too died. But that ghostly grin continued to float in the national consciousness, as if to indicate that its owner was meditating a reappearance. I first became aware of the power behind the grin in Washington, in February of 1976. The National Theater was trying out an ill-fated musical by Alan Lerner and Leonard Bernstein, *1600 Pennsylvania Avenue.* For two and a half hours Ken Howard worked his way through a chronological series of impersonations of historic Presidents. The audience sat on its hands, stiff with boredom, until the very end, when Mr. Howard clamped on a pair of pince-nez and a false mustache, and bared all his teeth in a grin. The entire theater burst into delighted applause.

From Edmund Morris, "Theodore Roosevelt, President," *American Heritage,* June/July 1981, Vol. 32, No. 4. Reprinted by permission of American Heritage, Inc. Copyright © Forbes, Inc., 1981.

What intrigued me was the fact that few people there could have known much about TR beyond the obvious clichés of San Juan Hill and the Big Stick. Yet somehow, subconsciously, they realized that here for once was a positive President, warm and tough and authoritative and funny, who believed in America and who, to quote Owen Wister, "grasped his optimism tight lest it escape him."

In [recent times] Theodore Roosevelt has made his long-promised comeback. He has been the subject of a *Newsweek* cover story on American heroes; Russell Baker has called him a cinch to carry all fifty states if he were running for the White House today; he's starring on Broadway in *Tintypes,* on television in *Bully,* and you'll . . . see him on the big screen in *Ragtime.* Every season brings a new crop of reassessments in the university presses, and as for the pulp mills, he figures largely in the latest installment of John Jakes's Kent Chronicles. No time like the present, therefore, to study that giant personality in color and fine detail.

When referring to Theodore Roosevelt I do not use the word "giant" loosely. "Every inch of him," said William Allen White, "was overengined." Lyman Gage likened him, mentally and physically, to two strong men combined; Gifford Pinchot said that his normal appetite was enough for four people, Charles J. Bonaparte estimated that his mind moved ten times faster than average, and TR himself, not wanting to get into double figures, modestly remarked, "I have enjoyed as much of life as any nine men I know." John Morley made a famous comparison in 1904 between Theodore Roosevelt and the Niagara Falls, "both great wonders of nature." John Burroughs wrote that TR's mere proximity made him nervous. "There was always something imminent about him, like an avalanche that the sound of your voice might loosen." Ida Tarbell, sitting next to him at a musicale, had a sudden hallucination that the President was about to burst. "I felt his clothes might not contain him, he was so steamed up, so ready to go, to attack anything, anywhere."

Reading all these remarks it comes as a surprise to discover that TR's chest measured a normal forty-two

inches, and that he stood only five feet nine in his size seven shoes. Yet unquestionably his initial impact was physical, and it was overwhelming. I have amused myself over the years with collecting the metaphors that contemporaries used to describe this Rooseveltian "presence." Here's a random selection. [Novelist] Edith Wharton thought him radioactive; Archie Butt and others used phrases to do with electricity, high-voltage wires, generators, and dynamos; Lawrence Abbott compared him to an electromagnetic nimbus; John Burroughs to "a kind of electric bombshell, if there can be such a thing"; James E. Watson was reminded of TNT; and Senator Joseph Foraker, in an excess of imagination, called TR "a steam-engine in trousers." There are countless other steam-engine metaphors, from Henry Adams' "swift and awful Chicago express" to Henry James's "verily, a wonderful little machine: destined to be overstrained, perhaps, but not as yet, truly, betraying the least creak." Lastly we have [western writer] Owen Wister comparing TR to a solar conflagration that cast no shadow, only radiance.

These metaphors sound fulsome, but they refer only to TR's physical effect, which was felt with equal power by friends and enemies. People actually tingled in his company; there was something sensually stimulating about it. They came out of the presidential office flushed, short-breathed, energized, as if they had been treated to a sniff of white powder. He had, as Oscar Straus once said, "the quality of vitalizing things." His youthfulness (he was not yet forty-three at the beginning of his first term, and barely fifty at the end of his second), his air of glossy good health, his powerful handshake—all these things combined to give an impression of irresistible force and personal impetus.

But TR was not just a physical phenomenon. In many ways the quality of his personality was more remarkable than its quantity. Here again, I have discovered recurrences of the same words in contemporary descriptions. One of the more frequent images is that of sweetness. "He was as sweet a man," wrote Henry Watterson, "as ever scuttled a ship or cut a throat." But most comments are kinder than that.

"There is a sweetness about him that is very compelling," sighed Woodrow Wilson. "You can't resist the man." Robert Livingstone, a journalist, wrote after TR's death: "He had the double gifts of a sweet nature that came out in every handtouch and tone . . . and a sincerely powerful personality that left the uneffaceable impression that whatever he said was right. Such a combination was simply irresistible." Livingstone's final verdict was that Theodore Roosevelt had "unquestionably the greatest gift of personal magnetism ever possessed by an American."

That may or may not be true, but certainly there are very few recorded examples of anybody, even TR's bitterest political critics, being able to resist him in person. Brand Whitlock, Mark Twain, John Jay Chapman, William Jennings Bryan, and Henry James were all seduced by his charm, if only temporarily. Peevish little Henry Adams spent much of the period from 1901 to 1909 penning a series of magnificent insults to the President's reputation. But this did not prevent him from accepting frequent invitations to dine at the White House and basking gloomily in TR's effulgence. By the time the Roosevelt era came to an end, Adams was inconsolable. "My last vision of fun and gaiety will vanish when my Theodore goes . . . never can we replace him."

It's a pity that the two men never had a public slanging match over the table, because when it came to personal invective, TR could give as good as he got. There was the rather slow British ambassador whom he accused of having "a mind that functions at six guinea-pig power." There was the State Supreme Court Justice he called "an amiable old fuzzy-wuzzy with sweetbread brains." There was that "unspeakable villainous little monkey," President Castro of Venezuela, and President Marroquin of Colombia, whom he described in one word as a "Pithecanthropoid." Woodrow Wilson was "a Byzantine logothete" (even Wilson had to go to the dictionary for that one); [retail magnate] John Wanamaker was "an ill-constitutioned creature, oily, with bristles sticking up through the oil," and poor Senator Warren Pfeffer never quite recovered from being called "a pinheaded anarchistic crank, of hirsute and slabsided

aspect." TR did not use bad language—the nearest to it I've found is his description of [jurist and statesman] Charles Evans Hughes as "a psalm-singing son of a bitch," but then Charles Evans Hughes tended to invite such descriptions. Moreover, TR usually took the sting out of his insults by collapsing into laughter as he uttered them. Booth Tarkington detected "an undertone of Homeric chuckling" even when Roosevelt seemed to be seriously castigating someone—"as if, after all, he loved the fun of hating, rather than the hating itself."

Humor, indeed, was always TR's saving grace. A reporter who spent a week with him in the White House calculated that he laughed, on average, a hundred times a day—and what was more, laughed heartily. "He laughs like an irresponsible schoolboy on a lark, his face flushing ruddy, his eyes nearly closed, his utterance choked with merriment, his speech abandoned for a weird falsetto. . . . The President is a joker, and (what many jokers are not) a humorist as well."

If there were nothing more to Theodore Roosevelt's personality than physical exuberance, humor, and charm, he would indeed have been what he sometimes is misperceived to be: a simple-minded, amiable bully. Actually he was an exceedingly complex man, a polygon (to use Brander Matthews' word) of so many political, intellectual, and social facets that the closer one gets to him, the less one is able to see him in the round. Consider merely this random list of attributes and achievements:

He graduated *magna cum laude* from Harvard University. He was the author of a four-volume history of the winning of the West which was considered definitive in his lifetime, and a history of the naval war of 1812 which remains definitive to this day. He also wrote biographies of Thomas Hart Benton, Gouverneur Morris, and Oliver Cromwell, and some fourteen other volumes of history, natural history, literary criticism, autobiography, political philosophy, and military memoirs, not to mention countless articles and approximately seventy-five thousand letters. He spent nearly three years of his life in Europe and the Levant, and had a wide circle of intellectual correspondents on both sides of the Atlantic. He habitually read one to three books a day, on subjects ranging from architecture to zoology, averaging two or three pages a minute and effortlessly memorizing the paragraphs that interested him. He could recite poetry by the hour in English, German, and French. He married two women and fathered six children. He was a boxing championship finalist, a Fifth Avenue socialite, a New York State Assemblyman, a Dakota cowboy, a deputy sheriff, a president of the Little Missouri Stockmen's Association, United States Civil Service Commissioner, Police Commissioner of New York City, Assistant Secretary of the Navy, Colonel of the Rough Riders, Governor of New York, Vice-President, and finally President of the United States. He was a founding member of the National Institute of Arts and Letters and a fellow of the American Historical Society. He was accepted by Washington's scientific community as a skilled ornithologist, paleontologist, and taxidermist (during the White House years, specimens that confused experts at the Smithsonian were occasionally sent to TR for identification), and he was recognized as the world authority on the big-game mammals of North America.

Now all these achievements *predate* his assumption of the Presidency—in other words, he packed them into his first forty-three years. I will spare you another list of the things he packed into his last ten, after leaving the White House in 1909, except to say that the total of books rose to thirty-eight, the total of letters to 150,000, and the catalogue of careers expanded to include world statesman, big game collector for the Smithsonian, magazine columnist, and South American explorer.

If it were possible to take a cross section of TR's personality, as geologists, say, ponder a chunk of continent, you would be presented with a picture of seismic richness and confusion. The most order I have been able to make of it is to isolate four major character seams. They might be traced back to childhood. Each seam stood out bright and clear in youth and early middle age, but they began to merge about the time he was forty. Indeed the white heat of the

Theodore Roosevelt, proudly displaying his specially-made Brooks Brothers cavalry uniform, prepares for battle. Morris describes the future president as a "militarist" who enjoyed "blood sports." In his Pulitzer-Prize winning biography, Morris quotes the toast Roosevelt gave to his Rough Riders before they departed for Cuba: "To the Officers—may they get killed, wounded, or promoted!" (Library of Congress)

Presidency soon fused them all into solid metal. But so long as they were distinct they may be identified as aggression, righteousness, pride, and militarism. Before suggesting how they affected his performance as President, I'd like to explain how they originated.

The most fundamental characteristic of Theodore Roosevelt was his aggression—conquest being, to him, synonymous with growth. From the moment he first dragged breath into his asthmatic lungs, the sickly little boy fought for a larger share of the world. He could never get enough air; disease had to be destroyed; he had to fight his way through big, heavy books to gain a man's knowledge. Just as the struggle for wind made him stretch his chest, so did the difficulty of relating to abnormally contrasting parents extend his imagination. Theodore Senior was the epitome of hard, thrusting Northern manhood; Mittie Roosevelt was the quintessence of soft, yielding Southern femininity. The Civil War—the first political phenomenon little Teedie was ever aware of—symbolically opposed one to the other. There was no question as to which side, and which parent, the child preferred. He naughtily prayed God, in Mittie's presence, to "grind the Southern troops to powder," and the victory of Union arms reinforced his belief in the superiority of Strength over Weakness, Right over Wrong, Realism over Romance.

Teedie's youthful "ofserv-a-tions" in natural history gave him further proof of the laws of natural selection, long before he fully understood [Charles] Darwin and Herbert Spencer. For weeks he watched in fascination while a tiny shrew successively devoured a mass of beetles, then a mouse twice her size, then a snake so large it whipped her from side to side of the cage as she was gnawing through its neck. From then on the rule of tooth and claw, aided by superior intelligence, was a persistent theme in Theodore Roosevelt's writings.

Blood sports, which he took up as a result of his shooting for specimens, enabled him to feel the "strong eager pleasure" of the shrew in vanquishing ever larger foes; his exuberant dancing and whooping after killing a particularly dangerous animal struck more than one observer as macabre. From among his own kind, at college, he selected the fairest and most unobtainable mate—"See that girl? I'm going to marry her. She won't have me, but I am going to have *her!*"—and he ferociously hunted her down. That was Alice Lee Roosevelt, mother of the late Alice Longworth.

During his first years in politics, in the New York State Assembly, he won power through constant attack. The death of Alice Lee, coming as it did just after the birth of his first child—at the moment of fruition of his manhood—only intensified his will to fight. He hurried West, to where the battle for life was fiercest. The West did not welcome him; it had

to be won, like everything else he lusted for. Win it he did, by dint of the greatest physical and mental stretchings-out he had yet made. In doing so he built up the magnificent body that became such an inspiration to the American people (one frail little boy who vowed to follow the President's example was the future world heavyweight champion, Gene Tunney). And by living on equal terms with the likes of Hashknife Simpson, Bat Masterson, Modesty Carter, Bronco Charlie Miller, and Hell-Roaring Bill Jones, he added another mental frontier to those he already had inherited at birth. Theodore Roosevelt, Eastern son of a Northern father and a Southern mother, could now call himself a Westerner also.

TR's second governing impulse was his personal righteousness. As one reviewer of his books remarked, "He seems to have been born with his mind made up." No violent shocks disturbed his tranquil, prosperous childhood in New York City. Privately educated, he suffered none of the traumas of school. Thanks to the security of his home, the strong leadership of his father, and the adoration of his brother and sisters, Teedie entered adolescence with no sexual or psychological doubts whatsoever. Or if he had any, he simply reasoned them out, according to the Judeo-Christian principles Theodore Senior had taught him, reached the proper moral decision, and that was that. "Thank heaven!" he wrote in his diary after falling in love with Alice Lee, "I am perfectly pure."

His three great bereavements (the death of his father in 1878, and the deaths of his mother and wife in the same house and on the same day in 1884) came too late in his development to do him any permanent emotional damage. They only served to convince him more that he must be strong, honest, clean-living, and industrious. "At least I can live," he wrote, "so as not to dishonor the memory of the dead whom I so loved," and never was a cliché more heartfelt. Experiment after experiment proved the correctness of his instincts—in graduating *magna cum laude* from Harvard, in marrying successfully, in defying the doctors who ordered him to live a sedentary life, in winning international acclaim as writer and politician long before he was thirty. (He received his first nomination for the Presidency, by the Baltimore *American,* when he was only twenty-eight; it had to be pointed out to the newspaper's editor that he was constitutionally debarred from that honor for the next seven years.)

In wild Dakota Territory, he proceeded to knock down insolent cowboys, establish the foundations of federal government, pursue boat thieves in the name of the law, and preach the gospel of responsible citizenship. One of the first things he did after Benjamin Harrison appointed him Civil Service Commissioner was call for the prosecution of Postmaster General William Wallace of Indianapolis—who just happened to be the President's best friend. "That young man," Harrison growled, "wants to put the whole world right between sunrise and sunset."

TR's egotistic moralizing as a reform Police Commissioner of New York City was so insufferable that the *Herald* published a transcript of one of his speeches with the personal pronoun emphasized in heavy type. The effect, in a column of gray newsprint, was of buckshot at close range. This did not stop TR from using the personal pronoun thirteen times in the first four sentences of his account of the Spanish-American War. In fact, a story went around that halfway through the typesetting, Scribner's had to send for an extra supply of capital *I's.*

The third characteristic of Theodore Roosevelt's personality was his sense of pride, both as an aristocrat and as an American. From birth, servants and tradespeople deferred to him. Men and women of high quality came to visit his parents and treated him as one of their number. He accepted his status without question, as he did the charitable responsibilities it entailed. At a very early age he was required to accompany his father on Sunday excursions to a lodging house for Irish newsboys and a night school for little Italians. It cannot have escaped his attention that certain immigrant groups lacked the intellectual and social graces of others. Extended tours of Europe and the Levant as a child, teen-ager, and young man soon taught him that this was not due to ethnic inferiority so much as to centuries of economic and political deprivation. Prosperous, independent countries like England and Germany were relatively free of slums and disease; but in Italy women and children scrabbled like chickens for scraps of his cake, and in Ireland people lay down in the road from sheer hunger. From what he read, things were no better in the Slavic countries.

Only in America, with its limitless economic opportunities and freedom from political bondage, might these peasants begin to improve their stock. And only in America could they revitalize their racial characteristics. His own extremely mixed ancestry proved that a generation or two of life in the New World was enough to blend all kinds of European blood into a new, dynamic American breed. (As President, he had a habit when shaking hands with ethnic groups of saying, "Congratulations, I'm German too!" and "Dee-lighted! I'm also Scotch-Irish, you know!" Newspapermen privately referred to him as "Old Fifty-seven Varieties.")

TR knew the value of an ethnic vote as well as the next man. There is a famous—alas, probably apocryphal—story of his appointment of Oscar Straus as the first Jewish Cabinet officer in American history. At a banquet to celebrate the appointment, TR made a passionate speech full of phrases like "regardless of race, color, or creed" and then turned to Jacob Schiff, the New York Jewish leader, and said, "Isn't that so, Mr. Schiff?" But Schiff, who was very deaf and had heard little of the speech, replied, "Dot's right, Mr. President, you came to me and said, 'Chake, who is der best Choo I can put in de Cabinet?'"

TR realized, of course, that the gap between himself and Joe Murray—the Irish ward-heeler who got him into the New York Assembly—was unbridgeable outside of politics. But in America a low-born man had the opportunity—the *duty*—to fight his way up from the gutter, as Joe had done. He might then merit an invitation to lunch at Sagamore Hill, or at least tea, assuming he wore a clean shirt and observed decent proprieties.

Here I must emphasize that TR was not a snob in the trivial sense. He had nothing but contempt for the [aristocratic] Newport set and the more languid members of the Four Hundred. When he said, at twenty-one, that he wanted to be a member of "the governing class," he was aware that it was socially beneath his own. At Albany, and in the [Dakota] Bad Lands, and as Colonel of the Rough Riders, he preferred to work with men who were coarse but efficient, rather than those who were polished and weak. He believed, he said, in "the aristocracy of worth," and cherished the revolution that had allowed such an elite to rise to the top in government. On the other hand (to use his favorite phrase) the historian John Blum has noted that he rarely appointed impoverished or unlettered men to responsible positions. He made great political capital, as President, of the fact that his sons attended the village school at Oyster Bay, along with the sons of his servants, of whom at least one was black; but as soon as the boys reached puberty he whisked them off to Groton.

Only the very young or very old dared call him "Teddy" to his face. Roosevelt was a patrician to the tips of his tapering fingers, yet he maintained till death what one correspondent called an "almost unnatural" identity with the masses. "I don't see how you understand the common people so well, Theodore," complained Henry Cabot Lodge. "No, Cabot, you never will," said TR, grinning triumphantly, "because I am one of them, and you are not." TR deluded himself. His plebeian strength was due to understanding, not empathy.

The fourth and final major trait of Theodore Roosevelt's character was his militarism. I will not deal with it in much detail because it is a familiar aspect of him, and in any case did not manifest itself much during his Presidency. There is no doubt that in youth, and again in old age, he was in love with war; but oddly enough, of all our great Presidents, he remains the only one not primarily associated with war (indeed, he won the Nobel Peace Prize in 1906).

He did not lack for military influences as a child; four of his Georgian ancestors had been military men, and stories of their exploits were told him by his mother. Two of his uncles served with distinction in the Confederate navy—a fact of which he

proudly boasts in his *Autobiography,* while making no reference to his father's civilian status. . . .

When TR learned to read, he reveled in stories "about the soldiers of Valley Forge, and Morgan's riflemen," and confessed, "I had a great desire to be like them." In his senior year at Harvard, he suddenly developed an interest in strategy and tactics and began to write *The Naval War of 1812;* within eighteen months he was the world expert on that subject. As soon as he left college he joined the National Guard and quickly became a captain, which stood him in good stead when he was called upon to lead a cavalry regiment in 1898. Throughout his literary years he made a study of classical and modern campaigns, and he would wage the great battles of history with knives and forks and spoons on his tablecloth. No doubt much of this fascination with things military related to his natural aggression, but there was an intellectual attraction too: he read abstract tomes on armaments, navigation, ballistics, strategy, and service administration as greedily as swashbuckling memoirs. Nothing is more remarkable about *The Naval War of 1812* than its cold impartiality, its use of figures and diagrams to destroy patriotic myths. Roosevelt understood that great battles are fought by thinking men, that mental courage is superior to physical bravado. Nobody thrilled more to the tramp of marching boots than he, but he believed that men must march for honorable reasons, in obedience to the written orders of a democratically elected Commander in Chief. In that respect, at least, the pen was mightier than the sword.

Now how much did these four character traits— aggression, righteousness, pride, and militarism—affect TR's performance as President of the United States? The answer is, strongly, as befits a strong character and a strong Chief Executive. The way he arrived at this "personal equation" is interesting, because he was actually in a weak position at the beginning of his first administration.

When TR took the oath of office on September 14, 1901, he was the youngest man ever to do so—a Vice President, elevated by assassination, confronted by a nervous Cabinet and a hostile Senate. Yet from the moment he raised his hand in that little parlor in Buffalo, it was apparent that he intended to translate his personal power into presidential power. The hand did not stop at the shoulder; he raised it high above his head, and held it there, "steady as if carved out of marble." His right foot pawed the floor. *Aggression.* He repeated the words of the oath confidently, adding an extra phrase, not called for in the Constitution, at the end: "And so I swear." *Righteousness.* His two senior Cabinet officers, [Secretary of State] John Hay and [Secretary of the Treasury] Lyman Gage, were not present at the ceremony, but TR announced that they had telegraphed promises of loyalty to him. Actually they had not; they were both considering resignation, but TR knew any such resignations would be construed as votes of no confidence in him, and he was determined to forestall them. By announcing that Hay and Gage would stay, out of loyalty to the memory of the dead President, he made it morally impossible for them to quit. *Pride.*

As for *militarism,* TR was seen much in the company of the New York State Adjutant General the next few days, and an armed escort of cavalrymen accompanied him wherever he went. This was perhaps understandable, in view of the fact that a President had just been assassinated, but it is a matter of record that more and more uniforms were seen glittering around TR as the months and years went on. Toward the end of his second administration, *Harper's Weekly* complained that "there has been witnessed under President Roosevelt an exclusiveness, a rigor of etiquette, and a display of swords and gold braid such as none of his predecessors ever dreamed of."

As the theatrical gestures at TR's Inauguration make plain, he was one of the most flagrant showmen ever to tread the Washington boards. He had a genius for dramatic entrances—and always was sure the spotlight was trained his way before he made one. The first thing he asked at Buffalo was, "Where are all the newspapermen?" Only three reporters were present. His secretary explained that there was no room for more. Ignoring him, TR sent out for the rest of the press corps. Two dozen

scribes came joyfully crowding in, and the subsequent proceedings were reported to the nation with a wealth of detail.

Here again we see a pattern of presidential performance developing. The exaggerated concern for the rights of reporters, the carefully staged gestures (so easy to write up, such fun to read about!)—it was as if he sensed right away that a tame press, and an infatuated public, were his surest guarantees of political security. To win election in his own right in 1904—his overriding ambition for the next three years—he would have to awake these two sleeping giants and enlist their aid in moral warfare against his political opponents, notably Senator Mark Hanna. (Hanna was chairman of the Republican National Committee and the obvious choice to take over McKinley's government after "that damned cowboy," as he called TR, had filled in as interim caretaker.)

The new President accordingly took his case straight to the press and the public. Both instantly fell in love with him. Neither seemed to notice that administratively and legislatively he accomplished virtually nothing in his first year in office. As David S. Barry of the *Sun* wrote, "Roosevelt's personality was so fascinating, so appealing to the popular fancy, so overpowering, so alive, and altogether so unique that . . . it overshadowed his public acts; that is, the public was more interested in him, and the way he did things . . . than they were about what he did."

This does not mean that TR managed, or even tried, to please all the people all the time. He was quite ready to antagonize a large minority in order to win the approval of a small majority. The swords had hardly stopped rattling on the top of McKinley's coffin when the following press release was issued: "Mr. Booker T. Washington of Tuskegee, Alabama, dined with the President last evening." Now this release, arguably the shortest and most explosive ever put out by the White House, has always been assumed to be a reluctant confirmation of the discovery of a reporter combing TR's guest book. Actually the President himself issued it, at two o'clock in the morning—that is, just in time for maximum exposure in the first edition of the newspapers. By breakfast time white

This famous photograph of Theodore Roosevelt was taken in 1912. The mustache and toothy grin, the laughing eyes crinkled shut behind wire-rimmed glasses, have become caricature symbols of TR that we recognize easily in our own day. Yet they are equally evidence of the personal charm and self-confidence that were the key to TR's enormous popularity, a popularity that, when combined with his aggression, his pride, and his patriotism, made him a successful president. (Brown Brothers)

supremacists all over the South were gagging over their grits at such headlines as ROOSEVELT DINES A NIGGER, and PRESIDENT PROPOSES TO CODDLE THE SONS OF HAM. This was the first time that a President had ever entertained a black man in the first house of the land. The public outcry was deafening—horror in the South, acclamation in the North—but overnight 9,000,000 Negroes, hitherto loyal to Senator Hanna, trooped into the Rooseveltian camp. TR never felt the need to dine a black man again.

Although we may have no doubt he had the redistribution of Southern patronage in mind when he

sent his invitation to Washington, another motive was simply to stamp a bright, clear, first impression of himself upon the public imagination. "I," he seemed to be saying, "am a man *aggressive* enough to challenge a hundred-year prejudice, *righteous* enough to do so for moral reasons, and *proud* enough to advertise the fact."

Again and again during the next seven years, he reinforced these perceptions of his personality. He aggressively prosecuted J. P. Morgan, Edward H. Harriman, and John D. Rockefeller (the holy trinity of American capitalism) in the Northern Securities antitrust case, threw the Monroe Doctrine at Kaiser Wilhelm's feet like a token of war in the Caribbean, rooted out corruption in his own administration, and crushed Hanna's 1904 presidential challenge by publicly humiliating the Senator when he was running for reelection in 1903. He righteously took the side of the American worker and the American consumer against big business in the great anthracite [coal] strike [in Pennsylvania], proclaimed the vanity of muckrake journalists, forced higher ethical standards upon the food and drug industry, ordered the dishonorable discharge of 160 Negro soldiers [charged with rioting and shooting in "the Brownsville Affair" in Texas], and to quote Mark Twain, "dug so many tunnels under the Constitution that the transportation facilities enjoyed by that document are rivalled only by the City of New York."

For example, when the anthracite strike began to drag into the freezing fall of 1902, TR's obvious sympathy for the miners, and for millions of Americans who could not afford the rise in fuel prices, began to worry conservative members of Congress. One day Representative James E. Watson was horrified to hear that the President had decided to send federal troops in to reopen the anthracite mines on grounds of general hardship. Watson rushed round to the White House. "What about the Constitution of the United States?" he pleaded. "What about seizing private property for public purposes without the due processes of law?"

TR wheeled around, shook Watson by the shoulder, and roared, "*To hell with the Constitution when the people want coal!*" Remarks like that caused old Joe Cannon to sigh, "Roosevelt's got no more respect for the Constitution than a tomcat has for a marriage license."

Pride, both in himself and his office, was particularly noticeable in TR's second term, the so-called imperial years, when Henry James complained, "Theodore Rex is distinctly tending—or trying to make a court." But this accusation was not true. Although the Roosevelts entertained much more elaborately than any of their predecessors, they confined their pomp and protocol to occasions of state. At times, indeed, they were remarkable for the all-American variety of their guests. On any given day one might find a Rough Rider, a poet, a British viscount, a wolf hunter, and a Roman Catholic cardinal at the White House table, each being treated with the gentlemanly naturalness which was one of TR's most endearing traits. His pride manifested itself in things like his refusal to address foreign monarchs as "Your Majesty," in his offer to mediate the Russo-Japanese War (no American President had yet had such global presumptions), and, when he won the Nobel Peace Prize for successfully bringing the war to a conclusion, in refusing to keep a penny of the forty-thousand-dollar prize money. This was by no means an easy decision, because TR could have used the funds: he spent all his presidential salary on official functions and was not himself a wealthy man. He confessed he was tempted to put the Nobel money into a trust for his children, but decided it belonged to the United States.

Pride and patriotism were inseparable in Theodore Roosevelt's character; indeed, if we accept Lord Morely's axiom that he "was" America, they may be considered as complementary characteristics. And neither of them was false. Just as he was always willing to lose a political battle in order to win a political war, so in diplomatic negotiations was he sedulous to allow his opponents the chance to save face—take all the glory of settlement if need be—as long as the essential victory was his.

As I have noted earlier, TR's militarism did not loom large during his Presidency. The organizational structure of the U.S. Army was revamped in such a way as to strengthen the powers of the Commander in Chief, but Secretary of war Elihu Root takes credit for that. TR can certainly take the credit for expanding the American Navy from fifth to second place in the world during his seven and a half years of power—an amazing achievement, but quite in keeping with his policy, inherited from Washington, that "to be prepared for war is the most effectual means to promote peace." The gunboat TR sent to Panama in 1903 was the only example of him shaking a naked mailed fist in the face of a weaker power; for the rest of the time he kept that fist sheathed in a velvet glove. The metaphor of velvet on iron, incidentally, was TR's own; it makes a refreshing change from the Big Stick.

If I may be permitted a final metaphor of my own, I would like to quote one from *The Rise of Theodore Roosevelt* in an attempt to explain why, on the whole, TR's character shows to better advantage as President than in his years out of power. "The man's personality was cyclonic, in that he tended to become unstable in times of low pressure." The slightest rise in the barometer outside, and his turbulence smoothed into a whir of coordinated activity, while a core of stillness developed within. Under maximum pressure Roosevelt was sunny, calm, and unnaturally clear. This explains why the first Roosevelt era was a period of fair weather. Power became Theodore Roosevelt, and absolute power became him best of all. He loved being President and was so good at his job that the American people loved him for loving it. TR genuinely dreaded having to leave the White House, and let us remember that a third term was his for the asking in 1908. But his knowledge that power corrupts even the man who most deserves it, his reverence for the Washingtonian principle that power must punctually revert to those whose gift it is, persuaded him to make this supreme sacrifice in his prime. The time would come, not many years hence, when fatal insolence tempted him to renege on his decision. That is another story. But the self denial that he exercised in 1908 gives us one more reason to admire Old Fifty-seven Varieties.

QUESTIONS TO CONSIDER

1 How would you describe Theodore Roosevelt's character and personality? To what extent was he shaped by the era in which he lived? What is your impression of his intellectual capabilities?

2 Morris suggests that TR's presidency was stamped by his four most salient character traits or governing impulses: aggression, self-righteousness, pride, and militarism. What does Morris see as the sources of each of these characteristics? How did each characteristic affect TR's presidency? How much did TR's charm influence his presidency and his effect on Americans?

3 What does Morris mean when he says that Theodore Roosevelt's presidency was a performance?

Do you think it was a successful or unsuccessful show, by and large? Was TR any the less sincere for all his showmanship?

4 In what ways do you think TR's was a potentially dangerous or risky personality for a president? How, for example, did he regard the Constitution when it got in the way of things he thought were important?

5 Can you think of any presidents to compare with Theodore Roosevelt? Could a Theodore Roosevelt be elected in the political climate of the twenty-first century? How would a modern-day electorate feel about a president with such an impenetrable ego or one who behaved with such highhandedness as Roosevelt exhibited in his gunboat diplomacy off Colombia? You may want to keep Theodore Roosevelt in mind when you read about Ronald Reagan in selection 29.

11 African Americans and the Quest for Civil Rights

SEAN DENNIS CASHMAN

During the Progressive era, African Americans launched a protest movement against legally enforced segregation and the whole philosophy of white supremacy and black inferiority that underlay it. Segregation was worse in the South, because that was where most African Americans lived. Indeed, by the beginning of the twentieth century, southern whites had turned their region into a bastion of white supremacy and racial discrimination. A farrago of state constitutional amendments, Jim Crow laws, and local ordinances shackled African Americans to the bottom of the South's racist social order. African Americans could not vote or run for political office; they had to attend separate and inferior "colored" schools, sit in segregated waiting rooms in southern depots, ride in segregated trains and streetcars, drink from separate water fountains, relieve themselves in separate restrooms, lodge only in "colored" hotels, and face humiliating "Whites Only" signs at public swimming pools, golf courses, and libraries. In Jackson, Mississippi, they were buried in a separate cemetery. Woe to African Americans who tried to cross the color line: they could expect a gunshot, incineration, or a lynching. Indeed, lynchings multiplied at an alarming rate in the Deep South. Meanwhile, in Plessy v. Ferguson (1896) the United States Supreme Court upheld "separate but equal" accommodations in Dixie. Never mind that facilities for African Americans were almost never equal to those for whites; the Court ruled that no discrimination was involved. Justice John Marshall Harlan, however, issued a ringing dissent, arguing that "our Constitution is color-blind, and neither knows nor tolerates classes among citizens."

Initially, especially in the South, African Americans submitted to living as third-class citizens in a white-dominated country. In that period of reaction, there was little else they could do. Most followed the advice of Booker T. Washington, the head of all-black Tuskegee Institute in Alabama, who had been born a slave. In 1895, in Atlanta, Washington urged African Americans to forget about political and social equality for now and to learn skills and trades to support themselves. By imitating white standards and values, perhaps they could earn white people's friendship and preserve racial peace. But as Martin Luther King Jr. noted later, it was "an obnoxious negative peace" in which "the Negro's mind and soul were enslaved."

In the following selection, historian Sean Dennis Cashman describes in lucid and eloquent detail what black Americans faced in this period of racial reaction. He offers trenchant insights, based on the best of modern scholarship, into the origins of segregation, and explains the two very different reactions to it by Booker T. Washington, a southern black, and W. E. B. Du Bois, a northern African American, who became Washington's ideological adversary. Du Bois exhorted the blacks' "Talented Tenth" to take the lead and find solutions to the misery of the black masses. In 1905, against a backdrop of spiraling racial violence, Du Bois met with a small band of well-educated, bold, and unhappy African American professionals and businessmen in the city of Niagara Falls, Canada (the blacks could not stay in a hotel on the American side of the falls). They drafted a blazing manifesto demanding justice and equality for African Americans. The Niagara platform became the blueprint for the National Association for the Advancement of Colored People (NAACP), established in 1909 in the centennial of Abraham Lincoln's birth. Du Bois and seven other Niagara leaders joined nineteen white racial progressives on the NAACP's original board (the racial imbalance reflected the paternalistic attitudes of the white founders). The first nationwide organization dedicated to gaining African Americans their rights as citizens, the NAACP concentrated on legal action and court battles. It won its first victory in 1915—the same year the twentieth-century Ku Klux Klan was founded on Stone Mountain in Georgia—when the United States Supreme Court outlawed the grandfather clause to the state constitutions of Oklahoma and Maryland. Those clauses had prohibited African Americans from voting unless their grandfathers had voted in 1860.

In Cashman's stirring pages, you will meet Du Bois and other significant figures who launched the "Negro rebellion" in Progressive America.

GLOSSARY

ACCOMMODATION Doctrine preached by Booker T. Washington calling for southern blacks to forget about racial equality, to accommodate themselves to the South's racist social order, and to learn skills and trades to support themselves.

ATLANTA COMPROMISE Speaking in Atlanta in 1895, Washington propounded the doctrine of accommodation, which later became known as the "Atlanta Compromise."

BROWN, HENRY BILLINGS Justice of the Supreme Court in the case of *Plessy* v. *Ferguson* (1896), who spoke for the majority in ruling that "if one race be inferior to the other socially, the Constitution of the United States cannot put them upon the same plane."

BROWNSVILLE "RIOT" Three companies of the black Twenty-Fifth Regiment of the U.S. Army allegedly rioted in Brownsville, Texas, in 1906 after some of the soldiers had retaliated against whites for racial insults. The charges were unproved, but President Theodore Roosevelt "arbitrarily" discharged the three companies in question.

BUCHANAN v. *WARLEY* (1917) The United States Supreme Court unanimously held that "all citizens of the United States shall have the same right in every state and territory, as is enjoyed by white citizens thereof, to inherit, purchase, lease, sell, hold and convey real and personal property." See also *Corrigan* v. *Buckley.*

CORRIGAN v. BUCKLEY (1926)   The *Buchanan* v. *Warley* decision resulted in "a spate of private restrictive covenants under which residents agreed to sell or rent their property to individuals of one race only." The court upheld the practice in *Corrigan* v. *Buckley.*

DU BOIS, W. E. B.   Reclusive professor of economics and sociology at Atlanta University who emerged as the leader of the African American elite, created the "myth of the Talented Tenth," helped found the NAACP, and served as first editor of the NAACP's official publication, *Crisis;* by his own reckoning, he was "the main factor in revolutionizing the attitude of the American Negro toward caste" between 1910 and 1930.

GRADUALISM   Another name for Booker T. Washington's doctrine of accommodation to the racial status quo; it stressed "patience, proposed submission, and emphasized material progress."

GREAT MIGRATION   During the 1910s and 1920s, blacks by the tens of thousands migrated from the South to the North. "The exodus," writes Cashman, "was mainly spontaneous and largely unorganized; whatever the personal motives for individual moves, the collective motive was bad treatment in the South."

HARLAN, JOHN MARSHALL   Justice of the United States Supreme Court who dissented from the majority decision in *Plessy* v. *Ferguson,* arguing that "our Constitution is color-blind, and neither knows nor tolerates classes among citizens."

JEFFERIES, JAMES J.   When black boxer Jack Johnson won the heavyweight title in 1908, white racists persuaded former world champion James J. Jefferies to come out of retirement and fight Johnson for the title. Johnson whipped this "great white hope" in Reno, Nevada, in 1912.

JIM CROW LAWS   Southern state and local laws that enforced segregation and discrimination against African Americans. They were called Jim Crow laws from the name of a song sung by Thomas Rice in a black minstrel show before the Civil War.

JOHNSON, JACK   An African American from Galveston, Texas, who won the heavyweight boxing title in 1908 and by doing so "aroused deep consternation throughout the white community." An excellent film about his life, *The Great White Hope* (1970) stars James Earl Jones as the legendary black boxer who was "the greatest heavyweight of his time."

NIAGARA MOVEMENT   In 1905, Du Bois and a cadre of other angry and unhappy black leaders met on the Canadian side of Niagara Falls and drafted a searing manifesto demanding justice and equality for African Americans. The Niagara platform became a blueprint for the National Association for the Advancement of Colored People (NAACP), established in 1909. It was the first nationwide organization dedicated to gaining African Americans their rights as citizens.

PLESSY v. FERGUSON (1896)   Decision of the United States Supreme Court that upheld "separate but equal" accommodations for whites and African Americans.

POLL TAX   A southern state tax on the right to vote, aimed at proscribing the poorer Negroes.

THE SOULS OF BLACK FOLK (1903)   Du Bois's brilliant collection of essays that summoned African Americans to resist Booker T. Washington's doctrine of accommodation.

TILLMAN, BEN "PITCHFORK"   Rabidly white supremacist governor of South Carolina and U. S. Senator.

TROTTER, WILLIAM   African American real-estate broker who in 1901 founded the *Boston Guardian* and devoted himself to destroying the teachings of Booker T. Washington.

VILLARD, OSWALD GARRISON   Grandson of William Lloyd Garrison, the great nineteenth-century abolitionist, Villard was a white journalist and pacifist who helped found the NAACP and served as chairman of its board.

WASHINGTON, BOOKER T.   Between 1903 and 1915, the champion of accommodation, who had once dined with President Theodore Roosevelt, found himself under a zealous ideological attack by Du Bois, Trotter, and other members of the radical African American elite.

WILLARD, JESS   Another "great white hope" chosen to defeat black heavyweight champion Jack Johnson, Willard was a former cowboy known for his strength. In a title fight in Havana, Cuba, in 1915, Willard knocked out a poorly conditioned Johnson, winning the title for the white race.

WILSON, WOODROW   President of the United States (1913–1921); his was "the most racist administration since the Civil War." Encouraged by his first wife and his postmaster general, Wilson "allowed systematic segregation in government offices, shops, restrooms, and lunchrooms. African Americans were even removed from appointments they had previously held."

The story of African-Americans and their quest for civil rights in the twentieth century . . . is a story with deep resonances. It is about nothing less than the transformation of African-American citizens' place in American society—constitutional, social and cultural—and it tells us something of the transformations white society had to ask of itself.

In a century where one of the primary themes of art has been the relationship of the individual and society, the continuously shifting fortunes of African-American citizens in American society have proved fertile subjects for argument and discussion. Moreover, the experience of African-Americans makes a stark comment on a central paradox of American history—how a nation composed of such diverse ethnic groups and beliefs could endure and survive. Thus novelist James Baldwin declared, "The story of the Negro in America is the story of America, or, more precisely, it is the story of Americans." His most fundamental point seems to have been that, as the African-American experience moved from slavery to incarceration to freedom and citizenship, African-Americans were, ironically enough, especially privileged to articulate the problems and preoccupations of men and women in modern society. . . .

The original circumstances for the development of a civil rights movement to restore their due dignity to African-American citizens had not been promising at the turn of the century and for several decades thereafter. Of the total American population of 76,094,000 in 1900, 8,833,000 were African-Americans—about 11.5 percent of the whole. Over 85 percent of them lived in the South—the eleven states of the old Confederacy and five others, Oklahoma and Kentucky to the west and Delaware, Maryland, West Virginia, and the District of Columbia to the north. Of the total population of 24,524,000 of this "Census South," 7,923,000 were African-Americans. Thus, whereas the ratio of African-Americans to whites

Sean Dennis Cashman, "African Americans and the Quest for Civil Rights," from *African Americans and the Quest for Civil Rights, 1900–1990* (New York: New York University Press, 1991). Reprinted by permission of the New York University Press.

across the country as a whole was, approximately, one in nine, in the South it was one in three. In two states, Mississippi and South Carolina, they predominated.

The abolition of slavery and the destruction of the rebel Confederacy in the Civil War (1861–1865) had led to the granting of equal social and political rights to African-Americans i the period of Reconstruction (1865–1877). The Thirteenth Amendment (1865) proscribed slavery. The first section of the Fourteenth Amendment (1866) defined American citizens as all those born or naturalized in the United States. It enjoined states from abridging their rights to life, liberty, property, and process of law. The second section of the amendment threatened to reduce proportionately the representation in Congress of any state denying the suffrage to adult males. Congress determined to protect African-American suffrage in the South by the Fifteenth Amendment (1869–1870), according to which the right to vote was not to be denied "on account of race, color, or previous condition of servitude." Yet forty years later these rights had been assailed or eroded by white racists. The abject position of African-Americans was such that historian Rayford Logan in *The Betrayal of the Negro* (1954; 1969) described the turn of the century as "the nadir" of African-American history, notwithstanding the existence of slavery up to 1865.

THE TYRANT CUSTOM—RACE RELATIONS AT THEIR NADIR

The regular intimacy of contact under slavery was being superseded by a caste system with next to no sustained contact, which resulted in an inexorable gulf between African-Americans and whites. Although African-Americans were the largest of America's ethnic minorities, they were segregated in schooling, housing, and places of public accommodation, such as parks, theaters, hospitals, schools, libraries, courts, and even cemeteries. The variety and fluidity of access of the late nineteenth century were abandoned as state after state adopted rigid segregation in a series of so-called Jim Crow laws. ("Jim Crow" was the title of a minstrel song in 1830 that presented African-Americans as childlike and inferior.)

In *The Strange Career of Jim Crow* (1955) historian C. Vann Woodward argues that cast-iron segregation was a product of the late nineteenth and early twentieth centuries and that the avalanche of Jim Crow laws began when poor white farmers came to power. Moreover, a new generation of African-Americans had grown up who had never known slavery. Previously, aristocratic southerners had shown a paternalistic attitude to African-Americans, protecting them from some overt racist attacks by poor whites. They knew that they did not need segregation laws to confirm their own privileged social position. Nevertheless, none of the states passed a single comprehensive segregation law. Instead, they proceeded piecemeal over a period of thirty to fifty years. Thus South Carolina segregated the races in successive stages, beginning with trains (1898) and moving to streetcars (1905), train depots and restaurants (1906), textile plants (1915 and 1916), circuses (1917), pool halls (1924), and beaches and recreation centers (1934). Georgia began with railroads and prisons (1891) and moved to sleeping cars (1899) and, finally, pool halls (1925), but refused to segregate places of public accommodation until 1954.

Another factor in turning the tide of white resentment was the move of African-Americans to new mining and industrial communities where, for the first time, white hillbillies were not only thrown into daily contact with them but also into competition for the same low-caste jobs at rockbottom wages. For low-class whites, social segregation was a means of asserting their superiority. As C. Vann Woodward puts it in his *The Origins of the New South* (1951), "It took a lot of ritual and Jim Crow to bolster the creed of white supremacy in the bosom of a white man working for a black man's wages." The South had made sure that African-Americans were socially and academically inferior by denying them a decent education. Southern legislatures starved African-American schools of adequate funds, thereby making it impossible

for them to approach anywhere near the same standards. In 1910 the eleven southern states spent an average of $9.45 on each white pupil but only $2.90 on each African-American pupil.

The South reacted against the natural tide of resentment by African-Americans to its new restrictive policies with more repression. Mississippi was the first state effectively to disfranchise African-American citizens by a constitutional convention in 1890. It was followed by South Carolina in 1895, Louisiana in 1898, North Carolina (by an amendment) in 1900, Alabama in 1901, Virginia in 1901 and 1902, Georgia (by amendment) in 1908, and the new state of Oklahoma in 1910. Four more states achieved the same ends without amending their constitutions: Tennessee, Florida, Arkansas, and Texas. Three pernicious and sophistical arguments were advanced by the proponents of disfranchisement. The removal of the African-American vote, they said, would end corruption at elections. It would prevent African-Americans from holding the balance of power in contests between rival factions of whites. Moreover, it would oblige African-Americans to abandon their false hopes of betterment and, instead, make them accept their true social place. As a result, race relations would steadily improve.

The Mississippi Constitution of 1890 set the pattern. It required a poll tax of two dollars from prospective voters at registration. Those who intended to vote at elections had to present their receipt at the polls. Thus anyone who mislaid his receipt forfeited his vote. More insidious was the requirement that, in order to register, prospective voters had to be "able to read the Constitution, or to understand the Constitution when read." It also excluded those convicted of bribery, burglary, theft, and bigamy. Racist officials used the various ordinances to discriminate in favor of poor, illiterate whites and against African-Americans.

The ruling elites in other states approved of the new Mississippi plan and several states borrowed from one another. In so doing they improved on previous attempts to disfranchise African-Americans. For example, Louisiana believed that the understanding clause was so obviously suspect that it could be invalidated in a court case. Thus it hit on the grandfather clause as being, legally, more secure. Only those who had had a grandfather on the electoral roll of 1867 could vote.

These devices were nothing if not effective. In Louisiana, 130,344 African-Americans were registered to vote in 1890; in 1900 there were 5,320. In 1909 there were only 1,342. In Alabama there were 181,000 African-American voters in 1890; in 1900 there were three thousand. In the South as a whole African-American participation fell by 62 percent. In 1900 Ben ("Pitchfork") Tillman of South Carolina boasted on the floor of the Senate, "We have done our best. We have scratched our heads to find out how we could eliminate the last one of them. We stuffed ballot boxes. We shot them. We are not ashamed of it." Despite concessions to poor whites, white participation in elections also declined—by 26 percent. Thus while, on average, 73 percent of men voted in the 1890s, only 30 percent did so in the early 1900s. Opposition parties dwindled away and the Democrats were left undisputed champions of the South.

Social segregation was also upheld by the Supreme Court. Its most notorious decision came in *Plessy* v. *Ferguson* in 1896. Louisiana state law required "separate but equal" accommodations for African-American and white passengers on public carriers and provided a penalty for passengers sitting in the wrong car. Homer Plessy was an octoroon so pale that he usually passed for white, but when he sat in a white car he was arrested. He argued that the state law of Louisiana violated the Fourteenth and Fifteenth Amendments. Justice John Marshall Harlan of Kentucky agreed with him, maintaining. "Our constitution is color-blind and neither knows nor tolerates classes among citizens." Moreover, "What can more certainly arouse race hate, what more certainly create and perpetuate a feeling of distrust between these races, than state enactments which in fact proceed on the ground that colored citizens are so inferior and degraded that they cannot be allowed to sit in public coaches occupied by white citizens?" However, he

was overruled by the other eight justices, who approved of the doctrine of "separate but equal." Justice Henry Billings Brown of Michigan, speaking for the majority on May 18, 1896, ruled with corrosive racial candor, "If one race be inferior to the other socially, the Constitution of the United States cannot put them upon the same plane." In *Williams* v. *Mississippi* on April 25, 1898, the Court went further and approved the Mississippi plan for disfranchising African-Americans. The Court unanimously upheld the opinion of Justice Joseph McKenna that "a state does not violate the equal protection clause of the fourteenth amendment when it requires eligible voters to be able to read, write, interpret, or understand any part of the Constitution."

Edgar Gardner Murphy, a humanitarian journalist, reported in *The Basis of Ascendancy* (1909) how extremists had moved "from an undiscriminating attack upon the Negro's ballot to a like attack upon his schools, his labor, his life—from the contention that no Negro shall vote to the contention that no Negro shall learn, that no Negro shall labor, and [by implication] that no Negro shall live." The result was an "all-absorbing autocracy of race," an "absolute identification of the stronger race with the very being of the state." In 1903 analyst Charles W. Chestnutt said that "the rights of the Negroes are at a lower ebb than at any time during the thirty-five years of their freedom, and the race prejudice more intense and uncompromising."

Racist scientists tried to prove that African-Americans were inferior to whites. In 1929 Lawrence Fick in the *South African Journal of Science* declared that Africans showed "a marked inferiority" to European whites and that the number who could benefit from education was limited. Americans measured intelligence on the basis of a test first developed by Frenchman Alfred Binet in 1905 and based on the skills expected of, and acquired by, educated children from the middle class. Not surprisingly, such a test found undereducated children, whether poor white, immigrant, or African-American, less intelligent. The final, conclusive "proof" of the inferiority of African-Americans came when

African-American soldiers scored worse than whites in intelligence tests given in World War I. Subsequent investigation showed that African-Americans from the North scored higher than southern whites. Here was disturbing proof of the inferiority of southern education as a whole. . . .

BOOKER T. WASHINGTON AND W. E. B. DU BOIS

Since African-Americans were being displaced from their traditional trades and confined to menial jobs in the towns, those who did succeed in entering the worlds of business and the professions were obliged by white society to adopt its attitudes in order to retain their hard-won position. Their undeclared leader was Booker T. Washington, head of Tuskegee Industrial Institute, Alabama.

Booker Taliaferro Washington was born at Hale's Ford, Franklin County, Virginia, in 1856, the son of a white father and an African-American mother who was enslaved. At the end of the Civil War he worked in a coal mine and salt furnace at Malden, West Virginia, while he attended school. From 1872 to 1875 he studied at Hampton Institute, the Negro vocational school in Virginia, where he earned his keep by working as a janitor. He also taught school at Malden (1875–1877) and subsequently studied at Wayland Seminary, Washington, D.C. In 1879 he returned to Hampton Institute, where he was in charge of the Indian dormitory and night school. In 1881 he was selected to organize an African-American normal school at Tuskegee chartered by the Alabama legislature.

Thereafter, his name was practically synonymous with African-American education. In fact, Booker T. Washington created three major institutions: the Normal and Industrial Institute for Negroes, the college in rural Alabama devoted primarily to agricultural and technical education; the Tuskegee Machine, a lobby of African-American intellectuals, politicos, and educators and white philanthropists who supported

Washington's political and economic aims; and the National Negro Business League, committed to establishing and consolidating a system of African-American entrepreneurs within the existing framework of white capitalism. Washington believed that the optimum strategy for the rural masses of African-Americans was to concentrate as much as possible on economic independence by thrift and the acquisition of property. For the time being they were to disregard disfranchisement and Jim Crow social segregation. The encouragement Washington and his school of thought gave to a new generation of African-American entrepreneurs and their clients to "buy black" and to think in terms of black nationalism allowed them to rise commercially at the expense of a different group of artisans, caterers, and porters who were essentially integrationists and who had had the lion's share of the market among African-Americans in the 1870s and 1880s.

Washington was as well known as a propagandist and polemicist as he was as an educational leader. He was invited to speak at the opening of the Cotton States and International Exposition in Atlanta on September 18, 1895, by businessmen who recognized his remarkable powers of expression. His address was one of the most effective political speeches of the Gilded Age, a model fusion of substance and style.

In what was later called the Atlanta Compromise he abandoned the postwar ideal of racial equality in favor of increased economic opportunity for African-Americans. "The wisest among my race understand that the agitation of questions of social equality is the extremist folly and that progress in the enjoyment of all the privileges that will come to us must be the result of severe and constant struggle rather than of artificial forcing." He preached patience, proposed submission, and emphasized material progress. Those African-Americans who rejected the Atlanta Compromise, such as rising activist W. E. B. Du Bois, considered his stance a capitulation to blatant racism. But Washington was telling white society exactly what it wanted to hear—that African-Americans accepted the Protestant work ethic. His most widely reported remark was a subtle metaphor about racial harmony: "In all things social we can be as separate as the fingers, yet one as the hand in all things essential to mutual progress."

Washington's emphasis on racial pride, economic progress, and industrial education encouraged white politicians and businessmen, such as steel tycoon Andrew Carnegie, to subsidize the institutions for African-Americans that he recommended. Through his close connections with business he was able to raise the funds necessary to create the National Negro Business League in 1900. Moreover, he used money not to advance acquiescence by African-Americans but to fight segregation. Others sought a more open insistence on racial pride. In 1890 T. Thomas Fortune, a journalist of New York, persuaded forty African-American protection leagues in cities across the country to join in a national body, the Afro-American League. Historian C. Vann Woodward assesses Washington's work thus: "Washington's life mission was to find a pragmatic compromise that would resolve the antagonisms, suspicions, and aspirations of 'all three classes directly concerned—the Southern white man, the northern white man, and the Negro.' It proved, he admitted 'a difficult and at times a puzzling task.' But he moved with consummate diplomacy, trading renunciation for concession and playing sentiment against interest."

Five weeks into his presidency (1901–1909), Theodore Roosevelt invited Booker T. Washington to the White House on October 18, 1901. Roosevelt was also committed to trying to reconcile the South to the Republican party. His invitation was intended as a symbolic gesture to African-Americans and was widely interpreted as such. There was terrible logic in the subsequent outrage of racist southerners when the story broke. The New Orleans *Times-Democrat* thought Roosevelt's action mischievous: "When Mr. Roosevelt sits down to dinner with a negro, he declares that the negro is the social equal of the White Man." Senator Benjamin ("Pitchfork") Tillman, declared, "The action of President Roosevelt in entertaining that nigger will necessitate our killing a thousand niggers in the South before they will learn their place again."

Despite Washington's insistence on patience, some African-Americans began to agitate fo desegregation on trains, a prime target of the protest movement that was the forerunner of civil rights. They reckoned that railroads would realize that it was more expensive to have segregated seating and would thus yield, if only for the sake of economy. In 1898 the Afro-American League called for a boycott of trains in protest of Jim Crow laws. In 1904 the Maryland Suffrage League began campaigning against the new Jim Crow law there and financed a successful lawsuit against segregated travel in 1905. Also in 1905, the Georgia Equal Rights League declared that African-Americans should be able "to travel in comfort and decency and receive a just equivalent for our money, and yet we are the victims of the most unreasonable sort of caste legislation." In 1909 the National Negro Conference denounced segregation and the oppression of African-Americans. Whites were taken aback by the effectiveness of boycotts when African-Americans either simply stopped using white-owned transport or established small companies of their own. White streetcar companies either ended segregation or went out of business, such as the streetcar company in Richmond, Virginia. However, the wave of protests was short lived.

Washington's approach of so-called gradualism could be justified as a necessary complement to the fearful atmosphere of prejudice and violence in the South. However, African-American intellectuals in the North grew impatient with his time-serving and ambiguity. William Trotter, son of Cleveland's recorder of deeds and a graduate of Harvard, founded the most vehemently critical paper, the *Boston Guardian,* in 1901, and roundly abused Washington for his association with Roosevelt, calling him a "self seeker" and a "skulking coward." Trotter criticized Washington at the 1903 annual convention of the Afro-American Council and created uproar at a meeting of the Boston Business League later the same year when he heckled Washington as he tried to speak. The uproar resulted in "the Boston riot" that ended with the imprisonment of Trotter for thirty days for having disturbed the peace. Nevertheless, Trotter and his creations were radical, vocal forces in the struggle for civil rights.

The publication of *The Souls of Black Folk* by W. E. B. Du Bois in 1903 solidified protest around a new spokesman. William Edward Burghardt Du Bois was born in Great Barrington, Massachusetts, in 1868, graduated from Fisk and Harvard, and attended the University of Berlin. After returning to America in 1894, he taught at Wilberforce University, Ohio, and Pennsylvania University before becoming professor of sociology at Atlanta. A handsome and invariably immaculately dressed man, Du Bois was also a creative writer who produced two novels, *The Quest of the Silver Fleece* (1911) and *The Dark Princess* (1928), and two volumes of essays and poems, *Dark Water* (1920) and *The Gift of Black Folk* (1924). One of Du Bois's early supporters, James Weldon Johnson, said of *The Souls of Black Folk* that "it had a greater effect upon and within the Negro race than any single book published in the country since *Uncle Tom's Cabin.*" One of the essays was a withering attack on what Du Bois considered Washington's acceptance of the heinous doctrine of racial inferiority. Du Bois insisted on an end to accommodation: "By every civilized and peaceful method we must strive for the rights which the world accords to men."

Deeply angered by Washington's counterrevolutionary tactics and intensely hostile to the strategy of accommodation, Du Bois invited like-minded activists to a national conference at Fort Erie in July 1905 that established the Niagara Movement. This was an elite cadre of about four hundred college-educated professional people. The Niagara Movement committed itself to continuing vocal protest against "the abridgment of political and civil rights and against inequality of educational opportunity." Du Bois and others published the *Moon* and, later, the *Horizon* as unofficial journals of the movement. Nevertheless, the Niagara Movement failed to establish itself as a distinctive national voice.

Moreover, it was becoming obvious to increasing numbers of African-Americans and sympathetic whites that a policy of accommodation was futile in the face of outright racist hostility. Despite Washington's supposed influence with Roosevelt, the president arbitrarily discharged three companies of African-Americans

W. E. B. Du Bois was the foremost member of a gifted group of African American leaders during the early years of the twentieth century. A "child of the black elite" and highly educated, with a bachelor's degree from Fisk and a Ph.D. from Harvard, he played a major role in the founding of the National Association for the Advancement of Colored People and raised the "black protest movement" to a new level of effectiveness. (Schomburg Center for Research in Black Culture, The New York Public Library; Astor, Lenox and Tilden Foundations)

of the Twenty-fifth Regiment on an unproven charge of rioting in Brownsville, Texas, on August 14, 1906, after some soldiers had retaliated against racial insults. For their part, Roosevelt and his successor, William Howard Taft, (1909–1913), had to hold together a diverse coalition of Republicans that included a section of gross racial bigots, the lily-whites, who wanted to establish an all-white Republican party in the South. To appease this faction both presidents limited the number of federal appointments of African-Americans, thereby contributing to racial prejudice.

JACK JOHNSON AND THE GREAT WHITE HOPE

White southerners came to accept without question the racist orthodoxy of such men as educator Thomas Pearce Bailey, as expressed in his article "Race Orthodoxy in the South" for *Neale's Monthly Magazine* (1903). He set forth a creed of fifteen points, including such statements as "the white race must dominate"; "The Teutonic peoples stand for race purity"; "The Negro is inferior and will remain so"; "Let there be such industrial education of the Negro as will best fit him to serve the white man"; and "Let the lowest white man count for more than the highest Negro." Even environmentalists who argued that nurture, rather than nature, determined human behavior were reluctant to challenge popular stereotypes. Progressive intellectual John R. Commons expressed the dominant reformist view in 1907. He claimed that African-Americans had opportunities "not only on equal terms, but actually on terms of preference over the whites." Their failure to rise "is recognized even by their partisans as something that was inevitable in the nature of the race at that stage of its development."

However, arguments about genetic inferiority were silenced when boxer Jack Johnson, an African-American and former stevedore from Galveston, Texas, won the world heavyweight boxing title from Canadian Tommy Burns in Sydney, Australia, on Boxing Day, December 26, 1908. Johnson's victory aroused deep consternation throughout the white community. Racists in Congress were so disturbed by the defeat of a white man by an African-American that they proposed, and had passed, a law forbidding the interstate transportation of motion picture films showing prize fights. Immediately after Johnson's sensational victory, former world champion James J. Jefferies, then living in retirement on a farm in California, was urged to come out of retirement to regain the title for the white race. He was eventually persuaded to do so and was defeated in a fifteen-round match at Reno, Nevada, on July 4, 1912.

Johnson was the greatest heavyweight of his time, standing over six feet tall and weighing over two hundred pounds. He moved with the swiftness and grace of a panther. He was widely known for his good nature, his "golden smile," which revealed numerous crowned teeth, and his badinage while in the ring. During the bout with Jefferies, Johnson stopped briefly to lean on the shoulders of his weary opponent and jeered at another, former fighter, Jim Corbett, at the ringside, saying, "Jim this big bum can't fight any better than you could." However, when a blow reached Johnson that really told, his veneer of good nature vanished and his killer instinct surfaced. He gloried in adulation and enjoyed provoking his numerous white critics. Johnson's prowess was a symbol of strength to African-Americans and his success could make him a rallying point for solidarity among them. In fact, he was inaugurating a mighty tradition of powerful African-American heavyweight champions extending through Joe Louis in the 1930s to Muhammad Ali in the 1960s and 1970s and then to Mike Tyson in the 1980s.

In the 1910s Jack Johnson's numerous white enemies determined to find a white challenger who could defeat him and restore the myth of white supremacy. The great white hope turned out to be Jess Willard of Kansas, a former cowpuncher who was known for feats of strength such as bending a silver dollar between his fingers. However, he was a mediocre fighter. Eventually Johnson, sated with European night life and adulation, became homesick and was keen to accept the suggestion of promoters that he should return and fight Willard. The venue would be Havana, Cuba. When Johnson arrived in poor condition, he disappointed his backers by doing next to no training and spending his days driving about the city with his white wife. The fight was held on April 5, 1915, with soldiers surrounding the stadium in order to prevent racial violence. The first twenty-two rounds were dull but in the twenty-third Johnson sank to the floor—though whether from a blow by Willard or from sunstroke, opinions differ. Thus fell the first of the great African-American stars of the worlds of entertainment and sports. Johnson returned to Chicago, attended subsequent boxing contests in which champions won millions, and in the 1930s became conductor of his own jazz orchestra.

THE NAACP AND THE EARLY CIVIL RIGHTS MOVEMENT

Not surprisingly, given the prevailing atmosphere of hysteria stroked by institutional racism and the pseudoscientific jargon of prejudiced scientists, African-Americans became helpless victims of race riots instigated by malicious, scared whites, such as the one in Atlanta, Georgia, in 1906, in which ten African-Americans were killed before martial law restored order. In 1908, after a white women claimed she had been raped, whites invaded the African-American section of Springfield, Illinois, lynched two African-Americans, and flogged several others. The white assailants escaped without punishment. However, on this occasion the North was influenced by an article denouncing the outrage, "Race War in the North," written by a southern socialist, William English Walling. Together with settlement workers Mary White Ovington and Dr. Henry Moskowitz, Walling persuaded Oswald Garrison Villard, editor of the *New York Evening Post* and grandson of the abolitionist leader [William Lloyd Garrison], to call a conference on race in 1909, the centenary of the birth of Abraham Lincoln.

At a meeting in New York on May 31 and June 1, 1909, African-American and white American radicals proposed a new national organization to protect the rights of African-Americans and a similar conference in 1910 established the National Association for the Advancement of Colored People (NAACP), with its declared goal of "equal rights and opportunities for all." Under its first president, Moorfield Storey, the NAACP formed several hundred branches. Under the editorship of W. E. B. Du Bois, The NAACP journal, the *Crisis,* reached a circulation of one hundred thousand. Du Bois's own column, "As

the Crow Flies," attacked white racism. Together with the *Chicago Defender,* the *Pittsburgh Courier,* and the *Baltimore African-American,* the *Crisis* made an ever-increasing spectrum of literate African-Americans aware of their national responsibilities and what the nation owed them.

The NAACP's distinctive strategy was litigation to challenge racist laws. For example, in 1917 the NAACP challenged a statute of Louisville, Kentucky, requiring "the use of separate blocks for residence, places of abode, and places of assembly by white and colored people respectively." Moorfield Storey took the case to the Supreme Court at a time when it was, in the terms of analyst Richard Kluger, peopled by men of Paleolithic perspective, notable Justices Willis van Devanter and James Clark McReynolds. Nevertheless, in the case of *Buchanan* v. *Warley* the Court unanimously, and surprisingly, decided on November 5, 1917, that "all citizens of the United States shall have the same right in every state and territory, as is enjoyed by white citizens thereof, to inherit, purchase, lease, sell, hold and convey real and personal property." However, the *Buchanan* decision resulted in a spate of private restrictive covenants under which residents agreed to sell or rent their property to individuals of one race only. The Court subsequently upheld this pernicious practice in *Corrigan* v. *Buckley* in 1926, maintaining that civil rights were not protected against discrimination by individuals.

Another sequence of NAACP cases tested the constitutionality of disfranchisement. In 1910 Oklahoma introduced its own grandfather clause to prevent African-Americans from voting. Two of its election officials, Guinn and Beal, were prosecuted by the NAACP for carrying out the new state law. When the officials were found guilty of violating the Fifteenth Amendment by a district court, they appealed to the Supreme Court. However, in the case of *Guinn* v. *United States* (1915), the Court unanimously declared that the grandfather clause was "an unconstitutional evasion of the 15th Amendment guarantee that states would not deny citizens the right to vote because of their

The 369th infantry regiment proudly displays the Croix de Guerre *medals won for bravery in World War I. A grateful French government had bestowed this honor on them. Fighting in segregated units "to make the world safe for democracy," African American troops returned home only to face continued racial prejudice and discrimination. (National Archives)*

race." On the same day the Court ruled by seven votes to one in the case of *United States* v. *Mosely* that it "upheld congressional power to relegate elections tainted with fraud and corruption." It seemed the law was on the side of civil rights for African-Americans.

Oklahoma reacted quickly. It passed a new election law, providing permanent registration for those entitled to vote according to the unconstitutional law and allowing African-Americans only twelve days to register or to be disqualified from voting for life. The new law was not contested in the Supreme Court for another twenty-two years. . . .

THE GREAT MIGRATION

The way racist whites openly flouted the basic rights of African-American citizens was now so flagrant as to be scarcely credible in a society moving through a phase of self-styled progressivism. For African-Americans, the notion of progressive reform was a joke in very bad taste. Ironically, the African-American community, like the white, was stronger economically than ever. In 1913 African-Americans owned 550,000 houses, worked 937 farms, ran forty thousand businesses, and attended forty thousand African-American churches. There were thirty-five thousand African-American teachers, and 1.7 million African-American students attended public schools.

The accession of Woodrow Wilson to the presidency (1913–1921) resulted in the most racist administration since the Civil War. Southern Democrats were dominant in Congress, the White House, and the Supreme Court. African-American needs were peripheral to Wilson's interests. Inasmuch as he had views on the subject, they were in the tradition of southern paternalism. As a result, and spurred on by his first wife, Ellen Axson Wilson, he acquiesced in the unrest of segregation. His postmaster general, Albert S. Burleson, introduced the subject of segregation at an early cabinet meeting, suggesting separation to reduce friction between white and African-American railway clerks. Convinced by this argument, Wilson and the cabinet allowed systematic segregation in government offices, shops, rest rooms, and lunchrooms. African-Americans were even removed from appointments they had previously held. The sum total of the Wilson policies was that only eight African-Americans out of thirty working in the federal government in Washington retained their appointments.

Emboldened, racists began to demand that Congress legislate for segregation throughout the civil service, forbid interracial marriages, and even repeal the Fourteenth and Fifteenth Amendments. The South extended its segregation to public transport. Thus, African-Americans were prevented from using taxis reserved for whites in the state of Mississippi in 1922 and in the cities of Jacksonville in 1929 and Birmingham in 1930.

Such discrimination, important in itself, had more momentous consequences because of the contemporary exodus of African-Americans [to the North from the South, where 85 percent of African-Americans lived]. For the 1910s and 1920s were also years of the Great Migration. The immediate reason for the exodus was the industrial requirements of World War I. Whites were being drawn increasingly into the armed services and newly created war industries. However, the war prevented European immigrants from coming to America and taking their place as laborers. Thus, in 1915 agents for northern employers began recruiting African-American labor from the South. However, at least four times as many African-Americans went north on word of mouth than did so at the prompting of labor agents. The exodus was mainly spontaneous and largely unorganized; whatever the personal motives for individual moves, the collective motive was bad treatment in the South. The Great Migration was facilitated by railroad transportation and continued after the war was over. In sum, the South lost 323,000 African-Americans in the 1910s and 615,000 in the 1920s—about 8.2 percent of its African-American population. At the outset white attitudes in both the North and the South to the migration were somewhat ambivalent. As time went on, they became alarmist: northerners resented another ethnic disruption following in the wake of the new immigration; southerners did not want to lose their ready supply of cheap labor. Some southern communities passed laws to prevent African-Americans from leaving. This happened in Montgomery, Savannah, Greenville, and elsewhere. Charleston editor William Watts Ball commented ruefully in 1925, "We have plenty of Southerners whose disposition is identical with that of the ancient Egyptians—they would chase the Negroes to the Red Sea to bring them back." However, nothing could reverse the tide.

Whereas the Great Migration is often interpreted as part of the inevitable progress of African-Americans to full citizenship because they were less likely to encounter political disfranchisement in the North than the South, some, such as playwright August Wilson, believe that it represented an incorrect cultural choice for African-Americans intent on capturing their legacy. In April 1990 he told the *New York Times,* "We were land-based agrarian people from Africa. We were uprooted from Africa, and we spend over 200 years developing our culture as Black Americans. Then we left the South. We uprooted ourselves and attempted to transplant this culture to the pavements of the industrialized North. And it was a transplant that did not take. I think if we had stayed in the South, we would have been a stronger people. And because the connection between the South of the '20s, '30s and '40s has been broken, it's very difficult to understand who we are."

Southern blacks who migrated North found to their dismay that the North was hardly the promised land, and migrants found themselves herded into city ghettos and kept there by a host of real estate and municipal codes. Thereafter when African Americans went north, as James Baldwin observed, they did not go to New York City, they went to Harlem; they did not go to Chicago, they went to the South Side; they did not go to Los Angeles, they went to Watts. As historian Leronne Bennett Jr. wrote, "Real estate became the principal dynamic in the ensemble of northern race relations," and the walls of segregation erected across the urban North in turn produced a new anger and militancy, indeed "a new and different black world." Black Muslim leaders Malcolm X and Louis Farrakhan (Louis X), among others, would be furious products of the northern black ghetto.

QUESTIONS TO CONSIDER

1 What were the basic principles and ideals of W. E. B. Du Bois, and how did they contrast with the program called for by Booker T. Washington? To which segments of the black and white population did each of them direct his concern, and to whom did it appeal?

2 What were the fundamental goals of the Niagara Movement? What did the movement accomplish, and what undermined it?

3 Why was Jack Johnson an important figure for black Americans? Why did he cause great consternation among white supremacists?

4 What is the NAACP? Who were its founders and what were their intentions? What methods did the NAACP use to gain advances for African-Americans?

5 What was the Great Migration? Do you think it was beneficial for black Americans to move north? What is the legacy of the Great Migration for the northern cities?

6 Consider America's social problems concerning race. What positive changes have there been since the Progressive era? What problems remain? Why do you think the issue of race continues to be a major problem in America? Can the problem be solved?

PART SIX

The Struggle for Justice at Home and Abroad (1914–1920)

12 Suffragists' Storm Over Washington

WILLIAM LAVENDER AND MARY LAVENDER

The women's rights movement actually began back in the Jacksonian period, when American women first organized to break the shackles of strict domesticity and to expand their rights and opportunities. Led by two brilliant crusaders, Elizabeth Cady Stanton and Susan B. Anthony, the early feminists rejected the notion of female inferiority and advocated full sexual equality with men. They demanded equal access to education, the trades, and the professions, and an end to the sexual double standard. They wanted the right to vote, too, not as an end in itself, but as a means of achieving their broader aim—to make women self-sufficient, equal partners with men in all areas of human enterprise.

A few feminists like Victoria Woodhull went even further than that to champion free love and licensed prostitution. That, of course, enraged the enemies of the movement, who charged that feminists were members of the lunatic fringe, out to destroy the nuclear family and wreck the moral fiber of America. As the nineteenth century drew to a close, most feminists rejected radical ideas like Woodhull's and became conspicuously conservative, placing renewed emphasis on feminine virtue, motherhood, and community service.

By 1900, a new generation of feminists had narrowed the vision of their predecessors mainly to one goal: the winning of the elective franchise. In the following selection, William and Mary Lavender recount the struggles of the indefatigable suffragists, who faced an uphill battle to gain the right to vote for women. When Woodrow Wilson, a Progressive Democrat, was elected president in 1912, the future seemed bleak indeed for the suffragists. Most Progressive reformers were male, white, and upper-middle-class and had little sympathy for equal rights for women or African Americans. The suffragists realized that they had to pressure Wilson and the other Progressives if the women's movement was ever to achieve more than token gestures. After the start of the Great War in 1914, the suffragists also faced a disapproving public, which viewed any form of protest as unpatriotic. Even so, suffragists Alice Paul and Lucy Burns continued the sisterhood of leadership that Stanton, Woodhull, and Susan B. Anthony had begun in the previous century. When Paul and Burns were unjustly imprisoned for picketing the White House, they had to endure scathing ridicule and horrible prison conditions. Still, they and their followers persevered. And they won in the end. They did so by identifying their movement with Progressivism and winning President Wilson and the entire nation to their cause. It is an inspiring story, and the Lavenders tell it brilliantly in "Suffragists' Storm Over Washington."

GLOSSARY

ANTHONY, SUSAN B. An eloquent champion of women's rights, Anthony helped found and lead the nineteenth century women's movement. She opposed the Fifteenth Amendment to the Constitution because it did not extend the elective franchise to women. Later, Anthony received a $100 fine (which she refused to pay) for attempting to vote in the 1872 presidential election. Because of her contributions to the women's movement, the proposed constitutional amendment that would grant women the right to vote was called the Susan B. Anthony Amendment.

BURNS, LUCY Like Alice Paul, Burns lived in England and observed the successful strategy employed by the British suffragists. Burns was more outgoing than Paul and felt comfortable participating in the street demonstrations that helped advance the women's movement in America. The notoriety associated with her imprisonment pressured the Wilson administration to support the Nineteenth Amendment.

MALONE, DUDLEY FIELD A friend of President Wilson and counsel to the National Woman's Party, Malone resigned his position as collector of the Port of New York because of the government's harsh treatment and imprisonment of suffragists. Along with fellow attorney Matthew O'Brien, Malone defended those women who peacefully protested for the right to vote.

NATIONAL AMERICAN WOMAN SUFFRAGE ASSOCIATION (NAWSA) Formed in 1890, NAWSA consisted mainly of middle-class women, with Susan B. Anthony and Elizabeth Cady Stanton among its early presidents. NAWSA helped influence Progressive leaders to include woman's suffrage on their agenda of reform. After the Nineteenth Amendment was ratified, NAWSA became the League of Women Voters.

NATIONAL WOMAN'S PARTY (NWP) This organization opposed the slow and generally unsuccessful strategy of pressuring individual states to support woman's suffrage through legislative initiatives and referenda. NWP's membership was more youthful and radical than the membership of NAWSA. In later years, the NWP championed the end to all forms of legal discrimination against women, and supported the Equal Rights Amendment to the United States Constitution.

NINETEENTH AMENDMENT Ratified in 1920, this Amendment guaranteed American women the right to vote, stating that "the right of citizens of the United States to vote shall not be denied or abridged by the United States or by any State on account of sex."

WHITTAKER, WILLIAM Superintendent of the Workhouse for Women in Occoquan, Virginia, Whittaker was responsible for the cruel treatment of the suffragists under his care.

ZINKHAN, LOUIS The warden in charge of the jail in Washington, D.C., Zinkhan was responsible for the inhumane conditions that suffragist prisoners had to endure.

Six well-bred women stood before a judge in the Washington, D.C., Police Court on June 27, 1917. Not thieves, drunks or prostitutes like the usual defendants there, they included a university student, an author of nursing books, a prominent campaign organizer and two former schoolteachers. All were educated, accomplished and unacquainted with criminal activity. But today they stood accused in a court of law. Their alleged offense: "obstructing traffic."

What they had actually done was to stand quietly outside the White House carrying banners urging President Woodrow Wilson to support their decades-long struggle to add one sentence to the Constitution: "The right of citizens of the United States to vote shall not be denied or abridged by the United States or by any State on account of sex."

The Susan B. Anthony Amendment was introduced in Congress in 1878. There it lay, regarded with fear and loathing, for almost 40 years. Some saw no point in women voting; with no understanding of politics, they would only vote as their menfolk told them. Others argued that after getting the vote, women would take over the government. With such opposition, the Anthony Amendment seemed doomed to lie dormant forever. The six accused of obstructing traffic that summer day in 1917 denied all charges, insisting that the crowd outside the White House had gathered only because police had announced that arrests would be made. Moreover, picketing had gone on since January without obstructing anything, and with no interference. It was, after all, entirely legal. Why the sudden crackdown now?

But the judge declared the ladies outside the White House were the "proximate cause" of the curious crowd, and must take the consequences. Besides, he added, "there are certain . . . people . . . who believe you ladies ought not have the vote."

Excerpts from this article, "Suffragists Storm Over Washington," by William Lavender and Mary Lavender are reproduced from the October 2003 issue of *American History Magazine* with the permission of PRIMEDIA Enthusiast Publications (History Group), copyright *American History Magazine*.

Unimpressed by the prisoners' spirited defense, the judge found them guilty as charged, and imposed a $25 fine or three days' imprisonment on each. Refusing to pay, which they saw as admitting guilt, they were led off unrepentant to the Washington jail.

Those six made a bit of history that day. All were members of the National Woman's Party (NWP). They were the first of a long procession of women jailed on trumped-up charges solely for demonstrating for their right to vote. NWP members came from all across the country and all levels of society, with little in common except dedication to obtaining that right. This was the exclusive goal of the NWP, whose driving force was a determined young woman named Alice Paul.

At 32, Paul was widely admired as one of the most daring and imaginative leaders the women's movement had ever seen—and just as widely denounced as a dangerous radical. The daughter of Quakers in Moorestown, N.J., she was petite, frail and soft-spoken—hardly a radical image. She never married, nor displayed romantic interest in any man or woman. All her energy was concentrated on her one obsessive passion: women's political rights. Even her closest associates never claimed to know her well, yet her magnetism inspired in them idolizing loyalty. Campaign strategy was her forte, and she planned with such military precision that some likened her to a general.

Paul arrived in Washington in December 1912 to take over the local office of the National American Woman Suffrage Association (NAWSA), headquartered in New York. Committed to a state-by-state approach, NAWSA considered the nation's capital so unimportant that the Washington office's budget for 1912 was $10. Paul was expected to raise her own operating funds.

With her came her chief assistant Lucy Burns. Tall, robust and flame-haired, at 38 the Brooklyn-born Burns was Paul's temperamental opposite, yet they complemented each other perfectly: Paul directing strategy from the background, while Burns was leading public demonstrations.

This banner-carrying woman was photographed at the gates of the White House in 1917. Later that year, forty-one women from fifteen states were arrested outside the White House for demanding the right to vote. In 1919, after women had rallied in support of President Wilson's wartime policies, he finally threw his support behind the Nineteenth Amendment. (© Bettmann/CORBIS)

In March 1913, Woodrow Wilson began his first term as president. Paul considered his support essential to the cause—but women's suffrage, it turned out, was not on this president's agenda. Repeated appeals for his support of the Anthony Amendment were just as repeatedly evaded, Wilson claiming that a president should not try to influence Congress, but should follow the dictates of his party (the Democratic Party, then dominated by arch-conservative Southerners). Women scoffed at this, since Wilson was known as an autocratic president, constantly exerting influence on Congress even in trivial matters. But the more they pressed him, the more he resisted, and the standoff lasted throughout his first term in office.

Meanwhile, Alice Paul's Washington-based group split from NAWSA in a fundamental dispute over strategy. NAWSA's conservative leadership, committed to patient, state-by-state campaigning, disdained action on the federal level and deplored Paul's tactics as far too aggressive. Paul insisted that the snail-paced, state-by-state approach was futile; victory could come only by passage of the Anthony Amendment, and the weak-kneed Congress would never pass it without the president's support. After the rupture, the indignant parent organization distanced itself from its unruly offspring as much as possible.

Headquarters for the Washington group was the handsome Cameron House, overlooking Lafayette Square, conveniently near the White House. There, on January 9, 1917, a fateful decision was made. Hours earlier President Wilson, recently elected for a second term, had walked out on a visiting suffrage delegation after angrily repeating his refusal to endorse their cause. This most brusque dismissal yet was the last straw. After years of polite appeals, it was time for direct action.

The next morning, 12 women carrying banners on long poles left Cameron House and took up positions outside the White House gates. In their movement's traditional colors—purple, white and gold—their banners demanded: "MR. PRESIDENT, HOW LONG MUST WOMEN WAIT FOR LIBERTY?"

They returned every day, in good weather and bad, silently directing this pointed question at the grand house behind them. No one quite knew what to think. Political picketing was uncommon in those days, and by women unheard of. Some passersby gawked, some hurled angry taunts, others were merely amused. The press was sharply divided. The president said nothing. Seemingly unperturbed, he sometimes smiled and tipped his hat at the pickets as his limousine drove through the White House gates. For long grueling weeks the women's severest challenge was a winter so bitingly cold that hands ached and feet felt like blocks of ice.

In March 1917, Alice Paul's organization joined an allied western group to form the National Woman's Party, and Paul, overwhelmingly elected chairwoman, became nationally prominent. A month later the United States entered World War I—and the NWP faced a major crisis.

At the outbreak of the Civil War, it was the nearly unanimous opinion of the leaders of the women's movement that they should suspend their work until peace was restored. Only Susan B. Anthony disagreed, fearing that what little progress they had made up until then would be lost. As Alice Paul

knew, Anthony had been right, and she was determined that the mistake made in that earlier time must not be repeated.

"We shall fight for the things we have always carried next to our hearts," President Wilson said in his war message to Congress. "For . . . the right of those who submit to authority to have a voice in their own governments." So shall we, declared the women of the NWP, hearing in Wilson's words an exact description of what they were striving for. The demonstrations would continue.

Public hostility toward the picketers dramatically increased. Rather than merely foolish and undignified, they were now branded as unpatriotic—even traitors. Some dropped out under the pressure. But the NWP's courage in the face of vilification also inspired a steady flow of eager recruits. The demonstrators became a peculiar kind of tourist attraction in Washington, objects of admiration, curiosity—or outrage. They were so quiet and orderly that the newspapers called them the "silent sentinels." But they were attracting attention—entirely the point in the eyes of master strategist Alice Paul.

For five months the White House siege continued, while Congress, controlled by the Democrats, refused to act without word from the president. Still Wilson remained silent. Finally, in late June, the stalemate broke. Public anger erupted and the administration's patience snapped when NWP pickets raised a banner highly critical of Wilson as a Russian delegation visited the White House. A hostile crowd ripped down the banner, and next morning Lucy Burns and another woman became the first picketers to be hustled away in a police patrol wagon. They were scolded for their behavior and released pending trial; four more later received the same treatment. Within a few days, those six women were convicted on the traffic obstruction charges and spent three days in jail—the first suffragists imprisoned for their cause. It was only the beginning. Early in July, 11 women—including Lucy Burns—were sent to jail. Two weeks later 16 women were stunned to get 60-day sentences, and not in the D.C. jail, but the more dreaded Workhouse for Women at Occoquan, Va.

But the picketers had their legal champions, attorneys who were well aware that demonstrating was entirely within the rights of any citizen, and that the arrests were blatantly illegal. One of these, Dudley Field Malone, collector of the Port of New York, was a friend of the president's. As counsel for the NWP, Malone argued with Wilson against the Occoquan sentences, threatening to resign his own position in protest. He believed, like many others, that Wilson was directing the crackdown from behind the scenes. Wilson professed to know nothing, but a few days later, all suffragists at Occoquan were suddenly pardoned. Partially mollified, Malone returned to New York—but he would be heard from again.

More troubles arose in mid-August, when picketers unfurled a banner referring to the president as "Kaiser Wilson." Congressmen often called the autocratic Wilson that, or worse, but doing so publicly, in the midst of rabid, wartime anti-German sentiment, ignited mob violence. For two days, the women could not set foot outside Cameron House without being physically assaulted. Attackers climbed to the second-floor balcony, grappling with defenders and ripping down banners. A shot was fired through one window, narrowly missing one of the women inside. After passively watching the melee for two days, police finally restored order. The next day, arrests of the picketers resumed. Six more women received 30 days in Occoquan—and this time there would be no pardons.

For six more tension-filled weeks, arrests and convictions on the transparently false obstructing traffic charge continued, with the luckless prisoners receiving 30 to 60 days in Occoquan. Yet women kept picketing, and in early September, Lucy Burns and 11 others drew 60-day sentences there. It was her second time behind bars.

Dudley Field Malone now carried out his threat to resign over the administration's use of such oppressive methods, making headlines and ending his already strained friendship with Wilson. Thereafter, Malone and Washington attorney Matthew O'Brien would comprise a formidable legal team for the embattled NWP.

Despite its quiet, rural setting, the workhouse at Occoquan was run like a concentration camp by its superintendent, William Whittaker. His name struck terror in all inmates, but the suffragist picketers aroused his special animosity—here were educated women, deliberately engaging in what he considered treasonable behavior.

Soon, in defiance of Whittaker's policy of suppressing his prisoners' contact with the outside world, horror stories began to leak out of Occoquan, mainly in the form of scribbled messages, cleverly smuggled to friends on the outside. "The worst misery was the food," one prisoner wrote, describing rancid meat, corn bread green with mold, grits containing worms, rat droppings and dead flies. "We tried to make sport of the worm hunt," reported another, but "when one prisoner reached fifteen worms during one meal, it spoiled our zest for the game." There was no sanitation, and the women were forced into intimate contact with regular inmates who, though obviously suffering from contagious diseases, received no medical attention. To many the worst punishment was the almost total isolation. Even their lawyers rarely got in, and then only under tight restrictions.

Armed with affidavits from former inmates and employees, attorney Malone demanded an investigation to expose "the rotten, filthy, depraved conditions at Occoquan under its present superintendent." But the investigative board only exonerated Whittaker, blaming all complaints on unruly prisoners. Whittaker was triumphant—for the time being.

Once, during a police court trial, a government attorney shook his finger at Alice Paul and said, "We'll get you yet." Although she had been directing battle strategy from behind the scenes until then, he was sure that sooner or later the general would go out to lead her troops—and be captured. It happened in October 1917, when Paul was hauled off the picket line twice in two weeks and hit with the heaviest sentence to date—seven months in the D.C. jail.

There she and her companions encountered hardships rivaling Occoquan's—no privacy; stifling, overcrowded vermin-infested cells; a near-starvation diet that left them almost too weak to stand; close to total isolation. Privileges enjoyed by regular inmates were denied the suffragists. Washington's Warden Louis Zinkhan was apparently competing with Occoquan's Whittaker for the title of "Most Ferocious."

Already detested by their jailers as troublemakers and traitors, the suffragists infuriated them further by demanding political prisoner status. Their claim contemptuously dismissed, they soon devised a form of resistance not so easily ignored. The moment of decision came, as Alice Paul told it:

At the end of two weeks of solitary confinement . . . without any exercise, without going outside of our cells, some of the prisoners were released, having finished their terms. . . . With our number thus diminished to seven . . . the doors were unlocked and we were permitted to take exercise. Rose Winslow fainted as soon as she got into the yard. . . . I was too weak to move from my bed. Rose and I were taken on stretchers that night to the hospital. . . . Here we decided upon . . . the ultimate form of protest left us—the strongest weapon left with which to continue . . . our battle. . . .

Their ultimate form of protest was the hunger strike. Having worked with English suffragists some years before, Paul knew from painful experience what terrors lay in that direction: "From the moment we undertook the hunger strike, a policy of unremitting intimidation began. 'You will be taken to a very unpleasant place if you don't stop this,' was a favorite threat of prison officials, as they would hint vaguely of the psychiatric ward, and the government insane asylum." Particularly frightening was examination by the "alienist" (a specialist in mental disorders), whose word was enough to commit anyone to the asylum.

Seriously weakened after three days of refusing food, Paul was taken to the psychiatric ward and subjected, along with some of her companions, to force-feeding three times daily. Between those feedings she endured solitary confinement in a tiny cell with boarded-up windows. This frail woman was, after all, the power behind the suffrage demonstrations. To crush them required breaking her spirit—and clearly, the authorities meant to break it.

But the government's heavy-handed tactics only made matters worse. As reports of the prisoners' experiences emerged, angry women flocked to Washington from across the country to join the fight and continue the picketing. In mid-November, 30 more demonstrators, drawing sentences ranging from six days to six months, were shipped to Occoquan. Grimly awaiting them was Superintendent Whittaker. Once, accused by a suffragist prisoner of practicing cruelty, he readily admitted, "Very well, I am willing to practice cruelty." His November 14 welcome for his latest group of picketers would live in NWP memory as the infamous "Night of Terror."

On Whittaker's order, one woman wrote later, "I was immediately seized by two heavy guards, dragged across the room, scattering chairs and furniture as I went . . . so fast that my feet could not touch the ground . . . to the punishment cells, where I was flung into a concrete cell with an iron-barred door."

"I saw Dorothy Day brought in," wrote Mary Nolan, at 73 the oldest of the suffragist prisoners. "The two men handling her were twisting her arms above her head. Then suddenly they lifted her up and banged her down over the arm of an iron bench—twice . . . and we heard one of them yell, 'The damned suffrager!'"

The feisty Lucy Burns, returning for the third time, got special treatment. Disobeying Whittaker's order to keep silent, she was handcuffed to the bars of her cell. Finally released from this torturous position, she was left handcuffed all night. But all this, and a near-sleepless night shivering on thin straw mattresses, only made the "suffragers" more defiant. They launched their own hunger strike. Undertaking Alice Paul's "ultimate form of protest" took courage. One faster described nausea and headaches, fever and dizziness, dry, peeling skin and swollen lips, and eventually, aphasia. "I could remember no names," she wrote, "and it was quite impossible to read." Many hallucinated and often fainted.

To crush the strike, prison officials tried everything from dire threats to tempting the strikers with fried chicken, mashed potatoes and all the trimmings. Nothing worked. After seven days, the fasters were dangerously weak. There was no escaping it—forced feeding was next. And facing that took the last ounce of courage they had left. One prisoner reported, "I was seized and laid on my back, where five people held me, [one] leaping upon my knees. . . . Dr. Gannon then forced the tube through my lips and down my throat, I was gasping and suffocating from the agony of it. I didn't know where to breathe from, and everything turned black. . . ."

A Washington prisoner later recalled:

Three times a day for fourteen days Alice Paul and Rose Winslow have been going through the torture of forcible feeding. I know what that torture is. The horrible griping and gagging of swallowing six inches of stiff rubber tubing—[it] is not to be imagined. That over, there is the ordeal of waiting while the liquids are poured through—then the withdrawal of that tube! With streaming eyes and parched, burning throat, one wonders how the people of this nation already tasting blood and pain can let this be done. . . .

The prisoners endured their punishment with unwavering resolve, but they were near collapse. If they meant to win or die, it seemed increasingly likely that dying would be their fate. But far away, the tide of their desperate war was turning, thanks to the NWP lawyers working overtime for the prisoners. Dudley Malone concentrated on the Washington jail, while Matthew O'Brien took on Occoquan, and their labors were producing results. Forcing their way into the prisons with court orders, both were outraged at what they found. In Washington, Alice Paul languished in a hellhole on the psychiatric ward, despite a clean bill of mental health from the alienist. The irate Malone demanded, and got, her prompt removal to the main jail. At Occoquan, O'Brien obtained a writ of habeas corpus ordering Superintendent Whittaker to produce all his suffragist prisoners for a hearing before the U.S. Court of Appeals in Alexandria, Va. Whittaker tried frantically to evade the writ—even hiding out in his own home in vain. The hearing was held November 23 and 24 before a packed house, including newspaper reporters from far and wide.

Both attorneys argued eloquently for justice for Americans who, as O'Brien declared, "were railroaded to Occoquan, where unspeakable brutalities occurred, for the sole purpose of terrorizing them and compelling them to desist from doing what . . . they have every legal right to do."

The sympathetic judge called the testimony given on the prisoners' behalf "blood-curdling." But more compelling than any evidence was the appearance of the prisoners themselves. Haggard, pale and disoriented, many with ugly bruises sustained during the Night of Terror, some barely able to walk or sit upright, their condition sent a wave of shocked disbelief throughout the courtroom. The sight of those mistreated women, vividly reported in newspapers, clinched their case. The judge ordered the prisoners' immediate transfer to the Washington jail pending further review—and the grim conflict took a startling turn.

For months the government had gone to extremes—even breaking the law—to suppress the picketing. But the movement only grew stronger as public opinion shifted toward the women. Clearly, the policy was not working. Perhaps in recognition of this, three days after the Alexandria hearing—and with no explanations—all suffragist prisoners were abruptly released.

On November 27, emerging from the jail to blink in the sunlight after five weeks of living death, Alice Paul could not stand without assistance. But her indomitable will was intact as she declared, "We were put out of jail as we were put in—at the whim of the government." She hoped that "no more demonstrations will be necessary, that the Federal Amendment is well on its way," but added, "What we do depends on what the Government does."

Things were peaceful along the White House sidewalks that Christmas season. The picketers were gone, the former prisoners having retreated to heal their wounds. It was only a truce: They would be back soon to continue the fight.

Several developments that took place in early 1918 were morale boosters. On January 10—40 years to the day since it was introduced into Congress—the Anthony Amendment was passed by the House of Representatives. In March the District Court of Appeals overturned as illegal all the arrests and jailings of the suffragists. And soon afterward—going almost unnoticed except by his former victims—William Whittaker's tenure as superintendent of the Occoquan workhouse was abruptly terminated.

Nevertheless, a long road lay ahead before the ultimate victory on August 26, 1920, when the Anthony Amendment finally took effect as the 19th Amendment to the Constitution. But for many who lived through it, the climatic battle took place in the fall of 1917, when Alice Paul and her courageous, half-starved band laid their lives on the line to defy a repressive government—and the government backed down.

QUESTIONS TO CONSIDER

1 What was the goal of the Susan B. Anthony Amendment to the Constitution? Why did it foment so much opposition that it took forty years to get the Amendment added to the Constitution?

2 How did the personalities of Alice Paul and Lucy Burns differ? What strengths did each of these women bring to the suffrage movement? Why would the author conclude that those two women "complemented each other perfectly"?

3 Explain President Wilson's position on the woman's suffrage issue at the start of his first administration? How did Alice Paul pressure him to recognize the importance of her cause?

4 After the start of the Great War of 1914–1918, what change took place in the public reaction to the suffragist demonstrations? Explain how growing patriotism and calls for unity during the Great War helped the federal government justify its harsh treatment of the White House picketers? Think of other wars where civil liberties have been sacrificed for the sake of national unity.

5 Describe the conditions endured by the suffragists in the Washington, D.C., jail and the Workhouse for Women at Occoquan, Virginia. How did Alice Paul and her fellow prisoners protest such harsh treatment?

6 Why did the Progressive reform movement need pressure before it supported women's suffrage? Do the personalities of Theodore Roosevelt (selection 10) and Woodrow Wilson (selection 13) offer clues as to why such pressure was necessary? Do those selections also help you better understand why the Progressives did not advocate equal rights for African Americans (see selection 11)?

13 "A Tragedy of Disappointment": Woodrow Wilson and the Treaty of Versailles

MARGARET MacMILLAN

The Great War of 1914–1918 was the most savage conflict ever fought up to that time. It was called the Great War then because nobody knew that an even more monstrous war lay in the future. The Great War began when Austria-Hungary declared war on a small Balkan country named Serbia, whose staunch ally was Russia. Because of entangling alliances among Europe's great powers, the war quickly spread until it engulfed much of Europe, with the Central Powers (Austria-Hungary,

Germany, and Turkey) fighting the Allied Powers (Russia, France, Britain, and Italy). It was the world's first "total war," in which whole societies battled one another. Before it was over, Russia had suffered almost 2 million casualties and collapsed in a Communist takeover; Germany had lost 2 million soldiers, France 1.5 million, and Britain almost 1 million.

The United States officially entered the war in April 1917, on the side of the Allies. The United States did so, in part, because the Germans had resorted to submarine war, torpedoing Allied warships without warning; to Americans, this seemed barbaric. The Allied blockade of the German coast, calculated to starve Germany into submission, did not strike most Americans the same way, because of their anti-German sentiment and sympathies for the Allies. When a German U-boat sank a British passenger ship, the Lusitania, with 128 Americans on board, the United States was enraged. President Woodrow Wilson warned the Germans that if they continued to commit such outrages, the United States would take the necessary action to protect its citizens traveling on non-military vessels. At first the Germans agreed not to sink any more enemy ships with Americans on board, but later withdrew the pledge on the grounds that Germany was already fighting American economic might—the United States was selling war materiel to the Allies—and had nothing to lose by attacking American merchant ships taking war supplies to Britain. "This means war," said Wilson. "The break that we have tried to prevent now seems inevitable." When the United States intercepted a secret telegram in which Germany invited Mexico to join the Central Powers, Wilson asked Congress to delcare war, and Congress did so with thunderous applause and cheering. "My message today," said Wilson, "was a message of death for our young men. How strange it seems to applaud that."

As that remark suggests, Woodrow Wilson had a horror of violence and war. Why, then, would he lead the United States into a savage conflict like the Great War? The answer lies in Wilson's complex and contradictory character. A former college professor and president of Princeton with a Ph.D. in political economy, Wilson was a conservative Democrat before he won the presidency. Once in office, however, he became a Progressive reformer who championed a program called the New Freedom that included substantial reforms in currency, anti-trust, and tariff legislation. Working well with Congress, Wilson went on to support women's political rights and engineered the most sweeping legislative program since the days of Alexander Hamilton. Despite his spectacular achievements, Wilson was a sensitive, lonely man who wanted "the people to love me." And yet he felt a powerful need, he said, to guard his emotions "from painful overflow." Although his intellectual tradition was British (he extolled the British system of parliamentary government and admired English leaders such as Edmund Burke and William Gladstone), his politics were rooted in his southern heritage. A learned, eloquent champion of democracy, he nevertheless shared the racial prejudice that prevailed among white Americans of his generation, and as president he began a policy of discrimination against African Americans in federal employment.

In many ways, Wilson's foreign policy was even more paradoxical. He abhorred violence, yet he was inclined to use moralistic, gunboat diplomacy in dealing with Latin America: he transformed Nicaragua into a veritable United States protectorate, twice sent American forces into Mexico, and ordered full-scale military occupation of Haiti and the Dominican Republic. Although Wilson convinced himself that high moral purpose justified such intervention, it left a legacy of bitterness and distrust in Latin America.

Finally, despite the pacific liberalism he had learned from British intellectuals, Wilson led the United States into the Great War on a messianic crusade to make that conflict "a war to end all wars." To achieve that goal, he devised the League of Nations, a kind of world parliament, which was the sanest blueprint for world peace anyone had yet contrived. But Wilson's noble dream ended *in a crushing defeat when the United States Senate rejected the League of Nations and America turned away from the idealism that had produced it.*

In the following selection, excerpted from her prize-winning book, Paris 1919, *Margaret MacMillan tells the story of Wilson and the League of Nations in an elegant narrative filled with trenchant insights. She not only describes Wilson's complex and contradictory personality, but also tells the rollicking story of his second marriage, to Edith Galt, while he was president. MacMillan goes on to explain how Wilson's ill health and inability to compromise, combined with the tenacity of his adversaries and the sentiment of the times, brought about America's rejection of the League of Nations. In the end, the United States was not prepared for the responsibilities of world leadership that Wilson had thrust upon it. Desperately ill from crippling strokes, Wilson viewed the rejection as a personal defeat. As historian Richard Hofstadter observed, the president's "sense of guilt hung over him like a cloud." Steeped in gloom, Wilson summarized his presidency with these words: "What I seem to see, with all my heart I hope that I am wrong, is a tragedy of disappointment."*

GLOSSARY

ARTICLE X   The most controversial part of the League of Nations covenant, Article X committed nations that were members of the League to defend any member nation when another power threatened its "territorial integrity" by "external aggression."

BAKER, RAY STANNARD   Wilson's press officer, friend, and admirer, Baker accompanied the president to Paris.

BLISS, TASKER   Bliss was America's representative on the Supreme War Council in Paris. He later became one of the commissioners to the peace conference at Versailles.

BULLITT, WILLIAM   Bullitt was an advisor to the American delegation that helped negotiate the Treaty of Versailles. He later served as the United States ambassador to Russia and then to France.

BURKE, EDMUND   President Wilson greatly admired this British statesman and political writer, who lived from 1729 to 1797. A thoroughgoing Anglophile, Wilson adopted a foreign policy that favored Great Britain and finally led the United States to enter the Great War on the side of Britain and the other Allies.

CLEMENCEAU, GEORGES   The French prime minister who wanted a peace treaty that would guarantee Germany could never again be a threat to France. An imperialist, he rejected President Wilson's idealism, saying: "God gave us the Ten Commandments, and we broke them. Wilson gave us the Fourteen Points. We shall see" about breaking them.

CREEL, GEORGE   Creel headed the Committee on Public Information (CPI) that publicized and, at times, propagandized American involvement in the Great War. Creel's committee issued pamphlets, posters, and speeches that addressed such issues as "Why We Are Fighting" and that portrayed the Germans as bloodthirsty aggressors; CPI funds produced a film entitled *The Kaiser, the Beast of Berlin*.

FOURTEEN POINTS   Wilson's idealistic blueprint for world peace that was generous to defeated Germany, but failed to satisfy the wartime goals of the allied nations. The last and most important point called for a League of Nations, a kind of parliament of humankind, which would resolve international conflicts and thus avoid future wars.

GALT, EDITH BOLLING   Wilson married this southern woman, seventeen years his junior, less than two years after the death of his first wife. Edith Galt was totally devoted to her husband. After the stroke that disabled him, she protected Wilson from perceived tormentors during his struggle with the Senate over the Treaty of Versailles.

GRAYSON, CARY TRAVERS   Wilson's personal physician and friend, Grayson opposed the President's final speaking tour in 1919, which caused a further deterioration of his health. A naval officer, Grayson had also served as a physician to Presidents Theodore Roosevelt and William Howard Taft.

HANKEY, SIR MAURICE   Secretary to the British cabinet and later to the Paris Peace Conference, Hankey fervently believed that Wilson's Fourteen Points were the "moral background" that would establish a new world order.

HITCHCOCK, GILBERT   A Democratic senator from Nebraska who led his party in the losing struggle to preserve

Wilson's League of Nations against those who wanted to alter or destroy it.

HOUSE, COLONEL EDWARD M. House was a close friend to Wilson, who called him "my alter ego." The Colonel was one of the President's most important advisors until his second wife, Edith Galt Wilson, persuaded her husband to disregard his counsel.

IRRECONCILABLES A group of about a dozen senators who opposed the League of Nations in any form.

LANSING, ROBERT Wilson's secretary of state, Lansing had doubts about the League of Nations that caused the President to lose confidence in him.

LEAGUE OF NATIONS An international organization of nations designed to prevent future wars. Without American participation, the League of Nations was largely ineffectual in the years following the Great War

LLOYD GEORGE, DAVID The British prime minister who pushed for a harsher peace treaty with defeated Germany and the other Central Powers. He once threatened that the Allies would squeeze Germany "until the pipes squeak."

LODGE, HENRY CABOT Lodge was the senior Republican member on the Senate Foreign Relations Committee who led the fight against Wilson's League of Nations.

RESERVATIONS Amendments to the League of Nations charter. Many United States senators believed them necessary to protect American sovereignty and to make the peace treaty consistent with the United States Constitution. Wilson adamantly opposed such changes to his cherished League. As a result, the Senate refused to ratify the Treaty of Versailles and thus rejected United States participation in the League, which proved too weak to preserve global peace and collapsed soon after the outbreak of World War II.

TAFT, WILLIAM HOWARD Rotund Republican president from 1909 to 1913, he lost to Wilson in the election of 1912. Taft believed that Wilson had slighted his party in the treaty negotiations that ended the Great War, and he subsequently opposed the League of Nations.

TREATY OF VERSAILLES (1919) Formally ended the Great War; only about four of the Fourteen Points found their way into the treaty. When Wilson refused to compromise on the League of Nations covenant, the Senate rejected United States participation in the world organization. As a result, America signed a separate treaty with Germany and the other Central Powers and never joined the international organization that Wilson had hoped would end all future wars and preserve democracy the world over.

WHITE, HENRY A retired diplomat, White was the only Republican member of the peace commission that accompanied Wilson to Paris.

On December 4, 1918, the *George Washington* sailed out of New York with the American delegation to the Peace Conference on board. Guns fired salutes, crowds along the waterfront cheered, tugboats hooted and Army planes and dirigibles circled overhead. Robert Lansing, the American secretary of state, released carrier pigeons with messages to his relatives about his deep hope for a lasting peace. The ship, a former German passenger liner, slid out past the Statue of Liberty to the Atlantic, where an escort of destroyers and battleships stood by to accompany it and its cargo of heavy expectations to Europe.

On board were the best available experts, combed out of the universities and the government; crates of reference materials and special studies; the French and Italian ambassadors to the United States; and Woodrow Wilson. No other American president had ever gone to Europe while in office. His opponents accused him of breaking the Constitution; even his supporters felt he might be unwise. Would he lose his great moral authority by getting down to the hurly-burly of negotiations? Wilson's own view was clear: the making of the peace was as important as the winning of the war. He owed it to the peoples of Europe, who were crying out for a better world. He owed it to the American servicemen. "It is now my duty," he told a pensive Congress just before he left, "to play my full part in making good what they gave their life's blood to obtain." A British diplomat was more

From *Paris 1919: Six Months that Changed the World* by Margaret MacMillan, copyright © 2001 by Margaret MacMillan. Used by permission of Random House, Inc.

cynical; Wilson, he said, was drawn to Paris "as a debutante is entranced by the prospect of her first ball."

Wilson expected, he wrote to his great friend Edward House, who was already in Europe, that he would stay only to arrange the main outlines of the peace settlements. It was not likely that he would remain for the formal Peace Conference with the enemy. He was wrong. The preliminary conference turned, without anyone's intending it, into the final one, and Wilson stayed for most of the crucial six months between January and June 1919. The question of whether or not he should have gone to Paris, which exercised so many of his contemporaries, now seems unimportant. From Franklin Roosevelt at Yalta to Jimmy Carter or Bill Clinton at Camp David, American presidents have sat down to draw borders and hammer out peace agreements. Wilson had set the conditions for the armistices which ended the Great War. Why should he not make the peace as well?

Although he had not started out in 1912 as a foreign policy president, circumstances and his own progressive political principles had drawn him outward. Like many of his compatriots, he had come to see the Great War as a struggle between the forces of democracy, however imperfectly represented by Britain and France, and those of reaction and militarism, represented all too well by Germany and Austria-Hungary. Germany's sack of Belgium, its unrestricted submarine warfare and its audacity in attempting to entice Mexico into waging war on the United States had pushed Wilson and American public opinion toward the Allies. When Russia had a democratic revolution in February 1917, one of the last reservations—that the Allies included an autocracy—vanished. Although he had campaigned in 1916 on a platform of keeping the country neutral, Wilson brought the United States into the war in April 1917. He was convinced that he was doing the right thing. This was important to the son of a Presbyterian minister, who shared his father's deep religious conviction, if not his calling.

Wilson was born in Virginia in 1856, just before the Civil War. Although he remained a Southerner in some ways all his life—in his insistence on honor and his paternalistic attitudes toward women and blacks—he also accepted the war's outcome. Abraham Lincoln was one of his great heroes, along with Edmund Burke and William Gladstone. The young Wilson was at once highly idealistic and intensely ambitious. After four very happy years at Princeton and an unhappy stint as a lawyer, he found his first career in teaching and writing. By 1890 he was back at Princeton, a star member of the faculty. In 1902 he became its president, supported virtually unanimously by the trustees, faculty and students.

In the next eight years Wilson transformed Princeton from a sleepy college for gentlemen into a great university. He reworked the curriculum, raised significant amounts of money and brought into the faculty the brightest and the best young men from across the country. By 1910, he was a national figure and the Democratic party in New Jersey, under the control of conservative bosses, invited him to run for governor. Wilson agreed, but insisted on running on a progressive platform of controlling big business and extending democracy. He swept the state and by 1911 "Wilson for President" clubs were springing up. He spoke for the dispossessed, the disenfranchised and all those who had been left behind by the rapid economic growth of the late nineteenth century. In 1912, at a long and hard-fought convention, Wilson got the Democratic nomination for president. That November, with the Republicans split by Teddy Roosevelt's decision to run as a progressive against William Howard Taft, Wilson was elected. In 1916, he was reelected, with an even greater share of the popular vote.

Wilson's career was a series of triumphs, but there were darker moments, both personal and political, fits of depression and sudden and baffling illnesses. Moreover, he had left behind him a trail of enemies, many of them former friends. "An ingrate and a liar," said a Democratic boss in New Jersey in a toast. Wilson never forgave those who disagreed with him. "He is a good hater," said his press officer and devoted admirer Ray Stannard Baker. He was also stubborn. As House said, with admiration: "Whenever a question is presented he keeps an absolutely open mind and welcomes all suggestion or advice which will lead to a correct decision. But he is receptive only during the period that he is weighing the question and preparing to make his decision. Once the decision is made it is final and there is an absolute end to all advice and suggestion. There is no moving him after that." What was admirable to some was a dangerous egotism to others. The French ambassador in Washington saw "a man who, had he lived a couple of centuries ago, would have been the greatest tyrant in the world, because he does not seem to have the slightest conception that he can ever be wrong.

This side of Wilson's character was in evidence when he chose his fellow commissioners—or plenipotentiaries, as the chief delegates were known—to the Peace Conference. He was himself one. House, "my alter ego," as he was fond of saying, was another. Reluctantly he selected Lansing, his secretary of state, as a third, mainly because it would have been awkward to leave him behind. Where Wilson had once rather admired Lansing's vast store of knowledge, his meticulous legal mind and his apparent readiness to take a back seat, by 1919 that early liking had turned to irritation and contempt. Lansing, it turned out, did have views, often strong ones which contradicted the president's. "He has," Wilson complained to House, who noted it down with delight, "no imagination, no constructive ability, and but little real ability of any kind." The fourth plenipotentiary, General Tasker Bliss, was already in France as the American military representative on the Supreme War Council. A thoughtful and intelligent man who loved to lie in bed with a hip flask reading Thucydides in the original Greek, he was also, many of the junior members of the American delegation believed, well past his prime. Since Wilson was to speak to him on only five occasions during the Peace Conference, perhaps that did not matter.

The president's final selection, Henry White, was a charming, affable retired diplomat, the high point of whose career had been well before the war. Mrs. Wilson was to find him useful in Paris on questions of etiquette.

Wilson's selection caused an uproar in the United States at the time and has caused controversy ever since. "A lot of cheapskates," said William Taft. "I would swear if it would do any good." Wilson had deliberately slighted the Republicans, most of whom had supported the war enthusiastically and many of whom now shared his vision of a League of Nations. "I tell you what," the humorist Will Rogers had him saying to the Republicans, "we will split 50–50—I will go and you fellows can stay." Even his most partisan supporters had urged him to appoint men such as Taft or the senior Republican senator on the important Committee on Foreign Relations, Henry Cabot Lodge. Wilson refused, with a variety of unconvincing excuses. The real reason was that he did not like or trust Republicans. His decision was costly, because it undercut his position in Paris and damaged his dream of a new world order with the United States at its heart.

Wilson remains puzzling in a way that Lloyd George and Clemenceau, his close colleagues in Paris, do not. What is one to make of a leader who drew on the most noble language of the Bible yet was so ruthless with those who crossed him? Who loved democracy but despised most of his fellow politicians? Who wanted to serve humanity but had so few personal relationships? Was he, as Teddy Roosevelt thought, "as insincere and cold-blooded an opportunist as we have ever had in the Presidency"? Or was he, as Baker believed, one of those rare idealists like Calvin or Cromwell, "who from time to time have appeared upon the earth & for a moment, in burst of strange power, have temporarily lifted erring mankind to a higher pitch of contentment than it was quite equal to"?

Wilson wanted power and he wanted to do great works. What brought the two sides of his character together was his ability, self-deception perhaps, to frame his decisions so that they became not merely necessary, but morally right. Just as American neutrality in the first years of the war had been right for Americans, and indeed for humanity, so the United States' eventual entry into the war became a crusade, against human greed and folly, against Germany and for justice, peace and civilization. This conviction, however, without which he could never have attempted what he did in Paris, made Wilson intolerant of differences and blind to the legitimate concerns of others. Those who opposed him were not just wrong but wicked.

Like the Germans. The decision to go to war had been agony for Wilson. He had worked for a peace of compromise between the Allies and the Central Powers. Even when they had rejected his offer to mediate, when German submarines had sunk American ships, when opponents such as Roosevelt had attacked his cowardice and when his own cabinet had been unanimous for war, he had waited. In the end he decided to intervene because, as he saw it, Germany left him no alternative. "It is a fearful thing," he told Congress in April 1917, when he went before it to ask for a declaration of war, "to lead this great peaceful people into war, into the most terrible and disastrous of all wars, civilization itself seeming to be in the balance." In Wilson's view Germany, or at the very least its leaders, bore a heavy burden of guilt. The Germans might be redeemed, but they also must be chastised.

The photographs taken in 1919 make him look like an undertaker, but in the flesh Wilson was a handsome man, with fine, straight features and a spare, upright frame. In his manner he had something of the preacher and of the university professor. He placed great faith in reason and facts, but he saw it as auspicious that he landed in Europe on Friday, December 13. Thirteen was his lucky number. A deeply emotional man, he mistrusted emotion in others. It was good when it brought people to desire the best, dangerous when, like nationalism, it intoxicated them. Lloyd George, who never entirely got his measure, listed his good qualities to a friend—"kindly, sincere, straightforward"—and then added in the next breath "tactless, obstinate and vain."

In public, Wilson was stiff and formal, but with his intimates he was charming and even playful. He was particularly at ease with women. He was usually in perfect control of himself, but during the Peace Conference he frequently lost his temper. (It is possible he

suffered a stroke while he was in Paris.) He loved puns and limericks and he liked to illustrate his points with folksy stories. He enjoyed doing accents: Scottish or Irish, like his ancestors, or Southern black, like the people who worked for him in Washington. He was abstemious in his habits; at most he would drink a small glass of whisky in an evening. He loved gadgets and liked the new moving pictures. On the voyage to Europe he generally went to the after-dinner picture shows. To general consternation the feature one evening was a melodrama called *The Second Wife*.

Wilson's relations with women had always caused a certain amount of gossip. During his first marriage he had close, possibly even romantic, friendships with several women. His first wife, whom he had loved deeply if not passionately, had died in 1914; by the end of 1915, he was married again, to a wealthy Washington widow some seventeen years his junior. That this caused gossip bewildered and infuriated him. He never forgave a British diplomat for a joke that went around Washington: "What did the new Mrs. Wilson do when the President proposed? She fell out of bed with surprise." Wilson's own family and friends were more charitable. "Isn't it wonderful to see Father so happy," exclaimed a daughter. House, who was later to become Mrs. Wilson's bitter enemy, wrote in his diary that it was a relief that Wilson had someone to share his burdens: "his loneliness is pathetic."

Edith Bolling, the new Mrs. Wilson, accompanied the president to Europe, a privilege not allowed lesser wives. She was warm and lively and laughed a great deal. She loved golf, shopping, orchids and parties. She had, everyone agreed, wonderful eyes, but some found her a bit plump and her mouth too large. She wore, they thought in Paris, her clothes a little too tight, the necks too low, the skirts too short. Wilson thought she was beautiful. Like him, she came from the South. She did not want to spoil her maid by taking her to London, she told a fellow American, because the British treated blacks too well. Although she had the easy flirtatious ways of a Southern woman, she was a shrewd businesswoman. After her first husband's death she had run the family

Woodrow Wilson and his wife Edith in 1920, when the President was recuperating from his near fatal stroke. Sheltering her husband from the outside world, Edith controlled most of the visitors and correspondence that Wilson saw. Gravely ill and clinging to his foreign policy goals, Wilson witnessed the Republican controlled Senate defeat his cherished League of Nations. (Library of Congress)

jewelry store. When she married Wilson, he made it clear that he expected her to share his work. She took up the offer with enthusiasm. No intellectual, she was quick and determined. She was also ferociously loyal to her new husband. Wilson adored her.

On board the *George Washington*, the Wilsons kept to themselves, eating most of their meals in their stateroom and strolling on the deck arm in arm. The American experts worked away on their maps and their papers, asking each other, with some disquiet, what their country's policies were to be. Wilson had said much about general principles but had mentioned

few specifics. A young man called William Bullitt boldly went up to the president and told him that they were all confused by his silence. Wilson was surprised but agreed pleasantly to meet with a dozen of the leading experts. "It is absolutely the first time," said one afterward, "the president has let anyone know what his ideas are and what his policy is." There were to be few other such occasions. The experts left the meeting heartened and impressed. Wilson was informal and friendly. He spoke about the heavy task ahead and how he was going to rely on them to provide him with the best information. They must feel free to come to him at any time. "You tell me what's right and I'll fight for it." He apologized for talking about his own ideas: "they weren't very good but he thought them better than anything else he had heard."

When it came to making peace, Wilson said, their country would rightly hold the position of arbiter. They must live up to the great American traditions of justice and generosity. They would be, after all, "the only disinterested people at the Peace Conference." What was more, he warned, "the men whom we were about to deal with did not represent their own people." This was one of Wilson's deep convictions, curious in a man whose own Congress was now dominated by his political opponents. Throughout the Peace Conference he clung to the belief that he spoke for the masses and that, if only he could reach them—whether French, Italian or even Russian—they would rally to his views.

He touched on another favorite theme: the United States, he assured his audience, had not entered the war for selfish reasons. In this, as in so much else, it was unlike other nations, for it did not want territory, tribute or even revenge. (As a sign that American participation in the war was different from that of the Europeans, Wilson had always insisted on the United States being an Associate and not an Ally.) . . .

In that meeting on the *George Washington*, Wilson also talked briefly about the difficulties that lay ahead with the nations emerging from the wreckage of central Europe: Poland, Czechoslovakia, Yugoslavia and many more. They could have whatever form of government they wanted, but they must include in their new states only those who wanted to be there. "Criterion not who are intellectual or social or economic leaders but who form mass of people," a member of his audience wrote down. "Must have liberty—that is the kind of government they want."

Of all the ideas Wilson brought to Europe, this concept of self-determination was, and has remained, one of the most controversial and opaque. During the Peace Conference, the head of the American mission in Vienna sent repeated requests to Paris and Washington for an explanation of the term. No answer ever came. It has never been easy to determine

what Wilson meant. "Autonomous development," "the right of those who submit to authority to have a voice in their own governments," "the rights and liberties of small nations," a world made safe "for every peace-loving nation which, like our own, wishes to live its own life, determine its own institutions": the phrases had poured out from the White House, an inspiration to peoples around the world. But what did they add up to? Did Wilson merely mean, as sometimes appeared, an extension of democratic self-government? Did he really intend that any people who called themselves a nation should have their own state? In a statement he drafted, but never used, to persuade the American people to support the peace settlements, he stated, "We say now that all these people have the right to live their own lives under governments which they themselves choose to set up. That is the American principle." Yet he had no sympathy for Irish nationalists and their struggle to free themselves from British rule. During the Peace Conference he insisted that the Irish question was a domestic matter for the British. When a delegation of nationalist Irish asked him for support, he felt, he told his legal adviser, like telling them to go to hell. His view was that the Irish lived in a democratic country and they could sort it out through democratic means.

The more Wilson's concept of self-determination is examined, the more difficulties appear. Lansing asked himself: "When the President talks of 'self-determination' what unit has he in mind? Does he mean a race, a territorial area, or a community?" It was a calamity, Lansing thought, that Wilson had ever hit on the phrase. "It will raise hopes which can never be realized. It will, I fear, cost thousands of lives. In the end it is bound to be discredited, to be called the dream of an idealist who failed to realize the danger until it was too late to check those who attempt to put the principle into force.". . .

Wilson spent most of his time in the meeting with his experts on the matter closest to his heart: the need to find a new way of managing international relations. This did not come as a surprise to his audience. In his famous Fourteen Points of January 1918, and in subsequent speeches, he had sketched out his ideas. The balance of power, he told the U.S. Congress in his "Four Principles" speech of February 1918, was forever discredited as a way to keep peace. There would be no more secret diplomacy of the sort that had led Europe into calculating deals, rash promises and entangling alliances, and so on down the slope to war. The peace settlements must not leave the way open to future wars. There must be no retribution, no unjust claims and no huge fines—indemnities—paid by the losers to the winners. That was what had been wrong after Prussia defeated France in 1870. The French had never forgiven Germany for the monies paid over and for the loss of their provinces of Alsace and Lorraine. War itself must become more difficult. There must be controls on armaments—general disarmament, even. Ships must sail freely across the world's seas. (That meant, as the British well knew, the end of their traditional weapon of strangling enemy economies by blockading their ports and seizing their shipping; it had brought Napoleon down, and, so they thought, hastened the Allied victory over Germany.) Trade barriers must be lowered so the nations of the world would become more interdependent.

At the heart of Wilson's vision was a League of Nations to provide the collective security that, in a well-run civil society, was provided by the government, its laws, its courts and its police. "Old system of powers, balance of powers, had failed too often," one expert jotted down, as the president spoke. The League was to have a council that could "butt in" in case of disputes. "If unsuccessful the offending nation is to be outlawed—'And outlaws are not popular now.'"

Wilson's was a liberal and a Christian vision. It challenged the view that the best way to preserve the peace was to balance nations against each other, through alliances if necessary, and that strength, not collective security, was the way to deter attack. Wilson was also offering a riposte to the alternative being put out by the Russian Bolsheviks, that revolution would bring one world, where conflict would no longer exist. He believed in separate nations and in democracy, both as the best form of government

and as a force for good in the world. When governments were chosen by their people, they would not, indeed they could not, fight each other. "These are American principles," he told the Senate in 1917. "We could stand for no others. And they are also the principles and policies of forward looking men and women everywhere, of every modern nation, of every enlightened community. They are the principles of mankind and they must prevail." He was speaking, he thought, for humanity. Americans tended to see their values as universal ones, and their government and society as a model for all others. The United States, after all, had been founded by those who wanted to leave an old world behind, and its revolution was, in part, about creating a new one. American democracy, the American constitution, even American ways of doing business, were examples that others should follow for their own good. As one of the younger Americans said in Paris: "Before we get through with these fellows over here we will teach them how to do things and how to do them quickly."

The Americans had a complicated attitude toward the Europeans: a mixture of admiration for their past accomplishments, a conviction that the Allies would have been lost without the United States and a suspicion that, if the Americans were not careful, the wily Europeans would pull them into their toils again. As they prepared for the Peace Conference, the American delegates suspected that the French and the British were already preparing their traps. . . .

American exceptionalism has always had two sides: the one eager to set the world to rights, the other ready to turn its back with contempt if its message should be ignored. The peace settlement, Wilson told his fellow passengers, must be based on the new principles: "If it doesn't work right, the world will raise hell." He himself, he added half-jokingly, would go somewhere to "hide my head, perhaps to Guam." Faith in their own exceptionalism has sometimes led to a certain obtuseness on the part of Americans, a tendency to preach at other nations rather than listen to them, a tendency as well to assume that American motives are pure where those of others are not. And Wilson was very American. He came to the Peace Conference, said Lloyd George, like a missionary to rescue the heathen Europeans, with his "little sermonettes" full of rather obvious remarks.

It was easy to mock Wilson, and many did. It is also easy to forget how important his principles were in 1919 and how many people, and not just in the United States, wanted to believe in his great dream of a better world. They had, after all, a terrible reference point in the ruin left by the Great War. Wilson kept alive the hope that human society, despite the evidence, was getting better, that nations would one day live in harmony. In 1919, before disillusionment had set in, the world was more than ready to listen to him.

What Wilson had to say struck a chord, not just with liberals or pacifists but also among Europe's political and diplomatic élites. Sir Maurice Hankey, secretary to the British War Cabinet and then the Peace Conference itself, always carried a copy of the Fourteen Points in the box he kept for crucial reference material. They were, he said, the "moral background." Across Europe there were squares, streets, railway stations and parks bearing Wilson's name. Wall posters cried, "We Want a Wilson Peace." In Italy, soldiers knelt in front of his picture; in France, the left-wing paper L'Humanité brought out a special issue in which the leading lights of the French left vied with each other to praise Wilson's name. The leaders of the Arab revolt in the desert, Polish nationalists in Warsaw, rebels in the Greek islands, students in Peking, Koreans trying to shake off Japan's control, all took the Fourteen Points as their inspiration. Wilson himself found it exhilarating but also terrifying. "I am wondering," he said to George Creel, his brilliant propaganda chief, who was on board the George Washington, "whether you have not unconsciously spun a net for me from which there is no escape." The whole world was turning to the United States but, he went on, they both knew that such great problems could not be fixed at once. "What I seem to see—with all my heart I hope that I am wrong—is a tragedy of disappointment."

The George Washington reached the French port of Brest on December 13, 1918. The war had been over for just a month. While the president stood on the bridge, his ship steamed slowly in through a great avenue of battleships from the British, French and American navies. For the first time in days, the sun was shining. The streets were lined with laurel wreaths and flags. On the walls, posters paid tribute to Wilson, those from right-wingers for saving them from Germany and those from the left for the new world he promised. Huge numbers of people, many resplendent in their traditional Breton costumes, covered every inch of pavement, every roof, every tree. Even the lampposts were taken. The air filled with the skirl of Breton bagpipes and repeated shouts of "Vive l'Amérique! Vive Wilson!" The French foreign minister, Stéphen Pichon, welcomed him, saying, "We are so thankful that you have come over to give us the right kind of peace." Wilson made a noncommittal reply and the American party boarded the night train for Paris. At three in the morning, Wilson's doctor happened to look out the window of his compartment. "I saw not only men and women but little children standing with uncovered head to cheer the passage of the special train."

Wilson's reception in Paris was an even greater triumph, with even greater crowds: "the most remarkable demonstration," said an American who lived in Paris, "of enthusiasm and affection on the part of the Parisians that I have ever heard of, let alone seen." His train pulled into the Luxembourg station, which had been festooned with bunting and flags and filled with great masses of flowers. Clemenceau, the French prime minister, was there with his government and his longtime antagonist, the president Raymond Poincaré. As guns boomed across Paris to announce Wilson's arrival, the crowds started to press against the soldiers who lined the route. The president and his wife drove in an open carriage through the Place de la Concorde and on up the Champs-Elysées to their residence, to the sound of wild cheers. That night, at a quiet family dinner, Wilson said he was very pleased with his reception. "He had carefully watched the attitude of the crowd," he reportedly told the table, "and he was satisfied that they were most friendly." . . .

The Peace Conference continued until January 1920, but it was like a theatrical production whose stars had gone. The foreign ministers and the diplomats took over again but they never regained their old grip on foreign relations. The important decisions were always referred back to their political superiors in Rome or London or Washington and the difficult issues were hammered out in special conferences, of which Lloyd George alone attended thirty-three between 1919 and 1922.

Between January and June 1919, the peacemakers had accomplished an enormous amount: a League of Nations and an International Labour Organization, mandates handed out, the Germany treaty finished, the treaties with Austria, Hungary, Bulgaria and Ottoman Turkey nearly done—but there were many loose ends. . . .

The peacemakers in 1919 felt that they had done their best, but they had no illusions that they had solved the world's problems. As he left Paris on June 28, Wilson said to his wife, "Well, little girl, it is finished, and, as no one is satisfied, it makes me hope we have made a just peace; but it is all in the lap of the gods." It was also in the laps of those who came next to lead the world, some of whom had been in Paris—such as Prince Konoe of Japan and Franklin Delano Roosevelt—some of whom had been watching from afar. In Italy, Mussolini was rising fast in nationalist politics, as the old liberal order crumbled. . . . The young Adolf Hitler was in Munich that June, taking congenial courses on the glories of German history and the evils of international Jewish capital. Already he was discovering his own talents as an ideologue and an orator. . . .

Wilson's end was the saddest. Exhausted by the Peace Conference, he plunged into a wrenching and debilitating fight with the Senate over ratification of the Treaty of Versailles and, more specifically, the League of Nations. His supporters and his opponents had both been busy while he was away. The League

to Enforce the Peace was energetically lobbying for ratification. Wilson, unfortunately, did not much care for them, dismissing them as "butters-in" and "wool-gatherers." The League for the Preservation of American Independence, inspired, so it frequently said, by George Washington's and Thomas Jefferson's repeated warnings against permanent or entangling alliances, did its best to thwart the president. As for the ninety-six members of the Senate, it became apparent that they were dividing into roughly four groups. At least six Republicans would not have the League in any form—they came to be known as the Irreconcilables. A few Democrat mavericks would probably vote with them. Some nine Republicans were Mild Reservationists who would have accepted the League so long as their reservations to protect American sovereignty were registered. (Reservations were the well-established diplomatic practice of accepting an international agreement with qualifications; so long as all parties to the treaty agreed, the reservations stood.) This left three dozen Republicans who were not yet fully committed. Most Democrats still followed their president, although many privately hoped he would come to terms with the Mild Reservationists. If Wilson did compromise, there was a good chance that there would be enough votes to get the treaty passed. Would the European powers accept reservations? Lloyd George claimed in his memoirs that they had always expected they might have to. But they were never put to the test.

Wilson could have built his own coalition. The Republicans only had a majority of two in the Senate and he could have won over the moderates among them by accepting some reservations. When Lansing urged him to compromise, the president was unmoved: "His face took on that stubborn and pugnacious expression which comes when anyone tells him a fact which interferes with his plans." His opponents, Wilson told an intimate, were moved by the basest instincts. "They are going to have the most conspicuously contemptible names in history."

The president arrived back in Washington at midnight on July 8, 1919. A crowd of 100,000, enormous

The Council of Four included from left to right: Vittorio Orlando of Italy, David Lloyd George of England, Georges Clemenceau of France, and Woodrow Wilson. During the negotiation of the Treaty of Versailles, Wilson lost all but four of his Fourteen Points. The victorious European leaders were never committed to *Wilson's noble goal of "a peace without victory." As Clemenceau sneered: "God gave us the ten commandments and we broke them. Wilson gave us the Fourteen Points—we shall see." (© Bettmann/CORBIS)*

for those days, waited at the train station. Two days later he presented the Treaty of Versailles, with the League covenant at its start, to the Senate in person. "Dare we reject it," he asked them, "and break the heart of the world?" His speech, it was generally agreed, was poor. Unusually, he read parts of it and he lost his thread in places. Washington, and the country, readied themselves for the next step—the Senate's consideration of the treaty.

At first Wilson chose to work largely behind the scenes, meeting with Republican senators in an effort to persuade them that American independence was not compromised by membership in the League or by Article X, in particular, which was the heart of collective security. (Signatories promised "to respect and preserve as against external aggression the territorial integrity and existing political independence of all Members of the League.") He was confident, he told a British diplomat, that the treaty would go through the Senate. He was not prepared, he reiterated, to accept any changes; the treaty must be ratified as they had written it in Paris.

At the end of his first week in Washington, Wilson escaped the summer heat with a cruise on the Potomac on the presidential yacht. He was already looking tired. The impending treaty fight was not the only problem facing his administration that summer. Food prices were going up sharply; racial tensions were exploding into race riots; key unions threatened strikes. The weather broke, with violent thunderstorms, and the president took to his bed for several days. A touch of dysentery, was Admiral Grayson's explanation. There has been much speculation since that it was in fact a minor stroke. Whatever the case, and we will never know for certain, Wilson was clearly not the man he had been. He was easily confused and forgot things he should have known. He lost his temper frequently, often over small matters. Wilson's deteriorating mental and physical health contributed, perhaps, to his refusal to face the reality that he did not have the votes to get the treaty as it stood through the Senate and also to making his well-known stubbornness something more like blind obstinacy. Grayson and Mrs. Wilson, loyal and protective to a fault, did their best to persuade him to rest. They also downplayed the problems with his health.

On July 14 a Democrat who supported the treaty made the first of what were to be five months of speeches in the Senate. On July 31 the Senate Foreign Relations Committee under Lodge's chairmanship started six weeks of hearings. Not surprisingly, the questioning from the Republican majority focused on the League's covenant, especially the by now notorious Article X. On August 19, in an extraordinary breach with convention, Wilson appeared before the committee. He gave no indication that he was prepared to compromise. Four days later, the committee voted on the first of what were to be numerous amendments and reservations to the treaty. The issue they chose was Shantung—to reverse its award to Japan and hand it back to China.

An angry Wilson decided the time had come to reach beyond the senators to the American people.

On September 2, 1919, he left Washington for a trip across the country. His closest advisers begged him not to go. Wilson was adamant. The treaty must be saved, even if he had to give his life for it. "In the presence of the great tragedy which now faces the world," he told them, "no decent man can count his personal fortunes in the reckoning." Grayson heard the decision with dread: "There was nothing I could do except to go with him and take such care of him as I could." As Wilson boarded his special train, he complained about the dreadful headaches that he had been having. For almost a month Wilson made speech after speech, sometimes two, even three a day. He hammered at the same themes. The treaty was a great document for peace and for humanity, dearly bought with the sacrifice of the young American men who had gone over to fight in Europe. Those who opposed it back in Washington were partisan, shortsighted, selfish, ignorant, perhaps something worse. "When at last in the annals of mankind they are gibbeted, they will regret that the gibbet is so high." He was glad, he told an audience in St. Louis, that he was away from the capital. "The real voices of the great people of America sometimes sound faint and distant in that strange city!" The crowds grew larger and more enthusiastic as he headed west. Supporters of the treaty grew moderately confident that it might get through if only Wilson would accept some of the milder reservations.

Wilson's headaches grew worse and he looked more and more exhausted. Bad news came in from Washington. Sentiment was growing in favor of reservations. . . . Grayson noticed with alarm that the president turned pale and saliva appeared in the corners of his mouth. In San Francisco, Wilson told an old friend, a woman whom he had once been close to, that the attacks on the treaty were simply personal. "If *I* had nothing to do with the League of Nations, it would go through just like that!"

On September 25 Wilson was in Colorado. By now he was having repeated coughing attacks which

Grayson attributed to asthma. He had to sit propped up at nights and could not sleep for more than two hours at a time. He spoke in Pueblo that afternoon, his fortieth speech in twenty-one days. "Disloyalty," he said of the League's opponents. There would be no compromise with them, no reservations to the covenant: "We have got to adopt it or reject it."

Wilson never spoke in public again. At two the next morning, Mrs. Wilson woke Grayson. He found the president in a pitiable state, ill, gasping for air, the muscles in his face twitching. Wilson feebly insisted that he must carry on. His wife and doctor overruled him. "The doctor is right," Wilson told his secretary with tears in his eyes. "I have never been in a condition like this, and I just feel as if I am going to pieces." The president was suffering, Grayson said in a public statement, from physical exhaustion and a nervous reaction affecting his stomach. The rest of the tour was canceled and the president's train headed back to Washington.

On October 2, at the White House, Wilson had a massive stroke that left him partly paralyzed on his left side. Although he would make a limited recovery over time, he was not physically or mentally the man he had been. He never effectively functioned as president again, although he continued to influence the battle over the treaty from his sickroom. Mrs. Wilson and Grayson took it upon themselves to conceal the full extent of his illness and to carry out his wishes. In the first weeks after the stroke, when it was not clear that Wilson would survive, they kept everyone except Wilson's daughters and the essential nurses and doctors from seeing the president. The leader of the Senate Democrats, Gilbert Hitchcock of Nebraska, was shocked when he finally saw Wilson on November 7. "As he lay in bed slightly propped up by pillows with the useless arm concealed beneath the covers I beheld an emaciated old man with a thin white beard which had been permitted to grow."

The treaty continued to make its way through the Senate for the rest of October and part of November 1919. Amendments, twelve in all, were defeated by a combination of Democrats and moderate Republicans.

Lodge managed, however, to hold most of the Republicans together, and their votes, along with those of the few Democrats who crossed party lines, were sufficient to attach a number of reservations to the treaty. The most crucial reservation involved Article X; the United States would not act to protect the territorial integrity or independence of any League member unless Congress approved. Lodge put forward a motion of ratification incorporating the reservation. When Hitchcock went to Wilson's bedside for a second time on November 17 to discuss this, he found the president significantly more alert—but also more determined than ever. Wilson adamantly opposed the reservation in any form. "That cuts the very heart out of the treaty." He told Hitchcock to let the Republicans take the responsibility for defeating the treaty; they would have to answer to the people of the United States. The following day Mrs. Wilson sent Hitchcock a letter she had written at her husband's dictation. The reservations of Senator Lodge and his cronies amounted to a nullification of the treaty. "I sincerely hope," Wilson said unequivocally, "that the friends and supporters of the League will vote against the Lodge resolution of ratification." The next day the Senate voted on Lodge's motion. It was defeated by a combination of those Democrats, the majority, who still followed Wilson's bidding and Republican Irreconcilables. Four weeks later, Wilson learned that he had won the Nobel Peace Prize.

Moderate Republicans and Democrats made a last-ditch effort to find a compromise. From the White House an embittered Wilson did his best to block them. Even so the moderates came close; when the Senate voted for the final time on March 19, 1920, on a fresh resolution to ratify the treaty, with slightly modified reservations, the new resolution passed. Twenty-three Democrats defied their president to vote in favor. The necessary two-thirds majority, however, remained just out of reach so the Senate failed to give its consent to the treaty. "Doctor," Wilson said to Grayson that night, "the devil is a busy man."

He never changed his view that he had been right to reject compromise. The United States later signed separate treaties with Germany, Austria and Hungary, but it never joined the League. Wilson, who had briefly contemplated running for president again, lingered on until 1924. Mrs. Wilson survived to go to John F. Kennedy's inauguration in 1961.

Wilson's efforts, and those of the many other peacemakers who shared his ideals, were not completely wasted. The Treaty of Versailles, and the other treaties with the defeated that used it as a model, certainly contained provisions about territory and reparations that could have been written in earlier centuries, but they were also imbued with a new spirit. . . . The provisions for an International Labour Organization, for treaties to protect minorities, to set up a permanent court of justice or to try men such as the kaiser for offenses against international morality, underlined the idea that there were certain things that all humanity had in common and that there could be international standards beyond those of mere national interest. And when those treaties were attacked in the interwar years it was generally because they had failed to match those standards.

Later it became commonplace to blame everything that went wrong in the 1920s and 1930s on the peacemakers and the settlements they made in Paris in 1919, just as it became easy to despair of democracy. Pointing the finger and shrugging helplessly are effective ways of avoiding responsibility. Eighty years later the old charges about the Paris Peace Conference still have a wide circulation. "The final crime," declared *The Economist* in its special millennium issue, was "the Treaty of Versailles, whose harsh terms would ensure a second war." That is to ignore the actions of everyone—political leaders, diplomats, soldiers, ordinary voters—for twenty years between 1919 and 1939.

Hitler did not wage war because of the Treaty of Versailles, although he found its existence a godsend for his propaganda. Even if Germany had been left with its old borders, even if it had been allowed whatever military forces it wanted, even if it had been permitted to join with Austria, he still would have wanted more: the destruction of Poland, control of Czechoslovakia, above all the conquest of the Soviet Union. He would have demanded room for the German people to expand and the destruction of their enemies, whether Jews or Bolsheviks. There was nothing in the Treaty of Versailles about that.

The peacemakers of 1919 made mistakes, of course. By their offhand treatment of the non-European world, they stirred up resentments for which the West is still paying today. They took pains over the borders in Europe, even if they did not draw them to everyone's satisfaction, but in Africa they carried on the old practice of handing out territory to suit the imperialist powers. In the Middle East, they threw together peoples, in Iraq most notably, who still have not managed to cohere into a civil society. If they could have done better, they certainly could have done much worse. They tried, even cynical old Clemenceau, to build a better order. They could not foresee the future and they certainly could not control it. That was up to their successors. When war came in 1939, it was a result of twenty years of decisions taken or not taken, not of arrangements made in 1919.

Of course things might have been different if Germany had been more thoroughly defeated. Or if the United States had been as powerful after the First World War as it was after the Second—and had been willing to use that power. If Britain and France had not been weakened by the war—or if they had been so weakened that the United States had felt obliged to step in. If Austria-Hungary had not disappeared. If its successor states had not quarreled with each other. If China had not been so weak. If Japan had been more sure of itself. If states had accepted a League of Nations with real powers. If the world had been so thoroughly devastated by war that it was willing to contemplate a new way of managing international relations. The peacemakers, however, had to deal with reality, not what might have been. They grappled with huge and difficult questions. How can the irrational passions of nationalism or religion be contained before they do more damage? How can we outlaw war? We are still asking those questions.

QUESTIONS TO CONSIDER

1 Explain MacMillan's conclusion that Wilson "remained a Southerner in some ways all his life." Describe how Wilson's background and character made it difficult for him to compromise.

2 Why did Woodrow Wilson personally lead the peace delegation to Paris? What risks did he take by leaving the United States when it was still recuperating from the war and was filled with anxieties about the upcoming peace settlement? Why did his peace delegation cause rancor among Republicans?

3 What role did women, especially Edith Bolling Galt, play in Wilson's life? How did the second Mrs. Wilson attempt to shield and protect her husband during those days when, gravely ill, he battled with the Senate over the League of Nations?

4 Why, at the peace negotiations at Versailles, was Wilson's goal of self-determination not consistently applied to all nations? For example, why did the Irish find unconvincing the President's appeal for self-determination? In what ways did the League of Nations challenge the old belief of world peace achieved through a balance of power? Explain the author's conclusion that Wilson's peace program incorporated the concept of "American exceptionalism."

5 When Wilson returned from France with the Treaty of Versailles, what dissension did he encounter in the United States Senate? Why was the President in no mood to compromise on any changes in the League covenant? How might Wilson's health problems have contributed to his intransigence on the peace treaty?

6 Why does MacMillan assert that the failures of the 1919 peacemakers did not cause the foreign policy problems of the next two decades or the outbreak of the Second World War? In what ways are twenty-first-century world leaders still trying to resolve threats to world peace that are similar to those faced by the diplomats of 1919?

PART SEVEN

The Twenties

14 Henry Ford: Symbol of an Age

RODERICK NASH

The election of Warren G. Harding as president reflected a massive popular reaction against the missionary idealism of Woodrow Wilson and the reformist zeal of the Progressive era. Harding would take the country back to "normalcy," so that Americans might continue their "normal, onward way." Essentially, this meant that federal regulation of industry would be reduced to a minimum, that the business of government, as Calvin Coolidge put it, would be big business.

The popular stereotype of the 1920s is that it was a decade of political corruption, speculative orgies, violence, and the last happy fling before the Great Depression crushed American innocence. But in reality this decade of "normalcy" was a good deal more complex than that. True, business consolidation under Republican rule continued throughout the decade. True, excessive and irresponsible speculation on the New York Stock Exchange culminated in the crash of 1929. True, organized crime was widespread, and gang wars rocked Chicago and New York. And true, a revolution in manners and morals challenged traditional standards and profoundly upset Americans who clung to the old morality.

Yet for many contemporaries, the 1920s were a time of exhilarating hope and high expectation for the United States. In fact, a number of intellectuals found much in American life to celebrate. Most optimistic of all were the businesspeople, who believed they were living in a new era—a time not only of conservative Republican leadership in Washington but of striking innovation and change in business itself. As industrial officials happily observed, corporate managers were bringing scientific procedures and efficient techniques to industry. This change, they contended, would raise production so high that poverty would soon be eliminated and the American dream of abundance for all would be attained at last. Their expectations, alas, perished in the crash of 1929 and the ensuing Depression, the worst the country had ever known.

During the 1920s, however, the United States seemed enormously prosperous, and the American businessperson enjoyed new preeminence in American life. One businessman became a leading figure of the decade. Indeed, his technological genius, love of country, and old-fashioned Americanism made him a folk hero to a large segment of American society. This was car maker Henry Ford, who introduced the first car built for the common person—the Model T—and whose technique of assembly-line production revolutionized American technology. What Ford wrought, as David Halberstam has said, also profoundly altered the way Americans lived: it made them far more mobile than they had been in the railroad age, and it created a culture of leisure in which people thought as much about recreation as they did about their jobs. The automobile dramatically changed American customs of courtship.

Ironically, Ford himself despised most of the social changes he helped bring about. A champion of the Protestant work ethic, he abhorred the very idea of leisure. "Work," he contended, "is the salvation of the race, morally, physically, socially. Work does more than get us our living; it gets us our life." He could be remarkably contradictory and unpredictable. He introduced the $5 wage for an eight-hour day (which revolutionized labor policy in industrial America) and yet opposed the union movement. He owned a fifty-six-room mansion and built the Ford Motor Company into what one author described as the biggest "family-owned industrial empire in the world," accumulating a total of $1 billion in profits, and yet he claimed to care little for material things and pleasures. "I have never known," he said, "what to do with money after my expenses were paid." In the end, he donated $40 million to philanthropic enterprises. He considered himself a pacifist, so much so that in 1915 he dispatched a "peace ship" to Europe in a futile if honorable attempt to stop the First World War. Yet this same man had what Roderick Nash calls a rural, "Bible-belt morality." He expatiated on the evils of jazz (it was all "monkey talk" and "jungle squeals") and blamed it and the new dances on a Jewish conspiracy. In fact, he published anti-Semitic diatribes in his Dearborn, Michigan, newspaper (he did retract his anti-Semitic statements in 1927).

The key to Ford's contradictory mind, as Nash says in the next selection, was ambivalence. He was both "old and new." He looked backward and forward at the same time, defending technology while extolling the old rural values and attitudes of a bygone era. In this respect, he symbolized the America of his age—a changing, industrial America that longed for the security of the old days as it struggled with the complexities of the new.

GLOSSARY

ALGER, HORATIO   Gilded Age author whose heroes rose from poverty to greatness and thus fulfilled the "American dream."

FORDISMUS   German word for Ford's "revolutionary mass-production techniques."

McGUFFEY READER   Its "moral-coated language lessons" in such stories as "The Hare and the Tortoise" were the staple of Ford's academic diet.

MODEL T   Ford's first automobile, introduced in 1908 and built for the masses.

ew names were better known to Americans from 1917 to 1930 than that of Henry Ford. Whether one read his publications,[1] or followed his headline-making public life, or merely drove the car his company manufactured, Ford was inescapable in the twenties. Indeed it is possible to think of these years as the automobile age and Henry Ford as its czar. The flivver, along with the flask and the flapper, seemed to represent the 1920s in the minds of its people as well as its historians.

Cars symbolized change. They upset familiar patterns of living, working, recreating, even thinking. Much of the roar of the twenties came from the internal combustion engine. While providing portable bedrooms in which to enjoy the decade's alleged sexual freedom, cars also assisted gangsters and bootleggers in getting away. The image of two of them in every garage helped elect a President in 1928. The rise of widespread use of the automobile, in a word, contributed significantly to setting the twenties apart. And Henry Ford, calling machinery the "new Messiah" (as he did in 1929), seemed to herald the new era.

Beneath the surface, however, such generalizations ring hollow. Neither Ford nor the twenties merited the clichés with which each has been so frequently discussed. In the case of the man, both old and new mingled in his mind. On the one hand Ford was a builder and bulwark of the modern, mechanized nation; on the other he devoted a remarkable amount of effort and expense to sustaining old-fashioned America. In fact, the nostalgic, backward-looking Henry Ford repeatedly deplored the very conditions that Ford the revolutionary industrialist did so much

Henry Ford at the peak of his power, about 1914. As Nash observed, Henry Ford was a "plain, honest, old-fashioned billionaire" and "technological genius" who fretted about the new morality of the Jazz Age, ridiculing jazz itself as "monkey talk" and "jungle squeals" and blaming illicit liquor on a Jewish conspiracy. Still, despite his rural outlook and biblical virtues, Ford was one of the most popular Americans of the Roaring Twenties. (Collection of Greenfield Village and Henry Ford Museum, Dearborn, Michigan)

From pp. 154–163 of *The Nervous Generation: American Thought, 1917–1930* by Roderick Nash. Published by Rand-McNally Publishing Company, Chicago. © 1970 by Roderick Nash. Reprinted by permission of Roderick Nash.

[1]In all probability Henry Ford did not actually write the numerous books, pamphlets, and articles associated with his name and attributed to him in this chapter. He was not a literary man; his critics even alleged he could not read! But Ford could pay people to express his opinions for him, and there is no reason to think that the ideas these writers recorded were not those of their employer.

to bring about. This ambivalence did not signify a lack of values so much as a superfluity. His faith was strong if bigoted and contradictory. His prescriptions for America were clear if simple-minded. He seemed to the masses to demonstrate that there could be change without disruption, and in so doing he eased the twenties' tensions. "The average citizen," editorialized the *New Republic* in 1923, "sees Ford as a sort of enlarged crayon portrait of himself; the man able to fulfill his own suppressed desires, who has achieved enormous riches, fame and power without departing from the pioneer-and-homespun tradition." In this nervous clinging to old values even while undermining them Ford was indeed a "crayon portrait" of his age.

But was Ford typical of the twenties? Can he really be said to symbolize the age? He was, after all, in his middle fifties when the decade began. However, a great many Americans were also middle-aged in the 1920s, far more in fact than the twenty-year-old collegians who have hitherto characterized these years. And at one point even a group of college students ranked Ford as the third greatest figure of all time, behind Napoleon and Jesus Christ.

The Dearborn, Michigan, into which Henry Ford was born in 1863 was a small farming community only a generation removed from the frontier. Both sides of the Ford family had agrarian backgrounds, and the children grew up on the farm. Henry's formal education began and ended in the Scotch Settlement School which he attended for eight years. The staple of his academic diet was the McGuffey reader with its moral-coated language lessons. When Ford left school to become an apprentice mechanic in Detroit, he also left the farm. But the farm never left Henry. Agrarian ideas and values shaped his thought even as he became an industrial king.

The 1880s for Ford were a time of aimlessness, his only real interest being in tinkering with watches and other engines. In 1892 he joined the Edison Company in Detroit as an engineer. During his spare time he struggled with the problem of building a gasoline engine compact enough to power a moving vehicle. By 1896 Ford had his automobile. Soon he had it doing ninety miles per hour! It required seven years more, however, for him to secure the necessary financial and administrative backing to launch the Ford Motor Company. The rest was pure Horatio Alger.

The first Model T appeared in 1908, and it soon made good Ford's boast that he could build a car for the masses. Six thousand sold the first year. Six years later, after the introduction of assembly line production, the figure was 248,000. From May to December 1920 almost 700,000 Model Ts rolled out of the Ford plants. The total for 1921 was one million.

In 1923, 57 percent of all cars manufactured in the United States were Fords. Three years later the Ford Motor Company produced its thirteen millionth car. From the perspective of efficient production the Ford organization was also something of a miracle. In 1913 it required twelve hours to make a car. The following year, after the introduction of the assembly line techniques, the figure dropped to ninety-three minutes. In 1920 Ford achieved his long-time dream of building one car for every minute of the working day. And still he was unsatisfied. On October 31, 1925, the Ford Motor Company manufactured 9,109 Model Ts, one every ten seconds. This was the high point, and competition was rising to challenge Ford's preeminence, but by the end of the twenties Henry Ford was a legend, a folk hero, and reputedly the richest man who ever lived. Transcending the role of automobile manufacturer, he had become an international symbol of the new industrialism. The Germans coined a word to describe the revolutionary mass production techniques: *Fordismus*. At home Ford's popularity reached the point where he could be seriously considered a presidential possibility for the election of 1924.

Fortunately for the historian of his thought, if not always for himself, Henry Ford had a propensity for forthrightly stating his opinions on a wide variety of subjects outside his field of competence. He also had the money to publish and otherwise implement his ideas. The resulting intellectual portrait was that of a mind steeped in traditional Americanism. For Ford agrarian simplicity, McGuffey morality, and Algerian determination were sacred objects. Nationalism was writ large over all Ford did, and America was great because of its heritage of freedom, fairness, and hard, honest work. Ford's confidence in the beneficence of old-fashioned virtues verged on the fanatical. The "spirit of '76," equal opportunity democracy, rugged individualism, the home, and motherhood were Ford's touchstones of reality. He deified pioneer ethics and values. "More men are beaten than fail," he declared in 1928. "It is not wisdom they need, or money, or brilliance, or pull, but just plain gristle and bone." A decade earlier "Mr. Ford's Page" in the

Dearborn Independent stated that "one of the great things about the American people is that they are pioneers." This idea led easily to American messianism. "No one can contemplate the nation to which we belong," the editorial continued, "without realizing the distinctive prophetic character of its obvious mission to the world. We are pioneers. We are pathfinders. We are the roadbuilders. We are the guides, the vanguards of Humanity." Theodore Roosevelt and Woodrow Wilson had said as much, but Ford was writing *after* the war that allegedly ended the nation's innocence and mocked its mission.

Ford's intense commitment to the traditional American faith led him to suspect and ultimately to detest whatever was un-American. The same loyalties compelled him to search for explanations for the unpleasant aspects of the American 1920s that exonerated the old-time, "native" citizen. The immigrant, and particularly the Jew, were primary targets of Ford's fire. In editorial after editorial in the *Dearborn Independent* and in several books Ford argued that aliens who had no knowledge of "the principles which have made our civilization" were responsible for its "marked deterioration" in the 1920s. They were, moreover, determined to take over the country if not the world. Spurred by such fears, Ford became a subscriber to the tired legend of an international Jewish conspiracy. When he couldn't find sufficient evidence for such a plot, Ford dispatched a number of special detectives to probe the affairs of prominent Jews and collect documentation. The search resulted in the "discovery" of the so-called "Protocols of the Learned Elders of Zion," an alleged exposition of the scheme by which the Jews planned to overthrow Gentile domination. Although the "Protocols" was exposed as a forgery in 1921, Ford continued to use the spurious document to substantiate his anti-Semitism until late in the decade. Everything wrong with modern American civilization, from the corruption of music to the corruption of baseball, was attributed to Jewish influence. Unable to admit that America as a whole might be blamed for its problems, unwilling to question the beneficence of time-honored ways, Ford searched for a

scapegoat. He found it in the newcomers who, he believed, had no conception of or appreciation for American ideals.

The tension in Henry Ford's thought between old and new, between a belief in progress and a tendency to nostalgia, is dramatically illustrated in his attitude toward farming and farmers. On the one hand he believed farm life to be a ceaseless round of inefficient drudgery. Indeed, he had abundant personal evidence, remarking at one point, "I have traveled ten thousand miles behind a plow. I hated the grueling grind of farm work." With the incentive of sparing others this painful experience, Ford addressed himself to the problem of industrializing agriculture. The farmer, in Ford's opinion, should become a technician and a businessman. Tractors (Ford's, of course) should replace horses. Mechanization would make it possible to produce in twenty-five working days what formerly required an entire year. Fences would come down and vast economies of scale take place. Ford's modern farmer would not even need to live on his farm but instead could commute from a city home. To give substance to these ideals Ford bought and operated with astonishing success a nine-thousand-acre farm near Dearborn.

Still Ford, the "Father of Modern Agriculture," as he has been dubbed, was only part of the man. He also retained a strong streak of old-fashioned, horse-and-buggy agrarianism. Farming, from this standpoint, was more than a challenge in production; it was a moral act. Constantly in the twenties, even while he was helping make it possible, Ford branded the modern city a "pestiferous growth." He delighted in contrasting the "unnatural," "twisted," and "cooped up" lives of city-dwellers with the "wholesome" life of "independence" and "sterling honesty" that the farm environment offered. In Ford's view the importance of cities in the nation's development had been greatly exaggerated. Early in the 1920s the *Dearborn Independent* editorialized: "when we all stand up and sing, 'My Country 'Tis of Thee,' we seldom think of the cities. Indeed, in that old national hymn there are no references to the city at all. It sings of rocks and rivers and hills—the great American Out-of-Doors.

And that is really The Country. That is, the country is THE Country. The real United States lies outside the cities."

As such a manifesto suggests, a bias toward nature and rural conditions was an important element in Henry Ford's thought. "What children and adults need," he told one reporter, "is a chance to breathe God's fresh air and to stretch their legs and have a little garden in the soil." This ideal led Ford to choose small towns instead of cities as the sites of his factories. "Turning back to village industry," as Ford put it in 1926, would enable people to reestablish a sense of community—with nature and with men—that urbanization had destroyed. Ford believed that cities were doomed as Americans discovered the advantages of country life.

Ford's enthusiasm for nature did not stop with ruralism. From 1914 to 1924 he sought a more complete escape from civilization on a series of camping trips with Thomas A. Edison. John Burroughs, the naturalist, and Harvey Firestone, the tire king, also participated. Although the equipment these self-styled vagabonds took into the woods was far from primitive, they apparently shared a genuine love of the outdoors. In the words of Burroughs, they "cheerfully endured wet, cold, smoke, mosquitoes, black flies, and sleepless nights, just to touch naked reality once more." Ford had a special fondness for birds. With typical exuberance he had five hundred birdhouses built on his Michigan farm, including one with seventy-six apartments which he called, appropriately, a "bird hotel." There were also electric heaters and electric brooders for Ford's fortunate birds. The whole production mixed technology and nature in a way that symbolized Ford's ambivalence. When he could not camp or visit his aviary, Ford liked to read about the natural world. Indeed he preferred the works of Emerson, Thoreau, and Burroughs to the Bible. Ford so admired Burroughs' variety of natural history that even before becoming acquainted with him he sent him a new Ford car.

As for roads and automobiles, Ford saw them not as a threat to natural conditions but rather as a way for the average American to come into contact with nature. The machine and the garden were not incompatible. "I will build a motor car for the great multitude . . . ," Ford boasted, "so low in price that no man . . . will be unable to own one—and enjoy with his family the blessings of hours of pleasure in God's great open spaces." In *My Life and Work* of 1923 Ford again confronted the tension between nature and modern civilization. He declared that he did not agree with those who saw mechanization leading to a "cold, metallic sort of world in which great factories will drive away the trees, the flowers, the birds and the green fields." According to Ford, "unless we know more about machines and their use . . . we cannot have the time to enjoy the trees and the birds, and the flowers, and the green fields." Such reconciliations only partially covered Ford's nervousness about the mechanized, urbanized future. Contradictions persisted in his thinking. The same man who envisaged fenceless bonanza farms could say, "I love to walk across country and jump fences." The lover of trees could state in utmost seriousness, "better wood can be made than is grown."

Ford's attitude toward history has been subject to wide misunderstanding. The principal source of confusion is a statement Ford made in 1919 at the trial resulting from his libel suit against the *Chicago Tribune*. "History," he declared, "is more or less the bunk. It is tradition. We don't want tradition. We want to live in the present, and the only history that is worth a tinker's dam is the history we make today." On another occasion he admitted that he "wouldn't give a nickel for all the history in the world." Complementing this sentiment is Ford's reputation as a forward-looking inventor and revolutionary industrialist unsatisfied with the old processes. Here seems a man fully at home in the alleged new era of the 1920s. But in fact Ford idolized the past. His "history . . . is bunk" remark came in response to a question about ancient history and Napoleon Bonaparte and had reference to written history. For history itself—what actually happened in his nation's past and its tangible evidence—Ford had only praise.

The most obvious evidence of Ford's enthusiasm for history was his collector's instinct. He began with the bastion of his own youth, the McGuffey readers. Sending agents out to scour the countryside and putting aside considerations of cost, Ford owned by 1925 one of the few complete collections of the many McGuffey editions. Hoping to share his treasures with his contemporaries, Ford had five thousand copies of *Old Favorites from the McGuffey Readers* printed in 1926. The book contained such classic stories as "Try, Try Again" and "The Hare and the Tortoise." It dispensed an ideal of individualism and self-reliance at the same time that Ford's assembly lines were making men cogs in an impersonal machine.

From books Ford turned to things, and during the 1920s amassed a remarkable collection of American antiques. He bought so widely and so aggressively that he became a major factor in prices in the antique market. Everything was fair game. Lamps and dolls, bells and grandfather clocks made their way to Dearborn. Size was no problem. Ford gathered enough machines to show the evolution of the threshing operation from 1849 to the 1920s. Another exhibit traced the development of wagons in America. Eventually the entire heterogeneous collection went into the Edison Museum at Dearborn, a pretentious building designed to resemble, simultaneously, Independence Hall, Congress Hall, and the old City Hall of Philadelphia. Ford delighted in showing visitors around the five-acre layout. Asked on one occasion why he collected, Ford replied, "so that they will not be lost to America." Later, on the same tour, Ford played a few bars on an antique organ and observed, "that takes me back to my boyhood days. They were beautiful days."

This sentiment undoubtedly figured in Ford's 1920 decision to restore his boyhood home. Everything had to be exactly as he remembered it. Furniture, china, and rugs were rehabilitated or reconstructed. Ford even used archaeological techniques to recover artifacts around the family homestead. The ground was dug to a depth of six feet and the silverware, wheels, and other equipment used by his parents in the 1860s were recovered. In 1922 Ford purchased the Wayside Inn at Sudbury, Massachusetts, to preserve it from destruction. Celebrated by the poet

Henry Wadsworth Longfellow, the old inn appealed to Ford as a symbol of pioneer days. He opened it for the public's edification in 1924. But a new highway ran too near. Roaring cars disturbed the horse-and-buggy atmosphere. So, turning against the age he helped create, Ford had the state highway rerouted around the shrine at a cost of $250,000. He also bought and restored the schoolhouse in Sudbury alleged to be the site where Mary and her little lamb gamboled. Naturally the shop of the "Village Blacksmith," also in Sudbury, had to be included in Ford's antique empire.

Beginning in 1926 with the construction of Greenfield Village near Dearborn, Ford embarked on a career of large-scale historical restoration. This time not a building but a whole community was the object of his attention. Greenfield, named after the Michigan hamlet in which Ford's mother grew up, was a monument to his agrarianism as well as his reverence for the past. "I am trying in a small way," Ford explained with unwarranted modesty, "to help America take a step . . . toward the saner and sweeter idea of life that prevailed in pre-war days." Greenfield Village had gravel roads, gas street lamps, a grassy common, and an old-fashioned country store. The automobile mogul permitted only horse-drawn vehicles on the premises. The genius of assembly line mass production engaged a glass blower, blacksmith, and cobbler to practice their obsolete crafts in the traditional manner. Ford dispatched his agents to seek out, purchase, and transport to Greenfield the cottages of Walt Whitman, Noah Webster, and Patrick Henry. In time they even secured the crowning glory: the log cabin in which William Holmes McGuffey had been born and raised.

History, then, was not "bunk" to Henry Ford. The speed of change seemed to increase proportionately to his desire to retain contact with the past. As Ford declared in 1928, a year before completing Greenfield Village, "improvements have been coming so quickly that the past is being lost to the rising generation." To counter this tendency Ford labored to put history into a form "where it may be seen and felt." But values and attitudes were also on display.

Ford looked back with nostalgia to the pioneer ethic. With it, he believed, the nation had been sound, wholesome, happy, and secure. "The Old Ways," as the *Dearborn Independent* declared, "Were Good."

Ford's opinion of the new morality of the jazz age was, not surprisingly, low. He deplored the use of tobacco and even went so far as to publish for mass circulation a tract, entitled *The Case Against the Little White Slaver,* which excoriated cigarettes. When Ford had the power he went beyond exhortation. "No one smokes in the Ford industries," their leader proclaimed in 1929. As for alcohol, Ford was equally unyielding. Twice he threatened to make his international labor force teetotalers at the risk of their jobs. In his American plants Ford enforced a policy of abstinence. Any workman detected drinking publicly or even keeping liquor at home was subject to dismissal. The prohibition policy of the 1920s, in Ford's estimation, was a great triumph. "There are a million boys growing up in the United States," he exulted in 1929, "who have never seen a saloon and who will never know the handicap of liquor." When confronted with evidence of widespread violation of the Eighteenth Amendment, Ford had a ready explanation. A Jewish conspiracy was to blame for illicit booze. The mass of real Americans, Ford believed, were, like himself, dry by moral conviction as well as by law.

Sex was too delicate a matter to be addressed directly, but Ford conveyed his opinions through a discussion of music and dancing. Few aspects of the American 1920s worried him more than the evils of jazz. The new music clashed squarely with his ruralism and Bible-belt morality. In 1921 Ford struck out in anger at "the waves upon waves of musical slush that invaded decent parlors and set the young people of this generation imitating the drivel of morons." Organized Jewry, once again, was blamed for the musical degeneracy. "The mush, the slush, the sly suggestion, the abandoned sensuousness of sliding notes," declared the Dearborn Independent, "are of Jewish origin." The problem, obviously, was not only musical but sexual as well. The loosening of morals in the 1920s appalled Ford. He expressed his feelings in reference to jazz: "monkey talk, jungle squeals, grunts and

squeaks and gasps suggestive of cave love are camouflaged by a few feverish notes." What Ford could only bring himself to call "the thing" appeared also in song titles such as *In Room 202* and *Sugar Baby.* Pointing to the Jewish origin of these tunes (Irving Berlin was a frequent target of attacks), Ford called on his countrymen to crush the serpent in their midst.

The reform of dancing fitted nicely into Ford's campaign to elevate the nation's morals to old-time standards. His interest began with the collection of traditional folk dances. Not only the scores but the backwoods fiddlers themselves were invited to Dearborn to play *Old Zip Coon* and *Arkansas Traveler.* To Ford's delight, here was something both wholesome and historical. He also manifested concern over social dancing, publishing in 1926 a guidebook entitled *"Good Morning": After a Sleep of Twenty-five Years Old-Fashioned Dancing is Being Revived by Mr. and Mrs. Henry Ford.* The book also endeavored to revive old-fashioned morality. It began by condemning as promiscuous the newer dances such as the Charleston and the whole flapper syndrome. "A gentleman," the book explained, "should be able to guide his partner through a dance without embracing her as if he were her lover." Proper deportment, according to Ford, minimized physical contact. "[The gentleman's] right hand should be placed at his partner's waist, thumb and forefinger alone touching her—that is, the hand being in the position of holding a pencil." There were also rules regarding gloves, handkerchiefs, and the way to request a partner for a dance. Ford's dance manual, in short, was a monument to the old conceptions of morality, decorum, and order, and the dances he and his wife hosted at Dearborn were implementations. Precisely at nine Ford's guests convened in evening dress in a lavish ballroom for a paean to Victorianism.

Ambivalence is the key to the mind of Henry Ford. He was both old and new; he looked both forward and backward. Confidently progressive as he was in some respects, he remained nervous about the new ways. The more conditions changed, the more the nostalgic Ford groped for the security of traditional values and institutions. He was not lost; on the contrary, he had too many gods, at least for consistency. Neither was he dissipated and roaring. And he hated jazz. But Ford was popular, indeed a national deity, in the twenties even if his senatorial and presidential bids fell short. As a plain, honest, old-fashioned billionaire, a technological genius who loved to camp out, he seemed to his contemporaries to resolve the moral dilemmas of the age. Like Charles A. Lindbergh, another god of the age, Ford testified to the nation's ability to move into the future without losing the values of the past.

QUESTIONS TO CONSIDER

1 Compare Henry Ford with "robber baron" Andrew Carnegie in selection 5. In what ways did each man symbolize the America of his age?

2 Analyze the sources of Ford's tremendous popularity in the 1920s. Was it true, as Nash argues, that despite the revolutionary social changes Ford's cars brought to American society, Ford's commitment to old-fashioned values comforted Americans who felt anxious about the effects of modernization?

3 Henry Ford was the symbol of the new industrial order of the 1920s, but he also reflected the urban-rural tensions of that decade, especially in his attitudes toward the "revolution in manners and morals" of the Jazz Age. Discuss Ford's attitudes toward alcohol, sex, music, and dancing and how they reflected the changes taking place in America in the 1920s.

4 In addition to being a technological genius, Ford was both an anti-Semite and a Victorian prude, but the American people loved him. Why do you think that was so?

15 Justice Denied: The Trial of Sacco and Vanzetti

JAMES WEST DAVIDSON AND MARK HAMILTON LYTLE

In the following selection, historians James West Davidson and Mark Hamilton Lytle examine the conflicting currents of the 1920s that produced "two nations" in this country. One "nation" consisted mainly of native-born white American Protestants. The other "nation" comprised the immigrants, most of them Jews and Catholics, who flooded into the country from Italy, Russia, and the rest of eastern Europe. Focusing on the nation of immigrants, the authors examine the notorious case of Nicola Sacco and Bartolomeo Vanzetti, "two Italian immigrants living on the fringe of American society." In 1921, a Massachusetts court convicted Sacco and Vanzetti of killing a paymaster and his guard and sentenced them to be executed. The jury had taken only five hours to find the two immigrants guilty. The trial provoked bitter national and international controversy. This was hardly the first execution in an American society that had long used the death penalty. So, the authors ask, "Why all the fuss?"

The answer, they believe, lies in the conflict between America's "two nations," which the trial of Sacco and Vanzetti symbolized. The "nation" of native-born white Anglo-Saxon Protestants was worried about the dark forces in the twenties that threatened their beloved country. Among these was a sexual revolution against the old Victorian moral code. This "revolution in manners and morals," as Frederick Lewis Allen described it, derived in part from the new consumer age, which afforded middle and upper-class Americans unbelievable luxuries and the time to indulge in them. One of those indulgences was Henry Ford's motor car, the topic of the previous selection, which proved to be more than an inexpensive means of transportation. When parked, the automobile allowed dating couples unprecedented privacy in sexual matters. As a result, new words like "petting" and "necking" entered the vocabulary. One disapproving journal called the automobile nothing more "than a house of prostitution on wheels." The twenties also witnessed the appearance of the legendary "flapper": an uninhibited young woman who wore her hair bobbed, dabbled rouge on her cheeks, wore shorter skirts, smoked in public, danced the Charleston, and dedicated herself generally to having fun and doing as she pleased. For a large percentage of native-born white Protestants, particularly those in the countryside, the youth-oriented sexual revolution posed a grave threat to traditional American values. So, too, did the teaching of Charles Darwin's theory of evolution in the nation's schools. Who was to blame for the dangerous moral threats to the traditional "American way of life"?

For many native-born Americans, the Catholic and Jewish immigrants from southern and eastern Europe were to blame. A new wave of anti-Semitic and anti-Catholic prejudice swept the land. Such prejudice prompted the federal government to set discriminatory immigration quotas. Worse still was the emergence of a new, more vicious, and more widespread Ku Klux Klan, which hated immigrants, Jews, and Catholics as well as African Americans.

For Attorney General A. Mitchell Palmer and millions of other native-born Protestant Americans, the increasing number of immigrants from eastern Europe posed a dangerous threat to the old values. Palmer declared that "out of the sly and crafty eyes of many of them, leap cupidity, cruelty, insanity, and crime; from their lopsided faces, sloping brows, and misshapen features may be recognized the unmistakable criminal types." In a flagrant violation of civil liberties, Palmer deported as many of these undesirables as he could. Few people protested. Indeed, as the authors point out, native-born Americans across the land were "alarmed that immigration threatened their cherished institutions."

It was their alarm, the authors believe, that brought about the trial and execution of Sacco and Vanzetti. As you read their sad and disquieting story, bear in mind that the courtroom has often served as a battleground between people with contrasting values. Do the have-nots of society still face discrimination under the American system of justice? Do people of Middle Eastern extraction in our day face some of the same prejudices that plagued Italian and eastern European immigrants in the 1920s? Do the ghosts of Sacco and Vanzetti still haunt us?

GLOSSARY

ANARCHISTS   Seeking to create a society where individuals voluntarily cooperate with each other, anarchists are against any form of imposed authority by the state. In the 1920s, class tensions and an opposition to capitalism produced a group of radicals who sought to overthrow the American government through a violent social upheaval. Many Americans believed that anarchists had infiltrated the labor movement and were among the wave of new immigrants who, following the Great War, came to American shores from southern and eastern Europe.

BOLSHEVIKS   In November, 1917, this group of Communist revolutionaries, led by V. I. Lenin, seized control of Russia. The new Bolshevik government made peace with

Germany and trumpeted an anticapitalist ideology that frightened many Americans.

COLLECTIVE BARGAINING   A process that permits negotiations between labor unions and employers on issues such as wages, hours, benefits, and working conditions. In 1935, the Wagner Act created a National Labor Relations Board that gave unions the support of the federal government in negotiating collective bargaining agreements.

DOS PASSOS, JOHN   In *Three Soldiers* (1921), novelist Dos Passos reflected the disillusionment of American writers that followed the Great War. Dos Passos was distressed by the executions of Sacco and Vanzetti. The fate of those immigrants symbolized, in Dos Passos's words, the presence of the "two nations"—immigrants and native citizens—in the post-war United States. The "two nations" had dramatically different values.

FRANKFURTER, FELIX A Harvard Law School professor, Frankfurter served as an advisor to Presidents Woodrow Wilson and Franklin Roosevelt. In 1939, FDR appointed Frankfurter to the Supreme Court, where he served until 1962.

HAYMARKET SQUARE RIOT On May 4, 1886, about three thousand workers gathered in Haymarket Square in downtown Chicago. They were protesting the death of two colleagues shot by policemen as they dispersed a group of strikers. Someone tossed a bomb that killed seven policemen. In the minds of many Americans, the ensuing riot linked the labor movement with radicalism and violence.

HOOVER, J. EDGAR During the "Red Scare" that followed the Great War, Hoover was an assistant to attorney general A. Mitchell Palmer. Hoover later earned a reputation as an outspoken anti-Communist. In 1924, he became the director of the Bureau of Investigations (renamed the Federal Bureau of Investigations in 1935). Hoover remained that agency's imperious director until his death in 1972.

IMMIGRATION ACTS OF 1921 AND 1924 A reaction to the immigrants who came to America following the Great War, these acts established a quota system. The quotas discriminated against Jews and Catholics in southern and eastern Europe who sought sanctuary in the United States. The 1924 legislation was blatantly racist against such immigrants and against migrants from Asia as well. By contrast, the acts set liberal quotas for immigrants from western Europe.

KATZMANN, FREDERICK The Massachusetts district attorney who prosecuted Sacco and Vanzetti, Katzmann based his case, not on solid legal evidence, but on character assassination and ethnic prejudice.

KU KLUX KLAN On Thanksgiving night in 1915, on Stone Mountain in Georgia, the twentieth-century Klan was born. Unlike the violent night riders of the post–Civil War years, the modern Klan had support outside the South, in urban as well as rural communities. Even more vicious than its nineteenth-century predecessor, the new Ku Klux Klan hated immigrants, Jews, and Catholics, as well as African Americans.

MOORE, FRED A Californian with an unorthodox style of life and radical sympathies, Moore served as the defense counsel for Sacco and Vanzetti until 1924. His casual dress and long hair alienated the judge and jury.

NATIVISM A "defensive nationalism," nativism was rooted in the Protestant Anglo-Saxon value system that defined American culture for most of the nineteenth century. "Native-born" Americans believed that the religion, language, and perceived radicalism of the immigrants from southern and eastern Europe represented a threat to the established values of the native-born.

PALMER, A. MITCHELL A Quaker and a progressive reformer, Palmer served as Woodrow Wilson's attorney general from 1919–1921. Following the Great War, Palmer launched a massive roundup of those immigrants he believed were foreign-born radicals. The government deported thousands of innocent people without hearings or trials. This was an unprecedented violation of civil liberties.

SINCLAIR, UPTON A muckraking author and socialist, Sinclair wrote *The Jungle* (1906) that exposed the Chicago meat packing industry's unsanitary practices and its harsh treatment of immigrant workers. He would later denounce the executions of Sacco and Vanzetti. In 1934, Sinclair ran for governor of California.

THAYER, WEBSTER The judge during the trial of Sacco and Vanzetti, Thayer later denied eight appeals of the convicted immigrants. On April 9, 1927, Thayer sentenced them to die. Thayer reflected the ethnic biases of his day and seemed predisposed to find the two defendants guilty. On August 22, 1927, Sacco and Vanzetti died in the electric chair.

In the years after World War I, crime statistics curved sharply upward. Armed robberies rose at an alarming rate, and anyone handling large sums of money had reason to exercise caution. On most paydays Frederick Parmenter, paymaster for the Slater and Morrill Shoe Company of South Braintree, Massachusetts, would have used a truck to deliver his money boxes to the lower factory building. Only a few months earlier, in December 1919, a brazen gang of bandits had attempted a daylight payroll heist in nearby Bridgewater. The bandits had fled empty-handed, and no one was hurt in the gunfight. Still, area businesses were uneasy. On the morning of April 15, 1920, however, the robbery attempt must have been far from Parmenter's mind. It was a mild spring day, and he set out on foot for the lower factory building with his assistant, Alessandro Berardelli, walking ahead.

Halfway to their destination, a man approached Berardelli from the side of the road, spoke to him briefly, and then suddenly shot him dead. As Parmenter turned to flee, the bandits fired again, mortally wounding him. A blue Buick pulled from its parking place. The two assailants and their lookout jumped into the car and fled toward Bridgewater. To discourage pursuers, the bandits threw tacks onto the streets. Two miles from Braintree they abandoned the Buick and escaped in another car.

Bridgewater Police Chief Michael Stewart thought he recognized a pattern in the Braintree crime. The same foreigners who bungled the December heist, he guessed, had probably pulled off the Braintree job. Stewart's investigation put him on the trail of Mike Boda, an Italian anarchist. Unable to locate Boda, Stewart kept watch on a car Boda had left at Simon Johnson's garage for repairs. Whoever came to get the car would, according to Stewart's theory, become a prime suspect in both crimes.

Edited excerpt from James West Davidson and Mark Hamilton Lytle. *After the Fact: The Art of Historical Detection*, 5th ed. (McGraw-Hill, 2005), pp. 262–279, 281–282, 284–286. Reproduced with permission of the McGraw-Hill Companies.

His expectations were soon rewarded. On May 5, 1920, Boda and three other Italians called for the car. Mrs. Johnson immediately slipped next door to alert the police, but the four men did not wait for her return. Boda and one friend, Riccardo Orciani, left on a motorcycle while their companions walked to a nearby streetcar stop. Apparently nervous, they moved on to another stop a half mile away. There they boarded the trolley for Brockton. As the trolley car moved down Main Street, Police Officer Michael Connolly climbed on. Having spotted the two foreigners, he arrested them. When they asked why, he replied curtly, "suspicious characters."

Thus began the epic story of Nicola Sacco and Bartolomeo Vanzetti, two obscure Italian aliens who became the focal point of one of the most controversial episodes in American history. Within little more than a year after their arrest a jury deliberated for just five hours before convicting both men of robbery and murder. Such a quick decision came as a surprise, particularly in a trial that had lasted seven weeks, heard more than 160 witnesses, and gained national attention.

Nor did the controversy end with the jury's decision. Six years of appeals turned a small-town incident of robbery and murder into a major international uproar. The Italian government indicated that it was following the case with interest. Thousands of liberals, criminal lawyers, legal scholars, civil libertarians, radicals, labor leaders, prominent socialites, and spokespersons for immigrant groups rallied to Sacco and Vanzetti's cause. Arrayed against them was an equally imposing collection of the nation's legal, social, academic, and political elite.

The case climaxed on April 9, 1927. Having denied some eight appeals, trial judge Webster Thayer sentenced Sacco and Vanzetti to die in the electric chair. His action triggered months of protests and political activities. Around Charleston Prison (where the two men were held) and the State House in Boston, Sacco and Vanzetti's supporters marched, collected petitions, and walked picket lines. Occasionally violence erupted between protesters and authorities, as mounted police attacked crowds in Boston and clubbed them off the streets in New York. On August 22, the morning

Nicola Sacco and Bartolomeo Vanzetti were two obscure Italian immigrants who were accused of committing murder during a payroll robbery. Immigration laws were controversial and their prosecution was tinged with ethnic prejudice. During a police line-up, Sacco and Vanzetti were forced to pose as bandits, alone in the middle of a room. (© Bettmann/CORBIS)

before Sacco and Vanzetti were scheduled to die, Charleston Prison appeared like an embattled fortress. Ropes circled the prison grounds to keep protesters at bay as eight hundred armed guards walked the walls. In New York's Union Square, 15,000 people gathered to stand in silent vigil. Similar crowds congregated in major European cities. All awaited the news of the fate of "a good shoemaker and a poor fish peddler."

The historian confronting that extraordinary event faces some perplexing questions. How did a case of robbery and murder become an international cause célèbre? How was it that two Italian immigrants living on the fringe of American society had become the focus of a debate that brought the nation's cherished legal institutions under attack? Or as one eminent law professor rhetorically posed the question:

Why all this fuss over a couple of "wops," who after years in this country had not even made application to become citizens; who had not learned to use our language even modestly well; who did not believe in our form of government; . . . who were confessed slackers and claimed to be pacifists but went armed with deadly weapons for the professed purpose of defending their individual personal property in violation of all the principles they preached?

THE QUESTION OF LEGAL EVIDENCE

Lawyers reviewing events might answer those questions by arguing that the Sacco and Vanzetti case raised serious doubts about the tradition of Anglo-Saxon justice so venerated in the United States. More specifically, many legal scholars then and since have asserted that the trial and appeals process failed to meet minimum standards of fairness, particularly for a criminal case in which the defendants' lives hung in the balance.

In the first flush of Sacco and Vanzetti's arrest, prosecutors seemed to have good reason to label the two men "suspicious characters." Both Sacco and Vanzetti were carrying loaded revolvers. Not only that, Sacco had twenty-three extra cartridges in his pockets, while Vanzetti carried several shotgun shells. When questioned, both men lied about their activities. They claimed not to know Mike Boda or to have been at the garage to pick up Boda's car. But suspicious behavior was one matter; proof that Sacco and Vanzetti had committed the Braintree murders was another. As the police and prosecutors went about making their case, they followed distinctly irregular procedures.

To be sure, in 1920 the police were allowed to conduct an investigation with far greater latitude than the law permits today. The Supreme Court decisions in *Miranda* (1966) and *Escobedo* (1964) established that criminal suspects have the right to remain silent, to be informed of their rights, and to stand in an impartial lineup for identification. None of those guarantees existed in 1920. Even so, District Attorney Frederick Katzmann and Chief Stewart showed unusual zeal in constructing a case against Sacco and Vanzetti. At no time during the first two days of

questioning did they tell either suspect why they had been arrested. Chief Stewart repeatedly asked them not about the robbery, but about their political beliefs and associates. The district attorney did obliquely inquire about their activities on April 15, though he never mentioned the Braintree crimes. Furthermore, when the police asked witnesses to identify the suspects, they did not use a lineup. Instead, they forced Sacco and Vanzetti to stand alone in the middle of a room posing as bandits.

As the investigation continued, the case came close to collapsing for lack of evidence. Of the five suspected gang members, all but Vanzetti could prove they had not been in Bridgewater during the December holdup attempt. Despite an intensive search of the suspects' belongings, including a trunk sent to Italy, Katzmann was never able to trace the money, even among radical political groups with whom the suspects were associated. Fingerprint experts found no matches between prints lifted from the abandoned Buick and those taken from the suspects.

Faced with those gaps in the evidence, Katzmann still decided, first, to prosecute Vanzetti for the December Bridgewater holdup and, second, to charge both Sacco and Vanzetti with the Braintree murders in April. Arguing the Bridgewater case in June 1920 before Judge Webster Thayer, Katzmann presented a weak case against Vanzetti on the charge of assault with intent to rob. Still, he did manage to make the jury aware of Vanzetti's anarchist views and persuade them to convict. Judge Thayer then meted out an unusually severe sentence (twelve to fifteen years) to a defendant with no criminal record for a crime in which no one was hurt and nothing was stolen.

That conviction allowed Katzmann to proceed with the second trial, to be held in the suburban town of Dedham. Since this trial would be a special session of the superior court, a judge had to be appointed to hear the case. Judge Thayer asked his old college friend, Chief Justice John Aiken, for the assignment, even though he had presided over Vanzetti's earlier trial and could scarcely consider himself impartial. Thus the second trial opened with a judge who already believed unequivocally in the defendants' guilt.

At Dedham, District Attorney Katzmann built his case around three major categories of evidence: (1) eyewitness identification of Sacco and Vanzetti at the scene, (2) expert ballistics testimony establishing Sacco's gun as the weapon that fired the fatal shot at Berardelli and Vanzetti's gun as one taken from Berardelli during the robbery, (3) the defendants' evasive behavior both before and after arrest as evidence of what is legally termed "consciousness of guilt."

The prosecution, however, had a difficult time making its case. Of the "eyewitnesses" claiming to place Sacco and Vanzetti at the scene, one, Mary Splaine, claimed to have observed the shooting from a window in the Slater and Morrill factory for no longer than three seconds at a distance of about 60 feet. In that time she watched an unknown man in a car traveling about 18 miles an hour. Immediately after the crime Splaine had difficulty describing any of the bandits, but one year later she picked out Sacco, vividly recalling such details as his "good-sized" left hand. She refused to recant her testimony even after the defense demonstrated that Sacco had relatively small hands.

Louis Pelzer testified for the prosecution that upon hearing shots, he had observed the crime from a window for at least a minute. He pointed to Sacco as the "dead image" of the man who shot Berardelli. Two defense witnesses, however, controverted Pelzer's story. Upon hearing the shots, they recalled, the intrepid Pelzer had immediately hidden under his workbench—hardly a vantage point from which to make a clear identification.

Lola Andrews, a third witness, claimed that on the morning of the crime she had stopped near the factory to ask directions from a dark-haired man working under a car. She later identified Sacco as that man. But a companion, Julia Campbell, denied that Andrews had ever spoken to the man under the car. Instead, Campbell testified, Andrews had approached a pale, sickly young man who was standing nearby. Other witnesses had recalled the same pale person. A second friend swore that he had heard Andrews say after she returned from police headquarters that "the government took me down and wanted me to recognize those men and I don't know a thing about them." Nor did Andrews's reputation as a streetwalker enhance her credibility. Yet in his summation, prosecutor Katzmann told the jury that in eleven years as district attorney he had not "ever before . . . laid eye or given ear to so convincing a witness as Lola Andrews."

Against Katzmann's dubious cast, the defense produced seventeen witnesses who provided the defendants with alibis for the day or who had seen the crime, but not Sacco or Vanzetti. One, an official of the Italian Consulate in Boston, confirmed Sacco's claim that he had been in Boston on April 15 acquiring a passport. The official remembered Sacco because he had tried to use a picture over 10 inches square for his passport photo. "Since such a large photograph had never been presented before," the official recalled, "I took it in and showed it to the Secretary of the Consulate. We laughed and talked over the incident. I remember observing the date . . . on a large pad calendar." Others said they had met Sacco at a luncheon banquet that day. Witnesses for Vanzetti claimed to have bought fish from him. Katzmann could only try to persuade the jury that the witnesses had little reason to connect such a mundane event with a specific date.

In the face of contradictory eyewitness testimony, the ballistics evidence might have decided the case. To prove murder, Katzmann wished to show that the fatal shot striking Berardelli had come from Sacco's gun. Ballistics specialists can often identify the gun that fired a bullet by characteristic marks, as distinct as fingerprints, that the barrel and hammer make on the projectile and casing. Two experts, Captains William Proctor and Charles Van Amburgh, connected the fatal bullet to a Colt pistol similar to and possibly the same as Sacco's. But neither of Katzmann's witnesses made a definitive link. "It is consistent with being fired by that pistol," Proctor replied to Katzmann. Van Amburgh also indicated some ambiguity: "I am inclined to believe that it was fired . . . from this pistol."

For unknown reasons defense attorneys never pursued the equivocation of those testimonies. Instead, they called their own ballistics specialists who stated with absolute certainty that the fatal bullet could not have come from Sacco's gun. In addition, they controverted the prosecutor's claim that Vanzetti had taken Berardelli's gun during the holdup. Shortly before his murder, Berardelli had left his pistol at a repair shop to have the hammer fixed. Shop records, though imprecise, indicated that the gun was .32 caliber, not a .38 such as Vanzetti was carrying. The records also supported Mrs. Berardelli's sworn testimony that her husband had never reclaimed his pistol. The defense then argued that the hammer on Vanzetti's gun had never been repaired.

Since the defense had weakened the ballistics evidence, Katzmann based his case primarily on "consciousness of guilt." To convict on those grounds, he had to convince the jury that Sacco and Vanzetti had behaved like men guilty of the crime, both before and after arrest. Here, Katzmann made his case with telling effect. Why had the defendants been carrying guns when they were arrested? They had gone hunting that morning, they claimed. But if that were the case, why were they still carrying hunting weapons and extra ammunition at night, when they set out to pick up Mike Boda's car? They were in such a hurry, Sacco and Vanzetti replied, that they forgot to leave their revolvers at home. But Katzmann continued his onslaught. Why did the two men lie at first about knowing Mike Boda or having visited the garage? Surely this evasion indicated a clear consciousness of guilt.

To explain such evasive behavior, defense lawyers were forced to introduce the inflammatory issue of Sacco and Vanzetti's political beliefs. For indeed, both men proudly proclaimed themselves to be anarchists, rejecting the authority of any government. Capitalism, they believed, was little more than an organized system of banditry under which the rich and powerful extorted the poor. Sacco and Vanzetti had both been active in the strikes and labor unrest of the era. As a result, they had been alarmed by the government crackdown on radicals that began in 1919. When Officer Connolly arrested them, the two men assumed that they, too, had been snared in the government's dragnet. They acted evasively, defense lawyers argued, not because they were criminals but because radicals were being persecuted and deported. Once arrested, Sacco and Vanzetti's fears were only confirmed by the police's constant questions about their political beliefs.

Similar worries accounted for their peculiar actions at Johnson's garage, the defense argued. Shortly before his arrest, Vanzetti had conferred with the Italian Defense Committee of New York, then inquiring into the fate of a fellow anarchist, Andrea Salsedo. The committee knew only that Salsedo was being held by Justice Department agents; members warned Vanzetti that he and his friends might be in danger of being jailed or deported. Only a week later, newspapers across the nation reported that Salsedo had fallen to his death from a twelfth-floor window. The police insisted the case had been a suicide, but many anarchists thought Salsedo had been pushed. Before he died, had he provided the government with the names of other anarchists? If so, Vanzetti and Sacco were at risk. Anyone found with anarchist literature could be arrested and deported. It was for that reason, Sacco and Vanzetti told the court, that they had gone to retrieve Mike Boda's car: they needed it to carry away the radical pamphlets stored in their homes—something they hardly wished to admit to police questioning them about radical activities.

The revelations of the defendants' radical politics could hardly have raised the jury's opinion of the two men. And their explanations did not stop Katzmann from focusing on consciousness of guilt in his final summation. Nor did Judge Thayer take into account their explanations in his charge to jury. In theory, a judge's charge guides the jury as it interprets conflicting evidence: in separating the relevant from the irrelevant and in establishing the grounds for an objective verdict. But Thayer made his sympathies all too clear. In discussing the ballistics testimony, he wrongly assumed that Katzmann's expert witnesses had unequivocally identified Sacco's gun as having fired the fatal shot. And he spent no time weighing the defense's argument that prosecution eyewitnesses had been unreliable. Only when he discussed consciousness of guilt did the judge become expansive and specific. He lingered over the evidence offered by the police and the garage owner while ignoring Sacco and Vanzetti's explanations.

Lawyers and legal historians have raised other telling criticisms—excesses in the trial procedures, prejudice on the part of both judge and prosecutor, bungling by the defense lawyer. Inevitably, these criticisms have influenced the way historians have approached the controversy. Most of them have centered on the issue of *proof* of guilt. Contrary to popular opinion, the courts do not determine whether a person is guilty or innocent of a crime. They decide merely whether the prosecutor has assembled sufficient evidence to establish guilt. The judge may even suspect a defendant is guilty, but if the evidence does not meet minimum standards of legal proof, the court must set the accused free. As one court concluded, "the commonwealth demands no victims . . . and it is as much the duty of the district attorney to see that no innocent man suffers, as it is to see that no guilty man escapes."

Thus lawyers tend to focus on narrow, yet admittedly important, questions. They are all the more crucial when human lives are at stake, as was the case with Sacco and Vanzetti. Believing that the legal system maintains vital safeguards of individual rights, lawyers in general seek to ensure that proper legal procedures have been followed, that evidence is submitted according to established rules, and, in accordance with those procedures, that guilt has been adequately determined. A lawyer answering the question, "Why all the fuss over the Sacco and Vanzetti case?" would most likely reply, "Because the trial, by failing to prove guilt beyond reasonable doubt, perpetrated a serious miscarriage of justice."

BEYOND GUILT OR INNOCENCE

. . . [H]istory affords far more latitude in weighing and collecting evidence than does the legal system. The law attempts to limit the flow of evidence in a trial to what can reasonably be construed as fact. A judge will generally exclude hearsay testimony, speculation about states of mind or motives, conjecture, and vague questions leading witnesses to conclusions. But those same elements are sources of information upon which historians can and do draw in their research. Historians can afford to speculate more freely, because their conclusions will not send innocent people to jail or let the guilty go free. In one instance, for example, appeals judges refused to act on defense claims that Judge Thayer had allowed his prejudices against Sacco and Vanzetti to influence his conduct of the trial. They ruled that remarks made outside the courtroom, no matter how inappropriate, had no bearing on what occurred inside. By contrast, the historian can accept the fact of Judge Thayer's prejudice regardless of where he revealed it.

Given their broader canons of evidence, historians might be tempted to go the lawyers one step further by establishing whether Sacco and Vanzetti actually did commit the robbery and murders at Braintree. To succeed in such an investigation would at least lay the controversy to its final rest. Yet that approach does not take us beyond the lawyers' questions. We are still dealing with only two men—Sacco and Vanzetti—and one central question—guilty or innocent?

We must remember, however, that when historians confront such either-or questions, their overriding obligation is to construct an interpretation that gives full play to *all* aspects of the subject being investigated, not just the question of guilt or innocence. They must look beyond Sacco and Vanzetti to the actions of the people and society around them. What political currents led the prosecutor to bring those two men to trial? How much were Judge Thayer, District Attorney Katzmann, and the men in the jury box representative of Massachusetts or of American society in general? Of just what crime did the jury actually convict the defendants? In answering those questions, historians must lift their drama out of the Dedham courtroom and into a larger theater of action. In short, we cannot answer our original question, "Why all the fuss?" merely by proving the defendants guilty or innocent. Historians want to know why this case provoked such sharp controversy for so many years.

Any historian who studies the climate of opinion in the early 1920s cannot help suspecting that those who persecuted Sacco and Vanzetti were far more concerned with who the defendants were and what they believed than with what they might have done. Throughout the nation's history, Americans have periodically expressed hostility toward immigrants and foreign political ideas that were perceived as a threat to the "American way of life." Nativism, as such defensive nationalism has been called, has been a problem at least since the first waves of Irish immigrants came ashore in the first half of the nineteenth century. Until then, the United States had been a society dominated by white Protestants with a common English heritage. The influx of the Catholic Irish and then political refugees from the 1848 German revolution diversified the nation's population. Native-born Americans became alarmed that immigration threatened their cherished institutions. Successive waves of newcomers from Asia, the Mediterranean, and eastern Europe deepened their fears.

In analyzing nativist ideology, historian John Higham has identified three major attitudes: anti-Catholicism, antiradicalism, and Anglo-Saxon nationalism. Anti-Catholicism reflected northern European Protestants' distrust of the Catholic Church, a rejection of its hierarchical and undemocratic structure, and a fear of the pope as a religious despot. Nativists often viewed Catholic immigrants as papal agents sent to bring the United States under the tyranny of Rome. Antiradicalism stemmed in part from an increasing rejection of America's own revolutionary tradition and in part from the American tendency to associate violence and criminal subversion with Europe's radical political creeds such as Marxism, socialism, and anarchism. Anglo-Saxon nationalism was a more amorphous blend of notions about the racial superiority of the northern European people and pride in the Anglo-Saxon heritage of legal, political, and economic institutions, one of the most cherished being the Anglo-Saxon belief in the rule of law.

The tides of nativism tend to rise and fall with the fortunes of the nation. During periods of prosperity, Americans often welcome immigrants as a vital source of new labor. In the 1860s, for example, many Californians cheered the arrival of the strange Chinese coolies, without whom the transcontinental railroad could not have been so quickly completed. In the 1870s, as the nation struggled through a severe industrial depression, nativism became a virulent social disease. The same Californians who once welcomed the Chinese now organized vigilante groups to harass them and clamored for laws to restrict the number of Asian immigrants.

The period following World War I, which Higham labeled the "Tribal Twenties," marked the high tide of nativism. No group more fully embodied the nativist impulse than the reborn Ku Klux Klan. By 1924 it claimed large chapters not only in its traditional southern strongholds but also in major cities, in Oregon and in the states of the upper Midwest—Indiana, Ohio, and Illinois in particular. The Klan's constitution unabashedly advertised the organization's commitment to all three nativist traditions:

to unite white, male persons, native born gentile citizens of the United States of America, who owe no allegiance of any nature to any foreign government, nation, institution, sect, ruler, person or people; whose morals are good, whose reputations and vocations are exemplary . . . ; to shield the sanctity of white womanhood; to maintain forever white supremacy.

Loyalty to the church, the pope, a motherland, Old World culture, or any other tie outside the United States eliminated almost all immigrants from possible Klan membership.

Several factors accounted for the resurgence of nativism. World War I had temporarily interrupted the flow of immigrants who, since the 1880s, had increasingly included a preponderance of Catholics and Jews from countries with strong radical traditions. In 1914 alone, more than 138,000 of a total of 1.2 million immigrants to the United States were Jews. During the war, the number fell to just 3,672 newcomers in 1918 (out of a total of 110,000), but then rose to 119,000 (out of 805,000) in 1921, the

If Sacco and Vanzetti represented one of the "two nations" of the 1920s, the Ku Klux Klan was the symbol of the other. The new KKK expanded its list of enemies to include blacks, Jews, and Catholics. Its prejudices reached into urban areas of the East and Midwest, where immigrants and African Americans competed for jobs and housing with native-born white Anglo-Saxon Protestants. (The New York Public Library, Astor, Lenox and Tilden Foundations)

last year of unrestricted immigration. A similar pattern occurred among Italians. In the entire decade of the 1870s fewer than 50,000 Italians came to the United States. In the first fifteen years of the twentieth century almost 3 million made the crossing. That torrent, which slowed to a trickle during the war years, swelled again with the return of peace. The approximately 221,000 Italians who immigrated in 1921 made up, with the Jews, more than 42 percent of the total immigrants. More than ever, nativists protested that these undesirable foreigners threatened to destroy cherished institutions, weaken the genetic pool, or in other ways undermine the American way of life.

The rocky transition to a peacetime economy only aggravated resentment toward immigrants. Returning veterans expected jobs from a grateful nation; instead, they found crowds of unemployed workers around factory gates. The army had discharged millions of soldiers almost overnight. The government dismissed hundreds of thousands of temporary wartime employees and canceled millions of dollars' worth of contracts with private businesses. As the economy plunged downward, native-born Americans once again looked on new immigrants as a threat to their livelihoods. Organized labor joined other traditional nativist groups in demanding new restriction laws.

Union leaders called for relief on another front. During the war they had cooperated with the government to control inflation by minimizing wage increases. At the same time, high wartime employment had attracted millions of new recruits to the union movement. The government had orchestrated labor-management harmony to ensure uninterrupted production schedules. Once the war ended, labor set out to consolidate its gains. Union leaders asked for higher wages, improved working conditions, and the recognition of collective bargaining.

Most business leaders were in no mood to compromise. They resented the assistance the government had given organized labor during the war. Now, they not only rejected even the mildest union demands but also sought to cripple the labor movement. Conservatives launched a national campaign to brand all organized labor as Bolsheviks, Reds, and anarchists. They called strikes "crimes against society," "conspiracies against the government," and "plots to establish communism." As the market for manufactures declined, employers had little reason to avoid a showdown. Strikes saved them the problem of laying off unneeded workers.

In 1919 American industry lost more labor hours to strikes than ever before in history. March brought 175 significant strikes, followed by 248 in April, 388 in May, 303 in June, 360 in July, and 373 in August. By September, strikes in the coal and steel industries alone had idled more than 700,000 workers and led to repeated violence. The average strike lasted thirty-four days, while some exceeded four months. Even employers who made minor concessions on wages or hours refused to yield on the question of collective bargaining.

Radicals played a minor role in the postwar labor unrest. Most union leaders were as archly conservative as the employers they confronted. Still, the constant barrage of anti-Red propaganda turned public opinion against the unions. And American radicals fed that hostility by adopting highly visible tactics. The success of a small band of Bolsheviks in capturing Russia's tottering government in October 1917 had rekindled waning hopes and at the same time startled most Americans. Two years later, the Bolsheviks boldly organized the Third Communist International to carry the revolution to other countries. Communist-led worker uprisings in Hungary and Germany increased conservative anxiety that a similar revolutionary fever might infect American workers, especially after a Comintern official bragged that the money spent in Germany "was as nothing compared to the funds transmitted to New York for the purpose of spreading Bolshevism in the United States."

Only a few shocks were needed to inflame the fears of Americans caught in the midst of economic distress, labor unrest, and renewed immigration from southern and eastern Europe. Those shocks were provided by a series of anarchist bombings inspired by Luigi Galleani, an Italian immigrant who had settled in New England. Although authorities at the time did not know it, members of Galleani's circle were the source of a series of thirty parcels mailed in April 1919 to eminent officials, including Attorney General A. Mitchell Palmer, Supreme Court Justice Oliver Wendell Holmes, members of Congress, mayors, as well as the industrial magnates John D. Rockefeller and J. P. Morgan. Only one of the deadly packages detonated (blowing off the hands of the unsuspecting servant who opened it), but in June a series of even more lethal explosions rocked seven cities. The most spectacular explosion demolished the entire front wall of Attorney General Palmer's home. The device exploded prematurely, blowing to bits the man who was crouching by the front steps.

The American public had already learned to associate such deeds with anarchists: the Haymarket Square explosion of 1886 as well as the assassination of President William McKinley in 1901 by radical Leon Czolgosz. ("The anarchist is the enemy of humanity, the enemy of all mankind," proclaimed McKinley's successor, Teddy Roosevelt.) Following the bombings of 1919 Attorney General Palmer reacted swiftly, launching a roundup of as many radicals as he could find, branding each "a potential murderer or a potential thief." That the majority were only philosophical anarchists who had never undertaken any violent acts toward the government did not deter Palmer. That the majority were foreign-born served only to raise his patriotic bile: "Out of the sly and crafty eyes of many of them leap cupidity, cruelty, insanity, and crime; from their lopsided faces, sloping brows, and misshapen features may be recognized the unmistakable criminal types."

For more than a year, Palmer and his young, Red-hunting assistant J. Edgar Hoover organized government raids on homes, offices, union halls, and alien organizations. Seldom did the raiders pay even passing attention to civil liberties or constitutional prohibitions against illegal search and seizure. One particularly spectacular outing netted more than 4,000 alleged subversives in some thirty-three cities. Most of those arrested, though innocent of any crime, were detained illegally by state authorities either for trial or Labor Department deportation hearings. Police jammed suspects in cramped rooms with inadequate food and sanitation. They refused to honor the suspects' rights to post bail or obtain a writ of habeas corpus.

The public quickly wearied of Palmer and the exaggerated stories of grand revolutionary conspiracies. Not one incident had produced any evidence of a serious plot. Palmer predicted that on May 1, 1920, radicals would launch a massive attempt to overthrow the government. Alerted by the Justice Department, local police and militia girded for the assault. But May Day passed without incident. The heightened surveillance did, however, have profound consequences for Nicola Sacco and Bartolomeo Vanzetti. Both men were on a list of suspects the Justice Department had sent to District Attorney Katzmann and Chief Stewart. Just four days after the May Day scare, Officer Connolly arrested the two aliens.

Sacco and Vanzetti fit the stereotypes that nativists held of foreigners. Sacco arrived in the United States in 1908 at the age of seventeen. Like so many other Italians, he had fled the oppressive poverty of his homeland with no intention of making a permanent home in America. Most of the young men planned to stay only until they had saved enough money to return home and improve their family fortunes. Although born into a modestly well-to-do family, Sacco was no stranger to hard labor. Shortly after his arrival he found steady work in the shoe factories around Milford, Massachusetts.

Sacco's resourcefulness and industry marked him as the kind of foreign worker whose competition American labor feared. Although he lacked formal schooling, Sacco understood that skilled labor commanded steadier work and higher wages, so he paid $50 out of his earnings to learn the specialized trade of edge trimming. His wages soon reached as high as $80 per week. By 1917 he had a wife and child, his own home, and $1,500 in savings. His employer at the "3 K" shoe factory described him as an excellent worker and recalled that Sacco often found time, despite his long workdays, to put in a few hours each morning and evening in his vegetable garden.

Vanzetti conformed more to the nativist stereotype of shiftless foreigners who drifted from one job to the next. Born in 1888 in the northern Italian village of Villafalletto, he had come to America in 1908 where, like many other immigrants, he found a limited range of jobs open to him. He took a job as a dishwasher in hot, stinking kitchens. "We worked twelve hours one day and fourteen the next, with five hours off every other Sunday," he recalled. "Damp food hardly fit for a dog and five or six dollars a week was the pay." Fearing an attack of consumption, Vanzetti migrated to the countryside in search of open-air work. "I worked on farms, cut trees, made bricks, dug ditches, and quarried rocks. I worked in a fruit, candy and ice cream store and for a telephone company," he wrote his sister in Italy. By 1914 he had wandered to Plymouth, where he took a job in a cordage factory.

If that sketch captured the essence of Sacco and Vanzetti's lives, they would most likely never have come to the attention of Justice Department agents. But because they were aliens and anarchists, they embodied the kind of foreign menace American nativists

A. Mitchell Palmer was Woodrow Wilson's Attorney General. He suspected that many of the new immigrants were importing radical ideas that threatened American democracy, and he deported as many of them as he could. Authorities even denied numerous immigrants the right to a hearing. This was a deliberate violation of their civil liberties. (© CORBIS)

most feared. Although not a student of politics like Vanzetti, Sacco was a rebel. He identified closely with the workers' struggle for better wages and the right to organize. In 1912 he and Vanzetti had independently participated in a violent textile strike at Lawrence, Massachusetts. Three years later plant owners around Plymouth had blacklisted Vanzetti for his role in a local strike. Sacco had walked off his job to express sympathy for the cordage workers. Soon after a local labor leader organized a sympathy strike to support workers in Minnesota, authorities arrested Sacco and convicted him of disturbing the peace. All this time, he and his wife regularly joined street-theater productions performed to raise money for labor and radical groups.

American entry into World War I created a crisis for both men. Their anarchist beliefs led them to oppose any war that did not work to overthrow capitalism. Sacco even refused the patriotic pressures to buy war bonds. He quit his job rather than compromise his principles. Both began to dread the law requiring them to register (though in fact as aliens they were ineligible for military service). They decided to join a group of pacifists who in May 1917 fled to

Mexico, where the two first became personal friends. The hard life and absence from his family finally drove Sacco to return home under an alias, though he did resume his name and former job after the war. Vanzetti returned to Plymouth and soon outfitted himself as a fish peddler.

So in the eyes of many Americans, Sacco and Vanzetti were guilty in at least one important sense. As self-proclaimed enemies of the capitalist system, they had opposed "the American way of life" that nativists cherished. Their suspicious behavior, which Katzmann successfully portrayed as consciousness of guilt, was all too real, for they knew that their radical beliefs might subject them to arrest and deportation, the fate hundreds of other friends and political associates had already faced.

Certainly, the trial record shows that nativism influenced the way judge and jury viewed the defendants. Almost all the eyewitnesses who identified Sacco and Vanzetti were native-born Americans. That they saw a resemblance between the Italian suspects and the foreign-looking criminals proved only, as Harvard law professor Felix Frankfurter remarked, that there was much truth in the popular racist song "All Coons Look Alike to Me." On the other hand, almost all the witnesses substantiating the defendants' alibis were Italians who answered through an interpreter. The jury, also all native-born Americans, would likely accept Katzmann's imputation that foreigners stuck together to protect each other from the authorities.

The choice of Fred Moore as chief defense counsel guaranteed that radicalism would become a central issue in the trial. . . . He spent the bulk of defense funds to orchestrate a propaganda campaign dramatizing the plight of his clients and the persecution of radicals. He gave far less attention to planning defense strategy, left largely in the hands of two local cocounsels, Thomas and Jeremiah McAnarney.

Yet in the courtroom Moore insisted on playing the major role. The McAnarneys soon despaired of making a favorable impression on the jury. An outsider from California, Moore wore his hair long and sometimes shocked the court by parading around in his shirtsleeves and socks. Rumors abounded about his unorthodox sex life. And at critical moments he sometimes disappeared for several days. Judge Thayer once became so outraged at Moore that he told a friend, "I'll show them that no long-haired anarchist from California can run this court." Not until 1924 did Moore finally withdraw in favor of William Thompson, a respected Massachusetts criminal lawyer.

Nativism, particularly antiradicalism, obviously prejudiced Judge Thayer and District Attorney Katzmann. We have already seen how Thayer used his charge to the jury to underscore Katzmann's construction of the evidence in the trial. Outside the courtroom, Thayer consistently violated the canons of judicial discretion by discussing his views of the case. George Crocker, who sometimes lunched with Thayer, testified that on many occasions the judge "conveyed to me by his words and manner that he was bound to convict these men because they were 'reds.'" Veteran court reporter Frank Silbey had been forced to stop lunching at the Dedham Inn to avoid Thayer and his indiscreet remarks. Silbey later recalled, "In my thirty-five years I never saw anything like it. . . . His whole attitude seemed to be that the jurors were there to convict these men."

From the moment the trial opened, Thayer and Katzmann missed few opportunities to strike a patriotic pose or to remind the jury that both defendants were draft dodgers. Thayer told the prospective jurors at the outset, "I call upon you to render this service . . . with the same patriotism as was exhibited by our soldier boys across the sea." Katzmann opened his cross-examination of Vanzetti with a cutting statement dressed up as a question: "So you left Plymouth, Mr. Vanzetti, in May 1917 to dodge the draft did you?" Since Vanzetti was charged with murder, not draft evasion, the question served to arouse the jury's patriotic indignation.

Katzmann struck hardest in his questioning of Sacco, whose poor command of English often left him confused or under a misapprehension. Judge Thayer never intervened to restrain the overzealous prosecutor, even when it became clear that Sacco could neither follow a question nor express his thoughts clearly. Playing again upon the residual patriotic war fervor,

Katzmann hammered away at the defendant's evident disloyalty:

> KATZMANN: And in order to show your love for this United States of America when she was about to call upon you to become a soldier you ran away to Mexico. Did you run away to Mexico to avoid being a soldier for the country that you loved?
>
> SACCO: Yes.
>
> KATZMANN: And would it be your idea of showing love for your wife that when she needed you, you ran away from her?
>
> SACCO: I did not run away from her.

When the defense objected, Thayer ruled that this line of questioning would help establish Sacco's character. But instead of showing Sacco's philosophical opposition to war, Katzmann made the defendant appear, as one critic expressed it, "an ingrate and a slacker" who invited the jury's contempt. With such skillful cross-examination Katzmann twisted Sacco's professed love of "a free country" into a preference for high wages, pleasant work, and good food.

The prosecutor summed up his strategy in his final appeal to the jury: "Men of Norfolk do your duty. Do it like men. Stand together you men of Norfolk." There was the case in a nutshell—native American solidarity against alien people and their values. Whether he had proved Sacco and Vanzetti guilty of murder mattered little, for he had revealed their disloyalty. In case the point was lost, Judge Thayer reiterated it in his charge:

> Although you knew such service would be arduous, painful, and tiresome, yet you, like the true soldier, responded to the call in the spirit of supreme American loyalty. There is no better word in the English language than "loyalty."

And just who were those "men of Norfolk" to whom the judge and prosecutor appealed? Could they put aside inflammatory rhetoric and render a just verdict? Not a single foreign name, much less an Italian one, appeared on the juror's list. Because Fred Moore had rejected any "capitalists" during jury selection, a few prospective jurors whom the McAnarneys knew to be fair-minded were kept off the jury. Those jurors selected were drawn from the tradespeople and other respectable Protestants of the town. None would share the defendants' antipathy to capitalism; few would have had any compassion for the plight of Italian immigrants or union members. Even worse, the jury foreman, Harry Ripley, was a former police chief who outdid himself in persuading his fellow jurors to convict. He violated basic rules of evidence in a capital case by bringing into the jury room cartridges similar to those placed in evidence. A short time before, he had told his friend William Daly that he would be on the jury in "the case of the two 'ginneys' charged with murder at South Braintree." When Daly suggested that they might be innocent, Ripley replied, "Damn them, they ought to hang anyway."

By using the concept of nativism to gain a broader perspective, the historian has come to understand the answer to a question lawyers need not even ask: what factors accounted for the conviction of Sacco and Vanzetti where legitimate evidence was so clearly lacking? Nativism explains many prejudices exhibited in the trial record. It also explains why those attitudes were so widespread in 1920–1921. We must accept the truth of law professor Edmund M. Morgan's assertion that it was "almost impossible to secure a verdict which runs counter to the settled convictions of the community." Sacco and Vanzetti symbolized for a majority of Americans and the "men of Norfolk" alien forces that threatened their way of life.

Yet, having answered one important question, the historian still faces another. Granted that a jury convicted two alien radicals of robbery and murder in 1921, but "why all the fuss," as we asked earlier, in the years that followed? After all, Sacco and Vanzetti were not sentenced until 1927, long after the virulent nativist mood had passed. Corruption and scandal had by then killed the Klan. Prohibition had closed that infernal den of immigrant iniquity, the saloon. The Immigration Acts of 1921 and 1924 had severely curbed the flow of newcomers from Italy and eastern Europe. The damage from unsuccessful strikes, management opposition, and government hostility had sent organized labor into a decline from which it would not recover until the New Deal years. The historian must still explain how a local case extended its impact beyond Norfolk County to the nation and even the international community.

No single answer, even one so broad as nativism, can account for the notoriety. Certainly, from the beginning the case had sent ripples across the nation. Socially prominent individuals, intellectuals, the American Federation of Labor, immigrant groups, and radicals had all contributed to the defense fund for the Dedham trial. Those people represented a small minority without great political influence. But by tracing out the appeals process, the historian discovers a series of events that enlarged the significance of the case, heightened the public's awareness of the crucial issues involved, and raised the stakes many groups risked on the judicial outcome.

A NATION STIRRED

In the American legal system, the right of appeal is designed to protect defendants against any miscarriage of justice rising out of the original trial. But in 1920 the appeals process in Massachusetts contained a provision that ultimately proved fatal to Sacco and Vanzetti. Any motion for a retrial based on new evidence had to be granted by the original trial judge. On each of eight motions made by the defense, including substantial evidence of prejudice on the part of the judge, the person who heard that appeal was none other than Webster Thayer! . . .

A mounting body of evidence seemed to indicate that the two men were innocent. Yet, as the courts remained deaf to the defense appeals, more and more reasonable people came to suspect that, indeed, powerful men and institutions were conspiring to destroy two people perceived as a threat to the social order. Thayer's sentence of death by electrocution seemed but a final thread in a web of legal intrigue to commit an injustice.

Sacco and Vanzetti played an important part in winning broad popular support for their cause. Steadfastly, in the face of repeated disappointments, they maintained their innocence. Sacco, the more simple and direct of the two, suffered deeply as a result of separation from his family. During the first trying years, he went on a hunger strike and suffered a nervous breakdown. From that point on, he stoically awaited the end, more preoccupied with saving his wife further anguish than with saving himself. To assist the defense effort, however, he had begun in 1923 to study English, though with little success. A letter written to his teacher in 1926 conveys his energetic, simple idealism. Sacco had wanted to explain to his teacher why he had been unable to master the language:

No, it isn't, because I have try with all my passion for the success of this beautiful language, not only for the sake of my family and the promise I have made to you—but for my own individual satisfaction, to know and to be able to read and write correct English. But woe is me! It wasn't so; no, because the sadness of these close and cold walls, the idea to be away from my dear family, for all the beauty and joy of liberty—had more than once exhaust my passion.

Vanzetti's articulate, often eloquent speeches and letters won him the respect of fellow prisoners, defenders, and literary figures drawn to the case, including Upton Sinclair, whose reformist instincts had not deserted him since writing *The Jungle* twenty years earlier. (Vanzetti was "one of the wisest and kindest persons I ever knew," Sinclair wrote, "and I thought him as incapable of murder as I was.") . . .

By the time all appeals were exhausted, the Sacco and Vanzetti case had brought to public attention not only issues of guilt and innocence, but more fundamental tensions in American society. On one side were arrayed immigrants, workers, and the poor for whom Sacco and Vanzetti stood as powerful symbols. On the other stood Thayer, the "men of Norfolk," the Protestant establishment, and those who believed that America should tolerate only certain peoples and ideas.

On the night of August 22, 1927, John Dos Passos, a young writer, stood with the crowd outside Charleston Prison waiting for news of Sacco and Vanzetti's fate. Shortly after midnight word came— the "good shoemaker and poor fish peddler" were dead. Grief and anger raked the crowd. Some wept, others cried out in the name of justice, and many tore their clothes in anguish. The scene outside the prison was repeated in New York and other cities around the world. Years later, Dos Passos expressed the outrage he felt against those who had persecuted Sacco and Vanzetti:

> they have clubbed us off the streets they are stronger they are rich they hire and fire the politicians the newspapereditors the old judges the small men with reputations the collegepresidents the ward heelers (listen collegepresidents judges America will not forget her betrayers). . . .
>
> all right you have won you will kill the brave men our friends tonight
>
> there is nothing left to do we are beaten. . . .
>
> America our nation has been beaten by strangers who have turned our language inside out who have taken the clean words our Fathers spoke and made them slimy and foul. . . .
>
> they have built the electricchair and hired the executioner to throw the switch
>
> all right we are two nations

Two nations—that was the reason for "all the fuss."

Will the real truth of the case ever be known? Perhaps not—at least not "beyond a reasonable doubt," to borrow the language of the courts. Yet historians have unearthed enough additional information to provide, if not the certainties of fact, at least a few ironies of probability. After Sacco and Vanzetti's execution, Upton Sinclair began to collect material for a novel about the case. As a socialist who had staunchly defended the two men during their years in prison, he was able to interview scores of friends and associates. While Sinclair remained convinced that Sacco and Vanzetti were innocent of the Bridgewater and Braintree robberies, he became less sure

whether the two men were merely philosophical anarchists. Both had "believed in and taught violence," he discovered. "I became convinced from many different sources that Vanzetti was not the pacifist he was reported to be under the necessity of defense propaganda. He was, like many fanatics, a dual personality, and when he was roused by the social conflict he was a very dangerous man."

Historian Paul Avrich, investigating the anarchist community of which the two men were a part, noted that Vanzetti was indeed a close friend of Luigi Galleani, the firebrand whose associates had launched the letter bombs of 1919 and dynamited Attorney General Palmer's home. "We mean to speak for [the proletariat through] the voice of dynamite, through the mouth of guns," announced the anarchist leaflet found nearby. Carlo Valdinoci, the man who was blown up carrying out his mission, had been a good friend of both Sacco and Vanzetti. Indeed, after Valdinoci's death, his sister Assunta moved in with Sacco and his family. Then, too, rumors within the anarchist community suggested that Vanzetti himself had assembled the bomb that demolished a judge's home in Boston the night Valdinoci had done his work in Washington.

"But my conviction is that I have suffered for things I am guilty of," Vanzetti told Thayer at the end. Perhaps there was pride as well as indignation in this response. What, in the end, was the guilt of which Sacco and Vanzetti were so conscious during the trial? Was it merely the knowledge that their radical pamphlets, if found, would get them deported? But both men had been preparing to flee the country anyway, before being arrested. (Recall Sacco's outsized passport photo.) Could their evasive behavior have resulted from the fact that they had more to conceal at home than a few pamphlets?

Upton Sinclair came to believe so. After the execution, Fred Moore confided to him that Sacco and Vanzetti had admitted "they were hiding dynamite on the night of their arrest, and that that was the real reason why they told lies and stuck to them." If true, Sacco and Vanzetti, like Valdinoci, had been willing to commit acts of anarchism that, by the laws of

American society, would have been punishable by death. Sacco made clear his own distinction between being tried for his beliefs and being arrested for mere bank robbery. "If I was arrested because of the Idea I am glad to suffer. If I must I will die for it. But they have arrested me for a gunman job."

Is the final irony that Sacco and Vanzetti were willing to die—perhaps even to kill others—for their Idea? Just as the "men of Norfolk" and the officials of Massachusetts were willing to execute Sacco and Vanzetti on behalf of *their* idea of what America should be? ("Damn them, they ought to hang anyway," remarked juror Ripley.) The historian must suspect that on that August night in 1927, citizens were not merely fighting over a matter of guilt or innocence, but (as Dos Passos put it) over the meaning of those "clean words our Fathers spoke." Sacco and Vanzetti had forced the nation to ask who in their own times best embodied the principles of freedom and equality inherited from 1776. Perhaps neither historians nor lawyers can resolve that question to the satisfaction of a divided nation.

QUESTIONS TO CONSIDER

1 Describe the crimes allegedly committed by Sacco and Vanzetti. When you consider the amount of evidence and the number of witnesses in their seven-week trial, explain why the jury came back with a guilty verdict in only five hours. Why did this trial of two lowly Italian immigrants generate such bitter controversy?

2 Why did the police label Sacco and Vanzetti as "suspicious characters"? Describe the unconventional investigation that attempted to link them to the Braintree murders. Given the lack of hard evidence (fingerprints, confiscated money), explain how the district attorney conducted his prosecution. Why would such a case have no credibility in the twenty-first-century American judicial system?

3 Why do the authors conclude "that those who prosecuted Sacco and Vanzetti were far more concerned with who the defendants were and what they believed than with what they might have done"? Define "nativism" and how it affected attitudes toward immigrants who came to America immediately after the Great War.

4 Who was A. Mitchell Palmer, and how did his actions reflect the ethnic prejudices of his day? How did Palmer violate the civil liberties of the people he suspected of radicalism? Following the Great War, what problems did the labor movement face? In what ways did labor unrest create an atmosphere in America that tolerated most of Palmer's excesses?

5 What factors transformed the trial of Sacco and Vanzetti into a national and international controversy? Explain why novelist John Dos Passos contended that the America of the 1920s consisted of "two nations."

6 What do the authors of this selection mean when they repeatedly contrast the rules of evidence that guide historians with the rules of evidence followed by judges and juries? How do these rules differ? How can historians explain why there was such acrimonious controversy over the trial of Sacco and Vanzetti?

PART EIGHT

Long Dark Night of the Depression

16 Under Hoover, the Shame and Misery Deepened

T. H. WATKINS

By the beginning of 1929, the nation seemed to have reached a permanent state of prosperity. Business and foreign trade both were expanding, the stock market was rising at a phenomenal rate, and national leadership appeared to be in expert hands. Republican Herbert Hoover had won the presidency the previous November, having easily defeated his Democratic opponent. "For the first time in our history," wrote two economists, "we have a President who, by technical training, engineering achievement, cabinet experience, and grasp of economic fundamentals, is qualified for business leadership."

"We in America today," Hoover himself had said, "are nearer to the final triumph over poverty than ever before in the history of any land. The poorhouse is vanishing from among us." Hoover was equally optimistic in his inaugural address in March 1929: "I have no fears for the future of our country," he proclaimed. "It is bright with hope."

Eight months later, the country plummeted into the most severe and protracted economic depression in American history. It started with the stock market crash in October 1929 and deepened slowly and inexorably until the entire economy and perhaps even the nation itself approached total collapse. It was the worst disaster the United States had faced since the Civil War, and there were voices of doubt everywhere. How had it happened? What would become of the American dream? Would the nation disintegrate? And who was to blame—President Hoover, the Republican party, or capitalism itself?

We now know that several factors caused economic collapse—chief among them underconsumption and overproduction, as consumer buying power lagged behind the quantity of goods being turned out. As factories and other businesses found themselves overextended, they began laying off workers, *which decreased consumer buying power, which in turn caused more layoffs and resulted in a vicious cycle. By 1932, some 12 million Americans were unemployed. At the same time, factories and businesses themselves shuttered their windows and closed their doors, and banks, unable to call in their loans, began failing at an alarming rate, taking people's savings down with them. In 1930 and 1931, a total of 3,646 banks failed, representing more than $2.5 billion in deposits. Never, in all the previous depressions and "panics," had the country been confronted with such statistics.*

The prosperity of the 1920s had turned into a nightmare. Unemployed men roamed the country in search of work, succumbing to feelings of guilt and worthlessness when they found nothing at all. In the following selection, excerpted from his prize-winning history of the Great Depression, a companion to the popular PBS series on that calamity, distinguished historian T. H. Watkins captures the human misery and the failure of early relief efforts through vignettes of common folk—whites, African Americans, and Mexican Americans. Watkins also offers an insightful discussion of President Hoover's approach to the crisis and why that failed.

As you read the next two selections, bear in mind that the Depression was a worldwide calamity that rocked industrial Europe and Japan as well as the United States. As historian John A. Garraty says, "While there were differences in its impact and in the way it was dealt with from one country to another, the course of events nearly everywhere ran something like this: By 1925, most countries had recovered from the economic disruptions caused by the Great War of 1914–18. There followed a few years of rapid growth, but in 1929 and 1930 the prosperity ended. Then came a precipitous plunge that lasted until early 1933. This dark period was followed by a gradual, if spotty, recovery. The revival, however, was aborted by the steep recession of 1937–38. It took a still more cataclysmic event, the outbreak of World War II, to end the Great Depression."

GLOSSARY

BLACK THURSDAY   The day the stock market crashed, October 24, 1929, causing a panic in the business world that presaged the Great Depression.

DEPRESSION   Called a "panic" in the nineteenth century, this was a severe downturn in the business cycle characterized by low business activity, bank and business failures, high unemployment, and want in the midst of plenty.

HOOVER, HERBERT   President of the United States, 1929–1933, who was widely blamed for the stock-market crash and the onset of the Great Depression.

HOOVERVILLES   Derogatory name for shantytowns, made of box crates, loose timber, and whatever else could be found that sprang up around many cities; unemployed families lived in them and called them Hoovervilles because they blamed a seemingly cold and remote president for their misery.

JIM CROW LAWS   State and local laws enacted in the South after Reconstruction, they denied African Americans the right to vote, hold political office, and sit on juries; relegated them to menial labor; restricted them to black sections of towns and cities; and excluded them from public accommodations. The laws took their name from a song, "Jim Crow," sung by Thomas Rice in a pre–Civil War black minstrel show.

MINEHAN, THOMAS   A sociologist who studied tramps and hoboes, roaming men and women who were unemployed.

RECONSTRUCTION FINANCE CORPORATION   Federal agency established by President Hoover that in 1932 started handing out federal funds to support agriculture and industry; later it was a powerful agency of the New Deal.

RED CROSS   International philanthropic organization that provided relief in war; national disasters like floods, pestilence, fires, storms; and other calamities like the Great Depression.

UNIVERSAL FEAR

Gordon Parks was sixteen years old in 1929, a young black man trying to work his way through high school in St. Paul, Minnesota, as a bellboy at a downtown club for white businessmen. One Wednesday afternoon, a notice was tacked to the employee bulletin board: "Because of unforeseen circumstances, some personnel will be laid off the first of next month. Those directly affected will be notified in due time." This puzzled Parks until the next day, Thursday, October 24, when the evening papers broke the news of the crash. "I read everything I could get my hands on," he recalled,

gathering in the full meaning of such terms as Black Thursday, deflation and depression. I couldn't imagine such financial disaster touching my small world; it surely concerned only the rich. But by the first week of November I . . . knew differently; along with millions of others across the nation, I was without a job. . . . Finally, on the seventh of November I went to school and cleaned out my locker, knowing it was impossible to stay on. A piercing chill was in the air as I walked back to the rooming house. The hawk had come. I could already feel his wings shadowing me.

While only a small percentage of the public was directly affected by the collapse of the stock market in October, 1929, it was still a moment of history shared by nearly every American. Like the Japanese attack of Pearl Harbor or the assassinations of John F. Kennedy, Martin Luther King, Jr., and Robert Kennedy in our own time, the crash was a point of reference for those of that time. People took the measure of their era by using the crash as an emotional baseline, and it became the one event on which tens of millions could fix their worry as the full dimensions of the debacle slowly began to be discerned. Gordon Parks was not the only one who felt the shadow of the hawk.

President Herbert Clark Hoover, though, apparently remained oblivious to that shadow—or if he felt it, did not want to acknowledge it. Unemployment had grown from about 1.5 million to at least 3.2 million in the five months since the crash, but on March 7, 1930, Hoover gave the American public the results of his own analysis of the situation. "All the evidences," he said, "indicate that the worst effects of the crash upon unemployment will have passed during the next sixty days."

A more accurate measure could have been found in an unnamed southern city that Sherwood Anderson visited that same month. The writer spent some time standing outside a big basement soup kitchen, where on a single day he watched seven hundred people go inside to get fed. He was struck by the number of those who did not want him to know their hunger. The man, for example, who approached the soup kitchen three times before swallowing his pride and going down the steps. "I am not here for soup," he told Anderson, who had not said a word. "I came here to meet a friend." Or the young woman who asked him where the soup kitchen was. "I do not want any soup," she assured him when he obliged. She just wanted to say hello to some of the women who were serving the needy. "They are friends of mine."

"They were Americans, such people as you and I," Anderson wrote. "I stood watching them. I was ashamed of my warm overcoat, my stout shoes.

"I made men ashamed standing there."

Most of those who were still coming to the soup kitchen six months later, as the first anniversary of the crash approached, probably would have put little or no faith in anything Herbert Hoover said on the subject of what was now being called, openly and increasingly, a depression. Unemployment had not declined; it had risen, implacably, and in another six months would hit at least 7.5 million. And they would have found plainly incomprehensible the confidence of Rome C. Stephenson, vice president of the American Bankers' Association, if they had heard the pep talk he gave his fellow bankers in downtown Cleveland on September 30. The bankers

Unemployment reached staggering levels during the long dark night of the Depression. To raise a little money, this man is forced to sell apples on West Street in New York City, 1932. In back of him is a "Hooverville," a collection of wrecked and abandoned buildings that became "home" for unemployed New Yorkers and their families. (Culver Pictures)

should not worry, Stephenson said, because business was about to get better. The slump, he insisted, was largely a matter of misperception:

The depression of the stock market impressed the general public with the idea that it would depress general business. Because of a psychological consequence, it did, but it should not have. There are 120,000,000 persons in the country and at the maximum not more than 10,000,000 were involved in stock-market transactions. The remaining 110,000,000 persons suffered no loss.

The bulk of the American population may not have suffered the loss of stock investments, but there were plenty of other ways to calculate loss, and by the end of 1929, with unemployment rising, with

shops and factories suddenly ornamented by Closed or Out of Business signs, and, perhaps most terrifying of all, with scores of banks failing and taking with them millions of dollars in deposits (which were at that time uninsured), the "general public's" confidence in the financial health of the country and the wisdom of its leaders was shaky at best. Confidence fell even further when 256 banks failed in the single month of November, 1930, and further yet on December 11, when the United States Bank, with deposits of more than $200 million, went under. It was the largest single bank failure in American history up to that time, and contributed no little portion to an economic hangover in which, in the words of banker J. M. Barker, "cupidity turned into unreasoning, emotional, universal fear."

FIGHTING FOR THE SCRAPS

There was reason enough for fear. The 1,352 banks that failed in 1930 represented more than $853 million in deposits. In 1931, 2,294 banks went under, with deposits of nearly $1.7 billion. In 1930, 26,355 businesses failed, and the rate of 122 failures per 10,000 was the highest ever recorded up to that time. Both numbers were surpassed in 1931 with 28,285 failures and a rate of 133. The 451,800 corporations still in business in 1932 had a combined deficit of $5.64 billion. The value of all farm property declined from $57.7 billion in 1929 (itself down from a high of $78.3 billion in 1920) to $51.8 billion in 1931. By the end of 1931 unemployment had climbed to 8 million and in a few months would be approaching 12 million.

There had never been such statistics in our history, and there have been none like them since. Their truest meaning, the effect they had on individual human lives, could be seen everywhere, as people struggled blindly and bravely to survive. Which is not to say that everyone was willing to see them for what they were. Like those who attempt to dismiss the homeless of our own day as aberrations, not indications, of the nation's economic condition, many of the pundits of the depression years spent a lot of time explaining away the presence of the poor and the hungry. These were temporary phenomena, it was said, transient indications of a momentary lapse in economic health. Many of the people were not even victims—they were just beggars too lazy or too ignorant to work. But the deprived of the depression years were even more difficult to ignore than the doorway sleepers and street-corner panhandlers of modern America. They could not be explained away, because they would not go away—and their numbers grew day by day, week by week. Like a plague, the disease of deprivation spread with such speed and across so many lines that there were few families in the United States who did not either experience or witness its pain.

When neighbors you had known all your life were found one morning with all their furniture stacked on the sidewalk, nowhere to go, no hope in sight, it did not take much imagination to see yourself standing there with them.

You did not even have to be especially vulnerable to feel the power of deprivation. Daniel Willard, president of the Baltimore & Ohio Railroad and in no danger of having his furniture stacked on anybody's sidewalk, for instance, received an honorary doctorate at the University of Pennsylvania in June, 1931, but instead of mouthing the usual platitudes on this happy occasion, burst out with a jeremiad against the very economic system that had made him rich:

A system—call it what you will—under which it is possible for 5,000,000 or 6,000,000 of willing and able-bodied men to be out of work and unable to secure work for months at a time, and with no other source of income, cannot be said to be perfect or even satisfactory. . . . I would be less than candid if I did not say in such circumstances I would steal before I would starve.

"No one is going hungry and no one need go hungry or cold," President Hoover still insisted in the winter of 1931. Willard would have disagreed. So would Louise V. Armstrong. "We saw the city at its worst," she wrote in *We, Too, Are the People* (1941). "One vivid, gruesome moment of those dark days we shall never forget. We saw a crowd of some fifty men fighting over a barrel of garbage which had been set outside the back door of a restaurant. American citizens fighting for scraps of food like animals!"

"Why does Every Thing have exceptional Value Except the Human being," one destitute person wrote the president, "—why are we reduced to poverty and starving and anxiety and Sorrow So quickly under your administration as Chief Executor. Can you not find a quicker way of Executing us than to starve us to death."

On Chicago's South Side, wandering reporter Edmund Wilson took a look at the old Angelus Building, a tottering, stinking wreck of a place whose owner would have demolished it if he had found the money to do so. It was now stuffed with black people who could afford to live nowhere else. The place, Wilson said, was

seven stories, thick with dark windows, caged in a dingy mess of fire-escapes like mattress-springs on a junk-heap, hunched up, hunchback-proportioned, jam-crammed in its dumbness and darkness with miserable wriggling life. . . . There is darkness in the hundred cells: the tenants cannot pay for light; and cold: the heating system no longer works. . . . And now, since it is no good for anything else, its owner had turned it over to the Negroes, who flock into the tight-packed apartments and get along there as best they can.

In an Appalachian Mountains school, a child who looked sick was told by her teacher to go home and get something to eat. "I can't," the girl replied. "It's my sister's turn to eat."

The city fathers over in Muncie, Indiana, did not like to think of people being that hungry in their all-American town. Muncie, after all, was the "Middletown" of the famous 1929 study of Robert S. and Helen Merrell Lynd, and was generally proud of it, too. But by the spring of 1932, the layer of confidence with which the city had consistently blanketed the depression began to grow a little tattered. That year, a Muncie businessman later told the Lynds, "people would go around saying in low tones, 'Have you heard that they're boarding up the so-and-so plant?' And a few days later, 'Have you heard that so-and-so-many trucks of machinery were moved out of town today? They say that half the floor at the plant is stripped already.' It got on our nerves as this went on!" The plant in question was a General Motors assembly plant, and by the end of the summer it had indeed stripped its floors of machinery, closed down, and left Muncie.

New Orleans did its best to keep reality from the door, too. Unemployment was greatly exaggerated, a writer to the letters column of the *Times-Picayune* said in February, 1930, a rumor spread by a "host of fly-speckers, calamity howlers and woe-be-tiders [who] are barnacles on prosperity," but a week later an estimated three to four hundred men showed up to answer a single classified advertisement for work available in Texas. When the advertisement turned out to be a fraud, the crowd started a small-scale riot and the police had to be brought in to put it down.

Out in Yavapai County, Arizona, depression was even harder to ignore for long. Hundreds of men who had been laid off from the copper mines in the southern part of the state wandered north to the vicinity of Prescott. During the summer of 1932, they spread "out into the hills and mountains in the hope of placer mining and getting a few cents a day out of the gravel-bars that were worked fifty years ago," Prescott poet Sharlot Hall wrote a friend in June. "Sometimes they really do pan out a few cents—or once in a while get a dollar or more—but the old diggings are very lean of gold. . . ." Others were trying the same thing up in Nevada, where in one lonely canyon a reporter found a man shoveling dirt into a primitive riffle chute to wash out gold. "Me a minin' man?" he replied when asked. "Yes, I'm a miner—all of ten weeks now. Before that, I'd been a sailor all my life. Now it's a simple case of 'root, hog, or die, so I'm rootin'.'"

Hundreds of thousands of people were on the move by then. The Southern Pacific Railroad estimated that its "railroad bulls" had thrown as many as 683,000 transients off its boxcars in a single year. At least 200,000 of the transients were adolescents, most of them male but with no small number of females among them. In the summer of 1932 sociologist Thomas Minehan began a study that took him on the road with young tramps and hoboes. Most of them, he noted, traveled in gangs for safety, an especially important consideration for the young women among them. "Girls in box cars," he wrote, "are not entirely at the mercy of any man on the road whatever their relations with the boys may be. In event of loneliness or illness, the boys and girls have friends to comfort and care for them."

One of the tramps with whom he traveled for a time was a Pennsylvania Dutch boy nicknamed Blink—so named because he had lost an eye when a live cinder blew into his face while he was riding an open car on the Santa Fe railroad. "A bloody socket forms a small and ever-weeping cave on the left side of his face," Minehan wrote. "Tears streak his cheek, furrowing the dirt and coal soot, leaving a strange moist scar alongside his nose." The boy showed Minehan a diary he had been keeping since August, 1932, when he had run away from an abusive father. The entry for September 10 was eloquently typical:

Slept in paper box. Bummed swell breakfast three eggs and four pieces meat. Hit guy in big car in front of garage. Cop told me to scram. Rode freight to Roessville. Small burg, but got dinner. Walked Bronson. N. G. Couple a houses. Rode to Sidell. N. G. Hit homes for meals and turned down. Had to buy supper 20 cents. Raining.

Young and old, male and female, the transient army drifted in a dark caravan of desperation from hobo jungle to hobo jungle, city mission to city mission, begging for leftovers at the back doors of homes, panhandling for pennies on city sidewalks, stealing chickens where chickens could be found, cooking up "mulligan" stews out of whatever could be boiled into edibility, being seduced and raped, thrown into jail, beaten by yard bulls. Those homeless who did not drift—and there were thousands in every city of any size at all—slept in lice-ridden and rat-infested flophouses when they could afford the ten or fifteen cents for a urine-stained mattress on the floor, and on park benches, under park shrubbery and bridge abutments, in doorways, packing crates, concrete pipes, culverts, construction sites, and abandoned automobiles when they could not afford it. The more ambitious among them contrived fragile shelters from scraps of wood and cardboard, old beer signs and fence posts, anything they could find that would keep off the wind and rain of winter and the direct sun of summer. They built them anywhere they could, but most of the time on the outskirts of cities and towns big enough to have outskirts, where outlandish villages began to coalesce like ramshackle suburbs. Everyone called them Hoovervilles; it was not a term of endearment.

THE LIMITS OF CHARITY

Like most of his contemporaries—and, indeed, most of the American middle class—if President Hoover believed in anything more profoundly than the virtues of self-reliance and individual initiative, it has not been recorded. This was, after all, the very ethos of a white, Protestant culture, the image that Hoover and his kind held up as the ideal of Americanism. Hard work, honesty, and independence, they believed utterly, had brought this country to the forefront of nations, had built a breed of men (and women, too, some conceded, though not often) who had taken the institutions of the founding fathers and made them the wonder of the world. Anything that might weaken the strength of that tradition would weaken the very character of America and was, by definition, evil. Government charity, especially, by robbing people of initiative, would be the very embodiment of error. The national government should stay out of the personal lives of its citizens, even if they were in trouble. For Hoover and for the millions of Americans who shared his convictions, the idea that people would turn to Washington, D.C., to help them out of a bad spot was nearly unthinkable.

It was a hard theory, but part of the accepted wisdom of the time and difficult for Hoover to abandon even in the face of the present situation. Still, when the dimensions of the crisis reached proportions that simply could not be ignored, he did not, as is often supposed, coldheartedly refuse to do anything about it. What he did do, for the most part, was call upon the natural generosity of the American people and the paternalism of local governments. Throughout his term he held to the firm belief that direct aid to the individual was not the business of the federal government—unless there were no other course, in which case he made it clear he would act, though almost certainly in great fear of permanently crippling the national character. "This is not an issue as to whether people shall go hungry or cold in the United States," he said in a statement to the press in the winter of 1931.

It is solely a question of the best method by which hunger and cold shall be prevented. . . . I am willing to pledge myself that if the time should ever come that the voluntary agencies of the country, together with the local and State governments, are unable to find resources with which to prevent hunger and suffering in my country, I will ask the aid of every resource of the Federal Government. . . . I have faith in the American people that such a day will not come.

In the meantime, Hoover authorized the expenditure of about $700 million on various public works projects. He also set up the Reconstruction Finance Corporation, which in early 1932 began doling out the $2 billion that Congress had appropriated to stimulate and prop up industry and agriculture in their time of need. The RFC was one of the few such efforts that amounted to much (it would survive to become one of the most powerful agencies in New Deal Washington). The National Business Survey Conference, for instance, was designed to "market" an optimistic feeling in the business community and as part of this goal its members took a solemn vow not to cut wages. Defections were almost immediate. The National Credit Corporation, for another example, was designed to set up a system whereby healthy banks would assist unhealthy banks; few did, and the NCC virtually collapsed in two years. The Federal Farm Board, created before the depression, was designed to stabilize farm prices through the temporary purchase of surplus farm produce; it managed to lose some $345 million and satisfied no one. The President's Emergency Committee for Employment (PECE) and its successor, the President's Organization for Unemployment Relief (POUR), were largely designed to promote the belief that things were not as bad as they appeared to be and even if they were they would soon get better; neither managed to get the message across with any great success—though the POUR was useful in helping local agencies and private charities raise money by getting pro bono advertisements placed in newspapers and magazines.

It must be said that many Americans tried to sustain self-reliance, as Hoover advised. Probably the best-known examples were the apple sellers who for a time appeared on the sidewalks of nearly every major city. In the fall of 1930, the hard-pressed International Apple Shippers Association came up with the idea of selling apples to the unemployed on credit at $1.75 a crate. The apples would retail on the street at a nickel apiece and if a seller got rid of all the apples in his or her crate, the net could be as much as $1.85. By the end of November, 1930, there were six thousand apple sellers on the streets of New York City alone, crouching, in the words of newspaperman Gene Fowler, "like half-remembered sins sitting upon the conscience of the town." Down in New Orleans, the same device was tried with Louisiana oranges—"Health for You—Help for the Needy," the *Times-Picayune* declared. While people at first responded with sympathy to these peddlers, they were altogether too visible a reminder of the nation's troubles; sales fell off drastically in a few months— not aided in the slightest by Hoover's peculiar public assertion at one point that "many persons left their jobs for the more profitable one of selling apples."

Many people tried to "maintain the spirit of charity" and the dogma of self-reliance in other ways, and many local governments struggled valiantly to meet the crisis themselves, as Hoover so fervently wished. Nothing worked for very long, even in the most successful instances. In Seattle, for example, a few Socialists got together and formed the Unemployed Citizens' League in July, 1931. The organization swiftly grew to a membership of somewhere between forty and fifty thousand. The UCL organized numerous self-help projects—cutting wood on donated land, picking unwanted fruit crops, fishing in Puget Sound, setting up commissaries for the distribution of food and wood, negotiating with landlords to prevent evictions, and putting together a kind of barter economy in which members exchanged services and goods. In response, Seattle mayor Robert Harlin formed the Mayor's Commission on Improved Employment to work with the UCL, and when a million-dollar bond issue was raised to finance it, put the leaders of the UCL in charge of the District Relief Organization. The UCL remained the principal distributor of food and work to the city's estimated forty-five thousand unemployed until the money began to run out.

In Philadelphia, it was the rich who organized, and for a time it seemed that the city would stand as the perfect model for Hoover's vision of private-public cooperation at the local level. On November 7, 1930, the Committee of One Hundred of the city's most influential people met for lunch at the Bellevue-Stratford Hotel and formed the Committee for Unemployment Relief, with Horatio Gates Lloyd, a partner in Drexel and Company, the Philadelphia branch of the House of Morgan, as its chairman. In order to "tide over the temporary distress" of the depression, the committee immediately raised $4 million, which Lloyd parceled out to various private charities. The committee also persuaded the Pennsylvania General Assembly to authorize the city to borrow $3 million for public relief. A municipal Bureau of Unemployment was established and Lloyd himself was put in charge of the distribution of its public funds. Like that of the Socialists in Seattle, the philanthropists' effort in Philadelphia was a great success—for as long as the money held out. The $7 million in private and public money was exhausted by November, 1931. A "United Campaign" raised another $10 million in cash and pledges; Lloyd's committee got $5 million of that, and in three months it, too, was gone, as was the remaining $5 million that had gone to other agencies. In April, 1932, the city got another $2.5 million in direct aid from the state; that was gone in two months. The Lloyd Committee, the *Philadelphia Record* reported on June 20, "is through. For fifty-seven thousand families to whom the Committee has meant life itself, it added, playing on the Hoover administration's assurances that "prosperity is just around the corner," "STARVATION is 'just around the corner.'"

Volunteerism had not worked in Philadelphia, and neither it nor self-reliance would be enough anywhere they were tried. They certainly were not enough in those states in which one of the worst droughts in history gave the overall economic calamity an almost biblical character. The hardest hit was Arkansas, which in July and August, 1930, received only 4.19 inches of rain—35 percent of what it had gotten during the same two months the previous year—but rainfall in another twenty-two states in the Midwest, Great Plains, and South also dropped by an average of nearly 40 percent in those two months. "The families that are suffering now, or on the verge of it," the Red Cross representative for Arkansas wrote national headquarters in August,

are not singled out as by flood or tornado or fire, but are just in their homes, with gardens ruined, sweet potatoes not making a crop, the prospect of being in debt to the landlord when the pitiable cotton crop is gathered instead of having money with which to buy food and clothing for the winter.

Hoover immediately formed another committee—several committees, in fact. At a conference of governors from the affected states on August 14, he told them that they should establish local and state drought committees to handle the problem. For the most part, he insisted, local communities were going to have to carry the burden alone. Furthermore, he believed that the Red Cross should provide the lion's share of any help beyond that. During the terrible floods in the southern Mississippi River Valley in 1927, the Red Cross had stepped in and brought relief to hundreds of thousands of people whose homes and lives had been devastated. The organization had sheltered the homeless, fed the hungry, had helped thousands of people to survive the disaster. Surely, it could do so again.

But the drought of these years was not a single, isolated event like a flood; it had gone on for a long time already and would go on for some time to come, and its disruptive effect was magnified by the larger economic situation which the Red Cross would not have been in a position to do anything about in any event. The organization's institutional inadequacy to accomplish what Hoover expected of it was compounded by the philosophy of its leader, national chairman Judge John Barton Payne. Payne was a close friend of Hoover's and shared the president's reverence for self-reliance. He made it clear from the start that the local and state Red Cross chapters would depend on volunteers and money from the local and state regions, and only under the most extreme circumstances would the national organization step in to help.

The system thus established was more efficient at withholding aid than in furnishing it. The state and local Red Cross chapters, like the state and local drought committees, usually were headed up by the "best people" who had been part of the oppressive plantation system for generations, and were prepared to think the worst of those who sought direct help. Many people worried that if food were distributed, workers might refuse to pick cotton at the wages plantation farmers were willing to pay. "Some, you know," the Red Cross chairman for Monroe County, Arkansas, wrote in early September,

are ready to let the Red Cross do it all, we think after the cotton is out we can raise some money, and as the worst is to come in the cold winter months, we think it best to postpone doing only what is absolutely necessary at this time, knowing that a person can get along on very little during warm weather.

By November even the planters were calling for direct aid, because they could not feed the families of their workers. Still, most local chapters continued to tell the national headquarters what it wanted to hear and people at headquarters ignored the streams of letters from the desperate, like that from an African-American farmer in Jefferson County, Arkansas:

There is thousands of collard farmers in Jefferson and Lincoln counties that has not bread. They are Bairfooted and thin closed many has went to the County Judge and to the local Red Cross they Both say that they has no Funds We are planning on sending a Collard men to Washington to lay our Trubles more clearly before you.

Stubbornly holding to his principles, Hoover himself continued to insist that the burden of relief should be carried by the Red Cross, not the government, and he did not even support legislation that would have provided $60 million for feed and seed loans from the Department of Agriculture. And Judge John Barton Payne continued to hold back the distribution of funds from the national Red Cross. But by January the situation was so terrible that even the local chapters had abandoned the pretense that local and state resources could provide sufficient relief, and national headquarters finally responded with a fund-raising drive that began on January 10 and ultimately raised a little over $10 million. Between then and the end of the program in the spring, 2,765,000 people had been fed just enough to get them through the winter. It was pinch-penny charity at best, and no one will ever know how many suffered how much during all the months in which virtually nothing had been handed out. And since records were as carelessly managed as the relief program itself, no one will know how many died.

Some "relief" efforts did not even pretend to charity. Chief among these was the attempted deportation of Mexican Americans, which managed to combine racism with selfishness and desperation in one of the least edifying episodes in American history. By the beginning of the thirties, there was a Mexican-American, or Chicano, population in the United States of about 1.5 million, much of it the result of immigration—some legal, some not (slovenly kept records and conflicting estimates between Mexican and U.S. officials made it impossible to say how many belonged in either category). Thousands of the immigrants had gone north to work the sugar-beet fields of Michigan and the other Great Lakes states, while others had refused stoop labor as a career, moving to Chicago, East Chicago, Gary, and Detroit to look for work in steel mills, automobile plants, and other industries. By 1930 there were 19,362 Mexican Americans living in Chicago, some 9,000 in East Chicago and Gary, and another 8,000 in Detroit, where the allure of the Ford Motor Company had reached into the towns of northern Mexico to call young workers to the "wonderful city of the magic motor."

Most of the immigrants, however, had spilled into the sugar-beet and cotton fields of Texas, Colorado, and Arizona, or on into the huge agribusiness farms of the Imperial and San Joaquin valleys of California. Those who had not joined the stream of migrant labor had gravitated toward the growing Mexican-American settlements in the larger cities. The biggest of these settlements was in Los Angeles, where the Chicano population had increased from 33,644 in 1920 to 97,116 in 1930, making the city the "Mexican capital" of the United States, exhausting the bounds of the older Chicano settlements and spreading out into the neighborhoods of East Los Angeles, where it would remain the largest single segment of the city's minority population.

The bigotry exercised against these people rivaled that endured by African Americans, and when the weight of the depression began to fall upon cities with large Chicano populations, unabashed racism was buttressed by the theory that unemployment among Anglo workers could be blamed on the presence of a labor force willing to work cheap and under conditions that "real" American workers would not tolerate—the Mexican Americans. The answer, some concluded, was deportation—or repatriation, as it was described more benignly. In Gary, Detroit, and other industrial centers, open discrimination, physical threats, racist propaganda campaigns, and free transportation helped to persuade thousands of Chicanos to return to Mexico.

Nowhere was the movement more vigorous than in Los Angeles, however, where the first consignment of 6,024 *repatriados* (songwriter-activist Woody Guthrie would call them "deportees" in one of his most famous songs) left Union Station aboard the cars of the Southern Pacific Railroad in February, 1931. At $14.70 a head, it cost the city and county of Los Angeles $77,249.29 to ship them out, but the savings in relief payments for that year amounted to $347,468.41—a net gain of $270,219.12. "In the last analysis," historian Rudolfo Acuña writes, "President Coolidge's maxim— 'the business of America is business'—was applicable, and repatriation proved profitable, at least in dollars and cents." Over the next three years, Los Angeles County would do a pretty good business, deporting 12,688 Chicanos back to Mexico—though Carey McWilliams, who had been

on hand to watch the first trainload leave Los Angeles in February, 1931, later pointed out, "Repatriation was a tragicomic affair: tragic in the hardships occasioned; comic because most of the Mexicans eventually returned to Los Angeles, having had a trip to Mexico at the expense of the county."

Elsewhere, there was little comedy, even dark comedy, to be found. In New York City, the apple sellers had vanished by the end of 1931 and by April, 1932, 750,000 people were living on city relief efforts that averaged $8.20 a month per person—about one-fifth of what it took to keep one human being decently—while an estimated 160,000 more waited to get on the rolls as soon as the money became available. In 1930, $6 million had gone for relief in New York; in 1931, $25 million; in 1932, it was estimated, the cost would be closer to $75 million. In Atlanta, the cost of relief for only thirty weeks was estimated at $1.2 million, but by December, 1931, only $590,000 had been raised and no more was forthcoming; in June, 1932, 20,000 people in Atlanta and Fulton County were simply removed from the relief rolls, most of them African Americans. In St. Louis, relief agencies were going through a quarter of a million dollars a month, and in July, 1932, the city had to drop 13,000 families off the rolls. In Fort Wayne, Indiana, the Allen County Emergency Unemployment Committee, formed in December, 1930, managed to raise enough money in its first two years to stay more or less even with the relief load. But in 1932, fund-raising targets were not met and the city's own relief expenditures began to slide. Like those in many other regions, Fort Wayne and other Allen County cities began printing their own scrip and using that as currency for goods and services within their own confines.

In Detroit, the Ford Motor Company was forced to shut down production lines on its spectacularly successful Model A. Introduced to a clamorous public in December, 1927, the Model A had taken the lead in sales away from Chevrolet, and even in 1930 the company had sold 1.4 million cars. But by August, 1931, sales were running at rates only half those of 1930, and Ford simply stopped production. Up to then, Detroit had been carrying a welfare budget of $14 million; it now was cut to $7 million, while the number of those in need of relief swelled. Similarly, a $17 million public works program was slashed to $6 million. Michigan Senator James Couzens offered to start a private relief fund with a personal donation of $1 million if Detroit's other rich people would come up with an additional $9 million; no one appeared interested.

A PRIVATE KIND OF SHAME

However desperate the measures taken against it by private and public agencies alike, nothing seemed powerful enough to lift the weight of the depression. For those in the middle class or those who might have hoped to work and save their way into the middle class, much of the weight was psychological. "What is surprising is the passive resignation with which the blow has been accepted," newsman Marquis Childs wrote, "this awful pretense that seeks to conceal the mortal wound, to carry on as though it were still the best possible of all possible worlds." Louis Adamic said of American workers, "I have a definite feeling that millions of them, now that they are unemployed, are licked," and many did seem to be finished, burdened beyond the bearing of it by a terrible load of guilt. They had been taught all their lives that hard work and thrift and honesty would be rewarded with at least security, if not wealth. That hope had failed them, and the fault must be in themselves; millions, Studs Terkel remembered, "experienced a private kind of shame when the pink slip came."

The architecture of despair could be seen everywhere, even among those, like most African Americans, who had been at the bottom so long that it might have seemed that nothing could possibly get any worse. But the hopes and psychic toughness of many black people, too, were tried as they had never been tried before—in the black working-class ghetto of Detroit's "Inkster," for example, where Ford Motor Company worker Odie Stallings scratched to keep his family alive.

Stallings, whose story was told in *American Odyssey,* Robert Conot's history of Detroit, had come to Detroit from Virginia after serving in World War I, joining an internal migration that had changed the face of urban America. If World War I had offered the wheat farmer of the Midwest the dream of avarice, it had given the African American of the South the dream of escape. Wartime America had needed bodies, and blacks had responded. Half a million had departed the rural South between 1916 and 1919 alone, and another million or more had migrated during the twenties. Most had found the promised land close to home—in such cities as Birmingham, Alabama, where the black population had nearly doubled in twenty years; or Memphis, Tennessee, where it had more than doubled; or Houston, Texas, where it had nearly tripled. But many of those who joined the Great Migration also had found opportunity winking at them from the Northeast and Midwest. "I'm tired of this Jim Crow," they sang, "gonna leave this Jim Crow town,/Doggone my black soul, I'm sweet Chicago bound," then had boarded trains by the carloads and headed north for Chicago, Detroit, Pittsburgh, Philadelphia, New York. "I should have been here 20 years ago," one transplant had written from Chicago to the folks back home in Hattiesburg, Mississippi.

I just begin to feel like a man. It's a great deal of pleasure in knowing that you got some privileges. My children are going to the same school with the whites and I don't have to umble to no one. I have registered—will vote the next election and there ain't any 'yes sir'—it's all yes and no and Sam and Bill.

Odie Stallings had been seduced by the same dream, settling in Inkster after finding work in the "black department" at the Ford Plant in River Rouge. He married, and he and his wife, Freda, soon produced two sons. She was pregnant with their third when Ford shut down operations in August, 1931. Shortly afterward, Freda gave birth to another boy. With no income, the Stallings family, like most of those in Inkster, lived on a diet that often was reduced to nothing but starches and water, and Odie dropped from 160 to 125 pounds. His wife was even more wasted, and her breasts were nearly dry; she fed the baby from a bottle filled with flour and water when she could not nurse him herself. Odie trudged the city streets and country roads all over Wayne County in search of any kind of work until his shoes were worn to less than shreds and he could no longer walk long distances. He patched his lightless and heatless shack with newspapers to keep out the cold, but when winter closed down on the ghetto like a fist, the children hacked and coughed incessantly, including the baby, who grew increasingly sick. The parents slept with the infant between them on a narrow bed to keep him warm, but nothing helped, and one morning when they woke he was dead. They put the tiny body in a cardboard box and walking close together under a gray morning sky the family carried their burden up the rutted muddy street and buried it in the makeshift cemetery next to the little community church.

So much, then, for belief in a system whose inherent strengths were supposed to prevent such misery from ever taking place—or if it could not guarantee that, would at least move swiftly and purposefully to repair the damage that had been done. That faith had been tested and had failed—in Detroit, in New York, Chicago, Philadelphia, Seattle, in the farm fields of the Midwest, the cotton plantations of the South, everywhere, resoundingly. What was left, then? Despair, certainly, the bleak anguish of a psychological depression whose dimensions matched the somber statistical dirge of the economic slump. But in human terms, depression often is just another form of anger. And in the end it would be anger, not despair, that would question conventional wisdom, dismantle comfortable assumptions about American society, challenge the machinery of government itself, and bring the first light to the long darkness of the Great Depression.

People everywhere protested their lot. In Arkansas, angry farmers invaded the town of England and demanded food for their hungry families. With reassurances from the Red Cross that they would be reimbursed, merchants distributed bread and other food to the farmers. In Oklahoma City, a mob of hungry men and women invaded a grocery store and seized what they needed. Despite tear gas fired by police, hundreds of workers staged a hunger march on Ford Motor Company at Dearborn, Michigan. In 1932, 20,000 veterans of the Great War marched on Washington after Hoover withheld bonuses promised them for their service in that savage conflict. Hoover sent in the army and six tanks to disperse these "dangerous radicals." That same year an angry and fearful electorate voted Hoover out of office, replacing him with a patrician Democrat who assured Americans that they had "nothing to fear but fear itself."

QUESTIONS TO CONSIDER

1 What economic conditions characterized the crash and the beginning of the Great Depression? The author cites a set of harrowing statistics to illustrate the gravity of the crisis. To what did they refer?

2 How did the Depression affect ordinary Americans, both economically and psychologically? Give examples from the text. What happened to Mexican Americans? Who was Odie Stallings? What does his story illustrate?

3 What was President Hoover's approach to the crisis? What were the beliefs that guided him in his attempt to solve it? What did he tell Americans they must do? What agencies did he rely on to provide relief? Did his approach succeed or fail?

4 What role did the Red Cross play in the early years of the Depression? If charity and volunteerism failed to solve the crisis, what do you think was needed?

5 Given the poverty, frustration, anger, and disillusionment of millions of Americans during the Depression, how can you explain the relative lack of violence or popular demands for radical change?

17 Government in Action: FDR and the Early New Deal

JAMES MacGREGOR BURNS

Franklin Roosevelt swept to power in 1932, carrying every state but six in the electoral college and gathering 23 million popular votes in contrast to Hoover's 16 million. It was a bitter defeat for the Republicans. But the election was even more disappointing for Norman Thomas and William Z. Foster, candidates for the Socialist and Communist parties, respectively. In this year of distress, with some 16 million people unemployed, Thomas collected 882,000 votes and Foster only 103,000.

Roosevelt was perhaps the most controversial president the United States ever had. For millions of Americans, he was a folk hero: a courageous statesman who saved a crippled nation from almost certain collapse and whose New Deal salvaged the best features of democratic capitalism while establishing unprecedented welfare programs for the nation. For others, he was a tyrant, a demagogue who used the Depression to consolidate his political power, whereupon he dragged the country zealously down the road to socialism. In spite of his immense popular appeal, Roosevelt became the hated enemy of much of the nation's business and political community. Conservatives denounced him as a Communist. Liberals said he was too conservative. Communists castigated him as a tool of Wall Street. And Socialists dismissed him as a reactionary. "He caught hell from all sides," recorded one observer, because few knew how to classify his political philosophy or his approach to reform. Where, after all, did he fit ideologically? Was he for capitalism or against it? Was his New Deal revolutionary or reactionary? Was it "creeping socialism" or a bulwark against socialism? Did it lift the country out of the Depression, or did it make the disaster worse?

In fact, as Roosevelt scholar James MacGregor Burns points out in the following selection, FDR was essentially nonideological. He rejected absolutes in favor of bold and practical experimentation. And the New Deal itself, as one scholar explained, was not a coherent, far-sighted program of reform, but "a series of improvisations" that reflected Roosevelt's empirical temper. He compared himself to a quarterback in a football game, "calling a new play after he saw how the last one turned out." There may not have been an ideology or philosophy behind FDR's New Deal. But "there was a loose collection of values," Burns says. These consisted of "Roosevelt's warm humanitarianism, his belief that the needy must be helped, that [the federal] government must step in when private institutions could not do the job."

And both private institutions and impoverished state governments were totally incapable of dealing with the Depression, the greatest economic disaster in American history, which threatened the very survival of the nation. As the winter of 1932–1933 approached, the crisis deepened. As Burns says elsewhere, "Business activity dropped to between a quarter and a third of 'normalcy' and one worker out of five—perhaps one out of four—was jobless." Those who had jobs were scarcely better off. In Manhattan sweatshops, women who lined slippers earned just over one dollar in a nine-hour day. Young women who sewed aprons made only twenty cents a day. "There is not a garbage-dump in Chicago which is not diligently haunted by the hungry," journalist and critic Edmund Wilson observed.

Out in the farmlands, rural families were also poverty-stricken and desperate. To stay warm, they burned their corn, which was cheaper than coal. When banks attempted to foreclose on farms, desperate rural folk brandished shotguns and hangman's nooses to drive the deputy sheriffs away. When a farm was auctioned, a neighbor would bid a dime and give the farm back to its owner. Farm leaders in Nebraska threatened to march thousands of protestors to the state capitol and destroy it if relief was denied. In Washington, D.C., officials warned that a revolution was building in the countryside.

Against this frightening background, fifty-one-year-old Franklin Delano Roosevelt prepared to speak to the nation in his inaugural address. Stricken by polio in 1921, the president-elect was unable to walk. He wore iron braces on his legs and gripped the arms of his sons in order to stand erect. This sets the scene for the gripping story Burns has to tell about the early New Deal, 1933–1934. It is the story of a crippled president who tried to save his crippled nation by bold and brilliant improvisations.

GLOSSARY

AGRICULTURAL ADJUSTMENT ADMINISTRATION (AAA) A New Deal agency designed to relieve Depression-wracked farmers, who suffered from falling prices and mounting crop surpluses. Established in 1933, the AAA subsidized farm prices until they reached a point of "parity." The AAA also sought to reduce agricultural surpluses by telling farmers how much to plant (acreage allotments) and paying them for what they did not grow. Declared unconstitutional by the Supreme Court in 1935, the AAA was superceded by the Soil Conservation and Domestic Allotment Act.

BERLE, JR., ADOLF A. A clergyman's son, Berle was a valuable member of FDR's Brain Trust. Berle was the author of *The Modern Corporation and Private Property* (1932) and worked to win the support of the business community for the New Deal.

BRAIN TRUST Special group of advisers led by eminent political economists Raymond Moley, Rexford Guy Tugwell, and Adolf A. Berle, Jr.

BYRD, HARRY F. Conservative Democratic senator from Virginia, Byrd often opposed the New Deal and advocated a return to a balanced budget and greater states' rights.

CIVILIAN CONSERVATION CORPS (CCC) Created in 1933, the CCC employed over two million young people, who came mainly from urban families on relief, to work in the nation's parks and recreational facilities. CCC employees received thirty dollars per month to plant trees, build trails, and work on soil conservation.

CIVIL WORKS ADMINISTRATION (CWA) Created in 1933, with Harry Hopkins at its head, the CWA put over four million people to work on "light" projects such as building roads and playgrounds. In its one-year existence, the CWA provided money for many unskilled workers who, because of the Depression, were unemployed and desperate.

CHURCHILL, WINSTON In the spring of 1940, when World War II in Europe was only seven months old, Churchill replaced the disgraced Neville Chamberlain as the United Kingdom's prime minister. Churchill's courage bolstered Great Britain during its darkest hours when the bombing of the German *Luftwaffe* almost destroyed the country.

GARNER, JOHN NANCE Former speaker of the House of Representatives, this Texan served as FDR's vice president from 1933 to 1941. Garner split with Roosevelt over the administration's failure to balance the budget and its refusal to oppose the labor movement's sit-down strikes.

GLASS, CARTER Conservative Democratic senator from Virginia, Glass frequently opposed FDR's monetary policies. Glass was a tenacious foe of the NRA, which he believed promoted monopolies and kept consumer prices high.

GREEN, WILLIAM President of the American Federation of Labor, Green was a respected leader of the organized labor movement in the 1930s.

HOPKINS, HARRY Director of the Works Progress Administration (WPA) and later secretary of commerce, Hopkins was one of Roosevelt's closest and most trusted advisors. Although weakened by cancer, Hopkins vigorously organized the Cabinet to prepare the nation for war.

HUGHES, CHARLES EVANS A former governor of New York and moderate Supreme Court justice, Hughes was the nominee of the Republican party in the presidential election of 1916. He later became President Harding's secretary of state and served as Chief Justice to the Supreme Court from 1930 to 1941.

ICKES, HAROLD "Honest Harold" served as Roosevelt's secretary of the interior and head of the Public Works Administration (PWA).

JOHNSON, HUGH Director of the National Recovery Administration (NRA), Johnson helped devise voluntary codes of fair competition and used public relations and propaganda to persuade employers to adhere to them.

LEWIS, JOHN L. Head of the United Mine Workers, Lewis was the driving force behind the creation of the Committee for Industrial Organization (CIO). Although a lifelong Republican, he campaigned for Roosevelt in 1936 and brought most of the labor movement into the Democratic camp. Lewis argued that "capitalism need not be uprooted, but its fruits must be more equally distributed."

MOLEY, RAYMOND A former Columbia University college professor, Moley was a shrewd and valuable member of FDR's Brain Trust. He also served as assistant secretary of state. Moley admired Roosevelt's courageous efforts to end the Depression, the greatest economic crisis in American history. Moley said FDR "was like the fairy-story prince who didn't know how to shudder."

NATIONAL RECOVERY ADMINISTRATION (NRA) Established in 1933, this New Deal agency sought to end unemployment by devising "industrial fair practice codes." It often impeded competition by authorizing production quotas and price fixing. In 1935, the Supreme Court declared the NRA unconstitutional.

PERKINS, FRANCES The first woman to serve in a presidential cabinet, Perkins was Roosevelt's secretary of labor from 1933 to 1945. She mediated bitter labor disputes and helped write the Social Security Act of 1935, the National Labor Relations Act of 1935, and other important New Deal legislation.

PUBLIC WORKS ADMINISTRATION (PWA) Created in 1933, with Harold Ickes at its head, the PWA focused on "heavy" projects such as building bridges and schools.

ROGERS, WILL This popular humorist was an astute observer of the American way of life. His sardonic assessments of political leaders made him into a legend.

TENNESSEE VALLEY AUTHORITY (TVA) In 1933, Congress created this public corporation, which focused on regional planning. The TVA completed a dam at Muscle Shoals, Alabama, on the Tennessee River, and improved or built many other dams, which all but ended flooding in the region. The TVA also generated and sold inexpensive electricity to thousands of rural Americans who had never had it before.

TUGWELL, REXFORD GUY A valuable member of Roosevelt's Brain Trust, Tugwell was an expert on agriculture.

Washington, D.C., March 4, 1933: Perched on the icy branches of the gaunt trees overlooking the Capitol's east front, they waited for the ceremony to which they had no tickets: an old man in ancient, patched-up green tweeds; a pretty young redhead in a skimpy coat; an older woman in rags, her face lined with worry and pain; a college boy whose father was jobless. They watched the crowd below as rumors drifted through that Roosevelt had been shot, that the whole area was covered by army machine guns. The older woman prayed on her tree limb: "No more trouble, please, God. No more trouble."

They watched as dignitaries straggled down the Capitol steps: Herbert Hoover, morose and stony-faced; Chief Justice Charles Evans Hughes, his white beard fluttering a bit in the cold wind; Vice President [John Nance] Garner, shivering without an overcoat; finally Franklin D. Roosevelt, moving down the steps with agonizing slowness on the arm of his son James. They watched as the new President took the oath of office, his hand lying on the 300-year-old Roosevelt family Bible, open at Paul's First Epistle to the Corinthians: "though I have faith . . . and have not charity, I am nothing." And they watched as, still unsmiling, he gripped the rostrum firmly and looked out at the crowd.

"I am certain that my fellow Americans expect that on my induction into the Presidency I will address them with a candor and a decision which the present situation of our Nation impels." The cold wind riffled the pages of his text.

"This great nation will endure as it has endured, will revive and will prosper." The President's words rang out across the plaza. "So, first of all, let me assert my firm belief that the only thing we have to fear is fear itself—nameless, unreasoning, unjustified terror which paralyzes needed efforts to convert retreat into advance."

The great crowd stood in almost dead silence. Chin outthrust, face grave, Roosevelt went on: "In every dark hour of our national life a leadership of frankness and vigor has met with that understanding and support of the people themselves which is essential to victory."

The crowd began to respond as it caught the cadence of the phrases: "The money changers have fled from their high seats in the temple of our civilization. . . .

"This Nation asks for action, and action now. Our greatest primary task is to put people to work." The throng stirred to these words. The President gave the core of what would become the first New Deal programs. He touched on foreign policy only vaguely and briefly.

"In the field of world policy I would dedicate this Nation to the policy of the good neighbor—the neighbor who resolutely respects himself and, because he does so, respects the rights of others. . . ."

He hoped that the Constitution, with its normal balance of presidential and congressional power, would be adequate to the crisis. But if Congress did not respond to his proposals or act on its own, and if the national emergency continued, "I shall ask the Congress for the one remaining instrument to meet the crisis—broad Executive power to wage a war against the emergency, as great as the power that would be given to me if we were in fact invaded by a foreign foe." The American people wanted direct, vigorous action.

"They have asked for discipline and direction under leadership. They have made me the present instrument of their wishes. . . ."

As Roosevelt ended, he was still grim; but his face lighted up when the crowd seemed to come to life. The old man in the tree had broken into tears. "It was very, very solemn, and a little terrifying," Eleanor Roosevelt said later to reporters in the White House. "The crowds were so tremendous, and you felt that they would do anything—if only someone would tell them what to do."

Someone would. The new President had no sooner reviewed the inaugural parade and hosted a White House reception for a thousand guests than he swore in his cabinet en masse upstairs in the Oval Room. Washington had come alive with rumor and hope. Even while couples waltzed gaily at the inaugural balls, haggard men conferred hour after hour in the huge marble buildings along Pennsylvania Avenue. Republican holdovers and Democrats newly arrived in Washington sat side by side, telephoning anxious bankers, drawing up emergency orders, all the while feeling the financial pulse of the nation and world. . . .

At the center of the action sat Franklin Roosevelt, presiding, instructing, wheedling, persuading, enticing, pressuring, negotiating, manipulating, conceding, horse-trading, placating, mediating—leading and following, leading and misleading. People marveled how the President, his cigarette holder deployed more jauntily than ever, appeared to bounce and skip through the day, despite his inability to walk, as he punctuated solemn conferences with jests, long and somewhat imaginary stories, and great booming laughter. While still in bed in the morning, his large torso looming over legs that hardly ribbed the sheets, he spouted ideas, questions, instructions to his aides. Wheeled over to the west wing, he swung into his office chair for long hours of visitors, letters, telephone calls, emergency sessions.

Calvin Coolidge had allegedly disposed of visitors by a simple formula: "Don't talk back to 'em." Roosevelt used talk as a tool of influence, outtalking his advisers, outtalking department heads, even outtalking visiting senators.

The President soon proved himself an artist in government—in his fine sense of timing, his adroit application of pressure, his face-to-face persuasiveness, his craft in playing not only foes but friends off against one another. Like a creative artist, Frances Perkins said, he would begin his picture "without a clear idea of what he intends to paint or how it shall be laid out upon the canvas, and then, as he paints, his plan evolves out of the material he is painting." He could think and feel his way into political situations with imagination, intuition, insight.

These traits dominated his policy thinking as well as his political calculating—and with less success. People close to Roosevelt were dismayed by his casual and disorderly intellectual habits. To Adolf Berle his judgments of people and ideas were "primarily instinctive and not rational," his learning came not from books but from people. He read not books but newspapers, perhaps half a dozen before breakfast—devoured them "like a combine eating up grain," a friend noted. He was not so much a creator of ideas as a broker of them. He did not assemble his ideas into a comprehensive and ordered program, with priorities and interconnections. Just as he lived each day for itself, as he liked to tell friends, so he appeared to flirt with each idea as it came along.

Everything seemed to conspire to fortify these intellectual habits of the new President—his eclectic education and reading, the ideologically divided party he led, the factionalized Congress he confronted, above all the advisers he had chosen and who had chosen him. His chief brain truster during 1933 was Ray Moley. Prickly and hard-driving, the former Columbia professor—now Assistant Secretary of State—shared some of his boss's political shrewdness and opportunism, intuitive judgment, and keenness in evaluating friend and foe. But Roosevelt also talked at length with Berle about banking, railroad, and monetary problems, and Berle's ideas for raising business to a higher level of efficiency and responsibility; with Tugwell about conservation, agriculture, and industrial discipline, and Tugwell's notions of democratic planning of the economy. . . .

Most remarkable of all was that one-woman brain trust, Eleanor Roosevelt—and all the more influential for not being viewed in that role. Through quick visits to her husband while he was still breakfasting in bed, little chits and memos, thick reports infiltrated into the executive offices, the visitors she invited to the White House, and her own influence on public opinion and Washington attitudes, she soon became a penetrating voice for the humanitarian liberal-left. Through a wide correspondence—she received 300,000 pieces of mail the first year—her press conferences and newspaper columns, her speeches and magazine articles, her widely advertised (and criticized) trips to CCC camps and coal mines, she began to build up a potentially powerful constituency of her own. Historian Mary Beard wrote admiringly of her ability to give "inspiration to the married, solace to the lovelorn, assistance to the homemaker, menus to the cook, and help to the educator, direction to the employer, caution to the warrior, and deeper awareness of its primordial force to the 'weaker sex.'" The First Lady also served as a model for other women in Washington government. Her close friend Frances Perkins, with her labor and urban concerns and constituencies, had special access to both Roosevelts, and women . . . learned that they could be, all at the same time, competent, caring, and controversial.

Such was the flux and flow of advice to the President that no one really knew which advisers were influential or why or when. Who was having the President's ear at the moment provoked jealousies worthy of the royal courts of old. The President's mind seemed awesomely accessible—to the kitchen cabinet, to department heads like Ickes and Perkins, to experts coming through Washington. The President would be seen talking animatedly with men regarded by the orthodox—though not necessarily by history—as quacks.

Roosevelt was following no set course, left, right, or center. He was leading by guess and by God. He not only admitted to playing by ear but boasted of it. He was a football quarterback, he told reporters, calling a new play after he saw how the last one turned out. Snap judgments had to be made. But Washington wondered what lay back of the snap judgments—some ideology or philosophy?

Neither of these, but rather a loose collection of values—Roosevelt's warm humanitarianism, his belief

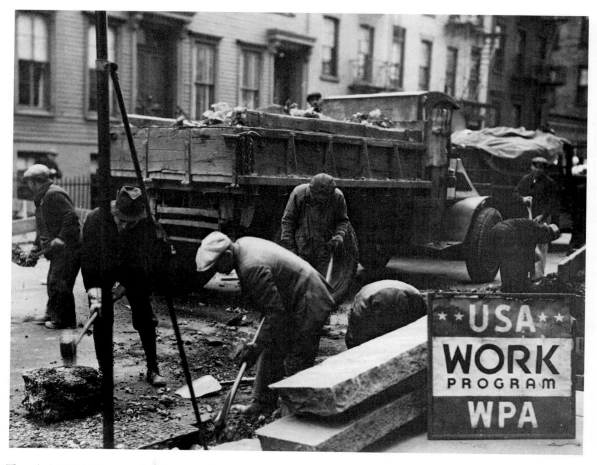

Through the Works Progress Administration, the New Deal put unemployed men like these to work on a variety of projects, from building bridges in the cities to blazing nature trails in the wilderness.

The workers shown here are widening a street. This creative agency also employed writers to do guidebooks to the states and artists to draw murals for government buildings. (The Bettmann Archive)

that the needy must be helped, that government must step in when private institutions could not do the job, and that now—in 1933—this meant the federal government. The President also had a fine grasp of political and governmental nuts and bolts. But between the two levels of grand philosophy and policy specifics he would be experimental, eclectic, nonprogrammatic, nondoctrinaire. He would be a broker of ideas as well as of interests and individuals.

As a master broker Roosevelt presided over a grand concert of interests. Labor, farmers, businessmen, investors, unemployed youth, some of the poor—all got a slice of the first New Deal, at least

on paper. FDR assumed the role of bipartisan leader, "president of all the people," virtually the national father. He happily cited a Nebraska congressman's definition of the New Deal as an effort "to cement our society, rich and poor, manual worker and brain worker, into a voluntary brotherhood of freemen, standing together, striving together, for the common good of all." Government, he told a convention of bankers, was "essentially the outward expression of the unity and the leadership of all groups." All this seemed a long cry from the "discipline and direction under leadership" he had promised in his inaugural address.

Congress, though more responsive to regional and special interests, quickened to the energy that radiated from the President. Even some Republicans fell over themselves to express support for the Democratic Roosevelt. In many respects the Chief Executive was Chief Legislator. Congress was by no means supine. Conservative Democratic senators like Carter Glass and Harry F. Byrd of Virginia usually opposed the President's bills. Congress as a whole, however, was more positive than even Roosevelt toward the New Deal. Many congressmen wanted more inflation than Roosevelt, ampler spending for people's needs, greater generosity to veterans and farmers, bigger public works, tougher policies toward Wall Street. The President skillfully brokered with the congressional left. For the conservative Democrats in the Senate he had growing hostility. Byrd opposed the AAA, FDR told Tugwell, because, as an apple grower, "he's afraid you'll force him to pay more than ten cents an hour for his apple pickers."

As master broker Roosevelt for a time could stay above the political and ideological battles raging around him. In the distribution of good things—whether government money or patronage jobs or social policy or his smile of approval—he could act as transactional leader within the existing system. He might give TVA to the left and economy to the right, but as a compromising broker rather than ideological leader he would not move decisively left or right. Social justice, he said, "ought not to consist of robbing Peter to pay Paul."

It all seemed to work beautifully for a time. Employment, prices, income all soared in the weeks after the Hundred Days. The industrial production index nearly doubled from March to July. Unemployment fell off from around 15 million at the time of Roosevelt's inaugural to about 11 million in October, a drop in the jobless rate from about 30 to about 22 percent.

Roosevelt's popularity floated high on this first gust of recovery. "If he burned down the capitol," said Will Rogers, "we would cheer and say, 'well, we at least got a fire started anyhow.'"

He won praise from Bertie McCormick's Republican Chicago *Tribune* and William Randolph Hearst's New York *American*. Daily, White House mailmen hauled in sacks of mail, most of it laudatory, some of it fulsome. An adviser found the President happily leafing through a sheaf of this mail. He was sorting letters he had received from British subjects addressing him as "Your Majesty" or "Lord Roosevelt" or in other monarchical terms. Why? He wanted to send them to King George V for his "amusement." History has not recorded that His Majesty was amused.

Psychology overwhelmed economics. In sad reality at least 10 million Americans remained jobless in 1933, and industrial production was still far below that of the prosperity years and even the first year of the depression. In October 3 million families—at least 12 million people—still depended on unemployment relief of about $23 a month, which covered food but left little or nothing for rent and utilities. But people *felt* better—and this was largely Roosevelt's doing. He exuded cheerfulness. He raised hopes and expectations. Above all, he *acted;* for several months he simply dominated the front pages of the nation's newspapers with his speeches, bill-signings, trips, executive orders, pronunciamentos.

His fireside chats carried his buoyant presence directly into home and hearth. "I want to talk for a few minutes with the people of the United States about banking," he said at the start of his first fireside chat in mid-March. "I want to tell you what has been done in the last few days, why it was done, and what the next steps are going to be." And he proceeded to do just that, in simple, human terms. Read later in cold print, the chats seemed a bit limp and pedestrian. Read by Roosevelt over the radio, they sounded warm, intimate, homely. Watching him deliver a fireside chat, Frances Perkins sensed that he could actually see the families listening at the other end. "His face would smile and light up as though he were actually sitting on the front porch or in the parlor with them." The President took care not to overuse this device, giving only four chats the first year, at two- or three-month intervals.

Nor did he overstrain the press conference as a way of reaching people. He held these twice a week, to the joy of the White House press corps, but the

FDR was the first president to effectively use mass communication. His radio "fireside chats" comforted Americans during the darkest moments of the Depression. Frances Perkins observed that Roosevelt's "face would smile and light up" when he delivered *these broadcasts to the American people. It was "as though he were actually sitting on the front porch or in the parlor with them," Perkins said. (Bettmann/CORBIS)*

sessions were often more frustrating than rewarding to the reporters. Roosevelt was a master at withholding information. He spent much of the half hour jovially fencing and parrying with the reporters, or offering them tidbits, or lecturing them. Crowding around the President's gadget-covered desk, the correspondents pressed him hard, with mixed results. Roosevelt wanted to control the flow of information, to create his own sensations, to set his own timing. He was not the first or the last President to do all this; he was simply more effective than most.

Nothing epitomized the New Deal in action better than the National Recovery Act and Administration—epitomized Roosevelt's Concert of Interests, his role of broker, the psychological impact of the Hundred Days, the fundamental problems of the "broker state" at work. As boss of NRA, Roosevelt chose General Hugh Johnson, who was a mass of contradictions himself—outwardly a tough old cavalryman with a leathery face, squint eyes, and a rough bark of a voice, inwardly an amalgam of public commitment, touchy ego, maudlin sentimentality, business savvy, and as clamorous and picturesque as a sideshow barker. The general's first job was to persuade employers to draw up codes of fair competition, a task he attacked like a cavalry charge. Once approved by the President and given the force of law, the codes were designed to discourage wasteful, junglelike competition by setting more orderly pricing and marketing policies, and to benefit workers by establishing higher wages, shorter hours, better working conditions, and the end of child labor. As part of the deal, anti-trust policies would be softened so that businessmen could cooperate in setting up the codes. Code signers could affix the "Blue Eagle" label to products and shopwindows.

With Johnson as bugler, the NRA galvanized the American people like a national call to arms. Suddenly the Blue Eagle was everywhere—on magazine covers, in the movies, on girls in chorus lines. (But not on Ford cars; Henry Ford perversely refused to sign the automobile code, then lived up to it anyway.) Rushing from city to city in an army plane, dishing out Boy Scout–style enthusiasm, biting criticism, and wisecracks at every stop, Johnson pressured and coaxed businessmen to endorse the codes, then gathered them in Washington for the signing and orating. As the very personification of recovery, the general staged a monster Blue Eagle parade on New York's Fifth Avenue. For hours he reviewed the parade of a quarter million persons, with another million and a half cheering from the sidewalks. Not since 1917 had Americans savored such a throbbing sense of marching unity.

As the months passed, though, the questions became more and more urgent: Unity for what? Marching to where? Under pressure for quick results, Johnson dealt with the business and labor leaders closest at hand, those who were most vocal, best organized, most skillful in dealing with bureaucrats and politicians. Inevitably he delegated crucial pricing and production decisions to the dominant interests, which often turned out to be the biggest corporations. . . .

Union labor, being organized, fared better under NRA. Section 7(a) of the act boldly proclaimed that employees "shall have the right to organize and bargain collectively through representatives of their own choosing, and shall be free from the interference, restraint, or coercion of employers" in choosing their representatives. No one seeking or holding a job "shall be required as a condition of employment to join any company union or to refrain from joining, organizing, or assisting a labor organization of his own choosing." Union leaders greeted this as labor's Magna Carta—comparable to Lincoln's Emancipation Proclamation, said John L. Lewis—and the message was clear: Organize. "THE PRESIDENT WANTS YOU TO JOIN A UNION," placards read. "Forget about injunctions, yellow dog contracts, black lists and the fear of dismissal." But there were complications. President William Green and the American Federation of Labor old guard wanted to organize workers into separate craft unions, even in huge auto plants, while Lewis and the rising young militants around him wanted to organize all the workers in a plant or company or industry into big, solid industrial unions.

Employers bridled at 7(a). Many set up company unions—or "employee representation plans"—which came to be run by company stooges. Labor responded with a rash of strikes during the summer of 1933; by September nearly 300,000 workers had walked out. The "concert of interests" seemed to be emitting discordant noises. "N.R.A. means National Run Around," read a sign hoisted on a picket line. The President set up special boards, trimmed NRA's power, eased Johnson out, and put in more domesticated chiefs, but to little avail; during 1934 the NRA eagle fluttered through heavy weather.

In the end the significance of the National Recovery Administration was not its impact on economic recovery, which was mixed, but its curbing of child labor, sweatshops, and unfair trade practices, its big boost to unionization and its modest protection to consumers. Why then was the NRA finally dismissed as a failure, even privately by Roosevelt himself? Largely because it failed in its highly touted supreme aim of bringing capital, labor, and other interests into a happy concert under the "Broker State," and by artificially raising prices and restricting production, it only marginally helped produce recovery.

If the Concert of Interests did not work, what would? Public works, the companion piece to the NRA, was launched with little of the drama of the Blue Eagle, under the leadership of one of the most committed and stout-hearted New Dealers, Secretary of the Interior Harold Ickes. Touchy and cantankerous, suspicious of friend and foe—and especially of government contractors— "Honest Harold" did not hesitate to use government snoopers to check on suspect PWA employees and their financial connections. Ickes was in no great hurry; his big projects needed careful planning and budgeting as well as laborious scrutiny by the secretary himself. When the public works program finally got underway it built gas and electric power plants, jails and hospitals, sewage and water systems, bridges, docks, and tunnels—and aircraft carriers, cruisers, destroyers, army and navy airplanes. But the $9 billion that PWA ultimately spent were not central to recovery during Roosevelt's first two years.

Much quicker to get underway was the federal relief program under a lanky young ex-director of private welfare programs named Harry Hopkins, who acted almost as fast as he talked. Appointed Federal Emergency Relief Administrator with a grant of half a billion dollars, Hopkins began authorizing millions of dollars in relief even while he was waiting in a hallway to be moved into his office. Since he could give money only to the state and local public relief agencies, which in turn administered relief programs, he could do little more than monitor the levels of compassion and competence with which programs were carried out. Behind his cynical, wisecracking façade Hopkins was deeply concerned with guarding the dignity, pride, and self-esteem of people on relief. Hence he was eager that the unemployed be given jobs and not merely handouts, but job programs cost more money. Late in 1933 Hopkins persuaded Roosevelt to launch a massive crash program to employ 4 million. In its brief existence, the Civil Works Administration undertook the building or rebuilding of vast numbers of roads, parks, schools, playgrounds, swimming pools, and other "light," short-term projects, in contrast to the PWA's "heavy" jobs.

It was this massive spending on work relief, supplemented by that of the PWA, the TVA, the CCC, the AAA, and other programs, that in 1933 and 1934 provided the central thrust of the early New Deal. It was not really planned that way; Roosevelt was responding not to grand ideology or to grand economics but to sheer human needs that he recognized and that Eleanor Roosevelt, Hopkins, Perkins, and the others brought to him. . . .

The public . . . saw a President who was doing his damnedest, quick to confront specific problems, brilliant at explaining his deeds and hopes, always positive, exuberant, seemingly on top of things. The public saw a leader.

For that public the ultimate test was economic recovery, and the flush of prosperity felt strong by fall 1934, compared to the miseries of March 1933. Could "bucks" be converted to ballots? A third of the senators and all the representatives were up for reelection. Roosevelt's tactic was to stand above the party battle, in line with his bipartisan posture of "leader of all the people." But he helped friendly candidates indirectly, and he posed the campaign issue by asking in a fireside chat, "Are you better off than you were last year? Are your debts less burdensome? Is your bank account more secure? Are your working conditions better? Is your faith in your own individual future more firmly grounded?"

The result was a resounding verdict for the President and his New Deal. Typically Presidents lost ground in midterm congressional elections, but in 1934 Democratic strength rose from 313 to 322 in the House and—incredibly—from 59 to 69 in the Senate. A clutch of highly conservative Republican senators was sacked. "Some of our friends think the majority top-heavy," Garner wrote the President, "but if properly handled, the House and Senate will be all right and I am sure you can arrange that."

Next month a late vote came in from Britain. "The courage, the power and the scale" of Roosevelt's effort, wrote Winston Churchill, "must enlist the ardent sympathy of every country, and his success could not fail to lift the whole world forward into the sunlight of an easier and more genial age." The British Conservative was seeking to place Roosevelt in the broadest sweep of history.

"Roosevelt is an explorer who has embarked on a voyage as uncertain as that of Columbus, and upon a quest which might conceivably be as important as the discovery of the New World."

With the early New Deal behind him, Roosevelt continued his bold experimentation throughout the 1930s. But the treacherous Depression continued to plague Americans. Too many teachers saw hungry children in their classrooms. Too many unemployed men committed "altruistic suicides" because they felt guilty about failing to feed their families. A man who had not had a steady job in over two years lamented: "Sometimes I feel like a murderer. What's wrong with me, that I can't protect my children?" In sum, the New Deal failed to end the Depression—America's entry into World War II would finally do that. Roosevelt had failed to devise a coherent strategy for dealing with the country's economic woes and to restore consumer purchasing power—the key to successful economic recovery.

Nevertheless, the New Deal accomplished many things. It provided relief for millions of Americans, protected the organizing and bargaining rights of labor, and saved the farmers through a system of price supports and acreage allotments. To those who were hurting, the New Deal represented a government that cared. And it made people feel better. Recall what Burns said: "This was largely Roosevelt's doing. He exuded cheerfulness. He raised hopes and expectations. Above all, he acted." And common Americans loved him for it. "He was my friend," said a man in Denver. Comparing Roosevelt's reforms to the relative inaction of the Hoover administration, historian William Manchester concluded that if FDR had "been another Hoover, the United States would have followed seven Latin American countries whose governments had been overthrown by Depression victims."

QUESTIONS TO CONSIDER

1 As FDR's inauguration day approached, what was the plight of the unemployed in American cities and the destitute farmers in the countryside? Why was Roosevelt's inaugural address, on that cold March day in 1933, one of the most important presidential speeches in American history?

2 Describe FDR's work habits and his approach toward problem solving. Why was Eleanor called FDR's "one woman brain trust"? Does the author believe that the early New Deal had an ideological focus? Or does he view it as emergency legislation designed to help those people who were hurting the most? Explain your answer by providing specific examples.

3 In describing America's mood in Roosevelt's first Hundred Days, Burns states that "psychology overwhelmed economics." Explain what his assessment means. What methods did FDR use to influence public opinion?

4 What were the goals of the NRA? What leadership qualities did Hugh Johnson bring to that New Deal agency? Describe the impact of the NRA, Section 7(a), on the labor movement.

5 Contrast the personalities and leadership styles of Harold Ickes and Harry Hopkins. What "heavy" jobs did the PWA undertake and what "light" tasks did the CWA initiate?

6 Describe how FDR was able to convert "bucks" into "ballots." How did most of the American people respond to the New Deal's first Hundred Days? How did Roosevelt's approach to solving the Depression compare to that of Herbert Hoover (selection 16)?

PART NINE

A World at War (1937–1945)

18 Franklin and Eleanor: The Early Wartime White House

DORIS KEARNS GOODWIN

For the first thirty-nine years of his life, success came easily to Franklin Delano Roosevelt. Born into a wealthy and prominent family in upstate New York (Theodore Roosevelt was a distant cousin), Franklin was a pampered only child who grew into a gregarious, handsome, and athletic young man. Educated at the finest private schools and graduated from Harvard, he chose politics for a career. With wealth and privilege, a famous name, powerful family connections, and a winning personality, he had every reason to believe that he would go far in politics, perhaps all the way to the White House. In 1905 he married his fifth cousin, Eleanor Roosevelt, a remarkably intelligent young woman who would prove to be as politically astute as her affable husband.

But in 1921 Roosevelt's world collapsed. He was stricken with polio, which left both legs paralyzed. He had to wear heavy metal braces on them and could get about only in a wheel chair or on crutches. For a man who had never had to struggle for success, Roosevelt could easily have submitted to his disability, left politics, and lived the rest of his life in the beautiful Roosevelt manor overlooking the Hudson River. Instead, his great inner strength enabled him not only to survive his "trial by fire," but also to continue and succeed brilliantly in politics. What is more, as Eleanor put it, his "great suffering" gave him "a greater sympathy and understanding of the problems of mankind."

In the following selection, prize-winning historian Doris Kearns Goodwin agrees with Eleanor's assessment. After his ordeal with polio, Franklin now "seemed less arrogant, less smug, less superficial, more focused, more complex, more interesting." Yet, as Goodwin reminds us, Roosevelt had his share of human frailties, which led him into an extramarital affair with his wife's social secretary, Lucy Mercer. If polio was the great test of Franklin's life, the discovery of his infidelity was

Eleanor's. Drawing on her own inner strength, Eleanor not only survived her husband's betrayal, but grew stronger from it and went on to become his indispensable political ally and the most influential first lady in American history.

Goodwin helps us understand the remarkable Roosevelt partnership against the backdrop of the early stages of the Second World War. That war began in Europe when powerful German forces invaded Poland in 1939. The United States, although theoretically neutral, was clearly sympathetic with the Allies, led by Britain and France. Indeed, Roosevelt was more preoccupied with the Nazi threat in Europe than with Japanese aggression in Asia. Time and again, he predicted that Hitler would eventually make war on the United States, and out of that belief flowed much of his European diplomacy: the destroyers-for-bases deal with Britain, Lend-Lease, and the Atlantic Charter. Still, through 1940 and 1941, as German planes bombed Britain and German armies swept into the Soviet Union, the Roosevelt administration often seemed adrift, as though the president and his advisers were confused, helplessly caught in a vortex of events over which they had no control.

Japanese intentions in the Pacific were especially perplexing. Since 1937, Japan had been laying waste to China, seizing its coastal territory and murdering its civilians—200,000 of them in Nanking alone. Did Japan's aggression against China constitute an immediate threat to United States security? Was a showdown with Japan inevitable, as American military leaders insisted? While the United States watched Japanese movements in Asia, Congress declared economic war against Germany with the controversial Lend-Lease program, which gave $7 billion in military aid to embattled Britain. Soon American convoys were carrying supplies across the Atlantic. When German submarines, called U-boats, torpedoed several American vessels, many observers contended that war with Hitler was only a matter of time.

Meanwhile, the Japanese question had become increasingly confusing. In Tokyo, a party led by General Hideki Tojo and the military demanded that the United States be driven from the Pacific so that Japan could establish an Asian empire free of Western influence. But Prime Minister Fumimaro, a moderate, wanted to negotiate with the United States and directed his ambassador in America to present Washington with a set of proposals that might avoid war. At the same time, the war party proceeded with a top-secret plan to attack the United States Pacific Fleet at Pearl Harbor if negotiations failed. By early December 1941, United States analysts knew that the Japanese were preparing to strike, but almost no one thought them capable of launching an air attack from aircraft carriers against distant Hawaii. When Japanese planes did exactly that, in a day that would "live in infamy," Americans from Pearl Harbor to Washington were caught completely by surprise.

Like the assassination of President John F. Kennedy and the terrorist attacks against the World Trade Center and the Pentagon, Pearl Harbor was one of those crises that mark the people who experience them for the rest of their lives. Americans of the war generation would recall exactly what they were doing when they first heard the news on that fateful Sunday. Roosevelt himself, Goodwin states, felt "great bitterness and anger toward Japan for the treachery involved in carrying out this surprise attack while the envoys of the two countries were still talking."

For years, Roosevelt detractors have charged that the president deliberately sent the Pacific fleet to Pearl Harbor so that the Japanese could attack it and give him an excuse to involve the United States in the war. There are those who still make this argument. But Gordon W. Prange's studies At Dawn We Slept *(1981) and* Pearl Harbor: The Verdict of History *(1985) and the bulk of modern scholarship exonerate Roosevelt of such a monstrous accusation. Goodwin concurs, "It is inconceivable that Roosevelt, who loved the navy with a passion, would have intentionally sacrificed the heart of the fleet, much less the lives of thirty-five hundred American sailors and soldiers, without lifting a finger to reduce the risk."*

On the Monday after Pearl Harbor, December 8, 1941, the United States declared war on the Japanese Empire. Three days later, Germany and Italy—Japan's Axis allies—declared war on the United States. Roosevelt and Congress reciprocated at once, thus placing America on the side of the Allied powers—Great Britain, the Soviet Union, and China. Franklin told Eleanor: "I never wanted to fight this war on two fronts." But now there was no choice. Fortunately for Franklin, the political partnership he had formed with Eleanor would serve him well in the terrible years ahead.

GLOSSARY

BULLITT, WILLIAM   Roosevelt's pessimistic ambassador to France who sent the president dramatic descriptions of the German invasion. On May 30, 1940, he wrote Roosevelt that he might "get blown up before I see you again."

CHAMBERLAIN, NEVILLE   British prime minister who resigned in the spring of 1940, shamed by his attempts to "appease" Hitler and by England's lack of military preparedness when the German military rolled through the Low Countries and France.

CHURCHILL, WINSTON   See glossary in previous selection.

CUDAHY, JOHN   Roosevelt's ambassador to Belgium who, in May of 1940, informed the president of Hitler's assault on the Low Countries. Goodwin writes that Cudahy "had almost been knocked down by the force of a bomb which fell three hundred feet from the embassy."

EARLY, STEPHEN   Roosevelt's press secretary from the South who helped manage the president's crowded schedule. He frequently disagreed with Eleanor's outspoken advocacy of civil rights and believed the first lady would harm the president among southern white voters, who traditionally voted for the Democratic ticket.

HOPKINS, HARRY   See glossary in previous selection.

HOWE, LOUIS   In the years that FDR struggled with polio, he was Roosevelt's closest political adviser and confidant. Howe eventually helped Roosevelt make a dramatic reentry into the political arena. He also encouraged Eleanor to become more actively involved in politics. The former newspaperman died in 1936.

KENNEDY, JOSEPH P.   A successful and ruthless businessman, ambassador to Great Britain, and father of a future president. Roosevelt eventually lost faith in Kennedy because of the diplomat's pessimism over the ability of England to resist Nazi aggression.

KNOX, FRANK   In 1940, Roosevelt appointed him secretary of the navy even though Knox was a Republican and a critic of the New Deal. One of Knox's fondest memories was charging up San Juan Hill with Theodore Roosevelt.

LeHAND, MARGUERITE "MISSY"   Roosevelt's personal secretary, who grew very close to the president after Eleanor's discovery of her husband's extramarital affair with Lucy Mercer. Missy shared FDR's private moments and became, in Goodwin's words, "his other wife."

MARSHALL, GEORGE   Roosevelt's army chief of staff and later, under Harry Truman, an influential and important secretary of state in the postwar years. When Hitler began his aggression against Germany's neighbors, this blunt, honest solider realized how unprepared the United States was to fight another world war.

McDUFFIE, IRVIN   Roosevelt's valet who lived in the White House and helped dress the president and prepare him for bed. He was friendly and talkative but was plagued with a drinking problem, and Eleanor worried that he would fail the president. The disabled chief executive, however, could not find it in his heart to dismiss him.

MERCER, LUCY PAGE   Eleanor's social secretary who had a love affair with Franklin. When Eleanor discovered their love letters, she gave her husband an opportunity for a divorce. Faced with disgrace and a lost inheritance, he refused, but their marriage was forever changed.

MORGENTHAU, HENRY   Roosevelt's secretary of the treasury who acted quickly to freeze the assets of those countries that Hitler's forces had overrun, making certain that those funds would not fall into the hands of the Nazis.

NEUTRALITY LAWS   In the isolationist 1930s, Congress passed this legislation designed to avoid the mistakes of the Great War and keep the United States out of future foreign conflicts. These measures prohibited loans and shipments of arms to belligerents and hampered Roosevelt's efforts to help England and France as those nations struggled against Nazi aggression.

PERKINS, FRANCES   See glossary in previous selection.

PHONY WAR   Many Americans used this term to describe the first part of World War II when little fighting was done. From the German attack on Poland in September of 1939 to the march of the German army through western Europe in May of 1940, the United States remained isolationist and hopeful that Nazi aggression would not threaten American national security.

RIBBENTROP, JOACHIM VON   Hitler's foreign minister who weakly argued that Nazi aggression against the Low Countries and France was a response to a threatened attack against Germany.

STIMSON, HENRY L.   In 1940, Roosevelt appointed this Republican as the secretary of war to give his cabinet a bipartisan direction as America prepared for global combat. This extremely intelligent head of the eastern establishment had served every president since William McKinley.

TULLY, GRACE   The White House secretary who, when Missy LeHand suffered a stroke, became a valued aide to Roosevelt. Nonetheless, in Goodwin's words, "she never enjoyed the intimacy, playfulness, and absolute trust Missy had."

WATSON, EDWIN "PA"   Roosevelt's secretary and military aide. He came to know the president's temperaments and did his best to channel FDR's busy schedule into productive directions.

WOODRING, HENRY   Roosevelt's first secretary of war. An isolationist from Kansas, he did not understand the need to strengthen the armed forces in response to increased aggression in Europe and Asia. Tension built when Louis Johnson, an internationalist, became assistant secretary of war.

O n nights filled with tension and concern, Franklin Roosevelt performed a ritual that helped him to fall asleep. He would close his eyes and imagine himself at Hyde Park as a boy, standing with his sled in the snow atop the steep hill that stretched from the south porch of his home to the wooded bluffs of the Hudson River far below. As he accelerated down the hill, he maneuvered each familiar curve with perfect skill until he reached the bottom, whereupon, pulling his sled behind him, he started slowly back up until he reached the top, where he would once more begin his descent. Again and again he replayed this remembered scene in his mind, obliterating his awareness of the shrunken legs inert beneath the sheets, undoing the knowledge that he would never climb a hill or even walk on his own power again. Thus liberating himself from his paralysis through an act of imaginative will, the president of the United States would fall asleep.

Reprinted with the permission of Simon & Schuster Adult Publishing Group and Sll/Sterling Lord Litenstic, Inc., from *No Ordinary Time: Franklin and Eleanor Roosevelt: The Home Front in World War II* by Doris Kearns Goodwin. Copyright © 1994 by Doris Kearns Goodwin. All rights reserved.

The evening of May 9, 1940, was one of these nights. At 11 p.m., as Roosevelt sat in his comfortable study on the second floor of the White House, the long-apprehended phone call had come. Resting against the high back of his favorite red leather chair, a precise reproduction of one Thomas Jefferson had designed for work, the president listened as his ambassador to Belgium, John Cudahy, told him that Hitler's armies were simultaneously attacking Holland, Luxembourg, Belgium, and France. The period of relative calm—the "phony war" that had settled over Europe since the German attack on Poland in September of 1939—was over.

For days, rumors of a planned Nazi invasion had spread through the capitals of Western Europe. Now, listening to Ambassador Cudahy's frantic report that German planes were in the air over the Low Countries and France, Roosevelt knew that the all-out war he feared had finally begun. In a single night, the tacit agreement that, for eight months, had kept the belligerents from attacking each other's territory had been shattered.

As he summoned his military aide and appointments secretary, General Edwin "Pa" Watson, on this spring evening of the last year of his second term, Franklin

Roosevelt looked younger than his fifty-eight years. Though his hair was threaded with gray, the skin on his handsome face was clear, and the blue eyes, beneath his pince-nez glasses, were those of a man at the peak of his vitality. His chest was so broad, his neck so thick, that when seated he appeared larger than he was. Only when he was moved from his chair would the eye be drawn to the withered legs, paralyzed by polio almost two decades earlier.

At 12:40 a.m., the president's press secretary, Stephen Early, arrived to monitor incoming messages. Bombs had begun to fall on Brussels, Amsterdam, and Rotterdam, killing hundreds of civilians and destroying thousands of homes. In dozens of old European neighborhoods, fires illuminated the night sky. Stunned Belgians stood in their nightclothes in the streets of Brussels, watching bursts of anti-aircraft fire as military cars and motorcycles dashed through the streets. A thirteen-year-old schoolboy, Guy de Liederkirche, was Brussels' first child to die. His body would later be carried to his school for a memorial service with his classmates. On every radio station throughout Belgium, broadcasts summoned all soldiers to join their units at once.

In Amsterdam the roads leading out of the city were crowded with people and automobiles as residents fled in fear of the bombing. Bombs were also falling at Dunkirk, Calais, and Metz in France, and at Chilham, near Canterbury, in England. The initial reports were confusing—border clashes had begun, parachute troops were being dropped to seize Dutch and Belgian airports, the government of Luxembourg had already fled to France, and there was some reason to believe the Germans were also landing troops by sea.

After speaking again to Ambassador Cudahy and scanning the incoming news reports, Roosevelt called his secretary of the Treasury, Henry Morgenthau, Jr., and ordered him to freeze all assets held by Belgium, the Netherlands, and Luxembourg before the market opened in the morning, to keep any resources of the invaded countries from falling into German hands.

The official German explanation for the sweeping invasion of the neutral lowlands was given by Germany's foreign minister, Joachim von Ribbentrop.

Germany, he claimed, had received "proof" that the Allies were engineering an imminent attack through the Low Countries into the German Ruhr district. In a belligerent tone, von Ribbentrop said the time had come for settling the final account with the French and British leaders. Just before midnight, Adolf Hitler, having boarded a special train to the front, had issued the fateful order to his troops: "The decisive hour has come for the fight today decides the fate of the German nation for the next 1000 years."

There was little that could be done that night— phone calls to Paris and Brussels could rarely be completed, and the Hague wire was barely working—but, as one State Department official said, "in times of crisis the key men should be at hand and the public should know it." Finally, at 2:40 a.m., Roosevelt decided to go to bed. After shifting his body to his armless wheelchair, he rolled through a door near his desk into his bedroom.

As usual when the president's day came to an end, he called for his valet, Irvin McDuffie, to lift him into his bed. McDuffie, a Southern Negro, born the same year as his boss, had been a barber by trade when Roosevelt met him in Warm Springs, Georgia, in 1927. Roosevelt quickly developed a liking for the talkative man and offered him the job of valet. Now he and his wife lived in a room on the third floor of the White House. In recent months, McDuffie's hard drinking had become a problem: on several occasions Eleanor had found him so drunk that "he couldn't help Franklin to bed." Fearing that her husband might be abandoned at a bad time, Eleanor urged him to fire McDuffie, but the president was unable to bring himself to let his old friend go, even though he shared Eleanor's fear.

McDuffie was at his post in the early hours of May 10 when the president called for help. He lifted the president from his wheelchair onto the narrow bed, reminiscent of the kind used in a boy's boarding school, straightened his legs to their full length, and then undressed him and put on his pajamas. Beside the bed was a white-painted table; on its top, a jumble of pencils, notepaper, a glass of water, a package of cigarettes, a couple of phones, a bottle of nose drops. On the floor beside the table stood a small basket—the Eleanor basket—in which the first lady regularly left memoranda, communications, and reports for the president to read—a sort of private post office between husband and wife. In the corner sat an old-fashioned rocking chair, and next to it a heavy wardrobe filled with the president's clothes. On the marble mantelpiece above the fireplace was an assortment of family photos and a collection of miniature pigs. "Like every room in any Roosevelt house," historian Arthur Schlesinger has written, "the presidential bedroom was hopelessly Victorian—old-fashioned and indiscriminate in its furnishings, cluttered in its decor, ugly and comfortable."

Outside Roosevelt's door, which he refused to lock at night as previous presidents had done, Secret Service men patrolled the corridor, alerting the guardroom to the slightest hint of movement. The refusal to lock his door was related to the president's dread of fire, which surpassed his fear of assassination or of anything else. The fear seems to have been rooted in his childhood, when, as a small boy, he had seen his young aunt, Laura, race down the stairs, screaming, her body and clothes aflame from an accident with an alcohol lamp. Her life was ended at nineteen. The fear grew when he became a paraplegic, to the point where, for hours at a time, he would practice dropping from his bed or chair to the floor and then crawling to the door so that he could escape from a fire on his own. "We assured him he would never be alone," his eldest son, Jimmy, recalled, "but he could not be sure, and furthermore found the idea depressing that he could not be left alone, as if he were an infant."

Roosevelt's nightly rituals tell us something about his deepest feelings—the desire for freedom, the quest for movement, and the significance, despite all his attempts to downplay it, of the paralysis in his life. In 1940, Roosevelt had been president of the United States for seven years, but he had been paralyzed from the waist down for nearly three times that long. Before he was stricken at thirty-nine, Roosevelt was a man who flourished on activity. He had served in the New York legislature for two years, been assistant secretary of the navy for seven years, and his party's candidate for vice-president in 1920. He loved to swim and to sail, to play tennis and golf; to run in the woods and ride horseback in the fields. To his daughter, Anna, he was always "very active physically," "a wonderful playmate who took long walks with you, sailed with you, could out-jump you and do a lot of things," while Jimmy saw him quite simply as "the handsomest, strongest, most glamorous, vigorous physical father in the world."

All that vigor and athleticism ended in August 1921 at Campobello, his family's summer home in New Brunswick, Canada, when he returned home from swimming in the pond with his children and felt too tired even to remove his wet bathing suit. The morning after his swim, his temperature was 102 degrees and he had trouble moving his left leg. By afternoon, the power to move his right leg was also gone, and soon he was paralyzed from the waist down. The paralysis had set in so swiftly that no one understood at first that it was polio. But once the diagnosis was made, the battle was joined. For years he fought to walk on his own power, practicing for hours at a time, drenched with sweat, as he tried unsuccessfully to move one leg in front of the other without the aid of a pair of crutches or a helping hand. That consuming and futile effort had to be abandoned once he became governor of New York in 1929 and then president in 1933. He was permanently crippled.

Yet the paralysis that crippled his body expanded his mind and his sensibilities. After what Eleanor called his "trial by fire," he seemed less arrogant, less smug, less superficial, more focused, more complex, more interesting. He returned from his ordeal with greater powers of concentration and greater self-knowledge. "There had been a plowing up of his nature," Labor Secretary Frances Perkins observed. "The man emerged completely warmhearted, with new humility of spirit and a firmer understanding of profound philosophical concepts."

He had always taken great pleasure in people. But now they became what one historian has called "his vital links with life." Far more intensely than before, he reached out to know them, to understand them, to pick up their emotions, to put himself into their shoes. No longer belonging to his old world in the same way, he came to empathize with the poor and underprivileged, with people to whom fate had dealt a difficult hand. Once, after a lecture in Akron, Ohio, Eleanor was asked how her husband's illness had affected him. "Anyone who has gone through great suffering," she said, "is bound to have a greater sympathy and understanding of the problems of mankind."

Through his presidency, the mere act of standing up with his heavy metal leg-braces locked into place was an ordeal. The journalist Eliot Janeway remembers being behind Roosevelt once when he was in his chair in the Oval Office. "He was smiling as he talked. His face and hand muscles were totally relaxed. But then, when he had to stand up, his jaws went absolutely rigid. The effort of getting what was left of his body up was so great his face changed dramatically. It was as if he braced his body for a bullet."

Little wonder, then, that, in falling asleep at night, Roosevelt took comfort in the thought of physical freedom.

The morning sun of Washington's belated spring was streaming through the president's windows on May 10, 1940. Despite the tumult of the night before, which had kept him up until nearly 3 a.m., he awoke at his usual hour of eight o'clock. Pivoting to the edge of the bed, he pressed the button for his valet, who helped him into the bathroom. Then, as he had done every morning for the past seven years, he threw his old blue cape over his pajamas and started his day with breakfast in bed—orange juice, eggs, coffee, and buttered toast—and the morning papers: *The New York Times* and the *Herald Tribune,* the *Baltimore Sun,* the *Washington Post* and the *Washington Herald.*

Headlines recounted the grim events he had heard at 11 p.m. the evening before. From Paris, Ambassador William Bullitt confirmed that the Germans had launched violent attacks on a half-dozen French military bases. Bombs had also fallen on the main railway connections between Paris and the border in an attempt to stop troop movements.

Before finishing the morning papers, the president held a meeting with Steve Early and "Pa" Watson, to review his crowded schedule. He instructed them to convene an emergency meeting at ten-thirty with the chiefs of the army and the navy, the secretaries of state and Treasury, and the attorney general. In addition, Roosevelt was scheduled to meet the press in the morning and the Cabinet in the afternoon, as he had done every Friday morning and afternoon for seven years. Later that night, he was supposed to deliver a keynote address at the Pan American Scientific Congress. After asking Early to delay the press conference an hour and to have the State Department draft a new speech, Roosevelt called his valet to help him dress.

While Franklin Roosevelt was being dressed in his bedroom, Eleanor was in New York, having spent the past few days in the apartment she kept in Greenwich Village, in a small house owned by her friends Esther Lape and Elizabeth Read. The Village apartment on East 11th Street, five blocks north of Washington Square, provided Eleanor with a welcome escape from the demands of the White House, a secret refuge whenever her crowded calendar brought her to New York. For decades, the Village, with its winding streets, modest brick houses, bookshops, tearooms, little theaters, and cheap rents, had been home to political, artistic, and literary rebels, giving it a colorful Old World character. . . .

The week before, at the Astor Hotel, Eleanor had been honored by *The Nation* magazine for her work in behalf of civil rights and poverty. More than a thousand people had filled the tables and the balcony of the cavernous ballroom to watch her receive a bronze plaque for "distinguished service in the cause of American social progress." Among the many speakers that night, Stuart Chase lauded the first lady's concentrated focus on the problems at home. "I suppose she worries about Europe like the rest of us," he began, "but she does not allow this worry to divert her attention from the homefront. She goes around America, looking at America, thinking about America . . . helping day and night with the problems

Crippled by polio in 1921, Roosevelt had to wear heavy metal braces on his legs and could not walk on his own. But in public, as this photograph shows, the president gave the impression that he was walking. He did this by using a cane with his right hand, clasping the arm of a supporter with his left arm, and then shifting his weight back and forth as he moved. In the White House, away from the public, he got about in a wheelchair. (UPI/Franklin D. Roosevelt Library)

of America." For, he concluded, "the New Deal is supposed to be fighting a war, too, a war against depression."

"What is an institution?" author John Gunther had asked when his turn to speak came. "An institution," he asserted, is "something that had fixity, permanence, and importance . . . something that people like to depend on, something benevolent as a rule, something we like." And by that definition, he concluded, the woman being honored that night was as great an institution as her husband, who was already being talked about for an unprecedented third term. Echoing Gunther's sentiments, NAACP head Walter White turned to Mrs. Roosevelt and said: "My dear, I don't care if the President runs for the third or fourth term as long as he lets you run the bases, keep the score and win the game."

For her part, Eleanor was slightly embarrassed by all the fuss. "It never seems quite real to me to sit at a table and have people whom I have always looked upon with respect . . . explain why they are granting me an honor," she wrote in her column describing the evening. "Somehow I always feel they ought to be talking about someone else." Yet, as she stood to speak that night at the Astor ballroom, rising nearly six feet, her wavy brown hair slightly touched by gray, her wide mouth marred by large buck teeth, her brilliant blue eyes offset by an unfortunate chin, she dominated the room as no one before her had done. . . .

It was this tireless commitment to democracy's unfinished agenda that led Americans in a Gallup poll taken that spring to rate Mrs. Roosevelt even higher than her husband, with 67 percent of those interviewed well disposed toward her activities. "Mrs. Roosevelt's incessant goings and comings," the survey suggested, "have been accepted as a rather welcome part of the national life. Women especially feel this way. But even men betray relatively small masculine impatience with the work and opinions of a very articulate lady. . . . The rich, who generally disapprove of Mrs. Roosevelt's husband, seem just as friendly toward her as the poor. . . . Even among those extremely anti-Roosevelt citizens who would regard a third term as a national disaster there is a generous minority . . . who want Mrs. Roosevelt to remain in the public eye."

The path to this position of independent power and respect had not been easy. Eleanor's distinguished career had been forged from a painful discovery when she was thirty-four. After a period of suspicion, she realized that her husband, who was then assistant secretary of the navy, had fallen in love with another woman, Lucy Page Mercer.

Tall, beautiful, and well bred, with a low throaty voice and an incomparably winning smile, Lucy Mercer was working as Eleanor's social secretary when the love affair began. For months, perhaps even years,

Franklin kept his romance a secret from Eleanor. Her shattering discovery took place in September 1918. Franklin had just returned from a visit to the European front. Unpacking his suitcase, she discovered a packet of love letters from Lucy. At this moment, Eleanor later admitted, "the bottom dropped out of my own particular world & I faced myself, my surroundings, my world, honestly for the first time."

Eleanor told her husband that she would grant him a divorce. But this was not what he wanted, or at least not what he was able to put himself through, particularly when his mother, Sara, was said to have threatened him with disinheritance if he left his marriage. If her son insisted on leaving his wife and five children for another woman, visiting scandal upon the Roosevelt name, she could not stop him. But he should know that she would not give him another dollar and he could no longer expect to inherit the family estate at Hyde Park. Franklin's trusted political adviser, Louis Howe, weighed in as well, warning Franklin that divorce would bring his political career to an abrupt end. There was also the problem of Lucy's Catholicism, which would prevent her from marrying a divorced man.

Franklin promised never to see Lucy again and agreed, so the Roosevelt children suggest, to Eleanor's demand for separate bedrooms, bringing their marital relations to an end. Eleanor would later admit to her daughter, Anna, that sex was "an ordeal to be borne." Something in her childhood had locked her up, she said, making her fear the loss of control that comes with abandoning oneself to one's passions, giving her "an exaggerated idea of the necessity of keeping all one's desires under complete subjugation." Now, supposedly, she was free of her "ordeal."

The marriage resumed. But for Eleanor, a path had opened, a possibility of standing apart from Franklin. No longer did she need to define herself solely in terms of his wants and his needs. Before the crisis, though marriage had never fulfilled her prodigious energies, she had no way of breaking through the habits and expectations of a proper young woman's role. To explore her independent needs, to journey outside her home for happiness, was perceived as dangerous and wrong.

With the discovery of the affair, however, she was free to define a new and different partnership with her husband, free to seek new avenues of fulfillment. It was a gradual process, a gradual casting away, a gradual gaining of confidence—and it was by no means complete—but the fifty-six-year-old woman who was being fêted in New York was a different person from the shy, betrayed wife of 1918.

Above the president's bedroom, in a snug third-floor suite, his personal secretary, Marguerite "Missy" LeHand, was already dressed, though she, too, had stayed up late the night before.

A tall, handsome woman of forty-one with large blue eyes and prematurely gray, once luxuriant black hair fastened by hairpins to the nape of her neck, Missy was in love with her boss and regarded herself as his other wife. Nor was she alone in her imaginings. "There's no doubt," White House aide Raymond Moley said, "that Missy was as close to being a wife as he ever had—or could have." White House maid Lillian Parks agreed. "When Missy gave an order, we responded as if it had come from the First Lady. We knew that FDR would always back up Missy." . . .

When Franklin contracted polio, Missy's duties expanded. Both Franklin and Eleanor understood that it was critical for Franklin to keep active in politics even as he struggled unsuccessfully day after day, month after month, to walk again. To that end, Eleanor adhered to a rigorous daily schedule as the stand-in for her husband, journeying from one political meeting to the next to ensure that the Roosevelt name was not forgotten. With Eleanor busily occupied away from home, Missy did all the chores a housewife might do, writing Franklin's personal checks, paying the monthly bills, giving the children their allowances, supervising the menus, sending the rugs and draperies for cleaning. . . .

By the time Roosevelt was president, she had become totally absorbed in his life—learning his favorite games, sharing his hobbies, reading the same books, even adopting his characteristic accent and patterns of speech. Whereas Eleanor was so opposed to gambling that she refused to play poker with Franklin's friends if even the smallest amount of money changed hands, Missy became an avid player, challenging Roosevelt at every turn, always ready to raise the ante. Whereas Eleanor never evinced any interest in her husband's treasured stamp collection, Missy was an enthusiastic partner, spending hours by his side as he organized and reorganized his stamps into one or another of his thick leather books. "In terms of companionship," Eliot Janeway observed, "Missy was the real wife. She understood his nature perfectly, as they would say in a nineteenth-century novel."

At 10:30 a.m., May 10, 1940, pushed along in his wheelchair by Mr. Crim, the usher on duty, and accompanied by his usual detail of Secret Service men, the president headed for the Oval Office. A bell announced his arrival to the small crowd already assembled in the Cabinet Room—Army Chief of Staff George Marshall, Navy Chief Admiral Harold Stark, Attorney General Robert Jackson, Secretary of Treasury Henry Morgenthau, Secretary of State Cordell Hull, and Undersecretary Sumner Welles. But first, as he did every day, the president poked his head into Missy's office, giving her a wave and a smile which, Missy told a friend, was all she needed to replenish the energies lost from too little sleep.

Of all the men assembled in the big white-walled Cabinet Room that morning, General George Catlett Marshall possessed the clearest awareness of how woefully unprepared America was to fight a major war against Nazi Germany. The fifty-nine-year-old Marshall, chief of operations of the First Army in World War I, had been elevated to the position of army chief of staff the previous year. The story is told of a meeting in the president's office not long before the appointment during which the president outlined a pet proposal. Everyone nodded in approval except Marshall. "Don't you think so, George?" the president asked. Marshall replied: "I am sorry, Mr. President, but I don't agree with that at all." The president looked stunned, the conference was stopped, and Marshall's friends predicted that his tour of duty would soon come to an end. A few months later, reaching thirty-four names down the list of senior generals, the

president asked the straight-speaking Marshall to be chief of staff of the U.S. Army. . . .

In 1940, the U.S. Army stood only eighteenth in the world, trailing not only Germany, France, Britain, Russia, Italy, Japan, and China but also Belgium, the Netherlands, Portugal, Spain, Sweden, and Switzerland. With the fall of Holland, the United States would rise to seventeenth! And, in contrast to Germany, where after years of compulsory military training nearly 10 percent of the population (6.8 million) were trained and ready for war, less than .5 percent of the American population (504,000) were on active duty or in the trained reserves. The offensive Germany had launched the morning of May 10 along the Western front was supported by 136 divisions; the United States could, if necessary, muster merely five fully equipped divisions.

In the spring of 1940, the United States possessed almost no munitions industry at all. So strong had been the recoil from war after 1918 that both the government and the private sector had backed away from making weapons. The result was that, while the United States led the world in the mass production of automobiles, washing machines, and other household appliances, the techniques of producing weapons of war had badly atrophied.

All through the winter and spring, Marshall had been trying to get Secretary of War Henry Woodring to understand the dire nature of this unpreparedness. But the former governor of Kansas was an isolationist who refused to contemplate even the possibility of American involvement in the European war. Woodring had been named assistant secretary of war in 1933 and then promoted to the top job three years later, when the price of corn and the high unemployment rate worried Washington far more than foreign affairs. As the European situation heated up, Roosevelt recognized that Woodring was the wrong man to head the War Department. But, try as he might, he could not bring himself to fire his secretary of war—or anyone else, for that matter.

Roosevelt's inability to get rid of anybody, even the hopelessly incompetent, was a chief source of the disorderliness of his administration, of his double-dealing and his tendency to procrastinate. "His real weakness," Eleanor Roosevelt observed, "was that—it came out of the strength really, or out of a quality—he had great sympathy for people and great understanding, and he couldn't bear to be disagreeable to someone he liked . . . and he just couldn't bring himself to really do the unkind thing that had to be done unless he got angry." . . .

The confusion multiplied when Roosevelt selected a staunch interventionist, Louis Johnson, the former national commander of the American Legion, as assistant secretary of war. Outspoken, bold, and ambitious, Johnson fought openly with Woodring, bringing relations to the sorry point where neither man spoke to the other. Paralyzed and frustrated, General Marshall found it incomprehensible that Roosevelt had allowed such a mess to develop simply because he disliked firing anyone. Years earlier, when Marshall had been told by his aide that a friend whom he had ordered overseas had said he could not leave because his wife was away and his furniture was not packed, Marshall had called the man himself. The friend explained that he was sorry. "I'm sorry, too," Marshall replied, "but you will be retired tomorrow."

Marshall failed to understand that there was a method behind the president's disorderly style. Though divided authority and built-in competition created insecurity and confusion within the administration, it gave Roosevelt the benefit of conflicting opinions. "I think he knew exactly what he was doing all the time," administrative assistant James Rowe observed. "He liked conflict, and he was a believer in resolving problems through conflict." With different administrators telling him different things, he got a better feel for what his problems were.

Their attitude toward subordinates was not the only point of dissimilarity between Roosevelt and Marshall. Roosevelt loved to laugh and play, closing the space between people by familiarity, calling everyone, even Winston Churchill, by his first name. In contrast, Marshall was rarely seen to smile or laugh on the job and was never familiar with anyone. . . .

As the officials sat in the Cabinet Room, at the great mahogany table under the stern, pinch-lipped stare of Woodrow Wilson, whose portrait hung above the fireplace, their primary reason for gathering together was to share the incoming information from Europe and to plan the American response. Ambassador John Cudahy in Brussels wired that he had almost been knocked down by the force of a bomb which fell three hundred feet from the embassy. From London, Ambassador Joseph P. Kennedy reported that the British had called off their Whitsun holiday, the long weekend on which Londoners traditionally acquired the tan that had to last until their August vacation—"tangible evidence," Kennedy concluded, "that the situation is serious."

Plans were set in motion for the army and navy to submit new estimates to the White House of what they would need to accomplish the seemingly insurmountable task of catching up with Germany's modern war machine. For, as Marshall had recently explained to the Congress, Germany was in a unique position. "After the World War practically everything was taken away from Germany in the way of materiel. So when Germany rearmed, it was necessary to produce a complete set of materiel for all the troops. As a result, Germany has an Army equipped throughout with the most modern weapons that could be turned out and that is a situation that has never occurred before in the history of the world." . . .

Seated at his desk with his back to the windows, Roosevelt faced the crowd that was now spilling into the Oval Office for his largest press conference ever. Behind him, set in standards, were the blue presidential flag and the American flag. "Like an opera singer about to go on the stage," Roosevelt invariably appeared nervous before a conference began, fidgeting with his cigarette holder, fingering the trinkets on his desk, exchanging self-conscious jokes with the reporters in the front row. Once the action started, however, with the doorkeeper's shout of "all-in," the president seemed to relax, conducting the flow of questions and conversation with such professional skill that the columnist Heywood Broun once called him "the best newspaperman who has ever been President of the United States."

For seven years, twice a week, the president had sat down with these reporters, explaining legislation, announcing appointments, establishing friendly contact, calling them by their first names, teasing them about their hangovers, exuding warmth and accessibility. Once, when a correspondent narrowly missed getting on Roosevelt's train, the president covered for him by writing his copy until he could catch up. Another time, when the mother of a bachelor correspondent died, Eleanor Roosevelt attended the funeral services, and then she and the president invited him for their Sunday family supper of scrambled eggs. These acts of friendship—repeated many times over—helped to explain the paradox that, though 80 to 85 percent of the newspaper publishers regularly opposed Roosevelt, the president maintained excellent relations with the working reporters, and his coverage was generally full and fair. "By the brilliant but simple trick of making news and *being* news," historian Arthur Schlesinger observed, "Roosevelt outwitted the open hostility of the publishers and converted the press into one of the most effective channels of his public leadership."

"History will like to say the scene [on May 10] was tense," Mark Sullivan wrote. "It was not. . . . On the President's part there was consciousness of high events, yet also complete coolness. . . . The whole atmosphere was one of serious matter-of-factness."

"Good morning," the president said, and then paused as still more reporters filed in. "I hope you had more sleep than I did," he joked, drawing them into the shared experience of the crisis. "I guess most of you were pretty busy all night." . . .

Asked if he would say what he thought the chances were that the United States could stay out of the war, the president replied as he had been replying for months to similar questions. "I think that would be speculative. In other words, don't for heaven's sake, say that means we may get in. That would be again writing yourself off on the limb and sawing it off." Asked if his speech that night would touch on the international situation, Roosevelt evoked a round of laughter by responding: "I do not know because I have not written it."

On and on he went, his tone in the course of fifteen minutes shifting from weariness to feistiness to playfulness. Yet, in the end, preserving his options in this delicate moment, he *said* almost nothing, skillfully deflecting every question about America's future actions. Asked at one point to compare Japanese aggression with German aggression, he said he counted seven ifs in the question, which meant he could not provide an answer. Still, by the time the senior wire-service man brought the conference to an early close, "partly in consideration of the tired newspaper men and partly in consideration of the President," the reporters went away with the stories they needed for the next day's news. . . .

[While Franklin was in his press conference, Eleanor was in the country.] Franklin called Eleanor his "will o' the wisp" wife. But it was Franklin who had encouraged her to become his "eyes and ears," to gather the grass-roots knowledge he needed to understand the people he governed. Unable to travel easily on his own because of his paralysis, he had started by teaching Eleanor how to inspect state institutions in 1929, during his first term as governor.

"It was the best education I ever had," she later said. Traveling across the state to inspect institutions for the insane, the blind, and the aged, visiting state prisons and reform schools, she had learned, slowly and painfully, through Franklin's tough, detailed questions upon her return, how to become an investigative reporter.

Her first inspection was an insane asylum. "All right," Franklin told her, "go in and look around and let me know what's going on there. Tell me how the inmates are being treated." When Eleanor returned, she brought with her a printed copy of the day's menu. "Did you look to see whether they were actually getting this food?" Franklin asked. "Did you lift a pot cover on the stove to check whether the contents corresponded with this menu?" Eleanor shook her head. Her untrained mind had taken in a general picture of the place but missed all the human details that would have brought it to life. "But these are what I need," Franklin said. "I never remembered things until Franklin taught me," Eleanor told a reporter. "His memory is really prodigious. Once he has checked something he never needs to look at it again."

"One time," she recalled, "he asked me to go and look at the state's tree shelter-belt plantings. I noticed there were five rows of graduated size. . . . When I came back and described it, Franklin said: 'Tell me exactly what was in the first five rows. What did they plant first?' And he was so desperately disappointed when I couldn't tell him, that I put my best efforts after that into missing nothing and remembering everything."

In time, Eleanor became so thorough in her inspections, observing the attitudes of patients toward the staff, judging facial expressions as well as the words, looking in closets and behind doors, that Franklin set great value on her reports. "She saw many things the President could never see," Labor Secretary Frances Perkins said. "Much of what she learned and what she understood about the life of the people of this country rubbed off onto FDR. It could not have helped to do so because she had a poignant understanding. . . . Her mere reporting of the facts was full of a sensitive quality that could never be escaped. . . . Much of his seemingly intuitive understanding—about labor situations . . . about girls who worked in sweatshops—came from his recollections of what she had told him."

During Eleanor's first summer as first lady, Franklin had asked her to investigate the economic situation in Appalachia. The Quakers had reported terrible conditions of poverty there, and the president wanted to check these reports. "Watch the people's faces," he told her. "Look at the conditions of the clothes on the wash lines. You can tell a lot from that." Going even further, Eleanor descended the mine shafts, dressed in a miner's outfit, to absorb for herself the physical conditions in which the miners worked. It was this journey that later provoked the celebrated cartoon showing two miners in a shaft looking up: "Here Comes Mrs. Roosevelt!"

At Scott's Run, near Morgantown, West Virginia, Eleanor had seen children who "did not know what it was to sit down at a table and eat a proper meal." In one shack, she found a boy clutching his pet rabbit,

which his sister had just told him was all there was left to eat. So moved was the president by his wife's report that he acted at once to create an Appalachian resettlement project.

The following year, Franklin had sent Eleanor to Puerto Rico to investigate reports that a great portion of the fancy embroidered linens that were coming into the United States from Puerto Rico were being made under terrible conditions. To the fury of the rich American colony in San Juan, Eleanor took reporters and photographers through muddy alleys and swamps to hundreds of foul-smelling hovels with no plumbing and no electricity, where women sat in the midst of filth embroidering cloth for minimal wages. Publicizing these findings, Eleanor called for American women to stop purchasing Puerto Rico's embroidered goods.

Later, Eleanor journeyed to the deep South and the "Dustbowl." Before long, her inspection trips had become as important to her as to her husband. "I realized," she said in a radio interview, "that if I remained in the White House all the time I would lose touch with the rest of the world. . . . I might have had a less crowded life, but I would begin to think that my life in Washington was representative of the rest of the country and that is a dangerous point of view." So much did Eleanor travel, in fact, that the *Washington Star* once printed a humorous headline: "Mrs. Roosevelt Spends Night at White House." . . .

When [Franklin] met with his Cabinet at two that afternoon, his concerns as he looked at the familiar faces around the table were . . . how to get a new and expanded military budget through the Congress, how to provide aid to the Allies as quickly as possible, how to stock up on strategic materials; in other words, how to start the complex process of mobilizing for war. . . .

Labor Secretary Frances Perkins, the only woman in the Cabinet, tended to talk a great deal at these meetings, "as though she had swallowed a press release." But on this occasion she remained silent as the conversation was carried by Harry Hopkins, the secretary of commerce, who was present at his first Cabinet meeting in months.

For the past year and a half, Hopkins had been in and out of hospitals while doctors tried to fix his body's lethal inability to absorb proteins and fats. His health had begun to deteriorate in the summer of 1939, when, at the height of his power as director of the Works Progress Administration, he was told that he had stomach cancer. A ghastly operation followed which removed the cancer along with three-quarters of his stomach, leaving him with a severe form of malnutrition. Told in the fall of 1939 that Hopkins had only four weeks to live, Roosevelt took control of the case himself and flew in a team of experts, whose experiments with plasma transfusions arrested the fatal decline. Then, to give Hopkins breathing space from the turbulence of the WPA, Roosevelt appointed him secretary of commerce. Even that job had proved too much, however: Hopkins had been able to work only one or two days in the past ten months.

Yet, on this critical day, the fifty-year-old Hopkins was sitting in the Cabinet meeting in the midst of the unfolding crisis. "He was to all intents and purposes," Hopkins' biographer Robert Sherwood wrote, "a finished man who might drag out his life for a few years of relative inactivity or who might collapse and die at any time." His face was sallow and heavy-lined; journalist George Creel once likened his weary, melancholy look to that of "an ill-fed horse at the end of a hard day," while Churchill's former daughter-in-law, Pamela Churchill Harriman, compared him to "a very sad dog." Given his appearance—smoking one cigarette after another, his brown hair thinning, his shoulders sagging, his frayed suit baggy at the knees—"you wouldn't think," a contemporary reporter wrote, "he could possibly be important to a President."

But when he spoke, as he did at length this day on the subject of the raw materials needed for war, his sickly face vanished and a very different face appeared, intelligent, good-humored, animated. His eyes, which seconds before had seemed beady and suspicious, now gleamed with light. Sensing the urgency of the situation, Hopkins spoke so rapidly that he did not finish half of his words, as though, after being long held back, he wanted to make up for lost time. It was as if the crisis had given him a renewed reason for living; it seemed, in reporter Marquis Childs' judgment at the time, "to galvanize him into life." From then on, Childs observed, "while he would still be an ailing man, he was to ignore his health." The curative impact of Hopkins' increasingly crucial role in the war effort was to postpone the sentence of death the doctors had given him for five more years.

Even Hopkins' old nemesis, Harold Ickes, felt compelled to pay attention when Hopkins reported that the United States had "only a five or six months supply of both rubber and tin, both of which are absolutely essential for purposes of defense." The shortage of rubber was particularly worrisome, since rubber was indispensable to modern warfare if armies were to march, ships sail, and planes fly. Hitler's armies were rolling along on rubber-tired trucks and rubber-tracked tanks; they were flying in rubber-lined high-altitude suits in planes equipped with rubber de-icers, rubber tires, and rubber life-preserver rafts. From stethoscopes and blood-plasma tubing to gas masks and adhesive tape, the demand for rubber was endless. And with Holland under attack and 90 percent of America's supply of rubber coming from the Dutch East Indies, something had to be done.

Becoming more and more spirited as he went on, Hopkins outlined a plan of action, starting with the creation of a new corporation, to be financed by the Reconstruction Finance Corporation, whose purpose would be to go into the market and buy at least a year's supply of rubber and tin. This step would be only the first, followed by the building of synthetic-rubber plants and an effort to bring into production new sources of natural rubber in South America. Hopkins' plan of action met with hearty approval.

While Hopkins was speaking, word came from London that Neville Chamberlain had resigned his post as prime minister. This dramatic event had its source in the tumultuous debate in the Parliament over the shameful retreat of the British Expeditionary Force from Norway three weeks earlier. . . .

The seventy-one-year-old prime minister had little choice but to step down. Then, when the king's first choice, Lord Halifax, refused to consider the post on the grounds that his position as a peer would make it difficult to discharge his duties, the door was opened for Winston Churchill, the complex Edwardian man with his fat cigars, his gold-knobbed cane, and his vital understanding of what risks should be taken and what kind of adversary the Allies were up against. For nearly four decades, Churchill had been a major figure in public life. The son of a lord, he had been elected to Parliament in 1900 and had served in an astonishing array of Cabinet posts, including undersecretary for the colonies, privy councillor, home secretary, first lord of the admiralty, minister of munitions, and chancellor of the Exchequer. He had survived financial embarrassment, prolonged fits of depression, and political defeat to become the most eloquent spokesman against Nazi Germany. From the time Hitler first came to power, he had repeatedly warned against British efforts to appease him, but no one had listened. Now, finally, his voice would be heard. "Looking backward," a British writer observed, "it almost seems as though the transition from peace to war began on that day when Churchill became Prime Minister."

Responding warmly to the news of Churchill's appointment, Roosevelt told his Cabinet he believed "Churchill was the best man that England had." From a distance, the two leaders had come to admire each other: for years, Churchill had applauded Roosevelt's "valiant efforts" to end the depression, while Roosevelt had listened with increasing respect to Churchill's lonely warnings against the menace of Adolf Hitler. In September 1939, soon after the outbreak of the war, when Churchill was brought into the government as head of the admiralty, Roosevelt had initiated the first in what would become an extraordinary series of wartime letters between the two men. Writing in a friendly but respectful tone, Roosevelt had told Churchill: "I shall at all times welcome it if you will keep me in touch personally with everything you want me to know about. You can always send sealed letters through your pouch or my pouch." Though relatively few messages had been exchanged in the first nine months of the war, the

seeds had been planted of an exuberant friendship, which would flourish in the years to come.

Once the Cabinet adjourned, Roosevelt had a short meeting with the minister of Belgium, who was left with only $35 since an order to freeze all credit held by Belgium, the Netherlands, and Luxembourg had gone into effect, earlier that morning. After arrangements were made to help him out, there began a working session on the speech Roosevelt was to deliver that night to a scientific meeting.

Then Roosevelt, not departing from his regular routine, went into his study for the cocktail hour, the most relaxed time of his day. The second-floor study, crowded with maritime pictures, models of ships, and stacks of paper, was the president's favorite room in the White House. It was here that he read, played poker, sorted his beloved stamps, and conducted most of the important business of his presidency. The tall mahogany bookcases were stuffed with books, and the leather sofas and chairs had acquired a rich glow. Any room Roosevelt spent time in, Frances Perkins observed, "invariably got that lived-in and overcrowded look which indicated the complexity and variety of his interests and intentions." Missy and Harry Hopkins were there, along with Pa Watson and Eleanor's houseguest, the beautiful actress Helen Gahagan Douglas. The cocktail hour, begun during Roosevelt's years in Albany, had become an institution in Roosevelt's official family, a time for reviewing events in an informal atmosphere, a time for swapping the day's best laughs. The president always mixed the drinks himself, experimenting with strange concoctions of gin and rum, vermouth and fruit juice.

During the cocktail hour, no more was said of politics or war; instead the conversation turned to subjects of lighter weight—to gossip, funny stories, and reminiscences. With Missy generally presiding as hostess, distributing the drinks to the guests, Roosevelt seemed to find complete relaxation in telling his favorite stories over and over again. Some of these stories Missy must have heard more than twenty or thirty times, but, like the "good wife," she never let her face betray boredom, only delight at the knowledge that her boss was having such a good time. And with his instinct for the dramatic and his fine ability to mimic, Roosevelt managed to tell each story a little differently each time, adding new details or insights.

On this evening, there was a delicious story to tell. In the Congress there was a Republican representative from Auburn, New York, John Taber, who tended to get into shouting fits whenever the subject of the hated New Deal came up. In a recent debate on the Wage and Hour amendments, he had bellowed so loudly that he nearly swallowed the microphone. On the floor at the time was Representative Leonard Schultz of Chicago, who had been deaf in his left ear since birth. As Mr. Taber's shriek was amplified through the loudspeakers, something happened to Mr. Schultz. Shaking convulsively, he staggered to the cloakroom, where he collapsed onto a couch, thinking he'd been hit in an air raid. He suddenly realized that he could hear with his left ear—for the first time in his life—and better than with his right. When doctors confirmed that Mr. Schultz's hearing was excellent, Mr. Taber claimed it was proof from God that the New Deal should be shouted down! . . .

While Franklin was mixing cocktails, Eleanor was on a train back to Washington from New York. For many of her fellow riders, the time on the train was a time to ease up, to gaze through the windows at the passing countryside, to close their eyes and unwind. But for Eleanor, who considered train rides her best working hours, there was little time to relax. The pile of mail, still unanswered, was huge, and there was a column to be written for the following day. Franklin's cousin Margaret "Daisy" Suckley recalls traveling with Eleanor once on the New York–to–Washington train. "She was working away the whole time with Malvina, and I was sitting there like a dumbbell looking out the window, and suddenly Mrs. Roosevelt said to Malvina, 'Now I'm going to sleep for fifteen minutes,' and she put her head back on the seat. I looked at my watch, and just as it hit fifteen minutes, she woke up and said, 'Now Tommy, let's go on.' It was amazing. I was stunned."

Even if Eleanor had reached the White House that evening in time for the cocktail hour, she would probably not have joined. Try as she might over the years, Eleanor had never felt comfortable at these relaxed gatherings. Part of her discomfort was toward alcohol itself, the legacy of an alcoholic father who continually failed to live up to the expectations and trust of his adoring daughter. One Christmas, Eleanor's daughter, Anna, and her good friend Lorena Hickok had chipped in to buy some cocktail glasses for Eleanor's Greenwich Village apartment in the hopes she would begin inviting friends in for drinks. "In a funny way," Anna wrote "Hick," as Miss Hickok was called, "I think she has always wanted to feel included in such parties, but so many old inhibitions have kept her from it."

But, despite Anna's best hopes, Eleanor's discomfort at the cocktail hour persisted, suggesting that beyond her fear of alcohol lay a deeper fear of letting herself go, of slackening off the work that had become so central to her sense of self. "Work had become for Eleanor almost as addictive as alcohol," her niece Eleanor Wotkyns once observed. "Even when she thought she was relaxing she was really working. Small talk horrified her. Even at New Year's, when everyone else relaxed with drinks, she would work until ten minutes of twelve, come in for a round of toasts, and then disappear to her room to work until two or three a.m. Always at the back of her mind were the letters she had to write, the things she had to do."

"She could be a crashing bore," Anna's son Curtis Dall Roosevelt admitted. "She was very judgmental even when she tried not to be. The human irregularities, the off-color jokes he loved, she couldn't take. He would tell his stories, many of them made to fit a point, and she would say, 'No, no, Franklin, that's not how it happened.'"

"If only Mother could have learned to ease up," her son Elliott observed, "things would have been so different with Father, for he needed relaxation more than anything in the world. But since she simply could not bring herself to unwind, he turned instead to Missy, building with her an exuberant, laughing relationship, full of jokes, silliness, and gossip."

"Stay for dinner. I'm lonely," Roosevelt urged Harry Hopkins when the cocktail hour came to an end. There were few others at this stage of his life that the president enjoyed as much as Hopkins. With the death in 1936 of Louis Howe, the shriveled ex-newspaperman who had fastened his star to Roosevelt in the early Albany days, helped him conquer his polio, and guided him through the political storms to the White House, the president had turned to Hopkins for companionship. "There was a temperamental sympathy between Roosevelt and Hopkins," Frances Perkins observed. Though widely different in birth and breeding, they both possessed unconquerable confidence, great courage, and good humor; they both enjoyed the society of the rich, the gay, and the well-born, while sharing an abiding concern for the average man. Hopkins had an almost "feminine sensitivity" to Roosevelt's moods, Sherwood observed. Like Missy, he seemed to know when the president wanted to consider affairs of state and when he wanted to escape from business; he had an uncanny instinct for knowing when to introduce a serious subject and when to tell a joke, when to talk and when to listen. He was, in short, a great dinner companion.

As soon as dinner was finished, Roosevelt had to return to work. In less than an hour, he was due to deliver a speech, and he knew that every word he said would be scrutinized for the light it might shed on the crisis at hand. Taking leave of Hopkins, Roosevelt noticed that his friend looked even more sallow and miserable now than he had looked earlier in the day. "Stay the night," the President insisted. So Hopkins borrowed a pair of pajamas and settled into a bedroom suite on the second floor. There he remained, not simply for one night but for the next three and a half years, as Roosevelt, exhibiting his genius for using people in new and unexpected ways, converted him from the number-one relief worker to the number-one adviser on the war. Later, Missy liked to tease: "It was Harry Hopkins who gave George S. Kaufman and Moss Hart the idea for that play of theirs, 'The Man Who Came to Dinner.'"

As the president was preparing to leave for Constitution Hall, he remembered something he had meant to ask Helen Gahagan Douglas during the cocktail hour. There was no time to discuss it now, but, stopping by her room, he told her he had an important question for her and asked if she would meet him in his study when he returned. "Certainly," she replied, and he left to address several thousand scientists and scholars at the Pan American Scientific Congress.

"We come here tonight with heavy hearts," he began, looking out at the packed auditorium. "This very day, the tenth of May, three more independent nations have been cruelly invaded by force of arms. . . . I am glad that we are shocked and angered by the tragic news." Declaring that it was no accident that this scientific meeting was taking place in the New World, since elsewhere war and politics had compelled teachers and scholars to leave their callings and become the agents of destruction, Roosevelt warned against an undue sense of security based on the false teachings of geography: in terms of the moving of men and guns and planes and bombs, he argued, every acre of American territory was closer to Europe than was ever the case before. "In modern times it is a shorter distance from Europe to San Francisco, California than it was for the ships and legions of Julius Caesar to move from Rome to Spain or Rome to Britain."

"I am a pacifist," he concluded, winding up with a pledge that was greeted by a great burst of cheers and applause, "but I believe that by overwhelming majorities . . . you and I, in the long run if it be necessary, will act together to protect and defend by every means at our command our science, our culture, our American freedom and our civilization."

Buoyed by his thunderous reception, Roosevelt was in excellent humor when he returned to his study to find Helen Gahagan Douglas waiting for him. Just as he was settling in, however, word came that Winston Churchill was on the telephone. Earlier that evening, Churchill had driven to Buckingham Palace, where King George VI had asked him to form a government. Even as Churchill agreed to accept the seals of office, British troops were pouring into Belgium, wildly cheered by smiling Belgians, who welcomed them with flowers. The change was made official at 9 p.m., when Chamberlain, his voice breaking with emotion, resigned. It had been a long and fateful day for Britain, but now, though it was nearly 3 a.m. in London, Churchill apparently wanted to touch base with his old letter-writing companion before going to sleep.

Though there is no record of the content of this first conversation between the new prime minister of England and the president of the United States, Churchill did reveal that when he went to bed that night, after the extraordinary events of an extraordinary day, he was conscious of "a profound sense of relief. At last I had the authority to give directions over the whole scene. I felt as if I were walking with Destiny, and that all my past life had been but a preparation for this hour and this trial."

"Therefore," Churchill concluded, "although impatient for morning, I slept soundly and had no need for cheering dreams. Facts are better than dreams." He had achieved the very position he had imagined for himself for so many years.

While Roosevelt was talking with Churchill, Helen Douglas tried to prepare herself for the important question the president wanted to ask her. Perhaps, she thought, it was related to her work with the farm-security program, or the National Youth Administration. Both Helen and her husband, fellow actor Melvyn Douglas, were ardent New Dealers, members of the National Advisory Commission for the Works Progress Administration and the California Advisory Commission for the NYA. Earlier that year, they had hosted Mrs. Roosevelt's visit to Los Angeles, accompanying her to the migrant-labor camps in the San Joaquin Valley.

"The day was unforgettable," Helen later recalled. "Soon after we started, Mrs. Roosevelt spotted a cluster of makeshift shacks constructed of old boards, tarpaper and tin cans pounded flat, one of the ditch bank communities that were commonplace in California then." She asked to stop the car and walked across the field toward some migrants. "One of the

bent figures straightened to see who was approaching and recognized her at once. 'Oh, Mrs. Roosevelt, you've come to see us,' he said. He seemed to accept as a natural event of American life that the wife of the President of the United States would be standing in a mucky field chatting with him."

Perhaps the president's question related to something his wife had told him about her journey. To be sure, Helen knew that Roosevelt loved movies and movie people, but not even that knowledge prepared her for the whimsical nature of the question the president posed to her that night.

"OK, Helen," Roosevelt began, his eyes flashing with good humor. "Now, I want you to tell me exactly what happened under the table at Ciro's between Paulette Goddard and Anatole Litvak." The juicy gossip Roosevelt wanted to hear involved the Russian-born director Anatole Litvak and Paulette Goddard, the vivacious brunette actress who was married first to the filmmaker Hal Roach and then to Charlie Chaplin. As Helen Douglas told the story, Goddard and Litvak were having dinner at the elegant nightclub, where the men had to wear tuxedos and the women long dresses, when the urge to make love became so strong that they eased themselves onto the floor under the table. As the moans were heard across the restaurant floor, waiters rushed to the scene with extra tablecloths to cover the sides of the table. Or so the story was told. "I love it, I love it," Roosevelt responded.

Returning to the White House from Union Station just as Helen was finishing her tale, Eleanor heard her husband's laughter and assumed that, as usual, he was with Missy, relaxing at the end of the day. At such times, she later admitted to her son Elliott, she felt terribly left out, wishing that she could let herself go and simply join in the frivolity. But as it was, she knew that if she opened the door she would be driven to talk business, to share the information and insights she had gleaned from her recent trip. Then, if her husband was tired and unresponsive, she would feel hurt and rejected. It had happened this way before. Better to go to her own bedroom and wait until morning to see her husband.

"All her life," her niece Eleanor Wotkyns observed, "Eleanor yearned to be more spontaneous, to relax more readily, but in the end how can one force oneself to be spontaneous?"

At ten after eleven that evening, according to the White House usher diary, both Eleanor and Franklin went to bed—Franklin settling into his small bedroom off his study, Eleanor into her own suite of rooms, next to her husband's, in the southwest corner of the mansion. But the separation by night belied the partnership by day—a partnership that would help change the face of the country in the years ahead.

At 1 p.m. on May 16, 1940, President Roosevelt was scheduled to address a joint session of Congress. It was the president's first appearance in the House Chamber since the war in Western Europe had begun. Despite the blinding rain falling steadily since early morning, a huge audience had gathered to hear him.

Here, on the floor of the House of Representatives, all the contending forces of American life had gathered over the years to argue their causes—abolitionists versus slaveowners, liberals versus conservatives, unions versus management, farmers versus city-dwellers. On a number of occasions, particularly in the nineteenth century, the debates had descended into physical violence as members brandished pistols, smashed one another's heads with tongs, canes, and brass spittoons, and pummeled each other with fists. The very size of the House Chamber, with large numbers of legislators, clerks, and page boys running from place to place, conspired to produce confusion and chaos.

As one o'clock neared, there was a stir among the audience, an air of expectation. Every face, not knowing for sure where the country was going, wore a look of nervousness. In the Congress in 1940, there were 526 men and five women, nearly three hundred lawyers, two dozen schoolteachers, sixty merchants, twenty bankers and insurance agents, nine newspaper publishers, five dentists, a half-dozen preachers, the owner of the largest cattle ranch in the world, an amateur magician, and a half-dozen or more aspirants to the presidency. There was one Negro.

At 12:59 p.m. the assistant doorkeeper announced the members of the Cabinet. The spectators responded with warm applause. But when the audience caught sight of the president himself, his right hand holding a cane, his left hand grasping the forearm of a Secret Service man, they jumped to their feet, applauding and cheering him as he had never been cheered in the Capitol before, a bipartisan ovation that could only be interpreted as a demonstration of national unity in a time of crisis.

It had been a week no one in the Western world would forget. After only five days of fighting, Holland, with tens of thousands of her citizens said to be dead, had surrendered; the Belgian army was almost totally destroyed, and France, reputed to possess the best army in all of Europe, was being overrun. The Germans seemed to have discovered a radically new style of air-ground warfare that was somehow free from ordinary constraints of time and distance. The speed and destructiveness of Germany's powerful tanks—able to cross rivers and canals as if they were paved boulevards, resisting all fire at normal ranges—were almost incomprehensible. Against these metal mastodons, French Premier Paul Reynaud lamented, the French defenses were like "walls of sand that a child puts up against waves on the seashore." Equally hard to fathom was the effectiveness of Germany's air force, roaring in ahead of advancing columns, bombing communication lines, strafing and terrorizing ground troops to the point of an almost total Allied collapse.

For many in the audience, Roosevelt's dramatic journey to the Hill awakened memories of Woodrow Wilson's appearance before Congress in the spring of 1917, when America entered the Great War. Now, once again, Europe was engaged in an expanding war that threatened to engulf the entire world, and emotions were running high. As the applause continued to swell, the president slowly maneuvered his body up the long ramp from the well of the House to the rostrum.

Standing at the podium, his leg braces firmly locked into place, the president looked at his audience, and an uncharacteristic wave of nervousness came upon him. Absent were both his conspicuous smile and the swaggering way he usually held his head; in their place, a slight slump of the shoulders and a grim expression that matched the gray day. Reporters seated behind the podium detected anxiety in his trembling hands and in the faltering way he tried and failed, not once but twice, to put on his glasses. . . .

The president had cause to feel apprehensive. He knew that both Britain and France were looking to the United States for help. Alone among the democratic nations, the United States possessed the potential resources—the abundance of raw materials, the oil fields, the bauxite mines, the assembly lines, the production equipment, the idle manpower, the entrepreneurial skills, the engineering know-how— necessary to wage technological war on a scale equal to that of Nazi Germany. "I trust you realize, Mr. President," Churchill had written earlier that week, "that the voice and force of the United States may count for nothing if they are withheld too long."

But when all was said and done, there was nothing "the most productive nation in the world" could do to save France. At dawn on the morning of June 14, German troops entered Paris. . . . A week later, Hitler laid down his terms for an armistice, and, in the same railroad car in a clearing in the woods at Compiègne where the Germans had capitulated to the Allies in 1918, a defeated and humiliated France concluded a truce. After the signing, Hitler ordered that the historic carriage and the monument celebrating the original French victory be conveyed to Berlin. Then, in an attempt to obliterate even the slightest physical memory of Germany's earlier defeat, he ordered that the pedestal of the carriage and the stones marking the site be destroyed. With the French surrender, Adolf Hitler was now the master of Austria, Czechoslovakia, Poland, Luxembourg, Belgium, Denmark, the Netherlands, Norway, and France. . . .

[Through 1940 and 1941 the European war intensified, with Germany fighting a mighty air war over Britain to clear the way for an invasion. But when the British won that war, Hitler turned to the East. In June 1941, he unleashed three million troops on the Soviet Union—the largest land invasion in the history of warfare. Meanwhile, in the Far East, militaristic Japan was waging its own war of aggression against hapless China. While Japanese warplanes bombed China's cities to rubble, Japanese troops seized coastal territory and murdered Chinese civilians—200,000 in Nanking alone—with unspeakable savagery. When Japanese forces struck southward against French Indochina, President Roosevelt retaliated by declaring an oil embargo against Japan, thus cutting off U.S. shipments of oil desperately needed by the Japanese war machine. When negotiations between the two countries faltered, the Japanese navy made plans for a surprise attack against the United States Pacific Fleet at Pearl Harbor, Hawaii. Final plans called for the attack to take place on Sunday morning, December 7, 1941.]

Shortly after 7:30 a.m., local time, while sailors were sleeping, eating breakfast, and reading the Sunday papers, the first wave of 189 Japanese planes descended upon Pearl Harbor, dropping clusters of torpedo bombs on the unsuspecting fleet. Half the fleet, by fortunate coincidence, was elsewhere, including all three aircraft carriers, but the ships that remained were tied up to the docks so "snugly side by side," Harold Ickes later observed, "that they presented a target that none could miss. A bomber could be pretty sure that he would hit a ship even if not the one he aimed at." Within minutes—before any anti-aircraft fire could be activated, and before a single fighter plane could get up into the air—all eight of the American battleships in Pearl Harbor, including the *West Virginia,* the *Arizona,* and the *California,* had been hit, along with three destroyers and three light cruisers.

Bodies were everywhere—trapped in the holds of sinking ships, strewn in the burning waters, scattered on the smoke-covered ground. Before the third wave of Japanese planes completed its final run, thirty-five hundred sailors, soldiers, and civilians had lost their lives. It was the worst naval disaster in American history.

United States battleships anchored at Pearl Harbor were sitting ducks. A torpedo has just struck the Oklahoma, kicking up a *towering geyser. Struck by four additional torpedoes, the great battleship quickly capsized. (U.S. Navy Photo)*

Knox relayed the horrifying news to the president shortly after 1:30 p.m. Roosevelt was sitting in his study with Harry Hopkins when the call came. "Mr. President," Knox said, "it looks like the Japanese have attacked Pearl Harbor." Hopkins said there must be some mistake; the Japanese would never attack Pearl Harbor. But the president reckoned it was probably true—it was just the kind of thing the Japanese would do at the very moment they were discussing peace in the Pacific. All doubt was settled a few minutes later, when Admiral Stark called to confirm the attack. With bloody certainty, the United States had finally discovered the whereabouts of the Japanese fleet. . . .

The first thing Eleanor noticed when she went into her husband's study was his "deadly calm" composure. While his aides and Cabinet members were running in and out in a state of excitement, panic, and irritation, he was sitting quietly at his desk, absorbing the news from Hawaii as it continued to flow in—"each report more terrible than the last." Though he looked strained and tired, Eleanor observed, "he was completely calm. His reaction to any event was always to be calm. If it was something that was bad, he just became almost like an iceberg, and there was never the slightest emotion that was allowed to show." Sumner Welles agreed with Eleanor's assessment. In all the situations over the years in which he had seen the president, he "had never had such reason to admire him."

Beneath the president's imperturbable demeanor, however, Eleanor detected great bitterness and anger toward Japan for the treachery involved in carrying out the surprise attack while the envoys of the two countries were still talking. "I never wanted to have to fight this war on two fronts," Franklin told Eleanor. "We haven't got the Navy to fight in both the Atlantic and the Pacific . . . so we will have to build up the Navy and the Air Force and that will mean that we will have to take a good many defeats before we can have a victory." . . .

"Within the first hour," Grace Tully recalled, "it was evident that the Navy was dangerously crippled." And there was no way of knowing where the Japanese would stop. The president's butler Alonzo Fields recalls overhearing snatches of a remarkable conversation between Harry Hopkins and the president that afternoon in which they imagined the possibility of the invading Japanese armies' driving inland from the West Coast as far as Chicago. At that point, the president figured, since the United States was a country much like Russia in the vastness of its terrain, we could make the Japanese overextend their communication and supply lines and begin to force them back.

Meanwhile, a little bit at a time, the public at large was learning the news. "No American who lived through that Sunday will ever forget it," reporter Marquis Childs later wrote. "It seared deeply into the national consciousness," creating in all a permanent memory of where they were when they first heard the news.

Churchill was sitting at Chequers with envoy Averell Harriman and Ambassador John Winant when news of the Japanese attack came over the wireless. Unable to contain his excitement, he bounded to his feet and placed a call to the White House. "Mr. President, what's this about Japan?" "It's quite true," Roosevelt replied. "They have attacked us at Pearl Harbour. We are all in the same boat now."

"To have the United States at our side," Churchill later wrote, "was to me the greatest joy." After seventeen months of lonely fighting, he now believed the war would be won. "England would live; Britain would live; the Commonwealth of Nations and the Empire would live." The history of England would not come to an end. "Silly people—and

there were many . . . ," Churchill mused, "—might discount the force of the United States," believing the Americans were soft, divided, paralyzed, averse to bloodshed. He knew better; he had studied the Civil War, the bloodiest war in history, fought to the last inch. Saturated with emotion, Churchill thought of a remark British politician Sir Edward Grey had made to him more than 30 years before. The U.S. was like "a gigantic boiler. Once the fire is lighted under it there is no limit to the power it can generate."

Shortly before 5 p.m., the president called Grace Tully to his study. "He was alone," Tully recalled, with two or three neat piles of notes stacked on his desk containing all the information he had been receiving during the afternoon. "Sit down, Grace. I'm going before Congress tomorrow. I'd like to dictate my message. It will be short."

He began to speak in the same steady tone in which he dictated his mail, but the pace was slower than usual as he spoke each word incisively, specifying every punctuation mark. "Yesterday comma December 7th comma 1941 dash a day which will live in world history . . . "

At eight-thirty on Sunday night, the Cabinet began to gather in the president's study. A ring of extra chairs had been brought in to accommodate the overflow. The president, Perkins noted later, was sitting silently at his desk; he was preoccupied, seemed not to be seeing or hearing what was going on around him. "It was very interesting," Perkins observed, "because he was always a very friendly and outgoing man on the personal side. He never overlooked people. . . . But I don't think he spoke to anyone who came in that night. He was living off in another area. He wasn't noticing what went on on the other side of the desk. He was very serious. His face and lips were pulled down, looking quite gray. His complexion didn't have that pink and white look that it had when he was himself. It had a queer gray, drawn look."

Finally, he turned around and said, "I'm thankful you all got here." He went on to say this was probably the most serious crisis any Cabinet had confronted since the outbreak of the Civil War. Then he told them what he knew. "I remember," Perkins

On December 9, 1941, Roosevelt solemnly signed the declaration of war against Japan, which Congress approved with one dissenting vote. Germany and Italy, Japan's Axis allies, responded by declaring war on the United States. These acts plunged America into the greatest war in history. (Franklin D. Roosevelt Library)

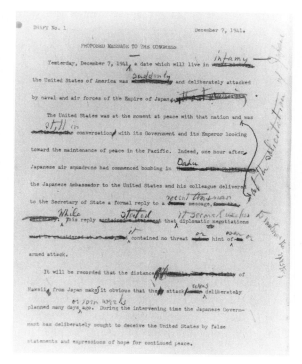

White House secretary Grace Tully was with the president just before 5 p.m. on the day the Japanese attacked Pearl Harbor. Roosevelt told her, "Sit down, Grace. I'm going before Congress tomorrow. I'd like to dictate my message. It will be short." The president made some handwritten changes to the original draft and the next day he received a thunderous ovation from a Congress now ready for war. (Franklin D. Roosevelt Library)

later said, "the President could hardly bring himself" to describe the devastation. "His pride in the Navy was so terrific that he was having actual physical difficulty in getting out the words that put him on record as knowing that the Navy was caught unawares. . . . I remember that he said twice to Knox, 'Find out, for God's sake, why the ships were tied up in rows.' Knox said, 'That's the way they berth them!' It was obvious to me that Roosevelt was having a dreadful time just accepting the idea that the Navy could be caught off guard."

By 10 p.m., congressional leaders had joined the Cabinet in the overcrowded study. The president told the gathering that he had prepared a short message to

be presented at a joint session of Congress the following day. The message called for a declaration by Congress that a state of war had existed between Japan and the United States from the moment of the attack Sunday morning. He then went on to describe the attack itself, repeating much of what he had told his Cabinet, including new information that Japanese bombs had also hit American airfields in Hawaii, destroying more than half the planes in the Pacific fleet. Apparently, the planes had been an easy mark, since they were grouped together on the ground, wing tip to wing tip, to guard against subversive action by Japanese agents. "On the ground, by God, on the ground," Roosevelt groaned.

"The effect on the Congressmen was tremendous," Stimson recorded. "They sat in dead silence and even after the recital was over they had very few words." Finally, Senator Tom Connally of Texas spoke up, voicing the question that was on everyone's mind. "How did it happen that our warships were caught like tame ducks in Pearl Harbor?" he shouted, banging the desk with his fist, his face purple. "How did they catch us with our pants down? Where were our patrols? They knew these negotiations were going on. They were all asleep."

"I don't know, Tom," the president muttered, his head bowed, "I just don't know."

Historians have focused substantial time and attention trying to determine who knew what and when before the 7th of December—on the theory that Roosevelt was aware of the Japanese plans to attack Pearl Harbor but deliberately concealed his knowledge from the commanders in Hawaii in order to bring the United States into hostilities through the back door. Unable to swing Congress and the public toward a declaration of war against Germany, critics contend, the president provoked Japan into firing the first shot and then watched with delight as the attack created a united America.

To be sure, Roosevelt was concerned that, if war came, the Japanese should be the ones to initiate hostilities. Stimson records a conversation on November 25 in which the president raised the possibility that Japan might attack without warning. The question Roosevelt asked "was how we should maneuver them into the position of firing the first shot without allowing too much danger to ourselves." But in the discussion, as in all others preceding Pearl Harbor, the reigning assumption was that Japan would attack from the south. Though Pearl Harbor was mentioned once, the previous January, in a report from the U.S. ambassador to Japan, Joseph Grew, to the State Department, it was assumed, again and again, right up to December 7, that the Philippines was the most likely target for Japanese aggression.

Moreover, "without allowing too much danger to ourselves," is the important phrase in the president's conversation with Stimson. Common sense suggests that, if the president had known beforehand about Pearl Harbor, he would have done everything he could to reposition the fleet and disperse the airplanes to ensure minimal damage. For the purposes of mobilizing the American people, one American ship torpedoed by the Japanese at Pearl Harbor would have sufficed. It is inconceivable that Roosevelt, who loved the navy with a passion, would have intentionally sacrificed the heart of its fleet, much less the lives of thirty-five hundred American sailors and soldiers, without lifting a finger to reduce the risk. It is an inquiry that obscures the more important question that Senator Connally posed: "How did it happen that our warships were caught like tame ducks in Pearl Harbor?"

It happened because the U.S. forces at Pearl Harbor were fatally unprepared for war on the morning of December 7. "Neither Army or Navy Commandants in Oahu regarded such an attack as at all likely," Secretary Knox explained to Roosevelt. "Both [General Walker Short and Admiral Husband Kimmel] felt certain that such an attack would take place nearer Japan's base of operations, that is, in the Far East." Lack of readiness characterized every aspect of the base—from the unmanned aircraft batteries to the radar station whose sentries went off duty at 7 a.m. that morning. . . .

Toward midnight, the meeting in the president's study drew to a close; and while every face wore an expression of regret and reproach, there was also relief. For Stimson, it was in the knowledge "that the indecision was over and that a crisis had come in a way which would unite our people." No matter how great the damage, at least, the matter was settled. "You know," Frank Knox whispered to Frances Perkins, "I think the boss must have a great load off his mind. I thought the load on his mind was just going to kill him, going to break him down. This must be a great sense of relief to him. At least we know what to do now."

"Monday was almost worse than Sunday," Marquis Childs observed. "A merciful kind of shock prevailed under the first impact and now as that wore off, the truth was inescapable." In Washington, the rumors of damage "hovered like a low-hanging gas, spreading the panic that seemed to infect the capital." On the same day as Pearl Harbor, the Japanese had attacked the Philippines, Malaya, Wake Island, Guam, and Hong Kong.

At noon, under heavy security, the president motored from the East Gate of the White House to the Capitol, where, to deafening applause, he delivered a brief but powerful speech. From his first words, commemorating the day that would "live in infamy," to his call upon Congress to declare that, since "the unprovoked and dastardly attack by Japan on Sunday, December 7th, a state of war has existed between the United States and the Japanese Empire," the president's anger and indignation burned through. His head held high, his chin thrust out, Roosevelt roused his audience to a standing ovation when he pledged that "this form of treachery shall never endanger us again. The American people in their righteous might will win through to absolute victory." The Congress responded unambiguously to the president's call; both chambers approved a declaration of war, with only one dissenting vote—that of white-haired Representative Jeanette Rankin of Montana.

Isolationism collapsed overnight. "American soil has been treacherously attacked by Japan," former President Herbert Hoover stated. "Our decision is clear. It is forced upon us. We must fight with everything we have." . . . After months of vacillation, confusion, and hesitation, the United States was committed at last to a common course of action.

QUESTIONS TO CONSIDER

1 Polio seemed to transform Roosevelt's life in many ways. What was his life like before crippling illness, and why would Goodwin conclude that FDR's disability "expanded his mind and his sensibilities"? Explain how Roosevelt's relationship with reporters provided him with favorable press coverage despite the opposition of most newspaper publishers? Would the media and the American people ignore a major political leader's disability today as they did then?

2 Goodwin's portrait of the Roosevelts is as complimentary to Eleanor as it is to Franklin. Why was this first lady so popular? What obstacles did she have to overcome in her personal life, including her marriage? How did her discovery of Franklin's infidelity free her to play a different role and become her husband's "eyes and ears" as she traveled around the country?

3 In the spring of 1940, was the United States militarily prepared to enter a major world war? In contrast, why were Germany's armed forces so modern? How did the Congress view aid to the struggling democracies of England and France?

4 Examine the personality of Franklin Roosevelt and how Missy LeHand and Harry Hopkins served his inner needs much better than Eleanor. How did the president relax and temporarily escape the overwhelming problems of the Depression and the foreign policy crisis abroad?

5 Describe the damage that the Japanese inflicted on the American fleet at Pearl Harbor. What was Churchill's reaction when he heard of the attack? Why does Goodwin believe that Roosevelt had no advance notice of the invasion, and why does she feel that our warships at Pearl Harbor were "like tame ducks"? Finally, how did Congress and the American people respond to the Japanese attack against Pearl Harbor?

19 America and the Holocaust

WILLIAM J. VANDEN HEUVEL

The Second World War was the deadliest conflict in human history. More than 53 million people perished, and whole towns and cities were annihilated in this roaring global inferno. The hardest hit was the Soviet Union, which felt the full fury of the invading Nazi war machine. Some 25 million Soviets were killed—by far the largest casualties of any other country. Compared to the destruction wrought in China, Japan, the Soviet Union, and Europe, the United States suffered relatively light casualties. There were no invasions of the American mainland, no bombing raids on American cities, no civilian massacres. Total American military deaths came to 408,000. By comparing statistics, we do not mean to slight those who died for our flag. Every American fighting man killed was a terrible sacrifice and a devastating blow to those who loved him.

As the next selection shows, the casualty rates of countries tell only part of the war's tragic story. The virulent anti-Semitism of Hitler and his Nazi henchmen led them to a "final solution" to the "Jewish question": the creation of hideous death camps, which systematically exterminated 6 million European Jews—men, women, and children alike. Winston Churchill called it "the most terrible crime ever committed in the whole history of the world."

How could the Allies have allowed this "terrible crime" to happen? Could the United States have stopped it? Did it even try? Many critics contend that American leaders did not do nearly enough to help the Jews of Europe, instead abandoning them to their fate. William J. vanden Heuvel disagrees. He points out that restrictive immigration laws limited the number of refugees America could accept before Hitler "put the lock on the most terrible dungeon in history." The author concedes that there were influential people in Congress and the State Department who were anti-Semitic. Even so, after anti-Semitic riots swept Germany in November 1938, more than half of all immigrants to the United States were Jewish.

Vanden Heuvel defends Roosevelt's Jewish policy, contending that the president and first lady were free of the prejudice that infected other Americans. Roosevelt knew about the death camps—he had read about them in a report from German refugee Gerhard Riegner, who warned that European Jews were being "exterminated in order to resolve, once and for all, the Jewish question in Europe." When a group of Jewish leaders called on Roosevelt, the president assured them: "We shall do all in our power to be of service to your people in this tragic moment." True, FDR refused to bomb railroad lines leading to the death camps, arguing that committing all military resources to defeating Germany as soon as possible would save more lives. Many Roosevelt critics question the validity of that argument, but not vanden Heuvel. He maintains that Roosevelt, given political realities and wartime priorities, did in fact do all he could to aid Europe's Jews. After reading this provocative essay, you will want to decide for yourselves if this argument is convincing and supported by the weight of evidence. For the opposing point of view, consult David S. Wyman's The Abandonment of the Jews: America and the Holocaust, 1941–1945 *(1984).*

GLOSSARY

AUSCHWITZ   The most notorious of the Nazi death camps. The Allies rejected any thought of bombing this concentration camp and the railroad tracks leading to it, and most mainstream Jewish groups agreed that the first victims of a bombing of Auschwitz would be the Jewish prisoners, who, if they survived the assault, would have no place to run. Moreover, the Germans could easily rebuild the railroad lines. The Allies believed that the best way to save Jewish lives was to end the war as soon as possible.

CHURCHILL, WINSTON   See glossary in selection 17.

DICKSTEIN, SAMUEL   Democrat who chaired the House subcommittee on immigration. Like Congressman Emanuel Celler of Brooklyn, he wanted to ease the quota restrictions to allow more Jewish immigrants to enter the United States, but he feared that such actions would provide reactionaries with an opportunity to further limit immigration.

EVIAN CONFERENCE   President Roosevelt helped organize this humanitarian effort "to facilitate the emigration from Germany and Austria of political refugees." It was largely a failure because of American immigration quotas and Hitler's refusal to permit refugees to keep some of their assets in order to start a new life.

GOEBBELS, JOSEF   Hitler's propaganda minister. Goebbels used radio and films to promote the Nazi cause at home, foment hatred toward European Jewry, and exaggerate German successes on the battlefield.

INTERNATIONAL RESCUE COMMITTEE   In 1933, Eleanor Roosevelt was one of the founders of this organization, which won sanctuary in America for many of the most prominent victims of Hitler's persecution.

KRISTALLNACHT   German word meaning "glass night," referring to the noise of breaking windows. In November 1938, anti-Semitic riots that resulted in looting and arson scarred much of Germany. Little was done to contain the senseless violence, which was a signal of much worse to come. In response, President Roosevelt extended the visas of twenty thousand Germans and Austrians in the United States so that they would not have to return home.

LONG, BRECKENRIDGE   Assistant secretary of state who allowed his biases to influence the restrictive immigration quotas established by Congress. These quotas limited the number of Jewish refugees who sought sanctuary in the United States.

MANN, THOMAS   Well-known humanist and German exile who believed that compromise was impossible in dealing with Hitler. He influenced policymakers in the United States to use the threat of force when negotiating with the Nazis.

NUREMBURG LAWS   In 1935, the Nazis severely restricted the rights of Jews through the Nuremburg Laws, a series of measures that limited the professions they could enter and barred marriage and sexual intercourse with gentiles. Hitler's purpose was to force German Jews to emigrate so that he could confiscate their property.

RIEGNER, GERHART   A representative of the World Jewish Congress whose telegram, in August of 1942, helped confirm the presence of Nazi death camps such as Auschwitz.

ST. LOUIS   In May of 1939, this ship carried 936 passengers, most of them Jewish, to Cuba, where all but 22 were refused sanctuary. Since the American government's strict immigration laws prevented their entry into the United States, American diplomats helped find temporary safety for them in other countries. However, most of those countries, like France and Belgium, eventually faced Nazi occupation and did not remain safe havens.

VICHY, FRANCE   After Hitler had overrun much of France, Marshal Pétain established a dictatorial government in the city of Vichy that collaborated with Germany. Pétain offered little resistance when the Nazis deported French Jews to extermination camps in eastern Europe.

WANNSEE CONFERENCE   In January 1942, the Nazi leadership formulated the "Final Solution" at this meeting in Berlin. Hitler's misguided belief in a pure master race of German "Aryans" resulted in a cruel plan to exterminate Europe's Jews.

WELLES, SUMNER   President Roosevelt's undersecretary of state who appreciated the plight of Jews trapped in Germany and the occupied countries. Welles urged the State Department to take more direct action to save them.

WISE, STEPHEN   A rabbi who was a friend of President Roosevelt and a respected leader of the American Jewish community. He spoke out against Hitler's atrocities, encouraged Jews to leave Germany, and pressured the American government to save as many lives as possible.

I t was Winston Churchill's judgment that the Holocaust "was probably the greatest and most terrible crime ever committed in the whole history of the world." The Holocaust, of course, was part of a colossal struggle in which fifty-three million people were killed, where nations were decimated, where democracy's survival was in the balance. In his campaign to exterminate the Jews of Europe, Hitler and his Nazi followers murdered six million men, women, and children for no other reason than that they were Jewish. This crime is of such profound proportions that it can never be fully understood; it must continue to be analyzed from every aspect as to how and why it happened, and its memory must unite all of us.

Nine million non-Jewish civilians were also murdered by the Nazis, as were three million Soviet prisoners of war, yet the Holocaust remains a uniquely horrible crime, and there can be no greater indictment than to allege complicity in it. Such an accusation was made against America in general and its leader, Franklin D. Roosevelt, in particular by a recent PBS documentary entitled "America and the Holocaust: Deceit and Indifference." The show drew on a substantial and growing body of scholarship that has caused many young American Jews to criticize and even condemn their grandparents and parents for being so absorbed in the effort to become assimilated in American society that they chose silence rather than voice outrage at the Nazi crimes and gave their overwhelming support to a President who was indifferent to the fate of Europe's Jews. Why did not the United States let the *St. Louis,* a German ship carrying Jewish refugees to Cuba in 1939, land at an American port when Cuba refused them admission? Also, perhaps the most frequently asked question of the last decade, why did the Allies not bomb Auschwitz and the railways that fed it? The people who pose these questions believe they know the answers. As one eminent spokesman for this viewpoint has written, "The Nazis were the murderers but we"—here he includes the American government, its President, and its people, Christians and Jews alike—"were the all too passive accomplices."

How much truth is there in these painful assertions? As we ask ourselves what more might have been done to save the innocent, we must frame our response in the context of the realities of World War II and the events and values of the years that preceded it.

Five weeks after Adolf Hitler became chancellor of Germany, in 1933, Franklin Roosevelt became President of the United States. Roosevelt's loathing for the whole Nazi regime was known the moment he took office; alone among the leaders of the world, he stood in opposition to Hitler from the very beginning. In a book published in 1937, Winston Churchill—to whom free humanity everywhere must be eternally indebted and without whose courage and strength the defeat of Nazi Germany could never have been achieved—described Hitler's treatment of the Jews, stating that "concentration camps pock-mark the German soil . . ." and concluding his essay by writing that "the world lives on hopes that the worst is over and that we may live to see Hitler a gentler figure in a happier age." Roosevelt had no such hopes. Thomas Mann, the most famous of the non-Jewish refugees from the Nazis, met with FDR at the White House in 1935 and confided that for the first time he believed the Nazis would be beaten because in Roosevelt he had met someone who truly grasped the evil of Adolf Hitler.

To comprehend the situation of European Jewry during those years, we must differentiate between the German Jews who were the immediate and constant subjects of Hitler's persecution and the Jews of Central Europe who were the principal victims of the Holocaust. The German Jews numbered about 525,000 in 1933. They were the yeast of Germany's great culture—leaders in literature, music, medicine, science, and financial and intellectual life. For the most part they wanted to be thought of as Germans. They had been a proud part of Germany's army in World War I. Anti-Semitism shadowed their lives, but they thought of Germany as *their* country and

William J. vanden Heuvel, "America and the Holocaust," *American Heritage,* vol. 50, no. 4 (July/August, 1999), pp. 34–37, 40–43, 46, 48, 50–53. Reprinted by permission of *American Heritage* magazine, a division of Forbes, Inc. © Forbes, Inc., 1999.

Nazi troops turn their rifles on helpless women and children in Poland's Warsaw Ghetto. The victims were caught "in a vast prison from which there was no escape and no possible rescue." The young, elderly, weak, and disabled were of limited use to the Germans in the cruel labor camps and were among the first to perish in the hideous gas chambers. (Yivo Institute for Jewish Research)

were deeply rooted in its existence. In the face of Nazi persecution, those who left Germany did so reluctantly, many seeking refuge in neighboring countries, from which they expected to return once the Hitler madness subsided. In the early years many, if not most, believed Hitler and his regime could not survive.

When, in 1933, Rabbi Stephen Wise, one of the most powerful and respected leaders of the American Jewish community during that era and a personal friend and close adviser of President Roosevelt, organized a New York rally to protest Nazi treatment of Jews, he received a message from leading German rabbis urging him to cut out such meetings and which, insultingly, indicated that American Jews were doing this for their own purposes and in the process were destroying the Germany that German Jews loved. Rabbi Wise never wavered in his belief

that the only option for Jews was to leave Germany. As the Nazi persecution intensified, as the Nuremberg Laws further degraded the Jews as had nothing before, as Hitler strove to make them emigrate and confiscated their property, the prospect of escape and exile had to shadow every Jewish family. In 1933 thirty-seven thousand Jews fled Germany, but in the relative calm of the next year, sixteen thousand returned. Every Jewish group affirmed the right of Jews to be German, to live in and love their country; they affirmed the legal right, the moral necessity, and the religious imperative of not surrendering to their persecutors. As important as any barriers to immigration in Western countries was the desire not to leave Germany until absolutely necessary. It is crucial to our understanding of these years to remember that at the time no one inside or outside Germany anticipated that the Nazi persecution would lead to the Holocaust. The actions of the German government were generally understood by both victims and by-standers as a return to the sorts of persecutions of prior centuries, not as steps on the road toward genocide.

Kristallnacht in November 1938 changed the situation dramatically. The assassination of a German diplomat in Paris by a seventeen-year-old Jewish youth whose father had been among the thousands of Polish Jews expelled from Germany and dumped across the Polish border just weeks before sparked a frenzy of arson and looting by Nazi thugs in almost every town and city. Huge, silent crowds looked on. The police did nothing to contain the violence. Many German Jews for the first time understood the hopelessness of their situation, and some looked west across the Atlantic.

The America that elected Franklin Delano Roosevelt its President in 1932 was a deeply troubled country. Twenty-five percent of its work force was unemployed—this at a time when practically every member of that work force was the principal support of a family. The economy was paralyzed, while disillusion after the sacrifices of the First World War fomented profound isolationist sentiments.

The nation's immigration laws had been established by legislation in 1921 and 1924 under Presidents Harding and Coolidge and by a Congress that had rejected the League of Nations. A formula assigned a specific quota to countries based on the population origins of Americans living in the United States in 1890. The law was aimed at Eastern Europe, particularly Russia and Poland, which were seen as seedbeds of bolshevism. Italians were targeted, and Asians practically excluded. The total number of immigrants who could be admitted annually was set at 153,774; the two countries of origin given the highest quotas were Great Britain (65,721) and Germany (25,957). The deepening Depression encouraged an unusual coalition of liberal and conservative forces, labor unions and business leaders, to oppose any enlargement of the immigration quotas. Because of the relatively large German quota, Jewish refugees from Germany had an easier time than anti-communist refugees from the Soviet Union, not to mention Chinese victims of Japan's aggression, or

Armenians. The Spanish who wanted to escape a civil war that between 1936 and 1939 killed half a million people faced an annual quota of 252.

The President and Mrs. Roosevelt were leaders in the effort to help those fleeing Nazi persecution. Eleanor Roosevelt was a founder, in 1933, of the International Rescue Committee, which brought intellectuals, labor leaders, and political figures to sanctuary in the United States. President Roosevelt made a public point of inviting many of them to the White House. In 1936, in response to the Nazi confiscation of personal assets as a precondition to Jewish emigration, Roosevelt greatly modified President Hoover's strict interpretation of the refugee laws, thereby allowing a greater number of visas to be issued. As a result the United States accepted twice as many Jewish refugees as did all other countries put together. As the historian Gerhard L. Weinberg has shown, Roosevelt acted in the face of strong and politically damaging criticism for what was generally considered a pro-Jewish attitude.

When, in March 1938, the Anschluss put Austria's 185,000 Jews in jeopardy, Roosevelt called for an international conference "to facilitate the emigration from Germany and Austria of political refugees." There was no political advantage to FDR in this; no other major leader in any country matched his concern and involvement. The conference, which met in Evian, France, tried to open new doors in the Western Hemisphere. At first things went well; the Dominican Republic, for example, offered to give sanctuary to 100,000 refugees. Then came a devastating blow: The Polish and Romanian governments announced that they expected the same right as the Germans to expel their Jewish populations. There were fewer than 475,000 Jews left in Germany and Austria at this point—a number manageable in an emigration plan that the twenty-nine participating nations could prepare—but with the possibility of 3.5 million more from Eastern Europe, the concern now was that any offer of help would only encourage authoritarian governments to brutalize any unwanted portion of their populations, expecting their criminal acts against their own citizens to force the democracies to give them haven. National attitudes then were not very different from today's; no country allows any and every refugee to enter without limitations. Quotas are thought even now to deter unscrupulous and impoverished regimes from forcing their unwanted people on other countries.

The Evian Conference failed to accomplish anything except organization of the Inter-Governmental Committee (IGC), which was to pressure the Germans to allow Jewish refugees to leave with enough resources to begin their new lives. It led to direct negotiations between Hjalmar Schacht, head of the Reichsbank, and George Rublee, a distinguished Washington lawyer personally designated by FDR. Schacht proposed that 150,000 Jews be allowed to emigrate, taking 25 percent of their assets with them, the rest to be impounded in a trust fund that would serve as collateral on bonds to be issued by the German state. Schacht was trying to resolve Germany's foreign exchange crisis, but Hitler ordered an end to the discussions. The negotiations, like all barter negotiations in the years ahead, failed because the Führer never allowed them to succeed.

America's reaction to *Kristallnacht* was stronger than that of any of the other democracies. Roosevelt recalled his ambassador from Germany and at his next press conference said, "I myself can scarcely believe that such things could occur in a twentieth-century civilization." He extended the visitors' visas of twenty thousand Germans and Austrians in the United States so they would not have to return. Americans in opinion polls showed anger and disgust with the Nazis and sympathy for the Jews; nevertheless, Roosevelt remained the target of the hard-core anti-Semites in America. He fought them shrewdly and effectively, managing to isolate them from mainstream America and essentially equating their anti-Semitism with treason destructive to both the national interest and national defense. Recognizing the inertia at the State Department, he entrusted Sumner Welles, the Undersecretary of State and a man wholly sympathetic to Jewish needs, to be his instrument of action.

Immigration procedures were complicated and sometimes harshly administered. The laws and quotas were jealously guarded by Congress, supported by a strong, broad cross section of Americans who were against all immigrants, not just Jews. Of course, there were racists and anti-Semites in the Congress and in the country, as there are today, only now they dare not speak their true attitudes. The State Department, deeply protective of its administrative authority in the granting of visas, was frequently more concerned with congressional attitudes and criticisms than with reflecting American decency and generosity in helping people in despair and panic. Roosevelt undoubtedly made a mistake in appointing as Assistant Secretary of State Breckenridge Long, who many allege was an anti-Semite. His presence at State was an assurance to Congress that the immigration laws would be strictly enforced. On the other hand there were countless Foreign Service officers who did everything possible to help persecuted, innocent people, just as they would today. There was an attitude that many sanctuaries besides the United States existed in the world, so the department, controlled by a career elite, conservative and in large part anti–New Deal and anti-FDR, was quite prepared to make congressional attitudes rather than those of the White House the guide for their administration of immigration procedures. Yet, between 1933 and 1941, 35 percent of all immigrants to America under quota guidelines were Jewish. After *Kristallnacht,* Jewish immigrants were more than *half* of all immigrants admitted to the United States. . . .

For his part, Roosevelt, knowing that he did not have the power to change the quota system of his own country, was constantly seeking havens for the refugees in other countries. His critics severely underestimate limitations on presidential power; clearly, the President could not unilaterally command an increase in quotas. In fact, the Democratic congressional leaders, including Rep. Samuel Dickstein, who chaired the House subcommittee on immigration, warned him that reactionary forces in Congress might well use any attempt to increase the quotas as an opportunity to reduce them. In 1939 Congressman

Emanuel Celler of Brooklyn, an outspoken defender of Jewish interests, gave a speech in which he warned that "it would be dangerous at this time because of public opinion in the South and West to press for the passage in Congress of [his own] bills to give asylum in the United States to refugees and to reallot for refugees the unused quotas of various countries." Congressman Celler said he had been warned by representatives from other parts of the country that if he pressed his proposals, other bills "to cut the quotas in half or to stop all immigration would be introduced and probably passed." Nor were the Jews the only refugees Congress was determined to bar. A few days later the Reverend Joseph Ostermann, executive director of the Committeee for Catholic Refugees from Germany, said that there were five hundred thousand actual or potential Catholic refugees whom "Goebbels and Rosenberg in Germany have attempted to identify with communism."

By the time the war made further emigration impossible, 72 percent of all German Jews had left the country—and 83 percent of all those under twenty-one. There are many reasons why the others did not get out: Some were too old to leave; some, like the brave chief rabbi of Berlin, Leo Baeck, believed it their religious duty to stay; some were in concentration camps and prisons; some just did not know what to do. Even after *Kristallnacht* nobody could foresee the events that became the Holocaust. Louis de Jong, an eminent Dutch historian and Holocaust survivor, said in his Erasmus lectures at Harvard University in 1989: "[There is] an aspect of the Holocaust which is of cardinal importance and which can never be sufficiently underlined: that the Holocaust, when it took place, was beyond the belief and the comprehension of almost all people living at the time, Jews included. Everyone knew that human history had been scarred by endless cruelties. But that thousands, nay millions, of human beings—men, women and children, the old and the young, the healthy and the infirm—would be killed, finished off, mechanically, industrially so to speak, would be exterminated like vermin—that was a notion so alien

to the human mind, an event so gruesome, so *new,* that the instinctive, indeed the natural, reaction of most people was: it can't be true."

Given the reality of the Holocaust, all of us in every country—and certainly in America—can only wish that we had done more, that our immigration barriers had been lower, that our Congress had had a broader world view, that every public servant had shared the beliefs of Franklin and Eleanor Roosevelt. If anyone had foreseen the Holocaust, perhaps, possibly, maybe . . . but no one did. Nevertheless, the United States, a nation remote from Europe in a way our children can hardly understand, took in double the number of Jewish refugees accepted by the rest of the world.

Among the anguishing events we read about is the fate of the ship *St. Louis* of the Hamburg-America Line, which left Germany and arrived in Cuba with 936 passengers, all but 6 of them Jewish refugees, on May 27, 1939. This was three months before the outbreak of the war and three years before the establishment of the death camps. Other ships had made the same journey, and their passengers had disembarked successfully, but on May 5 the Cuban government had issued a decree curtailing the power of the corrupt director general of immigration to issue landing certificates. New regulations requiring five-hundred-dollar bonds from each approved immigrant had been transmitted to the shipping line, but only 22 passengers of the *St. Louis* had fulfilled the requirements before leaving Hamburg on May 13. Those 22 were allowed to land; intense negotiations with the Cuban government regarding the other passengers—negotiations in which American Jewish agencies participated—broke down despite pressure from our government. It was not an unreported event. Tremendous international attention focused on the *St. Louis,* later made famous as the "Voyage of the Damned." Secretary of State Cordell Hull, Secretary of the Treasury Henry Morgenthau, Jr., and others, including Eleanor Roosevelt, worked to evade the immigration laws—for example, by attempting to land the passengers as "tourists" in the Virgin Islands. One survivor of the *St. Louis* whom I interviewed—a retired professor of human genetics at the University of Washington in Seattle—described its commander, Capt. Gustav Schroeder, as a compassionate man who ordered decent treatment for his Jewish passengers and who told them that he would run his ship aground off England rather than return them to Germany if Cuba refused admission. In the end, despite the legal inability of the United States to accept the passengers as immigrants, our diplomats were significantly helpful in resettling them. Not one was returned to Nazi Germany. They all went to democratic countries—288 in the United Kingdom, the rest in France, the Netherlands, Belgium, and Denmark. And who, in that spring of 1939, was prescient enough to foretell that in little more than a year all but one of those countries would be held by Nazi troops?

What were FDR's own attitudes toward Hitler and the Jews? Did he reflect the social anti-Semitism that was endemic in the America of that era? Contemporary Jews certainly didn't think so. Roosevelt opened the offices of government as never before to Jews. Henry Morgenthau, Jr., Samuel Rosenman, Felix Frankfurter, Benjamin Cohen, David Niles, Anna Rosenberg, Sidney Hillman, and David Dubinsky were among his closest advisers in politics and government. Rabbi Stephen Wise, the pre-eminent spokesman for American Zionism, said, "No one was more genuinely free from religious prejudice and racial bigotry."

Nazi policy changed radically after the outbreak of war. The Holocaust took place between 1941 and 1945. Hitler's conquest of the European continent let loose the full force of his psychopathic obsession about Jews. With the start of the war, on September 1, 1939, emigration from Germany was prohibited. Nevertheless, hundreds, perhaps thousands, of German Jews managed to escape across borders into Holland, Belgium, and Switzerland. But by June 1940, with the fall of France, Europe became a prison for Jews. Unoccupied France still offered an escape route, and despite intense criticism from the political left, FDR maintained diplomatic relations with Vichy, France, allowing that route to remain open. The International Rescue Committee, a group of which Eleanor Roosevelt remained very supportive, sent a team headed by Varian Fry that helped countless refugees find sanctuary in Spain and Portugal. But the vise was tightening. The invasion of Russia in June 1941 put the lock on the most terrible dungeon in history. Special squads of the German SS—the *Einsatzgruppen*—began the slaughter of 1.5 million Jews behind the German lines in Russia. The Wannsee Conference, which structured the "Final Solution," was held in a Berlin suburb in January 1942.

The Jews of Central Europe, the Jews from the occupied nations of Western Europe, the Jews of the Soviet Union—the principal victims of the Holocaust—were not refugees; they were prisoners in a vast prison from which there was no escape and no possible rescue. . . .

The doors had been closed not by the United States or its allies but by Hitler. On January 30, 1942, Hitler, speaking to the Reichstag, said, "This war can end in two ways—either the extermination of the Aryan peoples or the disappearance of Jewry from Europe." Since the mid-1920s Hitler had never voluntarily spoken to a Jew. He was the most determined ideologue of racial superiority and racial conflict who ever led a country. Nothing diminished his mission—not the defeat of his armies, not the destruction of his country. As Germany lay in ruins, as its dictator prepared to end his life in his bunker in Berlin, his Nazi acolytes continued his campaign, diverting even urgently needed reinforcements for his retreating armies in order to complete the Final Solution.

The prisoners of Hitler could be saved only by the total, unconditional surrender of Nazi Germany, and that was a task that required four years and the unprecedented mobilization of all the resources, human and material, of Great Britain, the Soviet Union, and the United States.

Some critics of American policy during these years maintain that the news of the annihilation of Europe's Jews was deliberately kept secret so that our people would not know about it and that if Americans had been aware of the Final Solution, they would have insisted on doing more than was done. The facts are otherwise. President Roosevelt, Winston Churchill, General Eisenhower, General Marshall, the intelligence services of the Allied nations, every Jewish leader, the Jewish communities in America, in Britain, in Palestine, and yes, anyone who had a radio or newspaper in 1942 knew that Jews in colossal numbers were being murdered. They may have received the news with disbelief; there was, after all, no precedent for it in human history. But the general information of the genocide was broadly available to anyone who would read or listen. The famous telegram from Gerhart Riegner, a representative of the World Jewish Congress, in Switzerland in August 1942, was not even the first knowledge of a death camp later to become known as Auschwitz when its gas chambers and crematoria had been built. Auschwitz, like every extermination camp, was treated as a top-secret project by the Nazis. The details and even the name of Auschwitz were not confirmed until the escape of two prisoners in April 1944, two years after its murderous processes had begun. But though the names, locations, and procedures of the death camps may not have been known—some not until the end of the war—the fact of the genocide and the Nazi determination to carry it out were not in doubt.

When Rabbi Wise was given the Riegner telegram, Sumner Welles asked him not to publicize it until its information could be confirmed by sources available to the Czech and Polish governments-in-exile. There was no video of this original version of "ethnic cleansing" such as we had available to us in Bosnia; there were no enterprising reporters who could photograph the Nazi butchery as there were in Rwanda. The experience of the First World War, in which atrocities attributed to the Germans turned out to be grossly inflated or Allied propaganda, caused many to wonder if the incredible reports coming from the continent of Europe would ultimately prove false as well.

When Sumner Welles confirmed the truth of the Riegner telegram to Rabbi Wise, the rabbi wept, as countless Jews and non-Jews would do in those terrible years when the Nazis lay beyond the reach of the armies that would defeat them. Encouraged by

Welles to hold a press conference to announce the news, Rabbi Wise did so, on November 28, 1942. Then he and his colleagues met with FDR and asked the President to warn Hitler and the Germans that they would be held individually responsible for what they were doing to the Jews. Roosevelt agreed immediately. An announcement to that effect in the name of the United Nations was made in Congress and in Britain's Parliament on December 17, 1942. It was repeated many times throughout the war. Parliament stood in silence for the first time in its history to mourn what was happening to the Jews and to pray for the strength needed to destroy their persecutors. In America the labor unions led the nation in a ten-minute period of mourning for the Jews of Europe. It is difficult to argue that there was a conspiracy of silence regarding the fate of Europe's Jews when the American broadcaster Edward R. Murrow, listened to throughout the nation, reported on December 13, 1942: "Millions of human beings, most of them Jews, are being gathered up with ruthless efficiency and murdered. . . . It is a picture of mass murder and moral depravity unequaled in the history of the world. It is a horror beyond what imagination can grasp. . . . The Jews are being systematically exterminated throughout all Poland. . . . There are no longer 'concentration camps'—we must speak now only of 'extermination camps.'"

American Jewry was no passive observer of these events. Despite issues that bitterly divided them, primarily relating to Palestine, the Jewish community in America spoke the same words in pleading to do whatever was possible for Europe's Jews. Jewish leaders lobbied Congress. Mass rallies were held across the country with overflow crowds throughout those years, praying, pleading for action to stop the genocide. The unremitting massacre continued because no one, no nation, no alliance of nations could do anything to close down the death camps—save, as Roosevelt said over and over again, by winning the war.

Had FDR followed the national will, Japan would have been our military priority, but understanding the Nazi threat to civilization, he ordered Germany to be the focus of our efforts. Had Roosevelt listened to General Marshall and his other military advisers, he would not have sent the few tanks we had in 1942 to help General Montgomery win at El Alamein, thereby probably saving Palestine from the same fate as Poland. Roosevelt gave frequent audience to Jewish leaders; he sent messages to rallies of Jews across the country; he listened to every plea and proposal for rescue that came to him. But he knew that the diversion of resources from the purpose of defeating the Nazi armies might palliate the anguish felt by so many, would rescue no one, and in all likelihood would kill the would-be rescuers. As Richard Lichtheim, a representative of the World Jewish Congress in Switzerland and a hero in informing the world of the genocide, said in December 1942, "You cannot divert a tiger from devouring his prey by adopting resolutions or sending cables. You have to take your gun and shoot him."

The historian Gerhard Weinberg answers those who question America's policy by suggesting that they consider how many more Jews would have survived had the war ended even a week or ten days earlier—and how many more would have died had it lasted an additional week or ten days. Given that the slaughter of the Jews went on into the final moments of the Third Reich, that every day until the surrender there were thousands of deaths by murder, starvation, and disease, the number of Jews saved by winning the war as quickly as possible was vastly greater than the total number who could have been saved by any rescue efforts proposed by anyone between 1941 and 1945. . . .

The proposal to bomb Auschwitz in 1944 has become the symbol for those who argue American indifference and complicity in the Holocaust. Some would have us believe that many American Jewish groups petitioned our government to bomb Auschwitz; in fact, there was considerable Jewish opposition in both the United States and Palestine. The focal center of the Holocaust Museum's exhibit on bombing Auschwitz is a letter from Leon Kubowitzki, head of the Rescue Department of the World Jewish Congress, in which he forwarded, without endorsement, a request from

the Czech State Council (in exile in London) to the War Department, in August 1944, to bomb the camp. Much is made of the Assistant Secretary John McCloy's response to Kubowitzki explaining the War Department's decision not to undertake such a mission. What is not on display and rarely mentioned is a letter dated July 1, 1944, from the same Leon Kubowitzki to the executive director of the War Refugee Board, arguing *against* bombing Auschwitz because "the first victims would be the Jews" and because the Allied air assault would serve as "a welcome pretext for the Germans to assert that their Jewish victims have been massacred not by their killers, but by Allied bombing."

Mainstream Jewish opinion was against the whole idea. The very thought of the Allied forces' deliberately killing Jews—to open the gates of Auschwitz so the survivors could run where?—was as abhorrent then as it is now. The Rescue Committee of the Jewish Agency in Jerusalem voted, at a meeting with the future Israeli prime minister David Ben-Gurion presiding, against even making the bombing request. Although only President Roosevelt or General Eisenhower could have ordered the bombing of Auschwitz, there is no record of any kind that indicates that either one ever heard of the proposal—even though Jewish leaders of all persuasions had clear access to both men.

A seemingly more reasonable proposal to bomb the railways to Auschwitz was made to Anthony Eden, the foreign minister of Great Britain, on July 6, 1944. Eden, with Churchill's immediate support, asked the RAF to examine the feasibility of doing so. The secretary of state for air, Sir Archibald Sinclair, replied several days later: "I entirely agree that it is our duty to consider every possible plan [to stop the murder of the Jews] but I am advised that interrupting the railways is out of our power. It is only by an enormous concentration of bomber forces that we have been able to interrupt communications in Normandy; the distance of Silesia from our bases entirely rules out doing anything of the kind." John McCloy had replied to a similar suggestion weeks earlier: "The War Department is of the opinion that the suggested air operation is impracticable for the reason that it could be executed only with the diversion of considerable air support essential to the success of our forces now engaged in decisive operations." Even the severest critics of America's response to the Nazi murder of the Jews acknowledge that successful interruption of railways required close observation of the severed lines and frequent rebombing, since repairs would take only a few days. Even bridges, which were costly to hit, were often back in operation in three or four days. Postwar studies of railway bombing totally vindicated the conclusion of the military authorities. Professor Istvan Deak of Columbia University asks in a recent article: "And if the rail lines had been bombed? The inmates of the cattle cars and those at the departure points would have been allowed to die of thirst, or of the heat, or of the cold, while the lines were being repaired."

It is often noted that American bombers were carrying out raids in the summer of 1944 on industrial targets only a few miles away from Auschwitz, suggesting how easy it would have been to bomb the gas chambers. They do not mention that preparation for the D-day invasion left only 12 percent of the U.S. Army Air Force available for the destruction of German fuel supplies, the primary mission as defined by Gen. Carl Spaatz. They point to the huge blowups of reconnaissance photographs at the Holocaust Museum that show not only the Farben synthetic-fuel plant, the target of the raids, but the outlines of Auschwitz and columns of prisoners. Yet the aerial photographs of Auschwitz on display were not developed until 1978, and their details were readable then only because advanced technology, developed by the CIA more than twenty years after the end of World War II, made it possible. *All* such strategic raids on military-industrial bases proceeded only after months of preparatory intelligence work, entailing the creation of a target folder with specific information about the size, hardness, structure placement, and defenses of the target and detailed aerial photography. These were costly, dangerous raids against heavily protected, frequently remote targets; the losses in men and planes

were tragically heavy. The Allied air forces simply lacked the intelligence base necessary to plan and execute a bombing raid against the Auschwitz extermination camp. It would have been a nonmilitary mission. Only Roosevelt or Eisenhower could have ordered it, and as we have seen, no one proposed it to them.

Yet many insist that anti-Semitism alone spared Auschwitz the wrath of the Army Air Force. With this in mind, it is worth considering the plight of northern Holland, where during the last seven months of the war more than eighty thousand citizens starved to death because the German occupiers wanted to punish the Dutch for insurrection and strikes following the failed assault on Arnhem. The Allies knew what was happening. Allied armies were everywhere around this occupied segment of the Netherlands; air rescue, or at least the capacity for organizing food drops, was minutes away. Still, eighty thousand men, women, and children died while the forces that could have saved them remained intent on their objective of a military engagement with the Germans that would lead to victory in the shortest possible time. Perhaps these military decisions were wrong, but they were not made because of any bias against the Dutch—or, regarding Auschwitz, because of anti-Semitism.

And what of those who managed to escape the Nazis once the war had started? President Roosevelt created the War Refugee Board in January 1944, immediately upon Henry Morgenthau's presenting the case for doing so. There were thousands of refugees stranded on the outer peripheries of Nazi Europe. With the invasion of Italy in 1943, thousands more had sought safety in camps in the south. Tito's success in Yugoslavia had enabled many to escape from Croat fascism and Serb hatred. But those were refugees who were already saved. They were not escapees from the death camps. Under pressure from Roosevelt and Churchill, Spain kept open its frontiers, stating as its policy that "all refugees without exception would be allowed to enter and remain." Probably more than forty thousand, many of them Jewish, found safe sanctuary in Spain. Makeshift transit camps there and in

This blowup of a reconnaissance photograph, taken in September 1944, shows Auschwitz and columns of condemned prisoners. The Holocaust Museum displays similar pictures with captions that read "thousands were gassed daily in this industrial killing center, but the Allies decided to ignore it." Vanden Heuvel maintains that it was not until 1978 that the CIA developed the technology to decipher the details in these arial photographs. (National Archives)

Portugal, Italy, and North Africa housed them in abysmal conditions. Those who fought for these people to come to America were right to do so; then, as now, refugees are generally powerless and voiceless. Governments have to be reminded constantly of their humanitarian responsibilities. But perhaps the Allied nations can be forgiven, in the midst of a war for survival, for not doing more for refugees whose lives had already been saved. . . .

Roosevelt's intervention with the government of Hungary, which by then understood that Nazi defeat was inevitable; the actions if the War Refugee Board,

such as retaining the heroic Raoul Wallenberg; the bombing of the Budapest area—all played a role in the rescue of half the Jewish community in Hungary. President Roosevelt was deeply and personally involved in this effort. Here is his statement to the nation on March 24, 1944: "In one of the blackest crimes of all history—begun by the Nazis in the day of peace and multiplied by them a hundred times in time of war—the wholesale systematic murder of the Jews of Europe goes on unabated every hour. As a result of the events of the last few days hundreds of thousands of Jews who, while living under persecution, have at least found a haven from death in Hungary and the Balkans, are now threatened with annihilation as Hitler's forces descend more heavily upon these lands. That these innocent people, who have already survived a decade of Hitler's fury, should perish on the very eve of triumph over the barbarism which their persecution symbolizes, would be a major tragedy. It is therefore fitting that we should again proclaim our determination that none who participate in these acts of savagery shall go unpunished. The United Nations have made it clear that they will pursue the guilty and deliver them up in order that justice be done. That warning applies not only to the leaders but also to their functionaries and subordinates in Germany and in the satellite countries. All who knowingly take part in the deportation of Jews to their death in Poland or Norwegians and French to their death in Germany are equally guilty with the executioner. All who share the guilt shall share the punishment." . . .

In December 1944 Anne O'Hare McCormick, a renowned foreign affairs reporter for *The New York Times,* wrote of a visit by a congressional delegation to the front in Italy. The congressmen expressed shock at the rigors of the campaign; they complained that this was one of the toughest battles of the war— and Americans were not being told about it. McCormick wrote: "The stories have been written and have been printed. They have even been overwritten and printed so many times that readers don't see the mud or blood anymore. They don't hear the screams of the shells or the thunder of the rockets. Congress either didn't read the accounts of the war in Italy or they couldn't take in the meaning of what they read. They had to see it. It is not their fault. It is because the thing is indescribable." How much more true is this insight regarding the death camps.

On April 12, 1945, General Eisenhower visited Ohrdruf Nord, the first concentration camp liberated by the American Army. "The things I saw beggar description," he wrote General Marshall. According to his biographer Stephen Ambrose, "Eisenhower had heard ominous rumors about the camps, of course, but never in his worst nightmares had he dreamed they could be so bad." He sent immediately for a delegation of congressional leaders and newspaper editors; he wanted to make sure Americans would never forget this. Five months later he dismissed his close friend and brilliant army commander Gen. George Patton for using former Nazi officials in his occupation structure and publicly likening "the Nazi thing" to differences between the Republicans and Democrats. (Patton had visited the Ohrdruf camp with Eisenhower and become physically ill from what he saw.)

Eisenhower got his first glimpse into the worst horrors at the heart of the Third Reich on the day death claimed the American who had done more than any other to bring them to an end. How ironic that Franklin Roosevelt—the man Hitler hated most, the leader constantly attacked by the isolationist press and derided by the anti-Semites, vilified by Goebbels as a "mentally ill cripple" and as "that Jew Rosenfeld"—should be faulted for being indifferent to the genocide. For all of us the shadow of doubt that enough was not done will always remain, even if there was little more that could have been done. But to say that "we are all guilty" allows the truly guilty to avoid that responsibility. It was Hitler who imagined the Holocaust and the Nazis who carried it out. We were not their accomplices. We destroyed them.

QUESTIONS TO CONSIDER

1 Would you agree with Winston Churchill that the Holocaust "was probably the greatest and most terrible crime ever committed in the whole history of the world"? After reading this selection, do you believe that the American government did all within its power to prevent it?

2 Why does vanden Heuvel argue that most German Jews, in spite of the anti-Semitism that they faced in their daily lives, were reluctant to abandon their homeland? When did emigration from Germany become virtually impossible?

3 Explain how immigration laws dictated the number of refugees who could enter the United States. Why did labor organizers, business leaders, and many members of Congress want to maintain those quotas? After *Kristallnacht,* about what percentage of immigrants who came to the United States were Jewish?

4 Why did both Cuba and the United States refuse to accept most of the Jewish passengers on the *St. Louis?* What did the future hold for most of those desperate travelers? Are you satisfied with vanden Heuvel's explanation that the United States did all it could given its restrictive immigration laws?

5 How do we know that, during the war years, President Roosevelt and the American people in general had knowledge of the senseless slaughter of Jews in the concentration camps? Why was there no attempt to bomb Auschwitz or the railroad lines leading to that death camp? What did Roosevelt believe was the most effective strategy to end the Holocaust?

6 What was the reaction of Generals Eisenhower and Patton when they liberated the death camps? In an age before instantaneous television film coverage, could the American people, Jews and gentiles, envision the horror of the Holocaust? Do you view this selection as an apology for American actions or a realistic appraisal of the response the United States adopted toward the Holocaust?

PART TEN

The Bomb

20 The Biggest Decision: Why We Had to Drop the Atomic Bomb

ROBERT JAMES MADDOX

Perhaps the most controversial episode of the Second World War was the decision of the American civilian and military leadership to drop atomic bombs on Japan in order to win the Pacific war. To place the debate in proper context, let us review what had transpired in the Pacific theater. In November 1943, American forces moved from a holding action to an aggressive, two-pronged island-hopping campaign, with Admiral Chester Nimitz's forces attacking at Tarawa and Kwajalein and General Douglas MacArthur's command breaking through the Japanese barrier on the Bismarck Archipelago, islands in the South Pacific. Eventually, MacArthur recaptured the Philippines while Nimitz pushed toward Japan itself from the central Pacific.

Japan fought back desperately, sending out kamikaze planes to slow the American advance with suicidal dives against United States warships. The kamikazes took a terrible toll: 34 American ships sunk and 288 damaged. But the "Divine Wind" vengeance that the kamikazes represented also cost the Japanese heavily: their losses were estimated at 1,288 to 4,000 planes and pilots. Moreover, they could not stop American army and naval forces, which moved on relentlessly, capturing Iwo Jima and then Okinawa, located just south of the Japanese home islands.

From Okinawa, the United States planned to launch an all-out invasion of the Japanese home islands, to begin sometime in November 1945. Army and naval leaders thought initial casualties would run from 31,000 to 50,000. But ultimately the losses could be staggering if it took a year to break Japanese resistance, as some experts predicted.

The invasion, however, never took place, because the United States soon had an awesome and terrible alternative. On July 16, 1945, after three years of top-secret development and production,

American scientists successfully detonated an atomic bomb in the New Mexico desert. Some scientists involved in the project urged privately that a demonstration bomb be dropped on an uninhabited island. But an advisory committee of scientists opposed any such demonstration and recommended that the bomb be used against Japan at once. Secretary of War Henry L. Stimson emphatically agreed: while the bomb would kill thousands of civilians, he said, it would shock Japan into surrendering and save thousands of American lives. Had the soldiers and marines in America's Pacific forces known about the bomb, they would have agreed, emphatically.

The final decision lay with Harry Truman, who became president after Roosevelt had died of a brain hemorrhage in April 1945. "I regarded the bomb as a military weapon and never had any doubt that it should be used," Truman later wrote. "The top military advisers to the president recommended its use, and when I talked to [British Prime Minister Winston] Churchill he unhesitatingly told me that he favored the use of the atomic bomb if it might aid to end the war." On July 25, Truman ordered that atomic bombs be dropped on or about August 3, unless Japan surrendered before that date. Then the United States, Great Britain, and China sent the Japanese an ultimatum that demanded unconditional surrender. The Japanese made an ambiguous reply. When August 3 passed and Japan fought on, Truman's orders went into effect, and American B-29s unleashed two of the "superhuman fireballs of destruction"—the first on Hiroshima, the other on Nagasaki—that forced Japan to surrender. Thus, the Pacific war ended as it had begun—with a devastating air raid. You may find it profitable to compare the Pearl Harbor air raid, a sneak attack against military targets (described in selection 18) with the nuclear blast at Hiroshima (covered in the following selection), which annihilated an entire city, including civilians and military installations.

Ever since, the use of the bomb has generated extraordinarily heated debate. Those against the bomb argue passionately that the monstrous weapon was not the only alternative open to Truman and his advisers in July and August. They point out that the invasion of Japan was not scheduled until November, so Truman had plenty of time "to seek and use alternatives." He could have sought a Russian declaration of war against Japan, or he could have ignored the advisory committee of scientists and dropped a demonstration bomb to show Japan what an apocalyptic weapon it was. He had another bomb to drop if the Japanese remained unimpressed. But Truman, in a remarkable display of "moral insensitivity," used the bomb because it was there to be used, and he never questioned his decision. To these critics, it is almost unthinkable that Truman and his advisers should ignore the entire moral question of dropping the bombs on civilians and ushering in a frightening and unpredictable atomic age. To this day, they point out with despair, America remains the only nation that has ever dropped an atomic bomb on another.

Other critics contend that Truman employed the bomb with an eye toward postwar politics. In their view, the president wanted to end the war in a hurry, before the Soviet Union could enter the conflict against Japan, seize territory, and threaten America's role in the postwar balance of power. Still others argue that the United States could have offered the Japanese conditional surrender, or found other ways to demonstrate the bomb, and so could have ended the war before the Soviets entered it.

Many analysts, however, defend Truman as passionately as his critics denounce him. Those for the bomb insist that his decision was a wise one that avoided a protracted land invasion in which hundreds of thousands of soldiers and civilians would have died. Sure, the bomb killed civilians, these critics say; it was unavoidable because the Japanese established military installations in residential areas of Hiroshima and Nagasaki. Besides, the Japanese could not complain: in their aggressions in Asia, the Japanese military had left 8 million civilians dead. "Did we have to drop the bomb?" asked a physicist who helped develop it. "You bet your life we did." He referred to a recent demonstration in the United States in memory of Hiroshima. "No one seems to realize," he said, "that without Pearl Harbor there wouldn't have been a Hiroshima."

In the following selection, historian Robert James Maddox of Pennsylvania State University presents the case for the bomb. Drawing on all available facts, he demolishes the "myths" of the anti-bomb school, one of which holds that several leading military advisers beseeched Truman not to use the bomb. As Maddox says, there is no evidence that a single one of them did so. After the war, Truman and others maintained that half a million American soldiers would have fallen if the United States had been forced to invade the Japanese home islands. Truman's critics have dismissed such claims as "gross exaggerations designed to forestall scrutiny of Truman's real motives." They point out that a war-plans committee estimated "only" 193,500 casualties. Maddox lampoons "the notion that 193,500 anticipated casualties were too insignificant to have caused Truman to resort to atomic bombs" and concludes that they were indeed necessary to end the war: the Japanese army, which ran the country, was preparing to fight to the last man, and the bomb was the only way to bring Japanese leaders to their senses and force them to surrender.

GLOSSARY

BOCK'S CAR   Nickname of the B-29 that dropped a second atomic bomb, called Fat Man, on Nagasaki.

ENOLA GAY   Nickname of the B-29 that dropped the first atomic bomb, called Little Boy, on Hiroshima.

GREW, JOSEPH   Truman's undersecretary of state; he had spent ten years in Japan as an ambassador and believed that the Japanese in the summer of 1945 were not even close to surrendering. Their "peace feelers," he claimed, were "familiar weapons of psychological warfare" whose purpose was to "divide the Allies."

HIROHITO   Emperor of Japan; the Japanese believed that the very soul of their nation resided in him.

JOINT WAR PLANS COMMITTEE (JWPC)   A report from this committee estimated that an American invasion of the Japanese home islands of Kyushu and Honshu would result in 193,500 total casualties in dead, wounded, and missing.

KAMIKAZES   Nickname for the Japanese pilots who flew suicide missions against United States naval forces toward the end of the Pacific war; the objective of the kamikazes was to crash their bomb-laden planes into American warships. The term *kamikaze* means "Divine Wind" in Japanese.

KONOYE, PRINCE FUMINARO   Sent to Moscow as a personal envoy of Emperor Hirohito. Prince Konoye sought to open negotiations that would lead to an end to the Pacific war.

MacARTHUR, GENERAL DOUGLAS   Commander of the army's half of the island-hopping campaign in the Pacific; it ran through the Carolinas and Solomons to the Philippines.

MARSHALL, GENERAL GEORGE C.   Army chief of staff during the Second World War and a close adviser to both Roosevelt and Truman. Warning that it was difficult to estimate battle casualties in advance, Marshall nevertheless thought that initial American losses from an invasion of Japan would be around 31,000 men. A subsequent medical report estimated that "total battle and non-battle casualties might run as high as 394,859" for the invasion of the southernmost Japanese island alone. Marshall not only supported Truman's decision to drop the atomic bomb on Japan, but considered using such bombs as tactical weapons during the land invasion.

NIMITZ, ADMIRAL CHESTER W.   Commander of the Pacific Ocean area; he headed the United States Navy's island-hopping campaign that led to the costly Battle of Okinawa; he believed that an invasion of Kyushu, the southernmost Japanese home island, ought to follow the operation at Okinawa.

OLYMPIC   Code name for the first phase of an American invasion of Japan, to commence at Kyushu, the southernmost home island, on November 1, 1945.

OPERATION CORNET   Code name for the United States invasion of Honshu, the main Japanese home island, on March 1, 1946.

SATO, NAOTAKI   Japanese ambassador to the Soviet Union in 1945.

TOGO, SHIGENORI   Japanese foreign minister in 1945; he made an overture to the Soviets asking that they initiate peace talks between Japan and the United States.

On the morning of August 6, 1945, the American B-29 *Enola Gay* dropped an atomic bomb on the Japanese city of Hiroshima. Three days later another B-29, *Bock's Car,* released one over Nagasaki. Both caused enormous casualties and physical destruction. These two cataclysmic events have preyed upon the American conscience ever since. The furor over the Smithsonian Institution's *Enola Gay* exhibit and over the mushroom-cloud postage stamp in the autumn of 1994 are merely the most obvious examples. Harry S Truman and other officials claimed that the bombs caused Japan to surrender, thereby avoiding a bloody invasion. Critics have accused them of at best failing to explore alternatives, at worst of using the bombs primarily to make the Soviet Union "more manageable" rather than to defeat a Japan they knew already was on the verge of capitulation.

By any rational calculation Japan was a beaten nation by the summer of 1945. Conventional bombing had reduced many of its cities to rubble, blockade had strangled its importation of vitally needed materials, and its navy had sustained such heavy losses as to be powerless to interfere with the invasion everyone knew was coming. By late June advancing American forces had completed the conquest of Okinawa, which lay only 350 miles from the southernmost Japanese home island of Kyushu. They now stood poised for the final onslaught.

Rational calculations did not determine Japan's position. Although a peace faction within the government wished to end the war—provided certain conditions were met—militants were prepared to fight on regardless of consequences. They claimed to welcome an invasion of the home islands, promising to inflict such hideous casualties that the United States would retreat from its announced policy of unconditional surrender. The militarists held effective power over the government and were capable of defying the emperor, as they had in the past, on the ground that his civilian advisers were misleading him.

Okinawa provided a preview of what invasion of the home islands would entail. Since April 1 the Japanese had fought with a ferocity that mocked any notion that their will to resist was eroding. They had inflicted nearly 50,000 casualties on the invaders, many resulting from the first large-scale use of kamikazes. They also had dispatched the superbattleship *Yamato* on a suicide mission to Okinawa, where, after attacking American ships offshore, it was to plunge ashore to become a huge, doomed steel fortress. *Yamato* was sunk shortly after leaving port, but its mission symbolized Japan's willingness to sacrifice everything in an apparently hopeless cause.

The Japanese could be expected to defend their sacred homeland with even greater fervor, and kamikazes flying at short range promised to be even more devastating than at Okinawa. The Japanese had more than 2,000,000 troops in the home islands, were training millions of irregulars, and for some time had been conserving aircraft that might have been used to protect Japanese cities against American bombers.

Reports from Tokyo indicated that Japan meant to fight the war to a finish. On June 8 an imperial conference adopted "The Fundamental Policy to Be Followed Henceforth in the Conduct of the War," which pledged to "prosecute the war to the bitter end in order to uphold the national polity, protect the imperial land, and accomplish the objectives for which we went to war." Truman had no reason to believe that the proclamation meant anything other than what it said.

Against this background, while fighting on Okinawa still continued, the President had his naval chief

Robert James Maddox, "The Biggest Decision: Why We Had to Drop the Atomic Bomb," *American Heritage,* vol. 46, no. 3 (May/June 1995), pp. 71–74, 76–77. Reprinted by permission of *American Heritage* magazine, a division of Forbes, Inc. © Forbes, Inc., 1995.

of staff, Adm. William D. Leahy, notify the Joint Chiefs of Staff (JCS) and the Secretaries of War and Navy that a meeting would be held at the White House on June 18. The night before the conference Truman wrote in his diary that "I have to decide Japanese strategy—shall we invade Japan proper or shall we bomb and blockade? That is my hardest decision to date. But I'll make it when I have all the facts."

Truman met with the chiefs at three-thirty in the afternoon. Present were Army Chief of Staff Gen. George C. Marshall, Army Air Force's Gen. Ira C. Eaker (sitting in for the Army Air Force's chief of staff, Henry H. Arnold, who was on an inspection tour of installations in the Pacific), Navy Chief of Staff Adm. Ernest J. King, Leahy (also a member of the JCS), Secretary of the Navy James Forrestal, Secretary of War Henry L. Stimson, and Assistant Secretary of War John J. McCloy. Truman opened the meeting, then asked Marshall for his views. Marshall was the dominant figure on the JCS. He was Truman's most trusted military adviser, as he had been President Franklin D. Roosevelt's.

Marshall reported that the chiefs, supported by the Pacific commanders Gen. Douglas MacArthur and Adm. Chester W. Nimitz, agreed that an invasion of Kyushu "appears to be the least costly worthwhile operation following Okinawa." Lodgment in Kyushu, he said, was necessary to make blockade and bombardment more effective and to serve as a staging area for the invasion of Japan's main island of Honshu. The chiefs recommended a target date of November 1 for the first phase, code-named Olympic, because delay would give the Japanese more time to prepare and because bad weather might postpone the invasion "and hence the end of the war" for up to six months. Marshall said that in his opinion, Olympic was "the only course to pursue." The chiefs also proposed that Operation Cornet be launched against Honshu on March 1, 1946.

Leahy's memorandum calling the meeting had asked for casualty projections which that invasion might be expected to produce. Marshall stated that campaigns in the Pacific had been so diverse "it is considered wrong" to make total estimates. All he would say was the casualties during the first thirty days on Kyushu should not exceed those sustained taking Luzon in the Philippines—31,000 men killed, wounded, or missing in action. "It is a grim fact," Marshall said, "that there is not an easy, bloodless way to victory in war." Leahy estimated a higher casualty rate similar to Okinawa, and King guessed somewhere in between.

King and Eaker, speaking for the Navy and the Army Air Forces respectively, endorsed Marshall's proposals. King said that he had become convinced that Kyushu was "the key to success of any siege operations." He recommended that "we should do Kyushu now" and begin preparations for invading Honshu. Eaker "agreed completely" with Marshall. He said he had just received a message from Arnold also expressing "complete agreement." Air Force plans called for the use of forty groups of heavy bombers, which "could not be deployed without the use of airfields on Kyushu." Stimson and Forrestal concurred.

Truman summed up. He considered "the Kyushu plan all right from the military standpoint" and directed the chiefs to "go ahead with it." He said he "had hoped that there was a possibility of preventing an Okinawa from one end of Japan to the other," but "he was clear on the situation now" and was "quite sure" the chiefs should proceed with the plan. Just before the meeting adjourned, McCloy raised the possibility of avoiding an invasion by warning the Japanese that the United States would employ atomic weapons if there were no surrender. The ensuing discussion was inconclusive because the first test was a month away and no one could be sure the weapons would work.

In his memoirs Truman claimed that using atomic bombs prevented an invasion that would have cost 500,000 American lives. Other officials mentioned the same or even higher figures. Critics have assailed such statements as gross exaggerations designed to forestall scrutiny of Truman's real motives. They have given wide publicity to the report prepared by the Joint War Plans Committee (JWPC) for the chiefs'

A Japanese soldier surrendering on Okinawa in May 1945. This was unusual. Most Japanese soldiers refused to surrender—it violated their sacred code of honor—and fought to the death. Robert James Maddox points out that "Okinawa provided a preview of what invasion of the [Japanese] home islands would entail. Since *April 1 the Japanese had fought with a ferocity that mocked any notion that their will to resist was eroding. . . . The Japanese could be expected to defend their sacred homeland with even greater fervor." (UPI/Corbis-Bettmann)*

meeting with Truman. The committee estimated that the invasion of Kyushu, followed by that of Honshu, as the chiefs proposed, would cost approximately 40,000 dead, 150,000 wounded, and 3,500 missing in action for a total of 193,500 casualties.

That those responsible for a decision should exaggerate the consequences of alternatives is commonplace. Some who cite the JWPC report profess to see more sinister motives, insisting that such "low" casualty projections call into question the very idea that atomic bombs were used to avoid heavy losses. By discrediting that justification as a cover-up, they seek to bolster their contention that the bombs really were used to permit the employment of "atomic diplomacy" against the Soviet Union.

The notion that 193,500 anticipated casualties were too insignificant to have caused Truman to resort to atomic bombs might seem bizarre to anyone other than an academic, but let it pass. Those who have cited the JWPC report in countless op-ed pieces in newspapers and in magazine articles have created a myth by omitting key considerations: First, the report itself is studded with qualifications that casualties "are not subject to accurate estimate" and that the projection "is admittedly only an educated guess." Second, the figures never were conveyed to Truman. They were excised at high military echelons, which is why Marshall cited only estimates for the first thirty days on Kyushu. And indeed, subsequent Japanese troop buildups on Kyushu rendered the

JWPC estimates totally irrelevant by the time the first atomic bomb was dropped.

Another myth that has attained wide attention is that at least several of Truman's top military advisers later informed him that using atomic bombs against Japan would be militarily unnecessary or immoral, or both. There is no persuasive evidence that any of them did so. None of the Joint Chiefs ever made such a claim, although one inventive author has tried to make it appear that Leahy did by braiding together several unrelated passages from the admiral's memoirs. Actually, two days after Hiroshima, Truman told aides that Leahy had "said up to the last that it wouldn't go off."

Neither MacArthur nor Nimitz ever communicated to Truman any change of mind about the need for invasion or expressed reservations about using the bombs. When first informed about their imminent use only days before Hiroshima, MacArthur responded with a lecture on the future of atomic warfare and even after Hiroshima strongly recommended that the invasion go forward. Nimitz, from whose jurisdiction the atomic strikes would be launched, was notified in early 1945. "This sounds fine," he told the courier, "but this is only February. Can't we get one sooner?" Nimitz later would join Air Force generals Carl D. Spaatz, Nathan Twining, and Curtis LeMay in recommending that a third bomb be dropped on Tokyo.

Only Dwight D. Eisenhower later claimed to have remonstrated against the use of the bomb. In his *Crusade in Europe,* published in 1948, he wrote that when Secretary Stimson informed him during the Potsdam Conference of plans to use the bomb, he replied that he hoped "we would never have to use such a thing against any enemy," because he did not want the United States to be the first to use such a weapon. He added, "My views were merely personal and immediate reactions; they were not based on any analysis of the subject."

Eisenhower's recollections grew more colorful as the years went on. A later account of his meeting with Stimson had it taking place at Ike's headquarters

in Frankfurt on the very day news arrived on the successful atomic test in New Mexico. "We'd had a nice evening at headquarters in Germany," he remembered. Then, after dinner, "Stimson got this cable saying that the bomb had been perfected and was ready to be dropped. The cable was in code . . . 'the lamb is born' or some damn thing like that." In this version Eisenhower claimed to have protested vehemently that "the Japanese were ready to surrender and it wasn't necessary to hit them with that awful thing." "Well," Eisenhower concluded, "the old gentleman got furious."

The best that can be said about Eisenhower's memory is that it had become flawed by the passage of time. Stimson was in Potsdam and Eisenhower in Frankfurt on July 16, when word came of the successful test. Aside from a brief conversation at a flag-raising ceremony in Berlin on July 20, the only other time they met was at Ike's headquarters on July 27. By then orders already had been sent to the Pacific to use the bombs if Japan had not yet surrendered. Notes made by one of Stimson's aides indicate that there was a discussion of atomic bombs, but there is no mention of any protest on Eisenhower's part. Even if there had been, two factors must be kept in mind. Eisenhower had commanded Allied forces in Europe, and his opinion on how close Japan was to surrender would have carried no special weight. More important, Stimson left for home immediately after the meeting and could not have personally conveyed Ike's sentiments to the President, who did not return to Washington until after Hiroshima.

On July 8 the Combined Intelligence Committee submitted to the American and British Combined Chiefs of Staff a report entitled "Estimate of the Enemy Situation." The committee predicted that as Japan's position continued to deteriorate, it might "make a serious effort to use the USSR [then a neutral] as a mediator in ending the war." Tokyo also would put out "intermittent peace feelers" to "weaken the determination of the United Nations to fight to the bitter end, or to create inter-allied dissension." While the Japanese people would be willing to make large concessions to end the war, "For a surrender to be acceptable to the Japanese army, it would be necessary for the military leaders to believe that it would not entail discrediting warrior tradition and that it would permit the ultimate resurgence of a military Japan."

Small wonder that American officials remained unimpressed when Japan proceeded to do exactly what the committee predicted. On July 12 Japanese Foreign Minister Shigenori Togo instructed Ambassador Naotaki Sato in Moscow to inform the Soviets that the emperor wished to send a personal envoy, Prince Fuminaro Konoye, in an attempt "to restore peace with all possible speed." Although he realized Konoye could not reach Moscow before the Soviet leader Joseph Stalin and Foreign Minister V. M. Molotov left to attend a Big Three meeting scheduled to begin in Potsdam on the fifteenth, Togo sought to have negotiations begin as soon as they returned.

American officials had long since been able to read Japanese diplomatic traffic through a process known as the MAGIC intercepts. Army intelligence (G-2) prepared for General Marshall its interpretation of Togo's message the next day. The report listed several possible constructions, the most probable being that the Japanese "governing clique" was making a coordinated effort to "stave off defeat" through Soviet intervention and an "appeal to war weariness in the United States." The report added that Undersecretary of State Joseph C. Grew, who had spent ten years in Japan as ambassador, "agrees with these conclusions."

Some have claimed that Togo's overture to the Soviet Union, together with attempts by some minor Japanese officials in Switzerland and other neutral countries to get peace talks started through the Office of Strategic Services (OSS), constituted clear evidence that the Japanese were near surrender. Their sole prerequisite was retention of their sacred emperor, whose unique cultural/religious status within the Japanese polity they would not compromise. If only the United States had extended assurances about the emperor, according to this view, much bloodshed and the atomic bombs would have been unnecessary.

A careful reading of the MAGIC intercepts of subsequent exchanges between Togo and Sato provides no evidence that retention of the emperor was the sole obstacle to peace. What they show instead is that the Japanese Foreign Office was trying to cut a deal through the Soviet Union that would have permitted Japan to retain its political system and its prewar empire intact. Even the most lenient American official could not have countenanced such a settlement.

Togo on July 17 informed Sato that "we are not asking the Russians' mediation in *anything like unconditional surrender* [emphasis added]." During the following weeks Sato pleaded with his superiors to abandon hope of Soviet intercession and to approach the United States directly to find out what peace terms would be offered. "There is . . . no alternative but immediate unconditional surrender," he cabled on July 31, and he bluntly informed Togo that "your way of looking at things and the actual situation in the Eastern Area may be seen to be absolutely contradictory." The Foreign Ministry ignored his pleas and continued to seek Soviet help even after Hiroshima.

"Peace feelers" by Japanese officials abroad seemed no more promising from the American point of view. Although several of the consular personnel and military attachés engaged in these activities claimed important connections at home, none produced verification. Had the Japanese government sought only an assurance about the emperor, all it had to do was grant one of these men authority to begin talks through the OSS. Its failure to do so led American officials to assume that those involved were either well-meaning individuals acting alone or that they were being orchestrated by Tokyo. Grew characterized such "peace feelers" as "familiar weapons of psychological warfare" designed to "divide the Allies."

Some American officials, such as Stimson and Grew, nonetheless wanted to signal the Japanese that they might retain the emperorship in the form of a constitutional monarchy. Such an assurance might remove the last stumbling block to surrender, if not when it was issued, then later. Only an imperial rescript would bring about an orderly surrender, they argued, without which Japanese forces would fight to the last man regardless of what the government in Tokyo did. Besides, the emperor could serve as a stabilizing factor during the transition to peacetime.

There were many arguments against an American initiative. Some opposed retaining such an undemocratic institution on principle and because they feared it might later serve as a rallying point for future militarism. Should that happen, as one assistant Secretary of State put it, "those lives already spent will have been sacrificed in vain, and lives will be lost again in the future." Japanese hard-liners were certain to exploit an overture as evidence that losses sustained at Okinawa had weakened American resolve and to argue that continued resistance would bring further concessions. Stalin, who earlier had told an American envoy that he favored abolishing the emperorship because the ineffectual Hirohito might be succeeded by "an energetic and vigorous figure who could cause trouble," was just as certain to interpret it as a treacherous effort to end the war before the Soviets could share in the spoils.

There were domestic considerations as well. Roosevelt had announced the unconditional surrender policy in early 1943, and it since had become a slogan of the war. He also had advocated that peoples everywhere should have the right to choose their own form of government, and Truman had publicly pledged to carry out his predecessor's legacies. For him to have formally *guaranteed* continuance of the emperorship, as opposed to merely accepting it on American terms pending free elections, as he later did, would have constituted a blatant repudiation of his own promises.

Nor was that all. Regardless of the emperor's actual role in Japanese aggression, which is still debated, much wartime propaganda had encouraged Americans to regard Hirohito as no less a war criminal than Adolf Hitler or Benito Mussolini. Although Truman said on several occasions that he had no objection to retaining the emperor, he understandably refused to make the first move. The ultimatum he issued from Potsdam on July 26 did not refer specifically to the emperorship. All it said was that occupation forces would be removed after "a peaceful and responsible" government had been established according to the "freely expressed will of the Japanese people." When the Japanese rejected the ultimatum rather than at least inquire whether they might retain the emperor, Truman permitted the plans for using the bombs to go forward.

Reliance on MAGIC intercepts and the "peace feelers" to gauge how near Japan was to surrender is misleading in any case. The army, not the Foreign Office, controlled the situation. Intercepts of Japanese military communication, designated ULTRA, provided no reason to believe the army was even considering surrender. Japanese Imperial Headquarters had correctly guessed that the next operation after Okinawa would be Kyushu and was making every effort to bolster its defenses there.

General Marshall reported on July 24 that there were "approximately 500,000 troops in Kyushu" and that more were on the way. ULTRA identified new units arriving almost daily. MacArthur's G-2 reported on July 29 that "this threatening development, if not checked, may grow to a point where we attack on a ratio of one (1) to one (1) which is not the recipe for victory." By the time the first atomic bomb fell, ULTRA indicated that there were 560,000 troops in southern Kyushu (the actual figure was closer to 900,000), and projections for November 1 placed the number at 680,000. A report, for medical purposes, of July 31 estimated that total battle and nonbattle casualties might run as high as 394,859 *for the Kyushu operation alone.* This figure did not include those men expected to be killed outright, for obviously they would require no medical attention. Marshall regarded Japanese defenses as so formidable that even after Hiroshima he asked MacArthur to consider alternate landing sites and began contemplating the use of atomic bombs as tactical weapons to support the invasion.

The thirty-day casualty projection of 31,000 Marshall had given Truman at the June 18 strategy meeting had become meaningless. It had been based on the assumption that the Japanese had about 350,000 defenders in Kyushu and that naval and air interdiction would preclude significant reinforcement. But the Japanese buildup since that time meant that the defenders would have nearly twice the number of troops available by "X-day" than earlier assumed. The assertion that apprehensions about casualties are insufficient to explain Truman's use of the bombs, therefore, cannot be taken seriously. On the contrary, as Winston Churchill wrote after a conversation with him at Potsdam, Truman was tormented by "the terrible responsibilities that rested upon him in regard to the unlimited effusion of American blood."

Some historians have argued that while the first bomb *might* have been required to achieve Japanese surrender, dropping the second constituted a needless barbarism. The record shows otherwise. American officials believed more than one bomb would be necessary because they assumed Japanese hard-liners would minimize the first explosion or attempt to explain it away as some sort of natural catastrophe, precisely what they did. The Japanese minister of war, for instance, at first refused even to admit that the Hiroshima bomb was atomic. A few hours after Nagasaki he told the cabinet that "the Americans appeared to have one hundred atomic bombs . . . they could drop three per day. The next target might well be Tokyo."

Even after both bombs had fallen and Russia entered the war, Japanese militants insisted on such lenient peace terms that moderates knew there was no sense even transmitting them to the United States. Hirohito had to intervene personally on two occasions during the next few days to induce hard-liners to abandon their conditions and to accept the American stipulation that the emperor's authority "shall be subject to the Supreme Commander of the Allied Powers." That the militarists would have accepted such a settlement before the bombs is farfetched, to say the least.

Some writers have argued that the cumulative effects of battlefield defeats, conventional bombing, and naval blockade already had defeated Japan. Even without extending assurances about the emperor, all the United States had to do was wait. The most frequently cited basis for this contention is the *United States Strategic Bombing Survey*, published in 1946, which stated that Japan would have surrendered by November 1 "even if the atomic bombs had not been dropped, even if Russia had not entered the war, and even if no invasion had been planned or contemplated." Recent scholarship by the historian Robert P. Newman and others has demonstrated that the survey was "cooked" by those who prepared it to arrive at such a conclusion. No matter. This or any other document based on information available only after the war ended is irrelevant with regard to what Truman could have known at the time.

What often goes unremarked is that when the bombs were dropped, fighting was still going on in the Philippines, China, and elsewhere. Every day that the war continued thousands of prisoners of war had to live and die in abysmal conditions, and there were rumors that the Japanese intended to slaughter them if the homeland was invaded. Truman was Commander in Chief of the American armed forces, and he had a duty to the men under his command not shared by those sitting in moral judgment decades later. Available evidence points to the conclusion that he acted for the reason he said he did: to end a bloody war that would have become far bloodier had invasion proved necessary. One can only imagine what would have happened if tens of thousands of American boys had died or been wounded on Japanese soil and then it had become known that Truman had chosen not to use weapons that might have ended the war months sooner.

QUESTIONS TO CONSIDER

1 What do you feel about Truman's decision to drop the atomic bomb on Japan? Do you think it was the right choice under the circumstances, or do you think it was wrong? What alternatives did he have? Would any of them have convinced the Japanese to accept America's terms of "unconditional surrender"?
2 Why did Truman and his advisers demand "unconditional surrender" by the Japanese? Why did

Japan's political and military leaders balk at accepting such terms? Why were they so determined to preserve the Emperor? What was the American view of him?

3 Much has been made of the estimated casualties the Americans would have suffered had they been forced to invade the Japanese homeland. To invade the first home island alone (this was Kyushu), Marshall came up with one casualty figure and Admiral Leahy with a somewhat higher figure for the first month of fighting. The Report of the Joint War Plans Committee estimated total losses from an invasion of the Japanese homeland at 193,500. After the war, Truman claimed that an invasion would have resulted in 500,000 American deaths. How do you explain such discrepancies? What does Professor Maddox say about them? Were Japanese forces on Kyushu and the main home island, Honshu, strong enough to inflict such losses? What is Maddox's opinion of critics who use the estimate of the Joint War Plans Committee to condemn Truman?

4 Why did the Japanese look to Stalin's regime in hopes of securing favorable peace terms? Why did the Soviet Union refuse to intercede in Japan's behalf in an effort to end the Pacific war? Had the Soviets approached the United States, asking for terms for Japan other than unconditional surrender, how do you think Truman and his advisers would have reacted?

5 What do you think might have happened had the Truman administration decided not to use its nuclear capacity against Japan?

21 Hiroshima: The Victims

FLETCHER KNEBEL AND CHARLES W. BAILEY II

One of our friends, who thinks that dropping the bomb was a necessity, believes nevertheless that the horrors it visited on Hiroshima and Nagasaki ought never to be forgotten. Indeed, perhaps the best argument against the bomb is what it did to its victims, which is the subject of the following selection. It and the previous selection ought to generate fiery discussions in every classroom in which Portrait of America *is read.*

For the people of Hiroshima and Nagasaki, the questions faced by Truman and his advisers did not matter. Nothing mattered to them but the searing flash of light that ultimately killed some 130,000 people in Hiroshima and 60,000 to 70,000 in Nagasaki and scarred and twisted thousands more. One scorched watch, found in the wreckage at Hiroshima, stopped at the exact moment of the atomic blast: 8:16 A.M. When the bomb exploded two thousand feet above the center of the city, thousands of people "were simply burned black and dead where they stood by the radiant heat that turned central Hiroshima into a gigantic oven." Some 60 percent of the city—roughly four square miles—was totally vaporized. "Beyond the zone of utter death and destruction," as one history puts it, "lightly built houses were knocked flat as far as three miles from ground zero, so that 80 percent of all buildings were destroyed and almost all the rest badly damaged." Nothing was left of Hiroshima but smoking, radioactive rubble. After the second bomb wrought similar destruction on Nagasaki, Emperor Hirohito spoke to his people by radio—the first time he had ever communicated with them. "The enemy," he said, "who has recently made use of an inhuman bomb, is incessantly subjecting innocent people to grievous wounds and massacre. The devastation is taking on incalculable proportions. To continue the war under these conditions would not only lead to the annihilation of Our Nation, but the destruction of human civilization as well."

Since then, a number of books have appeared about the atomic explosions at Hiroshima and Nagasaki. Among the best are J. Samuel Walker's Prompt and Utter Destruction *(1997), John Hersey's* Hiroshima *(1946), available in a new edition, and* No High Ground *(1960), by Fletcher Knebel and Charles W. Bailey II. The latter recounts the entire history of the first atomic bomb at Hiroshima, from Truman's decision to use it, to the flight of the* Enola Gay *(which dropped "Little Boy," as the bomb was called), up to the actual explosion and its cataclysmic results. In this selection, Knebel and Bailey describe that explosion with telling details, narrating the experiences of several people who somehow lived through that "fireball of destruction." Telling the personal side of Hiroshima is what makes this such a powerful account, with implicit lessons about the horror of nuclear war that have universal resonance. We can all identify with the people here, with Mr. Nukushina, Mrs. Susukida, and Dr. Imagawa, as the atomic blast swept over their city and changed the world forever.*

GLOSSARY

ENOLA GAY   Nickname of the B-29 that dropped the atomic bomb called "Little Boy" on Hiroshima.

HIRANO, MAJOR TOSAKU   Staff officer stationed in Hiroshima, he had gone up to Tokyo, and his decision to stay there a couple of extra nights saved his life; later, he persuaded Japan's leading nuclear scientist, who already suspected that the bomb dropped on Hiroshima was a nuclear weapon, to fly there and investigate.

DR. IMAGAWA   Visiting a patient's home when the bomb burst, he found himself "standing on top of a five-foot pile of rubble" with his clothes shredded; he made for his home in a suburb, helping the wounded along the way.

KINOSHITA, HIDEO   An officer at the monitoring station of the Japanese quasi-governmental news agency near Tokyo, he reported to his boss the news from America that an atomic bomb had been dropped on Hiroshima, and the boss relayed that report to the chief secretary of the Japanese cabinet.

NAKAMURA, BIN   Subchief of the Hiroshima bureau of Japan's news agency, he was eating breakfast when the explosion "lifted him off the straw mat on which he was sitting and sent a wave of 'immense' heat washing over his face"; miraculously unhurt, he spent the day interviewing survivors and got a story out on a suburban radio station.

NUKUSHINA, MICHIYOSHI   Fire-truck driver at the Hiroshima Army Ordnance Supply Depot, he had just returned home when the bomb exploded, flattening his home and blowing him into a corner where two safes prevented the falling roof from crushing him; he eventually found himself at an emergency aid station on Ninoshima Island.

OPPENHEIMER, J. ROBERT   Scientist and director of the top-secret project at Los Alamos, New Mexico, that built the first atomic bomb.

SAKAMOTO, CHINAYO   A mother who was mopping her kitchen floor when the *Enola Gay* droned by overhead, she and her family escaped "the blast and fire," because their home was situated behind a high protective hill.

SAKAMOTO, MIHO   Chinayo Sakamoto's daughter-in-law, who, after learning that her husband and his entire military unit had been wiped out, slit her throat with a razor in front of a little altar.

SUSUKIDA, HAYANO   Picking up salvaged roof tiles with other volunteers, she found herself suddenly slammed to the ground, her back severely burned, and her watch blown off; she made it to the emergency aid station on Ninoshima Island.

YAMAGUCHI, YUKO   She lived with her children in a rented farmhouse in a suburb and was just cleaning up after breakfast when the walls exploded in a black cloud of soot; unhurt, she went into the wrecked city and found her father and mother, both dying, in a Red Cross hospital; she never did find her husband's parents.

The sounding of the all-clear signal in Hiroshima at 7:13 A.M. on August 6 made little change in the tempo of the city. Most people had been too busy, or too lazy, to pay much attention to the alert. The departure of the single, high-flying B-29 caused no more stir than its arrival over the city twenty-two minutes earlier.

As the plane flew out over the sea, Michiyoshi Nukushina, a thirty-eight-year-old fire-truck driver at the Hiroshima Army Ordnance Supply Depot, climbed onto his bicycle and headed for home. He had received special permission to quit his post half an hour before his shift ended. Wearing an official-duty armband to clear himself through the depot gates, and carrying a new pair of wooden clogs and a bag of fresh tomatoes drawn from the depot commissary, he headed home through the narrow streets of Hiroshima.

Nukushina crossed two of the seven river channels that divided the city into fingerlike islands and finally arrived at his home in Kakomachi precinct a little more than half an hour after leaving the firehouse. Propping his bicycle by an entrance to his small combination home and wineshop he walked inside and called to his wife to go get the tomatoes.

At this same instant, in a comfortable house behind the high hill that made Hijiyama Park a welcome variation in the otherwise flat terrain of Hiroshima, a mother named Chinayo Sakamoto was mopping her kitchen floor after breakfast. Her son Tsuneo, an Army captain fortunately stationed right in his home town, had left for duty with his unit. His wife Miho had gone upstairs. Tsuneo's father lay on the straw mat in the living room, reading his morning paper.

Off to the east and south of the city, a few men in air defense posts were watching the morning sky or listening to their sound-detection equipment. At the Matsunaga lookout station, in the hills east of Hiroshima, a watcher filed two reports with the air defense center. At 8:06, he sighted and reported two planes, headed northwest. At 8:09, he saw another, following some miles behind them, and corrected his report to include it.

At 8:14, the telephone talker at the Nakano searchlight battery also made a report. His sound equipment had picked up the noise of aircraft engines. Unidentified planes were coming from Saijo, about fifteen miles east of Hiroshima, and were heading toward the city.

The anti-aircraft gunners on Mukay-Shima Island in Hiroshima harbor could now see two planes, approaching the eastern edge of the city at very high altitude. As they watched, at precisely seventeen seconds after 8:15, the planes suddenly separated. The leading aircraft made a tight, diving turn to the right. The second plane performed an identical maneuver to the left, and from it fell three parachutes which opened and floated slowly down toward the city.

The few people in Hiroshima who caught sight of the two planes saw the parachutes blossom as the aircraft turned away from the city. Some cheered when they saw them, thinking the enemy planes must be in trouble and the crews were starting to bail out.

For three quarters of a minute there was nothing in the clear sky over the city except the parachutes and the diminishing whine of airplane engines as the B-29's retreated into the lovely blue morning.

Then suddenly, without a sound, there was no sky left over Hiroshima.

For those who were there and who survived to recall the moment when man first turned on himself the elemental forces of his own universe, the first instant was pure light, blinding, intense light, but light of an awesome beauty and variety.

In the pause between detonation and impact, a pause that for some was so short it could not register on the senses, but which for others was long enough for shock to give way to fear and for fear in turn to yield to instinctive efforts at self-preservation, the sole impression was visual. If there was sound, no one heard it.

To Nukushina, just inside his house, and to Mrs. Sakamoto, washing her kitchen floor, it was simply sudden and complete blackness.

For Nukushina's wife, reaching for the bag of tomatoes on her husband's bicycle, it was a blue flash streaking across her eyes.

For Dr. Imagawa, at his patient's city home, it again was darkness. For his wife, in the suburban hills to the west, it was a "rainbow-colored object," whirling horizontally across the sky over the city.

To Yuko Yamaguchi, cleaning up after breakfast in the rented farmhouse where she and her in-laws now lived, it was a sudden choking black cloud as the accumulated soot and grime of decades seemed to leap from the old walls.

Hayano Susukida, bent over to pick up a salvaged roof tile so she could pass it down the line of "volunteer" workers, did not see anything. She was merely crushed to the ground as if by some monstrous supernatural hand. But her son Junichiro, lounging outside his dormitory at Otake, saw a flash that turned from white to pink and then to blue as it rose and blossomed. Others, also at a distance of some miles, seemed to see "five or six bright colors." Some saw merely "flashes of gold" in a white light that reminded them—this was perhaps the most common description—of a huge photographic flashbulb exploding over the city.

The duration of this curiously detached spectacle varied with the distance of the viewer from the point in mid-air where the two lumps of U-235 were driven together inside the bomb. It did not last more than a few seconds at the most.

For thousands in Hiroshima it did not last even that long, if in fact there was any moment of grace at all. They were simply burned black and dead where they stood by the radiant heat that turned central Hiroshima into a gigantic oven. For thousands of others there was perhaps a second or two, certainly not long enough for wonder or terror or even recognition of things seen but not believed, before they were shredded by the thousands of pieces of shattered

This scorched watch, found in the rubble at Hiroshima, stopped at the exact moment of the atomic blast: 8:16 A.M. When the bomb exploded, thousands of people "were simply burned black and dead where they stood by the radiant heat that turned central Hiroshima into a gigantic oven." (John Launois/Black Star; Hiroshima: National Archives)

window glass that flew before the blast waves or were crushed underneath walls, beams, bricks, or any other solid object that stood in the way of the explosion.

For everyone else in history's first atomic target, the initial assault on the visual sense was followed by an instinctive assumption that a very large bomb had scored a direct hit on or near the spot where they were standing.

Old Mr. Sakamoto, who a moment before had been lounging on the living-room floor with his newspaper, found himself standing barefoot in his back yard, the paper still in his hand. Then his wife staggered out of the house, and perhaps half a minute later, his daughter-in-law Miho, who had been upstairs, groped her way out also.

Dr. Imagawa had just reached for his medical satchel to begin the examination of his patient. When the blackness lifted from his senses, he found himself standing on top of a five-foot pile of rubble that had been the sickroom. With him, surprisingly, were both the sick man and the patient's young son.

Mrs. Susukida, flat on the ground amid the pile of old roof tiles, was left all but naked, stripped of every piece of outer clothing and now wearing only her underwear, which itself was badly torn.

Mrs. Nukushina had just time to throw her hands over her eyes after she saw the blue flash. Then she was knocked insensible. When she recovered consciousness, she lay in what seemed to her to be utter darkness. All around her there was only rubble where a moment earlier there had been her home and her husband's bicycle and the bag of fresh tomatoes. She too was now without clothing except for her underwear. Her body was rapidly becoming covered with her own blood from dozens of cuts. She groped around until she found her four-year-old daughter Ikuko. She saw no trace of her husband. Dazed and terrified, she took the child's hand and fled.

But Michiyoshi Nukushina was there, and was still alive, though buried unconscious inside the wreckage of his home. His life had been saved because the blast blew him into a corner where two big, old-fashioned office safes, used in the family wine business, took the weight of the roof when it fell and thus spared him from being crushed. As he came to, raised his head and looked around, everything seemed strangely reddened. He discovered later that blood from cuts on his head had gushed down over his eyelids, forming a sort of red filter over his eyes. His first conscious thought was that the emergency water tank kept on hand for fire-bombing protection was only one-third full. As his head cleared, he called for his wife and daughter. There was no reply. Getting painfully to his feet—his left leg was badly broken—he found a stick for a crutch and hobbled out of the rubble.

Hold out your left hand, palm down, fingers spread, and you have a rough outline of the shape of Hiroshima. The sea is beyond the fingertips. The back of the hand is where the Ota River comes down from the hills to the north. The spot where the bomb exploded is about where a wedding ring would be worn, just south of the main military headquarters and in the center of the residential-commercial districts of the city. Major Ferebee's aim was nearly perfect. Little Boy was detonated little more than two hundred yards from the aiming point on his target chart, despite the fact that it was released from a fast-moving aircraft over three miles to the east and nearly six miles up in the air.

Dropped with such precision, the bomb performed better than its makers had predicted. Several factors combined by chance to produce even more devastation than had been expected.

First was the time of the explosion. All over Hiroshima, thousands of the charcoal braziers that were the stoves in most households were still full of hot coals after being used for breakfast cooking. Almost every stove was knocked over by the massive blast wave that followed the explosion, and each became an incendiary torch to set fire to the wood-and-paper houses. In addition, where [J. Robert] Oppenheimer had estimated casualties on the assumption that most people would be inside their air-raid shelters, almost no one in Hiroshima was sheltered when the bomb actually fell. The recent all-clear, the fact that it was a time when most people were on their way to work, the mischance by which there had been no new alert when the *Enola Gay* approached the city, the fact that small formations of planes had flown over many times before without dropping bombs, all combined to leave people exposed. Thus more than seventy thousand persons instead of Oppenheimer's estimate of twenty thousand were killed outright or so badly injured that they were dead in a matter of hours.

The initial flash spawned a succession of calamities.

First came heat. It lasted only an instant but was so intense that it melted roof tiles, fused the quartz crystals in granite blocks, charred the exposed sides of telephone poles for almost two miles, and incinerated nearby humans so thoroughly that nothing remained except their shadows, burned into asphalt pavements or stone walls. Of course the heat was most intense near the "ground zero" point, but for thousands of yards it had the power to burn deeply. Bare skin was burned up to two and a half miles away.

A printed page was exposed to the heat rays a mile and a half from the point of explosion, and the black letters were burned right out of the white paper. Hundreds of women learned a more personal lesson in the varying heat-absorption qualities of different colors when darker parts of their clothing burned out while lighter shades remained unscorched, leaving skin underneath etched in precise detail with the flower patterns of their kimonos. A dress with blue polka dots printed on white material came out of the heat with dark dots completely gone but the white background barely singed. A similar phenomenon occurred in men's shirts. Dark stripes were burned out while the alternate light stripes were undamaged. Another factor that affected injury was the thickness of clothing. Many people had their skin burned except where a double-thickness seam or a folded lapel had stood between them and the fireball. Men wearing caps emerged with sharp lines etched across their temples. Below the line, exposed skin was burned, while above it, under the cap, there was no injury. Laborers working in the open with only undershirts on had the looping pattern of shoulder straps and armholes printed on their chests. Sometimes clothing protected the wearer only if it hung loosely. One man standing with his arm bent, so that the sleeve was drawn tightly over his elbow, was burned only around that joint.

The heat struck only what stood in the direct path of its straight-line radiation from the fireball. A man sitting at his desk writing a letter had his hands deeply burned because the heat rays coming through his window fell directly on them, while his face, only eighteen inches away but outside the path of the rays, was unmarked. In countless cases the human body was burned or spared by the peculiarity of its position at the moment of flash. A walking man whose arm was swinging forward at the critical instant was burned all down the side of his torso. Another, whose moving arm happened to be next to his body, was left with an unburned streak where the limb had blocked out the radiation. In scores of cases

people were burned on one side of the face but not on the other because they had been standing or sitting in profile to the explosion. A shirtless laborer was burned all across his back—except for a narrow strip where the slight hollow down his spine left the skin in a "shadow" where the heat rays could not fall.

Some measure of the heat's intensity can be gained from the experience of the mayor of Kabe, a village ten miles outside the city. He was standing in his garden and even at that distance distinctly felt the heat on his face when the bomb exploded.

After the heat came the blast, sweeping outward from the fireball with the force of a five-hundred mile-an-hour wind. Only those objects that offered a minimum of surface resistance—handrails on bridges, pipes, utility poles—remained standing. The walls of a few office buildings, specially built to resist earthquakes, remained standing, but they now enclosed nothing but wreckage, as their roofs were driven down to the ground, carrying everything inside down under them. Otherwise, in a giant circle more than two miles across, everything was reduced to rubble. The blast drove all before it. The stone columns flanking the entrance to the Shima Surgical Hospital, directly underneath the explosion, were rammed straight down into the ground. Every hard object that was dislodged, every brick, every broken timber, every roof tile, became a potentially lethal missile. Every window in the city was suddenly a shower of sharp glass splinters, driven with such speed and force that in hundreds of buildings they were deeply imbedded in walls—or in people. Many people were picking tiny shards of glass from their eyes for weeks afterward as a result of the shattering of their spectacles, or trying to wash out bits of sand and grit driven under their eyelids. Even a blade of grass now became a weapon to injure the man who tended it. A group of boys working in an open field had their backs peppered with bits of grass and straw which hit them with such force that they were driven into the flesh.

Many were struck down by a combination of the heat and the blast. A group of schoolgirls was working on the roof of a building, removing tiles as the structure was being demolished for a firebreak. Thus completely exposed, they were doubly hurt, burned and then blown to the ground. So quickly did the blast follow the heat that for many they seemed to come together. One man, knocked sprawling when the blast blew in his window, looked up from the floor to see a wood-and-paper screen across the room burning briskly.

Heat and blast together started and fed fires in thousands of places within a few seconds, thus instantly rendering useless the painfully constructed firebreaks. In some spots the ground itself seemed to spout fire, so numerous were the flickering little jets of flame spontaneously ignited by the radiant heat. The city's fire stations were crushed or burned along with everything else, and two-thirds of Hiroshima's firemen were killed or wounded. Even if it had been left intact, the fire department could have done little or nothing to save the city. Not only were there too many fires, but the blast had broken open the city's water mains in seventy thousand places, so there was no pressure. Between them, blast and fire destroyed every single building within an area of almost five square miles around the zero point. Although the walls of thirty structures still stood, they were no more than empty shells.

After heat, blast, and fire, the people of Hiroshima had still other ordeals ahead of them. A few minutes after the explosion, a strange rain began to fall. The raindrops were as big as marbles—and they were black. This frightening phenomenon resulted from the vaporization of moisture in the fireball and condensation in the cloud that spouted up from it. As the cloud, carrying water vapor and the pulverized dust of Hiroshima, reached colder air at higher altitudes, the moisture condensed and fell out as rain. There was not enough to put out the fires, but there was enough of this "black rain" to heighten the bewilderment and panic of people already unnerved by what had hit them.

After the rain came a wind—the great "fire wind"—which blew back in toward the center of the catastrophe, increasing in force as the air over Hiroshima grew hotter and hotter because of the great fires.

The wind blew so hard that it uprooted huge trees in the parks where survivors were collecting. It whipped up high waves on the rivers of Hiroshima and drowned many who had gone into the water in an attempt to escape from the heat and flames around them. Some of those who drowned had been pushed into the rivers when the crush of fleeing people overflowed the bridges, making fatal bottlenecks of the only escape routes from the stricken islands. Thousands of people were simply fleeing, blindly and without an objective except to get out of the city. Some in the suburbs, seeing them come, thought at first they were Negroes, not Japanese, so blackened were their skins. The refugees could not explain what had burned them. "We saw the flash," they said, "and this is what happened."

One of those who struggled toward a bridge was Nukushina, the wine seller turned fireman whose life had been saved by the big office safes in his house just over a half mile from "zero," the point over which the bomb exploded. Leaning on his stick, he limped to the Sumiyoshi bridge a few hundred yards away, where, with unusual foresight, he kept a small boat tied up, loaded with fresh water and a little food, ready for any possible emergency.

"I found my boat intact," he recalled later, "but it was already filled with other desperate victims. As I stood on the bridge wondering what to do next, black drops of rain began to splatter down. The river itself and the river banks were teeming with horrible specimens of humans who had survived and come seeking safety to the river."

Fortunately for Nukushina, another boat came by, operated by a friend who offered to take him on board.

"With his assistance, I climbed into the boat. At that time, they pointed out to me that my intestines were dangling from my stomach but there was nothing I could do about it. My clothes, boots and everything were blown off my person, leaving me with only my loincloth. Survivors swimming in the river shouted for help, and as we leaned down to pull them aboard, the skin from their arms and hands literally peeled off into our hands.

Their homes destroyed, city dwellers huddle on the Miyuki Bridge near the heart of Hiroshima. After the heat of the explosion came the "black rain," with drops as big as marbles, and then the "fire wind." Swept with conflagration, Hiroshima grew hotter and hotter.

Many refugees, attempting to escape the heat, drowned in the rivers, and the "crush of fleeing people overflowed the bridges, making fatal bottlenecks of the only escape routes." (Culver Pictures)

"A fifteen- or sixteen-year-old girl suddenly popped up alongside our boat and as we offered her our hand to pull her on board, the front of her face suddenly dropped off as though it were a mask. The nose and other facial features suddenly dropped off with the mask, leaving only a pink, peachlike face front with holes where the eyes, nose and mouth used to be. As the head dropped under the surface, the girl's black hair left a swirling black eddy. . . ."

Here Nukushina mercifully lost consciousness. He came to five hours later as he was being transferred into a launch that carried him, with other wounded, to an emergency first-aid station set up on the island of Ninoshima in the harbor. There he found safety, but no medical care. Only twenty-eight doctors were left alive and able to work in a city of a quarter million people, fully half of whom were casualties.

When Hayano Susukida tried to get up off the ground onto which she and the other members of her tile-salvaging labor gang had been thrown, she thought she was going to die. Her whole back, bared by the blast, burned and stung when she moved. But the thought of her four-year-old daughter Kazuko, who had been evacuated from the city after Hayano's husband was sent overseas and the family home had been marked for destruction in the firebreak program, made her try again. This time she got to her feet and staggered home. The blast had not leveled her house, about a mile and a quarter from the zero point, and the fire had not yet reached it. Hurriedly she stuffed a few things—a bottle of vegetable oil, some mosquito netting, two quilts, a small radio—into an old baby carriage, and started wheeling it toward the nearest bomb shelter. After going a few feet, she had to carry the carriage, for the street was choked with debris. She reached the shelter and passed the oil around to those inside, using the last of it to salve her own burns, which had not blistered or peeled but were nevertheless strangely penetrating and painful. She wondered what time it was. Her wrist watch was gone, so she walked home again to get her alarm clock. It was still running; it showed a little after ten. Back at the shelter, she just sat and waited. At noon someone handed out a few rice balls. As the survivors ate, an Army truck miraculously appeared and carried them to the water front, just beyond the edge of the bomb's destruction. Then they were ferried over to the emergency hospital on Ninoshima Island.

Dr. Imagawa, a little further from the center of the blast, was not seriously injured, although he was cut by flying glass in a number of places. His first reaction was annoyance. His clothes were in tatters, and he wondered how he would find the new pair of shoes which he had left at his patient's front door. Helping the small boy down off the five-foot rubble pile that had been the sickroom, he asked the youngster to take him to the front door. Oddly enough, they could not even find where the front of the house had been. Imagawa, much to his disgust, was out a new pair of shoes. At an artesian well with a pump that was still operating, he washed as best he could and set out for suburban Furue where his wife and children should be. He stopped frequently in response to appeals for help from the injured. One was a woman who wandered aimlessly in the street holding her bare breast, which had been split open. She pleaded with him to tell her whether she would live. The doctor, although positive she could not survive, assured her that a mere breast injury would not be fatal. Later, he drew water for a score of wounded from another well pump. Down the street, a trolley car burned briskly. Finally he got clear of the city and climbed the hill to Furue, where he found his family safe and uninjured. The walls of the house had cracked, in some places fallen, but his wife and the two little children had escaped injury, while the

oldest girl had walked home from school without a scratch after the blast. The doctor ate, washed thoroughly, painted his cuts with iodine and worked till dark with his wife cleaning up their house. That evening the somewhat sybaritic physician sat down to dinner and then relaxed, as he had done the night before in Hiroshima—twenty-four hours and an age earlier—over a few cups of wine.

The doctor sipping his wine that night had one thing in common with Mrs. Susukida and Michiyoshi Nukushina, both lying injured and untended in the emergency hospital on Ninoshima Island. None of them knew what it was that had destroyed their city. Nor did they yet have either time or inclination to wonder.

But others, outside Hiroshima, were anxiously trying to find out what the Enola Gay had dropped on the city. The search for information was a frustrating one.

At first there had been no indication that anything unusual had happened in Hiroshima. A moment after 8:16 A.M., the Tokyo control operator of the Japanese Broadcasting Corporation noticed that his telephone line to the radio station in Hiroshima had gone dead. He tried to re-establish his connection, but found that he could not get a call through to the western city.

Twenty minutes later the men in the railroad signal center in Tokyo realized that the mainline telegraph had stopped working. The break seemed to be just north of Hiroshima. Reports began to come in from stations near Hiroshima that there had been some kind of an explosion in the city. The railroad signalmen forwarded the messages to Army General Headquarters.

It was almost ten o'clock when Ryugen Hosokawa, managing editor of the Asahi vernacular newspaper in Tokyo, received a telephone call at his home. It was the office, reporting that Hiroshima had "almost completely collapsed" as the result of bombing by enemy planes. Hosokawa hurried to the office and sifted through the reports collected by Asahi's relay room. Every one of them sounded to him like something quite different from any previous bombing.

This must have been caused, he thought to himself, by very unusual bombs.

At about the same time Major Tosaku Hirano, a staff officer of the II Army Corps, was in General Headquarters in Tokyo. He had come up from Hiroshima a week earlier to report on the status of military supplies in the port city, and had been scheduled to fly back on Sunday. But he had put his departure off for a day or two and thus was still in the capital.

Now his telephone rang. It was a call from Central Command Headquarters in Osaka, an installation under the control of the II Army Corps in Hiroshima, reporting that its communications to Hiroshima and points west had failed.

Tokyo GHQ tried several times to raise the Hiroshima communications center, in the earth-and-concrete bunker next to the moat of the old castle, but could not get through. There was no explanation. The succession of reports from the radio network, from the railroad signal center, from *Asahi*'s newsroom and from Osaka indicated that something serious had happened, but no one could find out what it was.

Then, shortly after 1 P.M., General Headquarters finally heard from the II Army Corps. The message was short but stunning: "Hiroshima has been annihilated by one bomb and fires are spreading."

This flash came not from Corps Headquarters but from the Army shipping depot on the Hiroshima water front, which was outside the blast area and was not reached by the fire that followed. There was considerable damage at the shipping depot, something in the neighborhood of 30 per cent, but officers there were able to get a message out as far as Kure, where the naval station relayed it to Tokyo. There was no word at all from the II Army Corps Headquarters at the old castle in the northern part of town.

Reports continued to trickle in. By the middle of the afternoon, the Army knew that only three enemy planes had been over Hiroshima when the bomb exploded. It had been told that two of these did not drop any bombs. This information supported the startling assertion in the first flash that there had been only one bomb exploded. Something very big, and very frightening, had hit Hiroshima.

In mid-afternoon the managing editors of the five big Tokyo newspapers, plus their counterpart in the Domei news agency, were called to the office of the government Information and Intelligence Agency, which had charge of press and radio censorship. An Army press officer addressed the little group of newsmen:

"We believe that the bomb dropped on Hiroshima is different from an ordinary one. However, we have inadequate information now, and we intend to make some announcement when proper information has been obtained. Until we issue such an announcement, run the news in an obscure place in your papers and as one no different from one reporting an ordinary air raid on a city."

In other words, the lid was on. The Army already had a strong suspicion that the Hiroshima bomb might be an atomic weapon. Japanese Naval intelligence had reported U.S. work on the bomb in late 1944, noting the interest of the American government in buying up all available pitchblende (uranium ore). Thus, although the best scientists in Japan had agreed that there was no chance of the United States producing a fission bomb in less than three to five years, there was now immediate suspicion that an atomic bomb had fallen. But the Army, anxious to keep the war going so it could fight a showdown hand-to-hand battle with the Americans on Japanese soil, was determined to withhold the news from the Japanese people as long as it could.

The editors protested mildly, but the decision stood. At six o'clock that evening, the radio gave the people of Japan their first hint that Hiroshima had been chosen for a place in history as the spot where man first proved he could tear apart the basic structure of his world. A listener, however, would have been hard put to deduce the true story from the first news item as it was read:

A few B-29s hit Hiroshima city at 8:20 A.M. August 6, and fled after dropping incendiaries and bombs. The extent of the damage is now under survey.

This cryptic item was repeated several times between six and nine o'clock without further explanation. On the nine o'clock program in Osaka, the sound of the musical chime that signaled the switch from national to local news was followed by this item:

An announcement by the Osaka railway bureau in regard to changes in various transportation organs and changes in handling of passenger baggage:

First of all, the government lines. Regarding the down train, trains from Osaka will turn back from Mihara on the Sanyo line. From Mihara to Kaitichi, the trains will take the route around Kure. . . .

Mihara was about halfway from Osaka to Hiroshima. Kaitichi was on the southeastern edge of Hiroshima. Trains headed there from Osaka on the main line ordinarily ran through the Hiroshima yards and station before swinging back to the smaller community.

The morning *Asahi* in Tokyo on August 7 carried a long front-page story with a sizable headline reporting "Small and Medium Cities Attacked by 400 B-29s." At the end of this story, there was a four-line item tacked on. It read:

Hiroshima Attacked by Incendiary Bombs
Hiroshima was attacked August 6th by two B-29 planes, which dropped incendiary bombs.
The planes invaded the city around 7:50 A.M. It seems that some damage was caused to the city and its vicinity.

Those who survived in Hiroshima still did not know what it was that had struck them so viciously the day before. They did not have much time for thinking about it. Merely keeping alive was a full-time job. Some thought, as they fled the burning city, that the Americans had deluged their homes with "Molotov flower baskets," as the unhappily familiar incendiary clusters were nicknamed. Others, sniffing the air and detecting a strong "electric smell," decided that some kind of poison gas had been dropped. Another explanation was that a magnesium powder had been sprayed on the city, exploding wherever it fell on trolley wires and other exposed electrical conductors.

The prefectural government did what it could to bring order in the city. Somehow almost two hundred policemen were found for duty on August 7. They set to work, with whatever help they could commandeer, to clear the streets of bodies and debris. Police stations became emergency food depots, doling out hastily gathered supplies of rice, salt, pickled radishes, matches, canned goods, candles, straw sandals, and toilet paper.

The governor of Hiroshima prefecture, Genshin Takano, issued a proclamation:

People of Hiroshima Prefecture: Although damage is great, we must remember that this is war. We must feel absolutely no fear. Already plans are being drawn up for relief and restoration measures. . . .

We must not rest a single day in our war effort. . . . We must bear in mind that the annihilation of the stubborn enemy is our road to revenge. We must subjugate all difficulties and pain, and go forward to battle for our Emperor.

But most people in Hiroshima, if they could overcome their pain on this second day of the atomic age, were more concerned with finding their loved ones than with battling for their Emperor.

Yuko Yamaguchi, waiting out the war in the rented suburban farmhouse while her husband served overseas in the Army, was unhurt. So were her three little children. But her father-in-law, who had driven into the city Sunday for the meeting of his gas company board of directors, and her mother-in-law, who had left early Monday morning to fetch more supplies from their requisitioned city house, had not been heard from since the bomb fell. Yuko had had no word, either, from her own parents.

So at 6:30 this Tuesday morning, she left her children and set out for the city, walking the whole way because the suburban rail lines were not running. It was a long walk. By the time she reached the Red Cross Hospital, where she thought her in-laws might have been taken, it was noon.

Yuko did not find her husband's parents there. But, by sheerest chance, she found her own father, lying untended on the floor with an ugly wound in the back of his head. He begged his grief-stricken daughter for some water. When she did her best and filled a broken cup with stagnant water from a nearby pond, the delirious eye specialist was furious, insisting that ice and a slice of lemon be added to make it more palatable. Somehow, she found both in the wrecked hospital kitchen and made him as comfortable as possible. Then she started through the littered, jammed wards and halls to search for her other relatives. Again she found no trace of her in-laws, but at five o'clock she came on her own mother, lying unconscious, her face smashed almost beyond recognition and her intestines bared by a savage stomach wound.

Daughter dragged mother through the corridors to her father's side so the two could at least be together. There was little enough time. Near dusk the mother died, and Yuko had to carry the body outside, build a crude pyre and cremate it herself. At about dawn her father also died. This time, there were enough other corpses on hand so the hospital arranged a makeshift mass cremation, and Yuko left. She spent the day searching again for her husband's parents, but there was no trace of them, and she finally walked home to the hills to join her children. It was to be more than a month before she found any trace of her in-laws. Then she got only the stub of a commutation ticket bearing her mother-in-law's name, recovered from the wreckage of the train she had been riding at 8:16 A.M. Monday. A few charred bones uncovered still later in the burned-out office of the gas company president were the only trace ever found of her father-in-law.

Some who survived seemed to accept with stoicism the death of their loved ones. Miho Sakamoto, who with her husband's parents had escaped the blast and fire because their home was protected by the city's only high hill, was told on August 7 that her husband's military unit had been completely wiped out. She shed no tears and showed no emotion. Four days later, she visited the ruins of the building in

which he had died, found a bent ash tray which she recognized as his and brought it home. That night, she seemed in good spirits when she went upstairs to the room she had shared with her Tsuneo. The next morning she did not come down to breakfast. Her mother-in-law found her lying in front of a little altar, the ash tray in front of her beside a photograph of her dead husband, the razor with which she had cut her throat still clutched in her hand. She left a note of apology to "My Honorable Father and Mother":

What I am about to do, I do not do on sudden impulse; nor is it due to temporary agitation. It is a mutual vow exchanged with my husband while he still lived. This is the road to our greatest happiness and we proceed thereon. Like a bird which has lost one wing, we are crippled birds who cannot go through life without one another. There is no other way. Please, do not bewail my fate. Somewhere both of us will again be living happily together as we have in the past. . . . My honorable Tsuneo must be anxiously awaiting me and I must rush to his side.

Sixteen-year-old Junichiro Susukida, at his factory-school dormitory in Otake, sixteen miles west of Hiroshima, had seen the fireball and the great cloud that rose over the city Monday morning. When the first refugees arrived with the news that the city had been badly hit, he was one of many students who demanded permission to go to their homes, and he was one of five finally allowed to go into the city to contact authorities at the main school building and seek news of the students' families.

By the time they reached Miya-jima, on the southwestern edge of the city, the students could see the fires still burning in the bright late afternoon. As they came closer, they began to realize the full extent of the calamity. It was dark before the boys reached their home neighborhood and began their search for relatives. Junichiro, though unable to find either his mother or younger brother, did at last encounter neighbors who told him his brother had survived, though wounded, and had been taken to the home of other relatives in Fuchu. He could learn nothing about his mother, however, and finally headed back to his dormitory in Otake. Dead tired when he arrived at 2 A.M., he was nevertheless too distraught to sleep. He sat in the school auditorium and incongruously played the piano until fatigue finally subdued his nerves just before dawn on Tuesday, August 7.

Junichiro was not the only one who did not sleep that night. In Tokyo, the truth about Hiroshima was beginning to be revealed in ways that made it clear that the facts could not be kept from the people of Japan much longer.

A little before midnight on the sixth, the Tokyo office of Domei, the quasi-governmental news agency that served the whole nation, much as the Associated Press or Reuters do in the West, received a bulletin from Okayama prefecture, just east of Hiroshima. It was followed by a longer dispatch: the first eye-witness account of the bombing by a professional newsman.

Bin Nakamura, subchief of Domei's Hiroshima bureau, had been eating breakfast in his suburban garden when the bomb's explosion lifted him off the straw mat on which he was sitting and sent a wave of "immense" heat washing over his face. Once Nakamura discovered that the concussion and heat had not been caused by the nearby explosion of a "blockbuster"—his first reaction had been the typical one—he went to work as a reporter. On his bicycle and on foot, he spent the day in the city and talking to the refugees who streamed through his suburb. Then, at 10 P.M., like the experienced press-association man he was, he found communications at the suburban Haramura radio station and dictated a story to Okayama, the only point he could reach. In his dispatch, he said there was no way to tell what kind of a bomb had caused such havoc.

But before the night was much older the editors of Domei, and the leaders of Japan, had a way of telling much more about the bomb. In Saitama prefecture outside Tokyo, Domei operated a big monitoring station where nearly fifty workers, many of them Nisei girls born in the United States, listened to broadcasts from American stations. About 1 A.M. on the 7th of August (noon on the 6th in Washington, D.C.), Hideo Kinoshita, chief of the monitoring room, was awakened by the Japanese youth who had charge of the operation that night. The boy reported that U.S. stations were all broadcasting a statement by President Truman, describing the weapon that had been dropped on Hiroshima as "an atomic bomb." Kinoshita listened to the account and the boy's explanation of what "atomic bomb" might mean. Then he quickly called his own superior, Saiji Hasegawa, Domei's foreign news chief. Hasegawa was asleep in his hotel. When he was told of an "atomic bomb," he had no idea what it was, but although he was irritated at being awakened he hustled to his office. When he saw the text transcripts that were beginning to come through from the Saitama monitors, he was glad he had come to work. He reached for his telephone and called Hisatsune Sakomizu, chief secretary of the cabinet.

Sakomizu sleepily answered his bedside telephone, then came suddenly wide awake as he listened to the Domei executive. He already knew, from the first confused reports on the 6th, that the Americans had used some kind of new weapon. Now, learning that it was an atomic bomb, something the cabinet had discussed briefly almost a year earlier, he knew it meant just one thing: the war was over.

Sakomizu quickly called Prime Minister Suzuki, with whom he had been working in the effort to arrange a peace settlement by negotiation. They knew immediately, he said later,

. . . that if the announcement were true, no country could carry on a war. Without the atomic bomb it would be impossible for any country to defend itself against a nation which had the weapon. The chance had come to end the war. It was not necessary to blame the military side, the manufacturing people, or anyone else—just the atomic bomb. It was a good excuse.

The Army, however, was unwilling to accept this attitude, despite the urgings of the peace group that the bomb gave military leaders a chance to save face by blaming the "backwardness of scientific research" for Japan's inability to counter the new American bomb. The generals, sitting in an emergency cabinet meeting on the seventh, pointedly recalled an old Japanese legend about an Army commander who became a laughingstock because he mistook the fluttering of a flight of birds for the sound of the approaching enemy and fled. They argued that the bomb was not atomic but was merely a huge conventional projectile. They flatly refused Foreign Minister Togo's proposal to take up for immediate consideration the possibility of surrender on the terms of the Potsdam ultimatum, and insisted on keeping the Truman atomic statement from the Japanese people until the Army could conduct an "investigation" on the ground at Hiroshima.

The military had already started such a check. Major Hirano, the staff officer from the Hiroshima headquarters whose desire to spend a couple of extra nights in Tokyo had saved his life, called Yoshio Nishina, the nation's ranking nuclear scientist. He told him of the Truman claims and asked him to ride down to Hiroshima in his little liaison plane to investigate the matter. Nishina agreed to make the trip. The scientist was already pretty well convinced, on the basis of Hirano's report and further excerpts from the Truman statement given him a few minutes later by a reporter, that the bomb had indeed been the fission weapon which he and his colleagues had believed the United States could not manufacture so quickly. Truman's claim of a destructive power equal to twenty thousand tons of TNT coincided exactly with theoretical calculations made recently by one of Nishina's laboratory associates on the yield of an atomic bomb.

But the Army high command was keeping the lid on tight. When the Tokyo managing editors met again with the Information Agency censors that afternoon, they all had seen the text of Truman's statement. But they got nowhere with requests for permission to print it. The Army grudgingly allowed use of the phrase "a new-type bomb," but not the word "atomic." The editors argued hard this time, but to no avail. The end result of the wrangle was

this communiqué from Imperial General Headquarters at 3:30 P.M. on Tuesday, August 7:

1 A considerable amount of damage was caused by a few B-29s which attacked Hiroshima August 6th.
2 It seems that the enemy used a new-type bomb in the raid. Investigation of the effects is under way.

By evening, the newsmen were stretching the Army embargo as far as they could. A home service broadcast at 7 P.M. amplified the cryptic communiqué by adding that "a considerable number of houses were reduced to ashes and fires broke out in various parts of the city . . . investigations are now being made with regard to the effectiveness of the bomb, which should not be regarded as light." The broadcast went on to attack the Americans for "inhuman and atrocious conduct" and to urge the Japanese not to be "misled" by "exaggerated propaganda" such as "an announcement regarding the use of a new-type bomb" by Truman.

One man who was not likely to be "misled" by any announcement that night was Major Hirano, who finally had started back to Hiroshima in his five-seater liaison plane late in the afternoon. He had arrived at the Tokyo airport with the hurriedly assembled team of investigators earlier in the day, but had been ordered to wait until afternoon to avoid the U.S. Navy fighter planes that were now operating over Japan daily. There was some top brass in the inspection group which apparently was not anxious to hasten the day of personal contact with American invaders. Thus it was almost seven in the evening when Hirano's plane came down over Hiroshima. It was still light, however, so he got the full picture with shocking suddenness:

Being a soldier, my eye had been inured to the effects of bombing by that time. But this was a different sight. *There were no roads in the wastes that spread below our eyes:* that was my first impression. In the case of a normal air raid, roads were still visible after it was over. But in Hiroshima, everything was flattened and all roads were undiscernibly covered with debris.

When Hirano stepped from his plane, the first person he saw was an Air Force officer who came out on the runway to meet the team from Tokyo. His face was marked by a sharp dividing line right down the middle. One side was smooth and unhurt. The other, the one that had been toward the explosion, was burned, blistered, blackened. The investigators picked their way through the city to the wreckage of II Army Corps headquarters. Nobody was there. They finally found what was left of the headquarters—a few officers holed up in a hillside cave. By the time they began their formal investigation the next morning, the men from Tokyo knew the truth anyway. Hirano, in fact, had known it the moment he caught sight of what was left of Hiroshima from his circling plane.

QUESTIONS TO CONSIDER

1 What chance factors at Hiroshima added to the inherent destructiveness of the atomic bomb and produced more deaths and devastation than American scientists had expected?

2 Describe the sequence of destruction caused by the bomb's explosion. What were the physical effects of the bomb on human beings?

3 What was the immediate reaction of the Japanese army and government to the news of what had happened at Hiroshima? Why was the true nature of the American attack kept from the Japanese people?

4 Discuss the responsibility of the Japanese high command for prolonging the war after the bombing of Hiroshima.

5 Given the present-day proliferation of atomic weapons, what lessons can we draw from the firsthand accounts of the Japanese who experienced the horrors at Hiroshima fifty years ago?

PART ELEVEN

Perils of the Cold War

22 Harry Truman: "One Tough Son-of-a-Bitch of a Man"

DAVID McCULLOUGH

When he learned that Roosevelt had died and that he was now president of the United States, Truman told a group of reporters: "Boys, if you ever pray, pray for me now. I don't know whether you fellows ever had a load of hay fall on you, but when they told me yesterday what had happened, I felt like the moon, the stars, and all the planets had fallen on me."

He did not want to be president, and he certainly did not look like one: though cheery and brisk and always dressed in a spotless suit "as if he had just stepped from a bandbox," as his wife said, he was short, slight, and plain looking, wore thick spectacles, spoke in a Missouri twang, and radiated ordinariness. But, as a friend said, behind that plain-looking façade was "one tough son-of-a-bitch." Though not privy to Roosevelt's war strategy and military secrets, Truman stepped into the job with alacrity and confidently made decisions that led the country to victory in the Second World War.

In the postwar world, he faced a vortex of difficulties that would have daunted a lesser man. At home, the United States had to demobilize its vast military forces and convert wartime industry back to peacetime production. Abroad, the Allied victory proved to be a victory without peace. For out of the muck and rubble of the Second World War emerged a Cold War between the Soviet Union and the West that threatened the very survival of humankind. The genesis of the Cold War, as Truman learned, went back to the early days of the Second World War and involved control of eastern Europe. Russia and the Western Allies clashed over that area, and their rival strategies for the domination of eastern Europe influenced most of the wartime conferences among the big three (the United States, Great Britain, and the Soviet Union). The West hoped to establish democratic regimes in eastern Europe, but it proved an impossible program, for the massive Red Army overran eastern

Europe, and Stalin vowed to maintain Russian supremacy there. He did so not to export world Communism but to ensure Soviet security from the West—to make certain no western army could ever sweep through Poland and invade Russia as the Germans had done. The Soviet Union had lost from 20 to 25 million people in the war against Germany; no other nation swept up in the war, not even Germany itself, had suffered such casualties. Dominating eastern Europe, Soviet leaders hoped, would prevent such a catastrophe from ever happening again.

Once the Red Army occupied eastern Europe, Roosevelt did the only thing he could do. At the Yalta Conference of February 1945, he acknowledged Soviet hegemony in the region but pressed Stalin to hold free elections in the countries he controlled. Mainly to hold the wartime alliance together, Stalin promised free elections for eastern Europe. But obsessed as he was with Russian security, the Soviet boss never kept his promise, instead setting up Soviet puppet states from the Baltic to the Adriatic.

The West felt betrayed. By the time Truman came to power, the United States and many of its allies increasingly saw Stalin as a mad and devious Marxist dictator out to spread Communism across the globe. In the United States especially, a profound suspicion of the Soviets and world Communism swept over Washington and the Truman White House. Unlike Roosevelt, who had tried to conciliate the Russians, Truman in 1947 adopted a get-tough containment policy designed to block Soviet expansion and save the "free world" from Communism. The purpose of containment was not to overthrow the Soviet regime or invade the Soviet sphere but to prevent the Soviets from expanding the influence of Communism. To do that, Washington poured billions of dollars in aid into Greece, Turkey, and western Europe and extended American military power around the globe. American aid to western Europe, called the Marshall Plan, rebuilt its war-torn countries and neutralized Communist parties there.

From 1947 on, containment formed the basis of United States foreign policy. When in 1948 the Soviets blockaded Allied-controlled West Berlin (Berlin was located in the Russian sector of occupied Germany), Truman ordered a massive airlift by B-29s that prevented West Berlin from falling to the Soviets. His containment policy dictated that the United States get tough with China, too, after the Communists took over there in 1949 and drove Chiang Kai-shek's Nationalist Chinese into exile on Formosa (now known as Taiwan). The fall of China whipped up a storm of outrage and fears of Communism in the United States. In this sinister turn of events, Americans once again saw the evil hand of Joseph Stalin. At home, a terrible Red scare swept the land, as Americans saw Communists everywhere, from Hollywood to Washington, D.C., plotting to overthrow the government and hand the country over to the Soviets. Truman himself contributed to the scare by instituting a sweeping loyalty oath program and beginning extensive security checks for federal employment.

The Red scare produced in 1950 a finger-pointing rabble-rouser named Joseph McCarthy, who claimed that the State Department itself was crawling with Reds. He even accused Truman and General George Marshall, secretary of state, of being Communists. His strident accusations, which the press published with relish under black headlines, destroyed the careers of many innocent Americans. Yet not once in his anti-Communist crusade did McCarthy expose a single bona fide Communist.

The year, 1950, brought another shock. China's neighbor, Korea, was divided at the 38th parallel between a Communist regime in the north and a pro-Western government in the south. That June, North Korean forces invaded South Korea in what Washington viewed as an act of naked Communist aggression instigated by the Kremlin. Under the auspices of the United Nations, Truman sent in American troops, who in a few months drove the North Koreans back across the 38th parallel. By September, however, Truman had changed the purpose of the war: instead of simply maintaining the integrity of South Korea, he resolved to invade North Korea and liberate it from Communist rule. When United Nations forces under General Douglas MacArthur drove to the Chinese borders, that was enough for the Red Chinese: 260,000 of them crossed the Yalu and inflicted on MacArthur one of the worst military defeats in American history, sending him in pell-mell retreat back toward the 38th parallel. With that, Truman again changed the purpose of the war: he gave up fighting to liberate North Korea and fell back on the original United States goal of simply ensuring the sovereignty of South Korea. At that point, the Korean War bogged down in stalemate. When a frustrated MacArthur issued public statements vehemently criticizing Truman's policies and went on to advocate an all-out war against China, the president relieved him of command on the grounds that the general was trying to force his policies on his civilian commander in chief, which violated the constitutional provision of civilian control of the military.

In the following selection, David McCullough, Truman's foremost biographer and winner of the Pulitzer Prize, brings the tough little man from Missouri brilliantly alive in a warm and sympathetic portrait. McCullough shows us how Truman's personality and character—his no-nonsense bluntness, honesty, determination, courage, sense of history, and love of people—affected his postwar decisions and made him an extremely effective president despite his flaws and mistakes.

GLOSSARY

ACHESON, DEAN Truman's third secretary of state (1949–1953); he was the principal force behind the creation of the North Atlantic Treaty Organization (NATO), which allied the western democracies against the Soviet Union and its eastern bloc. Acheson implemented Truman's decision to send United States troops to South Korea, which had been invaded by Communist North Korea. Though Acheson was a diehard anti-Communist, Republicans accused him of being soft on Communism and blamed him for the Communist takeover of China in 1949.

BYRNES, JIMMY A conservative Democrat and "avowed segregationist," he was Truman's friend and adviser and served as his secretary of state from 1945 to 1947. He was one of the most vigorous advocates of dropping the atomic bomb on Japan. After the war, he tried to reconcile the United States and the Soviet Union but then became a harsh critic of Soviet designs.

CLIFFORD, CLARK Truman's special adviser from 1945 to 1950, he helped to formulate Truman's policy of containment and to create the Department of Defense.

DEWEY, THOMAS E. Republican nominee for president in 1948; he was universally expected to defeat Truman, so much so that before all the votes were counted, one newspaper ran a front-page headline: "DEWEY DEFEATS TRUMAN." As it turned out, Truman won the election, defying the pollsters and the odds.

FORRESTAL, JAMES Served as secretary of the navy from 1944 to 1947 and became the first secretary of defense when the Truman administration established the Department of Defense in 1947. He advocated a powerful military to contain Soviet aggression and persuaded the federal government to institute a peacetime draft.

HARRIMAN, W. AVERELL American businessman turned statesman; he served as United States ambassador to the Soviet Union from 1943 to 1946 and as Truman's secretary of commerce from 1946 to 1948.

KENNAN, GEORGE Historian and diplomat who helped formulate Truman's policy of containment toward the Soviet Union; he served as United States ambassador to Moscow until the Soviets demanded his removal.

LILIENTHAL, DAVID A long-time director of the Tennessee Valley Authority, which provided hydroelectric power for the Tennessee Valley. In 1946, Truman appointed him to chair of the United States Atomic Energy Commission, which stressed "civilian control and government monopoly of atomic energy."

LOVETT, ROBERT Influential undersecretary of state during Truman's presidency.

MARSHALL PLAN Also known as the European Recovery Program, it was the brainchild of George C. Marshall, Truman's second secretary of state (1947–1949) and former army chief of staff. The program distributed $12 billion in American aid that helped rebuild war-ravaged western Europe.

McCARTHY, JOSEPH   Republican senator from Wisconsin who earned his reputation by making fantastic accusations of Communist infiltration into the federal government, particularly the State Department. The cartoonist Herbert Block coined the term *McCarthyism* to describe the senator's Cold War witch-hunt to ferret out alleged Communists.

MUNICH, LESSON OF   In 1938, in Munich, Germany, the British and the French reached an accord with Adolf Hitler allowing Germany to possess an area of Czechoslovakia called the Sudetenland in exchange for Hitler's promise not to seize any more European territory. British Prime Minister Neville Chamberlain flew home to London, where he proclaimed that the Munich Pact had achieved "peace in our time." It had done nothing of the kind. A year later, Hitler's mighty mechanized army invaded Poland, thus setting off the Second World War. The "lesson of Munich" was that aggressors must never be appeased.

PENDERGAST, TOM   Boss of Missouri's Democratic political machine, through which Truman rose from judge of a county court to the United States Senate.

VAUGHAN, HARRY   Lifelong friend of Harry Truman who furnished him "comic relief." He was "Truman's Falstaff"—Falstaff being the bawdy, brazen, good-natured rascal in Shakespeare's *Henry IV, Parts 1 and 2*, and *The Merry Wives of Windsor*.

Harry Truman was President of the United States for not quite eight years. Looking back now we see him standing there in the presidential line, all of five foot nine, in a double-breasted suit, between two heroic figures of the century, Franklin Delano Roosevelt and Dwight D. Eisenhower. It's hard to convey today the feeling Americans had about General Eisenhower, the aura of the man, after World War II. He was charismatic, truly, if anyone ever was. Truman was not like that, not glamorous, not photogenic. And from the April afternoon when Truman took office, following the death of Franklin Roosevelt, he would feel the long shadow of Roosevelt, the most colossal figure in the White House in this century. He had none of Roosevelt's gifts—no beautiful speaking voice, no inherited wealth or social standing, no connections. He is the only president of our century who never went to college, and along with his clipped Missouri twang and eyeglasses thick as the bottom of a Coke bottle, he had a middlewestern plainness of manner, that, at first glance, made him seem "ordinary."

He had arrived first in Washington in the 1930s as a senator notable mainly for his background in the notorious Pendergast machine of Kansas City. He was of Scotch-Irish descent, and like many of Scotch-Irish descent—and I know something of this from my own background—he could be narrow, clannish, short-tempered, stubborn to a fault. But he could also be intensely loyal and courageous. And deeply patriotic. He was one of us, Americans said, just as they also said, "To err is Truman."

He was back in the news again after the Republican sweep in November 1994, the first such Republican triumph since 1946, and so naturally comparisons were drawn. Like Bill Clinton, Truman had been humiliated in his mid-term election of 1946, treated with open scorn and belittlement by Republicans, and seldom defended by his fellow Democrats. He was written off.

But how Truman responded is extremely interesting and bears directly on our subject, character in the presidency. It was as if he had been liberated from the shadow of Roosevelt. "I'm doing as I damn please for the next two years and to hell with all of them," he told his wife, Bess. And what's so remarkable and fascinating is that the next two years were the best of Truman's presidency. The years 1947 and 1948 contained most of the landmark achievements of his time in office: the first civil rights message ever sent to Congress, his executive order to end segregation in the armed forces, the Truman Doctrine, the recognition of Israel, the Berlin Airlift, and the

David McCullough, "Harry Truman: One Tough Son-of-a-Bitch" originally titled "Harry S Truman: 1945–1953" from *Character Above All*, edited by Robert A. Wilson. Reprinted by permission of Robert A. Wilson, Wilson Associates, Dallas, TX.

President Harry Truman, the tough little man from Missouri who made the decision to use atomic bombs against Japan, put forth the Truman Doctrine to contain the spread of Communism and sent American troops into the Korean War. Gruff and direct though he was, Truman also had "a resilient sense of humor" and particularly enjoyed "the good stories of politics." (Stock Montage)

Marshall Plan, which saved Western Europe from economic and political ruin and stands today as one of the great American achievements of the century.

He showed again and again that he understood the office, how the government works, and that he understood himself. He knew who he was, he liked who he was. He liked Harry Truman. He enjoyed being Harry Truman. He was grounded, as is said. He stressed, "I tried never to forget who I was, where I came from, and where I would go back to." And again and again, as I hope I will be able to demonstrate, he could reach down inside himself and come up with something very good and strong. He is the seemingly ordinary American who when put to the test, rises to the occasion and does the extraordinary.

Now by saying he knew himself and understood himself and liked himself, I don't mean vanity or conceit. I'm talking about self-respect, self-understanding. To an exceptional degree, power never went to his head, nor did he ever grow cynical, for all the time he spent in Washington. He was never inclined to irony or to grappling with abstract thoughts. He read a great deal, enjoyed good bourbon—Wild Turkey preferably—he was a good listener. His physical, mental, and emotional stamina were phenomenal. . . . There's much to be seen about people in how they stand, how they walk. Look at the photographs of Harry Truman, the newsreels—backbone American.

In the spring of 1945, the new untested President of the United States sat in the Oval Office. Across the desk, in the visitor's chair, sat a grim-looking old friend, Sam Rayburn, the Speaker of the House. They were alone in the room, just the two of them, and they were, in many ways, two of a kind. Rayburn knew he could talk straight from the shoulder to Truman, who had been in office only a few days.

"You have got many great hazards and one of them is in this White House. I've been watching this thing a long time," Rayburn began. "I've seen people in the White House try to build a fence around the White House and keep the very people away from the president that he should see. That is one of your hazards, the special interests and the sycophants who will stand in the rain a week to see you and will treat you like a king. They'll come sliding in and tell you you're the greatest man alive. But you know, and I know, you ain't."

Truman knew he wasn't Hercules, he knew he wasn't a glamour boy, he knew he didn't have—and this is so important—the capacity to move the country with words, with eloquence. He had none of the inspirational magic of his predecessor. If Roosevelt was Prospero, Truman was Horatio.

. . . Character counts in the presidency more than any other single quality. It is more important than how much the President knows of foreign policy or economics, or even about politics. When the chips are down—and the chips are nearly always down in the presidency—how do you decide? Which way do you go? What kind of courage is called upon? Talking of his hero Andrew Jackson, Truman once said, it takes one kind of courage to face a duelist, but it's nothing like the courage it takes to tell a friend, no.

In making his decision to recognize Israel, Truman had to tell the man he admired above all others, no—but more on that shortly.

Truman had seen a lot of life long before he came to Washington. He was born in 1884. He was a full-grown, mature, nearly middle-aged man by the time of the Great War, as his generation called World War I, which was the real dividing line between the nineteenth and the twentieth centuries and the turning point in his life. Everything changed in the period after World War I, which in retrospect may be seen as the first, hideous installment of a two-part world catastrophe. Even the same characters—Hitler, Churchill, Roosevelt, Truman, MacArthur, Marshall—reappear in World War II. Growing up in Victorian middle America, Truman came to maturity with much of the outlook, good and bad, of that very different time.

At heart he remained a nineteenth-century man. He never liked air-conditioning, hated talking by telephone. (And thank goodness, for he wrote letters instead, thousands as time went on, and as a result it is possible to get inside his life, to know what he thought and felt, in a way rarely possible with public figures, and presidents in particular.) He disliked Daylight Saving Time and time zones. (He liked wearing two watches, one set on Eastern Standard Time, the other on Missouri time "real time," as he called it.)

He was also a farmer, a real farmer let it be remembered, not a photo opportunity or a gentleman farmer like FDR or Tom Dewey. With his father, he *worked* on the farm, facing all the perils of bad weather, failing crops, insect plagues, and debt. Truman & Son, of Grandview, Missouri, were never out of debt. He was there for eleven years, until he went off to war in 1917, and as he used to say, "It takes a lot of pride to run a farm." Certainly on a family farm, you don't "do your own thing." Let down your end and the whole enterprise may fall. And every morning there's your father at the foot of the stairs at five-thirty, no matter the weather, no matter the season, telling you it's time to be up and at it.

There was no running water on the Truman farm, no electricity. When his mother had to have an emergency appendectomy, she was operated on by a country doctor on the kitchen table, and it was young Harry who stood beside her through all of it holding the lantern.

He was, as his pal Harry Vaughan, once said, "one tough son-of-a-bitch of a man. . . . And that," said Vaughan, "was part of the secret of understanding him." He could take it. He had been through so much. There's an old line, "Courage is having done it before."

It's been often said that Truman was poorly prepared for the presidency. He came to office not knowing any of the foreign policy establishment in Washington. He had no friends on Wall Street, no powerful financial backers, no intellectual "brain trust." When Winston Churchill came to Washington in the early 1940s and busied himself meeting everybody of known influence, no one suggested he look up the junior senator from Missouri.

But Truman had experienced as wide a range of American life as had any president, and in that sense he was well prepared. He had grown up in a small town when the small town was the essence of American life. He'd been on the farm all those years, and he'd gone to war. And the war was the crucible. Captain Harry Truman returned from France in 1919 having led an artillery battery through the horrific Battle of the Argonne and having discovered two vitally important things about himself. First, that he had courage, plain physical courage. Until then he had never been in a fight in his life. He was the little boy forbidden by his mother to play in roughhouse games because of his glasses. He was a bookworm—a sissy, as he said himself later on, using the dreaded word. But in France he'd found he could more than hold his own in the face of the horrors of battle and, second, that he was good at leading people. He liked it and he had learned that courage is contagious. If the leader shows courage, others get the idea.

Often he was scared to death. One of the most endearing of his many letters to Bess was written after his first time under fire in France, to tell her how terrified he was. It happened at night in the rain in the Vosges Mountains. The Germans had opened fire with a withering artillery barrage. Truman and his green troops thought it could be the start of a gas attack and rushed about trying frantically not only to get their own gas masks on, but to get masks on the horses as well. And then they panicked, ran. Truman, thrown by his horse, had been nearly crushed when the horse fell on him. Out from under, seeing the others all running, he just stood there, locked in place, and called them back using every form of profanity he'd ever heard. And back they came. This was no Douglas MacArthur strutting the edge of a trench to inspire the troops. This was a man who carried extra eyeglasses in every pocket because without glasses he was nearly blind. He had memorized the eye chart in order to get into the Army. And there he was in the sudden hell of artillery shells exploding all around, shouting, shaming his men back to do what they were supposed to do.

Now flash forward to a night thirty years later, in 1948, at the Democratic National Convention in Philadelphia, when Democrats on the left and Democrats on the right had been doing everything possible to get rid of President Harry Truman for another candidate. The Dixiecrats had marched out of the convention. The liberals, who had tried to draft General Eisenhower, were down in the dumps as never before, convinced, after Truman was nominated, that all was lost. Truman was kept waiting backstage hour after hour. It was not until nearly two in the morning that he came on stage to accept the nomination. That was the year when the conventions were covered by television for the first time and the huge lights made even worse the summer furnace of Philadelphia. The crowd was drenched in perspiration, exhausted. For all the speeches there had been, nobody had said a word about winning.

Truman, in a white linen suit, walked out into the floodlights and did just what he did in the Vosges Mountains. He gave them hell. He told them, in effect, to soldier up—and that they were going to win. It was astounding. He brought the whole hall to its feet. He brought them up cheering. Old-hand reporters, even the most diehard liberals who had so little hope for him, agreed it was one of the greatest moments they had ever witnessed in American politics.

So there we have it, courage, determination, call it as you will. Dean Acheson, his Secretary of State, much later, searching for a way to describe the effect Truman could have on those around him, and why they felt as they did about him, quoted the lines from Shakespeare's *Henry V,* when King

Henry—King Harry—walks among the terrified, dispirited troops the night before the Battle of Agincourt:

> . . . every wretch, pining and pale before,
> Beholding him, plucks comfort from his looks. . . .
> His liberal eye doth give to every one . . .
> A little touch of Harry in the night.

Acheson was remembering one of the darkest times of the Truman years, when unexpectedly 260,000 Chinese Communist troops came storming into the Korean War. Through it all, as Acheson and others saw at close hand, Truman never lost confidence, never lost his essential good cheer, never lost his fundamental civility and decency toward those who worked with him. He was never known to dress down a subordinate. "Give 'em hell, Harry" never gave anybody hell behind the scenes, on the job.

His decision to go into Korea in June 1950 was the most difficult of his presidency, he said. And he felt it was the most important decision of his presidency—more difficult and important than the decision to use the atomic bomb, because he feared he might be taking the country into another still more horrible world war, a nuclear war. Yet at the time, it was a very popular decision, a point often forgotten. The country was waiting for the President to say we would go to the rescue of the South Koreans, who were being overrun by the Communist North Korean blitzkrieg. The lesson of Munich weighed heavily on everyone. In Congress, the President had strong support on both sides of the aisle, at the start at least. He was applauded by the press across the country. It was only later that summer of 1950 when the war went so sour that it became "Truman's War."

But you see, there was no corollary between popularity and the ease or difficulty of the decision. His most popular decision was, for him, his most difficult decision, while his least popular decision was, he said, not difficult at all. That was the firing of General Douglas MacArthur, by far the most unpopular, controversial act of his presidency. Attacked by all sides, torn to shreds in editorials and by radio commentators, a potent force then as today, Truman went on with his work as usual, just riding it out. He seemed to have a sort of inner gyroscope for such times. Those around him wondered how it was possible. He said he was sure that in the long run the country would judge him to have done the right thing. Besides, he had only done his duty. The Constitution stated clearly that there will be civilian control over the military and he had taken an oath to uphold the Constitution. "It wasn't difficult for me at all," he insisted.

Truman's profound sense of history was an important part of his makeup. He believed every president should know American history at the least, and world history, ideally. A president with a sense of history is less prone to hubris. He knows he is but one link in the long chain going all the way back to the first president and that presumably will extend far into the future. He knows he has only a limited time in office and that history will be the final judge of his performance. What he does must stand the test of time. If he is blasted by the press, if his polls are plummeting as Truman's did during the Korean War, these are not the first concerns. What matters—or ought to matter—is what's best for the country and the world in the long run.

Truman probably understood the history of the presidency as well as or better than any president of this century with the exception of Woodrow Wilson, and in his first years in the White House he felt acutely the presence of the predecessors. He was sure the White House was haunted. This was before restoration of the old place, when it creaked and groaned at night with the change of temperature. Sometimes doors would fly open on their own. Alone at night, his family back in Missouri, he would walk the upstairs halls, poke about in closets, wind the clocks. He imagined his predecessors arguing over how this fellow Truman was doing so far.

His reputation seems to grow and will, I believe, continue to grow for the reason that he not only faced difficult decisions and faced them squarely, if not always correctly, but that the decisions were so often unprecedented. There were no prior examples to go by. In his first months in office, he made more difficult and far-reaching decisions than any

In April 1951, President Truman sacked General Douglas MacArthur (shown in this photograph) as commander of United Nations forces in Korea. McCullough concedes that it was the most "unpopular" and "controversial act" of Truman's presidency. But the president was confident, McCullough says, "that in the long run the country would judge him to have done the right thing." Today most American historians agree that Truman, in his capacity as commander in chief, was justified in relieving the contentious and insubordinate general. (© Carl Mydans, Time & Life Pictures-Getty Images).

president in our history, including Franklin Roosevelt and Abraham Lincoln. This much belittled, supposed backwater political hack, who seemed to have none or certainly very few of the requisite qualities of high office, turned out to do an extremely good job. And it is quite mistaken to imagine that nobody saw this at the time. Many did, and the closer they were to him, the more clearly they saw. Churchill, Marshall, and especially, I would say, Acheson, who was about as

different from Harry Truman in background and manner as anyone could be. Acheson once remarked that he had great respect for Franklin Roosevelt, but that he reserved his love for another president, meaning Harry Truman. Acheson didn't much like Roosevelt, I suspect, because Roosevelt was condescending toward him. I imagine that if Acheson were to tolerate condescension, it would have to be Acheson being condescending toward someone else.

In the course of more than one hundred interviews for my biography of Truman, I found no one who had worked with him, no one who was on the White House staff, or the White House domestic staff, or his Secret Service detail, who did not like him. He knew everybody by name on the White House staff and in the mansion itself. He knew all the Secret Service people by name. He knew all about their families— and this wasn't just a politician's trick. If he could have picked his own father, one former Secret Service man told me, it would have been Truman.

John Gunther, in a wonderful interview with Truman when Truman was Vice President, asked him what he was most interested in. "People," Truman said without hesitation.

He had a further quality, also greatly needed in the presidency: a healthy, resilient sense of humor. He loved especially the intrinsic humor of politics, the good stories of politics. Campaigning in Texas by train in 1948, he had nothing but blue skies and huge, warm crowds everywhere he stopped. It was the first time a Democratic candidate for President had ever come to Texas to campaign. That had never been necessary before. The reason now was his civil rights program, which was anything but popular in Texas. There had been warnings even of serious trouble if ever he were to show his face in Texas. But his reception was good-natured and approving the whole way across the state and Truman loved every moment. It was probably his happiest time of the whole 1948 whistle-stop odyssey. On board the train were Sam Rayburn and young Lyndon Johnson, who was running for the Senate, as well as Governor Beaufort Jester, who had earlier called Truman's civil rights program a stab in the back.

But all that was forgotten in the warmth of the days and the warmth of the crowds, and at the last stop, Rayburn's home town of Bonham, Rayburn invited the President to come by his little house on the highway, outside of the town. When the motorcade arrived, hundreds of people were on the front lawn. Rayburn told them to form a line and he would see they met the President. The Secret Service immediately objected, saying they had no identifications for anyone. Rayburn was furious. He knew every man, woman, and child on that lawn, he said, and could vouch for each and every one. So the line started for the house where Governor Jester offered greetings at the door and the President, a surreptitious bourbon within reach, shook hands with "the customers," as he called them. All was going well until Rayburn, who never took his eye off the line, shouted, "Shut the door, Beaufort, they're coming through twice."

Yet for all that it is mistaken to picture Harry Truman as just a down-home politician of the old stamp. The Harry Truman of Merle Miller's *Plain Speaking,* or of the play *Give-em Hell, Harry,* is entertaining and picturesque, but that wasn't the man who was President of the United States. He wasn't just some kind of cosmic hick.

Now he did make mistakes. He was not without flaw. He could be intemperate, profane, touchy, too quick with simplistic answers. In private conversation, he could use racial and religious slurs, old habits of the mouth. In many ways his part of Missouri was more like the Old South than the Middle West, and he grew up among people who in so-called polite society commonly used words like "nigger" and "coon."

Yet here is the man who initiated the first civil rights message ever and ordered the armed services desegregated. And let's remember, that was in 1948, long before Martin Luther King, Jr., or *Brown v. Board of Education,* the landmark Supreme Court decision on the desegregation of schools, or the civil rights movement. When friends and advisers warned him that he was certain to lose the election in 1948

if he persisted with the civil rights program, he said if he lost for that, it would be for a good cause. Principle mattered more than his own political hide. His courage was the courage of his convictions.

Truman's greatest single mistake was the loyalty oath program, requiring a so-called loyalty check of every federal employee. It was uncalled for, expensive, it contributed substantially to the mounting bureaucracy of Washington and damaged the reputations and lives of numbers of people who should never have had any such thing happen to them. He did it on the advice that it was good politics. He let his better nature be overcome by that argument. It was thought such a move could head off the rising right-wing cry of Communists in government, the McCarthy craze then in its early stages. But it didn't work. It was shameful.

His Supreme Court appointments weren't particularly distinguished. His seizure of the steel industry during the Korean War to avert a nationwide strike was high-handed and rightly judged unconstitutional, though his motives were understandable. We were at war and a prolonged shutdown of the production of steel threatened the very lives of our fighting forces in Korea.

He himself thought one of his worst mistakes was to have allowed the pell-mell demobilization that followed World War II. Almost overnight American military might had all but vanished. When we intervened in Korea, we had little to fight with, except for the atomic bomb. That Truman refused to use the atomic bomb in Korea, despite tremendous pressure from General MacArthur and others, stands as one of his most important decisions and one for which he has been given little credit.

The idea that Harry Truman made the decision to use the bomb against Japan and then went upstairs and went to sleep is an unfortunate myth for which he is largely accountable. I think he gave that impression because he came from a time and place in America where you were not supposed to talk about your troubles. "How are you?" "I'm fine." You might be dying of some terrible disease—"I'm fine. And you?" He refused ever to talk of the weight of the decision except to say that he made it and that it was his responsibility. . . .

With the return of peace, Truman's political troubles began. The year 1946 was particularly rough. He seemed hopelessly ineffectual. He seemed to be trying to please everybody at once, willing to say to almost anybody whatever they most wanted to hear. He wasn't at all like the Harry Truman I've been describing. He had never wanted the job and for some time appeared willing to give it up as soon as possible. He tried twice to get General Eisenhower to agree to run as a Democrat in the next election, saying he would gladly step aside. According to one account, he even offered to run as Vice President with Ike at the head of the ticket. But then after the setback in the '46 congressional elections, he became a different man.

Fire-in-the-belly for presidential glory was never part of his nature. He wasn't in the job to enlarge his estimate of himself. He didn't need that. He didn't need the limelight or fawning people around him in order to feel good about being Harry Truman.

On that note, it is interesting to see whom he did choose to have around him, as a measure of his character. There were Omar Bradley and Matthew Ridgway at the Pentagon, Eisenhower at the head of NATO. George C. Marshall served as Secretary of State and later as Secretary of Defense. There were Dean Acheson, Averell Harriman, Robert Lovett, George Kennan, Chip Bohlen, David Lilienthal, James Forrestal, Sam Rosenman, Clark Clifford—the list is long and very impressive. That most of them had more distinguished backgrounds than he, if they were taller, handsomer, it seemed to bother him not at all. When it was suggested to him that General Marshall as Secretary of State might lead people to think Marshall would make a better president, Truman's response was that yes, of course, Marshall would make a better president, but that he, Harry Truman, was President and he wanted the best people possible around him.

As no president since Theodore Roosevelt, Truman had a way of saying things that was so much his own, and I would like to quote some of them:

"I wonder how far Moses would have gone, if he had taken a poll in Egypt."

"God doesn't give a damn about pomp and circumstance."

"There are more prima donnas in Washington than in all the opera companies."

He is also frequently quoted as having said, "If you want a friend in Washington, buy a dog," and, "If you want to live like a Republican, vote Democratic." I doubt he said the first, but the second does sound like him.

"The object and its accomplishment is my philosophy," he said. Let me say that again. "The object and its accomplishment is my philosophy." And no president ever worked harder in office. At times, a little discouraged, he would say, "All the President is, is a glorified public relations man who spends his time flattering, kissing and kicking people to get them to do what they are supposed to do anyway."

Where were his strengths and his weaknesses in conflict? In interviews with those who knew him, I would ask what they believed to have been the President's major flaw. Almost always they would say he was too loyal to too many people to whom he should not have been so loyal—not as President. They were thinking mainly of the cronies—people like Harry Vaughan. Or remembering when Boss Tom Pendergast died and Vice President Harry Truman commandeered an Air Force bomber and flew to Kansas City for the funeral. "You don't forget a friend," was Truman's answer to the press.

Tom Pendergast had made Truman, and the Pendergast machine, though colorful and not without redeeming virtues, was pretty unsavory altogether.

But Truman was also, let us understand, the product of the smoke-filled room in more than just the Kansas City way. He was picked at the 1944 Democratic Convention in Chicago in a room at the Blackstone Hotel thick with smoke. He was tapped as Roosevelt's running mate and almost certain successor by the party's big-city bosses, the professional polls, who didn't want Henry Wallace, then the Vice President, because Wallace was too left wing, and didn't want Jimmy Byrnes, another Roosevelt favorite, because Byrnes was too conservative, an avowed segregationist and a lapsed Roman Catholic. They wanted Harry Truman, so Truman it was. They knew their man. They knew what stuff he was made of. And remember, this was all in a tradition of long standing. Theodore Roosevelt had been picked by a Republican machine in New York, Woodrow Wilson by the Democratic machine in New Jersey. For Franklin Roosevelt, such "good friends" as Ed Kelly of Chicago, Boss Crump of Memphis, Ed Flynn of the Bronx were indispensable. And because a candidate had the endorsement of a machine, or as in Truman's case owed his rise in politics to a corrupt organization, it didn't necessarily follow that he himself was corrupt. John Hersey, who did one of the best of all pieces ever written about Harry Truman, for *The New Yorker,* said he found no trace of corruption in Truman's record. Nor did I. Nor did the FBI when it combed through Truman's past at the time Pendergast was convicted for an insurance fraud and sent to prison. Nor did all the Republicans who ran against him in all the elections in his long political career.

I think he was almost honest to a fault. Still he understood, and felt acutely, the bargain he made with loyalty to the likes of Pendergast, and he understood why he was so often taken to task by the Republicans or the press or just ordinary citizens who didn't care for the kind of political company he kept.

Harry Vaughan was for comic relief, Truman's Falstaff. Among the delights of Truman as a biographical subject is that he enjoyed both Vaughan and Mozart. He loved a night of poker with "the boys," and he loved the National Symphony, which he attended as often as possible. If the program included Mozart or Chopin, he would frequently take the score with him.

This same Harry Truman, who adored classical music, who read Shakespeare and Cicero and *Don Quixote,* comes out of a political background about as steamy and raw as they get. And at times, this would get to him and he would escape to the privacy of a downtown Kansas City hotel room. There

he would pour himself out on paper, an innermost anguish in long memoranda to himself, and these amazing documents survive in the files of the Truman Library in Independence, Missouri, along with thousands of his letters and private diaries.

Here is a striking example written when Truman was a county judge (a county commissioner really) and one of his fellow commissioners had made off with $10,000 from the county till:

This sweet associate of mine, my friend, who was supposed to back me, had already made a deal with a former crooked contractor, a friend of the Boss's . . . I had to compromise in order to get the voted road system carried out . . . I had to let a former saloonkeeper and murderer, a friend of the Boss's, steal about $10,000 from the general revenues of the county to satisfy my ideal associate and keep the crooks from getting a million or more out of the bond issue.

He is not exaggerating with the million-dollar figure. When the Pendergast organization collapsed and its ways of operation were revealed, a million dollars was found to be about standard. But then, importantly, Truman goes on:

Was I right or did I compound a felony? I don't know. . . . Anyway I've got the $6,500,000 worth of roads on the ground and at a figure that makes the crooks tear their hair. The hospital is up at less cost than any similar institution in spite of my drunken brother-in-law [Fred Wallace], whom I'd had to employ on the job to keep peace in the family. I've had to run the hospital job myself and pay him for it. . . . Am I an administrator or not? Or am I just a crook to compromise in order to get the job done? You judge it, I can't.

This is all very painful for him. He writes of being raised at his mother's knee to believe in honor, ethics, and "right living." Not only is he disgusted by the immorality he sees behind the scenes, he doesn't understand it.

But let me return to 1948, where I think we see Truman, the President, at his best. Consider first the crisis over Berlin. That spring the Russians had suddenly clamped a blockade around the city, which was then under Allied control though within the Russian zone of East Germany. Overnight, without warning, Berlin was cut off. Other than by air, there was no way to supply it. Two and a half million people were going to be without food, fuel, medical supplies. Clearly Stalin was attempting to drive the Allies out. The situation was extremely dangerous.

At an emergency meeting in the Oval Office, it was proposed that the Allies break through with an armored convoy. It looked as though World War III might be about to start. It was suggested that Berlin be abandoned. Nobody knew quite what to do. Truman said, "We stay in Berlin, period." He didn't know how that could be done any more than anyone else, but he said, "We stay in Berlin." Backbone.

An airlift had already begun as a temporary measure. Truman ordered it stepped up to the maximum. It was said by experts, including the mayor of Berlin, that to supply the city by air would be impossible, given the size of the planes and the calculated number of landings possible per day. The whole world was on edge.

"We'll stay in Berlin," Truman said again, "come what may." The supposedly insoluble problem of the limit of the plane landings per day was nicely solved: they built another airport. The airlift worked. The Russians gave up the blockade. The crisis passed.

Among the most difficult and important concepts to convey in teaching or writing history is the simple fact that things never had to turn out as they did. Events past were never on a track. Nothing was foreordained any more then than now. Nobody knew at the start that the Berlin Airlift would work. It was a model, I think, of presidential decision making, and of presidential character proving decisive.

All this, I should also remind you, was taking place in an election year. Yet at no time did Truman include any of his political advisers in the discussions about Berlin. Nor did he ever play on the tension of the crisis for his own benefit in the speeches he made.

With the question of whether to recognize Israel, Truman faced an equally complex situation but one greatly compounded by emotion. Of particular difficulty for him, personally and politically, was the position of his then Secretary of State, George Marshall, who was gravely concerned about Middle Eastern oil supplies. If Arab anger over American support for a new Jewish state meant a cut-off of Arab oil, it would not only jeopardize the Marshall Plan and the recovery of Europe but could prove disastrous should the Berlin crisis indeed turn to war.

Marshall was thinking as a military man, determined to hold to a policy that was in the best interest of the United States. It was by no means a matter of anti-Semitism, as was sometimes charged, or any lack of sympathy for the idea of a Jewish homeland. But the fact that Marshall was against an immediate recognition put Truman in an extremely difficult position. No American of the time counted higher in Truman's estimate than Marshall. He saw Marshall as the modern-day equivalent of George Washington or Robert E. Lee and valued his judgment more than that of anyone in the cabinet. Further, Marshall was far and away the most widely respected member of the administration, and if Truman were to decide against him and Marshall were then to resign, it would almost certainly mean defeat for Truman in November. He could lose the respect of the man he most respected and lose the presidency.

Truman did recognize Israel—immediately, within minutes—and he never doubted he was doing the right thing. His interest in the history of the Middle East was long standing. He had been a strong supporter of a homeland for Jewish refugees from Europe from the time he had been in the Senate. But he also knew George Marshall and was sure Marshall would stand by him, as of course Marshall did.

I have spent a sizable part of my writing life trying to understand Harry Truman and his story. I don't think we can ever know enough about him. If his loyalty was a flaw, it was his great strength also, as shown by his steadfast loyalty to Dean Acheson when Joe McCarthy came after Acheson or the unflinching support he gave David Lilienthal when Lilienthal, Truman's choice to head the Atomic Energy Commission, was accused as a "pink," a Communist. Franklin Roosevelt had not been willing to stand up for Lilienthal. Truman did. And Lilienthal was approved by the Senate.

Perhaps Truman's greatest shortcoming was his unwillingness to let us know, to let the country know then, how much more there was to him than met the eye, how much more he was than just "Give 'em hell, Harry"—that he did have this love of books, this interest in history, his affection for people, his kindness, his thoughtfulness to subordinates, the love of music, the knowledge of music, his deep and abiding love for his wife, his bedrock belief in education and learning. Though he had never gone beyond Independence High School, this was a president who enjoyed Cicero in the original Latin. We should have known that. It's good to know now, too.

A few words about the '48 campaign, which will always be part of our political lore. It's a great American metaphor, a great American story. The fellow who hasn't got a chance comes from behind and wins. Nobody in either party, not a professional politician, not a reporter, not even his own mother-in-law doubted that Tom Dewey would be the next president. The result of a *Newsweek* poll of fifty top political commentators nationwide who were asked to predict the outcome was Dewey 50, Truman 0.

No president had ever campaigned so hard or so far. Truman was sixty-four years old. Younger men who were with him through it all would describe the time on the train as one of the worst ordeals of their lives. The roadbed was rough and Truman would get the train up to 80 miles an hour at night. The food was awful, the work unrelenting. One of them told me, "It's one thing to work that hard and to stay the course when you think you're going to win, but it's quite another thing when you *know* you're going to lose." The only reason they were there, they all said, was Harry Truman.

For Truman, I think, it was an act of faith—a heroic, memorable American act of faith. The poll takers, the political reporters, the pundits, all the sundry prognosticators, and professional politicians—it didn't matter what they said, what they thought. Only the people decide, Truman was reminding the country. "Here I am, here's what I stand for—here's what I'm going to do if you keep me in the job. You decide."

Was he a great president? Yes. One of the best. And a very great American. Can we ever have another Harry Truman? Yes, I would say so. Who knows, maybe somewhere in Texas she's growing up right now.

QUESTIONS TO CONSIDER

1 Describe Truman's character. How did his character affect his political career, especially his presidency? How was Truman's "profound sense of history" an important part of his makeup? Compare him as a man to Franklin D. Roosevelt, the subject of selection 18.

2 What was the most difficult decision Truman had to make as president? What did he fear his decision might lead to? What was "the lesson of Munich"? What controversial move did Truman make to uphold his oath to the Constitution? Why did he insist that the move was "not difficult" for him?

3 What was Truman's "greatest single mistake" as president? Why did he make it? Why did David McCullough say it was "shameful"? According to McCullough, what were some of President Truman's other mistakes?

4 What crisis showed Truman, as president, at his best? How did his character affect his decision to stand firm in that crisis?

5 How did Truman make evident America's resolve to maintain the global status quo and yet avoid precipitating a third world war? When during his presidency did nuclear war seem probable?

23 Eisenhower and Kennedy: Contrasting Presidencies in a Fearful World

MICHAEL R. BESCHLOSS

Dwight David Eisenhower, the supreme commander of Allied forces in Europe during 1944 and 1945, was America's greatest hero in the postwar years. In 1952, the Republicans chose this balding, avuncular, mild-mannered soldier to win the White House back for the GOP after twenty straight years of Democratic chief executives. No Republican had occupied the White House since Herbert Hoover, whom much of the country had blamed for the crash and Depression. In the 1952 election, Eisenhower soundly defeated liberal Democrat Adlai E. Stevenson and went on to serve two terms in the White House. He left such a mark that the 1950s became popularly known as the Eisenhower years, or "the Ike Age."

For some contemporary critics, his mark was entirely negative, for they thought him an inept president who spent more time on the golf course than in tending to affairs of state. When he did attend to his job, such critics contended, his policies only worsened Cold War tensions. He ended up adopting Truman's containment policy and even announced "the domino theory," which held that if the West allowed the Communists to take over one country, they would seize its neighbors, then their neighbors, and so on until they had conquered the world. Other contemporary critics, however, regarded Ike as a masterful statesman who ended the Korean War, opposed military intervention in the internal struggles of other nations, and presided over a period of domestic prosperity.

In the years after his presidency, historians tended to side with Eisenhower's hostile critics and rated him a poor chief executive. But more recently, with new evidence and new perspectives, scholars took another look at Eisenhower and liked what they saw. Their "revisionist" view has had a considerable influence on the current generation, so much so that a recent poll of historians and presidential scholars ranked Ike ninth on the list of presidents.

As for his young successor, John F. Kennedy, presidential scholars tend to place him in the bottom tier of chief executives. Such a low ranking probably reflects a negative scholarly reaction to the "myth of Camelot," created by First Lady Jacqueline Kennedy, which compared Kennedy and his men to legendary King Arthur and his Knights of the Round Table; the King's palace and court were known as Camelot. In sharp contrast to presidential scholars, the American public has had an ongoing love affair with the slain president. Public opinion polls have consistently ranked Kennedy as the best chief executive America has ever had.

In the following selection, presidential scholar Michael R. Beschloss eschews numerical ratings and assesses Eisenhower and Kennedy solely on the basis of their strengths and weaknesses, accomplishments and failures. He argues that Eisenhower, who wanted to be "a calm unifying national symbol," was "magnificently suited" to the 1950s. On the positive side, "Ike" accepted the New Deal and tried to administer it with typical Republican efficiency. For most of the fifties, "he balanced the budget, kept inflation low, and presided over a postwar boom." On the negative side, Beschloss gives Eisenhower demerits for his failure to grasp the importance of civil rights, for his refusal to speak out against McCarthyism, and for his inability to make the Republican party a moderate one. Even so, "with his impeccable reputation for character and integrity," Beschloss writes, "he was as much a national father figure as George Washington."

Assessing Kennedy, the youngest elected president in American history and the first born in the twentieth century, is a difficult task given the relatively brief period—"two years, ten months, and two days"—that he held office. Beschloss says nothing about Kennedy's notorious philandering, which deeply hurt his wife and threatened their marriage. But Beschloss does describe the young president's "embarrassing defeat" in the 1961 Bay of Pigs fiasco—the invasion of Cuba by CIA-trained Cuban exiles, which ended in disaster. On the positive side, Beschloss contends that Kennedy excelled at "crisis management—hour to hour to hour." The "paramount moment" of his presidency was the Cuban missile crisis of October 1962, when a nuclear war almost broke out between the United States and the Soviet Union. It was the closest the world has ever come to a nuclear holocaust. Kennedy's restrained and intelligent management of that crisis, Beschloss believes, "may have saved the world." Kennedy also gets high marks for the nuclear test ban treaty he negotiated with the Soviets in 1963. On the domestic front, the author praises Kennedy for sending a powerful new civil rights bill to Congress, where it met bitter southern white opposition.

One of the most vexing problems of Kennedy's presidency was the war in distant Vietnam. Some Kennedy scholars, on the basis of declassified government documents, believe that he planned to pull American military "advisers" out of Vietnam after the 1964 election. Beschloss, however, is skeptical of that contention. He concedes that JFK might have been more willing to withdraw from Vietnam than his successor, Lyndon Johnson. But "the fact is we will never know."

After reading this clear, concise, and well-argued essay, decide for yourselves who was the more effective president—the beloved Old Warrior with bad syntax and a passion for golf (Lyndon Johnson claimed that "Ike" often wore his golf shoes in the Oval Office, leaving cleat marks on the floor) or the handsome, articulate young statesman who suffered from Addison's disease and back pain and who spoke with a Boston accent, pronouncing Cuba as "Cuber" and party as "pahty."

GLOSSARY

BAY OF PIGS   In 1961, this represented Kennedy's greatest mistake in foreign policy. It was an ill-fated invasion of Fidel Castro's island that resulted in the death or capture of Cuban refugees whom the United States had inspired, trained, and armed. The young president learned a hard lesson and never again placed his full trust in the advice of the military and intelligence communities.

BROWN v. BOARD OF EDUCATION OF TOPEKA (1954)   Chief Justice Earl Warren stated in this landmark case that "separate educational facilities are inherently unequal" and that to segregate children by race "generates a feeling of inferiority as to their status in the community that may affect their hearts and minds in a way unlikely ever to be undone." Eisenhower did not put the moral weight of the presidency behind this decision and allowed southern governors to impede integration in the public schools.

CASTRO, FIDEL   In 1959, he led a successful revolution against the dictatorial government of Fulgencio Batista in

Cuba. A Communist who developed close ties with the Soviet Union, Castro remained a threat to the United States and a potential exporter of subversive doctrines that might afflict other nations in the Caribbean and Latin America.

DIRKSEN, EVERETT   A Republican leader of the Senate from Illinois, he supported Lyndon Johnson's 1964 civil rights initiatives. Johnson, unlike Kennedy, was able to artfully manipulate key political leaders to accomplish his domestic goals.

DOMINO THEORY   First voiced by President Eisenhower, it became a reason for America's reluctance to leave Vietnam. It argued that if Vietnam fell to Communism so would its neighbors. The tumbling process would eventually threaten Japan and the Philippines and thus would endanger the national security of the United States.

EXECUTIVE COMMITTEE (EX COMM)   The group of Kennedy advisers who brainstormed possible solutions to the Cuban missile crisis. They were a diverse group of doves (Adlai Stevenson) and hawks (Curtis LeMay). Ultimately, they recommended a blockade or "quarantine" of Cuba that provided Khrushchev with a way to remove the Soviet missiles and still save face (the United States promised not to invade the tiny island and informally agreed to remove its missiles from Turkey and Italy).

GAGARIN, YURI   In the spring of 1961, this Russian was the first man in space. Kennedy, under pressure to win the space race, promised that the United Sates by the end of the decade would put a man on the moon and return him safely to earth.

GOLDWATER, BARRY   A leading Republican senator from Arizona, he was the presidential nominee of his party in 1964. Lyndon Johnson easily defeated him, mainly because many Americans feared that Goldwater might too hastily use nuclear weapons in a confrontation with the Soviet Union.

KENNEDY, ROBERT F.   The president's brother, attorney general, and closest adviser. As a member of Ex Comm, he argued against military action. He ran for president in 1968 but like his brother, was cruelly assassinated.

KHRUSHCHEV, NIKITA   The bellicose and emotional Soviet premier who frightened many Americans with his boast that "we will bury you." He would accelerate the space race with the first orbiting satellite *Sputnik* and bring the world to the brink of nuclear annihilation by placing offensive missiles in Cuba.

KOREAN WAR   It started during the Truman administration when North Korean forces invaded South Korea across the 38th parallel in June 1950. Sixteen member nations of the newly formed United Nations fought this aggression. Eisenhower pledged to end the war when he ran for president in 1952, and an armistice was signed soon after his election.

MANSFIELD, MIKE   The Senate majority leader and a Kennedy friend who felt that the president would withdraw from Vietnam after he won a mandate from the American people in the 1964 election.

McCARTHYISM   A political philosophy, named after a Wisconsin senator, that frightened Americans in the 1950s and destroyed the careers of many innocent people. The demagogue Joseph McCarthy argued that Communism had infiltrated the army, the State Department, and even Hollywood.

MORROW, E. FREDERICK   The only significant African American within the Eisenhower administration, he was repeatedly frustrated in his attempt to convince the president to adopt a vigorous and proactive position that would help his race achieve a measure of equality.

O'DONNELL, KENNETH   One of Kennedy's closest advisers who, along with David Powers, wrote a moving tribute to the president entitled *Johnny, We Hardly Knew Ye*. He argued that Kennedy would have withdrawn from Vietnam after winning the presidential election of 1964.

PT 109   Kennedy's boat that was rammed by a Japanese destroyer during World War II. The future president showed courage in bringing his crew to safety. He paid a heavy price for his heroism by incurring an injury to his back that caused him great pain for the rest of his life.

RESTON, JAMES   The *New York Times* columnist who was not certain that Kennedy had a grand vision of the presidency. Yet, when the young chief executive died in Dallas, Reston wrote that what was killed "was not only the president, but the promise."

SORENSEN, THEODORE   Kennedy's speech writer and friend who was responsible for some of the president's most memorable statements, such as "Ask not what your country can do for you, ask what you can do for your country." Soon after the tragic assassination, he wrote a firsthand book about the murdered president entitled *Kennedy*.

SPUTNIK   The first orbiting satellite that the Russians put into space in 1957. This panicked many Americans and resulted in educational initiatives in science and math so that the United States could catch up with the Soviets in the space race. The assumption was that the nation that controlled space would have an enormous advantage in a nuclear war.

STEVENSON, ADLAI   Eisenhower defeated this former Illinois governor in presidential elections in 1952 and 1956. A liberal and an idealist, he did not capture the imagination of the American people as much as the World War II hero, who represented stability and continued prosperity.

TAFT, ROBERT A.   Isolationist leader of the Republican party from Ohio who might have won the Republican nomination for president in 1952 had he assured Eisenhower that defeating the Soviets and maintaining a significant American presence in the world community was a high priority.

U-2   A high-altitude spy plane that was shot down over the Soviet Union in 1960. It accelerated Cold War tensions and ruined a summit meeting in Paris that Eisenhower had planned with Khrushchev.

For most of American history, the presidency has been a weak office—and that was very much in keeping with what the framers intended. They did not want another king of England; they didn't want a dictator. They made sure that there were checks against presidential power, one of them being impeachment, and they were very worried about the idea of a president who would do too much. So a lot of the power of the presidency comes not at all from what's in the Constitution but from two other factors.

The first is the president's ability to go to the American people and ask them for something—especially sacrifice. One very good example would be Franklin Roosevelt in 1940, saying, "You may not want to get prepared for a possible war in Europe and Asia, but this is something I've thought a lot about and this is a sacrifice that we may have to make." Another example would be a president's appeal for a painful tax increase to achieve a balanced budget.

The second source of presidential power is a president's ability to get things out of Congress. The founders hoped that presidents would have such moral authority and people would think they were so wise that members of Congress would be intimidated. If a president went to Congress and asked for something like civil rights, members would take heed. That's one reason why Lyndon Johnson was a much more powerful president in 1964, 1965, and 1966 than I think others might have been: Because of his experience as one of the most canny and powerful leaders in the history of Congress, he was extraordinarily effective at getting what he wanted.

For most of our lifetimes, we have been in a situation that is something of an aberration. When I was ten years old, hoping to be able to write history about presidents when I grew up, it seemed very glamorous. I thought these people were, to crib a phrase from Leonardo DiCaprio, "kings of the world." The president was the centerpiece of the American political solar system, the center of our foreign and domestic policy, the most powerful person in the American government—and America was astride the world. That was the case from Franklin Roosevelt until the last year of George Bush.

In the 1930s Congress and the American people granted Roosevelt extraordinary influence over domestic affairs. In the wake of Pearl Harbor, they extended that power into foreign affairs. After 1945, Americans thought it was a good idea for power to flow to Washington. That enhanced the power of presidents. People liked federal action and federal programs. Congress was inclined to defer to the chief executive in foreign policy because we had to win the cold war. Then in the late 1960s and early 1970s, Americans grew more skeptical about Big Government. Power began to flow away from Washington. Then the cold war ended, and foreign policy seemed less urgent. The result is that now we are returning to a moment in which presidents don't have the kind of power that they had between the 1930s and the 1980s.

Dwight Eisenhower became president of the United States in 1953, at the apex of presidential power. But that power was enhanced by the man himself and the situation in which he found himself. It is hard to imagine a leader in a more commanding position. As the hero of World War II in Europe, Eisenhower enjoyed as august a national and world reputation as anyone who has ever entered the White House. With his impeccable reputation for character and integrity, he was as much a national father figure as George Washington.

Eisenhower had been elected by a landslide, and in that election he took both houses of Congress back from the Democrats. He could fairly argue that his ample coattails had made the difference. This was a new president with enormous reservoirs of political strength but also limited ambitions—much more limited than those of Woodrow Wilson, Franklin Roosevelt, or Lyndon Johnson.

Michael R. Beschloss, "Dwight D. Eisenhower and John F. Kennedy: A Study in Contrasts," from *Power and the Presidency* by Robert A. Wilson. Copyright © 1999 by Robert A. Wilson. Reprinted by permission of PublicAffairs, a member of Perseus Books, L.L.C.

Dwight David Eisenhower was the most popular Republican of his era. In the presidential elections of 1952 and 1956, huge cheering crowds chanted "We like Ike" and helped the World War II hero easily defeat Democratic candidate Adlai Stevenson. (© UPI / Bettmann / Corbis)

Although he would never have alienated conservatives in his party by saying so in public, Eisenhower had no desire to turn back the clock on the New Deal. Instead, he wanted to consolidate those reforms and do what Republicans do: administer the programs more efficiently and economically. Beyond that he saw himself—among the conflicting demands of labor, business, finance, and other engines of the American economy—as a balance wheel poised to let postwar prosperity roar ahead under a balanced budget.

He wanted to eliminate isolationism from the Republican Party and postwar America. We sometimes forget how close Republicans came to nominating the isolationist senator Robert Taft of Ohio in 1952. Ike had such deep convictions about this issue that in the winter of 1952 he went to Taft and said, "I feel so strongly about defending the Free World against the Soviets that I will make you a deal. If you renounce isolationism, I won't run against you for president."

Taft easily could have accepted, and Eisenhower never would have been president. It shows you how deeply he felt about this. He wanted to use his office to make sure that no postwar national leader could come to power without vowing to ensure that the United States would remain permanently engaged in the world. That comes about as close as anything Eisenhower had to a deep political conviction.

He hoped that by the end of his eight years in office he would be able somehow to reduce the harshness of the cold war. As a military man, he knew the danger of nuclear war. Once, sitting through a briefing by a civil defense official who was blithely describing how the federal government could survive underground after a Soviet nuclear attack, Ike told him to stop. "We won't be carrying on with government," he barked. "We'll be grubbing for worms!" He was disgusted that the United States had to spend billions of dollars on what he called "sterile" military programs, when it could have invested in schools and hospitals and roads.

To hold down the arms race as much as possible, he worked out a wonderful tacit agreement with Soviet premier Nikita Khrushchev. Khrushchev wanted to build up his economy. He didn't want to spend a lot of money on the Soviet military because he wanted to start feeding people and recover from the devastation of World War II. But he knew that to cover this he would have to give speeches in public that said quite the opposite. So Khrushchev would deliver himself of such memorable lines as, "We Soviets are cranking out missiles like sausages, and we will bury you because our defense structure is pulling ahead of the United States."

Eisenhower dealt with this much as an adult deals with a small boy who is lightly punching him in the stomach. He figured that leaving Khrushchev's boasts unanswered was a pretty small price to pay if it meant that Khrushchev would not spend much money building up his military.

The result was that the arms race was about as slow during the 1950s as it could have been, and Eisenhower was well on the way to creating an atmosphere of communication. Had the U-2 not fallen down in 1960 and had the presidential campaign taken place in a more peaceful atmosphere, I think you would have seen John Kennedy and Richard Nixon competing on the basis of who could increase

the opening to the Soviets that Eisenhower had created. Whether or not that would have sped the end of the cold war is open to argument.

In 1953 Eisenhower was disheartened by the bitterness and exhaustion in the American political climate. We had been through a stock market crash, a Great Depression, five years of global war, a growing Soviet threat, full-fledged cold war, the Korean War, McCarthyism and the backlash against it—all in the space of less than a generation. Our nerves were frayed. Ike wanted to be the calming, unifying national symbol who could give us a little bit of breathing space.

What personal qualities did Eisenhower bring to the Oval Office? The most obvious: He was the most popular human being in America and probably the most popular human being in the world. But he was also a much more intelligent man than people understood at the time. People who watched his press conferences—filled with those sentences that lacked verbs and never seemed to end—thought Ike was a wonderful guy but not too bright. Now, almost a half-century later, we have access to his letters and diaries and records of his private meetings. When you take Ike off the public platform and put him in a small room where he's talking candidly to his aides and friends, you find a leader much in command of complex issues—very different from the caricature of the time.

Harry Truman once predicted that when Ike became president he would be frustrated. Truman said that as a general, Eisenhower would shout, "Do this!" and "Do that!"—but that in the White House, when he did that, nothing would happen. Indeed, Ike had never been in domestic politics. But what people overlooked was that in the army for almost forty years he had been operating in large, bureaucratic organizations, not least the Allied Expeditionary Force in Europe. This was good experience for a president who had to deal with a rapidly growing CIA and Pentagon—and with ballooning domestic bureaucracies like the new Department of Health, Education, and Welfare.

What qualities did Eisenhower lack? Well, as an orator, he was no Franklin Roosevelt. He seemed to design his language to make sure that no one would remember—or in some cases, understand—what he said. Some scholars, like Fred Greenstein of Princeton, think that Eisenhower was often deliberately boring or opaque as a ploy, to keep from polarizing people. Maybe so, but the inability to use what Theodore Roosevelt called the "bully pulpit" is a big problem for a president. I think it robbed Eisenhower of considerable power that, used in the right way, could have been very important for this country.

Imagine if Eisenhower had been president in 1939. That was when FDR was making the case to the American people that we had to build our own defense forces because we might have to fight a war. His oratorical skills helped to move opinion in Congress and among the American people enough so that when war came, we were prepared. Had Roosevelt been mute, we would have lost World War II.

The ability to move a nation is essential if a president wants to ask Congress and the American people for something. It is just as essential if things are going bad. That's when a president needs to reassure the public. In 1958 America was plunging into recession. Eisenhower refused to improve things by unbalancing the budget. The Republicans lost badly in the 1958 midterm elections, largely because Ike could not or would not explain to Americans why it was necessary to stay the economic course. He allowed his critics to take the initiative, saying, "Eisenhower is tired and washed up and so obsessed with a balanced budget that he doesn't care about people who are suffering."

Another example came the previous year, with the Soviet launching of Sputnik, the first earth satellite. Eisenhower's foes said, "Ike is so lazy and asleep at the switch that he's allowed the Russians to be first to launch a satellite. Now the Russians can drop nuclear weapons on Chicago or Detroit—or Hanover, New Hampshire." In fact, sending up Sputnik was not the same thing as being able to drop a bomb precisely on a target by missile. The Soviets were still years away from being able to do that. But Eisenhower was unable to make that case to the American people. The result was near national hysteria.

Another of Ike's shortcomings was as a horse trader. He once said, "I don't know how to do what you have to do to get something out of a congressman." You wouldn't have heard Lyndon Johnson saying such a thing. Getting members of Congress to do things they don't want to do is a crucial part of being president.

On one of the tapes LBJ made of his private conversations as president, you hear Johnson in 1964. He knows that the key to getting his civil rights bill passed will be Everett Dirksen of Illinois, Republican leader of the Senate. He calls Dirksen, whom he's known for twenty years, and essentially says, "Ev, I know you have some doubts about this bill, but if you decide to support it, a hundred years from now every American schoolchild will know two names—Abraham Lincoln and Everett Dirksen." Dirksen liked the sound of that. He supported the bill, and the rest was history. You will never find an example of a conversation like that in the annals of Dwight Eisenhower. And his diffidence about Congress limited his ability to get things done.

If Eisenhower were president in a time requiring a leader standing in the epicenter of heroic change—like Roosevelt in the 1930s and 1940s, for example—he probably would have been a disaster because he lacked the ambitions and the skills that kind of presidential leadership requires. Yet Eisenhower was magnificently suited to the 1950s. He got people to accept Social Security and other controversial reforms as a permanent way of American life. For much of the decade, he balanced the budget, kept inflation low, and presided over a postwar boom. He fathered the interstate highway system. He was the very image of a chief of state. He made Americans feel happy about themselves and their country. He killed isolationism. He muted the U.S.–Soviet arms race as much as any president could have.

To use the parlance of West Point, I'd suggest three demerits in Ike's record as president. The first: Joseph McCarthy. Eisenhower was a civil libertarian. He knew what Senator McCarthy's reckless charges about internal communism were doing to this country. Imagine if Eisenhower had stood up in 1953 and said, "McCarthyism is a poison in this society. Believe me, of all people, I'll be the last to let this country be injured by communists within, but we can't tear this nation apart." That could have changed history. Instead, Ike was stunningly quiet, although some recent revisionists argue that he tried to tunnel against McCarthy behind the scenes.

The most coherent statement Ike made against McCarthy was at Dartmouth in June 1953. He had been chatting about the virtues of playing golf. He urged Dartmouth men to have fun in their lives. They didn't seem to need the advice. But toward the end of that speech, he got serious. He had been told how McCarthy's agents had tried to have certain "subversive" books removed from U.S. embassy libraries abroad. He told the Dartmouth graduates, "Don't join the book burners. Instead, go to the library and read books on communism so you'll know what you're fighting against." Nicely said, but these two paragraphs got little attention. They leave you feeling that Eisenhower could and should have said so much more.

Demerit two: civil rights. Ike never understood how vital it was to integrate American society after World War II. Imagine how he could have used that great moral authority and world reputation. He could have said in 1953, "I went to Europe and helped win the Second World War, but that was just part of the job. Now we have to finish what we fought for by bringing equal rights to all Americans." No other political figure would have carried so much weight.

But Ike had something of a blind spot on civil rights. He had spent a lot of his life in the South and, I think, overestimated the degree of resistance to a civil rights bill. We now know that in 1954, when the Supreme Court in *Brown* v. *Board of Education* ordered the desegregation of public schools, Eisenhower privately thought it a bad idea.

Ike had an aide named Frederic Morrow, who was the first African American to serve on a president's staff. Morrow would talk to the president about civil rights on occasion and would come away feeling that he had made some headway. Then Ike

would fly to Georgia for a hunting weekend with southern friends. And when he came back, it was almost as if his conversation with Morrow had never occurred.

Civil rights was a case where Eisenhower's instincts of compromise and moderation served him badly. Segregation was a moral issue. I think that the president's foot-dragging caused the civil rights revolution, when it reached full force in the 1960s, to be more bitter and violent.

The final demerit: One test of leaders is how they make sure that their ideas and programs will live on after they're gone. One way they do that is by building a political movement like a political party. Eisenhower tried to recreate his party in the image of what he called "modern Republicanism." But he failed. Four years after he left office, Republicans scorned his moderation as a "dime-store New Deal" and nominated Barry Goldwater. The Republican Party we see today is far more the party of Goldwater than of Eisenhower.

Another way you make sure your policies survive is with your words. But so unable or unwilling was Eisenhower to use his powers of persuasion that some of the basic tenets of his political credo vanished almost as soon as he left the White House. Because Ike failed to make the case for a balanced budget, his Democratic successors were able to start the great inflation of the 1960s. Because Ike failed to make the case for a moderate arms race, John Kennedy started what was at that time the largest arms buildup in human history.

Another way is to make sure you are followed by leaders who will carry on your purposes. Here Eisenhower failed. He once said that one of the biggest disappointments of his life was that in the race to succeed him, John Kennedy defeated his vice president, Richard Nixon. He called that "a repudiation of everything I've stood for for eight years."

It is hard to imagine two more different men than Dwight Eisenhower and John F. Kennedy—and perhaps in no way more so than this: Eisenhower in 1953 had access to vast amounts of power; Kennedy in 1961 had access to little.

This 1962 photograph shows the Kennedy brothers at the height of the "Camelot" era. Robert, the attorney general, is on the left; Ted, the new senator from Massachusetts, is in the center; and John, the president, is on the right. They brought glamour, wealth, and the inimitable "Kennedy style" to the political arena. The Kennedys were also fortunate that the press corps, in the early 1960s, ignored the private indiscretions of public figures. (Cecil Stoughton, White House/John Fitzgerald Kennedy Library, Boston)

Kennedy had been elected president by a margin of only 100,000 votes. Congress remained Democratic, but since most members had run well ahead of the new president, they felt they owed him little. As Kennedy saw it, he was faced by a House and Senate dominated by hostile coalitions of conservative Republicans and southern Democrats. Many of those who had known him as a fellow congressman or senator found it hard to get out of the habit of thinking of him as a distracted, absentee backbencher.

The American people had voted for Kennedy—narrowly—but they didn't really know him. Unlike Eisenhower, from the moment he was elected, Kennedy had to work hard to make an impression. He was always worried that he looked too young for people to think of him as a president. And when you look at videotape and newsreels of the period, you notice how stiff and formal Kennedy is on the platform.

JFK came to the presidency devoid of executive experience. The biggest organizations he had ever run were his Senate office and the PT-109 he commanded during World War II. What's more, he had been seeking the presidency for so long that he had only vague instincts about where he wanted to take the country. He did want to do something in civil rights. In the 1960 campaign, he promised to end discrimination "with the stroke of a pen." On health care, education, the minimum wage, the other social issues, he was a mainstream Democrat. He hoped to get the country through eight years without a nuclear holocaust and to improve things with the Soviets, if possible. He wanted a nuclear test ban treaty.

But as he was riding to the inaugural ceremonies with Kennedy in 1961, James Reston, the great *New York Times* columnist, asked what kind of country Kennedy wanted to leave his successor. Kennedy looked at him quizzically, as if he were looking at the man in the moon. Kennedy's method was never the grand vision of a Wilson or Reagan. It was crisis management—hour to hour to hour.

Kennedy's vow to land a man on the moon before 1970 is a perfect example. When he became president, he had no intention of launching a crash moon program. Advisers told him it would be too expensive and would unbalance a space program that was divided among communications, military, weather, exploration, and other projects.

But in the spring of 1961, the Russians injured American pride by launching the first man, Yuri Gagarin, into space. Then Kennedy suffered an embarrassing defeat when he and the CIA tried to use Cuban exiles to invade Cuba at the Bay of Pigs and seize the country from Fidel Castro. In the wake of that botched invasion, he badgered his aides for some quick fix that would help to restore American prestige. The moon-landing program was rolled out of mothballs.

People at the time often said Eisenhower was responsible for the Bay of Pigs, since it was Eisenhower's plan to take Cuba back from Castro. I think that has a hard time surviving scrutiny. Eisenhower would not necessarily have approved the invasion's going forward, and he would not necessarily have run it the same way. His son once asked him, "Is there a possibility that if you had been president, the Bay of Pigs would have happened?" Ike reminded him of Normandy and said, "I don't run no bad invasions."

Unlike Eisenhower, who almost flaunted his affinity for paperback westerns, Kennedy was a voracious reader of high intelligence. And we also remember JFK as one of the great orators of American history, which is only half right. Extemporaneously, he tended to speak too fast and with language that did not last for long. The great utterances we think of as coming from Kennedy—"Ask not what your country can do for you"; "We choose to go to the moon";

"Ich bin ein Berliner"—were almost all in prepared speeches, usually written by his gifted speechwriter Theodore Sorensen. If you read Kennedy's speeches from his earliest days as a congressman in 1947, you can see the difference at the instant Sorensen signs on in 1953. It's almost like the moment in *The Wizard of Oz* when the film goes from black and white to color. Suddenly, Kennedy had found his voice.

And when he used that voice, he was amazingly successful in moving public opinion. Think of the impact of Kennedy's inaugural or his Oval Office speech in October 1962, announcing Soviet missiles in Cuba and what he planned to do about them, or his civil rights address in June 1963, when he finally declared—as no president had ever declared—that civil rights was a "moral issue" that was "as old as the Scriptures and as clear as the Constitution."

JFK may never have run a large bureaucratic organization, but he was terrific at managing small groups. Look at the paramount moment of the Kennedy presidency—the Cuban missile crisis. How did he deal with the problem? He formed a small group of trusted officials, the Ex Comm (Executive Committee), which met in the Cabinet Room under the close supervision of the president and his brother Robert. Robert Kennedy was probably the most powerful member of a presidential entourage that we've seen in this century. That cut both ways. On the one hand, John Kennedy had someone he could rely upon as absolutely loyal, someone who totally shared his purposes. But on the other hand, it was virtually impossible for the president to distance himself from anything his attorney general did, since people assumed that when Robert Kennedy spoke, the message came from his brother.

The tape recordings of the Ex Comm meetings over thirteen days make it clear how enormously important it was to have Kennedy and his brother massaging the discussion. During the first week, the group moved from an almost certain intention to bomb the missile sites and invade Cuba to what JFK finally did: throw a quarantine around the island and demand that Nikita Khrushchev haul the missiles out. We now know that had Kennedy bombed, it might have easily escalated to a third world war. If Eisenhower had been running those meetings, with his Olympian approach, they might have been not nearly so effective. Here, Kennedy's talent for crisis management may have saved the world.

He had less success in his day-to-day dealings with Congress. One senator observed that the president would call him and say, "I sure hope I can count on your help on this bill." And he'd reply, "Mr. President, I'd love to help you, but it would cause me big problems in my state." If Lyndon Johnson had been president, he would have said, "Tough luck!" and pulled every lever he could to get his bill, even if it meant phoning the senator's bank and having his mortgage called. But Kennedy would say, "I understand. Perhaps you'll be with me the next time."

A good example is civil rights. Whatever he had pledged in the 1960 campaign, he was too overwhelmed by the opposition on Capitol Hill to do much to integrate American society. Voters who remembered his promise to end racial separation with a stroke of his pen angrily sent bottles of ink to the White House. Privately, he kept saying, "Wait until 1965. I've got to get reelected in a big way. If I'm lucky enough to run against Barry Goldwater, I'll win in a landslide with a big margin in Congress. Then on all the legislation I want, I can let 'er rip."

But the "Negro revolution," as people called it then, would not wait. In June 1963, with the South erupting in flames, Kennedy sent Congress a civil rights bill that was radical for its time. It was late, and he was pushed into it by events, but this was genuinely a profile in courage. JFK's public approval ratings dropped about twenty points. Southern states that had helped him win the presidency in 1960 turned against him. When Kennedy went to Texas in November 1963, he was by no means a shoo-in for reelection, and the reason was civil rights.

Unlike Eisenhower, Kennedy never had the eight years he had hoped for. Only two years, ten months, two days. And he never got that landslide in 1964. That went to Lyndon Johnson, who did have the good luck to run against Barry Goldwater. Thus to understand JFK's use of power, we have to ask two final questions about what might have happened had he lived.

First, what would have happened to his civil rights bill? I think that there is a good chance the Senate would have defeated it. In the aftermath of Kennedy's murder, Johnson was able to say, "Pass this bill as the memorial to our beloved late president." As I've mentioned, the Johnson tapes show that he used his monumental abilities to squeeze members of Congress to get the bill passed. Had Kennedy lived, neither of those things would have been possible. If you have to pull something redeeming out of the tragedy of Dallas, then, it is fair to say that because JFK gave his life, 20 million African Americans gained their rights sooner than they might have.

The other question is what Kennedy would have done in Vietnam. Some of Kennedy's champions, like Senate majority leader Mike Mansfield and his aide Kenneth O'Donnell, quote him as having said privately that he couldn't pull out before the 1964 election because he would be vilified as soft on communism. According to them, he planned to keep the troops in until after he was safely reelected, get the Saigon government to ask us to leave, and then withdraw.

I tend to be skeptical of this. If true, it means that Kennedy cynically would have kept young Americans in harm's way for fourteen months or more merely to help himself through the next election, then surrendered the commitment for which they'd been fighting.

Nor am I convinced by the notion that a reelected Kennedy in 1965, suddenly would have thrown caution to the winds. He still would have to serve as president for four years, and if he seemed to cave in on Vietnam in those times in which most Americans believed in the domino theory, there would have been a national backlash that would have undercut his ability to get anything he wanted from Congress, foreign or domestic.

And there was always in his mind the possibility that Robert Kennedy, or other Kennedys, might run for president. I doubt that he would have done something that might so injure his family's durability in American politics.

A greater possibility is that if Kennedy had escalated the war for two years and found himself as frustrated as Lyndon Johnson was, he might have been more willing than LBJ to pull out. Throughout his political career, Kennedy was adept at cutting losses.

The fact is, we will never know.

QUESTIONS TO CONSIDER

1 Did the framers of the Constitution want an all-powerful presidency? What two factors from the 1930s through the 1980s have increased the power of the men who have occupied the Oval Office? What roles did Franklin Roosevelt and Lyndon Johnson play in increasing the power of the presidency?

2 What made Dwight David Eisenhower a man with a "national and world reputation" by the time he became president? What were his views on the continuation of the New Deal, the role that the United States should play in world affairs, and the handling of Nikita Khrushchev?

3 What personal qualities did Eisenhower have that made him an effective president, and what qualities

did he lack that made his administration less notable than it might have been? Why does Beschloss conclude that Eisenhower was "magnificently suited to the 1950s" in the goals he accomplished?

4 What "three demerits" does Beschloss give Eisenhower's presidential record? Were these negative measures more important than Eisenhower's achievements? What did Eisenhower mean when he stated that the outcome of the 1960 presidential election was "a repudiation of everything I've stood for"?

5 Compare the impressions that the American people had of Eisenhower and Kennedy at the start of their presidential administrations. Why does Beschloss conclude that Kennedy's strength was "crisis management"? How did Kennedy display this talent during the Cuban missile crisis?

6 Compare Kennedy's dealings with Congress with those of Lyndon Johnson. Explain why Beschloss believes that Kennedy would not have been able to drive his civil rights legislation through Congress or remove American troops from Vietnam. Is it fair to evaluate a president who lived for only one thousand days in office?

24 Trapped: Lyndon Johnson and the Nightmare of Vietnam

LARRY L. KING

The Vietnam War was one of the most controversial episodes in United States history. American involvement in that conflict began with Truman and persisted through Democratic and Republican administrations alike, although the largest escalation took place under Lyndon Johnson—the subject of this selection.

To place Larry King's account in proper context, let us review what had gone on in Vietnam before the Johnson escalation. For more than twenty years, war had racked that distant Asian land. Initially, Communist and nationalist forces under Ho Chi Minh had battled to liberate their homeland from French colonial rule. The United States was suspicious of Ho, who was an avowed Communist trained in Moscow. But Ho was also an intense nationalist: he was determined to create a united and independent Vietnam and never wavered from that goal. Suspicious of Ho because of his Communist connections, the United States sided with the French against Ho and the Vietnamese; by 1954, when Dwight D. Eisenhower was president, the United States was footing 70 percent of the French cost of prosecuting a war that was highly unpopular in France. When Vietnamese forces surrounded and besieged twelve thousand French troops at Dien Bien Phu, Eisenhower's closest personal advisers urged armed American intervention to save the French position. Admiral Arthur Radford, chairman of the Joint Chiefs, even recommended dropping the atomic bomb on the Vietnamese. But Eisenhower would have none of it.

The Eisenhower administration, however, continued using American aid and influence to combat Communism in Indochina. In 1955, after suffering a humiliating defeat at Dien Bien Phu, the French withdrew from Vietnam, whereupon the United States acted to prevent Ho Chi Minh from gaining complete control there. Eisenhower and his secretary of state, John Foster Dulles, ignored an international agreement in Geneva that called for free elections and helped install a repressive, anti-Communist regime in South Vietnam, supplying it with money, weapons, and military advisers. From the outset, American policymakers viewed Ho Chi Minh's government in North Vietnam as part of a world Communist conspiracy directed by Moscow and Beijing. If Communism was not halted in Vietnam, they feared, then all Asia would ultimately succumb. Eisenhower himself repeated the analogy that it would be like a row of falling dominoes.

American intervention aroused Ho Chi Minh, who rushed help to nationalist guerrillas in South Vietnam and set out to unite all of Vietnam under his leadership. With civil war raging across South Vietnam, the Eisenhower administration stepped up the flow of American military aid to the government there, situated in the capital city of Saigon. Under President John F. Kennedy, an enthusiast for counterinsurgency (or counterguerrilla warfare), the number of American advisers rose from 650 to 23,000. But Kennedy became disillusioned with American involvement in Vietnam and devised a disengagement plan before he was assassinated in November 1963. Whether he would have implemented the plan cannot be stated with certainty. When Vice President Johnson succeeded Kennedy, he nullified the disengagement plan and (with the encouragement of Kennedy's own advisers) continued American assistance to South Vietnam. Then, in the Gulf of Tonkin Resolution in August 1964, Congress empowered the president to use armed force against "Communist aggression" in Vietnam. But Johnson repeatedly vowed, "We are not going to send American boys nine or ten thousand miles away from home to do what Asian boys ought to be doing for themselves."

Over the next winter, however, all that changed. In November and December 1964, South Vietnamese guerrillas of the National Liberation Front (or Vietcong) killed seven United States advisers and wounded more than a hundred others in mortar and bomb attacks. Johnson's Texas blood was up: he wasn't going to let them "shoot our boys" out there, fire on "our flag." He talked obsessively about Communist "aggression" in Vietnam, about Munich and the lesson of appeasement, about how his enemies would call him "a coward," "an unmanly man," if he let Ho Chi Minh run through the streets of Saigon. He couldn't depend on the United Nations to act—"It couldn't pour piss out of a boot if the instructions were printed on the heel." In February 1965, the administration became convinced that the coup-plagued Saigon government was about to collapse and that the United States had to do something drastic or South Vietnam would be lost and American international prestige and influence severely damaged. Accordingly, Johnson and his advisers moved to Americanize the war, sending waves of United States warplanes roaring over North Vietnam and 3,200 marines into the South.

The Americanization of the war took place with such stealth that people at home were hardly aware of the change. As reporter David Halberstam later wrote, United States decision makers *"inched across the Rubicon without even admitting it," and the task of their press secretaries was "to misinform the public." The biggest misinformers were Johnson and his spokesmen, who lied about costs (which were staggering), casualties, victories, and build-ups. By June, more than 75,000 American soldiers were in Vietnam, and combat troops were fighting Vietcong and North Vietnamese regulars in an Asian land war that Johnson had sworn to avoid. Soon troops were pouring in, and the war reeled out of control as each American escalation stiffened Vietcong and North Vietnamese resistance, which in turn led to more American escalation. By 1968, more than 500,000 American troops were fighting in that fire-scarred land. In the eyes of the administration and the Pentagon, it was unthinkable that America's awesome military power could fail to crush tiny North Vietnam and the Vietcong.*

But the unthinkable came true. America's military forces failed to smash their Vietnamese foe, and the war bogged down in stalemate. How Johnson trapped himself and his country in the quagmire of Vietnam is the subject of the following selection, written by Larry L. King, a native Texan and an eminent author, historian, and journalist. As a member of Johnson's political staff, King had occasion to observe his fellow Texan up close, and it shows in the stunning story he has to tell. To help us understand Johnson, King recounts the president's Texas background, personality, and political career in prose so stirring and full of insight and wit that you will not believe you are reading history. You will hear Johnson speak, see the world through his eyes, and feel his hurts and anger. You will think with Johnson as a combination of factors—his Cold War assumptions about a world Communist conspiracy and the domino theory, his belief in American invincibility, his emulation of mythical forebears, and his own deep-seated insecurities—drives him ever deeper into a war he never wanted to fight.

Finally, as King says, Johnson's manhood got tangled up in that horrendous conflict. To illustrate, King describes an episode that is shocking, hilarious, and sad all at the same time, an episode that captures perfectly Johnson's agony over Vietnam. This is surely one of the great portraits in literature.

GLOSSARY

ACHESON, DEAN   As Harry Truman's secretary of state, he was one of the principal architects of the policy of containing Communism that the United States developed in the early years of the Cold War.

ALAMO   The famous battle of the Texas revolution where 187 rebels held off a much larger force of Mexicans for more than a week. Lyndon Johnson saw this as a symbol of the willpower and macho determination that characterized the American spirit.

BUNDY, McGEORGE   The former dean of the arts and sciences faculty at Harvard, he was a "hawk" on the war in Vietnam when he served as national security adviser for both Kennedy and Johnson.

CHIANG KAI-SHEK   The leader of the Chinese Nationalists, who, despite American support, lost to the Communist forces under Mao Tse-tung. In 1949, the Nationalists

retreated to Formosa, where they hoped to mount an assault to regain control of the mainland.

CLIFFORD, CLARK   He replaced Robert McNamara as President Johnson's secretary of defense. Along with other trusted "wise men" (Dean Acheson and Omar Bradley among them), Clark recommended limiting the bombing of North Vietnam.

DIEM, NGO DINH   After the French left Vietnam in 1954, the United States provided economic and military support to Diem, who led the new government in South Vietnam. However, he was unable to unite his people or effectively fight the Communists. In November 1963, Diem died in a coup that had the approval of the American government.

DOMINO THEORY   First voiced by President Eisenhower, it became a reason for America's reluctance to leave Vietnam. It argued that if Vietnam fell to Communism so would its neighbors. The tumbling process would eventually threaten Japan and the Philippines and thus endanger the national security of the United States.

DULLES, JOHN FOSTER Eisenhower's secretary of state (1953–1959) and a militant cold warrior, he believed that threats of "massive nuclear retaliation" were the best way to deal with the Communist world.

FULBRIGHT, WILLIAM J. An Arkansas senator and chairman of the Foreign Relations Committee, he became an increasingly vocal critic of Johnson's escalation of the war in Vietnam. LBJ began referring to him as "Halfbright."

GOLDWATER, BARRY A conservative Republican senator from Arizona and a leading "hawk," Johnson easily defeated him in the presidential election of 1964.

GREAT SOCIETY Johnson's domestic reform agenda, which he saw as a fulfillment of FDR's New Deal. Many of the programs (civil rights, Medicaid, Medicare) were part of Kennedy's New Frontier. The war in Vietnam took both the focus and the funding of LBJ's administration away from the Great Society.

GULF OF TONKIN In August of 1964, the American destroyer *Maddox* opened fire on what it believed were enemy gunboats. When Johnson addressed Congress, he stated that the Communists had initiated an unprovoked attack. Since American ships had shelled the North Vietnamese coast and there was no evidence that Communist gunboats had attacked the *Maddox*, the president's statements were clearly misleading. Not knowing the true facts of the case, Congress empowered Johnson to use "all measures to repel any armed attack against the forces of the United States." The Gulf of Tonkin Resolution gave LBJ a virtual blank check to fight an undeclared war in Vietnam.

HALBERSTAM, DAVID A Pulitzer Prize–winning journalist who wrote a best-selling book entitled *The Best and the Brightest*. It examined the talented and intelligent advisers who made so many poor decisions while leading both Kennedy and Johnson into the war in Vietnam.

HO CHI MINH A Communist and a nationalist, he fought the French and then the Americans to establish a unified and independent Vietnam.

HUMPHREY, HUBERT LBJ's vice president who ran for president in 1968 only to lose to Richard Nixon. King concludes that Johnson abused Humphrey by publicly embarrassing him, and even kicking the proud Minnesotan.

KEARNS, DORIS (Now Doris Kearns Goodwin) As a White House fellow, she came to know Johnson on a personal basis. In the president's retirement years, she helped him with his memoirs, *Vantage Point,* and later wrote a biography entitled *Lyndon Johnson and the American Dream.*

McCARTHY, EUGENE A liberal senator from Minnesota who challenged LBJ for the presidential nomination of the Democratic party in 1968. McCarthy won almost half of the New Hampshire primary on a platform that called for American withdrawal from Vietnam. Johnson realized his vulnerability and how much the war had hurt his popularity. In March 1968, the president announced that he would not seek another term.

McCARTHY, JOSEPH R. The demagogic senator from Wisconsin who argued during the Cold War of the 1950s that the Communists had not only infiltrated the American government but also had gained power abroad. He blamed Truman's weak foreign policy based on containment. King argues that LBJ's "Texas was a particularly happy hunting ground" for McCarthyism.

McGOVERN, GEORGE A liberal Democratic senator from South Dakota who opposed the war in Vietnam, he lost the presidential election of 1972 to Richard Nixon.

McNAMARA, ROBERT He served as secretary of defense in the Kennedy and Johnson administrations. Near the end of Johnson's presidency, McNamara began to doubt whether America could win the war in Vietnam. He left the administration to head the World Bank.

MONOLITHIC COMMUNISM The belief that all Communists—Russian, Chinese, Vietnamese—were bent on world domination and cooperated with each other to achieve that goal.

MOYERS, BILL A former Peace Corps official and a close friend of Johnson whom the president treated like "a surrogate son." Moyers eventually left the administration to become an editor of *Newsday.*

PLEIKU In February of 1965, the North Vietnamese attacked Pleiku, killing nine Americans and destroying five aircraft. This resulted in an escalating program of air assaults against Communist targets above the 17th parallel.

PUEBLO An American warship seized by North Korea in 1968. There was also a crisis in Berlin that year. Johnson realized that Cold War tensions were not limited to Vietnam.

RAYBURN, SAM Powerful speaker of the House of Representatives and a Texan, he became one of LBJ's closest associates. When Johnson was a congressman, Rayburn assigned him to powerful committees that helped the future president learn about the importance of military preparedness.

RUSK, DEAN   Secretary of state in the Kennedy and Johnson administrations, he was an ardent cold warrior and a "hawk" on the war in Vietnam.

TET OFFENSIVE   Although Johnson continued to boast that "the enemy had been defeated in battle after battle" and that America was winning the war, the Vietcong on the last day of January 1968 launched the massive Tet Offensive. The Communists assaulted most of the major cities in South Vietnam and even temporarily occupied the American embassy in Saigon. This seemed undeniable proof that Johnson's military solution was a failure and that the claims of the president and his generals could not be believed.

WESTMORELAND, WILLIAM   American commander in Vietnam who devised "search and destroy" missions that the general hoped would help the United States win a war of attrition where "body counts" meant more than territory taken from the enemy.

He was an old-fashioned man by the purest definition. Forget that he was enamored of twentieth-century artifacts—the telephone, television, supersonic airplanes, spacecraft—to which he adapted with a child's wondering glee. His values were the relics of an earlier time; he had been shaped by an America both rawer and more confident than it later would become; his generation may have been the last to believe that for every problem there existed a workable solution; that the ultimate answer, as in old-time mathematics texts, always reposed in the back of the book.

He bought the prevailing American myths without closely inspecting the merchandise for rips or snares. He often said that Americans inherently were "can-do" people capable of accomplishing anything they willed. It was part of his creed that Americans were God's chosen; why, otherwise, would they have become the richest, the strongest, the freest people in the history of man? His was a God, perhaps, who was a first cousin to Darwin; Lyndon B. Johnson believed in survival of the fittest, that the strong would conquer the weak, that almost always the big 'uns ate the little 'uns.

There was a certain pragmatism in his beliefs, a touch of fatalism, and often a goodly measure of common sense and true compassion. Yet, too, he could be wildly romantic or muddle-headed. Johnson

King's portrait of Lyndon Johnson, shown above, reveals a complex man with manifold contradictions. He could be crude yet caring, overbearing yet insecure, committed to a moral cause yet deceitful and mendacious. Like his mentor, Franklin Roosevelt, Johnson wanted to make "people's lives a little brighter." He was a skillful manipulator of Congress and a bold advocate of civil rights. But in the end, the war in Vietnam destroyed his dream of building the Great Society in America. (LBJ Library Photo by Franke Wolfe)

Larry L. King, "Trapped: Lyndon Johnson and the Nightmare of Vietnam," from *Outlaws, Con Men, Whores, Politicians, and Other Artists*, Viking Press, 1980. Reprinted by permission of Sterling Lord Literistic, Inc. Copyright © 1980 by Larry L. King.

truly believed that any boy could rise to become President, though only thirty-five had. Hadn't he—a shirt-tailed kid from the dusty hardscrabble of the

Texas outback—walked with royalty and strong men, while reigning over what he called, without blushing, the Free World? In his last days, though bitter and withering in retirement at his rural Elba, he astonished and puzzled a young black teenager by waving his arms in windmill motions and telling the youngster, during a random encounter, "Well, maybe someday all of us will be visiting *your* house in Waco, because *you'll* be President and your home will be a national museum just as mine is. It'll take a while, but it'll happen, you'll see. . . ." Then he turned to the black teenager's startled mother: "Now, you better get that home of yours cleaned up spick-and-span. There'll be hundreds of thousands coming through it, you know, wanting to see the bedroom and the kitchen and the living room. Now, I hope you get that dust rag of yours out the minute you get home. . . ."

Doris Kearns, the Harvard professor and latter-day LBJ confidante, who witnessed the performance, thought it a mock show: "almost a vaudeville act." Dr. Johnson peddling the same old snake oil. Perhaps. Whatever his motives that day, Lyndon Johnson chose his sermon from the text he most fervently believed throughout a lifetime; his catechism spoke to the heart of American opportunity, American responsibility, American good intentions, American superiority, American destiny, American infallibility. *Why, hell, boy*—he was saying to the black teenager— *this country's so goddamn great even a nigger's gonna be President! And you and others like you got to be ready!*

Despite a sly personal cynicism—a suspicion of others who might pull their dirks on him; the keen, cold eye of a man determined not to be victimized at the gaming tables—he was, in his institutional instincts, something of a Pollyanna in that, I think, he somehow believed people in the abstract to be somewhat better than they are. He expected they would *do* more, and more things could be done *for* them, than probably is true. There *was* such a thing as a free lunch; there *was* a Santa Claus; there *was*, somewhere, a Good Fairy, and probably it was made of the component parts of Franklin Roosevelt, Saint Francis, and Uncle Sam.

There were certain thoroughly American traits— as LBJ saw them—which constituted the foundation stone upon which the Republic, and his own dream castle, had been built; he found it impossible to abandon them even as the sands shifted and bogged him in the quagmire of Vietnam. If America was so wonderful (and it *was;* he had the evidence of himself to prove it), then he had the obligation to export its goodness and greatness to the less fortunate. It would not do to limit this healing ministry merely to domestic unfortunates—to the tattered blacks of Mississippi or to the bombed and strafed disadvantaged of the South Bronx—because man, *everywhere,* deserved the right to be just like us! Yessir! This good he would accomplish at any cost; it was why we had no choice but "to nail the coonskin to the wall." For if Lyndon B. Johnson believed in God and America and its goodness and greatness, he also believed in guts and gunpowder.

All the history he had read, and all he had personally witnessed, convinced him that the United States of America—if determined enough, if productive enough, if patriotic enough—simply could not lose a war. We have evidence from his mother that as a boy his favorite stories were of the Minutemen at Lexington and Concord, of the heroic defenders of the Alamo, of rugged frontiersmen who'd at once tamed the wild land and marauding Indians. He had a special affinity for a schoolboy poem proclaiming that the most beautiful sight his eyes had beheld was "the flag of my country in a foreign land." He so admired war heroes that he claimed to have been fired on "by a Japanese ace," though little evidence supported it; he invented an ancestor he carelessly claimed had been martyred at the Alamo; at the Democratic National Convention in 1956 he had cast his state's delegate votes for the vice presidential ambitions of young John F. Kennedy, "that fighting sailor who bears the scars of battle."

On a slow Saturday afternoon in the late 1950s, expansive and garrulous in his Capitol Hill office, Johnson discoursed to a half dozen young Texas staffers in the patois of their shared native place. Why—he said—you take that ragtag bunch at Valley

Forge; who'd have given them a cut dog's chance? There they were, barefoot in the snow and their asses hanging out, nothing to eat but moss and dead leaves and snakes, not half enough bullets for their guns, and facing the soldiers of the most powerful king of his time. Yet they sucked it up, wouldn't quit, went on to fight and win. Or take the Civil War, now; it had been so exceptionally bloody because you had aroused Americans fighting on *both* sides; it had been something like rock against rock, or two mean ol' pit bulldogs going at each other and both of 'em thinking only of taking hunks out of the other. He again invoked the Alamo: a mere handful of freedom-loving men, knowing they faced certain death; but they'd carved their names in history for all time, and before they got through with ol' General Santa Anna, he thought he'd stumbled into a swarm of bumblebees.

Fifteen years later Johnson would show irritation when Clark Clifford suggested that victory in Vietnam might require a sustaining commitment of twenty to thirty years. No—LBJ said—no, no, the thing to do was get in and out quickly, pour everything you had into the fight, land the knockout blow; hell, the North Vietnamese *had* to see the futility of facing all that American muscle! If you really poured it on 'em, you could clean up that mess within six months. We had the troops, the firepower, the bombs, the sophisticated weaponry, the oil—everything we needed to win. Did we have the resolve? Well, the Texas Rangers had a saying that you couldn't stop a man who just kept on a-coming. And that's what we'd do in Vietnam, Clark, just keep on a-coming. . . .

Always he talked of the necessity to be strong; he invoked his father's standing up to the Ku Klux Klan in the 1920s, Teddy Roosevelt's carrying that big stick, FDR's mobilizing the country to beat Hitler and Tojo. He had liked ol' Harry Truman—tough little bastard and his own man—but, listen, Harry and Dean Acheson had lost control when they failed to prosecute the Korean War properly. They lost the public's respect, lost control of General MacArthur,

lost the backing of Congress, lost the *war* or the next thing to it. Next thing you know, they got blamed for losing China, and then there was Joe McCarthy accusing them of being soft on communism and everybody believed it. Well, it wouldn't happen to him, no, sir. *He* hadn't started the Vietnam War— Jack Kennedy had made the first commitment of out-and-out combat troops in force, don't forget— but *he* wouldn't bug out no matter how much the Nervous Nellies brayed. Kennedy had proved during the Cuban missile crisis that if you stood firm, then the Reds would back down. They were bullies, and he didn't intend to be pushed around any more than Jack Kennedy had. When a bully ragged you, you didn't go whining to the teacher but gave him some of his own medicine.

Only later, in exile, when he spoke with unusual candor of his darker secretions, did it become clear how obsessed with failure Lyndon Johnson always had been. As a preschool youngster he walked a country lane to visit a grandfather, his head stuffed with answers he knew would be required ("How many head of cattle you got, Lyndon? How much do they eat? How many head can you graze to the acre?") and fearing he might forget them. If he forgot them, he got no bright-red apple but received, instead, a stern and disapproving gaze. LBJ's mother, who smothered him with affection and praise should he perform to her pleasure and expectations, refused to acknowledge his presence should he somehow displease or disappoint her. His father accused him of being a sleepyhead, a slow starter, and sometimes said every boy in town had a two-hour head start on him. Had we known those things from scratch, we might not have wondered why Lyndon Johnson seemed so blind for so long to the Asian realities. His personal history simply permitted him no retreats or failures in testings.

From childhood LBJ experienced bad dreams. As with much else, they would stay with him to the shadow of the grave. His nightmares were of being paralyzed and unable to act, of being chained inside a cage or to his desk, of being pursued by hostile forces. These and other disturbing dreams haunted his White House years; he could see himself stricken and ill on a cot, unable even to speak—like Woodrow Wilson—while, in an adjoining room, his trusted aides squabbled and quarreled in dividing his power. He translated the dreams to mean that should he for a moment show weakness, be indecisive, then history might judge him as the first American President who had failed to stand up and be counted. Johnson's was a benign translation; others might see a neurotic fear of losing power—*his* power—to subordinates he did not, at least subconsciously, trust.

These deep-rooted insecurities prompted Lyndon Johnson always to assert himself, to abuse staff members simply to prove that he held the upper hand; to test his power in small or mean ways. Sometimes, in sending Vice President Hubert Humphrey off on missions or errands with exhortations to "get going," he literally kicked him in the shins. "Hard," Humphrey later recalled, pulling up his trouser leg to exhibit the scars to columnist Robert Allen. Especially when drinking did he swagger and strut. Riding high as Senate Majority Leader, Johnson one night after a Texas State Society function, in the National Press Club in Washington—in the spring of 1958—repaired to a nearby bar with Texas Congressmen Homer Thornberry and Jack Brooks.

"I'm a powerful sumbitch, you know that?" he repeatedly said. "You boys realize how goddamn *powerful* I am?"

Yes, Lyndon, his companions uneasily chorused. Johnson pounded the table as if attempting to crack stout oak. "Do you know Ike couldn't pass the Lord's Prayer without me? You understand that? Hah?" Yes, Lyndon. "Hah? Do you? Hah?" Sitting in an adjoining booth, with another Capitol Hill aide, James Boren, I thought I never had seen a man more desperate for affirmations of himself.

Lyndon Johnson always was an enthusiastic Cold Warrior. He was not made uncomfortable by John Foster Dulles's brinkmanship rhetoric about "rolling back" communism or "unleashing" Chiang Kai-shek to "free" the Chinese mainland—from which the generalissimo earlier had been routed by the Reds.

LBJ was, indeed, one of the original soldiers of the Cold War, a volunteer rather than a draftee, just as he had been the first member of Congress to rush to the recruiting station following Japan's attack on Pearl Harbor. Immediately after World War II he so bedeviled Speaker Sam Rayburn about his fears of America's dismantling its military machine that Rayburn, in vexation, appointed him to the postwar Military Policy Committee and to the Joint Committee on Atomic Energy. Johnson early had a preference for military assignments in Congress; he successfully campaigned for a seat on the House Naval Affairs Committee in the 1930s and, a decade later, the Senate Armed Services Committee. He eventually chaired the Senate Preparedness Committee and the Senate Space Committee. Perhaps others saw the exploration of outer space in scientific or peaceful terms; Johnson, however, told Senate Democrats that outer space offered "the ultimate position from which total control of the earth may be exercised. Whoever gains that ultimate position gains control, total control, over the earth."

He was a nagger, a complainer, a man not always patient with those of lesser gifts or with those who somehow inconvenienced him. Sometimes he complained that the generals knew nothing but "spend and bomb"; almost always, however, he went along with bigger military spending and, in most cases, with more bombing or whatever tough military action the brass proposed. This was his consistent record in Congress, and he generally affirmed it as President. On November 12, 1951, Senator Johnson rattled his saber at the Russians:

We are tired of fighting your stooges. We will no longer sacrifice our young men on the altar of your conspiracies. The next aggression will be the last. . . . We will strike back, not just at your satellites, but at you. We will strike back with all the dreaded might that is within our control and it will be a crushing blow.

Even allowing for those rhetorical excesses peculiar to senatorial oratory, those were not the words of a man preoccupied with the doctrine of peaceful coexistence. Nor were they inconsistent with John-son's mind-set when he made a public demand—at the outbreak of the Korean War, in June 1950—that President Truman order an all-out mobilization of all military reserve troops, National Guard units, draftees, and even civilian manpower and industry. He told intimates that this Korean thing could be the opening shot of World War III, and we had to be ready for that stark eventuality. In a Senate debate shortly thereafter, Senator Johnson scolded col-leagues questioning the Pentagon's request for new and supplementary emergency billions: "Is this the hour of our nation's twilight, the last fading hour of light before an endless night shall envelop us and all the Western world?"

His ties with Texas—with its indigenous xeno-phobic instincts and general proclivities toward a raw yahooism—haunted him and, in a sense, may have made him a prisoner of grim political realities dur-ing the witch-hunting McCarthy era. "I'm damned tired," he said, "of being called a Dixiecrat in Washington and a communist in Texas"; it perfectly summed up those schizophrenic divisions uneasily compartmentalizing his national political life and the more restrictive parochial role dictated by conditions back home. He lived daily with a damned-if-I-do-and-damned-if-I-don't situation. Texas was a par-ticularly happy hunting ground for Senator Joe McCarthy, whose self-proclaimed anticommunist crusade brought him invitation after invitation to speak there; the Texas legislature, in the 1950s con-trolled beyond belief by vested interests and showing the ideological instincts of the early primates, whooped through a resolution demanding that Sena-tor McCarthy address it despite the suggestion of State Representative Maury Maverick, Jr., that the resolution be expanded to invite Mickey Mouse also. Both Johnson's powerful rightist adversaries and many of his wealthy Texas benefactors were enthusi-astic contributors to the McCarthy cause and coffers.

Privately, LBJ groused of McCarthy's reckless showboat tactics and, particularly, of the Texas-directed pressures they brought him. Why—he said—Joe McCarthy was just a damn drunk, a blowhard, an incompetent who couldn't tie his own shoelaces, probably the biggest joke in the Senate. But—LBJ reminded those counseling him to attack McCarthy—people *believed* him; they were so afraid of the communists they would believe anything. There would come a time when the hysteria died down, and then McCarthy would be vulnerable; such a fellow was certain to hang himself in time. But right now anybody openly challenging Mc-Carthy would come away with dirty hands and with his heart broken. "Touch pitch," he paraphrased the Bible, "and you'll be defiled."

By temperament a man who coveted the limelight and never was bashful about claiming credit for pop-ular actions, Johnson uncharacteristically remained in the background when the U.S. Senate voted to cen-sure McCarthy in late 1954. Though he was instru-mental in selecting senators he believed would be effective and creditable members in leading the cen-sure effort, Johnson's fine hand was visible only to insiders. A correspondent for Texas newspapers later would remember it as "the only time we had to hunt to find Johnson. He almost went into hiding."

Johnson believed, however—and probably more deeply than Joe McCarthy—in a worldwide, mono-lithic communist conspiracy. He believed it was di-rected from Moscow and that it was ready to blast America, or subvert it, at the drop of a fur hat. LBJ never surrendered that view. In retirement he sug-gested that the communists were everywhere, hon-eycombing the government, and he told astonished visitors that sometimes he hadn't known whether he could trust even his own staff; *that's* how widespread spying and subversion had become. The communists (it had been his first thought on hearing the gunshots in Dallas, and he never changed his mind) had killed Jack Kennedy; it had been their influence that turned people against the Vietnam War. One of LBJ's former aides, having been treated to that angry lecture, came away from the Texas ranch with the sad and reluctant conclusion that "the Old Man's ab-solutely paranoid on the communist thing."

In May 1961 President Kennedy dispatched his Vice President to Asia on a "fact-finding" diplomatic trip. Johnson, who believed it his duty to be a team player, to reinforce the prevailing wisdom, bought without qualification the optimistic briefings of military brass with their charts and slides "proving" the inevitable American victory. "I was sent out here to report on the *progress* of the war," he told an aide, as if daring anyone to bring him anything less than good news. Carried away, he publicly endowed South Vietnam's President Ngo Dinh Diem with the qualities of Winston Churchill, George Washington, Andrew Jackson, and FDR. Visiting refugee camps, he grew angry at communist aggressions "against decent people" and concluded: "There is no alternative to United States leadership in Southeast Asia. . . . We must decide whether to help to the best of our ability or throw in the towel [and] pull back our defenses to San Francisco and a 'Fortress America' concept." Yes, sir, the damned dirty Reds would chase us all the way to the Golden Gate! LBJ believed then—and always would believe—in the domino theory first stated by President Eisenhower. Even after announcing his abdication, he continued to sing the tired litany: If Vietnam fell, then the rest of Asia might go, and then Africa, and then the Philippines. . . .

When Lyndon Johnson suddenly ascended to the presidency, however, he did not enter the Oval Office eager to immediately take the measure of Ho Chi Minh. Although he told Ambassador Henry Cabot Lodge, "I am not going to be the President who saw Southeast Asia go the way China went," he wanted, for the moment, to keep the war—and, indeed, all foreign entanglements—at arm's length. His preoccupation was with his domestic program; here, he was confident, he knew what he was doing. He would emulate FDR in making people's lives a little brighter. To aides he talked eagerly of building schools and houses, of fighting poverty and attaining full employment, of heating the economy to record prosperity. The honeymoon with Congress—he said—couldn't last; he had seen Congress grow balky and obstinate, take its measure of many Presidents, and he had to assume it would happen again. Then he would lean forward, tapping a forefinger against someone's chest or squeezing a neighboring knee,

and say, "I'm like a sweetheart to Congress right now. They love me because I'm new and courting 'em, and it's kinda exciting, like that first kiss. But after a while the new will wear off. Then Congress will complain that I don't bring enough roses or candy and will accuse me of seeing other girls." The need was to push forward quickly, pass the civil rights bill in the name of the martyred John F. Kennedy, then hit Capitol Hill with a blizzard of domestic proposals and dazzle it before sentiment and enthusiasms cooled. Foreign affairs could wait. Even war could walk at mark-time speed.

Lyndon B. Johnson at that point had little experience in foreign affairs. Except for his showcase missions accomplished as Vice President, he had not traveled outside the United States save for excursions to Mexico and his brief World War II peregrinations. He probably had little confidence in himself in foreign affairs; neither did he have an excessive interest in the field. "Foreigners are not like the folks I am used to," he sometimes said—and though it passed as a joke, there was the feeling he might be kidding on the level.

Ambassadors waiting to present their credentials to the new President were miffed by repeated delays—and then angrily astonished when LBJ received them in groups and clumps, seemingly paying only perfunctory attention, squirming in his chair, scowling or muttering during the traditional ceremonies. He appeared oblivious to their feelings, to their offended senses of dignity. "Why do I have to see them?" the President demanded. "They're Dean Rusk's clients, not mine."

Defense Secretary Robert McNamara was selected to focus on Vietnam while LBJ concocted his Great Society. McNamara should send South Vietnam equipment and money as needed, a few more men, issue the necessary pronouncements. But don't splash it all over the front pages; don't let it get out of hand; don't give Barry Goldwater Vietnam as an issue for the 1964 campaign. Barry, hell, he was a hip shooter; he'd fight Canada or Mexico—or give that impression anyhow—so the thing to do was sit tight, keep the lid on, keep all Asian options open. Above all, "Don't let it turn into a Bay of Pigs." Hunker down; don't gamble.

The trouble—Johnson said to advisers—was that foreign nations didn't understand Americans or the American way: They saw us as "fat and fifty, like the country-club set"; they didn't think we had the steel to act when the going got rough. Well, in time they'd find out differently. They'd learn that Lyndon Johnson was not about to abandon what other Presidents had started; he wouldn't permit history to write that he'd been the only American President to cut and run; he wouldn't sponsor any damn Munich. But for right now—cool it. Put Vietnam on the back burner, and let it simmer.

But the communists—he later would say—wouldn't permit him to cool it. There had been that Gulf of Tonkin attack on the United States destroyer *Maddox,* in August of 19-and-64, and if he hadn't convinced Congress to get on record as backing him up in Vietnam, why, then, the Reds would have interpreted it as a sign of weakness and Barry Goldwater would have cut his heart out. And in February of 19-and-65, don't forget, the Vietcong had made that attack on the American garrison at Pleiku, and how could he be expected to ignore that? There they came, thousands of 'em, barefoot and howling in their black pajamas and throwing homemade bombs; it had been a damned insult, a calculated show of contempt. LBJ told the National Security Council: "The worst thing we could do would be to let this [Pleiku] thing go by. It would be a big mistake. It would open the door to a major misunderstanding."

Twelve hours later, American aircraft—for the first time—bombed in North Vietnam; three weeks later, Lyndon Johnson ordered continuing bombing raids in the north to "force the North Vietnamese into negotiations"; only 120 days after Pleiku, American ground forces were involved in a full-scale war and seeking new ways to take the offensive. Eight Americans died at Pleiku. Eight. Eventually 50,000-plus Americans would die in Asia.

Pleiku was the second major testing of American will, within a few months, in LBJ's view. In the

spring of 1965 rebels had attacked the ruling military junta in the Dominican Republic. Lives and property of U.S. citizens were endangered, as Johnson saw it, but—more—this might be a special tactic by the Reds, a dry run for bigger mischief later on in Vietnam. The world was watching to see how America would react. "It's just like the Alamo," he lectured the National Security Council. "Hell, it's like you were down at that gate, and you were surrounded, and you damn well needed somebody. Well, by God, I'm going to *go*—and I thank the Lord that I've got men who want to go with me, from McNamara right down to the littlest private who's carrying a gun."

Somewhat to his puzzlement, and certainly to his great vexation, Lyndon Johnson would learn that not everybody approved of his rushing the Marines into the Dominican Republic, and within days building up a 21,000-man force. Congress, editorials, and some formerly friendly foreign diplomats blasted him. Attempting to answer these critics, he would claim thousands of patriots "bleeding in the streets and with their heads cut off"; paint a false picture of the United States ambassador cringing under his desk "while bullets whizzed over his head"; speak of howling Red hordes descending on American citizens and American holdings; and, generally, open what later become known as the Credibility Gap.

By now he had given up on his original notion of walking easy in Vietnam until he could put across the Great Society. Even before the three major "testings" of Tonkin Gulf, the Dominican Republic, and Pleiku, he had said—almost idly—"Well, I guess we have to touch up those North Vietnamese a little bit." By December 1964 he had reversed earlier priorities: "We'll beat the communists first; then we can look around and maybe give something to the poor." Guns now ranked ahead of butter.

Not that he was happy about it. Though telling Congress, "This nation is mighty enough, its society is healthy enough, its people are strong enough, to pursue our goals in the rest of the world while still building a Great Society here at home," he knew, in his bones, that this was much too optimistic an out-look. He privately fretted that his domestic program would be victimized. He became touchy, irritable, impatient with those who even timorously questioned America's increasing commitment to the war. Why should *I* be blamed—he snapped—when the communists are the aggressors, when President Eisenhower committed us in Asia in 19-and-54, when Kennedy beefed up Ike's efforts? If he didn't prosecute the Vietnam War now, then later Congress would sour and want to hang him because he hadn't—and would gut his domestic programs in retaliation.

He claimed to have "pounded President Eisenhower's desk" in opposing Ike's sending 200 Air Force "technicians" to assist the French in Indochina (though those who were present in the Oval Office later recalled that only Senators Russell of Georgia and Stennis of Mississippi had raised major objections). Well, he'd been unable to stop Ike that time, though he *had* helped persuade him against dropping paratroopers into Dienbienphu to aid the doomed French garrison there. And after all *that,* everybody now called Vietnam "Lyndon Johnson's War"! It was unfair: "The only difference between the Kennedy assassination and mine is that I am alive and it is more torturous."

Very well, if it was his war in the public mind, then he would personally oversee its planning. "Never move up your artillery until you move up your ammunition," he told his generals—a thing he'd said as Senate Majority Leader when impatient liberals urged him to call for votes on issues he felt not yet ripe. Often he quizzed the military brass, sounding almost like a dove, in a way to resemble courtroom cross-examinations. He forced the admirals and generals to affirm and reaffirm their recommendations as vital to victory. Reading selected transcripts, one might make the judgment that Lyndon Johnson was a most reluctant warrior, one more cautious in Vietnam than not. The larger evidence of Johnson's deeds, however, suggests that he was being a crafty politician—making a record so that later he couldn't be made the sole scapegoat.

He trusted Robert McNamara's computers, perhaps more than he trusted men, and took satisfaction when their printouts predicted that X amount of bombing would be needed to damage the Vietcong by Y or that X number of troops would be required to capture Z. Planning was the key. You figured what you had to do, you did it, and eventually you'd nail the coonskin to the wall. Johnson devoutly believed that all problems had solutions; in his lifetime alone we'd beaten the Great Depression, won two world wars, hacked away at racial discrimination, made an industrial giant and world power of a former agrarian society, explored outer space. This belief in available solutions led him, time and again, to change tactics in Vietnam and discover fresh enthusiasm for each new move; he did not pause, apparently, to reflect on why given tactics, themselves once heralded as practical solutions, had failed and had been abandoned. If counterinsurgency failed, you bombed. If bombing wasn't wholly effective, then you tried the enclave theory. If *that* proved disappointing, you sent your ground troops on search-and-destroy missions. If, somehow, your troops couldn't find the phantom Vietcong in large numbers (and therefore couldn't destroy them), you began pacification programs in the areas you'd newly occupied. And if *this* bogged down, if the bastards still sneaked up to knife you in the night, you beefed up your firepower and sent in enough troops simply to outmuscle the rice-paddy ragtags: Napalm 'em bomb 'em, shoot 'em; burn 'em out, and flush 'em out. Sure it would work! It always had! Yes, surely, the answer was there somewhere in the back of the book, if only you looked long enough. . . .

He sought, and found, assurances. Maybe he had only a "cow-college" education; perhaps he'd not attended West Point; he might not have excessive experience in foreign affairs. But he was surrounded by the good men David Halberstam later, and ironically, would label "the best and the brightest," and certainly they were unanimous in their supportive conclusions. "He would look around him," Tom Wicker later said, "and see in Bob McNamara that [the war] was technologically feasible, in McGeorge

Bundy that it was intellectually respectable, and in Dean Rusk that it was historically necessary." It was especially easy to trust expertise when the experts in their calculations bolstered your own gut feelings— and when their computers and high-minded statements and mighty hardware all boiled down to reinforce your belief in American efficiency, American responsibility, American destiny. If so many good men agreed with him, then what might be wrong with those who didn't?

He considered the sources of dissatisfaction and dissent: the liberals—the "red-hots," he'd often sneeringly called them; the "pepper pots"—who were impractical dreamers, self-winding kamikazes intent on self-destruction. He often quoted an aphorism to put such people in perspective: "Any jackass can kick down a barn, but it takes a carpenter to build one." He fancied, however, that he knew all about those queer fellows. For years, down home, Ronnie Dugger and his *Texas Observer* crowd, in LBJ's opinion, had urged him to put his head in the noose by fighting impossible, profitless fights. They wanted him to take on Joe McCarthy, slap the oil powers down, kick Ike's tail, tell everybody who wasn't a red-hot to go to hell. Well, he'd learned a long time ago that just because you *told* a fellow to go to hell, he didn't necessarily have to go. The liberals just didn't understand the communists. Bill Fulbright and his bunch—the striped-pants boys over at the State Department; assorted outside red-hots, such as the goddamn Harvards—they thought you could *trust* the communists. They made the mistake of believing the Reds would deal with you honorably when—in truth—the communists didn't respect anything but force. You had to fight fire with fire; let them know who had the biggest guns and the toughest hide and heart.

Where once he had argued the injustice of Vietnam's being viewed as "his" war, Lyndon Johnson now brought to it a proprietary attitude. This should have been among the early warnings that LBJ would increasingly resist less than victory, no matter his periodic bombing halts or conciliatory statements inviting peace, because once he took a thing personally,

his pride and vanity and ego knew no bounds. Always a man to put his brand on everything (he wore monogrammed shirts, boots, cuff links; flew his private LBJ flag when in residence at the LBJ Ranch; saw to it that the names of Lynda Bird Johnson and Luci Baines Johnson and Lady Bird Johnson—not Claudia, as she had been named—had the magic LBJ; he even named a dog Little Beagle Johnson), he now personalized and internalized the war. Troops became "my" boys; those were "my" helicopters; it was "my" pilots he prayed might return from their bombing missions as he paid nocturnal calls to the White House situation room to learn the latest news from the battlefields; Walt Rostow became "my" intellectual because he was hawkish on LBJ's war.

His machismo was mixed up in it now, his manhood. After a Cabinet meeting in 1967 several staff aides and at least one Cabinet member—Stewart Udall, Secretary of the Interior—remained behind for informal discussions. Soon LBJ was waving his arms and fulminating about his war. Who the hell was Ho Chi Minh, anyway, that he thought he could push America around? Then the President of the United States did an astonishing thing: He unzipped his trousers, dangled a given appendage, and asked his shocked associates, "Has Ho Chi Minh got anything like that?"

By mid-1966 he had cooled toward many of his experts: not because they'd been wrong in their original optimistic calculations, no, so much as that some of them had recanted and now rejected *his* war. This Lyndon Johnson could not forgive; they'd cut and run on him. Nobody had deserted Roosevelt—he gloomed—when FDR had been fighting Hitler. McGeorge Bundy, deserting to head the Ford Foundation, was no longer the brilliant statesman but merely "a smart kid, that's all." Bill Moyers, quitting to become editor of *Newsday* and once almost a surrogate son to the President, suddenly became "a little puppy I rescued from sacking groceries"—a reference to a part-time job Moyers held while a high school student in the long ago. George Ball, too, was leaving? Well, George had always been a chronic bellyacher.

This photograph shows the anguish and exhaustion of a president worn down by a seemingly endless war and the chants of protesters: "Hey hey LBJ/How many kids did you kill today?" Johnson moaned: "The only difference between the Kennedy assassination and mine is that I am alive and it is more torturous." (LBJ Library Photo by Jack Kightlinger)

When Defense Secretary McNamara doubted too openly (stories of his anguish leaked to the newspapers), he found it difficult to claim the President's time; ultimately he rudely was shuttled to the World Bank. Vice President Hubert Humphrey, privately having second thoughts, was not welcomed back to high councils until he'd muffled his timid dissent and shamelessly flattered LBJ. Even then, Johnson didn't wholly accept his Vice President; Hubert, he said, wasn't a real man, he cried as easily as a woman, he didn't have the weight. When Lady Bird Johnson voiced doubts about the war, her husband growled that *of course* she had doubts; it was *like* a woman to be uncertain. *Has Ho Chi Minh got anything like that?*

Shortly after the Tet offensive began—during which Americans would be shocked when the Vietcong temporarily captured a wing of the American Embassy in Saigon—the President, at his press conference of February 2, 1968, made such patently false statements that even his most loyal friends and supporters were troubled. The sudden Tet offensive had been traumatic, convincing many Americans that our condition was desperate, if not doomed. For years the official line ran that the Vietcong could not hang on, would shrink by the attritions of battle and an ebbing of confidence in a hopeless cause. Stories were handed out that captured documents showed the enemy to be of low morale, underfed, ill-armed. The Vietcong could not survive superior American firepower; the kill ratio favored our side by 7 to 1, 8 to 1; more. These and other optimisms were repeated by the President, by General Westmoreland, by this ambassador and that fact-finding team. Now, however, it became apparent that the Vietcong had the capability to challenge even our main lair in Asia—and there to inflict serious damage as well as major embarrassments. It dawned on the nation that we were a long way from defanging those rice-paddy ragtags.

It was a time demanding utmost candor, and LBJ blew it. He took the ludicrous position that the Tet offensive—which would be felt for weeks or months to come—had abysmally failed. Why, we'd known about it all along—had, indeed, been in possession of Hanoi's order of battle. Incredible. To believe the President, one also had to believe that American authorities had simply failed to act on this vital intelligence, had wittingly and willingly invited disaster. The President was scoffed at and ridiculed; perhaps the thoughtful got goose bumps in realizing how far Lyndon Johnson now lived from reality. If there was a beginning of the end—of Lyndon Johnson, of hopes of anything remotely resembling victory, of a general public innocence of official razzmatazz—then Tet, and that Looney Tunes press conference, had to be it.

Even the stubborn President knew it. His presidency was shot, his party ruined and in tatters; his credibility was gone; he could speak only at military bases, where security guaranteed his safety against the possibility of mobs pursuing him through the streets as he had often dreamed. The old nightmares were real now. Street dissidents long had been chanting their cruel *"Hey Hey LBJ/How many kids did you kill today?";* Senator Eugene McCarthy soon would capture almost half the vote in the New Hampshire primary against the unpopular President. There was nothing to do but what he'd always sworn he would not do: quit.

On March 31, 1968, at the end of a televised speech ordering the end of attacks on North Vietnam in the hope of getting the enemy to the negotiating table, Johnson startled the nation by announcing: ". . . I do not believe that I should devote an hour or a day of my time to any personal partisan causes or to any duties other than the awesome duties of this office—the presidency of your country. Accordingly, I shall not seek, and I will not accept, the nomination of my party for another term. . . ."

"In the final months of his Presidency," a former White House aide, and Princeton professor, Eric Goldman, wrote, "Lyndon Johnson kept shifting in mood. At times he was bitter and petulant at his repudiation by the nation; at times philosophical, almost serene, confidently awaiting the verdict of the future." The serenity always was temporary; he grew angry with Hubert Humphrey for attempting to disengage himself from the Johnson war policy and, consequently, refused to make more than a token show of support for him. He saw Richard Nixon win on a pledge of having "a secret plan" to end the war—which, it developed, he did not have. LBJ never forgave George McGovern for opposing "his" war and let the world know it by a lukewarm endorsement of the South Dakota senator in 1972 which pointedly was announced only to LBJ's little hometown weekly newspaper.

In his final White House thrashings—and in retirement—Lyndon Johnson complained of unfinished business he had wanted to complete: Vietnam peace talks; free the crew of the *Pueblo;* begin talks with the Russians on halting the arms race; send a

man to the moon. But the war, the goddamned war, had ruined all that. The people hadn't rallied around him as they had around FDR and Woodrow Wilson and other wartime Presidents; he had been abandoned, by Congress, by Cabinet members, by old friends; no other President had tried so hard or suffered so much. He had a great capacity for self-pity and often indulged it, becoming reclusive and rarely issuing a public statement or making public appearances. Doris Kearns has said that she and others helping LBJ write his memoirs, *The Vantage Point,* would draft chapters and lay out the documentation—but even then Lyndon Johnson would say no, no, it wasn't like that; it was like *this.* And he would rattle on, waving his arms and attempting to justify himself, invoking the old absolutes, calling up memories of the Alamo, the Texas Rangers, the myths, and the legends. He never seemed to understand where or how he had gone wrong.

When President Nixon assumed command of the war, he seemed to take up where Johnson left off. Like his predecessors, Nixon worried about "American credibility," about what would happen to American prestige if the United States sold out its South Vietnamese ally, and in 1970 he sent American troops into contiguous Cambodia to exterminate Communist hideouts there. The Cambodian invasion brought antiwar protest to a tragic climax, as Ohio national guard troops opened fire on protesting students at Kent State University and killed four of them. With the campuses in turmoil and the country divided and adrift, Nixon gradually disengaged American ground troops in Vietnam and sought détente with both Russia and China.

Although the Nixon administration continued to speak of "peace with honor" in Indochina, and although it continued to bomb Hanoi, it was clear nevertheless that American involvement in the Vietnamese civil war was a tragic and costly mistake. Indeed, the signs were unmistakable that the original premise for American intervention in Indochina was erroneous. The domino theory, based as it was on the assumption of a worldwide monolithic Communist conspiracy directed by Moscow, appeared more and more implausible. For one thing, China and Russia developed an intense and bitter ideological feud that sharply divided the Communist world, and they almost went to war over their disputed boundary. The Sino-Soviet split exploded the notion of a Communist monolith out for world domination, and so did the fierce independence of North Vietnam itself. Although Hanoi continued to receive aid from both Russia and China, North Vietnam apparently never asked China to intervene in the struggle (and apparently China never offered to do so). The truth was that North Vietnam was fighting to unite the country under Hanoi's leadership rather than under Beijing's or Moscow's.

At last, in top-secret negotiations in Paris, United States Secretary of State Henry Kissinger and North Vietnam's Le Duc Tho worked out a peace agreement. Eventually, the United States removed its combat forces, and in 1975 South Vietnam's regime fell to the North Vietnamese and the National Liberation Front. After almost two decades of bitter civil war and the loss of more than 1 million lives, Vietnam was united under Hanoi's Communist government, something that would probably have happened without further violence had general elections been held in 1956, according to the Geneva agreements of two years before.

QUESTIONS TO CONSIDER

1 Describe Johnson's background, personality, and vision of America. Do you think that LBJ, in retirement, was sincere when he called out to a young African American in Waco, Texas, that he and his mother better prepare for the day when the teenager would become president? Or, as Doris Kearns stated in her biography of Johnson, was it just "a vaudeville act"?

2 Explain King's assessment that Johnson's "personal history simply permitted him no retreats or failures in testings." Were there other reasons why LBJ could not conceive of an American defeat in Vietnam? Did the president generally support the military and its requests for manpower?

3 Why would King call Johnson an "enthusiastic Cold Warrior"? Why did Johnson view the space race as a vital element of America's national security? Although he despised Joseph McCarthy, why did LBJ fail to attack him?

4 When he first became president, did Johnson place more value in domestic or foreign policy goals? Had he much experience in dealing with foreign affairs or even much interest in the conduct of diplomacy?

5 King concludes that Johnson usually overreacted when he perceived a foreign policy threat. Do the president's actions after Pleiku, the rebel attacks in the Dominican Republic, and the Gulf of Tonkin incident support that assessment? At about what point in his presidency did he start believing that "guns now ranked ahead of butter"?

6 Was Johnson correct in assuming that the Eisenhower and Kennedy administrations committed him to the war in Vietnam? Explain how LBJ's character and background made it difficult for him to appreciate the position of his antiwar opponents or the significance of the Tet Offensive.

PART TWELVE

A New Birth of Freedom

25 Trumpet of Conscience: Martin Luther King Jr.

STEPHEN B. OATES

For most African Americans, the Depression had been an unmitigated calamity. An impoverished group to begin with, African Americans, especially southern sharecroppers, suffered worse than any other minority. World War II, however, offered African Americans relief, and they made considerable progress during the conflict. The war accelerated their exodus to the North, as southern blacks sought employment in war-related industry there. At first, white employers refused to hire African American workers, and the Roosevelt administration did little to stop such discrimination until A. Philip Randolph—the celebrated African American labor leader—threatened to lead a massive protest march. Roosevelt responded with an executive order that prohibited racial discrimination in defense plants and government agencies alike. By the close of 1944, two million African American men and women were working in shipyards, aircraft factories, steel mills, and other defense plants. At the same time, almost one million African Americans served in the United States armed forces—half of them overseas in segregated outfits. By war's end, however, some of the army bases at home were partly integrated, and African American sailors were serving on ships with whites.

Alas, African American soldiers and sailors who fought in a war against Nazi racists returned home to confront massive racial discrimination against them, especially in segregated Dixie. Many of those veterans joined the National Association for the Advancement of Colored People (NAACP), which now had chapters across the South, and became civil rights activists. In the postwar years, President Harry Truman proved to be sympathetic to the plight of African Americans and did much to help them: he established a special committee on civil rights, which worked out an agenda for attacking segregation that continued for two decades. Truman also issued an executive order that ended *segregation in the armed forces. Ironically, the military would become the most integrated institution in the United States.*

The NAACP, meanwhile, continued to battle segregation in case-by-case litigation in the federal courts and marked hard-earned victories against southern white primaries and segregated law schools in the border states. In May 1954, the NAACP Legal Defense Fund won its most spectacular triumph before the United States Supreme Court. In Brown v. Board of Education of Topeka, *the High Court outlawed segregation in public schools, thus reversing the doctrine of "separate but equal" that had prevailed since* Plessy v. Ferguson *fifty-eight years earlier. Said the Court: "Separate educational facilities are inherently unequal" and created "a feeling of inferiority" in African American students "that may affect their hearts and minds in a way unlikely ever to be undone." In one historic blow, the Supreme Court smashed the whole legal superstructure for the idea of racial separateness, knocking down a century and a half of devious rationalizations in defense of the doctrine that African Americans must be kept apart because they were inferior.*

But the white South obstructed the school decision at every turn. The Alabama legislature "nullified" the Court decision, vowing to preserve white supremacy come what may. Fiery crosses burned against Texas and Florida skies, and random Klan terrorism broke out against African Americans in many parts of Dixie. Faced with stiffening white resistance, the Supreme Court did not order immediate compliance with the Brown *decision and called instead for desegregation of public schools "with all deliberate speed." But the Court offered no guidelines and set no timetable. In 1956, more than one hundred southern members of Congress signed a "manifesto" that damned the Court decision and summoned the white South to defy it to the bitter end. Mustering its own legal forces, white officialdom promised to tie up the* Brown *decision in "a century of litigation."*

For African Americans, the road to freedom's land was elusive indeed. Most African Americans in the South languished in searing poverty and a rigid racial caste system that relegated them to the gutters of southern society and kept them away from the polls and out of politics.

How did African Americans feel about segregation? What did they say alone among themselves? "Lawd, man!" an elevator operator once told an African American writer. "Ef it wuzn't fer them polices n' them ol' lynch-mobs, there wouldn't be nothin' but uproar down here."

In 1955, African Americans in the South created an uproar despite the police and the lynchings. That was the year of the Montgomery bus boycott, an event that launched the nonviolent civil rights protest movement of the 1950s and 1960s. Many people rose to prominence in the movement, but Martin Luther King Jr. became its most popular and most eloquent spokesman. In this selection, you will walk with King from his birth in Atlanta and his intellectual odyssey in college to the great and impassioned days of the civil rights movement in the 1960s. As you ponder King's life and significance, consider what writer-historian Garry Wills said of King in The Kennedy Imprisonment *(1982), "While Washington's 'best and brightest' worked us into Vietnam," Wills wrote, "an obscure army of virtue arose in the South and took the longer spiritual trip inside a public bathroom or toward the front of a bus. King rallied the strength of broken [men and women], transmuting an imposed squalor into the beauty of chosen suffering. No one did it for his followers. They did it for themselves. Yet, in helping them, he exercised real power, achieved changes that dwarf the moon shot as an American achievement. The 'Kennedy era' was really the age of Dr. King."*

GLOSSARY

BLACK POWER In 1966, angry, disaffected young militants in the Student Nonviolent Coordinating Committee (SNCC) and the Congress of Racial Equality (CORE) turned away from nonviolence and racial integration; inspired by the earlier teachings of Malcolm X, a famous Black Muslim, they started advocating Black Power—the need for African Americans to organize themselves and consolidate their economic and political resources—as well as black separatism and even violent resistance.

CIVIL RIGHTS ACT OF 1964 Outlawed segregated public accommodations—the goal of King's civil rights campaign in Birmingham.

CONGRESS OF RACIAL EQUALITY (CORE) Founded in 1942, it staged sit-ins and applied Gandhian direct-action techniques to the American scene; in 1961, under the leadership of James Farmer, CORE sponsored the freedom rides to call attention to segregated busing facilities in the South, and the federal government responded by desegregating interstate bus stations.

CONNOR, EUGENE "BULL" City police commissioner who gained worldwide notoriety when he turned firehoses and police dogs on King's followers during the Birmingham demonstrations in 1963.

GANDHI, MOHANDAS The father of modern India whose teachings on nonviolent resistance and love for the oppressor profoundly influenced King.

MONTGOMERY BUS BOYCOTT (1955–1956) King rose to prominence as leader of this protest demonstration against segregated seating on Montgomery city buses; the Supreme Court finally nullified the Alabama laws that enforced the practice.

RAY, JAMES EARL King's assassin and a petty crook; subsequent evidence linked Ray to two white men in the St. Louis area who had offered "hit" money for King's life.

SOUTHERN CHRISTIAN LEADERSHIP CONFERENCE (SCLC) King's civil rights organization, which worked through African American churches to effect social and political change.

STUDENT NONVIOLENT COORDINATING COMMITTEE (SNCC) Established with King's help in 1960, SNCC organized sit-ins and voter-registration drives in segregated Dixie; many of its leaders were jealous of King, calling him "De Lawd."

VOTING RIGHTS ACT OF 1965 Passed in response to the Selma campaign, the measure outlawed barriers to voting by African Americans and authorized the attorney general to supervise federal elections in seven southern states where African Americans were kept off the voting rolls.

He was M.L. to his parents, Martin to his wife and friends, Doc to his aides, Reverend to his male parishioners, Little Lord Jesus to adoring churchwomen, De Lawd to his young critics in the Student Nonviolent Coordinating Committee, and Martin Luther King, Jr., to the world. At his pulpit or a public rostrum, he seemed too small for his incomparable oratory and international fame as a civil rights leader and spokesman for world peace. He stood only five feet seven, and had round cheeks, a trim mustache, and sad, glistening eyes—eyes that revealed both his inner strength and his vulnerability.

From "Trumpet of Conscience," by Stephen B. Oates. In *American History Illustrated* (April 1988), 18–27, 52. Reprinted through courtesy of Cowles Magazines, publisher of *American History Illustrated*.

He was born in Atlanta on January 15, 1929, and grew up in the relative comfort of the black middle class. Thus he never suffered the want and privation that plagued the majority of American blacks of his time. His father, a gruff, self-made man, was pastor of Ebenezer Baptist Church and an outspoken member of Atlanta's black leadership. M.L. joined his father's church when he was five and came to regard it as his second home. The church defined his world, gave it order and balance, taught him how to "get along with people." Here M.L. knew who he was— "Reverend King's boy," somebody special.

At home, his parents and maternal grandmother reinforced his self-esteem, praising him for his precocious ways, telling him repeatedly that he was *somebody*. By age five, he spoke like an adult and had such a prodigious memory that he could recite whole

Biblical passages and entire hymns without a mistake. He was acutely sensitive, too, so much so that he worried about all the blacks he saw in Atlanta's breadlines during the Depression, fearful that their children did not have enough to eat. When his maternal grandmother died, twelve-year-old M.L. thought it was his fault. Without telling anyone, he had slipped away from home to watch a parade, only to find out when he returned that she had died. He was terrified that God had taken her away as punishment for his "sin." Guilt-stricken, he tried to kill himself by leaping out of his second-story window.

He had a great deal of anger in him. Growing up a black in segregated Atlanta, he felt the full range of southern racial discrimination. He discovered that he had to attend separate, inferior schools, which he sailed through with a modicum of effort, skipping grades as he went. He found out that he—a preacher's boy—could not sit at lunch counters in Atlanta's downtown stores. He had to drink from a "colored" water fountain, relieve himself in a rancid "colored" restroom, and ride a rickety "colored" elevator. If he rode a city bus, he had to sit in the back as though he were contaminated. If he wanted to see a movie in a downtown theater, he had to enter through a side door and sit in the "colored" section in the balcony. He discovered that whites referred to blacks as "boys" and "girls" regardless of age. He saw "WHITES ONLY" signs staring back at him in the windows of barber shops and all the good restaurants and hotels, at the YMCA, the city parks, golf courses, swimming pools, and in the waiting rooms of the train and bus stations. He learned that there were even white and black sections of the city and that he resided in "nigger town."

Segregation caused a tension in the boy, a tension between his parents' injunction ("Remember, you are *somebody*") and a system that constantly demeaned and insulted him. He struggled with the pain and rage he felt when a white woman in a downtown store slapped him and called him "a little nigger" . . . when a bus driver called him "a black son-of-a-bitch" and made him surrender his seat to a white . . . when he stood on the very spot in Atlanta where whites had lynched

a black man . . . when he witnessed nightriding Klansmen beating blacks in the streets. How, he asked defiantly, could he heed the Christian injunction and love a race of people who hated him? In retaliation, he determined "to hate every white person."

Yes, he was angry. In sandlot games, he competed so fiercely that friends could not tell whether he was playing or fighting. He had his share of playground combat, too, and could outwrestle any of his peers. He even rebelled against his father, vowing never to become a preacher like him. Yet he liked the way Daddy King stood up to whites: he told them never to call him a boy and vowed to fight this system until he died.

Still, there was another side to M.L., a calmer, sensuous side. He played the violin, enjoyed opera, and relished soul food—fried chicken, cornbread, and collard greens with ham hocks and bacon drippings. By his mid-teens, his voice was the most memorable thing about him. It had changed into a rich and resonant baritone that commanded attention whenever he held forth. A natty dresser, nicknamed "Tweed" because of his fondness for tweed suits, he became a connoisseur of lovely young women. His little brother A.D. remembered how Martin "kept flitting from chick to chick" and was "just about the best jitterbug in town."

At age fifteen, he entered Morehouse College in Atlanta, wanting somehow to help his people. He thought about becoming a lawyer and even practiced giving trial speeches before a mirror in his room. But thanks largely to Morehouse President Benjamin Mays, who showed him that the ministry could be a respectable forum for ideas, even for social protest, King decided to become a Baptist preacher after all. By the time he was ordained in 1947, his resentment toward whites had softened some, thanks to positive contact with white students on an intercollegiate council. But he hated his segregated world more than ever.

Once he had his bachelor's degree, he went north to study at Crozer Seminary near Philadelphia. In this mostly white school, with its polished corridors and quiet solemnity, King continued to ponder the plight of blacks in America. How, by what method and means, were blacks to improve their lot in a white-dominated country? His study of history, especially of Nat Turner's slave insurrection, convinced him that it was suicidal for a minority to strike back against a heavily armed majority. For him, voluntary segregation was equally unacceptable, as was accommodation to the status quo. King shuddered at such negative approaches to the race problem. How indeed were blacks to combat discrimination in a country ruled by the white majority?

As some other blacks had done, he found his answer in the teachings of Mohandas Gandhi—for young King, the discovery had the force of a conversion experience. Nonviolent resistance, Gandhi taught, meant noncooperation with evil, an idea he got from Henry David Thoreau's essay "On Civil Disobedience." In India, Gandhi gave Thoreau's theory practical application in the form of strikes, boycotts, and protest marches, all conducted nonviolently and all predicated on love for the oppressor and a belief in divine justice. In gaining Indian independence, Gandhi sought not to defeat the British, but to redeem them through love, so as to avoid a legacy of bitterness. Gandhi's term for this—*Satyagraha*—reconciled love and force in a single, powerful concept.

As King discovered from his studies, Gandhi had embraced nonviolence in part to subdue his own violent nature. This was a profound revelation for King, who had felt much hatred in his life, especially toward whites. Now Gandhi showed him a means of harnessing his anger and channeling it into a positive and creative force for social change.

At this juncture, King found mostly theoretical satisfaction in Gandhian nonviolence; he had no plans to become a reformer in the segregated South. Indeed, he seemed destined to a life of the mind, not of social protest. In 1951, he graduated from Crozer and went on to earn a Ph.D. in theology from Boston University, where his adviser pronounced him "a scholar's scholar" of great intellectual potential. By 1955, a year after the school desegregation decision, King had married

A pensive King stands beside a portrait of Mohandas Gandhi, the Indian spiritual and political leader. "As King discovered from his studies, Gandhi had embraced nonviolence in part to subdue his own violent nature. This was a profound revelation for King, who had felt much hatred in his life, especially toward whites. Now Gandhi showed him a means of harnessing his anger and channeling it into a positive and creative force for social change." (Bob Fitch/Black Star)

comely Coretta Scott and assumed the pastorship of Dexter Avenue Baptist Church in Montgomery, Alabama. Immensely happy in the world of ideas, he hoped eventually to teach theology at a major university or seminary.

But, as King liked to say, the *Zeitgeist,* or spirit of the age, had other plans for him. In December 1955, Montgomery blacks launched a boycott of the city's segregated buses and chose the articulate twenty-six-year-old minister as their spokesman. As it turned out, he was unusually well prepared to assume the kind of leadership thrust on him. Drawing on Gandhi's teachings and example, plus the tenets of his own Christian faith, King directed a nonviolent boycott designed both to end an injustice and redeem his white adversaries through love. When he exhorted blacks to love their enemies, King did not mean to love them as friends or intimates. No, he said, he meant a disinterested love in all humankind, a love that saw the neighbor in everyone it met, a love that sought to restore the beloved community. Such love not only avoided the internal violence of the spirit, but severed the external chain of hatred that only produced more hatred in an endless spiral. If American blacks could break the chain of hatred, King said, true brotherhood could begin. Then posterity would have to say that there had lived a race of people, of black people, who "injected a new meaning into the veins of history and civilization."

During the boycott King imparted his philosophy at twice-weekly mass meetings in the black churches, where overflow crowds clapped and cried as his mellifluous voice swept over them. In these mass meetings King discovered his extraordinary power as an orator. His rich religious imagery reached deep into the black psyche, for religion had been the black people's main source of strength and survival since slavery days. His delivery was "like a narrative poem," said a woman journalist who heard him. His voice had such depths of sincerity and empathy that it could "charm your heart right out of your body." Because he appealed to the best in his people, articulating their deepest hurts and aspirations, black folk began to idolize him; he was their Gandhi.

Under his leadership, they stood up to white Montgomery in a remarkable display of solidarity. Pitted against an obdurate city government that blamed the boycott on Communist agitators and resorted to psychological and legal warfare to break it, the blacks stayed off the buses month after month, and walked or rode in a black-operated carpool. When an elderly woman refused the offer of a ride, King asked her, "But don't your feet hurt?" "Yes," she replied, "my feet is tired but my soul is rested." For King, her irrepressible spirit was proof that "a new Negro" was emerging in the South, a Negro with "a new sense of dignity and destiny."

That "new Negro" menaced white supremacists, especially the Ku Klux Klan, and they persecuted King with a vengeance. They made obscene phone calls to his home, sent him abusive, sickening letters, and once even dynamited the front of his house. Nobody was hurt, but King, fearing a race war, had to dissuade angry blacks from violent retaliation. Finally, on November 13, 1956, the U.S. Supreme Court nullified the Alabama laws that enforced segregated buses, and handed King and his boycotters a resounding moral victory. Their protest had captured the imagination of progressive people all over the world and marked the beginning of a southern black movement that would shake the segregated South to its foundations. At the forefront of that movement was a new organization, the Southern Christian Leadership Conference (SCLC), which King and other black ministers formed in 1957, with King serving as its president and guiding spirit. Operating through the southern black church, SCLC sought to enlist the black masses in the freedom struggle by expanding "the Montgomery way" across the South.

The "Miracle of Montgomery" changed King's life, catapulting him into international prominence as an inspiring new moral voice for civil rights. Across the country, blacks and whites alike wrote him letters of encouragement; *Time* magazine pictured him on its cover; the National Association for the Advancement of Colored People (NAACP) and scores of church and civic organizations vied for his services as a speaker. "I am really disturbed how fast all this has happened to me," King told his wife. "People will expect me to perform miracles for the rest of my life."

But fame had its evil side, too. When King visited New York in 1958, a deranged black woman stabbed him in the chest with a letter opener. The weapon was lodged so close to King's aorta, the main artery from the heart, that he would have died had he sneezed. To extract the blade, an interracial surgical team had to remove a rib and part of his breastbone; in a burst of inspiration, the lead surgeon made the incision over King's heart in the shape of a cross.

That he had not died convinced King that God was preparing him for some larger work in the segregated South. To gain perspective on what was happening there, he made a pilgrimage to India to visit

Gandhi's shrine and the sites of his "War for Independence." He returned home with an even deeper commitment to nonviolence and a vow to be more humble and ascetic like Gandhi. Yet he was a man of manifold contradictions, this American Gandhi. While renouncing material things and giving nearly all of his extensive honorariums to SCLC, he liked posh hotels and zesty meals with wine, and he was always immaculately dressed in a gray or black suit, white shirt, and tie. While caring passionately for the poor, the downtrodden, and the disinherited, he had a fascination with men of affluence and enjoyed the company of wealthy SCLC benefactors. While trumpeting the glories of nonviolence and redemptive love, he could feel the most terrible anger when whites murdered a black or bombed a black church; he could contemplate giving up, turning America over to the haters of both races, only to dedicate himself anew to his nonviolent faith and his determination to redeem his country.

In 1960, he moved his family to Atlanta so that he could devote himself fulltime to SCLC, which was trying to register black voters for the upcoming federal elections. That same year, southern black students launched the sit-in movement against segregated lunch counters, and King not only helped them form the Student Nonviolent Coordinating Committee (SNCC) but raised money on their behalf. In October he even joined a sit-in protest at an Atlanta department store and went to jail with several students on a trespassing charge. Like Thoreau, King considered jail "a badge of honor." To redeem the nation and arouse the conscience of the opponent, King explained, you go to jail and stay there. "You have broken a law which is out of line with the moral law and you are willing to suffer the consequences by serving the time."

He did not reckon, however, on the tyranny of racist officials, who clamped him in a malevolent state penitentiary, in a cell for hardened criminals. But state authorities released him when Democratic presidential nominee John F. Kennedy and his brother Robert interceded on King's behalf. According to many analysts, the episode won critical black votes for Kennedy and gave him the election in November. For King,

the election demonstrated what he had long said: that one of the most significant steps a black could take was the short walk to the voting booth.

The trouble was that most blacks in Dixie, especially in the Deep South, could not vote even if they so desired. For decades, state and local authorities had kept the mass of black folk off the voting rolls by a welter of devious obstacles and outright intimidation. Through 1961 and 1962, King exhorted President Kennedy to sponsor tough new civil rights legislation that would enfranchise southern blacks and end segregated public accommodations as well. When Kennedy shied away from a strong civil rights commitment, King and his lieutenants took matters into their own hands, orchestrating a series of southern demonstrations to show the world the brutality of segregation. At the same time, King stumped the country, drawing on all his powers of oratory to enlist the black masses and win white opinion to his cause.

Everywhere he went his message was the same. *The civil rights issue,* he said, *is an eternal moral issue that will determine the destiny of our nation and our world. As we seek our full rights, we hope to redeem the soul of our country. For it is our country, too, and we will win our freedom because the sacred heritage of America and the eternal will of God are embodied in our echoing demands. We do not intend to humiliate the white man, but to win him over through the strength of our love. Ultimately, we are trying to free all of us in America—Negroes from the bonds of segregation and shame, whites from the bonds of bigotry and fear.*

We stand today between two worlds—the dying old order and the emerging new. With men of ill-will greeting this change with cries of violence, of interposition and nullification, some of us may get beaten. Some of us may even get killed. But if you are cut down in a movement designed to save the soul of a nation, no other death could be more redemptive. We must realize that change does not roll in "on the wheels of inevitabilty," but comes through struggle. So "let us be those creative dissenters who will call our beloved nation to a higher destiny, to a new plateau of compassion, to a more noble expression of humaneness."

That message worked like magic among America's long-suffering blacks. Across the South, across

America, they rose in unprecedented numbers to march and demonstrate with Martin Luther King. His singular achievement was that he brought the black masses into the freedom struggle for the first time. He rallied the strength of broken men and women, helping them overcome a lifetime of fear and feelings of inferiority. After segregation had taught them all their lives that they were *nobody,* King taught them that they were *somebody.* Because he made them believe in themselves and in "the beauty of chosen suffering," he taught them how to straighten their backs ("a man can't ride you unless your back is bent") and confront those who oppressed them. Through the technique of nonviolent resistance, he furnished them something no previous black leader had been able to provide. He showed them a way of controlling their pent-up anger, as he had controlled his own, and using it to bring about constructive change.

The mass demonstrations King and SCLC choreographed in the South produced the strongest civil rights legislation in American history. This was the goal of King's major southern campaigns from 1963 to 1965. He would single out some notoriously segregated city with white officials prone to violence, mobilize the local blacks with songs, scripture readings, and rousing oratory in black churches, and then lead them on protest marches conspicuous for their grace and moral purpose. Then he and his aides would escalate the marches, increase their demands, even fill up the jails, until they brought about a moment of "creative tension," when whites would either agree to negotiate or resort to violence. If they did the latter, King would thus expose the brutality inherent in segregation and . . . stab the national conscience so [much] that the federal government would be forced to intervene with corrective measures.

The technique succeeded brilliantly in Birmingham, Alabama, in 1963. Here Police Commissioner Eugene "Bull" Connor, in full view of reporters and television cameras, turned firehoses and police dogs on the marching protesters. Revolted by such ghastly scenes, stricken by King's own searching eloquence

and the bravery of his unarmed followers, Washington eventually produced the 1964 Civil Rights Act, which desegregated public facilities—the thing King had demanded all along from Birmingham. Across the South, the "WHITES ONLY" signs that had hurt and enraged him since boyhood now came down.

Although SNCC and others complained that King had a Messiah complex and was trying to monopolize the civil rights movement, his technique worked with equal success in Selma, Alabama, in 1965. Building on a local movement there, King and his staff launched a drive to gain southern blacks the unobstructed right to vote. The violence he exposed in Selma—the beating of black marchers by state troopers and deputized possemen, the killing of a young black deacon and a white Unitarian minister—horrified the country. When King called for support, thousands of ministers, rabbis, priests, nuns, students, lay leaders, and ordinary people—black and white alike—rushed to Selma from all over the country and stood with King in the name of human liberty. Never in the history of the movement had so many people of all faiths and classes come to the southern battleground. The Selma campaign culminated in a dramatic march over the Jefferson Davis Highway to the state capital of Montgomery. Along the way, impoverished local blacks stared incredulously at the marching, singing, flag waving spectacle moving by. When the column reached one dusty crossroads, an elderly black woman ran out from a group of old folk, kissed King breathlessly, and ran back crying, "I done kissed him! The Martin Luther King! I done kissed the Martin Luther King!"

In Montgomery, first capital and much-heralded "cradle" of the Confederacy, King led an interracial throng of 25,000—the largest civil rights demonstration the South had ever witnessed—up Dexter Avenue with banners waving overhead. The pageant was as ironic as it was extraordinary, for it was up Dexter Avenue that Jefferson Davis's first inaugural parade had marched, and [it was] in the portico of the capitol [that] Davis had taken his oath of office as president of the slave-based Confederacy. Now, in the spring of 1965, Alabama blacks—most of them descendants of slaves—stood massed at the same statehouse, singing a new rendition of "We Shall Overcome," the anthem of the civil rights movement. They sang, "Deep in my heart, I do believe, We have overcome—*today*."

Then, watched by a cordon of state troopers and the statue of Jefferson Davis himself, King mounted a trailer. His vast audience listened, transfixed, as his words rolled and thundered over the loudspeaker: "My people, my people listen. The battle is in our hands. . . . We must come to see that the end we seek is a society at peace with itself, a society that can live with its conscience. That day will be a day not of the white man, not of the black man. That will be the day of man as man." And that day was not long in coming, King said, whereupon he launched into the immortal refrains of "The Battle Hymn of the Republic," crying out, "Our God is marching on! Glory, glory hallelujah!"

Aroused by the events in Alabama, Washington produced the 1965 Voting Rights Act, which outlawed impediments to black voting and empowered the attorney general to supervise federal elections in seven southern states where blacks were kept off the rolls. At the time, political analysts almost unanimously attributed the act to King's Selma campaign. Once federal examiners were supervising voter registration in all troublesome southern areas, blacks were able to get on the rolls and vote by the hundreds of thousands, permanently altering the pattern of southern and national politics.

In the end, the powerful civil rights legislation generated by King and his tramping legions wiped out statutory racism in America and realized at last the social and political promise of emancipation a century before. But King was under no illusion that legislation alone could bring on the brave new America he so ardently championed. Yes, he said, laws and their vigorous enforcement were necessary to regulate destructive habits and actions, and to protect blacks and their rights. But laws could not eliminate the "fears, prejudice, pride, and irrationality" that were barriers to a truly integrated society, to peaceful intergroup and interpersonal living. Such a society could be achieved only when people accepted that inner, invisible law that etched on their hearts the conviction "that all men are brothers and that love is mankind's most potent weapon for personal and social transformation. True integration will be achieved by true neighbors who are willingly obedient to unenforceable obligations."

Even so, the Selma campaign was the movement's finest hour, and the Voting Rights Act the high point of a broad civil rights coalition that included the federal government, various white groups, and all the other civil rights organizations in addition to SCLC. King himself had best expressed the spirit and aspirations of that coalition when, on August 28, 1963, standing before the Lincoln Memorial, he electrified an interracial crowd of 250,000 with perhaps his greatest speech, "I Have a Dream," in which he described in rhythmic, hypnotic cadences his vision of an integrated America. Because of his achievements and moral vision, he won the 1964 Nobel Peace Prize, at thirty-four the youngest recipient in Nobel history.

Still, King paid a high price for his fame and his cause. He suffered from stomachaches and insomnia, and even felt guilty about all the tributes he received, all the popularity he enjoyed. Born in relative material comfort and given a superior education, he did not think he had earned the right to lead the impoverished black masses. He complained, too, that he no longer had a personal self and that sometimes he did not recognize the Martin Luther King people talked about. Lonely, away from home for protracted periods, beset with temptation, he slept with other women, for some of whom he had real feeling. His sexual transgressions only added to his guilt, for he knew he was imperiling his cause and hurting himself and those he loved.

Alas for King, FBI Director J. Edgar Hoover found out about the black leader's infidelities. The director already abhorred King, certain that Communist spies influenced him and masterminded his demonstrations. Hoover did not think blacks capable of organizing such things, so Communists had to be behind them and King as well. As it turned out, a lawyer in King's inner circle and a man in SCLC's New York office did have Communist backgrounds, a fact that only reinforced Hoover's suspicions about King. Under Hoover's orders, FBI agents conducted a ruthless crusade to destroy King's reputation and drive him broken and humiliated from public life. Hoover's men tapped King's phones and bugged his hotel rooms; they compiled a prurient monograph about his private life and showed it to various editors, public officials, and religious and civic leaders; they spread the word, Hoover's word, that King was not only a reprobate but a dangerous subversive with Communist associations.

King was scandalized and frightened by the FBI's revelations of his extramarital affairs. Luckily for him, no editor, not even a racist one in the South, would touch the FBI's salacious materials. Public officials such as Robert Kennedy were shocked, but argued that King's personal life did not affect his probity as a civil rights leader. Many blacks, too, declared that what he did in private was his own business. Even so, King vowed to refrain from further affairs—only to succumb again to his own human frailties.

As for the Communist charge, King retorted that he did not need any Russians to tell him when someone was standing on his neck; he could figure that out by himself. To mollify his political friends, however, King did banish from SCLC the two men with Communist backgrounds (later he resumed his ties with the lawyer, a loyal friend, and let Hoover be damned). He also denounced Communism in no uncertain terms. It was, he believed, profoundly and fundamentally evil, an atheistic doctrine no true Christian could ever embrace. He hated the dictatorial Soviet state, too, whose "crippling totalitarianism" subordinated everything—religion, art, music, science, and the individual—to its terrible yoke. True, Communism started with men like Karl Marx who were "aflame with a passion for social justice." Yet King faulted Marx for rejecting God and the spiritual in human life. "The great weakness in Karl Marx is right here," King once told his staff, and he went on to describe his ideal Christian commonwealth in Hegelian terms: "Capitalism fails to realize that life is social. Marxism fails to realize that life is

individual. Truth is found neither in the rugged individualism of capitalism nor in the impersonal collectivism of Communism. The kingdom of God is found in a synthesis that combines the truths of these two opposites. Now there is where I leave brother Marx and move on toward the kingdom."

But how to move on after Selma was a perplexing question King never successfully answered. After the devastating Watts riot in August 1965, he took his movement into the racially troubled urban North, seeking to help the suffering black poor in the ghettos. In 1966, over the fierce opposition of some of his own staff, he launched a campaign to end the black slums in Chicago and forestall rioting there. But the campaign foundered because King seemed unable to devise a coherent anti-slum strategy, because Mayor Richard Daley and his black acolytes opposed him bitterly, and because white America did not seem to care. King did lead open-housing marches into segregated neighborhoods in Chicago, only to encounter furious mobs who waved Nazi banners, threw bottles and bricks, and screamed, "We hate niggers!" "Kill the niggers!" "We want Martin Luther Coon!" King was shocked. "I've been in many demonstrations all across the South," he told reporters, "but I can say that I have never seen—even in Mississippi and Alabama—mobs as hostile and as hate-filled as I've seen in Chicago." Although King prevented a major riot there and wrung important concessions from City Hall, the slums remained, as wretched and seemingly unsolvable as ever.

That same year, angry young militants in SNCC and the Congress of Racial Equality (CORE) renounced King's teachings—they were sick and tired of "De Lawd" telling them to love white people and work for integration. Now they advocated "Black Power," black separatism, even violent resistance to liberate blacks in America. SNCC even banished whites from its ranks and went on to drop "nonviolent" from its name and to lobby against civil rights legislation.

Black Power repelled the older, more conservative black organizations such as the NAACP and the

Urban League, and fragmented the civil rights movement beyond repair. King, too, argued that black separatism was chimerical, even suicidal, and that nonviolence remained the only workable way for black people. "Darkness cannot drive out darkness," he reasoned: "only light can do that. Hate cannot drive out hate: only love can do that." If every other black in America turned to violence, King warned, then he would still remain the lone voice preaching that it was wrong. Nor was SCLC going to reject whites as SNCC had done. "There have been too many hymns of hope," King said, "too many anthems of expectation, too many deaths, too many dark days of standing over graves of those who fought for integration for us to turn back now. We must still sing 'Black and White Together, We Shall Overcome.'"

In 1967, King himself broke with the older black organizations over the ever-widening war in Vietnam. He had first objected to American escalation in the summer of 1965, arguing that the Nobel Peace Prize and his role as a Christian minister compelled him to speak out for peace. Two years later, with almost a half-million Americans—a disproportionate number of them poor blacks—fighting in Vietnam, King devoted whole speeches to America's "immoral" war against a tiny country on the other side of the globe. His stance provoked a fusillade of criticism from all directions—from the NAACP, the Urban League, white and black political leaders, *Newsweek, Life, Time,* and the *New York Times,* all telling him to stick to civil rights. Such criticism hurt him deeply. When he read the *Times*'s editorial against him, he broke down and cried. But he did not back down. "I've fought too long and too hard now against segregated accommodations to end up segregating my moral concerns," he told his critics. "Injustice *anywhere* is a threat to justice everywhere."

That summer, with the ghettos ablaze with riots, King warned that American cities would explode if funds used for war purposes were not diverted to emergency antipoverty programs. By then, the Johnson administration, determined to gain a military victory in Vietnam, had written King off as an antiwar

agitator, and was now cooperating with the FBI in its efforts to defame him.

The fall of 1967 was a terrible time for King, the lowest ebb in his civil rights career. Everybody seemed to be attacking him—young black militants for his stubborn adherence to nonviolence, moderate and conservative blacks, labor leaders, liberal white politicians, the White House, and the FBI for his stand on Vietnam. Two years had passed since King had produced a nonviolent victory, and contributions to SCLC had fallen off sharply. Black spokesman Adam Clayton Powell, who had once called King the greatest Negro in America, now derided him as Martin Loser King. The incessant attacks began to irritate him, creating such anxiety and depression that his friends worried about his emotional health.

Worse still, the country seemed dangerously polarized. On one side, backlashing whites argued that the ghetto explosions had "cremated" nonviolence and that white people had better arm themselves against black rioters. On the other side, angry blacks urged their people to "kill the Honkies" and burn the cities down. All around King, the country was coming apart in a cacophony of hate and reaction. Had America lost the will and moral power to save itself? he wondered. There was such rage in the ghetto and such bigotry among whites that he feared a race war was about to break out. He felt he had to do something to pull America back from the brink. He and his staff had to mount a new campaign that would halt the drift to violence in the black world and combat stiffening white resistance, a nonviolent action that would "transmute the deep rage of the ghetto into a constructive and creative force."

Out of his deliberations sprang a bold and daring project called the poor people's campaign. The master plan, worked out by February 1968, called for SCLC to bring an interracial army of poor people to Washington, D.C., to dramatize poverty before the federal government. For King, just turned thirty-nine, the time had come to employ civil disobedience against the national government itself. Ultimately, he was projecting a genuine class movement that he hoped would bring about meaningful changes in American society—changes that would redistribute economic and political power and end poverty, racism, "the madness of militarism," and war.

In the midst of his preparations, King went to Memphis, Tennessee, to help black sanitation workers there who were striking for the right to unionize. On the night of April 3, with a storm thundering outside, he told a black audience that he had been to the mountaintop and had seen what lay ahead. "I may not get there with you. But I want you to know tonight that we as a people *will* get to the promised land."

The next afternoon, when King stepped out on the balcony of the Lorraine Motel, an escaped white convict named James Earl Ray, stationed in a nearby building, took aim with a high-powered rifle and blasted King into eternity. Subsequent evidence linked Ray to white men in the St. Louis area who had offered "hit" money for King's life.

For weeks after the shooting, King's stricken country convulsed in grief, contrition, and rage. While there were those who cheered his death, the *New York Times* called it a disaster to the nation, the *London Times* an enormous loss to the world. In Tanzania, Reverend Trevor Huddleston, expelled from South Africa for standing against apartheid, declared King's death the greatest single tragedy since the assassination of Gandhi in 1948, and said it challenged the complacency of the Christian Church all over the globe.

On April 9, with 120 million Americans watching on television, thousands of mourners—black and white alike—gathered in Atlanta for the funeral of a man who had never given up his dream of creating a symphony of brotherhood on these shores. As a black man born and raised in segregation, he had had every reason to hate America and to grow up preaching cynicism and retaliation. Instead, he had loved the country passionately and had sung of her promise and glory more eloquently than anyone of his generation.

They buried him in Atlanta's South View Cemetery, then blooming with dogwood and fresh green boughs of spring. On his crypt, hewn into the marble, were the words of an old Negro spiritual he had often quoted: "Free at Last, Free at Last, Thank God Almighty I'm Free at Last."

QUESTIONS TO CONSIDER

1 Martin Luther King Jr. was an angry young man who hated the segregated world of the American South and the injustices he saw inflicted on African Americans all over the nation. In adulthood, he came to feel that anger offered no solution to the problems that he and other African Americans faced. What made him change his mind? What were the roots of the philosophy that he adopted and used to lead the civil rights movement of the 1950s and 1960s? How did King give African Americans a sense of self-worth and the tools to achieve their aims?

2 What were SNCC and SCLC? How did these organizations differ from each other? In what ways were they alike? What changes took place in SNCC after the mid-1960s? How did Black Power differ from the civil rights movement under King?

3 What were the two major accomplishments of the civil rights movement in the mid-1960s? What specific actions did King and his followers undertake to influence public opinion and effect legislative change, and at what cost?

4 Describe the internal and external difficulties that beset King and the civil rights movement in the late 1960s. How did King defuse charges that he was a Communist? How did he react to the FBI crusade against him? To white and black backlashes? To the attacks on his policies that seemed to come from all sides? What did his support of the anti–Vietnam War movement cost him?

5 Why do you think Americans were receptive to King's pacifist message and nonviolent approach in the 1960s? Do you think similar tactics would be effective against oppression in a country such as the People's Republic of China?

26 Betty Friedan Destroys the Myth of the Happy Housewife

MARCIA COHEN

The Nineteenth Amendment, which gave American women the right to vote, did not bring them into the center of the nation's political life, and suffragists like Eleanor Roosevelt accepted a separate and subordinate "gender" role in their political work. During the Great Depression, as one feminist scholar has said, women "were partners in the struggle for survival." They also became involved in social and political activity; indeed, a "women's network" emerged within the New Deal and the Democratic party, allowing women for the first time to become a grassroots force. But women's achievements in the thirties proved to be short-lived, as historian Sara Evans has said, and women as a whole "were not empowered."

During the Second World War, women made significant economic advances as workers in America's defense plants. But after the war, as Marcia Cohen points out in this selection, the industrial establishment tended to push women back into the home because it recognized "the housewife's valuable role as the prime consumer of household products." At the same time, women's magazines such as Redbook *and* McCall's, *many of them published and edited by men, popularized the image of the happy housewife and stressed the old female virtues of passivity, marriage, and motherhood.*

The image of the happy homemaker and contented "auxiliary" troubled Betty Friedan, who in the mid-1950s was living in the suburb of Rockland County, New York, and trying to combine marriage and motherhood with freelance journalism. Back in the 1940s, she had been a brilliant student at Smith College and had done such outstanding work in psychology that she won a fellowship from the University of California at Berkeley. There she studied with the famous analyst Erik Erikson and won an even more prestigious grant that would have carried her into a professional career. But for some incredible reason—perhaps because a young man she was dating complained about the fellowship—she turned it down. Almost at once she suffered a protracted attack of asthma. Wheezing, gasping for breath, she left academe and the young man and fled to New York, where she sought relief in psychoanalysis.

When she felt better, she secured an editorial position at a small labor newspaper, married an amusing, ambitious man named Carl Friedan, and started raising a family. When she became pregnant with her second child, her employer decided that one pregnancy leave was enough; the paper fired her, ignoring the stipulation in her contract that guaranteed her maternity leave. She protested, but the Newspaper Guild refused to support her. Meanwhile, her marriage to Carl was becoming stormy; when they argued, she said, books and sugar bowls seemed to fly. Racked again by asthma, she resumed psychoanalysis.

Now living in a suburban Victorian house, Friedan did occasional freelance writing for women's magazines. She was increasingly attracted to stories about women who wanted the same things she did—an integrated life that used all of a woman's talents. She noted that prosperity offered the American woman an education and a living standard her grandmother would have envied, but it brought frustration too. By the 1950s, the American woman had been educated as never before, but to what end? When Friedan sent out a questionnaire for an article she was writing for McCall's, *she was astounded to learn that many women felt as unhappy as she did. Worse, their discontents were hidden behind the pervasive image of the happy housewife.*

In 1963, after years of struggling, Friedan published a book that demolished that image, The Feminine Mystique; *it galvanized millions of female readers, rocketed Friedan to national fame, and led to the modern feminist movement. Friedan's achievements were as important as those of many of the famous men we have studied thus far, and yet most of you would probably be hard pressed to identify her. You will get to know her well in the following selection, written by journalist Marcia Cohen, author of* The Sisterhood *(1988). Cohen recounts Friedan's extraordinary story, describing how she came to write* The Feminine Mystique *and to challenge a whole generation's assumptions and practices relating to women. An epilogue tells how Friedan initiated the "second wave" of organized feminism and founded and became the first president of the National Organization for Women, the first mainstream women's organization and the most successful one in history.*

GLOSSARY

BROCKWAY, GEORGE Editor at W. W. Norton who signed Friedan on to write *The Feminine Mystique,* which grew out of her article "The Togetherness Woman."

BROWN, HELEN GURLEY Author of *Sex and the Single Girl* (1962) and editor of *Cosmopolitan* who played a "pioneering role" in the sexual liberation of women in the 1960s and 1970s.

STEIN, BOB Editor of *Redbook* who agreed to publish an article ("The Togetherness Woman") based on Friedan's Smith class questionnaire if she expanded it to include younger women; he rejected the completed article on the

ground that it would appeal only to "the most neurotic housewife."

"THE TOGETHERNESS WOMAN" An article Friedan wrote for *McCall's* magazine that the male editor refused to publish. Based on a questionnaire Friedan had sent to her Smith College classmates, the article attacked woman's "homemaking role" as dull and unrewarding.

WOMEN'S WORLD (1952) Motion picture that stressed how much the home was a "woman's world" in which women buried their ambitions and subordinated themselves to their husbands.

It was a strange stirring, a sense of dissatisfaction, a yearning that women suffered in the middle of the twentieth century in the United States. Each suburban wife struggled with it alone. As she made the beds, shopped for groceries, matched slipcover material, ate peanut butter sandwiches with her children, chauffeured Cub Scouts and Brownies, lay beside her husband at night, she was afraid to ask even of herself the silent question—"Is this all?"

BETTY FRIEDAN, *The Feminine Mystique,* 1963

Her so-called "brilliant career"! Not much had come of that, Betty thought miserably as she trudged back to her beloved Smith College for her fifteenth reunion. The great promise her professors had seen—that eager, whirling intellectual energy—had come to nothing more than a

couple of women's magazine articles. Hardly "brilliant." Hardly even worthy of the term "career."

Betty—the class of 1942's hortatory, patriotic, tough tomato, always ready to take on an argument and, more often than not, *win* it. That same plump little girl who was so determined, way back in Peoria, to make her snooty contemporaries "respect her," who had set out, in her younger brother Harry's words, "to be somebody important . . ."

She was now, in 1957, returning to the alma mater that had been for her, such a glory, an affirmation,

Marcia Cohen, "Betty Friedan Destroys the Myth of the Happy Housewife," from *The Sisterhood: The True Story of the Women Who Changed the World.* © 1988 by Marcia Cohen.

"that whole thing," as she would put it years later in her gruff, gravelly voice, "of the *passion* of the mind." And she was coming back not as the professional psychologist they must all have expected, but as, well, "just a housewife" with a few articles to her credit.

"It rankled me," she would remember, "because I hadn't lived up to my brilliant possibilities."

But the undergraduates on campus, she found, were not the slightest bit interested in such "possibilities," and she was shocked by their distracted answers to her questions. Questions about, naturally, their scholarly interests, what ideas or professors they were "passionately excited about."

"They looked at me," she would recall, "as if I were speaking a foreign language. 'We're not excited about things like that,' they said. 'All we want to do is to get married and have children and do things with them, like go ice skating . . .'"

But it was now, of course, the quiet Eisenhower era, the gritrock pit of what would be viewed in retrospect as the heavy-duty husband-hunting years. "I chased her until she caught me," was a standard husband's joke, though the truth probably lay as much in the male youth's intent on settling down as the female's. The house in the suburbs, the station wagon bursting with kids and collie dogs, the ability to provide for a family proved manhood as much as homemaking proved femininity, and testified as well to those most important virtues of the decade: "adjustment," "maturity."

By now psychology was a preoccupation. Freud's vaunted theory of "penis envy" and [Dr. Helene] Deutsch's interpretation of the achieving, intellectual woman as "masculinized . . . her warm, intuitive knowledge . . . [having] yielded to cold unproductive thinking," hinted of maladjustments to be avoided at all costs. The idea that woman's true nature, reflecting her anatomy, was passive and could be fulfilled only through renouncing her goals and "sublimating" to a male had taken firm root in the American ethic.

The women's magazines, growing ever more powerful as advertising pages and circulations mounted, had been pounding the message home for nearly a decade. Women, as [Ferdinand] Lundberg and

[Dr. Marynia F.] Farnham had written [in *Modern Woman: The Lost Sex*], needed propaganda to keep them *in* traditional homemaking tasks, such as cooking or decorating, and *out* of those "fields belonging to the male area"—that is, "law, mathematics, physics, business, industry and technology." And indeed, the magazines invariably portrayed women as, above and beyond all else, housewives and mothers. If an interview subject happened to be an actress or dancer (two acceptably feminine undertakings), the editors quickly clarified: She was merely dabbling, taking a breather from her real work—and life—at home.

Nor was this notion purely the province of the popular press. Great citadels of learning were equally convinced and convincing. In most eastern women's schools, "gracious living" was the order of the day. This meant, on the whole, little more than learning to pour tea from a silver-plated samovar. But to carry out this future mission, give or take a samovar, you had to have a life of gentility, with, of course, a husband. Most college women, even those who never stood their turn at the tea kettle, knew beyond a shadow of a doubt that marriage—not a career—was their primary goal in life. Running a close second was the psychological health of their children, who were likely to erupt into neurotic misfits, psychologists warned, should Mother attempt any serious work outside the home.

Admittedly, the female's focus on marriage had an extra edge. The birth rate was soaring and given their dependent condition, women needed to be supported financially. The status gap of the thirties—between the gracious, respected matron, cared for by her breadwinner husband, and the lonely, forlorn working girl—was revived and slickly refurbished. Rare indeed was the college counselor who, by discussing the job market, would damn a female graduate to the latter state.

Some women left college without graduating. (Might as well get on with it. What's the point of waiting, anyhow?) Most collected a "Mrs." after or with their undergraduate degrees. You understood that you were marrying not just a husband but "a life," and this wholesale effort seemed at the time to blur class distinctions. Women cooked pot roast everywhere.

The idealized housewife from 1955, shown here on the cover of the Saturday Evening Post *for May 21, was well dressed and fashionably coiffed, even at home. Surrounded by modern appliances in her impeccable kitchen, she looks just as discontented as Betty Friedan found her a few years later—although the problem was a great deal more complex than runny chocolate icing.*

That there were, in fact, differences—in both class and interests—would eventually create knotty problems for feminists of the future. Many women, not only working-class women but also those with less defined intellectual appetites, very much enjoyed their roles as homemakers, household decision makers, disciplinarians, or managers, preferences that would eventually set them at odds with the revolutionaries of the sixties.

At the moment, though, like it or not, most women were preparing for the esteemed role of "auxiliary."

If, for instance, a woman was married to a doctor, she would join the hospital "auxiliary," have dinner ready when the doctor got home, and subscribe to a magazine called *Doctor's Wife.*

It was a given, in those days, that a young woman with a burning interest in the law should marry a lawyer. She would help him develop his practice and live the life of a lawyer's wife, mother of a lawyer's children. Or an engineer's, or a writer's, or a pharmacist's, or a retailer's—or especially a corporate executive's. That the deportment of an executive's wife had a major influence on her husband's advancement was a lesson clearly delivered, not just in an announcement from Radcliffe College of an Institute for Executive Wives, but in Jean Negulesco's popular film pointedly entitled *Women's World.*

In this 1952 movie, Lauren Bacall—no longer the sultry siren of the forties—played a devoted wife who, along with two others, June Allyson and Arlene Dahl, was summoned to corporate headquarters in New York, where their husbands were about to audition for top honcho.

"The best couple for the job," the company owner frankly informed the men, "will win. Your wife is under observation. She must never compete with the company. If there is a choice between wife and work, it must be work."

As the husbands in this "women's world" proceeded with their unmemorable politicking, the motivations (and "qualifications") of the wives were quickly established. June was frightfully anxious to rush home to her kids in the Midwest. Lauren fretted that the job might exacerbate her husband's ulcer. Arlene, on the other hand, was so delighted by the prospect of life in New York that she overreached by flirting with the owner, thus proving that she had missed not just one, but several commandments dosed out in the dialogue.

I "What's important to him is important to me."

II "You must convince him that you're perfectly happy even if you feel like screaming."

III "The man who gets the job must have a wife who loves him very much."

IV (the overriding theme): "A man is working for the children, and they're your children so it's a *woman's world.*"

And if, in the end, it's Arlene's man who does win the job, this plot twist occurs only after her restrained, expressionless husband has impressed the owner by dispensing with his "handicap": his ambitious, brazen, childless (and therefore dispensable) wife.

Though heavy-handed, the movie accurately reflected a large segment of the women's world of the fifties, where back in the suburbs wives quickly buried ambitions of the sort (vicarious or not) that plagued the unfortunate Arlene.

Few could imagine, in the expanding economy of the post–Korean War years, that among these selfless wives would be many who would find themselves, twenty and thirty years hence, in the wake of defunct marriages or financial belt-tightening, pounding the pavements, or training for jobs that could bring in much-needed cash or restore flagging self-esteem.

There were, of course, exceptions. A few remarkable college graduates *did* pursue professional careers. Among them, ironically—though barely noticed at the time—was an assertive, achieving Illinois woman who, in 1952, ran for Congress. Phyllis Schlafly, who would eventually stand forth as the new feminism's most vocal enemy, who would sound the alarm for women's return to the home, was among those who were not, at the moment, at home.

For even then, in spite of the social propaganda, many women, including those from middle-income families, were quietly moving into the workforce—so many, in fact, that they soon accounted for 60 percent of its growth in that decade. Among them were many single women, including college graduates who, as they waited for Mr. Right, took jobs as "Gal Fridays" in ad agencies, or as researchers, "helping" a reporter on a news magazine. Many took speed-writing or shorthand courses so they could be secretaries and thus avoid the typing pool, jobs for which there was plenty of call under "Female" in the help-wanted columns. The men who ran America's industries knew better than to give their girls (as in "Call my girl, she'll make an appointment for you") dangerous notions about careers. "Gal Fridays," summa cum laude be damned, ran errands and made coffee. They were lucky, they were told, to be hired at all, since it was a given that they wouldn't be around for long. If they were

"normal," they would soon drop out to get married, have babies.

And if they were "normal," they were known to be emotionally delicate as well, not cut out for the rough-and-tumble of the business world. . . .

If, for example, a wife was working outside the home, she retained her auxiliary, ladylike status by referring to her job as unimportant and transitory, a diversion, never a "career." She was helping out—just for the moment—with the family finances. She was subdued and modest. She strolled, seldom ran, let alone worked up a sweat. She knew better than to enter one of those rare girls' track meets, where young men guffawed to each other on the sidelines: "Nice tits" or "Some ass." She aspired, if not to June Allyson's saccharine self-sacrifice, to the controlled charm of Doris Day, the elfin poise of Audrey Hepburn, the serene aristocracy of Grace Kelly.

Any sign of ambition was disaster. What would be known in the seventies as "abrasive" in the fifties was a "castrating bitch."

Simone de Beauvoir's *The Second Sex,* a brilliant feminist polemic, was published in this country in 1953, but nobody in America talked about it much. The revolutionary Kinsey Report on *Sexual Behavior in the Human Female,* documenting the fact that women enjoyed sex both emotionally and physically pretty much the same way men did, went barely noticed in America's heartland. As the lure of television swept the country, people watched "Ozzie and Harriet" and "Father Knows Best," images of the perfect American family. Blacks appeared on the screen almost solely as servants; women, as wives and mothers. It was the age of "conformity," or, as probably suited best, the "silent generation."

And yet . . .

Anyone with an ear to the quiet, frozen lake of the mid-fifties might have heard the rumble, the growl and surge of a riptide beneath the ice. In the late forties, Holden Caulfield, J. D. Salinger's sensitive hero of *Catcher in the Rye,* inspired thousands of young fans by limning the hypocrisy he saw around him. (No one yet used the term "drop out," but Holden seemed destined to do it.) In 1954, the Supreme Court ordered desegregation in all public schools, an act that would not only change the paper-white face of the country, but may well have precipitated the enormous upheavals to come. In 1955, the sensitive, introspective James Dean struck a chord of disaffection in *Rebel Without a Cause.* Elvis Presley had begun to heat up and transform the soul of pop music. Writers Jack Kerouac in *On the Road* and Allen Ginsberg in "Howl" were giving voice to a strange youthful ennui, a rough-timbered, off-balance sense of disillusionment.

In 1953, *Playboy* magazine—with a nude calendar photo of Marilyn Monroe—was launched. Being the "party organ," as feminist writer Barbara Ehrenreich would one day call it, of the male, hedonistic rebellion, it had nothing good to say about collie dogs, station wagons, church picnics, or the family. It was billed as Hugh Hefner's answer to conformity, to "home, family and all that jazz," as he put it, and to "togetherness"—the resoundingly successful advertising slogan of *McCall's* magazine, the symbol of the happy, glorified home with Daddy at work, Mommy in the kitchen, and 2.5 children as total fulfillment.

"The Togetherness Woman" was, in fact, the title of the article Betty had promised *McCall's.* She had taken the assignment simply to justify the months and months she had spent on a questionnaire that Smith had asked her to prepare for her class reunion.

Betty had labored mightily over the thing, even brought a couple of her friends in to hash over the questions. She had worked so hard, in fact, that her classmates at the reunion had giggled about how *long* the form was. How involved, how detailed the questions.

"What difficulties have you found in working out your role as a woman?" "What are the chief satisfactions and frustrations of your life today?" "How do you feel about getting older?" Leave it to Betty, the psychology buff, they joked, to dream up all that stuff!

Yet all she had been trying to do was prove one little point, just a corollary to the women's home-is-all psychology of the day, a sort of reassurance to her classmates and herself.

"All I was trying to do with that questionnaire," Betty would remember, "was to show that an

education wasn't *bad* for a woman, it didn't make her *maladjusted* in her role as wife and mother." That academic learning was not, in short—as so many psychologists were then implying—an actual hindrance to femininity.

"I didn't realize it at the time," she would recall, "but I was asking the questions that were beginning to concern me." For indeed, skilled as she was in social science, and guiltily restless, Betty had designed the sort of query that took dead aim at the secrets of the heart—including her own.

"How have you changed inside?" she asked. "What do you wish you had done differently?"

And when, finally, she sat down to analyze the results for *McCall's,* she discovered that the responses raised more questions than they answered. Why was it, for example, that those of her classmates who were not active outside their homes were not especially happy at all? That they seemed, in fact, just as restless as she was?

They had written about a strange sense of emptiness—how like her own!—or a gnawing guilt, or shame, an uncertainty about who, exactly, they were: Jim's wife? Sally's mother? Betty found turmoils of indecision among these stay-at-home moms, and ennui, feelings of failure, despair, depression—even, for some, alcohol and drugs. And, most striking of all, from those isolated posts in suburbia, the uneasy sense that, because they had these feelings, they were unquestionably "neurotic."

So clearly Betty was not, as she had once thought, alone with these feelings. She was not, as she had also thought, a "freak."

But was education the villain, as all the psychologists and anthropologists and social scientists and magazine writers were more or less subtly suggesting?

That was, quite simply, a premise that the intense, verbal, thirty-six-year-old sometime writer, with her longings for intellectual achievement, could not accept. And as Betty read and reread and searched and analyzed, she discovered yet another piece to the puzzle.

"I found," she would remember at a later, much calmer time of her life, "that the women who seemed the strongest were not quite living this complete image of the housewife and feminine fulfillment. And that education had made them not willing to settle. . . ."

She was on to something!

Slowly but passionately, she began to write. Words and sentences began to fill the pages, words that bore no resemblance to "Millionaire's Wife," or "Two Are an Island," or anything she had ever written before. No panaceas, no hopeful methods of adjusting to the status quo, of finding total fulfillment in the home, poured forth from her pen. Instead of praising the homemaking role, she attacked the endless, monotonous, unrewarding housework it demanded. Instead of soothing her potential readers into the "feminine role" prescribed by the magazine she was writing for, she blasted the notion of vicarious living through husband and children. Rather than touting the "togetherness" so precious to *McCall's,* she indicted the slogan as a fraud.

She had to be kidding.

The male editor of *McCall's* summarily rejected "The Togetherness Woman."

A nasty shock for Betty Friedan. Never in her life had anything she had written been turned down. Quickly, she interviewed more women, then sent the piece to *Ladies' Home Journal.* There, sure enough, it was accepted, but . . .

"They rewrote it," she would remember years later, with the anger and dismay still in her voice, "to make the opposite point! That education *did* make women maladjusted in their role as women!"

Betty refused to allow the magazine to publish the article, retrieved it, and made one last try.

Bob Stein, then editor of *Redbook,* said he would indeed be interested in a piece based on Betty's Smith class questionnaire if it was greatly expanded to include younger women, and other, more extensive data.

Betty was already talking to younger married women and they weren't changing her view of the problem at all. In fact, she was beginning to think, the situation for women who graduated from college after 1942 seemed to be even worse than it was for her classmates. Given that domestic fantasy she had already seen among members of Smith's graduating class, even fewer women in their twenties and early thirties were active outside their homes; even *more* seemed vaguely unhappy.

She hadn't yet been paid for the article, of course, and she was violating that "enough-money-to-pay-the-maid" pact with herself. But still, since Bob Stein had asked—and since she was fascinated herself—she did more interviews. She rewrote the piece, integrating the new material, and shipped it off to the editor.

Who was, he would remember, stunned.

"I liked Betty a lot," Bob Stein would recall. "She was a solid, trustworthy writer, a bit argumentative maybe, but so were most writers worth their salt. I had been looking forward to 'The Togetherness Woman,' but when I read it, I could only wonder what in God's name had come over Betty Friedan. It was a very angry piece. I didn't think that our readers would identify with it at all."

The *Redbook* editor—like all successful editors of women's magazines—was fully aware of the link binding readers to *their* magazine, the great umbilical, as some called it, the trust which, if broken, could doom both magazine and its boss. And Betty was, Bob Stein would remember, "very sensitive about her writing. . . . Luckily, I'd never had to reject her work before." But this?

In years to come, Bob Stein would find himself on television and radio talk shows with Betty, defending her, if only because, as he would put it, "the opposition was so impossible," but admitting, too, that he hadn't realized "that the feelings dammed up out there were so strong." At the moment, though, he could only call Betty's agent and report regretfully: "Look, we can't print this. Only the most neurotic housewife would identify with this."

And that, perhaps, might have been the end of it.

Redbook had been Betty's last hope, and in the weeks that followed, she was very depressed. She wrote nothing and dropped out of an important writer's seminar because it met the same night of the week that she served as assistant den mother for her son's Cub Scout troop. She had already chastised herself, had an asthma attack, in fact, over missing some of those Scout meetings.

One night, though, just as a prop to her ego, just to make herself feel like a professional writer again, she made the trek in from Rockland County to hear the successful author Vance Packard talk about his book *The Hidden Persuaders,* an exposé of the sinister effects of advertising. Packard had written it, he said, after an article on the subject had been turned down by every major magazine.

And then—not long afterward, as Betty would remember it—she was riding the bus into Manhattan, taking the kids to the dentist, mulling it over . . . The juggernaut women's magazines, with their fingers on the commercial pulse, had been feeding the domestic palate to ever-rising profit margins . . .

"Damn it all," Betty suddenly realized, "I was right! Somehow what I was saying had gone against the grain of the women's magazines."

And now she knew she couldn't let it go.

In some deep place in the psyche of this impatient, demanding, worrisome, dedicated, prickly, volatile woman, a quiet vision was forming. Inside, as she would later write, she felt "this calm, strange sureness, as if in tune with something larger, more important than myself that had to be taken seriously."

It would be a book. Like *The Hidden Persuaders,* "The Togetherness Woman" could be a book. She would call that editor who had wanted her to expand "The Coming Ice Age," and this time she would tell him yes. Yes, she would write a book for W. W. Norton. But just as she had said before, it would not be about someone else's work. It would be hers. Her own research, her own social science, her own accomplishment in her field.

The Togetherness Woman.

And why not? said [Norton Editor] George Brockway, who immediately saw the potential.

The affluence of the fifties had permitted—even stimulated—critical examinations of contemporary life. *The Man in the Grey Flannel Suit, The Hucksters, Executive Suite, The View from the 40th Floor* had all been big sellers. *The Togetherness Woman,* the editor thought, would make a fine parallel to the latest sharp attack on the rage for conformity, William H. Whyte's *The Organization Man.*

And this woman had the fire in the belly.

"She was incredibly ambitious," Brockway would remember. "The most ambitious woman I had ever met. She said that she didn't know what to call the subject exactly, but that it had something to do with a lack of identity, that women weren't being told . . . they aren't being allowed . . ."

Betty talked on and on at that meeting, half her thoughts, as usual, dropping off mid-sentence, her mind going even faster than her tongue. She had been interviewing so many women. She didn't know quite how to put it, but . . .

There was *something* very wrong with the way women were feeling these days.

And, over the barrage, the furtive insights, the distress, George Brockway honed in.

"Ride it," he told Betty. "You've got the idea, now ride it, ride it!"

How long did she think it would take?

Well, she said, it took her about a month to do an article, so figure a chapter a month . . .

"A year," she said. "I'll have it done in a year." Oh, and yes, she supposed [an advance of] a thousand dollars now would be okay, with the rest of the $3,000 [advance] to come in installments.

It was years later—more research was required, a mysterious block arose—before Betty even *began* to write. She worked three days a week in the Frederick Lewis Allen Room of the New York Public Library and then, when her allotted time there ran out (and the maid quit), in her favorite spot at home, the beautiful dining room with windows on the garden.

"Neither my husband nor my publisher nor anyone else who knew about it thought I would ever finish it," she would write. "When the writing of it took me over completely . . . I wrote every day on the dining room table, while the children were in school, and after they went to bed at night. (It didn't do any good to have a desk of my own; they used it for their homework anyhow.)"

She worked against patronizing jokes about a "woman's book." Against guilt. Against fear. Given the resistance she had already encountered to her views, there must be *no* holes in her argument or her documentation, *no* room for attack.

But slowly, if not steadily, the chapters, scribbled on a legal pad, began to pile up in an old china cupboard in the corner of the dining room. In them, her thesis emerged.

At rock bottom, it was economics, if not to say greed. After World War II, women had been pushed back into the home as industrialists assessed the housewife's valuable role as the prime consumer of household products. The marketing of toasters, washing machines, cosmetics, and the like was the true purpose behind the hard sell of "femininity." Educators, sociologists, psychologists—and, of course, the women's magazines, with their hunger for the advertising dollar—followed suit.

One by one, Betty took them all on, both the current crop and their historical forebears.

Freud and his "sexual solipsism": "It is a Freudian idea . . . hardened into apparent fact, that has trapped so many American women today." Freud and his Victorian bias had perpetrated the greatest sin in psychotherapy; he had infantilized women, denied them their ability to grow, cut them off from "the zest that is characteristic of human health."

[Anthropologist] Margaret Mead: "The role of Margaret Mead as the professional spokesman of femininity would have been less important if American women had taken the example of her own life, instead of listening to what she said in her books."

Contemporary educators: They induced women into the superficial comfort of the home, thus depriving them of their function in society, consigning millions of women "to spend their days at work an eight-year-old could do."

As for the women's magazines, which offered that fraudulent home-as-religion editorial content: "I helped create this image. I have watched American women for fifteen years try to conform to it. But I can no longer deny its terrible implications. It is not a harmless image. There may be no psychological terms for the harm it is doing."

And, of course, "togetherness": "The big lie . . . the end of the road . . . where the woman has no independent self to hide even in guilt; she exists only for and through her husband and children."

It was this vicarious existence that caused educations to "fester," caused housewife's fatigue, ennui, depression. Not neurosis. It was society—not women—that was sick!

Like Lundberg and Farnham, Betty resurrected earlier feminists, but instead of damning them as sick souls, she sang their praises as heroines. Mary Wollstonecraft, Margaret Fuller, Elizabeth Cady Stanton, Lucy Stone, Susan B. Anthony. Anatomy, she agreed, with a somewhat cursory bow to Simone de Beauvoir's evocative phrasing in *The Second Sex,* is not destiny. Women were not simply their biology. They also had *minds.* And, "as if waking from a coma," they were beginning to ask, "Where am I? What am I doing here?"

She answered the hyperbole of Lundberg and Farnham with some of her own. The isolated suburban home, she wrote, was a "comfortable concentration camp," the women trapped within them cut off, like prisoners, from past adult interests and their own identities. It was a new neurosis, this modern ache, and you could read it in the hundreds of interviews and psychological tests she had accumulated—among them, one test that must have been reassuring, since it suggested that "the high-dominance woman was more psychologically free" than one who was "timid, shy, modest, neat, tactful, quiet, introverted, retiring, more feminine, more conventional." And perhaps, Betty herself speculated, only an "ugly duckling adolescence" or an unhappy marriage could fuel the ambition to resist the deadening, conformist pressure.

For "the problem lay buried, unspoken, for many years in the minds of American women." It was a problem, she wrote, "that had no name," a problem that was caused by the pervasive social pressure relegating women to the four walls of their homes, a pressure whose weapon was an image: "the feminine mystique."

Five years from the time Betty had signed the contract, four years late, *The Feminine Mystique* was published.

It was February 1963, and the New York newspapers, including the *Times,* were on strike. With no review in the *Times,* the chances that a book—even this thunderous polemic—would reach a substantial

The photographer has captured Betty Friedan in a moment of profound weariness. In the years after the publication of The Feminine Mystique, *Friedan worked zealously for women's rights: she organized demonstrations, lobbied for antidiscrimination legislation, and struggled to hold the women's movement together in the face of internal dissension. "In truth, she paid a high personal price for her cause." (Michael Ginsburg/Magnum Photos)*

public were practically nil. And there was plenty of competition. Morton Hunt had just published a gentle, affectionate paean to women's role *outside* as well as in the home. His book was called *Her Infinite Variety,* and it was moving off the bookstore shelves at a frighteningly rapid pace.

Betty was beside herself. And so, for that matter, was Carl. Never had the state of their marriage been worse, never stormier than during the last year she was writing, when, Carl would complain to friends, he would come home from work and "that bitch," instead of cooking dinner, was writing away at the dining-room table. Betty, friends would whisper, was writing out the problems of her marriage, writing a book instead of leaving Carl. His one-man advertising

and public relations firm was far from a booming success, and now this. Who would even hear of *The Feminine Mystique,* let alone buy it? Where, after all these years, was the payoff?

"Betty would come in with ideas to promote the book," George Brockway would recall. "You could tell Carl was behind them, saying, 'Tell 'em to do this, tell 'em to do that.'

"One day she told me that Carl wanted to know what could be done to make *The Feminine Mystique* as big a seller as *Gifts from the Sea.*" (This popular book was written by Anne Morrow Lindbergh, the wife of the heroic aviator.)

"'Tell Carl,' I told her, 'that he can fly the Atlantic solo.'"

Irascible Carl, George would call him—the low-key editor being far from charmed by what he regarded as Carl Friedan's "sharp and nasty" tongue.

But Betty thought her husband knew his business. She would always remember that it was Carl who had persuaded Norton to hire a publicist. Eventually, in fact, she would switch to another publishing house, leaving Brockway entirely.

"I remember him pleading with me," Betty would tell a reporter, "and I remember looking him right in the eye and saying, 'George, you made me feel Jewish for trying to sell that book. Go fuck yourself.'"

But, with the help of the publicist, excerpts from the book began to appear, and articles ran in major news magazines about Betty as an "angry battler for her sex." She began bouncing around the country for speaking engagements, crusaded enthusiastically on radio and that potent new vehicle, the television talk show.

After one of these appearances—outside Rockefeller Center—she met another author who had just taped a show herself. She was just about Betty's age, a former copywriter who had performed the remarkable feat of hitting the nonfiction best-seller list the year before.

The woman was Helen Gurley Brown, and her book, *Sex and the Single Girl,* aimed, obviously, at the burgeoning singles market, had actually set down in print the startling notion that it was perfectly all right to have "an affair." Even with a married man.

For those who would, in retrospect, regard the sexual revolution as either intrinsic to or actually the wellspring of the Golden Age of Feminism, it would be hard to ignore the pioneering role of Helen Brown. Most feminists, however, would manage to do just that.

It was a matter, in part, of philosophy. In even greater part, perhaps, of style.

Sex and the Single Girl was a typical how-to of the women's magazine genre. It offered advice on decorating your apartment, diet, clothes, and money—not, however, for the purpose of hooking a man into marriage, but for getting him into your bed.

Helen Brown didn't protest much of anything—least of all society's ills. She only wrote about, as she herself insisted, what was already going on anyhow. Single women having sex with men, married or not. She simply made them feel better about doing it. Like the women's magazines, and in a similarly blithe, not to say giddy style, she was reassuring and helpful. The major difference—the shocker—was that while the women's magazines were still righteously committed to the double standard, continually warning their readers of the dire consequences of sex without marriage, Helen Gurley Brown wrote that this was perfectly okay. "Nice single girls *do* have affairs and they don't necessarily die of them." *Sex and the Single Girl*—aimed, unlike underground erotica, at a mass audience—was undoubtedly something of a relief.

The single life the book touted was one of supreme independence, satisfying work, fashion and success and money—a life, in short, that most married women were bound to envy. The single woman was sexy, Helen had written, "because she lives by her wits." She was not "a parasite, a dependent, a scrounger, a sponger or a bum." And when, in 1965, Helen would take over the Hearst Corporation's ailing *Cosmopolitan,* the appeal of that view, and the skill of its pragmatic, meticulous editor, would eventually triple the magazine's circulation.

On television, Helen was, from the beginning, flirtatious, supremely tactful, frankly manipulative, an open disciple of male-flattering femininity. "Helen Gurley Girly," some viewers called her. She was a former secretary who had never gone to college and didn't plan to, a "girl" for whom *work* was the given, the man in one's life the pleasure to be sought. She had written her book at the suggestion of her husband, movie producer David Brown, and she had no hesitation about saying so.

And yet, in spite of Helen's flirtatiousness, and the focus on sex, which, Betty had written, was totally irrelevant, actually damaging to women's struggle for independence, the two women liked each other.

"We talked about business, promotion, all that," Helen would remember. "We became friends . . . and we've been friends ever since." They differed, but, in spite of her passionate nature, Betty would often differ with someone and still remain a loyal friend.

Unlike Helen Brown, however, Betty wasn't "cool"; her personality was not tailor-made for television. Often, in impatient, enthusiastic pursuit of an idea, she would talk so fast that hardly anyone could understand her. Or leave sentences dangling. Or angrily demand time. Her publicist would remember her screaming at hostess Virginia Graham on "Girl Talk": "If you don't let me have my say, I'm going to say orgasm ten times."

But Betty had been provoked.

Virginia Graham, Betty would one day explain, had coaxed the camera: "Girls, how many of us really need bylines? What better thing can we do with our lives than to do the dishes for those we love?"

"Well, I knew that her agent fought for every foot of the size of her byline on the television screen, and I wondered when the last time was she'd done the dishes for someone she loved. I turned to the camera and said, 'Women, don't listen to her. She needs you out there doing the dishes, or she wouldn't have the captive audience for this television program, whose byline she evidently doesn't want you to compete for.'"

Betty never was, never would be, any talk show host's favorite guest. She was confrontational, often tactless, and not—by any standard—a TV beauty.

But neither was she a phony. And there was something about this woman, who looked like everyone's . . . Aunt Minnie, something about what she proclaimed, in her hell-for-leather style, that made hundreds of viewers attend.

Scores of Americans, of course, including many women, were outraged. They could scarcely believe what they were hearing. A woman's career could be as important as a man's? A woman should go out in the world and compete with men?. . .

One Smith alumna, writing in *Reader's Digest* about "the feminine *mistake*," saluted the housewife's "small acts of domesticity" with the good Scout cheer: "Well, sure! That's what we signed up for!" And when the *New York Times* got around to reviewing the book—in a short blurb under "Digest"—Lucy Freeman, who had written a best-seller on her own conquest of mental illness, zapped it as "superficial. . . . The fault, dear Mrs. Friedan, is not in our culture, but in ourselves."

"*Where*," wailed a letter writer in *Commonweal* magazine, "are all these women to go, having fled their homes? And *what* are they to do?"

In the midst of it all, Betty brought Carl and the kids back to Peoria for her twenty-fifth high school reunion. There, instead of praise, she found herself sitting alone at the banquet table. She stayed with a friend, and the next morning found the tree outside her door festooned with toilet paper.

Yet the sales of *The Feminine Mystique* were beginning to climb, and there was no stopping Betty now. Especially since hundreds of letters, expressing enormous gratitude, were starting to pour in. Letters from women who said they had no idea, until they read her book, that anyone else had such strange feelings. They had felt, they wrote, like sexual freaks, or like "appliances," insecure in their dependence, unable, much longer, to keep up the "act" of selflessness. She had given them courage, they wrote, to go back to school, to begin careers.

For threaded through the social criticism of *The Feminine Mystique* was also a message of Emersonian self-reliance and responsibility. This message was not, at bottom, altogether unlike Helen Brown's, but it was one that would set Betty at odds with many women who might have been her allies. Since, as Betty wrote, the women she was addressing were not

those beset by dire poverty or disease, they were not, therefore, *completely* at the mercy of an unjust society.

"In the last analysis," Betty had written, "millions of able women in this free land choose themselves not to use the door education could have opened for them. The choice—and the responsibility—for the race back [to the] home was finally their own."

The Feminine Mystique *reached women very much like Friedan herself: white, educated wives and mothers mainly of the middle class. "Inspired and validated by finding their own truth presented as truth," as writer Marilyn French has said, "many of them changed their lives, returning to school, entering the work force." The Feminine* Mystique *also aroused professional and single women, both white and African American, for it exposed the attitudes and practices that blocked their own advancement. Along with Helen Gurley Brown and Gloria Steinem, Friedan helped liberate younger women, too, especially on the college campuses. Had Friedan done nothing more than write her book, she would be historically significant.*

But for her, The Feminine Mystique *was only the beginning. Thrust into national prominence as the voice of the new American woman, Friedan initiated the "second wave" of organized feminism, the first wave having ended with women's suffrage. In 1966, with the help of Dr. Kay Clarenbach, a Wisconsin women's leader, Friedan founded and became the first president of the National Organization for Women (NOW), the first mainstream women's organization and the most successful in history. "It is a mystery," Betty would say later, "the whole thing—why it happened, how it started. What gave any of us the courage to make that leap?" Under NOW's banners, the new women's movement sought equality for women through political means, for the 1960s civil rights movement had shown Friedan and her colleagues how effective antidiscrimination legislation could be. Employing the civil rights methods of picket lines, marches, political pressure, and media exposure, NOW set out to gain full citizenship for women: it challenged federal guidelines that sanctioned discrimination against them in employment, initiated lawsuits against companies refusing to hire women in positions traditionally occupied by men, sought legal abortion, and campaigned for the Equal Rights Amendment (ERA), which had languished since 1923. NOW helped to bring about a body of laws and rulings that prohibited sexual discrimination in education and in hiring and promotion; NOW was also instrumental in gaining congressional approval of the Equal Rights Amendment. In the 1980s, however, the ERA went down to defeat when it failed to be ratified by three fourths of the states. Even so, NOW was strong enough by 1984 to pressure the Democratic presidential candidate into selecting a woman as his running mate.*

Meanwhile, the women's movement had splintered into various dissenting groups; one of them even advocated lesbianism as the ultimate expression of feminism and demanded that NOW affirm this by publicly avowing, "We are all lesbians." This shocked Friedan, who with other NOW leaders argued that such a stance would alienate men and would be a tactical blunder. Feminism, she said, regarded men not as eternal foes but also as victims of a repressive, dehumanizing society.

Struggling to hold the movement together wore Friedan out. In truth, she had paid a high personal price for her cause: she had lectured and traveled everywhere in its behalf, living out of suitcases in lonely motel rooms; she had missed her children fiercely and the warmth and intimacy of family life. Too, her marriage to Carl had failed—he had beaten her more than once. In 1970, divorced and exhausted, she resigned as NOW president and turned to writing, lecturing, and teaching. She remained faithful to feminism's larger vision, a vision of "human wholeness" that liberated men as well as women. It did so by repudiating the laws and customs that prevented men from expressing their own nurturing qualities and caused them to deny women their birthright as Americans—an equal opportunity to better themselves, to realize their full potential as their talent and industry allowed.

QUESTIONS TO CONSIDER

1 Describe the American cultural ideal of womanhood in the 1950s. What does Marcia Cohen think were some of the sources of our culture's "home-is-woman's-all" psychology? Explain the role that consumerism, the press, and the American educational system played in perpetuating prevailing assumptions about women. Was anyone rebelling against all this conformity?

2 Betty Friedan did not deliberately set out to start a feminist revolution. Describe the steps she took in raising her own consciousness and the series of revelations and reversals that led her to write *The Feminine Mystique*.

3 *The Feminine Mystique* was not a political book, but just a few years after its publication Friedan found herself at the head of a reform movement and president of NOW. At what point did the yearning for self-awareness and self-fulfillment that Friedan aroused in American women become transformed into political activity? Why did women feel they needed a political movement to achieve personal gains?

4 Discuss the basic thesis of *The Feminine Mystique*. Whose ideas did Betty Friedan attack? Specifically, how did she feel about Sigmund Freud and Margaret Mead? About "togetherness"? About suburbia? About women's magazines? How did Friedan's ideas differ from those of Helen Gurley Brown? What underlying message did the two writers have in common? Did Friedan feel the sexual revolution was compatible with the new feminism?

5 Friedan's book was addressed to educated, white, upper- and middle-class women. She herself was aware that she had not tackled the problems of uneducated or poor or African American or immigrant women. Is it possible to apply all or part of Friedan's analysis to this second group? What additional complications might issues of race and social class bring to women's lives?

6 What strides has feminism made since the publication of *The Feminine Mystique*? Has true equality been achieved? What do you see as the future of the historic "women's rights" movement as we enter the twenty-first century?

PART THIRTEEN

The Seventies

27 "I Have Never Been a Quitter": A Portrait of Richard Nixon

OTTO FRIEDRICH

As his biographer Stephen Ambrose has said, Richard Nixon wanted to be one of the great presidents, even a modern-day Lincoln. But the flaws in Nixon's character prevented him from leaving that kind of legacy. He did accomplish many positive things during his tenure in the White House (1969–1973): though an ardent and dedicated anti-Communist during his entire political career, he effected a rapprochement with Communist China, established détente with the Soviet Union, and finally ended America's disastrous involvement in the Vietnam War. These were spectacular achievements for "the world's No. 1 anti-Communist," as Ambrose describes him. But Nixon above all was a pragmatist: his objective was to strengthen the United States in world affairs by playing the Soviets and Chinese off against one another through "triangular diplomacy."

At home, he reduced military spending and signed the measure that lowered the voting age to eighteen, but he was not much interested in getting legislation enacted on Capitol Hill. What occupied most of his time and energy was the antiwar movement and other enemies of his administration; he was obsessed with them and with what he perceived to be a liberal, anti-Nixon slant among the nation's major newspapers. Before long, a bunker mentality pervaded the Nixon White House: it viewed domestic politics as a desperate battlefield between "them" and "us," with the Nixon administration increasingly identifying "them" as traitors and "us" as the only patriots and true saviors of America. In the name of "national security," the Nixon administration flagrantly violated the law and the Constitution in its zeal to suppress dissent, defeat opponents, and uphold administration politics. Nixon himself compiled a list of his "enemies" and not only had their phones tapped, but also ordered the Internal Revenue Service to audit them. Most frightening of all,

Nixon's "campaign of subversion" produced the Watergate scandal. It began in June 1972, when five men associated with the Committee to Re-Elect the President (CREEP) broke into the Democratic National Committee headquarters in Washington, D.C., and were arrested on a charge of burglary. For a time, Nixon successfully covered up his complicity in the break-in and the abuse of executive power it represented. When reporters Carl Bernstein and Bob Woodward of the Washington Post exposed the Watergate scandal, it precipitated what one historian called "the greatest constitutional crisis the country had faced since the Civil War." The crisis shook Americans of every political persuasion and eventually brought down Nixon's presidency. In August 1973, he resigned his office—the first American President ever to do so—and flew back to California in disgrace.

Some historians have linked Watergate to the growth of an "imperial presidency," which resulted in an imbalance of power, tilted to the executive branch. Lyndon Johnson had hastened the process by waging his undeclared war in Vietnam and pressuring Congress into endorsing and funding it. In the Watergate crisis, as historian William H. Chafe put it, the country rallied against the excesses of the imperial presidency, insisting on "a government of laws rather than personal whim."

Nixon's only crime was not, as many Americans still contend, that he simply got caught doing what other presidents have done. Historian C. Vann Woodward observes in Responses of the Presidents to Charges of Misconduct (1974): "Heretofore, no president has been proved to be the chief coordinator of the crime and misdemeanor charged against his own administration. . . . Heretofore, no president has been held to be the chief personal beneficiary of misconduct in his administration or of measures taken to destroy or cover up evidence of it. Heretofore, the malfeasance and misdemeanor have had no confessed ideological purpose, no constitutionally subversive ends. Heretofore, no president has been accused of extensively subverting and secretly using established government agencies to defame or discredit political opponents and critics, to obstruct justice, to conceal misconduct and protect criminals, or to deprive citizens of their rights and liberties. Heretofore, no president has been accused of creating secret investigative units to engage in covert and unlawful activities against private citizens and their rights."

In "a post-Watergate backlash," as one historian termed it, American voters in 1974 gave the Democrats the second-biggest congressional victory in their entire history. Two years later, they sent Democrat Jimmy Carter to the White House, ousting Republican Gerald Ford, whom Nixon had chosen as his successor.

In the following selection, Otto Friedrich describes Nixon's painful and impoverished early years, which did so much to shape the angry, ambitious man he became. Though highly intelligent and gifted, as Friedrich shows, Nixon made his reputation by smearing political opponents, accusing them of being soft on Communism. He rationalized such tactics on the grounds that he had to win. "Of course I knew Jerry Voorhis wasn't a communist," he said of one defeated opponent, "but I had to win. That's the thing you don't understand. The important thing is to win." Friedrich goes on to show how Nixon kept rising and falling, rising and falling, and finally rising again, in a political career that spanned more than a quarter of a century.

GLOSSARY

AGNEW, SPIRO Nixon's vice president (1969–1973); he resigned after being indicted for graft and corruption.

BREZHNEV, LEONID Soviet leader (first secretary of the Communist party) who with Nixon signed the 1972 SALT I treaty. In it, the United States and the Soviet Union agreed to limit antiballistic missiles and reached "an interim accord" on restricting offensive nuclear weapons.

BROWN, PAT Incumbent governor of California who defeated Nixon in the gubernatorial election of 1962. Afterward Nixon held his "final press conference," in which he told reporters: "Think of what you've lost. You won't have Nixon to kick around anymore."

CHECKERS SPEECH Nixon's maudlin speech on television during the presidential election of 1952; in that speech, Nixon sought to clear his name after news of his $18,000 slush fund donated by California businessmen had come to the surface. As he spoke, he told the story of the Nixon family dog, Checkers; hence the speech's name.

COX, ARCHIBALD Appointed special prosecutor in the Watergate case; he was fired during the "Saturday night massacre" for insisting that Nixon turn over the tapes he had made of his conversations in the Oval Office.

DEAN, JOHN Nixon's legal counsel; he was one of three top Nixon officials involved in the cover-up of the Watergate break-in. The other two officials were Attorney General John Mitchell and Mitchell's deputy, Jeb Stuart Magruder. Dean pleaded guilty when he was indicted for obstructing justice in the Watergate investigations.

DOUGLAS, HELEN GAHAGAN Nixon defeated this former movie actress in the 1950 election in California for a seat in the United States Senate. She gave him his pejorative nickname, "Tricky Dick." Nixon won this mud-slinging election by calling Douglas "the pink lady"—that is, a Communist—and insisting that she was "pink right down to her underwear."

EHRLICHMAN, JOHN Nixon's chief domestic adviser who was indicted by a grand jury for obstructing justice in the investigation of Watergate. He resigned his office, stood trial for his part in the Watergate scandal, and served time in a federal prison.

FORD, GERALD United States congressman and House minority leader from Michigan who in 1973 replaced Spiro Agnew as Nixon's vice president; Ford became president when Nixon resigned the office in 1974. One month later Ford pardoned Nixon for his crimes in the Watergate scandal.

HALDEMAN, H. R. Nixon's chief of staff. Like John Ehrlichman, Haldeman was indicted by a grand jury for obstructing justice in the Watergate investigations. He, too, resigned from the White House, stood trial for his role in the Watergate scandal, and was confined to a federal prison.

HISS, ALGER Served in the State Department from 1936 to 1947; in that capacity he helped coordinate United States foreign policy. In 1948, Whittaker Chambers, an editor and confessed Communist courier, charged that Hiss had passed on confidential government documents to the Soviets. HUAC, led by Nixon, accused Hiss of espionage; he vigorously denied the charges and found himself indicted by a grand jury for perjury. He was later found guilty of that charge and sentenced to forty-four months in prison. He was never found guilty of espionage. The Hiss case "made Nixon a national figure."

HOOVER, J. EDGAR Powerful head of the Federal Bureau of Investigation from 1924 to 1972. Hoover advised Nixon to order illegal wiretaps on his alleged enemies, as Lyndon Johnson had done.

HUAC Acronym for the House Un-American Activities Committee (its official name was the House Committee on Un-American Activities), originally established in 1938 to uncover "malign foreign influences in the United States." It was taken over by conservative Republicans who, in 1947, launched widely publicized investigations into the extent of Communist subversion in this country.

HUMPHREY, HUBERT Lyndon Johnson's vice president (1965–1969) and Democratic nominee for president in the 1968 election; Nixon defeated him by a narrow margin.

KISSINGER, HENRY Nixon's national security adviser and second secretary of state (1973–1974); he arranged Nixon's visit to Communist China in 1972 and negotiated with the North Vietnamese a cease-fire agreement in North Vietnam that called for an American withdrawal.

McGOVERN, GEORGE Democratic nominee for president in 1972; Nixon soundly defeated him.

MITCHELL, JOHN Nixon's attorney general (1969–1972), who was implicated in the cover-up of the Watergate break-in.

SALT I TREATY See *Leonid Brezhnev.*

SATURDAY NIGHT MASSACRE On the night of October 20, 1973, a Saturday, Nixon ordered Attorney General Elliot

Richardson to fire special prosecutor Archibald Cox, who was investigating the Watergate case. Richardson refused Nixon's order and resigned; so did Deputy Attorney General William Ruckelshaus. General Alexander Haig, Nixon's new chief of staff, then persuaded Solicitor General Robert Bork to fire Cox. The "massacre" left the Nixon administration "a shambles."

STEVENSON, ADLAI Democratic presidential nominee who lost to Eisenhower in the elections of 1952 and 1956. As Eisenhower's running mate, Nixon spent much of his time in the 1952 campaign accusing Stevenson of being soft on Communism.

TEAPOT DOME SCANDAL President Warren G. Harding (1921–1923), at the urging of Albert Fall, secretary of the interior, transferred control of the navy's oil reserves in Wyoming to Fall's Interior Department. Fall leased the oil reserves to a couple of wealthy businessmen in return for almost $500,000 in "loans." Tried and convicted of bribery, Fall served a year in prison.

VOORHIS, JERRY The liberal Democrat Nixon defeated in the congressional election of 1946 in the Twelfth Congressional District east of Los Angeles.

Richard Nixon's first conscious memory was of falling—falling and then running. He was three years old, and his mother had taken him and his brother out riding in a horse-drawn buggy, and the horse turned a corner too fast on the way home. The boy fell out. A buggy wheel ran over his head and inflicted a deep cut. "I must have been in shock," Nixon recalled later, "but I managed to get up and run after the buggy while my mother tried to make the horse stop." The only aftereffect, Nixon said, was a scar, and that was why he combed his hair straight back instead of parting it on the side.

In a sense, Nixon spent his whole life falling and running and falling again. A symbol of the politics of anger, he was one of the most hated figures of his time, and yet he was also the only man in U.S. history ever to be elected twice as Vice President and twice as President. In the White House, he achieved many major goals: the U.S. withdrawal from Vietnam, restored relations with China, the first major arms agreement with the Soviet Union and much more. But he will always be remembered . . . as the chief perpetrator—and chief victim—of the Watergate scandal, the only President ever to resign in disgrace.

Despite all his gifts—his shrewd intelligence, his dedication and sense of public service, his mastery

of political strategy—there was a quality of self-destructiveness that haunted Nixon. To an admiring aide he once acknowledged, "You continue to walk on the edge of the precipice because over the years you have become fascinated by how close to the edge you can walk without losing your balance."

He kept losing it, tumbling to great depths, then grimly climbing back. After being defeated in the presidential race of 1960 and then the California gubernatorial race of 1962, he bitterly told reporters, "You won't have Nixon to kick around anymore." Six years later, he fought his way to another Republican presidential nomination, which he spoke of as "the culmination of an impossible dream." But at his last meeting with his Cabinet in August 1974, after what seemed like the final defeat in a lifetime devoted to the idea of winning, he burst into tears. "Always remember," he said, "others may hate you, but those who hate you don't win unless you hate them—and then you destroy yourself."

From anyone else, that might have served as a public farewell, but the disgraced Nixon spent more than a dozen years in climbing once more out of the abyss and re-creating himself as an elder statesman. He wrote his memoirs in 1978, then eight more books largely devoted to international strategy. He moved to the wealthy suburb of Saddle River, New Jersey (where he stayed until 1990, moving a mile away to Park Ridge), and began giving discreet dinners for movers and shakers. President Reagan called to ask his advice. So did President Bush. In November 1989, he became the first important American to

---

Otto Friedrich, "I Have Never Been a Quitter," *Time*, May 2, 1994. Copyright © 1994 Time Inc. Reprinted by permission.

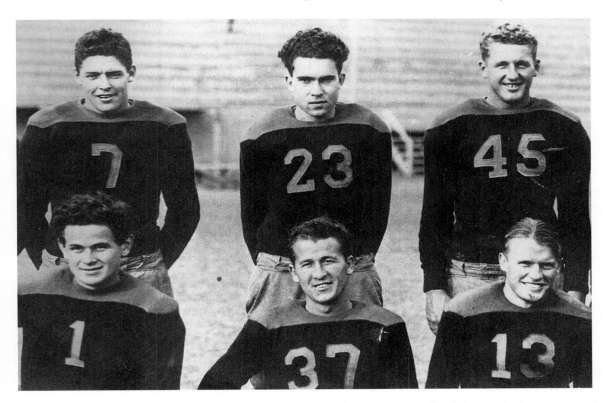

Richard Nixon (number 23), the second son of Frank and Han-nah Nixon, was named after the English King Richard the Lion-Hearted. He attended Whittier College and wanted to play *football, but was "too small and slow to make the starting team," writes Otto Friedrich, so "he showed up every day for practice in the line." (UPI/Corbis-Bettmann)*

make a public visit to Beijing after the massacre at Tiananmen Square.

The hallmark of Nixon's youth had been poverty— poverty and family illness and endless work. His father Frank, who had dropped out of school and run away from home after the fourth grade, was a combative and quarrelsome Ohioan. After running through a string of jobs, Frank moved to California in 1907, built a house in the desert-edge town of Yorba Linda and tried to grow lemons. There Frank's pious Quaker wife Hannah gave birth on Jan. 9, 1913, to a second son. She named him Richard, after the English King Richard the Lion-Hearted, plus Milhous, her own family name. The newborn baby, an attendant nurse later recalled, had a "powerful, ringing voice."

His mother sent him to school every day in a starched white shirt and a black bow tie, and he worked hard for his good grades. He liked to recite long poems and play the piano. One of his favorite forms of competition was debating, which he did well. Another was football. Too small and slow to make the starting team in Fullerton or Whittier High School or at Whittier College, he showed up every day for practice in the line. "We used Nixon as a punching bag," one of his coaches recalled. "What starts the process, really," Nixon later said of his life-long passion for winning, "are the laughs and slights and snubs when you are a kid. But if . . . your anger is deep enough and strong enough, you learn that you can change those attitudes by excellence, personal gut performance."

Nixon grew up in Whittier because his father had given up on citrus farming and found a new job there as an oil-field worker, then started a gas station, then expanded it into a general store. Hannah Nixon liked Whittier because it was largely a Quaker town where nobody drank or smoked or carried on. But life was not easy. All through high school, Nixon had to get up at 4 every morning and drive to the Seventh Street markets in Los Angeles to buy fresh vegetables for the family store.

When Dick Nixon was 12, his younger brother Arthur, the fourth of the five boys, complained of a headache; a month later he was dead of meningitis. Nixon wrote later that he cried every day for weeks. When Harold, the eldest son, was stricken with tuberculosis, Hannah left the rest of the family to take him to the drier air in Prescott, Arizona. She could pay for this only by operating a clinic where other TB patients waited out their last weeks of life. In the summers Dick found jobs nearby as a janitor, a chicken plucker, a carnival barker. After five years, Harold died. "We all grew up rather fast in those years," Nixon recalled.

Harold's illness was also a great financial drain. Nixon had to turn down a scholarship offer from Harvard (Yale was also interested in him) and save money by attending tiny Whittier College. Duke University Law School was just starting when it offered Nixon one of the 25 scholarships available to a class of 44. At first he lived in a $5-a-month room. Later he shared a one-room shack that had no plumbing or electricity; he shaved in the men's room of the library. In three years at Duke, he never once went out on a date. He finished third in the class of 1937.

Nixon had shown an interest in politics since the age of six, when he began reading news of current events and talking about them with his father. When he was 11, the Teapot Dome scandal prompted him to announce to his mother, "I'll be a lawyer they can't bribe." The practice of law in Whittier was hardly so inspiring. Taken into the firm of a family friend, he spent his first day dusting the books in the office library, then bungled his first case, losing all his client's money in a real estate deal. But he persevered, began joining various clubs, making speeches. He even joined a local theater group, where he met a schoolteacher named Thelma ("Pat") Ryan.

Driving her home from the theater, he said, "I'd like to have a date with you."

"Oh, I'm too busy," she replied. An orphan, she was not only working but attending classes as well. The second time Nixon drove her home, he again asked for a date, again was shrugged off. The third time it happened, Nixon said, "Someday I'm going to marry you." It took two years of courtship before she agreed in 1940; she converted to the Quaker faith and used her own savings to buy the wedding ring.

Nixon probably would not have been content to stay in Whittier forever, but Pearl Harbor uprooted his whole generation. He knew that if he was ever to have a political career, he would have to join the armed forces. So despite the Quaker belief in pacifism, he won a commission in the Navy in June 1942. He served creditably as a supply officer in New Caledonia, then the Solomon Islands. His most remarkable activity, though, was to become a master at bluffing in stud poker. By the end of the war, he had won and saved a stake estimated at as much as $10,000. He invested half of it in the following year in launching his political career.

Jerry Voorhis, a popular liberal Democrat, had won five straight elections in the 12th Congressional District east of Los Angeles, but a group of local businessmen hoped to unseat him. Nixon promised them "an aggressive and vigorous campaign." He began working up to 20 hours a day, making speeches about his war experiences, denouncing the New Deal. When Pat gave birth to their first daughter Patricia (Tricia), Nixon was out campaigning. (Confident of re-election, he stayed home when Julie was born two years later.)

Nixon implied—falsely—that Voorhis was virtually a communist. "Remember," said one of Nixon's ads, "Voorhis is a former registered Socialist and his voting record in Congress is more socialistic and communistic than Democratic." This kind of smear was to become a Nixon trademark. To one of Voorhis' supporters, Nixon later offered a very personal rationale: "Of course I knew Jerry Voorhis wasn't a communist, but I had to win. That's the thing you don't understand. The important thing is to win."

Win he did, with 56% of the vote. This was part of the end-of-the-war landslide that gave the G.O.P. control of both houses for the first time since the election following the Great Crash of 1929. Nixon asked to be put on the Education and Labor Committee, which was going to rewrite the rules of labor relations through the Taft-Hartley Act. In return, he was asked to serve on an eccentric committee [the House Committee on Un-American Affairs] that devoted its time to noisy investigations of "un-American activities." It was to be the making of his career.

Nixon began looking for experts on communist influence in labor unions. This led him to a Maryknoll priest whose report on the subject included the fact that a *Time* senior editor named Whittaker Chambers had told the FBI that he had belonged to a communist cell in Washington, and that it included Alger Hiss. It seemed incredible. A lawyer who had once clerked for Justice Oliver Wendell Holmes, Hiss had served as a State Department adviser at the Yalta conference, had helped organize the United Nations and was being touted as perhaps its first Secretary-General.

Hiss, then president of the Carnegie Endowment, denied ever having met anyone named Whittaker Chambers. Nixon had both men summoned before the committee to confront each other. Hiss finally admitted knowing Chambers slightly under a different name. Chambers insisted that they had been "close friends . . . caught in a tragedy of history." But nothing could be proved until Chambers produced the "pumpkin papers," microfilms of State Department documents that he said Hiss had given him for transmission to Moscow. Hiss was convicted of perjury in January 1950, served 44 months in prison and has spent the rest of his long life denying guilt.

The Hiss case made Nixon a national figure and launched him into a run for the Senate in 1950 against Helen Gahagan Douglas, a former actress who had served six years in the House as an ardent New Dealer. Since red hunting was a national mania in these Korean War days, Douglas foolishly tried to accuse Nixon of being soft on communism, and invented the name that haunted him for the rest of his life: Tricky Dick. But when it came to mudslinging, she was up against a champion. He called her the "pink lady" and declared that she was "pink right down to her underwear." He won by the biggest plurality of any Senate candidate that year.

Nixon had hardly begun serving in the Senate before the Republican leadership started fighting over whether the 1952 presidential nomination should go to conservative Senator Robert Taft or to the immensely popular General Dwight Eisenhower. The convention was in danger of deadlocking, in which case it might turn to California Governor Earl Warren. That was certainly Warren's plan, and all the California delegates, including Nixon, were pledged to back him. In some complicated maneuvering, though, the Eisenhower forces put forward a resolution that would give them a number of disputed Southern delegations. Nixon, who had already been sounded out as a running mate for Eisenhower, persuaded the California delegates to back this resolution, and so Eisenhower won. Warren never forgave Nixon for what he considered a betrayal.

Once nominated as Vice President, Nixon was assigned to play hatchet man on "communism and corruption" while Eisenhower remained statesmanlike. Nixon was all too eager to comply. He described Democratic nominee Adlai Stevenson as one who "holds a Ph.D. from [Secretary of State Dean] Acheson's College of Cowardly Communist Containment."

The Democrats got their revenge when the press discovered and trumpeted that Nixon had a secret slush fund of $18,000 provided by California businessmen to help finance his activities. Nixon insisted that the fund was perfectly legal and was used solely for routine political expenses, but the smell of scandal thickened. At Eisenhower's urging, Nixon went before a TV audience estimated at 58 million with an impassioned defense of his honesty. "Pat and I have the satisfaction that every dime we've got is honestly

Nixon and Dwight Eisenhower. "Once nominated as Vice President," Friedrich points out, "Nixon was assigned to play hatchet man on 'communism and corruption' while Eisenhower"—the Republican nominee for President—"remained statesmanlike."

During the scandal over the secret slush fund provided for Nixon by California businessmen, Nixon gave his famous Checkers speech, after which Eisenhower proclaimed in public, "You're my boy!" (UPI/Corbis-Bettmann)

ours," he said. The only personal present he had received was "a little cocker spaniel dog in a crate. Black-and-white spotted. And our little girl—Tricia, the six-year-old—named it Checkers. And you know, the kids love that dog." Hundreds of thousands of listeners cabled or wrote their support of Nixon, and Eisenhower settled his future by saying publicly, "You're my boy!"

Eisenhower won 55% of the vote, and the freshman Senator from California, still only 39, found himself the second youngest Vice President. He also found that a President and Vice President rarely like each other very much, because the latter's only real job is to wait for the former's death. Nixon faced the

great test of this uneasy relationship when Eisenhower suffered a heart attack in September 1955. It was up to Nixon to chair Cabinet meetings and generally run the White House machinery without ever seeming to covet the power that lay just beyond his fingertips. He did the job tactfully and skillfully throughout the weeks of Eisenhower's recovery.

One major function of modern Vice Presidents is to travel, and Nixon turned himself into a latter-day Marco Polo: nine trips to 61 countries. Everywhere he went, he conferred, orated, debated, press-conferenced. In Moscow to open a U.S trade exhibit in 1959, Nixon got into a finger-pointing argument on communism with Soviet Party Secretary Nikita Khrushchev in the kitchen of an American model home.

To some extent, Vice Presidents' tasks are defined by their own skills and experiences. Nixon knew more about politics than almost anyone else in Eisenhower's Administration, so he became the G.O.P.'s chief campaigner. When Eisenhower's second term expired, Nixon was the inevitable successor; he was nominated to run against the Democrats' John F. Kennedy.

Eisenhower and others warned Nixon not to accept Kennedy's challenge to a televised debate—Nixon was the Vice President, after all, and far better known than the junior Senator from Massachusetts—but Nixon took pride in his long experience as a debater. He also ignored advice to rest up for the debate and went on campaigning strenuously until the last minute. So what a record 80 million Americans saw on their TV screens was a devastating contrast. Kennedy looked fresh, tanned, vibrant; Nixon looked unshaven, baggy-eyed, surly. The era of the politics of TV imagery had begun, and the debates were a major victory for Kennedy.

The vote was incredibly close, with Kennedy winning 50.4% of the popular vote and Nixon 49.6%. He accepted the bitter defeat and returned to California. Then Nixon's legendary political shrewdness abandoned him. He let himself be talked into running for Governor of California against the popular Edmund G. ("Pat") Brown, and tried to imply that Brown was a dangerous leftist. It was after his crushing defeat that Nixon blew up at reporters and announced that this was his "last press conference."

Still only 49, he decided to move to New York City and make some money by practicing corporate law. He joined a prosperous Wall Street firm, which thereupon became Nixon, Mudge, Rose, Guthrie and Alexander. But he never really retired from politics. He was just biding his time. He thought Jack Kennedy would be unbeatable in 1964, and Lyndon Johnson soon appeared almost as much so. Nixon played elder statesman, letting Barry Goldwater and Nelson Rockefeller fight for the G.O.P. nomination.

Nixon stumped loyally for Goldwater, and when that campaign ended in disaster, he became the logical man to reunite the splintered party in 1968.

Following the advice of a young advertising man named H. R. Haldeman, he finally learned how to make effective use of television: not in speeches or press conferences but answering questions from "typical voters" and then carefully editing the results. If that was artificial, so in a way was the whole 1968 campaign. Democratic candidate Hubert Humphrey dared not repudiate Johnson's doomed Vietnam policy and talked instead about "the politics of joy." Nixon, who had agreed with Johnson's escalation of the war and hoped to court segregationist votes in the South, spoke mainly in code words about "peace with honor" in Vietnam and "law and order" at home. In a year of assassinations and ghetto riots, Nixon sounded reassuring, or enough so to defeat Humphrey and the war-torn Democrats. But it was close: 43.4% for Nixon, 42.7% for Humphrey, 13.5% for George Wallace.

Nixon's first term included sweeping innovations, often surprisingly liberal. He was the first President in years to cut military spending; the first to tie Social Security increases to the cost of living. He instituted "revenue sharing" to funnel $6 billion a year in federal tax money back to the states and cities. He signed the act lowering the voting age to 18. And he benefited from Kennedy's decision to go to the moon. When Neil Armstrong landed there in 1969, Nixon somewhat vaingloriously declared that "this is the greatest week in the history of the world since the Creation."

His imaginative measures were shadowed, however, by Vietnam. Nixon, who had supported each previous escalation—and indeed repeatedly demanded more—had campaigned on a promise to end the war "with honor," meaning no surrender and no defeat. He called for a cease-fire and negotiations, but the communists showed no interest. And while U.S. casualties continued at a rate of about 400 a month, protests against the war grew in size and violence.

To quiet antiwar demonstrators, Nixon announced that he would gradually withdraw U.S. forces, starting with 25,000 in June 1969. From now on, the war would be increasingly fought by the Vietnamese themselves. When, from their sanctuaries in Cambodia, the North Vietnamese began harassing the retreating Americans in the spring of 1970, Nixon ordered bombing raids and made a temporary "incursion" into the country. The main effect of this expansion of the war was an explosion of new anti-war outcries on college campuses.

These were fiercely contentious times, and Nixon was partly to blame for that. He had always been the fighter rather than the conciliator, and though he had millions of supporters among what he liked to call "the Silent Majority" in "middle America," the increasing conflicts in American politics made it difficult to govern at all. Nixon, as the nation learned later when it heard the Watergate tapes, brought to the White House an extraordinarily permanent anger and resentment. His staff memos were filled with furious instructions to fire people, investigate leaks and "knock off this crap."

Together with this chronic anger, the mistrustful Nixon had a passion for secrecy. He repeatedly launched military operations without telling his own Defense Secretary, Melvin Laird, and major diplomatic initiatives without telling his Secretary of State, William Rogers. All major actions went through his White House staff members, particularly National Security Adviser Henry Kissinger and Nixon's two chief domestic aides, Bob Haldeman and John Ehrlichman.

Just as he loved secrecy, Nixon hated leaks to the press (though he himself was a dedicated leaker to favored reporters). And so when he first ordered an unannounced air raid against communist bases in Cambodia in April 1969, he was furious to read about it in a Washington dispatch in the *New York Times*. FBI chief J. Edgar Hoover told the President that the only way to find the leaker was to start tapping phones. When Nixon entered the White House and dismantled the elaborate taping system that Johnson had installed, Hoover told him that the FBI, on Johnson's orders, had bugged Nixon's campaign plane.

Now Nixon started down the same path, getting Attorney General John Mitchell to sign the orders for 17 taps.

When a series of secret Vietnam documents known as the Pentagon Papers began appearing in the *New York Times* in June 1971, Kissinger persuaded Nixon that the leaker, Daniel Ellsberg, "must be stopped at all costs." The FBI turned balky at extralegal activities, so Nixon told Ehrlichman, "Then by God, we'll do it ourselves. I want you to set up a little group right here in the White House."

Thus was born the team of "plumbers." Its only known job involving Ellsberg was to break into his psychiatrist's office that September in search of evidence against him. But once such a team is created, other uses for it tend to be found. The following June, seven plumbers (five of them wearing surgical rubber gloves) were arrested during a burglary of Democratic national headquarters in the Watergate office and apartment complex.

They admitted nothing, and nobody connected them with Nixon. The White House itself was already doing its best to block any FBI investigation, but it formally denied any involvement in what press secretary Ron Ziegler dismissed as "a third-rate burglary attempt." Nobody has ever disclosed exactly what the burglars were looking for or what they found, if anything.

The Watergate burglary quickly faded from the front pages. Nixon was campaigning hard for re-election, portraying himself as a global peacemaker. In February 1972 he had reversed nearly 30 years of American policy by flying to Beijing, ending restrictions on trade with China and supporting China's entry into the U.N. In May he had signed the first arms-control agreement with Soviet leader Leonid Brezhnev, placing sharp restrictions on antiballistic missiles. And although Kissinger's protracted secret negotiations with the Vietnamese communists had not yet brought a truce agreement, Nixon pulled out the last U.S. combat troops in August.

Nixon trounced Senator George McGovern that fall, capturing nearly 61% of the vote. Then, after one last spasm of belligerence in the carpet bombing of

Hanoi at Christmas, Nixon announced in January 1973, "We today have concluded an agreement to end the war and bring peace with honor to Vietnam."

But the Watergate mystery remained. In court, five of the burglars pleaded guilty in January 1973 (the other two were quickly convicted), but they still admitted nothing. Federal Judge John Sirica angrily sentenced them to long prison terms (up to 40 years) and indicated that he might reduce the punishment if they confessed more fully. One of the seven, James McCord, wrote Sirica on March 20 that "others involved in the Watergate operation were not identified during the trial." In two secret sessions with Watergate committee counsel Sam Dash, he later named three top Nixon officials: Attorney General Mitchell; Mitchell's deputy, Jeb Stuart Magruder; and White House counsel John Dean.

Caught lying—but still denying any wrongdoing—Nixon said he was ordering a new investigation of the situation. Two federal grand juries were also investigating. So was the press. Though a lot of this probing was only loosely connected to the burglary, the term Watergate began to apply to a whole series of misdeeds that seriously tainted Nixon's great election victory. Not only did more than $100,000 donated to Nixon's campaign end up in the bank account of one of the plumbers, but the entire fundraising operation was marked by illegalities, irregularities and deceptions. Congress decided to investigate all this too. It chose a select committee to be headed by North Carolina's folksy Senator Sam Ervin.

Two and a half weeks before the committee was scheduled to open televised hearings in May 1973, Nixon made a stunning announcement: his two chief White House aides, Haldeman and Ehrlichman, were resigning, as were Attorney General Richard Kleindienst (who had succeeded Mitchell) and White House attorney Dean. "There can be no whitewash at the White House," Nixon said.

The Senate hearings soon showed otherwise. Magruder testified that Mitchell and Dean had been deeply involved. Then the dismissed Dean took the stand in June and testified that Nixon himself had been lying, that he had known about the White

House cover-up attempts since at least September 1972. He also disclosed that the White House kept hundreds of names on an "enemies list" and used tax investigations and other methods to harass them. But how could anyone prove such charges? That question received an astonishing answer a month later when a former White House official named Alexander Butterfield almost offhandedly told the committee that Nixon had installed voice-activated recorders that secretly taped all his White House conversations.

When the senate committee promptly demanded the tapes, Nixon refused, claiming Executive privilege. The new Attorney General, Elliot Richardson, had appointed Harvard law professor Archibald Cox as a special prosecutor in the whole case, and Cox sent a subpoena for tapes he wanted to hear. Nixon refused him too. Judge Sirica upheld Cox's demand, so Nixon resisted him in the U.S. Court of Appeals, which backed Sirica.

Nixon then offered to produce an edited summary of the tapes. When Cox rejected that idea, Nixon on Oct. 20 angrily told Richardson to fire Cox. Richardson refused and resigned instead. Nixon told Deputy Attorney General William Ruckelshaus to fire Cox; he too refused and resigned. General Alexander Haig, Haldeman's successor as White House chief of staff, finally got Solicitor General Robert Bork to do the job, and so the "Saturday Night Massacre" ended, leaving the Nixon Administration a shambles. (In the midst of all this, it was almost incidental that Vice President Spiro Agnew resigned under fire for having taken graft and that he was replaced by Michigan Congressman Gerald Ford.)

The House began on Oct. 30 to look into the possibilities of impeachment. Inside the besieged White House, Nixon raged like a trapped animal. There were unconfirmed reports that he was drinking heavily, that he couldn't sleep, that he even wandered around late at night and spoke to the paintings on the walls. To a meeting of Associated Press editors, he piteously declared, "I am not a crook."

Special prosecutor Cox had by now been replaced by a conservative Texas attorney, Leon Jaworski, who

On August 9, 1974, having resigned the Presidency in the wake of Watergate, Nixon bade good-bye to his staff and Cabinet in the East Room of the White House. To his right is his son-in-law, David Eisenhower. (Gene Forte/Consolidated News Pictures/Getty)

appeared no less determined to get the tapes. Still resisting inch by inch, Nixon released 1,254 pages of edited transcript. They were a revelation of the inner workings of the Nixon White House, a sealed-off fortress where a character designated as P in the transcripts talked endlessly and obscenely about all his enemies. "I want the most comprehensive notes on all those who tried to do us in," P said to Haldeman at one point, for example. "We have not used . . . the Justice Department, but things are going to change now." The edited tapes still left uncertainties about Nixon's involvement in the Watergate cover-up, however, so Jaworski insisted on the unedited originals of 64 specific tapes, transcripts and other documents. Nixon refused. Jaworski filed suit. The Supreme Court ruled unanimously that a President cannot withhold evidence in a criminal case (Mitchell,

Haldeman, Ehrlichman and others were by now under indictment, and Nixon himself had been named by the grand jury as an "unindicted co-conspirator").

During all this, the House Judiciary Committee, headed by New Jersey's Democratic Congressman Peter Rodino, had been conducting hearings on impeachment. It soon decided to impeach Nixon on three counts: obstruction of justice, abuse of presidential powers and defiance of the committee's subpoenas.

Nixon meanwhile sat out in his beach house in San Clemente, California, reading a biography of Napoleon and staring at the ocean. But he had also been listening to some of the disputed tapes, and he had found one—the "smoking gun"—that threatened to destroy his whole case. It was a talk with Haldeman on June 23, 1972, a time when Nixon had long pretended to know virtually nothing about the Watergate break-in just six days earlier. This tape recorded Nixon talking with Haldeman about Mitchell's involvement, ordering a cover-up, planning to use the FBI and CIA to protect himself. For good measure, the tape also included presidential slurs on Jews, women, homosexuals, Italians and the press. The reaction to the new tape, when Nixon finally released it, was disastrous. Even conservatives like Ronald Reagan and Barry Goldwater demanded Nixon's resignation, as did G.O.P. chairman George Bush. A congressional delegation told the President he had no more than 15 votes in the Senate, about the same in the House. Shortly after, Nixon told his family, "We're going back to California." His daughters burst into tears; his wife did not.

Two days later, on Aug. 8, 1974, Nixon made his last televised statement from the White House: "I have never been a quitter. To leave office before my term is completed is abhorrent to every instinct in my body. But as President I must put the interest of America first . . . Therefore, I shall resign the presidency effective at noon tomorrow." There remained then only a series of farewells. He spoke once again of winning and losing. "We think that when we suffer a defeat, that all is ended. Not true. It is only a beginning, always."

And so it was, once again, for Nixon. When he left Washington, there was a chance he might yet be prosecuted. Gerald Ford fixed that a month later by issuing a presidential pardon protecting Nixon from legal penalties for anything he had done in connection with Watergate. But Nixon's health was poor, his psychic shock obvious. An attack of phlebitis nearly killed him. He later told friends that he heard voices calling, "Richard, pull yourself back." And so he did.

His first public appearance came in 1978, and then the long, slow process of self-rehabilitation. Perhaps, in his last years, having regained a certain amount of public respect and even some grudging admiration, having acquired four grandchildren and all the comforts of leisurely wealth, Nixon finally found a little peace, finally got over that mysterious anger that had fueled his ambition throughout his long life. Perhaps.

QUESTIONS TO CONSIDER

1 What in Richard Nixon's background shaped him into the angry, ambitious man he became? How did his character traits affect his political career? What did he tell a supporter of Jerry Voorhis the most important thing was? What does this tell you about Nixon's character?

2 What was Nixon's favorite issue in his campaign against Jerry Voorhis for a seat in the national House and his campaign against Helen Douglas for a seat in the United States Senate? Describe the political atmosphere at the time that made that issue such a successful one for Nixon. What was Nixon's role on HUAC? What famous case rocketed him to national prominence?

3 What were Nixon's greatest successes as president? Why was he able to achieve momentous diplomatic breakthroughs with Communist China and the Soviet Union when nobody else could do so? We saw in selection 24 that Lyndon Johnson's policies trapped the United States in a stalemated war in Vietnam. How was Nixon able to end American involvement there? Why did he do so?

4 Discuss the Watergate scandal. How was the Nixon White House involved? Why did Nixon lie about his knowledge of the Watergate break-in and with the help of his aides try to cover it up? Why didn't Nixon simply tell the public the truth? What finally brought down the Nixon presidency, causing him to become the first American president ever to resign his office? Do you think that Gerald Ford should have pardoned Nixon?

5 Nixon's political career has been described as one of rising and falling, rising and falling, rising and falling, and rising again. How do you account for his resiliency? Do you think the nickname, "Tricky Dick," was appropriate or inappropriate? How would you rate him as president compared with Roosevelt, Truman, and Eisenhower?

28 How the Seventies Changed America

NICHOLAS LEMANN

To many Americans, it was the "loser" decade, a ten-year hangover from the excesses of the sixties, a time of bitter disillusionment, what with Watergate and the withdrawal from Vietnam, the only war America ever lost. It was a plastic era, to use Norman Mailer's term, that featured polyester suits and disco music. Many Americans still regard the 1970s as a vague interim between the liberal idealism and social upheaval of the sixties and the conservative individualism of the eighties. But to journalist Nicholas Lemann, looking back from today's vantage point, the seventies can no longer be dismissed as "the runt decade" in which relatively nothing significant occurred. On the contrary, he finds profound importance in terms of several "sweeping historical trends" that began or were acceler-ated in the seventies and that went on to shape what American society has become in our time.

First, he says, it was the decade in which geopolitics started revolving less around ideology than around oil and religion. He cites the 1973–1974 oil embargo of the oil-producing Arab-Muslim states as the "epochal event" of the decade, one that dashed the 1960s assumption of endless eco-nomic growth and prosperity for all in the United States. The oil embargo spurred the growth of the Sun Belt, initiated a period of staggering inflation, and marked the end, maybe forever, of "the mass upward economic mobility of American society." And that in turn fragmented the country into squabbling interest groups that cared more about looking out for themselves than about sacrificing for the national good.

Second, the presidential electorate became conservative and Republican, a trend that would last throughout the eighties, ending in the election of Democrat Bill Clinton in 1992. In reaction to the seeming paralysis and weakness of Jimmy Carter's liberal Democratic administration, 1977–1981, American voters sent Republican Ronald Reagan to the White House because he preached "pure strength" in foreign affairs and promised to reduce taxes at home (the Reagan presidency is treated in selection 29). Thus, Reagan capitalized on a third sweeping trend of the seventies—the middle-class tax revolt, which Lemann describes as "an aftershock" of the Arab oil embargo. For the first time, he says, the American middle class, once considered uniquely fortunate, perceived itself as an op-pressed group, the victim of runaway inflation, and revolted against the use of federal funds to help the less privileged.

A reporter for the Washington Post *during the seventies, Lemann draws an arresting portrait of this oft-disparaged decade. Indeed, Lemann believes that the seventies witnessed "the working of the phenomena of the sixties into the mainstream of American life." Lemann also contends that the six-ties' obsession with self-discovery became "a mass phenomenon" in the seventies and that the ethic of individual freedom as the "highest good," converging with the end of the American economy as an "expanding pie," led Americans to look out mainly for themselves.*

GLOSSARY

DÉTENTE   Relaxing of international tensions.

EST (ERHARD SEMINARS TRAINING)   System of encounter groups designed to help people "get in touch with themselves."

ORGANIZATION OF PETROLEUM EXPORTING STATES (OPEC)   Bargaining unit for the oil-exporting states in the Middle East and Africa; OPEC's oil embargo of 1973 quadrupled the price of oil and caused soaring inflation.

PROPOSITION 13   Initiative on the California state ballot that called for a significant reduction in property taxes; it passed overwhelmingly and led to similar tax revolts across the country.

That's it," Daniel Patrick Moynihan, then U.S. ambassador to India, wrote to a colleague on the White House staff in 1973 on the subject of some issue of the moment. "Nothing will happen. But then nothing much is going to happen in the 1970s anyway."

Moynihan is a politician famous for his predictions, and this one seemed for a long time to be dead-on. The seventies, even while they were in progress, looked like an unimportant decade, a period of cooling down from the white-hot sixties. You had to go back to the teens to find another decade so lacking in crisp, epigrammatic definition. It only made matters worse for the seventies that the succeeding decade started with a bang. In 1980 the country elected the most conservative President in its history, and it was immediately clear that a new era had dawned. (In general the eighties, unlike the seventies, had a perfect dramatic arc. They peaked in the summer of 1984, with the Los Angeles Olympics and the Republican National Convention in Dallas, and began to peter out with the Iran-contra scandal in 1986 and the stock market crash in 1987.) It is nearly impossible to engage in magazine-writerly games like discovering "the day the seventies died" or "the spirit of the seventies"; and the style of the seventies—wide ties, sideburns, synthetic fabrics, white shoes, disco—is so far interesting largely as something to make fun of.

But somehow the seventies seem to be creeping out of the loser-decade category. Their claim to importance is in the realm of sweeping historical trends, rather than memorable events, though there were some of those too. In the United States today a few basic propositions shape everything: The presidential electorate is conservative and Republican. Geopolitics revolves around a commodity (oil) and a religion (Islam) more than around an ideology (Marxism-Leninism). The national economy is no longer one in which practically every class, region, and industry is upwardly mobile. American culture is essentially individualistic, rather than communitarian, which means that notions like deferred gratification, sacrifice, and sustained national effort are a very tough sell. Anyone seeking to understand the roots of this situation has to go back to the seventies.

The underestimation of the seventies' importance, especially during the early years of the decade, is easy to forgive because the character of the seventies was substantially shaped at first by spillover from the sixties. Such sixties events as the killings of student protesters at Kent State and Orangeburg, the original Earth Day, the invasion of Cambodia, and a large portion of the war in Vietnam took place in the seventies. Although sixties radicals (cultural and political) spent the early seventies loudly bemoaning the end of the revolution, what was in fact going on was the working of the phenomena of the sixties into the mainstream of American life. Thus the first Nixon

---

"How the Seventies Changed America" by Nicholas Lemann, *American Heritage*, XLII (July/August 1991), 39–42, 44, 46, 48–49. Reprinted by permission of *American Heritage* magazine, a division of Forbes, Inc. © Forbes, Inc., 1991.

administration, which was decried by liberals at the time for being nightmarishly right-wing, was actually more liberal than the Johnson administration in many ways—less hawkish in Vietnam, more free-spending on social programs. The reason wasn't that Richard Nixon was a liberal but that the country as a whole had continued to move steadily to the left throughout the late sixties and early seventies; the political climate of institutions like the U.S. Congress and the boards of directors of big corporations was probably more liberal in 1972 than in any year before or since, and the Democratic party nominated its most liberal presidential candidate ever. Nixon had to go along with the tide.

In New Orleans, my hometown, the hippie movement peaked in 1972 or 1973. Long hair, crash pads, head shops, psychedelic posters, underground newspapers, and other Summer of Love–inspired institutions had been unknown there during the real Summer of Love, which was in 1967. It took even longer, until the middle or late seventies, for those aspects of hippie life that have endured to catch on with the general public. All over the country the likelihood that an average citizen would wear longish hair, smoke marijuana, and openly live with a lover before marriage was probably greater in 1980 than it was in 1970. The sixties' preoccupation with self-discovery became a mass phenomenon only in the seventies, through home-brew psychological therapies like EST. In politics the impact of the black enfranchisement that took place in the 1960s barely began to be felt until the mid- to late 1970s. The tremendously influential feminist and gay-liberation movements were, at the dawn of the 1970s, barely under way in Manhattan, their headquarters, and certainly hadn't begun their spread across the whole country. The sixties took a long time for America to digest; the process went on throughout the seventies and even into the eighties.

The epochal event of the seventies as an era in its own right was the Organization of Petroleum Exporting Countries' oil embargo, which lasted for six months in the fall of 1973 and the spring of 1974.

Everything that happened in the sixties was predicated on the assumption of economic prosperity and growth; concerns like personal fulfillment and social justice tend to emerge in the middle class only at times when people take it for granted that they'll be able to make a living. For thirty years—ever since the effects of World War II on the economy had begun to kick in—the average American's standard of living had been rising, to a remarkable extent. As the economy grew, indices like home ownership, automobile ownership, and access to higher education got up to levels unknown anywhere else in the world, and the United States could plausibly claim to have provided a better life materially for its working class than any society ever had. That ended with the OPEC embargo.

While it was going on, the embargo didn't fully register in the national consciousness. The country was absorbed by a different story, the Watergate scandal, which was really another sixties spillover, the final series of battles in the long war between the antiwar liberals and the rough-playing anti-Communists. Richard Nixon, having engaged in dirty tricks against leftish politicians for his whole career, didn't stop doing so as President; he only found new targets, like Daniel Ellsberg and [Democratic Party chairman] Lawrence O'Brien. This time, however, he lost the Establishment, which was now far more kindly disposed to Nixon's enemies than it had been back in the 1950s. Therefore, the big-time press, the courts, and the Congress undertook the enthralling process of cranking up the deliberate, inexorable machinery of justice, and everybody was glued to the television for a year and a half. The embargo, on the other hand, was a non-video-friendly economic story and hence difficult to get hooked on. It pertained to two subcultures that were completely mysterious to most Americans—the oil industry and the Arab world—and it seemed at first to be merely an episode in the ongoing hostilities between Israel and its neighbors. But in retrospect it changed everything, much more than Watergate did.

By causing the price of oil to double, the embargo enriched—and therefore increased the wealth, power,

"Steer clear of that one. Every day is always the first day of the rest of his life."

Charles Saxon's spirited sketch is good social history. In 1972 this is what a lot of Americans looked like. (© The New Yorker

and confidence of—oil-producing areas like Texas, while helping speed the decline of the automobile-producing upper Midwest; the rise of OPEC and the rise of the Sunbelt as a center of population and political influence went together. The embargo ushered in a long period of inflation, the reaction to which dominated the economics and politics of the rest of the decade. It demonstrated that America could now be "pushed around" by countries most of us had always thought of as minor powers.

Most important of all, the embargo now appears to have been the pivotal moment at which the mass upward economic mobility of American society ended, perhaps forever. Average weekly earnings, adjusted for inflation, peaked in 1973. Productivity—that is, economic output per man-hour—abruptly stopped growing. The nearly universal assumption in the post–World War II United States was that children would do better than their parents. Upward

mobility wasn't just a characteristic of the national culture; it was the defining characteristic. As it slowly began to sink in that everybody wasn't going to be moving forward together anymore, the country became more fragmented, more internally rivalrous, and less sure of its mythology.

Richard Nixon resigned as President in August 1974, and the country settled into what appeared to be a quiet, folksy drama of national recuperation. In the White House good old Gerald Ford was succeeded by rural, sincere Jimmy Carter, who was the only President elevated to the office by the voters during the 1970s and so was the decade's emblematic political figure. In hindsight, though, it's impossible to miss a gathering conservative stridency in the politics of the late seventies. In 1976 Ronald Reagan, the retired governor of California, challenged Ford for the Republican presidential nomination. Reagan lost the opening primaries and seemed to be about to drop out of the race when, apparently to the surprise even of his own staff, he won the North Carolina primary in late March.

It is quite clear what caused the Reagan campaign to catch on: He had begun to attack Ford from the right on foreign policy matters. The night before the primary he bought a half-hour of statewide television time to press his case. Reagan's main substantive criticism was of the policy of détente with the Soviet Union, but his two most crowd-pleasing points were his promise, if elected, to fire Henry Kissinger as Secretary of State and his lusty denunciation of the elaborately negotiated treaty to turn nominal control of the Panama Canal over to the Panamanians. Less than a year earlier Communist forces had finally captured the South Vietnamese capital city of Saigon, as the staff of the American Embassy escaped in a wild scramble into helicopters. The oil embargo had ended, but the price of gasoline had not retreated. The United States appeared to have descended from the pinnacle of power and respect it had occupied at the close of World War II to a small, hounded position, and Reagan had hit on a symbolic way of expressing rage over that change. Most journalistic and academic opinion at the time was fairly cheerful about the course of American foreign policy—we were finally out of Vietnam, and we were getting over our silly Cold War phobia about dealing with China and the Soviet Union—but in the general public obviously the rage Reagan expressed was widely shared.

A couple of years later a conservative political cause even more out of the blue than opposition to the Panama Canal Treaty appeared: the tax revolt. Howard Jarvis, a seventy-five-year-old retired businessman who had been attacking taxation in California pretty much continuously since 1962, got onto the state ballot in 1978 an initiative, Proposition 13, that would substantially cut property taxes. Despite bad press and the strong opposition of most politicians, it passed by a two to one margin.

Proposition 13 was to some extent another aftershock of the OPEC embargo. Inflation causes the value of hard assets to rise. The only substantial hard asset owned by most Americans is their home. As the prices of houses soared in the mid-seventies (causing people to dig deeper to buy housing, which sent the national savings rate plummeting and made real estate prices the great conversation starter in the social life of the middle class), so did property taxes, since they are based on the values of the houses. Hence, resentment over taxation became an issue in waiting.

The influence of Proposition 13 has been so great that it is now difficult to recall that taxes weren't a major concern in national politics before it. Conservative opposition to government focused on its activities, not on its revenue base, and this put conservatism at a disadvantage, because most government programs are popular. Even before Proposition 13, conservative economic writers like Jude Wanniski and Arthur Laffer were inventing supply-side economics, based on the idea that reducing taxes would bring prosperity. With Proposition 13 it was proved—as it has been proved over and over since—that tax cutting was one of the rare voguish policy ideas that turn out to be huge political winners. In switching from arguing against programs to arguing against taxes, conservatism had found another key element of its ascension to power.

The tax revolt wouldn't have worked if the middle class hadn't been receptive to the notion that it was oppressed. This was remarkable in itself, since it had been assumed for decades that the American middle class was, in a world-historical sense, almost uniquely lucky. The emergence of a self-pitying strain in the middle class was in a sense yet another sixties spillover. At the dawn of the sixties, the idea that *anybody* in the United States was oppressed might have seemed absurd. Then blacks, who really were oppressed, were able to make the country see the truth about their situation. But that opened Pandora's box. The eloquent language of group rights that the civil rights movement had invented proved to be quite adaptable, and eventually it was used by college students, feminists, Native Americans, Chicanos, urban blue-collar "white ethnics," and, finally, suburban homeowners.

With fleeting success, Jimmy Carter brings moral pressure to bear on a troubled world in a 1977 cartoon by Edward Sorel.

(Courtesy of Edward Sorel)

Meanwhile, the social programs started by Lyndon Johnson gave rise to another new, or long-quiescent, idea, which was that the government was wasting vast sums of money on harebrained schemes. In some ways the Great Society accomplished its goal of binding the country together, by making the federal government a nationwide provider of such favors as medical care and access to higher education; but in others it contributed to the seventies trend of each group's looking to government to provide it with benefits and being unconcerned with the general good. Especially after the economy turned sour, the middle class began to define its interests in terms

of a rollback of government programs aimed at helping other groups.

As the country was becoming more fragmented, so was its essential social unit, the family. In 1965 only 14.9 percent of the population was single; by 1979 the figure had risen to 20 percent. The divorce rate went from 2.5 per thousand in 1965 to 5.3 per thousand in 1979. The percentage of births that were out of wedlock was 5.3 in 1960 and 16.3 in 1978. The likelihood that married women with young children would work doubled between the mid-sixties and the late seventies. These changes took place for a variety of reasons—feminism, improved birth control, the legalization of abortion, the spread across the country of the sixties youth culture's rejection of traditional mores—but what they added up to was that the nuclear family, consisting of a working husband and a nonworking wife, both in their first marriage, and their children, ceased to be the dominant type of American household during the seventies. Also, people became more likely to organize themselves into communities based on their family status, so that the unmarried often lived in singles apartment complexes and retirees in senior citizens' developments. The overall effect was one of much greater personal freedom, which meant, as it always does, less social cohesion. Tom Wolfe's moniker for the seventies, the Me Decade, caught on because it was probably true that the country had placed relatively more emphasis on individual happiness and relatively less on loyalty to family and nation.

Like a symphony, the seventies finally built up in a crescendo that pulled together all its main themes. This occurred during the second half of 1979. First OPEC engineered the "second oil shock," in which, by holding down production, it got the price for its crude oil (and the price of gasoline at American service stations) to rise by more than 50 percent during the first six months of that year. With the onset of the summer vacation season, the automotive equivalent of the Depression's bank runs began. Everybody considered the possibility of not being able to get gas, panicked, and went off to fill the tank; the result was hours-long lines at gas stations all over the country.

It was a small inconvenience compared with what people in the Communist world and Latin America live through all the time, but the psychological effect was enormous. The summer of 1979 was the only time I can remember when, at the level of ordinary life as opposed to public affairs, things seemed to be out of control. Inflation was well above 10 percent and rising, and suddenly what seemed like a quarter of every day was spent on getting gasoline or thinking about getting gasoline—a task that previously had been completely routine, as it is again now. Black markets sprang up; rumors flew about well-connected

people who had secret sources. One day that summer, after an hour's desperate and fruitless search, I ran out of gas on the Central Expressway in Dallas. I left my car sitting primly in the right lane and walked away in the hundred-degree heat; the people driving by looked at me without surprise, no doubt thinking, "Poor bastard, it could have happened to me just as easily."

In July President Carter scheduled a speech on the gas lines, then abruptly canceled it and repaired to Camp David to think deeply for ten days, which seemed like a pale substitute for somehow setting things aright. Aides, cabinet secretaries, intellectuals, religious leaders, tycoons, and other leading citizens were summoned to Carter's aerie to discuss with him what was wrong with the country's soul. On July 15 he made a television address to the nation, which has been enshrined in memory as the "malaise speech," although it didn't use that word. (Carter did, however, talk about "a crisis of confidence . . . that strikes at the very heart and soul and spirit of our national will.")

To reread the speech today is to be struck by its spectacular political ineptitude. Didn't Carter realize that Presidents are not supposed to express doubts publicly or to lecture the American people about their shortcomings? Why couldn't he have just temporarily imposed gas rationing, which would have ended the lines overnight, instead of outlining a vague and immediately forgotten six-point program to promote energy conservation?

His describing the country's loss of confidence did not cause the country to gain confidence, needless to say. And it didn't help matters that upon his return to Washington he demanded letters of resignation from all members of his cabinet and accepted five of them. Carter seemed to be anything but an FDR-like reassuring, ebullient presence; he communicated a sense of wild flailing about as he tried (unsuccessfully) to get the situation under control.

I remember being enormously impressed by Carter's speech at the time because it was a painfully honest and much thought-over attempt to grapple with the main problem of the decade. The American economy had ceased being an expanding pie, and by unfortunate coincidence this had happened just when an ethic of individual freedom as the highest good was spreading throughout the society, which meant people would respond to the changing economic conditions by looking out for themselves. Like most other members of the word-manipulating class whose leading figures had advised Carter at Camp David, I thought there *was* a malaise. What I didn't realize, and Carter obviously didn't either, was that there was a smarter way to play the situation politically. A President could maintain there was nothing wrong with America at all—that it hadn't become less powerful in the world, hadn't reached some kind of hard economic limit, and wasn't in crisis—and, instead of trying to reverse the powerful tide of individualism, ride along with it. At the same time, he could act more forcefully than Carter, especially against inflation, so that he didn't seem weak and ineffectual. All this is exactly what Carter's successor, Ronald Reagan, did.

Actually, Carter himself set in motion the process by which inflation was conquered a few months later, when he gave the chairmanship of the Federal Reserve Board to Paul Volcker, a man willing to put the economy into a severe recession to bring back price stability. But in November fate delivered the *coup de grâce* to Carter in the form of the taking hostage of the staff of the American Embassy in Teheran, as a protest against the United States' harboring of Iran's former shah.

As with the malaise speech, what is most difficult to convey today about the hostage crisis is why Carter made what now looks like a huge, obvious error: playing up the crisis so much that it became a national obsession for more than a year. The fundamental problem with hostage taking is that the one sure remedy—refusing to negotiate and thus allowing the hostages to be killed—is politically unacceptable in the democratic media society we live in, at least when the hostages are middle-class sympathetic figures, as they were in Iran.

There isn't any good solution to this problem, but Carter's two successors in the White House demonstrated that it is possible at least to negotiate for the release of hostages in a low-profile way that will cause the press to lose interest and prevent the course of the hostage negotiations from completely defining the Presidency. During the last year of the Carter administration, by contrast, the hostage story absolutely dominated the television news (recall that the ABC show *Nightline* began as a half-hour five-times-a-week update on the hostage situation), and several of the hostages and their families became temporary celebrities. In Carter's defense, even among the many voices criticizing him for appearing weak and vacillating, there was none that I remember willing to say, "Just cut off negotiations and walk away." It was a situation that everyone regarded as terrible but in which there was a strong national consensus supporting the course Carter had chosen.

So ended the seventies. There was still enough of the sixties spillover phenomenon going on so that Carter, who is now regarded (with some affection) as having been too much the good-hearted liberal to maintain a hold on the presidential electorate, could be challenged for renomination by Ted Kennedy on the grounds that he was too conservative. Inflation was raging on; the consumer price index rose by 14.4 percent between May 1979 and May 1980. We were being humiliated by fanatically bitter, premodern Muslims whom we had expected to regard us with gratitude because we had helped ease out their dictator even though he was reliably pro–United States. The Soviet empire appeared (probably for the last time ever) to be on the march, having invaded Afghanistan to Carter's evident surprise and disillusionment. We had lost our most recent war. We couldn't pull together as a people. The puissant, unified, prospering America of the late 1940s seemed to be just a fading memory.

I was a reporter for the *Washington Post* during the 1980 presidential campaign, and even on the *Post*'s national desk, that legendary nerve center of politics, the idea that the campaign might end with Reagan's being elected President seemed fantastic, right up to

Brian Basset saw Carter lying helpless while the 1980 election bore down; the polls never did let him loose. (© Brian Basset)

the weekend before the election. At first [Ted] Kennedy looked like a real threat to Carter; remember that up to that point no Kennedy had ever lost a campaign. While the Carter people were disposing of Kennedy, they were rooting for Reagan to win the Republican nomination because he would be such an easy mark.

He was too old, too unserious, and, most of all, too conservative. Look what had happened to Barry Goldwater (a sitting officeholder, at least) only sixteen years earlier, and Reagan was so divisive that a moderate from his own party, John Anderson, was running for President as a third-party candidate. It was not at all clear how much the related issues of inflation and national helplessness were dominating the public's mind. Kennedy, Carter, and Anderson were all, in their own way, selling national healing,

that great post-sixties obsession; Reagan, and only Reagan, was selling pure strength.

In a sense Reagan's election represents the country's rejection of the idea of a sixties-style solution to the great problems of the seventies—economic stagnation, social fragmentation, and the need for a new world order revolving around relations between the oil-producing Arab world and the West. The idea of a scaled-back America—husbanding its resources, living more modestly, renouncing its restless mobility, withdrawing from full engagement with the politics of every spot on the globe, focusing on issues of internal comity—evidently didn't appeal. Reagan, and the country, had in effect found a satisfying pose to strike in response to the problems of the seventies, but that's different from finding a solution.

Today some of the issues that dominated the seventies have faded away. Reagan and Volcker did beat inflation. The "crisis of confidence" now seems a long-ago memory. But it is striking how early we still seem to be in the process of working out the implications of the oil embargo. We have just fought and won [the Gulf War] against the twin evils of Middle East despotism and interruptions in the oil supply, which began to trouble us in the seventies. We still have not really even begun to figure out how to deal with the cessation of across-the-board income gains, and as a result our domestic politics are still dominated by squabbling over the proper distribution of government's benefits and burdens. During the seventies themselves the new issues that were arising seemed nowhere near as important as those sixties legacies, minority rights and Vietnam and Watergate. But the runt of decades has wound up casting a much longer shadow than anyone imagined.

QUESTIONS TO CONSIDER

1 What, according to Nicholas Lemann, is the long-term influence of the 1960s on American politics and culture? In what way were "the phenomena of the sixties" worked into the cultural mainstream?

2 Lemann sees the OPEC oil embargo of 1973–1974 as "the epochal event" of the 1970s. What were its economic and practical effects? What were the psychological effects on Americans' confidence in their country and their culture? How did the cultural trends of the 1970s make this reaction even more critical at the end of the decade?

3 According to Lemann, the 1970s were characterized by a "gathering conservative stridency." Discuss the events and developments underlying this trend. In what ways was it fed by trends from the 1960s, and in what ways was it a reaction against the sixties?

4 What is Lemann's judgment of Jimmy Carter and Ronald Reagan as men and as politicians? Does he find Reagan's presidency more successful than Carter's?

5 What to Lemann is the long-term importance of the 1970s? Do you see any signs of change, or do you think we are still working out the legacy of the 1970s?

PART FOURTEEN

The End of the Cold War

29 Reagan: His Place in History

RICHARD BROOKHISER

The collapse of the Soviet Union and the end of the Cold War came with such speed and surprise that the pace of events was almost too much to comprehend. It began in 1985 when Mikhail Gorbachev acceded to power as Soviet general secretary. To the utter astonishment of the West, he became "the most revolutionary figure in world politics in at least four decades," as one historian put it. Gorbachev not only launched glasnost, *which ended many of the Soviet Union's most repressive practices, but started* perestroika, *or the restructuring of the Soviet Union, in order to end decades of economic stagnation and backwardness under Communism. Gorbachev sought to remake the Soviet economy by introducing such elements of capitalism as the profit motive and private ownership of property. His policies set the Soviet Union down the road toward a market economy; severely weakened the Soviet Communist party, which lost its monopoly of political power in 1990; and brought about détente with the West and the pioneering Intermediate Nuclear Forces Treaty (INF) with the United States, which led the two countries to jettison their intermediate-range missiles.*

In 1989, meanwhile, world Communism itself appeared to collapse. Our television sets brought us the stunning spectacle of eastern Europeans, subjected to decades of violent repression, demonstrating in the street in favor of individual freedom and democratic government. Every nation in the eastern bloc—East Germany, Bulgaria, Romania, Hungary, Czechoslovakia, and Poland—overthrew its Communist regime or made that regime reform itself into a non-Communist government. Most dramatic of all was the dismantling of the Berlin Wall, long the preeminent symbol of Cold War between East and West, and the reunification of Germany itself. At long last, the troubled legacy of the Second World War appeared to be over, leaving our planet a safer place. For those of us who lived through World War II and the entire length of the Cold War, the events of the late 1980s and early 1990s defied belief. Few thought we would ever live to see the downfall of the Soviet Communist state and the end of the Cold War at the same time.

In the following selection, Richard Brookhiser gives Ronald Reagan much of the credit for these dramatic changes. This former governor of California, one-time movie actor, and New Deal Democrat turned conservative Republican was an eloquent and dedicated foe of Communism. He made international headlines when he called the Soviet Union "the Evil Empire." During his eight years as president (1981–1989), Reagan greatly increased defense spending, so much so, his supporters argue, that the Soviet Union collapsed in a desperate but futile effort to keep pace with the United States. As Professor Garry Wills has said, Reagan brought about the end of "the Evil Empire" by spending so much on America's military that the national debt more than doubled, to $2.3 trillion, the deficit almost tripled, and the trade deficit more than quadrupled. In addition to augmenting conventional weapons, Reagan embarked on the futuristic and inordinately expensive Strategic Defense Initiative (SDI, nicknamed Star Wars after George Lucas's phenomenally successful science-fiction movie). The Reagan administration claimed that SDI, "through the use of lasers and satellites, would provide an impenetrable shield against incoming missiles and thus make nuclear war obsolete." The SDI program provoked something close to hysteria among Soviet leaders because the U.S.S.R. lacked the financial resources and the technical expertise to keep up with the United States in an escalation of the arms race into space. Perhaps this was a major reason why Gorbachev sought détente with the West, agreed to a ban on intermediate-range missiles, and set about restructuring the Soviet system. But Brookhiser argues that Reagan was the lead player in bringing about these momentous events.

To help us understand Reagan and his place in history, Brookhiser examines the salient traits of his personality that helped shape his performance in office. Brookhiser stresses that Reagan was upbeat, witty, and supremely optimistic. Even when John Hinckley shot him in a failed assassination attempt, Brookhiser says, Reagan "reacted to actual gunfire with better humor than many politicians do to bad headlines." The story goes that when he met the physicians at George Washington University Hospital, he was cracking one-liners. "Please tell me you're all Republicans," the President said.

Because of his basic optimism, Reagan never doubted America's ultimate victory over the forces of evil symbolized by Communism and the Soviet Union. But, as Brookhiser reminds us, there was a "black velvet backdrop behind his cheerfulness," which reveals another of Reagan's "salient traits": his coldness. Behind his "bonhomie," he was inaccessible. Even people who worked closely with him for years believed that they never really knew him.

In Brookhiser's view, Reagan was a classic "hedgehog"—historian Isaiah Berlin's term for one who thinks only about the big picture and thus misses crucial details. Even so, Reagan lived to witness the collapse of the Berlin Wall, the relegation of Communism to "the ash-heap of history," and the end of the Cold War that had plagued the planet for almost a half century. Brookhiser gives Reagan the credit for ending that war. Bestselling novelist Tom Clancy agrees. He dedicated his novel, Executive Orders *(1996), "To Ronald Wilson Reagan, fortieth president of the United States: The man who won the war."*

GLOSSARY

BRADY, JAMES   Reagan's press secretary, Brady was shot in the spray of bullets when John Hinckley tried to assassinate the President with a handgun. Brady's wounds were so severe that he had to be confined to a wheelchair. Later, the Brady Bill, named in honor of Reagan's stricken aide, placed restrictions on the purchase of handguns and assault weapons.

BUCHANAN, PATRICK J.   Previously a speech writer for Richard Nixon, Buchanan was Reagan's communications director. He ran for president on a conservative third-party ticket in 1992, 1996, and 2000.

CHAMBERS, WHITTAKER   A repentant Communist, Chambers gained notoriety in 1948 when he accused State Department official Alger Hiss of spying for the Soviets.

GORBACHEV, MIKHAIL   When he became the Soviet general secretary in 1985, Gorbachev represented a younger generation of leaders who wanted to move the Soviet Union away from the repressive political practices of the past and toward a market economy that included the ownership of private property. Gorbachev embraced détente and signed a treaty with the United States that banned intermediate-range missiles.

HINCKLEY, JOHN   On March 30, 1981, Hinckley attempted to assassinate Reagan. The president had just finished a speech at a Washington, D.C., hotel. Hinckley's shots hit a police officer and press secretary James Brady. One bullet ricocheted and struck Reagan in the chest. Declared mentally incompetent, Hinckley was institutionalized at St. Elizabeth's Hospital in Washington, D.C.

LAFFER, ARTHUR   A proponent of the supply-side theory of economics, Laffer believed that lower taxes would stimulate the economy and increase federal government revenue.

MORAL MAJORITY   Paul Weyrich and the Reverend Jerry Falwell helped establish this organization whose base consisted of "born again" evangelical Christians. The Moral Majority championed a return to prayer in public schools and opposed abortion, homosexuality, and the Equal Rights Amendment to the Constitution.

MORRIS, EDMUND   While still in office, Reagan selected Morris, a white person born and educated in Kenya, to be his official biographer. The president was impressed with Morris's Pulitzer Prize–winning biography of Theodore Roosevelt. Morris went on to write *Dutch: A Memoir of Ronald Reagan* (1999), which was highly controversial.

NOONAN, PEGGY   A White House speech writer, Noonan is best known for crafting Reagan's address at Normandy Beach in 1984, in a ceremony commemorating the fortieth anniversary of the Allied invasion of German-occupied France during World War II.

NORTH, OLIVER   A marine lieutenant colonel, North was a central figure in the Iran-Contra affair. The trading of arms for American hostages in Iran resulted in funds that North secretly diverted to support the anti-Communist Contra forces in Nicaragua. North argued that he did this to defend democracy. In fact, his actions were illegal and unconstitutional, and they embarrassed the Reagan administration.

O'NEILL, THOMAS P. (TIP)   A politically astute Massachusetts congressman, O'Neill served as the Democratic majority leader from 1973 to 1977 and speaker of the House of Representatives from 1977 to 1987.

STRATEGIC DEFENSE INITIATIVE (SDI)   Also known as "Star Wars," SDI was Reagan's program of lasers and satellites in space that in theory would provide the United States with a protective shield against nuclear missiles.

Contemporary judgments of presidents are notoriously erratic. Consider the four who decorate Mount Rushmore, the stony seal of posterity's approval. Although Washington retired with almost universally good reviews, Benjamin Franklin's grandson did say he had "debauched" the nation. Jefferson left the White House with the joy of an escaping prisoner and a stress-induced migraine condition. The Senate was so angry with Theodore Roosevelt in his last days in office that it refused to accept his communications. Lincoln, who tops every historian's rating of Presidents, was murdered.

When Ronald Reagan left office in 1989, he truly retired, intending no Nixonian or Carteresque codas, and the onset of Alzheimer's was soon setting his agenda in any case. Journalists and historians could thus get an early start on their posthumous shiftings. But their work will go on for years. . . .

Whatever the writers finally come up with, all their labors, like all the events of their subject's career, will be distilled by the national memory into two or three facts or phrases, maybe only one. My childhood history of the Presidents, which had to find something important and moderately good to say about every Chief Executive, could at least say of Millard Fillmore that he sent Commodore Perry to Japan.

Here is a preliminary list of six aspects of Ronald Reagan—three personal, three political—from which those in the year 2075 may make their selection.

Like notable predecessors—Jefferson, FDR—Reagan had an optimistic view of things. Also like them, he had demons and enemies. But he was serenely confident that he would prevail. His political optimism came from a buoyant temperament. The command performance for his personality was the moment when, at the age of 70, one of John Hinckley's bullets lodged an inch from his heart. He spent his time, before and after the operation that

saved his life, cracking jokes almost as old as himself. We often use military metaphors to describe normal political controversy—for instance, a "barrage" of criticism. Ronald Reagan reacted to actual gunfire with better humor than many politicians do to bad headlines.

In normal circumstances, Reagan's favorite story about his sunny worldview concerned two boys who were told to clean out a stable. The task proved so Augean that one of them gave up. The other kept going. With so much excrement, he reasoned, there had to be a pony in there somewhere.

That story conveyed a truth about Reagan's optimism: It was willed, sometimes contrary to all reason. Another story, which he told on the opening pages of his first memoir, the 1965 *Where's the Rest of Me?*, supplies the psychological background of his determined hopefulness. Reagan describes finding his father, Jack, a genial, but alcoholic, shoe salesman, collapsed on the front porch one night after a binge. The scene was pure Frank Capra, down to the weather conditions: Jack Reagan's "hair [was] soaked with melting snow." As in some Frank Capra movies, there was also a dark subtext beneath a sentimental gloss. Ronald remembered helping his father, pityingly, to bed: "I could feel no resentment." If he couldn't feel any, why does he mention it? Any drunk's child feels a host of negative emotions: resentment, anger, betrayal. Each child then deals with them in his own way. Ronald Reagan's way was to dismiss his pain and to focus on the bright side: "In a few days" his father "was the bluff, hearty man I knew and loved." In later life, Reagan would blot out both real problems and false obstacles, as well as bullets.

The black velvet backdrop behind his cheerfulness explains a second salient trait of Reagan's: his coldness. Yes, he had a funny story for everyone, including Tip O'Neill and Mikhail Gorbachev, and he laughed at other people's funny stories, not just his own. But behind the bonhomie, there was nothing accessible. "Even as a teenager," wrote Edmund Morris, "he had taken no personal interest in people. They were, and remained, a faceless audience to his

Excerpts from Richard Brookhiser, "Reagan, His Place in History," *American Heritage* (August/September, 2004), pp. 35–38. Reprinted by permission of the author.

Ronald Reagan and his wife Nancy as they appeared on inauguration day, January 20, 1981. The photographer captures Reagan's winning smile and movie-star appeal. Brookhiser praises him for his "sunny worldview" and his unflinching confidence in America's future. (Courtesy Ronald Reagan Library)

perpetual performance." Certainly Morris felt faceless in Reagan's presence, which seems to have driven the biographer to distraction. But he was not the only one. People who worked with Reagan closely for years felt they never penetrated. According to his speechwriter Peggy Noonan, White House staffers made jokes of his elusiveness: "Who was that masked man?"

Reagan's coldness allowed him to be stubborn. He used all the resources of public relations, from marks on the floor to theme-of-the-day spin control to movie-star looks, to make his case. But after he had done all that he could do, he did not care what

people thought of him. He had his message; when he became President, he had his programs; that was that. He often settled for less than he wanted, but he never stopped wanting it. His stubbornness helped him reach the White House despite one of the more discouraging pre-victory political records. Some politicians have won second contests after previously losing runs for the Presidency: Andrew Jackson, Richard Nixon. Some have won, after one failed attempt to secure their party's nomination: James Monroe, George H. W. Bush. Reagan failed twice to get the Republican nomination—in 1968 and 1976—before lightning struck. Repeat losers, from Henry

Clay to Bob Dole, usually go on losing. Only Reagan broke the pattern.

Reagan's third important personal trait was simplicity. The literature of management is filled with variations on the polarity between big-picture men and detail men; in the realm of philosophy, Isaiah Berlin taught us to think of hedgehogs (the thinkers who see in the universe one big thing) and foxes (the thinkers who see multiplicity). The characteristic mistake of big-picture hedgehogs is to ignore details that are in fact crucial; the characteristic mistake of detail foxes is to assume that hedgehogs see nothing at all. John Quincy Adams, the first Boylston Professor of Rhetoric at Harvard, called Andrew Jackson a "barbarian" who "hardly could spell his own name"; this was five years after Jackson had cleaned Adams's clock in the election of 1828.

Tip O'Neill, no Boylston Professor of Rhetoric but a Massachusetts politician, like Adams, said Reagan knew "less than any president I've ever known" (O'Neill, like Adams, also had his clock cleaned by his ignoramus enemy). Reagan indeed was about as far over in the direction of the big picture and hedgehog as it is possible to be. In his book *The Presidential Difference,* the political scientist Fred I. Greenstein made a useful movie-industry analogy to Reagan's intellectual and management style. Reagan obviously was the star of his own administration, but he was also its producer. The writing, even the directing, could always be left to someone else. He was responsible for Reaganism.

What was that? The most concentrated (Reaganesque?) summary of its leading heads was made by the journalist R. Emmett Tyrrell, Jr.: "The Evil Empire; cut taxes; the pieties." The economist Milton Friedman daydreams about an income tax return so simple it could be printed on a postcard. Reaganism could be jotted down on the back of a business card.

What fell off the card, Reagan believed, could safely be ignored. Pat Buchanan, another speechwriter, remembered sitting in on a cabinet-level debate between Secretary of State George Shultz and Secretary of Agriculture John Block on grain exports. While it raged, Reagan reached for a bowl of jellybeans, his favorite snack food, and began picking out his favorite colors. "My God," Buchanan thought, "what in heaven's name is with this guy?" Reagan, who caught Buchanan's eye, winked. Buchanan interpreted the wink to mean: "They're having an argument here, and I'm not getting into it." Maybe that is what the wink meant. Or maybe—the coldness kicking in—it was Reagan's way of averting an intrusive gaze. In either case, Mr. Shultz and Mr. Block were not attended to. That was safe enough when the subject was grain exports; less safe when it was the money shuffling of Lt. Col. Oliver North.

On the issues that constituted Reaganism, Reagan batted two for three. It became the fashion, after their collapse, to dismiss Communism and the Soviet Union as threats. It is easy to be wise after the fact. In the late seventies, Cuban soldiers patrolled the former Portuguese empire in Africa. The Soviets had acquired two new client states in the Western Hemisphere, Nicaragua and Grenada, and had invaded Afghanistan. Western Europe was rocked by a pro-Communist peace movement, terrified by the introduction of Soviet and American intermediate-range missiles on European soil.

Reagan's distrust of Communism was deep and long-standing. As a president of the Screen Actors Guild, he had seen Communist attempts to take over Hollywood crafts unions; when the guild's position on these turf wars shifted from neutral to anti-Communist, Reagan got an anonymous phone call on a movie set threatening that his face would be "fix[ed]." Early in the fifties, he read *Witness,* by the former Communist spy Whittaker Chambers. *Witness* was more than an espionage memoir; in one passage, Chambers recalled that the delicate folds of his baby daughter's ears persuaded him that the universe was divinely designed and that scientific socialism was false. Three decades later, Reagan cited the passage on the baby's ear to White House speechwriter Tony Dolan. Reagan was not well read, but what he read lodged in his mind.

Because of his optimism, he never adopted the defensive power-sharing strategy of longtime anti-Communists like Richard Nixon and Henry Kissinger.

He thought Communism was bad, and he thought it was doomed. When he became President, he confidently declared that freedom and the West would "transcend" Communism, that it would end "on the ash-heap of history," that the Berlin Wall should be torn down.

The steps he took to bring this about included rolling back Communist gains at the margins, invading Grenada, supporting a counterrevolution in Nicaragua, and sending Stinger missiles to the Afghan resistance. (As in all wars, there were unintended consequences, as the Taliban and Osama bin Laden demonstrate.) He announced that he would take advantage of America's lead in high tech by producing a missile defense system. Critics derided the Strategic Defense Initiative as a fantasy from *Star Wars;* Reagan embraced the pop-culture reference. He never deployed the system, and tests of its effectiveness continue to this day, as do arguments over the results. But the threat worried the Soviets; Gorbachev's foreign minister, Aleksandr Bessmertnykh, told a 1993 conference of Cold Warriors at the Woodrow Wilson School of Public and International Affairs that SDI caused a tug of war inside the Soviet bureaucracy that was reflected in the divided purposes of the Gorbachev regime. Former Defense Secretary Frank Carlucci said at the same press conference that he "never believed" in SDI, and his skepticism may prove to be justified. On the other hand, the Cold War postmortem at which Bessmertnykh and Carlucci spoke was hosted by the victors, in Princeton, New Jersey, not Leningrad.

No one thing wins a war by itself. But Reagan's appearance at the end of the Cold War was crucial. When he came into office, the Soviet Union was an aggressive hard-line state; when he left, it was a reforming, improvising one partly in response to his pressures. Less than a year after he retired, the Berlin Wall was torn down; two years after that, the Soviet Union was no more. It is hard to think of a comparably rapid collapse of a major power without major bloodletting. Woodrow Wilson helped beat the Central Powers in World War I, and Franklin Roosevelt played a far larger role in beating the

Axis in World War II. World War III—the Cold War—was less cataclysmic but longer, and the role of the United States was even more central. Ronald Reagan helped guarantee an American victory, without fighting a Second Battle of the Marne or a D-day.

When Reagan came into office, the American economy seemed as weak as the Yeltsin-era Russian army. The oil shock of the early seventies had hit it hard, and a combination of high inflation and high unemployment known as "stagflation"—which the reigning economists' paradigm of the Phillips curve declared to be impossible—seemed impervious to the best efforts of Presidents Nixon, Ford, and Carter to massage it.

Reagan's remedy was as theological as the passage on the baby's ear. A school of economists, called "supply-siders," had studied the economic impact of tax rates (Robert Mundell, the school's founder, was awarded the Nobel Prize in economics in 1999). They too had a curve, shaped like a croquet wicket and named after one of their number, Arthur Laffer, which they said showed the diminishing returns of revenue that resulted from ever-higher rates. If you cut tax rates, they argued, the economy would be stimulated, and the federal government would collect more money in tax revenues. Making use of a post-shooting wave of good feeling, Reagan was able to persuade Congress to implement something like their program.

In the event, the Laffer curve, like the Phillips curve, had some kinks in it. The great tax-rate cut was followed by two short, sharp recessions, one at the beginning of Reagan's first term, the other at the end of George H. W. Bush's only one. Both Bush and then Bill Clinton repudiated supply-side doctrine, though they did not in fact raise tax rates that much. The deficit, contrary to predictions, rose alarmingly, until the late nineties, when politicians began talking of surplus.

Still, the eighties and nineties were economically vastly different from the seventies. Americans worried less about OPEC or the potency of Asian models of capitalism and profited from their own. Success has many fathers. The Federal Reserve, which always goes its own way, deserves credit. So, more recently, does the computer economy, which was a spinoff of high-tech military spending. But Reagan was on the bridge when the twenty-year boom began.

On the third item of his agenda, "the pieties," more commonly known as the social issues, Reagan was completely defeated. After signing an expansive abortion-rights bill as governor of California, Reagan came to oppose the practice. When he was elected President, abortion opponents spoke hopefully of a constitutional amendment returning jurisdiction on abortion to the states or banning abortion outright or of a congressional act (per Article III, Section 2) removing the issue from the sway of the courts. Nothing happened. When Reagan addressed audiences of gun owners as a fellow NRA member, they helped him in Republican primaries. Gun-control supporters made little progress during his administration, but recently they have made lots, aided in no small part by the crippled presence of former press secretary James Brady, shot by one of John Hinckley's bullets. Sex continues to rock and roll through popular entertainment and, not so very long ago, even the Oval Office. Come to think of it, Reagan was the first divorced man to be elected President.

In 1979 the Washington political operative Paul Weyrich helped the Reverend Jerry Falwell found the Moral Majority, the organization's name confidently assuming that there was such a thing, as Weyrich and Falwell defined it. In 1999 Weyrich gloomily announced that religious and social conservatives should retreat to their families and communities since the political and cultural situation was hopeless. . . .

Perhaps the pieties fell victim to simplicity. It may be that a hedgehog's agenda maxes out at two big ideas. Abortion opponents were told during the early Reagan years to wait patiently while Communism and high tax rates were attended to; their turn would come. It never did.

Great generals and politicians often preside over social transformations they deplore. Washington's Farewell Address deplores the party spirit, yet partisan politics became an unshakable aspect of American life in his administration. Thomas Jefferson was the harbinger of the new era, yet as Henry Adams argued in stout volumes, that era was not the republican, country party ideal of Jefferson's youth. If posterity accords Reagan some measure of their success—a world war and a twenty-year boom—it will also accord him their failure.

Reagan's Presidency came at the end of the twentieth century—the actual one, not the calendrical one. The twentieth century, as many historians have noted, was a short century, running from 1914 to 1991. It was also an evil century, defined by tyranny and bloodshed. The United States came through it less badly scarred than any other major power and than many small ones. Ronald Reagan, who was born in 1911, before the Evil Century began, lived to see and understand its end—which he, as much as anyone else, assured would be relatively successful. Mount Rushmore is full, and that kind of pantheon should probably be reserved for those who speak to America's spirit (then what's TR doing there?). But when historians and children have to think of Ronald Reagan at the end of the twenty-first century, they won't have to scratch around for some Commodore Perry.

QUESTIONS TO CONSIDER

1 Describe how Ronald Reagan reacted to the assassination attempt. What does his reaction tell you about his temperament? How did Reagan view the episode in his youth when he had to help his alcoholic father to bed?

2 What is Brookhiser's evidence that there was a "coldness" beneath Reagan's cheerful demeanor? How does Reagan's political record before his presidency provide clues to his determination and tenacity?

3 Describe the difference between "hedgehogs" and "foxes." Why did Reagan fit perfectly into one of these categories? What were the three major goals of "Reaganism"? Why does Brookhiser conclude that

the President "batted two for three" with reference to the three goals?

4 Describe the origin of Reagan's "deep and long standing disdain" for Communism. Explain what Reagan did as president to place Communism "on the ash-heap of history." Why did Brookhiser conclude that Reagan "helped generate an American victory" in the Cold War without the bloodletting that ended the previous world wars? Do you agree with the author's conclusions?

5 Describe the economic theory of the "supply-siders." Why did Reagan believe that they would restore health to the American economy? Why does Brookhiser conclude that "the eighties and nineties were economically vastly different from the seventies"?

6 How does President Reagan's record on social issues measure up to the goals that he established at the start of his first administration? What grades would abortion opponents, NRA members, and the Moral Majority give to him?

30 Some Lessons from the Cold War

ARTHUR M. SCHLESINGER JR.

It is too soon to know what the demise of the Soviet Union and the end of the Cold War means for the future of humankind. But it is not too soon to reflect on some lessons of the Cold War, which on at least one occasion—the Cuban missile crisis of October 1962—almost exploded into a nuclear holocaust and the end of the world as we know it. How did humankind survive the Cold War? What caused and sustained it? The experts do not agree. Some see the Cold War as fundamentally an ideological struggle between the forces of freedom and the forces of autocracy. Still others view the Cold War as a geopolitical and military contest that involved not just a Soviet–United States confrontation but a western Europe–Soviet confrontation as well. While some specialists maintain that the Cold War strengthened hard-liners in the Soviet Union and sustained Communist rule there, others, such as Ronald Steel, believe that American policymakers exaggerated the military capacity of the Soviet Union throughout the Cold War, thus creating a bogus enemy that justified huge American defense build-ups.

In the selection that follows, Arthur M. Schlesinger Jr., one of our greatest historians, argues that it is irrelevant to allocate blame for the Cold War. It emerged, he says, from the efforts of the United States and the Soviet Union to fill the "power vacuum" left by World War II, and it developed into "a holy war" because of very real ideological differences between the two new superpowers and their allies. At bottom, Schlesinger believes, the Cold War was a "fundamental debate" between Communism and liberalism, including democratic socialism, and that debate charged the Cold War with its religious intensity.

Now that the holy war is over, Schlesinger suggests six fallacies that helped make it so long, so dark, and so dangerous. These fallacies, Schlesinger suggests, resulted from the perception of events by both sides. Yes, the perception of reality is the crucial element in understanding the past. How people perceive events and the motives of an alleged enemy determine how they act, and how they act in turn affects the course of subsequent events. When it comes to the Cold War, human error, exaggeration, misunderstanding, overinterpretation—all played a key role in shaping and sustaining tensions between East and West. Schlesinger hopes that his six fallacies, or errors of perception, judgment, and action, will benefit future policymakers, so that the world can avoid another Cold War, another "intimate brush with collective suicide." In the end, he argues, "Democracy won the political argument between East and West" and "the market won the economic argument." Yet in retrospect, Schlesinger says, the Cold War can only remind us "of the ultimate interdependence of nations and of peoples."

GLOSSARY

QUISLING Someone who betrays his country by helping enemy invaders and going on to serve in a puppet government; named after pro-Nazi Norwegian Vidkun Quisling (1887–1945).

STALIN, JOSEPH Soviet dictator from the 1920s until his death in 1953, he ruled the Soviet Union with a brutal hand, resorting to massive purges in the 1930s and again in the post–World War II years; he viewed the West as a devious menace (several times in its history Russia had been invaded by western European powers) and clamped an iron hand on eastern Europe, using it as a bulwark against Western "aggression."

WALLACE, HENRY A. FDR's vice president, 1941–1945, and Truman's secretary of commerce, 1945–1946; Wallace was forced to resign as commerce secretary after he publicly attacked Truman's "get tough" policy toward the Soviets; in 1948, Wallace made an unsuccessful bid for the presidency as the candidate of the Progressive party.

ZERO-SUM GAME Cold War notion that "a gain for one side was by definition a defeat for the other."

In those faraway days when the Cold War was young, the English historian Sir Herbert Butterfield lectured at Notre Dame on "The Tragic Element in Modern International Conflict." Historians writing about modern wars, Butterfield said, characteristically start off with a "heroic" vision of things. They portray good men struggling against bad, virtue resisting evil. In this embattled mood, they see only the sins of the enemy and ignore the underlying structural dilemmas that so often provoke international clashes.

As time passes and emotions subside, history enters the "academic" phase. Now historians see "a terrible human predicament" at the heart of the story, "a certain situation that contains the element of conflict irrespective of any special wickedness in any of the parties concerned." Wickedness may deepen the predicament, but conflict would be there anyway.

Perspective, Butterfield proposed, teaches us "to be a little more sorry for both parties than they knew how to be for one another." History moves on from melodrama to tragedy.

Butterfield made a pretty good forecast of the way Cold War historiography has evolved in the more than forty years since he spoke. In the United States the "heroic" phase took two forms: the orthodox in the 1940s and 1950s, with the Russians cast as the villains, and the revisionist in the 1960s, with the Americans as the villains. By the 1980s, American Cold War historians discerned what one of the best of them, John Lewis Gaddis, called an "emerging post-revisionist synthesis." History began to pass from a weapon in the battle into a more analytical effort to define structural dilemmas and to understand adversary concerns. *Glasnost* permitted comparable historiographical evolution in the former Soviet Union.

Quite right: The more one contemplates the Cold War, the more irrelevant the allocation of blame seems. The Second World War left the international order in acute derangement. With the Axis states vanquished, the Western European allies spent, the

"Some Lessons from the Cold War," by Arthur M. Schlesinger, Jr. From Michael J. Hogan (ed.), *The End of the Cold War: Its Meaning and Implications*, Cambridge University Press, 1992, 53–62. Copyright © 1992 by Arthur M. Schlesinger, Jr. Reprinted with the permission of Cambridge University Press.

colonial empires in tumult and dissolution, great gaping holes appeared in the structure of world power. Only two nations—the United States and the Soviet Union—had the military strength, the ideological conviction, and the political will to fill these vacuums.

But why did this old-fashioned geopolitical rivalry billow up into a holy war so intense and obsessive as to threaten the very existence of human life on the planet? The two nations were constructed on opposite and profoundly antagonistic principles. They were divided by the most significant and fundamental disagreements over human rights, individual liberties, cultural freedom, the role of civil society, the direction of history, and the destiny of man. Each state saw the other as irrevocably hostile to its own essence. Given the ideological conflict on top of the geopolitical confrontation, no one should be surprised at what ensued. Conspiratorial explanations are hardly required. The real surprise would have been if there had been no Cold War.

And why has humanity survived the Cold War? The reason that the Cold War never exploded into hot war was surely (and by providential irony) the invention of nuclear weapons. One is inclined to support the suggestion (Elspeth Rostow's, I think) that the Nobel Peace Prize should have gone to the atomic bomb.

At last this curious episode in modern history is over, and we must ask what lessons we may hope to learn from a long, costly, dark, dreary, and dangerous affair; what precautions humanity should take to prevent comparable episodes in the future. I would suggest half a dozen fallacies that the world might well forego in years to come.

The first might be called the fallacy of overinterpreting the enemy. In the glory days of the Cold War, each side attributed to the other a master plan for world domination joined with diabolical efficiency in executing the plan. Such melodramatic imagining of brilliant and demonic enemies was truer to, say, Sax Rohmer, the creator of Dr. Fu Manchu, than to shuffling historical reality.

No doubt Soviet leaders believed that the dialectic of history would one day bring about the victory of

In late 1988, Gorbachev announced that he would reduce Soviet military presence in the eastern bloc nations. Five months later, the first of the military units scheduled for withdrawal—thirty-one Soviet T.64 tanks—pulled out of Hungary and returned to the Soviet Union. (Jean Gaumy/Magnum)

communism. No doubt Western leaders believed that the nature of man and markets would one day bring about the victory of free society. But such generalized hopes were far removed from operational master plans.

"The superpowers," as Henry Kissinger well put it, often behave like two heavily armed blind men feeling their way around a room, each believing himself in mortal peril from the other whom he assumes to have perfect vision. Each side should know that frequently uncertainty, compromise, and incoherence are the essence of policymaking. Yet each tends to ascribe to the other a consistency, foresight, and coherence that its own experience belies. Of course, over time, even two blind men can do enormous damage to each other, not to speak of the room.

The room has happily survived. But the blind men meanwhile escalated the geopolitical/ideological confrontation into a compulsively interlocked heightening of tension, spurred on by authentic differences in principle, by real and supposed clashes of interest, and by a wide range of misperception, misunderstanding, and demagoguery. Each superpower undertook for what it honestly saw as defensive reasons actions that the other honestly saw as unacceptably threatening and requiring stern countermeasures. Each persevered in corroborating the fears of the other. Each succumbed to the propensity to perceive local conflicts in global terms, political conflicts in moral terms, and relative differences in absolute terms. Together, in lockstep, they expanded the Cold War.

In overinterpreting the motives and actions of the other, each side forgot Emerson's invaluable precept: "In analysing history, do not be too profound, for often the causes are quite simple." Both superpowers should have known from their own experience that governments mostly live from day to day responding to events as they come, that decisions are more often the result of improvisation, ignorance, accident, fatigue, chance, blunder, and sometimes plain stupidity than of orchestrated master plans. One lesson to be drawn from the Cold War is that more things in life are to be explained by cock-up, to use the British term, than by conspiracy.

An accompanying phenomenon, at first a consequence and later a reinforcing cause of overinterpretation, was the embodiment of the Cold War in government institutions. Thus our second fallacy: The fallacy of overinstitutionalizing the policy. The Soviet Union, a police state committed to dogmas of class war and capitalist conspiracy and denied countervailing checks of free speech and press, had institutionalized the Cold War from the day Lenin arrived at the Finland Station. In later years the Cold War became for Stalin a convenient means of justifying

his own arbitrary power and the awful sacrifices he demanded from the Soviet peoples. "Stalin needed the Cold War," observed Earl Browder, whom Stalin purged as chief of the American Communist party, "to keep up the sharp international tensions by which he alone could maintain such a regime in Russia."

In Washington by the 1950s the State Department, the Defense Department, the Central Intelligence Agency, the Federal Bureau of Investigation, and the National Security Council developed vested bureaucratic interests in the theory of a militarily expansionist Soviet Union. The Cold War conferred power, money, prestige, and public influence on these agencies and on the people who ran them. By the natural law of bureaucracies, their stake in the conflict steadily grew. Outside of government, arms manufacturers, politicians, professors, publicists, pontificators, and demagogues invested careers and fortunes in the Cold War.

In time, the adversary Cold War agencies evolved a sort of tacit collusion across the Iron Curtain. Probably the greatest racket in the Cold War was the charade periodically enacted by generals and admirals announcing the superiority of the other side in order to get bigger budgets for themselves. As President John F. Kennedy remarked to Norman Cousins, the editor of the *Saturday Review,* in the spring of 1963, "The hard-liners in the Soviet Union and the United States feed on one another."

Institutions, alas, do not fold their tents and silently steal away. Ideas crystallized in bureaucracies resist change. With the Cold War at last at an end, each side faces the problem of deconstructing entrenched Cold War agencies spawned and fortified by nearly half a century of mutually profitable competition. One has only to reflect on the forces behind the anti-Gorbachev conspiracy of August 1991 [which sought in vain to overthrow him].

A third fallacy may be called the fallacy of arrogant prediction. As a devotee of a cyclical approach to American political history, I would not wish to deny that history exhibits uniformities and recurrences. But it is essential to distinguish between those phenomena that are predictable and those that are not.

Useful historical generalizations are mostly statements about broad, deep-running, long-term changes: the life-cycle of revolutions, for example, or the impact of industrialization and urbanization, or the influence of climate or sea power or the frontier. The short term, however, contains too many variables, depends too much on accident and fortuity and personality, to permit exact and specific forecasts.

We have been living through extraordinary changes in the former Soviet Union and in Eastern Europe, in South Africa and in the Middle East. What is equally extraordinary is that *no one foresaw these changes*. All the statesmen, all the sages, all the savants, all the professors, all the prophets, all those bearded chaps on "Nightline"—all were caught unaware and taken by surprise; all were befuddled and impotent before the perpetual astonishments of the future. History has an abiding capacity to outwit our certitudes.

Just a few years back some among us were so absolutely sure of the consequences if we did not smash the Reds at once that they called for preventive nuclear war. Had they been able to persuade the U.S. government to drop the bomb on the Soviet Union in the 1950s or on China in the 1960s . . . but, thank heaven, they never did; and no one today, including those quondam preventive warriors themselves, regrets the American failure to do so.

The Almighty no doubt does know the future. But He has declined to confide such foresight to frail and erring mortals. In the early years of the Cold War, [theologian] Reinhold Niebuhr warned of "the depth of evil to which individuals and communities may sink . . . when they try to play the role of God to history." Let us not fall for people who tell us that we must take drastic action today because of their conjectures as to what some other fellow or nation may do five or ten or twenty years from now.

Playing God to history is the dangerous consequence of our fourth fallacy—the fallacy of national self-righteousness. "No government or social system is so evil," President Kennedy said in his American University speech in 1963, "that its people must be condemned as lacking in virtue," and he called on Americans as well as Russians to reexamine attitudes toward the Cold War, "for our attitude is as essential as theirs." This thought came as rather a shock to those who assumed that the American side was so manifestly right that self-examination was unnecessary.

Kennedy liked to quote a maxim from the British military pundit Liddell Hart: "Never corner an opponent, and always assist him to save his face. Put yourself in his shoes—so as to see things through his eyes. Avoid self-righteousness like the devil—nothing is so self-blinding." Perhaps Kennedy did not always live up to those standards himself, but he did on great occasions, like the Cuban missile crisis, and he retained a capacity for ironical objectivity that is rare among political leaders.

Objectivity—seeing ourselves as others see us—is a valuable adjunct to statesmanship. Can we be so sure that our emotional judgments of the moment represent the last word and the final truth? The angry ideological conflicts that so recently obsessed us may not greatly interest our posterity. Our great-grandchildren may well wonder what in heaven's name those disagreements could have been that drove the Soviet Union and the United States to the brink of blowing up the planet.

Men and women a century from now will very likely find the Cold War as obscure and incomprehensible as we today find the Thirty Years War—the terrible conflict that devastated much of Europe not too long ago. Looking back at the twentieth century, our descendants will very likely be astonished at the disproportion between the causes of the Cold War, which may well seem trivial, and the consequences, which could have meant the veritable end of history.

Russians and Americans alike came to see the Cold War as a duel between two superpowers, a Soviet-American duopoly. But the reduction of the Cold War to a bilateral game played by the Soviet Union and the United States is a fifth fallacy. The nations of Europe were not spectators at someone else's match. They were players too.

Revisionist historians, determined to blame the Cold War on an American drive for world economic hegemony, have studiously ignored the role of Europe. Washington, they contend, was compelled to demand an "open door" for American trade and investment everywhere on the planet because American capitalism had to expand in order to survive. The Soviet Union was the main obstacle to a world market controlled by the United States. So, by revisionist dogma, American leaders whipped up an unnecessary Cold War in order to save the capitalist system.

No matter that some fervent open door advocates, like Henry A. Wallace, were also fervent opponents of the Cold War. No matter that the republics of the former Soviet Union now want nothing more than American trade and investment and full integration into the world market. And no matter that most Western European nations in the 1940s had Socialist governments and that the democratic socialist leaders—Clement Attlee and Ernest Bevin in Britain, Leon Blum and Paul Ramadier in France, Paul-Henri Spaak in Belgium, Kurt Schumacher, Ernst Reuter, and Willy Brandt in West Germany—had powerful reasons of their own to fear the spread of Stalinist influence and Soviet power.

Such men could not have cared less about an open door for American capitalism. They cared deeply, however, about the future of democratic socialism. When I used to see Aneurin Bevan, the leader of the left wing of the British Labour party, in London in 1944, he doubted that the wartime alliance would last and saw the struggle for postwar Europe as between the democratic socialists and the Communists. "The Communist party," Bevan wrote in 1951, "is the sworn and inveterate enemy of the Socialist and Democratic parties. When it associates with them it does so as a preliminary to destroying them." Many in the Truman administration in the 1940s espoused this view and, dubbing themselves (in private) NCL, favored American support for the non-Communist Left.

The democratic socialists, moreover, were in advance of official Washington in organizing against the Stalinist threat. Despite his above-the-battle stance at Notre Dame, Herbert Butterfield himself wrote in 1969, "A new generation often does not know (and

does not credit the fact when informed) that Western Europe once wondered whether the United States could ever be awakened to the danger from Russia." The subsequent opening of British Foreign Office papers voluminously documents Sir Herbert's point.

Far from seeing President Truman in the revisionist mode as an anti-Soviet zealot hustling a reluctant Europe into a gratuitous Cold War, the Foreign Office saw him for a considerable period as an irresolute waffler distracted by the delusion that the United States could play mediator between Britain and the Soviet Union. Ernest Bevin, Britain's Socialist foreign secretary, thought Truman's policy was "to withdraw from Europe and in effect leave the British to get on with the Russians as best they could." A true history of the Cold War must add European actors to the cast and broaden both research nets and analytical perspectives.

The theory of the Cold War as a Soviet-American duopoly is sometimes defended on the ground that, after all, the United States and the Soviet Union were in full command of their respective alliances. But nationalism, the most potent political emotion of the age, challenged the reign of the superpowers almost from the start: Tito [of Yugoslavia], Mao, and others vs. Moscow; De Gaulle, Eden and others vs. Washington. Experience has adequately demonstrated how limited superpowers are in their ability to order their allies around and even to control client governments wholly dependent on them for economic and military support. Far from clients being the prisoners of the superpower, superpowers often end as prisoners of their clients.

These are lessons Washington has painfully learned (or at least was painfully taught; has the government finally learned them?) in Vietnam, El Salvador, Israel, Saudi Arabia, Kuwait. As for the Soviet Union, its brutal interventions and wretched Quislings in Eastern Europe only produced bitterness and hatred. The impact of clients on principals is another part of the unwritten history of the Cold War. The Cold War was *not* a bilateral game.

Nor was it—our sixth and final fallacy—a zero-sum game. For many years, Cold War theology decreed

The Berlin Wall, a symbol of the Cold War for nearly three decades, separated Communist East Berlin from West Berlin. With the easing of Cold War tensions, "the wall" was torn down in 1989 and Germany itself was reunited under western rule. (Guy Le Querrec/Magnum)

that a gain for one side was by definition a defeat for the other. This notion led logically not to an interest in negotiation but to a demand for capitulation. In retrospect the Cold War, humanity's most intimate brush with collective suicide, can only remind us of the ultimate interdependence of nations and of peoples.

After President Kennedy and Premier Khrushchev stared down the nuclear abyss together in October 1962, they came away determined to move as fast as they could toward détente. Had Kennedy lived, Khrushchev might have held on to power a little longer, and together they would have further subdued the excesses of the Cold War. They rejected the zero-sum approach and understood that intelligent negotiation brings mutual benefit. I am not an unlimited admirer of Ronald Reagan, but he deserves his share of credit for taking Mikhail Gorbachev seriously, abandoning the zero-sum fallacy he had embraced for so long, and moving the Cold War toward its end.

And why indeed has it ended? If the ideological confrontation gave the geopolitical rivalry its religious intensity, so the collapse of the ideological debate took any apocalyptic point out of the Cold War. The proponents of liberal society were proven right. After seventy years of trial, communism turned out—by the confession of its own leaders—to be an economic, political, and moral disaster. Democracy won the political argument between East and West. The market won the economic argument. Difficulties lie ahead, but the fundamental debate that created the Cold War is finished.

QUESTIONS TO CONSIDER

1 What are the six fallacies of judgment and action that aggravated the tensions between East and West after World War II, according to Arthur Schlesinger, and why did the two sides fall into them? What are the overarching lessons Schlesinger would like nations and peoples to learn from the mistakes of the Cold War?

2 Schlesinger says that democracy and the market economy won the Cold War, but do we know for certain what the future holds for the former Soviet Union and for eastern Europe? What do you think are the lasting effects of the Cold War on the United States and our future?

3 What have been the general trends in Cold War historiography? How are historians influenced by the traditions from which they come and the times in which they live? Do you think they may in turn influence those times?

4 As you reflect on Schlesinger's selection, what do you think is the relative influence of general social and political factors and the actions of individuals on the course of history? How have people's perceptions affected subsequent events?

5 Arthur Schlesinger calls himself a "devotee of a cyclical approach to American political history." In your general experience in American history, do you see certain recurring historical themes, trends, or concerns? What might these tell you about the basic principles and character of the American experience?

PART FIFTEEN

From the Technological Revolution to Modern Terrorism

31 Bill Gates: Enigmatic Genius of Microsoft

WALTER ISAACSON

We are living in the midst of a technological revolution whose historical significance has already eclipsed that of the Industrial Revolution. Such technological innovations as television, fax and photocopy machines, communications satellites, cell phones, teleconferencing, telecommuting, and computers with email and Internet capabilities have profoundly altered our lives. The advent of the computer is perhaps the most important technological achievement of all. The computer has made space programs and missile and air-defense systems possible; it has revolutionized the armed services and their weapons of war. It has completely transformed our methods of literary composition, book publishing, and filmmaking. It is the nerve center of governments, economies, educational institutions, and transportation and business operations the world over. The computer and the World Wide Web have helped convert our planet into a community of interconnected and interdependent nations. The computer has changed the way we work, play, think, and speak. Indeed, it has added a new nomenclature (megabyte, software, surf, browser, laptop, user-friendly, RAM) to our vocabulary.

In the last two decades, we have also witnessed a revolution in personal computers (PCs). The leading spirit of the PC revolution is William ("Bill") Henry Gates III, co-founder of Microsoft and the subject of the following selection by Time *writer Walter Isaacson. At age fourteen, Gates established his first company, Traf-o-Data, which sold systems that counted traffic flow; young Gates earned $20,000 from that venture. In 1973, he entered Harvard with plans to become a lawyer. Two years later he dropped out, moved to Albuquerque, New Mexico, and with Paul Allen* *formed Microsoft (Allen soon left the company because of a personality clash with Gates). Microsoft's first important contract, negotiated with the Tandy Corporation, was to create software for its Radio Shack computers. In 1980, now relocated in Seattle, Washington, Microsoft began an association with International Business Machines (IBM), which was starting to build personal computers meant for home use. In the late 1980s, Gates's company introduced the Windows operating system, which provided a "user-friendly" method of operating IBM-compatible computers with a hand-operated "mouse." By the late 1990s, Bill Gates had thoroughly "thrashed competitors in the world of desktop operation systems and application software," so much so that Microsoft had a near monopoly in the field, with a market value of $160 billion. And Microsoft's ruling genius, Bill Gates, was earning $30 million a day, which made him "by far" the richest person and most famous businessman on earth. Says Ann Winblad, a friend and fellow software entrepreneur: "We share our thoughts about the world and ourselves. And we marvel about how, as two young overachievers, we began a great adventure on the fringes of a little-known industry and it landed us at the center of an amazing universe."*

What follows is an intimate portrait of Bill Gates, described by Isaacson as "one of the most important minds and personalities of our era." A plump man in his mid-forties, Gates is something of an enigma. Isaacson says he possesses "an awesome and at times frightening blend of brilliance, drive, competitiveness and personal intensity." Associates describe him in the vocabulary of the computer age: he has "incredible processing power" and "unlimited bandwidth." He is agile at "parallel processing" and "multitasking." The richest person in the world often speaks in youthful slang: a good strategy is "really neat," "supercool," and "hardcore." A bad strategy is "really dumb" and "random to the max." Above all, Gates is fiercely competitive and has cutthroat instincts. Such traits helped him build Microsoft into "a media and Internet behemoth." In sum, Isaacson says, "He has become the Edison and Ford of our age. A technologist turned entrepreneur, he embodies the digital era."

For years, competitors have accused Gates of unfair and even illegal business practices: they claim that he has tried to eliminate competition in desktop operating systems, so that he can dominate everything "from word processing and spreadsheets to Web browsers and content." After investigating Microsoft's operations, the Federal Department of Justice agreed with Gates's critics and brought an antitrust suit against his Microsoft empire. In 2000, a federal court found Microsoft "liable for maintaining an illegal monopoly in personal computer operating systems." Two years later, after an appeal and several court hearings, the United States District Court for the District of Columbia ordered Gates's company to stop specific practices that destroyed competition in the desktop computer market. But the software giant successfully avoided a breakup and also avoided federal government interference in the company's efforts in product development. Insiders regarded this as "a big win" for Microsoft. Like Andrew Carnegie (selection 5) and John D. Rockefeller (selection 8), his innovative and cunning predecessors, Bill Gates continued to thrive, earning enormous profits for himself and giving much of it away in philanthropic donations.

GLOSSARY

ALLEN, PAUL   A boyhood friend of Gates. They met at the exclusive Lakeside School in Seattle and shared an enthusiasm for computers. In 1975, they formed Microsoft. Although the two men remain close, Allen left the new software company because, in Isaacson's words, the personalities of the youthful founders clashed; Allen was a "dreamy visionary" while Gates was the "workaholic code writer and competitor."

BALLMER, STEVE   A former Harvard classmate and friend of Gates who, in 1980, left Procter & Gamble to join the management team at Microsoft.

BUFFETT, WARREN   A multibillionaire Omaha, Nebraska, investor who became close friends with Gates. Although their business interests and areas of expertise are different, both men share an unpretentious style and enjoy each other's company.

MICROSOFT   In 1975, Gates and Allen formed this company to develop computer operating systems. Originally based in Albuquerque, New Mexico, its first big contract was with the Tandy Corporation to create software for Radio Shack computers. In 1980, with the company now in Seattle, Washington, Microsoft began a business relationship with IBM, which was starting to build personal computers. In the late 1980s, Gates introduced the "Windows" operating system, which provided a "user-friendly" way to operate IBM-compatible computers with a hand-held "mouse." By the late 1990s, the stock market valuation of Microsoft was $160 billion. Its dominance of the software market resulted in a federal antitrust suit.

MYHRVOLD, NATHAN   He earned a doctorate in physics from Princeton and managed Microsoft's advanced research group.

SOFTWARE   Computer operating systems such as BASIC, MS-DOS, and Windows. These systems became increasingly easier to understand and apply. Microsoft's versatile Windows product, with its on-screen symbols, dominated the market and overwhelmed competitors such as Apple Computer, with its more expensive Macintosh model.

He's the most famous businessman in the world. Reams have been written about how he dominated the revolution in personal computing and is now poised to turn Microsoft into a media and Internet behemoth. But we know little about him as a person. What beliefs and values drive this man who, as much as anyone, will determine the way we look not only at computers but at ourselves and our world? Here's an intimate look at one of the most important minds and personalities of our era.

When Bill Gates was in the sixth grade, his parents decided he needed counseling. He was at war with his mother Mary, an outgoing woman who harbored the belief that he should do what she told him. She would call him to dinner from his basement bedroom, which she had given up trying to make him clean, and he

wouldn't respond. "What are you doing?" she once demanded over the intercom.

"I'm thinking," he shouted back.

"You're thinking?"

"Yes, Mom, I'm thinking," he said fiercely. "Have you ever tried thinking?"

The psychologist they sent him to "was a really cool guy," Gates recalls. "He gave me books to read after each session, Freud stuff, and I really got into psychology theory." After a year of sessions and a battery of tests, the counselor reached his conclusion. "You're going to lose," he told Mary. "You had better just adjust to it because there's no use trying to beat him." Mary was strong-willed and intelligent herself, her husband recalls, "but she came around to accepting that it was futile trying to compete with him."

A lot of computer companies have concluded the same. In the 21 years since he dropped out of Harvard to start Microsoft, William Henry Gates III, [now 46], has thrashed competitors in the world of desktop operating systems and application software.

Walter Isaacson, "In Search of the Real Bill Gates," *Time,* vol. 149, no. 2 (January 13, 1997), pp. 44–52. © 1997 Time Inc. Reprinted by permission.

Now he is attempting the audacious feat of expanding Microsoft from a software company into a media and content company.

In the process he has amassed a fortune worth (as of last Friday) $23.9 billion. The 88 percent rise in Microsoft stock in 1996 meant he made on paper more than $10.9 billion, or about $30 million a day. That makes him the world's richest person, by far. But he's more than that. He has become the Edison and Ford of our age. A technologist turned entrepreneur, he embodies the digital era.

His success stems from his personality: an awesome and at times frightening blend of brilliance, drive, competitiveness and personal intensity. So too does Microsoft's. "The personality of Bill Gates determines the culture of Microsoft," says his intellectual sidekick Nathan Myhrvold. But though he has become the most famous business celebrity in the world, Gates remains personally elusive to all but a close circle of friends.

Part of what makes him so enigmatic is the nature of his intellect. Wander the Microsoft grounds, press the Bill button in conversation and hear it described in computer terms: he has "incredible processing power" and "unlimited bandwidth," an agility at "parallel processing" and "multitasking." Watch him at his desk, and you see what they mean. He works on two computers, one with four frames that sequence data streaming in from the Internet, the other handling the hundreds of E-mail messages and memos that extend his mind into a network. He can be so rigorous as he processes data that one can imagine his mind may indeed be digital: no sloppy emotions or analog fuzziness, just trillions of binary impulses coolly converting input into correct answers.

"I don't think there's anything unique about human intelligence," Gates says over dinner one night at a nearly deserted Indian restaurant in a strip mall near his office. Even while eating, he seems to be multitasking; ambidextrous, he switches his fork back and forth throughout the meal and uses whichever hand is free to gesture or scribble notes. "All the neurons in the brain that make up perceptions and emotions operate in a binary fashion," he

Bill Gates, shown in this photograph, built Microsoft into a corporate behemoth worth $160 billion. "His success," Isaacson says, "stems from his personality: an awesome and at times frightening blend of brilliance, drive, competitiveness, and personal intensity." His employees at Microsoft describe his intellect in computer terms: "he has 'incredible processing power'" and "unlimited bandwidth, an agility at 'parallel processing' and 'multitasking.'" (©Reuters NewMedia, Inc./Corbis)

explains. "We can someday replicate that on a machine." Earthly life is carbon based, he notes, and computers are silicon based, but that is not a major distinction. "Eventually we'll be able to sequence the human genome and replicate how nature did intelligence in a carbon-based system." The notion, he admits, is a bit frightening, but he jokes that it would also be cheating. "It's like reverse-engineering someone else's product in order to solve a challenge."

Might there be some greater meaning to the universe? When engaged or amused, he is voluble, waving his hands and speaking loudly enough to fill the restaurant. "It's possible, you can never know, that the universe exists only for me." It's a mix of Descartes' metaphysics and Tom Stoppard's humor. "If so," he jokes, "it's sure going well for me, I must admit." He laughs; his eyes sparkle. Here's something machines can't do (I don't think): giggle about their plight in the cosmos, crack themselves up, have fun.

Right? Isn't there something special, perhaps even divine, about the human soul? His face suddenly becomes expressionless, his squeaky voice turns toneless, and he folds his arms across his belly and vigorously rocks back and forth in a mannerism that has become so mimicked at Microsoft that a meeting there can resemble a round table of ecstatic rabbis. Finally, as if from an automaton, comes the answer: "I don't have any evidence on that." Rock, rock, rock. "I don't have any evidence on that."

The search for evidence about the soul that underlies Bill Gates' intellectual operating system is a task that even this boyish man might find a challenge.

"As a baby, he used to rock back and forth in his cradle himself," recalls Gates' father, a man as big and huggable as his son is small and tightly coiled. A retired lawyer, he still lives in the airy suburban Seattle house overlooking Lake Washington where Bill III—the boy he calls "Trey"—grew up. (The name comes from the card term for three, though the father is now resigned to being called Bill Sr.)

His mother Mary was "a remarkable woman." Bill Sr. says. A banker's daughter, she was adroit in both social and business settings, and served on numerous boards, including those of the University of Washington, the United Way, USWest and First Interstate Bancorp. After her death in 1994, the city council named the avenue leading into their neighborhood after her.

"Trey didn't have a lot of confidence in social settings," says his father. "I remember him fretting for two weeks before asking a girl to the prom, then getting turned down. But Mary did. She was a star at social intercourse. She could walk into a room . . ." He has the same toothy smile as his son, the same smudgy glasses covering twinkling eyes. But now, for just a moment, he is starting to tear up. His mind does not seem like a computer. He folds his arms across his stomach and starts to rock, gently.

He gets up to show some more pictures of Mary and of her mother. Both loved cards, and they would organize bridge games, as well as Password and trivia contests, after the big family dinners they held every Sunday. "The play was quite serious," Bill Sr. recalls. "Winning mattered."

As he wanders through the house, he points out more framed pictures of his son: Trey, the towheaded Cub Scout; Trey with sister Kristi, a year older, who now has the joy of being his tax accountant; and with Libby, nine years younger, who lives a few blocks away raising her two kids; with Bill Sr. and his new wife Mimi, the director of the Seattle Art Museum; and hugging his wife Melinda while listening to Willie Nelson play at their New Year's Day 1994 wedding in Hawaii.

"He's a busy guy," says Bill Sr., "so we don't see him a lot, but we spend holidays together." Thanksgiving was in Spokane, Washington, at Kristi's house, Christmas playing golf in Palm Springs, California, where Bill Sr. and Mimi have a place. They communicate mainly by E-mail. Just this morning he got one describing a photocopier Trey bought him for his birthday.

He lumbers over a table where he has gathered some pictures of summer vacations they used to take with friends at a cluster of rental cabins known as Cheerio on the Hood Canal, about two hours away. There were nightly campfires, family skits and the type of organized competitive games the Gates family loved. "On Saturdays there was a tennis tournament, and on Sundays our Olympics, which were a mixture of games and other activities," Bill Sr. recalls. "Trey was more into the individual sports, such as water skiing, than the team ones."

In 1986, after Microsoft became successful, Gates built a four-house vacation compound dubbed Gateaway for his family. There his parents would help him replicate his summer activities on a grander scale for dozens of friends and co-workers in what became known as the Microgames. "There were always a couple of mental games as well as performances and regular games," says Bill Sr. as he flips through a scrapbook. These were no ordinary picnics: one digital version of charades, for example, had teams competing to send numerical messages using smoke-signal machines, in which the winners devised their own 4-bit binary code.

"We became concerned about him when he was ready for junior high," says his father. "He was so small and shy, in need of protection, and his interests were so different from the typical sixth grader's." His intellectual drive and curiosity would not be satisfied in a big public school. So they decided to send him to an elite private school across town.

Walking across the rolling quad of the Lakeside School, Bill Sr. points out the chapel where his son played the lead in Peter Shaffer's Black Comedy. "He was very enthusiastic about acting. But what really entranced him was in there," he says, pointing to a New England-style steepled classroom building. With the proceeds from a rummage sale, the Mothers' Club had funded a clunky teletype computer terminal.

Learning BASIC language from a manual with his pal Paul Allen, Trey produced two programs in the eighth grade: one that converted a number in one mathematical base to a different base, and another (easier to explain) that played tic-tac-toe. Later, having read about Napoleon's military strategies, he devised a computer version of Risk, a board game he liked in which the goal is world domination.

Trey and Paul were soon spending their evenings at a local company that had bought a big computer and didn't have to pay for it until it was debugged. In exchange for computer time, the boys' job was to try (quite successfully) to find bugs that would crash it. "Trey got so into it," his father recalls, "that he would sneak out the basement door after we went to bed and spend most of the night there."

The combination of counseling and the computer helped transform him into a self-assured young businessman. By high school he and his friends had started a profitable company to analyze and graph traffic data for the city. "His confidence increased, and his sense of humor increased," his father says. "He became a great storyteller, who could mimic the voices of each person. And he made peace with his mother."

"In ninth grade," Gates recalls over dinner one night, "I came up with a new form of rebellion. I hadn't been getting good grades, but I decided to get all A's without taking a book home. I didn't go to math class, because I knew enough and had read ahead, and I placed within the top 10 people in the nation on an aptitude exam. That established my independence and taught me I didn't need to rebel anymore." By 10th grade he was teaching computers and writing a program that handled class scheduling, which had a secret function that placed him in classes with the right girls.

His best friend was Kent Evans, son of a Unitarian minister. "We read FORTUNE together; we were going to conquer the world," says Gates. "I still remember his phone number." Together with Paul Allen, they formed the official-sounding Lakeside Programmers Group and got a job writing a payroll system for a local firm. A furious argument, the first of many, ensued when Allen tried to take over the work himself. But he soon realized he needed the tireless Gates back to do the coding. "O.K., but I'm in charge," Gates told him, "and I'll get used to being in charge, and it'll be hard to deal with me from now on unless I'm in charge." He was right.

To relieve the pressures of programming, Evans took up mountain climbing. One day Gates got a call from the headmaster: Evans had been killed in a fall. "I had never thought of people dying," Gates says. There is a flicker of emotion. "At the service, I was supposed to speak, but I couldn't get up. For two weeks I couldn't do anything at all."

After that he became even closer to Paul Allen. They learned an artificial-intelligence language together and found odd jobs as programmers. "We were true partners," Gates says. "We'd talk for hours every day." After Gates went off to Harvard, Allen drove his rattletrap Chrysler cross-country to continue their collaboration. He eventually persuaded Gates to become that university's most famous modern dropout in order to start a software company, which they initially dubbed Micro-Soft (after considering the name Allen & Gates Inc.), to write versions of BASIC for the first personal computers. It was an intense relationship: Gates the workaholic code writer and competitor, Allen the dreamy visionary.

Over the years they would have ferocious fights, and Allen would, after a Hodgkin's disease scare, quit the company and become estranged. But Gates worked hard to repair the relationship and eventually lured Allen, who is now one of the country's biggest high-tech venture-capital investors (and owner of the Portland Trail Blazers), back onto the Microsoft board. "We like to talk about how the fantasies we had as kids actually came true," Gates says. Now, facing their old classroom building at Lakeside is the modern brick Allen/Gates Science Center. (Gates lost the coin toss.)

Steve Ballmer, big and balding, is bouncing around a Microsoft conference room with the spirit of the Harvard football-team manager he once was. "Bill lived down the hall from me at Harvard sophomore year," he says. "He'd play poker until 6 in the morning, then I'd run into him at breakfast and discuss applied mathematics." They took graduate-level math and economics courses together, but Gates had an odd approach toward his classes: he would skip the lectures of those he was taking and audit the lectures of those he wasn't, then spend the period before each exam cramming. "He's the smartest guy I've ever met," says Ballmer, 40, continuing the unbroken sequence of people who make that point early in an interview.

Ballmer nurtured the social side of Gates, getting him to join one of the college's eating clubs (at his initiation Gates gave a drunken disquisition on an artificial-intelligence machine), playing the video game Pong at hamburger joints and later wandering with him to places like the old Studio 54 during visits to New York City. "He was eccentric but charismatic," says Ballmer.

When Microsoft began to grow in 1980, Gates needed a smart nontechie to help run things, and he lured Ballmer, who had worked for Procter & Gamble, to Seattle as an equity partner. Though he can be coldly impersonal in making business decisions, Gates has an emotional loyalty to a few old friends. "I always knew I would have close business associates like Ballmer and several of the other top people at Microsoft, and that we would stick together and grow together no matter what happened," he says. "I didn't know that because of some analysis. I just decided early on that was part of who I was."

As with Allen, the relationship was sometimes stormy. "Our first major row came when I insisted it was time to hire 17 more people," Ballmer recalls. "He claimed I was trying to bankrupt him." Gates has a rule that Microsoft, rather than incurring debt, must always have enough money in the bank to run for a year even with no revenues. (It currently has $8 billion in cash and no long-term debt.) "I was living with him at the time, and I got so pissed off I moved out." The elder Gates smoothed things over, and soon the new employees were hired.

"Bill brings to the company the idea that conflict can be a good thing," says Ballmer. "The difference from P&G is striking. Politeness was at a premium there. Bill knows it's important to avoid that gentle civility that keeps you from getting to the heart of an issue quickly. He likes it when anyone, even a junior employee, challenges him, and you know he respects you when he starts shouting back." Around Microsoft, it's known as the "math camp" mentality: a lot of cocky geeks willing to wave their fingers and yell with the cute conviction that all problems have a right answer. Among Gates' favorite phrases is "That's the stupidest thing I've ever heard," and victims wear it as a badge of honor, bragging about it the way they do about getting a late-night E-mail from him.

The contentious atmosphere can promote flexibility. The Microsoft Network began as a proprietary online system like CompuServe or America Online. When the open standards of the Internet changed the game, Microsoft was initially caught flat-footed. Arguments ensued. Soon it became clear it was time to try a new strategy and raise the stakes. Gates turned his company around in just one year to disprove the maxim that a leader of one revolution will be left behind by the next.

During the bachelor years in the early '80s, the math-camp mentality was accomplished by a frat-boy

Bill Gates and his wife Melinda built this luxurious $97 million home with a 30-car garage on the shores of Lake Washington.

(© Reuters NewMedia, Inc. / Corbis)

recreational style. Gates, Ballmer and friends would eat out at Denny's, go to movies and gather for intellectual games like advanced forms of trivia and Boggle. As friends started getting married, there were bachelor parties involving local strippers and skinny-dipping in Gates' pool. But eventually, after Gates wed, he took up more mature pursuits such as golf. "Bill got into golf in the same addictive way he gets into anything else," says Ballmer. "It gets his competitive juice flowing."

It's a rainy night, and Gates is bombing around in his dark blue Lexus. He loves fast cars. When Microsoft was based in Albuquerque, New Mexico, in its early years, he bought a Porsche 911 and used to race it in the desert; Paul Allen had to bail him out of jail after one midnight escapade. He got three speeding tickets—two from the same cop who was trailing him—just on the drive from Albuquerque the weekend he moved Microsoft to Seattle. Later he bought a Porsche 930 Turbo he called the "rocket," then a Mercedes, a Jaguar XJ6, a $60,000 Carrera Cabriolet 964, a $380,000 Porsche 959 that ended up impounded in a customs shed because it couldn't meet import emission standards, and a Ferrari 348 that became known as the "dune buggy" after he spun it into the sand.

Despite this record, Gates is not wearing a seat belt. (A dilemma: Is it too uncool to use mine?) He rarely looks at you when he talks, which is disconcerting, but he does so when he's driving, which is doubly disconcerting. (I buckle up. As his mother and others have learned, it's not always prudent to compete.) . . .

Gates met Melinda French [his wife] 10 years ago at a Microsoft press event in Manhattan. She was working for the company and later became one of the executives in charge of interactive content. Their daughter Jennifer was born last April. Melinda, 32, is no longer at Microsoft, and she is active in charity work and on the board of Duke, where she studied computer science as an undergraduate and then got a graduate degree in business. Like Gates, she is smart and independent. Like his mother, she is also friendly and social, with an easy manner of organizing trips and activities. But she zealously guards her privacy and doesn't give interviews.

"I used to think I wouldn't be all that interested in the baby until she was two or so and could talk," says Gates as he shows off the more intimate family quarters. "But I'm totally into it now. She's just started to say 'ba-ba' and have a personality."

Melinda is Catholic, goes to church and wants to raise Jennifer that way. "But she offered me a deal," Gates says. "If I start going to church—my family was Congregationalist—then Jennifer could be raised in whatever religion I choose." Gates admits that he is tempted, because he would prefer she have a religion that "has less theology and all" than Catholicism, but he has not yet taken up the offer. "Just in terms of allocation of time resources, religion is not very efficient," he explains. "There's a lot more I could be doing on a Sunday morning."

If Ballmer is Gates' social goad, his intellectual one is Nathan Myhrvold (pronounced Meer-voll), 37, who likes to joke that he's got more degrees than a thermometer, including a doctorate in physics from Princeton. With a fast and exuberant laugh, he has a passion for subjects ranging from technology (he heads Microsoft's advanced-research group) to dinosaurs . . . to cooking. He sometimes moonlights as a chef at Rover's, a French restaurant in Seattle.

When he arrives there for dinner, owner Thierry Rautureau comes out to hug him and pour champagne. There follows a procession of a dozen courses, from black truffles and pureed celery root in smoked game consomme to venison with obscure types of mushrooms, each with different vintage wines. (The bill for two comes to $390, and picking it up assuages my discomfort that Gates had insisted on putting the previous evening's $37 tab at the Indian restaurant on his MasterCard.)

"There are two types of tech companies," Myhrvold says in between pauses to inhale the aroma of the food. "Those where the guy in charge knows how to surf, and those where he depends on experts on the beach to guide him." The key point about Gates is that he knows—indeed loves—the intricacies of creating software. "Every decision he makes is based on his knowledge of the merits. He doesn't need to rely on personal politics. It sets the tone."

Myhrvold describes a typical private session with Gates. Pacing around a room, they will talk for hours about future technologies such as voice recognition (they call their team working on it the "wreck a nice beach" group, because that's what invariably appears on the screen when someone speaks the phrase "recognize speech" into the system), then wander onto topics ranging from quantum physics to genetic engineering. "Bill is not threatened by smart people," he says, "only stupid ones."

Microsoft has long hired based on I.Q. and "intellectual bandwidth." Gates is the undisputed ideal: talking to most people is like sipping from a fountain, goes the saying at the company, but with Gates it's like drinking from a fire hose. Gates, Ballmer and Myhrvold believe it's better to get a brilliant but untrained young brain—they're called "Bill clones"—than someone with too much experience. The interview process tests not what the applicants know but how well they can process tricky questions: If you wanted to figure out how many times on average you would have to flip the pages of the Manhattan phone book to find a specific name, how would you approach the problem?

Gates' intellect is marked by an ability, as he puts it, to "drill down." On a visit to Time Inc.'s new-media facility, he answered questions from a collection of magazine editors as if by rote, but on his way out he asked to see the Internet servers and spent 45 minutes grilling the claque of awed techies there. Broad discussions bore him, he shows little curiosity about other people, and he becomes disengaged when people use small talk to try to establish a personal rapport.

Even after spending a lot of time with him, you get the feeling that he knows much about your thinking but nothing about such things as where you live or if you have a family. Or that he cares.

In that regard he is the opposite of, say, Bill Clinton, who brackets the other end of the baby boom: Gates analytically rigorous and emotionally reserved, the President equally smart but intellectually undisciplined and readily intimate. They played golf on Martha's Vineyard once, and the President, as usual, worked hard at bonding emotionally and being personally charming and intimate. He expressed sorrow about the death of Gates' mother, shared the pain of the recent death of his own mother and gave golfing tips to Melinda. But Gates noticed that Clinton never bore in or showed rigorous curiosity about technological issues. Though he vaguely considers himself a Democrat, Gates stayed neutral in the presidential election.

Warren Buffett, the Omaha, Nebraska, investor whom Gates demoted to being merely the second richest American, seems an unlikely person to be among his closest pals. A jovial, outgoing 66-year-old grandfather, Buffett only recently learned to use a computer. But as multibillionaires go, both are unpretentious, and they enjoy taking vacations together. Buffett's secretary apologetically explains that Buffett isn't giving interviews these days and at the moment is traveling, but she promises to pass along the request. Less than three hours later, Buffett calls to say he happens to be in the Time & Life Building with some free time between meetings in Manhattan, and he would be happy to come by to be interviewed. He likes to talk about Gates. . . .

When Gates decided to propose to Melinda in 1993, he secretly diverted the chartered plane they were taking home from Palm Springs one Sunday night to land in Omaha. There Buffett met them, arranged to open a jewelry store that he owned and helped them pick a ring. That year Gates made a movie for Buffett's birthday. It featured Gates pretending to wander the country in search of tales about Buffett and calling Melinda with them from pay phones. After each call, Gates is shown checking the coin slot for loose change. When she mentions that Buffett is only the country's second richest man, he informs her that on the new Forbes list Buffett had (at least that one year) regained the top spot. The phone suddenly goes dead. "Melinda, Melinda," Gates sputters, "you still there? Hello?"

Last October Gates brought Melinda and their new daughter to visit Buffett and his wife in San Francisco. They ended up playing bridge for nine hours straight. Another marathon session in Seattle started in the morning and lasted—with a break for Melinda to pick up lunch at Burger King—until guests started arriving for dinner. "He loves games that involve problem solving," Buffett says. "I showed him a set of four dice with numbers arranged in a complex way so that any one of them would on average beat one of the others. He was one of three people I ever showed them to who figured this out and saw the way to win was to make me choose first which one I'd roll." (For math buffs: the dice were nontransitive. One of the others who figured it out was the logician Saul Kripke.) . . .

Another of Gates' vacation companions is Ann Winblad, the software entrepreneur and venture capitalist he dated during the 1980s. They met in 1984 at a Ben Rosen–Esther Dyson computer conference and started going on "virtual dates" by driving to the same movie at the same time in different cities and discussing it on their cell phones. For a few years she even persuaded him to stop eating meat, an experiment he has since resolutely abandoned.

They were kindred minds as well as spirits. On a vacation to Brazil, he took James Watson's 1,100-page textbook, *Molecular Biology of the Gene,* and they studied bioengineering together. On another vacation, to a Santa Barbara, California, ranch, she took tapes of Richard Feynman's lectures at Cornell, and they studied physics. And on a larger excursion with friends to central Africa, which ended at some beach cottages on an island off Zanzibar, among their companions was anthropologist Donald Johanson, known for his work on the human ancestor Lucy, who helped teach them about human evolution. In the evenings on each trip they would go to the beach with four or five other couples for bonfires, Hood Canal-style games and a tradition they called the sing-down, where each team is given a word and has to come up with songs that feature it. Winblad remembers Gates disappearing on a dark beach after his group had been given the word *sea,* and then slowly emerging from the mist singing a high-pitched solo of *Puff, the Magic Dragon.*

They broke up in 1987, partly because Winblad, five years older, was more ready for marriage. But they remain close friends. "When I was off on my own thinking about marrying Melinda," Gates says, "I called Ann and asked for her approval." She gave it. "I said she'd be a good match for him because she had intellectual stamina." Even now, Gates has an arrangement with his wife that he and Winblad can keep one vacation tradition alive. Every spring, as they have for more than a decade, Gates spends a long weekend with Winblad at her beach cottage on the Outer Banks of North Carolina, where they ride dune buggies, hang-glide and walk on the beach. "We can play putt-putt while discussing biotechnology," Gates says. Winblad puts it more grandly. "We share our thoughts about the world and ourselves," she says. "And we marvel about how, as two young overachievers, we began a great adventure on the fringes of a little-known industry and it landed us at the center of an amazing universe."

After a recent whirl of travel that included a speech in Las Vegas and a meeting in Switzerland, Gates detoured to a secluded resort in New York's Adirondacks to spend a weekend with Melinda and Jennifer. There they played with 1,000-piece jigsaw puzzles from a craftsman in Vermont who makes them for customers like Gates. Melinda has helped broaden her husband. Instead of studying biotechnology together, they find time to take singing lessons.

Gates is ambivalent about his celebrity. Although he believes that fame tends to be "very corrupting," he is comfortable as a public figure and as the personification of the company he built. Like Buffett, he remains unaffected, wandering Manhattan and Seattle without an entourage or driver. Nestled into a banquette one Sunday night at 44, a fashionable Manhattan restaurant, he is talking volubly when another diner approaches. Gates pulls inward, used to people who want his autograph or to share some notion about computers. But the diner doesn't recognize him and instead asks him to keep his voice down. Gates apologizes sheepishly. He seems pleased to be regarded as a boyish cutup rather than a celebrity.

The phone in Gates' office almost never rings. Nor do phones seem to ring much anywhere on the suburban Microsoft "campus," a cluster of 35 low-rise buildings, lawns, white pines and courtyards that resemble those of a state polytechnic college. Gates runs his company mainly through three methods: he bats out a hundred or more E-mail messages a day (and night), often chuckling as he dispatches them; he meets every month or so with a top management group that is still informally known as the boop (Bill and the Office of the President); and most important, taking up 70 percent of his schedule by his own calculation, he holds two or three small review meetings a day with a procession of teams working on the company's various products.

There is a relaxed, nonhierarchical atmosphere as the seven young managers of the "WebDVD" group, all in the standard winter uniform of khakis and flannel shirts, gather in a windowless conference room near Gates' office. They have been working for almost a year on a digital videodisc intended to provide content along with Web browsing for television sets, and he wants to review their progress before leaving for Japan, where he will meet with such potential partners as Toshiba.

Craig Mundy, the veteran Microsoft exec who oversees all noncomputer consumer products, lets the younger team members lead the discussion. Gates quickly flips ahead through the deck of papers and within minutes has the gist of their report. He starts rocking, peppering them with questions that segue from the politics of their potential partners, the details of the technology, the potential competition and the broad strategy. The answers are crisp, even as Gates drills down into arcane details. No one seems to be showing off or competing for attention, but neither do any hesitate to speak up or challenge

Gates. To a man (and they all are), they rock when they think.

"Does this allow scripting in HTML?" he asks, referring to the authoring language used to create Websites. They explain how. He challenges them about why it requires four megabytes of memory. They explain; he drills down more; they finally prevail. There is an intense discussion of layers, sectors, modes, error corrections and mpeg-2 video-compression standards. "Our basic strategy must be processor agnostic," Gates decrees. Everyone nods. Then he shifts without missing a beat to corporate tactics. "Are we going to get Philips and other manufacturers and the moviemakers to agree on a standard?" We'll get to that in a minute, he's told. He wants to get to it now. There is a rapid discussion of the internal politics of Philips, Sony, Time Warner (the corporate parent of this magazine), Matsushita and Toshiba, along with their respective Hollywood alliances.

Gates doesn't address anyone by name, hand out praise or stoke any egos. But he listens intently, democratically. His famous temper is in check, even when he disagrees with someone's analysis of the DVD's capability to handle something called layering. "Educate me on that," he says in challenging the analysis, and after a minute or so cuts off the discussion by saying, "Send me the specs."

Gates does not hide his cutthroat instincts. "The competitive landscape here is strange, ranging from Navio to even WebTV," he says. He is particularly focused on Navio, a consumer-software consortium recently launched by Netscape and others designed to make sure that Windows and Windows CE (its consumer-electronics cousin) do not become the standard for interactive television and game machines. "I want to put something in our product that's hard for Navio to do. What are their plans?" The group admits that their intelligence on Navio is poor. Gates rocks harder. "You have to pick someone in your group," he tells Mundy, "whose task it is it to track Navio full time. They're the ones I worry about. Sega is an investor. They may be willing to feed us info." Then he moves on to other competitors. "What about the Planet TV guys?" Mundy explains that they are focusing on video games, "a platform we haven't prioritized." Gates counters: "We can work with them now, but they have other ambitions. So we'll be competitive with them down the line."

Though the videodisc is not at the core of Microsoft's business, this is a competition Gates plans to win. The group argues that the $10-per-unit royalty is too low. "Why charge more?" he asks. They explain that it will be hard to make a profit at $10, given what they are putting in. Gates turns stern. They are missing the big picture. "Our whole relationship with the consumer-electronic guys hangs in the balance," he declares. "We can get wiped." Only the paranoid survive. "The strategic goal here is getting Windows CE standards into every device we can. We don't have to make money over the next few years. We didn't make money on ms-dos in its first release. If you can get into this market at $10, take it." They nod.

His mother may have come to terms with this competitive intensity, but much of the computer world has not. There are Websites dedicated to reviling him, law firms focused on foiling him and former friends who sputter at the mention of his name. Companies such as Netscape, Oracle and Sun Microsystems publicly make thwarting his "plan for world domination" into a holy crusade.

The criticism is not just that he is successful but that he has tried to leverage, unfairly and perhaps illegally, Microsoft's near monopoly in desktop operating systems in ways that would let him dominate everything from word processing and spreadsheets to Web browsers and content. The company is integrating its Internet Explorer browser and Microsoft Network content into its Windows operating system, a process that will culminate with the "Active Desktop" planned for Windows 97, due out in a few months. Critics see a pattern of Microsoft's playing hardball to make life difficult for competing operating systems and applications: Microsoft Word has been buggy on Macintosh operating systems, users have found it tricky to make Netscape their default browser when going back and forth from Windows to the Microsoft Network, and application developers have complained that they don't get the full specs for new releases of Windows as quickly as Microsoft's own developers do.

"They are trying to use an existing monopoly to retard introduction of new technology," says Gary Reback, the Silicon Valley antitrust lawyer representing Netscape and other Microsoft competitors. The stakes are much higher than whose Web browser wins. Netscape is enhancing its browser to serve as a platform to run applications. "In other words," says Reback, "if Netscape is successful, you won't need Windows or a Microsoft operating system anymore." On the other hand, if Microsoft is allowed to embed its Web browser into its operating system in a manner that maintains its monopoly, Reback warns, "where will it stop? They'll go on to bundle in content, their Microsoft Network, financial transactions, travel services, everything. They have a game plan to monopolize every market they touch."

Gates makes no apologies. "Any operating system without a browser is going to be f——— out of business," he says. "Should we improve our product, or go out of business?" Later, on his trip to Japan, he returns to the subject in a two-page E-mail. "Customers are benefiting here in the same way they benefited from graphical interfaces, multitasking, compressions and dozens of other things," he writes. "If improving a product based on customer input is willful maintenance of trying to stay in business and not have Netscape turn their browser into the most popular operating system, then I think that is what we are supposed to do."

Though the stakes are clear, the law (which was developed in the era of railway barons) is not. After deadlocking, the Federal Trade Commission in 1993 surrendered jurisdiction over Microsoft to the Justice Department. FTC Commissioner Christine Varney, an expert in the field, says it's hard to apply antitrust law in a fluid situation. "My concern is with the law's ability to keep pace with market conditions in fields that change so rapidly," she says. "Once it's clear a practice is anticompetitive, the issue may already be moot."

Longtime competitors raise a more philosophical issue about Gates: his intensely competitive approach has poisoned the collaborative hacker ethos of the early days of personal computing. In his book *Startup*, Jerry Kaplan describes creating a handwriting-based system. Gates was initially friendly, he writes, and Kaplan trusted him with his plans, but he eventually felt betrayed when Gates announced a similar, competing product. Rob Glaser, a former Microsoft executive who now runs the company that makes RealAudio, an Internet sound system, is an admirer who compliments Gates on his vision. But, he adds, Gates is "pretty relentless. He's Darwinian. He doesn't look for win-win situations with others, but for ways to make others lose. Success is defined as flattening the competition, not creating excellence." When he was at Microsoft, for example, Glaser says the "atmosphere was like a Machiavellian poker game where you'd hide things even if it would blindside people you were supposed to be working with."

It comes down to the same traits that his psychologist noted when Gates was in sixth grade. "In Bill's eyes," says Glaser, "he's still a kid with a startup who's afraid he'll go out of business if he lets anyone compete." Esther Dyson, whose newsletter and conferences make her one of the industry's fabled gurus, is another longtime friend and admirer who shares such qualms. "He never really grew up in terms of social responsibility and relationships with other people," she says. "He's brilliant but still childlike. He can be a fun companion, but he can lack human empathy." "If we weren't so ruthless, we'd be making more creative software? We'd rather kill a competitor than grow the market?!?" Gates is pacing around his office, sarcastically repeating the charges against him. "Those are clear lies," he says coldly. "Who grew this market? We did. Who survived companies like IBM, 10 times our size, taking us on?" He ticks off the names of his rivals at Oracle, Sun, Lotus, Netscape in an impersonal way. "They're every bit as competitive as I am."

"We win because we hire the smartest people. We improve our products based on feedback, until they're the best. We have retreats each year where we think about where the world is heading." He won't even cop a plea to the charge that Microsoft tends to react to competitors' ideas—the graphical interface of Apple, the Web browser of Netscape—more than it blazes new trails of its own. "Graphical interfaces were done first at Xerox, not Apple. We bet on them early on, which is why Microsoft Office applications became the best."

Gates is enjoying this. Intellectual challenges are fun. Games are fun. Puzzles are fun. Working with smart people is superfun. Others may see him as ruthless, cold or brutal; but for him the competition is like a sport, a blood sport perhaps, but one played with the same relish as the summer games at Hood Canal. He sprawls on a couch, uncoils and pops open a Fresca. Though rarely attempting the social warmth of his mother (he doesn't actually offer me a Fresca but acquiesces when I ask), Gates has an intensity and enthusiasm that can be engaging, even charming. He takes a piece of paper and draws the matrix of strategies he faced when creating applications to compete with WordPerfect and Lotus. See what an exciting puzzle it was? His language is boyish rather than belligerent. The right stuff is "really neat" and "supercool" and "hardcore," while bad strategies are "crummy" and "really dumb" and "random to the max."

His office is rather modest, sparsely decorated and filled with standard-issue furniture. The biggest piece of art is a huge photo of a Pentium processor chip. There are smaller pictures of Einstein, Leonardo da Vinci and Henry Ford, though he admits that he has little admiration for the latter. The few personal pictures include one of the original dozen Microsoft employees (most with scruffy beards, except him), one of Ann Winblad on a trip to Germany, and one with Melinda and nine friends on a 1995 vacation to Indonesia. There are no pictures of Jennifer displayed, but he pulls a snapshot out of his desk showing him proudly cradling her.

He hopes to be running Microsoft for another 10 years, he says, then promises to focus as intensely on giving his money away. He says he plans to leave his children about $10 million each. "He will spend time, at some point, thinking about the impact his philanthropy can have," Buffett says. "He is too imaginative to just do conventional gifts." Already he's given $34 million to the University of Washington, partly to fund a chair for human genome-project researcher Leroy Hood; $15 million (along with $10 million from Ballmer) for a new computer center at Harvard; and $6 million to Stanford. An additional $200 million is in a foundation run by his father, and he has talked about taking over personally the funding of Microsoft's program to provide computers to inner-city libraries, to which he's donated $3 million in book royalties. "I've been pushing him gently to think more about philanthropy," his father says. "I think his charitable interests will run, as they do now, to schools and libraries."

Asked about his regrets, Gates talks about not getting a Microsoft E-mail application to the market quickly enough. "We were too busy, and at a retreat where I wrote our next priorities on a board, everyone said I had to take one off, so we took off E-mail."

It is hard to get him to delve more personally. But especially since Jennifer's birth, friends say, he has begun to reflect more on his life and what he might end up contributing. He speaks of the promise of computing, not just in business terms but in social ones. "Everyone starts out really capable," he says. "But as you grow and turn curious, either you get positive feedback by finding answers or you don't, and then this incredible potential you have is discouraged. I was lucky. I always had a family and resources to get more and more answers. Digital tools will allow a lot more people to keep going the next step rather than hitting a wall where people stop giving them information or tell them to stop asking questions."

He has also become less enamored with pure intelligence. "I don't think that I.Q. is as fungible as I used to," he says. "To succeed, you also have to know how to make choices and how to think more broadly."

So has family life dulled Gates' intensity? "Well, predictably, he's pumped and focused on Jennifer," says Ballmer. "He showed a picture of her at our last sales conference and joked that there was something other than Netscape keeping him awake at nights. He may be a bit less exhausting and a bit more civil.

But he still pushes as hard, still keeps score." Gates likes repeating Michael Jordan's mantra—"They think I'm through, they think I'm through"—and the one Intel's CEO Andrew Grove used as a book title, "Only the paranoid survive." As Ballmer says, "He still feels he must run scared." Gates puts another spin on it: "I still feel this is superfun."

And what about his feeling that there is nothing unique about the human mind, that intelligence can someday be replicated in binary code? Has watching a daughter learn to smile at a father's face changed that at all? At our last meeting, these questions don't seem to engage him. As I wander out of his office, he offers none of life's standard see-you-again-someday pleasantries, but he agrees that I should feel free to E-mail him. So I pose the questions, along with some more mundane technical ones, in a message a few days later. Answers to the tech issues come promptly. But he ignores the philosophical ones. Finally, weeks later, a note pops up in my mailbox, dispatched from storm-swept Seattle:

Analytically, I would say nature has done a good job making child raising more pleasure than pain, since that is necessary for a species to survive. But the experience goes beyond analytic description. . . . Evolution is many orders of magnitude ahead of mankind today in creating a complex system. I don't think it's irreconcilable to say we will understand the human mind someday and explain it in software-like terms, and also to say it is a creation that shouldn't be compared to software. Religion has come around to the view that even things that can be explained scientifically can have an underlying purpose that goes beyond the science. Even though I am not religious, the amazement and wonder I have about the human mind is closer to religious awe than dispassionate analysis.

QUESTIONS TO CONSIDER

1 Explain how the technological revolution has changed your lives. Make your own list of how it has profoundly transformed our world. Do you agree that the technological revolution has eclipsed the Industrial Revolution in historical significance?

2 Compare Bill Gates to earlier portraits in this volume of Andrew Carnegie and Henry Ford. Do you agree with Isaacson that Gates "has become the Edison and Ford of our age"? Does Gates possess the "cutthroat instinct" that made those previous business leaders a threat to their competitors? On the more positive side, has Gates, like those earlier entrepreneurs, attempted to give something back to society and to those people less fortunate than himself?

3 How would you describe Gates's personality, work habits, and intellectual curiosity? Does he seem more interested in other people or in himself? Is religion an important force in his life? Why did he and fellow baby boomer Bill Clinton fail to develop a close relationship on their golf outing?

4 Do you think that we can better understand Gates by examining his youth and family background? Gates's father maintained that "winning mattered" even in family games after Sunday dinner. What influence did this have on young Gates? As a boy, was Gates more interested in team or individual sports?

5 Why does Microsoft prefer to hire people based on their intelligence rather than their experience? In what ways does the work environment at Microsoft reflect its founder's personality? How would you describe Gates's management style and his relationship with his employees?

6 Although this selection originally appeared in *Time* before the federal government's antitrust action against Microsoft, what evidence does Isaacson provide to suggest that Gates "tried to leverage, unfairly and perhaps illegally, Microsoft's near monopoly in desktop operating systems"? Does Gates encourage cooperation among his employees at Microsoft? Does he encourage an environment there that rewards an open sharing of information?

32 The Lessons of September 11

JOHN LEWIS GADDIS

"Good of an unpredictable sort can come out of evil."

PAULINE MAIER

Americans of the current generation will never forget the September 11, 2001, terrorist attacks on the twin towers of the World Trade Center in New York City and the Pentagon near Washington, D.C. As President Roosevelt said of Pearl Harbor, September 11 is "a date which will live in infamy." For the rest of our lives, we will remember the scenes of unbelievable horror flickering on our television screens—scenes that were played over and over again that day. The TV cameras first showed one of the Trade Center towers with a gaping hole in it—caused, we initially thought, when a passenger jet accidentally crashed into it. But soon another jet airliner appeared at the corner of our TV screens, suddenly veered, and crashed into the second tower in an explosion of flame and smoke. Then, one by one, the great buildings collapsed, sending enormous clouds of dust, ash, and debris boiling through the streets and engulfing people who were running for their lives. What remained of the twin towers, once masterpieces of modern architecture, engineering, and construction, were mountains of smoldering rubble with an untold number of victims trapped inside. When the TV cameras swept the New York City skyline, there was a huge, haunting hole where the twin towers had once stood.

Thanks to television, we also saw the terrible damage caused by another passenger jet when it crashed into the Pentagon. We soon learned that the three jet airliners, with passengers on board, had been hijacked by Muslim terrorists from the Middle East, who turned the planes into guided missiles. A fourth hijacked airliner, heading for Washington (probably to hit the White House or the Capitol), crashed in Pennsylvania. Investigators believe that some heroic passengers wrested control of the aircraft from the terrorists and crashed the plane in order to thwart their murderous objective.

The strikes against the Pentagon and the World Trade Center were the worst hostile acts by foreign terrorists ever carried out on United States soil. Officials estimate that the attacks killed more than 3,000 people—the exact total may never be known—and wounded and maimed a great many more.

The events of September 11 have forever marked our generation, just as Pearl Harbor marked an earlier generation. Those murderous acts unified the country as no events had done in more than a generation. The inspirational leadership of Mayor Rudolph Giuliani of New York City brought us even closer together. So did the courage and sacrifice of the New York City firefighters and police, many of whom were killed when the towers collapsed. The country gave President George W. Bush an extraordinarily high approval rating when he vowed to bring the guilty parties to justice and to battle terrorists wherever they could be found. He called it "the first war of the twenty-first century."

When American intelligence identified Osama bin Laden and his al-Qaeda terrorist network, based in Afghanistan, as the culprits, President Bush acted swiftly. By his orders, American air and ground forces invaded Afghanistan, vanquished the brutal Taliban regime that had harbored the terrorists, obliterated al-Qaeda training camps, killed countless numbers of al-Qaeda and Taliban fighters, and drove the survivors into mountain hideouts. The vast majority of Americans resolutely supported the war and President Bush's handling of it.

In March, 2003, Bush expanded his war on terrorism by sending American forces to conquer Iraq and depose its dictator, Saddam Hussein. They and their British allies swiftly accomplished that mission in a stunning display of military power. Bush contended that he had to overthrow Saddam Hussein by force of arms, because the president believed that the Iraqi dictator had ties with al-Qaeda terrorists and was secretly developing weapons of mass destruction. Bush never produced evidence that Saddam Hussein had any connections with al-Qaeda terrorists. Nor did American troops ever discover any weapons of mass destruction or the facilities for producing them. Two years later, a commission appointed by the President investigated U.S. intelligence briefings, on which Bush had based his decision to make war on Iraq. The commission's lengthy report concluded that the briefings were "dead wrong" in most of their pre-war assessments of Iraq's arsenal. If the report distressed Bush, he showed no signs of it in public. In fact, he announced that he was implementing some of the commission's recommendations, which included expanding the authority of the newly created director of national intelligence, reorganizing the FBI, and establishing "a directorate of human intelligence based at the CIA."

In the meantime, American troops did capture Saddam Hussein, thus ridding both Iraq and the world of a monstrous tyrant. American and British occupation soldiers went on to supervise free elections of public officials in Iraq, in an effort to convert that long-oppressed country into a democracy. But as this volume goes to press, fighting still rages in Iraq, with pro-Hussein insurgents battling the Americans and British in a perplexing guerrilla war.

Meanwhile, in the aftermath of September 11, Americans across the country were frightened and insecure, all the more so when administration officials warned us to expect further terrorist acts on United States soil. "It's still America the beautiful," said Tom Brokaw of NBC, "but now it is also America the vulnerable, and it will take another great generation to bind up the wounds." The attacks of September 11 were so overwhelming, so unspeakably evil, that they still defy comprehension. How do we find meaning in that cataclysmic day? How did it happen? What does it portend for the future? Can history help us understand it?

In the following selection, John Lewis Gaddis, an expert on the history of foreign policy, discusses the lessons of September 11 from a historical perspective. Focusing on the post–Cold War decade, he explains how the failures and shortcomings of American foreign policy created anti-American feelings in much of the world. Washington officials, in particular, were too insensitive to the fact that American power and wealth "were being blamed" for the inequities caused by the globalization of capitalism. He warns us that September 11 was a historic turning point, thrusting us into a new era that is "bound to be more painful than the one we've just left."

Gaddis believes—and the editors of Portrait of America *agree—that a knowledge of history can ease our fears and help us endure the difficult days ahead. As Civil War historian James M. McPherson reminds us, the United States has been tested many times in the past and has "emerged from the trauma stronger and better than before." Historian Pauline Maier finds a lesson in the American Revolution that speaks to us across the centuries. "Americans joined arms and became a nation in the wake of an outside attack. Good of an unpredictable sort can come out of evil."*

GLOSSARY

BIN LADEN, OSAMA The son of a Saudi Arabian billionaire and an extremely wealthy man in his own right, bin Laden created an international terrorist network with bases in Afghanistan. He was responsible for the September 11 terrorist attacks on the Untied States. His hatred for America stems, in part, from the presence of United States troops in Saudi Arabia, where his family fortune was acquired and where the Muslim holy cities of Mecca and Medina are located.

BUSH, GEORGE W.   The former Texas governor and son of the forty-first president, he narrowly defeated Al Gore in the presidential election of 2000. He showed courage and leadership following the terrorist attacks of September 11 and rallied the American people behind what he called "the first war of the twenty-first century."

GLOBALIZATION   The movement toward universally accepted concepts and values that are a product, in part, of mass communication, interdependent economies, and a common cyberspace vocabulary that diminishes the importance of the borders between nations.

HUSSEIN, SADDAM   Iraq's dictator who in 1990 invaded neighboring Kuwait. That action resulted in the Persian Gulf War between Iraq and an international coalition led by the United States. Although the coalition drove Iraqi troops out of Kuwait, inflicting terrible losses in men and equipment, it left Saddam Hussein in power.

MARSHALL PLAN   Also known as the European Recovery Program, it was the brainchild of George C. Marshall, Truman's second secretary of state (1947–1949) and former army chief of staff. The program distributed $12 billion in American aid that helped rebuild war-ravaged western Europe.

MARX, KARL   He and Friedrich Engels wrote the *Communist Manifesto* (1848), which predicted the fall of capitalism and the creation of a workers' state that would control the means of production.

McCARTHYISM   A term that cartoonist Herbert Block ("Herblock") coined to describe the demagogic behavior of Senator Joseph R. McCarthy of Wisconsin and the anti-Communist fervor that plagued the United States in the 1950s.

MILOSEVIC, SLOBODAN   The brutal leader of Serbia whose terror-driven regime resulted in the murder of thousands of Bosnian Muslims and Croatians. This so-called ethnic cleansing forced NATO to intervene to ease tensions and prevent Milosevic from killing yet more innocent victims. Although eventually deposed and later imprisoned for his crimes, the Serbian president remained an awful reminder of the ethnic and religious hatreds that had long plagued the Balkans. He died of a heart attack in his cell in March 2006.

NORTH ATLANTIC TREATY ORGANIZATION (NATO)   Organized in 1949, NATO was a collective security agreement to protect the West from Soviet aggression. Part of the containment strategy that President Truman devised following World War II, NATO committed the United States to the defense of member nations that faced an "armed attack." The first countries to commit to NATO were Belgium, Canada, Denmark, France, Great Britain, Iceland, Italy, Luxembourg, the Netherlands, Norway, Portugal, and the United States.

RWANDA   Horrible famine and disease, a product of a vicious civil war, struck this poverty-ravaged nation in central Africa. In the summer of 1994, the Clinton administration offered humanitarian aid but refused to intervene in Rwanda, where political tension had produced one million refugees. Gaddis concludes that "we responded to the greatest atrocities of the decade by simply averting our eyes."

SMITH, ADAM (1723–1790)   An Enlightenment thinker who believed in *laissez-faire* economics that would allow individuals free access to world markets. He felt that tariffs and trade monopolies were destructive and that governments should not hinder private enterprise.

SOMALIA   Factional tension and hunger, the result of severe droughts, plagued this small African nation bordering the Indian Ocean. At first, the United States supported the relief efforts of the United Nations and sent troops to Somalia to help capture a recalcitrant warlord. But when, in the summer of 1993, guerrillas killed twelve American soldiers, President Clinton withdrew the American troops. Gaddis believes that "our reluctance to take casualties of our own revealed how little we were prepared to sacrifice for the rights of others."

UNILATERALISM   A foreign policy based on national self-interest that often ignores the concerns and insecurities of other nations. Gaddis argues that this was a failure of American diplomacy in the post–Cold War years. "We seemed to have assumed, perhaps because we were the greatest of the great powers, that we no longer needed the cooperation of the others to promote our interests."

UNITED STATES COMMISSION ON NATIONAL SECURITY IN THE 21ST CENTURY   Six months before the terrorist attacks on New York City and Washington, this commission and its chairpersons, Gary Hart and Warren Rudman, warned of the need for "homeland" security.

WARSAW PACT   Created in May 1955 in response to NATO, this was a Soviet-dominated alliance of the nations of eastern Europe. It collapsed after the end of the Cold War.

W e've never had a good name for it, and now it's over. The post–cold war era—let us call it that for want of any better term—began with the collapse of one structure, the Berlin Wall on November 9, 1989, and ended with the collapse of another, the World Trade Center's twin towers on September 11, 2001. No one, apart from the few people who plotted and carried out these events, could have anticipated that they were going to happen. But from the moment they did happen, everyone acknowledged that everything had changed.

It's characteristic of such turning points that they shed more light on the history that preceded them than on what's to come. The fall of the Berlin Wall didn't tell us much about the post–cold war world, but it told us a lot about the cold war. It suddenly became clear that East Germany, the Warsaw Pact, and the Soviet Union itself had long since lost the authority with which the U.S. and its NATO allies had continued to credit them right up to the day the wall came down. The whole history of the cold war looked different as a result. Having witnessed the end, historians could never again see the middle, or even the beginning, as they once had.

Something similar seems likely to happen now to the post–cold war era. For whatever we eventually settle on calling the events of September 11—the Attack on America, Black Tuesday, 9/11—they've already forced a reconsideration, not only of where we are as a nation and where we may be going, but also of where we've been, even of who we are. Our recent past, all at once, has been thrown into sharp relief, even as our future remains obscure. To paraphrase an old prayer, it's obvious now that we have done some things which we ought not to have done, and that we have not done other things which we ought to have done. How much health there is in us

John Lewis Gaddis, "And Now This: Lessons from the Old Era to the New One," from *The Age of Terror* by Strobe Talbott. Copyright © 2001 by Strobe Talbott and Nayan Chanda. Reprinted by permission of Basic Books, a member of Perseus Books, L.L.C.

will depend, to a considerable degree, on how we sort this out.

1.

But first things first. No acts of commission or omission by the U.S. can have justified what happened on September 11. Few if any moral standards have deeper roots than the prohibition against taking innocent life in peacetime. Whatever differences may exist in culture, religion, race, class, or any of the other categories by which human beings seek to establish their identities, this rule transcends them.

The September 11 attacks violated it in ways that go well beyond all other terrorist attacks in the past: first by the absence of any stated cause to be served; second by the failure to provide warning; and finally by the obvious intent to time and configure the attack in such a manner as to take as many lives as possible—even to the point, some have suggested, of the airplanes' angle of approach, which seemed calculated to devastate as many floors of the twin towers as they could. Let there be no mistake: this was evil, and no set of grievances real or imagined, however strongly felt or widely held, can excuse it.

At the same time, though, neither our outrage nor the patriotic unity that is arising from it relieves us of the obligation to think critically. Would anyone claim, in the aftermath of September 11, that the U.S. can continue the policies it was following with respect to its national defense or toward the world before September 11? Americans were not *responsible* for what happened at Pearl Harbor; but they would have been *irresponsible* in the extreme if they had not, as a consequence of that attack, dramatically altered their policies. Nobody—given the opportunity to rerun the events leading up to that catastrophe—would have handled things again in just the same way.

It's in that spirit, I think, that we need a reconsideration of how the U.S. has managed its responsibilities in the decade since the cold war ended, not with a view to assigning blame, indulging in recrimination, or wallowing in self-pity, but rather for the purpose—now urgent—of determining where we go from here. Patriotism demands nothing less.

—————

2.

The clearest conclusion to emerge from the events of September 11 is that *the geographical position and the military power of the U.S. are no longer sufficient to ensure its security.*

Americans have known insecurity before in their homeland, but not for a very long time. Except for Pearl Harbor and a few isolated pinpricks like Japanese attempts to start forest fires with incendiary bombs in the Pacific Northwest in 1942, or the Mexican guerrilla leader Pancho Villa's raid on Columbus, New Mexico, in 1916, the U.S. has suffered no foreign attack on its soil since British troops captured Washington and burned the White House and the Capitol in 1814. There's a macabre symmetry in the possibility that the fourth plane hijacked on September 11—which crashed presumably after an uprising among the passengers—probably had one of these buildings as its target.

Few other nations have worried so little for so long about what is coming to be called "homeland security." The late Yale historian C. Vann Woodward even went so far as to define this lack of concern as a central feature of the American character. "Free security," he insisted, had done as much to shape Americans' view of themselves as had the availability of free, or almost free, land.

The 20th century, to be sure, eroded that sense of safety, but this happened as a result of the larger role the U.S. had assigned itself in world affairs, together with ominous shifts in the European balance of power. It did not arise from any sense of domestic insecurity. We entered World War I to ensure that Germany did not wind up dominating Europe, and we were preparing to do the same thing again in World War II when the Japanese attack, followed by Hitler's own declaration of war, removed any choice in the matter from us.

Even so, the continental U.S. remained secure throughout the long and bloody conflict that followed. Neither the Germans nor the Japanese could bomb our cities or occupy our territory, as we eventually would do to them. And despite the incarceration of some 120,000 Japanese Americans during the war, the only significant fifth-column network operating within the U.S. at the time was that of an ally, the Soviet Union—a fact not discovered until after the war had ended. The world might be unsafe, but homeland security could be taken for granted almost as easily during the total wars of the 20th century as it had been throughout most of the 19th century.

The cold war made the American homeland seem less secure in two ways: when spies working on behalf of the Soviet Union were shown to have betrayed the country; and as the prospect arose that Soviet long-range bombers and later intercontinental ballistic missiles might soon be capable of reaching American soil. The spies were mostly rounded up by the time McCarthyism reached its peak in the early 1950s, a fact that helps to account for why that season of paranoia went away as quickly as it did. The nuclear danger never entirely went away, and for a while it was a palpable presence for Americans who saw their public buildings designated as fallout shelters even as they were being encouraged, for a while, to build their own in their own backyards.

Despite moments of genuine fear, however, as during the Berlin and Cuban missile crises, the only images we had of destroyed American cities were those constructed by the makers of apocalypse films and the authors of science fiction novels. Real danger remained remote. We had adversaries, but we also had the means of deterring them.

Even cold war insecurities, therefore, never meant that Americans, while living, working and traveling within their country, had to fear for their lives. Dangers to the American homeland were always vague and distant, however clear and present overseas dangers may have been. The very term "national security," invented during World War II and put to such frequent use during the cold war, always implied that both threats and vulnerabilities lay *outside* the country.

A second jet airliner commandeered by extremist Muslim terrorists prepares to crash into the World Trade Center's twin towers. Gaddis suggests that the "airplanes' angle of approach" assured maximum devastation. "Let there be no mistake," he says, "this was evil, and no set of grievances real or imagined, however strongly felt or widely held, can excuse it." (AP Photo/Anthony Cotsifas)

Our military and intelligence forces were configured accordingly.

That's why the U.S. Commission on National Security in the 21st Century—often known, for its co-chairs Gary Hart and Warren Rudman, as the Hart-Rudman Report—distinguished between "national" and "homeland" security when it warned of our domestic vulnerabilities, with uncanny prescience, in March 2001. In the aftermath of September 11, we have not only adopted the concept of "homeland security"—it has become synonymous with national security. Such is the revolution in our thinking forced upon us by the events of that day. It means that Americans have entered a new stage in their history in which they can no longer take security for granted: it is no longer free—anywhere, or at any time.

What was striking about September 11 was the success with which the terrorists transformed objects we had never before regarded as dangerous into weapons of lethal potency. There was nothing exotic here like bombs or even firearms. They used instead the objects of everyday life: pocket knives, twine, box-cutters and, of course, commercial aircraft. The terrorists also combined what may seem to us to be a primitive belief in the rewards of martyrdom with the most modern methods of planning, coordination, and execution. We confront, therefore, not only a new category of easily available weaponry, but a new combination of skill and will in using it.

The attack's cost-effectiveness was equally striking. No previous act of terrorism came close to this one in lives lost and damage inflicted. The dead were almost twice the number killed in some three decades of violence in Northern Ireland. They are ten times the toll on both sides in the most recent round of the Israeli-Palestinian *intifada*. They exceed, in deaths suffered on a single day, the most violent battles of the American Civil War. The operation required the lives of nineteen terrorists and expenditures of about $500,000. The "payoff," if we can use such a term for such a brutal transaction, was approximately 5,000 dead and perhaps as much as $100 billion in recovery costs. Ratios like these—some 263 victims for every terrorist, and $2,000 in damages for every dollar expended—cannot help but set a standard to which future terrorists will aspire.

The whole point of terrorism is leverage: to accomplish a lot with a little. This operation, in that sense, succeeded brilliantly—even allowing for the fact that one of the four planes failed to reach its target, and that more planes may have been in danger of being hijacked. As a consequence, the images of terrified New Yorkers running through the streets of their city to escape great billowing clouds of ash, dust, and building fragments; or of the government in Washington forced to seek shelter; or of several days of skies devoid of the contrails we have come to expect aircraft to add to the atmosphere over our heads—these memories will remain in our minds just as vividly as the images, from six decades earlier, of American naval vessels aflame, sinking at their own docks within an American naval base on American territory.

Security, therefore, has a new meaning, for which little in our history and even less in our planning has prepared us.

———

3.

That leads to a second conclusion, which is *that our foreign policy since the cold war ended has insufficiently served our interests.*

National security requires more than just military deployments or intelligence operations. It depends ultimately upon creating an international environment

Billowing smoke engulfs the Pentagon on "Black Tuesday," a day that the current generation of Americans will never forget. Gaddis states: "What was striking about September 11 was the success with which the terrorists transformed objects we had never before regarded as dangerous into weapons of lethal potency." (© Reuters NewMedia, Inc./Corbis)

congenial to the nation's interests. That's the role of foreign policy. Despite many mistakes and diversions along the way, the U.S. managed to build such an environment during the second half of the 20th century. The Soviet Union's collapse stemmed, in no small measure, from its failure to do the same.

As a consequence, the world at the end of the cold war was closer to a consensus in favor of American values—collective security, democracy, capitalism—than it had ever been before. President George H. W. Bush's talk of a "new world order" reflected a convergence of interests among the great powers which, while imperfect, was nonetheless, unprecedented. Differences remained with the European

Union, Russia, China and Japan over such issues as international trade, the handling of regional conflicts, the management of national economies, the definition and hence the protection of human rights; but these were minor compared to issues that had produced two world wars and perpetuated the cold war. Americans, it seemed, had finally found a congenial world.

What's happened since, though? Can anyone claim that the world of 2001—even before September 11—was as friendly to American interests as it had been in 1991? It would be silly to blame the U.S. alone for the disappointments of the past decade. Too many other actors, ranging from Saddam Hussein to Slobodan Milosevic to Osama bin Laden, have helped to bring them about. But the question that haunted Americans after Pearl Harbor is still worth asking: given the opportunity to rerun the sequence, what would we want to change in our foreign policy and what would we leave the same?

The question is not at all hypothetical. The administration of George W. Bush has already undertaken, in the wake of September 11, the most sweeping reassessment of foreign policy priorities since the cold war ended. Its results are not yet clear, but the tilt is far more toward change than continuity. That is an implicit acknowledgment of deficiencies in the American approach to the world during the post–cold war era that are clearer now than they were then.

One of these, it seems, was unilateralism, an occupational hazard of sole surviving superpowers. With so little countervailing power in sight, such states tend to lead without listening, a habit that can cause resistance even among those otherwise disposed to follow. The U.S. managed to avoid this outcome after its victory in World War II because we had, in the Soviet Union, a superpower competitor. Our allies, and even our former adversaries, tolerated a certain amount of arrogance on our part because there was always "something worse" out there; we in turn, fearing their defection or collapse, treated them with greater deference and respect than they might have expected given the power imbalances of the time.

With our victory in the cold war, though, we lost the "something worse." American ideas, institutions, and culture remained as attractive as ever throughout much of the world, but American policies began to come across as overbearing, self-indulgent, and insensitive to the interests of others. Our own domestic politics made things worse: with the White House in the control of one party and the Congress in the hands of another during most of this period, it was difficult to get a consensus on such matters as paying United Nations dues, participating in the International Criminal Court, or ratifying the Comprehensive Test Ban Treaty, the Land Mines Convention, or the Kyoto Protocol on Climate Change. During most of the cold war, knowing what our enemies would make of our failure to do these things, it would have been easy.

A second problem arose, largely as a result of this unilateralism: we neglected the cultivation of great power relationships. We seemed to have assumed, perhaps because we were the greatest of the great powers, that we no longer needed the cooperation of the others to promote our interests. We therefore allowed our relations with the Russians and the Chinese to deteriorate to the point that by the end of that decade we were barely on speaking terms with Moscow and Beijing. We failed to sustain one of the most remarkable achievements of American foreign policy during the cold war—the success of Richard Nixon and Henry Kissinger in creating a situation in which our adversaries feared one another more than they feared us. . . .

This happened chiefly as the result of a third characteristic of our post–cold war foreign policy, which was a preference for justice at the expense of order. We had never entirely neglected the demands of justice during the cold war, but we did tend to pursue these by working with the powerful to get them to improve their treatment of the powerless. We sought to promote human rights from the inside out rather than from the outside in: sometimes we succeeded, sometimes we did not.

With the end of the cold war, however, we changed our approach. We enlarged NATO against the wishes of the Russians, not because the Poles, the Czechs, and the Hungarians added significantly to the alliance's military capabilities, but rather because these states had suffered past injustices and therefore "deserved" membership. We then used the expanded alliance to rescue the Kosovars and bomb the Serbs, despite the fact that in doing so we were violating the sovereignty of an internationally recognized state without explicit United Nations approval. Unsurprisingly, this angered not just the Russians but also the Chinese, both of whom had discontented minorities of their own to worry about. . . .

A fourth aspect of our post–cold war foreign policy followed from the third: it was the inconsistency with which we pursued regional justice. We were, as it turned out, by no means as adamant in seeking justice for the Chechens or the Tibetans as we were for the Kosovars: Moscow and Beijing, despite their nervousness, had little to fear. But by applying universal principles on a less than universal basis, Washington did open itself to the charge of hypocrisy. It was worse elsewhere, as in Somalia, where our reluctance to take casualties of our own revealed how little we were prepared to sacrifice for the rights of others, or in Rwanda, where we responded to the greatest atrocities of the decade by simply averting our eyes.

Meanwhile, in the Middle East, we tolerated the continuing Israeli dispossession and repression of Palestinians even as we were seeking to secure the rights of the Palestinians; and we did nothing to adjust policy in response to the fact that an old adversary, Iran, was moving toward free elections and a parliamentary system even as old allies like Saudi Arabia were shunning such innovations. There was, in short a gap between our principles and our practices: we proclaimed the former without linking them to the latter, and that invited disillusionment. There are several reasons why the rantings of bin Laden resonate to the extent that they do in so many parts of North Africa, the Middle East, and Asia; but surely this is one of them.

A fifth problem was our tendency to regard our economic system as a model to be applied throughout the rest of the world, without regard to differences in local conditions and with little sense of the effects it would have in generating inequality. The problem was particularly evident in Russia, where we too easily assumed a smooth transition to market capitalism. Our efforts to help came nowhere near the scope and seriousness of the programs we'd launched to rebuild the economies of our defeated adversaries after World War II.

Meanwhile, Washington officials were less sensitive than they should have been to the extent to which American wealth and power were being blamed, throughout much of the world, for the inequities the globalization of capitalism was generating. Capitalism would have expanded after the cold war regardless of what the U.S. did. By linking that expansion so explicitly with our foreign policy objectives, however, we associated ourselves with something abroad that we would never have tolerated at home: the workings of an unregulated market devoid of a social safety net. Adam Smith was right in claiming that the pursuit of self-interest ultimately benefits the collective interest; but Karl Marx was right when he pointed out that wealth is not distributed to everyone equally at the same time, and that alienation arises as a result. . . .

Finally, and largely as a consequence, the U.S. emphasized the advantages, while neglecting the dangers, of globalization. There was a great deal of talk after the cold war ended of the extent to which that process had blurred the boundary between the domestic and the international: it was held to be a good thing that capital, commodities, ideas and people could move more freely across boundaries. There was little talk, though, of an alternative possibility: that danger might move just as freely. That's a major lesson of September 11: the very instruments of the new world order—airplanes, liberal policies on immigration and money transfers, multiculturalism itself in the sense that there seemed nothing odd about the hijackers when they were taking their flight training—can be turned horribly against it. It was as if we had convinced ourselves that the new world of global communication had somehow transformed an old aspect of human nature, which is the tendency to harbor grievances and sometimes to act upon them.

What connects these shortcomings is a failure of strategic vision: the ability to see how the parts of one's policy combine to form the whole. This means avoiding the illusion that one can pursue particular policies in particular places without their interacting with one another. It means remembering that actions have consequences: that for every action there will be a reaction, the nature of which won't always be predictable. It means accepting the fact that there's not always a linear relationship between input and output: that vast efforts can produce minimal results in some situations, and that minimal efforts can produce vast consequences in others. . . . Finally, it requires effective national leadership, a quality for which American foreign policy during the post–cold war era is unlikely to be remembered.

So what might we have done differently in the realm of foreign policy? Quite a lot, it's now clear, as we look back on a decade in which it appears that our power exceeded our wisdom.

4.

Where do we go from here? Will the events of September 11 bring our policies back into line with our interests? Can we regain the clarity of strategic vision that served us well during the cold war, and that seemed to desert us during its aftermath? Shocks like this do have the advantage of concentrating the mind. Those of us who worried, during the 1990s, about the difficulty of thinking strategically in an age of apparent safety need no longer do so. As was the case with Pearl Harbor, a confusing world has suddenly become less so, even if at horrendous cost.

What's emerging is the prospect, once again, of "something worse" than an American-dominated world—perhaps something much worse. The appalling nature of the attacks on New York and Washington forged a new coalition against terrorism overnight. The great power consensus that withered after 1991 is back in place in expanded form: the U.S., the European Union, Russia, China and Japan

are all on the same side now—at least on the issue of terrorism—and they've been joined by unexpected allies like Pakistan, Uzbekistan, and perhaps even, very discreetly, Iran. Terrorism can hardly flourish without some state support; but September 11 brought home the fact that terrorism challenges the authority of all states. Everybody has airplanes, and everything that lies below them must now be considered a potential target. Just as fear of the Soviet Union built and sustained an American coalition during the cold war—and just as the prospect of nuclear annihilation caused the Soviets themselves ultimately to begin cooperating with it—so the sudden appearance of "something much worse" is a paradoxical but powerful ally in the new war that now confronts us.

Maintaining this coalition, however, will require tolerating diversity within it. That was one of our strengths during the cold war: the U.S. was far more successful than the Soviet Union in leading while listening, so that those we led felt that they had an interest in being led. NATO survived, as a consequence, while the Sino-Soviet alliance and the Warsaw Pact did not. If the global coalition against terrorism is to survive, it will demand even greater flexibility on the part of Americans than our cold war coalition did. We'll have to give up the unilateralism we indulged in during the post–cold war era: the Bush administration, prior to September 11, had seemed particularly to relish this bad habit. We'll have to define our allies more in terms of shared interests, and less in terms of shared values. We'll have to compromise more than we might like in promoting human rights, open markets, and the scrupulous observance of democratic procedures. We'll have to concentrate more than we have in the past on getting whatever help we can in the war against terrorism wherever we can find it. Our concerns with regional justice may suffer as a result: we're not likely to return soon to rescuing Kosovars, or to condemning oppression against Chechens and Tibetans. The compensation, one hopes, will be to secure justice on a broader scale; for terrorism will offer little justice for anyone.

Even as we pursue this path, we'll need to address the grievances that fuel terrorism in the first place.

Once again, there are cold war precedents: with the rehabilitation of Germany and Japan after World War II, together with the Marshall Plan, we fought the conditions that made the Soviet alternative attractive even as we sought to contain the Soviets themselves. . . . Can we apply the same strategy now against the conditions that breed terrorists in so many parts of what we used to call the "third" world? We'd better try, for some of these regions are at least as much at risk now as Europe and Japan were half a century ago.

The era we've just entered—whatever we decide to call it—is bound to be more painful than the one we've just left. The antiterrorist coalition is sure to undergo strains as its priorities shift from recovery to retaliation. Defections will doubtless occur. Further terrorist attacks are unavoidable, and are certain to produce demoralization as well as greater resolve.

But it does seem likely, even at this early stage in the war they have provoked, that the terrorists have got more than they bargained for. "What kind of a people do they think we are?" Winston Churchill asked of the Japanese in the aftermath of Pearl Harbor. It's worth asking the same of our new enemies, because *it can hardly have been their purpose to give the U.S. yet another chance to lead the world into a new era, together with the opportunity to do it, this time, more wisely.*

QUESTIONS TO CONSIDER

1 Why does Gaddis view the events of September 11 as an example of pure evil, which existed at a level "well beyond all other terrorist attacks in the past"? What must the United States now reevaluate, in a manner similar to the reassessment after the Japanese attack on Pearl Harbor?

2 Do you agree with Gaddis that "the geographical position and the military power of the U.S. are no longer sufficient to ensure security"? Why has America, throughout its history, failed to place "homeland security" as a high priority? During the Cold War, why did many Americans feel vulnerable to outside attack and realize that the era of "free security" was over?

3 Why does Gaddis state that the "striking" thing about the events of September 11 was that the terrorists changed "objects we had never before regarded as dangerous into weapons of lethal potency"? Explain his conclusion that the attacks were cost effective and helped America's enemies gain "leverage."

4 The author claims that at the end of the Cold War the United States "had finally found a congenial world" that supported American interests and values. Why does he feel that America's foreign policy in the post–Cold War years "insufficiently served our interests"?

5 Since the end of the Cold War, how has unilateralism resulted in an American foreign policy that tends "to lead without listening"? Why has it failed to cultivate positive relationships with other significant nations like Russia and China? Do you agree with the author that recent U.S. diplomacy promotes "justice at the expense of order" and has inconsistencies between "principles and practices"?

6 How has globalization made the United States more vulnerable to terrorism? Does Gaddis's essay help you understand why many less fortunate people in the world might resent America's wealth and power? How have the events of September 11 helped develop new bonds between the United States and other nations?

ADDITIONAL MATERIAL

ADDITIONAL MATERIAL

APPENDIX

3

Were the Puritans Puritanical?

CARL N. DEGLER

The original Puritans were sixteenth-century English Christians who sought to "purify" the Anglican church, England's sole established church, by forcing it to adopt the tenets of Calvinism (see the glossary in selection 2). Some Puritans, called Separatists, defied English law and formed their own churches in order to worship as they wished. Because they were ruthlessly persecuted, were imprisoned, and even put to death, many Puritans sought refuge in North America. One Separatist group settled in Virginia. Another — the celebrated Pilgrims — came over on the Mayflower in 1620 and established Plymouth Plantation just north of present-day Cape Cod. Ten years later, a third Puritan group founded Massachusetts Bay Colony, comprising most of what is now Massachusetts and New Hampshire.

Led by even-tempered John Winthrop, their first governor, the Massachusetts Puritans sought to create a model Christian commonwealth — "a city on a hill" — that would stand as a beacon of inspiration for others to emulate. Each town had its own congregation and its own minister, whose sermons rang with Calvinist precepts. The system of local congregations that selected their ministers and ran their own affairs became known as the Congregational church. In their wilderness Zion, ministers and government officials worked together to maintain holiness, purity, and order. Only church members — the elect — could vote and hold political office. The government, in turn, protected the church by levying taxes to support it on members and nonmembers alike and by making church attendance compulsory. The Puritans, as Edmund S. Morgan said, "not only endeavored themselves to live a 'smooth, honest, civil life,' but tried to force everyone within their power to do likewise."

2

The Puritans were pious, sedate folk, but were they puritanical? Alas for them, they have received a bad rap in American popular culture. In Playboy some years ago, Hugh Hefner summed up the popular misconception, referring to the Puritans as grim bigots who hated pleasure in any form and who turned America into a land of rigid sexual repression, censorship, and conformity. As do many others, Hefner confused the Puritans with the custodians of the Victorian moral code of the nineteenth and early twentieth centuries. They were the ones who forbade discussion of sexual matters. They were the ones who cringed at the very notion of sex for pleasure and demanded that it be restricted to the marriage bed solely for purposes of procreation. Those who subscribed to the Victorian moral code were so prudish that they referred to piano legs as limbs, because the word legs was too licentious for them.

In the selection that follows, Carl N. Degler, an eminent social historian, sets the record straight as far as the Puritans were concerned. As he points out, they proscribed excesses of enjoyment, not enjoyment itself. What was more, Puritan Massachusetts had the highest educational standard in the English colonies. Bay Colony Puritans were the first to attempt public-supported and -controlled local schools, and their innovation, as Degler says, was "the American prototype of a proper system of popular education."

GLOSSARY

ANABAPTISTS Widely persecuted Christian sects that opposed infant baptism, holding that only believers should be baptized.

COMSTOCK, ANTHONY American moral crusader of the late nineteenth and early twentieth centuries who organized the New York Society for the Suppression of Vice and secured federal laws against obscene material.

COTTON, JOHN Puritan clergyman and leader in Massachusetts who played a part in the expulsion of Roger Williams and Anne Hutchinson.

HUTCHINSON, ANNE Brilliant Puritan who emigrated to Massachusetts Bay in 1634, she was branded a heretic and expelled for preaching what the religious and secular authorities deemed unorthodox doctrine.

LAUDIANS Following of Archibishop William

Laud of England, who believed in the supremacy of the Church of England and who persecuted and imprisoned religious nonconformists.

MASSACHUSETTS CODE OF 1648 Puritan measure requiring that children be taught to read.

MENCKEN, H. L. Baltimore journalist, author, and social critic, 1880–1956, who lampooned middle-class complacency.

MORISON, SAMUEL ELIOT Twentieth-century Harvard historian who wrote a history of the institution.

REFORMATION Sixteenth-century religious revolution in Western Europe, which began as a movement to reform the Roman Catholic Church and led to the rise of Protestantism.

WILLIAMS, ROGER Puritan minister who was banished from Massachusetts Bay in 1633 for asserting that the king of England had no authority

3

to seize Indian land without paying for it; Williams went on to found the colony of Rhode Island, where he established the separation of church and state and welcomed religious dissenters.

WINTHROP, JOHN Principal lay leader of Massachusetts Bay, he served as its first governor for ten years and as deputy governor for nine; he presided over Anne Hutchinson's trial and approved of her expulsion.

WINTHROP, MARGARET The governor's wife, "a very gracious woman" who "epitomized the Puritan marital ideal."

To most Americans — and to most Europeans, for that matter — the core of the Puritan social heritage has been summed up in [English historian Thomas Babington] Macaulay's well-known witticism that the Puritans prohibited bearbaiting not because of torture to the bear, but because of the pleasure it afforded the spectators. And as late as 1925, H. L. Mencken defined Puritanism as "the haunting fear that someone, somewhere, may be happy." Before this chapter is out, much will be said about the somber and even grim nature of the Puritan view of life, but quips like those of Macaulay and Mencken distort rather than illumine the essential character of the Puritans. Simply because the word "Puritan" has become encrusted with a good many barnacles, it is worth while to try to scrape them off if we wish to gain an understanding of the Puritan heritage. Though this process is essentially a negative one, sometimes it is clarifying to set forth what an influence is *not* as well as what it is.

Fundamental to any appreciation of the Puritan mind on matters of pleasure must be the recognition that the typical, godly Puritan was a worker in the world. Puritanism, like Protestantism in general, resolutely and definitely rejected the ascetic and monastic ideals of medieval Catholicism. Pleasures of the body were not to be eschewed by the Puritan, for, as Calvin reasoned, God "intended to provide not only for our necessity, but likewise for our pleasure and delight." It is obvious, he wrote in his famous *Institutes*, that "the Lord have endowed flowers with such beauty . . . with such sweetness of smell" in order to impress our senses; therefore, to enjoy them is not contrary to God's intentions. "In a word," he concluded, "hath He not made many things worthy of our estimation independent of any necessary use?"

It was against excess of enjoyment that the Puritans

Carl N. Degler, "Were the Puritans Puritanical?" from Carl N. Degler, *Out of Our Past: The Forces That Shaped Modern America* (Harper & Row, 1970).

Puritan women in Sunday dress. As Degler points out, Puritan dress was not drab and severe, but was rather "in the English Renaissance style." Puritan ladies like those above wore masks to protect their faces from the sun and wind, and wore chicken skin gloves in bed to keep their hands white. (Reproduced from Hollar, Ornatus Muliebris Anglicanus, 1640; Courtesy of the Trustees of the Boston Public Library)

cautioned and legislated. "The wine is from God," Increase Mather warned, "but the Drunkard is from the Devil." The Cambridge Platform of the Church of 1680 prohibited games of cards or dice because of the amount of time they consumed and the encouragement they offered to idleness, but the ministers of Boston in 1699 found no difficulty in condoning public lotteries. They were like a public tax, the ministers said, since they took only what the "government might have demanded, with a more *general imposition* . . . and it employes for the welfare of the publick, all that is raised by the *lottery.*" Though Cotton Mather at the end of the century condemned mixed dancing, he did not object to dancing as such; and his grandfather, John Cotton, at the beginning saw little to object to

in dancing between the sexes so long as it did not become lascivious. It was this same John Cotton, incidentally, who successfully contended against Roger Williams' argument that women should wear veils in church.

In matters of dress, it is true that the Massachusetts colony endeavored to restrict the wearing of "some new and immodest fashion" that was coming in from England, but often these efforts were frustrated by the pillars of the church themselves. [John] Winthrop reported in his *History*, for example, that though the General Court instructed the elders of the various churches to reduce the ostentation in dress by "urging it upon the consciences of their people," little change was effected, "for divers of the elders' wives, etc., were in some measure partners in this general disorder."

We also know now that Puritan dress — not that made "historical" by Saint-Gaudens' celebrated statue — was the opposite of severe, being rather in the English Renaissance style. Most restrictions on dress that were imposed were for purposes of class differentiation rather than for ascetic reasons. Thus long hair was acceptable on an upper-class Puritan like [Oliver] Cromwell or Winthrop, but on the head of a person of lower social status it was a sign of vanity. In 1651 the legislature of Massachusetts called attention to that "excess of Apparell" which has "crept in upon us, and especially amongst people of mean condition, to the dishonor of God, the scandall of our profession, the consumption of Estates, and altogether unsuitable to our poverty." The law declared "our utter detestation and dislike, that men and women of mean condition, should take upon them the garb of Gentlemen, by wearing Gold or Silver Lace, or Buttons, or Points at their knees, or to walk in great Boots; or Women of the same rank to wear Silk or Tiffany hoods, or Scarfes, which tho allowable to persons of greater Estates, or more liberal education, is intolerable in people of low condition." By implication, this law affords a clear description of what the well-dressed Puritan of good estate would wear.

If the Puritans are to be saved from the canard of severity of dress, it is also worth while to soften the charge that they were opposed to music and art. It is perfectly true that the Puritans insisted that organs be removed from the churches and that in England some church organs were smashed by zealots. But it was not music or organs as such which they opposed, only music in the meetinghouse. Well-known American and English Puritans, like Samuel Sewall, John Milton, and Cromwell, were sincere lovers of music. Moreover, it should be remembered that it was under Puritan rule that opera was introduced into England — and without protest, either. The first English dramatic production entirely in music — *The Siege of Rhodes* — was presented in 1656, four years before

the Restoration. Just before the end of Puritan rule, John Evelyn noted in his diary that he went "to see a new opera, after the Italian way, in recitative music and scenes. . . ." Furthermore, as Percy Scholes points out, in all the voluminous contemporary literature attacking the Puritans for every conceivable narrow-mindedness, none asserts that they opposed music, so long as it was performed outside the church.

The weight of the evidence is much the same in the realm of art. Though King Charles' art collection was dispersed by the incoming Commonwealth, it is significant that Cromwell and other Puritans bought several of the items. We also know that the Protector's garden at Hampton Court was beautified by nude statues. Furthermore, it is now possible to say that the Puritan closing of the theaters was as much a matter of objection to their degenerate lewdness by the 1640's as an objection to the drama as such. As far as American Puritans are concerned, it is not possible to say very much about their interest in art since there was so little in the seventeenth century. At least it can be said that the Puritans, unlike the Quakers, had no objection to portrait painting.

Some modern writers have professed to find in Puritanism, particularly the New England brand, evidence of sexual repression and inhibition. Though it would certainly be false to suggest that the Puritans did not subscribe to the canon of simple chastity, it is equally erroneous to think that their sexual lives were crabbed or that sex was abhorrent to them. Marriage to the Puritan was something more than an alternative to "burning," as the Pauline doctrine of the Catholic church would have it. Marriage was enjoined upon the righteous Christian; celibacy was not a sign of merit. With unconcealed disapprobation, John Cotton told a recently married couple the story of a pair "who immediately upon marriage, without ever approaching the *Nuptial* Bed," agreed to live apart from the rest of the world, "and afterwards from one another, too. . . ." But, Cotton advised, such behavior was "no other than an effort of blind zeal, for they are the dictates of a blind mind they follow therein and

6

not of the Holy Spirit which saith, *It is not good that man should be alone.*" Cotton set himself against not only Catholic asceticism but also the view that women were the "unclean vessel," the tempters of men. Women, rather than being "a necessary Evil are a necessary Good," he wrote. "Without them there is no comfortable Living for Man. . . ."

Because, as another divine said, "the Use of the Marriage Bed" is "founded in man's Nature" the realistic Puritans required that married men unaccompanied by wives should leave the colony or bring their wives over forthwith. The Puritan settlements encouraged marriages satisfactory to the participants by permitting divorces for those whose spouses were impotent, too long absent, or cruel. Indeed, the divorce laws of New England were the easiest in Christendom at a time when the eloquence of a Milton was unable to loosen the bonds of matrimony in England.

Samuel Eliot Morison in his history of Harvard has collected a number of examples of the healthy interest of Puritan boys in the opposite sex. Commonplace books, for example, indicate that Herrick's poem beginning "Gather ye rosebuds while ye may" and amorous lines from Shakespeare, as well as more erotic and even scatological verse, were esteemed by young Puritan men. For a gentleman to present his affianced with a pair of garters, one letter of a Harvard graduate tells us, was considered neither immoral nor improper.

It is also difficult to reconcile the usual view of the stuffiness of Puritans with the literally hundreds of confessions to premarital sexual relations in the extant church records. It should be understood, moreover, that these confessions were made by the saints or saints-to-be, not by the unregenerate. That the common practice of the congregation was to accept such sinners into church membership without further punishment is in itself revealing. The civil law, it is true, punished such transgressions when detected among the regenerate or among the nonchurch members, but this was also true of contemporary non-Puritan Virginia. "It will be seen," writes historian Philip A.

Bruce regarding Virginia, "from the various instances given relating to the profanation of Sunday, drunkenness, swearing, defamation, and sexual immorality, that, not only were the grand juries and vestries extremely vigilant in reporting these offences, but the courts were equally prompt in inflicting punishment; and that the penalty ranged from a heavy fine to a shameful exposure in the stocks . . . and from such an exposure to a very severe flogging at the county whipping post." In short, strict moral surveillance by the public authorities was a seventeenth-century rather than a Puritan attitude.

Relations between the sexes in Puritan society were often much more loving and tender than the mythmakers would have us believe. Since it was the Puritan view that marriage was eminently desirable in the sight of God and man, it is not difficult to find evidence of deep and abiding love between a husband and wife. John Cotton, it is true, sometimes used the Biblical phrase "comfortable yoke mate" in addressing his wife, but other Puritan husbands come closer to our romantic conventions. Certainly. John Winthrop's letters to his beloved Margaret indicate the depth of attachment of which the good Puritan was capable. "My good wife . . . My sweet wife," he called her. Anticipating his return home, he writes, "So . . . we shall now enjoy each other again, as we desire. . . . It is now bed time; but I must lie alone; therefore I make less haste. Yet I must kiss my sweet wife; and so, with my blessing to our children . . . I commend thee to the grace and blessing of the lord, and rest. . . ."

Anne Bradstreet wrote a number of poems devoted to her love for her husband in which the sentiments and figures are distinctly romantic.

To my Dear and loving Husband
I prize thy love more than whole Mines
of gold
Or all the riches that the East doth hold.
My love is such that Rivers cannot quench,
Nor aught but love from thee give recompense.

In another poem her spouse is apostrophized as

> My head, my heart, mine Eyes, my life, nay more
> My joy, my Magazine of earthly store

and she asks:

> If two be one, as surely thou and I,
> How stayest thou there, whilst I at Ipswich lye?

Addressing John as "my most sweet Husband," Margaret Winthrop perhaps epitomized the Puritan marital ideal when she wrote, "I have many reasons to make me love thee, whereof I will name two: First, because thou lovest God and, secondly, because thou lovest me. If these two were wanting," she added, "all the rest would be eclipsed."

It would be a mistake, however, to try to make these serious, dedicated men and women into rakes of the Renaissance. They were sober if human folk, deeply concerned about their ultimate salvation and intent upon living up to God's commands as they understood them, despite their acknowledgment of complete depravity and unworthiness. "God sent you not into this world as a Play-House, but a Workhouse," one minister told his congregation. To the Puritan this was a world drenched in evil, and, because it truly is, they were essentially realistic in their judgments. Because the Puritan expected nothing, Perry Miller has remarked, a disillusioned one was almost impossible to find. This is probably an exaggeration, for they were also human beings; when the Commonwealth fell, it was a Puritan, after all, who said, "God has spit in our faces." But Professor Miller's generalization has much truth in it. Only a man convinced of the inevitable and eternal character of evil could fight it so hard and so unceasingly.

The Puritan at his best, Ralph Barton Perry has said, was a "moral athlete." More than most men, the Puritan strove with himself and with his fellow man to attain a moral standard higher than was rightfully to be expected of so depraved a creature. Hence the di-

aries and autobiographies of Puritans are filled with the most tortuous probing of the soul and inward seeking. Convinced of the utter desirability of salvation on the one hand, and equally cognizant of the total depravity of man's nature on the other, the Puritan was caught in an impossible dilemma which permitted him no rest short of the grave. Yet with such a spring coiled within him, the Puritan drove himself and his society to tremendous heights of achievement both material and spiritual.

Such intense concern for the actualization of the will of God had a less pleasant side to it, also. If the belief that "I am my brother's keeper" is the breeding ground of heightened social conscience and expresses itself in the reform movements so indigenous to Boston and its environs, it also could and did lead to self-righteousness, intolerance, and narrow-mindedness, as exemplified in another product of Boston: Anthony Comstock. But this fruit of the loins of Puritanism is less typical of the earthy seventeenth-century New Englander than H. L. Mencken would have us think. The Sabbatarian, antiliquor, and anti-sex attitudes usually attributed to the Puritans are a nineteenth-century addition to the much more moderate and essentially wholesome view of life's evils held by the early settlers of New England.

To realize how different Puritans could be, one needs only to contrast Roger Williams and his unwearying opponent John Cotton. But despite the range of differences among Puritans, they all were linked by at least one characteristic. That was their belief in themselves, in their morality and in their mission to the world. For this reason, Puritanism was intellectual and social dynamite in the seventeenth century; its power disrupted churches, defied tyrants, overthrew governments, and beheaded kings.

The Reformation laid an awesome burden on the souls of those who broke with the Roman Church. Proclaiming the priesthood of all believers, Protestantism made each man's relationship to God his own terrifying responsibility. No one else could save him; therefore no one must presume to try. More concerned about his salvation than about any mundane matter, the Puritan was compelled, for the sake of his immortal soul, to be a fearless individualist.

It was the force of this conviction which produced the Great Migration of 1630–40 and made Massachusetts a flourishing colony in the span of a decade. It was also, ironically, the force which impelled Roger Williams to threaten the very legal and social foundations of the Puritan Commonwealth in Massachusetts because he thought the oligarchy wrong and himself right. And so it would always be. For try as the rulers of Massachusetts might to make men conform to their dogma, their own rebellious example always stood as a guide to those who felt the truth was being denied. Such individualism, we would call it today, was flesh and bone of the religion which the Puritans passed on. Though the theocracy soon withered and died, its harsh voice softened down to the balmy breath of Unitarianism, the belief in self and the dogged resistance to suppression or untruth which Puritanism taught never died. Insofar as Americans today can be said to be individualistic, it is to the Puritan heritage that we must look for one of the principal sources.

In his ceaseless striving for signs of salvation and knowledge of God's intentions for man, the Puritan placed great reliance upon the human intellect, even though for him, as for all Christians, faith was the bedrock of his belief. "Faith doth not relinquish or cast out reason," wrote the American Puritan Samuel Willard, "for there is nothing in Religion contrary to it, tho' there are many things that do transcend and must captivate it." Richard Baxter, the English Puritan, insisted that "the *most Religious*, are the *most truly, and nobly rational.*" Religion and reason were complementary to the Puritan, not antithetical as they were to many evangelical sects of the time.

Always the mere emotion of religion was to be controlled by reason. Because of this, the university-trained Puritan clergy prided themselves on the lucidity and rationality of their sermons. Almost rigorously their sermons followed the logical sequence of "doctrine," "reasons," and "uses." Conscientiously they shunned the meandering and rhetorical flourishes so beloved by Laudian preachers like John Donne, and in the process facilitated the taking of notes by their eager listeners. One of the unforgivable crimes of Mistress Anne Hutchinson was her assertion that one could "feel" one's salvation, that one was "filled with God" after conversion, that it was unnecessary, in order to be saved, to be learned in the Bible or in the Puritan writers. It was not that the Puritans were cold to the Word — far from it. A saint was required to testify to an intense religious experience — almost by definition emotional in character — before he could attain full membership in the Church. But it was always important to the Puritans that mere emotion — whether it be the anarchistic activities of the Anabaptists or the quaking of the Friends — should not be mistaken for righteousness or proper religious conduct. Here, as in so many things, the Puritans attempted to walk the middle path — in this instance, between the excessive legalism and formalism of the Catholics and Episcopalians and the flaming, intuitive evangelism of the Baptists and Quakers.

Convinced of reason's great worth, it was natural that the Puritans should also value education. "Ignorance is the mother (not of Devotion but) of Heresy," one Puritan divine declared. And a remarkably well-educated ministry testified to the Puritan belief that learning and scholarship were necessary for a proper understanding of the Word of God. More than a hundred graduates of Cambridge and Oxford Universities settled in New England before 1640, most of them ministers. At the same date not five men in all of Virginia could lay claim to such an educational background. Since Cambridge University, situated on the edge of Puritan East Anglia, supplied most of the graduates in America, it was natural that Newtown, the site of New England's own college, would soon be renamed in honor of the Alma Mater. "After God had carried us safe to New-England," said a well-known tract, some of its words now immortalized in metal in Harvard Yard, "one of the next things we longed and looked after, was to advance learning, and perpetuate it to posterity; dreading to leave an illiterate ministry to the churches, when the present ministers shall lie in the dust." "The College," founded in 1636, soon to be named Harvard, was destined to remain the only institution of higher learning in America during almost all the years of the seventeenth century. Though it attracted students from as far away as Virginia, it remained, as it began, the fountainhead of Puritan learning in the New World.

Doubt as one may Samuel Eliot Morison's claims for the secular origins of Harvard, his evidence of the typically Renaissance secular education which was available at the Puritan college in New England is both impressive and convincing. The Latin and Greek secular writers of antiquity dominated the curriculum, for this was a liberal arts training such as the leaders had received at Cambridge in England. To the Puritans the education of ministers could be nothing less than the best learning of the day. So important did education at Harvard seem to the New Haven colony in 1644 that the legislature ordered each town to appoint two men to be responsible for the collection of contributions from each family for "the mayntenaunce of scolars at Cambridge. . . ."

If there was to be a college, preparatory schools had to be provided for the training of those who were expected to enter the university. Furthermore, in a society dedicated to the reading of the Bible, elementary education was indispensable. "It being one chief project of that old deluder Satan to keep men from the knowledge of the Scriptures" began the first school laws of Massachusetts (1647) and Connecticut (1650). But the Puritans supported education for secular as well as religious reasons. The Massachusetts Code of 1648, for instance, required children to be taught to read inasmuch "as the good education of children is of singular behoof and benefit to any Commonwealth."

The early New England school laws provided that each town of fifty families or more was to hire a teacher for the instruction of its young; towns of one hundred families or more were also directed to provide grammar schools, "the master thereof being able to instruct youths so far as they may be fitted for the University." Though parents were not obliged to send their children to these schools, if they did not they were required to teach their children to read. From the evidence of court cases and the high level of literacy in seventeenth-century New England, it would appear that these first attempts at public-supported and public-controlled education were both enforced and fruitful.

No other colony in the seventeenth century imposed such a high educational standard upon its simple farming people as the Puritans did. It is true, of course, that Old England in this period could boast of grammar schools, some of which were free. But primary schools were almost nonexistent there, and toward the end of the seventeenth century the free schools in England became increasingly tuition schools. Moreover, it was not until well into the nineteenth century that the English government did anything to support schools. Primary and secondary education in England, in contrast with the New England example, was a private or church affair.

Unlike the Puritans, the Quakers exhibited little impulse toward popular education in the seventeenth and early eighteenth centuries. Because of their accent on the Inner Light and the doctrine of universal salvation, the religious motivation of the [Quakers] for learning was wanting. Furthermore, the Quakers did not look to education, as such, with the same reverence as the Puritans. William Penn, for example, advised his children that "reading many books is but a taking off the mind too much from meditation." No Puritan would have said that.

Virginia in the seventeenth century, it should be said, was also interested in education. Several times in the course of the century, plans were well advanced for establishing a university in the colony. Free schools also existed in Virginia during the seventeenth century, though the lack of village communities made them inaccessible for any great numbers of children. But, in contrast with New England, there were no publicly supported schools in Virginia; the funds for the field schools of Virginia, like those for free schools in contemporary England, came from private or ecclesiastical endowment. Nor was Virginia able to bring its several plans for a college into reality until William and Mary was founded at the very end of the century.

Though the line which runs from the early New England schools to the distinctly American system of free public schools today is not always progressively upward or uniformly clear, the connection is undeniable. The Puritan innovation of public support and control on a local level was the American prototype of a proper system of popular education.

QUESTIONS TO CONSIDER

1.   Discuss the reality of the widely held belief that Puritan society was grim, colorless, bigoted, and repressed. How would Degler respond to H. L. Mencken's 1925 definition of Puritanism as "the haunting fear that someone, somewhere, may be happy"? How did Puritan social and moral standards and ideals compare with those of Catholics, Quakers, and others in the seventeenth century?

2.   What does Degler mean by saying the Puritan at his or her best was a "moral athlete"? How did Puritanism and Quakerism embody the bourgeois spirit that historian Max Weber called the "Protestant Ethic"? Was this ethic merely a religious justification for ruthless materialism, or was it something more? How was the Protestant ethic transformed into the American work ethic?

3.   How did the Puritans' belief in their duty to God influence their view of the responsibility of individuals to themselves and to society? What have been the lasting influences of this view on American attitudes as they have developed since the seventeenth century?

4.   What was the Puritan position on the traditional juxtaposition of emotion and reason? How did they compare in this matter with their contemporaries of different religions?

5.   What was the educational background of the Puritans who settled in New England, and how did it compare with that of the Virginians? What did the New England Puritans see as the role and importance of education in society? How did they go about realizing their ideal, and how did their achievements compare with those of England and Virginia? What has been their lasting influence on the American educational ideal and system?

A Midwife's Tale:
The Life of Martha Moore Ballard
1785–1812

LAUREL THATCHER ULRICH

The study of everyday life is one of the most fascinating new fields of American history. Like biography, it is firmly grounded in specific experience; it allows us to see ordinary people of the past going about the daily business of living, and it invites us to compare their patterns of behavior with our own. By allowing us to reach back and touch the people of a bygone time, and be touched by them, the new social history does much to preserve the human continuum.

The next selection is an example of the new social history at its best. Here, a gifted historian uses a seemingly mundane document, the daily diary of a woman who lived in Maine during Jefferson and Washington's time, as the basis for recreating her life and neighborhood. While previous historians dismissed the diary as nothing but trivia, Laurel Thatcher Ulrich finds it an extraordinary chronicle, an "earnest, steady, gentle, and courageous record" that affords us a window into another way of life that no longer exists. The diary contains no profound meditations, no notes about sensational murders, no trenchant reactions to national events. But there is drama here and a quiet dignity. "It is in the very dailiness," Ulrich believes, "the exhaustive, repetitive dailiness, that the real power of Martha Ballard's book lies." By explicating Ballard's entries and sketching in rich background detail, Ulrich reconstructs both a woman and a mood, a sense of time and place, that is the very antithesis of the presentism Douglas Wilson laments in his discussion of

Jefferson (selection 8). Ballard's diary transports us back into "'a lost substructure of eighteenth-century life,'" where we meet her on her own terms, without the intrusion of present-day assumptions and moralizing.

We can appreciate Ballard all the more if we remember that women in her day were excluded from the republican idea of government for "the people" and were denied legal and political rights. Indeed, republican theory relegated women to the home. To solve the problem of female citizenship, the idea of Republican Motherhood came into vogue. That concept linked motherhood to the state by summoning women to raise virtuous, patriotic, republican sons. Ballard, however, did not identify with political ritual and never subscribed to Republican Motherhood. As Ulrich writes, her values belonged "to an older world, in which a woman's worth was measured by her service to God and her neighbors rather than to a nebulous and distant state." Within her neighborly activities, she found a deep sense of personal fulfillment and left a mark on the history of her community through the traditional woman's role of midwife. In her day, the midwife was one of the most important figures in American family and social life. Summoned to the bedside of a woman in labor, the midwife took full charge, with the assistance of other women. The midwife comforted the expectant woman, gave her hard liquor or wine, and helped her as she gave birth, which she did by squatting on a midwife's stool, kneeling on a pallet, or sitting on another woman's lap. In addition to her work in childbirth, the midwife might serve as the mother's confidante and even attend her child's baptism. In those days, people regarded childbearing as something that women must suffer through with the help and encouragement of other women while the menfolk stayed away.

As Ulrich emphasizes, Ballard's diary corrects the implications of male records — that by 1787 the new science of obstetrics had replaced the midwife in Hallowell. The diary shows that the physicians (all physicians were male in her day) merely supplemented the midwives — Ballard alone delivered more than half the local babies that year. What is more, the midwives "provided much of the medical care as well."

Ballard's diary also reveals the important role that she, her daughters, and other women played in Hallowell's economic life beyond the home. As Ulrich points out, the diary "forces us to consider midwifery in the broadest possible context, as one specialty in a larger neighborhood economy, as the most visible feature of a comprehensive and little-known system of early health care, as a mechanism of social control, a strategy for family support, and a deeply personal calling." As you read Ballard's story, think of her as "an archetypical pioneer," a frontier heroine who brought nobility to the unyielding dailiness of her life. For her, as Ulrich says, "living was to be measured in doing. Nothing was trivial."

GLOSSARY

BALLARD, CYRUS Son of Martha Ballard.

BALLARD, DOROTHY "DOLLY" Daughter of Martha Ballard.

BALLARD, EPHRAIM Husband of Martha Ballard.

BALLARD, JONATHAN Son of Martha Ballard.

BALLARD, LUCY Only one of Martha Ballard's first four daughters to survive.

BARTON, CLARA Granddaughter of Stephen Barton; pioneering battelfield nurse in the Civil War and founder of the American Red Cross (and the subject of a later selection).

BARTON, DOROTHY Younger sister of Martha Ballard.

BARTON, STEPHEN Brother-in-law of Martha Ballard, the husband of her sister Dorothy; a physician.

CONY, DANIEL Hallowell's most prominent physician.

HOWARD, WILLIAM Town's richest man, a trader.

LEARNED, EBENEZER Cousin of Martha Ballard; resident of Maine.

LEARNED, HANNAH Grandmother of Martha Ballard.

MOORE, ABIJAH Uncle of Martha Ballard; a Yale graduate and a physician.

MOORE, DOROTHY Mother of Martha Ballard.

MOORE, JONATHAN ("BROTHER JONATHAN") Harvard-educated younger brother of Martha Ballard.

MOORE, RICHARD AND MARY MOORE Uncle and aunt of Martha Ballard.

TORY An American who sided with England during the Revolution.

14

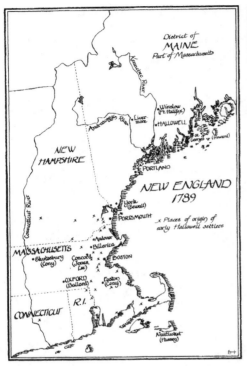

Map of New England, 1789

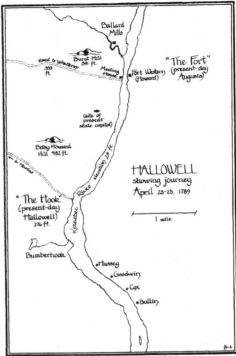

Map of Hallowell, 1789

Eight months of the year Hallowell, Maine, was a seaport. From early April to late November, ocean-going vessels sailed up the Kennebec, forty-six miles from the open Atlantic, bringing Pennsylvania flour, West Indian sugar, and English cloth and hardware, returning with shingles, clapboards, hogshead and barrel staves, white ash capstan bars, and pine boards destined for Boston or Bristol or Jamaica. In late autumn, ice blockaded the river, sometimes so suddenly that though a man had been expecting it for weeks, he was caught unprepared. One year, on November 25, after the last ships had sailed from the town, Jonathan Ballard pushed off from his father's sawmill with a raft of boards destined for Long Reach on the coast. He got no farther than

KENNEBEC
RIVER
REGION

Winslow

Vassalboro

Sidney

Hallowell

KENNEBEC RIVER

Pitts ton

Bowdoin ham

Pownal boro

Merry
Meeting
Bay

Swan
Ia.

Long Reach

Portland

Casco Bay

ATLANTIC OCEAN

Map of Kennebec River Region

Bumberhook Point, three miles below, before the Kennebec closed around him. It didn't open again until April 1.

Hallowell folks remembered openings and closings of the river the way people in other towns remembered earthquakes or drought. In 1785, the year of the long winter, the ice was still firm enough on April 22 to hold a sleigh bearing the body of Samuel Howard, one of the original settlers of the town, to his burying place at Fort Western. Not until May 3 did the first vessels arrive from "the westward," bringing

corn and pork to the straitened town. People both welcomed and feared the opening of the river. In bad years ice jams made ponds of fields and rafts of fences, backing up water in the mill creeks that cut through the steep banks on both sides. In good years, the opening water sent mill hands flying through April nights, ripping logs and securing lumber unlocked by the spring thaw. Sometimes the greatest danger was not from the river itself, though high water might pitch a man from a raft to his death before his fellows could reach him, but from the raging creeks on the shore.

In 1789, the river opened on April 7 in a heavy rain that took away the bridge over Ballard's brook, made a breach in the mill dam, and washed out the underpinning of the north side of the house. "But we are yet alive & well for which we ought to be thankful," Martha Ballard told her diary. She was fifty-four years old, a midwife. She and her family had lived at the mills since 1778, seven years after the incorporation of the town. Though she knew little of the sea, she had traveled much on the Kennebec, by water, by ice, and, during those treacherous seasons when the river was neither one nor the other, by faith.

The year Old Lady Cony had her stroke, Martha Ballard crossed the river in a canoe on December 2, pushing through ice in several places. On December 30 of another year, summoned by a woman in labor, she walked across, almost reaching shore before breaking through to her waist at Sewall's Eddy. She dragged herself out, mounted a neighbor's horse, and rode dripping to the delivery. Necessity and a fickle river cultivated a kind of bravado among Hallowell folks. "People Crost the river on a Cake of ice which swong round from the Eddy East side & stopt at the point below Mr Westons," Martha wrote on December 15 of one year. On April 1 of another she reported walking across on the ice after breakfast, adding drily in the margin of the day's entry, "the river opened at 4 hour pm."

Martha Moore was born in 1735 in the small town of Oxford, near the Connecticut border in Worcester

County, Massachusetts, but the real story of her life begins in Maine with the diary she kept along the Kennebec. Without the diary her biography would be little more than a succession of dates. Her birth in 1735. Her marriage to Ephraim Ballard in 1754. The births of their nine children in 1756, 1758, 1761, 1763, 1765, 1767, 1769, 1772, and 1779, and the deaths of three of them in 1769. Her own death in 1812. The *American Advocate* for June 9, 1812, summed up her life in one sentence: "Died in Augusta, Mrs. Martha, consort of Mr. Ephraim Ballard, aged 77 years." Without the diary we would know nothing of her life after the last of her children was born, nothing of the 816 deliveries she performed between 1785 and 1812. We would not even be certain she had been a midwife.

In the spring of 1789, Martha faced a flooding river and a rising tide of births. She attended seven deliveries in March and another seven before the end of April, twice her monthly average. On April 23 she went down the Kennebec to visit several families on the west side of the river opposite Bumberhook. This is how she told her story:

[*April 23*] Clear & very Pleasant. I sett out to go to Mr Bullins. Stept out of the Canue & sunk in the mire. Came back & Changd my Cloaths. Maid another attempt & got safe there. Sett out for home. Calld at Capt Coxes & Mr Goodins. Was Calld in at Mrs Husseys. Tarried all night. A sever storm before morn.

[*April 24*] A severe Storm of rain. I was Calld at 1 hour pm from Mrs Husseys by Ebenzer Hewin. Crosst the river in their Boat. A great sea A going. We got safe over then sett out for Mr Hewins. I Crost a stream on the way on fleeting Loggs & got safe over. Wonder full is the Goodness of providence. I then proseeded on my journey. Went beyond Mr Hainses & a Larg tree blew up by the roots before me which Caused my hors to spring back & my life was spared. Great & marvillous are thy sparing mercies O God. I was assisted over the fallen tree by Mr Hains. Went on. Soon Came to a stream. The Bridg was gone. Mr Hewin took the rains

waded thro & led the horse. Asisted by the same allmighty power I got safe thro & arivd unhurt. Mrs Hewins safe delivd at 10 h Evn of a Daughter.

After great deliverances came small annoyances. In the margin of that day's narrative, she wrote, "My Cloak was burnt while there so that it is not wareable." In all the excitement, someone had apparently allowed the midwife's sodden wrap to hang too near the fire. The story continued:

[*April 25*] Rainy. I came from Mr Hewins to Mr Pollards. My hors mired & I fell off in the mud but blessed be God I receivd no hurt. Mr Hewins attended me to Mrs Husseys. We arivd at 11 hour morning. Mrs Norcross was in Travill. Her women were immediately Calld & Shee was Safe Delivrd at 5 hour 30 minutes Evening of a fine son. Her Husband & Mrs Delino & her Childn went on board bound for Nantucket Early this morn.

[*April 26*] A very Cold morn. Snowd. I took my leav of Mrs Hussey & family. Came to Mr Herseys. He & William Howard brot me from fort Western by water. I left my patients Cleverly & found my famely well. It is the greatest freshet in this river that has been this many years.

Reading such a story, we can easily imagine Martha as an archetypical pioneer. Indeed, the rhythms of her story echo the seventeenth-century captivity narratives that gave New England its first frontier heroines. One thinks of Mary Rowlandson crossing the Ware River in Vermont on a makeshift raft in the early spring of 1676 or of Hannah Swarton traveling into Maine "over Steep and hideous Mountains one while, and another while over Swamps and Thickets of Fallen Trees." The religious language in Martha Ballard's diary strengthens the affinity with her Puritan progenitors. Dramatizing the dangers of her journey, she both glorified God and gave meaning and dimension to her own life. Mr. Hewins led her horse and Mr. Hains walked beside her, but Providence rescued her from the violence of the spring freshet.

17

"A great sea A going" — Martha knew how to suggest an entire landscape, or in this case a riverscape, in a phrase. Her description of the river crossing is part psalm, part tale. She understood instinctively, if not self-consciously, the importance of repetition and the uses of convention. Notice how in the April 24 passage she alternated spare, but vivid, action sentences with formulaic religious phrases:

I Crost the stream on the way on fleeting Loggs & got safe over. *Wonder full is the Goodness of providence.* I then proseeded on my journey. Went beyond Mr Hainses & a Larg tree blew up by the roots before me which Caused my hors to spring back & my life was spared. *Great & marvillous are thy sparing mercies O God.* I was assisted over the fallen tree by Mr Hains. Went on. Soon Came to a stream. The Bridg was gone. Mr Hewin took the rains waded thro & led the horse. *Asisted by the same allmighty power* I got safe thro & arivd unhurt.

Here the religious sentiments become a kind of refrain, punctuating and accentuating each stage in the narrative. Such a passage reveals a storyteller, if not a writer, at work.

There are other passages of similar quality in the diary. Yet most of Martha's entries are more mundane. The structure of her diary derives from two workaday forms of record-keeping, the daybook and the interleaved almanac. In eighteenth-century New England, farmers, craftsmen, shopkeepers, ship's captains, and perhaps a very few housewives kept daybooks, running accounts of receipts and expenditures, sometimes combining economic entries with short notes on important family events and comments on work begun or completed. Other early diarists used the blank pages bound into printed almanacs to keep their own tally on the weather, adding brief entries on gardening, visits to and from neighbors, or public occurrences of both the institutional and the sensational sort. Martha Ballard did all these things.

The extant diary, which begins in January of 1785, may have been preceded by an almanac of some sort,

since she ruled the margins of her homemade booklets and numbered the days of the month and week, using a "dominical letter" for Sundays, according to the almanac form. Whatever its origins, the diary functioned as a kind of daybook. Martha recorded debts contracted and "rewards" received, and some of the time she noted numbers of yards "got out" of the loom and varieties of beans put into the ground. Her midwifery accounts are even more methodical. She carefully labeled and numbered each delivery, adding an XX to the margin when the fee was paid.

Those few historians who have known about the diary have not known quite what to do with it. In his *History of Augusta* published in 1870, James W. North quoted several passages, including the one for April 24, 1789, but he pronounced most of the entries "brief and with some exceptions not of general interest." Although Charles Elventon Nash devoted more than a third of his 600-page *History of Augusta* to an abridgment of the journal, carefully extracting birth records and a sample of almost everything else except unsavory medical details or anything tainted with sex, he too found much of it "trivial and unimportant . . . being but a repetition of what has been recited many times." Curiously, a feminist history of midwifery published in the 1970s repeated the old dismissal: "Like many diaries of farm women, it is filled with trivia about domestic chores and pastimes."

Yet it is in the very dailiness, the exhaustive, repetitious dailiness, that the real power of Martha Ballard's book lies. To extract the river crossings without noting the cold days spent "footing" stockings, to abstract the births without recording the long autumns spent winding quills, pickling meat, and sorting cabbages, is to destroy the sinews of this earnest, steady, gentle, and courageous record. Martha sometimes slipped the folded half-sheets from which she constructed her diary into her bag when she crossed the river or waded through snow to sit out a tedious labor, and when she felt overwhelmed or enlivened by the very "trivia" the historians have dismissed, she said so, not in the soul-searching manner of a Puritan nor with the literary self-consciousness of a sentimentalist, but in a plain, matter-of-fact, and in the end unforgettable voice. For more than twenty-seven years, 9,965 days to be exact, she faithfully kept her record. Martha was not an introspective diarist, yet in this conscientious recording as much as in her occasional confessions, she revealed herself. "And now this year is come to a close," she wrote on December 31, 1800, "and happy is it if we have made a wise improvement of the time." For her, living was to be measured in doing. Nothing was trivial.

Because so few New England women of her generation left writing in any form, one searches for an explanation for the diary. Though her grandmother, Hannah Learned, was able to muster a clear but labored signature on the one surviving document bearing her name, her mother, Dorothy Moore, signed with a mark. On the male side of the family, however, there is a record of education. Martha's uncle Abijah Moore, who graduated from Yale in 1726, was the first college graduate from the town of Oxford. Martha's younger brother, Jonathan Moore, was the second. Jonathan graduated from Harvard College in 1761, serving for a time as librarian of the college before accepting a call as pastor of the First Congregational Church in Rochester, Massachusetts. Throughout her life Martha Ballard corresponded with "Brother Jonathan."

Although her handwriting is crude in comparison with her brother's and less certain than that of her husband, who was a surveyor and mapmaker as well as a miller, her ability to write cursive in any form is itself evidence that someone in Oxford in the 1740s was interested in educating girls. Judging from the diary, that education was quite conventional. Although Martha occasionally "perused" newspapers, she mentioned only one book other than the Bible. One June 25, 1786, a Sunday, she wrote, "I have Red in Mr Marshalls gospel Mystery of Sanctification." The book was Walter Marshall's *Gospel-Mystery of Sanctification,* a work of popular piety first published in London in 1692, though reprinted many times

in the eighteenth century. Her concern with the spelling of the title is intriguing; normally, she showed little interest in such matters. Obviously having the book in her hand elevated her consciousness, though it had little effect on the rest of the passage. *Read* remained *Red.*

Martha's choice of reading material was conservative, at least on that Sunday in 1786. She was aware of more modern forms of English literature, however. Her younger sister, Dorothy Barton, had two daughters named after characters in the novels of Samuel Richardson. *Pamela* and *Clarissa Harlowe* Barton were frequent visitors to and sometime inhabitants of the Ballard house, as was their sister *Parthenia.* Classical or pseudo-classical names were still rare in New England in the 1760s, though they became more popular after the Revolution. The Ballards succumbed to the same impulse and displayed an uncharacteristic bit of whimsy when they named their third daughter *Triphene.*

By Oxford standards, the Moores were well educated and ambitious. The family also seems to have had a medical bent. Martha's uncle Abijah Moore was a physician, as were two of her brothers-in-law, including Stephen Barton, the father of Pamela, Parthenia, and Clarissa. The one hint that Martha herself was involved in caring for the sick in Oxford comes from a Barton family story recorded many years later. It survives in two versions.

One explains that during the pre-Revolutionary boycotts, when Stephen Barton was on a committee to see that no tea was bought in the town, he "was wont to put on his hat and go without while his sympathetic wife and her sister, Martha Moore Ballard, made a cup of tea in the cellar for some sick mother in the neighborhood whose sufferings patriotism and loyalty failed to heal." The other version comes from Dorothy and Stephen's granddaughter, a woman christened Clarissa Harlowe Barton, but known to millions of Americans by her nickname, Clara. Clara Barton, the founder of the American Red Cross, later recalled being entertained by her "interesting, precise and intelligent grandmother Barton, telling us of the tea parties she and her sister Aunt Ballard held in the cellar when grandfather was out or *up* and didn't know what was going on in his own disloyal and rebellious home." Although the neighborly ministrations of the first story become "tea parties" in this one, both emphasize Dorothy Barton's independence. According to Clara, the two sisters "hung blankets inside the cellar door to prevent the savory fumes of the tea from reaching the loyal and official olfactories of 'Pater familias.' " Martha's rebellion may have been less serious than her sister's. As we shall see, Ephraim Ballard was himself a reluctant supporter, at best, of the Revolution.

The best evidence of the practical side of Martha's education comes from the diary itself. When it opened in 1785, she knew how to manufacture salves, syrups, pills, teas, and ointments, how to prepare an oil emulsion (she called it an "oil a mulge"), how to poultice wounds, dress burns, treat dysentery, sore throat, frostbite, measles, colic, "hooping Cough," "Chin cough," "St. Vitas dance," "flying pains," "the salt rhume," and "the itch," how to cut an infant's tongue, administer a "clister" (enema), lance an abscessed breast, apply a "blister" or a "back plaster," induce vomiting, assuage bleeding, reduce swelling, and relieve a toothache, as well as deliver babies.

She later wrote that she delivered her first baby in July of 1778, less than a year after her arrival in Maine. This statement should not be taken entirely at face value. She no doubt officiated as a midwife for the first time in 1778, but she had probably assisted in dozens of births in Oxford. This was the era of "social childbirth," when female relatives and neighbors, as well as midwives, attended births. Most midwives began as observers, gradually assuming a more active role, until one day, when the old midwife was delayed or willing, they "performed." For Martha, moving to Maine probably accelerated this process. In Oxford, even if she had the ability to practice she may have had little opportunity, since there were many older women in the town. Her own Grandmother

Learned was alive until 1777. In Hallowell, by contrast, she was one of the older women in a young and rapidly growing town.

Giving birth to nine babies was also a part of her preparation as a midwife. As one eighteenth-century midwifery manual expressed it, "There is a tender regard one woman bears to another, and a natural sympathy in those that have gone thro' the Pangs of Childbearing; which, doubtless, occasion a compassion for those that labour under these circumstances, which no man can be a judge of." Martha's "natural" sympathy had also been developed through death. Between 1767 and 1770, Oxford lost 12 percent of its population in one of the worst diphtheria epidemics in New England's history. One hundred forty-four persons died, mostly children ages two to fourteen. Martha's uncle and aunt, Richard and Mary Moore, buried eight of their eleven children. Martha and Ephraim lost three of their six children in less than ten days. A row of tiny headstones in the burying ground behind the Oxford Congregational Church commemorates the Moore deaths. There are no Ballard stones. Martha memorialized her little girls in the diary she kept along the Kennebec.

June 17, 1786: "this is 17 years since the Death of my Daughter Triphene who Deceast AE 4 years & 3 months."

July 1, 1788: "It is 19 years this Day since the Death of my Daughter Dorothy." (Dorothy had been two.)

July 5, 1789: "20 years since my daughter Martha's death." (Martha was "8 years & 2 months & 28 days" when she died.)

Both of the Ballard sons, Cyrus, twelve, and Jonathan, six, survived the throat distemper. Of the four daughters, only Lucy, age ten, remained. "It was a very hott day & Continued so thro the sumer," Martha recalled in one of the entries remembering Triphene's death. She had reason to feel the heat in that summer of sorrow. She was seven and a half months pregnant when the first of her daughters died.

On August 6, 1769, amidst death, she gave birth.

The baby was named Hannah, for Mother Ballard. Two years later another baby girl was born. She became Dorothy, or "Dolly," for Grandmother Moore, for her Aunt Dorothy Barton, and for the sister who had died of diptheria. Perhaps there would have been another Triphene or Martha in 1773, but in that year Ephraim Ballard was in Maine searching out a new home. As a consequence, the last Ballard baby, named Ephraim for his father, was born in Hallowell in 1779.

When Ephraim Ballard ascended the Kennebec in 1775 in search of new land, he was doing what his great-grandfather had done more than a century before when he left Lynn, Massachusetts, to build mills in the new town of Andover and what his own father had done when he left Andover for Billerica and then Oxford. The Ballards had been millers for four generations in New England, and in three of those four they helped to settle new towns.

The French and Indian wars first led Oxford men to Maine. Martha's cousin Nathan Moore, a veteran of the invasion of Canada, was settled in Vassalboro on the Kennebec by 1768. Another cousin, Ebenezer Learned, also a veteran, became a proprietor of the new township of Livermore on the Androscoggin River, though he continued to live in Oxford. Ephraim went to Maine for the first time as a surveyor and agent for Cousin Ebenezer, though his interest soon turned from the Androscoggin to the Kennebec. By 1775 his brother Jonathan, his brother-in-law Thomas Towne, Martha's brother Ebenezer Moore, and her brother-in-law Stephen Barton had all settled on lands laid out by the Kennebec Proprietors. Removing to Maine became another way of remaining in Oxford.

In 1775, there were six incorporated townships along the Kennebec above Long Reach — Pownalboro, Gardinerstown, Hallowell, Winthrop, Vassalboro, and Winslow — the town names reflecting the family connections and political power of the Kennebec Proprietors, also known as the Plymouth Company because they traced their land claims to

seventeenth-century Pilgrim grants. Unlike the pioneer settlements of early Massachusetts, these Maine towns were laid out by merchant speculators, who, having no intention of migrating themselves, gave away some of the land to early settlers, looking for a return on their investment from later land sales and rents and from the proceeds of mills, ships, and stores run by hired agents, who were themselves often paid in land. In 1775 the Kennebec Proprietors owned more than 600,000 acres of wild land, though the exact boundaries of their grants were in dispute. Here indeed was work for a good surveyor, and opportunity perhaps to acquire land and mills.

On April 6, 1775, Ephraim secured a lease from Silvester Gardiner of Boston, one of the wealthiest of the Kennebec Proprietors, to "Fort Hallifax and all the land adjoining." The Fort, originally built by the Massachusetts government, stood on a peninsula between the Kennebec and Sebasticook rivers. Surrounded by 400 acres of timber, it was described by one contemporary as "a great Salmon fishery in the summer and a bass fishery in the Winter."

It was an impressive site, but the timing was bad. In April of 1775, as Ephraim was sailing up the Kennebec toward the Fort, Martha was in Oxford watching her cousin Ebenezer Learned muster troops to meet the Lexington and Concord alarm. In June, when Ephraim applied to the Lincoln County Court for a tavern license, the Oxford Minutemen were at Bunker Hill. When an advance party of Benedict Arnold's army reached Fort Halifax in September of 1775, they disdained the accommodations of the Fort, not only because it was in a "ruinous state" but because the proprietor (who was without question Ephraim Ballard) was reputed a "rank tory." Still, they were pleased with the man's willingness to exchange "a barrel of smoke-dried salmon for a barrel of pork, upon honest terms."

A year later, relations between Ephraim and the patriots were less cordial. In a petition to the General Court, the Winslow Committee of Safety complained that "Mr Ballard with a Number of People (supposed to be unfriendly to the grand American Cause) from the next Town were cutting and haling Mill Logs" on Fort lands. (The "next Town" was Vassalboro, where Ephraim's brother and a bevy of Moore relatives lived.) The General Court empowered the committee to take the Gardiner property "under their care."

Having lost one Tory property, Ephraim went downriver to Hallowell and acquired another, taking up the management of land and mills owned by John Jones, a longtime resident of the Kennebec and a Plymouth Company agent. Jones was a loyalist who had already been declared "inimical to the liberties and privileges of the United States" by a Hallowell town meeting, but he was foresighted enough to deed his property to his wife's relatives before fleeing to Canada. Ephraim's lease was secure. His own sympathies may have been with his landlord, but he knew how to make peace with a revolution. When he too was accused of "Treasonable & Enimical Conduct Against the United States of America," he not only managed to get the charges dropped but soon after was elected moderator of the Hallowell town meeting. According to ' surer's account, he contributed 200 pounds (a standard assessment in this period of inflation) toward the support of a soldier at Fort Halifax.

Martha had joined her husband in Hallowell in October of 1777. "I first set my feet on the Kenebeck shore . . . at Mr John Jones' landing below the Hook," she later recalled, adding, "I spent 1 year and 17 days, then removed to his mill at Boman's brook." Jones's landing and his mills at Bowman's Brook were in opposite corners of the town. The landing was on the east side of the river in the southern half of the settlement, the section usually referred to as "the Hook," for Bumberhook Point, its most prominent feature. The mills were on the west side of the river in the northern half of the town (the part that separated in 1797 to become the town of Augusta). This area was called "the Fort," after old Fort Western, built by the Plymouth Company in 1754 as part of its line of defense on the Kennebec. Since 1769, the Fort

had been owned by James Howard, who used it as a dwelling house and store. (The restored Fort is now a museum owned and maintained by the city of Augusta.)

In 1777 there were 100 families in Hallowell, spread out along ten miles of river. Most people still lived in their first log houses, though a few, perhaps including John Jones, had managed to build frame houses and barns. The settlers had come from more than thirty different towns, some from Rhode Island and Nantucket, a few from New Hampshire, several from the British Isles, most from Massachusetts and Maine. They had come in small clusters of kin. There were two Howard brothers with their progeny, three Sewall cousins, two generations of Conys, strings of Savages and Clarks, and so on. Although most of the Ballard and Moore relatives were in other Kennebec towns, Ephraim's nephew and namesake, Ephraim Towne, was also a tenant of John Jones in Hallowell. In 1778, Towne married his cousin Lucy Ballard, Martha and Ephraim's oldest daughter.

Letters from John Jones to Towne provide the only glimpse we have of these years. "I have had an acompt of what you have met with or had your House serched for me," Jones wrote in the autumn of 1778. "I am very sorry that they should trouble themselves concerning me. I hant dun them no ronge. I sincear wish Everybody would miend their own business." When Kennebec patriots continued to mind Jones's business, he joined the British resistance at Fort George. His military forays into the region gave new point to his old nickname, "Black Jones." In one exploit he kidnapped Colonel Charles Cushing of Pownalboro, dragging him from his house barefoot in the night. His letters to Towne say less about politics, however, than about their common interest in the farm. "I am afraid there will be a famin for bread if the war continues," he wrote in February of 1779. He urged his tenant to "buy sum oxen or furrow cows" while he could, to set out apple trees on the hill behind the barn, and to "git a Salmon net maide, for Provisions is intolerable Dear." When shearing time came he hoped Towne would take care of his wool, though "if you need of it before I come you or your father Ballard may use what you stand in need of."

Ten years later, Jones had not yet come. He made an attempt in 1785, the first year Martha kept her diary, but was soon spirited out of town. "A gang went to Samuel Duttuns & took John Jones, brought him to Pollards, tarried till morn when they Set out with him for Wiscasset," Martha wrote. Characteristically, she offered no judgment on the behavior either of Jones or of his attackers. Nor does her diary open in time to record what may have been a last vigilante action against her own family. In 1784 Lucy and Ephraim Towne moved from Hallowell to Winslow, the place where Ephraim Ballard had had his first encounter with the Revolution. According to an oral tradition preserved in the Towne family, the young couple transported their household goods upriver on a flatboat, leaving their furniture on the wharf overnight. "Somebody tied one of the chairs to the top of a birch tree," their great-granddaughter recalled, "and when they went to get the furniture in the morning, here was a chair in the top of a tree." In her mouth the incident is an amusing but inexplicable event. Was tying furniture in trees some species of frontier humor, a folk form of welcome? The political context suggests otherwise. Apparently somebody in Winslow resented Ephraim Towne's association with John Jones, and perhaps, too, with that "rank tory" who had once cut timber at Fort Halifax.

When the diary opened, there were seven Ballards living in John Jones's house on Bowman's Brook — Martha and Ephraim and five unmarried children — Cyrus, Jonathan, Hannah, Dolly, and Ephraim. There were usually one or two hired helpers as well. All these people crowded into an unfinished house that had two rooms on the main floor (Martha called them simply the "east room" and the "west room") and two unfinished chambers above, which were unusable in winter. In addition there were a "seller," a barn, and various "yards," some fenced, some defined only by their proximity to a significant structure or natural barrier, as in "I sowd parsnip & Carrot seed *in the gardin by the Barn*." Or "I howd the Beans & Cucumbers *in the yard by the Brook*." Or "Houghed the plants *before the door*." Or "Cutt Aulders and maid a sort of a fence part round *the yard By the mill Pond*."

Housework extended from the west room to the yards. Martha Ballard and her daughters bleached newly spun thread on the grass and hung laundry on such fences as they had, though there were risks in such a practice. "Hannah washt Daniels Blankett & our swine tore it into strips," Martha wrote on one fateful day. (No matter, the girls cut up the remnants and made a warm petticoat for one of Lucy's children.) There were no sheep yet, but Ephraim owned a horse and a pair of oxen and Martha milked both a red and a "speckled" cow. Chickens pecked in a dooryard cluttered with wood chips and animal droppings, giving a comforting domesticity to a setting that was still wilderness beyond the clearings for hay and corn. "There was a moose by our gardin this afternoon," Martha wrote into the margin of her diary on one April day. In November of 1787, she noted, "Hannah & Dolly were fritened by a Baire between here & Neighbor Savages." In such a setting an errant calf — or a neighbor's child — might wander "up the crik" and disappear.

Yet for all its wildness there was a motion, a life, in Hallowell that had been missing in Oxford. There were ships on the river and a continuous movement of settlers through the town and into the back country. Ephraim's mill was a ram against the wilderness, an engine for transforming woods into towns. On good days the saw kept a steady rhythm, the vertical blade moving up and down 120 times a minute, striking a rapid trochee ("Faaa-sher, Faaa-sher") that echoed through the trees as log after log inched along the wooden track. Weather and the changing seasons, as much as the availability of timber, regulated the operation, too much water being as much of a problem as too little. "Our saw mills go Briskly," Martha wrote on one day after a heavy rain, but on another, "The mills have been stopt from going by the freshet."

Ephraim and his sons operated a gristmill as well as a sawmill, both perhaps housed in the same building, the saw or saws in the story above, the grinding mechanism below. There is a fitting symbolism in the division of responsibility for the two. Cyrus, the quiet older son who into his forties moved in and out of his father's household, never marrying, never achieving full independence, was assigned the grinding. Jonathan, the flamboyant and rebellious younger brother, did the rafting and ripping. One wonders if Cyrus was impaired in some way, though his mother never wrote of it in her diary. His shoulders, at least, were powerful, since it was his job to "pick mill," that is, to work with a mallet and chisel to restore and maintain grooves on the granite millstones. "Son Town" too had a role in the family operation. Having carried away the eldest daughter to Winslow, he returned every week or so, rafting logs to the mill.

When conditions were right the mills went day and night, though mechanical and human failure as well as the weather could bring silence. "The cornmill ceast grinding till finisht repairing," Martha would write, or "Thee swoap of one of the mills got off thee Crank so neither of them were tended this night." Still the sounds of sawing were as much a part of spring on Bowman's Brook as the songs of birds, such an omnipresent part of Martha's world that she usually did not notice them unless they were gone, as one May evening, after the hired hand had gone to bed ill and Jonathan had returned late from two days on the river searching for logs that had gone adrift, when she noted quietly, "The mill Lies still."

Perhaps it was a sense of history or a craving for stability, perhaps only a practical need to keep birth records, that first motivated Martha to keep a diary. "Thee number of childn I have Extracted since I came to Kennebeck I find by written account & other Calculations to be 405," she wrote on December 31, 1791. The demands of a practice that averaged almost forty births a year even in the prediary period may

eventually have made a "written account" essential. The diary opens on January 1, 1785, with short, choppy entries nineteen to the page. Gradually the entries become fuller and more regular. (The diary's overall average is six entries per page.) From the beginning she ruled a margin at the left of her page where she entered the day of the month. Soon she added a second column for the day of the week. By the end of 1787 she had added a right-hand margin where she summarized each day's events. A year or two later she began keeping a running head at the top of each page. Such changes suggest that she too could get lost in a stream of days. One delivery, one April day, could so easily fuse with another.

April 24, 1785: "I was Calld at 2 O Clock in the Morn to go to thee hook to Mrs Blake in travil."

April 18, 1786: "A rainy day. I was calld to Mr Gillmans at the hook to see his wife in Travil."

April 22, 1787: "I Was calld to Mr Welmans at 9 this morn. His wife Safe Delivd at 7 Evn of a son . . . it rained this Evinng."

April 28, 1788: "Rain, Snow & Haill & Cold [but this time no deliveries!]"

And then on April 24, 1789, the dramatic encounter with the spring freshet. "A sever Storm of rain. I was Calld at 1 h pm from Mrs Husseys by Ebenzer Hewin. . . . "

Both the difficulty and the value of the diary lie in its astonishing steadiness. Consider again that sequence of entries for April 23 through 26, 1789. The central story — Martha's crossing and recrossing of the Kennebec — is clear enough, but on first reading the reader is unlikely to notice a subplot being played out at the Hussey house while Martha was traveling through the April storm to the Hewins delivery. In fact, it is not even apparent at first that she has left one pregnant woman to attend another. Recall that she initially crossed the river on April 23 "to go to Mr Bullins," that a few hours later as she was about to return home after stopping in at "Capt Coxes & Mr Goodins," she was "Calld in at Mrs Husseys." She

"Tarried all night" at the Husseys', leaving about one the next afternoon when Ebenezer Hewins came through the storm to fetch her to his wife's delivery. She did not, however, return home after leaving the Hewins house, which was on the same side of the river as her own, but crossed the Kennebec once again to the Husseys.

In the entry for November 25 we find out why: "Mr Hewins attended me to Mrs Husseys. We arivd at 11 h morn. Mrs Norcross was in Travill. Her women were immediately Calld & Shee was Safe Delivrd at 5 hours 30 minutes Evening of a fine son." Then she added as a kind of aside: "Her Husband & Mrs Delino & her Childn went on board bound for Nantucket Early this morn." With some attention to context (and a quick search of family records), the characters in this little drama can be straightened out — Mrs. Norcross and Mrs. Delano were Mrs. Hussey's daughters.

Now look at the sequence of events so casually described in the entry. The ship bound for Nantucket left "Early" in the morning; the midwife arrived at eleven; the baby was born at 5:30 that afternoon. What we don't know is whether Mrs. Norcross was already in labor when her husband and sister sailed down the river, having risen early to catch the northwest wind that would make for easy sailing to Long Reach. Probably not. Earlier entries for the month suggest that Mr. Norcross had been waiting in port for almost two weeks anticipating the birth of his child. Martha first went to the Hussey house on April 9 and was still there two days later when "Captain Norcross came home" with the first ships of the season. She left on the eleventh, returned on the thirteenth, left again on the eighteenth, and was back the next day, remaining until April 20. When she was finally "called in" at the Hussey house on April 23, she had already spent a total of nine days waiting for a baby that would not arrive. It is doubtful she would have left Mrs. Norcross again for the Hewins delivery if there had been any sign of labor. That flat entry,

"Her Husband & Mrs Delino & her Childn went on board bound for Nantucket Early this morn" was an ironic commentary on a month's frustration. The watched pot would not boil.

Here the more interesting point may not be the departure of the seafaring father (for men the conflict between work and family is an old and continuing one) but the presence of the distant sister. Betsy Delano, whose husband was also a mariner, lived in Nantucket. Did she sail up the river with Philip Norcross on April 11 hoping to attend her sister's delivery? Or had she spent the winter months in Hallowell with her mother while her own husband was at sea?

A second subplot is suggested by a clue so subtle that without long acquaintance with Martha Ballard's habits of deference, it is easily missed. She wrote of going to *Mrs* rather than to *Mr* Hussey's house, though in the same section she spoke of going to *Mr* Bullins, *Capt* Coxes, and *Mr* Goodins. In Martha Ballard's world, houses belonged to men. That in April of 1789 the Hussey house seemed to belong to a wife is significant. Obed Hussey was in Wiscasset jail, imprisoned for debt. She alluded to his situation on April 18, during one of her many visits to Mrs. Norcross. "Mrs Hussey Gone to see her Husband," she wrote, though with typical restraint she said nothing more. Obed Hussey was eighty years old that year. He never again saw his warehouses and fishing seines along the Kennebec. "Esquire Hussey expired in prison," Martha noted on June 17, 1790.

A different kind of adversity is suggested in the dramatic journey across swollen streams and deep gullies to the Hewinses' delivery. That Ebenezer Hewins was trying to carve out a farm in the second mile of settlement suggests something about his own status. Earlier arrivals, like the Husseys and the Ballards, lived near the river. There is a kind of disorder as well as excitement suggested by Ebenezer Hewins's precipitous fetching of the midwife, a feeling compounded later by the entry regarding the burning of the cloak, and by the knowledge that Martha Ballard had delivered the Hewinses' first baby in 1787 just two months after the couple were married.

The problem is not that the diary is trivial but that it introduces more stories than can easily be recovered and absorbed. It is one thing to describe Martha's journey across the Kennebec, another to assess the historical significance of Nancy Norcross's lingering labor, Obed Hussey's sojourn in jail, or Zilpha and Ebenezer Hewins's hasty marriage. Taken alone, such stories tell us too much and not enough, teasing us with glimpses of intimate life, repelling us with a reticence we cannot decode. Yet, read in the broader context of the diary and in relation to larger themes in eighteenth-century history, they can be extraordinarily revealing.

Each of the subplots in the April 1789 passage relates to a larger question in social history. Nancy Norcross suffered lingering labor in an era when old childbirth practices were being challenged in both England and America by a new "scientific" obstetrics promoted by male physicians. Obed Hussey languished in debtor's prison in an age when debtor petitions and even debtor insurrections were convulsing the nation and when some men were taking to the streets or the woods to preserve their property. Ebenezer and Zilpha Hewins married at a time of high premarital pregnancy rates in America, a period when political essayists as well as novelists were obsessed with the theme of seduction. The late eighteenth century was not only an era of political revolution but of medical, economic, and sexual transformation. Not surprisingly, it was also a time when a new ideology of womanhood self-consciously connected domestic virtue to the survival of the state. The nature of these phenomena is still being debated in the literature, yet few scholars would disagree that the period of Martha's diary, 1785–1812, was an era of profound change, or that in some still dimly understood way, the nation's political revolution and the social revolutions that accompanied it were related. It is not as easy as it once was to dismiss domestic concerns as "trivia."

Martha Ballard's diary connects to several prominent themes in the social history of the early Republic, yet it does more than reflect an era. By restoring a lost substructure of eighteenth-century life, it transforms the nature of the evidence upon which much of the history of the period has been written. The point can be illustrated by comparing evidence from her book with three documents left by prominent Hallowell men, Daniel Cony, William Howard, and Henry Sewall.

Daniel Cony was the Kennebec's best-known physician. He was studying medicine with his brother-in-law, Dr. Samuel Curtis of Marlborough, Massachusetts, at the time of the Lexington alarm. He marched with the Minutemen, served as adjutant of the regiment of infantry with General Horatio Gates at Saratoga, and according to the town historian "was at the surrender of Burgoyne, but not in any of the battles which preceded that event." He arrived in Hallowell in 1778, the same year as Martha, and became, in the words of a contemporary, a "faithful labourer in the medical field," and, we might add, an earnest promoter of medical organization. Though he practiced 150 miles into the hinterland, Cony was an early member of the Massachusetts Medical Society centered in Boston, and he continued that membership even after he became president of a new Kennebec Medical Society founded in 1797.

Cony was one of a handful of Maine physicians mentioned in James Thacher's *American Medical Biography*, published in Boston in 1828. He was, by all accounts, a leader in his profession, an associate if not a peer of New England's most progressive physicians, the very group of men who were promoting the new scientific obstetrics. Significantly, his only contribution to the literature of the Massachusetts Medical Society was an obstetrical paper, a one-page account of "a circumstance which I had never before met with" in a delivery he performed in August of 1787. Since this brief paper makes no mention of a midwife, or of any woman other than the patient, it might seem that the obstetrical revolution was complete in

Hallowell by that date, that doctors had supplanted midwives.

Martha's diary confirms that Cony delivered at least one woman in August 1787 — his own wife — but it reduces his obstetrical career to its proper place in the medical history of the town. Several doctors, including some from neighboring towns, occasionally attended births in Hallowell, but their work was supplementary to that of the midwives. Martha herself attended 60 percent of the births in Hallowell in the year Cony presented his paper to the Massachusetts Medical Society, and she was not the only female practitioner active at the time. Martha and her peers were not only handling most of the deliveries, they were providing much of the medical care as well. In Martha's diary, it is doctors, not midwives, who seem marginal.

William Howard, the man who helped Martha Ballard across the river on April 26 when she was returning from the Hussey house, was the wealthiest man in the town. The son and son-in-law of Hallowell's earliest settlers, he lived and traded at Fort Western in partnership with his brother Samuel, a mariner. A surviving account book listed under the names of William and Samuel Howard provides rich material for assessing the external economy of the Kennebec in the last decade of the eighteenth century. A standard merchant's ledger with debit and credit entries for each customer listed on opposite pages, it begins in 1788, though it carries some balances forward "from another Book," now lost. Most entries date from 1788 through 1792, though a few go to 1800 or beyond. Almost all, including those for the Ballards, are listed under the name of a male head of household. Male products — lumber, fish, and furs — dominate the credit side of the ledger.

One might conclude from such a record that Kennebec women had no role in economic life beyond their own households. An intriguing page at the very end of the account book lists flaxseed sold by the Kennebec Agricultural Society, yet there is little evidence in the account book itself of any sort of textile production in the town. Martha's diary tells us what happened to the seed. It not only records when Ephraim Ballard planted the flax, but when she and her daughters weeded and harvested it. It not only identifies the male helpers who turned and broke it, but the many female neighbors who assisted her and her daughters with the combing, spinning, reeling, boiling, spooling, warping, quilling, weaving, bucking, and bleaching that transformed the ripe plant into finished cloth. Martha's diary fills in the missing work — and trade — of women.

It also provides additional detail on the day-to-day operation of the male economy. Like most merchants, Howard served as a kind of banker, settling third-party debts with store goods or cash. Ephraim Ballard's accounts are typical, listing salt, rum, molasses, and nails on the debit side, several thousand feet of "clear" and "merchantable" boards among the credits, and on both sides of the ledger "notes" or "orders" on other men. On May 3, 1790, for example, the Howards debited Ephraim's account for "Willard Spoldings order dated 9 of June 1786" and "John Spoldings order dated 1 of July 1786." The diary shows where those orders came from. Early in April of 1786, Martha had noted, "Mr Ballard Been out to purchase Loggs." Twice in the next few weeks she wrote that "the Spolldings" had brought timber into the "Crik." She made no mention of the Spoldings on June 9 or on July 1, the dates given on the orders brought to William Howard, but she did note that Ephraim had gone to Pownalboro court on one of those days and to Vassalboro to "assist Brother Moore Rais his hous" on the other. Together the account book and the diary tell us how Ephraim Ballard "purchaced" logs for his sawmill. Contracting with men like the Spoldings, he paid in credit at the local stores, settling debts at court days and house-raisings, eventually balancing his own accounts with sawn boards.

Martha had a part in all this, as she noted on April 25: "Thee Spolldings brot Loggs. We had 9 men dind beside our own famely." But she did far more than

27

support Ephraim's efforts. During that same week, she noted that a hired hand had performed an errand for her at one of the stores at the Hook, bringing home "6 galn of Rhum, 2 lb Coffee, 5 lb sugar, & some Tobacco & 1 bushl ¼ of salt from Joseph Williams for me for assisting his wife in travil with her Last Child." A few days later, she reported sending twenty-one skeins of tow yarn to Mrs. Chamberlain to weave. The Howard account book tells us a great deal about the male economy of eighteenth-century Hallowell. Martha's diary shows how women and men worked together to sustain this eighteenth-century town.

The comparisons with Henry Sewall are more direct, since he, too, kept a diary. Like Cony, Sewall was a veteran of the Continental Army. He had come to Hallowell from York, Maine, in 1784, shortly after experiencing an intense religious conversion. Appointed clerk of the U.S. District Court in 1789, he was also for thirty-two years the town clerk of Hallowell and Augusta and for seventeen years the registrar of deeds for Kennebec County. His clear, almost mechanically even handwriting fills the pages of town and county records. The diary he kept from 1776 to 1842 is as remarkable in its own way as Martha's (though less steady).

In April of 1789, while she was fighting the spring freshet in Hallowell, he was far away in New York City attempting to establish himself in business. His diary entry for April 23, the day she sank in the mire while stepping out of her canoe, marks the distance between her world and his. He wrote:

About 2 o'clock P.M. Genl Washington, the illustrious President of the United States, arrived in this city. He approached in a barge which was built here for his use. On his passing the Battery, a federal salute was fired, which was followed by an instantaneous display of colors from all the shipping in the harbour. On his landing, the federal salute was repeated and all the bells in the city rang peals of joy upon the glad occasion.

For Sewall this was an especially joyous moment, for he had served under Washington. "I took a stand on the roof of Mr. Rob. Hunter's house," he continued, "where I had the satisfaction of seeing once more my quondam General; now advanced to the chief magistracy of the empire, which his valour & magnanimity (under providence) protected and established under the most trying circumstances."

It is not easy to bring together the heroism of Sewall's "quondam General" with the heroism of Martha Ballard as she journeyed back and forth across the Kennebec that same week. The Revolution, the ratification of the Constitution, and the election of Washington certainly affected her life (if only in providing her with grandsons named George, Samuel Adams, and DeLafayette), but the political events that inhabit so much of the foreground in Sewall's diary are only a hazy background, if that, in hers. Yet the converse is also true. In fact, we can learn far more about the world of war and politics from Martha's diary than we can about domestic life from Henry's. Eight times Martha Ballard crossed the river to deliver Tabitha Sewall. Not until the fourth delivery did Henry note her presence, and then only twice after that. Nor did he once mention the fees he paid her, nor the names of the other women present, nor the complications (social and medical) that attended the births. Sewall had little to say about the women of Hallowell, including his own wife. It is Martha's diary, not his, that tells us Tabitha was a bonnetmaker.

Yet it is his diary rather than Martha's that describes the symbolic importance of women in the new republic. On February 22, 1800, he helped organize a parade to commemorate the death of his former commander, General Washington. At the head, following a military escort, were "16 Misses, clad in white, with black hats & cloaks, & white scarfs," representatives of the then sixteen states in the Union. (According to a later account, based on oral tradition, the white scarfs were "fastened on the right shoulder with a black and white rosette; tied under the left arm, with long ends falling to the bottom of the dress.") Led by the young women, the memorial procession passed into the meeting house, the militia companies followed by judges, lawyers, physicians, members of the fire society, and other dignitaries, "the music playing a dead march, & a detachment from Captain Bowman's artillery firing minute guns during the whole." For the young Daughters of Columbia it must have been an impressive occasion, a ritual identification of their own lives with the survival of the new nation.

Martha attended the service at the meeting house "to commemorate the Death of General George Washington." Significantly, she said nothing at all about the parade of young women, though she noted the presence of "the Lodg of Hallowell, Captain Casts Company of militia, and a larg concoarce of people." Her life had been altered by the Revolution, but her identity was unrelated to the rituals of republicanism. In 1800, she was far more concerned with the death of Nabby Andros, a neighbor's daughter, than with the demise of General Washington. Her values had been formed in an older world, in which a woman's worth was measured by her service to God and her neighbors rather than to a nebulous and distant state. For Martha, politics was what men did at town meetings — necessary perhaps, but often troublesome and divisive. Though she lived through a Revolution, she was more a colonial goodwife than a Republican Mother. Her story allows us to see what was lost, as well as what was gained, in the political, economic, and social transformations of the eighteenth and early nineteenth centuries.

To understand Martha's world we must approach it on its own terms, neither as a golden age of household productivity nor as a political void from which a later feminist consciousness emerged. Martha's diary reaches to the marrow of eighteenth-century life. The trivia that so annoyed earlier readers provide a consistent, daily record of the operation of a female-man-aged economy. The scandals excised by local historians provide insight into sexual behavior, marital and extramarital, in a time of tumult and change. The remarkable birth records, 814 deliveries in all, allow the first full accounting of delivery practices and of obstetrical mortality in any early American town. The family squabbles that earlier readers (and abridgers) of the diary found almost as embarrassing as the sexual references show how closely related Martha's occupation was to the life cycle of her own family, and reveal the private politics behind public issues like imprisonment for debt. The somber record of her last years provides rare evidence on the nature of aging in the preindustrial world, and shows the pull of traditional values in an era of economic and social turmoil.

The heroism is there, too. In the last decade of her life, when the world seemed to be falling apart around her — armed settlers attacking surveyors in the woods, husbands and fathers killing themselves, and, in the case of her neighbor Captain Purrinton, his wife and children as well — Martha found the courage to continue her work. On April 4, 1812, she rode "on horsback without a pillion" to a delivery. On April 26, 1812, just a month before her death, she attended her last birth.

The structure of the diary forces us to consider midwifery in the broadest possible context, as one specialty in a larger neighborhood economy, as the most visible feature of a comprehensive and little-known system of early health care, as a mechanism of social control, a strategy for family support, and a deeply personal calling. One might wish for more detail, for more open expressions of opinion, fuller accounts of medical remedies or obstetrical complications, more candor in describing physicians or judges, and less circumspection in recording scandal, yet for all its reticence, Martha's diary is an unparalleled document in early American history. It is powerful in part because it is so difficult to use, so unyielding in its dailiness.

QUESTIONS TO CONSIDER

1. Ulrich says that earlier historians thought Martha Ballard's diary too trivial to be of real interest. Why did they think so? Has she shown it to be more rewarding? If so, how has she done so?

2. What important role did Martha Ballard, her daughters, and other women play in Hallowell's economic life beyond the home?

3. What can you learn from Ulrich's comparison of the ordinary records left by men and those left by women?

4. Ulrich describes Martha Ballard as being from an older world, one already disappearing in revolutionary America. What does she mean by this and how was the world in which Ballard moved different from the one growing up around her?

5. What role did a midwife play in eighteenth-century America and how important was it? Was the midwife's status already being challenged?

24

The Myth of the
Southern Lady

ANNE FIROR SCOTT

The man of antebellum America was an enterprising builder of farms and plantations, factories and railroads, hard at work making his fortune in a bustling, materialistic society. For most white men of the period, the opportunities for individual advancement and self-fulfillment became increasingly plentiful. But it was not so for women. They were barred from polls and politics, most professions and occupations; if they were married, their earnings legally belonged to their husbands. As we saw in "The Lords and the Mill Girls" (selection 19), farm and immigrant women might secure low-paying, low-skill jobs in mills and factories, but the only place for the "true woman" was the home — or at least so said the nineteenth-century women's magazines and religious journals, which reflected the pervasive attitudes of a male-dominated world. Most men — and a great many women — firmly held that the ideal woman was pious, pure, submissive, and domesticated, caring for her husband and rearing her children with a fragile, unquestioning sweetness. As historian Barbara Welter has wryly observed, "It was a fearful obligation, a solemn responsibility, which the nineteenth-century American woman had — to uphold the pillars of the temple with her frail white hand." Those who nurtured the cult of true womanhood thundered at those who questioned the old virtues, branding them all as enemies of God, of the Republic, of civilization itself.

This viewpoint especially prevailed in antebellum Dixie, where preachers, planters, novelists, and other molders of opinion were fanatical in idealizing and idolizing southern women. The southern belle, in fact, became an exaggeration of the ideal woman so cher-

31

ished in antebellum (or pre–Civil War) America. In the spirited essay that follows, historian Anne Firor Scott examines the myth of the southern lady as it flourished in the patriarchal South and explains that the need to preserve the slave system contributed in large part to the insistence on perfect yet submissive women. As Scott points out, southern writers also created "the myth of the southern gentleman" — he was honorable, firm, and authoritative, "a perfect patriarch" — which complemented the image of the ideal southern lady as devoted, domesticated, and submissive. Readers may want to compare the idealized role of the southern lady with the role of the pioneer women discussed in selection 22.

GLOSSARY

FITZHUGH, GEORGE   Virginia proslavery theorist who held that women and children must "recognize their proper and subordinate place" and must be utterly obedient to "lord and master," the male head of the family.

HUNDLEY, DANIEL   Alabama lawyer and social analyst who insisted that southern women "content themselves with their humble household duties"; Hundley also mythologized the southern gentleman as the ideal patriarch.

LONGSTREET, AUGUSTUS BALDWIN Southern minister, educator, lawyer, and author of "realistic" stories about life in middle Georgia.

TUCKER, BEVERLY   Antebellum southern novelist who supported the image of the southern lady.

PAGE, THOMAS NELSON   Summed up the image of the ideal southern lady: "her life was one long act of devotion. . . . "

I f talking could make it so antebellum southern women of the upper class would have been the most perfect examples of womankind yet seen on earth. If praise could satisfy all of woman's needs, they would also have been the happiest. Literary journals, sermons, novels, commencement addresses — wherever men spoke there was praise of Woman, and exhortation to further perfection.

This marvelous creation was described as a submissive wife whose reason for being was to love, honor, obey, and occasionally amuse her husband, to bring up his children and manage his household. Physically weak, and "formed for the less laborious occupations," she depended upon male protection. To secure this protection she was endowed with the capacity to "create a magic spell" over any man in her vicinity. She was timid and modest, beautiful and graceful, "the most fascinating being in creation . . . the delight and charm of every circle she moves in."

Part of her charm lay in her innocence. The less a woman knew of life, Ellen Glasgow once remarked bitterly, the better she was supposed to be able to deal

Selection from Anne Firor Scott, *The Southern Lady, from Pedestal to Politics*, pages 4–21, copyright © 1970 by The University of Chicago. Reprinted by permission of the publisher.

with it. Her mind was not logical, but in the absence of reasoning capacity her sensibility and intuition were highly developed. It was, indeed, to her advantage that "the play of instincts and of the feelings is not cramped by the controlling influence of logic and reason." She was capable of acute perceptions about human relationships, and was a creature of tact, discernment, sympathy, and compassion. It was her nature to be self-denying, and she was given to suffering in silence, a characteristic said to endear her to men. Less endearing, perhaps, but no less natural, was her piety and her tendency to "restrain man's natural vice and immorality." She was thought to be "most deeply interested in the success of every scheme which curbs the passions and enforces a true morality." She was a natural teacher, and a wise counselor to her husband and children.

Thomas Nelson Page, writing many years after the Civil War, summed up the image:

Her life was one long act of devotion, — devotion to God, devotion to her husband, devotion to her children, devotion to her servants, to the poor, to humanity. Nothing happened within the range of her knowledge that her sympathy did not reach and her charity and wisdom did not ameliorate. She was the head and font of the church. . . . The training of her children was her work. She watched over them, inspired them, led them, governed them; her will impelled them; her word to them, as to her servants, was law. She reaped the reward . . . their sympathy and tenderness were hers always, and they worshipped her.

Even a realist like Augustus Baldwin Longstreet was obviously influenced by the image when he came to describe a southern matron in one of his stories:

. . . pious but not austere, cheerful, but not light; generous but not prodigal; economical, but not close; hospitable but not extravagant. . . . To have heard her converse you would have supposed she did nothing but read, to have looked through the departments of her household you would have

Painting by Alice Ravenal Huger Smith of a southern lady and her daughter in the "stack-yard" of the plantation. In patriarchal Dixie, the perfect lady was regal in bearing but submissive in all things to her husband; she was the mistress of her household, her slaves, and her children but not of herself. Living up to the idealized image of southern womanhood required intense inner struggle and self-repression, yet few women questioned the reality of the image or the need to maintain it. (The Gibbes Museum of Art/Carolina Art Association)

supposed she never read. . . . Everything under her care went on with perfect system.

Oddly enough this paragon of virtue was thought to need the direction and control of some man. A person identified only as "president of the oldest college in Virginia" published a letter to his newly married daughter in an early issue of the *Southern Literary Messenger*. The wife's conduct alone, he asserted, determined the happiness or misery of a marriage. She must resolve at the outset never to oppose her husband, never to show displeasure, no matter what he might do. A man had a right to expect his wife to place perfect confidence in his judgment and to believe that he always knew best. "A difference with your husband ought to be considered the greatest calamity," wrote the father, adding that a woman who permitted differences to occur could expect to lose her husband's love and all hope of happiness. He concluded with the usual injunctions that she should be amiable, sweet, prudent, and devoted, that she should regulate her servants with a kind but firm hand, cultivate her mind by reading history and not corrupt it with novels, and manage her domestic concerns with neatness, order, economy, and judgment.

A novelist echoed the opinions of the college president. "In the heart of woman, uncorrupted by a false philosophy which would unfit her for her proper sphere, the proudest feeling is that of admiration for her husband. . . . this is as God meant it should be. To this state the natural feelings of a woman's heart will tend, let quacks in education do what they will."

From earliest childhood girls were trained to the ideals of perfection and submission. A magazine for children published in Charleston, recording the death of a seven-year-old, spoke of her as "peculiarly amiable and engaging; her behaviour marked with a delicate sense of propriety, happily mingled with an artless innocence." She was praised for being kind and considerate to her servants. The fiction in the same magazine was filled with pious, obedient little girls. Boarding schools for young ladies, to which more and more girls were sent as the century wore on, emphasized correct female behavior more than intellectual development. In at least one school the girls wrote their English compositions on such subjects as modesty, benevolence, and the evils of reading novels.

By the time they arrived at their teens most girls had absorbed the injunctions of the myth. One young woman wrote in her diary that she longed to die because she had not found a husband, adding, "I know I would make a faithful, obedient wife, loving with all my heart, yielding entire trust in my husband."

The image of the submissive woman was reinforced by evangelical theology. Daniel R. Hundley, a young Alabama lawyer who wrote a sociological analysis of the antebellum South, relied on Saint Paul's authority for asserting that women should "content themselves with their humble household duties." Southern pulpits repeated the apostle's injunction that women should keep silent in the churches. One minister argued that women needed "the hope and prospects of religion more . . . than the other sex" to soften the pains of living and help women bear with patience and submission the inevitable trials of life, among which he suggested might be "a husband of acid temper." A North Carolina doctor wrote that "God in his inscrutable wisdom has appointed a place and duty for females *out of which* they can neither accomplish their destiny nor secure their happiness!!"

Southern women sought diligently to live up to the prescriptions, to attain the perfection and the submissiveness demanded of them by God and man. John Donald Wade, whose researches into the life of Augustus Baldwin Longstreet reinforced his understanding of the social history of middle Georgia, concluded that "men found intelligence in woman a quality that in general distressed more than it pleased. When they did not openly condemn they treated it with insulting condescension. *The women proved themselves marvelously adaptable.*" A woman novelist suggested something about the ongoing struggle to live up to the expectations of men:

To repress a harsh answer, to confess a fault, and to stop (right or wrong) in the midst of self-defence, in gentle submission, sometimes requires a struggle like life and death; but these *three* efforts are the golden threads with which domestic happiness is woven; once begin the fabric with this woof, and trials shall not break or sorrow tarnish it.

Men are not often unreasonable; their difficulties lie in not understanding the moral and physical structure of our sex. . . . How clear it is, then, that woman loses by petulance and recrimination! Her first study must be self-control, almost to hypocrisy. A good wife must smile amid a thousand perplexities, and clear her voice to tones of cheerfulness when her frame is drooping with disease or else languish alone.

Women made heroic efforts to live up to what was expected of them. One, who could hardly bear the sound of her husband tuning his violin, bit her lip and said nothing, murmuring about self-abnegation. There was no rest for the conscience. "We owe it to our husbands, children and friends," wrote a Louisiana housewife, "to represent as nearly as possible the ideal which they hold so dear." " 'Tis man's to act, 'tis woman's to endure," reflected an Alabama novelist in the midst of trials with a husband she did not much respect, and financial problems beyond her power to solve. Women were made, indeed, the long-suffering wife of the violinist concluded, "to suffer and be strong." "Give me a double portion of the grace of thy Spirit that I may learn meekness," wrote the self-flagellating wife of a minister.

Even more effort, if possible, went into the struggle to live up to what God was presumed to expect of women. A young bride laid down a program for herself:

1. To read the Bible and pray after rising in the morning and sometime after breakfast.

2. To pray again before dinner and read the Bible in the evening and pray before bed.

3. To obey my husband in all things reasonable.

4. "I will endeavor to use patience and forebearance towards my son [her husband's son by an earlier marriage] and correct him in a spirit of mildness for every offense of which he may be guilty.

5. "I will endeavor to offend not with the tongue, but hold it in with bit and bridle and speak charitably of all persons."

6. "I will endeavor to do good unto all as far as it is in my power, especially unto the household of faith."

7. "I will endeavor to subdue every evil propensity by the assistance of Divine Grace, and by practicing

that degree of fasting and abstinence which my health will admit of."

This same woman kept a religious diary devoted entirely to daily meditations and painful examination of her progress in the endless struggle for religious perfection. Shortly after her marriage she begged God to cleanse her of secret faults, to save her from impatience and hastiness of temper, and to give her "perfect resignation to Thy Holy Will concerning me." In succeeding entries she deplored her own hardness of heart and expressed guilt when she did not bear severe pain with Christian fortitude.

This was not just one aberrant perfectionist. There are numerous similar letters and diaries. "I feel this day heavy and sad and I would ask myself why and the answer is I feel cold in religious matters oh why am I thus?" "I feel that I am worthless and through the merits of Christ's all-atoning blood alone can I be saved." "Mr. B. [her husband] says we must try to live holier. Oh that I could. Spent some time today reading, weeping and praying." "Help me O Lord for I am poor and weak, help me for I am desolate, in Thee alone have I hope." "As for myself I find my heart so full of sinful feelings that I am ready to say 'I am chief of sinners.' " "Lord I feel that my heart is a cage of unclean beasts." "I see so much of sin, so many things to correct, that I almost despair of being a perfect christian." "Oh! for an increased degree of peace to know and do my redeemers will, to live more as I should."

The biblical verse most frequently quoted in southern women's diaries was from Jeremiah: "The heart is deceitful above all things and desperately wicked: who can know it?" There are references to sins too awful even to be recorded in a private journal, accompanied by allusions to cold hearts.

Many women assumed that if they were unhappy or discontented in the "sphere to which God had appointed them" it must be their own fault and that by renewed effort they could do better. "My besetting sins are a roving mind and an impetuous spirit," wrote one woman whose diary is filled with admonitions to herself to be systematic, diligent, prudent, economical, and patient with her servants. Josephine Clay Habersham was a gentle and gifted woman who presided with skill and dignity over a large plantation in eastern Georgia. A devoted mother who could write, "I wish always to have a sweet babe to mind, care for and love," she still felt it necessary to make a constant effort to cultivate a cheerful spirit, to ask God for help with her "dull and wayward heart," and to ask forgiveness for not being a more faithful servant. A girl of eighteen prayed to be useful and bemoaned the "vain desires that every now and then trouble this prevailing one [to love God] and my flesh is so weak, I am always failing."

Women whose families and friends thought them "spotless" were themselves convinced that their souls were in danger. One prayed to God to be delivered from the "serpent whose folds are around my limbs; his sting in my heart." A Mississippi woman found her mind "sunk in a state of apathy from which I can with difficulty arouse myself" and was sure that this was because she had neglected her duty and transgressed God's holy laws. She was constantly concerned lest "the world and its cares have too large a share of my time and affections."

For many of these women the brief span of earthly life was chiefly important as preparation for eternity, and much of their self-exhortation centered on being ready to die. They prayed for the will to "overcome every evil propensity . . . to be calm and collected at all times," so as to be ready to depart from the world at a moment's notice in a state of grace, or for the power to bring other sinners to the "throne of peace." Such women were cast into deep depression when they gave way to temper, slapped a child, or admonished a slave. One woman scolded herself, "I am not as much engaged in religion as I should be . . . too worldly." An unattainable perfection was the only standard.

There is little doubt that religious faith served an important function at a time when many children and adults died for no apparent reason. A firm belief that death was a manifestation of God's will made it easier to bear what otherwise would have been an intolerable burden. It is also clear that the requirements for salvation dovetailed neatly with the secular image of women. Religious women were persuaded that the very qualities which made any human being a rich, interesting, assertive personality — a roving mind, spirit, ambition — were propensities to be curbed. No matter what secret thoughts a woman might have about her own abilities, religion confirmed what society told her — namely, that she was inferior to men.

The language of piety and the desire for salvation, the belief in an eternal life, were not, of course, confined to women. The same phrases abound in the letters, diaries, and sermons of many men. The significant difference was that for men submission to God's will in spiritual matters was considered to be perfectly compatible with aggressive behavior and a commanding position in life. Men expected to be obeyed by women, children, and slaves, to be the decision makers and the ultimate source of secular authority.

Daniel Hundley's myth of the southern gentleman complements the image of the southern lady. The gentleman, Hundley insisted, in addition to being finely formed and highly educated, was firm, commanding, and a perfect patriarch. "The natural dignity of manner peculiar to the southern gentleman is doubtless owing to his habitual use of authority from his earliest years." The weakness and dependence of women was thrown into bold relief by his virility and mastery of his environment. Husbands were frequently referred to in the words used for God: Lord and Master.

The rigid definition of the proper role and behavior of southern women requires explanation. It is not that the constellation of ideas which constituted the image of the southern lady was peculiar to the American South; men in Victorian England conjured up a similar myth in poems like Coventry Patmore's "The Angel in the House." Harriet Martineau was speaking of all American women, not just those of the South, when she described them as lying down at night "full of self-reproach for the want of piety which they do not know how to attain." But, as William R. Taylor has noted, southern plantation novelists were "fanatical" in idolizing and idealizing southern women. The evidence adduced in this chapter bears out his observation with respect to southern men in general.

Such men continued an old tradition in Western history. The myth of the lady was associated with medieval chivalry. Books of advice on proper behavior for both men and women dated back to the invention of printing. Castiglione's *The Courtier,* a sixteenth-century book of etiquette, set the style for such books, and by the eighteenth century books specifically directed to women were widely read in England and in America. Usually written by men, they emphasized the softness, purity, and spirituality of women while denying them intellectual capacity. Women were instructed to please their husbands, attend to their physical needs, cover up their indiscretions, and give them no cause for worry. All such descriptions and injunctions were included in the southern creed.

But the fact that such ideas had been around for a long time does not explain why they were so enthusiastically embraced by antebellum southerners. Other models were available for a sparsely settled rural society. The good woman of Proverbs, for example, who worked willingly with her hands, got up early and set all in her household to work, bought and sold land, and didn't worry about her appearance might have been an excellent ideal. Why was she not chosen?

We know very little about the relationship of ideology to social structures and understand very little about the social consequences of unconscious needs.

Even so, it is possible to speculate that, as with so much else in the antebellum South, slavery had a good deal to do with the ideal of the southern lady. Because they owned slaves and thus maintained a traditional landowning aristocracy, southerners tenaciously held on to the patriarchal family structure. The patriarchy had been the norm in seventeenth-century England. Transported to Virginia and adopted as a social pattern by the planters there, it lived on into the nineteenth century in the whole South. A future officer of the Confederacy explained the theory of the family common among his contemporaries, and related it directly to the institution of slavery:

The Slave Institution of the South increases the tendency to dignify the family. Each planter is in fact a Patriarch — his position compels him to be a ruler in his household. From early youth, his children and servants look up to him as the head, and obedience and subordination become important elements of education. . . . Domestic relations become those which are most prized.

Women, along with children and slaves, were expected to recognize their proper and subordinate place and to be obedient to the head of the family. Any tendency on the part of any of the members of the system to assert themselves against the master threatened the whole, and therefore slavery itself. It was no accident that the most articulate spokesmen for slavery were also eloquent exponents of the subordinate role of women. George Fitzhugh, perhaps the most noted and certainly among the most able of these spokesmen, wrote, for example:

So long as she is nervous, fickle, capricious, delicate, diffident and dependent, man will worship and adore her. Her weakness is her strength, and her true art is to cultivate and improve that weakness. Woman naturally shrinks from public gaze, and from the struggle and competition of life . . . in truth, woman, like children, has but one right and that is the

right to protection. The right to protection involves the obligation to obey. A husband, a lord and master, whom she
should love, honor and obey, nature designed for every
woman. . . . If she be obedient she stands little danger of
maltreatment.

If the need to maintain the slave system contributed
to the insistence upon perfect, though submissive,
women, so did the simple fact that a male-dominated
society was good for men. Some of the characteristics
demanded of the southern lady were also expected
of women in other parts of the United States and
require no more complex explanation than that
any ruling group can find a theory to justify its
position. Like aristocrats, Communists, and bourgeois businessmen, southern men had no trouble
finding theoretical support for a way of life that was
decidedly to their advantage. Obedient, faithful, submissive women strengthened the image of men who
thought themselves vigorous, intelligent, commanding leaders.

Such women also contributed considerably to
manly creature comforts. Ellen Glasgow put it this
way in one of her novels:

The cares she met with such serenity had been too heavy for
her strength; they had driven the bloom from her cheeks
and the lustre from her eyes; and, though she had not faltered at her task, she had drooped daily and grown older
than her years. The master might live with lavish disregard
of the morrow, not the master's wife. For him were the
open house, the shining table, the well-stocked wine cellar
and the morning rides over the dewey fields; for her the
care of her home and children, and of the souls and bodies
of the black people that had been given into her hands.

Despite the vigor of their statements, there is some
evidence that southern men did not feel altogether secure in their self-proclaimed position of lord and
master of the whole patriarchy. Fear lay beneath the
surface of the flowery praise of woman and the insistence that God had made her the way men wanted

her to be. Otherwise it is hard to see why men spent
so much time and energy stating their position. One
of Beverly Tucker's leading characters discussed the
way he proposed to educate his daughter. She must
be raised, he said, to take for granted her husband's
superiority, to rely on his wisdom, to take pride in his
distinction. "Even should her faculties be superior to
his, he cannot raise her so high but that she will still
feel herself a creature of his hands."

What were they afraid of, these would-be patri-
archs who threatened to withdraw their love from
women who disagreed with them or aspired to any
forbidden activity? Partly, perhaps, that the women to
whom they had granted the custody of conscience
and morality might apply that conscience to male behavior — to sharp trading in the market place, to in-
ordinate addiction to alcohol, to nocturnal visits to
the slave quarters. Men were aware, too, that the
woman who had been so firmly put in her place, the
home, often showed unusual power within that restricted domain. She raised the children; she set the
standards for behavior. In 1802 a visiting Englishman
commented that in North Carolina "the legislative
and executive powers of the house belong to the mistress, the master has nothing to do with administration; he is a monument of uxoriousness and passive
endurance." Two decades later a North Carolinian
wrote to a friend contemplating matrimony that he
must be "prepared to have his nose occasionally
ground . . . and that he must not drink or play cards."
If women could exert so much power even in their
restricted position who could tell what they might do
with more freedom?

The omens were there to see. Southern men often
identified the work of the hated abolitionists with the
work of "strong-minded" northern women. A Virginian wrote to a friend in 1853:

You have doubtless seen in the newspapers the struggle we
had with the strong-minded women as they call themselves
in the World Temperance Convention. If you have seen a
true account of the matter you will see that we gained a

perfect triumph, and I believe have given a rebuke to this most impudent clique of unsexed females and rampant abolitionists which must put down the petticoats — at least as far as their claim to take the platforms of public debate and enter into all the rough and tumble of the war of words.

His college professor correspondent replied: "I most heartily rejoice with you in the defeat of those shameless amazons." It was a paradox that men who asserted that God made woman as they wished her to be, or that the feminine qualities they admired were given by nature, were afraid that women would break out of the God-given and natural mode of behavior.

If these speculations ring true, one pressing question still remains. Since the ideal of perfection placed a great strain upon women, why did they tolerate their role? One reason is suggested by the early indoctrination already mentioned: the institutions and mores of the society all pointed in the same direction. Churches, schools, parents, books, magazines, all promulgated the same message: be a lady and you will be loved and respected and supported. If you defy the pattern and behave in ways considered unladylike you will be unsexed, rejected, unloved, and you will probably starve.

The persistence of the complementary images of the soft, submissive, perfect woman and of the strong, commanding, intelligent, and dominant man in the face of an exigent reality that often called for quite different qualities suggests that these images had deep significance for the men and women who believed in them. A society increasingly threatened from the outside had every reason to try to diminish internal threats to its stability. George Fitzhugh made this quite explicit when he equated any change in the role of women *or* in the institution of slavery with the downfall of the family and the consequent demise of society. If the distance between the myth and reality became so great that it could not be overlooked, then the situation might be threatening indeed.

Though many southern women were worried about slavery, few had any vision of a society different from the one they knew. Perhaps they, too, sensed a threat of social disorganization inherent in any challenge to male dominance. For whatever reasons, most of them tried to live up to the Sisyphean task expected of them.

QUESTIONS TO CONSIDER

1. Compare the role of the southern lady with that of the mill girl (selection 19) and the pioneer woman (selection 22). How does the reality of each female's life square with the image of the "true woman"?

2. Examine the role of evangelical Protestantism in reinforcing the passive image of women. What similarities do you see with Christianity's role in supporting black slavery?

3. The cult of true womanhood was an ideal of female behavior. What evidence does Scott present that real southern women took this ideal seriously and attempted to live up to its exacting standards? What were the costs and gains of these attempts?

4. Examine the words of southern writers such as George Fitzhugh and Beverly Tucker on the subject of women. What fears and threats lurk behind their glorified praise of southern womanhood?

5. Why did southern whites, male and female, regard the maintenance of the feminine domestic ideal as crucial for the present and future stability of their slave-based society?

4

How the West Was Really Won

Miriam Horn

With the Indians out of the way, Americans were free at last to conquer the vast Great Plains that reached from Texas to the Canadian border in the center of the country. Westering farmers had stopped at the edge of this enormous grassland, because its arid climate and shallow topsoil seemed unsuited to agricultural techniques devised in the East. But after the Civil War came the development of new farming techniques and new machinery such as the windmill, the chilled-iron plow, and the combine, all of which made agriculture feasible on the windy prairies. As a consequence, farmers from east of the Mississippi swarmed there during the postwar years, some claiming 160 acres free under the 1862 Homestead Act, most buying their land from speculators or the railroads. In the 1880s alone, more than 1 million people poured onto the Great Plains from the Great Lakes states. Meanwhile, after the failure of Reconstruction, African Americans headed west as well; they were sodbusters, cowboys, speculators, miners, lawmen, desperadoes, and cavalrymen. Asian and Mexican Americans were present, too, all contributing to the drama of frontier conquest. The pioneers lived in all manner of homes — from dugouts to sod houses — battling tornadoes, hail, dust storms, blizzards, prairie fires, and grasshopper plagues in an endless struggle to make new lives for themselves on the nation's last frontier.

In 1890, the United States Census Bureau reported that the frontier was now settled. What had the frontier experience meant? How had it affected the national character? In 1893, a young history professor named Frederick Jackson Turner answered that question in a seminal essay, "The Significance of the Frontier in American History." The Turner thesis, as it would be known, argued that the American was a unique national type made that way by the frontier experience. According to Turner, a new society had sprung up in

40

America, one that borrowed from the Old World but was distinctly different because of its inexorable march westward. A significant consequence of that march was "the formation of a composite nationality," as the "crucible of the frontier" Americanized wave after wave of immigrants. Turner asserted, "To the frontier, the American intellect owes its striking characteristics. That coarseness and strength combined with acuteness and inquisitiveness; that practical, inventive turn of mind, quick to find expedients; that masterful grasp of material things, lacking in the artistic but powerful to effect great ends; that restless, nervous energy, that dominant individualism, working for good and for evil, and withal that buoyancy and exuberance which come with freedom — these are traits of the frontier, or traits called out elsewhere because of the existence of the frontier." As the country marched west, frontier types emerged, all of them, in the Turner pantheon, men: the explorer, the trapper, the trader, the soldier, the rancher, the farmer, and finally the town builder, each contributing in his distinct way to "the advance of civilization." Not only did the frontier produce "rugged individualism," the prime trait of Turner's all-American man, but it also carved democracy itself out of a virgin wilderness, producing the free political institutions that made America unique.

The Turner thesis had the force of myth, and its staying power in American popular culture may be attributed to its mythic quality. By myth, we do not mean some preposterous story. We mean the wishful, grandiose way a culture views its past. "Myths tell us of the exploits of the gods," says X. J. Kennedy, "all on a scale of magnificence larger than our life. We envy their freedom and power; they enact our wishes and dreams." Our wishes and dreams, projected onto the history of the West, reveal our deepest longing as a people.

If the Turner thesis, popularized in novels and motion pictures, has captured the popular imagination, it has also been the subject of heated controversy, especially in academe. While western historians such as Ray Allen Billington and Martin Ridge accepted Turner's basic argument and refined and updated it, others disputed his theory as romantic nonsense and fraught with error. Never, however, has the Turner argument been more assailed than today, what with the emergence of a younger generation of western historians who have placed the Turner hypothesis under siege. For them, as Miriam Horn says, "the West was not some rough-hewn egalitarian democracy, where every man had a piece of land and the promise of prosperity, but a world quickly dominated by big money and big government." The new western historians take Turner to task, too, for ignoring America's brutal treatment of the Indians and for the greed and destruction that characterized so much of the westering experience. They chastise Turner for omitting women, blacks, Asians, and Mexican Americans from the frontier equation. Disputing the notion of westerners as self-sufficient individualists, the new historians point out that the frontier in fact gave birth to the welfare state, thanks to federal irrigation projects, crop subsidies, and drought aid. Indeed, the example of supreme rugged individualism, the cattleman, enjoyed a huge *federal subsidy in the form of free range on government land. But perhaps the worst aspect of the westward movement, the new historians believe, was the ecological devastation that accompanied it. "The settlement of the Great Plains," one of them asserted, "was a world-class environmental catastrophe," the effects of which are still being felt.*

In the selection that follows, Miriam Horn summarizes the findings of the new western historians and reflects on what their work has done to our cherished western myths. Note, in particular, how these historians, using the techniques of the new social history, which focuses on everyday life, have shed new light on the role and experience of women on the frontier. Note, too, the western experiences of African, Asian, and Mexican Americans. If the new western historians sometimes overstate their case, concentrating too much on the negative side of the frontier story and its "legacy of conquest," they have forced us to reconsider that story, to acknowledge and benefit from its mistakes and its tragedies. As you study this selection, ask yourself how much you agree with the new western historians. Do you think that they have created a countermyth of the West, born of their disillusionment over Vietnam and the anti-imperialist views of the sixties? Why do you think the old myths of the West — which constitute America's only national mythology — have had such enduring appeal?

GLOSSARY

BECKWOURTH, JIM African American fur trapper.

DAWES ACT (1887) Broke up Indian reservations into individually owned plots of land; its goal was to make the Indians into "imitation white" farmers.

CROCKETT, DAVY Legendary hero of the Alamo, the famous "last stand" in Texas's war for independence against Mexico (1836); historian Dan Kilgore stirred up a storm of protest when he suggested that Crockett might not have died as mythology claims.

GOETZ, BERNHARD Manhattan citizen who in 1984 shot four African American teenagers in a New York City subway when they asked him for money; Goetz said that he packed a pistol in self-defense — he had been mugged in New York City in 1981; he was acquitted of homicide but was sentenced to five months in jail for carrying an unlicensed gun.

LAMAR, HOWARD Yale historian who regards the near-extermination of the buffalo "as one of the biggest ecological changes in North American history."

LIMERICK, PATRICIA Her book, *The Legacy of Conquest,* is "the most comprehensive summary of the new view" of western history.

NORTH, OLIVER American army colonel who was involved in the Iran-Contra scandal of the second Reagan administration (see selection 31); segments of the American public celebrated him as a hero, although he admitted to having lied to Congress and destroying incriminating documents; in 1994, he ran for the U.S. Senate.

PICKETT, BILL African American cowboy who felled steers by biting them on the lip and forcing them to the ground.

I t is our Book of Genesis. Our legend of Romulus and Remus. The story of the frontier is America's myth of creation. In those rolling prairies and gold-rich mountains, a new, freer man was born, unhindered by tradition, restless and independent, endlessly optimistic, hard-working and unafraid. Living on the "hither edge" of wilderness, in historian Frederick Jackson Turner's phrase, the pioneer had "broken the cake of custom" to forge the headstrong young nation that would become America.

Or so we were told by generations of historians. But the Turnerian view of the West is falling apart these days, dismantled by a group of young scholars raised on the disillusionments of Vietnam and the anti-imperialist rhetoric of the '60s. Turner himself understood that "each age writes the history of the past anew with reference to the conditions uppermost in its own time." So this new group of historians sifts through the evidence with an eye toward race, gender and class. They are turning away from Great Men and Great Events to ordinary people and daily life, poring over diaries and letters and the evidence left in the land itself.

Read the new studies, and you discover that the West was not some rough-hewn egalitarian democracy, where every man had a piece of land and the promise of prosperity, but a world quickly dominated by big money and big government. It was not Walt Whitman's "newer garden of creation," where the sodbuster might dwell in sweet harmony with nature, but a nearly unmitigated environmental catastrophe. Nor was the pioneer family, so often invoked by nostalgic politicians urging a return to fundamental American values, a close-knit little household facing down hardship. Often, it was torn apart by the great desert emptiness of the West.

Frederick Jackson Turner was right to locate the

From Miriam Horn, "How the West Was Really Won," *U.S. News & World Report*, May 21, 1990, 57–65.

roots of the American character on the frontier. But that legacy, say the new historians, is one of rapaciousness and environmental plunder, of fragmented families, racial strife, vast disparities between rich and poor. Though the frontier was "closed" 100 years ago, when the 1890 census showed settlement from sea to sea, that date did not mark a decisive break in history, as Turner and his followers argued. The new historians see a continuous story, with the issues that consumed the old West remaining central concerns in America today.

Still, these historians struggle to be taken seriously. Their more traditional colleagues are mildly critical, charging that they sometimes overstate their case. "Not all of their work is necessarily so new," says Martin Ridge, author with Ray Billington of the pre-eminent college text on Western history, *Westward Expansion*. "But they are without question innovative and committed scholars, and everybody welcomes new approaches to the region's history." A respectful hearing outside the field is more elusive. University of Colorado Prof. Patricia Limerick, author of the most comprehensive summary of the new view, *The Legacy of Conquest*, likens the "stereotypes of noble savages and noble pioneers struggling quaintly in the wilderness" to the aura of moonlight and magnolias that long shrouded Southern history, handicapping scholars in their efforts to excavate the realities of slavery and Reconstruction. With the mountain man and cowboy "the domain of mass entertainment and lighthearted national escapism," says Limerick, Western historians are relegated to a quaint regionalism.

They must also do battle with a deep ideological attachment to the fantasies of the frontier. In 1985, Ronald Reagan spoke of the men of the Alamo calling out encouragement to one another, the settler pushing west and singing his song: "It is the American sound: Hopeful, bighearted, idealistic; daring, decent and fair. That's our heritage . . . there is always a better tomorrow. We believed then and now there are no limits to growth." That faith in limitless bounty,

Homesteaders on the plains, with their sod house in the background. *"Most homesteaders," writes Miriam Horn, "went broke when* *their fields dried up, and were forced to sell to the handful of* *landowners lucky enough to have water." (The Bettmann Archive)*

say these historians, has been nothing but trouble for the American West.

Economic success was the ordained lot of frontier settlers; men and women had only to apply themselves to achieve wealth and an elevated social status. . . . The wide dispersal of land ownership mitigated against control by the few or the distant. If people fell by the wayside they had only themselves to blame.

— BILLINGTON AND RIDGE,
Westward Expansion, 1949

The idea of the self-sufficient individual is the most elevated tenet in the American gospel, codified by none other than Thomas Jefferson. With a vast conti-

nent before him, Jefferson foresaw a nation of yeoman farmers, each in possession of 160 acres carved out of the wilderness or liberated from indolent natives to be made productive by the sweat of the American brow. [Jefferson's vision was incorporated in the 1862 Homestead Act, which offered adult citizens and aliens alike, regardless of their sex or race, free 160-acre tracts of government land in the West; they would receive final titles to their farms after they had lived on them for five years and paid nominal fees.]

Unfortunately, what worked in the lush valleys of Virginia was doomed to fail in the arid reaches of the Far West. This was a land of deserts that were fiercely hot and fiercely cold, streams that flooded a few weeks each year and went dry the rest, grasshopper plagues, hail followed by drought followed by hail, sterile salt beds and relentless winds. A rancher might survive with 2,500 acres to run his livestock, but expecting a farmer to make it on 160 acres, wrote Ian Frazier in *Great Plains,* published last year [1989], "was like expecting a fisherman to survive on a little square of ocean." Most homesteaders went broke when their fields dried up, and were forced to sell to the handful of landowners lucky enough to have water.

Those men accumulated massive holdings, sometimes exceeding a million acres, despite feeble legal efforts to constrain their empire building. According to Marc Reisner, whose 1987 *Cadillac Desert* examines the role of federal and urban bureaucracies in the competition for water, the West presented endless opportunities for fraud. A speculator might meet the requirement for a domicile on each section, for instance, by scattering birdhouses across his land. Consequently, by the 1890s, seven eighths of the farmland west of the Mississippi was owned by nonfarmers, and agribusiness was born. Organized around large-scale water management, the West had become a "land of authority and restraint, of class and exploitation, and ultimately of imperial power," says University of Kansas historian Donald Worster, author of *Rivers of Empire.*

Monopoly enterprise came quickly to ranching and mining, as well, turning the "rugged individualist" into an impoverished wage laborer. In 1855, 157 Eastern-based corporations ran cattle in Colorado, and the Scotland-based Prairie Land & Cattle Company owned a strip 50 miles wide from the Arkansas River to New Mexico. The cowboy, that icon of freedom, wrote Wallace Stegner in 1987, "was and is an overworked, underpaid hireling, almost as homeless and dispossessed as a modern crop worker." Prospectors, too, soon exhausted the surface gold in the mountains and became virtually indentured to the Eastern financiers who owned the machines, mills and smelters necessary for underground mining.

Ironically, notes Limerick, the myth of self-suffi-

ciency deprived miners of recourse. Compensation for injury was typically denied by courts, which deemed the individual responsible for his own safety. Despite lung-clogging dust and temperatures often exceeding 120 degrees, unionization was long blocked on the ground that it would compromise the independence of the solitary miner.

And it was in the ostensibly self-reliant West, say the new historians, that the modern welfare state was born, beginning with mass federal irrigation projects in 1902 and evolving to include the crop subsidies and drought assistance of modern times. Though he had been lured to barren land by politicians and railroad marketeers, still the farmer was flogged for requiring aid. In the 1870s, Governor Pillsbury of Minnesota warned that assistance to farmers would "sap and destroy the vital energies of self-reliance."

Oh, faith rewarded! Now no idle dream,
The long-sought Canaan before him lies;
He floods the desert with the mountain stream,
And Lo! It leaps transformed to paradise.
— TRADITIONAL MORMON HYMN

The Romantic sensibility of the 19th century was fertile ground for the idea of "Natural Man" — an innocent fleeing dark, corrupted cities to settle in the promised land and bring forth its God-given bounty. In fact, says Worster, "the settlement of the Great Plains was a world-class environmental catastrophe, one we still refuse to admit, given our pride in our agricultural expertise."

Historians are now tapping geologists, biologists, botanists and environmental scientists to perform an autopsy on the land. Where alder trees have replaced Douglas fir, it means there was clearcutting and the land was burned over several times. An abundance of sage and juniper indicates overgrazing well in the past. The damage is vast: Ground water contaminated or depleted; plowed-up topsoil lost to drought and the merciless winds; entire species destroyed.

Yale historian Howard Lamar, who taught many of

the new historians and laid the foundation for their work with his *Reader's Encyclopedia of the American West,* describes the slaughter of the buffalo as one of the biggest ecological changes in North American history. In just 30 years, some 60 million animals were destroyed and replaced by cattle, disrupting the native ecology and leaving the land overgrazed and exhausted. "The rancher is a man who supplants the native grasses with tumbleweed, snakeweed, mud, dust and flies," wrote environmental activist and novelist Edward Abbey. "He drives off elk and antelope, shoots eagles, bears and cougars on sight. And then leans back and grins at the TV cameras and talks about how much he loves the American West." The problem has always been greed, argues Worster. The 1880s were a veritable free-for-all on the grasslands. Cattle barons eager to get rich quick built their herds to untenable size, leading finally to the collapse of the cattle kingdom. Miners, too, gutted the countryside to get out the minerals as fast as possible, heedless of the wasted land they left behind.

Cow country was man's country, but a cowboy was obliged to protect decent Christian women. Sometimes he would get a hankerin' to hit town, where he would spend his cash on liquor, gambling and women of ill repute. The ranch boss knew the cowboy had worked hard, felt isolated, built up tension and needed a binge.

— ROBERT HEIDE AND JOHN GILMAN, *Box Office Buckaroos,* 1990

Until recently, Western history has been by and about men. Now, as scholars reconstruct the lives of frontier women and children, they dismantle nostalgic notions of the prairie family. Again, individualism emerges as a decidedly mixed blessing. "Our national celebration of separation and autonomy has given us the justification for taking families apart," says historian Lillian Schissel, co-author of *Far from Home; Families of the Westward Journey.*

Drawing on diaries, letters and reminiscences, Schissel traces the sagas of pioneer families. A family

of Colorado prospectors buries all but one of seven children. A widow on an Oregon homestead is abandoned by her only son and must contend on her own with a failing farm, one daughter gone mad and another whose husband threatens to cut her throat. In South Dakota, two families of Russian immigrants live their first winter on the plains with all 12 people crowded into a boxcar "worse than a coyote hole" and so little food the children howl constantly with hunger.

The private records of this misery are richer than any fiction. One of the Russian men writes: "We were so lacking in tools for changing the rugged prairies into productive farmland that when I think back to our first year on that coyote land, I can hardly keep from crying." Things got better the second year, but "my wife Sophie, with seven children and all sleeping in a shanty that became a pond when it rained, loathed everything about America. It is odd we even slept together, but we had no other choice."

Given high mortality rates and the economic advantages of having numerous children, frontier women were nearly always pregnant and worked even in their ninth month hauling buckets of mud or armfuls of wheat to the threshing floor. The men were often drunk and occasionally violent. One frontier ditty advised: "A woman, a dog, a hickory tree, The more you beat them the better they be." Worst of all was the endless isolation. Tied to their homes and often miles from the nearest neighbor, says Schissel, the women would walk down to the tracks to catch a glimpse of human faces when the train passed by. Some went mad in their loneliness, listening to nothing but the incessant wailing of the wind. One prairie daughter recalled often "finding my mother crying, and wondering whether she cried of fatigue, craving a word of recognition, gratitude or praise."

Children, too, worked as soon as they were able. In *Growing up with the Country: Childhood on the Far Western Frontier,* historian Elliott West unearths a Kansas farmer's letter home about his son: "Little Baz

Backbreaking toil was the lot of women and men on the frontier. "Worst of all was the isolation. Tied to their homes and often miles from the nearest neighbor, women would walk down to the tracks to catch a glimpse of human faces when the train passed by." (The Bettman Archive)

can fetch up cows out of the stock fields, or oxen, carry in stove wood and climb in the corn crib and feed the hogs and go on errands down to his grandma's." At the time, Little Baz was just over 2 years old. Another boy, at age 11, was breaking horses for 50 cents apiece. "His father tied him to the horse, and tied his hat to his head, and after the kid had flopped around for a bit he got to be an expert," says West.

In the positive view he takes of frontier childhood, West is unusual among the new historians. He emphasizes the youngsters' closeness to the land, a sense of home never fully achieved by their displaced parents. Though to some degree perplexed by their wild prairie children, says West, these parents were extremely loving, if for no other reason than that they couldn't afford to have their children run away. That benign view is disputed by Schissel and others, who argue that frontier children were often emotionally neglected and physically abused. These more pessimistic historians stress the torments of childhood, the bedbugs and pinworms and cholera and fevers, the filth and starvation and death.

Anglo-American pioneers were uniquely equipped to capitalize on frontier opportunity for self-betterment.

— BILLINGTON AND RIDGE

For decades, Western history was not only male but white. The Indian was an object for Western heroism: A savage to be conquered or a noble primitive waiting to be civilized. The Hispanic was the enemy — remember the Alamo. Blacks and Chinese were simply left out. "The migration from the East was only one of many in the 19th century," says University of Utah historian Richard White, who [was in 1990] writing a text to replace Billington and Ridge. "There were also large migrations from the South and from Asia, both of which were periodically blocked and both of which continue to this day."

The approach of the 500th anniversary of the landing of Columbus . . . spurred extensive scholarship on the southern migration, much of it aimed at reclaiming Spain's status as the first to settle the American West. Coronado was already exploring western North America in 1539, hundreds of years before Anglos arrived there. In 1598, Don Juan de Onate led 400 colonists across the Rio Grande, and on April 30, they formally claimed the land for Spain. Last month [April 1990], the Texas House of Representatives passed a resolution declaring that day the first Thanksgiving in America, and asked Massachusetts to concede defeat.

Even before 1821, the year Mexico won independence, trappers and prospectors had begun encroaching on Mexican land. They were the "illegal aliens" of their day, says Limerick, but were tolerated and assimilated into Mexican culture. By the 1830s, however, distinguished Anglo writers were championing the notion of "the white man's burden" to civilize the more savage races and lamenting the waste of such rich territory. "In the hands of an enterprising people, what a country this might be," wrote Richard Dana in *Two Years Before the Mast* (1840). Historian Francis Parkman, touring the Rockies and Plains in 1846, described Hispanics as "slavish-looking, stupid, squalid, miserable and mean." That same year, America went to war [against Mexico]. Mexico lost half its territory. And though the Treaty of Guadalupe Hidalgo guar-

anteed Hispanics rights to their land, says Limerick, 80 percent ultimately went to American lawyers and settlers. As the final blow, in 1850 California passed the Foreign Miners' Tax, driving Hispanics out of the mines.

Writing Hispanic-American history is tricky business: The issues of the 19th century — bilingualism, cultural assimilation, immigration and labor competition — remain so volatile today that accounts of the past are inevitably highly politicized. Black Western history suffers an additional handicap — an acute lack of sources. In the few accounts that have been written, some remarkable heroes emerge, men like Jim Beckwourth, a fur trapper who lived with the Crow Indians; Britt Johnson, who rode alone hundreds of miles beyond the frontier to retrieve his wife and two children from their Kiowa captors, and cowboy Bill Pickett, who could drop a steer by biting its front lip and dragging it to the ground.

The first historians of the black West found in the frontier the seeds of racial equality. "Americans need to remember that the Wyoming pioneers desegregated their first school; that the West once approached the democracy they are still striving to achieve," wrote Philip Durham in *The Negro Cowboys* (1965). But the current crop of historians tells a more sorrowful story.

They write, for instance, of the migration of 40,000 blacks to Kansas in the 1870s, lured by the railroads to a false paradise. Homeless and jobless, they set up shantytowns and began to die at the rate of 50 a day. Within a few years, two thirds were dead or gone. Other states put provisions in their constitutions excluding free blacks: Blacks would intermarry with Indians, explained Oregon's delegate to Congress, and "led on by the Negro, these savages would become much more formidable. The fruits of their commingling would be long and bloody wars."

The new Asian historians tell equally bleak tales. The internment of the Japanese during World War II and the current increase in anti-Asian violence, they say, have their roots in the murderous attacks on Chinese railroad workers in the 1870s and in the chilling denial of civil rights in the California Constitution: "No native of China, no idiot or insane person . . . shall ever exercise the privileges of an elector."

We made this country. We found it and we made it.
                                    RUFE, in *Shane*, 1953

Once it was clear in the early part of this century that the conquest of the Native American was complete, it became fashionable to lament the beautiful tragedy of nature's wise child. "White people love to watch Indians die," says Ian Frazier. "They love to stand around and say things like 'the red man joins his ancestors' or talk about the 'end of the trail' for the noble brave. The problem is that the real end of the trail was usually smallpox or murder then and alcoholism or car accidents or diabetes now."

The noble-savage mythology has been terribly destructive. Settlers convinced of the natives' barbarism were mistrustful and aggressive, provoking violent confrontation that might have been avoided. The myth of the Indian's primitive purity has been equally destructive: When a tribe adapts to modern life, it is branded as "inauthentic" and therefore unworthy of the rights guaranteed by treaty.

But most damaging for the Indian has been the cult of individualism. Early 20th-century reformers saw Indian loyalty to the tribe as un-American, even socialist. One supporter of the 1887 Dawes Act, aimed at breaking up reservations into individually owned tracts of land, suggested the Indian needed to be "touched by the wings of the divine angel of discontent . . . to get the Indian out of the blanket and into trousers, trousers with a pocket that ached to be filled with dollars."

The new historians borrow the methods of anthropology to trace the evolution of the many Indian cultures. They are finding, says White, that many tribes were in fact the creation of European settlers, who herded disparate groups onto a reservation and required them to act as a single people. The Utes, as well as the Navajos, were originally scattered over a huge area with vastly divergent cultures. The Cheyenne were a group of autonomous bands brought together out of necessity as clan members fell to smallpox. These groups often shared no previous political affiliation, and in some cases didn't even speak the same language, but "the whites needed to invent a tribe so someone could sign the treaties," says White.

Surprisingly, the picture of Indian history now emerging is quite positive, focusing on the ability of the Indian, against all odds, to maintain semisovereign status. America's founders felt a deep moral obligation to treat Indians fairly, explains White, and chose treaty negotiations over genocide, the favored solution in Argentina and Chile, or the denial of all legal rights, as in Guatemala and Peru. For a century, the treaties were violated in every way possible: Tribal landholdings were broken up, Indians were denied the right to practice their religion, children were removed from their families to assimilationist schools. But the last two decades [since the 1970s] have seen a resurgence of Indian power in the courts and legislatures, and as severe water shortages have developed in the West, tribal leaders have begun to make use of the "mortgage on Western development" their water rights represent. Historian Vine Deloria, a member of the Sioux tribe, makes the highly controversial argument that "American Indians have actually been treated considerably better than any other aboriginal group on any continent."

A fiery horse with the speed of light, a cloud of dust and a hearty hi-ho Silver!
                        Introduction to "The Lone Ranger"

Times are tough for the classic hero of the American West. Howard Lamar brands General Custer "a foolish general who got himself into a spot where he was roundly defeated," and objects to "turning that defeat into a kind of moral victory or martyrdom." Frazier describes the William Edwards biography of "the gun-nut" Col. Samuel Colt "as stupider than any biography of Lenin," and notes that the heroes of Dodge City were all kingpins in gambling, prostitution and alcohol. In the words of Wallace Stegner, "Our principal folk hero, the frontiersman, was an antisocial loner, impatient of responsibility and law, ferocious, coarse, selfish, ready to violence."

Such hero-bashing can have nasty consequences. In 1978, historian Dan Kilgore published an essay — "How Did Davy Die?" — that disputed the heroic account of Davy Crockett's defense of the Alamo (he was supposed to have died with dozens of the enemy at his feet). Drawing on a diary of one of Gen. Santa Anna's officers, Kilgore revealed that Crockett hid during the battle, possibly under a mattress. When discovered, he claimed to be a tourist who had taken refuge in the Alamo on the approach of the Mexican Army. Texans were furious. One newspaper branded Kilgore's essay a "Communist plan to degrade our heroes." And in a remarkable display of the power of myth over reality, *People* ran a photo of diary translator Carmen Perry alongside one of John Wayne — as Crockett in the 1960 movie *The Alamo* — and invited the public to decide who was more credible.

The mythic West, it appears, has a tenacious hold on the national imagination. "America has always thought of the West as an escape from history," says Donald Worster, "an escape from Europe, corruption, evil, greed, failure, lust, tragedy." No such escape was possible, then or now, and the legacy of the frontier past remains fully alive today. The welfare state persists in the growing Western dependency on federal aid — farm supports, military installations, defense contracts, public land management and water projects. Right alongside it persists the dream of the self-reliant individual, the sage-brush rebel shaking his fist at Eastern corporations and politicians. The idea of a nation without limits endures in the unchecked growth of cities like Denver and Los Angeles. Both continue to import water from politically weaker agricultural areas, and both have lately begun effectively exporting their pollution by relying on power sources outside the state. "We persist in the fantasy," says White, "that we can transform a desert into a garden."

Most enduring is the idea of the lone ranger, the solitary hero, mistrustful of authorities and ready to take matters in his own hands. Oliver North was nicknamed a cowboy by his admirers, and subway vigilante Bernhard Goetz was cheered as a hero in the mold of Billy the Kid. Perhaps America isn't yet ready to give up its frontier vision — of a world where you can always tell the good guys from the bad guys, a world where complexity gives way to blissful simplicity.

QUESTIONS TO CONSIDER

1. Miriam Horn says that according to the new western historians the "faith in limitless bounty . . . has been nothing but trouble for the American West." How do they show the idea of individual self-sufficiency to have been harmful for western settlers? How was the idea that the "Great American Desert" could be made to bloom harmful to both settlers and the land?

2. How do the new historians differ from other historians in their view of the effect of westward migration on the family? Do the new historians agree with one another?

3. There has been much emphasis by the new historians on nonwhite settlers of the West — African, Mexican, and Asian Americans. How have evaluations of the experiences of these groups changed over time? How do the new historians evaluate the effect of European settlement of the West on the Indians and its consequences up to the present? How does this fit with the view given in selection 3?

4.   Why has the myth of the taming of the American West been so enduring? How was it created, and is it the view Americans have always held of the West? What are some of the legacies of this myth, according to Miriam Horn? Do you think there are others? Why have the new histories often been badly received?

5.   Frederick Jackson Turner said that "each age writes the history of the past anew with reference to the conditions uppermost in its own time." What conditions have influenced the new western historians? How might this influence your evaluation of these historians? Can there ever be such a thing as "the definitive history" of any subject?

7 Sam Adams, Firebrand of the American Revolution

ALEXANDER WINSTON

Until 1765, Benjamin Franklin remained an ardent defender of the British Empire. Most other colonists shared his pride in the empire and saw no reason to break away from it. But after 1765—and the date is significant, as we shall see—Franklin and many others marched steadily down the path toward revolution. By 1775, as one historian has noted, the relationship between the American colonials and their English rulers had become "so strained, so poisoned, so characterized by suspicion and resentment that the once seemingly unbreakable bonds of empire were on the verge of dissolution." That same year, in fact, Minutemen at Lexington and Concord fired the opening shots of the war that resulted in American independence.

What were the causes of the American Revolution? What had so poisoned American-English relations that armed conflict broke out? Most experts agree that the roots of the Revolution are to be found in the previous century, when American colonists began developing their own institutions and ideas—particularly ideas about constitutions, taxation, and representation—that significantly diverged from those in England. This "first American revolution," as Clinton Rossiter called it, took place during a period of "salutary neglect," when the British imperial government allowed the colonies to develop without rigid and consistent government control. After 1763, however, all that changed. Reacting to new circumstances inside England and to the enormous cost of a recent war with France (the French and Indian War) for supremacy in North America, the imperial government abandoned salutary neglect and attempted to do what it had every legal right to do: rule the empire, including the North American colonies, forcefully and consistently for the benefit of the mother country. Among other measures, the Stamp Act of 1765 reflected the new imperial approach: it taxed newspapers, pamphlets, and other printed documents in the colonies for the purpose of making the colonies pay a third of the cost of England's protecting them. Unaccustomed to such interference from faraway London, colonial Americans protested, first with restraint, then with rising anger and bitterness, every new measure imposed on them from abroad. By 1775, a sizable and outspoken group of colonists had become profoundly disillusioned with imperial rule, and in 1776 they struck for independence.

In the following selection, Alexander Winston, a specialist in Revolutionary history, tells the story of the coming of the Revolution through the life and deeds of Sam Adams, leader of Boston's hot-headed radicals and one of the foremost opponents to perceived British tyranny in all the colonies. Winston's biographical approach personalizes events; it elicits from cold fact the warmth of a living man of action, a true agitator who was in the thick of colonial resistance to the hated Stamp Act, the Townshend Acts, and the

Five Intolerable Acts and who led his "boys" in the Boston Tea Party, in which he was "in his glory." As an energetic member of the Continental Congresses, Winston tells us, "Sam was ready for independence when most Congress members still clung to compromise." When the break for independence finally came, no one had worked harder for it than the firebrand from Boston. In summing up Sam's significance, John Randolph of Roanoke called him "The Father of the Revolution."

GLOSSARY

BERNARD, FRANCIS   Tory governor of Massachusetts who opposed the boycotts against the Townshend Acts and begged the British for military protection, which made him overnight the most hated man in Massachusetts. The English recalled him, leaving Thomas Hutchinson as acting governor.

BOSTON MASSACRE (1770)   An angry Boston mob converged on the Customs House and taunted the nine English guards, throwing snowballs and brickbats at them. The guards panicked and fired their muskets into the crowd, killing five citizens.

BOSTON TEA PARTY (1773)   When Parliament allowed the East India Company to dump its stockpile of tea on the American colonies, Adams signaled his "boys," and a band of them disguised as Mohawk Indians boarded the ship and dumped the entire cargo into the bay. Parliament retaliated by closing Boston's port and ordering other harsh changes, all of which became known as the Intolerable Acts.

CONTINENTAL CONGRESS (1774)   Delegates from all colonies except Georgia attended this assembly in Philadelphia in 1774. Sam and John Adams were among the Massachusetts delegates. The Congress pledged not to obey the Intolerable Acts and, while promising obedience to the king, denied Parliament's right to tax the colonies.

FRENCH AND INDIAN WAR (ALSO CALLED THE GREAT WAR FOR THE EMPIRE) Anglo-French and Iroquois war (1754–1763) fought for control of North America. In the treaty ending the war, the French ceded Canada to Great Britain, along with all other French possessions east of the Mississippi except New Orleans.

GAGE, GENERAL THOMAS   Commander in chief of English forces in America who, as part of England's retaliation for the Boston Tea Party, replaced Hutchinson as governor of Massachusetts. Not long after, four regiments of redcoats encamped on the Boston Common.

HUTCHINSON, THOMAS   Conservative, pro-English lieutenant governor and then acting governor of Massachusetts whom Adams smeared by reading to the Massachusetts House passages of Hutchinson's letters out of context.

STAMP ACT (1765)   Enacted by the English Parliament, the measure levied fees on all legal documents, customs papers, newssheets, and pamphlets that were disseminated in the colonies. The purpose of the act was to raise money with which to pay for the recent French and Indian War, which had benefited the colonists, and to pay for the expense of protecting them with English troops.

TORIES   Colonists who supported the English government and wished to retain a colonial relationship with the mother country.

TOWNSHEND ACTS (1767)   Parliamentary law, named after the English chancellor of the exchequer, that imposed new taxes on glass, tea, printer's supplies, and paper in the colonies; the taxes were to help pay for the defense of the North American colonies. Sam Adams and his fellow patriots resisted the acts by boycotting the importation of the taxed items.

Members of the British Parliament who voted approval of the Stamp Act late one night in 1765 and went yawning off to bed had never heard, it would seem, of Boston's "Man of the Town Meeting," Samuel Adams. It was a fatal lapse. From that moment until the Declaration of Independence, Sam Adams pounced on Britain every time she moved to impose her will on the colonies. He made politics his only profession and rebellion his only business. He drove two royal governors out of Massachusetts and goaded the British government into open war. New England Tories branded him the "grand Incendiary," the "all-in-all" of colonial turmoil, and neatly capsuled Boston resistance as "Adams' conspiracy." In the opinion of his astute cousin John Adams, Sam was "born and tempered a wedge of steel to split the knot of *lignum vitae* that tied America to England."

"Born and tempered," as Cousin John put it, was more than rhetorical flourish. Sam's father—also named Samuel—made an avocation of politics, and was suspected of republican leanings. The boy got a taste for public affairs almost with his milk; while he was but a toddler his father was deep in the Caucus Club, the same radical brotherhood that Sam was to use with such adroitness. Sam senior clashed with the royal governors, and in 1741 saw his Land Bank venture—an effort to aid debtors by putting negotiable paper money into circulation—outlawed by Parliament. Father and son shared the bitter conviction that Britain's colonial policy was both arbitrary and unjust.

From his parents Sam also inherited a strenuous Calvinism that was to make his vision of the conflict with Britain resemble a huge and murky illustration for *Paradise Lost*. The American patriots, Sam was

sure, were children of light who fought England's sons of Belial in a struggle decisive for the future of mankind. Everyone knew where God stood on that. Sam saw England through a glass, darkly: her government venal, her manners effeminate and corrupt, her religion popish. In saving the colonies from her tyranny Sam hoped to save their manly virtues as well, and make of Boston a "Christian Sparta"— chaste, austere, godly. By 1765 three dominant strains were firmly fixed in his character: puritanism, political acumen, and hatred of British rule. He laced them together tight as a bull whip and, as Parliament was to discover, twice as deadly.

Any calm appraisal of his life up to that point, however, would surely have rated him among those least likely to succeed. After Harvard (M.A., 1743) he had dabbled at the study of law and later spent a few fruitless months as apprentice in a countinghouse. His father loaned him a thousand pounds to make a try at business—any business. The money ran through his fingers like water. Appointed Boston's tax collector in 1756, he combined softheartedness and negligence so ably that he ended at least four thousand pounds in arrears and faced court action. The prosperous little malt works that his father had left the family fell to ruins. The sheriff threatened to sell his house for debts. When the Stamp Act was passed in 1765, Sam was forty-two; he looked prematurely old, his hands trembled, his head shook with a palsied tremor.

But while his private affairs were in a perpetual state of collapse, Sam was making himself the gray eminence of Boston politics. The base of his power was the Caucus Club, a judicious mixture of shipyard laborers ("mechanics") and uptown intellectuals. They met in a garret to drink punch, turn the air blue with pipe smoke, and plot the next political move. Their decisions were passed quietly along to other radical cells—the Merchants' Club (which met in the more genteel Boston Coffee House), the contentious Monday Night Club, the Masons, the Sons of Liberty. With tactics mapped out and support solidified, the

Alexander Winston, "Sam Adams, Firebrand of the American Revolution," *American Heritage,* vol. 18, no. 3 (Apr. 1967), pp. 61–64, 105–108. Reprinted by permission of *American Heritage* Inc. 1967.

Samuel Adams, engraved from the portrait by John Singleton Copley in 1773. "He made politics his only profession," writes *Alexander Winston, "and rebellion his only business." (North Wind Picture Archives)*

action was rammed—or finessed, if need be—through town meeting. Nothing was left to chance; Sam and his tight coterie of patriots simply outworked, outmaneuvered, and, on occasion, outlasted the opposition.

At first rumor of the Stamp Act, Sam cried that "a deep-laid and desperate plan of imperial despotism has been laid, and partly executed, for the extinction of all civil liberty." But Parliament considered its act perfectly just. England's recent conquest of Canada [in the French and Indian War] which had removed an armed threat to the colonies from the French, had also run up a burdensome debt. Obviously the colonies, who had benefited most from the costly Canadian expedition, should not mind paying part of the bill. Passed in the spring of 1765, the Stamp Act required that after November 1 of that year validating stamps be bought from government offices and affixed to all legal documents, customs papers, newssheets, and pamphlets. To enforce the act Parliament decreed that offenders be tried in admiralty courts, where there were no juries, and pay their fines in silver coin, which was hard to get.

Sam rolled out his artillery months before the act went into effect. The instructions from the Boston town meeting to its representatives in the Massachusetts House constituted one of the first formal protests made in the colonies against the act, and one of the first appeals for united resistance. Sam declared that since the act imposed taxation by a body in which the taxed were not represented it flouted the Massachusetts charter, violated the established rights of British subjects, and was therefore null and void.

On the morning of August 14, 1765, the effigy of old Andrew Oliver, Boston distributor of stamps, hung from the Liberty Tree, a great oak in Hanover Square. Sam inspected the stuffed figure with care and wondered aloud how it got there. That night a mob knocked down the frame of the stamp office and built a fire of the debris in front of Oliver's house. After burning the decapitated effigy, they made the real Oliver swear to resign at the Liberty Tree—which he did, finally, under the added humiliation of a driving December rainstorm.

Sam was pleased. The event, he announced, "ought to be for ever remembered in America," for on that day "the People shouted; and their shout was heard to the distant end of this Continent." Two weeks later rioters racked and gutted the mansion of Lieutenant Governor Thomas Hutchinson, emptying his wine cellar and scattering his papers in the street.

On November 1, 1765, the day the Stamp Act went into effect, church bells tolled as for the dead. Flags hung at half-mast; from the harbor rolled the dull boom of minute guns. For the next six weeks the people of Boston refused to buy stamps. Port business came to a halt, law courts tried no cases. Sam had warned the farmers: "If our Trade may be taxed why not our Lands? Why not the Produce of our Lands and in short everything we possess or make use of?" He doubly damned the stamp revenue by prophesying that it would be used to fasten an episcopacy on puritan New England. In the provincial House, to which he had been elected in

September, Sam had a gallery installed to bring waverers under the accusing eye of his patriots. He and his colleague James Otis published a black list of those House members whose antagonism to the act lacked proper vigor. Frightened stamp officials fled for protection to Castle William in the harbor. Enforcement collapsed, and early in the next year Parliament repealed the act. But Sam did not join in Boston's celebration. Why rejoice, he grimly demanded, when Parliament has only granted us our just due?

The defeat of the Stamp Act suggested that no one in the colonies could hatch and execute a scheme with half Sam's cunning. His strategy was to let Britain make all the moves and then give her a bloody nose. "It is a good maxim in Politicks as well as War," he counselled, "to put and keep the enemy in the wrong." Britain soon obliged again. In May, 1767, Parliament launched a series of colonial bills named for their sponsor, Charles Townshend, Chancellor of the Exchequer. The Townshend Acts placed import duties on painters' colors, glass, lead, paper, and tea. At the same time they set up Commissioners of Customs with broad powers, authorized search warrants, and specified that the revenue would be used to pay Crown officials previously salaried (and therefore in part controlled) by the colonies.

Sam worked hard at nonimportation as the chief weapon against the Townshend Acts. By 1769 all the colonies had joined in the boycott. Sam revelled in their unity: "The *tighter* the cord of unconstitutional power is drawn round this bundle of arrows, the *firmer* it will be."

To enforce the boycott in Boston, gangs ranged outside the homes of Tory merchants by night, and small boys pelted their customers with dirt and dung by day. One shopkeeper, more obstinate than the rest, was ridden out of town to the gallows and loosed only when he swore never to return. Tories slept with loaded pistols by their beds. Governor Francis Bernard pleaded for military protection, and in September of 1768 two regiments of soldiers sailed in from Halifax. They set up guardposts, and levelled a pair of cannon at the town hall.

Overnight Governor Bernard became the most hated man in Massachusetts. The House demanded his removal; at Harvard, students slashed his portrait. Sam denounced him as "a Scourge to this Province, a curse to North America, and a Plague on the whole Empire." Recalled to England, Bernard sailed at the end of July, 1769, leaving Hutchinson to act as governor in his place. Despite Sam's outraged cry that Boston was now an occupied town, the troops remained, and he began sending a periodic *Journal of Events* to other colonies, accusing the redcoats of beating defenseless boys and raping women.

Early in March, 1770, a soldier was injured in a scuffle with dockmen. One morning soon after, the town was plastered with forged notices, allegedly signed by redcoats, promising a broad-scale attack on the townspeople. That night, March 5, as a bright moon shone on the late snow, a crowd gathered in front of the Custom House. It began to taunt the nine-man guard; snowballs and brickbats flew, the guard fired, and five citizens were left dead or dying. [The colonists called it "The Boston Massacre."]

The town was in a frenzy of anger. On the following afternoon an immense rally of excited citizens massed in and around Old South Church. Hutchinson told a committee of protest that he was willing to send the one offending regiment to the fort at Castle William but that he had no military authority to send the other as well. At dusk Sam came to the State House to deliver his ultimatum: "If you . . . have the power to remove *one* regiment you have the power to remove *both*. It is at your peril if you refuse. The meeting is composed of three thousand people. They are become impatient. A thousand men are already arrived from the neighborhood, and the whole country is in motion. Night is approaching. An immediate answer is expected.

Both regiments or none!" Hutchinson caved in and ordered the two regiments out of town.

Sam relished his moment of triumph. "If Fancy deceive me not," he reported, "I observ'd his Knees to tremble. I thought I saw his face grow pale (and I enjoy'd the Sight)." Copley's fine portrait . . . catches Sam at the moment of confrontation: broad forehead, heavy eyebrows, steady blue-gray eyes, nose like the prow of a ship, stubborn mouth, a chin you could plow with.

Sam wanted the soldiers who had fired the fatal shots to be tried immediately, while indignation still flamed white-hot, but the judges put it off for six months. He acquiesced when two patriots, his cousin John and Josiah Quincy, volunteered to be defense attorneys, sure that they would not press too hard on prosecution witnesses. The two proved more honorable than he had counted on; they argued their case ably and the sentence was light—a pair of soldiers were branded on the thumb. Sam was disgusted. He retried the case in the Boston *Gazette,* over the signature "Vindex," the avenger. . . .

After that, to Sam's chagrin, things quieted down. The blood of the "massacre" had washed away with the melting snow. In England a liberal government had assumed power and in April it repealed the Townshend Acts, except for the duty on tea. A majority of the colonists were tired of agitation, and the radical patriots temporarily lost control of the Massachusetts House. John Hancock courted the royalists; John Adams shook the dust of politics from his shoes and went back to pastoral Braintree. James Otis, who had been bludgeoned in a brawl, sank into recurrent fits of dementia.

Only Sam never let up. "Where there is a Spark of patriotick fire," he vowed, "we will enkindle it." Between August, 1770, and December, 1772, he wrote more than forty articles for the *Gazette.* Night after night, a lamp burned late in the study off his bedroom. Friends, passing in the small hours, could look up at the yellow square of window light and comfort themselves that Sam Adams was busily at work against the Tories. Sam alternately stated the fundamentals of colonial liberty (based on the charter, British law, and, finally, natural right) and whiplashed the British for transgressing it. His style in this period was at times severely reasoned, more often impassioned; the content was unfailingly polemical, partisan, and, on occasion, willfully inaccurate. As the conflict with Britain deepened, his accusations became more violent. "Every dip of his pen," Governor Bernard had once said, "stung like a horned snake." As clerk of the House (to which office he had been elected in 1765) Sam poured out a stream of remonstrances, resolves, and letters to the colony's London agents; but beyond their effect as propaganda he expected them to do little good. When his daughter expressed awe that a petition to the King might be touched by the royal hand, he growled that it would more likely be spurned by the royal foot.

In November, 1772, Sam managed to set up a Boston Committee of Correspondence to link the Massachusetts towns. Within a few months other towns had followed suit, and he had a taut organization poised to act at his command. A discerning Tory declared it the "foulest, subtlest, and most venomous serpent ever issued from the egg of sedition."

In fact, everything Sam did for a decade smacked of sedition. As early as 1768 Hutchinson had secretly sent depositions to England to see if there might be grounds for his arrest. Parliament dusted off a neglected statute of Henry VIII that would bring all treasonable cases to London for trial. Tories were sure that Sam would now end on the gibbet, where he belonged. They gloated that he "shuddered at the sight of hemp." A Londoner wrote jubilantly to Hutchinson: "The talk is strong of bringing them over and trying them by impeachment. Do you write me word of their being seized, and I will send you an account of their being hanged." But the British solicitor general took a long look at the evidence and decided that it was not sufficient—yet.

Meanwhile Sam was out to ruin Hutchinson, and didn't care how he did it. To beat the devil any stick would do. The chance came in 1772 when Ben Franklin, then in London as an agent for the Massachusetts House, laid hands on a bundle of letters written by Hutchinson and Andrew Oliver to correspondents in England. Franklin sent them to Boston with instructions to share them among the trusted inner circle of patriots and return them uncopied and unpublished. Whether he meant these instructions to be strictly obeyed, or issued them for his self-protection, we do not know. The patriots brooded over the letters for several months; then Sam announced that "a most shocking scene would soon open," and that a vicious plot against American liberties would be disclosed.

Expectation of horrifying news was raised to a fever pitch. In June, 1773, Sam ordered the House galleries cleared. He told the members in grave tones that he had letters vital to their concern, but that they must first swear neither to copy them nor make them public. At this Hancock rose to say that someone unknown to him had thrust copies of letters into his hand on the street. Might they be the same as those held by Mr. Adams? If so, were the letters not already abroad? Yes, to be sure, they were the same; obviously they were abroad. The House decided that the letters should no longer be concealed.

Hutchinson's correspondence was really fairly mild, and said little that he had not already stated openly, but Sam managed to put it in the worst possible light. When the letters were published, passages had been slyly snipped from the context, and an outraged commentary had been so mixed with the text that the unwary reader was easily led to see an evil purpose when none was intended. Other letters in the packet were more damaging than Hutchinson's, but he was neatly smeared with their brush. He suffered great discredit even in the rural villages, where most of his conservative support lay. The House petitioned the King, asking that Hutchinson be removed from office.

Now the storm was gathering. Alone of the revenue acts, the duty on tea remained. For years Boston matrons had boycotted the rich English brew, and instead had concocted somewhat unsavory beverages of catnip and mint. Prompted by the desperate straits of the East India Company, Parliament tried in 1773 to help the company unload its embarrassing stockpile of tea on the colonies. Boston patriots decided that the flesh should not be so tempted. While ships bearing 342 chests of tea lay at the wharfs, Sam gave the signal and a band of his mechanics disguised as Mohawk Indians whooped off toward the harbor. As every schoolboy knows, they dumped the whole cargo into Massachusetts Bay [in what became know as "the Boston Tea Party"]. "Sam Adams is in his glory," said Hutchinson; and he was.

Parliament retaliated in a rage. In March, 1774, it ordered the port of Boston clamped shut. It decreed that after August 1 the Provincial Council, which formerly had been elected by the House, would be named by the governor, as would the higher judges. The royal sheriff would select all juries; town meetings throughout the province would assemble only with the governor's consent, and discuss only what he authorized. General Thomas Gage, commander in chief of His Majesty's forces in America, supplanted Hutchinson as governor. By June, four regiments of redcoats were encamped on the Common. This was the showdown; it was knuckle under or risk war.

Sam knew that to pit Boston (population 17,000) against British power was to place the mouse beneath the lion's paw. "I wish we could arouse the continent," he had written to a fellow patriot the year before. Now, in the spring of 1774, the continent was awakening: a Continental Congress was in the making. How could this matter be discussed and delegates elected before Gage got wind of it and prorogued the Massachusetts legislature? He already had moved the House temporarily from troublesome Boston to the Tory stronghold of Salem; the town swarmed with redcoats.

For ten days the House dispatched routine business with disarming amiability while Sam lined up votes behind the scenes. On June 17, when all was ready, he suddenly ordered the doors of the meeting hall locked. Sensing a plot, one Tory member slipped past the doorkeeper and hurried away to alert Gage. Sam put the key in his pocket and presented a slate of delegates (of which he was one) to attend the Congress, set for Philadelphia in September. Gage scratched off a hurried order to dissolve the House, but the messenger beat on the door in vain. Inside, the House leisurely elected the delegates and assessed the towns for their expenses.

For the first time in his life Sam Adams was to leave the shores of Massachusetts Bay. He still lived in the crumbling ancestral home on Purchase Street, with land running down to the harbor, where he had a small dock. The household consisted of his second wife, Elizabeth Wells Adams (his first wife had died in 1757), a son and a daughter by his earlier marriage, a servant girl, and a shaggy dog famed for biting redcoats. Elizabeth Adams was devoted and above all frugal, for since their marriage his only earnings had been the meager allowance granted him as clerk of the House of Representatives. Fortunately he had few personal wants, and would live on bread and milk and dress in threadbare clothes, if the cause of liberty were thereby served. "He says he never looked forward in his Life," recorded Cousin John, with Yankee amazement at such carelessness, "never planned, laid a scheme, or formed a design of laying up any Thing for himself or others after him."

Friends put together the money to outfit him for the journey to Philadelphia. He was resplendent in new suit, wig, hose, shoes, and cocked hat; he swung a gold-topped cane, and in his pocket there was a much-needed purse of money. On August 10, 1774, the delegation—John Adams, Sam Adams, Thomas Cushing, and Robert Treat Paine—rolled out of Boston in full array—coach, coachmen, and mounted servants.

They were received with great honor along the route, but friendly patriots in Philadelphia advised them that the other colonies were suspicious of Boston's hot-headed radicals. John Adams summed up their warning: "You must not utter the word independence, not give the least hint or insinuation of the idea, either in Congress, or any private conversation; if you do, you are undone, for independence is as unpopular in all the Middle and South as the Stamp Act itself. No man dares speak of it. . . ."

During the seven-week session the Massachusetts delegation stayed discreetly in the background. When Sam urged that an Anglican clergyman be permitted to open the sessions with prayer, southerners decided that the dour Calvinist might have some good in him after all. But he was bold in opposing any concessions to Britain: "I should advise persisting in our struggle for liberty, though it was revealed from heaven that nine hundred and ninety-nine should perish, and only one of a thousand survive and retain his liberty. One such freeman must possess more virtue and enjoy more happiness than a thousand slaves; and let him propagate his like, and transmit to them what he hath so nobly preserved."

From 1774 to 1781 Sam Adams' public life was bound up with successive Congresses. He brought to them the same stubborn energy and forehandedness that had worked so well in Boston. "He was constantly holding caucuses of distinguished men," Jefferson recalled, ". . . at which the generality of the measures pursued were previously determined on, and at which the parts were assigned to the different actors who afterwards appeared in them." His name bobs up almost daily in the congressional journal. Joseph Galloway, leader of the conciliatory wing in the Congress, recognized him as one to keep a wary eye on, "a man who, though by no means remarkable for brilliant abilities, yet is equal to most men in popular intrigue and the management of a faction. He eats little, drinks little, sleeps little, thinks much, and is most decisive and inde-

fatigable in the pursuit of his objects. It was this man, who, by his superior application, managed at once the faction in Congress at Philadelphia and the factions in New England."

Sam was ready for independence when most Congress members still clung to compromise. Philadelphia Quakers were for leaving the issue to Providence; he tartly replied that Providence had already decided for liberty. To James Warren in Plymouth he wrote during the spring of 1776: "The Child Independence is now struggling for Birth. I trust that in a short time it will be brought forth, and, in Spite of Pharaoh, all America will hail the dignified Stranger."

In July he signed the Declaration of Independence, and with that stroke of the pen signed away his real vocation. Success put him out of business. America no longer needed an agitator; now it had to defeat an army in the field and build a new nation.

Sam admitted that he was unfit for "founding Empires," and in various ways he proved it. In Congress he favored a citizen militia until forced to concede that the war could be fought only with a more permanent army and a unified command. Frankly critical of Washington's Fabian tactics, Sam was widely accused of involvement in a cabal to replace him, but there is no evidence to support the charge. He disapproved of any social gaiety in so grave an hour, and had Congress pass rules forbidding members to attend balls or entertainments. They voted the rules, and diligently ignored them. His weakness for government by committee led the French minister to lament over the man "whose obstinate, resolute character was so useful to the Revolution at its origin, but who shows himself so ill-suited to the conduct of affairs in an organized government."

Yet Sam worked with his old doggedness through the dark years of war. Jefferson considered him "more than any other member, the *fountain* of our more important measures." At the low ebb of American fortunes in October, 1777, he was one of only twenty members who stuck with Congress. "Though the smallest," Sam remarked, "it was the truest Congress we ever had." He was on the committee that framed the Articles of Confederation in 1777. Four years later, when Congress celebrated their ratification with a keg of wine and some biscuits, Sam alone remained of the original drafters. In April, 1781, he went home and never crossed the borders of Massachusetts again.

He returned, like Ulysses, to find his hall full of strangers—the young, the new postwar merchants: unfamiliar faces, other times. John Hancock, who had been elected first governor of independent Massachusetts, led Boston on a merry romp of feasts and revels; it was far from the "Christian Sparta" of which Sam still dreamed. The old radical was elected to the state Senate and became its president, but he was no longer invincible. In 1783 and again in 1787 he lost the race for the rather empty and unsalaried office of lieutenant governor; in 1788 a youngster defeated him for the first Congress under the federal Constitution. But in 1789, when he teamed with Hancock to become lieutenant governor, some enthusiasts wrote his name on their ballots in gold. At Hancock's death in 1793 he succeeded to the governor's chair, and was re-elected by solid majorities for three more one-year terms.

Changing times even forced the revolutionary into the camp of reaction. As president of the Senate, which under the state constitution required its members to have an estate of four hundred pounds, he headed a body designed to check the democratic excesses of the House. Some Bostonians thought the town's growth warranted a change to representative government; Sam reported for his committee that the town-meeting system had no defects in it. Debtors in the western counties who in 1786, under a Revolutionary War veteran named Daniel Shays, resorted to mob violence discovered in the former rebel an implacable foe. He branded them "banditti"

and urged the execution of their leaders. Popular opinion was more merciful; Hancock commuted the death penalty. As governor, Sam vetoed a bill to permit stage performances, and Bostonians howled that he was robbing them of their natural rights. Toward the dispossessed Tories, others softened, but Sam's hatred burned with its old fierceness. He would not have a British subject left on American soil nor, indeed, admitted by naturalization.

But Sam had not really changed at all, and that was his misfortune. He earned the lasting enmity of Federalists by his opposition to the new federal Constitution proposed in 1787. Shocked to discover that it would set up "a National Government instead of a Federal Union of Sovereign States," he declared himself "open & decided" against it. But he also insisted that the state convention called in 1788 to ratify the federal Constitution give the document the careful paragraph-by-paragraph discussion that it deserved. Antifederalists who wanted a quick vote while their hostile majority was intact pleaded financial inability to stay for a long session. Sam dryly remarked that if they were so pressed he would dig up funds for their living expenses.

Very likely some of the fight went out of him with the death of his doctor-son while the convention was going on. According to one story, the Federalists finally swung him around by a shrewd move. They staged a meeting of Sam's beloved mechanics at the Green Dragon Inn, where resolutions were passed urging ratification. Daniel Webster wrote a dramatized account of how Paul Revere brought Sam the news:

"'How many mechanics,' said Mr. Adams, 'were at the Green Dragon when the resolutions were passed?'

"'More, sir,' was the reply, 'than the Green Dragon could hold.'

"'And where were the rest, Mr. Revere?'

"'In the streets, sir.'

"'And how many were in the streets?'

"'More, sir, than there are stars in the sky.'"

Sam, Webster tells us, thought that over a while. To him, the voice of the common man was as close to the voice of God as one could get. "Well," he mused, "if they must have it, they must have it."

He retired from public life in 1797, and lived six years more in a yellow frame house on Winter Street. Its parlor was hung with engravings of the great champions of liberty. He liked to sit on the doorstep or wander in the little garden, talking about old times. Death came on October 2, 1803, when he was 81 years of age.

The Federalist regime in Massachusetts was embarrassed about full burial honors for its political foe. The governor was absent; no subordinate dared risk a misstep, and the first suggestion was a modest cortege of school children. Aroused at this, friends rallied a fitting processional of state and town officials, dressed out with a muster of cadets. But eulogies delivered in the Massachusetts House were whittled down for public consumption. In Congress no member from Sam's state rose to memorialize him. It fell to Virginia's John Randolph of Roanoke to remind the House that a great patriot had died. With these small honors "The Father of the Revolution" went to his last sleep in the soil of a free and independent America.

QUESTIONS TO CONSIDER

1 Discuss Adams's personality and character traits. In light of his career as an anti-English agitator, is it significant that Adams lived in Boston? Could he have met with similar success had he been from another colonial city, such as Philadelphia, New York, or Richmond?

2 What was the French and Indian War? How did it set the stage for the coming of the Revolution? Do you think that the Stamp Act and Townshend Acts were justifiable? What, after all, was the English Parliament attempting to do through such enactments? Why did Adams rebel against them? Why was the Boston Tea Party such a powerful symbol?

3 How would you assess the role that Adams played in the coming of the Revolution? Does his career demonstrate that an individual can affect the course of historical events—that people, not abstract forces, make history?

4 Describe Adams's activities in the Continental Congresses. At what point, according to the author, did Adams "sign away his real vocation"? Why did he argue that he was not fit "for founding Empires"? Why did he oppose the new federal Constitution of 1787?

Appendix

Declaration of Independence

IN CONGRESS, JULY 4, 1776

The Unanimous Declaration of the Thirteen United States of America

When, in the course of human events, it becomes necessary for one people to dissolve the political bands which have connected them with another, and to assume, among the powers of the earth, the separate and equal station to which the laws of nature and of nature's God entitle them, a decent respect to the opinions of mankind requires that they should declare the causes which impel them to the separation.

We hold these truths to be self-evident: That all men are created equal; that they are endowed by their Creator with certain unalienable rights; that among these are life, liberty, and the pursuit of happiness; that, to secure these rights, governments are instituted among men, deriving their just powers from the consent of the governed; that whenever any form of government becomes destructive of these ends, it is the right of the people to alter or to abolish it, and to institute new government, laying its foundation on such principles, and organizing its powers in such form, as to them shall seem most likely to effect their safety and happiness. Prudence, indeed, will dictate that governments long established should not be changed for light and transient causes; and accordingly all experience hath shown that mankind are more disposed to suffer, while

evils are sufferable, than to right themselves by abolishing the forms to which they are accustomed. But when a long train of abuses and usurpations, pursuing invariably the same object, evinces a design to reduce them under absolute despotism, it is their right, it is their duty, to throw off such government, and to provide new guards for their future security. Such has been the patient sufferance of these colonies; and such is now the necessity which constrains them to alter their former systems of government. The history of the present King of Great Britain is a history of repeated injuries and usurpations, all having in direct object the establishment of an absolute tyranny over these states. To prove this, let facts be submitted to a candid world.

He has refused his assent to laws, the most wholesome and necessary for the public good.

He has forbidden his governors to pass laws of immediate and pressing importance, unless suspended in their operation till his assent should be obtained; and, when so suspended, he has utterly neglected to attend to them.

He has refused to pass other laws for the accommodation of large districts of people, unless those people would relinquish the right of representation in the legislature, a right inestimable to them, and formidable to tyrants only.

He has called together legislative bodies at places unusual, uncomfortable, and distant from the depository of their public records, for the sole purpose of fatiguing them into compliance with his measures.

He has dissolved representative houses repeatedly, for opposing, with manly firmness, his invasions on the rights of the people.

He has refused for a long time, after such dissolutions, to cause others to be elected; whereby the legislative powers, incapable of annihilation, have returned to the people at large for their exercise; the state remaining, in the mean time, exposed to all the dangers of invasions from without and convulsions within.

He has endeavored to prevent the population of these states; for that purpose obstructing the laws of naturalization of foreigners; refusing to pass others to encourage their migration hither, and raising the conditions of new appropriation of lands.

He has obstructed the administration of justice, by refusing his assent to laws for establishing judiciary powers.

He has made judges dependent on his will alone, for the tenure of their offices, and the amount and payment of their salaries.

He has erected a multitude of new offices, and sent hither swarms of officers to harass our people and eat out their substance.

He has kept among us, in times of peace, standing armies, without the consent of our legislatures.

He has affected to render the military independent of, and superior to, the civil power.

He has combined with others to subject us to a jurisdiction foreign to our constitution, and unacknowledged by our laws, giving his assent to their acts of pretended legislation:

For quartering large bodies of armed troops among us;

For protecting them, by a mock trial, from punishment for any murders which they should commit on the inhabitants of these states;

For cutting off our trade with all parts of the world;

For imposing taxes on us without our consent;

For depriving us, in many cases, of the benefits of trial by jury;

For transporting us beyond seas, to be tried for pretended offenses;

For abolishing the free system of English laws in a neighboring province, establishing therein an arbitrary government, and enlarging its boundaries, so as to render it at once an example and fit instrument for introducing the same absolute rule into these colonies;

For taking away our charters, abolishing our most valuable laws, and altering fundamentally the forms of our governments;

For suspending our own legislatures, and declaring themselves invested with power to legislate for us in all cases whatsoever.

He has abdicated government here, by declaring us out of his protection and waging war against us.

He has plundered our seas, ravaged our coasts, burned our towns, and destroyed the lives of our people.

He is at this time transporting large armies of foreign mercenaries to complete the works of death, desolation, and tyranny already begun with circumstances of cruelty and perfidy scarcely paralleled in the most barbarous ages, and totally unworthy of the head of a civilized nation.

He has constrained our fellow-citizens, taken captive on the high seas, to bear arms against their country, to become the executioners of their friends and brethren, or to fall themselves by their hands.

He has excited domestic insurrection among us, and has endeavored to bring on the inhabitants of our frontiers the merciless Indian savages, whose known rule of warfare is an undistinguished destruction of all ages, sexes, and conditions.

In every stage of these oppressions we have petitioned for redress in the most humble terms; our repeated petitions have been answered only by repeated injury. A prince, whose character is thus marked by every act which may define a tyrant, is unfit to be the ruler of a free people.

Nor have we been wanting in our attentions to our British brethren. We have warned them, from time to time, of attempts by their legislature to extend an unwarrantable jurisdiction over us. We have reminded them of the circumstances of our emigration and settlement here. We have appealed to their native justice and magnanimity; and we have conjured them by the ties of our common kindred, to disavow these usurpations, which would inevitably interrupt our connections and correspondence. They, too, have been deaf to the voice of justice and of consanguinity. We must, therefore, acquiesce in the necessity which denounces our separation, and hold them, as we hold the rest of mankind, enemies in war, in peace friends.

We, therefore, the representatives of the United States of America, in General Congress assembled, appealing to the Supreme Judge of the world for the rectitude of our intentions, do, in the name and by the authority of the good people of these colonies, solemnly publish and declare, that these United Colonies are, and of right ought to be, FREE AND INDEPENDENT STATES; that they are absolved from all allegiance to the British crown, and that all political connection between them and the state of Great Britain is, and ought to be, totally dissolved; and that, as free and independent states, they have full power to levy war, conclude peace, contract alliances, establish commerce, and do all other acts and things which independent states may of right do. And for the support of this declaration, with a firm reliance on the protection of Divine Providence, we mutually pledge to each other our lives, our fortunes, and our sacred honor.

JOHN HANCOCK [*President*]
[*and fifty-five others*]

Constitution of the United States of America

PREAMBLE

We the people of the United States, in order to form a more perfect union, establish justice, insure domestic tranquility, provide for the common defense, promote the general welfare, and secure the blessings of liberty to ourselves and our posterity, do ordain and establish this CONSTITUTION for the United States of America.

ARTICLE I

Section 1.   All legislative powers herein granted shall be vested in a Congress of the United States, which shall consist of a Senate and a House of Representatives.

Section 2.   The House of Representatives shall be composed of members chosen every second year by the people of the several States, and the electors in each State shall have the qualifications requisite for electors of the most numerous branch of the State Legislature.

No person shall be a Representative who shall not have attained to the age of twenty-five years, and been seven years a citizen of the United States, and who shall not, when elected, be an inhabitant of that State in which he shall be chosen.

Representatives and direct taxes shall be apportioned among the several States which may be included within this Union, according to their respective numbers, *which shall be determined by adding to the whole number of free persons, including those bound to service for a term of years and excluding Indians not taxed, three-fifths of all other persons.* The actual enumeration shall be made within three years after the first meeting of the Congress of the United States, and within every subsequent term of ten years, in such manner as they shall by law direct. The number of Representatives shall not exceed one for every thirty thousand, but each State shall have at least one Representative; *and until such enumeration shall be made, the State of New Hampshire shall be entitled to choose three, Massachusetts eight, Rhode Island and Providence Plantations one, Connecticut five, New York six, New Jersey four, Pennsylvania eight, Delaware one, Maryland six, Virginia ten, North Carolina five, South Carolina five, and Georgia three.*

When vacancies happen in the representation from any State, the Executive authority thereof shall issue writs of election to fill such vacancies.

The House of Representatives shall choose their Speaker and other officers; and shall have the sole power of impeachment.

Section 3.   The Senate of the United States shall be composed of two Senators from each State, *chosen by the legislature thereof,* for six years; and each Senator shall have one vote.

Immediately after they shall be assembled in consequence of the first election, they shall be divided as equally as may be into three classes. The seats of the Senators of the first class shall be vacated at the expiration of the second year, of the second class at the expiration of the fourth year, and of the third class at the expiration of the sixth year, so that one-third may be chosen every second year; and if vacancies happen by resignation or otherwise, during the recess of the legislature of any State, the Executive thereof may make

---

NOTE: Passages no longer in effect are printed in italic type.

temporary appointments *until the next meeting of the legislature, which shall then fill such vacancies.*

No person shall be a Senator who shall not have attained to the age of thirty years, and been nine years a citizen of the United States, and who shall not, when elected, be an inhabitant of that State for which he shall be chosen.

The Vice President of the United States shall be President of the Senate, but shall have no vote, unless they be equally divided.

The Senate shall choose their other officers, and also a President *pro tempore,* in the absence of the Vice President, or when he shall exercise the office of the President of the United States.

The Senate shall have the sole power to try all impeachments. When sitting for that purpose, they shall be on oath or affirmation. When the President of the United States is tried, the Chief Justice shall preside: and no person shall be convicted without the concurrence of two-thirds of the members present.

Judgment in cases of impeachment shall not extend further than to removal from the office, and disqualification to hold and enjoy any office of honor, trust or profit under the United States; but the party convicted shall nevertheless be liable and subject to indictment, trial, judgment and punishment, according to law.

Section 4. The times, places and manner of holding elections for Senators and Representatives shall be prescribed in each State by the legislature thereof; but the Congress may at any time by law make or alter such regulations, except as to the places of choosing Senators.

The Congress shall assemble at least once in every year, and such meeting *shall be on the first Monday in December, unless they shall by law appoint a different day.*

Section 5. Each house shall be the judge of the elections, returns and qualifications of its own members, and a majority of each shall constitute a quorum to do business; but a smaller number may adjourn from day to day, and may be authorized to compel the attendance of absent members, in such manner, and under such penalties, as each house may provide.

Each house may determine the rules of its proceedings, punish its members for disorderly behavior, and with the concurrence of two-thirds, expel a member.

Each house shall keep a journal of its proceedings, and from time to time publish the same, excepting such parts as may in their judgment require secrecy; and the yeas and nays of the members of either house on any question shall, at the desire of one-fifth of those present, be entered on the journal.

Neither house, during the session of Congress, shall, without the consent of the other, adjourn for more than three days, nor to any other place than that in which the two houses shall be sitting.

Section 6. The Senators and Representatives shall receive a compensation for their services, to be ascertained by law and paid out of the treasury of the United States. They shall in all cases except treason, felony and breach of the peace, be privileged from arrest during their attendance at the session of their respective houses, and in going to and returning from the same; and for any speech or debate in either house, they shall not be questioned in any other place.

No Senator or Representative shall, during the time for which he was elected, be appointed to any civil office under the authority of the United States, which shall have been created, or the emoluments whereof shall have been increased, during such time; and no person holding any office under the United States shall be a member of either house during his continuance in office.

Section 7. All bills for raising revenue shall originate in the House of Representatives; but the Senate may propose or concur with amendments as on other bills.

Every bill which shall have passed the House of Representatives and the Senate, shall, before it become a law, be presented to the President of the United States; if he approve he shall sign it, but if not he shall return it with objections to that house in which it originated, who shall enter the objections at large on their journal, and proceed to reconsider it. If after such reconsideration two-thirds of that house shall agree to pass the bill, it shall be sent, together with the objections, to the other house, by which it shall likewise be reconsidered, and, if approved by two-thirds of that house, it shall become a law. But in all such cases the votes of both houses shall be determined by yeas and nays, and the names of the persons voting for and against the bill shall be entered on the journal of each house respectively. If any bill shall not be returned by the President within ten days (Sundays excepted) after it shall have been presented to him, the same shall be a law, in like manner as if he had signed it, unless the Congress by their adjournment prevent its return, in which case it shall not be a law.

Every order, resolution, or vote to which the concurrence of the Senate and House of Representatives may be necessary (except on a question of adjournment) shall be presented to the President of the United States; and before the same shall take effect, shall be approved by him, or being disapproved by him, shall be repassed by two-thirds of the Senate and House of Representatives, according to the rules and limitations prescribed in the case of a bill.

Section 8. The Congress shall have power

To lay and collect taxes, duties, imposts, and excises, to pay the debts and provide for the common defense and general welfare of the United States; but all duties, imposts and excises shall be uniform throughout the United States;

To borrow money on the credit of the United States;

To regulate commerce with foreign nations, and among the several States, and with the Indian tribes;

To establish an uniform rule of naturalization, and uniform laws on the subject of bankruptcies throughout the United States;

To coin money, regulate the value thereof, and of foreign coin, and fix the standard of weights and measures;

To provide for the punishment of counterfeiting the securities and current coin of the United States;

To establish post offices and post roads;

To promote the progress of science and useful arts by securing for limited times to authors and inventors the exclusive right to their respective writings and discoveries;

To constitute tribunals inferior to the Supreme Court;

To define and punish piracies and felonies committed on the high seas and offenses against the law of nations;

To declare war, grant letters of marque and reprisal, and make rules concerning captures on land and water;

To raise and support armies, but no appropriation of money to that use shall be for a longer term than two years;

To provide and maintain a navy;

To make rules for the government and regulation of the land and naval forces;

To provide for calling forth the militia to execute the laws of the Union, suppress insurrections, and repel invasions;

To provide for organizing, arming, and disciplining the militia, and for governing such part of them as may be employed in the service of the United States, reserving to the States respectively the appointment of the officers, and the authority of training the militia according to the discipline prescribed by Congress;

To exercise exclusive legislation in all cases whatsoever, over such district (not exceeding ten miles square) as may, by cession of particular States, and the acceptance of Congress, become the seat of government of the United States, and to exercise like authority over all places purchased by the consent of the legislature of the State, in which the same shall be, for erection of forts, magazines, arsenals, dock-yards, and other needful buildings;—and

To make all laws which shall be necessary and proper for carrying into execution the foregoing powers, and all other powers vested by this Constitution in the government of the United States, or in any department or officer thereof.

Section 9. *The migration or importation of such persons as any of the States now existing shall think proper to admit shall not be prohibited by the Congress prior to the year 1808; but a tax or duty may be imposed on such importation, not exceeding $10 for each person.*

The privilege of the writ of habeas corpus shall not be suspended, unless when in cases of rebellion or invasion the public safety may require it.

No bill of attainder or ex post facto law shall be passed.

No capitation, or other direct, tax shall be laid, unless in proportion to the census or enumeration herein before directed to be taken.

No tax or duty shall be laid on articles exported from any State.

No preference shall be given by any regulation of commerce or revenue to the ports of one State over those of another; nor shall vessels bound to, or from, one State, be obliged to enter, clear, or pay duties in another.

No money shall be drawn from the treasury, but in consequence of appropriations made by law; and a regular statement and account of the receipts and expenditures of all public money shall be published from time to time.

No title of nobility shall be granted by the United States: and no person holding any office of profit or trust under them, shall, without the consent of the Congress, accept of any present, emolument, office, or title, of any kind whatever, from any king, prince, or foreign state.

Section 10. No State shall enter into any treaty, alliance, or confederation; grant letters of marque and reprisal; coin money; emit bills of credit; make anything but gold and silver coin a tender in payment of debts; pass any bill of attainder, ex post facto law, or law impairing the obligation of contracts, or grant any title of nobility.

No State shall, without the consent of Congress, lay any imposts or duties on imports or exports, except what may be absolutely necessary for executing its inspection laws: and the net produce of all duties and imposts, laid by any State on imports or exports, shall be for the use of the treasury of the United States; and all such laws shall be subject to the revision and control of the Congress.

No State shall, without the consent of Congress, lay any duty of tonnage, keep troops or ships of war in time of peace, enter into any agreement or compact with another State, or with a foreign power, or engage in war, unless actually invaded, or in such imminent danger as will not admit of delay.

ARTICLE II

Section 1. The executive power shall be vested in a President of the United States of America. He shall hold his office during the term of four years, and, together with the Vice President, chosen for the same term, be elected as follows:

Each state shall appoint, in such manner as the legislature thereof may direct, a number of electors, equal to the whole number of Senators and Representatives to which the State may be entitled in the Congress; but no Senator or Representative, or person holding an office of trust or profit under the United States, shall be appointed an elector.

The electors shall meet in their respective States, and vote by ballot for two persons, of whom one at least shall not be an inhabitant of the same State with themselves. And they shall make a list of all the persons voted for, and of the number of votes for each; which list they shall sign and certify, and transmit sealed to the seat of government of the United States, directed to the President of the Senate. The President of the Senate shall, in the presence of the Senate and the House of Representatives, open all the certificates, and the votes shall then be counted. The person having the greatest number of votes shall be the President, if such number be a majority of the whole number of electors appointed; and if there be more than one who have such majority, and have an equal number of votes, then the House of Representatives shall immediately choose by ballot one of them for President; and if no person have a majority, then from the five highest on the list said house shall in like manner choose the President. But in choosing the President the votes shall be taken by States, the representation from each State having one vote; a quorum for this purpose shall consist of a member or members from two-thirds of the States, and a majority of all the States shall be necessary to a choice. In every case, after the choice of the President, the person having the greatest number of votes of the electors shall be the Vice President. But if there should remain two or more who have equal votes, the Senate shall choose from them by ballot the Vice President.

The Congress may determine the time of choosing the electors and the day on which they shall give their votes; which day shall be the same throughout the United States.

No person except a natural-born citizen, *or a citizen of the United States at the time of the adoption of this Constitution,* shall be eligible to the office of President; neither shall any person be eligible to that office who shall not have attained to the age of thirty-five years, and been fourteen years a resident within the United States.

In case of the removal of the President from office or of his death, resignation, or inability to discharge the powers and duties of the said office, the same shall devolve on the Vice President, and the Congress may by law provide for the case of removal, death, resignation, or inability, both of the President and Vice President, declaring what officer shall then act as President, and such officer shall act accordingly, until the disability be removed, or a President shall be elected.

The President shall, at stated times, receive for his services a compensation, which shall neither be increased nor diminished during the period for which he shall have been elected, and he shall not receive within that period any other emolument from the United States, or any of them.

Before he enter on the execution of his office, he shall take the following oath or affirmation:—"I do solemnly swear (or affirm) that I will faithfully execute the office of the President of the United States, and will to the best of my ability preserve, protect and defend the Constitution of the United States."

Section 2.   The President shall be commander in chief of the army and navy of the United States, and of the militia of the several States, when called into the actual service of the United States; he may require the opinion, in writing, of the principal officer in each of the executive departments, upon any subject relating to the duties of their respective offices, and he shall have power to grant reprieves and pardons for offenses against the United States, except in cases of impeachment.

He shall have power, by and with the advice and consent of the Senate, to make treaties, provided two-thirds of the Senators present concur; and he shall nominate, and by and with the advice and consent of the Senate, shall appoint ambassadors, other public ministers and consuls, judges of the Supreme Court, and all other officers of the United States, whose appointments are not herein otherwise provided for, and which shall be established by law: but Congress may by law vest the appointment of such inferior officers, as they think proper, in the President alone, in the courts of law, or in the heads of departments.

The President shall have power to fill up all vacancies that may happen during the recess of the Senate, by granting commissions which shall expire at the end of their next session.

Section 3.   He shall from time to time give to the Congress information of the state of the Union, and recommend to their consideration such measures as he shall judge necessary and expedient; he may, on extraordinary occasions, convene both houses, or either of them, and in case of disagreement between them, with respect to the time of adjournment, he may adjourn them to such time as he shall think proper; he shall receive ambassadors and other public ministers; he shall take care that the laws be faithfully executed, and shall commission all the officers of the United States.

Section 4. The President, Vice President and all civil officers of the United States shall be removed from office on impeachment for, and on conviction of, treason, bribery, or other high crimes and misdemeanors.

ARTICLE III

Section 1. The judicial power of the United States shall be vested in one Supreme Court, and in such inferior courts as the Congress may from time to time ordain and establish. The judges, both of the Supreme and inferior courts, shall hold their offices during good behavior, and shall, at stated times, receive for their services a compensation which shall not be diminished during their continuance in office.

Section 2. The judicial power shall extend to all cases, in law and equity, arising under this Constitution, the laws of the United States, and treaties made, or which shall be made, under their authority;—to all cases affecting ambassadors, other public ministers and consuls;—to all cases of admiralty and maritime jurisdiction;—to controversies to which the United States shall be a party;—to controversies between two or more States;—*between a State and citizens of another State;*—between citizens of different States;—between citizens of the same State claiming lands under grants of different States, and between a State, or the citizens thereof, and foreign states, citizens or subjects.

In all cases affecting ambassadors, other public ministers and consuls, and those in which a State

shall be party, the Supreme Court shall have original jurisdiction. In all the other cases before mentioned, the Supreme Court shall have appellate jurisdiction, both as to law and fact, with such exceptions, and under such regulations, as the Congress shall make.

The trial of all crimes, except in cases of impeachment, shall be by jury; and such trial shall be held in the State where said crimes shall have been committed; but when not committed within any State, the trial shall be at such place or places as the Congress may by law have directed.

Section 3. Treason against the United States shall consist only in levying war against them, or in adhering to their enemies, giving them aid and comfort. No person shall be convicted of treason unless on the testimony of two witnesses to the same overt act, or on confession in open court.

The Congress shall have power to declare the punishment of treason, but no attainder of treason shall work corruption of blood, or forfeiture except during the life of the person attainted.

ARTICLE IV

Section 1. Full faith and credit shall be given in each State to the public acts, records, and judicial proceedings of every other State. And the Congress may by general laws prescribe the manner in which such acts, records, and proceedings shall be proved, and the effect thereof.

Section 2. The citizens of each State shall be entitled to all privileges and immunities of citizens in the several States.

A person charged in any State with treason, felony, or other crime, who shall flee from justice, and be found in another State, shall on demand of the executive authority of the State from which he fled, be delivered up, to be removed to the State having jurisdiction of the crime.

No person held to service or labor in one State, under the laws thereof, escaping into another, shall, in consequence of any law or regulation therein, be discharged from such service or labor, but shall be delivered up on claim of the party to whom such service or labor may be due.

Section 3. New States may be admitted by the Congress into this Union; but no new State shall be formed or erected within the jurisdiction of any other State; nor any State be formed by the junction of two or more States, or parts of States, without the consent of the legislatures of the States concerned as well as of the Congress.

The Congress shall have power to dispose of and make all needful rules and regulations respecting the territory or other property belonging to the United States; and nothing in this Constitution shall be so construed as to prejudice any claims of the United States, or of any particular State.

Section 4. The United States shall guarantee to every State in this Union a republican form of government, and shall protect each of them against invasion; and on application of the legislature, or of the executive (when the legislature cannot be convened), against domestic violence.

ARTICLE V

The Congress, whenever two-thirds of both houses shall deem it necessary, shall propose amendments to this Constitution, or, on the application of the legislatures of two-thirds of the several States, shall call a convention for proposing amendments, which, in either case, shall be valid to all intents and purposes, as part of this Constitution, when ratified by the legislatures of three-fourths of the several States, or by conventions in three-fourths thereof, as the one or the other mode of ratification may be proposed by the Congress; provided *that no amendments which may be made prior to the year one thousand eight hundred and eight shall in any manner affect the first and fourth clauses in the ninth section of the first article;* and that no State, without its con-

sent, shall be deprived of its equal suffrage in the Senate.

ARTICLE VI

All debts contracted and engagements entered into, before the adoption of this Constitution, shall be as valid against the United States under this Constitution, as under the Confederation.

This Constitution, and the laws of the United States which shall be made in pursuance thereof; and all treaties made, or which shall be made, under the authority of the United States, shall be the supreme law of the land; and the judges in every State shall be bound thereby, anything in the Constitution or laws of any State to the contrary notwithstanding.

The Senators and Representatives before mentioned, and the members of the several State legislatures, and all executive and judicial officers, both of the United States and of the several States, shall be bound by oath or affirmation to support this Constitution; but no religious test shall ever be required as a qualification to any office or public trust under the United States.

ARTICLE VII

The ratification of the conventions of nine States shall be sufficient for the establishment of this Constitution between the States so ratifying the same.

Done in Convention by the unanimous consent of the States present, the seventeenth day of September in the year of our Lord one thousand seven hundred and eighty-seven and of the Independence of the United States of America the twelfth. In witness whereof we have hereunto subscribed our names.

[Signed by]
G° WASHINGTON
Presidt and Deputy from Virginia
[*and thirty-eight others*]

Amendments to the Constitution

ARTICLE I*

Congress shall make no law respecting an establishment of religion, or prohibiting the free exercise thereof; or abridging the freedom of speech, or of the press; or the right of the people peaceably to assemble, and to petition the government for a redress of grievances.

ARTICLE II

A well-regulated militia being necessary to the security of a free State, the right of the people to keep and bear arms shall not be infringed.

ARTICLE III

No soldier shall, in time of peace, be quartered in any house without the consent of the owner, nor in time of war, but in a manner to be prescribed by law.

ARTICLE IV

The right of the people to be secure in their persons, houses, papers, and effects, against unreasonable searches and seizures, shall not be violated, and no warrants shall issue but upon probable cause, supported by oath or affirmation, and particularly describing the place to be searched, and the persons or things to be seized.

ARTICLE V

No person shall be held to answer for a capital, or otherwise infamous crime, unless on a presentment or indictment of a grand jury, except in cases arising in the land or naval forces, or in the militia, when in actual service in time of war or public danger; nor shall any person be subject for the same offense to

be twice put in jeopardy of life or limb; nor shall be compelled in any criminal case to be a witness against himself, nor be deprived of life, liberty, or property, without due process of law; nor shall private property be taken for public use without just compensation.

ARTICLE VI

In all criminal prosecutions, the accused shall enjoy the right to a speedy and public trial, by an impartial jury of the State and district wherein the crime shall have been committed, which district shall have been previously ascertained by law, and to be informed of the nature and cause of the accusation; to be confronted with the witnesses against him; to have compulsory process for obtaining witnesses in his favor, and to have the assistance of counsel for his defense.

ARTICLE VII

In suits at common law, where the value in controversy shall exceed twenty dollars, the right of trial by jury shall be preserved, and no fact tried by a jury shall be otherwise reexamined in any court of the United States, than according to the rules of the common law.

ARTICLE VIII

Excessive bail shall not be required, nor excessive fines imposed, nor cruel and unusual punishments inflicted.

ARTICLE IX

The enumeration in the Constitution, of certain rights, shall not be construed to deny or disparage others retained by the people.

*The first ten Amendments (Bill of Rights) were adopted in 1791.

ARTICLE X

The powers not delegated to the United States by the Constitution, not prohibited by it to the States, are reserved to the States respectively, or to the people.

ARTICLE XI   [Adopted 1798]

The judicial power of the United States shall not be construed to extend to any suit in law or equity, commenced or prosecuted against one of the United States by citizens of another State, or by citizens or subjects of any foreign state.

ARTICLE XII   [Adopted 1804]

The electors shall meet in their respective States, and vote by ballot for President and Vice President, one of whom, at least, shall not be an inhabitant of the same State with themselves; they shall name in their ballots the person voted for as President, and in distinct ballots the person voted for as Vice President, and they shall make distinct lists of all persons voted for as President, and of all persons voted for as Vice President, and of the number of votes for each, which lists they shall sign and certify, and transmit sealed to the seat of government of the United States, directed to the President of the Senate;—the President of the Senate shall, in the presence of the Senate and House of Representatives, open all the certificates and the votes shall then be counted;—the person having the greatest number of votes for President shall be the President, if such number be a majority of the whole number of electors appointed; and if no person have such majority, then from the persons having the highest numbers not exceeding three on the list of those voted for as President, the House of Representatives shall choose immediately, by ballot, the President. But in choosing the President, the votes shall be taken by States, the representation from each State having one vote; a quorum for this purpose shall consist of a member or members from two-thirds of the States, and a majority of all the States shall be necessary to a choice.

And if the House of Representatives shall not choose a President whenever the right of choice shall devolve upon them, before *the fourth day of March* next following, then the Vice President shall act as President, as in the case of the death or other constitutional disability of the President.

The person having the greatest number of votes as Vice President shall be the Vice President, if such a number be a majority of the whole number of electors appointed; and if no person have a majority, then from the two highest numbers on the list the Senate shall choose the Vice President; a quorum for the purpose shall consist of two-thirds of the whole number of Senators, and a majority of the whole number shall be necessary to a choice. But no person constitutionally ineligible to the office of President shall be eligible to that of Vice President of the United States.

ARTICLE XIII   [Adopted 1865]

Section 1. Neither slavery nor involuntary servitude, except as a punishment for crime whereof the party shall have been duly convicted, shall exist within the United States, or any place subject to their jurisdiction.

Section 2. Congress shall have power to enforce this article by appropriate legislation.

ARTICLE XIV   [Adopted 1868]

Section 1. All persons born or naturalized in the United States, and subject to the jurisdiction thereof, are citizens of the United States and of the State wherein they reside. No State shall make or enforce any law which shall abridge the privileges or immunities of citizens of the United States; nor shall any State deprive any person of life, liberty, or property, without due process of law; nor deny to any person within its jurisdiction the equal protection of the laws.

Section 2. Representatives shall be apportioned among the several States according to their respective numbers, counting the whole number of persons in each State, excluding Indians not taxed. But when the right to vote at any election for the choice of Electors for President and Vice President of the United States, Representatives in Congress, the executive and judicial officers of a State, or the members of the legislature thereof, is denied to any of the male inhabitants of such State, being twenty-one years of age and citizens of the United States, or in any way abridged, except for participation in rebellion, or other crime, the basis of representation therein shall be reduced in the proportion which the number of such male citizens shall bear to the whole number of male citizens twenty-one years of age in such State.

Section 3. No person shall be a Senator or Representative in Congress or Elector of President and Vice President, or hold any office, civil or military, under the United States, or under any State, who, having previously taken an oath, as a member of Congress, or as an officer of the United States, or as a member of any State legislature, or as an executive or judicial officer of any State, to support the Constitution of the United States, shall have engaged in insurrection or rebellion against the same, or given aid and comfort to the enemies thereof. Congress may, by a vote of two-thirds of each house, remove such disability.

Section 4. The validity of the public debt of the United States, authorized by law, including debts incurred for payment of pensions and bounties for services in suppressing insurrection or rebellion, shall not be questioned. But neither the United States nor any State shall assume or pay any debt or obligation incurred in aid of insurrection or rebellion against the United States, or any claim for the loss or emancipation of any slave; but all such debts, obligations, and claims shall be held illegal and void.

Section 5. The Congress shall have the power to enforce, by appropriate legislation, the provisions of this article.

ARTICLE XV   [*Adopted 1870*]

Section 1. The right of citizens of the United States to vote shall not be denied or abridged by the United States or by any State on account of race, color, or previous condition of servitude.

Section 2. The Congress shall have power to enforce this article by appropriate legislation.

ARTICLE XVI   [*Adopted 1913*]

The Congress shall have power to lay and collect taxes on incomes, from whatever source derived, without apportionment among the several States, and without regard to any census or enumeration.

ARTICLE XVII   [*Adopted 1913*]

Section 1. The Senate of the United States shall be composed of two Senators from each State, elected by the people thereof, for six years; and each Senator shall have one vote. The electors in each State shall have the qualifications requisite for electors of [voters for] the most numerous branch of the State legislatures.

Section 2. When vacancies happen in the representation of any State in the Senate, the executive authority of such State shall issue writs of election to fill such vacancies: Provided, that the Legislature of any State may empower the executive thereof to make temporary appointments until the people fill the vacancies by election as the Legislature may direct.

Section 3. This amendment shall not be so construed as to affect the election or term of any Senator chosen before it becomes valid as part of the Constitution.

ARTICLE XVIII   [*Adopted 1919; repealed 1933*]

Section 1. *After one year from the ratification of this article the manufacture, sale, or transportation of intoxicating liquors within, the importation thereof into,* or the exportation thereof from the United States and all territory subject to the jurisdiction thereof, for beverage purposes, is hereby prohibited.

Section 2.   The Congress and the several States shall have concurrent power to enforce this article by appropriate legislation.

Section 3.   This article shall be inoperative unless it shall have been ratified as an amendment to the Constitution by the legislatures of the several States, as provided by the Constitution, within seven years from the date of the submission thereof to the States by the Congress.

ARTICLE XIX   [Adopted 1920]

Section 1.   The right of citizens of the United States to vote shall not be denied or abridged by the United States or by any State on account of sex.

Section 2.   The Congress shall have the power to enforce this article by appropriate legislation.

ARTICLE XX   [Adopted 1933]

Section 1.   The terms of the President and Vice President shall end at noon on the 20th day of January, and the terms of Senators and Representatives at noon on the 3d day of January, of the years in which such terms would have ended if this article had not been ratified; and the terms of their successors shall then begin.

Section 2.   The Congress shall assemble at least once in every year, and such meeting shall begin at noon on the 3d day of January, unless they shall by law appoint a different day.

Section 3.   If, at the time fixed for the beginning of the term of the President, the President-elect shall have died, the Vice President-elect shall become President. If a President shall not have been chosen before the time fixed for the beginning of his term, or if the President-elect shall have failed

to qualify, then the Vice President-elect shall act as President until a President shall have qualified; and the Congress may by law provide for the case wherein neither a President-elect nor a Vice President-elect shall have qualified, declaring who shall then act as President, or the manner in which one who is to act shall be selected, and such persons shall act accordingly until a President or Vice President shall have qualified.

Section 4.   The Congress may by law provide for the case of the death of any of the persons from whom the House of Representatives may choose a President whenever the right of choice shall have devolved upon them, and for the case of the death of any of the persons from whom the Senate may choose a Vice President whenever the right of choice shall have devolved upon them.

Section 5.   Sections 1 and 2 shall take effect on the 15th day of October following the ratification of this article.

Section 6.   This article shall be inoperative unless it shall have been ratified as an amendment to the Constitution by the Legislatures of three-fourths of the several States within seven years from the date of its submission.

ARTICLE XXI   [Adopted 1933]

Section 1.   The eighteenth article of amendment to the Constitution of the United States is hereby repealed.

Section 2.   The transportation or importation into any State, Territory, or Possession of the United States for delivery or use therein of intoxicating liquors, in violation of the laws thereof, is hereby prohibited.

Section 3.   This article shall be inoperative unless it shall have been ratified as an amendment to the Constitution by conventions in the several States, as provided in the Constitution, within seven years from the date of submission thereof to the States by the Congress.

ARTICLE XXII   [*Adopted 1951*]

Section 1.   No person shall be elected to the office of President more than twice, and no person who has held the office of President, or acted as President, for more than two years of a term to which some other person was elected President shall be elected to the office of President more than once. But this article shall not apply to any person holding the office of President when this article was proposed by the Congress, and shall not prevent any person who may be holding the office of President, or acting as President, during the term within which this article becomes operative from holding the office of President or acting as President during the remainder of such term.

Section 2.   This article shall be inoperative unless it shall have been ratified as an amendment to the Constitution by the legislatures of three-fourths of the several States within seven years from the date of its submission to the States by the Congress.

ARTICLE XXIII   [*Adopted 1961*]

Section 1.   The District constituting the seat of Government of the United States shall appoint in such manner as the Congress may direct:

A number of electors of President and Vice President equal to the whole number of Senators and Representatives in Congress to which the District would be entitled if it were a State, but in no event more than the least populous State; they shall be in addition to those appointed by the States, but they shall be considered for the purposes of the election of President and Vice President, to be electors appointed by a State; and they shall meet in the District and perform such duties as provided by the twelfth article of amendment.

Section 2.   The Congress shall have the power to enforce this article by appropriate legislation.

ARTICLE XXIV   [*Adopted 1964*]

Section 1.   The right of citizens of the United States to vote in any primary or other election for President or Vice President, for electors for President or Vice President, or for Senator or Representative in Congress, shall not be denied or abridged by the United States or any State by reason of failure to pay any poll tax or other tax.

Section 2.   The Congress shall have the power to enforce this article by appropriate legislation.

ARTICLE XXV   [*Adopted 1967*]

Section 1.   In case of the removal of the President from office or of his death or resignation, the Vice President shall become President.

Section 2.   Whenever there is a vacancy in the office of the Vice President, the President shall nominate a Vice President who shall take office upon confirmation by a majority vote of both Houses of Congress.

Section 3.   Whenever the President transmits to the President pro tempore of the Senate and the Speaker of the House of Representatives his written declaration that he is unable to discharge the powers and duties of his office, and until he transmits to them a written declaration to the contrary, such powers and duties shall be discharged by the Vice President as Acting President.

Section 4.   Whenever the Vice President and a majority of either the principal officers of the executive departments or of such other body as Congress may by law provide, transmit to the President pro tempore of the Senate and the Speaker of the House of Representatives their written declaration that the President is unable to discharge the powers and duties of his office, the Vice President shall immediately assume the powers and duties of the office as Acting President.

Thereafter, when the President transmits to the President pro tempore of the Senate and the

Speaker of the House of Representatives his written declaration that no inability exists, he shall resume the powers and duties of his office unless the Vice President and a majority of either the principal officers of the executive department[s] or of such other body as Congress may by law provide, transmit within four days to the President pro tempore of the Senate and the Speaker of the House of Representatives their written declaration that the President is unable to discharge the powers and duties of his office. Thereupon Congress shall decide the issue, assembling within forty-eight hours for that purpose if not in session. If the Congress, within twenty-one days after receipt of the latter written declaration, or, if Congress is not in session, within twenty-one days after Congress is required to assemble, determines by two-thirds vote of both Houses that the President is unable to discharge the powers and duties of his office, the Vice President shall continue to discharge the same as Acting President; otherwise, the President shall resume the powers and duties of his office.

ARTICLE XXVI   [Adopted 1971]

Section 1.   The right of citizens of the United States, who are eighteen years of age or older, to vote shall not be denied or abridged by the United States or by any State on account of age.

Section 2.   The Congress shall have power to enforce this article by appropriate legislation.

ARTICLE XXVII*   [Adopted 1992]

No law, varying the compensation for services of the Senators and Representatives, shall take effect, until an election of Representatives shall have intervened.

---

*Originally proposed in 1789 by James Madison, this amendment failed to win ratification along with the other parts of what became the Bill of Rights. However, the proposed amendment contained no deadline for ratification, and over the years other state legislatures voted to add it to the Constitution; many such ratifications occurred during the 1980s and early 1990s as public frustration with Congress's performance mounted. In May 1992 the Archivist of the United States certified that, with the Michigan legislature's ratification, the article had been approved by three-fourths of the states and thus automatically became part of the Constitution. But congressional leaders and constitutional specialists questioned whether an amendment that took 202 years to win ratification was valid, and the issue had not been resolved by the time this book went to press.

RAND McNALLY

Atlas of
American
History

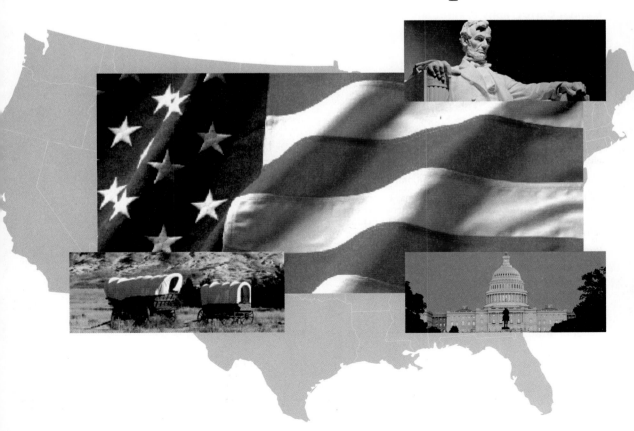

2

Project Manager
Carole Wicklander

Book Production Editor
Louise Frederiksen

Map Production Editor
Charles J. MacDonald

Managing Editor
Margaret McNamara

Digital Cartographers
Barbara Benstead-Strassheim
Elizabeth A. Hunt
Amy L. Troesch

Digital Cartography Project Manager
Thomas Vitacco

Cartographic Editorial
Robert K. Argersinger
Gregory P. Babiak
Jill M. Stift

Cartographic Production
Norma Denny
Jim Purvis

Manual Cartography Project Manager
David Zapenski

Designer
Donna McGrath

Production Manager
Robert Sanders

Typesetting
Yvonne Rosenberg

Photo Credit
Images provided by ©1999 PhotoDisc, Inc.

Printed in the United States of America

Rand McNally & Company
Skokie, Illinois 60076-8906

2000 printing

ISBN 528-84500-4

**For information about ordering *Atlas of American History*,
call 1-800-678-7263, or visit our website at www.k12online.com.**

Table of Contents

Introducing Atlas of American History

The features of *Atlas of American History* described below enhance understanding of America's past. They support and extend information from textbooks and primary sources. They provide additional links between history and geography.

Features of *Atlas of American History*

▲ Historical Maps

Maps are arranged chronologically. Each map includes a title that describes its content and dates that indicate the period of history it shows. Compare maps of the same area in different time periods to view historical changes.

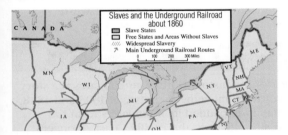

▲ Map Legends and Labels

A map legend explains the colors and symbols used on a map. Historical maps often use solid or dashed lines to indicate routes of explorers or other groups of people. These routes may be labeled on the map. Labels also identify sites of historical events.

Captions

Each map has a caption that helps explain the content of the map. It may provide information about the historical context of the map or point out an important feature of the map. Legends, labels, and captions help tell the story of American history.

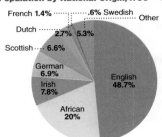

Population by National Origin, 1790

◀ Graphs

Some graphs in *Atlas of American History* illustrate information from the maps. Others provide additional information about American history. They may compare data or show changes over time.

Populations of United States Colonies and States, 1650-1990

States	1650	1700	1750	1770
Alabama				
Alaska				
Arizona				
Arkansas				
California				
Colorado				
Connecticut	4,139	25,970	111,280	183,881
Delaware	185	2,470	28,704	35,496

▲ Databank

The databank is a reference section on pages 72-75 of the atlas. It provides tables of information about the United States and its people.

People 1776
Juan Bautista de Anza establishes a presidio at San Francisco.

Events 1776
Declaration of Independence is signed in Philadelphia.

Literature 1776
"To His Excellency, General Washington," by a slave named Phillis Wheatley, is printed in the Pennsylvania Magazine.

◀ Chronologies

Each section of *Atlas of American History* includes a chronology. It lists people, events, and literature associated with the time period represented on the maps in that section. These listings provide connections that aid understanding of history.

I
Idaho, **46**
Illinois, **35a, 37, 41, 42, 43, 46**
Illinois (American Indians), **11**
immigration
   U.S., 1820-1870, **38**
   U.S., 1860-1919, **g45**
   U.S., 1880-1920, **48**
   U.S., 1910, **49**
   U.S., 1960s-1990s, **61**
Inca Empire, South America, **11,**
Inchon, South Korea, **59a**

◀ Index

The index is an alphabetical listing of the places and topics included in *Atlas of American History*. The index shows the page number(s) on which each entry appears. It provides explanatory information about many entries and refers to related entries when appropriate.

Periods of American History

Historians may divide American history into time periods in many different ways. Some periods may center around a theme, such as exploration. Others may center around an important event, such as the American Revolution.

Rand McNally *Atlas of American History* is divided into sections based on time periods described below. Some periods overlap to provide coverage of political and social history. Maps are organized chronologically within each section.

1. Beginnings (prehistory-1620)

Thousands of years ago, hunters from Asia migrated to the lands now called the Americas. These people, now referred to as American Indians or Native Americans, settled throughout the continents. They developed many different cultures, depending upon the environments in which they lived. They remained the only people in the Western Hemisphere until about A.D. 1000, when Vikings from Norway migrated to the coast of North America.

During the 1400s, European demand for Asian goods led Columbus to sail west across the Atlantic Ocean in search of a route to Asia. His discovery of a world previously unknown to Europeans touched off an age of exploration. During the 1500s, Europeans explored and claimed land in the Americas.

2. Establishing Colonies (1600-1775)

During the 1600s and early 1700s, Europeans came to the Americas for many different reasons. English settlers came seeking the freedom to wor-

ship as they pleased. Spaniards came to find gold and to spread Christianity. French trappers came to establish fur trade. Dutch settlers came for the promise of land. In addition, many Africans were brought to the Americas as slaves.

By the mid-1700s, English claims extended along the Atlantic coast, and the French controlled the vast interior of North America. Britain and France competed for control of the continent. As a result of the French and Indian War (1754-1763), Britain gained Canada and all of North America east of the Mississippi River.

3. Forming a New Nation (1775-1800)

English settlers in North America developed a prosperous economy and a way of life that differed from that in Great Britain. They began to resent Britain's control. They declared their independence and fought a revolution to win their freedom. As a result, the United States became an independent nation.

The original thirteen states stretched along the Atlantic coast. The western boundary of the new nation extended to the Mississippi River. Americans began to settle lands west of the Appalachian Mountains. The national government passed laws providing for the sale of western lands and the addition of new states.

4. The Nation Expands and Changes (1790-1870)

Much of the history of the United States is a story of westward movement. Between 1803 and 1848, the nation expanded its boundaries from the Mississippi River to the Pacific Coast. Pioneers had settled most of the land east of the Mississippi River by 1840.

	1769	1804	1933
People	Junípero Serra starts first Spanish mission in what is now California.	Meriwether Lewis and William Clark lead expedition from St. Louis to the Pacific Ocean.	President Franklin Roosevelt creates TVA to develop the natural resources of the Tennessee Valley
	about 700 B.C.	**1565**	**1787**
Events	The Adena (early North American Indians) build mounds in what is now Ohio.	Spaniards establish St. Augustine, FL, first permanent European settlement in what is now the United States.	Founders write the U.S. Constitution in Philadelphia, PA.
	1608	**1704**	**1868**
Literature	*A True Relation of Occurrences in Virginia*, by John Smith, describes the founding of Jamestown.	Sarah Kemble Knight's *Journal* describes the author's horseback journey from Boston to New York.	*Little Women*, by Louisa May Alcott, tells the story of four sisters growing up in New England in the mid-1800s.

In the early 1800s, fur trappers, traders, and miners pushed west of the Mississippi River, seeking economic opportunities. Soon they were followed by farmers and ranchers who settled the land. The promise of land and the hope of a better life also attracted millions of European immigrants to the United States.

5. A Nation Divided (1850-1865)

Different ways of life developed in the North and the South. Southern agriculture was based on slave labor. Industrial states in the North outlawed slavery. As settlers moved westward, new states were created. The question of whether to allow slavery in the new states led to conflict between the North and the South.

Debate and compromise failed to solve the problems. Eleven southern states withdrew from the Union. Between 1861 and 1865, the North and the South fought against each other in the Civil War.

6. Emerging as a Modern Nation (1860-1920)

Within 25 years after the Civil War ended, the process of settling the United States from coast to coast was completed. The settlement of the West also brought an end to the Native American way of life. The federal government sent soldiers to stop uprisings and move Indians onto reservations.

As the United States became an industrial nation, people moved to cities to work in factories. Millions of European immigrants also came to the United States seeking jobs.

The nation acquired territories overseas and began to emerge as a modern nation. By fighting in World War I, the United States also proved that it had become a world power.

7. Challenges and Changes in the 20th Century (1920-1990)

A period of prosperity followed World War I. However, the stock market crash in 1929 plunged the nation into an economic depression that lasted throughout the 1930s. During those years, the actions of powerful dictators in Europe led to World War II.

The United States fought in World War II from 1941 to 1945. It emerged as the leader of the free world, and the Soviet Union emerged as the leader of the Communist world. During the following decades, the United States intervened in many parts of the world to stop the spread of Communism.

8. Entering a New Millennium (1990 and beyond)

The United States has compiled information about the American population every ten years since 1790, when the first census was taken. According to the 1990 census, more than three-fourths of the country's 250 million people lived in cities. Americans born in 1990 could expect to live longer than any previous generation. Although many Americans lived in poverty in 1990, the United States had one of the world's highest standards of living.

The United States faces many challenges as it enters a new millennium. It must meet the needs of its diverse population. It must also continue its role of leadership in a rapidly changing world. The story of America is ongoing because today's events will become tomorrow's history.

1955 Rosa Parks protests segregation in Montgomery, AL by refusing to give up bus seat to white passenger.

1969 U.S. astronaut Neil Armstrong becomes first person to walk on the moon.

1989 Colin Powell, son of Jamaican immigrants, becomes first African American to head Joint Chiefs of Staff.

1848 Discovery of gold in California brings settlers to the West.

1941 Japanese bombing of Pearl Harbor, Hawaii, brings U.S. into World War II.

1970 Americans participate in Earth Day, a nationwide demonstration of concern for the environment.

1932 *Little House in the Big Woods*, by Laura Ingalls Wilder, describes life in the Midwest in the 1870s and 1880s.

1976 *Roots: The Saga of an American Family*, by Alex Haley, traces the author's ancestry back to the African slave trade.

1989 *The Joy Luck Club*, by Amy Tan, tells the experiences of Chinese women in San Francisco after World War II.

Benefits of Using Rand McNally *Atlas of American History*

Events gain fuller meaning.

Knowing where events took place gives them fuller meaning and often explains causes and effects. For example, the map of the final campaign of the American Revolution, on page 27, shows how American and French forces trapped the British at Yorktown. It helps explain why Cornwallis surrendered.

Connections among events are clarified.

Through the visual power of historical maps, the links between and among events become clear. The maps on pages 12 and 13 show international trade routes, 1350-1450, and Portuguese routes to India in the 1400s. They help explain why Europeans wanted to find an all-water route to Asia. They provide the background to understanding the age of exploration that followed Columbus's discovery of the Americas.

Similarities and differences become apparent.

The maps in *Atlas of American History* provide an opportunity to compare and contrast places over time. Compare the map of North America in 1763, on page 23, with the map of North America in 1783 on page 28. These maps show the emergence of the United States on a continent claimed by Britain and Spain.

The maps in this atlas also provide an opportunity to compare and contrast regions of the United States. The map titled "A Quarreling People," on page 41, indicates differences between the North and the South at the time of the Civil War.

The influence of sense of place is conveyed.

Maps in *Atlas of American History* convey people's sense of place at a particular time in history. The map titled "Opportunities and Uncertainties," on page 58, is a good example. The map's polar projection emphasizes how near the Soviet Union is to the United States. It reflects Americans' fear of nuclear attack from the north during the postwar period of tension between the United States and the Soviet Union.

Trends emerge.

The maps in this atlas show trends in American history. The map of Westward Expansion, on pages 36-37, shows the sequence in which the United States acquired land. It indicates the westward movement of settlement patterns. The maps on pages 38, 48, and 61 indicate changing trends in immigration.

The story of American history is communicated.

The text in *Atlas of American History* presents a chronological overview of American history and summarizes key events. It provides cross curricular connections by listing literature that clarifies or expands historical understandings. It highlights people whose accomplishments reflect American ideals.

The *Did You Know?* feature on each section opening page provides an interesting sidelight to history. Like the example below, each of these features demonstrates how history has influenced the American experience.

A picture of the Greek god Atlas, supporting the earth on his shoulders, appeared on the title page of an early book of maps. Later, people began to call a collection of maps an *atlas*.

Section 1   *(Prehistory-1620)*

Beginnings

To learn about **prehistory**, or the time before human beings learned to write, scientists study the physical evidence that early people left behind. This evidence suggests the first Americans migrated from Asia between 25,000 and 8,000 years ago. The descendants of these people, now called Native Americans or American Indians, spread throughout the Americas and developed different cultures.

◀ *The Cliff Palace in Mesa Verde, Colorado, was built by the Anasazi around 1100.*

Historical evidence indicates that Vikings from Norway established a settlement in North America about A.D. 1000. During the 1400s, increased demand for Asian goods led European nations to seek a water route to Asia. Columbus was attempting to achieve this goal when he discovered a world previously unknown to Europeans.

In 1524 Verrazano ▶ *explored the Atlantic coast of what is now North Carolina.*

During the 1500s, European explorers who came to the Americas found continents inhabited by native peoples of diverse cultures, from hunters and gatherers to advanced civilizations. Although figures vary greatly, the graph at the right indicates estimates of Native American populations around that time.

Did You Know ?

Scientists discovered a spearhead among bones of ancient bison near Folsom, New Mexico. These animals became extinct about 10,000 years ago. This discovery proved people had migrated to the region by about 8000 B.C.

Estimates of Native American Populations in 1492

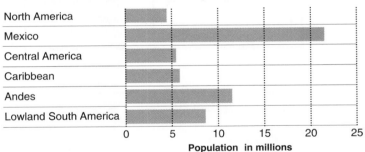

North America	
Mexico	
Central America	
Caribbean	
Andes	
Lowland South America	

0   5   10   15   20   25

Population in millions

	about A.D. 1000	**1492**	**1587**
People	Leif Ericson establishes a Viking settlement on the east coast of North America.	Christopher Columbus lands on San Salvador.	Virginia Dare, first English child born in America, is born on Roanoke Island.
	about 23,000 B.C.	**1325**	**about 1570**
Events	First Americans probably migrate from Asia to North America.	Aztecs build Tenochtitlán on site of present-day Mexico City.	Five Indian tribes in what is now New York form League of the Iroquois.
	1298	**1504**	**1552**
Literature	*Description of the World*, by Marco Polo, tells of the Italian trader's journey from Venice to China.	*New World*, a letter by Amerigo Vespucci, becomes the basis for naming America.	*In Defense of the Indian*, by Bartolomé de Las Casas, criticizes the Spanish for abusing Indians on Hispaniola.

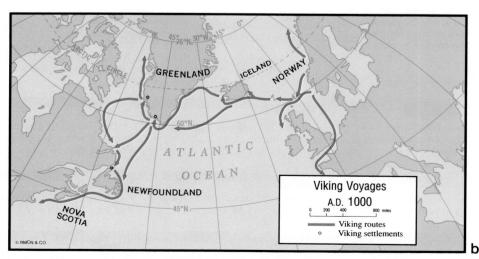

◀ During the Ice Ages, much of Earth's water was frozen in glaciers. These huge ice sheets covered much of what is now Canada and the northern United States. Scientists believe a land bridge existed where the Bering Strait now separates Asia and Alaska. Between 25,000 and 10,000 years ago, people from Asia may have migrated across the land bridge and spread throughout North America and South America.

Routes of the First Americans
23,000–8,000 B.C.

0   200   400   800   1200   miles at equator

Known routes
Probable route
Extent of ice

© RMCN & CO.

a

Viking Voyages
A.D. 1000

0   200   400   800   miles

Viking routes
o   Viking settlements

© RMCN & CO.

b

▲ About A.D. 1000, Norwegian Vikings, who had settled in Greenland, explored the coast of North America. They established a settlement in what is now Newfoundland, Canada.

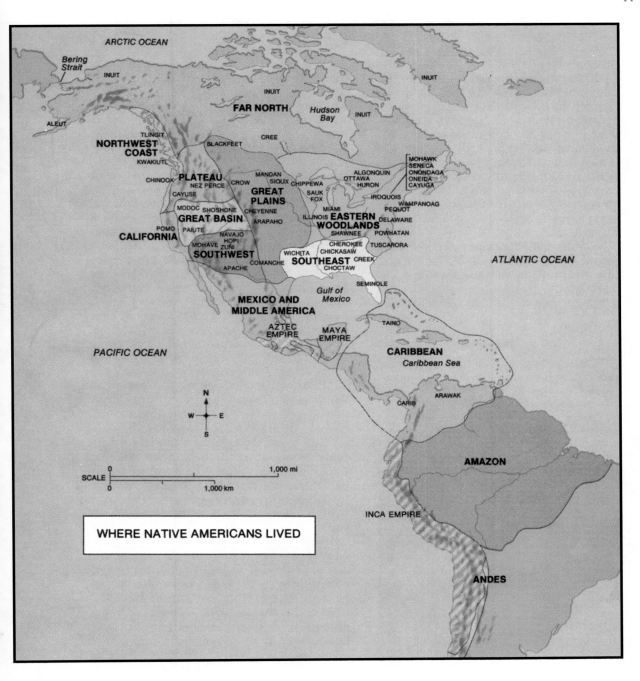

ARCTIC OCEAN

Bering Strait

INUIT

INUIT

INUIT

FAR NORTH

Hudson Bay

INUIT

ALEUT

CREE

TLINGIT

BLACKFEET

NORTHWEST COAST

KWAKIUTL

CHINOOK

PLATEAU

NEZ PERCE

CAYUSE

CROW

MANDAN

SIOUX

CHIPPEWA

ALGONQUIN

OTTAWA

HURON

MOHAWK

SENECA

ONONDAGA

ONEIDA

CAYUGA

MODOC

SHOSHONE

GREAT BASIN

PAIUTE

GREAT PLAINS

CHEYENNE

ARAPAHO

SAUK

FOX

MIAMI

ILLINOIS

EASTERN WOODLANDS

IROQUOIS

PEQUOT

WAMPANOAG

DELAWARE

POMO

CALIFORNIA

MOHAVE

NAVAJO

HOPI

ZUNI

SOUTHWEST

APACHE

COMANCHE

SHAWNEE

POWHATAN

WICHITA

CHEROKEE

CHICKASAW

SOUTHEAST

CHOCTAW

CREEK

TUSCARORA

ATLANTIC OCEAN

SEMINOLE

MEXICO AND MIDDLE AMERICA

Gulf of Mexico

AZTEC EMPIRE

MAYA EMPIRE

TAINO

PACIFIC OCEAN

CARIBBEAN

Caribbean Sea

ARAWAK

CARIB

N W E S

AMAZON

INCA EMPIRE

SCALE 0 — 1,000 mi
0 — 1,000 km

ANDES

WHERE NATIVE AMERICANS LIVED

▲ *Environments in which tribes of Native Americans or American Indians followed a similar way of life are called culture areas. The culture areas shown on the map existed around 1500, when Europeans began to arrive in the Americas. The map also lists major tribes of Native Americans within each culture area.*

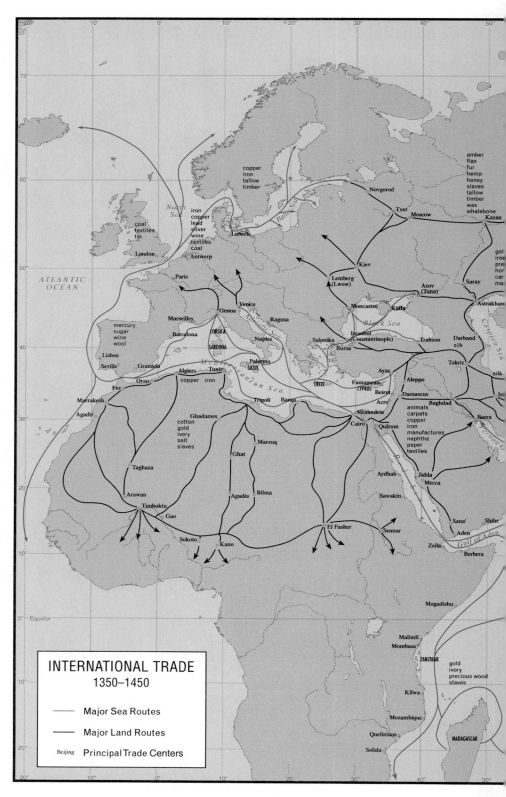

amber
flax
fur
hemp
honey
slaves
tallow
timber
wax
whalebone

copper
iron
tallow
timber

Novgorod

Tver

Moscow

Kazan

North Sea

iron
copper
lead
silver
wine
textiles
coal

Lübeck

Baltic Sea

gol
iro
pre
hor
car
ma

coal
textiles
tin

Antwerp

London

Kiev

Lemberg
(Lwow)

Azov
(Tana)

Saray

Astrakhan

Caspian Sea

ATLANTIC
OCEAN

Paris

Venice

Genoa

Adriatic Sea

Ragusa

Moncastro

Kaffa

Black Sea

Istanbul
(Constantinople)

Trabzon

Darband
silk

Marseilles

Barcelona

CORSICA

Naples

Salonika

Bursa

Tabriz

silk

mercury
sugar
wine
wool

SARDINIA

Palermo
SICILY

Ayas

Aleppo

Iss

Lisbon

Seville

Granada

Oran

Algiers   Tunis

Mediterranean Sea

CRETE

Famagusta
CYPRUS

Beirut

Damascus

copper iron

Tripoli

Barqa

Acre

Alexandria

Baghdad

Basra

Fez

Marrakesh

Agadir

Ghadames
cotton
gold
ivory
salt
slaves

Marzuq

Cairo

Quzum

animals
carpets
copper
iron
manufactures
naphtha
paper
textiles

Persian G

Ghat

Taghaza

Agadès   Bilma

Aydhab

Jidda
Mecca

Arawan

Timbuktu

Gao

Sawakin

Sana'

Shihr

Aden

Zeila

Gulf of Aden

Berbera

Sokoto

Kano

El Fasher

Sennar

Mogadishu

Equator

Malindi

Mombasa

ZANZIBAR

gold
ivory
precious wood
slaves

Kilwa

Mozambique

Quelimane

Sofala

MADAGASCAR

INTERNATIONAL TRADE
1350–1450

— Major Sea Routes

— Major Land Routes

Beijing Principal Trade Centers

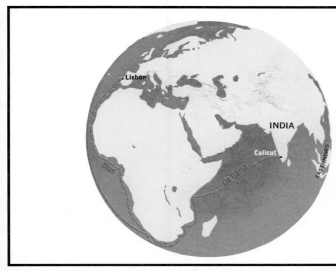

Portuguese Routes
to India
1488-1498

Between 1350 and 1450, Italian cities controlled trade through the Mediterranean, and Turkish Muslims controlled the main overland routes between Europe and Asia. Demand for Asian goods led European nations to seek a water route to Asia. The globe shows the routes of Portuguese explorers who accomplished this goal. In 1488 Bartholomeu Dias sailed around the southern tip of Africa. Ten years later, Vasco da Gama sailed around Africa to India.

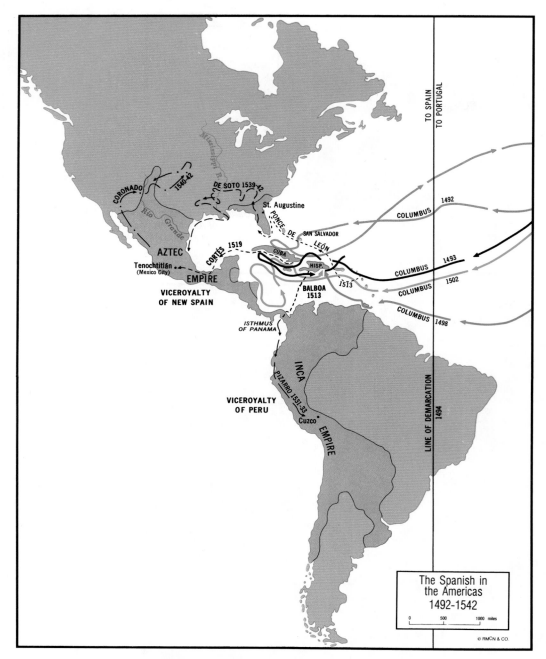

The voyages of Christopher Columbus led other Europeans to explore the Americas.
Pope Alexander VI established the Line of Demarcation to prevent disputes between
Spain and Portugal over lands their explorers claimed. The Spanish conquered
Indian empires in Mexico and Peru.

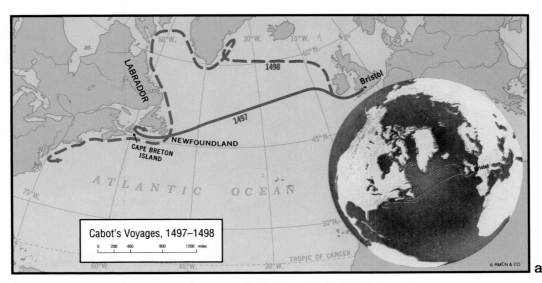

▲ John Cabot attempted to reach Asia by a northwest route across the Atlantic Ocean. In 1497 and 1498, Cabot explored the coasts of present-day Labrador, Newfoundland, and Cape Breton Island (Nova Scotia). His voyages gave England a claim to North America.

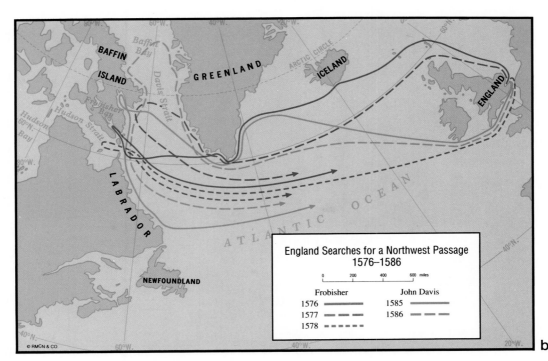

▲ In the 1570s and 1580s, England renewed its search for a water route to Asia through North America. Martin Frobisher and John Davis explored the Atlantic coast of what is now Canada and the area between Greenland and Baffin Island.

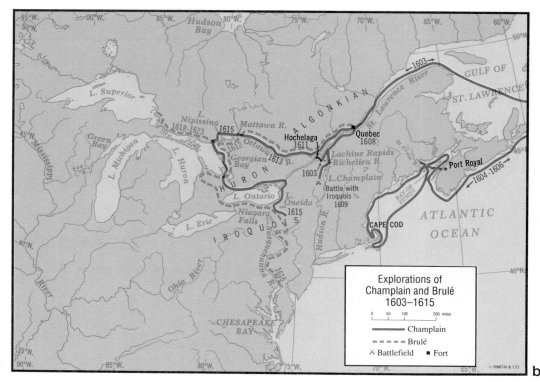

▲ France also sent explorers in search of a water route through North America. Giovanni da Verrazano explored the Atlantic coast from what is now North Carolina to Newfoundland. Jacques Cartier explored the St. Lawrence River and claimed the region for France.

▲ Samuel de Champlain extended French claims in North America. In 1608 he founded the city of Quebec. He then helped the Algonquin and Huron Indians defeat the Iroquois. Etienne Brulé lived among the Huron Indians and explored the river systems of northeastern North America for France.

Section 2   (1600-1775)

Establishing Colonies

Between 1600 and 1775, Europeans established **colonies**, or settlements ruled by their homelands, in North America. The English settled along the Atlantic coast and eventually took over Dutch and Swedish colonies established there. By 1732 thirteen English colonies stretched along the east coast of the present United States from New Hampshire to Georgia.

The French claimed the vast interior of North America. English attempts to settle west of the Appalachians led to conflict between France and Britain. The French and Indian War gave Britain control of all land east of the Mississippi River.

The colonial population grew rapidly due to a high birth rate and increased immigration. People came to America seeking religious freedom and economic opportunities. Slave traders also brought thousands of unwilling immigrants from Africa.

◄ *This stone canopy stands near the Massachusetts shore. It covers Plymouth Rock, which marks the spot near which the Pilgrims are believed to have stepped ashore.*

Reproductions of ► *ships that brought the first settlers to Jamestown are on the James River in Virginia. They are near the site of the first permanent English settlement in America.*

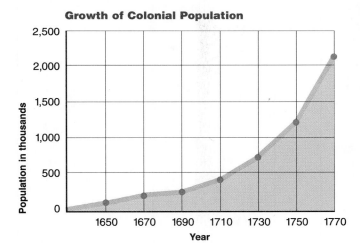

Growth of Colonial Population

(Graph: Population in thousands vs. Year, from 1650 to 1770, showing growth from near 0 to over 2,000 thousand)

Did You Know

?

Swedish settlers introduced log cabins in America. They built these houses along the Delaware River in the 1640s.

People	**1614** Pocahontas, daughter of Chief Powhatan, marries Jamestown colonist John Rolfe.	**1626** Peter Minuit purchases Manhattan Island from local Indians.	**1682** LaSalle claims Mississippi River Valley for France.
Events	**1607** Jamestown is founded.	**1620** Pilgrims settle Plymouth Colony.	**1754** French and Indian War begins at Fort Necessity.
Literature	**1640** The *Bay Psalm Book* is the first book written and published in the American colonies.	**1650** *The Tenth Muse Lately Sprung Up in America*, by Anne Bradstreet, describes home life in colonial New England.	**1733** *Poor Richard's Almanac*, by Ben Franklin, is published in Philadelphia.

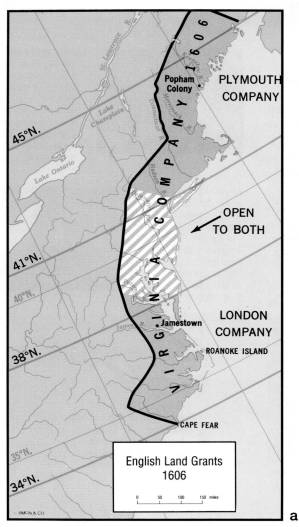

English Land Grants
1606

0   50   100   150 miles

a

▲ *The Plymouth Company and the London Company were groups of stockholders within the Virginia Company. Each group obtained a land grant from the English king to establish a colony in America. Land between 38° and 41° north latitude was open to both groups. Neither group was allowed to settle within 100 miles of the other.*

The Dutch bought Manhattan Island from Native Americans and established a fortified trading center called New Amsterdam. They established other settlements along the Hudson River and later took over Swedish settlements along the Delaware River.

▼

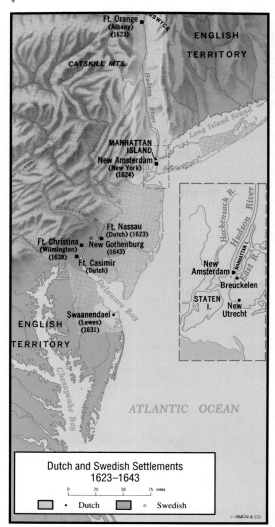

Dutch and Swedish Settlements
1623–1643

0   25   50   75 miles

☐ • Dutch   ☐ ○ Swedish

b

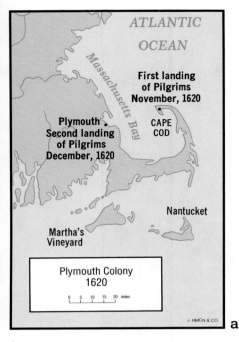

▲ The Pilgrims named their colony Plymouth, after the English port from which they had sailed.

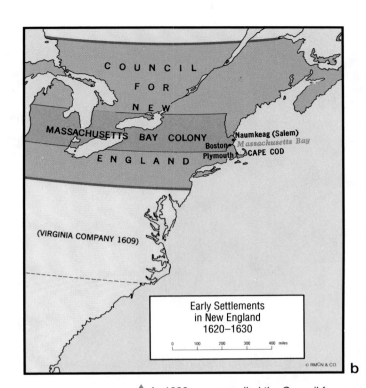

▲ In 1620 a group called the Council for New England received a land grant from the English king. The Massachusetts Bay Colony was established on this land in 1628.

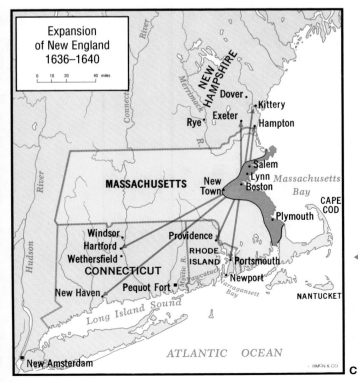

◀ The Puritans established settlements in the eastern part of Massachusetts, shown in blue on the map. Plymouth became part of the Massachusetts Colony. People who disagreed with Puritan views left Massachusetts and established new colonies.

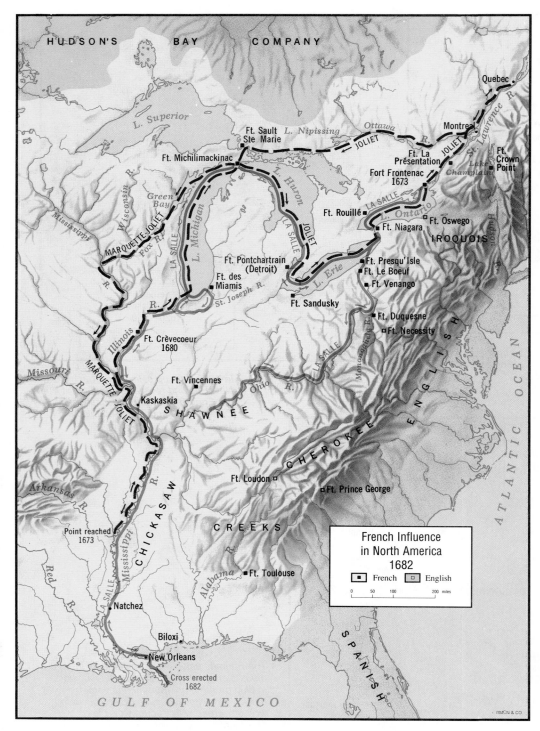

HUDSON'S   BAY   COMPANY

L. Superior

Quebec

Montreal

Ft. Sault
Ste Marie   L. Nipissing

Ottawa R.   JOLIET

St. Lawrence R.

JOLIET

Ft. La
Présentation

Ft. Crown
Point

Ft. Michilimackinac

Fort Frontenac
1673

Lake
Champlain

Wisconsin R.

Green
Bay

L. Huron

L. Michigan

Ft. Rouillé

L. Ontario

Ft. Oswego

LA SALLE

MARQUETTE-JOLIET

Fox R.

LA SALLE

JOLIET

Ft. Niagara

IROQUOIS

Hudson R.

Mississippi R.

Ft. Pontchartrain
(Detroit)

LA SALLE

Ft. Presqu'Isle
Ft. Le Boeuf
Ft. Venango

Ft. des
Miamis

St. Joseph R.

L. Erie

Ft. Sandusky

Ft. Duquesne

R.

Illinois R.

Ft. Crèvecoeur
1680

Ft. Necessity

Missouri R.

MARQUETTE-
JOLIET

Ft. Vincennes

Ohio R.

LA SALLE

Monongahela R.

ENGLISH

Kaskaskia

S H A W N E E

C H E R O K E E

ATLANTIC OCEAN

Ft. Loudon

Ft. Prince George

SALLE

LA

Arkansas R.

Point reached
1673

C R E E K S

CHICKASAW

Mississippi R.

Red R.

Alabama R.

Ft. Toulouse

SPANISH

Natchez

Biloxi

New Orleans

Cross erected
1682

GULF   OF   MEXICO

RMCN & CO

**French Influence
in North America
1682**

■ French   □ English

0   50   100   200 miles

▲ *France claimed the vast interior of North America, but it had little control over
the region because of a lack of settlers.*

The Thirteen Original British Colonies, 1750

0   200   400 Miles

Copyright by Rand McNally & Company. Made in U.S.A.

▲ *In about 150 years, the British established the 13 colonies that would become the United States. By 1750 the British colonies had a population of more than 1 million.*

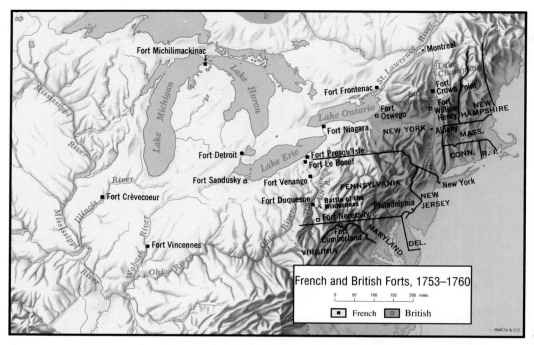

To keep the British east of the Appalachians, the French built a string of forts from Lake Erie to the Ohio River.

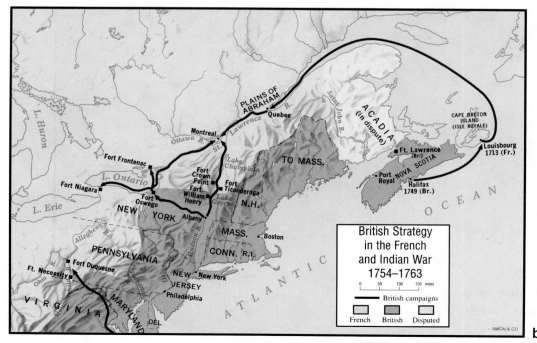

The British captured French forts in the St. Lawrence Valley and the eastern Great Lakes region.

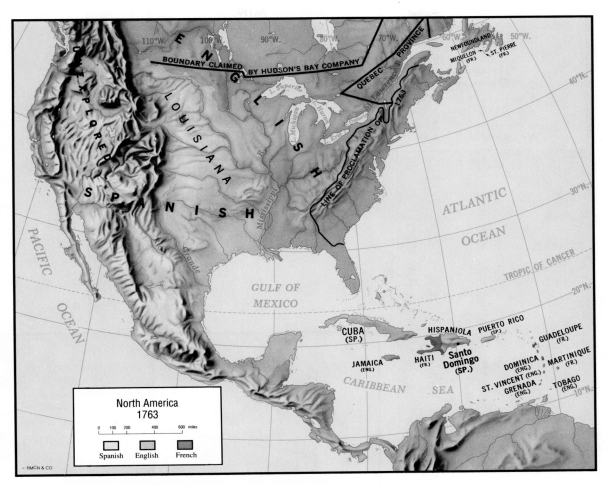

North America
1763

| 0 | 100 | 200 | 400 | 600 miles |

Spanish   English   French

▲ *The French and Indian War ended French control in North America. According to the Treaty of Paris in 1763, France kept only a few islands in the Caribbean. Britain acquired Canada and all French lands east of the Mississippi River. From Spain, France's ally in the war, Britain acquired Florida. To make up for the loss of Florida, France gave Spain the vast land between the Mississippi River and the Rocky Mountains.*

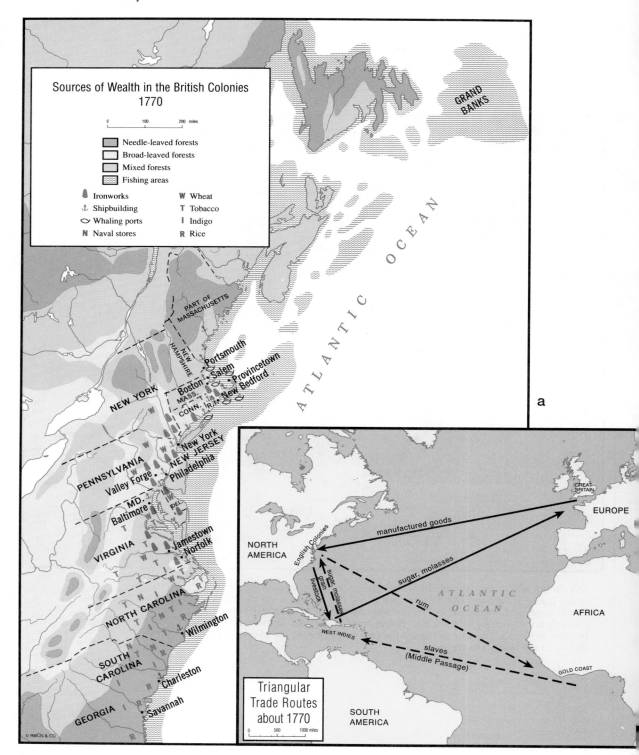

Sources of Wealth in the British Colonies 1770

0   100   200 miles

Needle-leaved forests
Broad-leaved forests
Mixed forests
Fishing areas

Ironworks
Shipbuilding
Whaling ports
Naval stores

W Wheat
T Tobacco
I Indigo
R Rice

GRAND BANKS

ATLANTIC OCEAN

PART OF MASSACHUSETTS

NEW HAMPSHIRE

Portsmouth
Salem
Provincetown
New Bedford

NEW YORK

Boston
MASS.
CONN. R.I.

New York

NEW JERSEY

PENNSYLVANIA

Valley Forge

Philadelphia

MD.
Baltimore

DEL.

VIRGINIA

Jamestown
Norfolk

NORTH CAROLINA

Wilmington

SOUTH CAROLINA

Charleston

GEORGIA

Savannah

a

Triangular Trade Routes about 1770

0   500   1000 miles

NORTH AMERICA

English Colonies

GREAT BRITAIN

EUROPE

manufactured goods

sugar, molasses

rum

grain, livestock

sugar, molasses

WEST INDIES

slaves (Middle Passage)

ATLANTIC OCEAN

AFRICA

GOLD COAST

SOUTH AMERICA

b

▲ Some colonial trade involved the exchange of goods for slaves. Thousands of unwilling immigrants from Africa suffered terribly during the voyage to America.

Section 3   (1775-1800)

Forming a New Nation

Between 1775 and 1800, the United States became an independent nation and established a new government. The Revolutionary War began when American minutemen clashed with British soldiers at Lexington and Concord in 1775. It ended in 1781 when Washington's troops, aided by French forces, defeated Cornwallis and his British troops at Yorktown.

◄ This statue in Boston honors Paul Revere's historic ride on April 18, 1775. Revere rode from Boston to Lexington to warn colonists that the British were coming.

The Treaty of Paris of 1783 recognized the independence of the United States and established its borders. The nation extended from the Atlantic Coast to the Mississippi River. The new states **ceded**, or gave up, their western lands to the federal government. The government created the Northwest Territory and provided for the sale of land to settlers.

During the 1700s, ► Spaniards built missions, like the one shown here, throughout the southwestern part of the present United States.

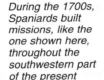

The Constitution, ratified in 1788, established the government that remains in effect today. The census in 1790 indicated the national origins of the American population.

Population by National Origin, 1790

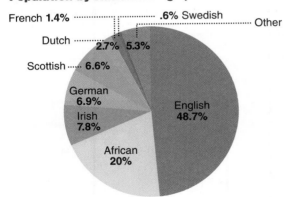

French 1.4%   .6% Swedish   Other
Dutch   2.7%   5.3%
Scottish   6.6%
German 6.9%
English 48.7%
Irish 7.8%
African 20%

Did You Know

?

The states carved from the Northwest Territory might be different if Thomas Jefferson had named them. He suggested such names as Dolypotamia, Assinisippia, and Metropotamia.

	1776	1789	1791
People	Juan Bautista de Anza establishes a presidio at San Francisco.	George Washington takes presidential oath of office in New York.	Benjamin Banneker, an African American surveyor, helps plan Washington, D.C.
	1776	1785	1800
Events	Declaration of Independence is signed in Philadelphia.	Land Ordinance provides plan for sale of land in the Northwest Territory.	Washington, D.C. becomes the national capital.
	1776	1782	1787
Literature	"To His Excellency, General Washington," by a slave named Phillis Wheatley, is printed in the Pennsylvania Magazine.	*Letters from an American Farmer*, by Jean de Crèvecoeur, describes social customs in the United States.	*The Federalist*, by Hamilton, Madison, and Jay, urges New York to ratify the Constitution.

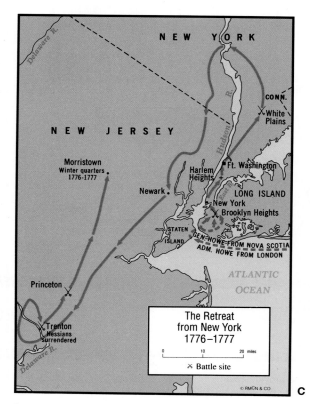

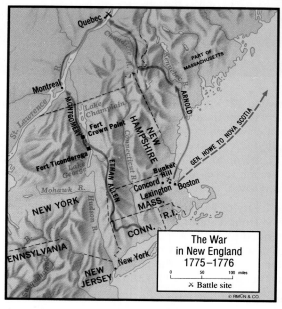

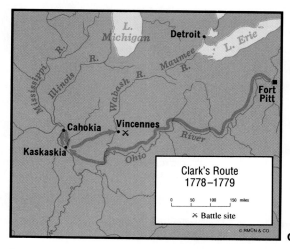

On the way to Concord, the British were met at Lexington by minutemen who had been warned by William Dawes and Paul Revere.

Americans captured British artillery at Forts Ticonderoga and Crown Point. They used the cannons in Boston, where they forced General William Howe and his troops to leave. An American invasion of Canada, led by General Richard Montgomery and Benedict Arnold, failed.

The British victory on Long Island forced George Washington and his troops to retreat from New York. After victories at Trenton and Princeton, American troops moved to winter quarters at Morristown.

Troops led by George Rogers Clark captured British settlements in the Ohio Valley.

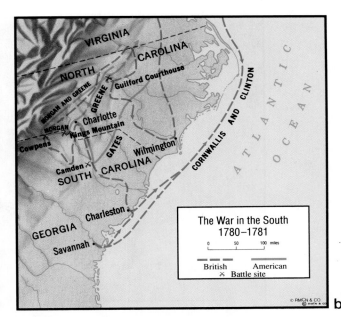

▲ British troops sailed to major ports in the South.

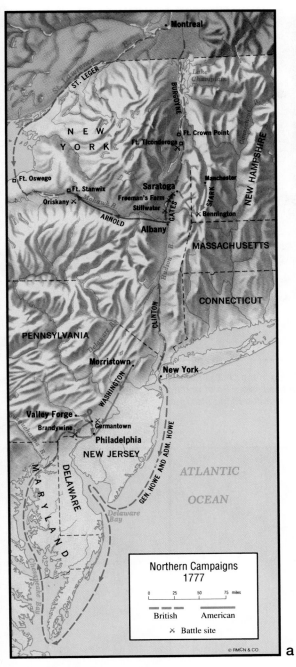

▲ Americans suffered heavy losses at Philadelphia and Germantown, but their victory at Saratoga convinced France to enter the war on the American side.

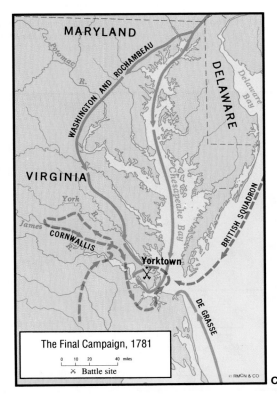

▲ The war ended at Yorktown when General Charles Cornwallis and his troops surrendered.

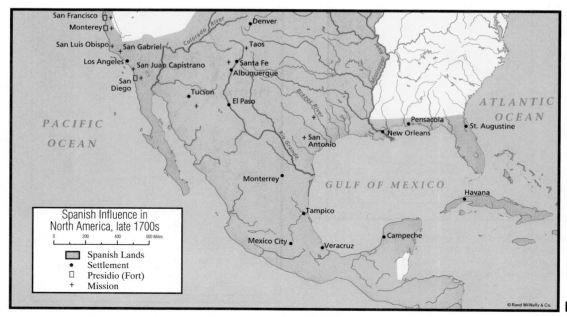

▲ The Treaty of Paris of 1783 established the boundaries of the United States. The new nation extended from the Atlantic Ocean to the Mississippi River and from 31° north latitude to the Canadian border. The treaty granted Florida to Spain.

▲ Spaniards established forts to protect their lands and missions to spread their faith.

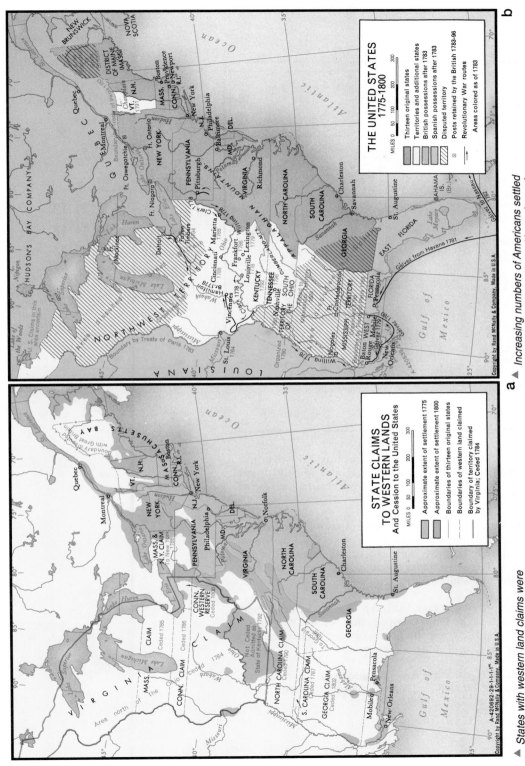

THE UNITED STATES 1775-1800

MILES 0 50 100 200 300

- Thirteen original states
- Territories and additional states
- British possessions after 1783
- Spanish possessions after 1783
- Disputed territory
- Posts retained by the British 1783-96
- Revolutionary War routes
- Areas colored as of 1783

Copyright by Rand McNally & Company. Made in U.S.A.

a ▲ Increasing numbers of Americans settled west of the Appalachians. Kentucky and Tennessee became states. Britain and Spain disputed areas of land added to the United States in 1783.

STATE CLAIMS TO WESTERN LANDS
And Cession to the United States

MILES 0 50 100 200 300

- Approximate extent of settlement 1775
- Approximate extent of settlement 1800
- Boundaries of thirteen original states
- Boundaries of western land claimed
- Boundary of territory claimed by Virginia; Ceded 1784

Copyright by Rand McNally & Company. Made in U.S.A.
A-420692-29-1-1-1-1▲

▲ States with western land claims were asked to put the good of the country above their own interests. Virginia was first to give up its claims. By 1802 all states had ceded their western lands to the United States.

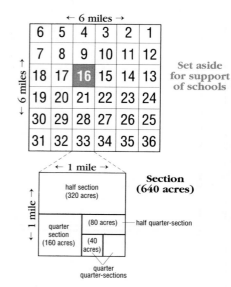

The Northwest Territory was land north of the Ohio River that later became the states of Ohio, Indiana, Illinois, Michigan, and Wisconsin. The Land Ordinance of 1785 provided a plan for the sale of this land.

Public lands were divided into townships that were six miles square. Each township was divided into 36 sections, as shown on the diagram. Each section consisted of 640 acres, and it sold for $1 per acre. The small white square in the grid on the map represents one township.

In the 1780s, few settlers could afford to buy a section of land. Companies such as the Ohio Company and Scioto Company bought land from the government and divided it into smaller lots. Then they sold it to settlers at a profit.

Section 16 in each township was set aside by the government for the support of education. Settlers could rent or sell this land to raise money for public schools.

Section 4   (1790-1870)

The Nation Expands & Changes

Between 1790 and 1870, the United States expanded its boundaries to the Pacific Coast. Through the Louisiana Purchase in 1803, it acquired the vast land between the Mississippi River and the Rocky Mountains. Through war with Mexico, 1846-1848, it gained land in the Southwest. Through a treaty with Britain in 1846, it gained land in the Pacific Northwest. Within 70 years after the United States became an independent nation, it had tripled in size.

Explorers, trappers, and traders blazed trails to the West. Pioneers rapidly settled new territories, pushing the **frontier**, or edge of settled land, west of the Mississippi River. Settlers followed the Oregon Trail to the Pacific Northwest. Mormons traveled to Utah in search of religious freedom. Gold seekers poured into California. Millions of immigrants from Europe came to the United States seeking a better life.

◄ The Gateway Arch stands along the Mississippi River in St. Louis. It honors the Louisiana Purchase and the pioneers who settled the West.

This monument ▶ marks the Oregon Trail, which thousands of pioneers traveled from Independence, Missouri, to the Oregon country.

Did You Know ?

Francis Scott Key wrote "The Star-Spangled Banner" during the War of 1812 as he watched the bombardment of Fort McHenry from a ship in Baltimore Harbor. The words were set to music and later became our national anthem.

Area of Selected Lands Added to the United States, 1803-1867

Year	Land	
1803	Louisiana Purchase	
1845	Texas Annexation	
1846	Oregon Treaty	
1848	Mexican Cession	
1867	Alaska Purchase	

0   200   400   600
Millions of acres

	1803	1847	1848
People	President Thomas Jefferson purchases Louisiana Territory from France.	Brigham Young leads Mormon migration from Illinois to the Great Salt Lake.	Elizabeth Cady Stanton and Lucretia Mott hold women's rights convention in New York.
	1819	**1825**	**1849**
Events	United States acquires Florida from Spain.	Erie Canal links the Great Lakes and Atlantic Ocean.	Gold rush brings thousands of people to California.
	1820	**1827**	**1854**
Literature	"Rip Van Winkle," by Washington Irving, is set in the Catskill Mountains.	*The Prairie*, by James Fenimore Cooper, describes frontier life on the western plains.	*Walden*, by Henry David Thoreau, describes the beauty of nature in Massachusetts.

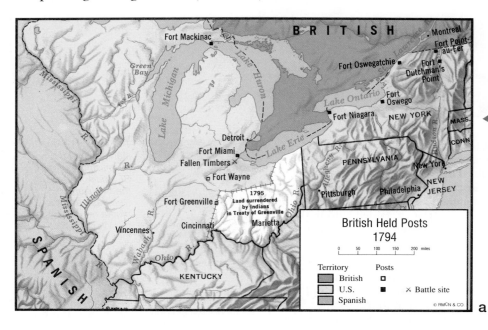

◀ *The British violated
the Treaty of Paris of
1783 by keeping
posts in U.S. territory.*

**British Held Posts
1794**

Territory
- British
- U.S.
- Spanish

Posts
- □
- ■
- ✕ Battle site

a

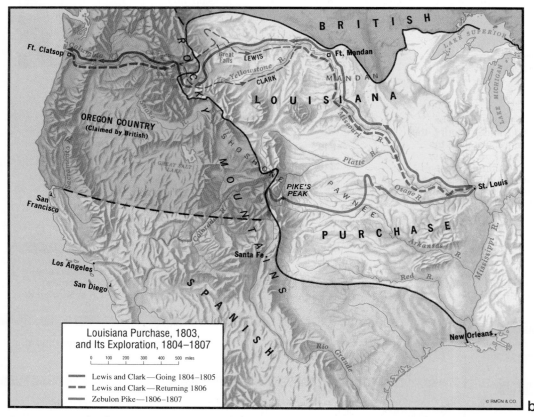

**Louisiana Purchase, 1803,
and Its Exploration, 1804–1807**

- Lewis and Clark—Going 1804–1805
- Lewis and Clark—Returning 1806
- Zebulon Pike—1806–1807

b

▲ *Explorations of the Louisiana Purchase by Lewis and Clark and Pike provided
valuable information about lands west of the Mississippi River.*

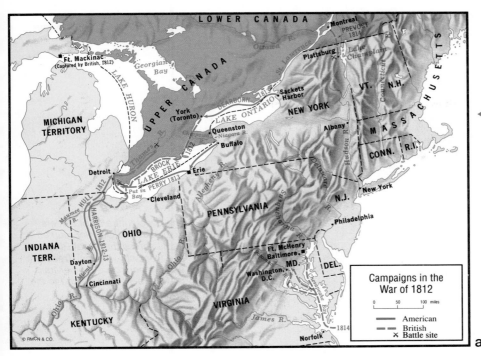

Campaigns in the
War of 1812 were
widely scattered.
They included a
decisive U.S.
victory on Lake
Erie as well as the
British capture and
burning of
Washington, D.C.

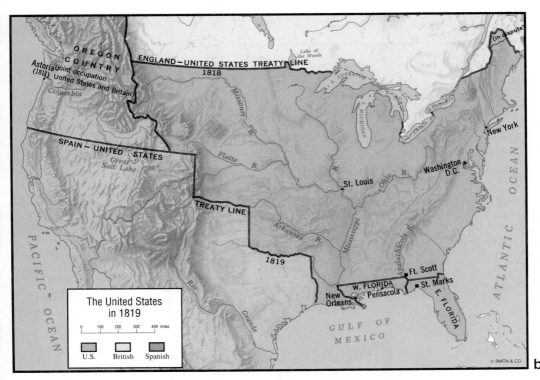

The Treaty of Ghent set a boundary between U.S. and British lands and allowed
both nations to settle the Oregon Country. The Adams-Onís Treaty set a
boundary between U.S. and Spanish lands and gave Florida to the United States.

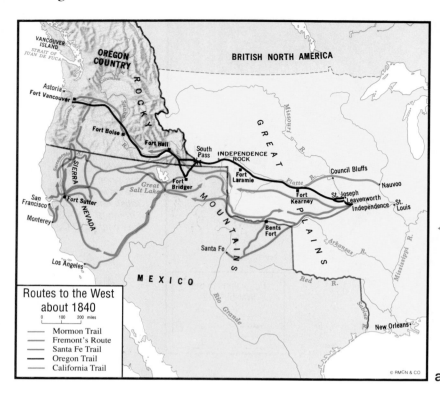

▶ The constant traffic of settlers to the Oregon Country marked a trail across the Great Plains and Rocky Mountains. Traders and trappers blazed other trails that settlers later followed to the Far West.

Routes to the West about 1840

0   100   200 miles

— Mormon Trail
— Fremont's Route
— Santa Fe Trail
— Oregon Trail
— California Trail

a

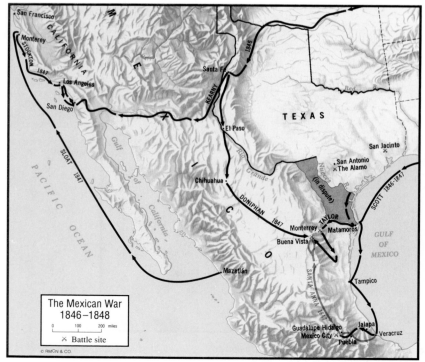

▶ The Mexican War began with a dispute over the southern boundary of Texas—the area shown in pink on the map. It ended when General Winfield Scott defeated Santa Anna and captured Mexico City. As a result of this war, the United States gained a large territory in the southwest.

The Mexican War 1846–1848

0   100   200 miles

× Battle site

b

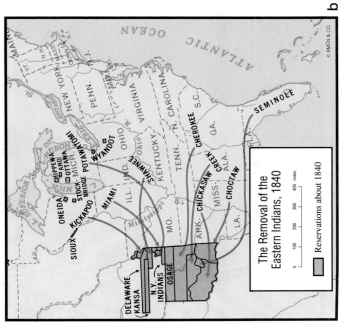

The U.S. government forced Native Americans to leave their lands in the East and move to reservations in the West. The journey of 15,000 Cherokees from Georgia to Oklahoma became known as the Trail of Tears. About 4,000 Indians died along the way.

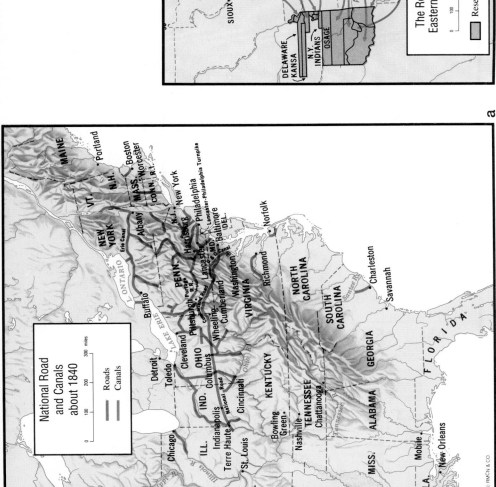

The Cumberland Road, also called the National Road, extended from Maryland to Illinois. The Erie Canal provided a link between the Great Lakes and the Atlantic Ocean.

WESTWARD EXPANSION
1800-1850

0 50 100   200   300   400

	U.S. Territory 1783
	Louisiana Purchase, 1803
	Texas, 1845
	Oregon Country
	Mexican Cession, 1848
IOWA 1846	States admitted 1800-1850
– – –	Mexican War Campaigns
——	Western Trails
✕	Battles of Mexican War
++++	Railroads of 1850
⌐⌐⌐	Major Canals of 1850

Copyright by Rand McNally & Company, Made in U.S.A.

Between 1800 ▶ and 1850, the United States added fifteen new states and extended its borders to the Pacific Coast.

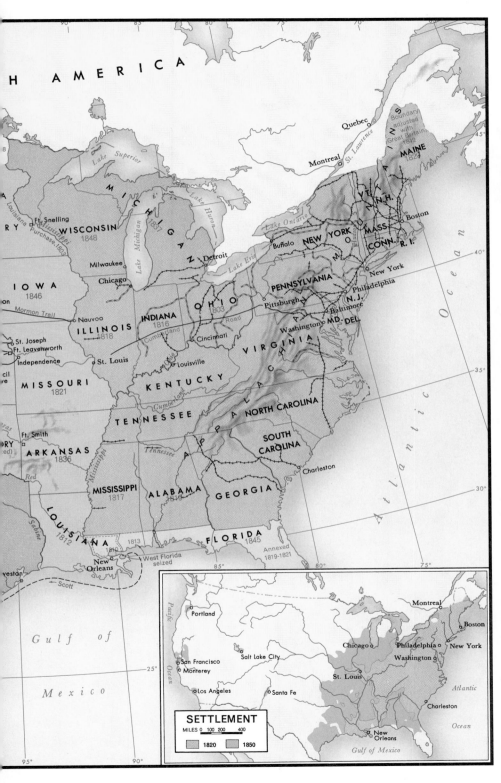

By 1850 settlement had spread west of the Mississippi River. Thousands of settlers also moved to the Far West.

SETTLEMENT

MILES 0 100 200 400

1820
1850

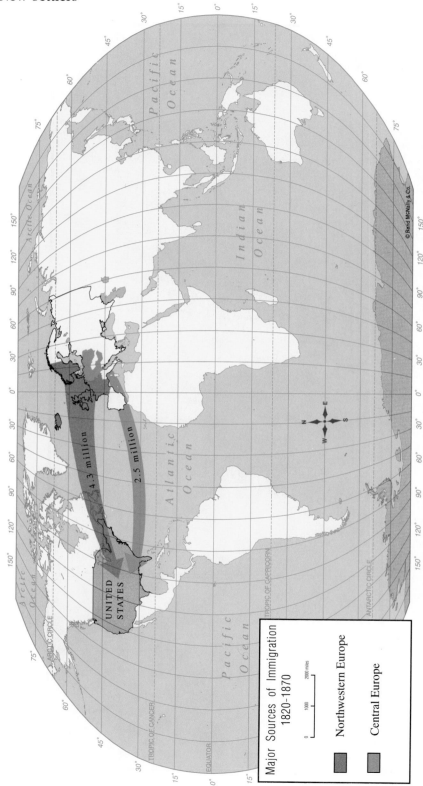

Major Sources of Immigration 1820–1870

0   1000   2000 miles

Northwestern Europe

Central Europe

▲ Between 1820 and 1870, about 7.5 million immigrants came to the United States. Most came from northern and western Europe. Crop failure and poverty led Irish, German, and Scandinavian immigrants to seek a better life in America.

Section 5 (1850-1865)

A Nation Divided

Between 1850 and 1860, differences between the North and the South widened. The agricultural economy of the South was based on slave labor. Many Northerners viewed slavery as wrong. **Abolitionists**, or people who demanded an end to slavery, operated the Underground Railroad to help slaves escape. The Compromise of 1850 and the Kansas-Nebraska Act attempted to settle the issue of slavery in the West.

When Abraham Lincoln was elected president in 1860, Southerners feared he would end slavery. Eleven southern states **seceded**, or withdrew, from the Union and formed the Confederacy. An attack on Fort Sumter in April 1861 marked the beginning of the Civil War. The war ended when Confederate general Robert E. Lee surrendered at Appomattox in April 1865.

The bitter war between the North and the South left lasting problems. Much of the South was destroyed. More Americans lost their lives in the Civil War than in any other war in which the United States has fought.

◄ The Battle of Gettysburg took place at this site in Pennsylvania in July 1863.

◄ This memorial to Confederate leaders is carved on Stone Mountain near Atlanta, Georgia.

American Deaths in Major Wars

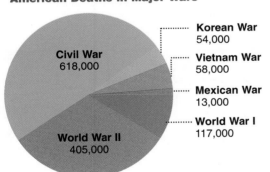

Korean War 54,000

Vietnam War 58,000

Mexican War 13,000

World War I 117,000

Civil War 618,000

World War II 405,000

Did You Know?

When Virginia seceded from the Union in 1861, 50 of its western counties separated from the state. These counties were admitted to the Union in 1863 as the state of West Virginia.

	1850	1863	1865
People	Harriet Tubman leads slaves from Maryland to freedom in the North.	Abraham Lincoln delivers Gettysburg Address on battlefield in Pennsylvania.	Robert E. Lee surrenders at Appomattox Court House, Virginia.

	1860	1861	1865
Events	South Carolina becomes first southern state to secede.	Civil War begins at Fort Sumter, South Carolina.	Thirteenth Amendment ends slavery in the United States.

	1850	1852	1865
Literature	*The Scarlet Letter*, by Nathaniel Hawthorne, is set in Puritan New England.	*Uncle Tom's Cabin*, by Harriet Beecher Stowe, highlights the cruelty of slavery in the South.	"Drum Taps," by Walt Whitman, describes scenes from Civil War battlefields.

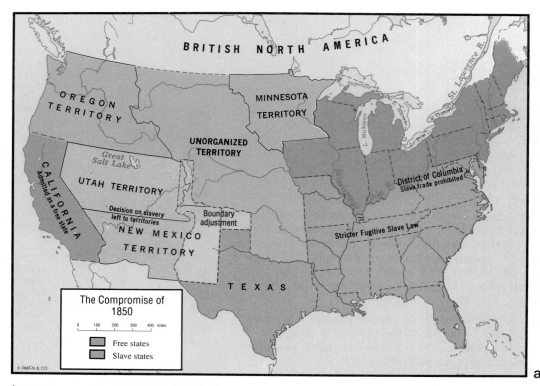

The Compromise of 1850 admitted California as a free state and ended slave trade in the District of Columbia. Utah and New Mexico Territories could decide the issue of slavery.

The Kansas-Nebraska Act allowed settlers in those territories to decide whether to allow slavery.

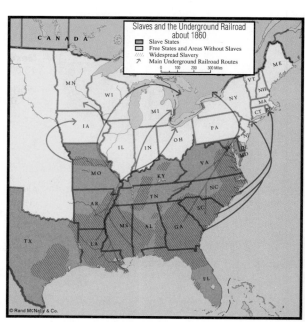

The Underground Railroad was a system of escape routes slaves followed to freedom.

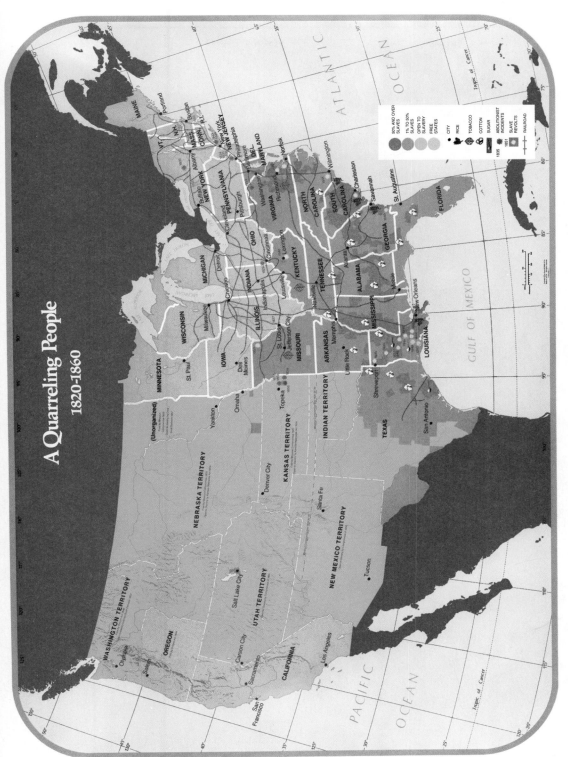

A Quarreling People
1820-1860

▲ *Economic differences created different ways of life in the North and the South. Plantation crops, such as tobacco, cotton, and sugar cane, supported an agricultural economy based on slavery in the South. Advances in mass production and transportation supported an economy based on industry and trade in the North. Northern abolitionists viewed slavery as wrong and began a movement to end it.*

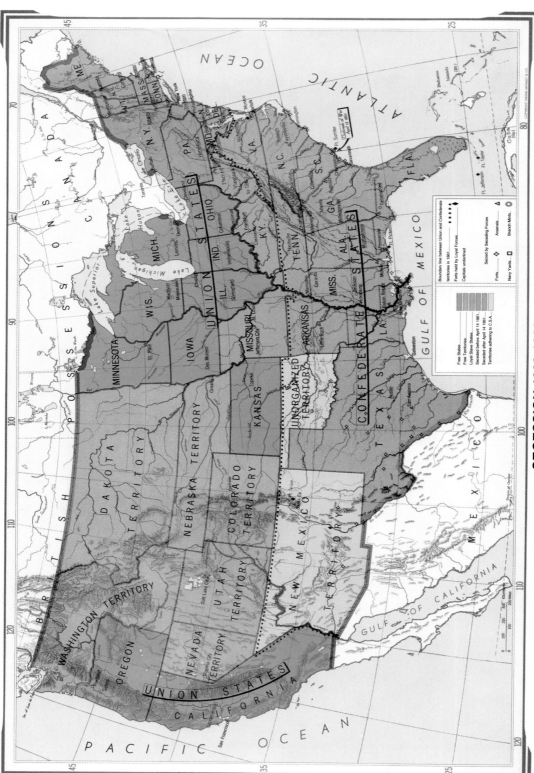

SECESSION 1860-1861

▲ The Confederate States of America consisted of eleven slave states that seceded from the Union in 1860 and 1861. The 23 remaining states and territories, including four slave states, fought for the Union during the Civil War.

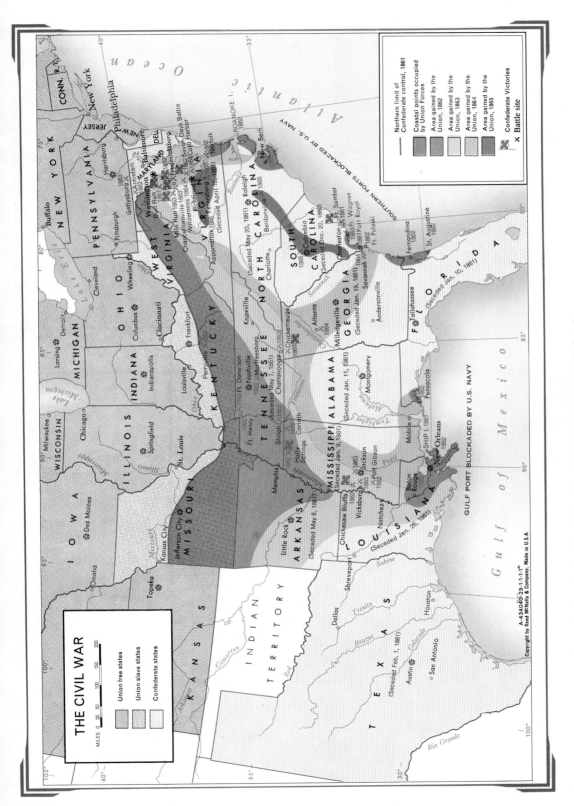

THE CIVIL WAR

MILES 0 25 50 100 150 200

- Union free states
- Union slave states
- Confederate states

Legend

- Northern limit of Confederate control, 1861
- Coastal points occupied by Union forces
- Area gained by the Union, 1862
- Area gained by the Union, 1863
- Area gained by the Union, 1864
- Area gained by the Union, 1865
- × Confederate Victories
- × Battle site

Copyright by Rand McNally & Company. Made in U.S.A.

A-434046-29-1-1-1-¹

▲ *Most of the fighting in the East took place in Virginia. Much of the fighting in the West took place in Tennessee and along the Mississippi River. The map legend indicates how Union strategy succeeded by dividing the Confederacy and blockading its ports.*

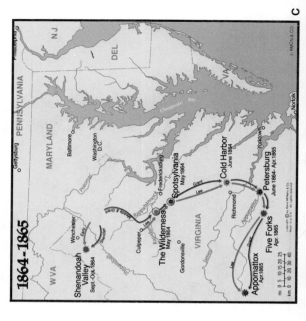

1861 - 1863

1864 - 1865

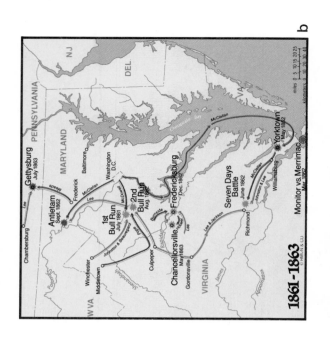

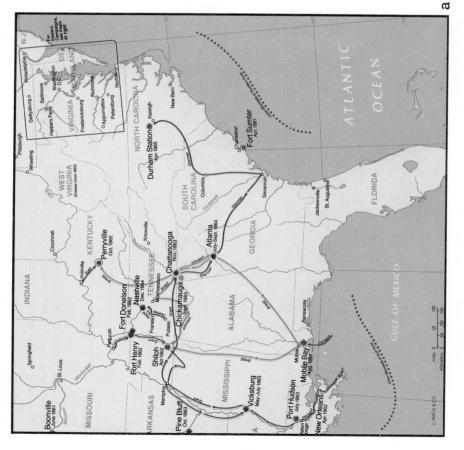

The Civil War 1861–1865

Union victory

Confederate victory

Battle indecisive

Union forces

Confederate forces

Union strategy involved blockading southern ports, splitting the Confederacy by gaining control of the Mississippi River Valley, and capturing Richmond. Confederate strategy involved defending the South from attack, breaking the Union blockade, and splitting the Union by gaining control of Washington, D.C., Maryland, and central Pennsylvania.

Section 6 (1860-1920)

Emerging as a Modern Nation

The years between 1860 and 1920 included the end of one era in American history and the beginning of another. The Great Plains opened to settlers as the U.S. Army defeated the Plains Indians and forced them onto reservations. Texas cattle ranchers drove their herds to railroads, which provided transportation to eastern markets. **Homesteaders**, or settlers who received free land from the government in exchange for farming it, moved to western territories. By 1890, the long process of settling the United States from coast to coast was complete. The American frontier had come to an end.

In the late 1800s, the United States began to emerge as a modern nation. Millions of immigrants came from Europe to farm the land or work in factories. The United States became an industrial nation and acquired territories overseas. It purchased Alaska and established naval bases on islands in the Pacific. It fought a war with Spain by which it acquired additional territories. The United States entered World War I in 1917 and assumed its role as a world power.

◀ This statue of Buffalo Bill Cody in Wyoming represents the Old West.

The Statue of Liberty ▶ in New York Harbor has welcomed immigrants since 1886. It was a gift to the United States from France.

Immigration to the United States, 1860-1919

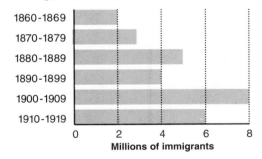

1860-1869	
1870-1879	
1880-1889	
1890-1899	
1900-1909	
1910-1919	

0   2   4   6   8
Millions of immigrants

Did You Know ?

In 1850 about 20 million bison, or buffaloes, roamed the Great Plains. The westward movement almost wiped out these animals. By 1890, only about 500 bison could be found in the West.

	1877	1889	1898
People	Chief Joseph leads Nez Percés on a retreat through Idaho and Montana.	Jane Addams opens Hull House to help immigrants in Chicago.	Theodore Roosevelt leads Rough Riders in Cuba during Spanish-American War.
	1867	**1892**	**1898**
Events	United States purchases Alaska from Russia.	Ellis Island, in New York Harbor, becomes an immigration station.	Hawaii becomes a U.S. territory.
	1876	**1881**	**1912**
Literature	*The Adventures of Tom Sawyer*, by Mark Twain, is set in Hannibal, Missouri.	*A Century of Dishonor*, by Helen Hunt Jackson, describes mistreatment of Native Americans in the U.S.	*Riders of the Purple Sage*, by Zane Grey, describes life in the West.

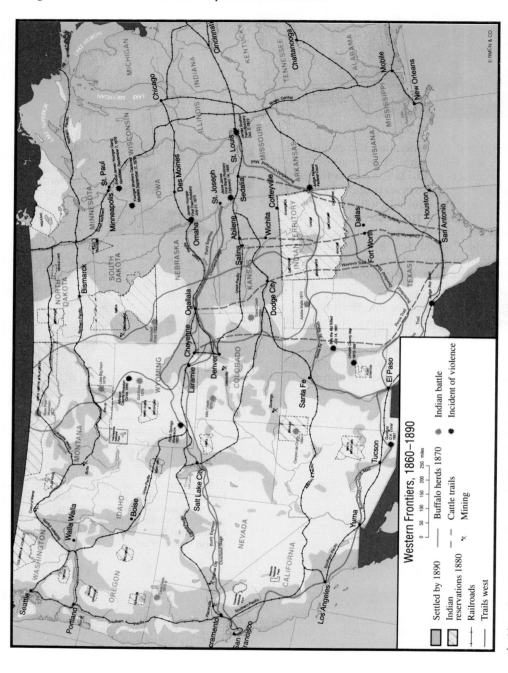

Western Frontiers, 1860–1890

☐ Settled by 1890	
☐ Indian reservations 1880	
┼ Railroads	
— Trails west	
— Buffalo herds 1870	
– – Cattle trails	
✕ Mining	
✸ Indian battle	
✸ Incident of violence	

0 50 100 150 200 250 miles

▲ *After 1860, the population west of the Mississippi River grew rapidly. Native Americans lost the battle to keep their lands, and the government moved them to reservations. Ranchers and farmers spread settlements throughout the Great Plains and the Far West. Although large areas of the West remained thinly populated, in 1890 the Census Bureau declared the frontier had come to an end.*

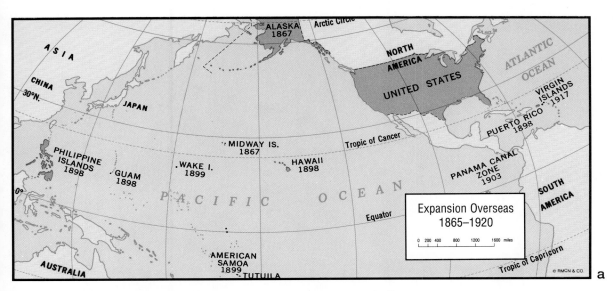

a

▲ The United States acquired islands in the Pacific Ocean that served as fueling stations for ships traveling to and from China and Japan. The Hawaiian Islands also provided raw materials for import or trade.

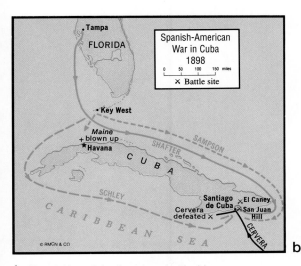

b

▲ The sinking of the American battleship Maine in Havana harbor brought the United States into war with Spain. The war was fought in both Cuba and the Philippines. As a result of the Spanish-American War, Spain granted freedom to Cuba and ceded Guam, Puerto Rico, and the Philippines to the United States.

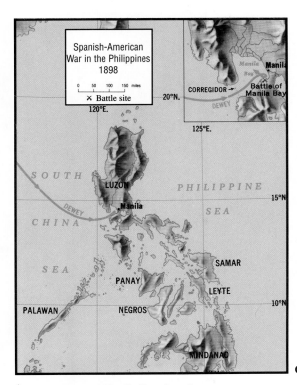

c

▲ In the Battle of Manila Bay, American ships commanded by Commodore George Dewey destroyed the Spanish fleet in the Philippines.

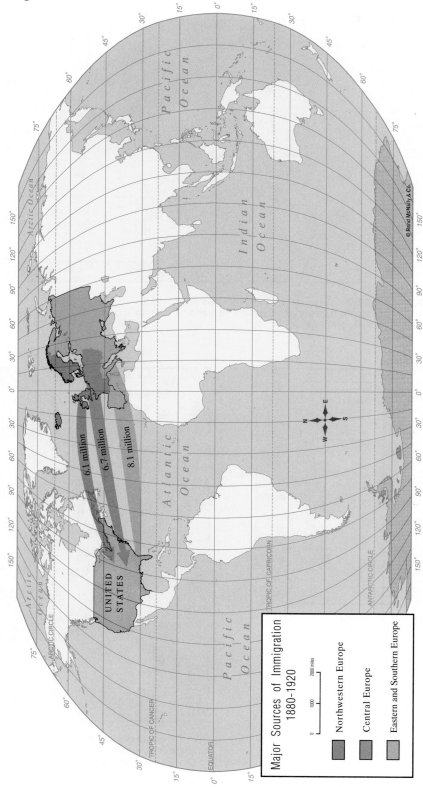

6.1 million

6.7 million

8.1 million

UNITED
STATES

Major Sources of Immigration
1880–1920

Northwestern Europe

Central Europe

Eastern and Southern Europe

0   1000   2000 miles

© Rand McNally & Co.

▲ Between 1880 and 1920, more than 20 million immigrants came to the United States. Unlike earlier
newcomers, who came mostly from northern and western Europe, these so-called "new immigrants"
came mostly from central, eastern, and southern Europe.

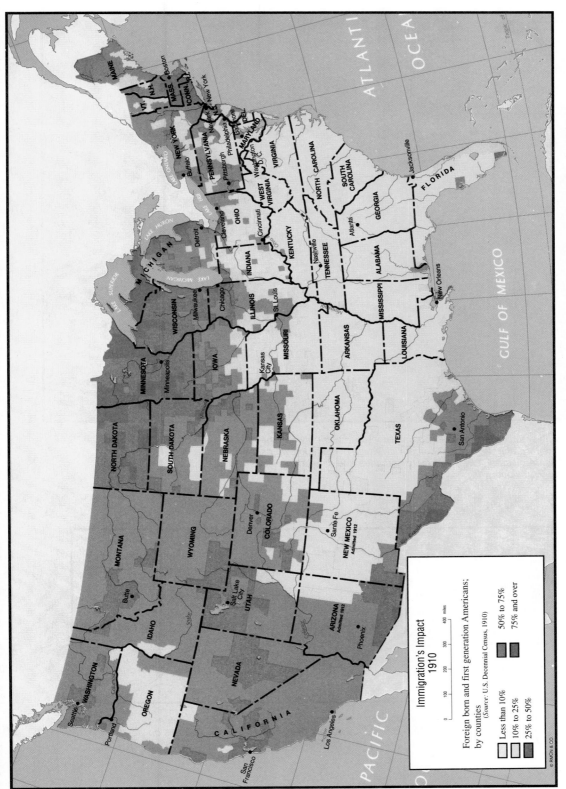

▲ Many immigrants settled in large cities in the East. Mining attracted newcomers to Montana, Colorado, and Nevada. Railroad companies encouraged European workers to settle in the West. Poor economic conditions in Mexico led thousands of immigrants to settle in the United States.

Immigration's Impact 1910

Foreign born and first generation Americans; by counties
(*Source:* U.S. Decennial Census, 1910)

- Less than 10%
- 10% to 25%
- 25% to 50%
- 50% to 75%
- 75% and over

0 100 200 300 400 miles

© RMCN & CO.

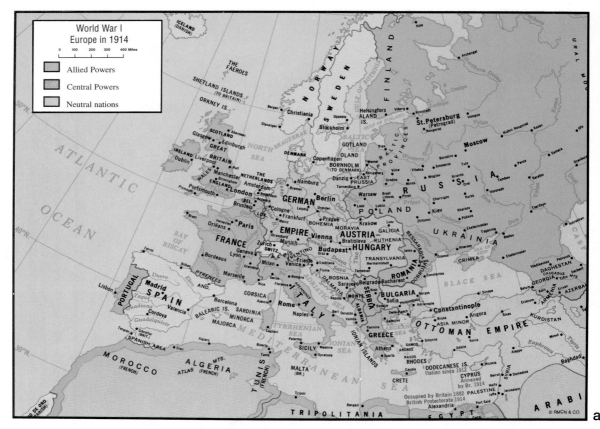

▲ In 1914, long-standing problems in Europe erupted in war between the Allied Powers and the Central Powers. The conflict, which became known as World War I, lasted four years. It involved more countries and caused more destruction than had any previous war.

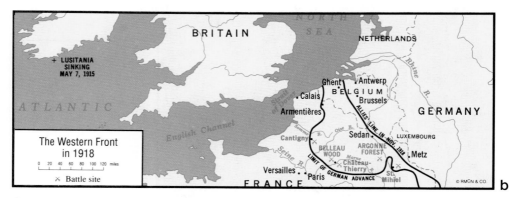

▲ The loss of American lives aboard the Lusitania helped draw the United States into the war in Europe. American troops helped the Allies defeat the Germans on the Western Front, which stretched through Belgium and France.

Section 7   (1920-1990)

Challenges & Changes in the 20th Century

During the decades between 1920 and 1990, the United States faced many challenges and experienced many changes. The economic prosperity of the 1920s ended with the stock market crash in 1929. Poverty and unemployment were widespread during the Great Depression of the 1930s. During World War II (1941-1945), United States troops fought in Europe and in the Pacific. After this war, the United States and the Soviet Union emerged as the world's leading powers.

The struggle between the Communist world, led by the Soviet Union, and the free world, led by the United States, was called the **Cold War**. Between 1950 and 1990, the United States intervened in Korea, in Southeast Asia, and in Central America and the Caribbean to stop the spread of communism.

Changes took place within the United States as Americans moved from one area of the country to another, and suburbs grew around major cities. The **gross domestic product** (GDP), or value of all goods and services produced within the country, rose sharply after 1940. Economic growth continued into the 1990s.

◄ The United States Marine Corps Memorial in Arlington, Virginia, honors the flag raising on Iwo Jima during World War II.

◄ In 1940 Houston, Texas, ranked 21st in population among U.S. cities. By 1990, it was among the nation's largest metropolitan areas.

Gross Domestic Product, 1920-1990

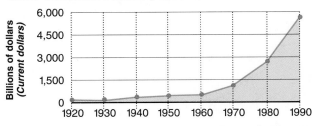

Billions of dollars (Current dollars): 0, 1,500, 3,000, 4,500, 6,000
Years: 1920, 1930, 1940, 1950, 1960, 1970, 1980, 1990

Did You Know ?

Between 1941 and 1945, one in every five **Americans moved from one part of the United States to another.**

	1927	1963	1981
People	Charles Lindbergh makes first nonstop flight from New York to Paris.	Dr. Martin Luther King, Jr., leads civil rights march on Washington, D.C.	Arizona judge Sandra Day O'Connor becomes first woman to serve on the Supreme Court.
	1959	1961	1973
Events	Alaska and Hawaii become states.	First American astronaut is launched into space from Cape Canaveral, Florida.	Native Americans seize Wounded Knee, South Dakota, to demand return of Indian lands.
	1939	1961	1971
Literature	*The Grapes of Wrath*, by John Steinbeck, tells of an Oklahoma family during the Great Depression.	*To Kill a Mockingbird,* by Harper Lee, explores racial prejudice in Alabama.	*Barrio Boy*, by Ernesto Galarza, describes Hispanic life in Sacramento, California.

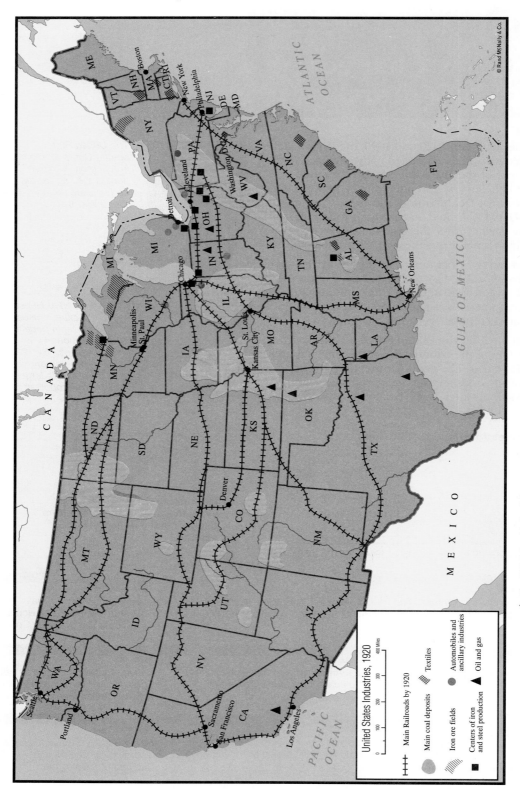

© Rand McNally & Co.

United States Industries, 1920

0 | 100 | 200 | 300 | 400 Miles

- ┼┼┼ Main Railroads by 1920
- Main coal deposits
- Iron ore fields
- ■ Centers of iron and steel production
- Textiles
- ● Automobiles and ancillary industries
- ▲ Oil and gas

▲ *By 1920 the United States was a leading industrial nation. Advances in technology enabled workers to produce more goods faster. The demand for petroleum and steel increased to meet the growing needs of new industries such as the automobile industry. Spectacular economic growth provided a high standard of living for many Americans.*

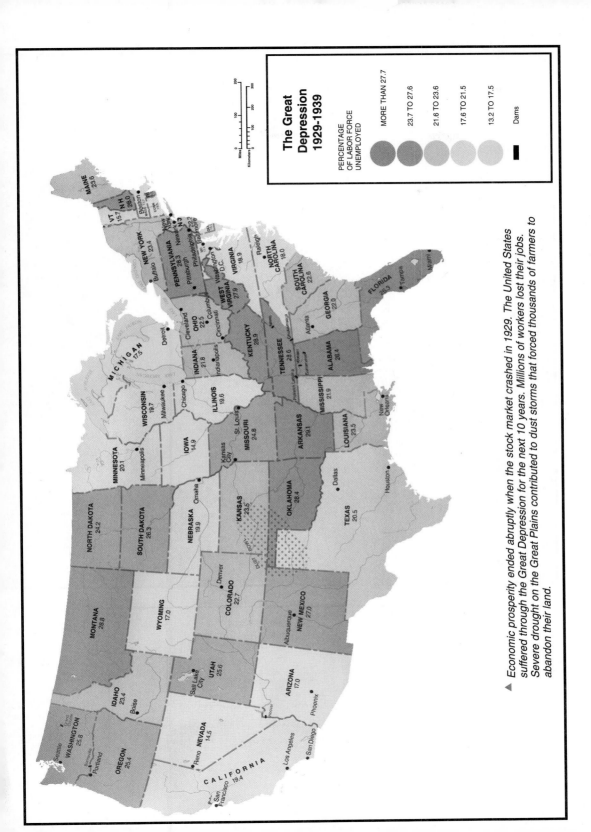

The Great Depression 1929-1939

PERCENTAGE OF LABOR FORCE UNEMPLOYED

MORE THAN 27.7

23.7 TO 27.6

21.6 TO 23.6

17.6 TO 21.5

13.2 TO 17.5

Dams

▲ Economic prosperity ended abruptly when the stock market crashed in 1929. The United States suffered through the Great Depression for the next 10 years. Millions of workers lost their jobs. Severe drought on the Great Plains contributed to dust storms that forced thousands of farmers to abandon their land.

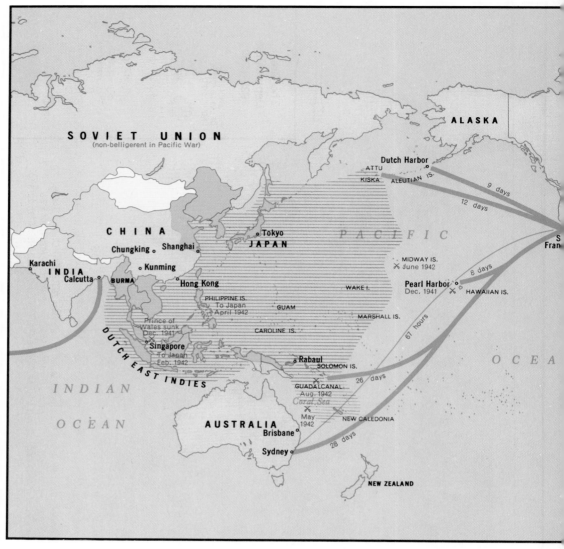

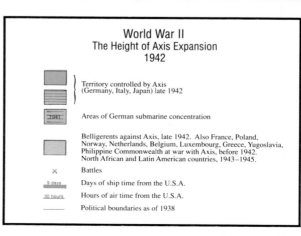

World War II
The Height of Axis Expansion
1942

Territory controlled by Axis
(Germany, Italy, Japan) late 1942

Areas of German submarine concentration

Belligerents against Axis, late 1942. Also France, Poland,
Norway, Netherlands, Belgium, Luxembourg, Greece, Yugoslavia,
Philippine Commonwealth at war with Axis, before 1942.
North African and Latin American countries, 1943–1945.

× Battles

Days of ship time from the U.S.A.

Hours of air time from the U.S.A.

Political boundaries as of 1938

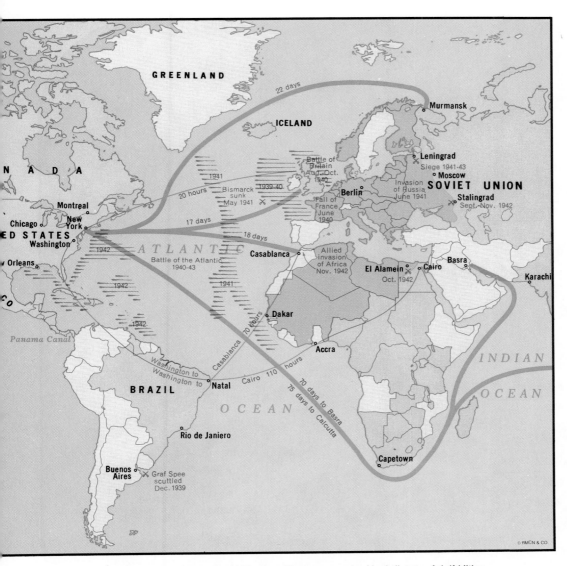

GREENLAND

22 days

ICELAND

Murmansk

Leningrad
Siege 1941-43

Moscow

Battle of
Britain
Aug.-Oct.
1940

1941

Bismarck
sunk
May 1941

1939-40

Berlin

Invasion
of Russia
June 1941

SOVIET UNION

Stalingrad
Sept.-Nov. 1942

NADA

Montreal

20 hours

17 days

Fall of
France
June
1940

Chicago
New
York

ED STATES

Washington

18 days

Orleans

1942

ATLANTIC

Casablanca

Allied
invasion
of Africa
Nov. 1942

El Alamein
Oct. 1942

Cairo

Basra

Karachi

CO

Battle of the Atlantic
1940-43

1942

1941

Panama Canal

1942

Dakar

70 hours

Accra

INDIAN

Washington to
Washington to

Casablanca 70 hours

Cairo 110 hours

70 days to Basra

OCEAN

BRAZIL

Natal

75 days to Calcutta

OCEAN

Rio de Janiero

Capetown

Buenos
Aires

Graf Spee
scuttled
Dec. 1939

© RMCN & CO.

▲ *World War II began in 1939 when Germany, under Nazi dictator Adolf Hitler, invaded Poland. The Axis powers (Germany, Italy, Japan, and their partners) fought against the Allied powers (shown in gold on the map). Few nations remained neutral. By 1942 the Axis controlled most of Europe, northern Africa, and parts of Asia and the Pacific. German submarines attacked Allied cargo ships in the Atlantic.*

The Japanese attack on Pearl Harbor, Hawaii, in December 1941 brought the United States into the war. American troops and supplies were sent to Europe and to the Pacific. The map indicates transportation time by air and by water from the United States to selected sites. During 1942, Allied forces halted Axis expansion in northern Africa, the Soviet Union, and the Pacific.

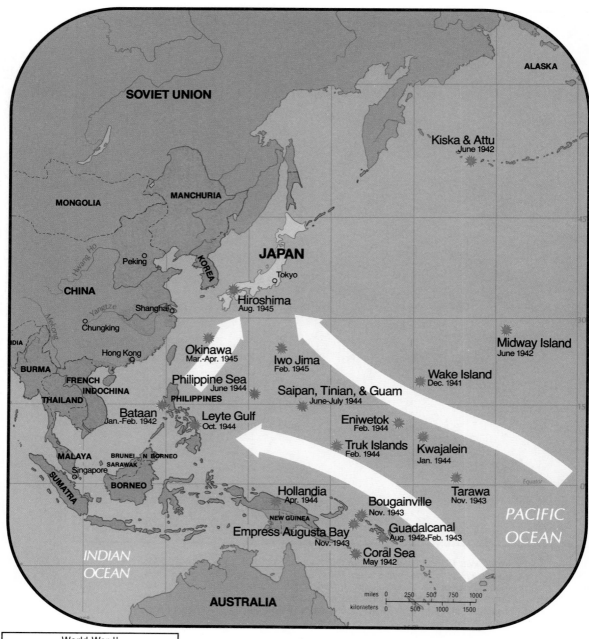

ALASKA

SOVIET UNION

Kiska & Attu
June 1942

MONGOLIA

MANCHURIA

JAPAN

Tokyo

Peking

KOREA

Hwang Ho

CHINA

Shanghai

Yangtze

Chungking

Hiroshima
Aug. 1945

Midway Island
June 1942

DIA

Hong Kong

Okinawa
Mar.-Apr. 1945

Iwo Jima
Feb. 1945

Wake Island
Dec. 1941

BURMA

FRENCH
INDOCHINA

Philippine Sea
June 1944

Saipan, Tinian, & Guam
June-July 1944

THAILAND

Mekong

PHILIPPINES

Bataan
Jan.-Feb. 1942

Leyte Gulf
Oct. 1944

Eniwetok
Feb. 1944

MALAYA

BRUNEI N BORNEO

SARAWAK

Truk Islands
Feb. 1944

Kwajalein
Jan. 1944

SUMATRA

Singapore

BORNEO

Equator

Hollandia
Apr. 1944

Tarawa
Nov. 1943

PACIFIC
OCEAN

Bougainville
Nov. 1943

NEW GUINEA

Empress Augusta Bay
Nov. 1943

Guadalcanal
Aug. 1942-Feb. 1943

INDIAN
OCEAN

Coral Sea
May 1942

miles 0   250   500   750   1000

kilometers 0   500   1000   1500

AUSTRALIA

World War II
1941–1945
Pacific Theater

Allied powers

Axis powers

Battles

Axis controlled
areas

Allied advances

▲ *In 1943 and 1944, the Allies captured
Japanese-held islands in the Pacific. In
August 1945, the United States dropped
an atomic bomb on Hiroshima, Japan.
World War II ended when the Japanese
surrendered in September 1945.*

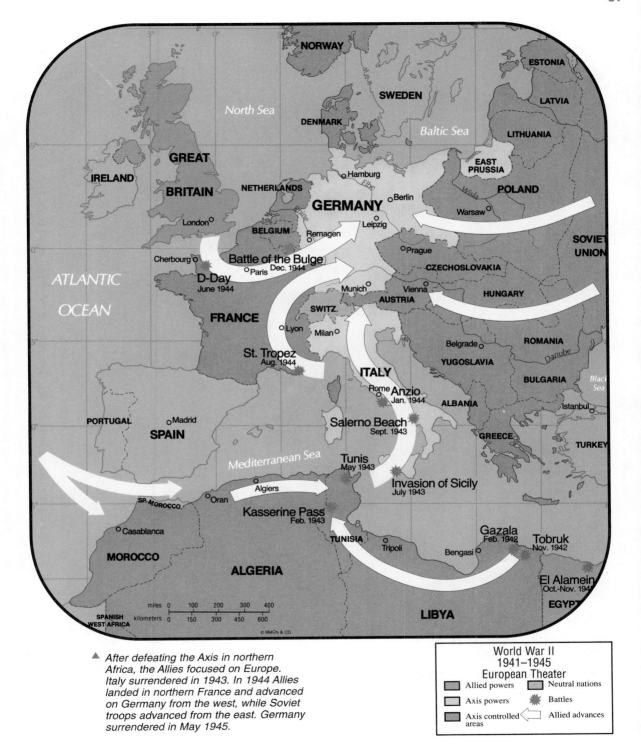

After defeating the Axis in northern Africa, the Allies focused on Europe. Italy surrendered in 1943. In 1944 Allies landed in northern France and advanced on Germany from the west, while Soviet troops advanced from the east. Germany surrendered in May 1945.

World War II
1941–1945
European Theater

▨	Allied powers	▨	Neutral nations
▨	Axis powers	✳	Battles
▨	Axis controlled areas	◁	Allied advances

Map labels:

NORWAY
SWEDEN
ESTONIA
LATVIA
LITHUANIA
DENMARK
North Sea
Baltic Sea
EAST PRUSSIA
POLAND
GREAT BRITAIN
IRELAND
Hamburg
Berlin
Warsaw
SOVIET UNION
NETHERLANDS
GERMANY
Leipzig
London
BELGIUM
Remagen
Prague
CZECHOSLOVAKIA
ATLANTIC OCEAN
Cherbourg
Battle of the Bulge Dec. 1944
Paris
D-Day June 1944
Munich
Vienna
AUSTRIA
HUNGARY
FRANCE
SWITZ.
Lyon
Milan
Belgrade
ROMANIA
Danube
St. Tropez Aug. 1944
YUGOSLAVIA
ITALY
BULGARIA
Black Sea
Rome
Anzio Jan. 1944
ALBANIA
Istanbul
PORTUGAL
Madrid
SPAIN
Salerno Beach Sept. 1943
GREECE
TURKEY
Mediterranean Sea
Tunis May 1943
Algiers
Invasion of Sicily July 1943
SP. MOROCCO
Oran
Kasserine Pass Feb. 1943
Casablanca
TUNISIA
Tripoli
Gazala Feb. 1942
Tobruk Nov. 1942
Bengasi
MOROCCO
ALGERIA
El Alamein Oct.-Nov. 194_
EGYPT
LIBYA
SPANISH WEST AFRICA

miles 0 100 200 300 400
kilometers 0 150 300 450 600
© RMCN & CO.

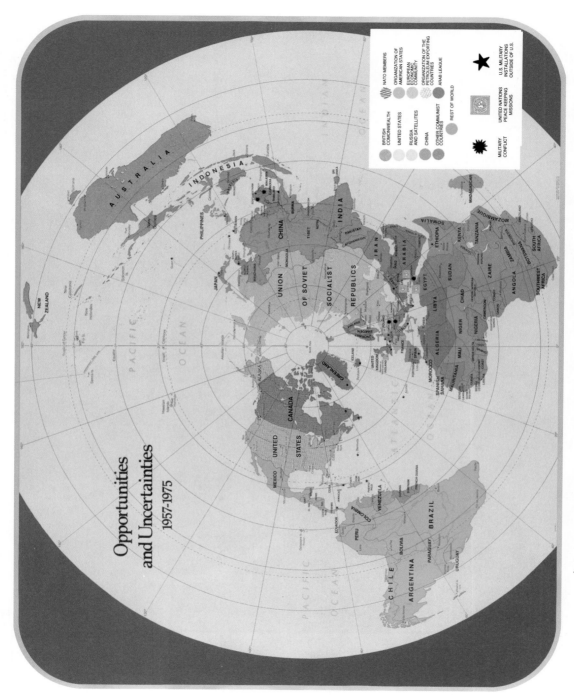

Opportunities and Uncertainties

1957–1975

▲ In 1949 the United States and other free nations formed a military alliance called the North Atlantic Treaty Organization (NATO) to prevent the spread of communism. The Soviet Union and other communist countries formed a competing alliance called the Warsaw Pact. This view indicates why Canada and the United States feared a possible Soviet attack from the north.

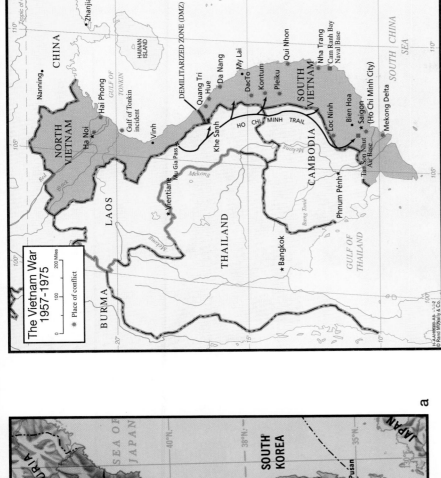

The Vietnam War 1957–1975

* Place of conflict

0 100 200 Miles

CHINA

Nanning

Zhanjiang

Tropic of Cancer

NORTH VIETNAM

Ha Noi

Hai Phong

GULF OF TONKIN

Gulf of Tonkin incident

Vinh

HAINAN ISLAND

DEMILITARIZED ZONE (DMZ)

Quang Tri

Hue

Da Nang

My Lai

DacTo

Kontum

Pleiku

Qui Nhon

Nha Trang

Cam Ranh Bay Naval Base

SOUTH VIETNAM

Khe Sanh

Mu Gia Pass

HO CHI MINH TRAIL

Loc Ninh

Bien Hoa

Saigon (Ho Chi Minh City)

Tan Son Nhut Air Base

Mekong Delta

SOUTH CHINA SEA

LAOS

Vientiane

Mekong

CAMBODIA

Phnum Pénh

Tonle Sap

THAILAND

Bangkok

GULF OF THAILAND

BURMA

Red

Black

▲ The United States entered the longest war in its history to prevent communist-ruled North Vietnam from taking over non-communist South Vietnam. The Ho Chi Minh Trail was a system of roads the North Vietnamese used as a supply route for the Viet Cong, or communist rebels in South Vietnam.

The War in Korea 1950

0 50 100 miles

CHINA

MANCHURIA

SEA OF JAPAN

40°N.

Chinese attack, Nov. 26, 1950

limit of UN advance, Nov. 24, 1950

NORTH KOREA

Pyongyang

Kaesong

Panmunjom

Seoul

Inchon

N. Korean invasion, June 25, 1950

Sept. 15, 1950

limit of N. Korean advance, Aug. 1950

38°N.

SOUTH KOREA

Pusan

35°N.

JAPAN

YELLOW SEA

125°E.

▲ United Nations members, including the United States, sent troops to defend South Korea from an invasion by communist-ruled North Korea. In 1950, UN forces halted the North Korean advance at Pusan and pushed to the Yalu River in the north. The war ended in 1953 when the UN and North Korea signed an armistice agreement.

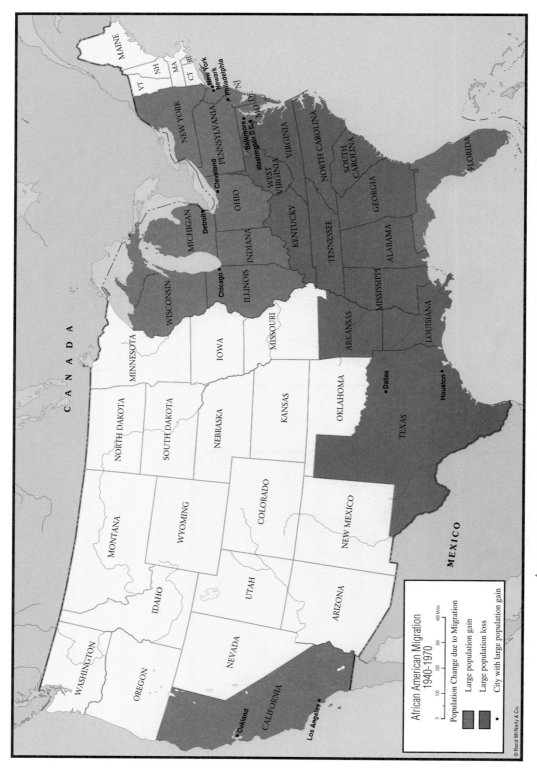

▲ Between 1940 and 1970, millions of African Americans moved out of the South. More than two-thirds of the total African American population relocated to cities. More than half the urban black population was concentrated in the twelve cities shown on the map.

African American Migration
1940–1970

Population Change due to Migration

Large population gain

Large population loss

City with large population gain

© Rand McNally & Co.

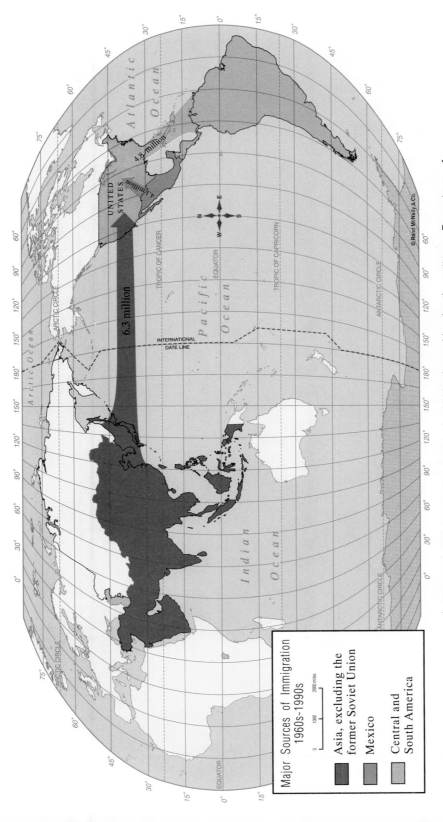

▲ Changes in U.S. immigration laws in the 1960s changed immigration patterns. Percentages of immigrants from Europe decreased. In the 1990s, most immigrants to the United States came from Mexico, the Philippines, Haiti, China, India, Vietnam, Jamaica, Cuba, and South Korea.

UNITED STATES

4.8 million

4.1 million

6.3 million

INTERNATIONAL DATE LINE

© Rand McNally & Co.

Atlantic Ocean

Pacific Ocean

Indian Ocean

Arctic Ocean

TROPIC OF CANCER

EQUATOR

TROPIC OF CAPRICORN

ANTARCTIC CIRCLE

ARCTIC CIRCLE

Major Sources of Immigration 1960s-1990s

Asia, excluding the former Soviet Union

Mexico

Central and South America

0   1000   2000 miles

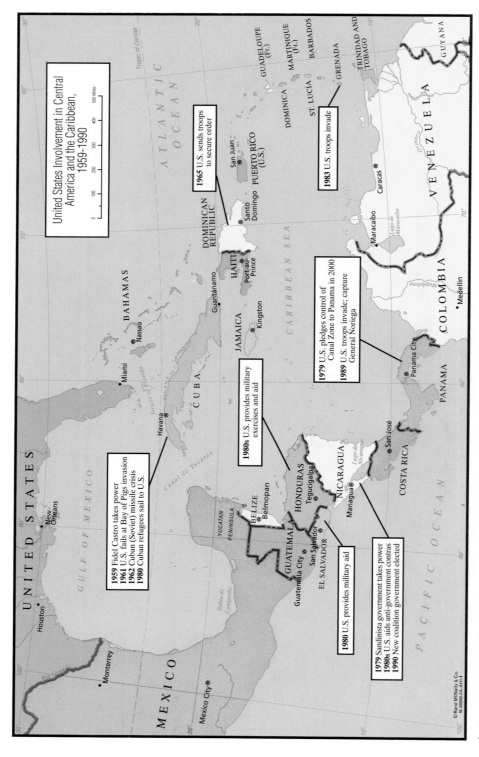

United States Involvement in Central America and the Caribbean, 1959-1990

0   100 200 300 400 500 Miles

1965 U.S. sends troops to secure order

1983 U.S. troops invade

1979 U.S. pledges control of Canal Zone to Panama in 2000
1989 U.S. troops invade; capture General Noriega

1980s U.S. provides military exercises and aid

1959 Fidel Castro takes power
1961 U.S. fails at Bay of Pigs invasion
1962 Cuban (Soviet) missile crisis
1980 Cuban refugees sail to U.S.

1980 U.S. provides military aid

1979 Sandinista government takes power
1980s U.S. aids anti-government contras
1990 New coalition government elected

© Rand McNally & Co.
M-390000-2A-AH-1

Houston
Monterrey
Rio Grande
MEXICO
Mexico City
New Orleans
UNITED STATES
GULF OF MEXICO
Bahía de Campeche
YUCATAN PENINSULA
Canal de Yucatán
Miami
Straits of Florida
Havana
CUBA
BAHAMAS
Nassau
Tropic of Cancer
ATLANTIC OCEAN
San Juan
PUERTO RICO (U.S.)
Santo Domingo
DOMINICAN REPUBLIC
HAITI
Port-au-Prince
Guantánamo
JAMAICA
Kingston
CARIBBEAN SEA
GUADELOUPE (Fr.)
MARTINIQUE (Fr.)
DOMINICA
ST. LUCIA
BARBADOS
GRENADA
TRINIDAD AND TOBAGO
GUYANA
Caracas
VENEZUELA
Maracaibo
Lago de Maracaibo
Orinoco
COLOMBIA
Medellín
Magdalena
Panama City
PANAMA
San José
COSTA RICA
NICARAGUA
Managua
Lago de Nicaragua
HONDURAS
Tegucigalpa
BELIZE
Belmopan
GUATEMALA
Guatemala City
San Salvador
EL SALVADOR
PACIFIC OCEAN

▲ *Communist activity in Central America and the Caribbean threatened U.S. security. In 1962 the Cuban missile crisis led the United States to the brink of nuclear war with the Soviet Union. The United States continued to intervene in the region to support democracy and to protect U.S. interests.*

Section 8   *(1990 & beyond)*

Entering a New Millennium

In 1990 the United States was one of the world's leading nations. Its resources and technology made it a leader in the production of goods and services. Its principles of freedom and opportunity provided its people with one of the world's highest standards of living.

The diverse population of the United States reflected the history of a nation settled by people from every part of the world. According to the 1990 census, most Americans lived throughout the country in large **metropolitan areas**, or cities surrounded by suburbs. They earned more money and lived longer than Americans in the past. In spite of widespread prosperity, however, many Americans lived in poverty.

As the United States enters a new millennium, it must consider ways to meet the needs of an aging population. It also faces challenges in a changing world. Defending human rights, supporting economic development, and protecting the environment have become global issues.

◀ *Skyscrapers tower over midtown Manhattan in New York – the largest U.S. city in population in 1990.*

Seattle, Washington, became an aerospace and technology center as well as a leading U.S. port for Pacific Rim trade. ▶

Did You Know ❓

More than half the people who lived in the Los Angeles metropolitan area in 1990 moved there from other countries or other parts of the United States.

Population Distribution by Age, 1990

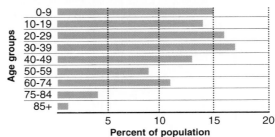

Age groups (vertical axis): 0-9, 10-19, 20-29, 30-39, 40-49, 50-59, 60-74, 75-84, 85+

Percent of population (horizontal axis): 5, 10, 15, 20

	1992	1992	1997
People	Mae Carol Jemison, of Illinois, becomes first African American woman to travel in space.	Ross Perot, of Texas, runs as independent candidate for President of the United States.	Madeleine Albright, who was born in Czechoslovakia, becomes first woman U.S. secretary of state.
	1991	**1992**	**1994**
Events	Collapse of the Soviet Union marks end of Cold War.	World leaders hold Earth Summit in Rio de Janeiro, Brazil.	United States, Canada, and Mexico sign North American Free Trade Agreement (NAFTA).
	1991	**1991**	**1993**
Literature	*There Are No Children Here*, by Alex Kotlowitz, describes social conditions in Chicago's inner city.	*The Lost Garden*, by Laurence Yep, describes how the author grew up as a Chinese American in San Francisco.	*Having Our Say*, by the Delany sisters, describes 100 years of African American life in North Carolina and New York, NY.

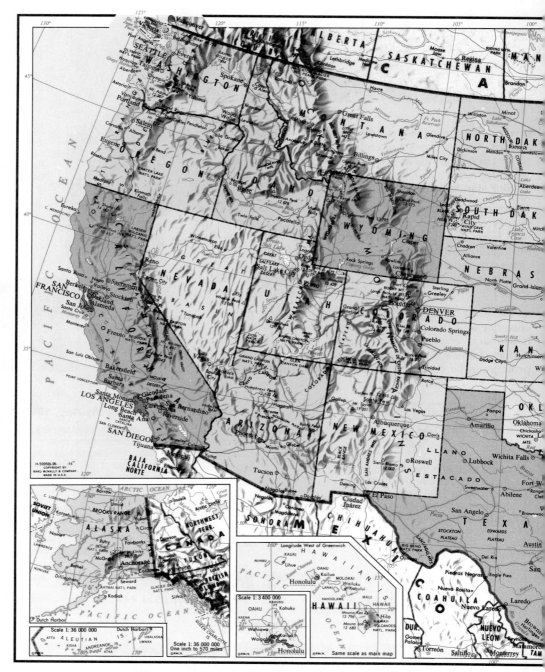

▲ *In 1990 the United States had more than 350 metropolitan areas. The largest of these areas are indicated in red on the map. Los Angeles-Long Beach had a 1990 population of almost 9 million, making it the country's largest metropolitan area in population.*

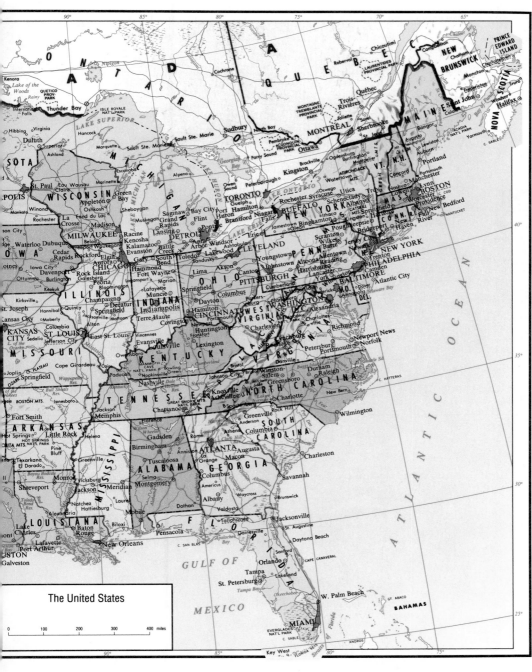

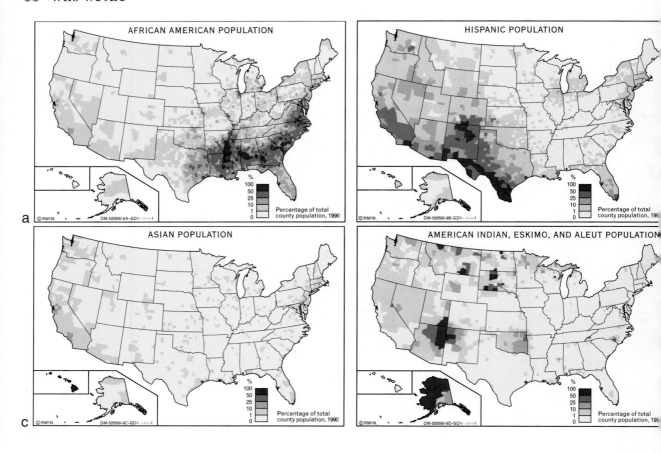

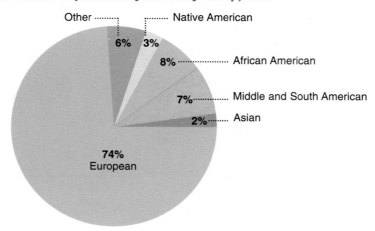

The maps show some major racial/ethnic groups in the United States in 1990 and where they lived. The graph shows the percentages of people of different ancestry groups within the United States population in 1990.

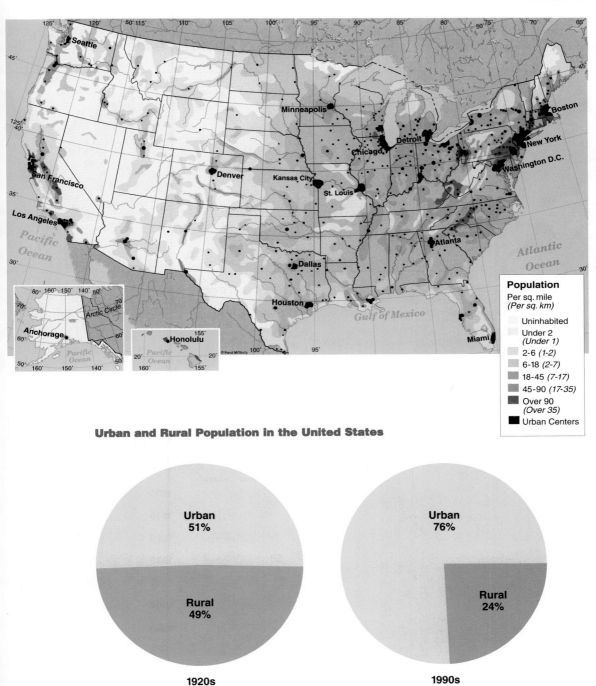

Population

Per sq. mile
(Per sq. km)

	Uninhabited
	Under 2 *(Under 1)*
	2-6 *(1-2)*
	6-18 *(2-7)*
	18-45 *(7-17)*
	45-90 *(17-35)*
	Over 90 *(Over 35)*
	Urban Centers

Urban and Rural Population in the United States

Urban
51%

Rural
49%

1920s

Urban
76%

Rural
24%

1990s

In 1990 more than three-fourths of all Americans lived in urban areas. The map shows the locations of the most densely populated parts of the United States. Notice that several metropolitan areas from Boston to Washington, D.C. had grown together to form a large, densely populated area called a megalopolis. The circle graphs compare the percentages of urban and rural population in the United States in the 1920s and 1990s.

Median Family Income, 1990

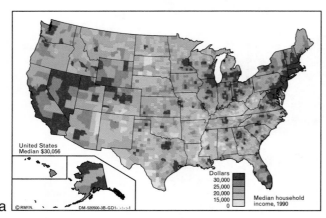

a

▲ The map shows median family income, or the middle value of all family incomes, in different parts of the United States in 1990.

Lifetime Expectance, 1990

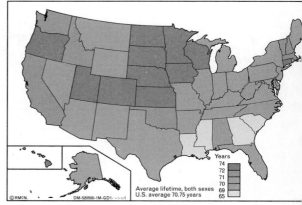

▲ The map shows the average lifetime of all Americans in different parts of the United States in 1990.

Median Family Income (in current dollars), 1960-1990

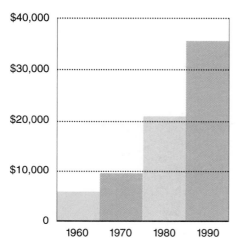

▲ The graph shows how median family income throughout the United States changed between 1960 and 1990.

Lifetime Expectance of Males and Females 1900-1990

Male - years	Year of Birth	Female - years
46	1900	48
48	1910	52
54	1920	55
58	1930	62
61	1940	65
66	1950	71
67	1960	73
67	1970	75
70	1980	77
72	1990	79

▲ The graph shows how average lifetimes of males and females in the United States changed between 1900 and 1990.

rcentage of U.S. Population
low Poverty Level, 1990

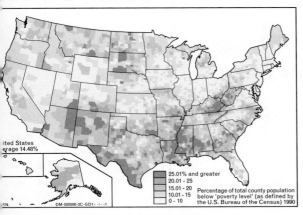

ited States
erage 14.48%

25.01% and greater
20.01 - 25
15.01 - 20   Percentage of total county population
10.01 - 15   below 'poverty level' (as defined by
0 - 10   the U.S. Bureau of the Census) 1990

DM-520500-3C-GD1- -:- -1

The map shows the percentages of people living below the poverty level in different parts of the United States in 1990. Poverty level is based on the income needed to feed a family adequately without spending more than a third of the family income on food.

U.S. Unemployment Rates, 1990

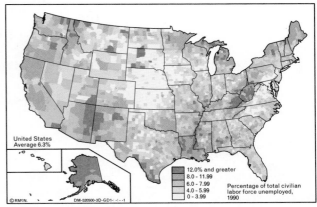

United States
Average 6.3%

12.0% and greater
8.0 - 11.99
6.0 - 7.99
4.0 - 5.99   Percentage of total civilian
0 - 3.99   labor force unemployed,
              1990

©RMGN.   DM-520500-3D-GD1- -:- -1

b

▲ *The map shows the percentages of unemployed workers in different parts of the United States in 1990.*

rcentage of U.S. Population
elow Poverty Level, 1960-1990

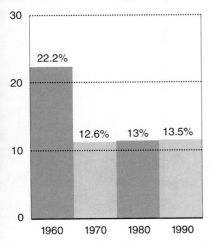

30

22.2%

20

12.6%   13%   13.5%

10

0
      1960   1970   1980   1990

The graph shows how the percentage of Americans below the poverty level changed between 1960 and 1990.

U.S. Unemployment Rates,
1960-1990

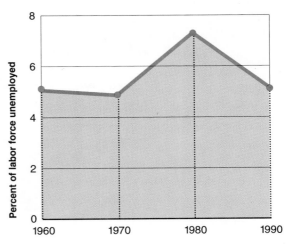

8

6

Percent of labor force unemployed

4

2

0
      1960   1970   1980   1990

▲ *The graph shows how the percentage of unemployed workers in the United States changed between 1960 and 1990.*

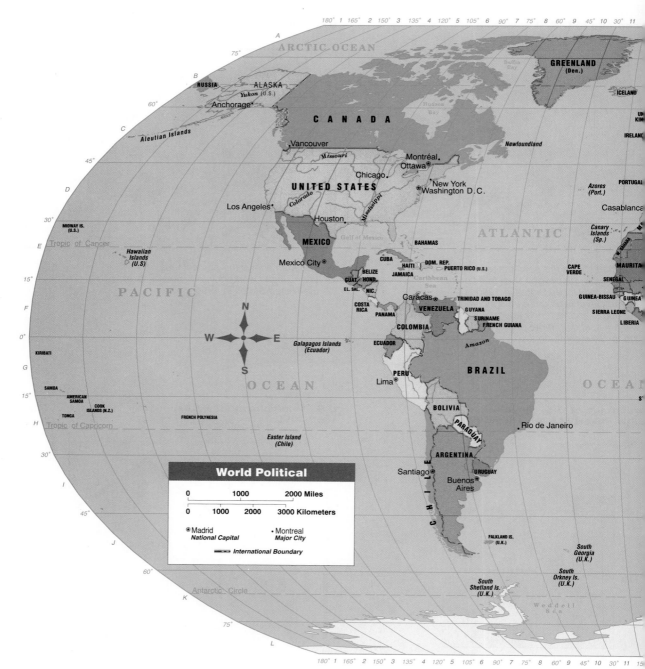

The 50 states that make up the United States cover an area of more than 3 1/2 million square miles. The United States is the world's fourth largest country in area.

14 30° 15 45° 16 60° 17 75° 18 90° 19 105° 20 120° 21 135° 22 150° 23 165° 24 180°

ARCTIC OCEAN

A

75°

Franz Josef Land

B

Novaya Zemlya

60°

FINLAND

SWEDEN
EST. LAT.
LITH.
POLAND BELARUS

Ob'

Yenisey

Lena

Bering Sea

C

R U S S I A

Moscow

.Novosibirsk

45°

NY CZ AUS. HUNG.
CRO. SLVA.
ITALY ALB. BUL. ROM.
GREECE
TURKEY

UKRAINE MOLD.

KAZAKHSTAN

MONGOLIA

Sea of Okhotsk

D

Black Sea
GEO.
ARM. AZER.

UZBEKISTAN

KYRG.

NORTH KOREA

Sea of Japan

JAPAN

Crete
CYPRUS LEB.
ISRAEL
JORDAN
SYRIA
IRAQ
KUWAIT

TURKMENISTAN

TAJIK.

Beijing⊛

SOUTH KOREA

Tōkyō

30°

iterranean Sea

IRAN

AFGHANISTAN

C H I N A

e⊛

UNISIA

LIBYA EGYPT

SAUDI ARABIA

QATAR
U.A.E.

PAKISTAN

Ganges

NEPAL

BHU.
BNGL.

Yangtze

.Shanghai

P A C I F I C

E

Cairo

OMAN

Mumbai (Bombay)

I N D I A

Calcutta.

MYANMAR

Guangzhou⊛

TAIWAN

Tropic of Cancer

NORTHERN MARIANA ISLANDS (U.S.)

WAKE ISLAND (U.S.)

15°

GER

CHAD

SUDAN

ERITREA

YEMEN
DJIBOUTI

Arabian Sea

LAOS
THAILAND

Bay of Bengal

Bangkok⊛

CAMBODIA

VIETNAM

South China Sea

PHILIPPINES

GUAM (U.S.)

RIA

CENTRAL AFRICAN REPUBLIC

Addis Ababa

ETHIOPIA

SRI LANKA

PALAU

O C E A N

F

CAMEROON

Congo

UGANDA

SOMALIA

MALDIVES

BRUNEI

MALAYSIA

FED. STATES OF MICRONESIA

MARSHALL ISLANDS

GABON

CONGO

RWANDA

KENYA

SINGAPORE

Borneo

New Guinea

Equator

0°

DEM. REP. OF THE CONGO

BURUNDI

SEYCHELLES

Sumatra

.Jakarta

INDONESIA

PAPUA NEW GUINEA

SOLOMON ISLANDS

G

TANZANIA

Java

ANGOLA

ZAMBIA

MOZAMBIQUE

COMOROS

I N D I A N

.Darwin

Coral Sea

VANUATU

15°

ZIMBABWE

MADAGASCAR

MAURITIUS

NEW CALEDONIA (Fr.)

FIJI

NAMIBIA

BOTSWANA

REUNION (Fr.)

A U S T R A L I A

Tropic of Capricorn

H

SWAZILAND

SOUTH AFRICA

LESOTHO

O C E A N

Perth.

Darling

Sydney

30°

pe Town.⊛

Melbourne.

NEW ZEALAND

I

Tasmania

Wellington⊛

Kerguelen Islands (Fr.)

45°

J

60°

K

75°

NTARCTICA

Copyright by Rand McNally & Co.
Made in U.S.A.
DM-510000-2A-CL1- -l-l-3

L

° 14 30° 15 45° 16 60° 17 75° 18 90° 19 105° 20 120° 21 135° 22 150° 23 165° 24 180°

In 1990 the United States had a population of about 250 million. It was the world's third largest country in population.

Populations of United States Colonies and States, 1650-1990

States	1650	1700	1750	1770	1790	1800	1820	1840
Alabama							127,901	590,756
Alaska								
Arizona								
Arkansas							14,273	97,574
California								
Colorado								
Connecticut	4,139	25,970	111,280	183,881	237,946	251,002	275,248	309,978
Delaware	185	2,470	28,704	35,496	59,096	64,273	72,749	78,085
District of Columbia						8,144	23,336	33,745
Florida								54,477
Georgia			5,200	23,375	82,548	162,686	340,989	691,392
Hawaii								
Idaho								
Illinois							55,211	476,183
Indiana						5,641	147,178	685,866
Iowa								43,112
Kansas								
Kentucky				15,700	73,677	220,955	564,317	779,828
Louisiana							153,407	352,411
Maine[4]				31,257	96,540	151,719	298,335	501,793
Maryland	4,504	29,604	141,073	202,599	319,728	341,548	407,350	470,019
Massachusetts[4]	16,603	55,941	188,000	235,308	378,787	422,845	523,287	737,699
Michigan							8,896	212,267
Minnesota								
Mississippi						8,850	75,448	375,651
Missouri							66,586	383,702
Montana								
Nebraska								
Nevada								
New Hampshire	1,305	4,958	27,505	62,396	141,885	183,858	244,161	284,574
New Jersey		14,010	71,393	117,431	184,139	211,149	277,575	373,306
New Mexico								
New York	4,116	19,107	76,696	162,920	340,120	589,051	1,372,812	2,428,921
North Carolina		10,720	72,984	197,200	393,751	478,103	638,829	753,419
North Dakota[3]								
Ohio						45,365	581,434	1,519,467
Oklahoma[5]								
Oregon								
Pennsylvania		17,950	119,666	240,057	434,373	602,365	1,049,458	1,724,033
Rhode Island	785	5,894	33,226	58,196	68,825	69,122	83,059	108,830
South Carolina		5,704	64,000	124,244	249,073	345,591	502,741	594,398
South Dakota[3]								
Tennessee				1,000	35,691	105,602	422,823	829,210
Texas								
Utah								
Vermont				10,000	85,425	154,465	235,981	291,948
Virginia[6]	18,731	58,560	231,033	447,016	691,737	807,557	938,261	1,025,227
Washington								
West Virginia[6]					55,873	78,592	136,808	224,537
Wisconsin								30,945
Wyoming								
Total[1]	50,368	250,888	1,170,760	2,148,076	3,929,214	5,308,483	9,638,453	17,069,453[2]

[1] All figures prior to 1890 exclude Indians unaffected by the pioneer movement. Figures for 1650 through 1770 include only the British colonies that later became the United States. No areas are included prior to their annexation to the United States. However, many of the figures refer to territories prior to their admission as states. U.S. total includes Alaska from 1880 through 1970 and Hawaii from 1900 through 1970.

[2] U.S. total for 1840 includes 6,100 persons on public ships in service of the United States not credited to any state.

[3] South Dakota figure for 1860 represents entire Dakota Territory. North and South Dakota figures for 1880 are for the parts of Dakota Territory which later constituted the respective states.

1860	1880	1900	1920	1940	1950	1960	1970	1980	1990
964,201	1,262,505	1,828,697	2,348,174	2,832,961	3,061,743	3,266,740	3,444,165	3,893,888	4,062,608
	33,426	63,592	55,036	72,524	128,643	226,167	302,173	401,851	551,947
	40,440	122,931	334,162	499,261	749,587	1,302,161	1,772,482	2,718,425	3,677,985
435,450	802,525	1,311,564	1,752,204	1,949,387	1,909,511	1,786,272	1,923,295	2,286,435	2,362,239
379,994	864,694	1,485,053	3,426,861	6,907,387	10,586,223	15,717,204	19,953,134	23,667,565	29,839,250
34,277	194,327	539,700	939,629	1,123,296	1,325,089	1,753,947	2,207,259	2,889,735	3,307,912
460,147	622,700	908,420	1,380,631	1,709,242	2,007,280	2,535,234	3,032,217	3,107,576	3,295,669
112,216	146,608	184,735	223,003	266,505	318,085	446,292	548,104	594,317	668,696
75,080	177,624	278,718	437,571	663,091	802,178	763,956	756,510	638,432	609,909
140,424	269,493	528,542	968,470	1,897,414	2,771,305	4,951,560	6,789,443	9,746,342	13,003,362
1,057,286	1,542,180	2,216,331	2,895,832	3,123,723	3,444,578	3,943,116	4,589,575	5,463,105	6,508,419
		154,001	255,881	422,770	499,794	632,772	769,913	964,691	1,115,274
	32,610	161,772	431,866	524,873	588,637	667,191	713,008	944,038	1,011,986
1,711,951	3,077,871	4,821,550	6,485,280	7,897,241	8,712,176	10,081,158	11,113,976	11,426,596	11,466,682
1,350,428	1,978,301	2,516,462	2,930,390	3,427,796	3,934,224	4,662,498	5,193,669	5,490,260	5,564,228
674,913	1,624,615	2,231,853	2,404,021	2,538,268	2,621,073	2,757,537	2,825,041	2,913,808	2,787,424
107,206	996,096	1,470,495	1,769,257	1,801,028	1,905,299	2,178,611	2,249,071	2,364,236	2,485,600
1,155,684	1,648,690	2,147,174	2,416,630	2,845,627	2,944,806	3,038,156	3,219,311	3,660,257	3,698,969
708,002	939,946	1,381,625	1,798,509	2,363,880	2,683,516	3,257,022	3,643,180	4,206,312	4,238,216
628,279	648,936	694,466	768,014	847,226	913,774	969,265	993,663	1,125,027	1,233,223
687,049	934,943	1,188,044	1,449,661	1,821,244	2,343,001	3,100,689	3,922,399	4,216,975	4,798,622
1,231,066	1,783,085	2,805,346	3,852,356	4,316,721	4,690,514	5,148,578	5,689,170	5,737,037	6,029,051
749,113	1,636,937	2,420,982	3,668,412	5,256,106	6,371,766	7,823,194	8,875,083	9,262,078	9,328,784
172,023	780,773	1,751,394	2,387,125	2,792,300	2,982,483	3,413,864	3,805,069	4,075,970	4,387,029
791,305	1,131,597	1,551,270	1,790,618	2,183,796	2,178,914	2,178,141	2,216,912	2,520,638	2,586,443
1,182,012	2,168,380	3,106,665	3,404,055	3,784,664	3,954,653	4,319,813	4,677,399	4,916,759	5,137,804
	39,159	243,329	548,889	559,456	591,024	674,767	694,409	786,690	803,655
28,841	452,402	1,066,300	1,296,372	1,315,834	1,325,510	1,411,330	1,483,791	1,569,825	1,584,617
6,857	62,266	42,335	77,407	110,247	160,083	285,278	488,738	800,493	1,206,152
326,073	346,991	411,488	443,083	491,524	533,242	606,921	737,681	920,610	1,113,915
672,035	1,131,116	1,883,669	3,155,900	4,160,165	4,835,329	6,066,782	7,168,164	7,364,823	7,748,634
93,516	119,565	195,310	360,350	531,818	681,187	951,023	1,016,000	1,302,981	1,521,779
3,880,735	5,082,871	7,268,894	10,385,227	13,479,142	14,830,192	16,782,304	18,241,266	17,558,072	18,044,505
992,622	1,399,750	1,893,810	2,559,123	3,571,623	4,061,929	4,556,155	5,082,059	5,881,813	6,657,630
	36,909	319,146	646,872	641,935	619,636	632,446	617,761	652,717	641,364
2,339,511	3,198,062	4,157,545	5,759,394	6,907,612	7,946,627	9,706,397	10,652,017	10,797,624	10,887,325
		790,391	2,028,283	2,336,434	2,233,351	2,328,284	2,559,253	3,025,290	3,157,604
52,465	174,768	413,536	783,389	1,089,684	1,521,341	1,768,687	2,091,385	2,633,149	2,853,733
2,906,215	4,282,891	6,302,115	8,720,017	9,900,180	10,498,012	11,319,366	11,793,909	11,863,895	11,924,710
174,620	276,531	428,556	604,397	713,346	791,896	859,488	949,723	947,154	1,005,984
703,708	995,577	1,340,316	1,683,724	1,899,804	2,117,027	2,382,594	2,590,516	3,121,833	3,505,707
4,837	98,268	401,570	636,547	642,961	652,740	680,514	666,257	690,768	699,999
1,109,801	1,542,359	2,020,616	2,337,885	2,915,841	3,291,718	3,567,089	3,924,164	4,591,120	4,896,641
604,215	1,591,749	3,048,710	4,663,228	6,414,824	7,711,194	9,579,677	11,196,730	14,229,288	17,059,805
40,273	143,963	276,749	449,396	550,310	688,862	890,627	1,059,273	1,461,037	1,727,784
315,098	332,286	343,641	352,428	359,231	377,747	389,881	444,732	551,456	564,964
1,219,630	1,512,565	1,854,184	2,309,187	2,677,773	3,318,680	3,966,949	4,648,494	5,346,818	6,216,568
11,594	75,116	518,103	1,356,621	1,736,191	2,378,963	2,853,214	3,409,169	4,132,180	4,887,941
376,688	618,457	958,800	1,463,701	1,901,974	2,005,552	1,860,421	1,744,237	1,950,279	1,801,625
775,881	1,315,497	2,069,042	2,632,067	3,137,587	3,434,575	3,951,777	4,417,933	4,705,521	4,906,745
	20,789	92,531	194,402	250,742	290,529	330,066	332,416	469,557	455,975
31,443,321	**50,189,209**	**76,212,168**	**106,021,537**	**132,164,569**	**151,325,798**	**179,323,175**	**203,235,298**	**226,547,346**	**249,632,692**

[4]Maine figures for 1770 through 1800 are for that area of Massachusetts which became the state of Maine in 1820. Massachusetts figures exclude Maine from 1770 through 1800, but include it from 1650 through 1750. Massachusetts figure for 1650 also includes population of Plymouth (1,566), a separate colony until 1691.

[5]Oklahoma figure for 1900 includes population of Indian Territory (392,060).

[6]West Virginia figures for 1790 through 1860 are for that area of Virginia which became West Virginia in 1863. These figures are excluded from the figures for Virginia from 1790 through 1860.

Facts About the States

State	Admission to the Union date (order)	Capital	Area in sq.mi. (rank in area)	Nickname	Postal Abbreviation
Alabama	1819 (22)	Montgomery	51,705 (29)	The Heart of Dixie	AL
Alaska	1959 (49)	Juneau	591,004 (1)	Last Frontier	AK
Arizona	1912 (48)	Phoenix	114,000 (6)	Grand Canyon State	AZ
Arkansas	1836 (25)	Little Rock	53,187 (27)	Land of Opportunity	AR
California	1850 (31)	Sacramento	158,706 (3)	Golden State	CA
Colorado	1876 (38)	Denver	104,091 (8)	Centennial State	CO
Connecticut	1788 (5)	Hartford	5.018 (48)	Constitution State	CT
Delaware	1787 (1)	Dover	2,044 (49)	First State	DE
Florida	1845 (27)	Tallahassee	58,664 (22)	Sunshine State	FL
Georgia	1788 (4)	Atlanta	58,910 (21)	Empire State of the South	GA
Hawaii	1959 (50)	Honolulu	6,471 (47)	Aloha State	HI
Idaho	1890 (43)	Boise	83,564 (13)	Gem State	ID
Illinois	1818 (21)	Springfield	56,345 (24)	Land of Lincoln	IL
Indiana	1816 (19)	Indianapolis	36,185 (38)	Hoosier State	IN
Iowa	1846 (29)	Des Moines	56,275 (25)	Hawkeye State	IA
Kansas	1861 (34)	Topeka	82,277 (14)	Sunflower State	KS
Kentucky	1792 (15)	Frankfort	40,409 (37)	Bluegrass State	KY
Louisiana	1812 (18)	Baton Rouge	47,752 (31)	Pelican State	LA
Maine	1820 (23)	Augusta	33,265 (39)	Pine Tree State	ME
Maryland	1788 (7)	Annapolis	10,460 (42)	Old Line State	MD
Massachusetts	1788 (6)	Boston	8,284 (45)	Bay State	MA
Michigan	1837 (26)	Lansing	58,527 (23)	Wolverine State	MI
Minnesota	1858 (32)	St. Paul	84,402 (12)	Gopher State	MN
Mississippi	1817 (20)	Jackson	47,689 (32)	Magnolia State	MS
Missouri	1821 (24)	Jefferson City	69,697 (19)	Show Me State	MO

State	Admission to the Union date (order)	Capital	Area in sq.mi. (rank in area)	Nickname	Postal Abbreviation
Montana	1889 (41)	Helena	147,046 (4)	Treasure State	MT
Nebraska	1867 (37)	Lincoln	77,355 (15)	Cornhusker State	NE
Nevada	1864 (36)	Carson City	110,561 (7)	Silver State	NV
New Hampshire	1788 (9)	Concord	9,297 (44)	Granite State	NH
New Jersey	1787 (3)	Trenton	7,787 (46)	Garden State	NJ
New Mexico	1912 (47)	Santa Fe	121,593 (5)	Land of Enchantment	NM
New York	1788 (11)	Albany	49,108 (30)	Empire State	NY
North Carolina	1789 (12)	Raleigh	52,669 (28)	Tar Heel State	NC
North Dakota	1889 (39)	Bismarck	70,702 (17)	Flickertail State	ND
Ohio	1803 (17)	Columbus	41,330 (35)	Buckeye State	OH
Oklahoma	1907 (46)	Oklahoma City	69,956 (18)	Sooner State	OK
Oregon	1859 (33)	Salem	97,073 (10)	Beaver State	OR
Pennsylvania	1787 (2)	Harrisburg	45,308 (33)	Keystone State	PA
Rhode Island	1790 (13)	Providence	1,212 (50)	Ocean State	RI
South Carolina	1788 (8)	Columbia	31,113 (40)	Palmetto State	SC
South Dakota	1889 (40)	Pierre	77,116 (16)	Mount Rushmore State	SD
Tennessee	1796 (16)	Nashville	42,114 (34)	Volunteer State	TN
Texas	1845 (28)	Austin	266,807 (2)	Lone Star State	TX
Utah	1896 (45)	Salt Lake City	84,899 (11)	Beehive State	UT
Vermont	1791 (14)	Montpelier	9,614 (43)	Green Mountain State	VT
Virginia	1788 (10)	Richmond	40,767 (36)	Old Dominion	VA
Washington	1889 (42)	Olympia	68,139 (20)	Evergreen State	WA
West Virginia	1863 (35)	Charleston	24,231 (41)	Mountain State	WV
Wisconsin	1848 (30)	Madison	56,153 (26)	Badger State	WI
Wyoming	1890 (44)	Cheyenne	97,809 (9)	Equality State	WY

In addition to place names that appear on the maps in this atlas, the Index also lists names of people, groups, events, and other topics related to American history. It provides explanatory information, such as dates, identifications, and geographic locations for many entries. When appropriate, entries are cross-referenced to related topics.

The Index lists boldfaced page numbers on which each entry appears. A small letter beside a page number identifies a specific map on the page on which the entry appears. Postal abbreviations are used for state names.

The following abbreviations also are used:

Ft.	Fort	St.	Saint
g	graph	t	table
Is.	Islands	terr.	territory
p	photograph	U.S.	United States
pop.	population		